Adventures

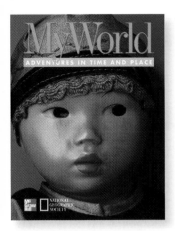

The nation's leading

in

Social Studies publisher

Time

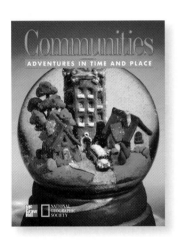

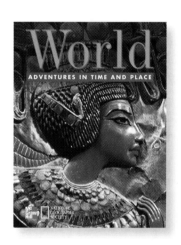

brings you the number one

and

K-7 Social Studies program.

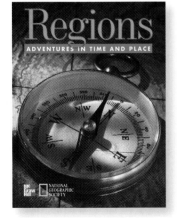

Place

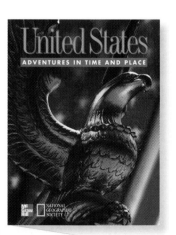

McGRAW-HILL

AUG 2002

D1401215

Program Philosophy

Each and every one of the educators, authors, editors, and designers who created McGraw-Hill's **Adventures in Time and Place** share a deep commitment to provide

- **rich, relevant content** in all areas of social studies at every grade level

- **geographic literacy skills** for all students, created in partnership with the National Geographic Society

- **easy-to-use teaching materials** with choices to accommodate diverse student learning styles and support various teaching styles

NATIONAL GEOGRAPHIC SOCIETY

Program Authorship

National Geographic Society, recognized as the world's premier authority on geography and geography education, joins seven of the nation's leading educators to bring you the nation's number one Social Studies program.

DR. BARRY BEYER
George Mason University
Fairfax, VA

DR. JAMES BANKS
University of Washington
Seattle, WA

JEAN CRAVEN
Albuquerque Public Schools
Albuquerque, NM

DR. GLORIA CONTRERAS
University of North Texas
Denton, TX

DR. MARY MCFARLAND
Parkway Public Schools
Creve Coeur, MO

DR. WALTER PARKER
University of Washington
Seattle, WA

DR. GLORIA LADSON-BILLINGS
University of Wisconsin-Madison
Madison, WI

Easy-to-use Program Options

Teaching Options

Grades K-2
Teachers can choose to:
- Teach with **Big Books (K-2)**
- Teach with **Pupil Editions (1-2)**
- Teach with **a combination (1-2)**

Use the same manageable Teacher's Edition for all three options.
Choose the activities that fit your classroom style!

Assessment Options

Adventures in Time and Place
provides a variety of methods to
check students' mastery of facts and
application of skills:
- **Standardized Test Format**
- **Written Response Format**
- **Performance Assessments
  with Scoring Rubrics**

For every child, there's an option to
provide accurate assessment.

Technology Options

Multimedia choices, correlated directly to the program, provide a variety of
extensions that meet your needs:
- **World Wide Web activities**
- **Lessons on videodisc and videotape**
- **National Geographic technology**
- **CD-ROM technology**

inter NET CONNECTION Visit our website:
www.mhschool.com

Adventures in Time and Place gives you the widest variety of choices to
meet your needs.

Adventures in Time and Place Components

	K	1	2	3	4	4/5	5	5/6	6/7	6/7	6/7
	HERE I AM	MY WORLD	PEOPLE TOGETHER	COMMUNITIES	REGIONS	A YOUNG NATION	UNITED STATES	A NATION GROWS	WORLD	LATIN AMERICA AND CANADA	WORLD REGIONS
Pupil Editions		•	•	•	•	•	•	•	•	•	•
Teacher's Multimedia Editions	•	•	•	•	•	•	•	•			•
Unit Theme Big Books	•	•	•								
Literature Big Books	•	•	•	•							
Theme Big Books Stickers	•	•	•								
Social Studies Anthology	•	•	•	•	•	•	•	•	•	•	•
Anthology Audiocassette	•	•	•	•	•	•	•	•	•	•	•
Language Support Handbook	•	•	•	•	•		•		•		
Classroom Library Trade Books and Teacher's Guide	•	•	•	•	•	•	•	•	•		
Adventure Books	•	•	•	•	•	•	•	•	•	•	•
Reading Social Studies Practice Book		•	•	•	•	•	•	•	•		
Word/Vocabulary Cards	•	•	•	•							
Pupil Edition on Audiocassette		•	•	•	•	•	•	•	•	•	•
Geo Adventures Pads		•	•	•	•	•	•	•	•	•	•
Desk Maps	•	•	•	•	•	•	•	•	•	•	•
Geo Big Books	•	•	•	•							
Outline Maps		•	•	•	•	•	•	•	•	•	•
Floor Maps	•	•	•	•							
Student Atlas	•	•	•	•	•	•	•				•
Posters	•	•	•	•	•		•		•		•
Inflatable Globe	•	•	•	•	•	•	•	•	•	•	•
Map Transparencies		•	•	•	•	•	•	•	•	•	•
Graphic Organizer Transparencies				•	•	•	•	•	•	•	•
Practice Books		•	•	•	•	•	•	•	•	•	•
Project Books	•	•	•	•							
Assessment Books		•	•	•	•	•	•	•	•	•	•
Social Studies Test Readiness	•	•	•	•	•	•	•	•	•	•	•
Videodiscs	•	•	•	•	•	•	•		•		•
Videotapes	•	•	•	•	•	•	•	•	•	•	•
Adventure Time! CD-ROM				•	•	•	•	•		•	•
Internet Projects		•	•	•	•	•	•	•	•	•	•

World

ADVENTURES IN TIME AND PLACE

PROGRAM AUTHORS

Dr. James A. Banks
Professor of Education and Director of the Center for Multicultural Education
University of Washington
Seattle, Washington
Related Publications: *An Introduction to Multicultural Education,* Allyn & Bacon, ©1994; *Multiethnic Education: Theory and Practice,* Allyn & Bacon, © 1981
Honors: Teachers of English to Speakers of Other Languages, Inc. 1998 Presidents' Award; National Association of Multicultural Education for the Handbook of Research on Multicultural Education

Dr. Barry K. Beyer
Professor Emeritus,
Graduate School of Education
George Mason University
Fairfax, Virginia
Related Publications: *Hints for Improving the Teaching Thinking in Our Schools: A Baker's Dozen* (Montclair State College: Institute for Critical Thinking) Resource Publication, Series 1#4, 1988; *Using Inquiry in the Social Studies Guidelines for Teaching,* Cooperative Center for Social Science Education, Ohio University, 1968; Guest editor, "Critical Thinking Revisited," Social Education, April 1985; Co-editor, Values of the American Heritage, 46th (Bicentennial) Yearbook of the National Council for the Social Studies, 1976

Dr. Gloria Contreras
Professor of Education
University of North Texas
Denton, Texas
Related Publications: Editor, *Latin American Culture Studies Handbook* Austin, Texas: The University of Texas Institute for Latin American Studies, 1988
Awards: University of North Texas Student Association Honor Professor Award, 1997; "Professing Women" Award, UNT Women's Studies Roundtable, 1996

Jean Craven
District Coordinator of Curriculum Development
Albuquerque Public Schools

Albuquerque, New Mexico
Related Publications: *Teacher's Manual for Government in the United States,* Macmillan Publishing, ©1984
Advisory Boards: Editorial Review Board, The Social Studies, 1994-1997; National Commission on Social Studies in the Schools, 1989-1990

Dr. Gloria Ladson-Billings
Professor of Education
University of Wisconsin
Madison, Wisconsin
Related Publications: *Dictionary of Multicultural Education,* Oryz Press, 1997; *The Dreamkeepers: Successful Teachers of African American Children,* Jossey Bass, 1994
Awards: Mary Ann Raywid Award for Distinguished Scholarship in Education, Society of Professors of Education, American Educational Research Association, 1997; Outstanding Educator Award Research Focus in Black Education, 1996

Dr. Mary A. McFarland
Instructional Coordinator of Social Studies, K-12, and Director of Staff Development
Parkway School District
Chesterfield, Missouri
Grants: Author of Block Grant Project in Social Studies, 1990; Director of Missouri Committee for the Humanities Project, 1985

Dr. Walter C. Parker
Professor and Program Chair for Social Studies Education
University of Washington
Seattle, Washington
Related Publications: *Social Studies in Elementary Education,* 10th ed. Merill/Prentice-Hall, 1997; editor, *Educating the Democratic Mind,* SUNY Press, 1996; *Renewing the Social Studies Curriculum;* Association for Supervision and Curriculum Development, 1991

NATIONAL
GEOGRAPHIC
SOCIETY
Washington, D.C.

HISTORIANS/SCHOLARS

Daniel Berman
Asian Studies Specialist,
Former Coordinator of Social Studies
Bedford Central Schools
Bedford, New York

Dr. John Bodnar
Professor of History
Indiana University
Bloomington, Indiana
Related Publications: *Remaking America: Public Memory, Commemoration, and Patriotism in the Twentieth Century,* (Pulitzer Prize Nominee) Princeton University Press, 1992
Awards: Teaching Excellence Award, Indiana University, 1997; Florence Chair in American History, Florence, Italy (selected by the Fulbright Commission)

Dr. Roberto Calderón
Assistant Professor
Department of Ethnic Studies
University of California at Riverside
Related Publications: *Mexican Coal Mining Labor in Texas and Coahuila, 1830-1930,* Texas A & M University Press, 1999; "All Over the Map: La Onda Tejana and the Making of Selena" in *Chicanos and Chicanas at the Crossroads: Literary and Cultural Change,* Editors: David Maciel, María Herrera-Sobeck and Isidro Ortiz, University of Arizona Press, 1999

Dr. Sheilah Clarke-Ekong
Professor, Department of Anthropology
University of Missouri, St. Louis
St. Louis, Missouri
Related Publications: "Ghana's Festivals: Celebrations of Life and Loyalty" *Journal of African Activist Association, Vol. 23,* 1997; "Traditional Festivals in the Political Economy," *Journal of Social Development in Africa*

Council on Islamic Education
Fountain Valley, California
Related Publications: *Muslim Holidays; Muslim Women Through the Centuries; The Crusades from Medieval European and Muslim Perspectives; Images of the Orient: 19th-century European Travelers to*

Muslim Lands; Beyond A Thousand and One Nights, A Sampler of Literature from Muslim Civilization; The Emergence of the Renaissance: Cultural Interactions Between Europeans and Muslims

Dr. John L. Esposito
Professor of Religion and
International Affairs
Georgetown University
Washington, D.C.
Related Publications: *The Islamic Threat: Myth or Reality,* Oxford University Press, 1992; Editor-in-Chief, *Encyclopedia of the Modern Islamic World,* 4 vols., Oxford University Press, 1995; *Islam: The Straight Path,* Oxford University Press, 1988

Dr. Darlene Clark Hine
John A. Hannah Professor of History
Michigan State University
East Lansing, Michigan
Related Publications: *A Shining Thread of Hope: The History of Black Women in America,* Broadway Books, 1998; *Speak Truth to Power: Black Professional Class in United States History,* Carlson Publishing, Inc. 1995
Awards: Doctor of Humane Letters, University of Massachusetts, 1998; Avery Citizenship Award, Avery Research Center, College of Charleston, 1997

Paulla Dove Jennings
Project Director
The Rhode Island Indian Council, Inc.
Providence, Rhode Island

Henrietta Mann
Professor of Native American Studies
University of Montana, Missoula
Missoula, Montana
Related Publications: *Cheyenne-Arapaho Education 1871-1982,* University Press of Colorado, 1998; "Native American Women of the Southern Plains" in *The Reader's Companion to U.S. Women's History,* Houghton Mifflin Company, 1998

Dr. Gary A. Manson
Department of Geography

Michigan State University
East Lansing, Michigan
Related Publications: *New Perspectives on Geographic Education: Putting Theory Into Practice,* Kendall-Hunt Publishing Company, 1977 (editor)
Grants: National Science Foundation, 1982

Dr. Juan Mora-Torrés
Professor of Latin American History
University of Texas at San Antonio
San Antonio, Texas
Related Publications: *The Making of the Mexican Border: The State, Capitalism and Society, Nuevo Leon, 1848-1970* (in progress)
Honors: Visiting Scholar, University of Chicago, Center for Latin American Studies, 1999

Dr. Valerie Ooka Pang
Professor, School of Teacher Education
San Diego State University
San Diego, California
Related Publications: Editor, *Struggling To Be Heard: The Unmet Needs of Asian Pacific American Children,* 1998, State University of New York
Awards: Senior Fellow, Annenberg Institute for School Reform, Brown University 1998-2000; Distinguished Scholar Award, American Educational Research Association, 1997

Dr. Joseph Rosenbloom
Professor, Classics Department
Washington University
St. Louis, Missouri
Related Publications: *Conversion to Judaism: From the Biblical Period to the Present,* Hebrew Union College Press, 1978; *The Dead Sea Isaiah Scrolls: A Literary Analysis,* William B. Eerdsmans Publishing Company, 1970

Dr. Joseph B. Rubin
Director of Reading/Reading Council
Leader, Fort Worth Independent
School District
Related Publications: "Language Arts Across the Curriculum," in Language Arts Today, Macmillan Publishing Company,

1989; "What Children Bring to School!"
Texas Reading Newsletter, Texas State Council, International Reading Association, 1985
Awards: Graduate School Teaching Award, University of Arizona, 1981

Dr. Robert Seltzer
Professor of Jewish History
Hunter College
City University of New York
Related Publications: *Jewish People, Jewish Thought: The Jewish Experience in History,* Macmillan, 1980; editor, *Judaism: A People and its History,* Macmillan, 1989

Dr. Peter Stearns
Dean, College of Humanities
and Social Studies
Carnegie Mellon University
Pittsburgh, Pennsylvania
Related Publications: *The Industrial Revolution in World History,* Westview, 1998; *World History: Patterns of Change and Continuity,* HarperCollins, 1998
Awards: 1998 finalist History Book of the Year Award; Robert Doherty Educational Leadership Award, Carnegie Mellon, 1995

Ensuring Success For All Learners
Facilitating a Child's Learning and Understanding of English

by Janice Wu
Student Achievement Specialist, Sacramento City Unified School District

Today, nearly one of every five students in the United States entering school (2.5-3.5 million children per year) knows a language other than English. Nearly half of these students are limited in English-language proficiency. According to demographers, in the near future, language-minority students and those acquiring a second language will compose an even larger proportion of our school-age population.

Many English Language Learners (ELL) come into the classroom with a wealth of prior knowledge and a strong oral language base. But some do not experience success in school. Many students who speak a language other than English face barriers that inhibit their learning. As a result, the role of the teacher as facilitator becomes one of nurturing and building upon what a child already knows.

In accessing the curriculum in **Adventures in Time and Place/Aventuras a través del tiempo**, you need to be skillful in utilizing the text to meet the needs of every individual learner. The instruction you provide your students will facilitate the understanding of the curriculum for English Language Learners. As you structure an environment that builds on students' strengths and English language learning, you will make learning a rewarding and meaningful experience for all your students. The information provided below will help you utilize the many resources available in **Adventures in Time and Place/Aventuras a través del tiempo** so that you can effectively meet the needs of every individual learner.

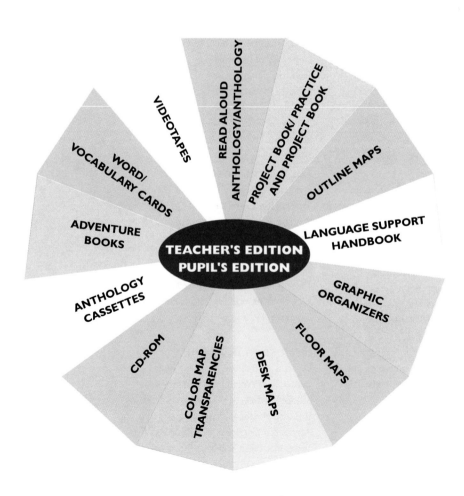

I   TEACHER'S EDITION

The *Adventures in Time and Place/Aventuras a través del tiempo* Teacher's Edition provides a variety of features that complement content lessons by offering teacher support and strategies for English Language Learners. These features include:

- **Specially Designed Academic Instruction in English (SDAIE)/Sheltered Instruction** is presented to you to help engage students in active learning. The focus of SDAIE is to provide curriculum content for all students—especially, but not only, those challenged by less than proficient English skills.

- **Second Language Support** offers strategies to help you customize instruction for the English Language Learner. These strategies are designed to help you contextualize the lessons to make them more understandable and meaningful to students who are acquiring English and to help you present lesson content while providing linguistic and conceptual support.

- **Meeting Individual Needs** allows you to re-teach, extend, and enrich the instruction for every child. Scaffolding the instruction for English Language Learners in this manner will foster positive and successful learning experiences in Social Studies.

- **Reading Strategies and Language Development** provides you with teaching suggestions aimed at understanding and clarifying concepts and vocabulary that could be confusing to the English Language Learner.

- **Extending the Lesson Activities** in Grades 1–2 and **Getting Ready for the Chapter** in Grades 3-6 provide activities in a variety of learning styles, such as auditory, kinesthetic, and visual, to satisfy the learning needs of students who are talented in art, language, and physical activity and who may better understand history/social science concepts connected to their own areas of interest.

- **Visual Literacy** is the integration of text with visuals. This integration is especially helpful to the English Language Learner. The Teacher's Edition offers strategies that provide you with opportunities for the teaching of important history/social science concepts by utilizing photographs, artwork, and maps in *Adventures in Time and Place/Aventuras a través del tiempo.*

- **Ongoing Unit Projects** set the stage for all learners by inviting them to participate in a cooperative setting that encourages language development in a natural environment. These projects also engage English Language Learners in high interest, hands-on experiences.

II   ADVENTURES IN TIME AND PLACE/AVENTURAS A TRAVÉS DEL TIEMPO COMPONENTS

In addition to the *Adventures in Time and Place/ Aventuras a través del tiempo* Teacher's Edition features mentioned above, there are a variety of supplementary program components that provide teacher support and strategies for English Language Learners. A description of these resources, in addition to suggested ELL classroom activities, is listed below:

• ADVENTURE BOOKS (Grades K-6)

Description: Adventure Books are supplementary "easy readers" that provide additional literacy experiences tailored to specific students' needs and interests. The range and simplicity of the stories allows for independent reading related to the Social Studies content. Students will read about special people, places, and events that reflect many people and cultures around the world.

ELL Strategy: Building Comprehension Skills

To encourage independent reading, set up a student reading center with the Adventure Books. Allow English Language Learners to select from the various stories and report on their favorite readers by making posters or charts with illustrations. Students at different levels of language proficiency in English can label and/or write brief descriptions retelling the story.

• ANTHOLOGY CASSETTES (Grades K-6)

Description: Students will be exposed to a variety of literature selections, songs, and poems that are read in an engaging and entertaining style.

ELL Strategy: Facilitate Listening Comprehension in English

Listening to songs and poetry read by others is a powerful way to provide models of fluent and dramatic reading. Set up a "Listening Post" or "Listening Center" for a small group of students. Model the use of the listening area with your class and assign a student monitor who will be in charge of rotating the cassettes as needed.

• CD-ROM (Grades 3-6)

Description: *The Adventure Time!* CD-ROM enables students to travel the world, meet people, and explore places. Students can experience historical events through photographs, maps, movies, charts, and climographs. The *Adventure Time!* CD-ROM program makes geography fun, puts history in context, and motivates children to learn map and globe skills.

ELL Strategy: Paired Reading

With a click of the computer mouse an English Language Learner can see, hear, and take world tours and experience environments from images on a CD-ROM. Pair an English Language Learner with an English-proficient learner and ask them to read the text in each frame together. Partners should take turns reading. At the end of each frame, the listener should relate back the main ideas of the text. Discussions can also include descriptions of sounds and visuals they are experiencing. Encourage students to work together to discuss these responses.

• COLOR MAP TRANSPARENCIES (Grades 1-6)

Description: Map transparencies support a student-centered map program and encourages active, hands-on geography practice. These maps are from Reviewing Geography Skills lessons, Skills Lessons, and the Atlas in the Pupil's Edition.

ELL Strategy: Using Visuals

The use of visuals like map symbols provides important support in building comprehension and establishing the context-rich environment that fosters language acquisition. Using an overhead projector, have students identify the different map symbols on each Map Transparency. Then have them describe the symbols shown on each map.

• DESK MAPS (GRADES 1-6)

Description: Students will gain a greater understanding of their community and the world around them by using Desk Maps of the United States and the world. These maps are useful in teaching map and globe skills in meaningful and concrete ways.

ELL Strategy: Building Geography Skills

Use of the Desk Maps will encourage students to develop their geography skills. Prompt students to work alone or in groups to use lesson content and other maps to search the text for illustrations and information to help them place details on the map, such as mountain ranges, deserts, oceans, etc. Encourage students to use as many details as possible. Pairing English Language Learners with partners that are fluent English speakers encourages mastery of the English language in a non-threatening environment.

• FLOOR MAPS (Grades K-3)

Description: Students can use a floor map as a base for building three-dimensional models of different types of communities or environments. Floor maps can help English Language Learners move from understanding simple, concrete materials to understanding more difficult and abstract concepts.

ELL Strategy: Using Manipulative Materials

Divide students into groups of four to six students. To encourage rich dialogue include students of different levels of English proficiency in each group. Have each group create simple three-dimensional buildings, cars, people, etc. to place on the floor maps in order to create a community. Students should describe the objects that they have created and discuss where they should be placed on the floor map. Encourage students to use geography and map-related terms and concepts to describe their community.

• GRAPHIC ORGANIZERS (Grades 3-6)

Description: Graphic Organizers provide visual tools to help English Language Learners organize the relationships between and among words, concepts, ideas, and events.

ELL Strategy: Organizing Information Using a Visual Tool

Have students organize information about the natural resources of their community. Encourage them to list on the chart some of the resources they have learned about and whether they are renewable or nonrenewable. Have students display and discuss their completed charts in class.

• LANGUAGE SUPPORT HANDBOOK (Grades K-6)

Description: In working with the English Language Learner it is important to recognize that each child enters the classroom with different levels of oral language proficiency. This means that the production of language may be receptive (absorbing the language but not producing verbally) or productive (verbally producing some English words or phrases). To help you have a better understanding of the various stages of second language acquisition, the Language Support Handbook lists the stages of language production with student behaviors and effective teaching strategies.

ELL Strategy: Shared Reading

It is important for English Language Learners to hear English read by a fluent English speaker. A useful strategy is to read aloud while students are able to read and follow along silently with their own text copies. Ask students to take notes as important concepts are discussed. They can then work with others to write a brief summary of the most important information they have learned.

• OUTLINE MAPS (GRADES 1-6)

Description: Outline Maps offer students the opportunity to improve their basic map skills, such as understanding hemispheres, using cardinal and intermediate directions, and identifying map keys and symbols.

ELL Strategy: Understanding Personal Perspectives

Have students use Outline Maps to locate their community in relation to their state and country. Then have them use the World Map to locate their community in relation to the country that they, or their parents or friends, may have come from. By understanding different geographic perspectives, English Language Learners can gain understanding and confidence in learning about different cultures and places.

• PROJECT BOOK (Grades K-3)
PRACTICE AND PROJECT BOOK (Grades 4-6)

Description: Your students will be actively involved in constructing a variety of projects related to the Social Studies content in their Pupil's Edition. These activities include tracing family ties, connecting their home to their communities, and understanding important dates and events relevant to them.

ELL Strategy: Facilitating Cooperative Learning and Interaction

Set aside an area in the classroom for a work station or center called "Our Projects." This work station should have ample working room for a group of four or five students to design and create projects listed in the Project Book. Projects can then be displayed in this area, as well as in other areas of the classroom. This activity encourages friendly dialogue and discussions among students and encourages positive language learning. Students of all language levels of proficiency will benefit.

• READ ALOUD ANTHOLOGY (Grades K-3)
ANTHOLOGY (Grades 4-6)

Description: Anthologies are rich resources filled with literature, stories, songs, poems, folktales, and more. They are useful in supporting lesson content and themes taught in the Pupil's Edition.

ELL Strategy: Paired Reading

Pair each English Language Learner with a fluent English partner. Tell each pair to choose a character from an Anthology selection in whose voice they will speak or write. Ask them to search the text and illustrations for pertinent information, then have them introduce themselves to their partners and talk about their experiences. Prompt them to expand their stories by suggesting a series of basic questions to which they can respond: *What is your name? Where do you live? What has been happening around you? What do you think will happen next?*

• VIDEOTAPES (Grades K-6)

Description: Videotapes of rich and relevant content covering topics such as communities and geographic location are available at every grade level. These short video presentations provide the teacher and students with another means of "experiencing" events in history.

ELL Strategy: Previewing/Reviewing

A preview/review strategy will facilitate students' understanding of the curriculum. Identify significant concepts and vocabulary that will be used in the video and teach them to students. After watching the video, check student comprehension by asking questions related to the initial concepts and vocabulary presented during the preview lesson. This activity will help reinforce concepts, build vocabulary, and expand students' knowledge.

• WORD/VOCABULARY Cards (Grades K-3)

Description: Word/Vocabulary cards are used to help teach challenging vocabulary words or phrases that appear in the Social Studies Pupil's Edition. Each word or phrase appears on one side of a card. A definition of the word or phrase appears on the other side of the card.

ELL Strategy: Building Vocabulary Skills

Select five important words from the appropriate Pupil's Edition lessons that might be difficult for the English Language Learner to comprehend. Write these words on the chalkboard. Then hand out five blank index cards to each student. Next, use gestures, props, illustrations, etc. to act out the meaning of the word for the students. Students should then write the word you are describing on their index cards. On the backs of the cards they should draw pictures or illustrations to help them remember the meaning of the word. Repeat this process for all five words. Students can learn the definitions of these words by using their index cards as flashcards.

III TIPS FOR CREATING AN EFFECTIVE LEARNING ENVIRONMENT FOR THE ENGLISH LANGUAGE LEARNER

School experiences are long-lasting and set the stage for future performance. By creating a positive, sensitive, and interactive learning environment, you can make a critical difference in preparing English Language Learners for the future. Remember that success for these students means more than acquiring good grades and high test scores. It also means having a positive image of themselves and confidence in their ability to embrace a second language and a new culture. Following is a list of useful tips for helping you create an effective learning environment for the English Language Learner.

• Praise Students' Efforts Regularly

Accept the "half rights" and "yes" and "no" responses from your English Language Learners. A nod of the head in agreement or a simple "yes" response from you will let your students know that they are on the right track.

• Accelerate Students' Learning

Maintaining high expectations for all English Language Learners will accelerate learning. Conveying the belief that all students have the ability and desire to succeed is your responsibility. Provide multiple opportunities for students to "take charge" and be responsible for the work that they produce.

• Encourage Students To Preview Or "Picture Walk"

Students will be eager and excited to learn about the lesson when they are allowed to explore and select information (e.g. picture, caption, word or phrase) that piques their interest. Direct students to share their findings in English or their primary language with a partner or partners. Sampling a lesson in this manner will lower the student's affective filter and make for a more comfortable and positive experience.

• Minimize Structural Error Correction

As students participate in class discussions, modeling appropriate structural responses can be done in a manner that does not directly bring attention to the error. For example, student states, "My country Central America. She country North America." Teacher may respond by modeling, "Yes, your country is in Central America," and "her [for "she"] country is in North America."

• Allow For Appropriate "Wait Time"

English Language Learners need "wait time" to process the information being taught. Give students sufficient time for a response. Keep in mind that responses will vary depending on the students' levels of oral language proficiency. A simple facial expression, physical gesture or short phrase may serve as a response.

• Use A Total Physical Response Approach

Use gestures and facial expressions (as dramatic as you need to be) to assist students in comprehending what is being conveyed. Allow students to respond in the same manner.

• Practice The 3 R's Of Instruction

Revisit, Review, and Repeat the material being taught as much as possible in different ways. Approaching the instruction from a different perspective provides the student with another opportunity to acquire the content being taught. When Social Studies content is familiar it allows students to be freed up to attend to new and challenging content.

• Speak Naturally

Students benefit greatly from having the teacher explain challenging content in clear and simplified speech. Clear enunciation and brief pauses assist the English Language Learner in hearing distinct pronunciation of vocabulary.

• Summarize Content Taught Frequently

For English Language Learners it is important to summarize the content at point of use. Briefly stating in simple sentences the content after one, two, or three paragraphs is a strategy that benefits all students by allowing them to reflect on what they have just read and enables you to check for understanding.

• Sheltered English Strategies

In order to make the content matter meaningful to students, it is important to provide many examples of the concepts being taught. Simplifying the language when presenting a concept is crucial, as is providing visuals (video clip, semantic web, or graphic organizer) to demonstrate the concept. For example, when teaching the concept of "community," rather than just defining the term, you might encourage students to draw, take photographs, or cut clippings from magazines or newspapers to construct a collage or mural of what they perceive as a community.

• Allow Students to Speak Their Native Languages

Encourage students to communicate with their peers who are speakers of the same language. Allow students to write in their primary language and seek others who are literate in that language to translate and provide feedback. Provide primary language resources such as dictionaries, storybooks, videos, audiocassettes, and computer software. Having access to resources that they can read and use independently builds students' confidence in learning.

• Word Walls to Build Vocabulary

A word wall is a designated wall in the classroom that displays a collection of words. Social Studies word walls provide a place to display important vocabulary words with illustrations to clarify definitions and concepts. The word wall can include important words from the curriculum as well as often-used words and/or commonly misspelled words that students can access and use when they write. Students should be encouraged to contribute to the "Social Studies Word Wall" whenever they feel that there are important words that they want clarified.

• Provide Opportunities for Students to Work Together

English Language Learners benefit from working in cooperative learning groups. Working in mixed ability groups, English Language Learners have the opportunity to use language for real communication as they solve problems assigned by the teacher. As English Language Learners work together they learn academic language while investigating new topics or exploring content areas.

• Encourage Classroom Participation

Give students opportunities to talk and interact. Also encourage them to express ideas, feelings, and opinions. Students' self-esteem and motivation are enhanced when teachers elicit their experiences in classroom discussions and validate what they have to say.

• Cross-Age Tutoring and Peer Tutoring

Research indicates that learning is enhanced both for those who are tutored and for the tutors themselves. English Language Learners working one-on-one with tutors develop listening, communication, and problem-solving skills. The tutor develops personal responsibility and self-esteem as he or she works to ensure the success of another child. The tutor becomes a model of success. Pairing intermediate grade students with primary grade students makes for positive and lasting friendships.

By utilizing the resources in the *Adventures in Time and Place/Aventuras a través del tiempo,* the instruction you provide will facilitate learning for English Language Learners. As you structure an environment that builds on students' strengths and English Language Learning, you will make the classroom experience rewarding and meaningful for all your students.

TEACHER'S *MULTIMEDIA* EDITION

VOLUME **2**

World

ADVENTURES IN TIME AND PLACE

James A. Banks

Barry K. Beyer

Gloria Contreras

Jean Craven

Gloria Ladson-Billings

Mary A. McFarland

Walter C. Parker

NATIONAL GEOGRAPHIC SOCIETY

THIS IMAGE WAS CARVED ON THE THRONE OF TUTANKHAMUN, WHO RULED ANCIENT EGYPT MORE THAN 3,000 YEARS AGO. THIS IS ONE OF THE MANY IMAGES THAT HELP TELL THE STORY OF OUR WORLD'S HISTORY.

THE PRINCETON REVIEW

McGraw-Hill School Division

New York   Farmington

PPROGRAM AUTHORS

Dr. James A. Banks
Professor of Education and
  Director of the Center for
  Multicultural Education
University of Washington
Seattle, Washington

Dr. Barry K. Beyer
Professor Emeritus, Graduate
  School of Education
George Mason University
Fairfax, Virginia

Dr. Gloria Contreras
Professor of Education
University of North Texas
Denton, Texas

Jean Craven
District Coordinator of
  Curriculum Development
Albuquerque Public Schools
Albuquerque, New Mexico

Dr. Gloria Ladson-Billings
Professor of Education
University of Wisconsin
Madison, Wisconsin

Dr. Mary A. McFarland
Instructional Coordinator of
  Social Studies, K–12, and
  Director of Staff Development
Parkway School District
Chesterfield, Missouri

Dr. Walter C. Parker
Professor and Program Chair for
  Social Studies Education
University of Washington
Seattle, Washington

NATIONAL
GEOGRAPHIC
SOCIETY
Washington, D.C.

PROGRAM CONSULTANTS

Daniel Berman
Asian Studies Specialist
Coordinator of Social Studies
Bedford Central Schools
Bedford, New York

Dr. Khalid Y. Blankinship
Affiliated Scholar, Council on Islamic
  Education
Fountain Valley, California
Assistant Professor of Religion
Temple University
Philadelphia, Pennsylvania

Dr. John Bodnar
Professor of History
Indiana University
Bloomington, Indiana

Dr. Roberto R. Calderón
Department of Ethnic Studies
University of California at Riverside
Riverside, California

Dr. Sheilah Clarke-Ekong
Asst. Professor, Department of
  Anthropology and Research Associate,
  Center for International Studies
University of Missouri, St. Louis
St. Louis, Missouri

Dr. John L. Esposito
Professor of Religion and International
  Affairs
Georgetown University
Washington, D.C.

Dr. Darlene Clark Hine
John A. Hannah Professor of History
Michigan State University
East Lansing, Michigan

Paulla Dove Jennings
Project Director
The Rhode Island Indian Council, Inc.
Providence, Rhode Island

Dr. Henrietta Mann
Professor of Native American Studies
University of Montana, Missoula
Missoula, Montana

Dr. Gary Manson
Professor, Department of Geography
Michigan State University
East Lansing, Michigan

Dr. Juan Mora-Torrés
Professor of Latin American History
University of Texas at San Antonio
San Antonio, Texas

Dr. Valerie Ooka Pang
Professor, School of Teacher Education
San Diego State University
San Diego, California

Dr. Joseph R. Rosenbloom
Professor, Classics Department
Washington University
St. Louis, Missouri

Dr. Joseph B. Rubin
Director of Reading
Fort Worth Independent School District
Fort Worth, Texas

Dr. Robert M. Seltzer
Professor of Jewish History
Hunter College of The City University
  of New York
New York, New York

Dr. Peter N. Stearns
Dean, College of Humanities and
  Social Studies
Carnegie Mellon University
Pittsburgh, Pennsylvania

CONSULTING AUTHORS

Dr. James Flood
Professor of Teacher Education,
  Reading and Language Development
San Diego State University
San Diego, California

Dr. Diane Lapp
Professor of Teacher Education,
  Reading and Language Development
San Diego State University
San Diego, California

GGRADE-LEVEL CONSULTANTS

Dianne C. Baker
Sixth Grade Teacher
Ingleside Middle School
Phoenix, Arizona

Maureen F. Barber
Sixth and Seventh Grade
  Social Studies Teacher
Center Based Gifted Program
Manchester Middle School
Chesterfield, Virginia

David H. Delgado
Sixth Grade Social Studies Teacher
Rogers Middle School
San Antonio, Texas

Martha Doster
Sixth Grade Teacher
Northwest Rankin Attendance Center
Brandon, Mississippi

Joyce Garbe Orland
Sixth–Eighth Grade Teacher and Chair-
  person, Social Studies Department
Pershing School
Berwyn, Illinois

CONTRIBUTING WRITERS

Ruth Akamine Wassynger
Winston-Salem, North Carolina

Spencer Finch
Brooklyn, New York

Linda Scher
Raleigh, North Carolina

CONSULTANTS FOR TEST PREPARATION

THE
PRINCETON
REVIEW
The Princeton Review is not affiliated
with Princeton University or ETS.

Acknowledgments

The publisher gratefully acknowledges permission to reprint the following copyrighted material:

From **Lost Civilizations: Sumer: Cities of Eden** by the editors of Time-Life Books. Copyright 1993 Time-Life Books, Inc. Reprinted by permission.
From **Tropical Rainforests** by Arnold Newman. Text copyright 1990 Arnold Newman. Reprinted with permission of Facts On File, Inc., New York.
From **The Iliad of Homer: The Wrath of Achilles**, translated by I.A. Richards, Translation copyright 1950 by W.W. Norton & Company, Inc.,
  renewed 1978 by I.A. Richards. Reprinted with permission of W.W. Norton & Company, Inc.
Excerpts from **Corpus of Early Arabic Sources for West African History.** Copyright University of Ghana, International Academic Union,
  Cambridge University Press 1981. Reprinted with the permission of Cambridge University Press.

(continued on page R79)

McGraw-Hill School Division

A Division of The McGraw-Hill Companies

McGraw-Hill School Division
Two Penn Plaza
New York, New York 10121

Printed in the United States of America

ISBN 0-02-149138-0

1 2 3 4 5 6 7 8 9 027/046 04 03 02 01 00

Teacher's Multimedia Edition
Copyright © 2001, 2000, 1999 McGraw-Hill School Division, a Division of the Educational and Professional Publishing
Group of The McGraw-Hill Companies, Inc.

ISBN 0-02-149149-6

2 3 4 5 6 7 8 9 073/046 03 02 01 00

Handbook for Reading Social Studies

One of the most important things you will do in your study of Social Studies this year is read this textbook. In order to understand important facts and ideas in any subject area—Social Studies, or Science, or even Mathematics—it is necessary to read in a certain way. This Reading Handbook will show you a few strategies for effectively reading social studies.

Lesson Overview

Actual passages from the student text are used to demonstrate the strategy of identifying main idea and details.

Lesson Objectives

★ Identify the main idea of passages.

★ Recognize the supporting details.

1 PREPARE

MOTIVATE Ask students:

● *What parts of a selection do you focus on to determine what it is about?*

● *How do you decide which details of a passage are important?*

SET PURPOSE Read the title of the lesson to students. Ask them what they think it means. Explain that they will be finding the main idea and supporting details in passages from their textbooks.

2 TEACH

Identifying MAIN IDEA and SUPPORTING DETAILS Guide students to see that the main idea is the most important idea of the paragraph or selection. Explain that supporting details are finer points that provide additional information about the main idea.

Read the sample paragraph aloud. Point out that it is from the lesson titled "Geography of Ancient Greece" in Chapter 8. Using the bubble callouts, guide students to state the main idea of the paragraph and the details that support it.

Main Idea and Supporting Details

As you read, remember to look for the **main idea** and **supporting details**. The main idea is what a paragraph or section is mostly about. The details support or expand the main idea. Keeping track of the main idea and supporting details will help you remember what you read.

■ The first sentence or two of a paragraph often—but not always—contains the main idea.

■ Use the titles and subheads as a guide in identifying the main idea.

■ Make an outline of the main idea and supporting details of a lesson to help you review.

To Find the Main Idea

Ask yourself:

• What is this paragraph or section mostly about?

To Find the Supporting Details

Ask yourself:

• What words give more information about the main idea?

In your book you will read about the agriculture and climate of Greece. Climate is the pattern of weather in a place over many years. Read this paragraph to find the main idea and supporting details.

> Besides having little fertile land, Greece has a climate that presents special challenges for farmers. Summers are hot and dry. Winters can be wet and fiercely windy. Fields can become parched in the summer but soaked with rain in the winter.
>
> *from page 194*

The main idea is how climate affects farming in Greece.

The supporting details include information about each season.

USING A GRAPHIC ORGANIZER

Draw a main idea and details supporting graphic organizer like the one below to help students identify main idea and details.

Main Idea	Climate affects farming in Greece.	
Details	hot, dry summers	wet, windy winters

READING SOCIAL STUDIES

TRY IT!

Read this paragraph about farming in ancient Greece. Copy and complete the main idea and supporting details chart below.

Ancient Greek farmers raised crops and animals that were well suited to this environment. They grew some wheat and barley to make bread, which was important to the Greek diet. Olives and grapes became Greece's other major crops. Both grew well in rocky and hilly areas. Shrubs on Greece's many hills and mountains provided food for herds of sheep, goats, and cattle.

from page 194

Main Idea
Ancient Greek farmers raised crops and animals suited to the environment.

Details

Olives and grapes grew well in rocky, hilly areas.

Sheep, goats, and cattle ate shrubs on hills and mountains.

• What steps did you take to find the main idea and details?

Practice Activities

❶ **READ** Read the first paragraph under the heading "A New Government" on page 237. Copy the chart above and record the main idea and supporting details of this paragraph.

❷ **WRITE** Write a paragraph describing one aspect of your local environment. Be sure to use a main idea sentence and supporting details.

Keep in Mind...

For more help in reading social studies, try these strategies:

☑ **Reread**
Review each sentence carefully. Make sure you understand what each sentence means before you read further.

☑ **Look up unknown words**
Use a dictionary or the glossary in your book to find the meaning of any unfamiliar words or terms.

☑ **Form a mental picture**
As you read, think about what your reading would look like.

EXTENDING BEYOND THE TEXTBOOK

Direct students to a local newspaper article to apply their understanding of main idea and details. Note that:

• the title will clearly state the topic of the article;

• the main idea will almost always be contained in the first paragraph;

• the supporting details follow the main idea.

TRY IT!

Ask students to silently read the selection on this page. Point out that this paragraph is also from their textbook. Have them copy and complete the graphic organizer to identify the main idea and details.

Direct students to the *Tip!* section on the preceding page to help them complete the main idea and details diagram.

• **What steps did you take to find the main idea in this paragraph?**

Encourage students to explain the method they used to find the main idea and supporting details.

⭐ 3 CLOSE

Discuss the importance of identifying the main idea and details when reading social studies. Point out that this strategy can help them organize, understand, and remember important events and ideas.

Direct students to the *Keep in Mind...* tab for general help in reading social studies.

Practice Activities

❶ **READ** Have students read the first paragraph under the heading "A New Government" on page 237 in their textbook and identify the main idea and details in a graphic organizer.
Main Idea: Julius Caesar made important changes. **Details:** He created a new calendar, gave land to soldiers, and grain to poor citizens, increased the number of senators, and granted citizenship to people not born in Rome.

Additional selections for practicing this skill include:

• page 84, first paragraph under *The Big Picture*

• page 54, first paragraph under "A New Kind Of Home"

❷ **WRITE** Have students apply what they have learned about main idea and details to their own writing.

The Reading Social Studies Practice Book provides students with additional practice in identifying main ideas and supporting details.

Lesson Overview

Actual passages from the student text are used to demonstrate the strategy of using context clues.

Lesson Objectives

★ Use context clues to find the meaning of new or unfamiliar words.

★ State the meaning of unfamiliar terms.

1 PREPARE

MOTIVATE Ask students:

● *What do you do when you come to a word or term that is unfamiliar in a selection?*

● *Why is it important to understand unfamiliar words and terms in social studies?*

SET PURPOSE Read the title of the lesson to students. Ask them what they think context clues means. Explain that as they read the following selections they will use clues from other words and phrases in the selection to help them figure out the meanings of unfamiliar words or terms.

2 TEACH

Using CONTEXT CLUES Explain that context clues are clues they can find in the text or words that they read. These context clues will help them understand unfamiliar words. Some context clues describe the purpose or effects of an unfamiliar term. Others are examples, descriptions, definitions, synonyms in parentheses, or antonyms.

Read the sample paragraph aloud. Point out that it is from the lesson titled "Geography of Arabia" in Chapter 10. Using the bubble call-outs, guide students to identify context clues for the word *cloudburst.* Then have volunteers tell what they think *cloudbursts* means based on the clues.

Context Clues

As you read a sentence or paragraph in your book, you may find a word or term that you do not know. One way to find the meaning of a new word is to look for **context clues.** Context clues are the words and sentences around the unfamiliar term. Using context clues helps you become a better reader.

To Use Context Clues

Ask yourself:

● **What word is unfamiliar to me?**

● **What might the word mean?**

● **What other words, phrases, and sentences help me figure out the meaning of the new word?**

● **What information do these other words, phrases, and sentences provide?**

In your book you will read about the climate of Arabia. Read the following paragraph and see how context clues can help you learn the meaning of the word *cloudbursts.*

TIP!

■ Have you heard this word before? How was it used?

■ Write down the context clues you used to find the meaning of the new word.

■ Use the new word in a sentence of your own to help you remember it.

> Some of Arabia's deserts contain stone cliffs. Others have huge hills of sand. The world's largest continuous body of sand is on the Arabian peninsula. This region, called the Empty Quarter, is uninhabitable. Some parts have no rain for 10 years or more. Other parts enjoy winter cloudbursts that allow desert plants to grow. All of Arabia's deserts have a lack of water and oven-like summer heat.
>
> from page 263

Clue:
Some parts don't have rain for 10 years.

Word:
cloudbursts

Clue:
Cloudbursts allow desert plants to grow.

HANDBOOK 4

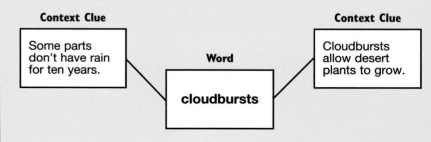

USING A GRAPHIC ORGANIZER

Draw a context clues graphic organizer like the one below to help students identify context clues.

Context Clue

Some parts don't have rain for ten years.

Word

cloudbursts

Context Clue

Cloudbursts allow desert plants to grow.

READING SOCIAL STUDIES

TRY IT!

Read this paragraph from your book. Copy and complete the chart below to list context clues for the term *treaty*.

The world had come dangerously close to a nuclear war. In the following year, 1963, the two superpowers signed a treaty banning most kinds of nuclear weapons testing. World leaders hoped that the treaty would reduce the chance that nuclear weapons would ever be used in war.

from page 561

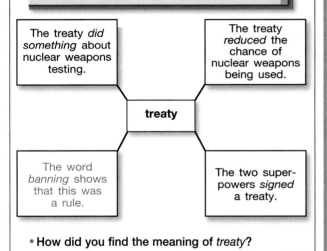

The treaty *did something* about nuclear weapons testing.

The treaty *reduced* the chance of nuclear weapons being used.

treaty

The word *banning* shows that this was a rule.

The two superpowers *signed* a treaty.

• **How did you find the meaning of *treaty*?**

Practice Activities

1 **READ** Read the section of your book titled "Cultural Expansion" on page 404 of your book. Tell how you understood the word *expeditions*.

2 **WRITE** Write a short paragraph about an expedition you have made.

Keep in Mind...

For more help in reading social studies, try these strategies:

☑ **Reread**
Review each sentence carefully. Make sure you understand what each sentence means before you read further.

☑ **Form the big picture**
As you read, think about the topic and the most important information in each paragraph section.

☑ **Make predictions**
As you read, think about what might happen next in your reading.

HANDBOOK 5

TRY IT!

Ask students to silently read the selection on this page. Point out that this paragraph is also from their textbook. Have them copy and complete the graphic organizer to identify context clues for the meaning of *treaty*. Have students then write their own definition of *treaty*.

Direct students to the *Tip!* section on the preceding page to help them complete the context clues diagram.

• **How did you find the meaning of *treaty*?**

Encourage students to explain how they used the context clues to determine the meaning.

3 CLOSE

Discuss the importance of using context clues when reading social studies. Point out that if students come across a term they do not understand, and do not correctly use context clues, they may miscomprehend the entire selection.

Direct students to the *Keep in Mind...* tab for general help in reading social studies.

Practice Activities

1 **READ** Read the section titled "Cultural Expansion" on page 404. Have students use context clues to tell the meaning of the word *expeditions*. **Word: expeditions Context Clues:** Large ships were built; trading

Additional selections for practicing this skill include:

● pages 264-265, second paragraph under "Trade Across Desert and Sea." Use context clues to tell the meaning of *journeyed*.

● page 293, the first paragraph under "The Olmec." Use context clues to tell the meaning of *flourished*.

2 **WRITE** Have students use what they have learned about context clues in their own writing.

The Reading Social Studies Practice Book provides students with additional practice in using context clues.

EXTENDING BEYOND THE TEXTBOOK

Have students use context clues to identify the meaning of an unfamiliar word or term in their science textbooks or in a science article. Have them do the following:

● write the term;

● list the clues;

● write the meaning of the term in their own words;

● check the dictionary to see if they are correct.

Lesson Overview

Actual passages from the student text are used to demonstrate the strategy of sequencing.

Lesson Objectives

★ Recognize clue words that show the sequence of events.

★ List important events in sequential order.

★ 1 PREPARE

MOTIVATE Ask students:

● *What do you do to determine the order of important events in social studies?*

● *Why is it important to understand the time order of events?*

SET PURPOSE Read the title of the lesson to students. Ask them what they think it means. Explain that they will read passages from their books to learn how to understand the sequence or order of events.

★ 2 TEACH

SEQUENCING Guide students to understand that sequencing means to correctly order events or steps in a process. Point out that not all selections or passages present events in the actual order in which they occurred. Students need to use clue words and dates to understand time relationship among different events.

Read the sample paragraph aloud. Point out that it is from the lesson titled "Iceman of the Alps" in Chapter 2. Using the bubble call-outs, guide students to list in order the steps the archaeologists had to follow. Direct students' attention to clue words in the passage such as *first* and *next*.

Sequencing

As you read, look for the order in which things happen. **Sequencing** events is listing them in the order in which they happen. Sequencing events helps you understand and remember what you read.

■ Look for dates—years, months, or centuries—that tell when events happened.

■ Look for words like *first, next, then, followed, finally, last, before,* and *later* to identify the order of events.

■ Use chapter time lines to help you remember the sequence of events.

To Use Sequencing
Ask yourself:

● Which event happened first?

● Which event happened next?

● Which order of events makes sense?

Read the following paragraph about archaeologists. Archaeologists study *artifacts*, or objects left by past groups of people. Pay attention to the sequence of events.

> The archaeologists' first task was to make a detailed map of the location. They also took photographs showing where each artifact was found. Next, they used steam blowers and even hair dryers to melt snow and ice around the artifacts. The melted water was filtered three times. Archaeologists wanted to make sure that even the tiniest specks of evidence were not lost.
>
> *from page 34*

First Event:
Make a map.

Second Event:
Take photographs.

Third Eve
Melt sn
and ice

Fourth Event:
Filter the melted water.

USING A GRAPHIC ORGANIZER

Draw a sequencing graphic organizer like the one below to help students sequence events.

First Event: Make a map.

Second Event: Take photographs.

Third Event: Melt snow and ice.

Fourth Event: Filter the melted water.

TRY IT!

Read this paragraph from your book about the Mogul Empire. Copy and complete the chart below to record the sequence of events.

> The Moguls were originally from Central Asia and may have been related to the Turks. In 1526 Moguls invaded the Indus plain. Within three years the Moguls controlled much of northern India . . . India's Mogul Empire would grow even bigger during its 235-year rule. At one time it would cover most of the Indian subcontinent. Much of that growth would take place under Akbar, the ruler whose name meant "Great" in Arabic.
>
> *from page 393*

1526 Moguls invaded Indus plain

↓

1529 they controlled northern India

↓

grew bigger during 235-year rule

- What steps did you take to determine the sequence of events?

Practice Activities

1 READ Read the second and third paragraphs under "Hatshepsut's Trading Journey" on page 87 of your book. List the key events in sequence.

2 WRITE Write what steps you take to prepare for a vacation. Include the words *first, then, next,* and *finally.*

Keep in Mind...

For more help in reading social studies, try these strategies:

☑ **Look up unknown words**
Use a dictionary or the glossary in your book to find the meanings of any words you do not know.

☑ **Reread**
Review each sentence carefully. Make sure you understand what each sentence means before you read further.

☑ **Summarize**
In your own words, briefly describe what your reading is about. Look for topic sentences that contain the main ideas.

HANDBOOK 7

EXTENDING BEYOND THE TEXTBOOK

Have students read the directions to a lab experiment in science and list the steps in correct sequence. Encourage them to use time words such as *first, next,* and *last* in their list.

TRY IT!

Ask students to silently read the selection on this page. Point out that this paragraph is also from their textbook. Have them copy and complete a graphic organizer to identify the sequence of events.

Direct students who are having difficulty completing the sequence diagram to the *Tip!* section on the preceding page.

- **What steps did you take to determine the sequence of events?**

Encourage students to explain how they identified the correct sequence.

3 CLOSE

Discuss the importance of understanding the sequence of events. Point out that this strategy can help students understand why certain events took place. Some events are the result of other events.

Direct students to the *Keep in Mind...* tab for help in reading social studies.

Practice Activities

1 READ Have students read the second and third paragraphs under "Hatshepsut's Trading Journey" on page 87. Have them list the events in time order.

Sequencing: First Event: Loaded cargo. **Second Event:** Sailed to Punt. **Third Event:** Displayed and traded goods. **Fourth Event:** Returned with several Punt leaders.

Additional selections for practicing this skill include:

- page 33, three paragraphs under "A Mystery in the Ice." Have students list in sequence the major events of the discovery of the Iceman.
- pages 98-99, last two paragraphs under "Children in Egypt." Have students list, in sequence, the steps of the work process

2 WRITE Have students apply what they have learned about sequence to their own writing.

The Reading Social Studies Practice Book provides students with additional practice in sequencing.

Lesson Overview
Actual passages from the student text are used to demonstrate the strategy of making predictions.

Lesson Objective
★ Combine background knowledge and what has been read to make predictions about what comes next.

1 PREPARE

MOTIVATE Ask students:

● *As you read, how do you get an idea of what might happen next?*

● *Besides what you learn from reading the passage, what other knowledge can you use to make predictions?*

SET PURPOSE Discuss the title of this lesson with students. Ask them what they think it means. Explain that they will be reading passages from their textbooks to make predictions about what happens next.

2 TEACH

MAKE PREDICTIONS Guide students to understand that they can identify clues in a passage that will help them predict what might happen next. Their own background knowledge can also help them make predictions.

Read aloud the sample paragraph. Point out that it is from the lesson titled "Early People of North America." Using the bubble call-outs, guide students to predict what will happen next.

Make Predictions

As you read a paragraph or section in your book, think about what might come next. What you think will happen is your **prediction.** A prediction does not have a correct or incorrect answer. Making predictions helps you to carefully consider what you are reading.

TIP!

■ Think about other things you know that will help you make an "educated guess."

■ Test your prediction: read further to see if you were correct.

■ Revise your prediction: read further to see if more information changes your prediction.

To Make a Prediction
Ask yourself:

● **What happened in this paragraph or section?**

● **What prior knowledge do I have about the events in the text?**

● **What similar situations do I know of?**

● **What do I think might happen next?**

The lessons in this book begin with a Read Aloud. These sections are sometimes poems or quotations that give you an idea of the lesson subject. Read this Read Aloud to make a prediction about the following lesson.

Text Information:
The Ojibwa moved each season. They used the resources in different environments.

Background Information:
I know that European settlers changed Native Americans' way of life.

In the summer the Ojibwa lived by the waters of Lake Superior. When summer changed to autumn, they moved to the marshes where wild rice grew. They left the marshes before the heavy snows fell, living now near the herds that could be hunted. In spring sap flowed in the maple trees, and the Ojibwa came to collect it.

Like many of the peoples of North America, the Ojibwa moved their villages each season. This way of living allowed them to use many of the resources of their environment.

from page 440

Prediction:
The Ojibwa way o life will be chang because of the arr of European settlers.

HANDBOOK 8

USING A GRAPHIC ORGANIZER

Draw a make predictions graphic organizer like the one below to help students make predictions.

Text Information

The Ojibwa moved each season. They used the resources in different environments.

Background Information

I know that European settlers changed Native Americans' way of life.

My Prediction

The Ojibwa way of life will be changed because of the arrival of European settlers.

TRY IT!

Read this paragraph about a struggle for independence. On a separate sheet of paper, copy and complete the prediction chart below.

> "The force generated by nonviolence is infinitely greater than the force of all the arms invented by man's ingenuity."
>
> Mohandas Gandhi wrote these words during a period when Britain ruled his nation, India. His words describe a way of working toward independence without fighting battles that would harm and kill people. For many years Gandhi led the people of India in a largely nonviolent struggle against Britain.
>
> *from page 580*

Text Information

Gandhi said nonviolence was stronger than weapons.

Background Information

India is now an independent nation.

My Prediction

The nonviolent struggle will make the British leave India.

• On what did you base your prediction?

Practice Activities

1 **READ** Read the paragraphs under the title "Working for Change" on page 608 of your book. Predict whether the sanctions will affect apartheid.

2 **WRITE** Write a short paragraph that predicts what high school might be like. Interview someone in high school to test your prediction.

Keep in Mind...

For more help in reading social studies, try these strategies:

☑ **Sequencing**
As you read, think about the order in which things happened.

☑ **Form the big picture**
As you read, find the most important information about the topic in the paragraph or section.

☑ **Relate to personal experience**
Think about how what you are reading about relates to your own life.

HANDBOOK 9

EXTENDING BEYOND THE TEXTBOOK

• Have students predict what will happen on next week's episode of their favorite television show. Ask them to write their prediction, save it and record how accurate their predictions were after they watch the show next week.
• Ask students to write an idea for a sequel to a movie they enjoyed.
• On what parts of the movie did they base their predictions?

TRY IT!

Ask students to read the selection on this page. Remind them that the paragraph is also in their textbook. Have them copy and complete the graphic organizer to make predictions.

Encourage students to refer to the *Tip!* section on the preceding page if they are unsure of how to complete the make predictions graphic organizer.

● **On what did you base your prediction?**

Invite students to discuss how they made their predictions.

3 CLOSE

Discuss with students the importance of being able to make predictions when reading social studies. Explain that when they make predictions as they read, they pay more attention to details and will remember more.

Direct students to the *Keep in Mind...* tab for general help in reading social studies.

Practice Activities

1 **READ** Have students test their prediction by reading *The Big Picture* on page 580.

Text Information: In the 1980's countries set up sanctions against the South African government because of its apartheid laws. **Background Information:** I know South Africa has taken steps toward integration. **My prediction:** Apartheid laws are abolished and sanctions are dropped.

Additional selections for practicing this skill include:

● page 508, section *Read Aloud*
● page 492, section *Read Aloud*

2 **WRITE** Have students apply what they have learned about making predictions to their own writing.

The Reading Social Studies Practice Book provides students with additional practice in making predictions.

Lesson Overview

Actual passages from the student text are used to demonstrate the compare and contrast strategy.

Lesson Objective

★ Identify similarities and differences in order to compare and contrast elements in a text.

1 PREPARE

MOTIVATE Ask students:

- *As you read, how can you determine how things are similar?*
- *How can you determine how things are different?*

SET PURPOSE Discuss the title of this lesson with students. Ask them what they think it means. Explain that they will be reading actual passages from their textbooks in order to compare and contrast people, things, or events.

2 TEACH

Using COMPARE and CONTRAST

Guide students to understand that they can compare things to see how they are alike and contrast things to see how they are different. Comparing and contrasting helps in understanding the relationship between things.

Read aloud the sample paragraph. Point out that it is from the section "Nations of the Americas" on page 623. Using the bubble call-outs, guide students to compare and contrast Anglo America and Latin America.

Compare and Contrast

This book often **compares** and **contrasts** people or events. To compare things is to see how they are alike. To contrast things is to see how they are different. Comparing and contrasting helps you understand the relationships between things.

To Compare
Ask yourself:

- **What are the things being compared?**

- **How are they alike?**

To Contrast
Ask yourself:

- **What are the things being contrasted?**

- **How are they different?**

In your book you will read about different parts of North and South America. Read this paragraph to compare and contrast parts of these continents.

TIP!

- To compare, look for clue words such as *like*, *similar*, *in common*, *same*, and *resemble*.

- To contrast, look for clue works such as *before*, *after*, *different from*, *unlike*, and *by contrast*.

> The Western Hemisphere includes two cultural regions. The United States and Canada make up Anglo-America. This region was influenced strongly by British culture. Latin America includes Mexico, Central America, the Caribbean Islands, and South America. It was influenced by Spain, Portugal, and France.

from page 623

Contrast:
The U.S. and Canada drew from British culture.

Compare:
Anglo America and Latin America are both cultural regions.

Compare:
Both regions were influenced by European countries.

Contrast:
Latin American countries drew from Spain, Portugal and France.

HANDBOOK 10

USING A GRAPHIC ORGANIZER

Draw a compare and contrast graphic organizer like the one below to help students compare and contrast.

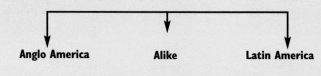

Anglo America · **Alike** · **Latin America**

The U.S. and Canada drew from British culture.

Anglo America and Latin America are both cultural regions influenced by European countries.

Latin American countries drew from Spain, Portugal and France.

READING SOCIAL STUDIES

TRY IT!

Read this paragraph about Europe in the early 1900s. Copy and complete the Venn diagram below, comparing and contrasting some European nations.

In the early 1900s Europe was like a huge jigsaw puzzle. The "pieces" were nations. Some, such as Britain and France, had existed for centuries. Others, such as Italy and Germany, had been unified only in the 1800s.

from page 527

Older Countries: Britain and France existed for centuries

Alike: European countries

Newer Countries: Germany and Italy became unified countries in 1800s

• What steps did you take to compare and contrast?

Practice Activities

❶ **READ** Read the first paragraph on page 577 of your book. Compare and contrast the two groups living in Palestine after World War II.

❷ **WRITE** Write a paragraph in which you compare and contrast the activities on two recent weekends.

Keep in Mind...

For more help in reading social studies, try these strategies:

☑ **Look up unknown words**
Use a dictionary or the glossary in your book to find the meaning of any unfamiliar words.

☑ **Form the big picture**
As you read, think about the most important information of the paragraph or section.

☑ **Summarize**
In your own words, briefly describe what your reading is about.

TRY IT!

Have students read the paragraph on this page from their textbook. Direct students to copy and complete the graphic organizer to compare and contrast.

If students are unsure of how to complete the compare and contrast graphic organizer, refer them to the *Tip!* section on the preceding page.

• **What steps did you take to compare and contrast?**

Ask students to discuss how they identified similarities and differences.

⭐ 3 CLOSE

Discuss with students the importance of using the compare and contrast strategy as they read social studies. Explain that they will need to identify similarities and differences to understand people and events in history.

Direct students to the *Keep in Mind...* tab for help in reading social studies.

Practice Activities

❶ **READ** Have students read the first paragraph on page 577 and compare and contrast the two groups living in Palestine after World War II.

Compare: Both groups lived in Palestine; **Contrast:** Arabs were native born, some Jews were immigrants; Arab population was twice as big as Jewish population; most Arabs were Muslim

Additional selections for practicing this skill include:

● page 318, section "From Forests to Farmland"
● page 384, section *Read Aloud*

❷ **WRITE** Have students apply what they have learned about the compare and contrast strategy to their writing.

The Reading Social Studies Practice Book provides students with additional practice in using the compare and contrast strategy.

EXTENDING BEYOND THE TEXTBOOK

Direct students to compare and contrast two of their favorite sports stars or animals. Note that:

● before they can compare and contrast, they will need to identify the characteristics of the subjects;

● there will be both similarities and differences between the two subjects.

Lesson Overview

Actual passages from the student text are used to demonstrate the strategy of summarizing.

Lesson Objectives

★ Identify the important information in a selection.

★ Briefly summarize the important information.

1 PREPARE

MOTIVATE Ask students:

● *How do you distinguish important from unimportant information?*

● *What information do you include in a summary?*

SET PURPOSE Read the title of the lesson to students. Ask them what they think it means. Explain that they will read passages from their books to learn how to summarize what they read.

2 TEACH

SUMMARIZING Guide students to see that writing a summary involves several skills. Students need to identify important ideas, organize them in a logical way and use their own words to summarize them.

Read the sample paragraph aloud. Point out that it is from the lesson titled "Maya Civilization" in Chapter 11. Using the bubble call-outs, guide students to summarize the selection in their own words.

Summarize

After you read a paragraph or section of this book, you can **summarize** what you have read. In a **summary**, you briefly tell in your own words about the most important information in the section. Summarizing is a way to help you understand what you read.

To Summarize

Ask yourself:

● **What is this paragraph or section about?**

● **What information is most important?**

● **How can I say this in my own words?**

In your book you will read about the ancient civilization of the Maya. Read this paragraph and sample summary about life in a Maya city.

TiP!

■ Look for titles, headings, and key words that identify important information.

■ Keep your summary brief, and organize the information in a clear way.

■ Don't include information and facts that are not the most important.

Boys and girls lived very differently in Copán. When boys were in their teens, they moved out of their family homes into large group homes. There they learned to play the ball game. Boys also learned to become soldiers. Girls stayed at home, where they were strictly raised by their mothers. They learned how to cook maize and other food and how to run a household.

from page 301

Summary:
Mayan teenage boys and girls lived in different homes. They learned different skills.

The important information is underlined.

HANDBOOK 12

USING A GRAPHIC ORGANIZER

Draw a summarize graphic organizer like the one below to help students write a summary.

Important Information

As teens, boys moved to large group homes.

Boys learned to play ball and become soldiers.

Girls learned to cook and run a household.

Summary

Mayan teenage boys and girls lived in different homes. They learned different skills.

READING SOCIAL STUDIES

TRY IT!

Read the following paragraph about an ancient Maya ball game. Copy and complete the diagram below to organize a summary of the paragraph.

> Among the impressive structures at Copán is the ball court. Here a fierce Maya ball game, called *pokta-pok* (POHK tuh POHK), was played. Players wore helmets and padding on their arms and legs, for the game was rough. They were not allowed to touch the five-pound rubber ball with their hands. The two teams rushed up and down the court trying to get the ball through a stone hoop. If they succeeded, they won the game. Excited spectators filled the stands and gave clothing to the winning team.
>
> *from page 299*

Important Information

| Players wore helmets and padding. |

| They could not use their hands. |

| Spectators gave clothing to the winning team. |

My Summary

| *Pokta-pok* was a fierce, exciting ball game. Fans rewarded the winners. |

• How did you choose what to include in your summary?

Practice Activities

1 READ Read and summarize the Legacy feature on page 304.

2 WRITE Think about a recent time when you went shopping. Write a summary of what happened.

Keep in Mind...

For more help in reading social studies, try these strategies:

☑ **Reread**
Review each sentence. Make sure you understand what each sentence means before you read further.

☑ **Form the big picture**
As you read, think about the topic and the main ideas of the paragraph or section.

☑ **Make an outline**
As you read, write an outline of the topic and the main ideas of the reading.

TRY IT!

Ask students to silently read the selection on this page. Point out that this paragraph is also from their textbook. Have them copy and complete the graphic organizer to make a summary.

Direct students to the *Tip!* section on the preceding page to help them complete the summarize diagram.

● **How did you choose what to include in your summary?**

Encourage students to explain how they decided which information they would include in their summary.

3 CLOSE

Discuss the importance of being able to summarize when reading social studies. Point out that this strategy helps students focus on the important ideas of a selection. By writing a summary of the ideas, students reinforce the concepts they must learn.

Direct students to the *Keep in Mind...* tab for general help in reading social studies.

Practice Activities

1 READ Important Information: The Maya liked to watch the stars and planets. They devised a calendar and predicted eclipses. **My Summary:** The Maya paved the way for modern astronomy.

Additional selections for practicing this skill include:

● page 76, first paragraph under "Religion In Egypt"

● pages 132-133, two paragraphs under "Working With The Environment"

2 WRITE Have students apply what they have learned about summarizing to their own writing.

The Reading Social Studies Practice Book provides students with additional practice in summarizing.

EXTENDING BEYOND THE TEXTBOOK

● Have students write a summary of a movie they saw. Have them share their summaries with the class.

● Have students interview a community helper or person in a career they are interested in. Have them summarize what they learn about the person.

Lesson Overview

Actual images from the student text are used to demonstrate the strategy of using visuals.

Lesson Objective

★ Clarify and supplement information in the main text by using visuals.

1 PREPARE

MOTIVATE Ask students:

● *How can a visual help you understand what you read?*

● *Drawings and captions are two kinds of visuals. Can you name others?*

SET PURPOSE Discuss the title of the lesson with students. Ask them what they think it means to use visuals.

2 TEACH

USE VISUALS Guide students to understand that they can use visuals to better understand the main text. Visuals such as captions, photos, maps, and headings can give information that isn't included in the main text.

Read aloud the caption and have students study the diagram. Point out that the diagram is in their textbook on page 256. Using the bubble call-outs, guide students to explain what the visual teaches them about the history of the modern alphabet.

Use Visuals

One way to learn from your reading is to use **visuals.** Visuals are the graphs, charts, pictures, and maps in your book. Visuals provide useful information in a clear, easy-to-study form.

TiP!

■ Read the caption and labels for information they provide.

■ Look for objects in the picture that might give additional information.

■ When looking at graphs, maps, or charts, be sure to read the legend or key to find the meanings of special symbols.

To Use Visuals

Look closely at the visual. Ask yourself:

● What does the graph, chart, picture, or map show?

● How does it help me to understand what I have read?

● How does it add to the information I have read?

● What information does the caption or labels provide?

You will read about the development of writing. Study this diagram showing the development of the Roman alphabet, which we use today.

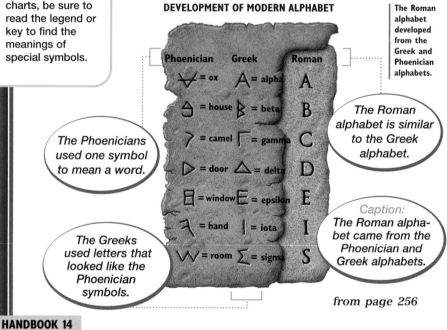

DEVELOPMENT OF MODERN ALPHABET

The Roman alphabet developed from the Greek and Phoenician alphabets.

Phoenician	Greek	Roman
⩔ = ox	A = alpha	A
⌂ = house	B = beta	B
7 = camel	Γ = gamma	C
▷ = door	Δ = delta	D
目 = window	E = epsilon	E
⇃ = hand	I = iota	I
W = room	Σ = sigma	S

The Phoenicians used one symbol to mean a word.

The Greeks used letters that looked like the Phoenician symbols.

The Roman alphabet is similar to the Greek alphabet.

Caption:
The Roman alphabet came from the Phoenician and Greek alphabets.

from page 256

HANDBOOK 14

USING A GRAPHIC ORGANIZER

Draw a using visuals graphic organizer like the one below to help students use visuals.

Caption: The Roman alphabet came from the Phoenician and Greek alphabets.

Visual: A chart comparing the Phoenician, Greek, and Roman alphabets.

Information: The Greeks used letters that resembled Phoenician symbols.

Information: The Phoenicians used one symbol to mean a word.

Information: The Roman alphabet is similar to the Greek alphabet.

READING SOCIAL STUDIES

TRY IT!

Study this picture of a crowd of people. On a sheet of paper, copy the chart below. Think about the information in the picture and complete the chart.

In the early days of television, not everyone was lucky enough to own their own set. Often, people would crowd sidewalks to watch.

from page 26

> **Caption Information:**
> Not everyone had a set so they watched where they could.

> **Visuals:** People watching a TV set that is in a store window

> **Visual Information:**
> People's clothes suggest late 1940s or early 1950s.

> **Visual Information:**
> The crowd has people of various ages and backgrounds.

Practice Activities

1 READ Study the photo on page 494 in your book. What information do the caption and the visual provide?

2 WRITE Copy the chart above, and write what you learn from the pictures and caption on page 505 of your book.

Keep in Mind...

For more help in reading social studies, try these strategies:

☑ **Use Visuals**
Photographs and drawings of people and places will help you understand the reading.

☑ **Study the charts and graphs**
Charts and graphs provide information in an easy-to-understand form.

☑ **Study the unit and chapter openers**
The first page of a unit or chapter often summarizes what you will read about. It also may contain useful maps and pictures.

TRY IT!

Ask students to study the picture on this page. Point out that the visual is also in their textbooks on page 26. Have students copy and complete the graphic organizer to use visuals.

Direct students to the *Tip!* section on the preceding page to help them complete the graphic organizer.

● **How did you get information from the visual?**

Invite students to discuss how they used details in the visual to get information.

3 CLOSE

Discuss with students that it is important to use visuals while they read social studies because this strategy will help them better understand the text. Visuals sometimes include details that are not in the main text.

Direct students to the *Keep in Mind...* tab for general help in reading social studies.

Practice Activities

1 READ Have students read page 494 in the textbook and study the visual. Have students list the ways the visual adds to the information in the main text.

Visual: The painting by Jose Orozco shows Miguel Hidalgo shouting in front of a group of Mexican citizens. **Visual Information:** The Mexicans were armed with guns, bows and arrows, but mostly with swords. They seem ready to fight. **Caption Information:** The Mexicans were fighting for independence from Spain.

Additional selections for practicing this skill include:

● page 334, map and captions
● pages 368-369, selection "Griots and Oral History"

2 WRITE Have students apply what they have learned about using visuals to their own writing.

The Reading Social Studies Practice Book provides students with additional practice in using visuals.

EXTENDING BEYOND THE TEXTBOOK

Have students write down directions describing the route from their house to school. Then have them make a map showing the route. Note that:

● the map makes the directions clearer and easier to follow;
● the map may include streets not mentioned in the written directions.

CONTENTS

iii

UNIT TWO *River Valley Civilizations*

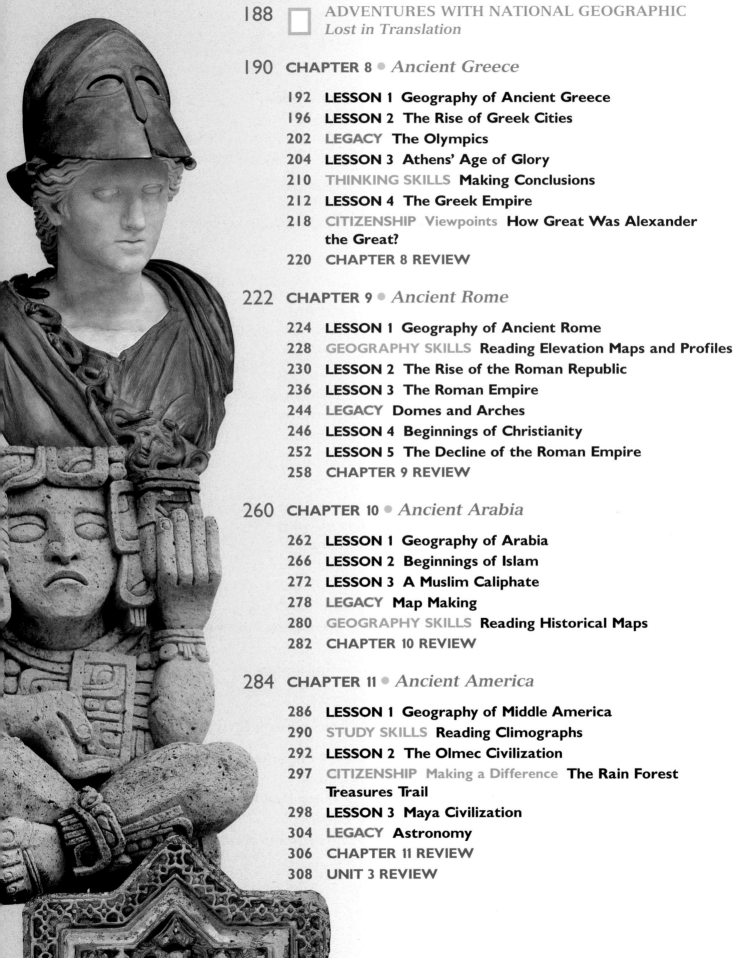

UNIT THREE New Ideas and New Empires
186

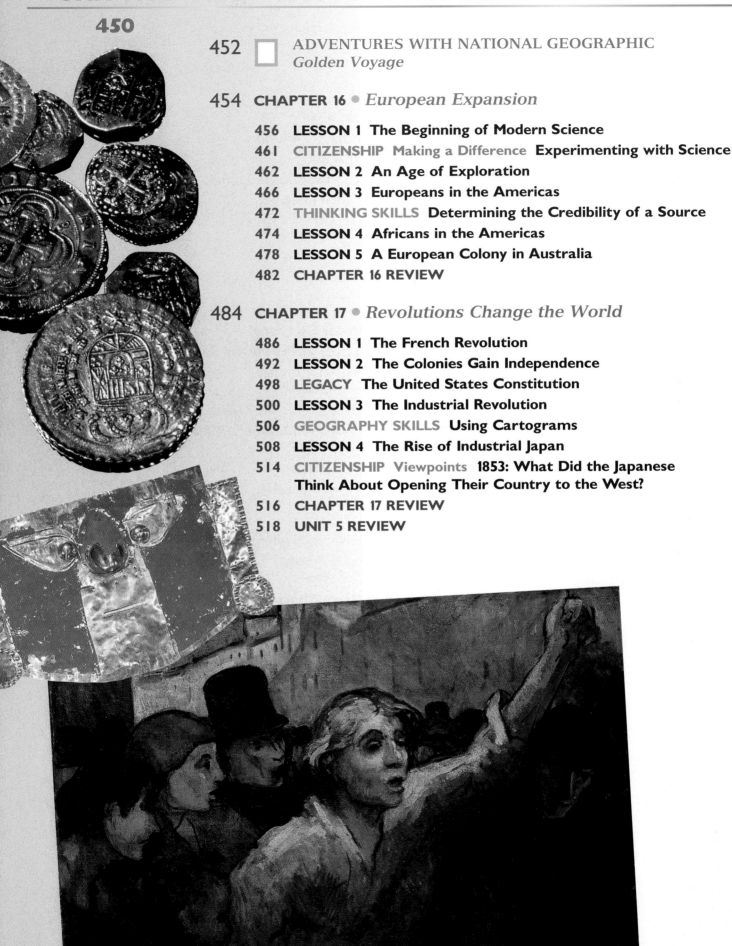

UNIT FIVE   *Dawn of the Modern World*

450

A Century of Conflict

REFERENCE SECTION

STANDARDIZED TEST SUPPORT

FEATURES

CHARTS, GRAPHS, & DIAGRAMS

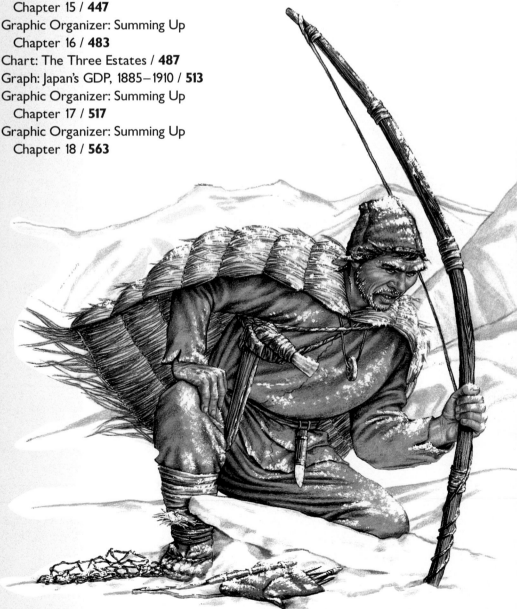

TIME LINES

MAPS

Note that the Table of Contents lists all the different parts of your textbook in page order.

Five Themes of Geography In each unit of *World: Adventures in Time and Place,* students will find a section that describes and illustrates five outdoor adventures for students. *Five Themes of Geography* introduces five key concepts that will help students describe their own adventures as they explore the different parts of *World*.

● **What are the five themes of geography?** *(Region, Human/Environment Interactions, Place, Location, and Movement)*

A Typical Lesson Have students examine the excerpt from Chapter 9, Lesson 2: *The Rise of the Roman Republic.*

● **How does Lesson 2 begin?** *(with a Read Aloud)*

Discussing Features Within Lessons Note that Lesson 2 includes a feature called *Many Voices* (Primary Sources or Literature). Explain that primary sources contain information from persons who were present at what they are describing. Diaries are primary sources.

Other features include *Links* (to different content areas like art or math) and *Did You Know?* (more facts of interest).

● **What is the Many Voices selection in this lesson?** *(an excerpt from Stories of Rome)*

Discussing Infographics Note that *Infographics* combine pictures and words.

● **What is the sample Infographic about?** *(treasures of an ancient tomb)*

Discussing Skills Lessons Note that your text also covers Thinking Skills, Geography Skills, and Study Skills.

YOUR TEXTBOOK
at a glance

Your textbook is called *World: Adventures in Time and Place.* It has 20 chapters, each with two or more lessons. There are also many special features for you to study and enjoy.

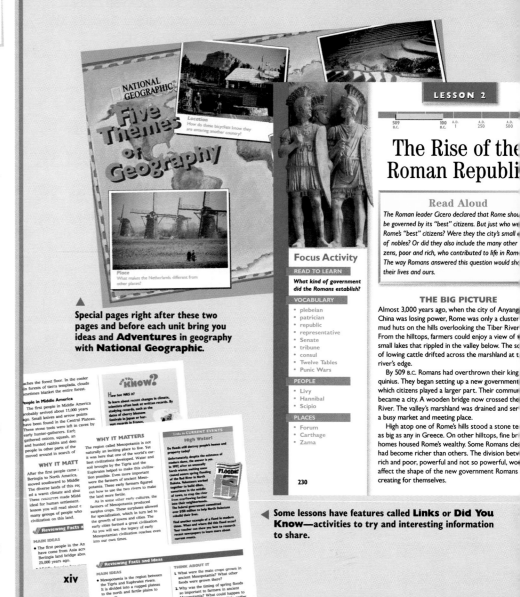

Special pages right after these two pages and before each unit bring you ideas and **Adventures** in geography with **National Geographic**.

Some lessons have features called **Links** or **Did You Know**—activities to try and interesting information to share.

ADDITIONAL FEATURES OF THE TEXTBOOK

UNIT OPENER Have students turn to the Unit Opener on pp. 186–187. Note how the visuals illustrate the Unit's theme.

CHAPTER OPENER Have students examine the Chapter 1 and 9 Openers on pp. 6–7 and 222–223. Ask students to distinguish the information shown in Chapter 1 from the information shown in Chapter 9.

VISUAL AIDS Have students identify visual aids included throughout the text such as: photographs, illustrations, charts, graphs, diagrams, time lines, and maps. (The last five items are also listed in the Table of Contents.)

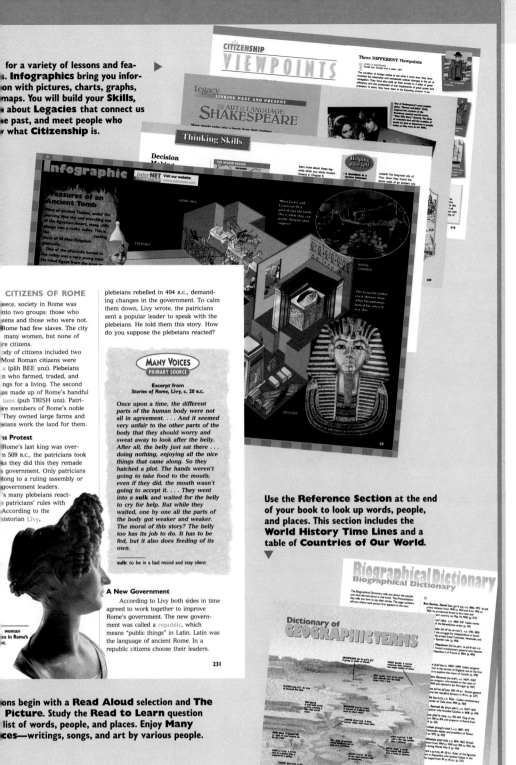

for a variety of lessons and fea-
s. **Infographics** bring you infor-
on with pictures, charts, graphs,
maps. You will build your **Skills**,
about **Legacies** that connect us
e past, and meet people who
what **Citizenship** is.

CITIZENS OF ROME

eece, society in Rome was
nto two groups: those who
zens and those who were not.
Rome had few slaves. The city
many women, but none of
re citizens.

ody of citizens included two
Most Roman citizens were
s (plih BEE unz). Plebeians
n who farmed, traded, and
ngs for a living. The second
as made up of Rome's handful
ians (puh TRISH unz). Patri-
re members of Rome's noble
They owned large farms and
eians work the land for them.

ns Protest

Rome's last king was over-
n 509 B.C., the patricians took
As they did this they remade
s government. Only patricians
long to a ruling assembly or
government leaders.

's many plebeians react-
e patricians' rules with
According to the
historian Livy,

woman
Rome's
st.

plebeians rebelled in 494 B.C., demanding changes in the government. To calm
them down, Livy wrote, the patricians
sent a popular leader to speak with the
plebeians. He told them this story. How
do you suppose the plebeians reacted?

MANY VOICES
PRIMARY SOURCE

Excerpt from
Stories of Rome, Livy, c. 20 B.C.

*Once upon a time, the different
parts of the human body were not
all in agreement. . . . And it seemed
very unfair to the other parts of the
body that they should worry and
sweat away to look after the belly.
After all, the belly just sat there . . .
doing nothing, enjoying all the nice
things that came along. So they
hatched a plot. The hands weren't
going to take food to the mouth;
even if they did, the mouth wasn't
going to accept it. . . . They went
into a **sulk** and waited for the belly
to cry for help. But while they
waited, one by one all the parts of
the body got weaker and weaker.
The moral of this story? The belly
too has its job to do. It has to be
fed, but it also does feeding of its
own.*

sulk: to be in a bad mood and stay silent

A New Government

According to Livy both sides in time
agreed to work together to improve
Rome's government. The new government was called a **republic**, which
means "public things" in Latin. Latin was
the language of ancient Rome. In a
republic citizens choose their leaders.

231

Use the **Reference Section** at the end
of your book to look up words, people,
and places. This section includes the
World History Time Lines and a
table of **Countries of Our World**.

ons begin with a **Read Aloud** selection and **The
Picture**. Study the **Read to Learn** question
list of words, people, and places. Enjoy **Many
ces**—writings, songs, and art by various people.

• **What kind of sample Skills Lesson
is shown?** *(a Thinking Skills lesson)*

Discussing Citizenship Have students examine the *Citizenship* features
in the Table of Contents. Note that
Citizenship features are of two types:
Viewpoints and *Making a Difference*.

• **Which type of Citizenship feature
is shown on this page?** *(Viewpoints)*

Exploring the Reference Section
Have students examine the reference
section that begins on p. R2.

• **What parts are in the reference
section?** *(Atlas, Country Tables,
Time Lines, Dictionary of Geographic
Terms, Gazetteer, Biographic Dictionary, Glossary, and Index)*

Explain that the *Biographical Dictionary*
alphabetically lists the names of the
people discussed in the textbook. The
Dictionary also provides a brief description and a page reference for each person. The *Dictionary of Geographic
Terms* is an illustration of the different
types of land and bodies of water,
along with a corresponding definition.

Sum up by noting that all these features
will help students better understand the
history and geography of the world.

• **Where would you look for information of people discussed in your
textbook?** *(in the* Biographical Dictionary*)*

• **Where would you look for definitions and illustrations of geographic words?** *(in the* Dictionary of
Geographic Terms*)*

**READING INSTRUCTION IN
YOUR TEACHER'S EDITION**

**READING STRATEGIES AND
LANGUAGE DEVELOPMENT**
A variety of strategies at the start
of each lesson helps you develop
student vocabulary and language
skills. Strategies access prior
knowledge and teach clues to
understanding the text and
improving writing skills.

READING COMPREHENSION
Questions at the end of the
lessons in the student book use
a variety of reading strategies to
assist students in summarizing,
interpreting, and analyzing the
main ideas of the lessons. Reading
strategies are identified after the
answers in the teacher's edition.

ADDITIONAL FEATURES OF THE TEXTBOOK

ADVENTURES WITH NATIONAL GEOGRAPHIC Have students look at
these features, such as on pp. 4–5, which follow the Unit Opener.

CHAPTER SUMMARIES AND REVIEWS Have students examine a typical Chapter Summary and Review, such as on pp. 182–183. Ask students to identify the types of information (for example, vocabulary and
facts) and skills (thinking and writing) they are asked to review.

UNIT REVIEWS Have students review a typical Unit Review, such as on
pp. 62–63. Explain to students that a Unit Review will help them re-
fresh their memories about information covered in the unit.

REFERENCE SECTION Have students examine the sections not covered
above: Atlas (R4–R19), Country Tables (R20–R35), Time Lines
(R36–R45), Dictionary of Geographic Terms (R46-R47), Gazetteer
(R48-R54), Biographical Dictionary (R55–R59), Glossary (R60–R69), and
Index (R70–R77).

4 UNIT ORGANIZER

World Regions in Transition

PAGES 310–449

UNIT OVERVIEW

From A.D. 600 to 1600, the Middle Ages, the Renaissance, and Reformation were pe of transition between ancient and modern times. The growth of cities and trade had important impact on world culture. Empires grew in Europe, Africa, Asia, and the Americas and spread new ideas about religion, the arts, and science and changed t way people viewed the world.

ADVENTURES WITH NATIONAL GEOGRAPHIC
City in the Sky **pp. 312–313**

UNIT PLANNING GUIDE

CHAPTER	SUGGESTED PACING	RESOURCES	ASSESSMENT
12 Cultures of Medieval Europe The feudal system predominated. The Renaissance saw a rebirth in art; the Reformation changed Christianity. pp. 314–351	10–11 days	• **Practice and Project Book, pp. 64–70** • **Anthology,** pp. 67–77 • **Transparency:** Graphic Organizer, Flow Chart • **Technology:** Videodisc/Video Tape 3 • **Technology:** *Adventure Time!* CD-ROM	• **Meeting Individual Needs,** pp. 319, 327, 335, 341, 347, 349 • **Write About It,** 319, 327, 335, 341, 349 • **Chapter Review,** pp. 350–351 • **Assessment Book:** *Assessing Think and Write, pp. T81–T83. Chapter 12 Tests: Content, Skills, Writing*
13 Empires and Cultures of Africa Ethiopia became independent. Timbuktu, Zanzibar, and the Kingdom of Zimbabwe became important trading centers. pp. 352–381	9–10 days	• **Practice and Project Book, pp. 71–77** • **Anthology,** pp. 78–92 • **Desk Map** • **Outline Map** • **Transparency: Map 16** • **Technology:** *Adventure Time!* CD-ROM	• **Meeting Individual Needs,** pp. 357, 361, 367, 369, 371, 375, 379 • **Write About It,** pp. 357, 361, 367, 3 375, 379 • **Chapter Review,** pp. 380–381 • **Assessment Book:** *Assessing Think and Write, pp. T84–T86. Chapter 13 Tests: Content, Skills, Writing*
14 Empires and Cultures of Asia Ottoman rulers and Kublai Khan united great empires. Temples were built at Angkor, Cambodia, and Agra, India. pp. 382–419	11–12 days	• **Practice and Project Book, pp. 78–85** • **Anthology,** pp. 93–103 • **Transparency:** Graphic Organizer, Main Idea Chart • **Technology:** Videodisc/Video Tape • **Technology:** *Adventure Time!* CD-ROM	• **Meeting Individual Needs,** pp. 387, 391, 397, 401, 407, 415, 417 • **Write About It,** pp. 387, 391, 397, 4 407, 415, 417 • **Chapter Review,** pp. 418–419 • **Assessment Book:** *Assessing Think and Write, pp. T87–T89. Chapter 14 Tests: Content, Skills, Writing*
15 Empires and Cultures of the Americas The Aztecs and Incas founded great empires. The Ojibwa established trade on the Great Lakes. pp. 420–447	9–10 days	• **Practice and Project Book, pp. 86–91** • **Anthology,** pp. 104–114 • **Desk Map** • **Transparency:** Maps 17, 18, Graphic Organizer, World Map • **Technology:** Videodisc/Video Tape • **Technology:** *Adventure Time!* CD-ROM	• **Meeting Individual Needs,** pp. 425, 431, 433, 439, 445 • **Write About It,** pp. 425, 431, 439, 44 • **Chapter Review,** pp. 446–447 • **Assessment Book:** *Assessing Think and Write, pp. T90–T92. Chapter 15 Tests: Content, Skills, Writing*
Unit 4 Review pp. 448–449	1–2 days	• **Geo Adventures Daily Geography Activities**	• **Unit 4 Project,** p. 449

The McGraw-Hill School's Home Page at
☞ **http://www.mhschool.com**
on the World Wide Web for projects related to this unit.

FOR FURTHER SUPPORT
• **Language Support Handbook**
• **Standardized Test Support**

McGraw-Hill Adventure Books

de Mauro, Lisa. **The Chinese Calendar.** The author traces the development of the Chinese calendar. **(Easy)**

Classroom Library

■ Clare, John D., ed. **Knights in Armor.** San Diego, CA: Harcourt Brace Jovanovich, 1992. This book describes the role of the knight during the Middle Ages.

Student Books

Corbishley, Mike. **The Medieval World.** New York: Peter Bedrick Books, 1992. Read about the world between A.D. 450 and 1500. **(Challenging)**

Fisher, Leonard Everett. **The Great Wall of China.** New York: Macmillan Publishing Co., 1986. Find out how one million people built the Great Wall. **(Easy)**

■ Lewis, Richard. **All of You Was Singing.** New York: Macmillan /McGraw-Hill School Publishing Company, 1991. This is a retelling of an Aztec myth. **(Easy)**

Lucas, Eileen. **The Ojibwas.** Brookfield, CT: The Millbrook Press, 1994. Read about the contemporary life of the Ojibwa. **(Average)**

Major, John S. **The Silk Route: 7,000 Miles of History.** New York: HarperCollins Publishers, 1994. Find out about China's precious cloth, A.D. 618-906. **(Average)**

McKissack, Patricia, and Fredrick McKissack. **Royal Kingdoms of Ghana, Mali, and Songhai: Life in Medieval Africa.** New York: Henry Holt and Co., 1994. Explore the Western Sudan. **(Challenging)**

■ Stanley, Diane. **Leonardo da Vinci.** New York: William Morrow, 1996. A beautifully illustrated picture book of this famous painter's life and art techniques. **(Average)**

■ Walker, Barbara K., reteller. **A Treasury of Turkish Folktales.** Hamden, CT: the Shoe String Press, 1988. This group of Turkish folktales is suited for reading aloud. **(Average)**

Wood, Tim. **The Aztecs.** New York: Viking, 1992. A description of the lifestyle of the Aztecs with detailed illustrations. **(Challenging)**

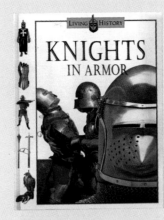

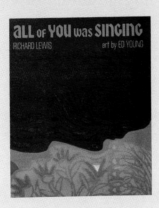

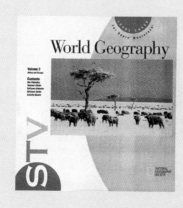

Teacher Books

Kranz, Rachel. **Across Asia by Land.** New York: Facts On File, 1991. This history of trade routes in Asia focuses on the Silk Route.

Zevin, Jack, ed. **The Kingfisher Illustrated History of the World: 40,000 BC to Present Day.** New York: Kingfisher Books, 1993. This useful resource starts in the ancient world and ends in 1993.

Read-Alouds

Chaucer, Geoffrey. **Canterbury Tales.** Adapted by Barbara Cohen. New York: Lothrop, Lee and Shepard, 1988. Four of Chaucer's tales are retold in narrative style.

Hodges, Margaret, and Margery Evernden. **Of Swords and Sorcerers.** New York: Macmillan Publishing Group, 1993. These tales of King Arthur and his knights are suited for reading aloud.

Lewis, Naomi. **Proud Knight, Fair Lady: The Twelve Lais of Marie de France.** New York: Viking, 1989. These tales illuminate twelfth century society.

Technology Multimedia

Exploring the Renaissance (1350 - 1650 A.D.) . Video. No. UL10301V. Explore the accomplishments of great masters from this time period. Knowledge Unlimited. (800) 356-2303.

The Monkey People. Video. An old African man transforms the villagers into monkeys for their laziness. **Peachboy.** Video. Momotaro, the Japanese warrior, rescues the captives who were stolen by the ogres years ago. Story Lane Theater, Macmillan/McGraw-Hill. (800) 442-9685.

☐ **STV: World Geography.** Videodisc. Students explore the continents. National Geographic Society. (800) 368-2728.

Free or Inexpensive Materials

For a Teacher's Resource Packet on North American Indians, send to: Smithsonian Institution; Anthropology Outreach; NHB 363, MRC 112; Washington, DC 20560.

■ *Book excerpted in the Anthology*

■ *Book featured in the student bibliography of the Unit Review*

☐ *National Geographic technology*

Ideas for Active Learning

BULLETIN BOARD

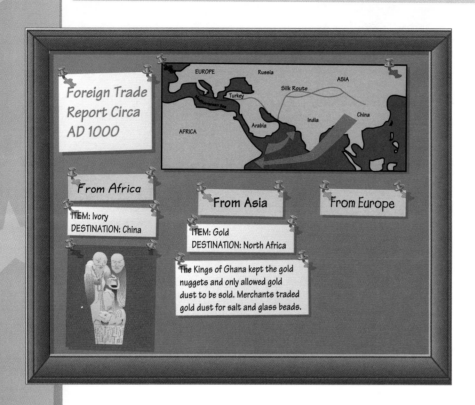

Foreign Trade Report Circa AD 1000

From Africa

ITEM: Ivory
DESTINATION: China

From Asia

ITEM: Gold
DESTINATION: North Africa

From Europe

The Kings of Ghana kept the gold nuggets and only allowed gold dust to be sold. Merchants traded gold dust for salt and glass beads.

World Regions in Transition

Help students to create a bulletin board titled "Foreign Trade Report, Circa A.D. 1000." Include a small map of Europe, Africa, and Asia. Label the Silk Route, and draw an arrow from eastern Africa to Asia and from Europe to China. Ask students to create three headings on construction paper: "From Africa," "From Asia," and "From Europe," and to place them in three columns beneath the map. For each export or trade that students learn about, have them fill out an index card that begins with the word "Item:" followed by the name of the commodity that was traded. On the second line of the card have them write the word "Destination:" followed by the name of the country to which the item was exported. On the remainder of the card, students can draw pictures or glue photographs of the item or country of origin or write information about the trade.

TEACHER EXCHANGE

Thanks to: Mark Palmer, Emerson Elementary, Midland, Texas

Make an Eyewitness Report

ON YOUR OWN

30 MINUTES OR LONGER

CURRICULUM CONNECTION   Language Arts/Art

Materials: yellow or off-white construction paper, oaktag, calligraphy or plain markers

1. Talk with students about how they have learned what our country and other countries look like. Talk with them about primary sources, and say that in earlier times, eyewitness reports were the only way to share facts.
2. Have students choose a region of the world that they would like to visit. Then have them use reference materials to look at pictures of the place and take notes about their first impressions.
3. After their research is complete, have them create an eyewitness scroll that describes the location as if they were seeing it for the first time, based on their first impression notes.
4. If possible, have students use calligraphic markers to create their old-fashioned scrolls. Then invite volunteer "eyewitnesses" to read aloud their descriptions.

Enriching with Multimedia

RESOURCE: McGraw-Hill School's Home Page

- Have students go to McGraw-Hill School's home page at http://www.mhschool.com on the World Wide Web for projects related to this unit.

RESOURCE: *Adventure Time! CD-ROM*

- Enrich Unit 4 with the *Time Lines* and the Unit 4 Activities on the *Adventure Time!* CD-ROM.

SCHOOL-TO-HOME

World Regions in Transition

- Throughout the unit, students will have the opportunity to learn about goods that were traded between countries as early as A.D. 1000, and how the new commodities enriched the lives of the people who imported them. With students, generate a list of items that were traded between continents in the years around A.D. 1000.

- Using the list as a starting-off point, students and their families can make a new list of goods that are commonly traded between the United States and other countries, or imported by the United States. Families can use the media and their own experiences to complete their lists. By comparing their two lists, families can notice if a country still produces and trades the same items today as in A.D. 1000—for example silk in China.

ONGOING UNIT PROJECT

Make a Global Time Line

CURRICULUM CONNECTION   Art

RESOURCE: Practice and Project Book p. 133.

Students will be working throughout this unit, individually and cooperatively, to make a picture time line like those on pages 282 and 306.

1. After the class has completed each chapter, have each student draw a picture that illustrates one of the main global historical events.
2. After all the drawings have been completed, guide students to work in small groups to select one drawing for each lesson.
3. Provide each group with yarn or string and some clothespins. Help group members to hang their drawings, with the date arrows provided, in lesson order on the time line.
4. Have a student from each group describe one of the time line's pictures.

Assessment suggestions for the activity appear on page 448.

UNIT FOUR

PAGES 310–449

Introducing the Unit

Once again, mention the social studies theme of change over time. Ask students to identify a word in the unit title that tells us that this unit will deal with change over time. (*Transition*) Give students time to read *Why Does It Matter?* on p. 311 and examine the pictures of artifacts.

Exploring Prior Knowledge Encourage students to try to identify any pictures they recognize.

- *Which of these artifacts have you seen before? What do you know about them?* (*Students may identify and describe any familiar items; invite other students to add what they know about any artifact named.*)

- *How many different world regions can you recognize in these artifacts?* (*Students should be able to identify Europe, Africa, Asia, and America.*)

★THINKING FURTHER: *Making Conclusions* **Based on these artifacts, what would you conclude is important in life to the peoples who produced them?** (*Possible answers: power, beauty, religion*)

Looking Ahead In this unit students will explore the period of the Middle Ages and the Renaissance, from about A.D. 600 to A.D. 1600, in four different settings—Europe, Africa, Asia, and the Americas. They will trace the emergence of new civilizations and the evolving of new civilizations out of old ones.

INCA KNIFE, PERU

ROSE WINDOW, THE CATHEDRAL OF NOTRE DAME, FRANCE
GOLD MASK, BENIN

MODEL OF MING DYNASTY SHIP, CHINA

310

BACKGROUND INFORMATION

ABOUT THE ARTIFACTS

- **ROSE WINDOW FROM THE CATHEDRAL OF NOTRE DAME, PARIS** Many great churches and cathedrals were constructed during this time period. This cathedral was completed in the early 1300s.

- **INCA KNIFE FROM PERU** The Inca civilization developed a high level of gold-working techniques, as seen in this knife from pre-Columbian Peru. Gold was considered to be "tears of the gods."

UNIT FOUR

World Regions in Transition

"To no one will we deny, or delay, rights or justice."

from the Magna Carta
See page 327.

Why Does It Matter?

The idea of protecting people's rights was just beginning to develop in the period covered in this unit. Many of the ways of life that we think of as "modern" began in the years between about a.d. 600 and a.d. 1600. In fact, many historians call this period the Middle Ages because they think of it as being between ancient and modern times. During these years, religious ideas spread and developed in Europe, Africa, Asia, and the Americas. These ideas affected the arts, science, and the ways people viewed the world and their place in it.

PORTRAIT OF
QUEEN ELIZABETH I,
ENGLAND

FIND OUT MORE!
Visit our website:
www.mhschool.com

*inter*NET
CONNECTION

311

Discussing the Artifacts Go back to students' conclusions about the aspects of life the artifacts reflect— beauty, religion, and so forth. Divide the class into six small groups and assign each group one of the artifacts. Tell each group to determine which of life's aspects its artifact reflects—perhaps more than one.

★THINKING FURTHER: *Making Conclusions* **Which aspect or aspects of life do you think your artifact reflects? Why?** *(Call on each group to offer its determination and invite other students to add their views.)*

Discussing WHY DOES IT MATTER? Have one student read the quote aloud and have the class discuss the paragraph.

● **Would you say that the idea put forth in this quote is important to our own society? Explain.** *(Students should recognize that basic human rights, including the right to justice, are the bedrock of American political beliefs.)*

● **Where was this idea stated, according to the text?** *(Have students turn to page 326 to identify England as the place where this statement appeared, in the* Magna Carta *in 1215.)*

● **What span of time will you explore in this unit?** *(A.D. 600–1600)*

★THINKING FURTHER: *Making Conclusions* **Why can you conclude that a great deal of cultural borrowing was taking place in the world at this time?** *(Possible answer: Religious ideas were spreading over the world and affecting civilizations as they did.)*

BACKGROUND INFORMATION

ABOUT THE ARTIFACTS
● **MODEL OF A MING DYNASTY SHIP** The Ming Dynasty in China was a period of growth and expansion in which shipping and trade played an important part.

● **AFRICAN GOLD MASK** Benin is noted for its extraordinary sculpture and gold work. This mask is an example of the triumph of skill in both metal-working and sculpture.

● **PORTRAIT OF QUEEN ELIZABETH I** The reign of Queen Elizabeth I (1558-1603) was a time of great growth and expansion of commerce and the arts in England.

Introducing
City in the Sky

Exploring Prior Knowledge Identify the pictured city as Machu Picchu and ask students if they have ever heard of it or seen pictures of it before. Encourage them to share any knowledge they already have of it with the class. Then, based on what they have already learned in this class, have them tell why it was obviously built by a technologically advanced society. (The high level of engineering is evident in its buildings and terraces.)

Links to the Unit As students work through Unit 4, they will continue to trace the development of high levels of civilization in different parts of the world. Often these civilizations had little or no knowledge of one another's existence—Machu Picchu shown here knew nothing of other civilizations across the oceans, which also knew nothing of it. Yet all were developing in ways that would one day bring them into contact.

City in the Sky After students read the text, help them to recognize how remote Machu Picchu was from the rest of the world, high atop its mountain—so remote that it would "disappear" from human knowledge for centuries. Have them pinpoint where it is located (atop the Andes Mountains running down South America's western coast), to help account for its remoteness.

Resource REMINDER

National Geographic Poster

Geo Adventures *Daily Geography Activities*

Technology: *Adventure Time!* CD-ROM

Adventures
with
NATIONAL GEOGRAPHIC

BACKGROUND INFORMATION

MORE ABOUT MACHU PICCHU

- It lies on a precipice between steep peaks nearly 8,000 feet above sea level on the eastern slope of the Andes Mountains. Though it lies only about 50 miles from the ancient Inca capital of Cuzco, which the Spanish conquered in 1533, the Spanish never located it.

- The Inca called it Vilcampapa. Perhaps its most dazzling feature is its carved stone, especially a carved natural stone known as the Intihuantana that is enclosed by stone walls in which trapezoidal windows have been carved.

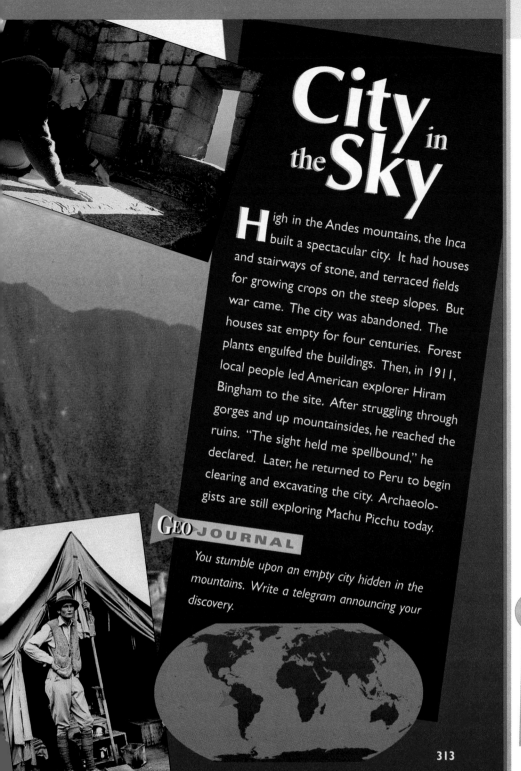

City in the Sky

High in the Andes mountains, the Inca built a spectacular city. It had houses and stairways of stone, and terraced fields for growing crops on the steep slopes. But war came. The city was abandoned. The houses sat empty for four centuries. Forest plants engulfed the buildings. Then, in 1911, local people led American explorer Hiram Bingham to the site. After struggling through gorges and up mountainsides, he reached the ruins. "The sight held me spellbound," he declared. Later, he returned to Peru to begin clearing and excavating the city. Archaeologists are still exploring Machu Picchu today.

GEO JOURNAL

You stumble upon an empty city hidden in the mountains. Write a telegram announcing your discovery.

313

Refer the class to the lefthand inset to get a close-up view of what has been uncovered at Machu Picchu. Help students to recognize that the Inca carved flat surfaces out of the steep mountainside to give themselves stair-like terraces on which to construct their houses. Help students note that the Inca did the same thing to produce farmfields.

Call students' attention to the lower righthand inset to see explorer Hiram Bingham at his tent site. Call on them to recall the name Howard Carter from their earlier study and have them look him up in the Index to find material on him. How was Howard Carter like Hiram Bingham? Encourage students to identify similarities between the two. (Both explorers operated at about the same time, the former finding Tutankhamun's tomb and the latter uncovering Machu Picchu— both major archaeological finds of this or any century.)

Using the Geo Journal To help students write their telegrams, urge them to picture themselves in the situation described—they are expecting something but they don't really know what. And then, there it is. What are their reactions?

 Technology CONNECTION

ADVENTURE TIME! CD-ROM
Have students use the *National Geographic Adventure* on the *Adventure Time!* CD-ROM.

CURRICULUM CONNECTION

LANGUAGE ARTS Explain to the class that major literary writers have written in praise and wonder at the sight of Machu Picchu. "The city upraised like a cup in our fingers," wrote one poet. "What a breath-taking place! You seem to be climbing into a larger world, a landscape built by titans," said another.

Have students write their own haikus or other short poems that describe what they see when they look upon Machu Picchu.

THEMES of GEOGRAPHY

As you work through Unit 4 with your students, consider the following themes:

Regions Regions are areas with common features that distinguish them from other areas. As you discuss Chapter 13, consider the geographical, cultural, historical, and economic characteristics that define the different regions of Africa.

Location Location is the position of a place on the earth's surface. Ask students to identify the relative and absolute locations of the following places: Normandy (Ch. 12, Lesson 2), Mount Kilimanjaro (Ch. 13, Lesson 1), Istanbul (Ch. 14, Lesson 2), Lake Texcoco (Ch. 15, Lesson 2), and Cuzco (Ch. 15, Lesson 3).

CHAPTER 12 Cultures of Medieval Europe

Pages 314–351

CHAPTER OVERVIEW

In the Middle Ages, most Europeans lived in a feudal system of knights and castles. In 1095, Pope Urban II began the Crusades to Jerusalem. During the Renaissance, there was a rebirth of interest in "classical" art. Martin Luther began the Reformation in 1517 with his 95 Theses.

GEO ADVENTURES DAILY GEOGRAPHY ACTIVITIES

Use **Geo Adventures** Daily Geography activities to assess students' understanding of geography skills.

CHAPTER PLANNING GUIDE

LESSON 1	LESSON 2	THINKINGSKILLS
SUGGESTED PACING: 2 DAYS	SUGGESTED PACING: 2 DAYS	SUGGESTED PACING: 1 DAY
Geography Of Europe pp. 316–319	**The Middle Ages** pp. 320–327	**Determining Point Of View** pp. 328–329
CURRICULUM CONNECTIONS Links to Music, p. 318	**CURRICULUM CONNECTIONS** Links to Language Arts, pp. 321, 325	**RESOURCES** Practice and Project Book, p. 66
RESOURCES Practice and Project Book, p. 64 Desk Map Outline Map	Links to Reading, p. 322	
	CITIZENSHIP Understanding Government, p. 336	
	RESOURCES Practice and Project Book, p. 65 Anthology, pp. 69–72, 73 ▭Anthology, p. 68	

LESSON 4	LESSON 5	Legacy
SUGGESTED PACING: 3 DAYS	SUGGESTED PACING: 2 DAYS	SUGGESTED PACING: 2 DAYS
The Renaissance pp. 336–341	**The Reformation** pp. 342–347	**The Art Of Language: Shakespeare** pp. 348–349
CURRICULUM CONNECTIONS Links to Art and Science, p. 339 Links to Language Arts, p. 339	**CURRICULUM CONNECTIONS** Links to Language Arts, p. 346 Links to Math, p. 346	**RESOURCES** ◑ Anthology, p. 77
INFOGRAPHIC Spread of the Renaissance, pp. 340–341	**RESOURCES** Practice and Project Book, p. 69	
RESOURCES Practice and Project Book, p. 68 Anthology, pp. 74–76 ◑TECHNOLOGY Adventure Time! CD-ROM		

LEARNING STYLE: Visual ON YOUR OWN 30 MINUTES OR LONGER

Write a "Once Upon a Time" Story

Objective: To acquaint students with medieval Europe.

Materials: paper

1. Write "Once upon a time..." on the chalkboard and ask students what these words bring to mind—perhaps fairy tales and kings, princesses, and castles.
2. Challenge students to write "Once upon a time..." stories using ideas and characters of their own.
3. Invite volunteers to share their stories with the class. Lead students to distinguish between story elements that may have been real in the Middle Ages and those that are purely imaginative.

LESSON 3

SUGGESTED PACING: 2 DAYS

The Church In The Middle Ages pp. 330–335

CURRICULUM CONNECTIONS
Links to Art, p. 332
Links to Reading, p. 332
Links to Science, p. 332

CITIZENSHIP
Monks and Nuns as Good Citizens, p. 331
Recognizing Cultural Perspectives, p. 333

RESOURCES
Practice and Project Book, p. 67

CHAPTER REVIEW

SUGGESTED PACING: 1 DAY

pp. 350–351

RESOURCES
Practice and Project Book, p. 70
🔵 TECHNOLOGY Videodisc/Video Tape 3
Assessment Book: Chapter 12 Test
Transparency: Graphic Organizer, Flow Chart

SHELTERED INSTRUCTION

READING STRATEGIES & LANGUAGE DEVELOPMENT

Rereading/Word History, p. 316, Lesson 1
Sequencing/Compound Words, p. 320, Lesson 2
Context Clues/Homophones, p. 328, Thinking Skills
Making and Supporting Generalizations/Word Roots, p. 330, Lesson 3
Using Visuals/Word Origins, p. 336, Lesson 4
Cause and Effect/Prefixes, p. 342, Lesson 5

SECOND-LANGUAGE SUPPORT

Reading Strategies, p. 318
Dramatization, pp. 325, 339
Taking Notes, pp. 331, 344
Medieval Festival, p. 350

MEETING INDIVIDUAL NEEDS

Reteaching, Extension, Enrichment, pp. 319, 327, 335, 341, 347, 349
McGraw-Hill Adventure Book

ASSESSMENT OPPORTUNITIES

Practice and Project Book, pp. 64–70
Write About It, pp. 319, 327, 335, 341, 347, 349
Assessment Book: Assessing Think and Write, pp. T81–T83; Chapter 12 Tests: Content, Skills, Writing

CHAPTER 12

PAGES 314–351

Introducing the Chapter

Begin by having students read the chapter title and asking them which civilizations in Europe they have already studied. Call on them to offer legacies that ancient Greece and Rome left behind, and invite them to explore what Europe later did with them.

THINKING ABOUT HISTORY AND GEOGRAPHY

Have students read the text on this page and identify three major characteristics of the Middle Ages in Europe (religious faith, struggle for power, creativity). Then have them trace highlighted map locations back to their panels and tell which characteristic each reflects.

1095 ROME

- **Which characteristic would you say this panel reflects? Why?** (The pope and Jerusalem, a Christian holy city, both reflect religious faith and a zeal to protect it.)

- **What is a crusade?** (a battle for a religious cause)

★THINKING FURTHER: *Making Conclusions* **What do you conclude took place in 1095?** (Europeans went on a crusade to Jerusalem.)

ABOUT 1200 CHARTRES

- **Where does the action in this panel take place?** (at Chartres, in western Europe, in what is now France)

★THINKING FURTHER: *Making Conclusions* **How might Chartres help to support the idea that for Europe the Middle Ages were an "Age of Faith"?** (Building such a structure reflects how important religious faith was to the Europeans.)

Resource REMINDER

 **Technology:** *Videodisc/Video Tape 3*

Cultures of Medieval Europe

THINKING ABOUT HISTORY AND GEOGRAPHY

In the period called the Middle Ages, most Europeans lived, worked, and worshiped in farming communities. During this "Age of Faith," Christianity spread throughout Europe. At the same time, rulers and nobles struggled for power. At the end of the Middle Ages came a time of great creativity in the arts, sciences, and religion.

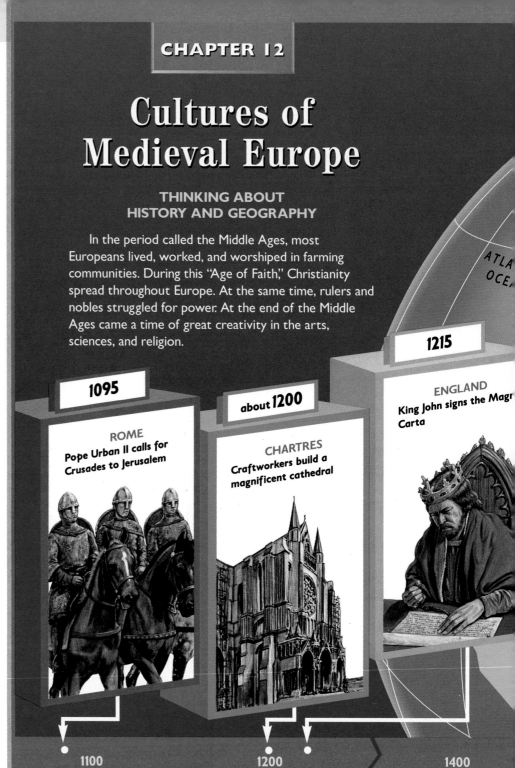

1095
ROME
Pope Urban II calls for Crusades to Jerusalem

about 1200
CHARTRES
Craftworkers build a magnificent cathedral

1215
ENGLAND
King John signs the Magna Carta

1100   1200   1400

BACKGROUND INFORMATION

LINKING THE MAP AND THE TIME LINE

- When Pope Urban II, in Rome (the seat of the Roman Catholic Church and the former capital of the Western Roman Empire), sounded the call for the Crusades he was responding to pleas from Constantinople, the seat of the Eastern Church and the former capital of the Eastern Roman Empire. The Byzantine emperor, threatened by the Muslims who held Jerusalem, had begged Western Christendom for help against the Muslims.

- Chartres Cathedral, located about 55 miles southwest of Paris, is actually the sixth church to stand on this site. It was begun soon after the fifth one burned down in 1194.

1503

FLORENCE
Leonardo da Vinci paints the Mona Lisa

1517

WITTENBERG
Martin Luther posts his 95 Theses

ENGLAND
Wittenberg
Chartres
EUROPE
Florence
Rome
ASIA
Mediterranean Sea
AFRICA
Red Sea

1500   1600   315

BACKGROUND INFORMATION

LINKING THE MAP AND THE TIME LINE

- The *Magna Carta* was signed at Runnymede, a meadow on the banks of the Thames River about 20 miles from London. Today a portion of this field is dedicated to former U.S. President John F. Kennedy.

- Florence, in the Tuscany region of Italy, was the birthplace of the Renaissance; today it attracts a million visitors a year to enjoy the rich artistic heritage that the city left the world.

- Wittenberg, located along the Elbe River in present-day Germany, was home to the University of Wittenberg, newly founded in 1502 when Martin Luther posted his 95 Theses on the door of the Wittenberg castle's church. Thus a university town became the birthplace of the Protestant Reformation.

 Technology CONNECTION

VIDEODISC/VIDEO TAPE 3
Enrich Chapter 12 with *The Renaissance* segment on the Videodisc.

Search Frame 6339 Side B

LESSON 1

PAGES 316–319

Lesson Overview

Europe's geographic features—long, jagged coastline, many harbors, temperate climate, fertile farmland, and navigable rivers—have contributed greatly to its development.

Lesson Objectives

★ Describe Europe's main geographic features.

★ Explain how they have contributed to the growth of civilization there.

1 PREPARE

MOTIVATE Have two students do the *Read Aloud,* one reading the quote, the other the narration. Use it and the photo of a canal to discuss a time before airplanes. Note how much slower and more difficult transportation was then and how vital waterways were to movement.

SET PURPOSE Refer students to the *Read to Learn* question. Encourage them to speculate on the use of waterways. Have them read the lesson to verify their speculations. Preview the *Vocabulary.*

2 TEACH

Understanding THE BIG PICTURE Refer the class to the map on p. 317.

● **How is Europe both a small and a big land mass?** *(Small: second smallest continent. Big: a part of Eurasia.)*

● **On what ocean does western Europe face?** *(the Atlantic)*

● **On what sea does much of southern Europe face?** *(the Mediterranean)*

★**THINKING FURTHER:** *Making Conclusions* **Why would you expect Europeans to use waterways extensively?** *(They are easily accessible.)*

Resource REMINDER

Practice and Project Book: *p. 64*

Desk Map

Outline Map

Geography of Europe

Read Aloud

"The great rivers and the strange number of canals . . . do not only lead to every great town, but almost to every village, and every farm-house in the country; and the [countless number] of sails are seen everywhere coursing up and down upon them."

These words were written by an English man named William Temple, after he visited the Netherlands 300 years ago. Like others before and after him, he was fascinated by the many rivers and canals throughout Europe.

Focus Activity

READ TO LEARN

What effects did the waterways of Europe have on the development of civilizations there?

VOCABULARY

- temperate
- deforestation
- navigable

PLACES

- Eurasia
- North Sea
- North European Plain
- Seine River

316

THE BIG PICTURE

You have already studied the geography of two parts of Europe—Greece and Italy. The Netherlands, often called Holland, is a small present-day country in northern Europe. In this chapter you will learn more about the European continent and its history.

Next to Australia, Europe is the world's smallest continent. Europe, however, connects with Asia to create the world's largest landmass, called Eurasia. Find the Ural (YUR ul) and Caucasus (KAW kuh sus) mountains on the map on the next page. They are considered to be the border between Europe and Asia.

In Europe you can find some of the most unusual features of geography—from spouting geysers in Iceland to huge glaciers in the Alps. Waterways are an important part of Europe's geography. Much human activity here has been shaped by rivers and canals, seas and bays, and harbors and channels.

 SHELTERED INSTRUCTION

READING STRATEGIES & LANGUAGE DEVELOPMENT

REREADING Remind students how useful it is to reread confusing passages. Point out how rereading helps readers understand and recall key facts. Explain that a good way to reread is by creating a question based on each subtitle in the text. Use a Think-Aloud to model the process. Read the subtitle "From Forests to Farmland" on p. 318 and ask, "How did forests become farmland?" Read the passage aloud, pausing to answer the question. Reread confusing sentences. **[SDAIE STRATEGY: MODELING/METACOGNITIVE DEVELOPMENT]**

WORD HISTORY Refer students to the word *fjord* on p. 317. Explain to them that the *fj* is a clue that this word comes from Norwegian, the language of Norway. Students might sometimes also see the word spelled *fiord,* which is an Anglicizing of the Norwegian.

EUROPE

Europe is shaped like a big peninsula jutting westward off Eurasia. The continent has many peninsulas and islands. Europe also has a long, jagged coastline. It is surrounded by the Atlantic Ocean, the Mediterranean Sea, the North Sea, and the Baltic Sea. The Scandinavian peninsula, located in the north, has narrow inlets called fjords (FYORDZ) where the sea surges in between cliffs.

The climate of Europe is temperate, or mild, because of the winds that blow over the warm currents of the ocean. Even some lands near the Arctic Circle are relatively temperate. Extreme temperatures are found mostly along the border with Asia and on the peaks of the Alps.

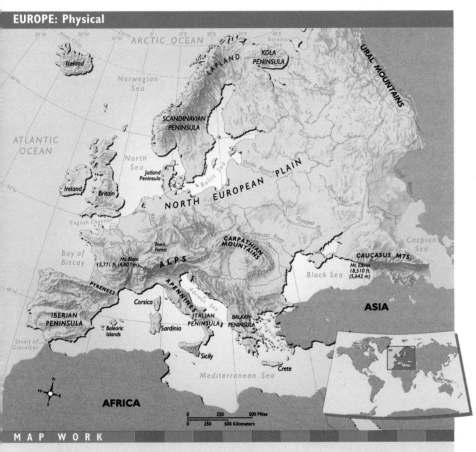

EUROPE: Physical

MAP WORK

The geography of Europe is varied. The continent has mountainous areas, plains, and rivers.

1. Which mountains separate the Iberian Peninsula from the rest of Europe?

2. Which is farthest north—the Aegean Sea, the Baltic Sea, or the Black Sea?

3. Which is the highest mountain in Europe?

MAP WORK: 1. Pyrenees 2. Baltic Sea 3. Mt. Elbrus

317

EUROPE

Call attention to Europe as a peninsula.

● **How does climate influence how people develop their culture?** (It affects what they can grow and the comfort or discomfort of their lives.)

● **What kind of climate does Europe have?** (generally temperate, or mild, but in some areas extremes prevail)

★THINKING FURTHER: *Cause and Effect* **How might a temperate climate benefit cultural development?** (good food production, pleasant to acceptable living conditions)

More MAP WORK

Refer students to the map. Encourage them to work between the map and text.

● **Trace your finger along the outline of Europe. What are the first things you notice?** (Students should note the long, jagged coastline, the many peninsulas and islands.)

● **What major islands do you spot?** (Britain, Ireland, Iceland)

● **What peninsulas can you identify?** (Iberian, Italian, Balkan, Jutland, Scandinavian, Kola)

● **What seas encircle Europe?** (North, Baltic, Norwegian, Barents, Caspian, Black, Aegean, Adriatic, Mediterranean)

● **What mountain ranges are Europe's highest?** (Alps, Pyrenees, Caucasus)

● **What river runs from the Black Forest to the Black Sea? from the Alps to the North Sea?** (the Danube; the Rhine)

★THINKING FURTHER: *Cause and Effect* **"Rivers and canals, seas and bays, harbors and channels"—What benefits do these geographic features bring to the development of culture and of civilization?** (Help students recognize that all these features encourage human movement, which in turn encourages trade among people in both goods and ideas, which in turn enriches cultures and furthers the growth of civilization.)

BACKGROUND INFORMATION

ABOUT EUROPE'S MINERAL RESOURCES

● Over time Europe has been well served by its mineral deposits.

● Europe provided considerable amounts of the two minerals—coal and iron ore—necessary for the modern Industrial Revolution. Although by now its iron ore resources have been largely depleted, Europe is still a major world coal producer.

● Petroleum resources were inadequate in Western Europe until oil was discovered in the North Sea in recent times. Now the North Sea has become a major source of crude oil, along with Russian fields around the Caspian Sea and fields in northern Russia.

● Bauxite (for making aluminum) and potash supplies are ample.

● Copper, lead, zinc, gold, and silver have been mined over time.

LAND AND WATER

As students discuss Europe's natural resources described on this page, talk about the mineral resources listed in the *Background Information* on p. 317.

Discussing From Forests to Farmland Refer the class to the map on p. 317.

● **What is deforestation and how does it relate to Europe?** *(The process of clearing forests from the land; it took place in Europe mostly after A.D. 1100.)*

● **Find the North European Plain on the map. Why might this be a major farming area?** *(Fairly temperate climate, fertile soil, and relatively flat land often means good farming.)*

⭐**THINKING FURTHER:** *Making Conclusions* **Why might a broad sweeping area like this also encourage warfare?** *(Remind the class of the peoples they learned about in Chapter 9, like the Huns and Visigoths, who marched across this plain, conquering those in their way. Such open land presents no natural barriers to invaders.)*

Exploring Bounty from Rivers and Seas Start a list on the board of benefits the waterways offer.

● **What benefits have Europe's rivers and seas brought its people?** *(fish, navigable waterways, water power, trade, busy port cities)*

⭐**THINKING FURTHER:** *Making Conclusions* **Why is it possible to travel from Britain to the Ural Mountains without ever leaving a boat?** *(Waterways, whether they are natural or human-built, connect all Europe from west to east.)*

More CHART WORK

As the class studies the chart on p. 319, have students use their desk maps to help identify the country or countries in which the city, river, and mountain are located.

⭐**THINKING FURTHER:** *Using Visuals* **In which country is Europe's highest mountain? its longest river? its largest city?** *(The answer to all three questions is Russia.)*

LAND AND WATER

The land and water of Europe are rich in natural resources. These resources have helped to make Europe a wealthy and productive region.

From Forests to Farmland

Two thousand years ago most of Europe lay under a blanket of dense forest. One group of Roman explorers is said to have walked through forests from Poland to France without ever seeing sunlight! Europeans began to clear forests to make room for farms and cities, especially after about A.D. 1100. The process of clearing forests is called deforestation. It has happened in many places around the world throughout history.

After forests were cleared, Europeans could farm more land. The most fertile farmland in Europe is found in a region called the North European Plain. Look at the map on page 317 to see this region. A long growing season helps farmers to grow crops like wheat in the plain's rich soil. In southern countries, like Greece and Spain, oranges and olives are grown.

Bounty from Rivers and Seas

Much of the European continent is within 300 miles of the sea. The jagged coastline creates natural harbors that help to protect boats. For these reasons, it is no surprise that fishing has always been important to the European economy. Fish are especially plentiful in the North Atlantic. Today nearly a third of all fish caught in the world come from waters around Europe.

Europe's rivers are also important to the economy. Over 2,000 years ago, Europeans began using river power to turn waterwheels that ground wheat. Traders transported goods on Europe's many long, navigable (NAV ih guh bul) rivers. Navigable rivers are deep

Today people still fish the waters near Iceland and herd cattle in mountainous Switzerland.

318

CURRICULUM CONNECTION

LINKS TO MUSIC Many European composers have written pieces about geographic features. Ask a music librarian to find some for the class.
● Johann Strauss: "Blue Danube Waltz," "Tales of the Vienna Woods"
● Richard Strauss: "The Alpine Symphony"
● Richard Wagner: "Siegfried's Rhine Journey"
● Bedrich Smetana: "My Country"

SECOND-LANGUAGE SUPPORT

READING STRATEGIES Summarizing may help second-language learners remember key information. Assign lesson sections to student pairs. Have them read and summarize the section and formulate a question about the main point. Have students challenge others to read the summary and answer the question, and record responses.

EUROPE AT A GLANCE

Total Land Area	3,800,000 sq. miles 9,900,000 sq. km
Highest Mountain	Mt. Elbrus, Russia 18,510 feet (5,642 m)
Longest River	Volga River, Russia 2,290 miles 3,687 km
Largest City	Moscow, Russia Population 10,769,000
Current Population	800,000,000
Percent of World Population	14%

Note: City population includes population for metropolitan area.
Source: 1997 Information Please Almanac and The World Almanac and Book of Facts 1997

GEO FACT
Though many of Europe's forests have been cleared, there are still large forests in Northern Europe. One of them is the Black Forest of Germany. This region gets its name from the dark fir and spruce trees.

CHART WORK

The chart provides information about the size and geography of Europe.

1. What is the largest city in Europe? What is its population?
2. How did the Black Forest get its name?

---

enough for boat travel. One important navigable river is the Seine River. Paris, France, one of Europe's largest cities, grew alongside the Seine River. Europeans have developed thriving economies by using rivers for power and transportation.

European engineers created more waterways by building canals. In fact, it is possible to travel by boat from the English Channel in the west to the Ural Mountains in the east. Locate these features on the map on page 317.

WHY IT MATTERS

Rivers and coasts were very important in the growth of European cultures. Waterways provided power and helped to make transportation and trade possible. Remember, though, that Europeans added to their natural river system.

Europe's rivers and coasts still affect the way people live. They are used for transport. The fishing trade helps feed millions of Europeans.

In upcoming lessons, you will read how Europeans used their continent's resources to build civilizations.

Reviewing Facts and Ideas

MAIN IDEAS

● Europe, Earth's second-smallest continent, has a long, jagged coastline.

● Closeness to the sea has had important effects on Europe's climate and economy.

● Europe's rivers and seas are great sources of fish. Waterways are also used for transportation and power.

THINK ABOUT IT

1. What makes the climate of Europe temperate?

2. Name a trade that has always been important to the European economy.

3. **FOCUS** How did the waterways of Europe affect life there?

4. **THINK** Explain why the following statement is a *fact* or why it is an *opinion*: "Europe's navigable rivers help in the transport of goods."

5. **GEOGRAPHY** Find the island of Corsica and the English Channel on the map on page 317. Trace two possible sailing routes between these places—one by sea and one by river. Which route is longer? How much longer?

319

Discussing WHY IT MATTERS
Review the importance of natural resources.

★**THINKING FURTHER:** *Cause and Effect How would you summarize the causes for the readiness of Europeans to establish their civilization?* (Have students review the natural resources that gave Europeans transportation, food, power, trade, and sites that helped them develop the cultures that would eventually lead to civilization.)

3 CLOSE

MAIN IDEAS

Call on students to answer the following questions.

● *Why, when Europe is among the smallest continents, does it have so many ports and so much shipping?* (It has long, jagged coastlines that provide many harbors.)

● *What effects has its closeness to the sea had on Europe?* (The sea tempers the climate and encourages trade.)

● *What are at least three benefits rivers and seas have given Europe?* (food fish, transportation, power)

EVALUATE
✓ **Answers to Think About It**

1. warming winds from the sea
Summarize

2. fishing
Draw Conclusions

3. They gave people food, power, transportation, trade, and cities.
Main Idea

4. It is a fact because it can be proven by information about the amount of shipping along rivers that is carried on each year.
Evaluate Fact/Opinion

5. Route One: from Mediterranean up through France by river. Route Two: west through Mediterranean, through Strait of Gibraltar, into Atlantic and north. Route 2 is more than five times as long.
Five Themes of Geography: Movement

Write About It Ask students to picture themselves as a river boat sailor in Europe, choose a river from the map on p. 317, and write a journal entry about their work on it.

MEETING INDIVIDUAL NEEDS

RETEACHING (Easy) Have students use an outline map of Europe and draw in major rivers and mountain ranges and the major plain.

EXTENSION (Average) Ask students to choose a geographic location in Europe that appeals to them, one where they might like to live for a while. Have them write a paragraph to describe the geographic features that attract them to this place.

ENRICHMENT (Challenging) Have students prepare a travelog about a trip from the source of a major European river to its mouth. First have them choose a river and use an encyclopedia or a travel book to research it and the surrounding land. In their travelog, students should describe the places they see and name some cities or landmarks that they pass along the way.

LESSON 2

Lesson Overview

During the *Middle Ages,* life in Europe revolved around the system of feudalism, which gradually grew weaker as trade re-emerged and towns grew into cities.

Lesson Objectives

★ Describe *feudalism* and life under it.

★ Explain how urban centers emerged.

★ Identify major events in the evolution of government.

1 PREPARE

MOTIVATE Have a student do the *Read Aloud* and discuss it as an "obituary" for the Roman Empire. You might draw a parallel to the breakup of the Soviet Union, to show the chaos that can result from government breakdown.

SET PURPOSE Refer students to the *Read to Learn* question, to introduce them to the Middle Ages, the period that followed the Roman Empire. Have them read to learn how Europeans found their way out of the chaos. Ask for meanings of *Vocabulary* terms.

2 TEACH

Understanding THE BIG PICTURE
Point out the photo of the castle and tell students that castles are characteristic of the Middle Ages.

● **When did the Middle Ages take place?** *(from about A.D. 500, following the fall of Rome, to about the 1500s.)*

★THINKING FURTHER: *Cause and Effect* **What effects did the breakdown of Roman rule have on Europe?** *(Small kingdoms replaced central rule; trade declined; wealthy nobles established manors; workers, or serfs, were bound to the manors.)*

Resource REMINDER

Practice and Project Book: *p. 65*

Anthology: *Sur le Pont d'Avignon, p. 68; Tale of King Arthur, pp. 69–72; A Contract Between a Vassal and Lord, p. 73*

Focus Activity

READ TO LEARN

What was life like in Europe during the Middle Ages?

VOCABULARY

- Middle Ages
- manor
- serf
- feudalism
- lord
- vassal
- fief
- guild
- Magna Carta

PEOPLE

- Charlemagne
- William the Conqueror
- King John I

PLACES

- Aachen
- Normandy
- England

320

---

400 · 500 · 1250 · 1300 · 1600

The Middle Ages

Read Aloud

"Woe to thee, Rome, that thou art crushed and trodden down by so many peoples; who has been seized by a northern king, and thy folk slaughtered and thy strength brought to nothing."

These words were written around A.D. 900 by a monk after an attack on Rome. The invaders were from England.

THE BIG PICTURE

Following the end of the western Roman empire around A.D. 500, Europe entered a new era of history. This period became known as the Middle Ages. It lies between the Roman period and about the 1400s.

The Roman empire left behind many legacies, including the Latin language and a large network of roads. The Christian religion also continued to grow and spread. However, the breakdown of Roman rule brought great changes for the people of Europe. Many small kingdoms developed.

Along with changes in government, the end of the Roman empire also brought about economic changes in Europe. Trade declined, after which ownership of land came to mean wealth and power. Large estates owned by wealthy nobles were called manors. Workers, called serfs, became bound to work on the manors. Serfs had little more freedom than slaves. Unlike slaves, however, serfs could not be bought or sold.

SHELTERED INSTRUCTION

READING STRATEGIES & LANGUAGE DEVELOPMENT

SEQUENCING Review sequence, the order in which events occur, and chronological order. To help students reexamine the lesson concept, have them create a flowchart tracing key events of the Middle Ages, from A.D. 500 to A.D.1500. Direct students to skim section headings and subheadings to find key events. Encourage students to add dates and brief descriptions as they read the chapter. **[SDAIE STRATEGY: TEXT RE-PRESENTATION/SCHEMA BUILDING]**

COMPOUND WORDS Refer the class to two compound words that appear on these pages: *breakdown* on this page and *set up* on p. 321. Have students identify *breakdown* as a noun and *set up* as a verb phrase. Explain that this is a common pattern for compound words— one word as a noun, but two words as a verb, as in *breakdown* (noun) and *break down* (verb), *setup* (noun) and *set up* (verb).

THE FRANKISH EMPIRE

Of the many small kingdoms in western Europe, one rose to great power in the 700s. This kingdom, ruled by a people called the Franks, was based in present-day France. You may remember from Chapter 9 that this region was the place the Romans called Gaul. The Franks built an empire that was the largest and richest in Europe since Roman times. Find it on the map.

A Powerful Ruler

The greatest leader of the Franks was called Charles the Great, or Charlemagne (SHAHR luh mayn). He conquered lands in southwestern parts of what is now France and in Italy and Germany. Charlemagne was a Christian. As his armies spread across Europe, they also spread Christianity.

Charlemagne's biggest achievement came in 800, when he arrived with his army in Rome. The leader of the Roman Church, Pope Leo III, placed a golden crown on Charlemagne's head and declared him Emperor. For a while, it appeared to western Europeans that the old Roman empire had risen again.

Charlemagne's Court

Charlemagne set up his capital in the city of Aachen (AH khun) in what is today Germany. His court became a lively political and cultural center.

Charlemagne was very tall for his time—over 6 feet. He loved to ride horses and swim in a pool he had built at Aachen. Perhaps most remarkably for his time, he also loved learning.

During the Middle Ages books were scarce and very few people could read. Charlemagne filled his court with scholars, poets, and musicians. One scholar at Charlemagne's court wrote this about the emperor:

> You know very well how sweet is arithmetic in its reasoning, and how pleasant is a knowledge of the heavenly stars in their courses. And yet how rare it is to find a man who takes the trouble to know these things!

FRANKISH EMPIRE, A.D. 800

MAP WORK

The Franks ruled an empire based in what is today France.

1. Which Mediterranean islands were part of the Frankish empire?

2. About how many miles was the city of Aachen from Rome?

Charlemagne established a school at his palace where scholars collected and copied Roman works.

321

LIFE IN THE MIDDLE AGES

Write *feudalism* on the board.

- **What was the system of feudalism?** *(a way of organizing and governing, based on land and service)*

> ★ **THINKING FURTHER:** *Making Connections* **How do you suppose the manor related to feudalism?** *(Help students see that the manor was the basic unit of feudalism.)*

Discussing Lords and Ladies As students work through these sections, have them draw a social pyramid on the board reflecting the information given.

- **What was the role of the lord and lady?** *(They were in charge of castle affairs.)*

> ★ **THINKING FURTHER:** *Making Conclusions* **Why might a lady of the manor have been quite powerful?** *(She often ran the manor.)*

Learning About the Lord's Vassals Develop the idea of reciprocity in the lord-vassal relationship.

- **What was a vassal?** *(a noble who was loyal to a manor lord and who served as a defender of the manor)*

- **How did the manor lord bind his vassals to him?** *(by giving them fiefs, separate manors to control)*

> ★ **THINKING FURTHER:** *Making Connections* **How did feudalism make lords and their vassals dependent on each other?** *(The lords needed soldiers, which the vassals provided, while vassals needed a means of support, which the lords provided.)*

LIFE IN THE MIDDLE AGES

During the Middle Ages, the manor was almost a world within itself. Some manors were so large that they included several villages as well as many acres of farmland. Often things that were needed were grown or made right on the manor. This meant that money was not needed to buy goods. It also meant that most people seldom left the manor during their entire lives.

Starting around A.D. 800 a system called feudalism developed in Europe. Feudalism is a way of organizing and governing society, based on land and service. Like the laws of ancient Rome, feudalism required that people behave in certain ways.

Lords and Ladies

At the top of feudal society was the noble, called the lord, who owned the manor. The lord had total control over his manor. In some parts of Europe, the lord also had to serve a king.

The lord's wife was the lady of the manor and was in charge of castle affairs. When the lord was away, she often led the defense of the castle if it was attacked.

As you can see on the diagram, the lord's castle was the center of all activity on the manor. The castle served both as a house for the lord's family and as a fort to protect the manor in case of attack.

The Lord's Vassals

Manor lords chose nobles who did not own land to serve

322

as vassals. Vassals took an oath of loyalty to the lord, pledging to serve him. In return, the lord gave each vassal a fief (FEEF). A fief was usually a separate manor. The vassal often did not own his fief, but he had authority over its serfs. Next to the lord, vassals were the most powerful people in feudal society.

The lady of a manor ran daily affairs, while knights defended the lord and his lands.

CURRICULUM CONNECTION

LINKS TO READING Suggest that students read David Macaulay's highly illustrated picture book *Castle* or watch the video based on it.

BACKGROUND INFORMATION

ABOUT KNIGHTHOOD
- Being a knight was an expensive proposition. A knight had to have at least three horses, complete armor, and a squire to serve him, all of which required means.
- Some knights tried to make a living by fighting in tournaments. A major event in tournaments was jousting, in which one fully armored knight galloped toward another with lance and shield raised in an effort to unseat the opponent and protect himself.

BACKGROUND INFORMATION

ABOUT THE STAGES IN A KNIGHT'S TRAINING
- Page—This stage began at age seven. One "textbook" for a page was a book of etiquette. Among its instructions: "Do not sigh, or belch, or with puffing and blowing cast foul breath upon your lord."
- Squire—This was the second stage. A short church ceremony marked taking this step. The squire was blessed by a priest and given a sword and a belt.
- Knight—Becoming a knight marked "graduation." On the eve of the ceremony that would make him a knight, the candidate spent the entire night in fasting and prayer. In the morning, the king dubbed him a knight by tapping him with a sword three times.

MANOR LIFE
The lord's castle was located at the center of a manor.

COMMON PASTURE

LORD'S CASTLE

WEST FIELDS

CHURCH

EAST FIELDS

MOAT

MILL

SERFS' HOUSES

The most important duty of a vassal was to serve as the lord's knight. Knights were soldiers who protected the manor. Sometimes they traveled with their lords to fight in distant lands.

A Knight's Training

The son of a noble began preparing for knighthood when he was young. First he learned to ride and care for horses. At the age of seven he left home to live and train in a knight's household. There he learned to behave with courtesy and to handle small weapons.

From the ages of 15 to 20, the young noble began to ride into battle alongside the knight. After this experience he was ready to become a knight himself. In a special ceremony he knelt before a lord and was declared a knight.

Life of a Serf

In Europe during the Middle Ages, only about one person in a hundred was a noble. Most Europeans were serfs or village craftworkers. Craftworkers were free, but they had to follow the rules of the nobles.

Serfs were given some land to farm for themselves, but they had to work the lord's land too. Serfs also had to pay rents and taxes to the lord. They even had to ask the lord's permission to get married.

Serfs usually lived in small one-room houses with a fire in the center for cooking and warmth. The whole family slept in one large, straw bed. Most shared their houses with animals. One observer said, "The livestock use the same entrances as the people, and they are not far from sleeping together."

Life was short and difficult—few serfs lived past the age of 40. Most people married while they were in their early teens. Serfs' lives revolved around work in the manor fields. Everyone, including young children, gathered wheat and picked vegetables. The village church bell rang every hour and signaled breaks for meals.

323

BACKGROUND INFORMATION

ABOUT THE LIFE OF A SERF
In the 1100s, a writer had this to say about a fictional serf:

• "I work hard. I go out at daybreak, driving the oxen to the field, and then I yoke them to the plow. Be the winter ever so [cold], I dare not linger at home for [fear] of my lord ... Every day I must plow a full acre or more ... I have a boy, driving the oxen with an iron [rod], who is hoarse with cold and shouting. Mighty hard work it is, for I am not free."

USING THE ANTHOLOGY

TALE OF KING ARTHUR, pages 69–72 After students read the selection ask them to explain its popular appeal over the centuries.

More **DIAGRAM WORK**

Refer students to the diagram and have them examine it carefully.

● **In what way was a manor self-supporting?** *(Everything needed to live was produced on the grounds.)*

● **What is at the center of the manor?** *(the lord's castle)*

● **What surrounds the castle?** *(Common pasture, church, east fields, serfs' houses, mill, moat, west fields)*

★THINKING FURTHER: *Making Conclusions* **Why do you think the castle is at the center of the manor?** *(Since the lord was at the center of manor life, it would make sense that his home would be at the center of the manor.)*

Exploring A Knight's Training
Have students draw a timetable on the board, showing the ages and stages in a knight's training and the duties and skills involved in each. Then have them match the facts in the *Background Information* note on p. 322 to these stages.

★THINKING FURTHER: *Making Conclusions* **Why would a young man want to go through the long training to become a knight?** *(Help students recognize that knighthood held high status and was one of a few options for a man of good family.)*

Discussing Life of a Serf Make sure that students understand that feudalism involved only the arrangement between lords and vassals. The arrangement between serfs and their feudal masters is known as *manorialism.*

● **What duties did serfs have to their feudal master?** *(work his land, pay him rents and taxes, get his permission to marry)*

★THINKING FURTHER: *Classifying* **The philosopher Thomas Hobbes called life "poor, nasty, brutish, and short." How does this description apply to the lives of serfs?** *(Have students match details from the text to these adjectives, for example, "short"—few lived past age 40.)*

GROWTH OF TOWNS

Have students work with this section by creating a cause and effect chart on the board.

> ★ THINKING FURTHER: *Cause and Effect* **How would you create a cause and effect chart to show the growth of towns?** *(more peaceful time → surpluses created → need for places to trade surpluses → towns developed as marketplaces → greater prosperity → people living longer → population growth → serfs attracted to towns by freedom → more town growth)*

Learning about Town Craftworkers Encourage students to examine the illustrations showing town life and craftworkers as part of it. Share the *Background Information* at the bottom of this page with students.

- **How would you describe a typical craftworker operation?** *(home-based, family-owned and run, with father making goods and all family members helping in making and selling)*

- **What was the role of the guilds?** *(These organizations of individual crafts made rules that set quality, prices, and training standards.)*

> ★ THINKING FURTHER: *Making Conclusions* **Why might guilds have helped both craftworkers and consumers?** *(If they set high standards, goods would be attractive and useful to buyers and thus increase sales for sellers.)*

Investigating Europe's Cities Examine the growth from town to city.

- **What was good about emerging city life?** *(glory, influence, wealth, trade)*

- **What was bad?** *(danger, evil, vice)*

> ★ THINKING FURTHER: *Compare and Contrast* **How would you compare town and city life of Europe during the Middle Ages with manor life there?** *(Help students recognize the usual urban vs. rural life differences in housing, crowding vs. open spaces, work done, different social activities.)*

GROWTH OF TOWNS

Around A.D. 1000 Europe's economy began to change. The nobles began to spend less time in battle and more time on the manors. Nobles increased their farmlands, clearing forests and draining swamps. This created crop surpluses for the manor lords. Towns developed to provide a marketplace for the surpluses.

European traders exchanged goods like grains, wool cloth, and wine for spices and silk from Asia and Africa. They also used coin money for the first time since the days of ancient Rome.

With more to eat, people lived longer and the population grew. So did the towns. By the 1200s many towns had become crowded and dirty. Houses were so close that upstairs neighbors could shake hands across the street. Many serfs saw towns as places where they could escape from the manors. They came to the towns because they said the "air was freer." In fact, serfs could win their freedom if they remained in a town without being caught for a year and a day.

Town Craftworkers

The narrow town streets were lined with shoemaking, saddle making, and other craft shops. Most shops were family-owned businesses on the ground floor of a house. The father might have been an expert craftsman, or master. He ran the business while his wife and children helped. If her husband died, the wife often took over the business.

Traders and craftworkers organized themselves into groups called guilds

324

Much trading took place in towns like Rothenburg, Germany (left). Food brought to town from manors was sold in busy markets (below).

(GILDZ). Each craft, such as carpentry, had its own guild that made rules about quality and prices. The guild also set the path by which an apprentice, or a beginner craftworker, became a master.

Europe's Cities

Some towns, such as London, grew into cities. In 1175 one London resident, William fitz Stephen, wrote:

> *Among the noble and celebrated cities of the world, London, the capital of the kingdom of the English, extends its glory farther than all others and sends its wealth and [goods] more widely.*

BACKGROUND INFORMATION

ABOUT THE PATH FROM APPRENTICE TO MASTER

- At around the age of 14, boys began an apprenticeship by going to live with a master's family and learning the craft. As apprentices, they received only food and lodging for pay.

- After from 3 to 12 years' training and work, the apprentice was made a journeyman. Now he was paid for his work but could not yet join the guild or open his own shop.

- For at least another three years, the journeyman had to work under a master. As a final step, he had to make an item of his trade—whether a shoe or a sword or a candlestick—that was so good it was judged a "master piece." Only then could the journeyman become a master, enter his guild, and open his shop.

Not everyone agreed that London was a glorious city. Some people thought that London was very dangerous. One trader from France who visited there said,

If you go to London pass through it quickly ... Every evil or [vicious] thing that can be found anywhere on earth you will find in that one city.

Popular Songs

Some of the people passing through Europe's towns and cities during this time were traveling musicians. These people of the 1100s and 1200s were called troubadours (TROO buh dawrz) and minstrels (MIN strulz). Troubadours and minstrels wrote and performed songs about love and life for Europe's nobles. These traveling musicians usually accompanied themselves on the guitar or lute. You may remember that both instruments had been introduced to Europe by Arab musicians in the 700s.

Carcassonne, a town in southern France, was protected by three rows of stone walls. The French restored the town beginning in the 1800s.

Although many troubadour songs praised the idea of love, some of them were funny. This song, by a woman troubadour named Isabella, tells about a man she once loved.

*Elias Cairel, you're a phony
if I ever saw one,
like a man who says he's sick
when he hasn't the slightest pain.
If you'd listen I'd give you good
    advice:
go back to your [home] and don't
dare pronounce my name again.*

Minstrels often had to wander from court to court looking for work.

325

Discussing Popular Songs Write *troubadour* and *minstrel* on the board.

● **Who were the troubadours and minstrels?** *(musicians who traveled through Europe during the 1100s and 1200s)*

● **What kind of music did they make?** *(songs of love and life)*

● **Who was their audience? Why might this group have been their audience?** *(Nobles; only the nobles would have the money to pay or house them.)*

● **What skills did troubadours and minstrels need to succeed?** *(good singing voices, the ability to play an instrument to accompany themselves, and the ability to make up tunes and write loving or comical lyrics to them)*

● **Why did these musicians find it necessary to travel?** *(They had to move around to find courts that would want to hear their songs and support them for a time.)*

★**THINKING FURTHER:** *Compare and Contrast* **How would you compare the life of a troubadour or minstrel with the life of a modern-day pop musician?** *(Encourage students to think in terms of song writing, travel, audience, and rewards for success.)*

BACKGROUND INFORMATION

ABOUT THE GROWTH OF UNIVERSITY TOWNS
● A major contributor to the rise of towns in the Middle Ages was a development in higher education.
● Centers of learning called universities emerged in France at Paris and in Italy at Bologna.
● With these universities as models, numerous others sprang up, for example, in England at Oxford and Cambridge.
● Universities today are direct descendants of these institutions. Traditions such as set courses of study, examinations, and the awarding of degrees are all legacies of the universities of the Middle Ages.

CURRICULUM CONNECTION

LINKS TO LANGUAGE ARTS Refer students to the troubadour's song in the text. Have them divide into groups and compose their own verse that a troubadour might have written. Encourage them to set it to music.

SECOND-LANGUAGE SUPPORT

DRAMATIZATION Role-playing helps second-language learners develop oral skills. Choose students to play Charlemagne, Charlemagne's court, lords and ladies, vassals, craftworkers, troubadours, kings, and serfs. Have students read about their roles in the Middle Ages and create skits to introduce themselves in character to the class. Be sure they explain the relationship to others.

CONQUERORS AND KINGS

Remind students that economic and social change is often accompanied by political change.

Discussing Invasions from the North Explain to the class that the Vikings held the same terror for Europeans of the Middle Ages that the Germanic barbarians had held for the Romans. In fact, Europeans had a prayer: "From the wrath of the Northmen, O Lord, deliver us!"

● **Who were the Vikings?** *(invaders from Scandinavia who attacked European towns)*

★**THINKING FURTHER:** *Sequencing* **How did some Vikings become Normans?** *(by settling down in France and adopting French culture)*

Learning how Normans Invade England Have students locate the English Channel on the map on p. 321.

★**THINKING FURTHER:** *Cause and Effect* **How did the Norman conquest change England?** *(It replaced Anglo-Saxon rule with strong, organized Norman rule and it blended Norman culture into Anglo-Saxon culture.)*

Exploring The Power of English Kings To expand students' understanding of the *Magna Carta*, share the *Citizenship* note at the bottom of the page with them.

● **Why did the lords oppose King John I?** *(They believed he was trampling on their rights as Englishmen.)*

● **How did they get him to change his ways?** *(by using knights to force him to sign the Magna Carta)*

MANY VOICES
PRIMARY SOURCE

Discussing the PRIMARY SOURCE

Have students read the Magna Carta excerpts aloud.

★**THINKING FURTHER:** *Making Conclusions* **Why might the Magna Carta be considered an early step toward fairer government?** *(It limits government power by stating the legal rights government must grant citizens.)*

CONQUERORS AND KINGS

The growth of towns and trade had greatly changed the economy and social life of Europe by the 1200s. At the same time, western Europe's political life was also undergoing developments.

Invasions from the North

At the end of Charlemagne's reign, in the early 800s, mainland Europe had come under attack by people from the north. These invaders were called Vikings, or Norsemen. The name Norsemen means "Northmen." The Norsemen sailed from Scandinavia in search of riches and land. For hundreds of years they made surprise attacks across Europe. Their invasions were part of the reason that the Frankish empire fell apart after Charlemagne's death.

By 900 some Norsemen began setting up villages around the mouth of the Seine River. Find this region on the map on page 321. These Norsemen became known as Normans. The region in which the Normans settled was called Normandy. The Normans adopted Christianity, the French language, and many Frankish customs.

Normans Invade England

In 1066 Norman forces crossed the English Channel and conquered the Anglo-Saxon people of England. The Norman leader became known as William the Conqueror.

William, the first Norman king of England, established a strong and well-organized rule in England. As a result, Norman and English cultures blended. In fact, the English language we speak today comes from a mix of French and the language of the Anglo-Saxons.

326

These Viking chess pieces were carved from walrus ivory.

The Power of English Kings

One of the kings who ruled England after William was King John I. King John was crowned in 1199. Like other kings before him, he tried to increase his power over England's lords. John demanded money from the lords to pay for wars. He also claimed the power to imprison a person without a trial.

In 1215 a group of lords took action to limit the king's power. They wrote a charter, or legal document, which stated that they had certain rights, such as the right to a fair trial. This charter was called the Magna Carta, which means "great charter" in Latin.

With the support of their knights, the lords forced the king to sign the Magna Carta. Some of the laws are shown on the next page. Which one guarantees that even the king would have to follow the laws?

CITIZENSHIP ★

UNDERSTANDING GOVERNMENT—ABOUT THE MAGNA CARTA
● The Magna Carta grew out of the feudal relationship between King John and England's lords, who were his vassals. As vassals, they owed allegiance to him, but they believed he demanded too much loyalty, such as having them go overseas to serve him or paying him exorbitant taxes.

● Because these lords outnumbered the king, and because they had their own vassals to join them in fighting him, John I had to give in and sign the document.

● Most of the clauses in the Magna Carta pertained only to the nobles, but later the rights they named were extended to all classes. One clause would eventually lead to the development of Parliament, England's representative governing body.

MANY VOICES
PRIMARY SOURCE

**Excerpts from
the Magna Carta,
by the lords of England, 1215.**

We have granted to all free men
of our kingdom for us and our
heirs forever, all the liberties written below.

No widow shall be forced to marry
so long as she wishes to live without a husband.

A free man shall not be fined for a
small offense.

No sheriff, or anyone else, shall
take horses or wagons of anyone
without permission.

No freeman shall be taken, or
imprisoned, or banished, or in anyway injured, except by the law of
the land.

To no one will we sell, to no one
will we deny or delay, rights or
justice.

All merchants shall be safe and
secure in leaving and entering England . . . both by land and by
water, for buying and selling.

All these customs and liberties . . .
shall be observed by all men of our
kingdom.

The Magna Carta (left)
contains 63 articles, or
parts. The charter has
influenced many
political leaders.

WHY IT MATTERS
The Magna Carta was a beginning
toward limiting the power of a ruler by
law. It gave rights mainly to nobles.
Eventually, it would serve as an example
of rights for all people. As you will read
in the next lesson, the Christian Church
also had great effects on the lives of
Europeans during the Middle Ages.

✓ Reviewing Facts and Ideas

MAIN IDEAS

● Charlemagne, a king of the Franks,
built an empire in Europe in the 800s.

● The manor was the center of life for
most Europeans in the Middle Ages.

● In the late Middle Ages towns grew
and trade expanded.

● Normans, a people from Scandinavia,
invaded many parts of Europe and
eventually conquered England.

● King John I was forced to sign the
Magna Carta in 1215, protecting certain rights of England's nobles.

THINK ABOUT IT

1. What did vassals promise to a lord
under feudalism? What did the lord
give in return?

2. What was the purpose of guilds in
European towns?

3. **FOCUS** How was life different for
serfs and town residents during the
Middle Ages?

4. **THINKING SKILL** What *effects* did the
Magna Carta have on the relationship
between England's lords and kings?

5. **WRITE** Suppose you are a visitor to a
manor during the Middle Ages. Write
three daily journal entries about what
you see at the manor.

327

Discussing WHY IT MATTERS
Have several students work together at
the board to complete this activity.

★**THINKING FURTHER:** *Sequencing*
**How would you construct a class
flow chart of important developments in European civilization
from A.D. 500 to 1500?** *(Chart
may include: fall of Rome, Charlemagne's court, feudalism, growth of
towns, Norman Conquest, Magna
Carta, end of Middle Ages)*

★ 3 CLOSE

MAIN IDEAS
Have students write their answers and
then exchange papers with a partner
for verification and correction.

● *What did Charlemagne accomplish?* (He built the Frankish empire,
the greatest since the Roman empire.)

● *What was the center of life for
most Europeans in the Middle
Ages?* (the manor)

● *What happened to towns and trade
during the late Middle Ages?* (Both
expanded greatly.)

● *How did the Normans change the
history of England?* (They conquered the nation and set up a new
government there.)

● *What was the Magna Carta?* (a
document protecting the rights of
English nobles, which they forced the
king to sign)

EVALUATE
✓ **Answers to Think About It**

1. military support; control of a fief
Summarize

2. to regulate the crafts
Recall Details

3. Serfs were bound to the land; townspeople were free. Living conditions
differed along urban/rural lines.
Main Ideas

4. The lords gained the protection of
laws, limiting the king's power.
Cause and Effect

5. Encourage students to think about
living and working conditions, physical layout, and the people.
Summarize

Write About It Have each student
choose someone from the Middle Ages
and write a paragraph describing life as
that person.

MEETING INDIVIDUAL NEEDS

RETEACHING (Easy) Divide the class in half and have one-half create
an illustrated flow chart showing the path from squire to knight and the
other the path from apprentice to master.

EXTENSION (Average) Have each student choose a role he or she
might have liked to play in the Middle Ages. Then have them write a
two- or three-paragraph journal entry describing that life.

ENRICHMENT (Challenging) Divide the class into groups and assign
each group one of the following areas of Viking life: life at home; boats
and sailing; soldiering—armor and weapons; areas of the world invaded. Have each group research their topic (there are several good young
adult books on the Vikings) and prepare a presentation of their findings for the class.

Lesson Overview

Point of view reveals how a speaker or a writer looks at a particular subject.

Lesson Objective

★ Determine points of view.

1 PREPARE

MOTIVATE Ask students if they have ever watched a news show in which several people discussed a topic. Help students see that the producer wanted several ways of looking at the subject. Then have students read *Why the Skill Matters* to help them determine points of view. Get students to see people's likes, dislikes, and backgrounds that help determine their points of view.

SET PURPOSE Discuss ways that background and feelings shape a point of view. Explore reasons we have to determine a person's point of view in evaluating what he or she says. Have students read *Helping Yourself* to preview ways to go about determining point of view.

2 TEACH

Using the Skill Remind students of the role feelings play in shaping a person's point of view.

● **Who is the subject of the poem?** *(the writer's lord)*

● **What clues can you find to show how the writer feels about his subject?** *(words like "dear" and statements of loyalty)*

● **Who is the writer?** *(the lord's knight)*

Resource REMINDER

Practice and Project Book: *p. 66*

Transparency: *Graphic Organizer*

Thinking Skills

Determining Point of View

VOCABULARY

point of view

WHY THE SKILL MATTERS

In the last lesson you read about some of the different people who made up European society in the Middle Ages—lords and ladies, serfs and craftworkers, troubadours and minstrels. All these people had different roles in society, with different jobs, rights, and duties. They also had different points of view.

A point of view is the position from which someone looks at the world. It is shaped by his or her background, concerns, likes and dislikes, interests, and fears. A person's point of view helps shape his or her opinion on many things. Different people have different points of view about the same subject. No one point of view presents that subject completely and accurately. In a classroom, for example, a teacher's point of view is usually different from a student's point of view. Determining a person's point of view helps us to understand how that person sees things. To understand something completely and accurately, you must look at it from a variety of points of view.

USING THE SKILL

One way to determine a person's point of view is to look carefully at a statement that he or she has made. The person's focus, the words he or she uses, and the opinions expressed often reveal his or her point of view.

The poem you will read was written during the Middle Ages. First identify the subject. The first line tells you that the writer was writing about his lord. Apparently, his

relationship to the lord was very important. As you read the poem, try to find clues that tell how the writer felt about his lord. These clues will help you to determine his point of view and who he was.

> If my dear lord is slain, his fate I'll
> share.
> If he is hanged, then hang me by his
> side.
> If to the stake he goes, with him I'll
> burn;
> And if he's drowned, then let me
> drown with him.

One clue that you might notice right away is the word *dear*. This word shows you the writer's opinion about his lord, which was that he cared for him very much. Other phrases also show that the writer felt that the lord was very important. In fact, the writer was willing to die with him. What kind of person wrote this poem? A knight? Remember that a knight was a lord's vassal. He pledged to serve his lord. This poem

The Bayeaux Tapestry, embroidered in the 1100s, is a Norman record of their invasion of England in 1066.

READING STRATEGIES & LANGUAGE DEVELOPMENT

CONTEXT CLUES Review with students the concept of a word's context, how its use and the words around it help us define an unfamiliar word and also expand our understanding of a familiar word. For example, refer students to the use of *stake* in the knight's poem. They probably know what a stake is—"a pointed piece of wood or other material driven into the ground," but its use in its context here tells us that it was used in executions by burning in the Middle Ages.

HOMOPHONES Set students on a homophone hunt in this *Skills Lesson*. Tell them to find words that have homophones and list them (some/sum, roles/rolls, rights/writes/rites, made/maid, stake/steak, dear/deer, die/dye, knight/night, sent/cent/scent, there/their). Remind students of the need to use the right homophone in writing. Most computer spelling checks do not catch homophones as misspellings.

*brave
**You must, you may be ordered; Charlemagne expects the lords to do as he commands, the knight feels such strong loyalty

shows *loyalty*, one of the most important qualities for a knight to have. Can you think of another word that might describe this knight's point of view?*

TRYING THE SKILL

Now read the following announcement that Charlemagne sent to all the lords in his empire. Remember that Charlemagne was a ruler of the Franks during the Middle Ages. As you read this announcement, use the Helping Yourself box to help you determine Charlemagne's point of view.

You must arrive at Strassfurt with your men on June 18, complete with supplies, so that you will be able to proceed from there in any direction in which you may be ordered to go.

Helping yourself

- **Point of view** is the position from which a person views something.
- First identify the subject or topic that the person is discussing.
- Identify words or phrases that tell how the person feels about the topic.
- Use this information to determine the point of view of that person.

that he is willing to do much more for his lord; Charlemagne does not use caring words such as *dear*.

What are some key words or phrases in this announcement that tell how Charlemagne felt about the lords? Compare this announcement with the earlier example. How was Charlemagne's point of view about the lords different from the knight's? How can you tell?**

REVIEWING THE SKILL

1. What is a point of view?
2. What shapes people's points of view? Explain your answer.
3. How does one's point of view influence how he or she sees things?
4. Why might learning about various points of view be important in a democracy?

BACKGROUND INFORMATION

USING THE GRAPHIC ORGANIZER You may want to have students work with this Graphic Organizer transparency to help them organize their information.

★**THINKING FURTHER: *Determining Point of View* How would you describe the point of view of the knight?** (highly admiring of his lord and fiercely loyal to him, willing to serve him under any circumstances)

Trying the Skill Have students review *Helping Yourself* before beginning this section.

- **What do you already know about the background of this speaker, Charlemagne?** (He was a powerful emperor, accustomed to command.)
- **What clues reveal his point of view?** ("You must," "you may be ordered")

★**THINKING FURTHER: *Determining Point of View* How would you describe Charlemagne's point of view?** (He expects others to follow his orders.)

Using Visuals Ask students to examine the Bayeux Tapestry.

★**THINKING FURTHER: *Determining Point of View* From whose point of view was the tapestry created? Who might have had a different point of view?** (the Normans; the English)

3 CLOSE

SUM IT UP

Have students listen to one another and to other people. Then have them list the kinds of things they believe they should know about people to determine their points of view. Encourage them to recognize differing points of view.

EVALUATE
✓ **Answers to Reviewing the Skill**

1. the position from which a person looks at the world
2. their backgrounds, concerns, likes and dislikes, interests, and fears
3. it shapes his or her opinions
4. Understanding various points of view could help people within a democracy make decisions that would be acceptable to a majority of the people.

LESSON 3

Lesson Overview
Christianity played a powerful role in European life during the Middle Ages.

Lesson Objectives
★ Describe the role of monasteries, convents, and cathedrals in society.
★ Analyze the Crusades and their effects on Europe.
★ Explain the effects of the Black Death on Europe.

1 PREPARE

MOTIVATE Ask students to identify the subject of the photo (a church). Remind them they have studied economic, social, and political developments in Europe during the Middle Ages. Ask the class to identify the development they will now study (religion). Have a student do the *Read Aloud.*

SET PURPOSE Review information about the beginnings of Christianity and its spread through the Roman Empire. Refer students to the *Read to Learn* question. Preview the *Vocabulary.*

2 TEACH

Understanding THE BIG PICTURE Help students recall the polytheism prevalent in Europe before Christianity.

● **How did Christianity expand after the Roman empire fell?** (*It spread across all Europe.*)

● **How would you describe its importance to life in Europe?** (*It was central, important even in small tasks.*)

★ **THINKING FURTHER: Predicting**
What role do you predict Christianity might play in European civilization during the Middle Ages? (*Help students recognize the power of a single set of religious beliefs on a civilization's values.*)

Resource REMINDER
Practice and Project Book: *p. 67*

400 500   1350   1600

The Church in the Middle Ages

Read Aloud
The overwhelming majority of people in Europe in the Middle Ages were Christian. In fact, Europe was a large part of what the Christians called Christendom—or "kingdom of the Christians." At the center of this "kingdom" was the Christian Church based in Rome. The Church leader was the Pope, who was as powerful as any king or lord.

Focus Activity

READ TO LEARN
How did Christianity affect life in Europe?

VOCABULARY
* monastery
* nun
* convent
* cathedral
* saint
* Crusade
* plague

PEOPLE
* Benedict
* Francis of Assisi
* Pope Urban II

PLACES
* Chartres

THE BIG PICTURE
During the Middle Ages Christianity spread throughout the entire continent of Europe. Kings, such as Charlemagne, brought Christianity to conquered lands. In other places, such as Ireland, priests brought the new religion. Eventually Christianity became central to life for almost everyone in Europe. People even measured a simple act like boiling an egg by the length of time it took to say a certain prayer.

Not all Europeans were Christian, however. Jews had lived in villages and towns throughout Europe since the early days of the Roman Empire. Muslims had come to Spain around A.D. 700. In this lesson you will read how the Christian Church in Rome affected Europe during the Middle Ages.

330

SHELTERED INSTRUCTION

READING STRATEGIES & LANGUAGE DEVELOPMENT

MAKING AND SUPPORTING GENERALIZATIONS Remind students that an effective way to understand what they read is to identify generalizations, conclusions drawn from details. Model the process by making a generalization based on information the Read Aloud contains. Then partner students to model how they would use reasoning and evidence to support the generalization. **[SDAIE STRATEGY: METACOGNITIVE DEVELOPMENT/MODELING]**

WORD ROOTS Refer the class to the word *manuscript* on p. 331 and write it on the board. Remind students that they have already encountered the word *script* in connection with scribes and writing. The word part *manu-* means "hand" and occurs also in *manufacture,* "to make by hand," and in *manual,* "using the hand."

AN "AGE OF FAITH"

The growth of Christianity in Europe happened gradually. Over time most people of other religions began to accept the Christian faith. Eventually Christian belief grew so strong that the later Middle Ages became known as the "Age of Faith."

Life in Monasteries and Convents

For several centuries, life in Europe revolved around religion. Some men, called monks, devoted their lives to religion. They lived in communities called monasteries. Women who vowed to devote their lives to religion were called nuns. Their communities were called convents. Many people entered convents and monastaries at a young age and stayed until death. In no place was faith stronger.

An Italian monk named Benedict wrote the first plan for monasteries in the A.D. 500s. Monks had to obey the head monk, who was called the abbot. Here are some of Benedict's rules:

No one, without permission of the abbot, shall presume to give, or receive, or keep as his own, anything whatever: neither book nor tablets, nor pen: nothing at all.... All things are to be common to all.

Monasteries and convents, like manors, were churches, farms, homes, and schools all rolled into one. Most monks and nuns spent much of the day in prayer. They also farmed and studied, and made wine, medicines, and craft goods.

Monasteries served as centers of learning in the Middle Ages. Most monasteries had a scriptorium, or a room for making books. Since no printing press existed, all books were carefully copied by hand. Monks wrote books of prayer and poetry. They also copied old Greek and Roman texts. These beautifully decorated books are called manuscripts. Some had such value that they were chained to desks. Today they are important records of ancient life and the Middle Ages.

In addition to praying, monks often spent time making illustrated books.

AN "AGE OF FAITH"

Help students to recognize that as greater numbers of people accepted Christianity others were more willing to become Christians.

Discussing Life in Monasteries and Convents If you have any monasteries or convents in your community or state, call students' attention to them. Write on the board the following words: *monastery, convent, monks, nuns.*

● **How would you pair these words and why?** *(Call on students to come up and link monastery with monk and convent with nuns and explain that monks lived in monasteries and nuns in convents.)*

● **What are monasteries and convents?** *(Monasteries: communities where religious men live and work; Convents: communities where religious women live and work)*

● **How were monasteries and convents similar to manors?** *(Both were self-contained worlds that could supply their own needs.)*

● **What kinds of work did the monks and nuns do?** *(prayed, farmed, studied, made wine, medicines, crafts, and produced hand-written books)*

★THINKING FURTHER: *Determining Point of View* **What attitude did monks have toward learning? How do you know?** *(They considered it important; they preserved ancient knowledge by copying it and recorded new knowledge that they developed.)*

CITIZENSHIP ★

MONKS AND NUNS AS GOOD CITIZENS During the Middle Ages, there were no hotels, restaurants, or hospitals as we know them. Often, only the monasteries and convents made such services available. Many had hostels where wayfarers could stop for a meal and bed for the night as well as facilities to treat the sick.

SECOND-LANGUAGE SUPPORT

TAKING NOTES As students read each section, have them create a personal log of terms and key words. At the end of each section, encourage peer discussion about the terms students included and their meanings. Have students keep their logs handy for later reference.

BACKGROUND INFORMATION

ABOUT ILLUMINATED MANUSCRIPTS
Refer the class to the manuscript pages illustrated on this page and explain that it shows an art form called *illumination.*

● The term comes from the Latin word *illuminare,* meaning "to light up."

● Illumination first appeared in the 600s and 700s and was developed by Christians, Jews, and Muslims to adorn manuscripts.

● Illuminated manuscripts required months of painstaking work. First, scribes copied the text onto vellum or paper. Then, artists drew and painted the illuminations, using paint as well as gold and silver.

Encourage students to show that they understand what happened to the Christian Church in 1054 by having them make a cause and effect diagram of events on the board (Cause: tensions between Pope in Rome and Church in Constantinople; Effect: split between the Eastern Orthodox Church and Roman Catholic Church).

- **What is a cathedral?** (a grand church)

- **Why did people of the Middle Ages want to build cathedrals?** (to express their religious beliefs)

★**THINKING FURTHER:** *Making Conclusions* **How might cathedral building have reflected both the pride of towns and rivalry among them?** (Cathedrals gave townspeople a way to show their success, and they strove to build a bigger, more beautiful cathedral than the next town.)

Discussing A Magnificent Cathedral Give the class time to study the illustration of the Cathedral of Notre Dame, its rose window, and the *Links to Art* scene of constructing a stained glass window.

- **Why is this a magnificent cathedral?** (Encourage students to note its soaring size, the engineering its building required, the skilled craft work it shows in its stained glass windows and its stone carvings.)

★**THINKING FURTHER:** *Making Connections* **Why do you suppose the cathedrals of the Middle Ages used so many stained glass windows and carvings of scenes in their design?** (You might hint at what they have already learned about widespread illiteracy in the Middle Ages, to help students appreciate that windows and carvings were often used to tell stories from the Bible in pictorial fashion, the only way the illiterate could "read" them.)

THE ROMAN CHURCH

For years there had been tension between the Pope in Rome and other Christian leaders in Constantinople. In 1054 these tensions led to a split in the Christian Church. The Church based in Constantinople was called the Eastern Orthodox Church. The Church based in Rome later became known as the Roman Catholic Church.

At around the same time as the split in the Christian Church, towns began to grow in size and wealth. Townspeople expressed their religious beliefs by building grand churches, or cathedrals. Skilled craftworkers created windows for the cathedrals out of pieces of colored glass. These stained-glass windows often showed scenes from Christian writings.

A Magnificent Cathedral

Suppose you are a traveler to Chartres (SHAHRT), France, in 1260. The road is narrow and muddy. As you emerge from the thick forest, you see the spires of the town's magnificent cathedral rising high into the sky.

Chartres Cathedral took about 36 years to build. Many workers never saw their cathedrals completed. Some took more than 400 years to build. Many cathedrals still stand as one of the great legacies of the Middle Ages.

Saints and Pilgrimages

Another way that Christians showed their devotion was through pilgrimages. Europe's Christian pilgrims traveled great distances to Rome or Jerusalem. Jerusalem was and is a holy city to Jews, Muslims, and Christians.

During the Middle Ages, pilgrims also traveled to shrines, or special buildings that had been built for saints.

332

The Cathedral of Notre Dame in Paris is known for its tall spires and many stained-glass windows (right). Sometimes knights on pilgrimage were women (below).

Saints are women and men considered to be especially holy.

One of the most honored saints of the Middle Ages was Francis of Assisi. He lived from about 1181 to 1226. Francis devoted his life to serving the poor and sick in Italy. His followers came to be called Franciscans.

The First Crusade

In 1095 Pope Urban II called for Christians throughout western Europe to make a pilgrimage to Jerusalem. He also urged the pilgrims to capture Jerusalem from the Seljuk Turks, who were Muslim. Thousands of Europeans responded to the Pope's call. This journey to gain control of Jerusalem was the first Crusade. Those who went were called Crusaders.

CURRICULUM CONNECTION

LINKS TO ART: DESIGN A STAINED-GLASS WINDOW, p. 333 Have on hand some picture books showing stained glass windows for the class to study before making their own models. An alternative to using craft sticks as the framework: Use black construction paper, folded over and cut into shapes.

LINKS TO READING Suggest that students read David Macaulay's highly illustrated book *Cathedral: The Story of Its Construction* or watch the video based on it.

LINKS TO SCIENCE In the illustration of the Cathedral of Notre Dame, call students' attention to the stone structures that line the outside walls. Explain that they are called "flying buttresses" and that they help support the walls and carry the heavy ceiling weight.

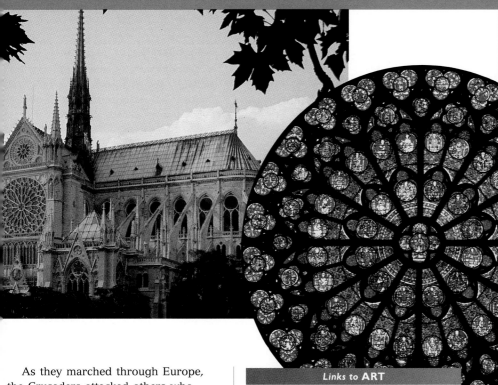

As they marched through Europe, the Crusaders attacked others who were not Christian. They raided Jewish communities in France and Germany. One shocked Christian wrote:

They should have traveled their road for Christ. Instead they turned to madness and shamefully, cruelly cut down the Jewish people in the cities and towns through which they passed.

About 100,000 knights, priests, and other pilgrims left for the "Holy Land," as the Crusaders called the land around Jerusalem. The Crusaders battled against Turkish armies even before they reached Jerusalem. The Crusaders suffered such great hunger and sickness that half died before they reached Jerusalem in 1099.

For two days the Crusaders attacked Jerusalem, killing many Muslims and Jews. The Crusaders captured Jerusalem, which would remain in Christian hands for about 100 years.

Links to ART

Design a Stained-Glass Window

The art of making stained-glass windows developed in western Europe during the Middle Ages. These windows are made of pieces of glass joined by strips of lead. At first the windows were small. By the 1200s, though, stained-glass windows were larger and had different shapes.

Many stained-glass windows in churches and cathedrals tell stories. Such windows helped people who did not know how to read to learn Bible stories.

Draw a design for a stained-glass window that you would like to see at the entrance of your school. As examples, look at stained-glass windows in churches and other buildings in your community. Then draw a sketch of the design and pieces of colored glass.

333

Discussing Saints and Pilgrimages
Help students see the link between saints and the pilgrimages to their shrines.

● **On what kinds of pilgrimages did Christians of the Middle Ages go?** *(to holy cities, like Rome or Jerusalem, or to shrines dedicated to holy people called saints)*

★THINKING FURTHER: *Making Generalizations* **What generalization can you make concerning ideas the pilgrimages, shrines, and saints reveal about life in Europe during the Middle Ages?** *(The period was marked by a strong drive to be holy and to do holy things.)*

Learning About The First Crusade Have students sit in pairs with one text opened to this page and the other to the map on p. 334.

● **Trace the routes of the Crusaders and tell how they show that the first Crusade was an all-European event.** *(They start at several different points in Europe and they probably gathered more troops as they proceeded on toward Constantinople.)*

● **What religious cause brought on the first Crusade?** *(the desire of Christians to capture control of Jerusalem from Muslim Turks)*

★THINKING FURTHER: *Making Generalizations* **How would you support the generalization that Crusaders were not always true to Christian teaching as they went on the march?** *(The recorded slaughter of Jews along the way does not seem to be in keeping with Jesus' teachings of love for all and obedience to the Ten Commandments, including "Thou shalt not kill.")*

CITIZENSHIP★

RECOGNIZING CULTURAL PERSPECTIVES For Christians, the Crusades represented a noble religious struggle to recapture the birthplace of Christianity. But the Holy Land was also important and sacred to both Jews and Muslims. Many Muslims viewed the Crusaders as little more than hostile invaders of their homeland. A Muslim poet, Usamah ibn-Munqidh, wrote of the Crusades:

● "When one comes to recount cases regarding the Franks [Europeans], he cannot but glorify Allah (exalted is He!) and sanctify Him, for He sees them as . . . possessing the virtues of courage, but nothing else . . ."

After reading the excerpt aloud, ask student to determine the differing points of view that could cause European Christians and Muslims to hold such differing opinions about the Crusades.

END OF THE MIDDLE AGES

Encourage students to see the cultural exchanges the Crusades introduced.

More MAP WORK

Refer to the map and encourage students to work with the text and map.

- **What Italian port cities did the Crusaders regularly pass through?** *(Genoa, Venice, Rome)*

- **What city of the Byzantine empire did they pass through?** *(Constantinople)*

- **How did all this travel promote cultural borrowing?** *(The Europeans were introduced to new products and knowledge from Asia and Africa.)*

- ★THINKING FURTHER: *Cause and Effect* **How would you construct a cause and effect diagram to show how the Crusades brought change to Europe?** *(knowledge of new goods→increased trade between Europe and the East→growth in the European economy→weakening of the feudal system in Europe)*

Discussing "Most Terrible of Terrors" To set the stage, have a student do a dramatic reading of the italicized description on p. 335.

- ★THINKING FURTHER: *Compare and Contrast* **How would you contrast Western Europe before and after the Black Death?** *(Before: bustling, growing in both wealth and population. After: brought to a standstill, one third of the population dead, people in sorrow and despair.)*

END OF THE MIDDLE AGES

Other Crusades took place over the next 200 years, but most of these failed. Despite their failure the effects of the Crusades were felt far beyond the Holy Land. Find the Crusade routes on the map on this page. As you can see, the Crusaders often passed through the Italian port cities on their way to the Holy Land. With more people passing through, trade began to grow in these cities. The Crusaders also returned to Europe, bringing products and new knowledge from Asia and Africa.

By the end of the Crusades in 1291, Europe had changed in many ways. With changes in Europe's economy, the system of feudalism was gradually breaking down.

"Most Terrible of Terrors"

One of Europe's cities bustling with activity was Siena, Italy. Here trade flourished and the people had been building a great cathedral since the 1100s. This cathedral remains unfinished to this day, however. Its construction was halted in 1348, when a plague struck Western Europe. A plague is a terrible disease that spreads quickly. This plague was caused by bacteria that was spread by rats and fleas. At that time, however, no one knew what caused the sickness. They just knew terrible misery and sadness. This plague, which was later called the Black Death, wiped out one third of the western European population. In Siena, two thirds of the people died. One man from that city described the horrible effects that the Black Death

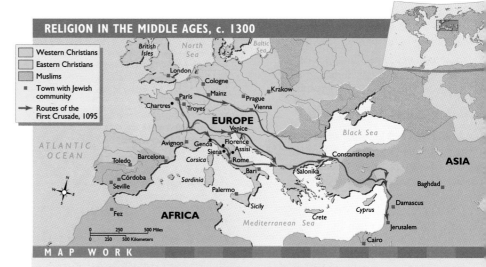

RELIGION IN THE MIDDLE AGES, c. 1300

- Western Christians
- Eastern Christians
- Muslims
- ■ Town with Jewish community
- → Routes of the First Crusade, 1095

ATLANTIC OCEAN

British Isles · North Sea · Baltic Sea
London · Cologne · Krakow
Paris · Mainz · Prague
Chartres · Troyes · Vienna
EUROPE
Venice
Avignon · Genoa · Florence · Assisi
Siena · Rome · Constantinople
Toledo · Barcelona · Corsica · Bari · Salonika
Córdoba · Sardinia · Palermo
Seville
Sicily · Crete · Cyprus · Damascus
Fez · AFRICA · Mediterranean Sea · Jerusalem
Cairo
Black Sea · ASIA · Baghdad

0   250   500 Miles
0   250   500 Kilometers

MAP WORK

Crusaders traveled throughout Europe on their way to Jerusalem.

1. Which towns east of Constantinople had a Jewish community?

2. Where did more Muslims live—in Europe or in northern Africa?

3. Which city did Crusaders pass through after they left Vienna?

MAP WORK: **1.** Baghdad, Damascus, Jerusalem, Cairo **2.** northern Africa **3.** Rome and Salonika

---

BACKGROUND INFORMATION

ABOUT THE CRUSADES AND EAST-WEST TRADE

- Among the new food products that Crusaders encountered in the East were rice, sugar, oranges, lemons, apricots, and melons.
- Spices too enticed their taste buds. The use of pepper, cinnamon, cloves, and nutmeg in Eastern food soon made many Crusaders prefer it to their own.
- Among the luxury goods they discovered were Persian rugs, Chinese silks, and fine steel from Damascus.
- The ships that brought the Crusaders from Italian ports began returning with these goods for trade. Demand for them in Europe skyrocketed, making Italian port cities the leading East-West traders in Europe.

GLOBAL CONNECTION

THE PATH OF THE BLACK DEATH The Black Death moved beyond Europe to Asia and Africa. In 1348 it struck Egypt, leaving thousands dead in Cairo. That same year it swept across western North Africa. In 1349 it moved from the Mediterranean eastward as far as the Persian Gulf, decimating Baghdad.

BACKGROUND INFORMATION

ABOUT "RING AROUND THE ROSIES" AND THE BLACK DEATH This children's rhyme grew out of the Black Death. The "ring" applied to the ring around the rash. The "posies" were flowers people carried hoping to ward off the disease. And the "all fall down" refers to dying.

These Crusaders are preparing to sail from Italy to Jerusalem.

had on people who became infected with the disease:

The plague began in Siena in May, a horrible and cruel event. They died almost immediately . . . they would swell up under the armpits and drop dead while talking. People brought members of their own household to the ditches as best they could, without priest or holy ceremony or ringing of bells. Nobody wept for the dead, since each was awaiting death; and so many died that everyone thought the end of the world had come.

Towns in France flew black flags from church towers to warn travelers of the plague. Nearly 130 years would pass before the plague was completely gone from Europe.

WHY IT MATTERS

Today the Roman Catholic Church and the Eastern Orthodox Church continue to be important to the lives of many Christians around the world. Some men and women still live in monasteries and convents. The splendid cathedrals of the Middle Ages remain as well. These creations of technology, imagination, and faith stand as stunning reminders of the achievements of the Middle Ages.

✔✔ Reviewing Facts and Ideas

MAIN IDEAS

- The Christian Church had a great influence on the lives of Europeans during the Middle Ages.
- Christians in Europe built magnificent cathedrals for worship.
- Monasteries across Europe served as centers of faith and learning.
- During the first Crusade, beginning in 1095, Christians conquered Jerusalem.
- In 1348 a plague struck Europe, killing one out of three people.

THINK ABOUT IT

1. What rule did Benedict give about property for monks?
2. For Pope Urban II, what was the main purpose of the Crusades?
3. **FOCUS** Why are the Middle Ages known as the "Age of Faith"?
4. **THINKING SKILL** Read the quote by the Christian writer on page 333. What shaped this person's *point of view*? What might have been the point of view of a Crusader?
5. **GEOGRAPHY** Study the map on page 334. What city was a stop along all Crusade routes shown? What empire ruled this city?

335

Discussing WHY IT MATTERS Use the *Curriculum Connection* note on p. 321 to remind students that the Middle Ages have also been called the Dark Ages.

★**THINKING FURTHER:** *Making Decisions* **Using what you have learned in this and the previous lesson, tell why the term Dark Ages does not properly apply to the Middle Ages.** *(Call on students for examples of achievements during the Middle Ages in knowledge, trade, cultural borrowing, art, and architecture.)*

⭐3 CLOSE

MAIN IDEAS

Call on students for answers.

- **What was the greatest religious influence on Europe during the Middle Ages?** *(the Christian Church)*
- **What architectural works remind us of the "Age of Faith"?** *(cathedrals)*
- **What did Christians accomplish in the first Crusade?** *(capturing Jerusalem from the Muslims)*
- **What did the Black Death do to the population of Europe?** *(killed a third)*

EVALUATE
✔ **Answers to Think About It**

1. no personal, only common, property
   Recall Details
2. to capture Jerusalem from the Muslims
   Summarize
3. because Christian belief was so strong among the people of Europe
   Main Idea
4. His point of view was a belief in following the teachings of Jesus; the point of view of other Crusaders may have been that non-Christians were fair game for attack.
   Point of View
5. Constantinople; the Byzantine empire
   Five Themes of Geography: Location

Write About It Ask students to write one generalization about how each of the following three categories affected life in Europe during the Middle Ages—(1) monasteries and convents, (2) places and ways of worship, and (3) the Crusades.

LESSON 4

PAGES 336–341

Lesson Overview

Thanks to renewed interest in ancient knowledge and arts, the Renaissance sparked a dazzling burst of creativity.

Lesson Objectives

★ Identify the roots of the *Renaissance.*

★ Explain the role of patrons in supporting Renaissance figures.

★ Describe the achievements of major Renaissance masters.

1 PREPARE

MOTIVATE Have two students do the *Read Aloud,* one doing a dramatic reading of the quote and the second the narration. What "powerful new way of thinking" does the quote express? Help students to see that the Renaissance was sparked by a belief that humankind was capable of more than had been thought.

SET PURPOSE What did this new period produce? Refer students to the photo of the head of Michelangelo's statue of David and to the *Read to Learn* question. Have them explore the lesson to find out. Preview the *Vocabulary.*

2 TEACH

Understanding THE BIG PICTURE Develop the concept of the rebirth of classical times.

● **In what ways was this new period a "rebirth"?** *(It renewed interest in the achievements of ancient times, and it made people feel more confident in their abilities and possibilities.)*

★ **THINKING FURTHER:** *Compare and Contrast* **How would you contrast the focus of thinking in the Middle Ages and the Renaissance?** *(Middle Ages: focus on the next world; Renaissance: focus on human possibilities in this world.)*

Resource REMINDER

Practice and Project Book: *p. 68*

Anthology: *Notebooks from the Renaissance, pp. 74–76*

 Technology: *AdventureTime!* CD-ROM

Focus Activity

READ TO LEARN

What were some major achievements of the Renaissance?

VOCABULARY

- Renaissance
- humanism
- patron

PEOPLE

- Lorenzo Medici
- Petrarch
- Michelangelo
- Leonardo da Vinci
- Nicolaus Copernicus

PLACES

- Florence

336

---

400   700   1000   1300 1350 1550 1600

The Renaissance

Read Aloud

"This is the supreme, marvelous truth of man. He can be that which he wills to be. God the Father endowed man, from birth, with the seeds of every possibility and every life."

These words are by Pico della Mirandola (PEE koh DAYL luh mee RAHN doh lah), an Italian scholar of the 1400s. He expressed a powerful new way of thinking that arose in Europe as the Middle Ages came to an end.

THE BIG PICTURE

Out of the misery of the Black Death came new ideas that stirred Europe. Starting around 1350 enthusiasm for art, literature, and trade increased throughout northern Italy. This was the beginning of a period called the **Renaissance** (REN uh sahns), from the French word meaning "rebirth." Many Europeans saw this time as a rebirth of the classical periods of Greece and Rome. Although the Renaissance began in Italy, within a century it had spread to the rest of Europe.

The Renaissance was a time of great creativity. Central to the ideas of the Renaissance was a powerful interest in **humanism** (HYOO muh niz um). Humanism meant concern with human interests and values. People in the Middle Ages had often turned their thoughts toward the "next world," or heaven. People of the Renaissance were still usually very religious. However, they began to focus more on what people could achieve in this world.

 SHELTERED INSTRUCTION

READING STRATEGIES & LANGUAGE DEVELOPMENT

USING VISUALS Review with students the different types of visuals and what each can reveal about a civilization. Arrange students in pairs to skim this lesson and select a painting, statue, or other piece of art they find especially striking, such as the Mona Lisa on p. 338. Then have partners imagine that they lived during the Renaissance. Have them write an eyewitness account of the work's creation, showing what it reveals about the values of the Renaissance. **[SDAIE STRATEGY: TEXT RE-PRESENTATION]**

WORD ORIGINS The text states that while the Renaissance began in Italy, it soon spread to the rest of Europe. Tell the class that France was probably the first place it spread, as reflected by the fact that the word *Renaissance* comes from French, as do this lesson's other two vocabulary terms—*humanism* and *patron.*

RENAISSANCE IN ITALY

Of course, the Renaissance did not happen overnight. Europeans did not wake up one morning and start a new era. Change came first to the city of Florence, in northern Italy. Why did the Renaissance begin in Florence?

The Glory of Florence

As you read in the last lesson, growth in trade, partly caused by the Crusades, benefited Italian cities. By 1400 Florence had become one of the richest cities in Europe. Find this city on the map on page 334. Traders from Florence journeyed to the towns of France and to the port cities of the Black Sea. They also traveled to Asia and Africa, returning with spices and silks. Florence was a busy craft-producing city. People worked in about 200 shops, turning out enormous amounts of woolen cloth.

Lorenzo the Magnificent

One of the wealthiest families in Florence was the Medici (MED ih chee) family. The Medicis gained great wealth through banking and trading. Although Florence had become a republic around 1300, by the 1400s the Medicis had gained control. The most famous member of the family was Lorenzo Medici. He came to power in 1469. Some considered him a tyrant—an all-powerful and often unjust ruler. One Florentine, however, said, "If Florence was to have a tyrant, she could never have a better or more delightful one."

Lorenzo Medici was a patron, or supporter, of the arts. He loved poetry and painting. Before long, scholars and artists flocked to Florence, where they were paid by Lorenzo to pursue their work. The city was soon bursting with art and learning, and its leader became known as "Lorenzo the Magnificent."

Lorenzo Medici (right) made Florence a powerful city in the late 1400s.

337

ARTS AND IDEAS
As you have read, the Renaissance was a time of looking back to achievements of earlier civilizations. During the 1300s humanists began to search the Italian countryside for Greek and Roman artifacts. They found examples of classical cultures such as manuscripts, coins, and statues to study for ideas.

European scholars, especially scientists, also learned from Arab scholars. As you read in Chapter 10, scholars in Baghdad preserved and developed Greek, Roman, and Indian scientific knowledge. As trade between Europe, Asia, and Africa grew during the Crusades, goods and knowledge spread.

The Power of Words
One of the earliest Italian humanists to study classics—works of literature from ancient Greece, Rome, and Arabia—was Petrarch (PEE trahrk). Petrarch was a poet who lived from 1304 to 1374. He loved learning, and he read every book he could find. Petrarch believed the classics were better than any works written later.

Petrarch became the most celebrated poet in all of Europe. He once described his love of writing as follows:

> There is no lighter burden, nor more agreeable, than a pen.... As there is none among earthly delights more noble than literature, so there was none more lasting, none gentler or more faithful.

Renaissance Artists
Artists as well as poets learned from ancient Romans and Greeks. One of the greatest Renaissance artists was Michelangelo. He used many classical ideas—such as balance of form—in his paintings, sculptures, and architecture.

338

You can see his *David* at the beginning of this lesson.

A very famous painter of Italy was the humanist Leonardo da Vinci (lee uh NAHR doh duh VIHN chee). He lived from 1452 to 1519. Like Michelangelo, Leonardo da Vinci was a painter, sculptor, and architect. However, Leonardo da Vinci was a scientist, engineer, and musician as well. Da Vinci's interests and talents were as broad as the Renaissance itself.

Leonardo da Vinci, the Painter
As a child, Leonardo da Vinci showed great ability in drawing. When he turned 15, his father took him to study with the greatest painter in

Mona Lisa, by Leonardo da Vinci, is one of the most famous paintings in the world.

Florence. Leonardo painted with such skill that his teacher put down his own paintbrushes and never picked them up again. Before long, Leonardo was invited to set up his studio in the garden of his patron, Lorenzo Medici.

Da Vinci loved the world of Florence. He would sometimes follow interesting townspeople for a whole day and then paint them from memory. Leonardo da Vinci's careful observation helped him create paintings that were so realistic they surprised viewers.

Leonardo da Vinci, the Inventor

Besides painting, da Vinci also kept hundreds of notebooks in which he wrote down all kinds of new ideas. Da Vinci always wrote backward to keep his ideas secret. He made plans for a submarine and a machine gun. He wrote this plan for a parachute:

If a man has a tent made of linen, of which the holes have all been stopped up, and it is 20 feet across and 20 in depth, he will be able to throw himself down from any great height without sustaining any injury.

Leonardo da Vinci studied carefully the flight of birds. His close observation helped him to design a flying machine. Four hundred years would pass before a human actually flew. Leonardo da Vinci's love of knowledge inspired future artists and inventors.

Earth, Sun, and Stars

In a small town in Poland, a young man named Nicolaus Copernicus (kuh PUR nih kus) studied books of Greek

Da Vinci drew this portrait of himself. He also made many sketches of his inventions such as a flying machine (below).

and Arab astronomy. He observed the night sky with a simple telescope and carefully recorded the positions of the stars he saw.

In 1514 Copernicus made a startling discovery. Earth seemed to orbit around the sun, once each year. This was a new idea. Since people first tracked the stars and moon, they believed that Earth was the center of the universe. Many European leaders, including officials of the Church in Rome, found this new theory unacceptable. They felt it went against Church teachings, which put Earth at the center of the universe. It was not until after Copernicus died that his book was published. It was called *On the Revolutions of the Heavenly Spheres*. Copernicus's ideas about the universe greatly changed our knowledge of astronomy.

339

Exploring Leonardo da Vinci, the Inventor Write the signature *Leonardo da Vinci* on the board and under it, "disciple of experiment." Explain to the class that this is how Leonardo proudly signed his name to one set of his works.

● **With what kinds of things did Leonardo experiment?** *(submarine, machine gun, parachute, flight. Tell students he also studied anatomy, botany, geology, and astronomy.)*

★**THINKING FURTHER:** *Classifying* **Leonardo has been classified as a genius and a visionary. What evidence can you give for each classification?** *(Genius: his early and amazing ability in art, his works of art, his breadth of study and knowledge; Visionary: his drawings of machines that would not appear for another 400 years)*

Discussing Earth, Sun, and Stars Remind the students that astronomy served religion in many cultures.

● **What revolutionary discovery did Copernicus make?** *(Earth is not the center of the universe.)*

● **Why was this discovery controversial at the time?** *(It contradicted Church teaching.)*

★**THINKING FURTHER:** *Making Conclusions* **Why might the Church have been upset about Copernicus's findings?** *(It might have feared that if this Church teaching were wrong, people might doubt other Church teachings as well.)*

CURRICULUM CONNECTION

LINKS TO ART AND SCIENCE For students who take a particular interest in art or science, you might recommend that they read the Horizon Caravel Book *Leonardo da Vinci*. It shows many of his paintings in full color as well as working models of some of his mechanical drawings.

LINKS TO LANGUAGE ARTS Explain to the class that two words are important in any discussion of the center of the universe—*geocentric* and *heliocentric*. Have them find the two words in the dictionary and explain why (*geo*- from the Greek for "earth" = "earth-centered" and *helio*- from the Greek for "sun" = "sun-centered").

GLOBAL CONNECTION

WHO WAS FIRST WITH HELIOCENTRIC THEORY? Heliocentric theory goes back at least as far as the 200s B.C. in Greece. There, Aristarchus of Samos, a mathematician and astronomer was among the first to propose it.

SECOND-LANGUAGE SUPPORT

DRAMATIZATION Have second-language learners work in heterogeneous groups to create skits about Lorenzo Medici, Petrarch, Leonardo da Vinci, and Copernicus. Group members should read the section about their character and do further research. All group members should have speaking parts.

Infographic

Briefly review with students the idea of cultural borrowing and how it can enrich human life. Help them appreciate the Renaissance as a shining example of a movement that freely borrowed from the past and that then spread quickly outward as people from different countries borrowed its ideas and eagerly gave them their own interpretations.

Discussing The Spread of the Renaissance Give students a few minutes to read the introduction, study the map, and relate the different works of art and learning with their captions to where they originated.

- *Which of the works shown here reflects classical Greece and Rome most clearly? How?* (probably Bramante's Tempieto in Rome, with its Greek columns and Roman dome)

- *Which work demonstrates that Renaissance craftworkers could raise even a mechanical device to the level of art? How?* (the French clock, utilitarian yet beautifully made)

- *Which work demonstrates that a great painting knew no national boundaries during the Renaissance?* (El Greco's painting from Spain—he came from Greece and went to Venice before continuing on to Spain.)

★**THINKING FURTHER:** *Making Generalizations* **"The Renaissance was an idea whose time had come." What evidence can you offer to support this generalization?** (examples of the intellectual and artistic excitement the Renaissance generated and its rapid spread across Europe)

Technology CONNECTION

ADVENTURE TIME! CD-ROM
Enrich this lesson with the *Infographic* and related Unit Activity on the *Adventure Time!* CD-ROM.

Infographic

inter**NET** CONNECTION — Visit our website: www.mhschool.com

Spread of the Renaissance

As you have read, the Renaissance began in Florence, Italy, around 1350 and later spread throughout Europe. Artists, writers, and scientists often traveled to different Europeans cities to study and work. How might exchanging ideas have led to achievements?

"All the world's a stage, And all the men and women merely players."

by William Shakespeare

Clock
This clock and its decorated cover were made in France around 1540. Powered by a coiled spring, the clock was portable.

El Greco "A View of Toledo"
El Greco was a Greek who studied art in Venice. He settled in Toledo, Spain, and painted many scenes of life in that city.

Tempietto
Donato Bramante designed Tempietto, a temple in Rome. Completed in 1502, the temple has features of classical architecture such as columns.

EXPANDING THE INFOGRAPHIC

RESEARCHING AND WRITING Have students create a class book of Renaissance art works. Have them do research in Renaissance art—its painting, sculpture, and architecture—and have each one choose a work that particularly appeals to him or her. Then have them draw it on a piece of construction paper and write a paragraph telling about it. Finally, have the students assemble the pages into "Our Class Book of Renaissance Art." You might suggest the following research sources:

- Encyclopedia entries for *Renaissance art and architecture.*
- A library catalog for entries under *Renaissance art and architecture* or under favorite Renaissance artists' names.

(Time-Life's *The Renaissance* and Gardiner's *Art Through the Ages* are good reference sources.)

Caterina Van Hemmessen

Painters in Europe often painted themselves, as in this self-portrait by a German woman.

WHY IT MATTERS

The Renaissance was a time of looking back to the classical achievements of Greece, Rome, and Arabia. It was also a time of looking forward, for much remained to be discovered.

Though the Renaissance began in Italy, it soon spread to the rest of Europe. The Renaissance brought about changes to many old ways of thinking. For this reason, historians often call it the beginning of the modern age.

In the next lesson you will read about the spread of new ideas into the Roman Catholic Church.

✓// Reviewing Facts and Ideas

MAIN IDEAS

- The Renaissance began in Italy, where an interest in humanism first developed.
- In Florence wealthy patrons like Lorenzo Medici supported artists and scholars.
- Renaissance scientists studied Greek, Roman, and Arab texts, and made new discoveries about the world.

THINK ABOUT IT

1. What did the people of the Renaissance mean by *humanism*?
2. How did Florence become one of the richest cities in Europe?
3. **FOCUS** How did Renaissance achievements reflect both the past and their own time?
4. **THINKING SKILL** Make and explain at least two *generalizations* about Renaissance thinkers.
5. **WRITE** Look at one of the Renaissance artworks in this lesson. Write a paragraph explaining what you like or dislike about the art.

341

Discussing WHY IT MATTERS Explain to the class that Janus was a Roman god (January was named for him) who was shown as having two faces back to back, thus looking to the past as well as the future.

> ★**THINKING FURTHER:** *Making Connections* **In what way was the Renaissance like Janus?** *(Like Janus, it looked backwards and forwards at the same time.)*

⭐ 3 CLOSE

MAIN IDEAS

Call on students for answers.

- *Where did the Renaissance begin and how did it change the focus of many people's thinking?* *(It began in Italy and it marked a change from a focus on the next world to a more humanistic focus on this world.)*
- *What role did people like Lorenzo Medici play in the Renaissance?* *(They served as patrons who supported the work of artists and scholars.)*
- *What effect did Renaissance scientists' study of ancient learning have on their work?* *(Past knowledge gave them a foundation on which to make new scientific discoveries.)*

EVALUATE
✓ **Answers to Think About It**

1. greater concern with human interests and values
   Make Inferences
2. by being a center of banking and trading
   Recall Details
3. Renaissance artists and scholars learned all they could of what the ancients had known and then used methods and tools available to them to build on and sometimes correct the past.
   Main Ideas
4. Generalizations will probably touch on Renaissance thinkers' quests for past knowledge and on the unique ways they interpreted and used it.
   Make Generalizations
5. Have students consider subject matter, composition, and execution.
   Make Judgements and Decisions

Write About It Have students write a paragraph in which they describe what they think was the greatest achievement of the Renaissance and explain why.

MEETING INDIVIDUAL NEEDS

RETEACHING (Easy) Have students review the examples of Renaissance painting in this lesson and have them do a drawing or painting of their own in a Renaissance style.

EXTENSION (Average) Have students picture themselves as struggling artists who would like to gain the support of a patron like Lorenzo Medici. Tell them to write a letter to him, making their case for why he should back them in their work.

ENRICHMENT (Challenging) For an experience in cooperative learning, divide the class into five groups. Have each group do research and create a presentation for the class on the work of one of these giants of the Renaissance in Italy—Botticelli, Donatello, Della Robbia, Raphael, and Tintoretto.

LESSON 5

PAGES 342–347

Lesson Overview
The Reformation divided the western Christian Church into Protestantism and Roman Catholicism.

Lesson Objectives
★ Describe Martin Luther's protests.

★ Identify the effects of the printing press.

★ Explain how the Reformation affected Europe.

★ 1 PREPARE

MOTIVATE Have two students rehearse and do a dramatic reading of the *Read Aloud,* one as Martin Luther (pictured in the illustration) and the other as the narrator. Remind students of the status of the Roman Catholic Church as the major religious power in western Europe, unifying European Christians under its authority.

SET PURPOSE Have a student ask the *Read to Learn* question. Write *Reformation* on the board and work with the class to get at its meaning of "change." Tell students to explore the lesson to find out what that change was. List *Vocabulary* terms on the board and fill in their meanings as they occur in the text.

★ 2 TEACH

Understanding THE BIG PICTURE
Help students to understand the split in thinking about religion that appeared as a result of the Renaissance.

★ **THINKING FURTHER:** *Classifying*
How did humanism raise questions about traditional beliefs? How did this in turn raise concerns among many Christians?
(Have students classify the two lines: (1) Everything is open to question; (2) Too much questioning can shake people's faith.)

Resource REMINDER
Practice and Project Book: *p. 69*

Focus Activity

READ TO LEARN

What changes did the Reformation bring to Europe?

VOCABULARY

- indulgence
- reform
- **Reformation**
- **Protestantism**
- armada

PEOPLE

- **Erasmus**
- **Martin Luther**
- **Johannes Gutenberg**
- **King Henry VIII**
- **Queen Elizabeth I**
- **William Shakespeare**

342

---

400   700   1000   1300   1450   1600

The Reformation

Read Aloud

"Here I stand; I can do no other. God help me. Amen."

These words were spoken in the 1500s by a German monk named Martin Luther. Luther had spoken out against the Church in Rome. Church leaders had called upon Luther to take back his criticisms. Luther's beliefs were too strong, however. He refused to back down.

THE BIG PICTURE

As humanism gained popularity among Europe's artists and scholars, people began to question everything around them. They studied books and started schools in an effort to find answers to their questions. Nicolaus Copernicus, you may recall, questioned the old belief that Earth was the center of the universe. The Renaissance had shaken many of Europe's established traditions and beliefs.

At the same time some Christians began to be concerned. They thought that some Renaissance artists and scientists had gotten too far away from their religious teachings. These Christians said that many artists and scientists were too worldly, or concerned about this world. Many also felt that the Church in Rome had become too worldly and rich. A few Christians began to question the authority of the Pope.

SHELTERED INSTRUCTION

READING STRATEGIES & LANGUAGE DEVELOPMENT

CAUSE AND EFFECT Remind students that writers often use cause and effect to analyze historical events. Review how causes show why something happened; effects show results. Then share the Read Aloud with the class. Using a Think-Aloud, find the causes and effects. [Causes: Luther speaks out against the Roman Catholic Church. Effects: Church orders him to recant; he refuses.] As they read, students can find causes and effects of the Reformation. **[SDAIE STRATEGY: METACOGNITIVE DEVELOPMENT/TEXT RE-PRESENTATION]**

PREFIXES Point out to the class that this lesson's title contains one of the most common prefixes in the English language and have them identify it *(re-).* Ask them for other examples of other *re*-words they know and have them define what the prefix means ("to do again or anew").

THE CHURCH OF ROME

By 1500 the Roman Church had become the most powerful institution in Europe. The Pope claimed authority over all of Europe's rulers. The Pope's power also brought great wealth to the Roman Church. Like the government of the Roman empire, the Roman Church taxed the people of Europe. Some of this money was spent on works of art.

Questions of Faith

Starting around 1500, humanists such as Erasmus (ih RAZ mus) began to criticize the Roman Church. He especially questioned the Church policy concerning indulgences (ihn DUL juns ez). An indulgence is a pardon, or forgiveness, from the Church. During the Middle Ages, some people began to pay to be forgiven by the priest for acting against Christian teachings. Erasmus believed that the indulgences were wrong. He hoped to reform, or change, the Roman Church.

In Wittenberg, Germany, the sale of indulgences also made a monk, Martin Luther, angry. He felt that the money, often given by people who were poor, should not be spent on the building of Saint Peter's, a great cathedral in Rome.

In 1517 Luther wrote 95 Theses (THEE seez), or statements, of protest. He placed his list on a Wittenberg church door. Luther had no idea that this simple act would soon shake beliefs across the entire continent.

Read the excerpts from Luther's Theses. How did he suggest that the Church pay for building Saint Peter's?

MANY VOICES
PRIMARY SOURCE

Excerpt from the 95 Theses, written by Martin Luther in 1517.

*O*ut of love and **zeal** for truth and the desire to bring it to light, the following theses will be publicly discussed at Wittenberg under the chairmanship of the Reverend Martin Luther.

Before long all the churches, palaces, walls, and bridges of Rome will be built out of our [indulgence] money. . . . We Germans can not attend Saint Peter's. Better it should never be built than that our **parochial** churches should be **despoiled**. . . . Why doesn't the pope build the **basilica** out of his own money?

---

zeal: eagerness
parochial: local
despoiled: robbed
basilica: cathedral

Martin Luther studied law before he became a monk in 1505.

343

BACKGROUND INFORMATION

ABOUT MARTIN LUTHER
- He was born in the German village of Eisleben in 1483 to a family of poor peasants. But his father's later success as a miner and then a small-time capitalist enabled Luther to spend four years studying law at Erfut University.
- A terrifying encounter with a violent thunderstorm made him decide to become a monk in 1505 and a priest two years later.
- In 1521 Pope Leo X excommunicated Luther from the Church.
- In 1525 Luther married a former nun, Katherina von Bora; they raised six children.
- In late 1545 he was called to arbitrate a dispute in Eisleben. On February 17, 1546, he had settled the quarrel, but the strain on him had been too great. He died the next day.

THE CHURCH OF ROME

Help students to recognize the power and wealth of the Roman Church in 1500 by identifying its sources (the Pope's authority over Europe's rulers and the Church's taxation of everyone in Europe). Have them compare this power with that of the Roman empire.

Discussing Questions of Faith
Point out that these criticisms did not attack the most basic religious beliefs.

- **What criticism did the humanist Erasmus raise about the Roman Church?** *(that its selling indulgences, forgiveness of sins, was wrong)*

- **What did he want the Roman Church to do?** *(to change itself to eliminate such practices)*

- **What criticism did Martin Luther raise about the sale of indulgences?** *(that if they were sold, the money should go to the local poor, not to cathedral building in far-off Rome)*

★**THINKING FURTHER:** *Cause and Effect* **What step did Luther's criticism cause him to take?** *(He posted the 95 Theses, or statements of protests, to the church door and demanded they be discussed.)*

MANY VOICES
PRIMARY SOURCE

Discussing the PRIMARY SOURCE

Have the same reader who read Luther in the *Read Aloud* read his statement here. Point out that here we have just one of his Theses but that it is representative.

- **What does Luther say his motive is in posting his 95 Theses?** *(to bring out the truth)*

★**THINKING FURTHER:** *Making Conclusions* **In the Thesis quoted here, what conflict of interest does Luther see between what the Pope wants in Rome and what the German people need?** *(He says that the Pope wants to beautify Rome with expensive structures like St. Peter's. But taking money from the Germans for this effort is not right; they live too far from Rome to visit St. Peter's and, besides, their churches need the money being taken from them.)*

A CALL FOR REFORM

Explain that Luther's act of defiance set off a chain reaction across Europe and encourage students to follow its movement to other places.

Discussing Spreading the Word

Point out that in Luther's pre-radio, pre-television days, his actions in an obscure German town might have gone unnoticed but for a new technological development.

- **How did Johannes Gutenberg revolutionize communications?** *(He developed a printing press.)*

- **How did this technology compare with the way books had been made?** *(Previously, books were laboriously hand-copied; now movable type and the printing press made the process much faster and cheaper.)*

★**THINKING FURTHER:** *Cause and Effect* **How did the printing press affect the spread of Luther's ideas? How did his translation of the Bible from Latin gain him more followers?** *(It put his ideas into the hands of virtually anyone who could read; it helped unite German-speaking people behind him.)*

Exploring Division of the Roman Church If you shared the *Background Information* on p. 337 with the class, remind them that Pope Leo X, mentioned here, was Lorenzo the Magnificent's son.

- **Why didn't the German rulers punish Luther, in obedience to the Pope's orders?** *(They saw an opportunity to break away from the Pope's authority and increase their own power and to stop the outward flow of tax money from their country to Rome.)*

★**THINKING FURTHER:** *Cause and Effect* **What effect did Luther's activities have on Western Christianity?** *(It split in two—between the Roman Church, later called Roman Catholicism, and the protesting followers of Luther, ushering in Protestantism.)*

A CALL FOR REFORM

Martin Luther's 95 Theses in Wittenberg started a movement called the Reformation (ref ur MAY shun). This movement brought reform to the Church in Rome. It would also lead to another division of Christianity.

Spreading the Word

News of Luther's bold action in Wittenberg spread with the help of a recent invention. In 1448 a man named Johannes Gutenberg (yoh HAHN uhs GOO tun burg) had built a printing press. It used metal letters called movable type to spell out words on a page.

Before 1448, each page had to be hand-carved. Now that letters could be

Johannes Gutenberg built the first printing press out of a device used to press grapes and cheese.

344

moved around, printing was cheaper and easier as well as faster. Gutenberg's press could print 300 pages a day. By 1500 several million books had been printed in Europe!

The new invention helped spread Luther's criticisms of the Roman Church and a translation of the Bible. In those days almost everything was printed in Latin. Luther wrote in German, which helped to unite many German-speaking people on his side.

Division of the Roman Church

In 1520 Pope Leo X (the Tenth) ordered that Luther's books be burned, but Luther did not stop his protest. A visitor from Rome reported: "All Germany is up in arms against Rome."

Although the leaders of the Roman Church in Rome wanted Luther punished, German rulers protected him. By this time their loyalty to their homeland had become stronger than their loyalty to the Pope. These rulers also hoped to keep taxes intended for Rome.

In 1529 the break in the Roman Church became permanent. Luther's followers were now called Protestants, because they protested against the Roman Church. Western Christianity was divided in two—Protestantism (PROT uh stun tiz um) and Roman Catholicism.

The Protestant Church

The indulgence issue was not the only Church policy with which Protestant leaders disagreed. These leaders taught that monasteries and convents were unnecessary. Protestants also thought that church decorations and services should be simpler. They worked to spread translated Bibles and have church services in local languages.

In time, new Protestant leaders arose, such as John Calvin in Switzerland. Calvin founded a separate Protestant group called the Calvinists. The new Protestant groups did not agree on every issue, but they were united in their refusal to follow the Pope.

Roman Catholic Reform

Even before the Protestants split from the Roman Church, Catholic leaders had begun making reforms. Between 1545 and 1563 a group of Catholic leaders met in the city of Trent, Italy. They ordered that parts of church services should be in the language of the people of a country, not just in Latin. They also tried to see that the Church's money was spent more carefully. These reforms helped to strengthen the Roman Catholic religion. Some critics, such as Erasmus, decided not to leave the Catholic Church.

During the 1500s most people in Germany, Scandinavia, Holland, and Switzerland became Protestant. As you can see on the map on this page, most of Spain, Italy, and France remained Catholic. Tensions between Protestants and Roman Catholics increased.

England's Break With Rome

At this time of religious conflict, a new ruler brought religious change to England. This ruler was King Henry VIII. Henry was building a strong monarchy, or a government ruled by a king or a queen.

At the beginning of his rule in 1509, Henry supported the Roman Church. His view, however, changed in 1527. Henry, who had one daughter, wanted a son to inherit his throne. His wife, Queen Catherine, was unable to have more children. So the king asked the

Pope to give him permission to divorce the Queen. The Pope refused.

Henry VIII stated that the Pope did not have authority over the English monarchy. He then took control of Church land and cut off payments to Rome. Henry started a new Protestant church, the Church of England, also called the Anglican Church. With control over England's church, Henry's monarchy became more powerful.

CHRISTIANITY IN WESTERN EUROPE, c. 1560

Legend:
- Roman Catholics
- Lutherans
- Calvinists
- Anglicans
- Eastern Christians
- Mixture of Catholics, Lutherans & Calvinists
- — Present-day boundaries

MAP WORK

By 1560 many different Christian groups had formed. Followers of these groups were spread throughout western Europe.

1. In which country was the Anglican religion common?

2. Which religion was most widespread?

345

BACKGROUND INFORMATION

ABOUT JOHN CALVIN

- He was born in Noyon, a cathedral city in northern France, in 1509, the son of a Roman Church employee. Like Luther, he studied law as a young man.

- At university, he converted to Protestantism. In 1535, suspected of heresy, he had to flee France for Switzerland.

- As a clergyman in Geneva, Switzerland, Calvin preached and wrote about a severe form of Christianity. He drew up stern laws both for his followers and for city government. Calvinists were urged to meet a very high moral standard and many pastimes—card playing, dancing, play going, or even wearing bright colors—were forbidden.

- He died in Switzerland in 1564.

- The Puritans who helped to found our country were Calvinists.

Discussing The Protestant Church Note that the Protestant groups were not centralized.

★**THINKING FURTHER:** *Compare and Contrast **In what ways did Protestantism differ from Roman Catholicism?*** *(opposed the issuing of indulgences; supported making church practices simpler, using local languages instead of Latin)*

Exploring Roman Catholic Reform Help students see that the Roman Catholic Church dealt with some of the criticism.

● ***In what ways did the Roman Church reform itself?*** *(using local languages, making sounder use of money)*

★**THINKING FURTHER:** *Cause and Effect **What effect did these reforms have on some Christians?*** *(Some decided to remain part of Roman Catholicism.)*

More **MAP WORK**

Help students see the generally north-south split on religious lines.

★**THINKING FURTHER:** *Making Conclusions **Looking at the map on this page, what can you conclude about the geographic division of Western Christianity?*** *(Roman Catholicism remained strong in much of Southern Europe; Protestantism found strength in Northern Europe.)*

Studying England's Break With Rome Lead students to recognize that England's break with Roman Catholicism came from its ruler.

● ***What issue caused King Henry VIII to break from the Roman Church?*** *(the Pope's refusal to grant him a divorce so he could remarry)*

● ***How did Henry benefit from the break?*** *(He gained control of the Church, ended taxes to Rome, was no longer under the Pope's authority.)*

★**THINKING FURTHER:** *Cause and Effect **The desire for religious reform was one cause of the Reformation. What was another?*** *(the desire of national leaders to increase their own power and wealth)*

QUEEN ELIZABETH I

Explain to the class that until 1952, there was no "I" after Elizabeth. Ask them why it might have been added (the crowning of a second Queen Elizabeth).

Discussing The Elizabethan Age
Help students identify Elizabeth's reign with the peak of the Renaissance in England.

> ★THINKING FURTHER: *Making Conclusions* **Why might England have been an exciting place to be during the Elizabethan Age?** *(Help students connect the prosperity of business and trade with the artistic creativity of the Renaissance.)*

Discussing The Spanish Armada
Stress the idea of Elizabeth as a leader.

● **Why did Spain put together the armada?** *(to deny England control of sea trade routes and to make it Catholic again)*

MANY VOICES
PRIMARY SOURCE

Discussing the PRIMARY SOURCE

Have a student rehearse this quote and do a dramatic reading of it for the class.

● **How does she make her subjects feel good about themselves?** *(references to their strength, loyalty, good will)*

● **How does she build up their faith in her?** *(by linking herself to strong symbols—English kings, her people—and by heaping scorn on the enemy)*

★THINKING FURTHER: *Making Decisions* **On a scale of 1 to 10, where would you rank this speech for effectiveness?** *(most likely high)*

Discussing Battle at Sea Discuss how a smaller sea force won.

> ★THINKING FURTHER: *Compare and Contrast* **How would you compare the advantages and disadvantages of each side?** *(English: fewer but faster and better armed ships; Spanish: more but poorer ships, bad luck of a storm)*

England's Queen Elizabeth I (below) stands on a map of her empire. England defeated the Spanish Armada (right).

QUEEN ELIZABETH I

In the years following the split with the Catholic Church, England was torn by religious differences. During this troubled time, Henry VIII's daughter, Elizabeth, came to the throne. In 1558 she became Queen Elizabeth I. Not only did the queen face conflict at home, but also there were threats of invasion from mainland Europe. Despite these problems, Elizabeth became one of the most powerful and popular monarchs England has ever known.

The Elizabethan Age

Under Elizabeth the anger between England's Protestants and Catholics cooled. London bustled with business and trade. Also during this time, the Renaissance arrived in England. Elizabeth enjoyed poetry and plays. Some-

times she watched the performances of a young writer and actor named William Shakespeare. Shakespeare was one of the greatest writers in the English language. You will learn more about him in the Legacy on page 348.

The Spanish Armada

Elizabeth hated war and worked hard to keep her country at peace. In 1588, however, Elizabeth faced the threat of a war with Spain.

The Spanish hoped to gain control of Atlantic trade routes. They also hoped to return England to the Catholic faith. Under King Philip II, Spain had gathered a huge and powerful fleet, called an armada, of 130 warships. They prepared to attack England.

Queen Elizabeth assembled her troops and delivered a stirring speech. How do you think the troops reacted?

CURRICULUM CONNECTION

LINKS TO LANGUAGE ARTS Have the class go through the *Many Voices* quote to find a word that would not be grammatically acceptable today. If necessary, say it involves the superlative (*chiefest*—we don't use the comparative or superlative form of the word *chief*).

LINKS TO MATHEMATICS Use the number of English ships (90) and Spanish ships (130) to work on ratios, fractions, and percentages.

● Ratio: 130 − 90 = 40; Spain had nearly one and one half as many ships as England.

● Fraction: 90 + 130 = 220, giving England 9/22 of the ships and Spain 13/22.

● Percentages: 90 + 130 = 220, 90 ÷ 220 = .41, giving England a little over 40%; 130 ÷ 220 = .59, giving Spain a little under 60%.

MANY VOICES
PRIMARY SOURCE

Excerpt from Queen Elizabeth's speech to her troops during the battle with the Spanish Armada, 1588.

*Let tyrants fear. I have always so behaved myself that, under God, I have placed my **chiefest** strength and **safeguard** in the loyal hearts and good will of my **subjects**; and therefore I am come.... to live or die amongst you all, and to lay down for my God and for my kingdom and for my people, my honor and my blood, even in the dust. I know I have the body of a weak and feeble woman, but I have the heart and stomach of a king, and a king of England too, and think **foul scorn** that ... Spain, or any prince of Europe should dare to invade the borders of my **realm**.*

chiefest: greatest
safeguard: protection
subjects: people of the kingdom
foul scorn: badly
realm: kingdom

Battle at Sea

With only 90 ships, England's fleet was smaller than the Spanish Armada. However, the English ships were faster and had better guns. This battle for the seas took place in the English Channel. After nine days the Spanish Armada was badly beaten. Not one English ship was sunk. Many Spanish ships escaped, only to be wrecked in a violent storm. Only half of the Spanish Armada made it back to Spain. England continued to build its fleet. The country would soon become the greatest naval power in the entire world.

WHY IT MATTERS

By 1600 the unity that had brought Europe together under the Roman Church had broken apart. The Pope was no longer the most powerful leader in Europe. Kings and queens began to act in the interest of their own countries. In coming years, these kingdoms would extend their power to places beyond Europe—to Africa, the Americas, and Asia.

The Christian Church remained split. Of the almost 2 billion Christians in the world today, over 1 billion are Roman Catholics. Almost 400 million are Protestants. In the United States alone, there are 59 million Roman Catholics and 90 million Protestants.

✓ Reviewing Facts and Ideas

MAIN IDEAS

- In 1517 Martin Luther put the 95 Theses on a church door in Germany.
- Luther's actions led to the Reformation. The Western Christian Church soon split into the Protestant and Roman Catholic Churches.
- Under Elizabeth I, England's culture and power flourished.

THINK ABOUT IT

1. What were indulgences? What did Martin Luther think about them?

2. What reforms did the Protestant and Catholic Churches make in the 1500s?

3. **FOCUS** How did the Reformation affect the unity of Europe?

4. **THINKING SKILL** What was the *point of view* of Queen Elizabeth toward Spain in her speech to her troops?

5. **GEOGRAPHY** Study the location of England and Spain on the map on page 345. Why did both countries need a powerful navy?

347

Discussing WHY IT MATTERS Point out that we have inherited the results of that time.

> ★**THINKING FURTHER:** *Compare and Contrast* **How would you contrast Europe before and after the 1500s?** *(Before: Pope was Europe's most powerful ruler, with authority over national leaders, taxes rolling into Roman Church; After: kings and queens ruled independent nations, wealth kept from Roman Church)*

⭐ 3 CLOSE

MAIN IDEAS
Have students write their answers on a piece of paper.

- *How did Martin Luther begin the Reformation?* (by posting the 95 Theses)

- *What ultimate effect did the Reformation have on Western Christianity?* (It split it in half.)

- *How would you describe England during the Elizabethan Age?* (prosperous, with business and trade, and rich with Renaissance arts)

EVALUATE
✓ **Answers to Think About It**

1. payments for forgiveness of sins; Luther thought the money they made was wrongly spent. *Recall Details*

2. Protestants: simplifyied religious practices, replaced Latin with local languages, altered certain religious beliefs; Catholics: replaced some use of Latin with local languages, changed how money was spent) *Make Conclusions*

3. It broke the central authority of the Pope and strengthened the monarchs of independent nations. *Main Idea*

4. She felt scorn for Spain for wanting to change and attack England. *Point of View*

5. They both have long seacoasts. *Five Themes of Geography: Place*

Write About It Have students picture themselves as either a Spanish or an English sailor. Have them write a journal entry describing the Armada sea battle they have just fought.

MEETING INDIVIDUAL NEEDS

RETEACHING (Easy) Have students review the lesson and choose a dramatic scene that it describes (for example, Luther's posting the 95 Theses or Elizabeth I addressing her forces). Have them use colored pens, pencils, or crayons to draw the scene.

EXTENSION (Average) Divide the class into groups and assign each group one of the names in *People* listed on p. 342. Have each group create an illustration of their subject and research some interesting facts about him or her, to be part of a "Movers and Shakers of the Reformation" bulletin board.

ENRICHMENT (Challenging) Divide the class into five groups and have each group write and perform a skit involving an event in the life of one of the following: Pope Leo X; Martin Luther; Johannes Gutenberg, Henry VIII, Elizabeth I.

LEGACY

Lesson Overview

Shakespeare's works enriched the English language and literature.

Lesson Objective

★ Appreciate the great value of Shakespeare's literary works.

1 PREPARE

MOTIVATE Refer the class to the quote from Shakespeare in the *Infographic* on p. 340. Have a student read it aloud, then have the class interpret its meaning. Help them to see and appreciate its basic truths and the grace with which they are stated.

SET PURPOSE What kind of man could write such a passage? What would he have to know about human nature? What language skills would he need? Tell students to explore the *Legacy* to find answers to questions like these.

2 TEACH

Understanding the Concept of a Legacy Have students read the text on this page. and think about Shakespeare's legacy.

- *Where and during what "age" did Shakespeare write his works? When was that?* (the Elizabethan Age in England; the late 1500s–1600s)

- *What kinds of works did he write?* (plays and poems)

- *Why do plays and poetry call for a broad knowledge of how human beings think, feel, and behave?* (Help students understand the importance to good playwriting of a knowledge of thought processes, emotions, and varieties of behavior and the importance to poetry of presenting vivid and compressed ideas.)

Resource **REMINDER**

Anthology: *This Scepter'd Isle*, p. 77

Legacy
LINKING PAST AND PRESENT

THE ART OF LANGUAGE: SHAKESPEARE

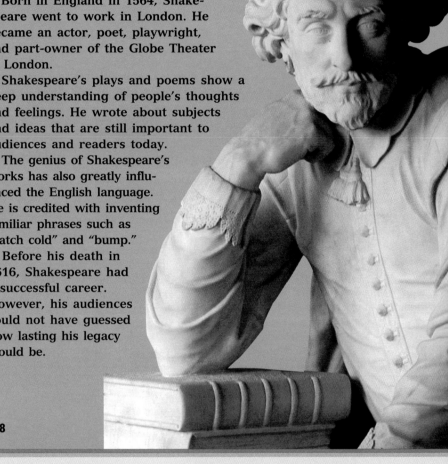

The Granger Collection

Many people today take a break from their routines to see a movie or a play. If you lived in London during the Elizabethan Age, you might have gone to a play by one of the greatest writers of all time, William Shakespeare. His plays are still performed today.

Born in England in 1564, Shakespeare went to work in London. He became an actor, poet, playwright, and part-owner of the Globe Theater in London.

Shakespeare's plays and poems show a deep understanding of people's thoughts and feelings. He wrote about subjects and ideas that are still important to audiences and readers today.

The genius of Shakespeare's works has also greatly influenced the English language. He is credited with inventing familiar phrases such as "catch cold" and "bump."

Before his death in 1616, Shakespeare had a successful career. However, his audiences could not have guessed how lasting his legacy would be.

348

BACKGROUND INFORMATION

ABOUT WILLIAM SHAKESPEARE AND THE GLOBE THEATRE

- Shakespeare's earliest plays began appearing in 1588, when he was 24 years old.

- As an actor and a playwright, he was part of a theatrical group known as the Lord Chamberlain's Men (later the King's Men), named after their patron. This group held shares in the business that built the Globe Theatre in 1599. Shakespeare wrote two plays a year to be performed there.

- Starting in the thatched roof, fire burned down the Globe Theatre in 1613. It was rebuilt but then demolished in 1649.

- In the 1990s a new Globe Theatre (built on the old plans, thatched roof and all) was erected near the original site.

One of Shakespeare's most popular plays, "Romeo and Juliet" (left), inspired the creators of the Broadway musical and hit movie, "West Side Story" (below). The ideas of romantic love and the troubles of youth are just as important to people today as they were in the 1500s.

Cornelius Visscher painted London in 1616, the year Shakespeare died. People enter the Globe Theater, shown in the bottom, right corner.

349

★ **THINKING FURTHER:** *Making Conclusions* **What do you think might be major evidence for Shakespeare's being one of the greatest writers of the English language?** *(perhaps that his plays are still being performed and his poems read 400 years after their writing)*

Examining the Illustrations Give the class a few minutes to examine the illustrations and read their captions.

● *Where were Shakespeare's plays performed in his time?* (the Globe Theater in London)

● *Why might actors and actresses find playing Shakespeare a real but rewarding challenge?* (Students have perhaps heard enough Shakespeare to know that his language often differs from what we speak today, so they might comment on the difficulty of memorizing and speaking his lines. But help them so see the pleasure players take in speaking his well-constructed lines and in portraying the rich characters he creates.)

● *How does a modern Broadway musical prove that Shakespeare's playwriting continues to be vital?* ("Everything old is new again"—the conflicts and emotions he portrayed are just as important in human life today.)

★ **THINKING FURTHER:** *Making Decisions* **On a scale of 1 to 10, where would you position Shakespeare for his contributions to English literature? Explain your choice.** (Students should rank him quite high, perhaps based on oft-quoted sayings he has added to English, and on his long-lived popularity.)

3 CLOSE

SUM IT UP
Encourage students to discuss reasons that some works of art endure for hundreds of years.

EVALUATE
Write About It Ask students to write a thank-you letter to Shakespeare for the works he left us.

MEETING INDIVIDUAL NEEDS

RETEACHING (Easy) Write these lines from *Romeo and Juliet* on the board: "What's in a name? That which we call a rose/By any other name would smell as sweet." Discuss them with the class and then tell students to rewrite them in their own words.

EXTENSION (Average) *Familiar Quotations,* collected by John Bartlett, is available at most libraries. Have students thumb through its pages of Shakespeare quotations and pick out one that appeals to them. Have them write the quotation on a piece of paper and write an explanation of what it means to them.

ENRICHMENT (Challenging) Divide the class in two. Have one half research *Romeo and Juliet* to get its story line. Have the other research *West Side Story's* story line. Have each group present its findings and then have the class compare the two.

DISCUSSING MAJOR EVENTS Use these questions to help students relate major events.

● **What two major events occurred in the 1000s? How did both involve fighting men on the move?** (the Norman Conquest and the First Crusade; the first had French troops on the move across the English Channel to conquer England and the second had Christian fighters on the move to control the Holy Land.)

● **What major event occurred in 1448 and how was it an early step in creating today's Information Age?** (Gutenberg's development of the printing press made producing books faster and cheaper and greatly increased the number in circulation.)

Answers to THINKING ABOUT VOCABULARY

1. C
2. I, indulgence
3. I, feudalism
4. C
5. C
6. I, Renaissance
7. C
8. C
9. C
10. C

Answers to THINKING ABOUT FACTS

1. Serfs lived difficult lives of hard work, crowded living conditions, duty to a master, payment of rents and taxes, and death usually by age 40.

2. a terrible plague that killed one third of the people of Western Europe

3. Earth orbited the sun, which meant Earth was not the center of the universe, as had been believed.

Resource REMINDER

Practice and Project Book: p. 70

Assessment Book: Chapter 12 Test

Technology: Videodisc/Video Tape 3

Transparency: Graphic Organizer, Flow Chart

350

CHAPTER 12 REVIEW

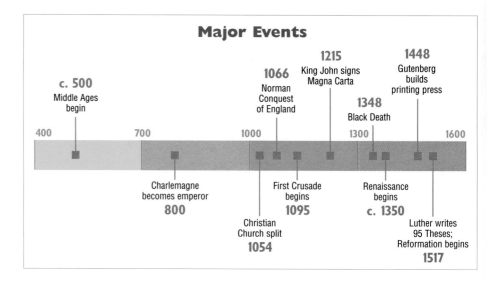

Major Events

1215 King John signs Magna Carta

1448 Gutenberg builds printing press

c. 500 Middle Ages begin

1066 Norman Conquest of England

1348 Black Death

400   700   1000   1300   1600

Charlemagne becomes emperor
800

First Crusade begins
1095

Renaissance begins
c. 1350

Christian Church split
1054

Luther writes 95 Theses; Reformation begins
1517

THINKING ABOUT VOCABULARY

Number a sheet of paper from 1 to 10. Decide whether the underlined word or term in each of the following statements correctly completes the sentence. If the word or term is correct, write **C** beside the number. If the word or term is incorrect, write **I** and then write the word or term that correctly completes the sentence.

1. A <u>patron</u> is a wealthy or influential supporter of art and artists.

2. <u>Feudalism</u> is a pardon or forgiveness from the Pope.

3. <u>Renaissance</u> is a way of organizing and governing society based on land and service.

4. A <u>guild</u> was a group of traders or craftworkers in a medieval town.

5. Protestantism was an attempt to <u>reform</u> the Roman Catholic Church.

6. The <u>indulgence</u> was the period of artistic and cultural rebirth.

7. A <u>monastery</u> is a place where monks devote their lives to religion.

8. A <u>fief</u> was part of a lord's manor given to a vassal to manage.

9. The period when many people lived on manors owned by lords is called the <u>Middle Ages</u>.

10. <u>Deforestation</u> is the clearing of forests to make room for farms and cities.

THINKING ABOUT FACTS

1. How did serfs live?

2. What was the Black Death?

3. What did Copernicus learn from observing the sky?

4. What major changes in the Christian Church did you read about in this chapter?

5. According to the time line above, how long after the beginning of the Renaissance did the Protestant Reformation begin? How were the Renaissance and Reformation different?

350

MEDIEVAL FESTIVAL Students will enjoy presenting a medieval festival in which they dress up as knights, ladies, minstrels, crafts makers, and peasants. They might pantomime a joust or sword fight, have minstrels play guitars and sing, or tell about life in medieval Europe in their own words. Inform students that modern-day admirers of the medieval and Renaissance periods in Europe enjoy participating in recreations of life in those times called Renaissance Faires. Challenge students to find information on Renaissance Faires and describe what they are like.

THINK AND WRITE

WRITING AN EXPLANATION
Write a paragraph about feudalism. Identify lords, ladies, vassals, and serfs and explain their roles in feudal society.

WRITING AN INTERVIEW
Suppose you could go back into the Middle Ages and interview a monk or a nun. Write at least three questions you would ask the person and the answers you think he or she might give.

WRITING A LIST
Make a list of three complaints some people had about the Roman church that led to the Protestant Reformation.

APPLYING THINKING SKILLS

DETERMINING POINT OF VIEW

1. What is a point of view?
2. What point of view do you think the lord of a manor might have toward his serfs? What point of view might a serf have toward the lord?
3. Reread the words of Petrarch on page 338. What is his point of view about writing? Why do you think he had that point of view?
4. How did the points of view of Protestant and Catholic leaders differ during the Reformation?
5. Why is it important to the study of history to be able to understand different points of view?

Summing Up the Chapter

Review the chapter. Then copy on a separate piece of paper the flow chart shown below. Using what you learned in the chapter, fill in the remaining events. Then use the chart to write a paragraph that answers the question "What led to the decline of the feudal system?"

- The Church calls for crusaders to capture the Holy Land.
- European trade expands to Asia and Africa.
- Towns and cities grow throughout Europe.
- The feudal system declines.
- King John is forced to sign the Magna Carta, giving people more rights.
- Traders and craftworkers organize into guilds.

351

4. It became divided into Roman Catholicism and Protestantism, and the Pope was no longer the leader of all of Western Christianity.
5. 167 years; the Renaissance was a burst of creativity and renewed interest in ancient learning and arts, while the Reformation was an attempt to reform the Christian Church that led to its division.

Answers to APPLYING THINKING SKILLS

1. the position from which someone looks at the world
2. A lord might look at serfs from the point of view of one who has complete power over their lives and to whom they are practically property. A serf might look at a lord from the point of view of one belonging to him and subject to his every whim.
3. Petrarch seems to have looked at writing from the point of view of one who found it art of the highest order and central to life, perhaps because he did it well and therefore had made it the center of his life.
4. Protestant leaders operated from a point of view that saw the Christian Church as desperately in need of change, while Catholic leaders operated from the point of view that whether or how the Church changed remained for them to decide.
5. The people who make history operate from different points of view, which need to be understood to understand why things happened as they did.

Technology CONNECTION

VIDEODISC/VIDEO TAPE 3
Enrich Chapter 12 with *The Renaissance* segment on the Videodisc.

Search Frame 6339 Side B

SUGGESTIONS FOR SUMMING UP THE CHAPTER

After students have copied the flow chart on a piece of paper, have them identify and discuss the first and last events in the chart. Have them find the date for the call for the Crusades on the time line on the facing page (1095) and look in Lesson 3 for when the feudal system began to decline (late 1300s). Encourage them to go back into the chapter for major events during that period that helped to bring on the final detail in the chart here. Possible answers appear on the reproduced pupil page above, and you may want to give students some hints to them as they conduct their search. When they have completed filling in the flow chart and begin writing their paragraphs, suggest that they weave their boxed answers together chronologically to answer the question posed.

ASSESSING THINK AND WRITE: *For performance assessment, see Assessment Book, Chapter 12, pp. T81–T83.*

CHAPTER 13 Empires and Cultures of Africa

Pages 352–381

CHAPTER OVERVIEW

In 1200 Ethiopia was independent and built magnificent Christian churches. Timbuktu became an important trading center for West Africa in 1300. Zanzibar developed trade between Arabs, Asians, and inland Africans in 1350. Great Zimbabwe became rich from the gold trade.

GEO ADVENTURES DAILY GEOGRAPHY ACTIVITIES

Use **Geo Adventures** Daily Geography activities to assess students' understanding of geography skills.

CHAPTER PLANNING GUIDE

LESSON 1	LESSON 2	LESSON 3
SUGGESTED PACING: 2 DAYS	SUGGESTED PACING: 2 DAYS	SUGGESTED PACING: 3 DAYS
Geography Of Africa pp. 354–357	**The Kingdoms Of Ethiopia** pp. 358–361	**Empires Of West Africa** pp. 362–367
CURRICULUM CONNECTIONS Links to Language Arts, p. 355	**CURRICULUM CONNECTIONS** Links to Science, p. 360	**CURRICULUM CONNECTIONS** Links to Reading, p. 366
RESOURCES Practice and Project Book, p. 71 ▦ Anthology, p. 78 Desk Map Outline Map	**RESOURCES** Practice and Project Book, p. 72 Anthology, pp. 79–81 Outline Map	**FIELD TRIP** Visit a Museum, p. 364 **INFOGRAPHIC** Timbuktu, p. 365 **RESOURCES** Practice and Project Book, p. 73 Anthology, pp. 82–83, 84 Desk Map ◉ TECHNOLOGY *Adventure Time!* CD-ROM

GEOGRAPHY SKILLS	LESSON 4	LESSON 5
SUGGESTED PACING: 1 DAY	SUGGESTED PACING: 2 DAYS	SUGGESTED PACING: 2 DAYS
Reading Distribution Maps pp. 370–371	**Africa's Eastern Coast** pp. 372–375	**Great Zimbabwe** pp. 376–379
RESOURCES Practice and Project Book, p. 74 Transparency Map 16 ◉ TECHNOLOGY *Adventure Time!* CD-ROM	**CURRICULUM CONNECTIONS** Links to Music, p. 374 **RESOURCES** Practice and Project Book, p. 75 ▦ Anthology, pp. 89–92 Desk Map Outline Map	**CURRICULUM CONNECTIONS** Links to Art, p. 377 **CITIZENSHIP** Understanding Government, p. 378 **RESOURCES** Practice and Project Book, p. 76 ◉ TECHNOLOGY *Adventure Time!* CD-ROM

LEARNING STYLE: Visual ON YOUR OWN 30 MINUTES OR LONGER

Write a Long-Ago Journal Entry

Objective: To introduce African empires and cultures.

Materials: paper

1. Ask students to imagine they are accompanying a trader to an African kingdom that developed after the civilizations of Kush and Punt. The trader might be Arabian, Chinese, or European.
2. Have students write a journal entry about their home region, the goods they want to trade and to obtain, and what they hope to learn about the African kingdom they will be visiting.
3. Ask students to share their journals with the class.

Legacy

SUGGESTED PACING: I DAY

Griots And Oral History
pp. 368–369

RESOURCES
Anthology, pp. 85–86, 87–88

CHAPTER REVIEW

SUGGESTED PACING: I DAY

pp. 380–381

RESOURCES
Practice and Project Book, p. 77
⊙ TECHNOLOGY Videodisc/Video Tape 3
Assessment Book: Chapter 13 Test
Transparency: Graphic Organizer, Main-Idea Map

SDAIE SUPPORT — SHELTERED INSTRUCTION

READING STRATEGIES & LANGUAGE DEVELOPMENT

Making Conclusions/Homographs, p. 354, Lesson 1
Main Ideas and Details/Words with Multiple Meanings, p. 358, Lesson 2
Classifying/Quotation Marks, p. 362, Lesson 3
Making Conclusions/Words with Multiple Meanings, p. 370, Geography Skills
Cause and Effect/Word Roots, p. 372, Lesson 4
Problem–Solution/Compound Words, p. 376, Lesson 5

SECOND-LANGUAGE SUPPORT

Working with Peers, p. 355
Using Visuals, p. 359
Dramatization, p. 363
Using Props/Taking Notes, p. 374
Dialogs, p. 377
Maps/Interviews, p. 380

MEETING INDIVIDUAL NEEDS

Reteaching, Extension, Enrichment, pp. 357, 361, 367, 369, 371, 375, 379
McGraw-Hill Adventure Book

ASSESSMENT OPPORTUNITIES

Practice and Project Book, pp. 71–77
Write About It, pp. 357, 361, 367, 369, 375, 379
Assessment Book: Assessing Think and Write, pp. T84–T86; Chapter 13 Tests: Content, Skills, Writing

CHAPTER 13

Introducing the Chapter

Refer students to the chapter title and have them identify the continent to which they are returning. Ask what civilization that they have already studied was located in Africa. On the map, have them locate Egypt on the African continent (northeast corner).

THINKING ABOUT HISTORY AND GEOGRAPHY

Have students look at the map and help them recognize how large a landmass Africa is and therefore the variety of geographic environments it must have. Have them read the text on this page to get a sense of different civilizations developing in different parts of Africa.

1200 LALIBELA

● **Where is Lalibela?** *(in eastern Africa, just above the hornlike peninsula jutting into the Indian Ocean)*

★THINKING FURTHER: *Making Conclusions* **Based on what is happening in the panel, what can you conclude about religion in this civilization?** *(Christianity must have taken hold here because Christian churches are being built.)*

1300 TIMBUKTU

● **Have you ever heard of Timbuktu before? Where is it?** *(Students may have heard "from here to Timbuktu"; have them locate Timbuktu as a real place in west Africa.)*

● **What does this panel show?** *(people in a marketplace with structures in the background)*

★THINKING FURTHER: *Making Conclusions* **What conclusions can you make about Timbuktu in 1300?** *(It was an important center for trade)*

 Resource **REMINDER**

● **Technology:** *Videodisc*

Empires and Cultures of Africa

THINKING ABOUT HISTORY AND GEOGRAPHY

The stories of Africa's cultures often take place on the continent's fertile grasslands. Following the time line, see how civilizations developed in different parts of the continent. The great amounts of gold and other trade goods in Africa made these civilizations wealthy. As different peoples came into contact, new religious and cultural traditions were born.

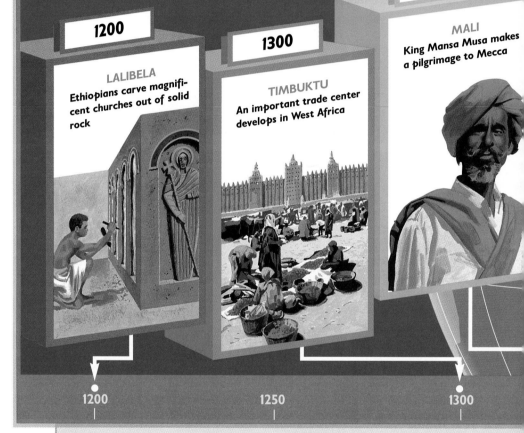

1200

LALIBELA
Ethiopians carve magnificent churches out of solid rock

1300

TIMBUKTU
An important trade center develops in West Africa

1324

MALI
King Mansa Musa makes a pilgrimage to Mecca

ATLANTIC OCEAN

1200   1250   1300

BACKGROUND INFORMATION

LINKING THE MAP AND THE TIME LINE

● Lalibela is located in the mountainous northern Eritrea region of modern-day Ethiopia. The eleven rock-hewn Christian churches here are of two types. Four are shrine-like grottoes, carved into cavities in the sides of mountains; seven are freestanding monoliths carved in the shape of crosses.

● Timbuktu became part of the African nation of Mali in 1960. Following its glory as a center of trade and scholarship (treated in the *Info-graphic* on page 365), it began a decline, brought on by constant raids by marauders. By 1828 it had become a "mass of ill-looking houses built of earth," according to one European visitor.

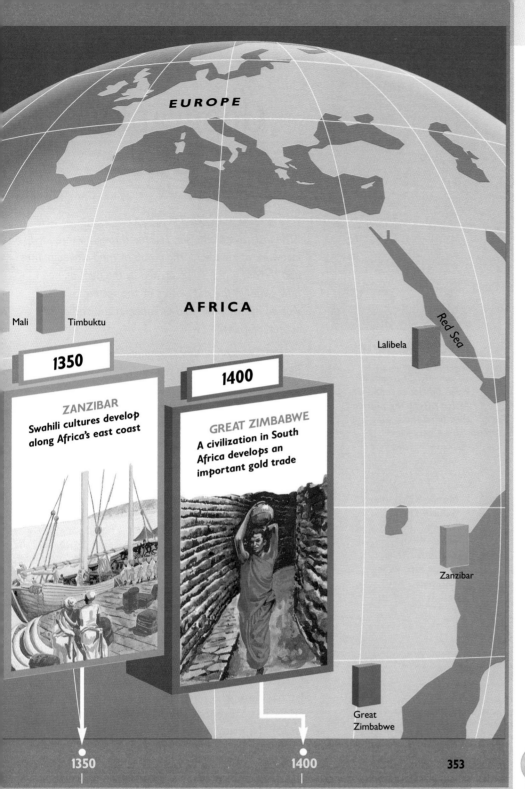

EUROPE

AFRICA

Mali Timbuktu

Red Sea

Lalibela

1350

1400

ZANZIBAR
Swahili cultures develop along Africa's east coast

GREAT ZIMBABWE
A civilization in South Africa develops an important gold trade

Zanzibar

Great Zimbabwe

1350   1400   353

● **Where is Mali?** *(in west Africa to the west of Timbuktu)*

● **What is happening in this panel?** *(King Mansa Musa, apparently king of Mali, is making a pilgrimage to Mecca.)*

★**THINKING FURTHER:** *Making Conclusions* **From this, what can you conclude about Islam and West Africa?** *(Islam must have spread to West Africa if one of its kings is on pilgrimage to Mecca.)*

● **Where is Zanzibar?** *(along the east coast of Africa, on the Indian Ocean)*

● **What language was spoken in Zanzibar and other east coast cities?** *(Swahili)*

★**THINKING FURTHER:** *Making Conclusions* **What economic activity would you conclude gave rise to these cities? Why?** *(The panel shows sea trade, and the coastal location also hints at it.)*

● **Where is Great Zimbabwe located in relation to Zanzibar?** *(southwest and inland from the Indian Ocean)*

★**THINKING FURTHER:** *Making Connections* **What important resource does Great Zimbabwe have?** *(gold)*

Technology CONNECTION

VIDEODISC
Enrich Chapter 13 with the *African Empires* segment on the Videodisc.

Search Frame 52846 Side A

BACKGROUND INFORMATION

LINKING THE MAP AND THE TIME LINE

● The empire of Mali has since lent its name to the modern-day African nation of Mali. The boundaries of modern Mali differ from those of the empire although the two have some territory in common.

● Zanzibar is an island in the Indian Ocean lying about 20 miles east of the mainland nation of Tanzania, of which it is now part. Zanzibar was founded around 1000 by African mainlanders, who were soon joined by Arab, Persian, and Indian traders.

● Great Zimbabwe, like the empire of Mali, has lent its name to a modern-day African nation, Zimbabwe. The impressive remains of Great Zimbabwe lie in the eastern part of the modern nation.

LESSON 1

Lesson Overview

The vast continent of Africa is highly diverse in its geographical features.

Lesson Objectives

★ Identify major geographical features of Africa.

★ Explain how early Africans adapted to and changed their environment.

1 PREPARE

MOTIVATE Have students close their eyes and recall scenes from the media of places where the sun burned so hot that the air seemed to ripple. Then ask them to picture the scene described as you do the *Read Aloud*.

SET PURPOSE Use the photo of animals grazing on the savanna to encourage students to name features that they may know of Africa's geography. Note the features on the board and add the *Vocabulary* term. Ask students to use the *Read to Learn* question to focus their reading.

2 TEACH

Understanding THE BIG PICTURE Refer students to their desk maps of the world and have them locate Africa, to see its comparative size, second only to Asia.

● **What major geographical feature of Africa have we already studied?** (the Nile River flowing through Egypt)

● **What other kinds of geographical features does Africa have?** (deserts, rain forests, vast plains)

★THINKING FURTHER: *Making Conclusions* **Why is it likely that Africa would have great geographical variety?** (It covers a vast area.)

Resource REMINDER

Practice and Project Book: *p. 71*

Anthology: *Fall Rain, Fall Rain, p. 78*

Desk Map

Outline Map

Focus Activity

READ TO LEARN

How did the savanna of Africa affect the people that lived there long ago?

VOCABULARY

● savanna

PLACES

● Mount Kilimanjaro
● Sahara Desert
● Sahel
● Niger River
● Zambezi River
● Great Rift Valley
● Red Sea

354

Geography of Africa

Read Aloud

"The last rays of the sun filtered through a shredded lacework of clouds . . . the group of mud-walled houses and the dry grass, still scorched by the heat of noon, now swam in the red waters of the setting sun. . . . It was an afternoon in mid-October, at the end of the season of rains."

West African author Ousmane Sembene (oos MAH nee sem BAY nee), from the country of Senegal, wrote these words describing the end of one day in Africa. Throughout this huge continent, and throughout history, the sun—along with rain and vast stretches of grassland—has shaped the pattern of millions of lives.

THE BIG PICTURE

Africa is larger than the United States and all of the countries of Europe put together. The history of this enormous continent is long and varied. In Chapter 3 you read about the early people who lived in places like Border Cave. Then in Chapter 4, you read about one of the most powerful civilizations of the ancient world, ancient Egypt.

Civilization in Egypt, you may recall, was made possible by the "gift of the Nile." The Nile River provided both water and fertile soil in a dry environment. Several other life-giving rivers flow through Africa. Africa also has deserts, rain forests, and vast plains. This great variety has presented special challenges and opportunities for the many peoples of the continent.

SHELTERED INSTRUCTION

READING STRATEGIES & LANGUAGE DEVELOPMENT

MAKING CONCLUSIONS Review with students how to make conclusions by using facts in the text and what they already know about a subject. Model how you make conclusions about Africa's geography by reading paragraph one of *The Big Picture*. Make your conclusion: Africa is a huge continent with a long, varied, and rich history. Arrange students in a jigsaw to find the information in the paragraph that you used to make the conclusion. **[SDAIE STRATEGY: MODELING]**

HOMOGRAPHS Briefly review what homographs are—words that have the same spelling but are different in meaning or word origin or pronunciation. Refer them on this page to the noun *deserts,* with the accent on the first syllable and ask how else this same spelling can be pronounced (as a verb, with the accent on the second syllable).

AFRICA

As you can see on the map, the equator runs through the middle of Africa. Mountains rise along Africa's eastern and northern edges. Snow lingers year round on Mount Kilimanjaro. In the Sahara Desert, though, temperatures can reach a sizzling 136°F! This is the world's largest desert. Dry grasslands of the Sahel (SA hihl) form a narrow belt along the Sahara's southern edge. *Sahel* is an Arabic word that means "shore." Find the Sahel on the map.

The Niger River and the Zambezi (zam BEE zee) River water thirsty lands. The Great Rift Valley extends nearly 3,000 miles, from the Mozambique Channel to the Red Sea.

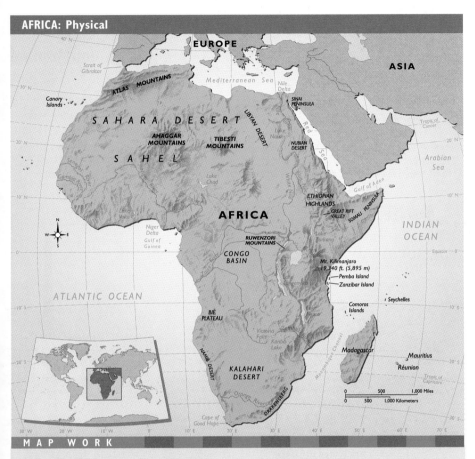

AFRICA: Physical

The varied geography of Africa includes dense rain forests and empty deserts where rain may not fall for years at a time.

1. Which desert is found on the southwestern coast of Africa?

2. In which direction would you travel to go from the Tibesti Mountains to Lake Victoria?

3. How is it possible to reach Kariba Lake from Lake Victoria without land travel?

MAP WORK: 1. Namib Desert **2.** southeast **3.** by traveling down the Nile River, through the Mediterranean Sea, around the West Coast of Africa, and up the Zambezi River

355

CURRICULUM CONNECTION

LINKS TO LANGUAGE ARTS Explain to the class that certain expressions are often used to refer to sections of Africa. The *horn of Africa* or the *African horn* describes the horn-shaped Somali peninsula extending into the Indian Ocean below the Gulf of Aden. The *hump of Africa* or the *African hump* is the western bulge that extends into the Atlantic Ocean.

SECOND-LANGUAGE SUPPORT

WORKING WITH PEERS Second-language learners may benefit by working with English-proficient peers to read assigned sections of various lessons. Have the mixed pairs present the content of their sections, retelling the most important information. Make sure that second-language learners take an active speaking role in the retellings.

AFRICA

Mention that Africa is divided into many countries, and their geography varies.

More MAP WORK

Refer students to the map. Encourage them to work back and forth between map and text. Have them locate the equator and the area between the Tropic of Cancer and the Tropic of Capricorn.

● *How much of Africa falls into this area? What does that tell you about Africa's climate?* (Most of the continent is in the tropics; therefore the climate must be hot.)

● *What geographical feature covers much of the northern part of the continent?* (the Sahara Desert)

● *What geographical feature runs along the Sahara Desert's southern edge?* (the Sahel)

● *What other large part of Africa is covered by desert?* (Much of the southwestern part is covered by the Namib and Kalihari deserts.)

● *How does the Great Rift Valley act as a sort of dividing line in Africa?* (It cuts a 3,000-mile path of cliffs and canyons through eastern Africa.)

● *On the map, find Mount Kilimanjaro near the equator. Why would it have snow on its top at this location?* (Help students recall "the higher, the colder" maxim concerning elevation and temperature.)

● *With your fingers, trace the courses of the Niger and Zambezi rivers. What part of Africa does each of them water?* (Niger: northwest; Zambezi: southeast)

★**THINKING FURTHER:** *Making Conclusions If you had to give someone a brief picture of the geography of Africa, how would you describe it?* (Possible answer: two dry regions north and south sandwiching a well-watered central region, with mountains along the northern tip and eastern edge and a deep cut, or rift, up and down the eastern half)

THE GRASSY PLAINS

Refer the class to the map on p. 355.

- **What are savannas?** *(grassy, tree-dotted plains)*

- **What area of Africa do savannas cover?** *(Have students trace with their fingers the area across north-central Africa down south to south-western Africa up around the Namib and Kalihari deserts to the west coast.)*

> ★**THINKING FURTHER:** *Compare and Contrast* **How would you contrast the dry season with the rainy season on the savannas?** *(Dry: brown grass, cracked dry ground. Rainy: sudden heavy rains, new growth everywhere.)*

Discussing Early Farmers As the class discusses farming, have a student write on the board the main crops.

- **Why would savannas be better for farming than many other areas of Africa?** *(Students should recognize that deserts are not suitable for farming nor are cliffs and canyons.)*

- **How long ago did farmers begin tilling the savannas?** *(4,000 years ago)*

- **What crops did they grow?** *(nourishing grains, like millet and sorghum, as well as vegetables)*

> ★**THINKING FURTHER:** *Making Conclusions* **How would you say that early Africans made good use of the land?** *(They found the crops that grew best in the thin, dry soil and concentrated on growing the most nourishing ones.)*

Exploring People and the Environment Review slash-and-burn agriculture.

- **Why did farmers set fire to the savannas?** *(to clear land or encourage growth of new grass for their herds)*

> ★**THINKING FURTHER:** *Making Connections* **What long-term effect did this have on the land? Where have you seen this effect earlier in your study of the world?** *(Help students to recognize a recurring theme in human land use—deforestation—which they have already seen in Europe and elsewhere.)*

356

THE GRASSY PLAINS

Grassy, tree-dotted plains called savannas cover a large area of Africa. This area is about the size of the entire United States. Savannas cover most of southern Africa and the region between Ethiopia and Senegal.

The savannas have a dry season and a rainy season. During the dry season, savanna grasses turn brown and the ground dries and cracks. This quickly changes, though, when the rainy season arrives. Author Bessie Head describes the effect of rain on the savanna of Botswana, in southern Africa.

> *Before the first rains fall, it gets so hot that you cannot breathe. Then one day the sky just empties itself in a terrible downpour. After this, the earth and sky [come] alive and there is magic everywhere. . . . With just a little rain everything comes alive all at once; over-eager and hungry. . . . Crickets and frogs appear overnight in the pools around the village: there is a heavy, rich smell of breathing earth everywhere.*

New grass and leaves sprout up across the savanna, providing a welcome feast for antelopes, zebras, and giraffes. The rains also bring needed water for crops and domestic animals.

Early Farmers

Africans began farming the savanna about 4,000 years ago. They domesticated grains called millet and sorghum (SAWR gum). These grains grew well in the thin, dry soil of the savannas. Both crops grew so quickly that they were ready for harvest before the dry season set in. Best of all, millet and sorghum contain vitamins, protein, and other nutrients needed for a healthy diet.

Modern equipment is used to harvest wheat on Kenya's savanna. **Zambian women grind grain traditionally.**

356

BACKGROUND INFORMATION

ABOUT AFRICA'S GEOGRAPHY
- The area to the north of the Gulf of Guinea and as far east of it as Zaire is covered by rain forest.
- As might be expected, much of Africa's northern tip has a Mediterranean climate, but so does much of its southern tip.

GLOBAL CONNECTION

THE COLUMBIAN EXCHANGE With recent interest in Cajun and Creole cooking, students may be familiar with okra. In Creole cooking, it is called *gumbo*. Explain that this vegetable was part of the Columbian exchange. It was brought from West Africa to the Americas.

CHART WORK: 1. large desert areas with little rain contrasted to rain forests with very heavy rainfall **2.** Nile River; 4,160 miles (6,671 kilometers)

AFRICA AT A GLANCE

	Total Land Area	11,704,000 sq. miles 30,312,999 sq. km
	Highest Mountain	Mt. Kilimanjaro, Tanzania 19,340 feet (5,895 m)
	Longest River	Nile River 4,160 miles 6,671 km
	Largest City	Cairo, Egypt Population 6,052,832
	Current Population	706,000,000
	Percent of World Population	13%

GEO FACT
More than half of Africa receives less than 20 inches (51 cm) of rain each year. In parts of the Sahara and Namib deserts, rain may not fall for six or seven years in a row. On the other hand, the rain forests of the Congo River Basin and the coastal region of western Africa receive more than 80 inches (203 cm) of rain each year.

CHART WORK

Africa is a continent of contrasts.

1. What, according to the chart, is one of Africa's greatest contrasts?
2. Which is Africa's longest river? How long is it?

These crops—along with okra, peas, and other vegetables—became the fuel for growing civilizations throughout Africa. The crops remain important today.

People and the Environment

In ancient times farmers set fire to the savannas and nearby areas to clear the land for farming or to make room for the growth of new grass for the herds. New grasses caused savannas to spread. Many historians believe that grasslands now ripple where forests once stood.

WHY IT MATTERS

The landforms of Africa are vast and varied. So are the continent's climate and bodies of water. All of these factors have affected the way Africans have lived. Ancient Africans farmed on the savannas. So do many Africans today.

Many people have worked to preserve and protect these important regions. Some savannas have become protected areas on which thousands of wild animals roam and feed.

You have learned how farming traditions shaped Africa's environment. In the next lesson you will read about a civilization that created unique religious legacies in a rocky environment.

Reviewing Facts and Ideas

MAIN IDEAS

- Africa's many climate regions range from the snow-covered top of Mount Kilimanjaro to the Sahara, the world's largest desert.
- Savannas cover much of southern Africa and are home to wildlife.
- Farmers began growing millet and sorghum about 4,000 years ago.

THINK ABOUT IT

1. What parts of Africa have hills and mountains?
2. What is the Sahel? Where is this region located?
3. **FOCUS** How have Africa's savannas shaped the lives of the people who have lived on them? How have people affected the savannas?
4. **THINKING SKILL** What are some *effects* of rainfall on the savanna?
5. **GEOGRAPHY** In what ways do people interact with the savanna environment in Africa?

357

More CHART WORK

- *What is Africa's largest city? In what country is it?* (Cairo; Egypt)

- ★**THINKING FURTHER:** *Making Conclusions* **Using what you know of history, why would that country's population be large?** *(Students should recall that Egypt was one of the world's earliest civilizations.)*

Discussing WHY IT MATTERS Have students review the role of geography in people's ways of life.

★**THINKING FURTHER:** *Making Conclusions* **How might Africa's geographical variety affect ways people adapt to their environments?** *(Geographical variety results in variety among the cultures in Africa.)*

3 CLOSE

MAIN IDEAS
Call on students for answers.

- *How would you describe the range of Africa's climate regions?* (Possible answer: from snow-capped mountain tops to sun-baked deserts)

- *Where are Africa's savannas and what role do they serve?* (They cover much of Africa south of the Sahara, and serve as farmland and home to wild animals.)

EVALUATE
✓ **Answers to Think About It**

1. the eastern edge and northern tip *Use Maps*

2. a narrow band of dry grasslands along the Sahara's southern edge *Recall Details*

3. The savannas furnished land that people could farm; people extended the savannas by burning forests. *Main Idea*

4. a burst of new plant life and water for animals who live on the savannas *Cause and Effect*

5. They use it for farming and herding and have changed it over time. *Five Themes of Geography: Human/Environment Interactions*

Write About It Have students write a description of Africa's geography.

MEETING INDIVIDUAL NEEDS

RETEACHING (Easy) On an outline map of Africa, have students draw in the Atlas Mountains, the Sahara, the Sahel, the Great Rift Valley, the savanna region, and the Namib and Kalihari.

EXTENSION (Average) Remind the class that some of Africa's savanna land has become protected so that wildlife can roam there freely. Have students write a statement entitled "The Benefits of Wildlife Refuges."

ENRICHMENT (Challenging) Divide the class into four groups and assign each one of the following African environments: desert, the Sahel, savanna, rain forest. Have the groups research the species of wildlife that live in their assigned environment and collect pictures of them, with identifying captions. Then have the class assemble their categories in a "Class Book of African Wildlife."

LESSON 2
PAGES 358–361

Lesson Overview
Following 500 B.C., independent kingdoms like Kush, Aksum, and Zagwe emerged and flourished in northeastern Africa.

Lesson Objectives
★ Describe the role trade played in the development of Kush, Aksum, and the Zagwe rulers.

★ Identify their accomplishments.

1 PREPARE

MOTIVATE Have students examine the stone churches here and on pp. 360–361 as you read the *Read Aloud*. Help them to appreciate what an incredible idea carving a church out of rock is and what a massive undertaking it must have been. Who could have conceived such a plan?

SET PURPOSE Refer students to the *Read to Learn* question and encourage them to explore the lesson to find out what led to the development of a level of civilization that produced such work.

2 TEACH

Understanding THE BIG PICTURE
Review what students have already learned about Egypt, Punt, and Kush.

● **What have you already learned that tells you northeastern Africa was a seedbed for civilizations?** *(Egypt, Punt, and Kush developed there.)*

★THINKING FURTHER: *Cause and Effect* **Why do you suppose the presence of one or more civilizations in an area encourages the development of others?** *(Help students to identify the value of cultural contact, through trade or other means, and of cultural borrowing.)*

Resource REMINDER

Practice and Project Book: *p. 72*
Anthology: *The Kingdom of Kush, pp. 79–81*
Outline Map

600　700　1225　1350　1600

The Kingdoms of Ethiopia

Read Aloud
It began with a cliff some four stories high. From the hard red stone, workers carved out a massive block. The carvers then hollowed out the block and gave it windows and doors. They carved elegant arches, columns, and designs into the rock. The stone cliff slowly turned into a beautiful church. Such carving took place in the 1200s, in the highlands of Ethiopia.

Focus Activity

READ TO LEARN

How did kingdoms develop in what is today Ethiopia?

VOCABULARY
- Queen Amanishakhete
- Lalibela

PLACES
- Ethiopia
- Kush
- Aksum

THE BIG PICTURE
While castles and churches were being built in Europe during its Middle Ages, communities and kingdoms in Africa flourished as well. One of them developed a rich culture in northeastern Africa, near the tip of the Arabian peninsula.

In Chapter 4 you read that the Egyptian pharaoh Hatshepsut sent trading ships to the wealthy kingdom of Punt. Punt may have been located in the present-day country of Ethiopia. You also read that ancient Egypt's army conquered Kush, located in what is now Sudan. Egypt, Punt, and Kush were just three of the early civilizations of northeastern Africa. In this lesson you will read about other kingdoms that developed there.

This painting of apostles is in a stone church in Ethiopia.

SHELTERED INSTRUCTION

READING STRATEGIES & LANGUAGE DEVELOPMENT

MAIN IDEAS AND DETAILS Remind students that finding main ideas and details in a passage can help them understand the author's point. On the board, create a diagram in the shape of an umbrella. At the top of the "umbrella," write main idea. On each of the spokes, write details. Guide students to see that a main idea can be a framework on which to hang details about a subject. As they read this lesson, have students complete the diagram with details about the kingdom of Ethiopia. [SDAIE STRATEGY: SCHEMA BUILDING]

WORDS WITH MULTIPLE MEANINGS Refer students to the word *network* on p. 359. Have them define it (an interconnected system of trade routes). Ask for other meanings of this word. (They should be familiar with television networks and perhaps with computer networks. Point out that the original meaning was "open-work fabric, or netting.")

CIVILIZATIONS IN NORTHEASTERN AFRICA

When Egyptian civilization declined, Kush became an independent kingdom. Kushite kings based their government at Meroe (MER oo ee), a city along the banks of the Nile.

The Kingdom of Kush

From about 500 B.C. to A.D. 150, Kush's rulers controlled a large trade network. This network stretched east to Arabia, north to the Mediterranean, and southwest toward the center of Africa.

Meroe's ruins give some clues to what life in Kush was like. There are remains of grand palaces, temples, and pyramid-shaped tombs. These remains show Kush's rulers had great wealth. Some of that wealth was found inside the tomb of Queen Amanishakhete (ah mahn uh SHAHK huh tee).

Queen Amanishakhete ruled Kush around 27 B.C. Archaeologists found gold bracelets, chains, rings, and statues within her tomb. The large amount of gold found in the tomb shows the richness of the Kush kingdom. The jewelry's beauty shows the skill of Kush's craftworkers.

The Kingdom of Aksum

By A.D. 350 the kingdom of Kush and its capital city had weakened. Historians are uncertain about the events that led to the decline of Kush. They know that Kush was conquered in 350 by Aksum, a powerful kingdom to the southeast.

Aksum was located high in the hills and mountains of what are today Eritrea and Ethiopia. Find Aksum on the map. Like Meroe, Aksum gained power and wealth by controlling important cities and trade routes. Traders traveled to the port city of Adula on the Red Sea.

There ships unloaded treasures from Arabia, Egypt, and India. People bought goods with gold coins or ivory.

Christianity in Africa

Many of Aksum's coins were stamped with signs of the Christian cross. Aksum's rulers became supporters of Christianity around A.D. 300. This early date makes ancient Ethiopia's Christian Church among the oldest in the world.

Christians in Ethiopia developed some beliefs that differed from those of Christians in Rome. For example, Ethiopians did not look to the Pope as their religious leader. Instead, Christians in Ethiopia follow a leader called a patriarch (PAY tree ark). Today nearly half of all Ethiopians are Christians.

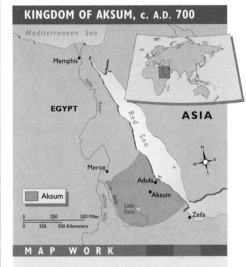

KINGDOM OF AKSUM, c. A.D. 700

MAP WORK

Trade thrived in cities within the kingdom of Aksum. Many traders crossed the Red Sea.

1. In which direction did Aksum's traders travel to reach the Red Sea?
2. About how far was Meroe from Adula?
3. Which rivers flowed along the western edge of Aksum?

MAP WORK: 1. east 2. about 400 miles (about 643 kilometers) 3. White Nile, Blue Nile   **359**

CIVILIZATIONS IN NORTH-EASTERN AFRICA

Remind students of the role of the Nile.

More   **MAP WORK**

Refer students to the map and the text.

- **On what river is Meroe?** *(Nile)*

- **Why would this be a good location for trade?** *(water transport)*

- **Where is the kingdom of Aksum in relation to Meroe? In what modern-day country is it?** *(southeast; Ethiopia)*

- **Why was Aksum also in a good position for trade?** *(It is on a river—the Nile—and a sea—the Red Sea.)*

Discussing The Kingdom of Kush
On the map, have students locate Meroe and the trade network from Kush.

- **To what points did Kush's trade network extend?** *(Arabia, the Mediterranean, central Africa)*

- **Why would control of such a network produce great wealth?** *(Help students see that trade is carried on to increase wealth and that control of trade would greatly increase wealth.)*

★**THINKING FURTHER:** *Cause and Effect* **What effect did great wealth have on Kush civilization?** *(It was used to create grand works—great palaces, temples, tombs, gold jewelry, and statues.)*

Exploring The Kingdom of Aksum
Call attention to gold and ivory as mediums of exchange.

★**THINKING FURTHER:** *Compare and Contrast* **Why might you say that Aksum was like Kush?** *(Aksum too controlled a vast trade network and so grew powerful.)*

Discussing Christianity in Africa
Stress the early Christianity in Aksum.

- **When did Aksum's rulers first support Christianity?** *(around A.D. 300)*

★**THINKING FURTHER:** *Compare and Contrast* **How did Ethiopian Christianity differ from the Roman Church?** *(Ethiopian Christians followed their patriarch, not the Pope.)*

BACKGROUND INFORMATION

ABOUT RELIGION IN MODERN ETHIOPIA
- Nearly half of Ethiopians are Christians, most of the rest, Muslims.
- About two percent of Ethiopians are Jews.

SECOND-LANGUAGE SUPPORT

USING VISUALS Second-language learners may benefit by creating a Venn diagram to compare and contrast different cultures.

Kush
500 B.C. to A.D. 350
Ethiopia

Both
Palaces, pyramids
temples, wealth
Tombs of rulers held gold
and jeweled
objects
Used Nile River

Ancient Egypt
5000 B.C. to 1200 B.C.
Egypt

A NEW KINGDOM

Give students a few minutes to go back to Chapter 10, Lesson 3, to review what they learned about the Baghdad caliphate, referred to in this section.

- **How long did Aksum's power as a trading center last?** (from around A.D. 350 to 700—350 years)

- **What caused Aksum to weaken?** (The Baghdad caliphate took control of Red Sea shipping.)

★**THINKING FURTHER:** *Making Conclusions* **How does Aksum's ultimate fate show that there always seems to be someone ready to pick up the reins of power?** (Local nobles—the Zagwe—overthrew Aksum's weakened leaders.)

Discussing Churches Carved in Rock Lead students to recall that major public works require powerful leadership.

- **Who was Lalibela?** (the most powerful Zagwe king, who ruled 1185–1225)

- **For what is he best remembered?** (sponsoring the carving of 11 stone churches out of solid rock)

★**THINKING FURTHER:** *Cause and Effect* **How do you think the carving of the stone churches might have affected the Zagwe kingdom?** (It may have heightened religious fervor, it must have provided a great deal of work, and it encouraged cultural contact as stone workers came from other regions of the world to take part.)

A NEW KINGDOM

Aksum's trading success came to an end around A.D. 700. The kingdom suffered when the growing Baghdad caliphate took control of all shipping on the Red Sea. The loss of this important source of trade and wealth caused Aksum's economy to weaken. Bronze coins began to replace the more valuable gold coins. Around A.D. 900 Aksum stopped making coins altogether. By that time, the capital of the kingdom had been moved to more fertile lands farther south. Then Aksum's rulers were overthrown by local nobles called the Zagwe (ZAHG we).

360

Churches Carved in Rock

The Zagwe nobles, like the rulers of Aksum, supported Christianity. The most powerful Zagwe king, Lalibela (LAH lee be lah), ruled Ethiopia from about 1185 to 1225. During his rule, workers carved 11 stone churches in Ethiopia's new capital city. The city was named Lalibela to honor the king.

Day after day, year after year, people of the city probably heard sounds of clanging and chipping. Stoneworkers from as far away as Palestine and Egypt came to work on the projects. Their different languages must have been heard throughout the city.

Rock churches carved from huge pieces of stone still stand in Lalibela (left, below). Some of the services (far left) in Christian churches there and in other parts of Ethiopia follow traditions that developed under the Zagwe rulers.

Historians believe that each church in Lalibela was designed to look like a famous earlier church in Aksum. Some of the churches in Aksum had wooden beams jutting from the buildings. Lalibela's stonecutters carved out similar structures in stone. Since many of the churches were carved out of a single piece of stone, the stoneworkers had to be very careful. One slip of the chisel could result in a mistake that could not be corrected!

WHY IT MATTERS

The churches of Lalibela show the importance of Christianity in ancient Ethiopia. They also brought fame and honor to their builder, Lalibela. While little is known about the Zagwe kingdom, the stone churches have provided clues about the people of Zagwe.

The Zagwe kingdom of Ethiopia was only one of many that developed in Africa. In the next lesson you will read about a rich and powerful empire in western Africa. It grew at about the same time as the Zagwe kingdom.

✓/// Reviewing Facts and Ideas

MAIN IDEAS

- Between 500 B.C. and A.D. 150, Kush grew wealthy from trade across the Mediterranean, in Arabia, and farther south in Africa.
- In A.D. 350 Kush was conquered by Aksum, a powerful trading state to the south. Christianity took root in Africa around this time.
- After 1100, Zagwe kings such as Lalibela created stone churches.

THINK ABOUT IT

1. How were Kush and Aksum similar? Describe one way in which the kingdoms were different.

2. Why were the churches of Lalibela so unusual and difficult to build?

3. **FOCUS** How was trade important to civilizations in ancient Ethiopia?

4. **THINKING SKILL** What _effects_ did the loss of Red Sea trade have on the kingdom of Aksum?

5. **WRITE** Write a short paragraph explaining what the artifacts in the tomb of Queen Amanishakhete reveal about Kush civilization.

361

LESSON 3

Lesson Overview
By the 700s A.D., empires rich in gold—Ghana, Mali, Songhai—began to emerge in western Africa.

Lesson Objectives
★ Classify information about each of these three kingdoms.

★ Analyze how their economies worked.

★ Describe life in Timbuktu.

1 PREPARE

MOTIVATE On a globe or desk map of the world, have students locate West Africa in relation to Europe and western Asia. Then have a student do the *Read Aloud* and ask the class to identify a tie that bound them all (African gold).

SET PURPOSE Briefly discuss with students the lure and value of gold; then refer them to the *Read to Learn* question and the photo of the gold mask. Preview the *Vocabulary*.

2 TEACH

Understanding THE BIG PICTURE
Make sure students realize the scene has shifted from northeast to West Africa.

● **What common product was needed in West Africa and why?** *(salt, to preserve foods)*

● **What did West Africa produce that could pay for salt?** *(gold)*

★THINKING FURTHER: *Making Conclusions* **Necessity is often called "the mother of invention." Why can it also be called "the mother of trade"?** *(A need that a location cannot provide for itself can be gained through trade.)*

Resource REMINDER

Practice and Project Book: *p. 73*

Anthology: *Observations of a 14th Century Traveler, pp. 82–83; The Empire of Mali, p. 84*

 Technology: *Adventures CD-ROM*

Desk Map

Focus Activity

READ TO LEARN

What resources helped the empires of West Africa to grow wealthy and powerful?

VOCABULARY
• supply
• demand
• griot

PEOPLE
• Sunjata
• Mansa Musa

PLACES
• Ghana
• Mali
• Timbuktu
• Songhai
• Morocco

---

600   750   1591 1600

Empires of West Africa

Read Aloud
What did jewelry and coins from such places as Morocco, Spain, and the storage rooms of the Medici family in Florence have in common? The answer is African gold. From 900 to 1500 most gold in western Asia and Europe came from the rich mines of West Africa. The resources from these mines would shape life throughout the Eastern Hemisphere—most of all in Africa—for hundreds of years.

THE BIG PICTURE
As new kingdoms grew in northeastern Africa, other civilizations developed on the savannas of western Africa. These civilizations flourished while Baghdad's caliphs ruled a vast area in western Asia and northern Africa. At the same time, the Renaissance and Reformation swept through Europe.

As you read in Lesson 1 of this chapter, the savannas were a challenging environment for raising crops. Farmers could usually raise the sorghum, millet, and other crops that people needed for food. They could not, however, grow a very important item—salt. Salt was important because it could be used to prevent food from spoiling in warm climates. In parts of western Africa, salt actually became worth its weight in gold! Gold was another important item in West Africa. Much gold was bought and sold in the region's trade centers. Trade routes grew because of the need for salt and gold. These trade routes linked the empires of West Africa with the rest of Africa, Asia, and Europe.

SHELTERED INSTRUCTION

READING STRATEGIES & LANGUAGE DEVELOPMENT

CLASSIFYING Remind students that a good way to make sense of information is to classify it. Explain that this lesson explores three West African empires. Have students skim the text to identify them [Ghana, Mali, Songhai]. Create a three-column chart. Down the left side, list the empires. Then have students brainstorm categories to classify the empires, write them across the top, and complete the chart as they read. **[SDAIE STRATEGY: SCHEMA BUILDING]**

QUOTATION MARKS Ask students to name the situations for which we use quotation marks (for words someone has written or spoken, for a word used as a name, for a characterization of something). Have students look at p. 363 to find an example of the first (the quote in the right column) and an example of the third ("Land of Gold") in the subtitle.

In the Ghana empire, people sold salt in solid blocks. In some African towns, salt is still sold in the same way (left). Other trade goods included spoons, boxes to hold gold dust, and shells (below).

GHANA: AN EARLY EMPIRE

By the 700s the empire of Ghana was already a major power in Africa. Ghana was located at the southwestern edge of the Sahara, between the Senegal and Niger rivers.

The "Land of Gold"

In the 700s Muslim traders from northern Africa first began arriving in Ghana. What they saw amazed them. One trader, named al-Bakri, described the king's court in Ghana's capital city, Kumbi Salei (KOOM bee sah LEH).

Behind the king stand ten helpers holding shields and swords decorated with gold; and on his right are the sons of his vassal kings, wearing splendid garments and with gold woven in their hair. At the door of the pavilion are dogs guarding him. Round their necks they wear collars of gold and silver.

Ghana's merchants were allowed to handle only gold dust. Nuggets of gold were kept by the king. Al-Bakri explained the reason for this practice. If all of Ghana's gold was allowed into the marketplace, he wrote, "the people would [collect] gold until it lost its value."

By keeping gold scarce, Ghana's kings followed an important rule of economics called supply and demand. Supply is a quantity of some good, product, or resource. Demand is people's desire for that particular item. According to the rule of supply and demand, items that are plentiful in supply do not have high value—because they are easy to get. Items that are scarce, however, are high in value—because they are *not* easy to get. By keeping gold scarce, Ghana's kings kept its demand—and price—high.

363

GHANA: AN EARLY EMPIRE

Refer students to the map on p. 364 and have them find Ghana on it.

> ★THINKING FURTHER: *Making Conclusions* **How does Ghana's location make it both a "port" on the Sahara and a river port?** *(It lies along the southern edge of the Sahara and near the Senegal and Niger rivers.)*

Discussing The "Land of Gold"
Ask students to try to envision a land with an abundance of gold.

- *What attracted Muslim traders to Ghana?* *(It was a "land of gold.")*

- *From where did these Muslim traders come and how did they reach Ghana?* *(from North Africa across the "sea" of the Sahara Desert.)*

- *What rule of economics did the kings of Ghana use in making gold available?* *(supply and demand)*

- *How would you define supply? demand?* *(the quantity of goods available; the desire for goods)*

> ★THINKING FURTHER: *Making Conclusions* **Suppose you made a product for which there was great demand but you could produce a very limited amount. What would you expect to happen to the price? Suppose you could suddenly increase production tenfold, what would happen to the price?** *(It would be high; it would probably go down.)*

BACKGROUND INFORMATION

ABOUT "SAILING THE SAHARA"
- To Muslim traders from northern Africa, the Sahara was a "sea" that they sailed mounted on camels—their "ships of the desert."
- They traveled in vast caravans, sometimes 12,000 camels strong, to protect themselves from bandits who acted as the "pirates of the desert."
- Because the desert was as trackless as the sea, each caravan was led by a pilot who could navigate the way based mainly on patterns of sun, stars, and wind.
- Along the way, caravans would stop at salt-mining villages in the desert to pick up slabs of salt for trade when they reached the "ports" to the south.

BACKGROUND INFORMATION

ABOUT THE RITUAL OF "THE SILENT TRADE"
- Along the Niger River, Muslim traders piled slabs of salt in a neat row. After pounding drums, they left.
- At this signal, gold traders emerged, judged the salt's worth, deposited that much gold, and also left.
- The traders returned; if they judged there was enough gold, they took it and left. If not, they began again.

SECOND-LANGUAGE SUPPORT

DRAMATIZATION Second-language learners may simulate the law of supply and demand. Distribute many ordinary paper clips and one red clip. Ask students how many ordinary clips they would trade for the red one.

THE RISE OF MALI

Two modern countries in Africa took the names *Ghana* and *Mali,* but they are not direct heirs to the ancient lands.

- **How long did Ghana's kings control the gold supply?** *(about 500 years)*

- **According to tradition, what happened to weaken their control?** *(Sunjata, a Mali prince, conquered Ghana and other areas to create the Mali empire.)*

★**THINKING FURTHER:** *Making Conclusions* **How does Sunjata prove the wisdom of the old saying, "Don't judge a book by its cover"?** *(In appearance, he seemed harmless.)*

More MAP WORK

Refer students to the map on this page. Have them identify much of the area it shows as the "hump" of Africa.

- **Where does Mali lie in relation to Ghana?** *(Mali includes most of Ghana and extends to the Atlantic as well as east beyond the bend in the Niger River.)*

- **What empire succeeded Mali? How far did it extend beyond Mali?** *(Songhai; farther north into the Sahara as well as farther east beyond the Niger)*

Discussing From Mine to Market
Follow the complex gold trade.

- **How would you design a flow chart to show the steps gold took "from mine to market"?** *(Have students draw steps in the process on the board.)*

- **On the map, find Timbuktu. Why was it a crossroads of major trade routes?** *(It lies on the Niger River "highway" and on the edge of the Sahara, making it a port on both.)*

★**THINKING FURTHER:** *Making Conclusions* **Which kind of trade good might you wish were not available in Timbuktu? Why?** *(Students will probably name slaves and offer objections to slavery.)*

364

MAP WORK: **1.** Songhai **2.** about 250 miles (about 402 kilometers) **3.** Niger River **4.** Songhai **5.** Kumbi Salei

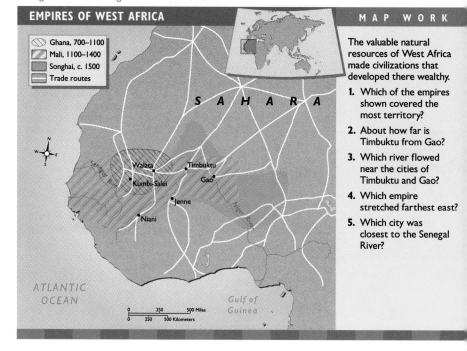

EMPIRES OF WEST AFRICA

MAP WORK

Ghana, 700–1100
Mali, 1100–1400
Songhai, c. 1500
Trade routes

SAHARA

Walata
Kumbi-Salei
Timbuktu
Gao
Jenne
Niani

Senegal River
Niger River

ATLANTIC OCEAN

Gulf of Guinea

0   250   500 Miles
0   250   500 Kilometers

The valuable natural resources of West Africa made civilizations that developed there wealthy.

1. Which of the empires shown covered the most territory?

2. About how far is Timbuktu from Gao?

3. Which river flowed near the cities of Timbuktu and Gao?

4. Which empire stretched farthest east?

5. Which city was closest to the Senegal River?

THE RISE OF MALI

Ghana's kings controlled western Africa's gold supply for over 500 years. Eventually, though, other empires began challenging Ghana's power. According to traditional African stories, all but one prince in an empire called Mali (MAH lee) were killed. Sunjata (sahn JAH tah) was spared because he was disabled and seemed harmless. The stories say that Mali's enemies, including Ghana, made a deadly mistake by misjudging Sunjata. He conquered his old enemies and all of Ghana as well. Sunjata died in 1255, but Mali continued to grow after his death. Look at the map to see how large Mali was at its peak in the 1300s.

From Mine to Market

Like Ghana, Mali grew very rich by controlling the gold trade. In the 1300s gold became more valuable than ever. Gold was mined in tunnels and pits throughout western Africa. Miners dug dirt and rock out of the ground.

Women sifted the gold dust. Grains they found were then poured into hollow feather quills or other containers and transported to Mali's market cities.

One of these cities was Timbuktu (tim buk TOO). It was located at a crossroads of major trade routes, near the Niger River. Timbuktu also bordered the Sahara and was a final stop for caravan routes that crossed the desert.

In Timbuktu's busy markets, farmers sold vegetables and grains. Some bargained over the price of gold, salt, and North African horses. Other traders settled the price of enslaved prisoners. Most of the enslaved people would be taken to Europe and Northern Africa.

364

FIELD TRIP

African art, like that produced in West African kingdoms like Benin, is often featured in traveling museum exhibits. If your local museum has an African art department or if an exhibition is available, plan a field trip to see it. Or make library books of African art available to students.

GLOBAL CONNECTION

CURRENCY IN EUROPE AND AFRICA While African gold went to Europe to make coins, Africans often used other forms of currency.

- Cowry shells, the high-gloss shells of warm-water marine gastropods, were a favored form of money. An agreed-upon number of shells could be used to buy anything from food to a bride.

- Metal objects, like molded copper ingots or spearheads, also served as money. So did beads brought by Muslim traders.

Infographic

interNET CONNECTION Visit our website: www.mhschool.com

Timbuktu

Timbuktu grew as a trading center near the great bend of the Niger River. Located at the end of Arab trade routes that crossed the Sahara, Timbuktu was the site of much cultural exchange during the Mali and Songhai empires. How did cultural influences combine in Timbuktu?

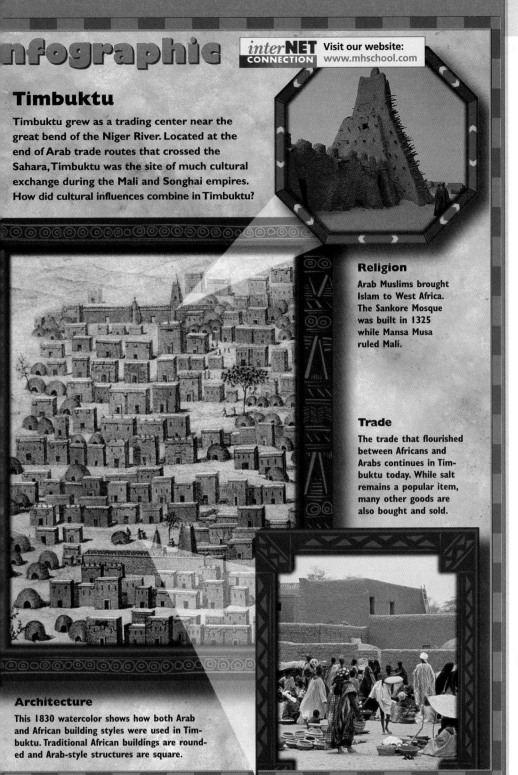

Religion

Arab Muslims brought Islam to West Africa. The Sankore Mosque was built in 1325 while Mansa Musa ruled Mali.

Trade

The trade that flourished between Africans and Arabs continues in Timbuktu today. While salt remains a popular item, many other goods are also bought and sold.

Architecture

This 1830 watercolor shows how both Arab and African building styles were used in Timbuktu. Traditional African buildings are rounded and Arab-style structures are square.

Infographic

Remind students of other cities they have studied—ancient Athens, ancient Rome—and have them discuss what life was like in them—the housing, the streets, the meeting places, the craft-workers making and selling their wares, for example. In general, help the class see cities as hubs of economic, political, and social activity, as Timbuktu was.

Discussing Timbuktu Have students identify the place and time span the *Infographic* covers and give them a few minutes to examine it. Tell them to write three headings on a piece of paper—Types of Trade, Architecture, and Religion—and then make notes under each heading to classify information about it.

● *What were the influences on Timbuktu's architecture?* (Arab and African styles)

● *How did Islam come to Timbuktu?* (It was brough by Arab Muslims)

★THINKING FURTHER: *Making Conclusions Why would Arab and African influences show at Timbuktu?* (The city was at a junction of Arab and African trade routes.)

Technology CONNECTION

ADVENTURE TIME! CD-ROM
Enrich the *Infographic* with the *Timbuktu* and the Time Lines on the *Adventure Time!* CD-ROM.

EXPANDING THE INFOGRAPHIC

RESEARCHING AND WRITING Explain to the class that the Timbuktu of 1300 shown here would, in the 1500s under the Songhai empire, grow into a renowned center of learning. Its university boasted numerous scholars, and merchants there made greater profits from books than from any other commodity. Tell students to do further research on Timbuktu's status as a cultural and educational center and write a report of their findings. You might suggest the following sources for research:

● Encyclopedia entries for *Africa: History* and *Timbuktu*.

● A library card catalog for entries for *Africa: History, Timbuktu,* and *Songhai* (Time-Life's *African Kingdoms* presents both text and illustration on the subject).

USING THE ANTHOLOGY

OBSERVATIONS OF A 14TH CENTURY TRAVELER, pages 82–83 Ibn Battutah, a Moroccan traveler, visited Mali during the rule of Mansa Sulayman, a grandson of Mansa Musa. His writings are some of the best primary sources we have for the places and period. Have students read the anthology selection and create illustrations of some of the sights the writer describes.

LIFE IN THE EMPIRES

List the various empires on the board.

- **When did Mali reach its height as an empire?** *(during the 25-year reign of Mansa Musa in the 1300s)*

★THINKING FURTHER: *Making Conclusions* **How can you tell that major cultural borrowing had taken place in western Africa prior to Mansa Musa's reign?** *(Many western Africans, including Mansa Musa, had adopted Islam as their religion after Muslim traders brought it with them from northern Africa.)*

Discussing the PRIMARY SOURCE

Help students to form a clear picture of empire government in West Africa.

- **What pomp and ceremony accompanied the king?** *(Flags, drums, guitars, and trumpets announced his arrival.)*

- **Why do you suppose pomp and ceremony are often part of government?** *(to impress people with its seriousness and power)*

- **How can you tell that the king wanted to know what was going on?** *(the attention he paid to reports by his men)*

★THINKING FURTHER: *Making Decisions* **On a scale of 1 to 10, how would you rank the king?** *(Students may rank him high for concern for his subjects or low for his tight hold on the land.)*

Discussing The Songhai Empire
Point out that we know about Songhai through an oral tradition.

- **How was Songhai a fitting successor to Mali?** *(Both were powerful.)*

- **Who were its griots?** *(storytellers who described historical events)*

★THINKING FURTHER: *Making Conclusions* **Why do you think the role of the griots was important in western Africa?** *(They transmitted the area's history to the ordinary people who couldn't read.)*

366

LIFE IN THE EMPIRES

In the early 1300s the best horses and goods were bought by a Mali king called Mansa Musa. During Mansa Musa's reign, from 1312 to 1337, Mali was at its peak of wealth and power. Mansa Musa ruled with great authority. Nevertheless, he recognized at least one power as being greater than himself: Allah. The religion of Islam had been spreading throughout western Africa ever since the first Muslim traders arrived there in the 700s.

In 1324 Mansa Musa fulfilled one of the Five Pillars of Islam. He made a pilgrimage to Mecca. During the year-long journey, the king gave away gifts of gold to rich and poor people alike. How does the following excerpt, by a northern African writer, reflect Mansa Musa's power?

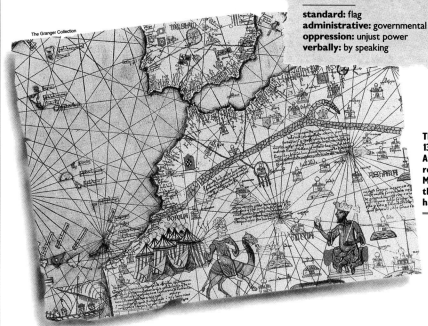
The Granger Collection

366

From the writings of Al-'Umari, about 1337-1338.

*When the king of this kingdom comes in from a journey an [umbrella] and a **standard** are held over his head as he rides, and drums are beaten and guitars and trumpets well made of horn are played in front of him.... When one whom the king has charged with a task or assignment returns to him he questions him in detail about everything which has happened to him from the moment of his departure until his return. Complaints and appeals against **administrative oppression** are placed before this king and he delivers judgment on them himself. As a rule nothing is written down; his commands are given **verbally**.*

standard: flag
administrative oppression: unjust governmental power
verbally: by speaking

This map made in 1375 shows West African trade routes. Find Mansa Musa in the bottom right-hand corner.

BACKGROUND INFORMATION

ABOUT MANSA MUSA'S PILGRIMAGE On his pilgrimage to Mecca, it is said that Mansa Musa traveled with a retinue of 60,000 attendants, including 500 slaves, each of whom carried a 4-pound bar of gold to pay travel expenses.

ABOUT ASKIA THE GREAT Askia Muhammad gained this title by being perhaps Songhai's greatest emperor (ruling 1493–1528). He reorganized the empire, redesigned its government, built up a professional army and enlarged the fleet of canoes that patrolled the Niger River, and made Timbuktu a world-renowned center of learning.

CURRICULUM CONNECTION

LINKS TO READING Students may enjoy reading *The Cow-Tail Switch and Other West African Stories*, collected by Harold Courlander and George Herzog—18 short tales that griots might have told.

This figure of an archer from Mali was found near the Niger River.

The Songhai Empire

As Mansa Musa ruled Mali, a small eastern territory called Songhai (SOHNG hi) was growing strong. In the next 150 years, Songhai rose to take Mali's place as the most powerful empire in western Africa. The empire of Songhai lasted from about 1490 until 1590.

Like the kings of Ghana and Mali, Songhai kings were all-powerful rulers. Among the most important assistants to the kings were griots (GREE ohs). Griots are people who tell stories that describe historical events. Such stories are told again and again so people can learn about the past. Kings also made use of scribes. Scribes wrote official documents in Arabic.

WHY IT MATTERS

In 1591 the Songhai empire collapsed when it was attacked by an army from the north. This army used guns against the arrows and spears of the Songhai empire. The army came from the African country of Morocco. Morocco had long had trading ties with West Africa. Its leader wanted to gain complete control of this trade and perhaps of the gold mines as well.

The great demand for gold affected life for many people in West Africa. Gold played a part in the lives of the miners who recovered it, the traders who brought it to market, and the kings who used it to bring glory to their rule. Africa's gold was also in demand in Europe. Gold coins in Venice and Florence helped pay for the great art projects of the European Renaissance.

The empires of western Africa were not the only civilizations to spread African wealth to far-off places. In the next lesson you will read about busy port cities on the continent's east coast. Those cities had contact with places as far away as China.

Reviewing Facts and Ideas

MAIN IDEAS

- The empire of Ghana lasted from before 700 until around 1200. It was nicknamed the "land of gold."
  - The empire of Mali ruled from about 1240 to 1400. Timbuktu became a major center of trade.
- Mansa Musa ruled Mali between 1312 and 1337. Islam spread in West Africa during this time.
- The empire of Songhai lasted from about 1490 to 1590. Oral historians, or griots, and scribes kept records of events in the empire.

THINK ABOUT IT

1. What did Sunjata do to build the empire of Mali?

2. How were griots and scribes important to rulers of the Songhai empire?

3. **FOCUS** What role did the gold trade play in West Africa's empires?

4. **THINKING SKILL** Explain the *effects* produced when Ghana's kings kept gold scarce in the marketplace.

5. **GEOGRAPHY** How might the Niger River have been important for trade in West Africa?

367

Discussing WHY IT MATTERS Place Songhai in the context of rising and falling empires.

- **Why did the Songhai empire collapse?** (conquest by an army from Morocco in northern Africa)

★**THINKING FURTHER:** *Making Conclusions* **How did the factor that made the succession of western African empires strong in the first place lead to their overthrow in the end?** (Being centers of trade had built them; outsiders wanting to take control of this advantage destroyed them.)

3 CLOSE

MAIN IDEAS
Call on students for answers.

- **What was the "land of gold" and how long did it last?** (Ghana; for 500 years from about 700 to 1200)

- **What empire replaced it and how long did it last?** (Mali, from about 1240 to 1400)

- **How does an event in Mansa Musa's life show us that Islam had become important in western Africa?** (His pilgrimage to Mecca shows that it had become the religion of its leaders and probably many more of its people.)

EVALUATE
√ **Answers to Think About It**

1. He conquered Ghana and surrounding territory as well to create Mali. *Summarize*

2. They recorded Songhai's historical events, orally and in writing. *Make Inferences*

3. It was a major good that helped to create powerful and wealthy centers of trade. *Make Conclusions*

4. It limited the supply of gold and thus kept the gold price high. *Cause and Effect*

5. It served as a "highway" for transporting goods to major trading centers like Timbuktu. *Five Themes of Geography: Movement*

Write About It Ask students to picture themselves visiting a trading city of West Africa during the 1400s, and write a journal entry in which they describe people they see and things taking place.

MEETING INDIVIDUAL NEEDS

RETEACHING (Easy) Have students reread the description of the Mali king's approach in the *Many Voices* quote. Tell them to use colored pens, pencils, or crayons to draw the scene described.

EXTENSION (Average) Have students reread the information about Sunjata on p. 364. Then have them write it as a story, as a griot might tell it.

ENRICHMENT (Challenging) Divide the class into three groups and give each group one of the following subjects: the "silent trade" for salt; Mansa Musa's pilgrimage to Mecca; Askia the Great (Askia Muhammad, king of Songhai). Have students do further research about their topics and use it to write a story as a griot might have told it. Have them present their stories, orally, to the class.

Lesson Overview

Griots played the important role of keeping Africa's oral history alive.

Lesson Objective

★ Appreciate the cultural contribution of griots, past and present.

⭐ 1 PREPARE

MOTIVATE Ask students if they have ever sat around a campfire or in a library room and listened to a story teller, or perhaps to stories that were read to them as small children. Discuss with them why people, young and old, throughout the world like to listen to stories.

SET PURPOSE Remind students that the African griots were storytellers but that their importance went far beyond simple entertainment. Encourage them to explore this *Legacy* to expand their knowledge of the griots' art and contribution to their people.

⭐ 2 TEACH

Understanding the Concept of a Legacy Have students read the text.

● *What were the subjects of the griots' stories and songs?* (their people's history, beliefs, and traditions)

● *Why were griots important in a society where many people could not read written languages?* (Speaking and listening were the main ways to give or get information.)

★THINKING FURTHER: *Making Conclusions Why was a griot's work of great value both to the kings and to the people they governed? (Griots carried information to the people from the kings and kept the people in touch with their family histories and with the beliefs and traditions of the society.)*

Resource REMINDER

Anthology: *Test of a Friendship, pp. 85–86; Ji-Nongo-Nongo, pp. 87–88*

Legacy
LINKING PAST AND PRESENT

GRIOTS
AND ORAL HISTORY

During the time when empires ruled West Africa, griots told stories and sang songs for traders, villagers, and kings alike. These special stories and songs described the history, beliefs, and traditions of African families and of the land. They became the oral history, or spoken record of events, of Africa.

Because many people could not read a written language, they depended upon the spoken words of the griots. African kings depended on griots to help keep people informed about happenings in the empire. In time the singing and speaking skills of the griots became an important West African legacy.

That legacy continues today. Modern griots tell African history and traditions to people around the world. Some have become teachers and historians. Others perform before audiences in order to entertain as well as educate.

368

Griots in ancient Africa told stories that taught people their history. Griots often know hundreds of events by heart.

BACKGROUND INFORMATION

ABOUT A MODERN GRIOT TALE

● If students are familiar with the book *Roots: The Saga of an American Family* (1976) or the television series based on it, they may be interested to know that its author, Alex Haley, went back to West Africa to search for his family line.

● There he found a griot who told a story of a family that Haley believed was his own family line in West Africa. The griot spoke of a man named Kunta Kinte—Haley's possible first ancestor in America—who was captured by slave catchers and marched west toward the Atlantic.

● Like a griot telling the story of a long family line, Haley went on to write the story of seven generations of his family, from the enslaved Kunta Kinte down to his own generation.

Some griots travel around the world telling the stories of their cultures. Many wear traditional clothing styles that griots have worn in Africa for more than 700 years.

The griot uses a *kora* during his performance. A kora is a hand-crafted instrument that is traditionally used by griots. Each year thousands of people attend performances in which griots tell stories about history, cultural traditions, and current events.

369

Examining the Illustrations Encourage students to appreciate the training and tradition that a griot must experience.

- ● *Who are shown in the illustration on p. 368? Why might it be fair to say that they were "walking encyclopedias"?* (Griots in Africa; they required prodigious memories. Help students to try to grasp how amazing it is for a person to hold so much information in his or her mind and the discipline necessary to be successful.)

- ● *Who is shown in the other illustrations? How do they keep the griot tradition alive?* (Modern griots can recreate the appearance and stories of the ancient griots and bring back a world and culture long gone.)

★THINKING FURTHER: *Making Conclusions Why can it be said that griots, both ancient and modern, have served as both entertainers and educators?* (They appeal to and serve people's desire for entertainment in the form of story telling, and they educate by making their information available to those who hear them.)

3 CLOSE

SUM IT UP
Have students summarize ways that griots enriched and facilitated life in the empires of West Africa.

EVALUATE
Write About It Tell students to write a paragraph telling how griots have served as educators.

MEETING INDIVIDUAL NEEDS

RETEACHING (Easy) Have students write a brief explanation of how African griots were the newscasters of their day.

EXTENSION (Average) Divide the class into several groups. Have each group pick a news event of today and make up a verse or two of a song that tells about it. Have the groups present their verses to the class.

ENRICHMENT (Challenging) Divide the class into several groups and have each group pick an American tradition, historical event, or current event. Tell each group to make up either a story or a song (perhaps sung to a familiar tune) that informs listeners about the topic. Have the groups present their stories or songs in class.

GLOBAL CONNECTION

THEODORE ROOSEVELT AND WEST AFRICAN TRADITION
- ● Griots did more than sing songs and tell stories. They also recited poems, posed riddles, spoke tongue-twisters, and recited proverbs.
- ● One West African proverb that crossed the Atlantic was popularized in the United States by President Theodore Roosevelt in the early 1900s: "Speak softly but carry a big stick; you will go far."

Encourage students to interpret the meaning of this proverb.

SKILLS LESSON
PAGES 370–371

Lesson Overview
A distribution map shows how a particular feature is spread over an area.

Lesson Objective
★ Interpret a distribution map.

★ 1 PREPARE

MOTIVATE Refer the class to the *Skills Lesson* title and have them define *distribution*. (the way something is spread out) What can a *distribution map* show? Have students read *Why the Skill Matters* to find out how population, climates, or language is spread out over an area. Work with them on the concept of *population density*—the more people in an area, the denser the population; the fewer people, the less dense.

SET PURPOSE How do we interpret distribution maps? Set students to answering this question by referring them to *Helping Yourself* and have them read its second item aloud.

★ 2 TEACH

Using the Skill Refer students to Map A.

- **What is the subject of this map? How do you know?** *(population density in Africa; indicated by the map's title)*

- **What symbol tells how many people are in different places?** *(dots that stand for 100,000 people each)*

- **Where in Africa is the population the densest? How do you know?** *(At the southern edge of the "hump"; that is where the dots are closest together.)*

- **In what areas is it the least dense?** *(the Sahara)*

Resource REMINDER

Practice and Project Book: *p. 74*
Transparency: *Map 16*
Technology: *Adventure Time!* CD-ROM

Geography Skills

Reading Distribution Maps

VOCABULARY
distribution map
population density

WHY THE SKILL MATTERS

In the last lesson you learned that West Africa's earliest known empires developed between the Senegal and Niger rivers. Some 25,000 people lived in Timbuktu, making it one of the region's biggest cities. Thousands more lived in the towns and villages that

Traders bargain at a busy market in Burundi.

370

developed on the nearby savannas and in forests.

Today much has changed in western Africa. The region's population as a whole has grown. So has the Sahara Desert, partly as a result of human interaction with the environment. The once-productive heartland of Ghana's empire, for example, is now part of the desert.

Looking at a distribution map can help you see how such changes have affected where people live in Africa today. A distribution map is a special purpose map. It shows how one particular feature is spread over an area. The maps on these pages show current population density in Africa. Population density is the number of people living in a given amount of space. Distribution maps can also show such features as climate, land use, products, and languages spoken in an area.

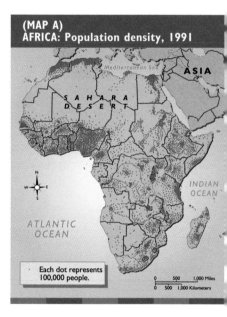

(MAP A)
AFRICA: Population density, 1991

Each dot represents 100,000 people.

SHELTERED INSTRUCTION
READING STRATEGIES & LANGUAGE DEVELOPMENT

MAKING CONCLUSIONS Remind students that they are often asked to make conclusions based on written evidence, but in this skill they are working with visual evidence. Have them identify the evidence they are offered (how dots or shading that stands for a given number of people is distributed over an area). Then have them identify the kind of conclusion they are supposed to draw from the evidence (how dense or sparse the population is in any part of the area).

WORDS WITH MULTIPLE MEANINGS Call students' attention to the word *density* and have them define it as it is used in this *Skills Lesson* (the closeness of something). In what other ways have you heard this word used? After students have offered their ideas, have them look up *density* in a dictionary to complete a list that includes "thickness," scientific meanings, and "stupidity."

USING THE SKILL

Study Map A. The title tells you that the map provides information about population density in Africa. The map key shows that each dot on the map represents 100,000 people. The closer together the dots, the more dense is the population. The more spread out and fewer the dots, the less dense is the population. The great bend of the Niger River is one of the most populated areas in West Africa. This is shown by the large number of dots in that area.

TRYING THE SKILL

Distribution Map B on this page shows the population density of the continent of Africa in another way. How many people per square mile live near the coast of present-

Helping yourself

- A **distribution map** shows how one kind of feature, such as **population density**, is spread over an **area**.
- Study the map title and key.

day Ghana? How many people per square mile live near the Nile River delta?*

REVIEWING THE SKILL

Use the map on this page to answer the following questions:

1. How do you know this is a distribution map?

2. Which city has more people, Nairobi or the western coastal city of Abidjan?

3. Which region has a higher population density today, the Sahara Desert or eastern lands along the coast of the Indian Ocean? How do you know?

4. What kind of distribution map could help you to better understand life in your own community?

(MAP B) AFRICA: Population density, 1991

Casablanca · Algiers · Mediterranean Sea · Cairo · ASIA · SAHARA DESERT · Lagos · Abidjan · GHANA · Addis Ababa · ATLANTIC OCEAN · Kinshasa · Nairobi · INDIAN OCEAN · Johannesburg · Cape Town

People per square mile	People per square kilometer
0–25	0–10
25–250	10–100
250–500	100–200
over 500	over 200

• Major city

0   500   1,000 Miles
0   500   1,000 Kilometers

PEARL · ICL

About 1.2 million people live in Harare, Zimbabwe's capital.

*250–500; over 500

371

★THINKING FURTHER: *Making Conclusions Which areas on the map would you say are urban? Which are rural? Why?* (Help students to relate high density with urban areas and low density with rural.)

Trying the Skill Remind students of the second item in *Helping Yourself.*

- *What does Map B show? How do you know?* (how population is distributed in Africa; the title)

- *What symbol tells you how many people there are in different areas?* (Remind students to use the map key. Discuss how shading to show density differs from dots in Map A.)

- *What is the population density along the northern coast of Africa?* (mostly 25–250 people per square mile)

- *How would you describe the population density in southwestern Africa?* (very light)

★THINKING FURTHER: *Making Connections Compare Map B with the map of Africa on p. 355. Why do you suppose population is so light in southwestern Africa?* (It is a desert area—Namib and Kalihari.)

3 CLOSE

SUM IT UP
Atlas maps pp. R5B-D offer more practice in reading distribution maps.

EVALUATE
✓ **Answers to Reviewing the Skill**

1. from the map title and key

2. Nairobi

3. lands along the coast of the Indian Ocean; the shading of the area

4. Students may suggest distribution maps showing population of school-age children, of fast-food stores, or of various other subjects.

Technology CONNECTION

ADVENTURE TIME! CD-ROM
Enrich this Skills Lesson with country information in *Symbols* on the *Adventure Time!* CD-ROM.

MEETING INDIVIDUAL NEEDS

RETEACHING (Easy) Tell students to make up three additional questions that can be answered from Map B. Have them write out their questions and exchange papers with a partner.

EXTENSION (Average) Have students picture themselves as the writer of a vacation advice column. Someone who loves crowds has written to ask for a good place to visit in Africa. So has someone who hates crowds. Have students write a response suggesting a place each of them might like to visit, and explain the reason for each.

ENRICHMENT (Challenging) Tell students to make up their own kingdom, name it and its cities and towns, and make up population densities for those places and the outlying areas. Have them draw a map of their kingdom showing these densities, giving the map an explanatory title and making a map key for it.

LESSON 4
PAGES 372-375

Lesson Overview
Beginning about A.D. 1000, busy trading cities emerged on Africa's east coast along the Indian Ocean.

Lesson Objectives
★ Locate and describe Swahili trading cities.

★ Explain why they emerged.

★ Analyze their interaction with other parts of Africa and the world.

1 PREPARE

MOTIVATE Tell students to contrast this lesson title with that of Lesson 3 to find that they have crossed the continent. Have a student do the *Read Aloud,* and encourage the class to compare the kingly splendor described and shown in the photo of the Kilwa palace with its counterpart in West Africa.

SET PURPOSE Present the *Read to Learn* question and call on students to make predictions about possible answers, based on what they learned about West Africa. Tell them to read the lesson to check their predictions.

2 TEACH

Understanding THE BIG PICTURE
On a wall map or desk map of the world, have students locate both eastern Africa and the area of western Africa they studied.

★**THINKING FURTHER:** *Making Conclusions* **Why might you expect eastern Africa to have different trading partners from western Africa? Who are those partners?** (*Students should relate western Africa to Atlantic and Mediterranean trading partners while eastern Africa, on the Indian Ocean, is on routes to Arabia, India, and China.*)

Resource REMINDER

Practice and Project Book: *p. 75*

Anthology: *Epic of Liyongo, pp. 89–92*

Desk Map

Outline Map

Focus Activity

READ TO LEARN

What was life like in the trading cities along the coast of the Indian Ocean?

PLACES

• Mombasa
• Zanzibar
• Mogadishu

372

---

600   850   1100   1300   1600

Africa's Eastern Coast

Read Aloud

The king of the city of Kilwa had a palace with over 100 rooms and a maze of courtyards. He even had an eight-sided pool built into a cliff overlooking the blue waters of the Indian Ocean. The immense palace was just a small part of the great wealth in eastern Africa during the 1300s. That wealth was the result of trade.

THE BIG PICTURE

Before A.D. 1100 the kingdom of Ghana was at its peak. Another powerful African civilization was growing some 2,500 miles to the east of Ghana. Actually, this civilization's villages, towns, and cities were closer to the Indus River valley of Asia than they were to the Niger River of western Africa. Yet the African civilizations had important things in common. For example, their many languages were rooted in an ancient language called Bantu. Both civilizations also profited from trade within Africa and with other continents.

In the last lesson you read that West African gold was transported to northern Africa and Europe. There it was made into coins. In eastern Africa, gold was shipped to cities in Arabia, India, and China. So were elephant tusks, which are the material called ivory.

Ivory from East Africa was used to make this jeweled lion. It was worn on the arm.

SHELTERED INSTRUCTION

READING STRATEGIES & LANGUAGE DEVELOPMENT

CAUSE AND EFFECT Remind students that identifying cause-and-effect relationships can help them understand why things happen. Write these categories on the board: location, resources, needs and wants. Invite volunteers to explain how these categories attract people to specific vacation areas such as camping sites, lakes, beaches, and resorts. Then point out that cause-and-effect relationships were important in the development of Africa's eastern coast. As they read, students can find these cause-and-effect relationships. [SDAIE STRATEGY: BRIDGING]

WORD ROOTS Point out to the class that they have met the word *port* many times and will meet it again on p. 374. Explain that it comes from the Latin word for "door." Have them discuss how a *port* is a kind of door for people and goods to enter and leave an area.

MAP WORK: **1.** Indian Ocean **2.** Kilwa Kisiwani **3.** Somali Peninsula
4. about 1,400 miles (about 2,253 kilometers) **5.** Lake Tanganyika

CHAPTER 13 • LESSON 4

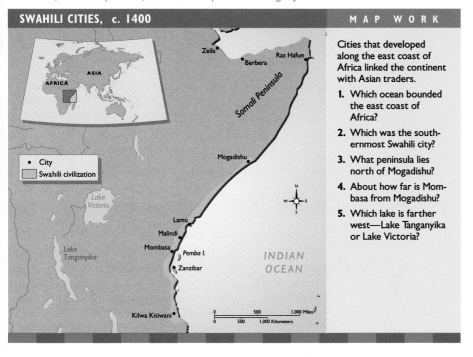

SWAHILI CITIES, c. 1400

MAP WORK

Zeila
Berbera
Ras Hafun
Somali Peninsula
ASIA
AFRICA
Mogadishu
Lake Victoria
Lamu
Malindi
Mombasa
Lake Tanganyika
Pemba I.
Zanzibar
INDIAN OCEAN
Kilwa Kisiwani

• City
☐ Swahili civilization

0   500   1,000 Miles
0   500   1,000 Kilometers

Cities that developed along the east coast of Africa linked the continent with Asian traders.

1. Which ocean bounded the east coast of Africa?

2. Which was the southernmost Swahili city?

3. What peninsula lies north of Mogadishu?

4. About how far is Mombasa from Mogadishu?

5. Which lake is farther west—Lake Tanganyika or Lake Victoria?

TRADE ALONG THE INDIAN OCEAN

The coastal cities of eastern Africa linked Africa to Asia. For hundreds of years, boats loaded with trade goods sailed the Indian Ocean. In the coastal cities, merchant-sailors from Asia eagerly bought African goods.

Many of the goods were brought from further inland. These goods included gold, leopard skins, rhinoceros horns, and ivory. Demand for East African ivory in Asia was high. This ivory was softer and easier to carve than West African ivory. Arabian craftworkers made chess pieces from ivory. Chinese used it to make beautiful artwork and containers.

In the coastal markets, African merchants were able to buy goods from Asia and other places. Metal tools, fine pottery, cloth, glass containers, and wheat were in great demand in the coastal cities of Africa.

The "People of the Shore"

Over time, some of the foreign merchants settled in Africa's eastern coastal cities. Many were Arab Muslims. They made important contributions to the civilization that became known as Swahili. *Swahili* means "people of the shore" in Arabic. Many Arabic words also became part of the Swahili language. Settlers from Arabia also shared the traditions of Islam with the Swahili people. Islam became an important religious heritage for many Africans in the busy port cities that developed on the east coast.

373

TRADE ALONG THE INDIAN OCEAN

Help students recall the importance of waterways to trade.

● **What goods from inland did the eastern coastal cities make available to Asian traders?** *(gold, leopard skins, rhinoceros horns, and ivory)*

● **What kinds of goods did African traders want in return?** *(metal tools, fine pottery, cloth, glass containers, and wheat)*

★THINKING FURTHER: *Cause and Effect* **What cause-and-effect relationship can you find between resources, needs and wants, and the development of trade?** *(Resources available:→traders come to buy; need for particular resource: →produce something to trade for it.)*

More MAP WORK

● **What ocean lies between eastern Africa and Asia?** *(the Indian Ocean)*

● **What major bodies of water lie to the west of the cities shown?** *(Lake Victoria, Lake Tanganyika)*

● **What is the "horn" of Africa called on this map?** *(the Somali Peninsula)*

★THINKING FURTHER: *Making Conclusions* **Find the area shown here on a desk map of the world. Why would the cities shown here be able to reach Arabia fairly easily?** *(The Arabian peninsula is just up the coast, just north of the Somali peninsula.)*

Discussing The "People of the Shore" Once again, remind students of the theme of cultural contacts.

● **Who were the original people of the eastern coast?** *(the Swahili)*

● **Who joined them?** *(Arab Muslims)*

★THINKING FURTHER: *Cause and Effect* **How did cultural contact change the culture of the eastern coastal cities?** *(The Swahili people took Arabic words into their language, and Islam became part of their religious heritage.)*

GLOBAL CONNECTION

ASIA TO AFRICA—RIDING THE WINDS Students will learn about monsoons in Chapter 14, but now point out that winds blow across the Indian Ocean from the northeast in winter and blow across it from the southwest in summer. Diagram this pattern on the board and explain that ships from Arabia, India, and China used these winds to reach Swahili cities in winter and to sail back home in summer.

BACKGROUND INFORMATION

ABOUT THE SWAHILI
● The Swahili are not a single people; rather, they are members of many different groups of coastal dwellers in eastern Africa.

● Each group speaks its own dialect in Swahili.

● "Swahili" now includes about a half million people of eastern Africa.

LIFE ALONG THE COAST

Reinforce the importance of trade to the well-being of these and other cities.

★THINKING FURTHER: *Compare and Contrast* **How were the fates of the West African and the Swahili trading cities similar? How were their ways of government different?** *(Similar: both tended to decline if they lost control of trade. Different: the West Africa trading cities were governed as part of one empire; the Swahili cities were never united.)*

Discussing Swahili Cities Have students sit in pairs with one text open to this page, the other to the map on p. 373.

● *Locate Mombasa and Zanzibar. On what kinds of landforms were both these trading cities located?* (islands)

● *How might this fact have contributed to making them good ports?* (Help students to see that an island might provide plenty of room for harbors where ships might dock.)

● *Find Mogadishu. It is located at the mouth of a river. How would that fact contribute to making it a trading city?* (Help students to see that the river could be a "highway" for shipping goods to Mogadishu from inland.)

★THINKING FURTHER: *Compare and Contrast* **How was Mogadishu like Timbuktu?** *(It was a center for trading gold.)*

Extending Did You Know? Bring in some whole cloves so that students can touch and smell them. Ask them how they have seen cloves used in cooking (Perhaps they have seen whole cloves stuck into ham for baking, or ground cloves used in pumpkin or mince pie.) Call on students to do some encyclopedia research on cloves and report on other uses for them (perfume, blends of spices, candles, and medicinal uses as an antiseptic or anesthetic, especially for toothaches).

LIFE ALONG THE COAST

Between 1000 and 1500, Swahili cities grew in size and strength. Like the trading cities of West Africa, Swahili cities grew when they controlled important trade routes. Cities often declined when that control slipped away. Unlike the empires to the northwest, Swahili cities and villages were each ruled by their own leaders.

Swahili Cities

Mombasa (mom BAH suh), located on an island of present-day Kenya, was one important trading center. The city had a port and crowded markets. Many ships were attracted to Mombasa each season. Another main Swahili city, Zanzibar (ZAN zuh bar), was located on a much bigger island about 100 miles to the south, in what is today the country of Tanzania (tan zuh NEE uh).

Mogadishu (mohg uh DISH oo), in present-day Somalia, was one of the largest of the coastal cities. Find Mogadishu on the map on page 373.

The people of Mogadishu lived by farming and fishing. Some used sailboats to transport gold to other trading centers. Mogadishu controlled much of Africa's gold trade from about 1000 to 1300. On days when the wind was still, the sailors sang songs. They often sang this one as they worked.

Plunge in the paddles,
Plunge in the paddles,
If the sail is against the mast,
Plunge in the paddles.

For much of the year Mogadishu's sailors shared their port with the larger sailboats that brought cargo and merchants from Asia. In the city's marketplaces, foreign merchants bought load after load of ivory, gold, and leopard

Sculpted elephant tusks arch over a main street in Mombasa, Kenya (above). The illustration (left) shows Mombasa during the 1300s.

374

CURRICULUM CONNECTION

LINKS TO MUSIC Refer the class to the lines of the work song the sailors sang in eastern Africa. Encourage students to make up a simple tune, setting these words to it. Then have the class sing their own work song.

SECOND-LANGUAGE SUPPORT

USING PROPS Second-language students may understand this lesson better if props or pictures representing the objects traded on the African coast are used to create a simulated marketplace.

TAKING NOTES Instruct students to work in pairs to turn the lesson headings into an outline about the Swahili cities. Have student pairs summarize information under each heading in a sentence or two.

skins. They also purchased tortoise shells, tools, and glass.

WHY IT MATTERS

Today some important legacies of early Swahili civilization remain in the countries of East Africa. Swahili has become the common language of Tanzania, Kenya, Zaire, and Uganda. Old Swahili ports such as Mombasa and Zanzibar still ship goods around the globe.

Once-powerful cities like Mombasa, however, are not as strong as they were long ago. The decline of these cities was a result of conflicts that broke out in the 1500s. These conflicts took place between Swahilis and newcomers to eastern Africa. You will read in Chapter 16 about how those newcomers came to explore Africa's east coast.

DID YOU KNOW?

What trade good from Zanzibar is commonly in demand today?

In the 1400s Zanzibar was known for its ivory, tortoise shells, and other goods. Today Zanzibar is the world's largest producer of tiny flowers from a special kind of evergreen tree. The unopened buds of these flowers are dried, then sold to buyers across the world. After being shipped and packaged, some of these buds eventually make their way into the spice sections of your local grocery stores. You will find them under the name "cloves." Cloves are used as spice in cooking.

✔✔ Reviewing Facts and Ideas

MAIN IDEAS

- Many eastern African coastal cities grew as a result of trade with Asian countries across the Indian Ocean.
- The coastal cities of Mogadishu, Mombasa, and Zanzibar were enriched by trade in ivory and gold.
- Eastern Africa's earliest Arab settlers contributed to Swahili civilization in the areas of language and religion.
- Swahili cities flourished mainly between 1000 and 1500, when a period of conflict began.

THINK ABOUT IT

1. Why was eastern African ivory a valuable trade item? What other items were traded in the coastal cities?

2. In what ways did Muslim Arabs who settled on Africa's eastern coast contribute to Swahili culture? Describe an important legacy of the Swahili civilization.

3. **FOCUS** How did life in Mogadishu reflect the importance of trade in Swahili cities?

4. **THINKING SKILL** Name one major _cause_ for the settlement of Arabs in eastern Africa. Describe two _effects_ of their settlement there.

5. **GEOGRAPHY** In what ways did the people of Africa's coastal cities interact with their environment?

375

MEETING INDIVIDUAL NEEDS

RETEACHING (Easy) On an outline map that shows Asia, Africa, and the Indian Ocean, have students label these areas and draw in possible trade routes from Arabia, India, and China to Africa, all of which they should also label.

EXTENSION (Average) Have students think about the work that an African trader in the Swahili cities must have done. Tell them to create a description of "A Day in the Life of an African Trader."

ENRICHMENT (Challenging) Ivory, rhinoceros horns, leopard skins— today there are groups and even governments that want to ban trade in all these goods that were once in great demand from the eastern African ports. Divide the class into three sections and assign each section one group or government. Have students research their topic to find out why they want to ban this trade and report to the class.

Discussing WHY IT MATTERS Help students recognize the continuing importance of location.

> ★ **THINKING FURTHER:** _Making Conclusions_ **Why do you suppose that the old Swahili ports will always remain important locations in the world, even if they are not as powerful as they once were?** _(their access to resources from inland Africa and role as shipping ports)_

3 CLOSE

MAIN IDEAS
Call on students for answers.

- _**Why did coastal cities emerge in eastern Africa?**_ _(They had access to African goods in demand in Asia.)_

- _**Name three of the Swahili cities that traded in ivory and gold?**_ _(Mogadishu, Mombasa, Zanzibar)_

- _**How did Arab settlers enrich Swahili civilization?**_ _(They enriched the language with Arabic words and brought the religion of Islam.)_

EVALUATE
✔ **Answers to Think About It**

1. It was soft and easy to carve; gold, leopard skins, rhinoceros horns, ivory, metal, cloth, wheat, and glass containers. _Recall Details_

2. They enriched its language and introduced Islam; religion and language. _Main Idea_

3. It was filled with sailors and merchants from Asia; Arab traders were among its leading citizens. _Draw Conclusions_

4. Cause: Arabs were drawn to the Swahili cities by the rich resources and fine locations for trade there. Effects: They affected the language and religion. _Cause and Effect_

5. They encouraged the bringing in of resources from inland Africa and they made good use of their coast to develop ports along it. _Five Themes of Geography: Human/ Environment Interactions_

Write About It Ask students to picture themselves as Asian sailors who have just arrived in Zanzibar and to write postcards home describing why they have come and what they have found.

LESSON 5

Lesson Overview

Beginning in A.D 1000 the mysterious Great Zimbabwe civilization emerged in southeastern Africa.

Lesson Objectives

★ Locate and describe Great Zimbabwe.

★ Explain how its economy operated.

⭐ 1 PREPARE

MOTIVATE Refer the class to the picture of the Great Zimbabwe ruins on this page and do the *Read Aloud* for them, stressing the sense of the continuing mystery. Have students list the various unsolved mysteries about Great Zimbabwe.

SET PURPOSE How can we ever solve these mysteries? Tell students to explore the lesson to find out what we have learned so far and how we have learned it—see the *Reading Strategies* below—and to find the answer to the *Read to Learn* question.

⭐ 2 TEACH

Understanding THE BIG PICTURE
Refer the class to the map on p. 377.

● **Where is Great Zimbabwe located in relation to the Indian Ocean?** *(Have students note its location inland rather than on the coast.)*

★**THINKING FURTHER:** *Making Conclusions* **Why might this location give Great Zimbabwe an advantage as a site for gathering trade goods?** *(It might be close to the sources of gold and other valuable goods.)*

Resource REMINDER

Practice and Project Book: *p. 76*

Technology: *Adventure Time!* CD-ROM

Focus Activity

READ TO LEARN

What effects did the growth of Great Zimbabwe have on southern Africa?

PLACES

• Great Zimbabwe
• Sofala

376

```
600      850     1100     1350        1500
                                  1400
```

Great Zimbabwe

Read Aloud

Around 1400 a powerful city surrounded by stone walls was located in a hilly region south of the Zambezi River. The city had covered passages that led through different sections within the walls.

One section of the city was once known as "the house of the great woman" by later neighbors. Who was that woman? What role did she play in the city? So far, the answers to those questions have remained unknown. They are just a few of the unsolved mysteries that surround the southern African civilization known as Great Zimbabwe.

THE BIG PICTURE

In the last lesson you read about wealthy cities that developed along the eastern African coast. These cities grew rich from trade in ivory, gold, and other goods. Much of the gold came from inland mines to the west, in present-day Zimbabwe.

Farming and herding villages had existed here for hundreds of years. Over time historians believe one village won control over the region's gold trade. During the 1300s this community grew in power.

Historians know very little about this community. Its people left behind no oral traditions or written documents. Historians are even unsure about the meaning of its name: Great Zimbabwe. In the Shona language, *Zimbabwe* can mean either "houses of stone" or "honored houses." By closely examining artifacts left by the peoples of Great Zimbabwe, however, archaeologists and historians have learned something about this community.

SHELTERED INSTRUCTION

READING STRATEGIES & LANGUAGE DEVELOPMENT

PROBLEM AND SOLUTION Explain that people in the past could not predict the outcome of their actions. Often they did not save documents or other articles from their civilization. Explain that there are no surviving written documents from the Great Zimbabwe. Invite volunteers to explain what problems this poses for historians. [It's hard to learn about the people's culture.] Have the class brainstorm possible solutions to this problem. [**SDAIE STRATEGY:** Contextualization]

COMPOUND WORDS Point out to the class that compound words are often used in naming people by the jobs they do, for example, *homemaker, bricklayer, gold miner*. Have students offer other examples and then have them scour this lesson for still more (*craftworker* and *stoneworker*, p. 377, and *metalworker*, p. 378).

THE PEOPLE OF GREAT ZIMBABWE

Between bare granite hills and rolling, tree-filled savannas are the ruins of Great Zimbabwe. Early farmers and herders made use of the region's fertile areas. Farmers raised crops year after year. Herds of cattle, sheep, and goats lived on nearby savannas.

People built their villages and cities near these areas. Craftworkers made jugs and other containers from clay. These pieces of pottery helped people cook, carry water, and collect grains. Pottery fragments in the area show that the community of Great Zimbabwe grew between about 1000 and 1500. During that time people built houses with walls that were made of mud. Archaeologists have found holes that held the main poles of the houses. They have also found the remains of thick stone walls. The walls, they say, were built around the city in the 1300s. What life was like within those walls, though, is a mystery.

Walls of Stone

For the people of Great Zimbabwe, of course, the stone walls and buildings of their city were not new and different. In fact, in southern Africa at the time, over 100 other stone towns are known to have existed. The walls of Great Zimbabwe, however, were by far the biggest. Many historians believe that trade helped make the construction of these walls possible. Who was responsible for building the walls around the growing city?

Great Zimbabwe's kings probably ordered workers to make the city's walls. To do this, stoneworkers used a material that was very close at hand. They used huge granite rocks that lay in and around the city to build the walls. Many of these rocks were larger than several homes put together. Workers heated sheets of the stone, then cracked them into pieces that had straight edges. Next they cut the stones into brick-sized pieces. The work was hard. Workers stacked the granite bricks to form walls as high as 30 feet. The heavy weight of the stones held the walls in place.

GREAT ZIMBABWE, c. 1400

MAP WORK

Great Zimbabwe was located in a fertile area that was rich in natural building materials.

1. Great Zimbabwe was located east of which desert?
2. Which river flowed to the north of Great Zimbabwe?
3. About how many miles did traders from Great Zimbabwe have to travel to reach the Indian Ocean?

This carved bird was found in an area used for ceremonies.

377

THE PEOPLE OF GREAT ZIMBABWE

Once again, point out that farming was a basis for creating a civilization.

● *How did people make their livings in Great Zimbabwe?* (as farmers, herders, craftworkers)

● *In what kind of houses did they live?* (houses made of mud)

★THINKING FURTHER: *Making Conclusions How do we know when the Great Zimbabwe community flourished and how the people built their houses?* (from artifacts—pottery fragments—and from holes left by house poles)

More ▸ MAP WORK

Refer the class to the map on this page.

● *What is the closest Indian Ocean port to Great Zimbabwe?* (Sofala)

● *About how far is it from Great Zimbabwe to Sofala?* (about 200 miles)

● *About how far is Great Zimbabwe from the Zambezi River?* (about the same distance)

★THINKING FURTHER: *Making Conclusions How do you suppose goods were transported from Great Zimbabwe to the coast?* (probably by human bearers or pack animals, if they were available)

Discussing Walls of Stone Refer the class again to the picture of the Great Zimbabwe ruins on p. 376.

● *On whose orders were the walls of Great Zimbabwe probably built?* (one or more kings)

● *What material did workers use to construct these walls?* (granite)

● *What process did they use?* (heating the stone and splitting it into brick-sized pieces)

★THINKING FURTHER: *Making Conclusions How do you suppose we know about this process?* (probably from what archaeologists and other scientists, such as geologists, know about how stone can be worked)

SECOND-LANGUAGE SUPPORT

DIALOGS Encourage second-language learners to hold conversations as if they are archaeologists to help them develop hypothetical language such as, *maybe, might,* and *could have.* Have students discuss the lesson content in this way.

CURRICULUM CONNECTION

LINKS TO ART Call for a team of volunteers to do some further research on the Zimbabwe ruins—encyclopedias are a ready source. Have them make a large drawing of the layout of the Great Enclosure, with labels of its main parts, and have them prepare and make a presentation of it to the class.

THE CITY ON A HILL

Use this opening paragraph for further discussion of how historians work.

- *What is the unsolved mystery of the walls of Great Zimbabwe?* (Why were they built?)

- *What are possible answers?* (to keep something in, to keep something out, to provide privacy or reflect power)

- *From where do these answers come?* (conclusions made by historians)

★THINKING FURTHER: *Making Conclusions* **On what kinds of factors do you suppose historians base their conclusions?** (Help students to identify such factors as what historians know about other societies, the variety of reasons that similar things have been done in the past, possible cause and effect.)

Discussing Controlling the Gold Trade Use this section to get at cause-and-effect relationships—the effects of gold on Great Zimbabwe.

- *Why did Great Zimbabwe become a trading center?* (its location near gold resources)

- *What effect did the refining of gold have on work done in the area?* (It must have drawn many workers into gold mining and gold processing.)

- *What effect did gold have on Great Zimbabwe's rulers?* (It made them very rich and increasingly powerful.)

- *What effect did gold have on farmers and herders in the area?* (They must have had to work harder to supply food to the gold workers and the growing number of city residents.)

- *What is the final unsolved mystery of Great Zimbabwe?* (Why was it abandoned?)

★THINKING FURTHER: *Predicting* **What kinds of things might be found to help archaeologists and historians solve the mysteries of Great Zimbabwe?** (perhaps some written records of visitors there or artifacts that provide new information)

THE CITY ON A HILL

Historians believe that most of the stone walls of Great Zimbabwe surrounded the large homes of the ruling families. Were the walls meant to keep something in—or out? The walls may have been built to keep the city safe from attack by other cities and villages. Or they may have given extra privacy to the lives of Great Zimbabwe's leaders. Maybe the walls reflected their great power in the community. There is no way to know for certain. Historians can only guess at what their lives may have been like. It is likely, however, that many of these ruling families became powerful by trading gold.

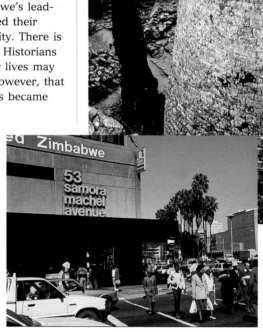

Controlling the Gold Trade

Some of southern Africa's richest gold fields are located around Great Zimbabwe. Sometime in the 1300s Great Zimbabwe began to trade with an important Swahili coastal city called Sofala. Miners probably worked hard to increase the gold supply that was brought to Sofala. They probably brought gold from the mines back to Great Zimbabwe. There, workers used a special furnace to melt the gold. Melted gold then was reshaped for shipment.

Great Zimbabwe's powerful families grew wealthy from the increase in the flow of gold among the mines, the city, and Sofala. Artifacts show that they used some of their new wealth to buy loads of glass beads, cloth, and pottery from China and Persia.

Most people, however, still used locally made pottery to carry water or for cooking. Metalworkers in the city coiled gold wire into bracelets for their customers. The people who lived in Great Zimbabwe liked to wear the gold and beaded jewelry they created. The city's metalworkers also made iron hoes and axes for farmers. Farmers used those tools to raise millet and sorghum at the edges of Great Zimbabwe. Those grains, along with milk and meat, were important items in the daily diet of the city's residents. During the period in which Great Zimbabwe thrived in the

---

CITIZENSHIP★

UNDERSTANDING GOVERNMENT Chiefs of a people called the Karanga ruled Great Zimbabwe. They themselves acted as traders, bartering gold and copper from outlying mines with traders from the eastern Africa coast. Scholars trace their success as rulers to two essential qualities: political skill and kinship loyalty.

BACKGROUND INFORMATION

ABOUT THE ZIMBABWE-SOFALA CONNECTION
- Today African bearers are no longer the link between Zimbabwe and Sofala.
- Now a passage called the Beira corridor links the port city with the nation of Zimbabwe. This important and well-used connection includes a road, a railroad, and a pipeline.

Great Zimbabwe (above) was a main trading center for 400 years. Today Harare (left) is the business center in the country of Zimbabwe.

early 1400s, about 18,000 people lived in the community. This meant that farmers and herders worked hard to provide food for the people of the walled city.

For reasons unknown to historians, Great Zimbabwe began to decline in the late 1400s. Most of its residents left and moved to other regions. Did too much farming wear out the land around the city and create hardship? Did some natural catastrophe happen? Archaeologists and historians are working to learn more about Great Zimbabwe. Even so, they may never be able to answer these questions.

WHY IT MATTERS

Events after Great Zimbabwe was abandoned are not such a mystery. In the late 1490s a small European ship sailed past Sofala. It was the first one ever to do so. In its wake would come many changes for all of Africa.

Meanwhile, a new group of peoples began to farm and trade in southern Africa. Today these distant relatives of the people of Great Zimbabwe continue to live in Zimbabwe, the country that is named after the ancient city.

✓ Reviewing Facts and Ideas

MAIN IDEAS

- Information about Great Zimbabwe is limited due to a lack of oral traditions and written documents.
- The city thrived in the 1300s and 1400s, due in part to its control of local gold trade routes.
- Great Zimbabwe's trade in gold tied it to Swahili cities and to Asia.

THINK ABOUT IT

1. What purposes might the walls of Great Zimbabwe have served?

2. Why was the coastal city of Sofala important to the growth and strength of Great Zimbabwe?

3. **FOCUS** How did Great Zimbabwe's involvement in the gold trade affect life in the city?

4. **THINKING SKILL** Based on your reading, make a _conclusion_ about why Great Zimbabwe's wealthy families may have needed the protection of the stone walls. Explain how you made your conclusion.

5. **GEOGRAPHY** How did the people of Great Zimbabwe make use of raw materials when they built their city?

379

Discussing WHY IT MATTERS Have students answer the _Read to Learn_ question.

> ★**THINKING FURTHER:** _Cause and Effect_ **What effects did the growth of Great Zimbabwe have on southern Africa?** (It built up the Great Zimbabwe civilization there, expanded gold mining and gold processing, and strengthened its trade.)

⭐ 3 CLOSE

MAIN IDEAS
As you ask the following questions, have students arrive at class answers and write them on the board.

- _Why is information about Great Zimbabwe limited?_ (the lack of oral traditions or written documents)

- _When did Great Zimbabwe thrive as a city and why?_ (in the 1300s and 1400s because of its control of gold trade routes)

EVALUATE
✓ **Answers to Think About It**

1. to keep something in or out or for protection or privacy
Make Inferences

2. It was their closest Indian Ocean port.
Make Conclusions

3. It enriched the rulers, made the city a trading center, and probably enlarged its population.
Make Inferences

4. Students' conclusions may reflect the idea that outsiders may have wanted to get at all that gold wealth.
Make Conclusions

5. They used its mud for ordinary houses and its granite for grander buildings.
Five Themes of Geography: Human/ Environment Interactions

Write About It Have students write a paragraph in which they describe housing, work, and diet in Great Zimbabwe.

 Technology CONNECTION

ADVENTURE TIME! CD-ROM
Have students _Explore_ the Zimbabwe map on the _Adventure Time!_ CD-ROM.

DISCUSSING MAJOR EVENTS Use the time line to have students identify in which parts of Africa the major events shown took place.

- *Which of the events in this time line took place in northeastern Africa?* (the two Kush events and Lalibela's reign)

- *Which took place in West Africa?* (Ghana, Mali, and Songhai events and supplying gold)

- *Which took place along or near Africa's eastern to southeastern coast?* (Swahili cities and Great Zimbabwe)

Answers to
THINKING ABOUT VOCABULARY

1. savanna
2. demand
3. supply
4. Sahel
5. griot

Answers to
THINKING ABOUT FACTS

1. Sahara

2. 3,000 miles

3. an area the size of the United States; there is a dry season when the grasses turn brown and a rainy season when terrible downpours flood the land and encourage growth.

4. millet and sorghum

5. Its rulers controlled a large trade network.

6. about 500 years; they controlled its supply, keeping it scarce to keep its price high.

7. 1312; Mali was at its peak of its wealth and power and king Mansa Musa controlled most of West Africa during this time period.

Resource **REMINDER**

Practice and Project Book: *p. 77*
Assessment Book: *Chapter 13 Test*
Transparency: *Graphic Organizer, Main-Idea Map*

CHAPTER 13 REVIEW

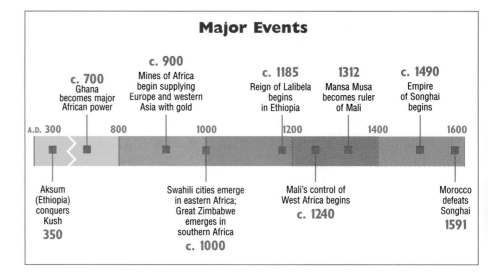

Major Events

THINKING ABOUT
VOCABULARY

Number a sheet of paper from 1 to 5. Beside each number write the word that best matches the statement.

demand   savanna
griot   supply
Sahel

1. A grassy plain dotted with trees
2. The people's desire for an item or service
3. A quantity of available goods, products, or resources
4. The dry southern edge of the Sahara
5. A person who tells stories that describe historical events

THINKING ABOUT FACTS

1. What is the world's largest desert?
2. How long is the Great Rift Valley?
3. How much of Africa is covered by savannas? What is the weather like on the savannas?

4. What grains have Africans been growing on the savannas for 4,000 years?
5. How did the ancient kingdom of Kush become wealthy?
6. How long did the empire of Ghana last? What did Ghana's kings do to keep the value of gold high?
7. According to the time line above, when did Mansa Musa become ruler of Mali? What important change took place in West Africa about that time?
8. Name three important Swahili cities. What two important products did they trade with Asia?
9. What was Great Zimbabwe? Why don't we know more about it?
10. According to the time line above, how many years were there between Aksum's conquest of Kush and the beginning of the Songhai empire? Name three African states that arose during that time.

SECOND-LANGUAGE SUPPORT

MAPS Using their Outline Maps and the text as sources of information, students can make a large classroom display map of Africa and explain its main features as a review.

INTERVIEWS Invite students to pretend that they are magazine writers assigned to write a story about interesting people in medieval Africa. They are going to interview King Lalibela of Ethiopia, Sunjata of Ghana, Mansa Musa of Mali, an African griot, and a Swahili trader. Student pairs will pick one person to interview and think of three questions to ask him. Then they will skim the chapter to see if it contains the answers. If they cannot find the answers in the chapter, encourage them to do some research to answer their own questions.

THINK AND WRITE ◀ ▭▶

WRITING A DIARY

Suppose you are Queen Amanishakhete of Kush. Write a diary entry about some of the things you did today.

WRITING A TRAVEL BROCHURE

Imagine you are a travel agent who wants to interest people in Timbuktu. Write a brief brochure about the city's history so people will want to visit it.

WRITING A DESCRIPTION

Write a paragraph describing the Swahili civilization of eastern Africa. Include information about Swahili cities and about trade on the Indian Ocean.

APPLYING GEOGRAPHY SKILLS

READING DISTRIBUTION MAPS

1. What is a distribution map?

2. What information do the two distribution maps on pages 370 and 371 provide?

3. What other features might distribution maps of Africa and West Africa show?

4. Look at Map B on page 371. Which is more densely populated, Timbuktu or Accra?

5. Why is a distribution map useful?

---

8. Mombasa, Zanzibar, Mogadishu; ivory and gold

9. a great stone community in south-eastern Africa; it left behind no oral tradition or written documents.

10. 1490 minus 350 = 1,140 years; Ghana, Great Zimbabwe, Mali

Answers to APPLYING GEOGRAPHY SKILLS

1. A distribution map is a special purpose map that shows how one particular feature is spread over an area.

2. population density in Africa

3. perhaps how climates are distributed over an area or what languages are spoken in different parts of an area

4. Accra

5. It can show where in an area a specific feature can be found and to what degree.

Summing Up the Chapter

Copy the main idea map below on a separate sheet of paper. Then review the chapter and fill in information for each region. After you complete the diagram, write a paragraph that answers the question "What helped to make ancient Africa diverse?"

Ethiopian Kingdoms

Kush
Aksum
Zagwe

Swahili Cities in East Africa

Mombasa
Zanzibar
Mogadishu

Civilization and Cultures Flourished in Sub-Saharan Africa

West African Empires

Ghana
Mali
Songhai

Southern Africa

Great Zimbabwe

381

SUGGESTIONS FOR SUMMING UP THE CHAPTER

Before students copy the main-idea diagram on a piece of paper, have them read the main idea aloud and identify what area sub-Saharan Africa takes in (all Africa south of the Sahara Desert). As they copy the diagram, point out that its four categories correspond to Lessons 2, 3, 4, and 5 and encourage them to review each of these lessons to identify the places they are called on to fill in. Possible answers appear on the reproduced pupil page above. Once they have completed their diagrams, have them read the question posed aloud. Suggest that they think about how each of the boxed areas differed from one another. Point out that the differences they identify can serve as the basis for their paragraph explaining Africa's diversity.

ASSESSING THINK AND WRITE: *For performance assessment, see Assessment Book, Chapter 13, pp. T84–T86.*

14 Empires and Cultures of Asia

Pages 382–419

CHAPTER OVERVIEW

In A.D. 800 Suryavarman II built the massive temple of Angkor, Cambodia. By 1279 all of China was united under Kublai Khan. The Ottoman empire ruled Anatolia, southeast Europe, the Arab Middle East, and North Africa in the 1300s. In 1631, the Shah Jahan began building the Taj Mahal in Agra, India.

GEO ADVENTURES DAILY GEOGRAPHY ACTIVITIES

Use **Geo Adventures** Daily Geography activities to assess students' understanding of geography skills.

CHAPTER PLANNING GUIDE

LESSON 1	**LESSON 2**	**LESSON 3**
SUGGESTED PACING: 2 DAYS	SUGGESTED PACING: 2 DAYS	SUGGESTED PACING: 2 DAYS
Geography Of Asia pp. 384–387	**The Ottomans** pp. 388–391	**India Under The Moguls** pp. 392–397
CURRICULUM CONNECTIONS Links to Language Arts, p. 386	**CURRICULUM CONNECTIONS** Links to Music, p. 389	**CURRICULUM CONNECTIONS** Links to Art, p. 395
RESOURCES Practice and Project Book, p. 78 Outline Map	**CITIZENSHIP** Understanding Government, p. 390	**CITIZENSHIP** Understanding Government, p. 393
	RESOURCES Practice and Project Book, p. 79 Anthology, pp. 93–95	**RESOURCES** Practice and Project Book, p. 80

LESSON 5	**THINKINGSKILLS**	**LESSON 6**
SUGGESTED PACING: 3 DAYS	SUGGESTED PACING: 1 DAY	SUGGESTED PACING: 2 DAYS
Great Empires Of China pp. 402–407	**Making Generalizations** pp. 408–409	**Feudal Japan** pp. 410–415
CURRICULUM CONNECTIONS Links to Reading, p. 403 Links to Reading and Viewing, p. 403	**RESOURCES** Practice and Project Book, p. 83	**CURRICULUM CONNECTIONS** Links to Reading, p. 413
CITIZENSHIP Understanding Government, p. 404		**CITIZENSHIP** Understanding Government, p. 412
INFOGRAPHIC Trade on the Silk Road, pp. 406–407		**RESOURCES** Practice and Project Book, p. 84 Anthology, pp. 102–103 Outline Map
RESOURCES Project and Practice Book, p. 82 Anthology, pp. 96–98, 99–101 ⊙ TECHNOLOGY *Adventure Time!* CD-ROM		

LEARNING STYLE: Visual

 ON YOUR OWN

 30 MINUTES OR LONGER

Create a City

Objective: To help students prepare to learn about the empires and cultures of Asia.

Materials: markers, scissors, glue, cartons, colored paper, aluminum foil

1. Invite students to imagine they are rulers of a long-ago empire. Ask them to think about where their empires are located, what laws they have, and what government buildings they would need.
2. What would their capital cities look like? Have students build models of their capitals, using cartons for the buildings and colored paper and foil for decorations.
3. Display the models around the room.

LESSON 4

SUGGESTED PACING: 2 DAYS

The Khmer Of Southeast Asia pp. 398–401

CURRICULUM CONNECTIONS
Links to Reading, p. 399

CITIZENSHIP
Preserving Our Heritage, p. 399

RESOURCES
Project and Practice Book, p. 81

Legacy

SUGGESTED PACING: 1 DAY

Printing And Calligraphy
pp. 416–417

CURRICULUM CONNECTIONS
Links to Art, p. 417

SDAIE SUPPORT SHELTERED INSTRUCTION

READING STRATEGIES & LANGUAGE DEVELOPMENT

Rereading/Place Names, p. 384, Lesson 1
Evaluating Accuracy/Synonyms, p. 388, Lesson 2
Using Visuals/Suffixes, Comparatives, and
  Superlatives, p. 392, Lesson 3
Predicting/Words Often Confused, p. 398, Lesson 4
Problem and Solution/Word Origin, p. 402, Lesson 5
Making Generalizations/Apostrophes in Possessives,
  p. 408, Thinking Skills
Sequencing/Words Often Confused, p. 410, Lesson 6

SECOND-LANGUAGE SUPPORT

Using Games, p. 385
Working with Peers, p. 389
Using Visuals, pp. 395, 405
Research, p. 400
Oral Practice/TV Quiz Game, p. 418

MEETING INDIVIDUAL NEEDS

Reteaching, Extension, Enrichment, pp. 387, 391,
  397, 401, 407, 415, 417
McGraw-Hill Adventure Book

ASSESSMENT OPPORTUNITIES

Practice and Project Book, pp. 78–85
Write About It, pp. 387, 391, 397, 401, 407, 415, 417
Assessment Book: Assessing Think and Write,
  pp. T87–T89; Chapter 14 Tests: Content, Skills,
  Writing

CHAPTER REVIEW

SUGGESTED PACING: 1 DAY

pp. 418–419

RESOURCES
Practice and Project Book, p. 85
TECHNOLOGY Videodisc
Assessment Book: Chapter 14 Test
Transparency: Graphic Organizer,
Main-Idea Chart

Introducing the Chapter

Have students read the chapter title to realize that they are returning to study Asia. Have them trace the panels to the map to see which of these locations concern places they have already studied (China, the Byzantine Empire, and India).

THINKING ABOUT HISTORY AND GEOGRAPHY

Have students read the text on this page and then identify three characteristics of Asia during the period under study (trade, use of military to increase power, great architecture). Then have them examine the panels to see which characteristic each reflects.

1100s ANGKOR

- *Where in Asia is Angkor? (in the southeastern part)*

- *What is happening in this panel? Which characteristic does it reflect? (Suryavarman II is building a massive temple; great architecture.)*

★THINKING FURTHER: *Making Conclusions Given the location in Asia and style of the temple, what religion might it reflect? (Hinduism or Buddhism)*

1279 BEIJING

- *Where in Asia is Beijing? (in the east, in China)*

- *Which characteristic would you say that this panel reflects? (the use of military to increase power)*

★THINKING FURTHER: *Cause and Effect How can conquest of an area lead to uniting it? (Since the time Menes of Egypt, conquerors often brought different groups under one government.)*

Resource REMINDER

🔘 **Technology:** *Videodisc*

CHAPTER 14

Empires and Cultures of Asia

THINKING ABOUT HISTORY AND GEOGRAPHY

For centuries, Asia has been home to many civilizations. The time line and map show where some of them developed. Asian peoples between A.D. 1100 and A.D. 1650 used trade and military power to increase their influence. Many also constructed buildings that remain among the world's finest architectural achievements.

1100s

ANGKOR

Suryavarman II builds Angkor Wat

1279

BEIJING

Kublai Khan conquers and unites China

1453

CONSTANTINOPLE

Turks conquer the Byzantine empire

1100   1250   1400

BACKGROUND INFORMATION

LINKING THE MAP AND THE TIME LINE

- Angkor, located in today's Cambodia, was reclaimed by the jungle after around 1200 and was unknown to the outside world until the 1860s. At that time, French missionaries working in Southeast Asia heard tales of a vast temple complex hidden in the jungle and went in search of it. Since then, French archaeologists off and on have directed expeditions (with interruptions for war) to uncover and study the site.

- Beijing, today the capital of China, served as the capital of many of China's past dynasties: the Chin (1126–1234), the Yuan (1279–1368), the Ming (1368–1644), and the Ch'ing (1644–1911).

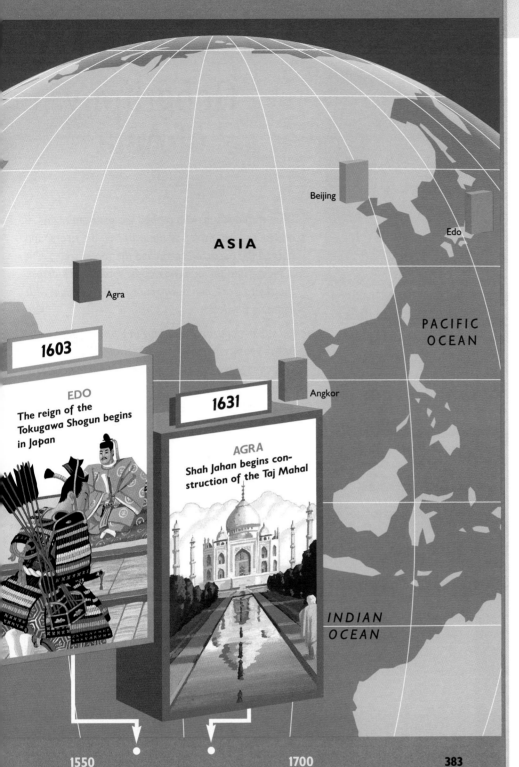

ASIA

Beijing

Edo

PACIFIC OCEAN

Agra

1603

EDO
The reign of the Tokugawa Shogun begins in Japan

1631

Angkor

AGRA
Shah Jahan begins con-struction of the Taj Mahal

INDIAN OCEAN

1550   1700   **383**

- *Where is Constantinople located?* (at a crossroads where Europe and Asia meet)

- *What have you already learned about the Byzantine Empire?* (It succeeded the Eastern Roman Empire and was home to the Eastern Orthodox Church.)

★THINKING FURTHER: *Making Conclusions* **Why do you think the Turks would have wanted to conquer Constantinople?** (Students may recall that the Crusades had been fought because Muslim Turks had taken control of much of the Byzantine Empire, so it makes sense that they would want its capital.)

1603 EDO

- *Where is Edo located in Asia?* (in the far eastern part of Asia, in Japan)

★THINKING FURTHER: *Making Conclusions* **How does this panel show that the use of the military is important in the development of Japan?** (Warriors appear to be prominent.)

1631 AGRA

- *Where is Agra located in Asia?* (in the southern part, in India)

★THINKING FURTHER: *Making Decisions* **Would you agree or disagree that the Taj Mahal is one of the most beautiful buildings ever built? Explain your opinion.** (Invite opinions and discussion.)

Technology CONNECTION

VIDEODISC
Enrich Chapter 14 with *The Indian Subcontinent* on the Videodisc.

Search Frame 13297 Side A

BACKGROUND INFORMATION

LINKING THE MAP AND THE TIME LINE
- Constantinople, now Istanbul in Turkey, was a contested prize since its founding in about 600 B.C. Before the Turks conquered it, Persians, Greeks, Romans, Arabs, Bulgars, and Russians all contended for it.
- Edo, now Tokyo (the capital of Japan), became the real seat of Japanese government in 1603, although the imperial court remained at Kyoto. The emperor moved his court to Edo in 1863 and renamed it Tokyo ("eastern capital").
- Agra, on the banks of the Jumna River in north central India, is today a predominantly Hindu city, but it retains its rich Muslim heritage. In addition to the Taj Mahal, it boasts the Agra Fort, a red sandstone fortress complex.

LESSON 1

PAGES 384–387

Lesson Overview

Asia, the largest continent, has a great diversity of geographical environments.

Lesson Objectives

★ Identify major regions of Asia.

★ Locate and describe major physical features of Asia.

⭐ 1 PREPARE

MOTIVATE Have the class look at the map on p. 385 as two students do the *Read Aloud,* one reading the quote, the other the narration. Use the quote and the photo of sunset in the Himalayas to help students get an idea of how dramatic Asia's geography can be.

SET PURPOSE Refer students to the *Read to Learn* question and ask if they know what the Himalayas are (world's highest mountains). How might the Himalayas affect a whole continent? Preview the *Vocabulary* and tell students to explore the lesson to learn more about Asia's other major physical features.

⭐ 2 TEACH

Understanding THE BIG PICTURE Again, refer students to the map. As they read the text, have them use their fingers to identify on it regions the text describes.

★**THINKING FURTHER:** *Making Conclusions Why would you expect Asia to have a great variety of climates, landforms, peoples, and histories? (Students should recognize that its size, and north-south extent would produce different environments and differences in how people adapted to them.)*

Resource REMINDER

Practice and Project Book: *p. 78*

Outline Map

Focus Activity

READ TO LEARN

How do the Himalayas affect the geography of Asia?

VOCABULARY

- archipelago
- monsoon

PLACES

- Himalayas
- Mount Everest
- Tibetan Plateau
- Gobi Desert

Geography of Asia

Read Aloud

"The summer sun, who robbed the pleasant nights, and plundered [stole] all the water of the rivers, and burned the earth, and scorched the forest trees, is now in hiding; and the autumn clouds, spread thick across the sky to track him down, hunt for the criminal with lightning flashes."

Indian poet Amaru, writing in Sanskrit, described India's yearly change of seasons over 1,000 years ago. This change is a big event for many people across Asia. Many, in fact, depend on it for their lives.

THE BIG PICTURE

Asia is the world's largest continent. It stretches from Saudi Arabia and Turkey in the west to the eastern parts of China and Japan. Asia has many regions. The continent is made up of areas called North, West, Central, South, Southeast, and East Asia. Each of these regions has a great variety of people and environments.

Asia includes many climates, landforms, peoples, and histories. Some of the ancient Asian civilizations you have already read about include Harappa, Mesopotamia, and Shang China.

A thin strip of land in northeastern Egypt is considered Asia's border with Africa. The Ural mountains separate North Asia from Europe. Asia has more mountains than any other continent. It also has the highest mountains. Not surprisingly, mountains greatly affect life on the continent. You will read about the world's highest mountain range in this lesson.

SHELTERED INSTRUCTION

READING STRATEGIES & LANGUAGE DEVELOPMENT

REREADING Review with students benefits of rereading new material to be certain that they understand its meaning. Then have students preview this lesson by forming a question about each Vocabulary and Places term. Model how to write the questions, leaving one line between each. As students read, have them answer the questions. Remind them to reread passages to find the information they need. [SDAIE STRATEGY: CONTEXTUALIZATION]

PLACE NAMES Students may wonder why Mount Everest, which is in Asia, has an English name. It has been called Mount Everest only since the late 1880s, when it was surveyed by a British surveyor, Sir George Everest. Older names for this peak include *Chomolungma* in the Tibetan language and *Sagarmatha* in Nepalese.

ASIA

The Himalayas (him uh LAY uz) and neighboring mountains make up the heart of Asia. Many of the world's highest peaks are here, including the tallest of all—Mount Everest. The Himalayas form the southern border of the vast Tibetan Plateau. This plateau is a high mountain plain where more than a half dozen of the continent's powerful rivers begin. Locate the Tibetan Plateau and the Himalayas on the map below.

Asia has several island chains off its shores. One of these chains is Japan. Find it on the map. Japan forms an archipelago (ahr kuh PEL ih goh). *Archipelago* is the word for such a group or chain of islands.

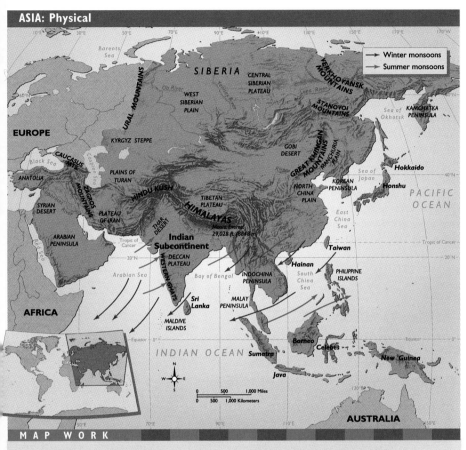

ASIA: Physical

→ Winter monsoons
→ Summer monsoons

MAP WORK

Asia is a land of extreme contrasts in geography. In addition to the highest mountains in the world, it has vast plains and deserts.

1. What mountain ranges border the Gobi Desert to the east and northeast?

2. What other deserts are in Asia?

3. Which coast of the Indian Subcontinent, the east or west, would be more likely to encounter flooding in the summer?

MAP WORK: **1.** Stanovoi and Great Khingan **2.** Syrian and Thar **3.** the West Coast, because the summer monsoons would be traveling toward the West Coast from the Arabian Sea

385

ASIA

Have a student list some of the major geographical features on the board.

More **MAP WORK**

Refer students to the map and have them work with both text and map.

- *In what region of Asia are the Himalayas? What world's record do they hold?* (the northern border of South Asia; the world's tallest peaks)

- *Where among them is Mount Everest? What world's record does it hold?* (in the center; the world's tallest peak)

- *What physical feature lies just north of the Himalayas? Why might it be called "the mother of rivers"?* (Tibetan Plateau; several major rivers—the Indus, Huang, Mekong, Chang, and Ganges—rise here.)

- *What major peninsulas can you find?* (Arabian, Indochina, Korean, Malay, Kamchatka)

- *What is an archipelago? What archipelagos can you locate on the map?* (a group or chain of islands; Japan, Indonesia, Malaysia, the Philippines)

- *What major plateau covers part of the Indian subcontinent?* (Deccan)

- *What places do you think make up East Asia?* (eastern China, the Korean Peninsula, and Japan)

- *What places make up Southeast Asia?* (Indochina Peninsula, Malaysia, Indonesia, the Philippines)

BACKGROUND INFORMATION

ABOUT THE TIBETAN PLATEAU

- At 15,000 feet, it is the highest and largest plateau on Earth.
- Because of its altitude, its climate varies little over the year, with temperatures ranging from a high of 45°F down to -8° F.
- Because the Himalayas block monsoon rains from reaching the plateau, it receives only about 10 inches of rainfall a year.
- Its status as "mother of rivers" stems from the runoffs that come down from the Himalayas.

SECOND-LANGUAGE SUPPORT

USING GAMES Second-language learners may benefit from a game using geographical place names. Have students read the geographical features, and create a game called "Looking for ___," using the name of a friend or a celebrity. Students should create clues such as "André hired a guide to climb the highest mountain in the world." Other students have to guess where André would be found.

A WALL OF MOUNTAINS

If possible, have the November 1988 issue of *National Geographic* available for students to examine. It contains sweeping pictures of the Himalayas.

- **What are the world's highest natural wall?** *(the Himalayas)*

- **How do they act as a barrier to movement?** *(They cut off the Indian subcontinent from Tibet and China.)*

- **How do they act as a climate barrier?** *(prevent rain clouds from the south from reaching land to the north)*

★**THINKING FURTHER: Summarizing** How would you summarize the effects the Himalayas have on Asia's geography? *(They discourage movements of people between north and south in Central Asia and they limit the rainfall of areas north of them.)*

Discussing Monsoons Remind students of the wind patterns over the Indian Ocean, (*Global Connections* p. 373). Have students diagram on outline maps the directions of winter and summer monsoons.

- **What are monsoons?** *(seasonal winds, from the northeast in winter, from the southwest and southeast in summer)*

- **How do winter monsoons differ from summer monsoons?** *(Winter: dry. Summer: moist.)*

- **Why are monsoons so important to farming in South Asia?** *(They bring the rain necessary to grow crops.)*

★**THINKING FURTHER: Compare and Contrast** What similarities can you see between monsoons and flooding in ancient river valley civilizations? *(Both were crucial to farming, but too much or too little water could be devastating.)*

More CHART WORK

Have students study the chart, p. 387.

★**THINKING FURTHER: Compare and Contrast** How does Asia's population compare with the population of the rest of the world combined? *(Asia's population is almost twice as large as that of the rest of the world combined.)*

A WALL OF MOUNTAINS

Himalaya means "snowy range" in Sanskrit. This vast range stretches across central Asia for 1,500 miles. Many of the peaks are over 25,000 feet high. Their immense heights form the world's highest natural wall.

The Himalayas and neighboring mountain ranges form a towering wall that divides India and Nepal from Tibet and China. The barrier makes movement through the region difficult.

The Himalayas have a big effect on the climate of much of Asia. They block clouds that blow north from the Indian Ocean. This causes large amounts of rainfall on the ocean-facing sides of the mountains and small amounts on their northern sides. In Cherrapunji, India, for example, an average of 38 feet of rain falls each year! By contrast, only a few inches fall on the other side, Tibet. Even less falls in the Gobi (GOH bee) Desert. This rocky, nearly treeless region in northern China is almost twice the size of Texas.

Monsoons

Plenty of rain is usually good news for Asia's many farmers. Throughout much of South Asia, though, most rain falls during only one season. The rest of the year remains dry. Rain clouds are brought to the region by seasonal winds called monsoons.

An Indian leader named Indira Gandhi once remarked, "for us in India scarcity [shortage of resources] is only a missed monsoon away." What she said is true for millions of people throughout Asia. Farmers count on the monsoons to bring water for their crops.

In India the months of November through May remain dry and, toward the end, intensely hot. During these months dry winter monsoons blow across South Asia from the northeast. From about June through October, however, moisture-bearing winds from the southeast and southwest sweep across the continent. These winds are the summer monsoons. Farmers joyfully

Rains brought by monsoon winds flood Dhaka, the capital of Bangladesh (left). In Tibet camps are built on the high, drier plains (below).

ASIA AT A GLANCE

Total Land Area	16,992,000 sq. miles 44,009,000 sq. km
Highest Mountain	Mt. Everest, Nepal 29,028 feet (8,848 m)
Longest River	Chang River, China 3,915 miles 6,300 km
Largest City	Tokyo, Japan Population 8,112,000
Current Population	3,389,000,000
Percent of World Population	61%

GEO FACT
Giant pandas live in bamboo forests in the high elevations of southwestern China. The bearlike animals eat bamboo shoots. Because there is often a shortage of bamboo for the pandas to eat, panda numbers are limited. In the late 1980s scientists estimated that only about 600 pandas were left in the wild.

CHART WORK

The chart provides information about the size and geography of Asia.

1. What is one condition that contributes to the limited population of the giant panda?

2. What percentage of the world's population lives in Asia?

greet the huge sheets of rain brought by summer monsoons that water their rice, sorghum, millet, and chickpeas, among other crops.

As long as the rain-bearing monsoon runs its normal course, farmers can count on successful harvests. An Indian proverb, however, warns "if the sky fails, the earth will fail." If too much rain falls, as often happens in some regions, flooding may result in loss of life and property.

CHART WORK: 1. shortage of a certain kind of bamboo **2.** 61%

WHY IT MATTERS

From the chart on this page you can see that Asia has a large population. People in the many regions of Asia have adapted to the great variety of geographical features on the continent.

Some of these features—mountains, river valleys, and monsoons—helped create rich farmland on which people could live. In the following lessons you will read about some of the people who lived in these different environments.

Reviewing Facts and Ideas

MAIN IDEAS

● Asia, the world's largest continent, has more mountains than any other. These mountain ranges include the awesome Himalayas.

● The Himalayas block clouds blowing north from the Indian Ocean. As a result, large amounts of rain fall south of the mountains while little falls to the north.

● Seasonal winds called monsoons affect many Asians' lives. Important crops depend on rain the summer monsoons bring each year.

THINK ABOUT IT

1. Why are monsoons important to farmers in South Asia?

2. How does the Tibetan plateau affect other regions of Asia?

3. FOCUS How is life in Asia affected by the Himalayas?

4. THINKING SKILL What _conclusions_ can you make about life in Asia from the information in this lesson? On what facts did you base your conclusions?

5. GEOGRAPHY Look at the map on page 385. What major rivers begin on the Tibetan Plateau?

387

LESSON 2

PAGES 388–391

Lesson Overview

In the 1300s the Ottoman empire emerged to rule Anatolia, southeastern Europe, the Arab Middle East, and North Africa.

Lesson Objectives

★ Locate and describe the area the Ottoman empire covered.

★ Describe the achievements of the Ottoman empire.

1 PREPARE

MOTIVATE Have one student do the *Read Aloud* quote and another the narrator's part. Point out that the quoted leader is known as "Süleyman the Magnificent" because he helped create an opulent Ottoman civilization. The illustration shows him and his army in 1588.

SET PURPOSE Read to the class a quote from an Italian ambassador visiting Süleyman's empire in the 1500s: "I know of no State which is happier than this one . . . It controls war and peace with all; it is rich in gold, in people, in ships, and in obedience; no State can be compared with it." Encourage students to explore the lesson to evaluate the statement and to answer the *Read to Learn* question. Preview the *Vocabulary*.

2 TEACH

Understanding THE BIG PICTURE
Stress the understanding that Constantinople is located in two continents.

★**THINKING FURTHER:** *Sequencing*
What various roles did Constantinople play as an important world city for 1,000 years? *(From the time of Constantine, it was a religious center. Later it became the capital of the Eastern Roman empire and, then the capital of the Muslim Turkish-led Ottoman empire.)*

Resource **REMINDER**

Practice and Project Book: *p. 79*
Anthology: *The Hoca, pp. 93–95*

Focus Activity

READ TO LEARN

What was life like in the Ottoman empire?

VOCABULARY

- sultan
- grand mufti

PEOPLE

- Osman
- Süleyman
- Sinan

PLACES

- Istanbul
- Anatolia

388

800	1050	1300	1566	1800

The Ottomans

Read Aloud

"In Baghdad I am the shah [king], in Byzantine realms the caesar, and in Egypt the sultan; who sends his fleets to the seas of Europe, North Africa, and India."

These words were written by a leader named Süleyman, who headed one of the world's biggest empires in the early 1500s. His capital was not Baghdad, nor was it a new city. Rather it was a city that had once been the capital of the Eastern Roman empire. That city was Constantinople.

THE BIG PICTURE

The city once known as Constantinople is located in present-day Turkey. Now called Istanbul, the city crosses two continents. It extends across both sides of the Bosporus Strait, which separates Asia from eastern Europe. Anatolia, as Turkey was known during the Byzantine empire, has been home to some of the world's oldest civilizations. In Chapter 3 you read about the prehistoric city of Catal Huyuk, which thrived there over 8,000 years ago. In Chapter 9 you learned about the Roman emperor Constantine. He built Constantinople and its many Christian churches around A.D. 330.

For 1,000 years after Constantine built this city, the Byzantine empire remained a center of Christianity. In the 1300s, though, Anatolia was settled by a people called Turks. The Turks were Muslims from Central Asia. Within 150 years the Turks had made the city of Constantinople the capital of a new Turkish-led empire.

SHELTERED INSTRUCTION

READING STRATEGIES & LANGUAGE DEVELOPMENT

EVALUATING ACCURACY Explain that it is important to evaluate or judge a reading to see if the information is correct. Read the Set Purpose aloud with the class and evaluate its accuracy. Is the Italian ambassador telling the truth? What motives would he have for flattering his audience? Together, create some guidelines to evaluate the speaker's words. As they read the lesson, have students apply what they learned. [SDAIE STRATEGY: METACOGNITIVE DEVELOPMENT]

SYNONYMS Refer the class to the number of different place-specific names Süleyman gives to his role as ruler in different places—*shah* in Baghdad, *caesar* in Byzantine, *sultan* in Egypt. Call on students for other names by which rulers have been known around the world—for example, *emperor, king, queen, pharaoh, tsar, kaiser, maharaja, mikado, chieftain.*

AN EXPANDING EMPIRE

In 1301 Turkish warriors rallied behind a leader named Osman (OHZ mahn). He led them to their first major victory against the Byzantine empire. In honor of Osman's great skill as a leader, his followers called themselves "Osmanlis." In the next 150 years the "Osmanlis" became known as Ottomans. Their growing empire eventually surrounded the city of Constantinople.

The Battle for Constantinople

In 1453 Constantinople had the strongest defense of any city in Europe. It was surrounded on three sides by the sea. Attackers had to break through massive stone walls to get inside the city. Moats and ditches were built between the walls. Defenders could shoot from the tops of these walls.

The Ottoman empire also had strengths, though. Ottoman soldiers had the newest and largest cannons in Europe. These cannons hurled half-ton cannonballs more than a mile.

In the pre-dawn hours of May 29, 1453, the Ottomans fired heavily on the walls of Constantinople. Before the morning was over, Constantinople had fallen into Ottoman hands. After more than 1,000 years, the Byzantine empire was no more.

The Christian rulers of Europe, who once waged crusades against Islam, now had Muslim neighbors to the east. Those neighbors would be a powerful force in Europe for years to come.

Leadership of the Empire

When Constantinople became the new capital of the Ottoman empire in 1453, the Turks called the city Istanbul. This name comes from a Greek word meaning "in the city." Istanbul remained the empire's center until 1918. Today it is the largest city in Turkey.

During the 500 years of Ottoman rule, sultans, or supreme rulers, governed the empire. They passed control to their oldest or favorite sons. Religious leaders called grand muftis interpreted the laws of Islam and applied them to life in the Ottoman empire.

The Mosque of Süleyman is a striking sight in the landscape of Istanbul.

AN EXPANDING EMPIRE

To reinforce students' understanding the origin of the term *Ottoman*, have them draw a flow chart on the board→ the leader Osman→his followers Osmanlis→the Ottomans.

Discussing The Battle for Constantinople Have students locate Constantinople on the map on p. 390 and identify it as a crossroads between Europe and Asia.

● *Why would the Ottomans have wanted to capture Constantinople?* (its strategic location)

● *In 1453 what advantages did Constantinople have to fight off attackers?* (the sea on three sides, massive stone walls, moats and ditches, heights from which to shoot)

● *What advantages did the Ottoman empire have?* (powerful and far-shooting cannons)

● *Who won the battle?* (the Ottomans)

★THINKING FURTHER: *Predicting What consequences might this Muslim victory have for Christian Europe?* (It positions the Ottoman empire well for movement farther into Europe.)

Exploring Leadership of the Empire Have students recognize the common tradition of hereditary rule.

● *What name change signaled the Ottoman victory?* (Constantinople became Istanbul.)

● *For how long did the Ottoman empire last after Osman captured Constantinople?* (465 years)

● *Who ruled the Ottoman empire? How was power passed on?* (sultans; through their sons)

● *Who were the grand muftis?* (religious leaders in the Ottoman empire who interpreted the laws of Islam)

★THINKING FURTHER: *Making Conclusions Under Islamic rule, the laws of Islam are also the laws of the government. Why would this fact have made the grand muftis powerful figures?* (They would have had political as well as religious power.)

CURRICULUM CONNECTION

LINKS TO MUSIC As an enjoyable way for your students to remember the Constantinople to Istanbul name change, you may want to play for them an amusing novelty song from the 1950s. It is called "Istanbul, Not Constantinople" and was recorded by the Four Lads.

SECOND-LANGUAGE SUPPORT

WORKING WITH PEERS Second-language learners may find this lesson more accessible in the present tense. Have students work with English-proficient partners to retell the fall of the Byzantine empire as current events. Encourage students to retell the events as if they were TV reporters covering the news firsthand.

THE AGE OF SÜLEYMAN

Write *1520–1566* on the board.

More

Refer the class to the map on this page.

- **What does this map show?** *(the Ottoman empire under Süleyman)*

- **How much of the Mediterranean coastline did the empire control?** *(all of it except that of western Europe)*

- **What large land masses did it cover?** *(much of eastern Europe and Anatolia—help students see that Anatolia includes Asia Minor and the area east to beyond the Black Sea and down nearly to Arabia)*

- **What long strips did the empire cover?** *(area along the Nile and along the Mediterranean coast)*

- ★**THINKING FURTHER:** *Making Conclusions* **What do you think the size of the Ottoman empire says about it being "rich ... in people"?** *(Students should see that this much territory would have many peoples.)*

Discussing Life in Istanbul Help students see that Istanbul was a true world capital at the time.

- **What similarities do you see between Istanbul and other major cities you have met—Athens, Rome, Alexandria, Timbuktu, the Swahili trading cities?** *(varied specialties of workers—craftworkers, traders, artists, government and religious officials; trade goods from other parts of the world; grand buildings; slaves)*

- ★**THINKING FURTHER:** *Making Conclusions* **What tells you that a person of simple birth could rise high in the Ottoman empire?** *(the rise of Sinan, son of a stoneworker and trained in architecture, who became chief architect to the sultan Süleyman)*

Extending Did You Know? Ask students to do research on the history of the Netherlands to learn how the introduction of the tulip changed the Dutch economy. Students should then prepare oral reports on their findings.

THE OTTOMAN EMPIRE OF SÜLEYMAN I, 1520–1566   M A P   W O R K

Under Sultan Süleyman I the Ottoman empire expanded its borders.

1. About how far is Istanbul from Jerusalem?

2. What major river in Asia runs along the eastern border of the Ottoman empire?

THE AGE OF SÜLEYMAN

Between 1520 and 1566 the Ottoman empire reached its peak under Sultan Süleyman (SOO lay mahn). As you can see from the map, Süleyman's empire sprawled over three continents. It included Jerusalem.

Life in Istanbul

If "all roads led to Rome" during the Roman empire, all routes in the Ottoman empire—whether on sea or land—led to Istanbul. Coffee flowed into the city's coffeehouses from southern Arabia. Ships from Egypt brought rice and African gold. Butter, cheese, grain, and wheat, which helped feed the Ottoman army, were shipped across the Black Sea from present-day Ukraine, along with Russian furs.

Jews who had fled persecution in Spain now lived and worked in the city. So did Christians from all over Europe. Jews, Christians, and other non-Muslims worshiped freely in Istanbul.

At times Istanbul's non-Muslim merchants did business in the vast outer courtyard of Süleyman's palace. There they blended with the thousands of guards, weavers, armor-makers, horsetenders, and gardeners who worked for the sultan. Few, however, could enter the beautiful, walled-off garden and palace beyond the courtyard. The sultan lived and worked within these walls, along with his grand mufti and advisors, court musicians, painters, and poets. Almost all of Süleyman's assistants, soldiers, and closest advisers were slaves.

Government workers chose boys who were 8 or older to be slaves at the palace. The boys were trained to do many jobs. Some became craftworkers, surgeons, and architects.

One of the boys drafted into service, Sinan (suh NAHN), was the son of an Anatolian stoneworker. After years of training he became Süleyman's chief architect. He designed dozens of libraries, hospitals, and colleges for the sultan. Sinan also built buildings for Süleyman's wife, Hürrem Sultan. Among these buildings were a school for orphans and a soup kitchen for the poor. Sinan's greatest achievement was the mosque he designed for Süleyman. It still stands in the center of Istanbul.

390

CITIZENSHIP ★

UNDERSTANDING GOVERNMENT Part of the tribute the Ottoman empire demanded in the 1300s was Christian boys from conquered lands in Eastern Europe. The boys were converted to Islam and trained to be Janissaries, a strictly disciplined and well-trained army elite corps and the sultan's bodyguard. Eventually the Janissaries became one of the world's finest fighting corps and a privileged group that became so elite that men who were born Muslims demanded admission to the corps.

BACKGROUND INFORMATION

MORE ABOUT SINAN An Eastern Orthodox Christian by birth, Sinan was one of those boys who was converted to Islam and drafted into military service. He learned architecture by converting Christian churches into mosques and built at least 300 buildings.

WHY IT MATTERS

The battle for Constantinople in 1453 marked an important turning point in world history. It brought to an end the Byzantine empire and its 1,000-year-old link with ancient Rome. That battle also caused the center of Eastern Orthodox Christianity to give way to the Islam of the Ottoman empire.

Under Süleyman, the Ottoman empire grew and prospered on three continents—Europe, Asia, and Africa. A large mix of goods came to Istanbul from the empire's vast lands. Many different peoples came to Süleyman's capital as well. Enslaved youths from all over the empire rose through the ranks to carry out the sultans' laws.

The Ottoman empire lasted until 1922. Soon after the empire dissolved, the Turkish Republic was formed. Today the legacy of the Ottoman empire lives on. It can be found in the people and the grand mosques of southeastern Europe and Istanbul.

DID YOU KNOW?

How did Süleyman's gardens change life in the Netherlands?

Süleyman, like most sultans, loved flowers. His favorites included flowers that European visitors had never seen before—tulips, named after the Turkish word for "turban." A turban is a Muslim head-covering that is made by wrapping material around the head.

In the 1560s Austria's ambassador to Süleyman's court gave a handful of tulip bulbs to a Dutch gardener. When they bloomed, the rare flowers sparked a huge demand. In the early 1600s one bulb could fetch the price of an entire home or business! As time went on, prices dropped, but Dutch farmers continued to grow the turban-like flowers. Today the Netherlands is the world's largest producer of tulips.

Reviewing Facts and Ideas

MAIN IDEAS

- The Ottoman victory at Constantinople in 1453 ended the Byzantine empire and began a new era of Muslim rule in part of Europe.
- The Ottomans renamed the city of Constantinople, calling it Istanbul.
- The Ottoman empire was governed by leaders called sultans.
- During Süleyman's rule Istanbul drew products and peoples from across the empire. Non-Muslims were allowed to worship freely.

THINK ABOUT IT

1. Who was Sinan? What were some of the buildings he designed?

2. Why was Constantinople a difficult city to conquer? What role did technology play in its defeat in 1453?

3. **FOCUS** How did Süleyman's palace in Istanbul affect life in the city?

4. **THINKING SKILL** Why was the battle for Constantinople a disaster from the *point of view* of the Byzantines? Why was it a triumph in the eyes of the Ottomans?

5. **WRITE** Write a paragraph explaining why the fall of Constantinople was an important event in history.

391

Discussing WHY IT MATTERS Have students turn to their notes on the Italian ambassador's statement (See p. 388, *Reading Strategies*.)

★**THINKING FURTHER:** *Making Generalizations* **How factual would you judge the Italian ambassador's statement to be?** *(There is evidence for the empire's vast military strength—affecting war and peace—and for its richness in gold and people. Evidence for happiness, obedience, or comparability are perhaps lacking.)*

3 CLOSE

MAIN IDEAS
Call on students for answers.

- **How did the battle of Constantinople end one era and start another?** *(It ended the Byzantine empire and began Muslim rule in eastern Europe.)*

- **How was Constantinople's name changed?** *(The Ottomans renamed it Istanbul.)*

- **What were Ottoman rulers called?** *(sultans)*

- **Why can Süleyman's Istanbul be considered a world city?** *(It attracted people and products from all parts of a three-continent empire.)*

EVALUATE
✓ **Answers to Think About It**

1. chief architect to Süleyman; libraries, hospitals, colleges, school for orphans, soup kitchen for the poor, a huge mosque. *Recall Details*

2. It had strong defenses, natural and human-built; powerful long-range cannons helped to defeat it. *Draw Conclusions*

3. It created thousands of jobs for guards, weavers, armor-makers, horse tenders, gardeners, musicians, painters, and poets. *Main Idea/Supporting Details*

4. The Byzantines lost control of their capital city; the Ottomans gained it. *Point of View*

5. Paragraphs should reflect the end of one era and beginning of another. *Make, Confirm or Revise Predictions*

Write About It Ask students to write three generalizations that they can make and support about what life was like in the Ottoman empire.

MEETING INDIVIDUAL NEEDS

RETEACHING (Easy) Have students reread the material on p. 390 that describes what went on in and around Süleyman's palace. Tell students to picture a scene from it and use colored pencils, pens, or crayons to illustrate it.

EXTENSION (Average) Tell students to review what they have learned about Süleyman's Istanbul. Have them write a journal entry describing what they did and saw on a day spent there.

ENRICHMENT (Challenging) Divide the class into four groups and assign each group one of the following roles of Süleyman—(1) as lawgiver and ruler, (2) as military leader, (3) as patron of the arts, (4) as leader of a splendid court. Have the groups research their topic (*National Geographic*, November 1987, is one excellent source) and prepare an illustrated presentation of it for the class.

LESSON 3

PAGES 392–397

Lesson Overview
During the 1500s and 1600s, the Moguls created an empire that covered most of the Indian subcontinent.

Lesson Objectives
★ Locate and describe the Mogul empire.

★ Identify and describe its greatest achievements.

1 PREPARE

MOTIVATE Do the *Read Aloud* for the class and have them identify the challenges the young prince—shown in the illustration on a tiger hunt—had to face early in life (born while his parents were on the run, seizures, reading disorder, a ruler at age 13). How can one person handle these challenges and succeed?

SET PURPOSE Encourage students to infer from the title who Akbar's people were (Moguls) and where they settled (India). Give them a few minutes to review what they learned earlier about India. Then refer them to the *Read to Learn* question and tell them to read the lesson to resume the story in India.

2 TEACH

Understanding THE BIG PICTURE Have students predict some coming changes.

● **What were the major religions in India when we left it in Chapter 6?** (Hinduism and Buddhism)

● **What religion did the Moguls bring with them?** (Islam)

★THINKING FURTHER: *Predicting* **What troubles do you foresee arising from this situation?** (Possible answer: Religious clashes might flare up.)

Resource **REMINDER**

Practice and Project Book: *p. 80*

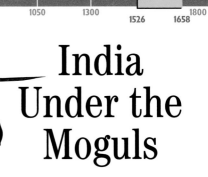

| 800 | 1050 | 1300 | | 1800 |
| | | | 1526 1658 | |

India Under the Moguls

Read Aloud
In 1543 a prince was born in a desert near the Indus River, where his parents were on the run from enemy leaders. In his youth he became an expert hunter. He also battled what may have been seizures and a reading disorder. At the age of 13 he became ruler of his father's battered territory in India. This prince, whose name meant "Great" in Arabic, would build a powerful empire.

Focus Activity

READ TO LEARN
Who were the Moguls and what did they achieve?

PEOPLE
• Akbar
• Shah Jahan
• Mumtaz Mahal

PLACES
• Agra
• Taj Mahal

392

THE BIG PICTURE
A powerful new empire began when Muslims from Central Asia began moving onto the Indian subcontinent. In Chapter 6 you read that Aryan princes gained control over much of the Indian subcontinent around 500 B.C. In the thousand years that followed, Hindu traditions became deeply rooted in India. Hindu rulers were challenged, however, by Muslim conquerors. By A.D. 1200 the fertile lands of the Indus plain had come under Muslim control.

The new sultans of the plain made Islam the law of the land. Hindus were called upon to pay a special tax, which cost ordinary workers as much as a month's wages. By law Hindus could no longer build any new temples. These and other rules caused anger among the large Hindu population. The result was more war, rather than peace. However, a new prince was about to bring big changes to the Indian subcontinent.

SHELTERED INSTRUCTION

READING STRATEGIES & LANGUAGE DEVELOPMENT

USING VISUALS Remind students how visuals such as paintings can teach us much about a civilization. Have small groups select a visual from this lesson they find especially dramatic, such as the painting from Mogul India on p. 395. Then have students create and share dialogues explaining what the visual suggests about the Moguls who ruled India.
[SDAIE STRATEGY: TEXT RE-PRESENTATION]

SUFFIXES, COMPARATIVES, AND SUPERLATIVES Remind the class that the suffix *-ly* signals an adverb, the part of speech that can modify a verb, an adjective, or another adverb. Have them find examples of *-ly* adverbs in the lesson (*originally*, p. 393 and *fairly*, p. 394). Point out that *fairly* is modified by another adverb, *more*. Explain that comparatives and superlatives of *-ly* adverbs are usually formed by adding *more* or *most*.

THE MOGUL EMPIRE

The conquerors you read about in the Big Picture were called Moguls. The Moguls were originally from Central Asia and may have been related to the Turks. In 1526 Moguls invaded the Indus plain. Within three years the Moguls controlled much of northern India. The map on this page shows you the region where the Moguls ruled. India's Mogul empire would grow even bigger during its 235-year rule. At one time it would cover most of the Indian subcontinent. Much of that growth would take place under Akbar, the ruler whose name meant "Great" in Arabic.

Akbar's Achievements

As you read in the Read Aloud, Akbar was made ruler of the Mogul empire when he was just 13. The year was 1556—when workers were completing Süleyman's mosque in Istanbul and shortly before Elizabeth I became queen of England.

At the age of 19, Akbar led an army into battle for the first time. Over the next 43 years he and his army fought many wars to expand the Mogul empire. During that time Akbar almost never lost a battle, and his fame as a brilliant commander grew.

Akbar offered no mercy to those who opposed him. At the same time he worked hard to improve life for those under his rule. He created a unified money system so that business would run smoothly throughout the empire. He varied the amount that farmers had to pay in taxes, based on how

Tiger hunting was a favorite sport of Akbar.

fertile their land was. Akbar also ordered government workers to build new canals and wells to help farmers.

Akbar's major changes, though, affected Hindus, the majority of people in India at that time. The changes helped to create a remarkable period of unity and power in Indian history.

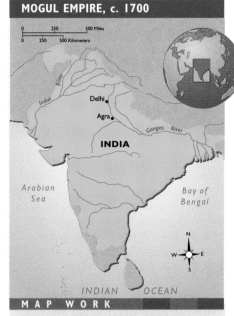

MOGUL EMPIRE, c. 1700

INDIA

Indus

Delhi

Agra

Ganges River

Arabian Sea

Bay of Bengal

INDIAN OCEAN

MAP WORK

By the year 1700 the Mogul empire had almost covered the entire Indian subcontinent.

1. What geographical features were near the Mogul empire's northern borders?

2. About how far is Delhi from Agra?

THE MOGUL EMPIRE

Reinforce the idea that Muslims—the Moguls—took control of Hindu India.

More **MAP WORK**

Refer students to the map. Encourage them to work with both text and map.

- *When did the Moguls invade the Indus plain? From where did they come?* (1526; Central Asia)

- *By what date had they created the empire shown in this map?* (1700)

- *How would you describe the extent of the Mogul empire at this point?* (most of the Indian subcontinent, except the southernmost tip)

★THINKING FURTHER: *Making Conclusions* **Why might the major conqueror of India have been given the name he received?** *(Someone who could conquer such a vast area might understandably be thought "great" or "Akbar.")*

Discussing Akbar's Achievements
Encourage students to assess Akbar's achievements by their own standards.

★THINKING FURTHER: *Classifying* **What "great" things did Akbar do as a military leader? as a ruler?** *(As military leader: expanded the empire while almost never losing a battle. As ruler: helped business with a unified money system, made taxes fairer, built public projects, promoted unity.)*

BACKGROUND INFORMATION

ABOUT AKBAR'S PREDECESSORS Akbar was the third of the first six emperors known as India's "Great Moguls."

- The first was Babur, whose name means "the Tiger." In 1526, outnumbered four to one, he used artillery, barricades, and cavalry to overcome the war elephants of the defending ruler of Delhi.

- Four years later, at his death, his son Humayan took the reins of power, but enemies—Hindus and Afghans—recaptured lands that Babur had taken and drove Humayan out of India. It was during this troubled time that Humayan's son Akbar was born. In 1555 Humayan recaptured the empire, but died just six months later after an accidental fall in his palace.

CITIZENSHIP★

UNDERSTANDING GOVERNMENT Explain to the class that Akbar's levying lower taxes on less productive soil and higher taxes on more productive soil is an example of what is called "progressive taxation." The rate of taxation goes up as the amount of income produced goes up. This is the principle on which the United States federal income tax has been based—the lower one's income, the lower the percentage of it taken in taxes; as incomes go higher, the percentages taken of them in taxes go higher too.

AN ERA OF HARMONY

In Chapter 10, p. 273, the *Background Information* explained that when Muslims conquered non-Muslim lands, they charged non-Muslims an annual fee if those people chose to retain their own religions. Remind students of it. In India, this tax was called a *jizya*.

- ● *What city did Akbar make his capital?* (Have students locate the city, Agra, on the map on p. 393.)

- ● *What were the first two steps Akbar took to encourage unity between Hindus and Muslims?* (marrying an important Hindu leader's daughter and making Hindus officials in his Muslim-led government)

- ● *What did he do about the jizya? What other religious freedom did he extend to the Hindus?* (removed it; the right to build temples again)

★**THINKING FURTHER:** *Making Conclusions* **Would you call Akbar a religiously tolerant leader? Why or why not?** (Akbar's interest in Muslim, Hindu, and Christian beliefs reflects a high level of religious tolerance.)

Discussing The Leader's Interests
Encourage the class to examine the illustrations on these pages and to work back and forth between them and the text.

- ● *How do you know that, in spite of his inability to read, Akbar was a great scholar?* (his library, his love of study, and his amazing memory)

- ● *How do you know he was a great patron of the arts and crafts?* (his intense interest in and support of them)

★**THINKING FURTHER:** *Making Conclusions* **Based on the text and the works shown here, what kinds of arts and crafts did Akbar love?** (music, painting, poetry, fine carpets, curtains, weapons, jewelry)

Today only official buildings like the Hall of Public Audience (left) remain in Fatehpur Sikri. Akbar had the city built in 1570.

AN ERA OF HARMONY

When he was 20, Akbar married the daughter of an important Hindu leader. The young emperor then hired his wife's father and other Hindus to work with him in his capital city of Agra. For the first time, Hindus became top officials in a Muslim-led government.

In 1579 the emperor passed a law that won him even more support among Hindus. That law did away with the tax that earlier Muslim leaders had forced all non-Muslims to pay. Akbar also allowed Hindus to build temples once more. These acts showed that the new emperor wanted Hindus to be treated more fairly under Mogul law.

Akbar himself had a strong interest in other religions. He had a special building constructed at his palace where Muslims, Hindus, Christians, and other religious leaders could meet and explain their beliefs. It is said that Akbar would pace back and forth on walkways above the building floor, listening to those sitting below. At times he would toss out questions that sparked heated debates.

The Leader's Interests

In addition to learning from such debates, Akbar learned from books in his library. The library included custom-made translations of Hindu, Persian, Arabic, and Greek classics. Since he could not read, Akbar had someone read to him every day. His legendary memory helped him to remember most of what he heard.

Akbar also loved the beauty of arts and crafts. He paid fortunes to bring Asia's best painters, poets, musicians, and craftworkers to his palace. During the day he often visited the palace's 100 workshops. There experts made carpets, curtains, weapons, jewelry, and paintings, among other things. It was not uncommon to see the emperor hammering iron, shaving camel hair, or discussing painting. At night musicians played for him and sometimes he joined in on drums.

394

Akbar oversaw the creation of many new buildings. Under his direction workers built several huge forts and new palaces.

In this painting an artist captured the creation of one of Akbar's palaces in Fatehpur Sikri. What does the painting tell you about how buildings were made in Akbar's time?

MANY VOICES
PRIMARY SOURCE

Painting from Mogul India depicting the building of Fatehpur Sikri, 1570

This painting is one of a series illustrating a biography of Akbar by his closest assistant. It shows ordinary people working together to create a lasting legacy of the Mogul empire.

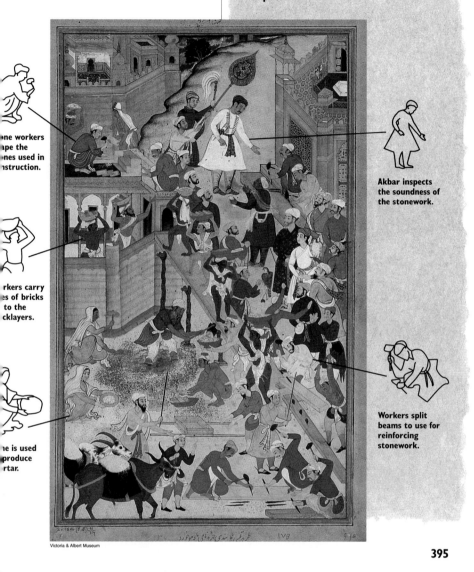

ne workers ape the nes used in nstruction.

rkers carry es of bricks to the cklayers.

ne is used produce rtar.

Akbar inspects the soundness of the stonework.

Workers split beams to use for reinforcing stonework.

Victoria & Albert Museum

395

★**THINKING FURTHER:** *Making Conclusions* **According to the text and illustration here, in what additional form of art was Akbar interested?** *(architecture, as shown by his hands-on involvement with building forts and palaces)*

MANY VOICES
PRIMARY SOURCE

Discussing the PRIMARY SOURCE

Give students a few minutes to study this painting and its captions. Encourage them to identify the many different jobs that are being done in it and to identify Akbar as the overseer of it all.

● *Why is all this work being done?* (Akbar had a new palace built at Fatehpur Sikri.)

● *Where is Akbar shown and what is he doing?* (in the upper center, giving directions to workers)

● *What different jobs can you identify as being involved in the building?* (stonecutting, stone grinding, mortar making, stone and mortar carrying, stone laying—and fanning the emperor)

★**THINKING FURTHER:** *Cause and Effect* **How do you think a grand, newly built palace might have affected life in the Mogul civilization?** *(It would have further encouraged the development of arts and crafts there, and it would have given citizens a new source of pride in their empire.)*

GLOBAL CONNECTION

MOVING A CAPITAL Moving a capital from one place to another happens time and again across the globe.

● In the early days of the United States, the national capital moved several times—from Philadelphia, Pennsylvania, to New York City to Washington, D.C.

● In more recent times, India moved its capital from Calcutta and built a new capital called New Delhi, alongside original Delhi. Building went on from 1912 to 1929, and New Delhi was inaugurated in 1931.

● In 1957 Brazil decided to move its capital from coastal Rio de Janeiro hundreds of miles inland. Built in the shape of a giant airliner, Brasília became Brazil's capital in 1960.

CURRICULUM CONNECTION

LINKS TO ART Call for a volunteer team to research art from Mogul India. Time-Life's *Historic India* contains an excellent color portfolio called "Exploits of Akbar," with a story line and illustrations from *Akbarnama,* a history of his reign that Akbar himself commissioned. Have the team prepare their findings to present to the class.

SECOND-LANGUAGE SUPPORT

USING VISUALS These students should be encouraged to use their English skills as they retell lesson events. Assign lesson sections to small groups to create a poster depicting the main events of their section. Then have students retell the events in their own words.

SHAH JAHAN

The Taj Mahal has made Shah Jahan one of the best-known emperors of India.

● **Who was Shah Jahan?** *(Akbar's grandson and a later emperor)*

★ **THINKING FURTHER:** *Making Conclusions* **Why might it be fair to say that Shah Jahan was one of the most extravagant people who ever lived?** *(Possible answer: The cost and design of his throne alone seems to give him claim to that title.)*

Discussing The Taj Mahal Tell students that the Taj Mahal is often mentioned as an example of both beauty and luxury.

● **Why did Shah Jahan build the Taj Mahal?** *(as a tomb for his beloved wife Mumtaz Mahal, who died in childbirth)*

● **In what ways is it an extravagant building?** *(No expense was spared to build it, and the building process took nearly 20 years.)*

★ **THINKING FURTHER:** *Making Conclusions* **The Taj Mahal has been called "the jewel in India's architectural crown." As you look at the illustration of it on this page, why do you think it deserves this description?** *(Help students to pick out and appreciate such details as the symmetry of its four towers, its use of large and smaller arches and domes, its simple yet elegant design.)*

Understanding Trading with Europe Once again trade fostered growth.

● **What was the state of India's economy under the Mogul emperors like Shah Jahan?** *(Its trade was booming, thanks in part to the demand of three continents for its cotton fabric and its supplies of silks and spices.)*

★ **THINKING FURTHER:** *Making Conclusions* **Why is it probably safe to assume that the Mogul emperors claimed a big cut of profits made from India's international trade?** *(Booming trade would have been a good source of the wealth spent on their costly arts and building projects.)*

SHAH JAHAN

In 1605 Akbar died at the age of 63. As his legacy, he left behind one of the wealthiest and most powerful empires in the world at that time.

Akbar's grandson, Shah Jahan (SHAH juh HAHN) ruled the Mogul empire from 1628 to 1658. His name meant "Emperor of the World" in Arabic. In addition to expanding the empire, Shah Jahan spent immense fortunes constructing spectacular objects and buildings. His throne alone cost twice as much to make as the palace of Akbar in which it sat! The throne took seven years to build and was made of diamonds, pearls, rubies, and other jewels set in gold.

The Taj Mahal

The tomb Shah Jahan had made for his wife, Mumtaz Mahal (mum TAHZ mah HAHL), or "Chosen One of the Palace," was even more amazing. Mumtaz Mahal died during childbirth in 1631. The grief-stricken emperor ordered his chief architect and thousands of workers to build a special tomb for her in Agra. No expense was spared. When it was completed nearly 20 years later, the Taj Mahal stood as one of the most beautiful buildings ever made.

The white marble dome of the Taj Mahal rises some 20 stories from the ground. Passages from the Koran elegantly carved over each gateway

396

describe the paradise said to await all Muslims upon death. In this way the Taj Mahal honors not only the life of Mumtaz Mahal and her husband, but also the beliefs of Islam.

Trading With Europe

The Taj Mahal was one of the costliest buildings ever built under Mogul rule. One reason Shah Jahan could afford to spend so much on it was because trade in India was booming as never before. India's cotton fabric now clothed many people in Asia and even Africa and Europe. For the first time, spices and silks were sold directly to eager merchants from Portugal, England, and the Netherlands. In Chapter 19 you will read about how Europeans took part in Indian life.

The Mogul empire is known for its beautiful jewelry and the Taj Mahal (left), built by Shah Jahan in honor of his wife (far left).

WHY IT MATTERS

During the 1500s and 1600s, the rulers of the Mogul empire united most of the Indian subcontinent under one government. That government in turn benefited from India's growing trade with the rest of the world. Akbar also changed life in India by passing laws that promoted harmony between the Hindu majority and India's small but powerful Muslim population. By this time, Hinduism had spread to other regions of Asia, especially Southeast Asia. You will read about its influence there in the next lesson.

✓// Reviewing Facts and Ideas

MAIN IDEAS

- By 1200 India's Indus plain was controlled by Muslims who had arrived from central Asia.
- Akbar expanded the large and wealthy Mogul empire. He gave Hindus rights which had been denied them by other Mogul leaders.
- Akbar's grandson Shah Jahan built the Taj Mahal in honor of his wife and the religion of Islam.

THINK ABOUT IT

1. What was the Mogul empire?
2. Why was it helpful to the Mogul empire that Akbar was a strong military commander?
3. **FOCUS** How did Akbar's rule affect Hindus in the Mogul empire?
4. **THINKING SKILL** Describe the main *cause* that led Akbar to construct a special building for religious meetings. What is one *effect* this building might have had on life in India?
5. **WRITE** Write a paragraph describing the Taj Mahal.

397

Discussing WHY IT MATTERS Review the great changes in India under Mogul rule.

> ★**THINKING FURTHER: Compare and Contrast How would you construct a before-and-after picture of India—pre-Mogul and post-Mogul?** *(Pre-Mogul: Hindu majority and Hindus in power; Post-Mogul: still Hindu majority but Muslims in power, Muslim art styles much in evidence, India more prominent in world trade)*

⭐ 3 CLOSE

MAIN IDEAS
Have students write their answers and exchange papers for correction.

- ***By 1200, who controlled the Indus plain?*** *(Muslims from central Asia)*

- ***How did Akbar affect the size of the Mogul empire and Hindu rights there during his reign?*** *(He expanded the empire to fill nearly all the Indian subcontinent and he expanded Hindu rights by removing a tax on them, letting them build temples, and giving them government positions.)*

- ***How does the Taj Mahal praise both love and Islam beliefs?*** *(Shah Jahan had it built in honor of his beloved late wife and Islam.)*

EVALUATE
✓ **Answers to Think About It**

1. an empire established on the Indian subcontinent by Muslims from central Asia *Summarize*

2. His conquests expanded the empire. *Make Inferences*

3. It gave Hindus more religious rights than previous Muslim rulers had. *Make Conclusions*

4. Cause: he wanted to learn about a variety of religious beliefs—Muslim, Hindu, Christian. Effect: it perhaps made some in India more tolerant of differences in religious beliefs. *Cause and Effect*

5. In their paragraphs, students should describe form and function. *Make Conclusions*

Write About It Have students write a postcard home describing their reactions to a visit they have made to the Taj Mahal.

LESSON 4

Lesson Overview

Like other cultures of Southeast Asia, the Khmer kingdom of the 1100s reflected strong influences from India and China.

Lesson Objectives

★ Locate and describe the Khmer kingdom.

★ Identify its major achievements.

⭐ 1 PREPARE

MOTIVATE Have students examine the photos of Angkor Wat on this page and pp. 400-401. Try to have the May 1982 issue of *National Geographic* ("The Temples of Angkor: Ancient Glory in Stone") available as you do the *Read Aloud*. Help them visualize its vast size.

SET PURPOSE Refer students to the *Read to Learn* question and invite them to predict the answer. (The reference to "famous Hindu stories" should suggest India.) Tell them to explore the lesson to verify or correct their predictions.

⭐ 2 TEACH

Understanding THE BIG PICTURE
Have the class sit in pairs with one text open to this page and the other to the map on p. 385.

● **In what part of Asia is Angkor Wat located?** *(Southeast Asia)*

● **How did Indian and Chinese influences reach this region?** *(Indian traders arrived on their way to China, and Chinese merchants came too.)*

★THINKING FURTHER: *Making Conclusions* **How might the location of the Khmer kingdom have contributed to its development?** *(It was on a trading route, opening it to trade and ideas from other cultures.)*

Resource **REMINDER**

Practice and Project Book: *p. 81*

Focus Activity

READ TO LEARN

What cultures influenced the Khmer of Southeast Asia?

PEOPLE

• Jayavarman II
• Suryavarman II

PLACES

• Mekong River
• Tonle Sap
• Angkor
• Phnom Penh

398

| 800 | | 1450 | 1550 | 1800 |

The Khmer of Southeast Asia

Read Aloud

The stone temple enclosed an area the size of 370 football fields. Its walls were covered with carvings of famous Hindu stories. At its center rose five towers shaped like the buds of water lilies. On the first day of spring, visitors standing at the temple's west gate could see the sun rise directly over the highest tower. This was fitting since the name of the temple's patron meant "one protected by the sun."

THE BIG PICTURE

The temple described above is called Angkor Wat (ANG kawr WAHT). Today it is a tourist attraction in the country of Cambodia. Some 700 years ago, however, it was the center of a great kingdom in Southeast Asia.

About 2,000 years ago, Indian merchants stopped at various places in Southeast Asia. The peninsula region of Southeast Asia includes what are now Vietnam, Cambodia, Thailand, Myanmar, and Laos. Some stopped at the mouth of the Mekong (MAY KAHNG) River, a highway of ships and goods since ancient times. Chinese merchants and diplomats also came, bringing their own traditions. As a result, Indian traditions of Hinduism and Buddhism began to take root in Southeast Asia.

Many civilizations were enriched by Chinese and Indian traditions. One of those, along the Mekong, was the Khmer (kuh MER) Kingdom. It occupied present-day Cambodia. Angkor Wat, built in the 1100s, was one of many amazing structures in the Khmer kingdom.

SHELTERED INSTRUCTION

READING STRATEGIES & LANGUAGE DEVELOPMENT

PREDICTING Tell students that what they learned about various civilizations in earlier lessons can help them make predictions about the Khmer of Southeast Asia. Review the cultural pattern they learned: the rise of a people (often led by a strong leader and assisted by strong trade), the achievement of great works, the weakening of the culture. Have students brainstorm predictions about the Khmer, based on what they learned about other civilizations. Note their ideas on the board. Encourage students to evaluate their predictions as they read this lesson. **[SDAIE STRATEGY: BRIDGING]**

WORDS OFTEN CONFUSED Point out to the class that Angkor Wat is a great tourist *sight*. What other words—homophones—are pronounced the same way? *(site and cite)*. Write the three words on the board and have students differentiate among the meanings and spellings of the three.

LIFE ALONG THE MEKONG

The Mekong, like many of the world's great rivers, provides needed water and silt to farmers of Southeast Asia. During the monsoon rains, torrents of rainwater fill the Mekong to overflowing. In fact, so much water pours into the river that a branch of it starts to flow *backward* into Tonle Sap (tahn LAY SAP) or "Great Lake." When the rains end, that branch of the Mekong flows forward again and the Tonle Sap returns to its normal size. Locate the Mekong and Tonle Sap on the map.

About 2,000 years ago, Khmer farmers were already using floods along the Mekong and Tonle Sap. Plentiful silt and water allowed them to grow large rice crops. Along with fish, rice became a mainstay of Khmer meals.

Farmers and God-Kings

A food surplus made it possible for a complex civilization to grow in Cambodia. Like their counterparts in ancient Egypt and medieval Europe, Khmer farmers often worked on land owned by religious or government officials. The rice, fruits, vegetables, and livestock that farmers raised fed temple workers, craftworkers, and nobles as well.

Much of the surplus supported the head of Khmer society, the king. The Khmer believed that their king was not only all-powerful, but a living god as well. One of Cambodia's first kings, Jayavarman II (jah yah VAHR mahn), ruled in the 800s. He, like many Khmer kings to come, observed Hindu traditions and claimed to be a human form of the god Shiva.

Khmer, whether farmers or nobles, were expected to do their part to support their god-king. In local markets women sold rice, fish, and fruits like bananas. Like other workers, they gave some of their goods to the king as taxes. Military leaders promised:

We will not revere another king. . . . If there is a war, we will strive to fight and disregard life, with all our soul, in devotion to the king. . . . The reward of those who are devoted to their masters, may we obtain it from this world into the next.

Kings, in return, built canals and roads in the kingdom. Canals watered the fields, producing better crops. Roads provided better means of transportation. Kings also led troops in war and judged disputes.

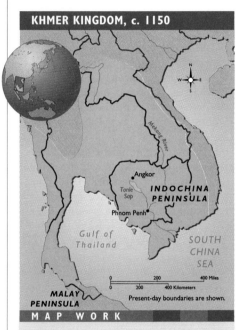

KHMER KINGDOM, c. 1150

Angkor

Tonle Sap

Phnom Penh

INDOCHINA PENINSULA

Gulf of Thailand

SOUTH CHINA SEA

Mekong River

MALAY PENINSULA

0 200 400 Miles
0 200 400 Kilometers
Present-day boundaries are shown.

MAP WORK

Trade and travel routes helped the cultures of southeast Asia to grow.

1. The Mekong River empties into which body of water?
2. On which peninsula is Phnom Penh located?

MAP WORK: 1. South China Sea **2.** Indochina Peninsula

399

CITIZENSHIP★

PRESERVING OUR HERITAGE Remind the students of the *Citizenship* note in Chapter 4, p. 75, dealing with the vandalism that scarred the Sphinx. Explain that Angkor Wat has also suffered from vandalism in recent years. Soldiers from several different regimes have passed through and aimed rifle fire on walls and great stone heads. Invite students to comment on how such behavior robs the entire world, not just Cambodia, of a priceless heritage.

CURRICULUM CONNECTION

LINKS TO READING To underscore the vandalism in Angkor, call for a volunteer to read the short "The Temples of Angkor: Will They Survive?" *National Geographic*, May 1982, and report to the class.

LIFE ALONG THE MEKONG

The 2,600 mile-long Mekong is one of Asia's ten longest rivers.

More **MAP WORK**

Refer students to the map and have them work with the text and map.

- *Follow the flow of the Mekong River with your finger. Through how much of the Indochina peninsula does it flow? Into what body of water does it empty?* (down the entire length of it; the South China Sea)

- *How does the Mekong encourage crop growing? How do monsoons over Southeast Asia help farming?* (by providing silt and water; by making the Mekong overflow with more water)

- *Locate Tonle Sap. What is it? How do monsoons help create it?* (A great lake; rain-laden monsoons make the Mekong overflow.)

★**THINKING FURTHER: Cause and Effect** *How did flooding and monsoons affect the diet of the Khmer?* (It gave them the great amounts of water needed to grow rice and watered the rivers where fish could grow in abundance.)

Discussing Farmers and God-Kings Help students understand the Khmer social structure.

- *For whom did Khmer farmers grow their crops?* (They often worked for landlords—religious or government officials—and raised surpluses to feed non-farmers as well as themselves.)

★**THINKING FURTHER: Compare and Contrast** *How were kings like Jayavarman II similar to the pharaohs of Egypt?* (The Khmer kings too claimed to be gods as well as supreme rulers, though they upheld Hindu rather than Egyptian beliefs; they started and supported major public works to improve production and transportation; they acted as military leaders and government officials.)

A CAPITAL CITY

Refer students to the map on p. 399 and have them trace the extent to which the Khmer empire grew, covering much of the Indochina peninsula and a good part of the Malay peninsula.

- **Why might location, amount of land, and a long coastline all have helped to enrich the Khmer kingdom?** *(All these elements contributed resources and shipping points to build up trade.)*

- **Why did the Khmer king Suryavarman II use the term "Angkor" in the name of his capital?** *(It means "holy city," and the giant stone temple he built there made it a "holy city.")*

★**THINKING FURTHER:** *Compare and Contrast* **What similarities can you identify between the building of Angkor Wat and the building of the pyramids in Egypt? What differences can you identify?** *(Similarities: both built of stones transported some distance by boat, use of farmers as labor. Differences: design—the shapes used—and style—slab-sided pyramids vs. carved stone figures.)*

Discussing The Walls of Angkor Thom Have students recognize the recurring theme of trying to outdo one's predecessors.

★**THINKING FURTHER:** *Compare and Contrast* **How would you compare and contrast Jayavarman VII to his great-grandfather Suryavarman II?** *(He too built a great stone temple, Angkor Thom, but his temple stressed Buddhism rather than his ancestor's Hindu beliefs.)*

Exploring The Decline of Angkor Discuss the forces that led to decline.

★**THINKING FURTHER:** *Predicting* **Did what eventually happened to the Khmer kingdom agree with or contradict your predictions for it? How?** *(Most students probably did predict eventual decline, but have them identify the reasons for it in this case—continual wars and building projects, all of which drained national wealth.)*

A CAPITAL CITY

Between 800 and 1200, Khmer forces expanded the borders of their kingdom into present-day Vietnam, Laos, and Thailand. The map on page 399 shows the territory of the Khmer. This expansion made the kingdom rich. In the early 1100s the king was Suryavarman II (sur yuh VAHR mun). He used a large part of this wealth to build a temple in the capital city of Angkor, on the north shore of Tonle Sap. You read about this temple, Angkor Wat, at the lesson's beginning. *Angkor* means "holy city" in the Khmer language.

Angkor Wat was the biggest temple built by the Khmer up to that time. Like the pyramids of ancient Egypt, it was built with thousands of stones from distant sources. Farmers working as laborers loaded the heavy stones onto boats. Stones were transported about 20 miles on canals. Architects designed the temple so that, in the spring, the sun shone on the walls, which told Hindu stories about the world's creation. At year's end, by contrast, the sun highlighted scenes that described death.

The Walls of Angkor Thom

One of the boys who watched Angkor Wat being built was the king's great-grandson, the future Jayavarman VII. When he became king in 1181, Jayavarman VII set out to create an even grander complex than his great-grandfather's. His Angkor Thom (ANG kawr TAWM) became just that. In 1296 a Chinese diplomat named Zhou Daguan visited the city. He wrote this description:

The city walls are approximately 2.5 miles in circumference. They have five gateways and each gate is a double one. On the outer side of the wall is a great moat. On either side of the moat's bridges are 54 stone gods like "stone generals;" they are gigantic and terrible to look at.

At the center of the city stood a large temple. This one honored Buddhist, rather than Hindu, beliefs. In this respect Jayavarman VII differed greatly from his forefathers. Over time many Khmer would adopt Buddhism as their religious belief. Today, as a sign of this change, Angkor Wat itself contains Buddhist as well as Hindu statues, and the people of Cambodia are mostly followers of Buddhism.

GLOBAL CONNECTION

KHMER ACHIEVEMENT AMONG CIVILIZATIONS IN THE WORLD Here is how one scholar ranks the temples of ancient Khmer: "a combination of physical and spiritual grandeur found elsewhere only in ancient Greece and Egypt, among the Maya and Aztecs, and in the medieval Europe of the Gothic cathedrals."

SECOND-LANGUAGE SUPPORT

RESEARCH Encourage students to do research to find more illustrations of Angkor Wat. With the illustrations and information they find, students will create a travel brochure describing the beauty and wonders of Angkor Wat. The brochure should point out the major sights to visit. Tell students to skim the lesson and other information for words and phrases to use in their travel brochure.

Angkor Wat (above) was built by the Khmer in the 1100s. Many of the statues at the temple (left) represent both Hindu and Buddhist figures.

The Decline of Angkor

The great building projects of Angkor drained Khmer resources. So did the constant wars that Khmer kings waged against neighboring kingdoms. Their strongest enemies were kingdoms that were in what are today Vietnam and Thailand. Jayavarman VII won control over both kingdoms, but they broke free of Khmer rule after his death. In the 1430s Thai soldiers attacked Angkor itself. The city was abandoned shortly thereafter. Khmer rulers moved their capital to a site farther south along the Mekong. Later the kingdom would become known as Kampuja and its capital as Phnom Penh (puh NOM PEN). It remains Cambodia's capital city today.

WHY IT MATTERS

The Khmer are just one of the many peoples who built a lasting civilization in the monsoon environment of Southeast Asia. As a reminder of their ancient heritage, today's Cambodians have put an image of Angkor Wat at the center of their flag. Each time they salute their flag, Cambodians honor the special blend of traditions that makes their country unique.

✓// Reviewing Facts and Ideas

MAIN IDEAS

- The Khmer kingdom of Southeast Asia was located along major shipping routes between India and China. For this reason, Indian and Chinese traditions became part of life in the Khmer kingdom.
- Khmer kings were considered to be living gods who deserved great power and respect.
- In the 1100s and 1200s, Khmer kings ordered the construction of great buildings and temples in the capital city of Angkor.

THINK ABOUT IT

1. Why was the Mekong River important to life in early Cambodia?

2. Explain why an advanced civilization was needed to build a place like Angkor Wat.

3. **FOCUS** How did Angkor Wat reflect what—or who—was most important to the Khmer?

4. **THINKING SKILL** What would you do to determine the *credibility* of the description of Angkor Thom quoted on page 400?

5. **GEOGRAPHY** How did monsoons affect life in early Cambodia?

401

Discussing **WHY IT MATTERS** Reinforce the lasting influence of Khmer civilization.

> ★**THINKING FURTHER:** *Summarizing* **For what reasons was Southeast Asia an environment that encouraged the development of lasting civilizations?** *(good place for growing crops, plenty of waterways, long coastline, location at an important crossroads of trade)*

★ 3 CLOSE

MAIN IDEAS
Have students give verbal responses.

- **Why did India and China heavily influence the Khmer of Southeast Asia?** *(The Khmer kingdom was located along major shipping routes between the two, so it had a great amount of contact with both.)*

- **What helped make Khmer kings powerful and respected?** *(They were considered living gods as well as kings.)*

- **Why is Angkor so well remembered today?** *(It is the site of great stone buildings and temples.)*

EVALUATE
✓ **Answers to Think About It**

1. It provided silt and water for growing crops. *Make Conclusions*

2. Construction demanded high levels of organization, technology, and art. *Make Inferences*

3. Angkor Wat reflected the power of the Khmer kings, and the buildings themselves reflected the beliefs in the Hindu and Buddhist religions. *Make Conclusions*

4. examination of the city walls today *Fact/Opinion*

5. They brought the rains that caused the Mekong River to flood and leave soil-enriching silt, and they watered crops. *Five Themes of Geography: Human/ Environment Interactions*

Write About It Have students write a paragraph in which they describe how Southeast Asia was enriched by India and China and how it adapted influences from them.

MEETING INDIVIDUAL NEEDS

RETEACHING (Easy) Have students reread the *Read Aloud,* and review the illustrations of Angkor Wat. Then have them use colored pens, pencils, or crayons to draw the scene described in the *Read Aloud.*

EXTENSION (Average) Have students choose to be either Suryavarman II or Jayavarman VII. Tell them to write a letter that the king they chose might have written to his architect explaining what he wanted in the buildings he was commissioning and why.

ENRICHMENT (Challenging) Refer the class to the *National Geographic* article mentioned on p. 398. As a class project, have students examine the illustrations of and plan for Angkor Wat in it and use them to make a model. Materials may include clay for the buildings and walls and green paper for the grass.

LESSON 5

PAGES 402–407

Lesson Overview

China continued to produce magnificent civilizations—the Yuan dynasty, (a result of Mongol invasions), and the Ming dynasty, (a return to Chinese rule).

Lesson Objectives

★ Explain and locate the spread of the Mongol empire.

★ Identify and describe the achievements of the Yuan and Ming dynasties.

1 PREPARE

MOTIVATE Have a student do the *Read Aloud* and point out the photo of the Great Wall. Ask students if they have ever heard of Genghis Khan and his mounted Mongol warriors who came thundering out of the steppes north of China. Tell them that they have already met one group who claimed descent from this group—the Moguls of India. *(Mogul is Persian for Mongol.)*

SET PURPOSE Refer the class to the *Read to Learn* question. Do students suppose the Mongols affected China in the same ways that the Moguls affected India? Tell students to explore the lesson to find out. Preview *Vocabulary.*

2 TEACH

Understanding THE BIG PICTURE Invite students to recall what they have already learned about China.

● **In what ways did the Chinese continue to prosper?** *(richer rice crops, busy international trade, continued inventiveness)*

★**THINKING FURTHER:** *Predicting*
What do you predict will happen at this point in history? *(unstoppable invasion from the north)*

Resource REMINDER

Practice and Project Book: *p. 82*

Anthology: *The Splendours of Hangzhou: pp. 96–98; The Travels of Marco Polo, pp. 99–101*

Technology: *Adventure Time!* CD-ROM

| 800 | 1050 | 1209 | 1525 | 1800 |

Great Empires of China

Read Aloud

The walls that Shihuangdi and the Qin dynasty built along China's northern border were meant to protect against invaders. In the 1200s, though, these walls did little to stop a fierce group of conquerors. These invaders from the grasslands north of China had conquered much territory in Asia. Then they focused their might on the biggest prize of all: China.

Focus Activity

READ TO LEARN

How did the Mongols affect life in China?

VOCABULARY

• Grand Canal

PEOPLE

• Genghis Khan
• Kublai Khan
• Marco Polo

PLACES

• Beijing
• Forbidden City

THE BIG PICTURE

In the 1100s—while the Khmer were building Angkor and Europeans were fighting the Crusades—China was prospering as never before. Chinese farmers began to grow a new kind of rice developed by the Khmer and their neighbors. They were able to grow more of this rice in less time, especially in southern China's warm and wet climate. Huge surpluses were shipped to faraway cities using a system of canals that kept water flowing for hundreds of miles.

Port cities such as Guangzhou (GWAHNG JOO)—later known as Canton—linked China to international trade. In those busy cities people made new kinds of printed books, paintings, compasses, and large ships that could carry as many as 500 people.

All of this was threatened in the 1200s, when invaders from the north set out to take over China. China's ancient border walls could not stop them. These invaders were called Mongols. They were herders and horse-riding experts from the grassy steppes north of China. Sheep provided much of what they needed. The Mongols also depended on trade for goods such as cloth and weapons.

SHELTERED INSTRUCTION

READING STRATEGIES & LANGUAGE DEVELOPMENT

PROBLEM AND SOLUTION Remind students that identifying problems and solutions is a good way to make sense of what they read. Share the first three paragraphs of *The Big Picture* and state the problem and solution. [China was prospering as never before, so the Mongols invaded to seize the country and plunder its wealth.] Have students create political cartoons that reflect the goals of the Chinese and the Mongols. Encourage students to look for problems and solutions as they read the lesson. **[SDAIE STRATEGY:** TEXT RE-PRESENTATION**]**

WORD ORIGIN Point out to the class that the term *khan* comes up in two names in this lesson—Genghis Khan and Kublai Khan. Explain that it comes from a Turkic word meaning "prince" or "local chieftain."

NORTHERN INVADERS

In 1209, Mongol leader Genghis Khan (JENG gihs KAHN) united Mongol communities to conquer China, their main source of supplies. The Mongols rode south into China. They were helped by Chinese military leaders who joined their side after being defeated. When Genghis Khan died in 1227 he controlled almost all of northern China.

Kublai Khan

In 1252 Genghis Khan's grandson Kublai Khan (KOO bli KAHN) invaded southern China. After 27 years, all of China yielded to Kublai Khan's rule. China's Mongol rulers were called the Yüan dynasty. How would Mongols, who lived neither on farms nor in cities, govern a land of both?

Kublai Khan's answer was to have Mongols oversee China's already vast government. Kublai Khan made tax collection easier, though, by establishing paper money. The world's first all-paper money system made things easier on people's pockets. One note replaced about 8 pounds of coins!

Kublai Khan also oversaw the expansion of the Grand Canal. This canal had been built many years earlier to connect the Huang and Chang rivers. With Kublai Khan's expansion, it connected the new capital city, Beijing (BAY JING), with cities over 1,000 miles to the south. The Grand Canal is still used for shipping today.

Kublai Khan assigned soldiers to protect merchants traveling on the ancient Silk Road that connected Asia with Europe. You will read more about the Silk Road and one man who traveled on it, Marco Polo, in the Info-graphic on page 406.

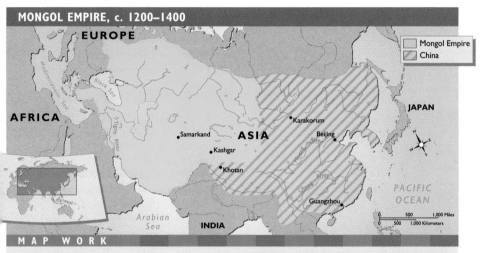

MONGOL EMPIRE, c. 1200–1400

EUROPE
AFRICA
ASIA
JAPAN
Karakorum
Samarkand
Beijing
Kashgar
Khotan
Guangzhou
PACIFIC OCEAN
Arabian Sea
INDIA
Mediterranean Sea
Black Sea
Tigris River

Legend:
☐ Mongol Empire
▨ China

500   1,000 Miles
500   1,000 Kilometers

MAP WORK

In the 1200s the Mongol empire extended west into eastern Europe.

1. Which river flowed near the westernmost Asian boundary of Mongol lands?

2. About how far from Beijing is the mouth of the Tigris River?

3. Which cities in the empire were *not* in China?

MAP WORK: **1.** Tigris River **2.** about 4,000 miles (about 6,436 kilometers) **3.** Kashgar, Samarkand

403

· CURRICULUM CONNECTION

LINKS TO READING Students who would like to learn more about Genghis Khan may want to read *Chingis Khan* by Demi, published by Henry Holt and Company in 1991. It has many beautifully executed illustrations while it is light on text. Interested students might prepare a presentation of the book to the class.

LINKS TO READING AND VIEWING ABOUT THE MONGOL ARMY The British Broadcasting Corporation (BBC) produced a multi-part television series called *Storm from the East: From Genghis Khan to Khubilai Khan* available on video. A book of the same name based on the series was prepared by Robert Marshall and was published by University of California Press in 1993.

NORTHERN INVADERS

Point out that Ghengis Khan had help from military leaders inside China.

● **Who were the Mongols?** *(herders and horse riders from the steppes north of China)*

● **Why did their leader, Genghis Khan, want to invade China?** *(Help students to recognize a recurring theme here—wanting resources one's neighbor has.)*

★**THINKING FURTHER:** *Making Conclusions* **What tells you that Genghis Khan and his army were fearsome warriors?** *(their capture of Chinese cities and their winning control over most of northern China)*

More **MAP WORK**

Refer the class to the map on this page.

● **From how far west to east did the Mongol empire stretch?** *(from the Black Sea and Arabia to the Pacific)*

● **How many continents were involved?** *(two, Europe and Asia)*

Discussing Kublai Khan Help students see that it was Kublai Khan who completed the invasion.

● **How did Genghis Khan's grandson continue the Mongol invasion of China?** *(Kublai Khan took the invasion to southern China and eventually controlled all of China.)*

● **What new dynasty did Kublai Khan establish to rule China?** *(the Yuan)*

● **What way did he, a nomadic Mongol, find to rule the ancient Chinese state?** *(He had mongols oversee China's already vast goverment.)*

★**THINKING FURTHER:** *Making Conclusions* **In what ways was Kublai Khan good for the Chinese economy?** *(He improved trade routes by building the Grand Canal and protecting travel along the Silk Road and made tax collection easier by establishing paper money.)*

Help students grasp changes in power.

- **What circumstances led to the Ming dynasty?** *(Mongol control weakened, Chinese rulers grew stronger.)*

More **MAP WORK**

Refer students to the map and have them work with both text and map.

- **How would you describe the extent of territory Ming China covered?** *(from the Great Wall in the north to the South China Sea and 1,500 miles inland from the East China Sea)*

- **At what major city does the Grand Canal begin? What two major rivers does it cross?** *(Beijing; Huang and Chang Jiang)*

Discussing Cultural Expansion
List the Ming accomplishments.

- **What was the Forbidden City and for whom was it built?** *(a walled city built to house the Ming emperors)*

- **Why was it called the "Forbidden City"?** *(Ming Emperors lived and ruled from within the walls of this city.)*

- **What luxury products did Ming China produce?** *(porcelain, silk)*

- **For whom were they produced?** *(emperor's palace, overseas trade)*

- **From what you learned earlier, how far from China did trade of these goods reach?** *(Help students recall silk going to ancient Rome and porcelain found as far away as Great Zimbabwe.)*

- **How did China operate as a sea power before the late 1400s?** *(Trading ships went as far as East Africa.)*

Discussing Looking Inward Have students focus on effects of isolation.

- **What happened to China as a sea power after the late 1400s?** *(Shipping expeditions ended, and China turned inward.)*

★**THINKING FURTHER: Cause and Effect What caused this reversal?** *(a shift of resources to extend the Great Wall against threats of a Mongol invasion)*

THE MING DYNASTY

After Kublai Khan's death in 1294, Mongol control over China began to weaken. Terrible floods along the Huang River, famine, and disease added to the country's distress. In 1368 the Mongols were driven out by rebel Chinese forces. Chinese rulers once again came to control China. The Ming Dynasty had begun.

Cultural Expansion

During the Ming dynasty's 276-year history, China prospered. Between 1417 and 1420 almost one million people worked to build the Forbidden City in Beijing. Stoneworkers and carpenters built almost 1,000 stately palaces, libraries, temples, and gardens. Ming emperors lived and ruled from within the walls of this city. Outside the poor

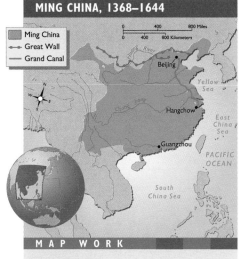

MING CHINA, 1368–1644

- Ming China
- Great Wall
- Grand Canal

0 400 800 Miles
0 400 800 Kilometers

Beijing
Yellow Sea
Hangchow
East China Sea
Guangzhou
PACIFIC OCEAN
South China Sea

MAP WORK

Ming rulers expanded the canal system to increase trade.

1. To which sea did the Grand Canal link Beijing?
2. The Great Wall extended along which of China's borders?

404 MAP WORK: 1. East China Sea 2. northern border

sang to passersby, asking for money. You can see one of their songs on the next page.

When the Forbidden City was completed, China's best porcelain, silk, and paintings were sent to fill its palaces and kitchens. The Ming government controlled thousands of porcelain workshops. They produced blue-and-white dishes that became world-famous. The government also controlled silk workshops. In those shops women and children over the age of 10 worked to produce China's valuable silk cloth.

Many of these luxury products went to the emperor's palace. Still more were bought by foreign merchants. Some merchants brought goods home along the Silk Road. Others shipped their goods from port cities like Guangzhou.

In 1405 large ships were built to take Ming officials on trading expeditions. The largest ship was about 400 feet long! Ming ships reached East Africa.

Looking Inward

With the new ships, China was well on its way to becoming the world's greatest sea power. That changed in the late 1400s, when Ming concerns shifted northward once again. Fears of another Mongol invasion grew. Ming emperors focused China's resources on the Great Wall as protection. They strengthened and extended the walls Shihuangdi had built almost 2,000 years earlier.

Because their resources were being used to protect their borders, the Ming abandoned efforts in shipbuilding. Expeditions were expensive and the Ming government was not interested in expansion. By the year 1525 it had given up all efforts in sea travel. China's interests turned inward for the next several centuries.

CITIZENSHIP ★

UNDERSTANDING GOVERNMENT Explain to the class that governments are often divided into two or more factions that disagree on what government policy should be. For example, in the American government, Democrats and Republicans often back different policies. Similarly, Ming China's government was divided into factions regarding shipping.

- One set of the emperor's advisers backed foreign trade and approved of the wealth it brought to them personally.

- The other set of advisers, the Confucians, directly opposed foreign trade. They questioned the benefit for the nation from the wealth brought by trade. They also argued that trade suggested that China needed things from the outside, hinting it was not self-sufficient—an idea unworthy of the dragon throne.

Have the class discuss the points of view of each set of advisers and ask students to be prepared to support their own point of view.

MANY VOICES
MUSIC

Fung Yang Song

Chinese Folk Song
Arranged by Marilyn Davidson

Pronunciation: jooaw shohoo looaw yoo shohoo goo
English: Sing the Fung Yang song. Sing it loud and long.

shohoo nah looaw goo lahee chahng guh
With drums and cym-bals we sing the Fung Yang song.

biheh dee guh ur waw yeh boo hway chahng
This is a song we can sing the whole day long.

juh hway chahng guh fung yahng guh
We strike the gong to the Fung——— Yang——— song.

405

MANY VOICES
PRIMARY SOURCE

**Discussing
"Fung Yang Song"**

Help students to learn this simple song and encourage them to use cymbals, drums, and gongs to beat out the rhythm as they sing, as called for by the song's lyrics.

● *Would you describe this as a simple or difficult song? Why?* (Students will probably find the melody and lyrics quite simple.)

★THINKING FURTHER: *Making Conclusions* **Why do you suppose the Chinese might like to sing songs like these?** (Possible answer: to pass the time on a long hike to the fields or as a work song while they are doing repetitive chores)

BACKGROUND INFORMATION

ABOUT CHINESE MUSIC
● Chinese music flourished under the Shang dynasty, but its roots go back much further.

● Its melody is usually based on a 5-tone scale.

● Standard Chinese musical instruments include lutes, fiddles (which have only two strings), zithers, a double-reed instrument that produces a buzzing sound, cymbals, gongs, clappers, and drums.

GLOBAL CONNECTION

THE INFLUENCE OF CHINESE MUSIC Both the styles and instruments of Chinese music have spread to Korea, Japan, and throughout Southeast Asia.

SECOND-LANGUAGE SUPPORT

USING VISUALS Second-language learners can use visuals for the epoch in this lesson. Work with students to create time lines of the events in each lesson in this chapter and compare simultaneous events.

1100s	China is a wealthy, advanced civilization.
1200s	Mongols conquer and rule China (*Genghis Khan, Kublai Khan*).
1368	Mongols are driven out by Chinese forces.
1368-1644	Ming Dynasty rules a rich and powerful China.

Infographic

Remind the class of the long history of the Silk Road. At one time, it bridged two great civilizations—ancient Rome and ancient China. Point out to students that during the time of the Roman emperors, the commodity for which the Silk Road was named was literally worth its weight in gold in Rome.

Discussing Trade on the Silk Road Have students use their fingers to trace the route of the Silk Road on the map. Use the *Infographic* to identify goods it carried.

- *Who was Marco Polo?* (a Venetian explorer who traveled the Silk Road during the 13th century)

- *Which dynasty ruled China at the time?* (the Yuan dynasty)

- *Who was the "Great Khan"?* (Kublai Khan, who ruled from 1252 to 1294)

- *What is the easternmost city he visited?* (Khanbalik, now known as Beijing)

- *Through what city in Turkey did he pass?* (Constantinople)

- *What kinds of goods did he see traded along the Silk Road?* (Besides silk, there were pearls, precious stones, porcelain, gold, and silver.)

- *What did he say about paper money?* (that the Great Khan's subjects were willing to be paid with paper money)

★THINKING FURTHER: *Making Conclusions* **Do you think that paper money was used for payment in Europe? Explain.** (Possible answer: probably not because Marco Polo would not have considered it unusual for the Chinese to accept paper money if it were used in Europe)

Technology CONNECTION

ADVENTURE TIME! CD-ROM
Enrich the *Infographic* with the *Discoveries Time Lines* activity on the *Adventure Time!* CD-ROM.

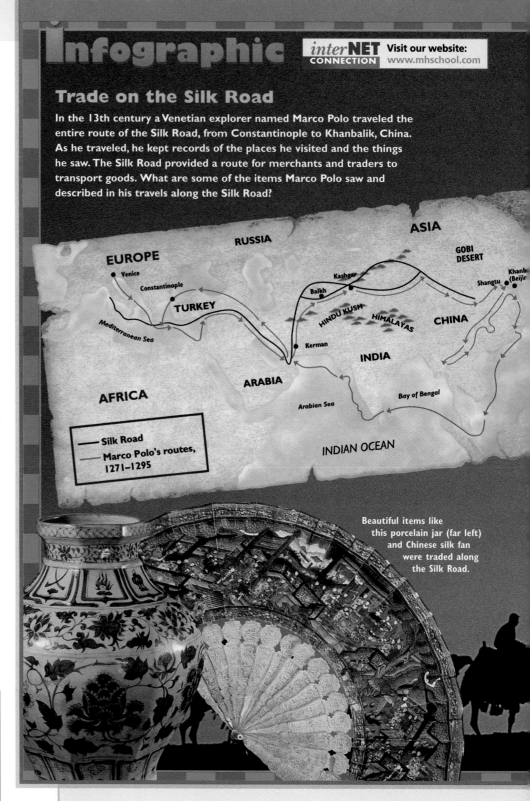

Trade on the Silk Road

In the 13th century a Venetian explorer named Marco Polo traveled the entire route of the Silk Road, from Constantinople to Khanbalik, China. As he traveled, he kept records of the places he visited and the things he saw. The Silk Road provided a route for merchants and traders to transport goods. What are some of the items Marco Polo saw and described in his travels along the Silk Road?

Silk Road
Marco Polo's routes, 1271–1295

Beautiful items like this porcelain jar (far left) and Chinese silk fan were traded along the Silk Road.

EXPANDING THE INFOGRAPHIC

RESEARCHING AND MAKING PRESENTATIONS Several aspects of Silk Road trade and of Marco Polo can be profitably explored. Divide the class into five groups and assign each group one of the following topics: the legendary city of Samarkand, Baghdad as a stop on the Silk Road, Marco Polo's journey to China, Marco Polo's years in China, Marco Polo's return to his native Italy. Have each group research its topic and make a presentation of their findings to the class. You might suggest the following sources:

- Encyclopedia and library catalog entries for *Silk Road, Samarkand, Baghdad,* and *Polo, Marco.*

- *National Geographic Index:* 1888-1988 entries for *Silk Road* and *Polo, Marco.*

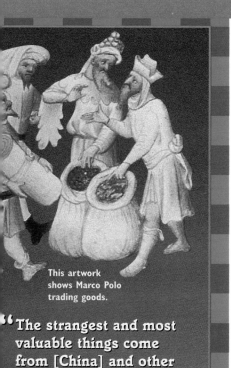

This artwork shows Marco Polo trading goods.

❝The strangest and most valuable things come from [China] and other provinces.... At least 1,000 cartloads of silk are sent [here] every day.❞

❝The Great Khan's subjects are perfectly willing to be paid in paper money since with it they can buy anything, including pearls, precious stones, gold, and silver.❞

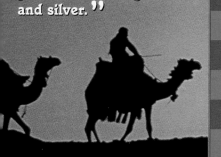

WHY IT MATTERS

Between the 1200s and 1500s, China underwent many changes. The Mongol invasions hurt once-bustling cities. Under Kublai Khan, though, China's cities and trade grew once again. In the Ming dynasty that followed, China became even stronger.

Wherever its trade goods went, China's ideas and traditions soon followed. China's influence was especially strong in the chain of islands that lay to the east. Those were the islands of Japan, which will be the focus of the next lesson.

✓∥ Reviewing Facts and Ideas

MAIN IDEAS

- Genghis Khan began the Mongol invasion of China in the 1200s.
- Kublai Khan ruled by using China's ancient government system. He also started the world's first all-paper money system and made the Silk Road safer for travel.
- Trade, cities, and sea travel grew under the early Ming dynasty. With the threat of foreign invasion, Ming emperors focused on defense projects such as the Great Wall.

THINK ABOUT IT

1. Why did Mongols invade China?
2. What did Kublai Khan do to govern China? Why might he have wanted to protect travelers?
3. **FOCUS** How did Kublai Khan improve life in China?
4. **THINKING SKILL** Make at least two _conclusions_ about the importance of trade in Ming China. On what facts did you base each conclusion?
5. **GEOGRAPHY** How did the Grand Canal affect movement in China?

407

Discussing WHY IT MATTERS Help students recognize the heritage of the Yuan dynasty for China.

> ★**THINKING FURTHER:** _Summarizing_ **How did Kublai Khan's Mongol rule contribute to the later achievements of the Ming dynasty?** (_Kublai Khan's achievements such as the development of paper money, expansion of the Grand Canal, and protection of Silk Road trade improved the infrastructure on which the Ming dynasty could build._)

⭐ 3 CLOSE

MAIN IDEAS

Call on students for answers.

- **Who invaded China in the 1200s?** (_Genghis Khan and the Mongols_)

- **What were some of Kublai Khan's achievements?** (_carrying on China's tried-and-true government system, developing a paper money system, and protecting Silk Road trade_)

- **Why did Ming emperors concentrate so heavily on defense and what defense was it?** (_The threat of another Mongol invasion from the north caused them to strengthen the Great Wall._)

EVALUATE
✓ **Answers to Think About It**

1. They wanted supplies that China had. _Summarize_

2. He kept China's ancient government structure in place; he wanted to build up China's trade. _Make Inferences_

3. paper money, expanding the Grand Canal, protecting Silk Road trade _Main Idea_

4. It provided jobs and wages for craftworkers; it provided income from trade. _Make Conclusions_

5. It made traveling and shipping goods the length of northeastern China easier.
Five Themes of Geography: Movement

Write About It Have students write a paragraph in which they compare Mongol rule of China with Mogul rule of India.

MEETING INDIVIDUAL NEEDS

RETEACHING (Easy) Have students make an illustrated chart of the great landmarks of Chinese civilization (such as the Great Wall, the Grand Canal, and the Forbidden City).

EXTENSION (Average) Tell students to picture themselves as Marco Polo first entering the court of Kublai Khan. Have them write a letter home describing Kublai Khan and his rule of China under the Yuan dynasty.

ENRICHMENT (Challenging) Divide the class into several groups and have them do research on the Forbidden City within Beijing, which has been open to the public as a museum since 1971 and has since spawned several picture books. Assign the groups topics such as size and surrounding walls, layout, the Hall of Supreme Harmony, shrines, and the gardens. Have them present their findings in class.

Lesson Overview
Making generalizations helps readers recognize similarities.

Lesson Objective
★ Make generalizations based on different pieces of evidence.

1 PREPARE

MOTIVATE Ask students if they have ever played a game (sometimes called *picture lotto*) in which they had to match pictures of objects such as flowers or animals. Point out to them that they were making generalizations then: they were recognizing similarities in objects. Have students read *Why the Skill Matters* to see why making generalizations is an important skill.

SET PURPOSE Point out to students that making generalizations is a process that follows certain steps. Have them read *Helping Yourself* to preview these steps.

2 TEACH

Using the Skill Lead students through the steps in this section.

- **What topic was chosen for making generalizations?** *(how people become powerful leaders)*

- **What three leaders are used as examples? Why?** *(Genghis Khan, Sunjata, and Alexander the Great: they became powerful leaders.)*

- **What differences do they show? What similarities?** *(Differences: time and place. Similarities: command of a strong military force, control over vast stretches of territory.)*

Resource **REMINDER**
Practice and Project Book: *p. 83*
Transparency: *Graphic Organizer*

Thinking Skills

Queen Elizabeth I (left) and Ghengis Khan were powerful leaders who ruled vast empires.

Making Generalizations

VOCABULARY
generalization

WHY THE SKILL MATTERS

In the last lesson you read about Ghengis Khan and the Mongols' rise to power in China. You have also read about other leaders and how they came to rule—Alexander the Great, Sunjata, and Elizabeth I, to name a few. If you compare their histories, you might notice certain similarities. As a result, you might make a general statement about what

things are necessary for people to become powerful leaders.

If you did so, you would be making a generalization. A generalization is a statement that points out a common feature shared among different things. A generalization shows how some things that might seem very different on the surface can actually be similar underneath.

Why are generalizations useful? Generalizations allow you to draw conclusions from specific examples. Once you make a generalization, you can better understand how

408

READING STRATEGIES & LANGUAGE DEVELOPMENT

MAKING GENERALIZATIONS Present this generalization to the class: "Many social studies skills, or thinking skills in general, involve making connections among pieces of information." As examples to support this point, mention cause and effect, comparing and contrasting, drawing conclusions, sequencing, as well as making generalizations. Discuss how making connections among various pieces of information helps us to understand why things happen as they do. This skill is as important in life as it is in social studies.

APOSTROPHES IN POSSESSIVES Use *the Mongols'* in *Why the Skill Matters* to reinforce the correct use of the apostrophe in possessives. Call on students to explain why the apostrophe is located after the *s* in this case (the noun is plural). Where would it be if the word were singular? (before the *s*)

things fit within a larger framework. You can see new relationships between separate things. This is very useful in the study of history. Use the Helping Yourself box to guide you in making generalizations.

USING THE SKILL

Suppose you wanted to make a generalization about how people become powerful leaders. To start, you might choose three leaders to serve as your examples. Say that you chose Ghengis Khan, Sunjata, and Alexander the Great.

Your next step would be to examine these different examples, looking for similarities. Ghengis Khan's great armies of soldiers and expert horsemen brought almost all of Northern China under his control in the 1200s. At roughly the same time in West Africa, the swift armies of the underestimated Sunjata helped him to rule the huge empire of Mali. Over 1,000 years earlier, Alexander the Great led his undefeated army to conquer vast lands from Asia Minor to Persia.

In order to make a generalization, think about what features or qualities these leaders may have shared. Recall that, by making the most of their powerful armies, all won control over vast stretches of land. The use of a strong military is therefore a feature that was common to all of these leaders.

More than one generalization might be made about this topic. Based on these facts, though, one possible generalization might be: Many leaders gain power as a result of control they have over a strong military force.

Helping yourself

- A generalization states a feature shared by a group of examples.
- Select a topic to make a generalization about.
- Identify a feature that relates to the topic and is common to all of the examples.
- Based on this common feature, make a generalization.

TRYING THE SKILL

You just made a generalization about leaders' rise to power. Now try making a generalization about how leaders can use their power to develop strong governments. Remember to look for common features with which to make a generalization.

Use as your examples the rules of Akbar, Elizabeth I, and Caesar Augustus. You may recall that Akbar faced religious conflict. Elizabeth I and Augustus were challenged by threats of war when they came to power. Akbar used his power to bring peace and religious tolerance to India. Elizabeth I faced down the Spanish Armada while England enjoyed the Renaissance. Augustus brought the Pax Romana to ancient Rome. How did their actions win these rulers special popularity, thereby strengthening their governments? What generalization can you make from these three examples?*

REVIEWING THE SKILL

1. What is a generalization?

2. How can generalizations help us to better understand history?

3. Consider whether or not generalizations are always true. Suppose you made the following statement: "Strong government results only when leaders address the greatest needs of their citizens." Do you think this generalization is always true? Explain.

4. What generalization can you make about leaders today? What facts did you use to make your generalization?

*They formed highly organized governments and found solutions to conflicts; their actions created peace and security for their subjects and therefore increased their popularity as leaders. **409**

★THINKING FURTHER: *Making Conclusions* **Why is comparing important in making generalizations?** *(Comparing points out common features shared by different examples; a generalization is a statement about shared features.)*

Trying the Skill Have students take another look at *Helping Yourself* before beginning this section. Also encourage them to use the index to refer to the leaders under discussion.

★THINKING FURTHER: *Making Generalizations* **What generalizations can you make from these three examples?** *(Generalizations will probably focus on leaders' personal style and substance, their courageous stands and actions, and an understanding of their people's wishes and needs.)*

⭐ 3 CLOSE

SUM IT UP
Have students write a paragraph in which they explain why being able to make sound generalizations is helpful in social studies and in life.

EVALUATE
✓ **Answers to Reviewing the Skill**

1. a statement which shows a common feature shared among different things

2. They show how things fit within a larger framework. They can show how historical events are related and can help us spot major themes and trends in history.

3. Answers may or may not support the generalization, but should be supported with facts.

4. Generalizations may vary, but should be supported with facts.

VISUAL LITERACY

ABOUT THE PORTRAIT OF QUEEN ELIZABETH I This portrait of Queen Elizabeth I was painted by George Gower, who was appointed as her royal portraitist in 1581. Queen Elizabeth I was a popular English monarch during her reign from 1558 until her death in 1603. She was a powerful public speaker and a devoted patron of the arts. She used her charm, grace, and intelligence to keep peace with the Spanish abroad and between the Protestants and Catholics at home. Her red hair reminded her subjects of her father, who was the popular King Henry VIII. Invite students to study the painting and share ideas about how it shows the character and stature of Queen Elizabeth I. Possible questions include: How has the artist brought the viewers' attention to her popular red hair? How does this portrait express her grace and royalty?

LESSON 6
PAGES 410–415

Lesson Overview
Japan emerged as a feudal society that emperors and shoguns ruled with religious and military power.

Lesson Objectives
★ Locate Japan and describe its feudal society.

★ Explain how the Tokugawa shoguns managed Japan's development in isolation from the rest of the world.

⭐ 1 PREPARE

MOTIVATE Have a student do the *Read Aloud.* Ask the class to identify the order of priorities it sets forth (first duty, then life, then money) and the group that accepted it (Japan's soldiers). Give students time to comment on these priorities and the values they reflect.

SET PURPOSE How did this order of priorities affect all of Japanese society? Encourage students to explore this lesson for answers to that question as well as to the *Read to Learn* question. Point out the typically Japanese torii gate in the photo. Preview the *Vocabulary*.

⭐ 2 TEACH

Understanding THE BIG PICTURE
Refer the class to the map of Asia on p. 385. Have them locate Japan.

● **What different kinds of cultural influences reached Japan?** *(Confucian teachings, Buddhism, Chinese writing and art, which came by way of Korea)*

● **With what native beliefs did these mingle?** *(Shinto religion, which held the Japanese emperor as god-king)*

★**THINKING FURTHER:** *Summarizing* **How would you characterize Japanese society?** *(one family headed by the emperor)*

Resource REMINDER
Practice and Project Book: *p. 84*
Anthology: *The Tale of Genji, pp. 102–103*
Outline Map

800 1050 1192 1867

Feudal Japan

Read Aloud
"Nothing is more important than duty. Second in importance comes life, and then money." To writer Muro Kyuso, who lived almost 300 years ago, these words described life for a certain group of people in Japan. They were Japan's soldiers.

Focus Activity

READ TO LEARN
What changes did the shoguns make in feudal Japan?

VOCABULARY
• Shinto
• shogun
• samurai

PEOPLE
• Yoritomo
• Tokugawa Ieyasu
• Lady Murasaki Shikibu

PLACES
• Edo
• Tokyo
• Kyoto

410

THE BIG PICTURE
As you read in Lesson 1, Japan is located in the Pacific Ocean east of mainland Asia. Its four main islands form a 2,000-mile-long archipelago. This arc stretches from Russia in the north toward the Korean Peninsula in the south. From ancient times Chinese and Korean people moved to the islands of Japan. They brought Confucian teachings with them. Immigrants from Korea also introduced Buddhism to Japan around A.D. 550, along with China's writing system and new forms of art.

These immigrants arrived in a region that already had ancient traditions of its own. Most important was the Japanese religion called Shinto (SHIN toh), or "the way of the gods." According to Shinto belief, everything on Earth has a spirit of its own, including the land and such crops as rice. As in ancient Greece, Japan's farmers tried to ensure good harvests by offering prayers before planting or harvesting. The most important prayers, though, were offered by Japan's emperor. The emperor's family was believed to be descended from the Shinto sun goddess.

In time Shinto, Buddhism, and Confucianism blended together in Japan to form a unique way of life. All Japanese were believed to be part of one big family, whose head was the emperor. As in all families, each member had duties to fulfill. Not all duties were the same, and not everyone had equal rank, as you will see.

SHELTERED INSTRUCTION
READING STRATEGIES & LANGUAGE DEVELOPMENT

SEQUENCING Review with students the sequence of events as civilizations develop and decline. Remind them that one stage grows out of another in chronological order. To help students review the lesson concept, have them skim the text and jot down the section headings and subheadings. Then have students predict the sequence of events in the development of feudal Japan. **[SDAIE STRATEGY: SCHEMA BUILDING]**

WORDS OFTEN CONFUSED Use the second sentence of *The Big Picture* on this page to reinforce the difference between *its* and *it's*. Have students identify the use of *its* here as a possessive pronoun and have them contrast this with the use of *it's* as a contraction of the pronoun *it* and the verb *is*.

A FEUDAL SYSTEM

The ruler of Japan was the emperor. However, powerful families fought for control over Japan's mountains and plains. One family won the long, fierce struggle for power in 1192. The emperor made the leader of this struggle, Yoritomo (yawr ee TOH moh), Japan's first shogun, or military commander. Yoritomo changed the way Japan was governed. While the emperor headed Japan in name, the shogun ruled the country as military dictator.

Samurai Warriors

Life in Japan, like life in Europe at this time, was shaped by a type of feudalism. Lords controlled large pieces of land, which were worked by farmers. Protecting the lords and their lands were soldiers called samurai. They believed their main duty was to remain loyal to their lord. "Nothing is so important in a warrior as loyalty," wrote one samurai in the 1400s.

Although lords held great power in their regions, they were considered vassals of the shogun. Lords had to serve the shogun. This service could mean providing rice or samurai for war. In return the shogun granted new lands or privileges to lords.

The shogun, his lords, and their samurai formed the upper part of Japan's social pyramid. Below them were farmers, craftworkers, and merchants. These commoners—non-nobles—had to show utmost respect to those above them in society. Whenever a lord and his samurai passed through a village, servants shouted "Down! Down!" This signal prompted commoners to fall face-down on the ground in respect. Those who did not do so risked death.

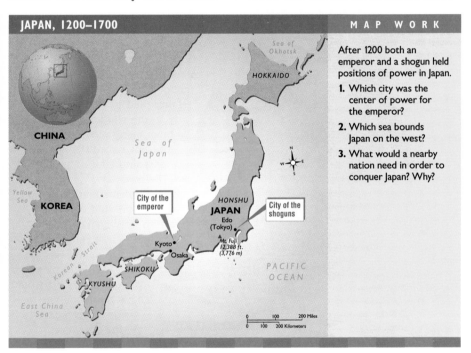

JAPAN, 1200–1700

MAP WORK

After 1200 both an emperor and a shogun held positions of power in Japan.

1. Which city was the center of power for the emperor?

2. Which sea bounds Japan on the west?

3. What would a nearby nation need in order to conquer Japan? Why?

MAP WORK: **1.** KYOTO **2.** SEA OF JAPAN **3.** A STRONG NAVY, BECAUSE JAPAN IS TOTALLY SURROUNDED BY WATER

411

GLOBAL CONNECTION

THE MONGOLS AND JAPAN The Mongols, led by Kublai Khan, tried to extend their empire to include Japan.

• In 1274 Kublai Khan ordered a force of 900 ships and 40,000 men to sail for Japan to invade the island of Kyushu, but a typhoon arose and sank 200 of his ships, taking the lives of 13,500 of his men. The surviving Mongols sailed back to the mainland.

• In 1281 Kublai Khan tried again, this time with 4,400 ships and 142,000 men. Once again, a typhoon arose and destroyed many ships and killed 10,000 men. Once again, the Mongols retreated.

• The Japanese called their savior typhoons *Kamikaze*, meaning "Divine Wind." They would use the same name for World War II suicide fighter planes, once again hoping for divine salvation.

A FEUDAL SYSTEM

Review the meaning of *feudal* as it applied in Europe of the Middle Ages.

★**THINKING FURTHER:** *Sequencing* **How did Japan become a military dictatorship?** *(powerful families struggle for control→Yoritomo's family wins→emperor makes Yoritomo shogun, or military commander→ supreme military command makes him military dictator)*

More **MAP WORK**

Refer the class to the map on this page, and have them label their outline maps.

• **Why is Japan called an archipelago?** *(It is a chain of islands.)*

• **How many major islands does it have and what are they?** *(four: Hokkaido, Honshu, Shikoku, Kyushu. You may want to inform students that Hokkaido officially became part of Japan in the early 1600s.)*

• **What modern city was once called Edo?** *(Tokyo)*

• **What sea separates Japan from Korea and China?** *(Sea of Japan)*

★**THINKING FURTHER:** *Making Conclusions* **Why might you expect Japan to be a seafaring nation?** *(It is made of many islands.)*

Discussing Samurai Warriors Review with the class what they learned about the feudal system as it operated in Europe during the Middle Ages. On the board, have volunteers draw a social pyramid of Europe's feudal society.

★**THINKING FURTHER:** *Compare and Contrast* **What parallels can you draw between feudal society in Japan and Europe?** *(Students should note the similar structure: shogun and king, samurai and knights, and common folk at the bottom. Both societies stressed loyalty and the duties of one group to another. Japanese common people had to show even more abject respect than European commoners were required to exhibit.)*

TOKUGAWA SHOGUN

Help students see that a shogun's power depended on his strength.

- **What weakened the shogun's powers?** *(rebellions of powerful lords and difficulty of ruling many islands)*

- **What gave the lords their power to go to war often?** *(Help students see that each lord had an army of samurai warriors and a warrior held a highly honored position in society.)*

- **Who finally emerged strong enough to restore order?** *(Tokugawa Ieyasu)*

★**THINKING FURTHER:** *Making Conclusions* **What powers do you think a dynasty would need to maintain control of Japan?** *(a strong military to put down or discourage rebellions, strong laws and ability to enforce them, the emperor's support)*

Discussing Ruling Japan Be sure students appreciate the major changes.

- **How many ways can you identify that the Tokugawa dynasty weakened the lords' ability to make war against it?** *(curbing the supply of weapons, displacing disloyal lords with loyal lords, holding lords and their families hostage, forcing lords to spend their money so that they would have none to finance rebellion)*

★**THINKING FURTHER:** *Making Decisions* **On a scale of 1 to 10, how would you rate the Tokugawa methods and chances for success?** *(Students will probably rank them high for effectiveness.)*

TOKUGAWA SHOGUN

Shoguns like Yoritomo were very powerful. However, they were not always strong enough to keep lords from rebelling and seizing more land for themselves. Remember, Japan is a very long archipelago. For this reason, keeping control over Japan's dozens of powerful lords proved almost impossible. By the early 1500s the shoguns had lost much of their power.

In 1603, though, the emperor made Tokugawa Ieyasu (toh koo GAH wah ee yeh YAH soo) Japan's ruler. Under the Tokugawa, Japan became not only unified but remained at peace for over 200 years. How did the Tokugawa leaders achieve what no one else had been able to do?

A samurai wore the decorated headdress and cloak shown. Samurai also carried two swords.

412

Ruling Japan

The Tokugawas became the unchallenged masters of Japan by ordering massive changes in society. To prevent rebellion, only samurai could own weapons. Lords who opposed the Tokugawa leaders were stripped of their lands. Those lands amounted to half the farmable land in Japan. These lands were given to loyal vassals.

Most importantly, all lords had to live in the Tokugawa capital city of Edo (ED oh), or what is today Tokyo. There the shogun's assistants could keep a close watch on the lords, making sure no rebellions were planned. Every two years the lords could return to their towns. Their wives and children, however, had to stay in Edo to insure that the lords would return.

Lords oversaw most everyday affairs in Japan, including collecting taxes from commoners. The lords were not taxed, but were expected to contribute whenever a new national road or castle was built. Lords had to prove their loyalty to the shoguns by giving them many gifts. Lords who did not risked the chance of losing land or privileges. The lords also had to obey strict rules about everything, from what kind of silk they wore to how many servants they had. These rules forced the lords to spend lots of money. Without plenty of money, no lord would have the resources to wage a war against the shoguns.

GLOBAL CONNECTION

EUROPEAN-JAPANESE CONTACTS One thousand years after Buddhist missionaries first reached Japan, Christian missionaries arrived there from Europe.

- A Spanish Jesuit named Francis Xavier, later to be canonized a saint, arrived there in 1549, with dreams of making Japan the first Christian land in eastern Asia.

- By the early 1600s, there were more than 300,000 converts to Christianity in Japan.

- By this time, though, Tokugawa Ieyasu had grown fearful of European contacts, so he ordered all European missionaries to leave the country and all Japanese Christians to become Buddhists.

CITIZENSHIP★

UNDERSTANDING GOVERNMENT Explain to the class that government under the Tokugawa regime was what we might today call a "police state."

- The government kept a close watch on the lordly class. As they traveled to and from Edo, they were searched for weapons at checkpoints along the way.

- The movements and activities of the samurai were also closely monitored and closely restricted.

- The peasants, the majority of the Japanese population, lost most of their rights and were taxed about half of the crops they grew.

Life in cities like Tokyo (left) has changed since feudal times, here painted by Hokusai (below).

Life in Villages and Cities

One road that Japan's lords helped pay for connected Edo with the emperor's capital city of Kyoto (KYOH toh). In time its 300-mile length became crowded with the shogun's servants carrying messages from the shogun to the emperor. Merchants also used the road on their way to market, as did lords traveling to and from Edo.

As the lords traveled with their servants and samurai, they passed through a Japan that was steadily changing. Peace had brought boom times. In farming villages, people leveled forests to clear new farmland. With improved irrigation more rice, cotton, and other crops could be grown. Village shrines and temples were also being expanded. Many of them started schools where children could study reading, writing, arithmetic, and religion.

More and more, older children of farmers were leaving their villages. They left to live in Japan's growing towns and cities. Some found work as servants or laborers on building projects. Others became maids in the homes of samurai families.

Development of Edo

No other city grew as big or as fast as Edo. After 1603 more than 200 lords and their families moved into stately city homes. These households required the services of thousands of maids, cooks, and other servants. Etsu Sugimoto described the maids who worked in her family's kitchen:

> Here the air was filled with the buzz of work mingled with chatter and laughter. In one corner, a maid was grinding rice for tomorrow's dumplings; another was making padded scrub-cloths out of an old kimono; . . . and a little apart from the others sat another whirling her spinning wheel.

Servants searched the city's markets each day for fresh goods. While the lords and samurai spent money to satisfy the shogun, merchants became rich. Some became far richer than many lords.

413

Discussing Life in Villages and Cities
Write the following heads on the board: *Road Building, Deforestation, Irrigation, Education, Urbanization.*

- **What evidence can you find that each of these processes was taking place in Japan?** *(Have students come up to the board and enter evidence under its appropriate head.)*

★ THINKING FURTHER: *Making Conclusions* **In what ways do you think these processes could change Japan?** *(probably by increasing farm production, trade, and population; by changing the environment; by raising Japan's educational level; by making the Japanese society more mobile; by increasing the urban dwellers)*

Exploring Development of Edo
Have students locate Edo on the map, p. 411.

- **What geographic factors might have contributed to Edo's rapid growth?** *(its location on a bay, in the center of the Japanese archipelago)*

- **Who was forced to move to Edo and whom did they in turn cause to move there?** *(More than 200 lords and their families moved there, and in turn they attracted thousands of builders and servants to supply their needs.)*

★ THINKING FURTHER: *Making Conclusions* **The term "conspicuous consumption" describes lavish or wasteful spending to enhance social prestige. How did conspicuous consumption in Edo make merchants grow richer and lords poorer?** *(Supporting lavish life styles was costly to the lords as it enriched the merchants from whom they bought goods.)*

BACKGROUND INFORMATION

ABOUT EDO
- Edo was first established in the 1100s as a village on the Kanta plain at the Sumida River.
- One reason the Tokugawa shogun chose Edo was that it was easily defensible and was far from the emperor's court at Kyoto, reducing the lords' contact with the emperor.
- Within a century of becoming the Tokugawa seat of government, Edo had a population of a half million, making it by far the largest city in Japan.

CURRICULUM CONNECTION

LINKS TO READING
- Author Katherine Paterson has written two story books about early Japan for young people—*The Sign of the Chrysanthemum* and *The Master Puppeteer.*
- Time-Life's *Early Japan* contains several excellent picture essays that students might enjoy examining to expand their knowledge of Japan.

  1) "Tales of Courtly Love" (original illustrations and story line of *The Tale of Genji*), pp. 43–53

  2) "The Way of the Warrior" (explanation of bushido, the warrior's code, and illustrations of the samurai arming himself), pp. 65–73

  3) "Kabuki—A Theater of Escapism," pp. 169–181

A FLOURISHING CULTURE

Encourage students to study the illustrations of Japanese art on pp. 414–415 and read the caption.

- **What do these visuals tell you about the arts that flourished in Japan?** *(Landscape art, prints, literature, and theater all were popular and accomplished.)*

- **What is Kabuki?** *(a popular form of Japanese drama)*

- **What was its usual subject matter?** *(the trials, tribulations, and loves of samurai and ordinary people, struggles between duty and freedom)*

- **How do you know that literature was popular in Japan?** *(Books could be rented.)*

- **What was Japan's, and perhaps the world's, first novel?** *(The Tale of Genji, written by a high-born lady)*

- **What does Genji seek?** *(a magical way to find friendship and joyfulness)*

★**THINKING FURTHER:** *Making Conclusions* **Judging from their arts, what do you think the Japanese people valued in life?** *(beauty, love, duty, samurai life, ordinary life, friendship, happiness)*

Discussing The Closing of Japan
Recall with students China's turning inward in the late 1400s.

- **For how long were the Tokugawa shoguns able to maintain their power over Japan?** *(264 years, 1603–1867)*

- **How did they view contact with other countries during this time?** *(They cut off contact, fearing that outside influences would threaten their rule.)*

- **What steps did they take to isolate themselves similar to the Ming dynasty's steps to isolate China?** *(no foreign contact and no shipbuilding)*

★**THINKING FURTHER:** *Making Conclusions* **A dictionary defines irony as "a fact, result, or happening that seems the opposite of what one would naturally expect." Why was Japan's choice of isolation an irony?** *(In the past, the Japanese welcomed cultural contacts and borrowed widely from them to develop their culture.)*

A FLOURISHING CULTURE

New traditions were being born in the heart of Edo. Actors playing in a new form of drama called Kabuki packed Edo's theaters each night. Their plays dealt with samurai heroes and ordinary people, often torn by love or by struggles between duty and freedom.

New technology also made book printing easier than ever before. Merchants carried huge stacks of books on their backs. Books were rented for next to nothing. Some people read adventure stories about the golden age of the samurai. Others read love stories or classics like Lady Murasaki Shikibu's *The Tale of Genji* (GEN JEE), from around the year 1000. It is thought to be the world's first novel. In this excerpt, the main character decides on a way to solve his problems.

For Genji life had become an unbroken string of problems. He must consider what to do next. If he went on pretending that all was well, then even worse things might lie ahead.

Genji thought of the Suma coast [near present-day Kobe]. People of great value had once lived there, he was told, but now it was deserted, save for the huts of fishermen. According to his attendants, however, Suma was known to be the home of one mysterious resident: a puppet. And the puppet had powers to make human beings a joyful lot.

Genji thought to himself, "Soon, I shall make the journey to Suma. Soon, a wonderful puppet shall rest on my arm. Soon, I shall turn to a puppet and gain the gifts of friendship and joyfulness."

This painting (right) shows a scene from *The Tale of Genji*. Today actors continue to perform Kabuki drama.

USING THE ANTHOLOGY

THE TALE OF GENJI, Pages 102–103 You may have students use their anthologies to read an additional excerpt from *The Tale of Genji*. After they read the excerpts on this page and in the anthology, begin a discussion of what details seem to be particular to Japanese culture and which details seem to apply to almost all cultures.

The Closing of Japan

The Tokugawa shoguns kept an iron-handed grip over life in Japan for over 200 years, between 1603 and 1867. During this time Japan had almost no contact with other countries. Like the emperors of Ming China, the shoguns of Tokugawa Japan saw outside influences as threats to their rule. Their response was to seal off their borders. Lords were forbidden to have any foreign contact or to build ships. Throughout most of its history, Japan had grown from contacts with the outside world; now it remained isolated.

WHY IT MATTERS

Japan was one of the few countries in Asia to remain largely untouched by outside forces in the 1600s and 1700s. Even without the benefits of interna-

tional trade and movement, though, life in Japan continued to grow and change. Most importantly, feudal society changed as lords moved to Edo.

Samurai no longer fought wars but instead often held desk jobs. Drawn to new economic and cultural opportunities, farmers set off for growing towns and cities. A new age had begun in Japan. That age, however, would be jolted in the 1800s, as foreign ships came to challenge Japan's closed borders. You will read about where the ships came from and why in Chapter 17.

✓/// Reviewing Facts and Ideas

MAIN IDEAS

- The Japanese religion of Shinto was changed by the arrival of Buddhism and Confucianism. Together they formed the belief that Japan was like a family, with the emperor as head.
- Feudal society in Japan was run by a military leader called a shogun.
- The Tokugawa shoguns held power for over 200 years. They forced lords to live in Edo and also shut off Japan to outside influence.

THINK ABOUT IT

1. Describe Japan's social pyramid during feudal times.

2. Why was the order for lords to move their families to Edo so important to Tokugawa rule?

3. **FOCUS** How did life change for people in Japan under shogun rule?

4. **THINKING SKILL** How might Tokugawa history support this *generalization*: "Strict rule can bring positive results."

5. **GEOGRAPHY** How did Japan's sheer length affect the early shoguns' ability to keep order in the country?

415

Discussing WHY IT MATTERS Help students recognize the change from within Japan.

- *What changes were taking place in Edo? (Both lords and farmers moved to the city.)*

★**THINKING FURTHER:** *Cause and Effect* **Why would the long Tokugawa peace cause the samurai to find a new occupation?** *(Japanese society no longer had a need for warriors.)*

⭐ 3 CLOSE

MAIN IDEAS
Have students write their answers and exchange papers for correction.

- *How did Shinto, Buddhism, and Confucianism blend to produce a model of Japanese society? (They created a belief that Japan was one family with the emperor as its head.)*

- *Who ran Japan's feudal society? (a military commander called a shogun)*

- *What two major steps helped the Tokugawa to hold power? (control of the lords and isolation)*

EVALUATE
✓ **Answers to Think About It**

1. from top to bottom: emperor and shogun, lords, samurai, commoners *Recall Details*

2. It kept the lords under Tokugawa control and it drew many servants and other workers to Edo. *Make Conclusions*

3. weakened feudalism, created more urban dwellers, expanded farmland and irrigation, expanded education, employed samurai differently *Confirm Predictions*

4. Strict Tokugawa rules unified Japan and brought it a long period of peace. *Make Generalizations*

5. Its length housed hundreds of different lords, and the Tokugawa had to find ways to control them all. *Five Themes of Geography: Human/Environment Interactions*

Write About It Have students write a paragraph in which they identify the major stages that Japan went through from pre-shogun times to 1867.

MEETING INDIVIDUAL NEEDS

RETEACHING (Easy) Have students design and execute posters that advertise a new Kabuki play being presented in Edo.

EXTENSION (Average) Have students write a newspaper feature in which they describe samurai life before and after the Tokugawa dynasty achieved control over the Japanese lords.

ENRICHMENT (Challenging) As a class activity, have students do research on Kabuki (*Kabuki* means "song, dance, acting") and then prepare and present their own Kabuki show. Perhaps the story might center on *The Tale of Genji* excerpt. Divide the class into committees to handle plot line and dialog, song (either original or new words to an old song) dance, costume, makeup, props, and backdrop. Invite other classes for an audience.

LEGACY

Lesson Overview

Over time, printing and calligraphy have developed into art forms.

Lesson Objective

★ Appreciate the beauty and art of printing and calligraphy.

⭐ 1 PREPARE

MOTIVATE Write *calligraphy* on the board and tell the class that it comes from a Greek word for "beautiful writing." Explain that all written languages lend themselves to calligraphy and remind students of examples they have already seen—the Arabic script in Chapter 11 and the illuminated manuscript in Chapter 12.

SET PURPOSE Remind students of the power of printing to spread knowledge, as evidenced by the great impact that Gutenberg's development of printing had on Europe, helping to bring on the Renaissance. Tell them to explore this lesson to see its power to make art available to just about everyone.

⭐ 2 TEACH

Understanding the Concept of a Legacy Have students read the text on this page.

● *How did the Japanese raise common handwriting to the art of calligraphy?* (by practicing writing characters until they could make them look like brush strokes in a painting)

● *How did printing make this art available to everyone?* (Printing made many copies of a single work of art.)

★**THINKING FURTHER:** *Making Conclusions* **Why do you think that calligraphy is pleasing to the eye?** (*Perhaps it appeals to our sense of order and beauty and to our appreciation of great skill.*)

Legacy
LINKING PAST AND PRESENT

PRINTING AND Calligraphy

Do you remember how difficult writing seemed when you first learned to do it? You probably practiced drawing letters over and over. Then you began to learn to write words and sentences.

Japanese of feudal times also worked hard at their writing. They used brush strokes similar to painting. They developed their written language, which they borrowed from the Chinese, into an art form called calligraphy (kuh LIHG ruh fee).

Advances in printing technology brought this art to many people. Printing made it possible for many people to own beautifully written works of art.

Calligraphy is still an important part of education for many Asian students. This Chinese girl practices her writing at school.

416

BACKGROUND INFORMATION

MORE ABOUT CALLIGRAPHY IN JAPAN
● Among the aristocrats of feudal Japan, mastery of calligraphy was an all-important social grace. A person's writing was thought to reveal his or her social standing, education, character, and even mood.
● Calligraphy remains a highly regarded skill in Japan today. Large calligraphy contests are held where school-age boys and girls compete to letter scrolls that are judged most beautiful and striking.

The woman in this Japanese print (above) is writing a letter using a calligraphy brush. The scroll (left) shows the following Japanese poem, titled "Waiting for the Cuckoo." The calligraphy, handwritten by the poet Yoshimasa, is still admired for its beauty.

Oh, cuckoo, crying for thy mate
Up in the sky, on mine own part,
I wait for thee tonight
With my whole heart.

417

Examining the Illustrations Allow students time to study the visuals.

- *What kinds of equipment did people use for writing?* (a brush and ink pad)

- *What evidence can you find that calligraphy is important in other parts of East Asia in addition to Japan?* (the example of a Chinese girl practicing calligraphy)

★**THINKING FURTHER:** *Making Conclusions* **Why do you think that any written language can lend itself to calligraphy?** (The strokes in any language can be written in a way to make them beautiful to the eye.)

3 CLOSE

SUM IT UP
Have students explain how the art of printing can serve the art of calligraphy.

EVALUATE
Write About It Have students write poems in praise of the art of printing or of calligraphy.

CURRICULUM CONNECTION

LINKS TO ART Libraries stock books for both adults and juveniles on "calligraphy made easy." Have a group of volunteers investigate such books and prepare a demonstration of calligraphy styles for the class. They may choose to use some markers that are made especially for calligraphy. They might even call for some hands-on participation of class members in doing some writing on the board.

LINKS TO ART Invite students to do some printing of their own. Have them use potatoes as "wood blocks" on which they sculpt their own cutouts or lettering. Then have them press their "blocks" on a sponge saturated with tempera paint and print them on paper.

MEETING INDIVIDUAL NEEDS

RETEACHING (Easy) After showing students examples of calligraphy styles, as shown in "how-to" calligraphy books, invite them to render their own names and the name of their school in their own calligraphy style.

EXTENSION (Average) Again, after showing students "how-to" calligraphy books, have them write a poem and then render it in calligraphy.

ENRICHMENT (Challenging) Invite students to design their own alphabet—A to Z—in calligraphy. Encourage them to think in terms of readability, a pleasant look, and a sense of letters that match one another in style. Display the alphabets around the room.

DISCUSSING MAJOR EVENTS Use the time line to remind students of the widespread conquest and empire-building that went on in Asia during this period.

- *What three major groups were on the march toward conquest in Asia during the period shown in the time line?* (Mongols, Turks, Moguls)

- *Where did the Mongols and Turks operate and what did they achieve?* (The Mongols' march took them to invade and control China, and the Turks eventually conquered the Byzantine empire and its capital at Constantinople.)

- *Where and by what time had the Moguls gained control of a major area?* (By 1556, they controlled the Mogul empire of India, with Akbar as its ruler.)

Answers to THINKING ABOUT VOCABULARY

1. samurai
2. sultan
3. archipelago
4. Grand Canal
5. shogun

Answers to THINKING ABOUT FACTS

1. Indus, Huang, Mekong, Ganges, Chang

2. an Ottoman empire architect who built magnificent mosques, libraries, hospitals, colleges, orphanages, and other buildings

3. He expanded the empire, unified the money system, reformed the tax system, built canals and wells to help farmers, promoted religious harmony, and encouraged scholarship and the arts.

4. Shah Jahan built it as a tomb for his beloved wife Mumtaz Mahal.

Resource REMINDER

Practice and Project Book: *p. 85*

Assessment Book: *Chapter 14 Test*

Technology: *Videodisc*

Transparency: *Graphic Organizer, Main-Idea Chart*

CHAPTER 14 REVIEW

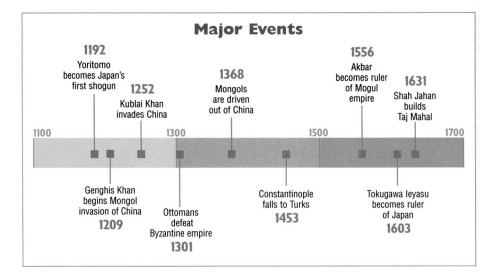

Major Events

1192 Yoritomo becomes Japan's first shogun

1252 Kublai Khan invades China

1368 Mongols are driven out of China

1556 Akbar becomes ruler of Mogul empire

1631 Shah Jahan builds Taj Mahal

1100 ... 1300 ... 1500 ... 1700

Genghis Khan begins Mongol invasion of China 1209

Ottomans defeat Byzantine empire 1301

Constantinople falls to Turks 1453

Tokugawa Ieyasu becomes ruler of Japan 1603

THINKING ABOUT VOCABULARY

Number a sheet of paper from 1 to 5. Beside each number write the word or term from the list below that best completes each sentence.

archipelago
Grand Canal
samurai
shogun
sultan

1. _____ were soldiers used by Japanese lords.

2. A _____ is a supreme ruler of a Muslim state.

3. _____ is a word meaning "a chain of islands."

4. The name of the human-made waterway in China that connects the Huang and Chang rivers is the _____.

5. A _____ was a military commander who governed Japan.

THINKING ABOUT FACTS

1. What Asian rivers begin on the Tibetan Plateau?

2. Who was Sinan and what were his accomplishments?

3. What did Akbar do to strengthen the Mogul empire in India?

4. Why was the Taj Mahal built?

5. What is Angkor Wat?

6. Why did the Mongols invade China?

7. Who was Kublai Khan? How did he govern China?

8. What was the effect of the Tokugawa dynasty on Japanese history?

9. What was the most significant achievement of Lady Murasaki Shikibu?

10. According to the time line above, how long after Ghengis Khan invaded China were the Mongols driven out?

418

SECOND-LANGUAGE SUPPORT

ORAL PRACTICE Second-language learners can get valuable oral practice by explaining the items they chose to include on their main idea charts on p. 419.

TV QUIZ GAME A quiz show is an enjoyable way to have students review the material in this chapter. Have students skim the chapter and note information about the important people, places, and vocabulary listed at the beginning of each lesson. They will then turn this information into questions to be asked on a "TV quiz show." Students will take turns quizzing each other using their favorite game show format.

THINK AND WRITE ◄▭▭▭)

WRITING A NEWS ARTICLE

Suppose you are a newspaper reporter sent back in time to cover the fall of Constantinople. Reread page 389. Then use the information to write an on-the-scene report about what happened.

WRITING A COMPARISON

Write a comparison of the Mogul empire in India and the Mongol empire in China. How were they similar? How were they different? Include the contributions made by Akbar and Kublai Khan.

WRITING DESCRIPTIONS

Write one paragraph each about two of the following places: (1) Taj Mahal, (2) Angkor Wat, and (3) the Forbidden City.

APPLYING THINKING SKILLS

MAKING GENERALIZATIONS

1. What is a generalization?
2. Review Lesson 2. Explain how using the example of the Mogul emperor Akbar helps to support this generalization: "Effective rulers make the people they govern feel they are being treated fairly."
3. Make a generalization about what is required to become ruler of a large area. Use information from this and other chapters you have read.
4. What generalization can you make about the ways rulers of the past governed? Use as examples the rulers you chose for number 3.
5. Why are generalizations useful?

Summing Up the Chapter

Copy the main-idea chart below on a separate sheet of paper. Then fill in each column with information from the chapter. When you have completed the chart, use the information to write a paragraph that answers the question "What contributions did peoples of Asia make to civilization?"

MAIN IDEA: Powerful civilizations were built in Turkey, India, Cambodia, China, and Japan.

Country	Dynasty	Rulers	Capital Cities	Achievements
Turkey	Ottoman	Sultan Suleyman	Istanbul	buildings by Sinan
India	Moguls	Akbar Shah Jahan	Agra	Taj Mahal
Cambodia	Khmer	Jayavarman II Suryavarman II	Angkor	Angkor Wat
China	Mongols Yuan	Genghis Kahn Kublai Khan	Bejing	Forbidden City Grand Canal
Japan	Tokugawa	Emperor Yoritomo Shogun Tokugawa Ieyasu	Edo (Tokyo) Kyoto	First Japanese novel

419

SUGGESTIONS FOR SUMMING UP THE CHAPTER

After students copy the main-idea chart on a piece of paper, have them read the main idea aloud and locate the horizontal column that pertains to each. Point out that Lessons 2, 3, 4, and 5 of the chapter correspond to these columns. Then have them identify the categories of information they are to enter in the verticle columns and ask for one answer for each category. Possible answers appear on the reproduced pupil page above. Encourage students to review the appropriate lesson as they work to complete each horizontal column. As they write their paragraphs answering the question posed, suggest that they not only weave together the contributions of Asians but also identify each contributor.

ASSESSING THINK AND WRITE: *For performance assessment, see Assessment Book, Chapter 14, pp. T87–T89.*

---

5. a huge stone Hindu temple complex in today's Cambodia
6. They wanted the supplies that China offered.
7. Genghis Khan's grandson who unified China, reformed its money system, used taxes for useful public works, and encouraged China's trade along the Silk Road by protecting it.
8. It brought Japan internal peace for 200 years, which brought boom times and rich cultural development.
9. She wrote *The Tales of Genji*, maybe the world's first novel.
10. The Mongols were driven out of China 159 years after Genghis Kahn's invasion: 1368 minus 1209 equals 159.

Answers to APPLYING THINKING SKILLS

1. a broad statement of observation applied to different kinds of examples
2. Taxing farmers according to the fertility of their land and ending Muslim discrimination against Hindus support the generalization.
3. Generalizations might focus on a powerful military, political savvy and a good system of laws, supporting business and trade, improving transportation and communication systems, and a sense of fairness.
4. Encourage students to choose rulers who exemplified the generalizations in answer 3 and tell how they did so.
5. Generalizations are useful because they help to uncover underlying similiarities among things that may otherwise have been missed.

Technology CONNECTION

VIDEODISC
Enrich Chapter 14 with the *Kublai Khan* segment on the Videodisc.

Search Frame 305, Side A

CHAPTER 15 Empires and Cultures of the Americas

Pages 420–447

CHAPTER OVERVIEW

In 1325 the Aztec founded their capital of Tenochtitlan and gradually gained control of the valley of Mexico. Meanwhile, Cuzco became the capital of the Inca, whose empire eventually spread throughout the Andes. The Ojibwa people of North America established trade on the Great Lakes in 1500.

GEO ADVENTURES DAILY GEOGRAPHY ACTIVITIES

Use **Geo Adventures** Daily Geography activities to assess students' understanding of geography skills.

CHAPTER PLANNING GUIDE

LESSON 1	LESSON 2	GEOGRAPHYSKILLS
SUGGESTED PACING: 2 DAYS	SUGGESTED PACING: 2 DAYS	SUGGESTED PACING: 1 DAY
Geography Of The Americas pp. 422–425	**The Aztec Empire** pp. 426–431	**Using Map Projections** pp. 432–433
CURRICULUM CONNECTIONS Links to Math, p. 424 Links to Science, p. 424 **RESOURCES** Practice and Project Book, p. 86 Desk Map Outline Map	**CURRICULUM CONNECTIONS** Links to Art, p. 430 **CITIZENSHIP** Understanding Government, p. 429 **RESOURCES** Practice and Project Book, p. 87 ⬛Anthology, pp. 104–105	**RESOURCES** Practice and Project Book, p. 88 Transparency Maps 17, 18 ⦿TECHNOLOGY Adventure Time! CD-ROM

LESSON 4	CHAPTER REVIEW
SUGGESTED PACING: 3 DAYS	SUGGESTED PACING: 1 DAY
Early People Of North America pp. 440–445	pp. 446–447
CURRICULUM CONNECTIONS Links to Science, pp. 442, 443 Links to Health, p. 443 **CITIZENSHIP** Understanding Government, p. 441 **INFOGRAPHIC** Native North Americans, pp. 444–445 **RESOURCES** Project and Practice Book, p. 90 ⬛Anthology, pp. 109–114 Desk Map ⦿TECHNOLOGY Adventure Time! CD-ROM	**RESOURCES** Practice and Project Book, p. 91 ⦿TECHNOLOGY Videodisc/Video Tape 5 Assessment Book: Chapter 15 Test Transparency: Graphic Organizer, Word Map

GETTING READY FOR THE CHAPTER

LEARNING STYLE: Visual

GROUP   30 MINUTES OR LONGER

Name the States

Objective: To prepare students to think about the empires and cultures of the Americas.

Materials: paper, crayons, markers, United States maps

1. Tell students that half the states in the United States have names that come from Native American languages. Do they know or can they guess some of those names?
2. Ask groups of students to research and write about the Native American names of at least five states, and to locate and color them in on a United States map.
3. Invite volunteers to point out these states on a wall map and encourage students to share what they learned.

LESSON 3

SUGGESTED PACING: 2 DAYS

The Inca Empire pp. 434–439

CURRICULUM CONNECTIONS
Links to Art, p. 436
Links to Reading, p. 436

CITIZENSHIP
Understanding Government, p. 437

RESOURCES
Project and Practice Book, p. 89
Anthology, pp. 106–108

SHELTERED INSTRUCTION

READING STRATEGIES & LANGUAGE DEVELOPMENT

Cause and Effect/Words with Multiple Meanings, p. 422, Lesson 1
Making and Supporting Generalizations/Synonyms, p. 426, Lesson 2
Compare and Contrast/Word History, p. 432, Geography Skills
Compare and Contrast/Idioms, p. 434, Lesson 3
Classifying/Words Often Confused, p. 440, Lesson 4

SECOND-LANGUAGE SUPPORT

Using Visuals, p. 423
Working with a Peer, p. 428
Using Props, p. 437
Dramatization, p. 442
Working with Peers/Oral Discussion, p. 446

MEETING INDIVIDUAL NEEDS

Reteaching, Extension, Enrichment, pp. 425, 431, 433, 439, 445
McGraw-Hill Adventure Book

ASSESSMENT OPPORTUNITIES

Practice and Project Book, pp. 86–91
Write About It, pp. 425, 431, 439, 445
Assessment Book: Assessing Think and Write, pp. T90–T92; Chapter 15 Tests: Content, Skills, Writing

CHAPTER 15

PAGES 420–447

Introducing the Chapter

After students read the title, call on them to recall things they remember from their study of the Americas in Chapter 11. Help them to remember aspects of Middle America and let them know that they will soon be returning there to start where they left off.

THINKING ABOUT HISTORY AND GEOGRAPHY

Have students read the text on this page and trace the panels to their locations on the map. Ask where in this chapter, in addition to Middle America, their studies will take them. (to western South America and to the Great Lakes area of North America)

1325 TENOCHTITLÁN

- *Where is Tenochtitlán located?* (in the Valley of Mexico in Middle America)

- *What earlier people have we met in this location?* (the early people who first cultivated corn)

- *What people will we meet now?* (the Aztec)

> ★THINKING FURTHER: *Making Conclusions* **By what earlier peoples might the Aztec have been influenced? Why?** (by the Olmec and the Maya; they preceded the Aztec in the general region.)

1350 CUZCO

- *Where is Cuzco in relation to Tenochtitlán?* (far to the southeast, in western South America)

- *How much later is this panel than the previous one? What people does it involve?* (25 years; the Inca)

Resource REMINDER

Technology: *Videodisc*

CHAPTER 15

Empires and Cultures of the Americas

THINKING ABOUT HISTORY AND GEOGRAPHY

In this chapter you will read about civilizations that developed in North America and South America. Follow the time line to see how empires developed in what are today Mexico and Peru. The peoples of these empires built unique and powerful civilizations. Near the Great Lakes of North America, Native Americans became skilled farmers who traded across a wide area.

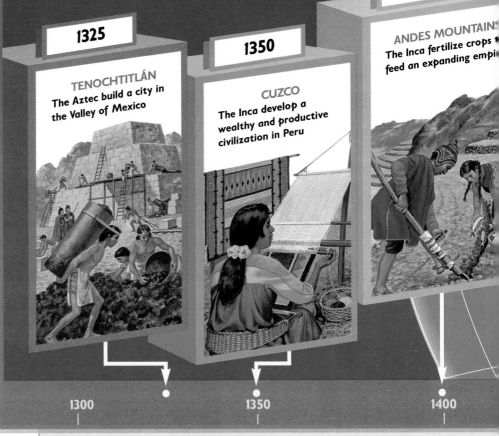

1325

TENOCHTITLÁN
The Aztec build a city in the Valley of Mexico

1350

CUZCO
The Inca develop a wealthy and productive civilization in Peru

1400

ANDES MOUNTAINS
The Inca fertilize crops feed an expanding empire

1300

1350

1400

BACKGROUND INFORMATION

LINKING THE MAP AND THE TIME LINE

- Tenochtitlán is the site of the capital of present-day Mexico City, Mexico. At its height, in the early 1500s, Tenochtitlán had a population of about 300,000, five times larger than London's population at that time, which made it one of the biggest cities of the 16th century.

- Cuzco is today the capital of the Cuzco province in southern Peru. It lies at the heart of a thickly populated agricultural region and its population is more than a quarter million. Known for its Inca ruins, the city is today a popular tourist center. The sturdy Inca stone walls withstood a severely damaging earthquake in 1950; when much of the Spanish architecture that used Inca walls as foundations did not.

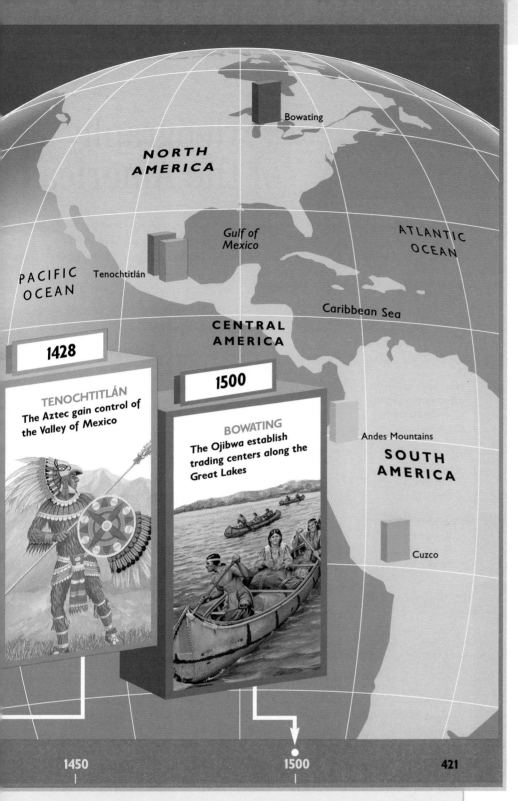

1428

TENOCHTITLÁN
The Aztec gain control of the Valley of Mexico

1500

BOWATING
The Ojibwa establish trading centers along the Great Lakes

Bowating

NORTH AMERICA

Gulf of Mexico

ATLANTIC OCEAN

PACIFIC OCEAN

Tenochtitlán

Caribbean Sea

CENTRAL AMERICA

Andes Mountains

SOUTH AMERICA

Cuzco

1450   1500   421

★**THINKING FURTHER:** *Making Conclusions* **What do these first two panels tell you about the development of civilization in the Americas?** *(Two civilizations, Aztec and Inca, developed at the same time)*

1400 ANDES MOUNTAINS

● **Trace the Andes Mountains on the map, p. 423, with your finger. How far down the west coast of South America do they run?** *(nearly the entire length)*

★**THINKING FURTHER:** Making Conclusions **Judging from information in the panel, do you think the Inca conquered new areas? Explain.** *(The panel refers to "an expanding empire," suggesting that the Inca were taking over new territories.)*

1428 TENOCHTITLÁN

● **How much time has passed since the Aztec founded a city here?** *(103 years)*

★**THINKING FURTHER:** Compare and Contrast **How does the area the Aztec controlled compare with the area the Inca controlled?** *(The Aztec territory is smaller.)*

1500 BOWATING

● **Where is Bowating located?** *(in the Great Lakes area of North America)*

● **What people lived there?** *(the Ojibwa)*

● **What does this panel say they accomplished?** *(They established trading centers along the Great Lakes)*

★**THINKING FURTHER:** Making Conclusions **Why would you conclude that the Ojibwa were in a good position to act as traders?** *(They had the Great Lakes as water highways on which to transport goods over a broad area.)*

Technology CONNECTION

VIDEODISC
Enrich Chapter 15 with *Aztec Lands* on the Videodisc.

BACKGROUND INFORMATION

LINKING THE MAP AND THE TIME LINE
● The Andes Mountains were well suited to settlement by the Inca because they do not form a single high range but rather a series of ranges, between which lie fertile valleys that receive plentiful rainfall.

● Tenochtitlán's influence spread as Aztec forces conquered outlying regions. There is evidence that its political control was enforced by armed settlers and priest-aristocrats who moved into newly conquered territories.

● Bowating's location today lies along the border between the United States and Canada, between Michigan's Upper Peninsula, which borders Wisconsin on the west and the Canadian province of Ontario.

LESSON 1

PAGES 422–425

Lesson Overview
Spanning 10,000 miles north to south, the Americas contain every possible physical feature and climate zone.

Lesson Objectives
★ Locate and describe major physical features of the Americas.

★ Describe adaptations people have made to the geography of the Americas.

1 PREPARE

MOTIVATE Try to have on hand picture books showing dramatic geographic scenes of the Americas for students to examine as you have two students do the *Read Aloud,* one as George Meegan, the other as the narrator.

SET PURPOSE On the map on p. 423, have students locate and trace the spine of mountains that runs down the west coasts of the Americas from Alaska to Argentina. Remind students how important the Himalayas are to Asia and call attention to the photo of the Andes. Refer them to the *Read to Learn* question and encourage them to explore this lesson to learn how these mountains have affected life in the Americas. Preview the *Vocabulary.*

2 TEACH

Understanding THE BIG PICTURE
As students read this section, have them trace Meegan's route on their desk maps.

● *What different physical features did Meegan have to cross in this journey?* (mountains, rain forests, deserts, plains, Great Lakes, tundra)

★**THINKING FURTHER:** *Making Conclusions* **What different kinds of gear must he have needed for his long journey?** *(Encourage students to think in terms of varied clothing and equipment.)*

Resource REMINDER

Practice and Project Book: *p. 86*

Desk Map

Outline Map

Focus Activity

READ TO LEARN

How have mountains affected the growth of civilizations in the Americas?

VOCABULARY

- tundra
- isthmus
- timberline

PLACES

- Andes Mountains
- Great Lakes
- Rocky Mountains
- Canadian Shield

422

Geography of the Americas

Read Aloud

"Here at the top of the continent, I felt that the Americas 'belonged' to me in a way that they belonged to no one else. . . . The fog's curtain slowly lifted. . . . This was the end. Great sobs shook my frame, and my tears mingled with frozen dust."

These words were written in 1976 by the Englishman George Meegan. Over a period of seven years, he walked from the southern tip of South America all the way north to the Arctic Ocean.

THE BIG PICTURE

Pulling his belongings in a cart, Meegan climbed up the Andes Mountains and down to the steamy rain forests of Central America. He also traveled across Mexico's dry deserts and through the Great Plains of North America. He walked along the shores of the Great Lakes, up and over the Rocky Mountains, and across the tundra, or treeless plain, of Alaska. After 19,000 miles, Meegan had crossed both North and South America—the two continents that form the Western Hemisphere.

Many civilizations have developed in the Americas during the past 10,000 years. Among the earliest of them, as you may recall, were the Olmec and the Maya of Middle America. In this lesson you will read about the geography of the Americas and the ways in which some people adapted to it.

SHELTERED INSTRUCTION

READING STRATEGIES & LANGUAGE DEVELOPMENT

CAUSE AND EFFECT Remind students that recognizing cause-and-effect relationships can help them understand why things happen as they do. Share the Read to Learn question and invite volunteers to explain what they might have done as explorers encountering mountains in their path. As they read, students can find these cause-and-effect relationships. **[SDAIE STRATEGY: BRIDGING]**

WORDS WITH MULTIPLE MEANINGS Point out that the word *people* can have a general meaning and a more specific meaning. It can refer to people in general or it can refer to a specific group of people—for example, Americans are a people as are the Japanese or the Khmer. Used to refer to a specific group, the word can be either singular or plural—a *people* or several *peoples.*

THE AMERICAS: Physical

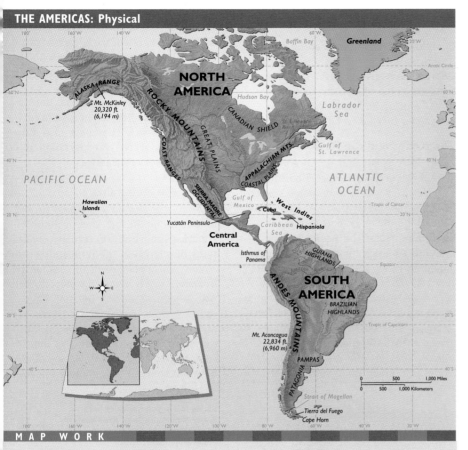

The Americas have many physical features.

1. Which mountain range extends along the western part of South America?

2. Which oceans bound the Americas?

3. Which are the two largest gulfs in the Americas?

4. Where are the Great Plains located?

5. In which mountain range is Mt. McKinley located?

THE AMERICAS

Many physical features in the Americas were shaped by glaciers during the Ice Age. The Canadian Shield is a huge rocky region in northern Canada where soil was removed by glaciers. Their crushing weight also carved the basins of the Great Lakes. When the Ice Age ended about 15,000 years ago, glaciers melted and filled the basins with water.

Melting glaciers also caused the ocean levels to rise. At the southern tip of Central America, rising waters covered land, leaving only an isthmus (IHS mus) between the continents. An isthmus is a narrow strip of land that connects two larger land masses.

MAP WORK: 1. Andes Mountains **2.** Arctic Ocean, Atlantic Ocean, Pacific Ocean **3.** Gulf of St. Lawrence and Gulf of Mexico **4.** central North America **5.** Alaska Range **423**

SECOND-LANGUAGE SUPPORT

USING VISUALS Second-language learners may benefit from demonstrations that trace formation of landforms and geographical features. As you read aloud *The Americas,* have volunteers trace the movement of glaciers, the shearing of mountains, formation of an isthmus, and other events on a relief map.

GLOBAL CONNECTION

THE WORLD'S MAJOR ISTHMUSES The two most important isthmuses in the world are the Isthmus of Panama and the Isthmus of Suez. Have students locate both on a desk map of the world and have them identify two things they have in common. (Both connect two continents: Panama—North America and South America, Suez—Africa and Asia; and both have had canals cut through them.)

THE AMERICAS

Suggest that glaciers were like a giant carving tool, giving shape to the land.

More **MAP WORK**

Refer students to the map on this page and encourage them to work back and forth between text and map. First have them review what they learned about glaciers on p. 286.

- *What are glaciers?* (great ice sheets that move, cutting into and scraping the land beneath them as they move)

- *Where is the Canadian Shield on the map? What did glaciers have to do with creating it?* (The area south of Hudson Bay; they scraped off its soil and left behind a huge rocky region.)

- *The Great Lakes are shown but not named on the map. Can you locate them?* (Help students identify the large bodies of water south of Hudson Bay and the Canadian Shield.)

- *What did the glaciers have to do with creating the Great Lakes?* (They carved out their basins and filled the basins with water when the glaciers melted.)

- *Where are the major plains and highland regions in the Americas?* (the Great Plains of North America and the Patagonia Pampas and Guiana Highlands and Brazilian Highlands of South America)

- *What is an isthmus?* (a narrow strip of land that connects two larger land masses)

- *Where is the Isthmus of Panama? What land masses does it connect?* (at the southern tip of Central America; North America and South America)

- *Where does the Amazon River flow?* (through northern South America)

★THINKING FURTHER: *Predicting What kind of climate would you expect to find near the Amazon? Why?* (a tropical climate because the equator runs through it)

MOUNTAINS OF THE AMERICAS

Review the map on p. 423.

- **What is the major mountain range along western North America? along western South America?** *(Rocky Mountains; Andes Mountains)*

★**THINKING FURTHER:** *Compare and Contrast* **Which range covers a broader strip of its continent?** *(Rockies are broader)*

Discussing The Andes and the Rockies Focus on the mountains.

- **Which range spans the greater length? by how much?** *(Andes: 4,500 miles, 1,500 miles greater)*

- **What is the timberline? What effect does it have on wildlife?** *(The line above which trees cannot grow; less wildlife above it, some wildlife in the fir and spruce below it.)*

★**THINKING FURTHER:** *Making Conclusions* **Prevailing winds blow from the west toward the Rockies. How might the Rockies affect the climate to their east?** *(Just as the Himalayas block rains from reaching north of them, so the Rockies make the climate east of them dry.)*

Investigating Life in the Mountains Help students recognize the special challenges of living in the mountains.

- **In what ways did early people of the Andes make changes to their environment?** *(They built irrigation systems, fertilized the soil, and stretched rope bridges from peak to peak)*

★**THINKING FURTHER:** *Compare and Contrast* **Why were the Andes easier to adapt to than the Rockies?** *(They had shorter winters, more fertile soil.)*

More **CHART WORK**

Refer to the chart on p. 425.

★**THINKING FURTHER:** *Compare and Contrast* **What is the population of the Americas? Is it larger or smaller than Europe? Africa? and Asia?** *(784 million; larger than Africa; smaller than Europe and Asia)*

MOUNTAINS OF THE AMERICAS

Climbing the tall mountains of the Americas was an exhausting part of George Meegan's journey. The mountains are some of the spectacular features—and great resources—of the continents that make up the Americas.

The Andes and the Rockies

North America and South America are similar in at least one important way. A great wall of mountains stretches along the western side of each continent. Huge plains extend to the east of these mountains. The Andes Mountains in South America make up the longest mountain range in the world. The range spans 4,500 miles. Mount Aconcagua (ak un KAH gwuh), the tallest mountain in the Americas, towers to 22,834 feet.

North America's Rocky Mountains extend over 3,000 miles, from Texas to Alaska. They are not quite as tall as the Andes. Mountain goats and bighorn sheep live on the steepest peaks above the timberline. Above this imaginary line on a mountain, trees cannot grow. Below the timberline, mountain lions and bears can be found living in forests of fir and spruce trees.

Like the Himalayas in Asia, the Andes and the Rockies have a great effect on climate. They have also influenced ways of life, transportation, and the history of civilizations.

Life in the Mountains

Many peoples have adapted to mountain life. In fact, one of South America's most advanced early civilizations developed in the highlands of the Andes. Early peoples of this region built irrigation systems and developed effective ways of fertilizing the soil. They found ways to farm crops such as maize, peppers, and potatoes on the slopes of the Andes. They also built rope bridges to make travel possible between some of the mountain peaks.

Hiking is a popular activity in the Rocky Mountains (left). Reed boats are used on Lake Titicaca in the Andes Mountains (below).

424

CURRICULUM CONNECTION

LINKS TO MATH Have students work out the ratio of the length of the Andes (4,500 miles) to the length of the Rockies (3,000 miles).

$4,500 \div 1,500 = 3 \qquad 3,000 \div 1,500 = 2$

The ratio is 3:2

LINKS TO SCIENCE No continuous vegetation can grow above the timberline. The vegetation above it is called *Alpine tundra*—plants that can survive extremely cold temperatures, gusting winds, lack of precipitation, and short growing seasons.

THE AMERICAS AT A GLANCE

	Total Land Area	16,236,000 sq. miles 42,051,000 sq. km
	Highest Mountain	Mt. Aconcagua, Argentina 22,834 feet (6,960 m)
	Longest River	Amazon River 4,000 miles 6,437 km
	Largest City	Mexico City, Mexico Population 10,263,275
	Current Population	757,000,000
	Percent of World Population	14%

GEO FACT
Northern Canada and Alaska make up part of the Arctic tundra. The climate of the tundra is so cold that the ground from 1 to 5 feet below the surface stays frozen all year. During the summer, the surface of the tundra thaws and moss and wildflowers grow.

CHART WORK

The Americas are rich not only in resources, but also in plants and minerals.

1. What is the longest river in the Americas?
2. How does the climate of the Arctic tunda affect the ground?

In North America's Rocky Mountains, early peoples had more difficult lives. Longer winters than those in the Andes, and less fertile soil, made farming a greater challenge.

WHY IT MATTERS

From the windy tip of South America to the icy rivers of Alaska, the Americas provide a 10,000-mile span of varied geography. Every possible climate zone can be found here, including polar, temperate, and tropical. Many physical

CHART WORK: 1. Amazon River, 4,000 miles (6,437 kilometers) **2.** The cold climate causes the ground 1 to 5 feet below the surface to stay frozen all year long, while allowing the surface to thaw in the summer.

features, such as North America's Grand Canyon and South America's Amazon River, which flows through the world's largest rain forest region, make these continents unique.

A study of this great land is incomplete, however, without meeting the people who live here. You have already read about the ancient civilizations of the Olmec and the Maya. Soon you will read about later peoples who lived in other parts of the Western Hemisphere.

✔// Reviewing Facts and Ideas

MAIN IDEAS

- Glaciers shaped much of the land of North America.
- The Isthmus of Panama connects North America and South America.
- The Andes Mountains and the Rocky Mountains are the two major mountain ranges of this region.
- North and South America contain a variety of landforms and climates.
- Early peoples of the Andes region built irrigation systems and developed ways of growing maize, peppers, and potatoes on the mountain slopes.

THINK ABOUT IT

1. How were the Great Lakes formed?
2. What is the timberline?
3. **FOCUS** How have mountains affected the growth of civilization in the Americas?
4. **THINKING SKILL** How might mountains such as the Andes and Rockies have *effects* on trade?
5. **GEOGRAPHY** Use the map on page 423 to determine at what degrees of latitude and longitude Lake Superior is located. At about what latitude is the Amazon River located?

425

Discussing WHY IT MATTERS Review the great variety of climate and terrain.

> ★**THINKING FURTHER:** *Classifying*
> ***Going from South Pole to North Pole, how would you classify the climate zones in the order that George Meegan traveled through them?*** *(polar, temperate, tropical, temperate, polar)*

★3 CLOSE

MAIN IDEAS
Call on students for answers.

- ***What action shaped the Canadian Shield and the Great Lakes?*** *(the movement of glaciers that scraped and scooped out the land)*
- ***What strip of land connects North and South America?*** *(the Isthmus of Panama)*
- ***What are the Americas' two major mountain ranges?*** *(Andes and Rockies)*
- ***What term might you use to describe America's landforms and climates?*** *(Possible answer: highly varied)*
- ***How did early people of the Andes adapt their environment to serve their food needs?*** *(They built irrigation systems and fertilized the soil.)*

EVALUATE
✔ **Answers to Think About It**
1. Glaciers scooped out their basins and, by melting, filled them with water. *Summarize*
2. the line above which trees cannot grow *Recall Details*
3. Early people of the Andes were able to develop civilization there. *Main Idea*
4. As barriers to movement, they would not encourage and would, in fact, hinder trade. *Make Inferences*
5. Lake Superior: about 40°N, 90°W; Amazon River: about 70°W *Five Themes of Geography: Location*

Write About It Have students write a postcard message that George Meegan might have written home at some place along his journey.

· MEETING INDIVIDUAL NEEDS

RETEACHING (Easy) On an outline map of the Americas, have students locate and label the *Places* listed on p. 422 as well as the Isthmus of Panama.

EXTENSION (Average) Have students create an illustrated map showing the chief landforms and climates of either North America or South America.

ENRICHMENT (Challenging) Have students choose one country in the Western Hemisphere and do research on it so that they can create a travel brochure advertising the geographic advantages of that country. Their brochures should describe physical features and climate as well as vegetation and resources.

LESSON 2

PAGES 426–431

Lesson Overview
After settling in the Valley of Mexico in the 1100s, the Aztec created a powerful empire.

Lesson Objectives
★ Describe ways the Aztec adapted their environment to their needs.

★ Trace the growth of the Aztec empire.

★ Identify and describe major achievements of the Aztec empire.

1 PREPARE

MOTIVATE Have one student rehearse the quote in the *Read Aloud* and another the narration. As they read to the class, invite students to close their eyes and try to visualize the scene described.

SET PURPOSE Refer to the photo of the Aztec mask. Remind the class of Middle American empires they have studied—Olmec and Maya. What influences might these older civilizations have had on the Aztec? What traditions will the Aztec carry on and perhaps expand upon? Encourage students to explore the lesson for answers to these questions as well as to the *Read to Learn* question and *Vocabulary*.

2 TEACH

Understanding THE BIG PICTURE
Have students turn back to the map on p. 287 and locate the Central Plateau, the site of the Valley of Mexico. Have them also recall what they have learned about the climates of Middle America.

★**THINKING FURTHER:** *Making Conclusions* **What geographic features might have drawn the Aztec here?** *(Help students to recall that it is an area of gently rolling hills and of tierra templada— temperate climate.)*

Resource REMINDER
Practice and Project Book: *p. 87*
Anthology: *Poetry of the Aztec, pp. 104–105*

1200   1325   1521   1600

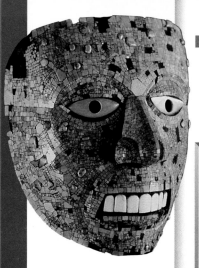

The Aztec Empire

Read Aloud
"The great city has many broad streets, though among these are two or three main ones. Of the remainder, half of each is hard earthlike pavement, and the other half is by water, so that the people leave in their canoes or barks, which are of wood hollowed out, although some of them are large enough to hold comfortably five persons. The residents go for a stroll, some in canoes and others along the land, and keep up conversations."

This is a description of a city in Middle America made by a Spanish soldier in 1519. The soldier was greatly impressed by the beautiful city and the people who lived there—the Aztec.

Focus Activity

READ TO LEARN

How did the Aztec build an empire?

VOCABULARY
- chinampas
- tribute
- Triple Alliance
- codex

PLACES
- Tenochtitlán
- Valley of Mexico
- Lake Texcoco

THE BIG PICTURE
As you have read, Middle America was the scene for the development of two great ancient civilizations— the Olmec and the Maya. As time passed, these civilizations lost their power. Other peoples carried on their traditions of farming and building. In the 1400s the Aztec built an empire that rivaled the achievements of the Maya hundreds of years earlier. The center of Aztec culture and power was the great capital city called Tenochtitlán (te noch tee TLAHN).

At the time the Spanish soldier observed it, Tenochtitlán was probably larger than any other city in the world. Today one of the world's largest cities, Mexico City, is located in the same area. That area is a fertile valley where the great drama of the Aztec unfolded.

426

SHELTERED INSTRUCTION

READING STRATEGIES & LANGUAGE DEVELOPMENT

MAKING AND SUPPORTING GENERALIZATIONS Remind students that they can make generalizations to better understand what they read. On the board, create a flowchart to model the process: decide on a topic, choose facts to support the topic, create a generalization from the information. Arrange students in cooperative groups to make an organizer to use as they read this lesson. Students can fill it in with generalizations about the Aztecs. **[SDAIE STRATEGY:** METACOGNITIVE **DEVELOPMENT/SCHEMA BUILDING]**

SYNONYMS Refer students to the word *marshland* on p. 427 and ask them to define it (an area of low, wet land). Ask students for synonyms they can think of for this term (perhaps *swamp, bog, wetland*).

THE AZTEC SETTLE IN MIDDLE AMERICA

According to legend, the Aztec, who called themselves *Mexica*, journeyed for years in Middle America, searching for a place to settle. In the 1100s the Aztec came to the Valley of Mexico. They were among many newcomers there seeking a home. In this high valley surrounded by mountains are several lakes. About 1325 the Aztec arrived at the shores of Lake Texcoco (tay SKOH koh).

The Aztec saw an island in the center of the lake. On that island, their historical accounts state, they received a sign. An eagle flew from the sky, perched atop a cactus, and began eating a snake. The Aztec took this to mean that they should build a city on the island. The Aztec named the city Tenochtitlán. *Tenochtitlán* means "place of the prickly pear cactus" in the Aztec language, Nahuatl (NAH wah tul).

Creating Farmland

At first Tenochtitlán was no more than a collection of reed huts surrounding a temple. Although their land was poor, the Aztec soon developed a system of agriculture similar to the ones used by other peoples of the area. They carved canals through the marshland. In the lake they piled up the lake's soil to make smaller islands. Most of these islands were about the size of a football field. These human-made islands, were known as chinampas (chin AHM pahz). Chinampas were held in place by wooden stakes and the roots of willow trees. Some chinampas actually floated. They could be moved from one part of the lake to another!

By carefully planting different crops year round, Aztec farmers created a constant supply of squash, tomatoes, chili peppers, and flowers. The most important crop, maize, was grown mostly in fields on the lake shore.

Building a City

Although three out of four Aztec worked as farmers, many worked at other jobs in Tenochtitlán. Some people worked to make stone buildings that gradually replaced the reed huts. Others built three long bridges, or causeways, that connected the island to the lake shore. Although most people lived in one-room stone or mud houses, Aztec rulers lived in grand palaces surrounded by luxurious gardens. A Spanish soldier described one of these palaces: "I walked until I was tired and never saw the whole of it." That palace even had its own zoo!

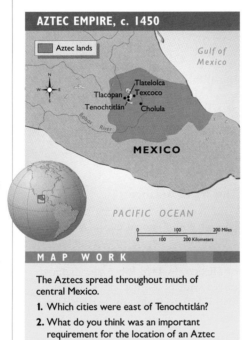

AZTEC EMPIRE, c. 1450

Aztec lands

Gulf of Mexico

Tlatelolca
Tlacopan • Texcoco
Tenochtitlán • Cholula

MEXICO

PACIFIC OCEAN

0   100   200 Miles
0   100   200 Kilometers

MAP WORK

The Aztecs spread throughout much of central Mexico.

1. Which cities were east of Tenochtitlán?
2. What do you think was an important requirement for the location of an Aztec city?

MAP WORK: 1. Cholula, Texcoco 2. about 200 miles (about 322 kilometers) 3. Balsas River **427**

THE AZTEC SETTLE IN MIDDLE AMERICA

Have students list the attractive features of the Valley of Mexico.

More   MAP WORK

Refer students to the map and have them work with both text and map.

● ***When and where did the Aztec settle after their search for a homeland?*** *(in the 1100s in the Valley of Mexico)*

● ***On what spot did they settle? Why?*** *(On an island in Lake Texcoco; they saw a sign—an eagle, perched on a cactus, was eating a snake.)*

● ***What did they call the island city they founded there?*** *(Tenochtitlán)*

★THINKING FURTHER: *Making Conclusions* **Why might an island be a good site for a city?** *(good natural defenses)*

Discussing Creating Farmland
Help students appreciate the Aztec ingenuity.

● ***What ingenious ways did the Aztec use to create farmland from marshland and lake water?*** *(carving canals through the marshland to drain it, and assembling floating farm fields called* chinampas*)*

★THINKING FURTHER: *Making Conclusions* **How did these methods and the climate affect their growing season?** *(The fields they created, crop rotation, and a temperate climate provided year-long crops.)*

Investigating Building a City Early Spanish explorers called Tenochtitlán the greatest city they had ever seen.

● ***How did the Aztec connect Tenochtitlán to the shore?*** *(with three long bridges, or causeways)*

★THINKING FURTHER: *Making Conclusions* **Why do you suppose the causeways were necessary to the growth and maintenance of a large city?** *(Help students recognize that heavy traffic would cross regularly to the city.)*

BACKGROUND INFORMATION

MORE ABOUT TENOCHTITLÁN

● According to legend, the Aztec god of the sun and of war set the Aztec on their quest for a place to settle, telling them, "Search until you find this sign—an eagle perched atop a cactus holding a snake in its beak." This sign they found in Lake Texcoco.

● The causeways the Aztec built to link Tenochtitlán to the surrounding shore had an ingenious feature. When an enemy, threatening to attack, appeared on shore, sections of the causeways could be lifted up, like a modern drawbridge, making it impossible for invaders to cross them.

USING THE ANTHOLOGY

POETRY OF THE AZTEC, pages 104–105 Have students read the poems and discuss how they reveal what was important to the Aztecs.

GROWTH
OF AN EMPIRE

Help students see that when the Aztec first arrived, they were not strong.

- **Did the Aztec pay or collect tribute at first?** *(They paid tribute.)*

★THINKING FURTHER: *Making Conclusions* **How do you suppose a people forced to pay tribute felt about those to whom they had to pay it?** *(Possible answer: angry and deeply resentful)*

Discussing The Triple Alliance
Have students sit in pairs with one text open to this page and the other to the map on p. 427.

- **How did the Aztec of Tenochtitlán turn the tables from being tribute payers to becoming tribute collectors?** *(by forming an alliance with two other cities and thus becoming stronger than everyone else)*

- **Looking at the map, how would you describe the extent of the area over which the Aztec spread their empire?** *(more than 200 miles east to west and north to south)*

- **How was this spread accomplished?** *(through warfare)*

- **How did the Aztec treat those they captured in war?** *(They sacrificed captives to their sun god, whom they believed could be nourished only by human blood.)*

- **How did they treat the peoples they conquered?** *(They demanded tribute from them. Point out to the class that this tribute included crops as well as young people to be sacrificed.)*

★THINKING FURTHER: *Making Generalizations* **What generalizations can you make about the Aztec attitude toward war and toward their place in the world?** *(Facts about how ready they were to go to war and the poet's comment show a prominent warlike streak; facts about their actions toward others show a strong belief that "might makes right.")*

GROWTH
OF AN EMPIRE

When the Aztec first arrived in the Valley of Mexico, they had to pay tribute, or taxes, to the rulers of nearby cities. This tribute was usually a part of their crops, which people carried by boat and on foot from Tenochtitlán to the other cities.

The Triple Alliance

Before long, though, tribute was pouring into Tenochtitlán instead of pouring out. The Aztec became one of the most powerful groups in the Valley of Mexico. In 1428 the Aztec joined forces with two other cities, Texcoco and Tlacopan (tlahk oh PAHN). They formed the Triple Alliance and worked together to strengthen their power. Soon the Triple Alliance gained control of the entire Valley of Mexico.

By 1450 Aztec power spread beyond the mountains surrounding the Valley of Mexico. Under the leadership of the Aztec ruler Ahuítzotl (ah WEE soht ul), the armies of the Triple Alliance conquered areas west to the Pacific Ocean and south to what is today Guatemala. Equipped with wooden shields and sharp stone spears, the Aztec army caused great fear among the peoples of Mexico.

One Aztec poet described the great respect paid to soldiers who died in battle, writing "There is nothing like death in war." Soldiers preferred, however, to capture enemies as prisoners. These prisoners were sacrificed to honor the Aztec god of the sun, Huitzilopochtli (weet si loh POHCH tlee). To sacrifice means to kill in a religious ceremony. The Aztec believed that only human blood could nourish the sun god.

GLOBAL CONNECTION

CONTRASTING THE EASTERN AND WESTERN HEMISPHERES Remind students that American civilizations developed in total isolation, in contrast to civilizations in the Eastern Hemisphere, where ancient Rome and ancient China had knowledge of one another. Ideas, knowledge, inventions, and goods circulated through Europe, Asia, and Africa for thousands of years, but people of the Eastern and Western hemispheres were unaware of one other.

SECOND-LANGUAGE SUPPORT

WORKING WITH A PEER Reduce the number of pages second-language learners must read to help their comprehension. Divide the class in thirds to cover lessons 2, 3, and 4. Work with each group to summarize its particular section and create an oral presentation.

This scene (far left) shows how the Great Plaza at Tenochtitlán may have looked. Aztec messengers carried feather fans like this one (left).

The tribute the conquered cities paid brought the Aztec great wealth. Workers brought more than one million loads of food for tribute to the Aztec capital each year. Tenochtitlán grew until it reached a population of about 150,000 people.

Governing the Empire

Like those of many other cultures you have read about, the Aztec social pyramid was made up of several levels. At the top was the emperor, who held great political and religious power. He was the richest person in Tenochtitlán. He also led the Aztec army. The emperor was worshiped by the Aztec people, who believed he had godlike powers. The emperor even had a special color—turquoise. No one else was allowed to wear clothing of this color.

Below the emperor were nobles and government workers. Nobles were in charge of running the Aztec empire. They made sure tributes were paid, temples were built, and streets were swept. Nobles also planned wars.

The majority of the population made up the family groups called *calpulli* (kahl POOL lee). *Calpulli* means "groups of houses" in Nahuatl. In Tenochtitlán there were 20 different calpulli. Each had its own leaders and was settled in a different part of the city. Each also had its own temple, school, and farmland. Members worked as farmers, craftworkers, merchants, and soldiers.

Near the base of Aztec society were poor farmers. They were among the poorest members of society, since they owned no land and had to work for others. Below the farmers were slaves. Only about 2 percent of the people in Tenochtitlán were enslaved. Most slaves were captured outside Aztec lands and brought to the capital by merchants. Slaves had no freedom and had to do whatever work their owners told them to do. Unlike those in most other cultures that practiced slavery, the children of Aztec slaves were free and could make choices about their lives.

This mosaic serpent was made to be worn on the chest. The serpent was a god to the Aztec.

Discussing Governing the Empire
As students work with this section, call them up to the board to draw the Aztec social pyramid described. (top to bottom: emperor → nobles and government workers → members of calpulli → poor farmers → slaves)

● **How was the Aztec emperor like the Egyptian pharaoh?** *(He had great religious and political power, was considered a god, and commanded great wealth.)*

● **What level of the social pyramid ran the government?** *(the nobles and government workers)*

● **What were the calpulli and where did they rank?** *(family groups who made up the majority of the population, lived together in their own neighborhoods, and worked as farmers, craftworkers, merchants, and soldiers; below nobles and government workers)*

● **What groups were at the base of the pyramid?** *(poor farmers who worked land owned by others, slaves)*

● **How were Aztec slaves different from slaves in other groups you have studied?** *(Their children were free.)*

★THINKING FURTHER: *Making Generalizations* **What generalizations can you make about social pyramids you have studied so far?** *(Students might use facts about the Egyptian, European Middle Ages, and Japanese social pyramids to comment, for example, on "rich at the top, poor at the bottom" and "power at the top, lessening as it moves down.")*

CITIZENSHIP★

UNDERSTANDING GOVERNMENT Aztec government made itself strongly felt throughout Aztec society, including enforcement of a strict moral code.

● Thieves and drunkards were punished by death. So were couples who broke their marriage vows.

● If they were commoners, their executions were carried out in public. Nobles were executed in private.

● Modern laws against child abuse would have been strange indeed to the Aztecs. Aztec parents believed in physical punishment for their children.

VISUAL LITERACY

ABOUT THE AZTEC MOSAIC SERPENT
This serpent ornament is a piece of Aztec jewelry designed to be worn on the chest. It is made of carved wood and covered with a mosaic of turquoise. The gums and nostrils of the serpent are made from red shell. The teeth are made of white shell. The entire piece is about seven inches tall. The serpent was a god to the Aztec and appears frequently in Aztec art from this period. Invite students to study the ornament and discuss it as a religious symbol for the Aztec. Possible questions include: Who might have worn this jewelry? How do you think the Aztecs felt about their serpent god? (Possible answer: fearful) How is this shown?

AZTEC CIVILIZATION

The year 1500 was shortly before the Europeans arrived in Mexico.

> ★ THINKING FURTHER: *Making Conclusions* **Why is it accurate to say that the Aztec were well advanced in science and art?** *(Medicine, astronomy, and skilled craft work were all in evidence in their society.)*

Discussing The Great Temple Refer students to the illustrations of the Great Plaza on p. 428 and of the pyramid on this page and give them a few moments to examine them.

● **What do these illustrations tell you about the importance of religion in Aztec life?** *(Religion was important to Aztec society.)*

● **What different kinds of structures were included here?** *(temples, priests' homes, religious schools, ball courts)*

> ★ THINKING FURTHER: *Making Conclusions* **Judging from this variety, what kinds of events do you assume were carried on here?** *(worship of gods, sacrifices to them, religious education, sports)*

Learning about Aztec Writing
The Spanish destroyed Aztec writings as well as Maya writings (see note on p. 302) because they considered both to be the work of the devil.

● **How would you describe Aztec writing?** *(colorful pictures and symbols, gathered in codices)*

● **What kinds of information did these codices present?** *(Aztec history, religion, government, and science)*

> ★ THINKING FURTHER: *Cause and Effect* **What effect would you say their destruction had on our knowledge about the Aztec?** *(It robbed us of much that we could have known but now never will.)*

AZTEC CIVILIZATION

By 1500 the city of Tenochtitlán bustled with trade and learning. Aztec doctors made more than 1,000 medicines from plants. Plants were used to heal wounds, reduce fevers, and cure stomachaches. Predicting eclipses and the movements of planets, Aztec astronomers built on Maya knowledge of the heavens. Craftworkers created beautiful feather headdresses, gold and copper jewelry, ceramic storage jars, and woven cloth.

The Great Temple

From birth until death, from morning until night, religion played a central role in the lives of the Aztec. The center of religious life in Tenochtitlán was the temple district. This district was located where three main streets came together. Here stood temples to

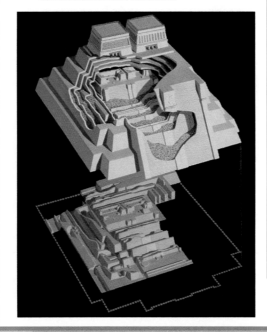

This model shows the outside of the Great Temple at Tenochtitlán. The inside is shown below the model.

different gods, homes for men and women priests, schools for young priests, and ball courts. Rising as high as an eight-story building was the Great Temple. Aztec built this temple to honor Huitzilopochtli, their sun god, and Tlaloc (TLAH lohk), their rain god.

Two staircases, decorated with carved and painted sculptures, led up to the top of the temple platform. It was here, on two massive stone blocks, that special priests sacrificed thousands of war prisoners every year.

Aztec Writing

In addition to performing temple ceremonies, priests kept a calendar that was used to predict the future. Some kept records using a special Aztec system of writing. Colorful pictures and symbols were drawn on a long folded sheet of paper. Each of these folded sheets was called a codex (KOH deks). Two or more of these sheets were called codices (KOH dih seez). Codices contained information about the history, religion, government, and science of the Aztec. Few

BACKGROUND INFORMATION

ABOUT AZTEC RITUAL GAMES Refer the class to the description of the Maya ball game called *pokta-pok* (p. 299) and its religious meaning.

● The Aztec also played a ritual ball game, which they called *lachtli*. In it, players struck a small rubber ball with their hips or thighs and knocked it across a special court.

● Another ritual game involved men who were dressed as birds, attached to ropes, and slung in a wide circle around a pole.

CURRICULUM CONNECTION

LINKS TO ART Students who would like to learn more about Aztec art should examine Francis F. Berdan's *The Aztecs*, part of the *Indians of North America* series. It contains a color art portfolio entitled "Art of the Aztec Empire."

The codex (far left) shows the god of spring. A statue of the god of flowers and song is at left.

remain because the Spanish destroyed most Aztec records in the 1500s.

The Aztec also had a strong oral tradition. People memorized many poems, songs, and speeches. Poems were often recited on special occasions, accompanied by drums and flutes. This is an Aztec poem:

> *An emerald fell to the ground,*
> *and a flower was born; this is your*
> *song!*
> *Whenever you sing your songs here*
> *in Mexico*
> *the sun shines eternally [forever].*

WHY IT MATTERS

Within only a hundred years, the Aztec built one of the most powerful empires in the Americas. Farming techniques and efficient government helped the empire to grow and run smoothly. Constant warfare brought many enemies under Aztec rule. In 1521 the Aztec fell to the European kingdom of Spain.

Aztec people and many of their traditions survived. Food such as maize, Aztec crafts, and even the Nahuatl language are all part of Mexican culture today. The name *Mexico* comes from the name the Aztec called themselves. Even the flag of Mexico celebrates the Aztec legacy. At its center the flag shows the Aztec symbol of an eagle with a snake in its beak.

✓// Reviewing Facts and Ideas

MAIN IDEAS

- The Aztec first settled in the Valley of Mexico in about 1325.
- The Aztec built a powerful empire centered at Tenochtitlán.
- The Aztec gained much knowledge in medicine and astronomy and created beautiful buildings and works of art.

THINK ABOUT IT

1. Why did the Aztec settle in the Valley of Mexico?

2. How did the people of nearby cities help make Tenochtitlán wealthy?

3. **FOCUS** How did the Aztec expand their empire to areas beyond the Valley of Mexico?

4. **THINKING SKILL** Make a *conclusion* about how the people of conquered villages were treated in the Aztec empire. Explain how you reached your conclusion.

5. **WRITE** Write a paragraph describing one major achievement of the Aztec. Explain why that achievement was important for the Aztec civilization.

431

Discussing WHY IT MATTERS Point out that Aztec heritage is still strong in Mexico.

★**THINKING FURTHER:** *Making Conclusions* **How did farming techniques, efficient government, and constant warfare contribute to building up the Aztec empire?** *(Successful farming fed a growing population; efficient government helped the society run smoothly, and a strong constant warfare extended Aztec territory.)*

⭐ 3 CLOSE

SUM IT UP
Have students write their answers and exchange papers for correction.

- *Where did the Aztec settle in 1325?* (the Valley of Mexico)

- *What did they make their capital city?* (Tenochtitlán)

- *What signs are there that the Aztec were advanced in science and art?* (the high level of their medicine and astronomy and the high quality of their architecture and art)

EVALUATE
✓ **Answers to Think About It**

1. They believed they saw a sign that told them to settle there. *Recall Details*

2. They had to pay tribute to it. *Make Inferences*

3. by forming an alliance with two other cities and then by conquest *Steps in a Process*

4. They were completed overwhelmed by the Aztec, forced to submit to them and pay tribute to them. Students should offer details to support their conclusions. *Make Conclusions*

5. Paragraphs may center on the development of chinampas, the establishment of Tenochtitlán, success in conquest, efficient government, Aztec science, or Aztec art.

Write About It Ask students to picture themselves as visitors to Tenochtitlán and write a diary entry describing what they have seen and done there.

MEETING INDIVIDUAL NEEDS

RETEACHING (Easy) Have students use colored pens, pencils, or crayons to illustrate a scene in which the Aztec ruler stands upon temple steps to receive tributes from conquered peoples. Remind students to be sure to put the emperor in the proper color clothing (turquoise) for the ceremony.

EXTENSION (Average) Tell students to design the itinerary for a tour of Tenochtitlán. Their itineraries should identify the stops on the tour and describe what the visitor will see at each stop.

ENRICHMENT (Challenging) As a class project, have students use the recreation of Tenochtitlán's Great Plaza on p. 428 and research other recreations of it to create their own cardboard or clay model of the Great Plaza.

SKILLS LESSON
PAGES 432–433

Lesson Overview
Map projections are attempts to show a spherical Earth as accurately as possible on a flat map.

Lesson Objective
★ Evaluate various map projections.

★ 1 PREPARE

MOTIVATE Roughly draw Earth's major continents with a felt pen on an orange. Then peel the orange and press the pieces down on a flat surface to show how flatness distorts shapes. What do cartographers do to try to solve this problem? Have students read *Why the Skill Matters* to find out. Work with them on the meanings of *distortion* and *projection* and on the idea that no projection is perfect.

SET PURPOSE How do we know which projection can give the most accurate picture of the area we need to study? Invite the class to explore this *Skills Lesson* to find out and to begin by reading the steps in *Helping Yourself*.

★ 2 TEACH

Using Map Projections Help students evaluate the features of each projection.

● **What kind of projection does both Map A and Map B show? What does this kind of projection show well?** *(an equal-area projection; the comparative sizes of land masses)*

● **What advantages does Map A have over Map B? Map B over Map A?** *(Map A gives a better idea of distances between places, except at the far edges; Map B shows actual shapes better.)*

Resource REMINDER

Practice and Project Book: *p. 88*
Transparency: *Maps 17 & 18*
Technology: *Adventure Time!* CD-ROM

Geography Skills

MAP A: EQUAL-AREA PROJECTION

MAP B: EQUAL-AREA PROJECTION

Using Map Projections

VOCABULARY
distortion
projection
equal-area projection
mercator projection
polar projection

WHY THE SKILL MATTERS

Only one tiny map fragment remains from Aztec times, but most historians believe that the Aztec commonly used maps. Maps would have been an important tool for keeping track of the widespread Aztec empire.

Today some maps are more accurate than others. Maps that show the entire world vary greatly in accuracy. Since Earth is a sphere, cartographers must stretch or cut parts of the globe, making it fit onto a flat map. This stretching and cutting causes distortion—errors that make the map less accurate.

When cartographers create a map of Earth's entire surface, they must use a

432

projection. A projection is a way of showing parts of Earth on a flat map.

USING MAP PROJECTIONS

One of the most common types of map projections is the equal-area projection. An example of this projection is shown on Map A. This map is especially useful for comparing sizes of land masses. However, it distorts the shapes of land. Distances between places at the edges of this map are distorted. It is also difficult to find north and south on this map, because these directions curve along meridians.

Map B is another kind of equal-area projection. The shapes on Map B are more accurate than the shapes on Map A. However, the cuts in this map make it very difficult to tell the distances between places.

Another kind of world map, the mercator projection, is shown on Map C. This projection was invented by a Flemish mapmaker in the 1500s. Near the equator there is little distortion and sizes are accurate, too. However, as you move farther from the equator, sizes become more distorted.

Polar projections are used to show the area around the North Pole or the South

---

READING STRATEGIES & LANGUAGE DEVELOPMENT

COMPARE AND CONTRAST Point out to the class that this *Skills Lesson* is based on carefully comparing and contrasting various map projections to evaluate their advantages, disadvantages, and usefulness. As students work through this lesson, encourage them go beyond the text questions to create their own compare and contrast questions about the material to pose to the class at the end of the lesson.

WORD HISTORY Call attention to the word *pilot* on p. 433. Point out that it was first used for ships and comes from a Greek word meaning "oar" or "rudder." In English, the word *pilot* first meant "a person who steers a ship." Later its meaning was extended to mean "one who flies a plane." Other meanings for *pilot* include "a model for a project," "a sample of a proposed television show" and "a stove's starting burner."

Pole. Most polar projections show only half the globe or less. Map D shows a polar projection of the North Pole. Sizes and shapes near the center are accurate. Near the edges, however, there is distortion.

Polar projections like Map D are used by pilots flying over the North Pole. The shortest distance between two points on a polar projection is a straight line.

TRYING THE SKILL

Suppose you are traveling on a long trip through the Americas. You want to use a map that will accurately show the distances you have traveled and how far you still have to go. Which kind of projection would you select? Would you have any use for a polar projection on this trip?*

REVIEWING THE SKILL

1. Why do all flat maps of the world have some distortion?

2. Where does distortion occur on a mercator projection map?

3. Look at the Atlas map of the world on page R18. Which type of projection is used for this map?

4. In what ways is a flat map better than a globe? In what ways is a globe better?

5. Why are there many different kinds of map projections?

Helping yourself

- Map **projections** are useful for studying and comparing parts of Earth.
- Since different projections have different uses, first decide what you want to learn.
- Select the type of projection that best serves your purpose.

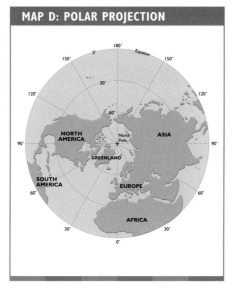

MAP C: MERCATOR PROJECTION

MAP D: POLAR PROJECTION

*mercator projection; yes, for planning travel in the northernmost parts of North America and in the southernmost parts of South America

433

- **What kind of projections does Map C show? For what purpose is this projection useful?** (mercator; navigation requiring straight-line compass directions)

- **What disadvantage does Map C have?** (severe distortion of size, especially at far north and south)

- **How does Map D's name describe its projection?** (It is a polar projection, showing Earth from one of the two poles, in this case, the North Pole.)

Trying the Skill Again refer students to *Helping Yourself* steps two and three.

★**THINKING FURTHER:** *Making Conclusions* **Why would you choose an equal-area projection to measure distance? a mercator projection to check direction? a polar projection on the trip?** (equal area: greatest accuracy in size of area; mercator: straight-line compass accuracy; polar projection: accurate sizes and shapes at beginning and end of the journey)

3 CLOSE

SUM IT UP

Invite students to pose for the class their compare and contrast questions and call on other students to answer.

EVALUATE

✓ **Answers to Reviewing the Skill**

1. A flat surface cannot accurately reflect a spherical surface.

2. farther from the equator

3. equal-area, Map A type

4. A flat map is more portable and easily reproduced; a globe is more accurate in showing actual sizes, shapes, and distances.

5. because there are so many different kinds of things to show accurately and different needs for using maps

 Technology CONNECTION

ADVENTURE TIME! CD-ROM

Encourage students to use *Grid* in *Build* on the World Map on the *Adventure Time!* CD-ROM.

MEETING INDIVIDUAL NEEDS

RETEACHING (Easy) Have students construct a summary table of the three projections, listing advantages and drawbacks of each as well as one particular use for each. They can turn the table into a bulletin board by illustrating each projection.

EXTENSION (Average) Divide the class into groups, each one to research one of the following "big names" in mapmaking: Claudius Ptolemy, Columbus, Martin Behaim, Mercator, and Mollweide. Have the groups report their findings to the class.

ENRICHMENT (Challenging) Divide the class into groups, each to do encyclopedia and atlas research into one of the following kinds of map projections: sinusoidal, cylindrical (other than Mercator), perspective, and conic projections. Have the groups analyze advantages and drawbacks of each and illustrate their report.

LESSON 3

PAGES 434–439

Lesson Overview
Along the rugged heights of the Andes Mountains, the Inca built a brilliant civilization of about 12 million people.

Lesson Objectives
★ Describe ways the Inca adapted the environment to their needs.

★ Trace the growth of the Inca empire.

★ Identify and describe major achievements of the Inca empire.

1 PREPARE

MOTIVATE Tell students to picture this: A band of landless warriors is searching for land on which to settle; they come upon a valley and a sign tells them this is the place; they displace the people there and begin a conquest of surrounding lands. Sound familiar? No, it's not the Aztec; it's the Inca. Do the *Read Aloud* to set the stage.

SET PURPOSE Tell students that the time for the founding of the two empires was roughly the same, but for the Inca, the place was the Valley of Cuzco, shown in the photo. Encourage them to explore the lesson for the rest of the story and to answer the *Read to Learn* question. Preview the *Vocabulary* terms.

2 TEACH

Understanding THE BIG PICTURE
Begin to help students develop a sense of the uniqueness of the Inca civilization.

> ★THINKING FURTHER: *Compare and Contrast* **What other similarities and differences were there between the Aztec and Inca?**
> *(Similarities: worship of sun god, dependence on maize, strong army, efficient government. Differences: South America, not North America, and extent of empire.)*

Resource REMINDER

Practice and Project Book: *p. 89*
Anthology: *The Glory of the Incas, pp. 106–108*

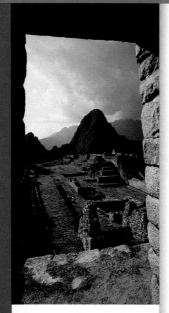

Focus Activity

READ TO LEARN

What were some of the major achievements of the Inca?

VOCABULARY
- terrace
- quipu

PEOPLE
- Pachakuti Inca

PLACES
- Cuzco
- Machu Picchu

434

1200　　　　　　　　　1531　1600

The Inca Empire

Read Aloud

I am rich in silver

I am rich in gold.

These words come from an Inca poem. They celebrate the wealth of the Inca civilization, which developed in the Andes Mountains of South America. In these mountains the Inca found the large amounts of metal and minerals that made their empire rich. They also found a place to develop traditions that made their culture rich as well.

THE BIG PICTURE
While the Aztec were extending their rule beyond the Valley of Mexico, another culture was expanding in the mountains of South America. This people, known as the Inca, built an empire along the Andes Mountains. The empire stretched from what is today Ecuador to central Chile. This distance is about equal to the distance from New York City to the Panama Canal. At its peak the Inca empire had about 12 million people. Although they had little contact with the Aztec, the Inca, too, worshiped the sun, depended on maize as a major crop, and organized a strong army. Like the Aztec to the north, the Inca also created a system of government in their empire. In many other ways, however, the Inca were unique in the Americas and in the world.

SHELTERED INSTRUCTION

READING STRATEGIES & LANGUAGE DEVELOPMENT

COMPARE AND CONTRAST To help students review the lesson concept, display two commonplace items and invite volunteers to compare and contrast them. Then divide the class in half. Have one half act as the Aztec; the other half, the Inca. Invite students to explain their similarities and differences. **[SDAIE STRATEGY: MODELING]**

IDIOMS Refer students to the sentence on p. 435 that refers to "People from all corners of the empire." Can an empire have *four corners?* Point out that this kind of expression is called an idiom, which means "an expression having a special meaning different from the usual meaning of the words." Such expressions add color to our use of language. Cite such common idioms as *cut and dried, make heads or tails of,* and *split hairs.* Call on students for other examples of idioms.

THE RISE OF THE INCA

The Inca empire rose out of a small village called Cuzco (KOOS koh) in a fertile valley in what is today Peru. About 1200 the Inca settled at Cuzco to grow maize and other crops. At first the word *Inca* was the name for the ruler. Later the word applied to all of the people. When drought reduced the amount of fertile farmland, the Inca took over their neighbors' land. During the 1300s the Inca ruled most of the Cuzco Valley and demanded tributes from the other people living there.

Building an Empire

In 1438 a ruler called Pachakuti (pah chah KOO tee) Inca greatly extended the Inca borders. Soon the Inca controlled land west to the Pacific Ocean and south to the area of Lake Titicaca. Find the Inca lands on the map on this page. The Inca army seemed unstoppable in its quest to conquer new areas. In the Inca language, the word *Quechua* (KECH oo uh) means "to fight" and "to enjoy oneself."

Pachakuti became known as Sapa Inca, or Supreme Inca. As emperor, Pachakuti set about organizing the new land he controlled. He forced conquered people off their land. Then he allowed people who

were loyal to the Inca to settle there. Pachakuti appointed governors in each region. People from all corners of the empire were required to do jobs for the government. Men built roads and raised crops; women made cloth.

Pachakuti also spread the Inca religion throughout the empire. Their religion was based on the worship of an ancient Inca god called Viracocha. According to Inca beliefs, this god had appeared in the emperor's dream during a war. Conquered people were forced to worship Viracocha and provide offerings of food. However, the Inca also let people continue to worship their own gods, as well.

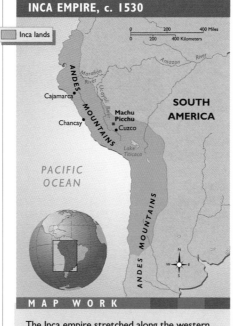

INCA EMPIRE, c. 1530

Inca lands

0   200   400 Miles
0   200   400 Kilometers

SOUTH AMERICA

Cajamarca

Chancay

Machu Picchu
Cuzco

Lake Titicaca

PACIFIC OCEAN

ANDES MOUNTAINS

ANDES MOUNTAINS

Amazon River

Marañón River

Ucayali River

This poncho was made of feathers by an Inca craftworker. It was worn during Inca ceremonies.

MAP WORK

The Inca empire stretched along the western edge of South America.

1. Which city was located along the Ucayali River?
2. About how far is Lake Titicaca from Machu Picchu?

435

THE RISE OF THE INCA

Encourage students to consider reasons for the rapid growth of the Inca empire.

More **MAP WORK**

Refer students to the map on this page and encourage them to work back and forth between text and map.

- *Find Cuzco on the map. Where in the Inca empire is it located?* (at about the center point)

- *About how far does it lie from Lake Titicaca?* (about 150 miles)

- *About how great a length down the Andes Mountains does the Inca empire extend?* (over 1,500 miles)

- *Why did the Cuzco settlers begin to conquer their neighbors?* (Drought reduced their fertile farmland.)

★**THINKING FURTHER:** *Compare and Contrast How would you compare the power of the Inca of the 1300s with the Aztec of the 1430s?* (Both controlled their valleys and demanded tributes.)

Discussing Building an Empire
Refer the class to the map once again.

- *In what directions from Cuzco did the Inca expand their empire? Under whose direction?* (north northwest and south southeast; Pachakuti, the Supreme Inca)

- *What government system did he set up?* (governors ruling regions from which conquered people were driven off, unless they were loyal to the Inca)

- *With what did he replace the tribute system?* (He demanded that the people work for the government.)

★**THINKING FURTHER:** *Compare and Contrast How would you compare and contrast the Inca with the Aztec on attitudes toward war and attitudes toward religion?* (The Aztec poet's quote and the fact that the Inca used the same word for making war and for enjoying oneself show both loved war; Aztec stress on religion appears stronger than the more lax Inca allowance of worship of non-Inca gods.)

CHILDREN OF THE SUN

For these two pages, have students sit in pairs with one text open here and the other to Lesson 2, on the Aztec. Invite students to find information there on which to base comparisons with the Inca.

- **Who was Inti?** *(the god of the sun whom the Inca considered their parent)*

- **How did Pachakuti show special reverence for Inti?** *(by building this god the most important temple in Cuzco, with a golden sun sculpture)*

★**THINKING FURTHER:** *Compare and Contrast* **How does Inti compare with the Aztec god Huitzilopochtli?** *(Both were their people's gods of the sun and both were honored by having great temples dedicated to them.)*

Discussing Life in Cuzco Help students develop an appreciation for Cuzco's technology. Tell students that the writing on the codex shown here is old Spanish.

- **What evidence is there in Cuzco of an advanced civilization?** *(solid building construction, well laid-out streets, a water channel)*

★**THINKING FURTHER:** *Compare and Contrast* **How would you compare and contrast living in and around Cuzco and Tenochtitlán?** *(Cuzco seems to have had stone, adobe, and mud huts along stone-paved streets and on slopes, but there is no sign that the people lived in separate groups in separate sections of city as the calpulli did in Tenochtitlán.)*

CHILDREN OF THE SUN

After his victory Pachakuti built a temple with a gold sculpture of the god Viracocha. This temple was located in the city of Cuzco. The most important temple in Cuzco, though, honored Inti, the sun god. In the center of this temple was a huge golden sculpture of the sun, decorated with precious stones. The Inca considered Inti to be their parent and often called themselves "Children of the Sun."

Life in Cuzco

Cuzco served as the center of government, religion, and trade in the Inca empire. The temples and government buildings at the center of Cuzco were constructed of stone blocks. These blocks fit together so well that it is impossible to put a knife between them!

Beyond the main plaza lived the emperor and wealthy nobles. These people were easy to recognize by the special headbands and earrings they wore. One of the first Spanish soldiers to visit the city was impressed by Inca building skill. He wrote the following description in the 1500s:

Cuzco is large enough and handsome enough to compare to any Spanish city. Most of the houses are of stone; others have stonework only halfway up; many are of adobe [clay bricks] and all are regularly built. The streets, all stone-paved and straight, cross each other at right angles, and have each a stone-lined water channel running down the middle. The city is placed on high ground, and many houses cling to the slopes above and many can be seen on the flat lands below.

The Inca were skilled at building with stone (left) and at farming, as the codex (below) shows.

Outside Cuzco, workers and farmers lived in small mud huts with high windows. Also outside the city were many government storage buildings. Some contained food, such as maize, dried fruit, or salt. Others contained neat piles of beautiful wool and cotton cloth. There was even a building just to hold the feathers of hummingbirds, which were used as decoration for clothing.

Inca Agriculture

Every year the Inca emperor, followed by a group of nobles, traveled to a field outside Cuzco and dug up the ground with a plow made of pure gold. This act signaled the importance of agriculture to all of Inca society.

Inca farmers grew potatoes, maize, and peppers. They adapted their farming methods to the geography of different parts of the empire. In hilly areas they built terraces, level platforms of earth that climbed each hill like a staircase. In rocky areas Inca farmers dug huge pits 20 feet deep. Farmers enriched the soil by placing fish in the pits. In dry areas the Inca brought water through a system of canals and aqueducts. One stone aqueduct crossed nearly 500 miles to bring water from a faraway mountain lake.

Although all farming was done by human labor, the Inca did raise animals for other uses. They used llamas as pack animals to carry many trade items through the empire. The best wool came from wild sheep. Only the nobles were allowed to wear the fine wool from these sheep. The Inca also hunted deer for food and clothing.

As in the past, llamas are still used to carry goods in the Andes Mountains.

DID YOU KNOW?

How did the Inca keep records of trade throughout the empire?

Although the Inca did not have a written language, they developed a method for recording important matters. The Inca used special cords called quipus (KEE pooz). A quipu was about 2 feet long and had threads of different colors hanging from it. White threads stood for silver, yellow stood for gold, and red stood for war. By tying knots in the string, a quipu keeper could record trade items, battles, or births and deaths in a village.

437

Discussing Inca Agriculture Help students appreciate the symbolism of using a gold plow.

- *What evidence do you find that the Inca valued agriculture very highly?* (Planting was ushered in yearly by a ceremony in which the Inca emperor plowed land with a solid gold plow.)

- *What inventive means did the Inca develop to extend farmland in their mountainous environment?* (Students should mention terrace farming. Invite them to come up to the board to diagram how the terraces must have been dug out of the sides of hills and mountains.)

★**THINKING FURTHER:** *Compare and Contrast* **How would you compare the degree of inventiveness that went into the Inca's developing terrace farming and the Aztec's developing chinampas?** (Students should give both peoples high marks for such successful adaptations to their environments.)

★**THINKING FURTHER:** *Compare and Contrast* **How would you compare Inca engineering skill with that of the Romans in transporting water?** (Both mastered the building of aqueducts.)

Extending Did You Know? Invite students to use different colored string or yarn to make up three of their own quipus—perhaps recording years in their ages, years spent in school, and number of subjects at school.

CITIZENSHIP★

UNDERSTANDING GOVERNMENT The efficient Inca government regulated agriculture for both production and taxes.

- Each year, Inca officials estimated the amount of land throughout the empire that could be cultivated.

- They set aside enough for the general population to grow enough to feed itself—larger families got more land than smaller families.

- The rest—generally over half—was set aside for the state and to support religion. Farmers had to cultivate state and church land before they could work the land allotted to them.

GLOBAL CONNECTION

INCA AND PILGRIMS Refer students to the mention of Inca enriching the soil by placing fish in it. Ask them if this reminds them of something they learned in American history in connection with the Pilgrims in New England. Perhaps they will recall that this is a method that Squanto taught the Pilgrims to use shortly after they arrived in the Americas.

SECOND-LANGUAGE SUPPORT

USING PROPS Encourage second-language learners to create drawings that depict the scenes of Inca life. For a class display, students should write narratives that describe their scenes.

TRAVELING THROUGH THE EMPIRE

If students are not familiar with the useful term *infrastructure,* this would be a good place to introduce it as "the basic framework of a transportation system—roads, bridges, tunnels essential to moving people and goods."

- **What evidence can you find that the Inca had a well-developed infrastructure?** *(its 19,000-mile network of often paved roads through a highly rugged, mountainous terrain)*

- **How did the Inca use this infrastructure?** *(for the passage of messengers, huge armies, and long trade caravans throughout the empire)*

★THINKING FURTHER: *Making Conclusions* **How does this infrastructure give further proof of Inca mastery of engineering?** *(It demanded major feats of cutting away rock, paving, and bridge building.)*

Discussing A City in the Clouds
Refer the class to the illustrations of Machu Picchu on this page and pp. 310-311. Have students locate it on the map on p. 435 and tell them the story of the discovery. (See the *Background Information* below.)

- **When did the outside world learn about the presence of Machu Picchu in the Andes? How?** *(in 1911; American explorer Hiram Bingham came upon it.)*

- **Why might Machu Picchu have been built?** *(perhaps as a religious center or for use as a fortress during war)*

★THINKING FURTHER: *Making Conclusions* **As you look at Machu Picchu, what more does it tell you about Inca engineering skill?** *(Help students recognize its perch atop a steep mountain ridge, its use of cut and close-fitting stone, its sturdy architecture, its terraces.)*

The Inca used decorated knives (below) in ceremonies at places such as Machu Picchu (above).

TRAVELING THROUGH THE EMPIRE

Nothing was more important to keeping the empire together than the huge network of roads. The Inca built more than 19,000 miles of roads—over some of the most rugged landscape in the world. One Spanish visitor wrote this report in the 1500s:

I believe there is no account of a road as great as this, running through deep valleys, high mountains, banks of snow, torrents of water, living rock, and wild rivers. Through some places it went flat and paved; it was dug out of steep rock in the mountains; it passed with walls along rivers, and had steps and resting spots in the snow.

Important quipu messages were carried through the empire by runners. Messengers stopped every few miles to pass on messages to the next runner. Huge armies and long trade caravans made up of hundreds of llamas also traveled along the useful stone highways.

A City in the Clouds

Roads connected all corners of the empire, but some places were still difficult to reach. One road wound high into the mountains north of Cuzco, through stone tunnels and along steep cliffs. The road ended on a mountaintop, at a town called Machu Picchu (MAHCH oo PEEK choo). Machu Picchu is so far from other towns that it was forgotten until an American

438

BACKGROUND INFORMATION

ABOUT HIRAM BINGHAM'S DISCOVERY OF MACHU PICCHU In 1911 Hiram Bingham climbed through the Andes in search of the final capital of the Inca civilization. Here is how he described his find:

- "Suddenly I found myself confronted with the walls of ruined houses built of the finest quality of Inca stone work. It was hard to see them for they were partly covered with trees and moss.... It fairly took my breath away. What could this place be?" His party continued their climb.

- "Surprise followed surprise in bewildering succession. We came to a great stairway of large granite blocks. [Continuing their climb] Suddenly we found ourselves standing in front of the ruins of two of the finest and most interesting structures in ancient America ... The sight held me spellbound."

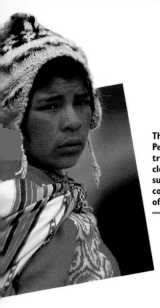

This girl from Peru wears traditional clothing suited to the cool climate of the Andes.

explorer named Hiram Bingham came across it in 1911.

Bingham found stone ruins of buildings, walls, and terraces at the mountaintop location. No one is sure why Machu Picchu was built or why it was forgotten. Some historians think that it may have been a special religious town, similar to a European monastery. There Inca may have worshiped at shrines. Many historians believe the town was built around 1438 by the Inca ruler Pachakuti, who wanted a place to worship. Another possibility is that the town was used as a fortress during war.

WHY IT MATTERS

The lost city of Machu Picchu is just one of many mysteries that surround the Inca. When Spanish soldiers conquered the Inca empire in the 1500s, they destroyed many Inca treasures. Fortunately, many quipu records remain, and some Spanish soldiers wrote down their thoughts about this civilization.

The few gold artifacts that remain show the skill of Inca craftworkers. Stone roads and city walls are evidence of great building knowledge. The songs and poems recorded by Spanish conquerors give a hint of the Inca's rich oral tradition. The language of the Inca is kept alive by millions of people today. People who speak Quechua still live in the Andes region of Peru. Through these sources historians can still get a sense of the brilliant culture created by the "Children of the Sun."

✔ Reviewing Facts and Ideas

MAIN IDEAS

- The Inca built a huge empire in the Andes Mountains in western South America.
- The Inca capital of Cuzco was the center of government, religion, and trade in the empire.
- Inca farmers used terraces and irrigation to grow crops.
- The vast Inca road system helped unite the empire. Roads allowed easy travel for armies, merchants, and messengers.

THINK ABOUT IT

1. Why did the Inca call themselves "Children of the Sun"?
2. How did terraces help the Inca expand their agriculture?
3. **FOCUS** List three major achievements of the Inca.
4. **THINKING SKILL** *Compare* the Inca empire with the Aztec empire. How were they similar? How were they different?
5. **GEOGRAPHY** Describe two ways in which the Inca interacted with their environment.

439

Discussing WHY IT MATTERS Tell students that the Spanish melted down many of the Inca gold artifacts.

- *Why is our knowledge of the Inca more limited than it could have been?* (destruction of Inca records and artifacts by the Spanish)
- *What do we still have of their legacy?* (language, some gold artifacts, remains of their infrastructure and architecture, oral tradition)

⭐ 3 CLOSE

MAIN IDEAS
Call on students for answers.

- *Where did the Inca build their empire?* (the Andes Mountains of western South America)
- *What was the Inca capital and what was centered there?* (Cuzco; center of government, religion, and trade)
- *What human-built devices did Inca farmers use for growing crops?* (irrigation and terraces)
- *Who used the Inca network of roads?* (armies, merchants, and messengers)

EVALUATE
✔ **Answers to Think About It**

1. They considered Inti, god of the sun, their parent. *Recall Details*
2. It gave them flat farm surfaces in their mountainous environment. *Problem and Solution*
3. Any three of the following: stone architecture, Cuzco, beautiful artifacts, terrace farming, quipu system, roads, Machu Picchu *Recall Details*
4. Similarities: worship of sun god, dependence on maize, liking for war, strong armies, efficient government, lavish capital building. Differences: location and size of empire, Inca use of terrace farming *Compare and Contrast*
5. Any two of the following: building irrigation canals, constructing terraces for farming, building a network of roads *Five Themes of Geography: Human/Environment Interactions*

Write About It Have students write a detailed journal entry that Hiram Bingham might have written after finding Machu Picchu.

LESSON 4

Lesson Overview

The Ojibwa of North America developed unique ways to adapt to their environment, following the seasons.

Lesson Objectives

★ Identify and describe the resources and changing seasons of the Ojibwa environment.

★ Analyze and describe ways the Ojibwa adapted their environment to their needs.

1 PREPARE

MOTIVATE As a student reads the *Read Aloud* slowly, invite students to close their eyes and visualize the movement described. How does it show that the Ojibwa are in harmony with the seasons and their environment?

SET PURPOSE Encourage students to explore this lesson to answer this question more fully and answer the *Read to Learn* question. Preview the *Vocabulary*.

2 TEACH

Understanding THE BIG PICTURE
Have students refer to the map on p. 423.

● **In what region of North America did the Ojibwa live?** *(Great Lakes)*

● **Locate the sites of the Aztec and the Inca empires. Where is Ojibwa territory in relation to them?** *(far to the north and northwest)*

★**THINKING FURTHER:** *Predicting*
How do you predict that the Great Lakes region will differ from the Aztec and Inca regions? *(Students should predict that it will differ in climate from the Aztec region because it is much farther north and from the Inca in not being mountainous.)*

Resource REMINDER

Practice and Project Book: *p. 90*

Anthology: *The Lakota and Nature, pp. 109–110; Kokoom, p. 111; Sugar Mapling, pp. 112–113; Loneliness Song, p. 114*

Technology: *Adventure Time!* CD-ROM

Desk Map

| 1200 | 1300 | 1400 | 1600 |

Early People of North America

Read Aloud

In summer the Ojibwa (oh JIHB wah) lived by the waters of Lake Superior. When summer changed to autumn, they moved to the marshes where wild rice grew. They left the marshes before the heavy snows fell, living now near the herds that could be hunted. In spring sap flowed in the maple trees, and the Ojibwa came to collect it.

Like many of the peoples of North America, the Ojibwa moved their villages each season. This way of living allowed them to use many of the resources of their environment.

Focus Activity

READ TO LEARN

How did the Ojibwa make use of their northern forest environment?

VOCABULARY

• diversity
• Three Fires Council
• wigwam

PLACES

• Bowating

THE BIG PICTURE

As you have read, North America and South America were home to many peoples before the arrival of Europeans. These peoples and their descendants are called Indians. Tremendous diversity has always existed among these peoples. Diversity refers to differences. Peoples who lived in what is now the United States, and their descendants, are also called Native Americans. All of these peoples had many things in common, but each group adapted to its environment in unique ways.

Around 1400, in the Great Lakes region of North America, a group of Native Americans called the Ojibwa learned to make use of the forest environment. The Ojibwa harvested wild rice, collected maple sap in the forest, and developed many cultural traditions based on the changing seasons of their region.

440

SHELTERED INSTRUCTION

READING STRATEGIES & LANGUAGE DEVELOPMENT

CLASSIFYING Review how classifying information can help readers understand text. Explain that this lesson explores how closely Ojibwa life was tied to changing seasons. Have students list the seasons in their region and classify their activities during each one. Then have students predict how the Ojibwa might make use of their environment. **[SDAIE STRATEGY: SCHEMA BUILDING]**

WORDS OFTEN CONFUSED Refer the class to the term *council* on p. 441. Write it on the board and have students define it ("a league or cooperative group"). Then write the word *counsel* on the board. How does this word differ in spelling and meaning from *council*? Have students define *counsel* as both a noun ("advice") and as a verb ("to give advice"). Help them to see that although a *council* can give advice, it is not advice, or *counsel,* itself.

PEOPLE OF THE WOODLANDS

About 500 years ago nearly all the land east of the Mississippi River was thick forest. The Native Americans who lived here used the forest as a source of fuel, tools, shelter, and food. The forest provided such things as wood and maple syrup. One group of Native Americans, the Seneca, praised the forest in this poem about the sugar maple tree:

> To The Tree:
> O we share your scents,
> You the forests!
> We beg you
> To continue as before,
> The flowing waters of the maple.

The Ojibwa

Among the other woodland groups living in the eastern part of North America was the Ojibwa. The Ojibwa lived in the Great Lakes area of what are today Canada and the United States. The Ojibwa called themselves Anishinabe (ahn ish uh NAH bee), which means "original people."

According to their traditions, the Ojibwa once lived near the mouth of the St. Lawrence River, near the Atlantic Ocean. They migrated to the Great Lakes region about 500 years ago. There the Ojibwa settled along the eastern end of Lake Superior, which they called Kitchigami. A tremendous lake, with cold, deep waters, Kitchigami was an object of wonder and worship for the Ojibwa.

Villages at the Shore

The Ojibwa lived in villages of a few hundred people each. Many of these villages were scattered along the shores of Kitchigami and on the north shore of the peninsula between Lakes Huron and

* at night

PEOPLES OF THE GREAT LAKES, c. 1500

Ojibwa lands
Present-day boundaries are shown.

MAP WORK

The Ojibwa were one of many groups who lived near the Great Lakes.

1. On which side of Lake Superior was the village of Bowating located?

2. Near which lake did the Winnebago and Miami groups live?

Michigan. Some of the larger villages served as trading centers. One trading center was the village of Bowating (BOH ah tihng). *Bowating* means "place at the falls." This village was located on an island in the river that connects Lake Superior and Lake Huron. As you can see on the map on this page, Bowating was centrally located for people who depended on boat travel.

Two neighboring Native American communities—the Potawatomi and the Ottawa—joined the Ojibwa to form the Three Fires Council. This council was a league, or cooperative group. Its main purpose was trade. People traveled among communities, bringing their trade goods in bark canoes. At what time of day does canoe travel take place in the song on the next page?*

441

GLOBAL CONNECTION

OJIBWA OR CHIPPEWA? The Native Americans featured in this lesson are known by both names, depending on the country. These people's territory spanned both Canada and the United States. In Canada, they are most often called Ojibwa; in the United States, Chippewa.

CITIZENSHIP ★

UNDERSTANDING GOVERNMENT At first the Ojibwa lived in small, self-governing bands without any tribal organization. But as they became more prominent in the fur trade and as they expanded their territory, they initiated institutions that ran across the separate bands. One was the Midewiwin, or Grand Medicine Societies, open to men and women who sought to become expert in the healing arts.

PEOPLE OF THE WOODLANDS

Remind students of what they learned in American history about Plains Indians, and of their reliance on the buffalo for so many of their basic needs.

★**THINKING FURTHER:** *Compare and Contrast* **How did Native Americans east of the Mississippi use the forests in much the same way?** *(Students should recognize that just as the Plains Indians used the buffalo skin for shelter, meat for food, buffalo chips for fuel, and bones for tools, so people east of the Mississippi used forest products to serve these needs.)*

Discussing The Ojibwa Help students understand the term "woodland group."

● **Why are the Ojibwa called a woodland group?** *(because they lived in and relied on the forests)*

More **MAP WORK**

Refer students to the map and have them work with text and map. They may also mark their desk maps.

● **Locate the Ojibwa lands. Trace the Ojibwa migration route from the St. Lawrence River to the Great Lakes. Through what bodies of water did the route pass?** *(up the St. Lawrence River from its mouth near the Atlantic through Lakes Ontario, Erie, and Huron and into Superior)*

★**THINKING FURTHER:** *Compare and Contrast* **How was the Ojibwa feeling about Lake Kitchigami like the Aztec and Inca feelings about the sun?** *(All reflected wonder and worship.)*

Understanding Villages at the Shore Help students understand the Ojibwa way of life.

● **In what kind of villages did the Ojibwa live?** *(lakeshore communities of a few hundred people each)*

★**THINKING FURTHER:** *Making Conclusions* **How do we know that trade was important to their economy?** *(the role of Bowating as a major trading center and the Three Fires Council founded to encourage trade with neighboring groups)*

441

PRIMARY VOICE

Discussing "My Bark Canoe"
Give students a few moments to examine the picture that accompanies the song on this page and encourage them to try to picture themselves in this scene. Might it make them happy? sad? frightened? at peace? Tell the class that the song is from the Ojibwa and have them sing or recite it.

● *What does the song tell us? (The singer is making a long journey through the night in a canoe made of bark.)*

● *Based on the artwork, through what kind of terrain is this journey taking the singer? (across long waters through forests)*

● *How is the terrain consistent with the Great Lakes region of 500 years ago? (It is well watered and heavily forested.)*

★THINKING FURTHER: *Making Conclusions* **Why do you suppose the canoeist might be singing this song?** *(Possible answer: to pass the time or to feel less alone or to measure the timing of his paddling or to let others know he is there. Point out that this might be considered an example of work songs, which often are used to make work pass more quickly and/or to set up a rhythm for it.)*

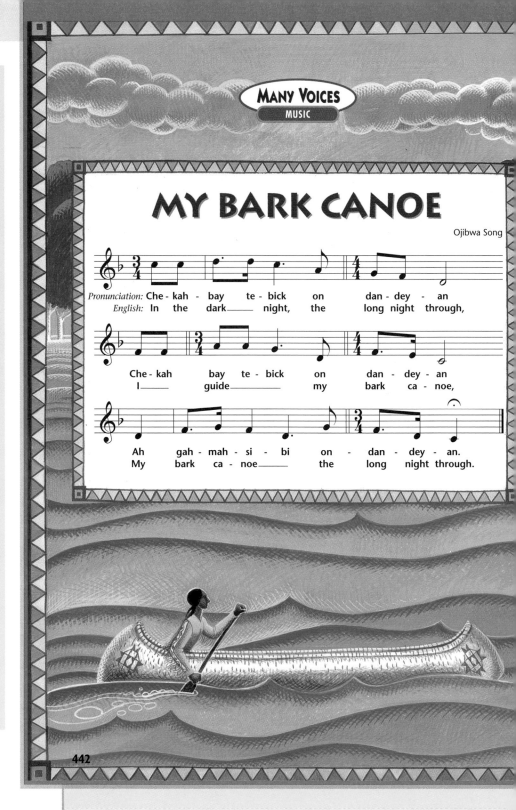

BACKGROUND INFORMATION

ABOUT BIRCHBARK CANOES Native Americans used canoes to hunt, fish, travel, and carry trade goods.

● They made their canoes in the spring using bark that they stripped from the white birches that grew in abundance in the Eastern Woodlands.

● They stripped large sheets of inner bark from a tree. Then they separated them into sheets of different thicknesses and placed the bark over a cedar wood frame.

● Finally, they heated gum from the black spruce tree until it had the consistency of thick syrup and used it to waterproof the seams of the canoe.

CURRICULUM CONNECTION

LINKS TO SCIENCE Have students research and report on the white birch. Topics might include the white birch's relationship to its surroundings, the characteristics that make the white birch suitable for canoes and other artifacts, and the ways in which current environmental pollution threatens the white birch's existence.

SECOND-LANGUAGE SUPPORT

DRAMATIZATION Second-language learners may enjoy and benefit from dramatizing seasonal life in an Ojibwa village. Have students reread and discuss the lesson content with a partner before preparing their scene.

CYCLE OF THE SEASONS

To make the best use of their environment, the Ojibwa followed the cycle of the seasons. This meant that the Ojibwa moved with the change of seasons during the year. In each village families built dome-shaped houses they called wigwams. The Ojibwa made these houses by placing sheets of birch bark and cattail reeds over a frame of wooden poles. Families could roll up the birch bark sheets, leaving the wood frame behind.

Summer and Fall

The Ojibwa settled near a lake during the summer months. However, they often traveled as far as 50 miles away to find food. Men fished in the lakes and rivers and hunted in the surrounding forests. Women and children gathered nuts and berries. They also grew corn, beans, and squash.

To relax, the Ojibwa sometimes played a game called baggataway. Villages competed against each other to drive a ball over a goal line, using sticks with nets attached. Today a modern version of this game, lacrosse, is still played in many parts of the United States and in Canada.

When fall came, the Ojibwa moved near the marshes and ponds where wild rice grew. There women and men worked together to harvest the rice. Men used poles to push birch bark canoes through the shallow lakes and streams. Women used special sticks to knock rice grains into the canoes. The Ojibwa also worked to spread wild rice to new areas.

Winter and Spring

During winter the Ojibwa moved to areas where they could hunt. To travel through the deep snow of their long winter season, they wore snowshoes and used toboggans, or sleds. The Ojibwa hunted deer, moose, bear, and fox. They used bows and arrows, spears, and special traps that dropped logs or other heavy weights on animals. Meat was roasted or boiled and then smoked so that it could be stored. The skins from animals were tanned and then sewn into clothing and moccasins.

In spring the Ojibwa moved to an area where many sugar maple trees grew. The Ojibwa collected the maple sap in birch bark buckets and then boiled it down to make maple sugar. This sugar was used to flavor rice, fish, and other food. The Ojibwa moved on to their summer villages after maple sugar season ended. They carried the maple sugar with them in containers decorated with pictographs. Pictographs are drawings of symbols that are used as a writing system. In fact, the name Ojibwa comes from a term that means "those who make pictographs."

People of the Great Lakes region still make products from maple sap.

BACKGROUND INFORMATION

ABOUT WILD RICE Though it is now very expensive, try to have some wild rice available for students to see and touch. Explain that it is not actually a form of rice but is an unrelated member of the grass family.

CURRICULUM CONNECTION

LINKS TO SCIENCE Explain that the tanning of animal skins is a chemical process that preserves skins and turns them into leather. The Ojibwa would have used salt, tannic acids extracted from chestnut, oak, or hemlock trees, and natural oils in the process.

LINKS TO HEALTH Divide the class into several groups and have each group design a healthful meal that the Ojibwa would have been able to serve, based on the resources available to them.

CYCLE OF THE SEASONS

Ask students how their lives are affected by the seasons and to compare that with Ojibwa seasonal life.

- *How did the Ojibwa "follow the cycle of the seasons"?* (They moved each season to find seasonal resources.)

> ★**THINKING FURTHER:** *Making Conclusions* **Why were wigwams an efficient form of housing for people who moved with the seasons?** (Their coverings were permanent; the Ojibwa just rolled them up and brought the birch bark "siding" along for a move.)

Discussing Summer and Fall Have students list summer and fall activities of the Ojibwa.

- *What types of foods did the Ojibwa gather and produce during summer?* (fish from lakes; game from forests; nuts, berries, and crops—corn, beans, and squash)

- *What game still played today did Ojibwa men and women play?* (baggataway, now called lacrosse)

- *What crop did the Ojibwa gather in the fall?* (wild rice)

Studying Winter and Spring Have students list Ojibwa winter and spring activities.

- *What did Ojibwa use to get around in winter?* (snowshoes and toboggans)

- *How many different uses did they make of the animals they hunted at this time?* (meat for food, skins for clothing and moccasins)

- *Where did the Ojibwa move in spring? Why?* (places where many maple trees grew; to harvest the sap and make maple sugar from it)

> ★**THINKING FURTHER:** *Making Conclusions* **How would you say that following the cycle of the seasons served the basic needs of the Objibwa and gave them a variety of goods for trade?** (Hunting, fishing, gathering, and growing crops gave them many different foods and resources for clothing as well as for trade goods such as wild rice, maple sugar, furs.)

Infographic

Help students to relate the wide variety of environments across North America to the wide variety of Native American groups that developed there and of adaptations made to the environments.

Discussing Native North Americans Refer students to the map and have them locate the Ojibwa on it.

- **In what area of North America did the Ojibwa live?** (Eastern Woodlands)

- **What other groups that you have already studied can you find on this map? In what area did they live?** (Maya, Aztec; Middle America)

- **Look at the picture at the upper left. From what group does the necklace come? In what area did they live?** (Hupa; California)

- **What natural resources were used?** (shells and feathers)

- **Why does it make sense that the Hupa wear seashells?** (They live along the Pacific coast.)

- **Look at the Friendship Bag. From what people does it come? In what area did they live?** (Menominee; Eastern Woodlands)

- **Why were these beaded bags called Friendship Bags?** (because they were given as gifts)

- **Look at the gold pendant. From what people does it come? In what area did they live?** (Aztec; Mexico)

★**THINKING FURTHER:** *Making Conclusions* **Locate the Subarctic and the Caribbean areas on the map. How would you expect their environments to differ? How would you expect artifacts from those environments to differ?** *(Students should recognize extremes of cold and warmth of the areas named and differences in natural resources from which artifacts would be made.)*

Technology CONNECTION

ADVENTURE TIME! CD-ROM
Have students do the Unit Activity on the *Adventure Time!* CD-ROM.

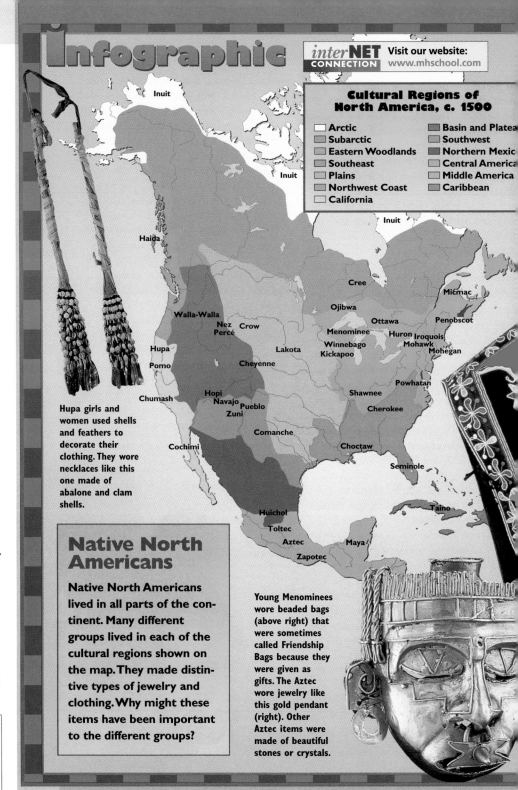

Infographic

interNET CONNECTION Visit our website: www.mhschool.com

Cultural Regions of North America, c. 1500

- Arctic
- Subarctic
- Eastern Woodlands
- Southeast
- Plains
- Northwest Coast
- California
- Basin and Plateau
- Southwest
- Northern Mexico
- Central America
- Middle America
- Caribbean

Inuit
Inuit
Inuit
Haida
Cree
Mićmac
Ojibwa
Walla-Walla
Ottawa
Penobscot
Nez Percé
Crow
Menominee
Huron Iroquois
Hupa
Lakota
Winnebago
Kickapoo
Mohawk
Mohegan
Pomo
Cheyenne
Chumash
Hopi Navajo Pueblo
Zuni
Powhatan
Shawnee
Comanche
Cherokee
Cochimi
Choctaw
Seminole
Huichol
Taino
Toltec
Aztec Maya
Zapotec

Hupa girls and women used shells and feathers to decorate their clothing. They wore necklaces like this one made of abalone and clam shells.

Native North Americans

Native North Americans lived in all parts of the continent. Many different groups lived in each of the cultural regions shown on the map. They made distinctive types of jewelry and clothing. Why might these items have been important to the different groups?

Young Menominees wore beaded bags (above right) that were sometimes called Friendship Bags because they were given as gifts. The Aztec wore jewelry like this gold pendant (right). Other Aztec items were made of beautiful stones or crystals.

EXPANDING THE INFOGRAPHIC

RESEARCHING AND MAKING PRESENTATIONS Divide the class into six small teams and assign each team two of the areas of North America shown on the map. Have the teams research their areas and at least one group that lived in the areas. Then have the teams prepare an illustrated report of one or more of the ways that their Native American groups used to adapt to the environment in which they lived. Have each team present its report to the class and assemble a bulletin board display of reports. You might suggest the following sources:

- Encyclopedia and library catalog listings for the individual Native American groups or for *Indians, North America.* (There is also a wealth of juvenile and adult books available.)

- *National Geographic Index:* 1888–1988 for same entries.

WHY IT MATTERS

The arrival of Europeans in North America in the 1600s brought great change for the Ojibwa and other Native American groups. Wars, disease, and European settlement all took a tremendous toll on the Ojibwa and their way of life. Still, the Ojibwa survived, and they continued many of the traditions of their people.

Today nearly 200,000 Ojibwa live in the Great Lakes region of the United States and Canada. Gerald Vizenor, an Ojibwa writer, recently described his feelings about his homeland:

The land is everything to me. The land is part of my language, part of the way I perceive [become aware of] the world. The water, the trees, the smell of pine, the smell of autumn, the smell of wet leaves in the spring. It is all part of my imagination, part of my dreams.

Today the Ojibwa continue to follow important cultural traditions. This Ojibwa dance group is performing at a Native American harvest festival in Wisconsin.

✓// Reviewing Facts and Ideas

MAIN IDEAS

- The woodlands of North America provided many resources for the Native Americans who lived there.
- The Ojibwa settled around the area of Lake Superior about 500 years ago.
- The Ojibwa moved with the seasons to hunt, fish, farm, and harvest food in different places.
- Many Ojibwa continue to live in the Great Lakes region and carry on their cultural traditions.

THINK ABOUT IT

1. According to tradition, from where did the Ojibwa migrate when they settled near Lake Superior about 500 years ago?

2. Why did the Ojibwa travel to different areas throughout the year?

3. **FOCUS** How did the Ojibwa use forest resources to make their homes?

4. **THINKING SKILL** What *conclusions* can you make from the fact that wigwams were easily taken apart?

5. **WRITE** Create a calendar that describes what the Ojibwa did during each season of the year.

445

DISCUSSING MAJOR EVENTS Use the time line to reinforce the areas of the Americas each group settled in.

- **Where in South America did a major group settle and when?** *(The Inca settled in Cuzco, in what is now Peru, around 1200.)*

- **Where and when did the Ojibwa settle in North America?** *(in the Great Lakes area in about 1400)*

- **Where did the Aztec make a settlement around 1325 and on which continent?** *(around Lake Texcoco, in what is now Mexico, on North America)*

Answers to THINKING ABOUT VOCABULARY

1. T

2. T

3. F, The cords that the Inca knotted to record numbers involved in important matters are called quipus.

4. T

5. F, A codex is a folded sheet on which Aztec writing appears.

6. T

7. F, Chinampas were the islands the Aztec made in a lake for farming.

8. F, During the last part of his walk from the southern tip of South America to the Arctic Ocean, George Meegan walked across the treeless plain, or tundra, of Alaska.

9. T

10. F, A timberline is an imaginary line on a mountain above which trees cannot grow.

Answers to THINKING ABOUT FACTS

1. They shaped the Canadian Shield and carved out and filled the Great Lakes.

Resource REMINDER

Practice and Project Book: *p. 91*

Assessment Book: *Chapter 15 Test*

Technology: *Videodisc*

Transparency: *Graphic Organizer, Word Map*

CHAPTER 15 REVIEW

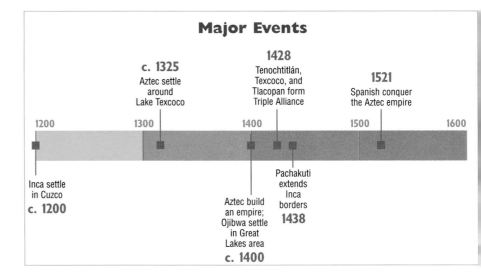

Major Events

c. 1325
Aztec settle around Lake Texcoco

1428
Tenochtitlán, Texcoco, and Tlacopan form Triple Alliance

1521
Spanish conquer the Aztec empire

1200 — 1300 — 1400 — 1500 — 1600

Inca settle in Cuzco
c. 1200

Aztec build an empire; Ojibwa settle in Great Lakes area
c. 1400

Pachakuti extends Inca borders
1438

THINKING ABOUT VOCABULARY

Each of the following statements contains an underlined vocabulary word or term. Number a sheet of paper from 1 to 10. Beside each number write **T** if the statement is true and **F** if the statement is false. If the statement is false, rewrite the sentence using the vocabulary word or term correctly.

1. Great <u>diversity</u> existed among various Native American peoples.

2. <u>Wigwams</u> were made by placing sheets of birch bark and cattail reeds over a frame of wooden poles.

3. The islands the Aztec made in a lake for farming were called <u>quipus</u>.

4. The Aztec had to pay <u>tribute</u> to the rulers of nearby cities when they arrived in the Valley of Mexico.

5. A <u>codex</u> is a weapon used by Ojibwa warriors.

6. Inca farmers planted crops on <u>terraces</u> that climbed up hills like stairs.

7. <u>Chinampas</u> was the name of the corn eaten by the Ojibwa people, who lived in the Great Lakes region.

8. During the last part of his seven-year walk from the southern tip of South America to the Arctic Ocean, George Meegan walked across the warm, swampy <u>tundra</u> of Florida.

9. North America and South America are connected by an <u>isthmus</u>.

10. A <u>timberline</u> separates Native American villages.

THINKING ABOUT FACTS

1. How did the Ice Age glaciers affect physical features of North America?

2. Describe the Aztec system of writing.

3. What role did Pachakuti play in Inca history?

4. What was the Three Fires Council? Why was it formed?

5. According to the time line above, how long did the Aztec empire last?

SECOND-LANGUAGE SUPPORT

WORKING WITH PEERS If students have read about only one of the three civilizations—Aztec, Inca, or Ojibwa (see p. 428)—have them present their section to other second-language learners orally so that they will all be prepared for the Chapter Review. Students should work with a partner to create the chart on p. 447 and work together to write the paragraph. Tell students to prepare for writing the paragraph by making a list that shows similarities and differences among the three cultures in geography, government, and achievements. They might begin by listing facts and marking + (plus sign) for similarities and − (minus sign) for differences.

ORAL DISCUSSION Ask second-language learners to compare the civilization of the Aztecs to that of ancient Egypt and the empire of the Incas to the empire of Rome. What similarities do they find?

THINK AND WRITE

WRITING A LETTER
Suppose you are George Meegan in 1976 and you have just finished your seven-year walk across the length of the Americas. Write a letter to a friend about your journey.

WRITING A SUMMARY
Write a paragraph summarizing the achievements of the Aztec civilization.

WRITING A DESCRIPTION
Write a paragraph describing how the Ojibwa of the Great Lakes region adapted to their forest environment.

APPLYING GEOGRAPHY SKILLS

USING MAP PROJECTIONS

1. What is a map projection?

2. Maps A and B on page 432 both show equal-area projections. What are some of the advantages and disadvantages of each map?

3. Place a ruler between North America and South America on Map C. Then find a globe and use a string to measure the same straight-line distance. Explain why that line would look curved on Map C.

4. Compare Maps A and D on pages 432–433. If you were exploring the North Pole, which map would you bring with you? Why?

5. Why are map projections useful?

2. The Aztec system of writing involves colorful pictures and symbols drawn on long folded sheets of paper called codices in the plural, codex in the singular.

3. He extended the Inca empire, organized and ran its government, and spread Inca religion throughout it.

4. The Potawatomi, Ottawa, and Ojibwa organized it as a cooperative group to encourage trade among themselves.

5. 1521 minus c. 1400 = about 121 years

Answers to
APPLYING GEOGRAPHY SKILLS

1. a way of placing parts of Earth onto a flat map

2. Map A gives a better idea than Map B of distances between places, except at the far edges, but Map B gives a better idea of actual shapes of land.

3. The line would look curved on Map C because it is a longer distance on the globe than it is on a flat map.

4. Map A shows the North Pole from the side while Map D shows it from the top. Map D would be the better map for exploration because it shows the North Pole area more accurately.

5. They present different ways of picturing Earth on a flat surface, each of which has its own advantages and disadvantages and is useful for a different purpose.

Summing Up the Chapter

Copy the word map below on a separate sheet of paper. Review the chapter to find at least two pieces of information to support each topic in the word map. When you have filled in the map, write a paragraph that answers the question "What made the Aztec, Inca, and Ojibwa civilizations similar and what made them different?"

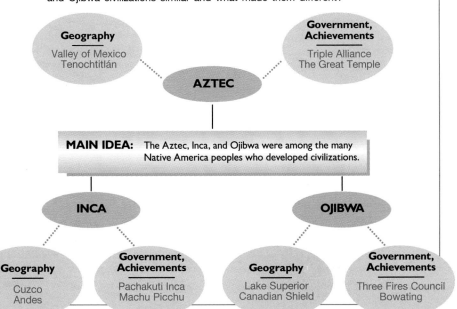

Geography
Valley of Mexico
Tenochtitlán

Government, Achievements
Triple Alliance
The Great Temple

AZTEC

MAIN IDEA: The Aztec, Inca, and Ojibwa were among the many Native America peoples who developed civilizations.

INCA

OJIBWA

Geography
Cuzco
Andes

Government, Achievements
Pachakuti Inca
Machu Picchu

Geography
Lake Superior
Canadian Shield

Government, Achievements
Three Fires Council
Bowating

447

SUGGESTIONS FOR SUMMING UP THE CHAPTER

Have students read the main idea in the diagram aloud and then have them copy the diagram on a piece of paper. Before they begin looking for information to fill in, you may want to suggest a few examples, to help them pinpoint the kinds of things they should look for. Possible answers appear on the reproduced pupil page above. When they have finished filling in the information, have them read the question posed aloud and suggest they break it down into three smaller questions to think about before writing their paragraphs: How were they alike and similar in geography? How were they alike and similar in government? How were they alike and similar in achievements? Urge them to weave their smaller answers together in their paragraphs.

ASSESSING THINK AND WRITE: *For performance assessment, see Assessment Book, Chapter 15, pp. T90–T92.*

Technology CONNECTION

VIDEODISC
Enrich Chapter 15 with the *Aztec Lands* segment on the Videodisc.

Search Frame 42677, Side B

Answers to
THINKING ABOUT VOCABULARY

1. savanna
2. monsoon
3. shogun
4. navigable
5. feudalism
6. monarchy
7. grand mufti
8. diversity
9. isthmus
10. griot

Suggestions for
THINK AND WRITE

1. Encourage students to look up their chosen subjects in the index, go back and reread everything about that person and his/her times in the text, and use any other knowledge gained to create a vivid profile showing how that person reflected his/her times and contributed to or changed them.

2. Have students review each selected civilization and take notes on its beliefs and values and on its experiences with war. Urge them to use these notes when describing differences between perspectives.

3. Paragraphs should explain the rise of the empires of Ghana, Mali, and Songhai, describe the function of gold and salt as valuable natural resources, include the effects of supply and demand on trade and the people of West Africa, mention Islam and griots, and include Sunjata and Mansa Musa.

Suggestions for
BUILDING SKILLS

1. Students should recognize that the Byzantine Christians and Turkish Muslims looked on each other as infidels. To the Byzantine, the fall of Constantinople would be a tragic defeat for Christian civilization. To the Turk, it would be a heroic victory over a corrupt empire.

2. The map on page G11 shows the distribution of vegetation in Russia and the map on page 548 shows the distribution of the time zones around the world. These are special-purpose maps that show how one particular feature is spread over an area and can help you see how this feature affects where people live. Distribution maps can also show such features as population, climate, or languages spoken in an area.

UNIT 4 REVIEW

THINKING ABOUT VOCABULARY

Number a sheet of paper from 1 to 10. Beside each number write the word or term from the list below that best matches the definition.

diversity	monarchy
feudalism	monsoon
grand mufti	navigable
griot	savanna
isthmus	shogun

1. A grassy, tree-dotted plain
2. A seasonal wind
3. A military ruler of Japan
4. Can be traveled by ships
5. A way of organizing and governing society based on land and service
6. A government by king or queen
7. A religious leader responsible for interpreting Islamic law
8. Made up of or showing different kinds
9. A narrow strip of land that connects two larger land masses
10. A special African storyteller and oral historian

THINK AND WRITE

WRITING ABOUT PEOPLE
Write about somebody you read about in the unit—Michelangelo, Queen Amanishakhete, Kublai Khan, Lady Murasaki Shikibu, or Pachakuti Inca, for example. Discuss the person's achievements and his or her importance in history.

WRITING ABOUT PERSPECTIVES
Choose two of the empires or civilizations in Europe, Africa, Asia, and the Americas that you have read about. Write about what someone from each culture would have thought about war. What might they consider to be important reasons for going to war? Explain why there might be differences in their perspectives.

WRITING AN EXPLANATION
Write two paragraphs about the rise of empires in West Africa. Explain how the area's natural resources played a role in the development of trade. Describe the effects of this trade on the people living in the area. Include facts about powerful rulers who led the empires.

BUILDING SKILLS

1. **Point of view** Reread the section about the fall of Constantinople on pages 388–389. Explain different points of view about the event. For example, how might a Turkish historian describe the fall of the city? How might a Byzantine historian describe it?

2. **Distribution maps** Look again at the population maps on pages 370–371 to review how distribution maps can show how something is spread out over an area. Then look through the book for at least two other distribution maps. What do they show?

3. **Making generalizations** From what you already know about the growth of civilizations, make a generalization about the types of environment civilizations require. What are some exceptions to your generalization?

4. **Making generalizations** Make a generalization about students. What do they have in common that would allow you to generalize about them as a group?

5. **Map projections** Look at the map of Marco Polo's journey on page 406. What kind of projection is used for this map?

ONGOING UNIT PROJECT

OPTIONS FOR ASSESSMENT
This ongoing project, begun on page 310D can be part of your assessment program, along with other forms of evaluation.

PLANNING Emphasize that students' drawings should show an important idea learned in each lesson. Explain that the way students describe in writing the picture on the time line will also be very important.

SIGNS OF SUCCESS

- Students' drawings should reflect the main idea of each lesson; that is, to show cultural contrast, for Lesson 2, Chapter 12, a knight in his manor, and for Lesson 2, Chapter 13, an Ethiopian queen.

- Group members should work well together choosing pictures.

- Information presented should be accurate and interesting.

 FOR THE PORTFOLIO Individual drawings can be included in students' portfolios.

YESTERDAY, TODAY & *TOMORROW*

Civilizations in Europe, Africa, Asia, and the Americas had very different cultures and languages. Today mass communication is helping people around the world understand each other better. Do you think people in different civilizations will be more similar in the future? Do you think someday everybody will speak the same language? Explain your answers.

READING ON YOUR OWN

Here are some books you might find at the library to help you learn more.

LEONARDO DA VINCI
by Diane Stanley
A beautifully illustrated picture book of this famous painter's life and art techniques.

KNIGHTS IN ARMOR
Edited by John D. Clare
A well-illustrated overview of the lifestyle and role of the knight during the Middle Ages.

ALL OF YOU WAS SINGING
by Richard Lewis
This is a retelling of an Aztec myth.

3. Generalizations may focus on the need for water nearby and for land that can be farmed, for a hospitable climate, and for natural resources to make tools and wares. Exceptions to this generalization would be the Bedouins with little farmland and without iron for weapons.

4. Common features on which to base generalizations might include age, occupation (students), sports and other activities.

5. The map is a Mercator projection, which allows us to calculate the distances that Marco Polo traveled.

Suggestions for
YESTERDAY, TODAY & TOMORROW

Have students turn back to the *Infographic* in Chapter 1 and identify the school subjects that these children from across the world have in common (English is one). Also suggest they think about the effects of worldwide television broadcasts and worldwide distribution of movies.

Suggestions for
READING ON YOUR OWN

The books listed here can enhance students' understanding of dangers that people living in the Middle Ages faced. You may also make available the books in the *Annotated Bibliography and Resources* in the Unit Organizer on page 301B. Ask each student to read one book and identify dangers that people in it faced.

UNIT 4 REVIEW PROJECT

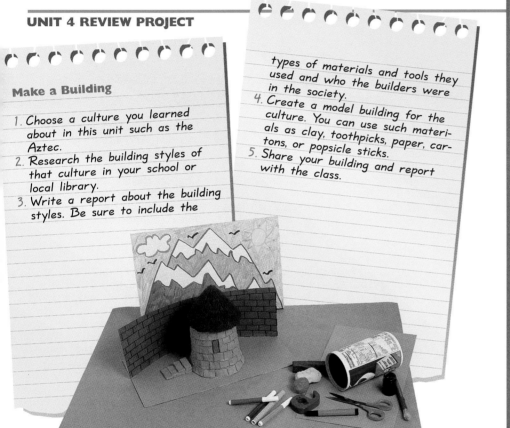

Make a Building

1. Choose a culture you learned about in this unit such as the Aztec.
2. Research the building styles of that culture in your school or local library.
3. Write a report about the building styles. Be sure to include the types of materials and tools they used and who the builders were in the society.
4. Create a model building for the culture. You can use such materials as clay, toothpicks, paper, cartons, or popsicle sticks.
5. Share your building and report with the class.

449

UNIT 4 REVIEW PROJECT *Make a Building*

COMPLETING THE BUILDING

 ON YOUR OWN   30 MINUTES OR LONGER

OBJECTIVE: Making a model building in the style of one of the cultures studied in the unit will reinforce facts they have learned in the unit.

MATERIALS: clay, toothpicks, paper, cartons, popsicle sticks, other building materials

• Have students return to the text to choose a culture and review what they learned in the unit. Then allow time for students to visit the library to do additional research on the building styles of the cultures they have chosen.

• Have students write their reports in class.

• Provide a variety of building materials for students to use for their model buildings.

• Schedule class time during which students can present their reports and model buildings to the class.

FOR THE PORTFOLIO Students reports can be part of their portfolios.

OPTIONS FOR ASSESSMENT

This project can be part of your assessment program.

For more performance assessment and portfolio opportunities, see Assessment Book, Unit 4, p. T93.

5 UNIT ORGANIZER

PAGES 450–519

Dawn of the Modern World

UNIT OVERVIEW

Explorers sailed to the Western Hemisphere and charted new courses around the world. Europeans settled in the Americas and colonized the native peoples. Revolutions erupted in France, Mexico, and South America as people fought for independence. Finally, capitalism and scientific advances brought about the industrial revolution in Europe.

☐ **ADVENTURES WITH NATIONAL GEOGRAPHIC**
Golden Voyage **pp. 452–453**

UNIT PLANNING GUIDE

CHAPTER	SUGGESTED PACING	RESOURCES	ASSESSMENT
16 European Expansion Ferdinand Magellan and Samuel de Champlain explored the Americas, and James Cook searched for Australia. Enslaved Africans were brought to the Caribbean, and Pizarro conquered Peru. pp. 454–483	10–11 days	• **Practice and Project Book,** pp. 92–98 • **Anthology,** pp. 116–132 • **Desk Map** • **Outline Map** • **Transparency:** Graphic Organizer, Main Idea Pyramid • ⊙ **Technology:** Videodisc/Video Tape	• **Meeting Individual Needs,** pp. 460, 465, 471, 477, 481 • **Write About It,** pp. 460, 465, 471, 477, 481 • **Chapter Review,** pp. 482–483 • **Assessment Book:** *Assessing Think and Write, pp. T94–T96. Chapter 16 Tests: Content, Skills, Writing*
17 Revolutions Change the World People revolted and fought for freedom and independence in France, Mexico, and Venezuela, while capitalism and science sparked the industrial revolution. pp. 484–517	8–9 days	• **Practice and Project Book,** pp. 99–104 • **Anthology,** pp. 133–140 • **Desk Map** • **Transparency:** Map 19, Graphic Organizer, Cause and Effect Map • ⊙ **Technology:** *Adventure Time!* CD-ROM	• **Meeting Individual Needs,** pp. 491, 497, 499, 505, 507, 513 • **Write About It,** pp. 491, 497, 499, 505, 513 • **Chapter Review,** pp. 516–517 • **Assessment Book:** *Assessing Think and Write, pp. T97–T99. Chapter 17 Tests: Content, Skills, Writing*
Unit 5 Review pp. 518–519	1–2 days	• **Geo Adventures Daily Geography Activities**	• **Unit 5 Project,** p. 519

McGRAW-HILL SCHOOL'S HOME PAGE at
☞ **http://www.mhschool.com**
contains on-line student activities related to this unit.

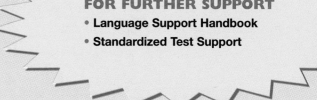

FOR FURTHER SUPPORT
• **Language Support Handbook**
• **Standardized Test Support**

450A

McGraw-Hill Adventure Books

Mike, Jan. **The Sun and the Kookaburra.** In this retelling of an Aboriginal folktale from Australia, a small bird asks the Sky Spirit for light at a time when the world is dark. **(Easy)**

Classroom Library

■ Avakian, Monique. **The Meiji Restoration and the Rise of Modern Japan**. Englewood Cliffs, NJ: Silver Burdett Press, Inc., 1991. This book details Japan's transformation to a modern industrial and military power.

Student Books

Blumberg, Rhoda. **Commodore Perry in the Land of Shogun**. New York: Lothrop, Lee & Shepard, 1985. This is a presentation of how Commodore Matthew Perry opened Japan to world trade. **(Challenging)**

■ Clare, John D., ed.**The Industrial Revolution.** San Diego, CA: Harcourt Brace, 1994. Informative text, detailed illustrations, and photos trace the technology that emerged from this time period. **(Average)**

Fernández, Jos. **José de San Martín.** Brookfield, CT: The Millbrook Press, 1994. Read about the Argentinian general who helped to liberate South America from Spanish rule. **(Average)**

■ Matthews, Rupert. **Explorer**. New York: Alfred A. Knopf, Inc., 1991. This photo essay is about explorations of land, sea, air, and space, beginning with ancient times. **(Challenging)**

Sis, Peter. **Starry Messenger: Galileo Galilei.** New York: Farrar Straus Giroux, 1996. A beautifully illustrated story about the life of Galileo, accompanied by Galileo's own notes and drawings. **(Easy)**

Stewart, Gail B. **Life During the French Revolution**. San Diego, CA: Lucent Books, 1995. A detailed account of life during the French Revolution is told from an ordinary person's point of view. **(Challenging)**

■ Whitney, Clara. **Clara's Diary: An American Girl in Meiji Japan.**

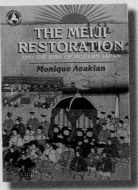

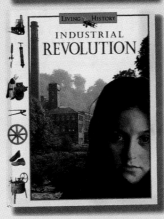

New York: Kodansha International Ltd., 1978. This is a young girl's account of her life when she went to live in Japan in the late nineteenth century. **(Average)**

Teacher Books

Blumberg, Rhoda. **The Remarkable Voyage of Captain Cook.** New York: Bradbury Press, 1991. A well-detailed account of the adventures of Captain Cook, the British explorer and discoverer.

Fritz, Jean. **Around the World in a Hundred Years: From Henry the Navigator to Magellan**. New York: Putnam, 1994. The achievements of ten explorers are chronicled in a compelling style, providing good background information.

Read-Alouds

Matthews, Sally S. **The Sad Night: The Story of an Aztec Victory and a Spanish Loss.** New York: Clarion Books, 1994. Read how Cortés's arrival in Tenochtitlán began the Aztecs' downfall.

Sadler, Catherine Edwards, reteller. **Heaven's Reward: Fairy Tales from China**. New York: Atheneum, 1985. Folktales that date back as far as the Confucian era illuminate China's culture.

Technology Multimedia

The Age of Exploration Series. Video Series No. 4845–106. Europe explores the Americas. Britannica Videos. (800) 554-9862.

Anansi. Video. Anansi, the feisty and tiny spider, was the holder of all the stories in Africa's jungle long ago. Story Lane Theater, Macmillan/McGraw-Hill. (800) 442-9685.

The Industrial Revolution in England. Video. No. 1740-106. (26 min.) Explore how the factory system transformed the economy in nineteenth century England. Britannica Videos. (800) 554-9862.

Free or Inexpensive Materials

For a kit on the American Revolution, send to: Jamestown-Yorktown Foundation; Education Dept., P. O. Drawer JF; Williamsburg, VA 23187.

■ *Book excerpted in the Anthology*

■ *Book featured in the student bibliography of the Unit Review*

☐ *National Geographic technology*

Ideas for Active Learning

BULLETIN BOARD

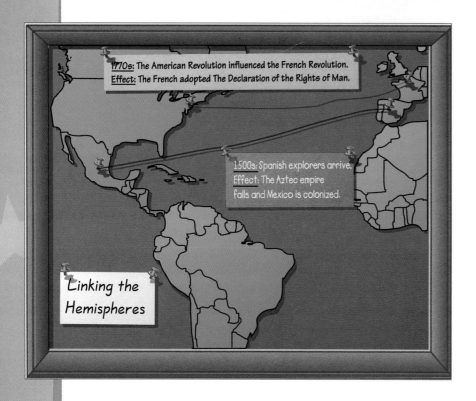

1770s: The American Revolution influenced the French Revolution.
Effect: The French adopted The Declaration of the Rights of Man.

1500s: Spanish explorers arrive.
Effect: The Aztec empire falls and Mexico is colonized.

Linking the Hemispheres

Dawn of the Modern World

Help students to create a bulletin board titled "Linking the Hemispheres." Begin by covering the bulletin board with a map. Use a portion of a world map that includes the Eastern United States, the West Indies, Mexico and South America, England, France, Spain, Portugal, and the western coast of Africa including Ghana. As students learn about the arrival of Europeans and Africans in the Americas, invite them to use different colors of yarn or markers to show the movement of people, goods, and ideas from Europe and Africa to the Americas and back. Have them choose a color for each country, and write information on a color-coordinated piece of construction paper to explain the trade or movement of peoples. Each piece of writing should include a date and an "Effect."

TEACHER EXCHANGE

Thanks to: Leah Taylor, Central Elementary, Smithtown, New York

Make an Independence Display

 GROUP 30 MINUTES OR LONGER

CURRICULUM CONNECTION Language Arts/Art

Materials: butcher paper, construction paper, markers, scissors, glue, thin dowels

1. Begin a discussion about the fight for independence in the colonies. Then have students share what they know about revolutions in other colonies and countries in the past and present.
2. Have students work in groups to choose a country from a list that you have brainstormed with them. Then instruct them to research how that country gained its independence.
3. Let students work with art materials to create the flag of the country and attach it to a dowel. Then have each group member create a construction paper triangle with a fact about that country's independence.
4. Display all the flagpoles around the room or on a bulletin board and ask group members to discuss their particular entry.

Enriching with Multimedia

RESOURCE: McGraw-Hill School's Home Page

- Have students go to McGraw-Hill School's home page at http://www.mhschool.com on the World Wide Web for projects related to this unit.

RESOURCE: *Videodisc/Video Tape*

- Enrich Unit 5 with the Videodisc *map* segments.

Search Frame 53299   Side B

SCHOOL-TO-HOME

Dawn of the Modern World

- Throughout the unit, students will have the opportunity to learn about the enslavement of African peoples and native peoples in the Americas, and the struggles for liberty and independence that later took place in the Americas and in France. Help students prepare a survey with questions about current issues of human rights and independence currently in the news.

- Ask students to conduct their survey among friends and family members to get their opinions on contemporary issues. Students and their families may wish to add further questions to the survey. When the survey is completed, students and their families can analyze the responses to the questions. Students may be interested in returning their surveys to the classroom in order to chart the results.

ONGOING UNIT PROJECT

Enact Short Historical Scenes

CURRICULUM CONNECTION   **Drama**

RESOURCE: Practice and Project Book p. 135.

Throughout this unit students will work individually and cooperatively to write and enact scenes about the beginnings of the modern world.

1. After each chapter, have students make a list of characters that they would like to create scenes for and present to the class in groups.
2. After the lessons are completed, guide students working in small groups to plan their choice of characters, setting, and time for one scene with the help of the planning sheet provided.
3. Each group can choose a director and decide who will play which character.
4. Allow time for students to rehearse the scene and then present it informally for the other groups.

Assessment suggestions for the activity appear on page 518.

UNIT FIVE

PAGES 450–519

Introducing the Unit

Refer students to the unit title and ask them what the term *modern* means to them. Explain that the period that began what we call "the modern world" goes back somewhat further than very recently. To help them absorb this, have them read *Why Does It Matter?* on p. 451 and examine the artifacts from "the dawn" of that world.

Exploring Prior Knowledge Encourage students to try to identify some of the artifacts shown on these pages.

● *Which of these artifacts do you recognize? What does the artifact represent or for what purpose was it used?* (Encourage students to offer any information they have about the items pictured and tell how they learned it—from reading, movies, television.)

● *What different parts of the world can you recognize in these artifacts?* (Europe— compass, coins; Americas—steam locomotive; Asia— the quote)

★**THINKING FURTHER:** *Making Conclusions* **What clue does this give you to the continents you will learn about in this unit?** (Possible answer: The modern age developed in many parts of the world.)

Looking Ahead In this unit students will explore the 400-year period from roughly 1500 to roughly 1900 as important events unfolded in Europe, the Americas, and Asia. They will follow the path of ground-breaking and world-transforming new ideas and new technologies.

UNIT CONTENTS

EXPLORER'S COMPASS, EUROPE; GOLD AND SILVER COINS, SPAIN

STEAM LOCOMOTIVE, UNITED STATES

450

BACKGROUND INFORMATION

ABOUT THE ARTIFACTS

● **GOLD AND SILVER SPANISH COINS** Spain used both newly mined gold and silver and melted-down artifacts to produce the coins that represented the wealth it gained from colonies in the Americas.

● **EXPLORER'S COMPASS** To this day, the magnetic compass remains the principle instrument of navigation, on land, sea, or air, and it was crucial to the period of exploring Earth.

UNIT FIVE

Dawn of the Modern World

"Knowledge shall be sought throughout the world."

from the Charter Oath
See page 511.

Why Does It Matter?

These words, from a Japanese document of 1889, express a yearning for new ideas and knowledge. During the period you will read about—when our modern world was just beginning to take shape—new ways of thinking spread among many peoples.

People began to learn more about the world around them. European explorers sailed to the Western Hemisphere, charting new courses and coming into contact with peoples of the Americas. Scientists learned about Earth and its position in the solar system. They invented new technologies. The changes that resulted created a world of new ideas and challenges.

FIND OUT MORE!
Visit our website:
www.mhschool.com

*inter*NET
CONNECTION

GALILEO'S ROOM, ITALY

451

Discussing the Artifacts Have students sit in pairs with one text opened to this spread and the other to the Unit Four Opener on pp. 310–311.

★THINKING FURTHER: *Compare and Contrast* **Which of these artifacts appear to be more "modern" than those on pages 310–311? How are they more modern?** *(Machine technology shown here should strike students as more modern than artifacts shown for Unit Four. Clearly, ideas for technology and knowledge of how it could be developed had advanced.)*

Discussing WHY DOES IT MATTER? Have a student read the quote aloud and have the class review the passage.

● *From what document does the quote come?* (the Charter Oath, a Japanese document of 1889)

● *What yearning do the Japanese express in this quote?* (a desire for new ideas and knowledge from wherever they can find them)

● *How much earlier had "the dawn of the modern world" begun?* (nearly 400 years earlier, before 1500)

● *How did the Japanese yearning reflect the yearnings of many others since the dawn of the modern world? What kinds of knowledge did these people seek?* (They too sought knowledge of the world around them—of Earth and its regions, of the solar system, of ways to develop new technologies.)

★THINKING FURTHER: *Making Conclusions* **The English thinker Francis Bacon, who lived early in the period under study, said, "Knowledge is power." How did the Japanese of 1889 show that they believed this statement?** *(Possible answer: They had come to believe that they had to have knowledge of the world since they swore an oath to seek it.)*

BACKGROUND INFORMATION

ABOUT THE ARTIFACTS

● **STEAM LOCOMOTIVE** The use of steam to power machinery was a hallmark of the dawn of the modern world. The steam locomotive was first invented and used in England, but the United States made great use of this mode of transportation to carry people and goods across vast distances.

● **GALILEO'S ROOM** Perhaps Galileo Galilei represents the dawn of modern thinking to a greater degree than any other scientist. His use of the scientific method initiated new ways of working with science.

Introducing
Golden Voyage

Exploring Prior Knowledge As students examine the views of the sailing ship pictured, encourage them to discuss how such ships differed from modern ocean-going ships. How was the way they were powered different? (sail vs. engines) What equipment did they lack that modern vessels would have? (ship-to-shore radio, electronic navigation, for example) Help students to picture themselves as passengers or crew aboard such ships, to sense the danger and adventure.

Links to the Unit As students work through Unit 5, they will be entering "a brave new world," much as Drake did on the *Golden Hind.* They will find that it is a world of discovery across the globe and a time of revolutions that truly changed the world.

Golden Voyage Give students a few minutes to read the text and examine all the pictures closely. On the pictured globe, have them trace the route the voyage followed with their fingers, starting with England and following the route westward. Have them identify the oceans crossed and the continents reached.

Refer students to the title of this Adventure and challenge them to identify reasons that "Golden Voyage" might have been chosen. Help them to see that not only did the ship have the word *Golden* in its name but it brought treasures in gold seized from the Spanish back to England, as evidenced by the inset at the far left.

Resource **REMINDER**

National Geographic Poster

Geo Adventures *Daily Geography Activities*

Technology: *Adventure Time!* CD-ROM

Adventures with NATIONAL GEOGRAPHIC

BACKGROUND INFORMATION

MORE ABOUT DRAKE'S GOLDEN VOYAGE

• Like other ships of its time, the *Golden Hind* was very small by modern standards, only a little over 100 feet long!

• The voyage began from Plymouth, England, in December 1577 with a fleet of five ships and 160 men. But through mutiny, abandonment, and sinking, only the *Golden Hind* remained by the time Drake reached the Pacific.

• As he sailed along the North America's western coast, Drake made landfall in what is today the San Francisco area. He claimed it for England and named it "New Albion" (Albion being another name for England).

Golden VOYAGE

Today, a reproduction of the *Golden Hind* sails off the coast of England. Four hundred years ago, the real *Golden Hind* carried explorer Francis Drake from England around the world. Surviving violent storms, Drake rounded South America and headed up its western coast. Along the way, he picked up a fortune in treasure—by raiding Spain's South American ports. Three years after his departure, Drake returned to England. Queen Elizabeth was so pleased by his feat—and by the treasure he brought home—that she knighted him right on the deck of the *Golden Hind*.

GEO JOURNAL

You're Queen Elizabeth's speechwriter. Compose a speech to welcome Drake home.

453

As students examine the lower right-hand inset, explain that it shows the *Golden Hind* struggling through what Drake called an "intolerable tempest." It occurred on the second of the 16 days it took the *Golden Hind* to get through the Strait of Magellan near the southern tip of South America. This storm lasted for nearly two months and Drake said that its winds tossed the ship and its crew "like a ball in a racket."

As students look at the proud Drake pictured in the upper righthand inset, point out that by this time he was known as Sir Francis Drake. Help them to make the connection between being knighted—and the right to be called "Sir." You might also explain that women who are knighted are called "Dame." Ask students how they suppose Spain felt about England's stealing its treasures by piracy at sea. Explain that Spain demanded that what was stolen be returned. Not only did England not return it, but Queen Elizabeth rewarded the captain who stole it, a slap in Spain's face.

Using the Geo Journal As students approach writing their welcoming speeches, urge them to take a few moments to think of reasons the Queen was grateful to Drake and weave their speeches around those reasons.

 Technology CONNECTION

ADVENTURE TIME! CD-ROM
Enrich the National Geographic Adventures with the *Discoveries* activity on the *Adventure Time!* CD-ROM.

CURRICULUM CONNECTION

ART Explain to the class that Sir Francis Drake had a life filled with adventure—he was an explorer, raider, pirate, and naval commander in war.

Encourage students to do further research on events in his life and then pick one to illustrate. They may choose to do a single dramatic color illustration of a scene from that event or they may want to do a cartoon strip that shows the progress of the event. Have them create a bulletin board display of their artwork.

 ## THEMES of GEOGRAPHY

As you work through Unit 5 with your students, consider the following theme:

Human-Environmental Interactions The surroundings in which we live influence and are influenced by people. Discuss these interactions as you read about the revolutions in Chapter 17. How did the environment help create the tension that led to the revolts of Latin American colonies? (by providing minerals and crops that were taken by Europeans from the colonists) What are some of the ways that people changed their environment during the Industrial Revolution? (As populations exploded, factories and cities developed.)

CHAPTER 16 European Expansion

Pages 454–483

CHAPTER OVERVIEW

Explorer Ferdinand Magellan sailed around the tip of South America in 1520. Francisco Pizarro founded Lima, Peru, in 1535. In the 1500s, enslaved Africans were brought to work on sugar plantations in the Caribbean. Samuel de Champlain established settlements and a fur trade in Quebec by 1608.

GEO ADVENTURES DAILY GEOGRAPHY ACTIVITIES

Use **Geo Adventures** Daily Geography activities to assess students' understanding of geography skills.

CHAPTER PLANNING GUIDE

LESSON 1	CITIZENSHIP	LESSON 2
SUGGESTED PACING: 2 DAYS	SUGGESTED PACING: 1 DAY	SUGGESTED PACING: 2 DAYS
The Beginning Of Modern Science pp. 456–460	**Making History In Space** p. 461	**An Age Of Exploration** pp. 462–465
CURRICULUM CONNECTIONS Links to Science, p. 457 Links to Math, p. 458 **CITIZENSHIP** Understanding Health and Environmental Concerns, p. 459 **RESOURCES** Practice and Project Book, p. 92 ◯ TECHNOLOGY Videodisc/Video Tape 5	**CITIZENSHIP** Experimenting with Science, p. 461	**CITIZENSHIP** Citizen of..., Sailing for.... p. 464 **RESOURCES** Practice and Project Book, p. 93 Anthology, pp. 116–117 Desk Map

THINKING SKILLS	LESSON 4	LESSON 5
SUGGESTED PACING: 1 DAY	SUGGESTED PACING: 2 DAYS	SUGGESTED PACING: 2 DAYS
Analyzing The Credibility Of A Source pp. 472–473	**Africans In The Americas** pp. 474–477	**A European Colony In Australia** pp. 478–481
RESOURCES Practice and Project Book, p. 95 Transparency: Graphic Organizer	**CURRICULUM CONNECTIONS** Links to Reading, p. 476 **RESOURCES** Practice and Project Book, p. 96 Anthology, pp. 124–125 Outline Map	**CURRICULUM CONNECTIONS** Links to Science, p. 480 **CITIZENSHIP** Recognizing Perspectives, p. 480 **RESOURCES** Practice and Project Book, p. 97 Anthology, pp. 126–132

LEARNING STYLE: Visual GROUP 30 MINUTES OR LONGER

Make a Modern Explorer's Poster

Objective: To prepare students to study European exploration and expansion.

Materials: oaktag, art supplies

1. Invite students to imagine they are modern-day explorers. What regions might they explore, including outer space and undersea?
2. In groups, have students choose regions they would like to explore. What equipment would they need?
3. Have each group create a poster showing their regions.
4. Share the posters with the class and discuss the benefits and risks of exploration.

LESSON 3

SUGGESTED PACING: 2 DAYS

Europeans In The Americas pp. 466–471

CURRICULUM CONNECTIONS
Links to Language Arts, p. 467

CITIZENSHIP
Understanding Government, p. 469

RESOURCES
Project and Practice Book, p. 94
Anthology, pp. 118–119, 120, 121–122, 123
Desk Map

CHAPTER REVIEW

SUGGESTED PACING: I DAY

483

RCES
tice and Project Book, p. 98
ECHNOLOGY Videodisc/Video
5
ssment Book: Chapter 16 Test
sparency: Graphic Organizer,
-Idea Pyramid

SDAIE SUPPORT — SHELTERED INSTRUCTION

READING STRATEGIES & LANGUAGE DEVELOPMENT

Context Clues/Word Origins, p. 456, Lesson 1
Sequence/Idioms, p. 462, Lesson 2
Making and Supporting Generalizations/Homographs, p. 466, Lesson 3
Problem and Solution/Suffixes, p. 472, Thinking Skills
Rereading/Word Roots and Prefixes, p. 474, Lesson 4
Compare and Contrast/Word Origin, p. 478, Lesson 5

SECOND-LANGUAGE SUPPORT

Reading Strategies, p. 457
Using Visuals, p. 463
Making Connections, p. 468
Working with a Peer, p. 476
Taking Notes, p. 480
Self-Assessment/Portrait Gallery, p. 482

MEETING INDIVIDUAL NEEDS

Reteaching, Extension, Enrichment, pp. 460, 465, 471, 477, 481
McGraw-Hill Adventure Book

ASSESSMENT OPPORTUNITIES

Practice and Project Book, pp. 92–98
Write About It, pp. 460, 465, 471, 477, 481
Assessment Book: Assessing Think and Write, pp. T94–T96; Chapter 16 Tests: Content, Skills, Writing

Introducing the Chapter

Refer students to the chapter title and call on them to tell the area into which Europe was expanding (into the Western Hemisphere). Have them briefly recall what was happening in the Americas at the end of the last chapter and the peoples who were flourishing there.

THINKING ABOUT HISTORY AND GEOGRAPHY

Have students read the text on this page and trace each panel's location to the map. Have them identify the peoples of the Americas they already know (Aztec, Inca, Great Lakes Ojibwa) whom the Europeans are about to meet.

1519 VALLEY OF MEXICO

- **What meeting of civilizations is about to take place?** (Spanish and Aztec)

- **When did this meeting take place and where?** (1519, the Valley of Mexico)

★THINKING FURTHER: *Predicting* **What predictions might you make about this meeting's effect on each civilization?** *(Give students free rein to offer predictions based on prior knowledge gained from other sources. Invite students to write down the predictions and to check them against what they learn in this chapter.)*

1520 STRAIT OF MAGELLAN

- **Where is the Strait of Magellan located on the map?** (near the southern tip of South America)

- **If Magellan has sailed to this point from Europe, in what direction has he sailed?** (southwest)

★THINKING FURTHER: *Making Conclusions* **Which ocean will he leave and which will he enter at this point?** (from Atlantic to Pacific)

Resource REMINDER

 **Technology:** *Videodisc/Video Tape 5*

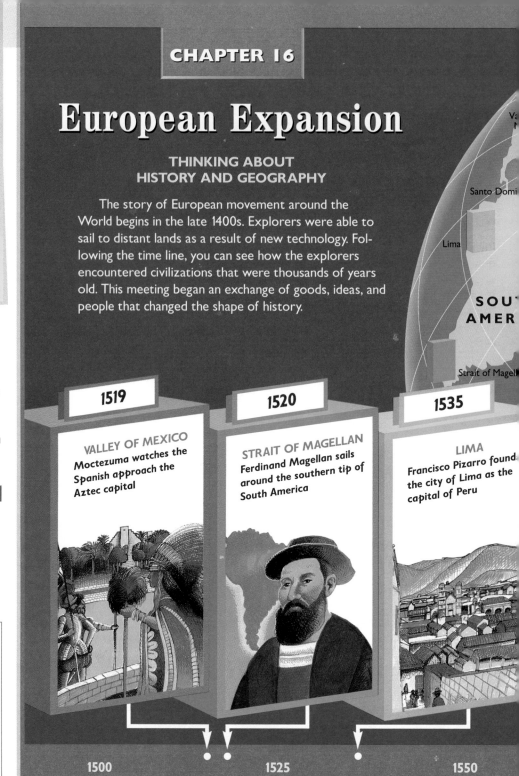

CHAPTER 16

European Expansion

THINKING ABOUT HISTORY AND GEOGRAPHY

The story of European movement around the World begins in the late 1400s. Explorers were able to sail to distant lands as a result of new technology. Following the time line, you can see how the explorers encountered civilizations that were thousands of years old. This meeting began an exchange of goods, ideas, and people that changed the shape of history.

Santo Domi

Lima

SOU
AMER

Strait of Magell

1519

VALLEY OF MEXICO
Moctezuma watches the Spanish approach the Aztec capital

1520

STRAIT OF MAGELLAN
Ferdinand Magellan sails around the southern tip of South America

1535

LIMA
Francisco Pizarro found. the city of Lima as the capital of Peru

1500   1525   1550

BACKGROUND INFORMATION

LINKING THE MAP AND THE TIME LINE
- The Valley of Mexico was not an easy place for the Spaniards, led by Hernando Cortés, to reach. After landing on the Gulf of Mexico coast, they had to climb from sea level to elevations of 12,000 feet and cross three series of mountains before finally reaching the Aztec capital of Tenochtitlán.

- The Strait of Magellan, surrounded by snow-covered mountains, is often difficult to navigate because of wind, fog, and riptides. It took Magellan a month to get through this treacherous passage, and by that time one of his ships had deserted and turned back to return to Spain.

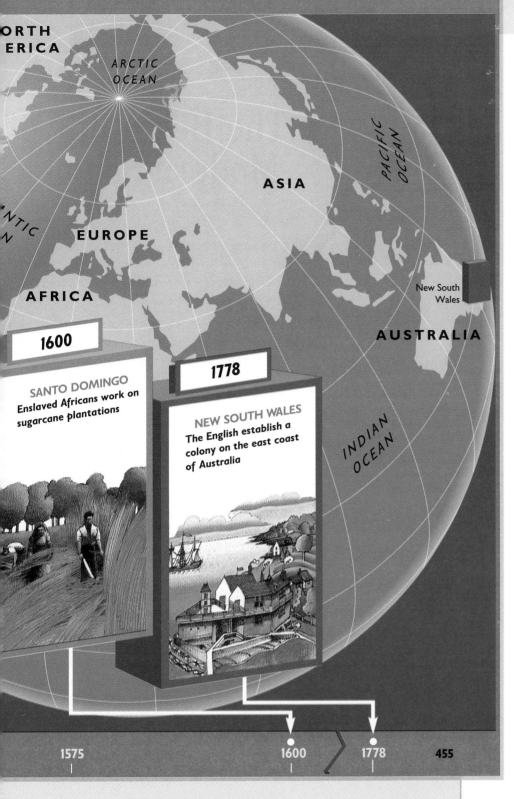

ORTH
ERICA
ARCTIC
OCEAN
ASIA
PACIFIC OCEAN
EUROPE
NTIC
N
New South
Wales
AFRICA
AUSTRALIA
INDIAN OCEAN

1600

SANTO DOMINGO
Enslaved Africans work on
sugarcane plantations

1778

NEW SOUTH WALES
The English establish a
colony on the east coast
of Australia

1575   1600   1778   455

- *Where is Lima located on the map?* (on the west coast of South America)

- *Whose territory was this when last you encountered it?* (the Inca's)

- *What is happening in this panel?* (A Spaniard is founding Lima as the capital of Peru.)

★THINKING FURTHER: *Making Conclusions* **What do you conclude has happened between the Spanish and the Inca to make this possible?** *(The Spanish must have been able to gain control there.)*

1600 SANTO DOMINGO

- *Where is Santo Domingo located on the map?* (on an island in the Atlantic Ocean)

- *Are the people pictured in this panel Native Americans or European? Explain.* (No, they are enslaved Africans.)

★THINKING FURTHER: *Making Conclusions* **What does this tell you about the Americas by 1600?** *(Enslaved Africans had been brought there.)*

1788 NEW SOUTH WALES

- *Where is New South Wales located on the map?* (in eastern Australia)

- *Who established a colony there in 1788?* (The English)

★THINKING FURTHER: *Making Conclusions* **What does the location and date of New South Wales say about European expansion?** *(European expansion started in the Americas and proceeded to other parts of the world.)*

 Technology CONNECTION

VIDEODISC/VIDEO TAPE 5
Enrich Chapter 16 with the *Aztecs and Conquistadors* segment on the videodisc.

Search 43579, Play To 45647

BACKGROUND INFORMATION

LINKING THE MAP AND THE TIME LINE

- "Lima" was not Francisco Pizarro's choice for his capital city's name. Because he founded it in 1535 on the Feast of the Epiphany, or Three Kings Day, he wanted to call it the City of Kings, but it became known as Lima, a corruption of the Indian name for the Rimac River, which ran through the site.

- Santo Domingo was one of the earliest Caribbean markets for enslaved Africans. In the decade from 1520 to 1530, 8,000 people were sold there. By 1600, a total 300,000 enslaved Africans had been brought there and elsewhere in the Americas.

- Quebec takes its name from an Algonkian term for "where the river narrows." This narrow stretch of river attracted Champlain to the site because it gave him strategic command of the waterway.

455

LESSON 1
PAGES 456–460

Lesson Overview
Modern science, with the ground-breaking work of Galileo and Newton, created clashes between the Church and science.

Lesson Objectives
★ Define *geocentric* and *heliocentric* views of the universe.

★ Explain the clash between Galileo and the Church.

★ Describe Newton's idea of gravity.

1 PREPARE

MOTIVATE Have two students read the *Read Aloud,* one as narrator, the other as Galileo. Refer to the photo of the telescope on this page. Ask students if they ever looked through a telescope. What new horizons did it open?

SET PURPOSE Mention the term *modern science,* as in "the wonders of modern science." Suggest that it is not as modern as we thought. Refer to the *Read to Learn* question and the *Vocabulary.* Invite students to explore the lesson to learn how Galileo and Newton helped set science on its modern course.

2 TEACH

Understanding THE BIG PICTURE
Write on the board the terms *geocentric* and *heliocentric* (which you may have introduced on p. 339). Ask students to differentiate between the terms.

● **When did the geocentric view of the universe originate?** *(in ancient times)*

★THINKING FURTHER: *Making Conclusions* **Why might saying that the geocentric idea was wrong have disturbed many Europeans?** *(It contradicted ideas that most people believed.)*

Resource REMINDER

Practice and Project Book: *p. 92*
 Technology: *Videodisc*

Focus Activity

READ TO LEARN

What were the achievements of Galileo Galilei and Isaac Newton?

VOCABULARY

- geocentric
- heliocentric
- telescope
- gravity
- scientific method

PEOPLE

- Galileo Galilei
- Isaac Newton

456

1400   1490   1700   1800

The Beginning of Modern Science

Read Aloud

In the early 1600s Galileo Galilei (gal uh LAY oh gah lee LE ee) used a new invention, the telescope, to look into space for the first time. He saw more stars than he could count. He wrote:

"Upon whatever part of the galaxy the telescope is directed, a crowd of stars is immediately presented to view. Many of them are rather large and quite bright, while the number of smaller ones is quite beyond calculation."

THE BIG PICTURE
Around 1500 Europeans were expanding their influence in other parts of the world. Explorers were making new connections between Europe and other continents. In the cities of Renaissance Italy, artists such as Leonardo da Vinci were painting the world around them in exciting new ways. As you read in Chapter 12, the Christian world was changing as well.

Scientists, too, began to take a fresh look at the world around them. Until this time most Europeans' understanding of the universe and how it worked came from ancient times. Most people believed that the universe was geocentric (jee oh SEN trihk), or centered around Earth. This view seemed to make sense. After all, it was the sun that seemed to "rise" and "set" each day, while Earth seemed not to move. In the early 1500s, however, a challenge to this belief would excite and disturb many Europeans.

SDAIE SUPPORT

SHELTERED INSTRUCTION

READING STRATEGIES & LANGUAGE DEVELOPMENT

CONTEXT CLUES Remind students that writers often give readers clues in a text to help them figure out the meaning of unfamiliar words. Review how the clue can be a synonym. Model how you define *astronomy* on p. 457 and *thermometer* on p. 458 by using synonyms as context clues. Then explain how writers often define a new word in a sentence or paragraph. Read the paragraph under the heading "Observing the World" on p. 457 and explain how the paragraph defines the word *experiment.* [SDAIE STRATEGY: CONTEXTUALIZATION/MODELING]

WORD ORIGINS Once again, refer students to the term *thermometer* on p. 458, and to *telescope* on p. 457. Explain that these words had to be made up to describe new inventions. As often happens in such cases, both words were formed from Greek elements. Have students look up the origins of both words in the dictionary.

NEW VIEWS

At this time scientists were talking about the ideas of Polish scientist Nicolaus Copernicus. In Chapter 12 you read that Copernicus suggested that Earth is not located at the center of the universe. He put forth a heliocentric (hee lee oh SEN trihk), or sun-centered, view. In this view, Earth and other planets move in orbits, or paths, around the sun. The heliocentric view caused a great stir. Was it really possible that Earth—and the people who lived on it—were not at the center of all things?

Copernicus spent much time studying the night sky. He also spent a great deal of time doing mathematics. Copernicus and many other scientists saw astronomy as a kind of mathematics. Astronomy is the science that deals with the sun, moon, stars, and planets. Scientists' ideas began to change when a new way of actually *seeing* the stars was invented. That invention was the telescope, which made faraway things appear close. As you will read, the telescope first became a useful scientific tool in the hands of Galileo Galilei.

Observing the World

Galileo was born in 1564 in the Italian city of Pisa, famous for its Leaning Tower. Like Copernicus, Galileo became interested in mathematics. Everywhere he looked, Galileo saw mathematics as part of daily life. A hailstorm made him wonder, do large hailstones fall faster than smaller ones? Ancient Greek thinkers such as Aristotle said that they do, because large hailstones are heavier than smaller ones. Yet when Galileo carefully watched hail falling from the sky, he thought Aristotle might have been wrong. A new age of testing ideas through observation had begun.

Galileo learned a great deal by looking closely at the world around him. In a cathedral one day, he saw an oil lamp swinging in a draft. Galileo made careful notes about the swinging lamp. Other inventors used Galileo's ideas to create clock pendulums. A pendulum is a weight hung so that it can swing back and forth—much like the oil lamp Galileo noticed!

Copernicus (right) studied the sky and made drawings of planets orbiting the sun (below).

The Granger Collection

457

NEW VIEWS

Review with the class what they learned about Copernicus in Chapter 12, p. 339.

- **What is the heliocentric view of the Universe?** *(a sun-centered view, where all the planets, including earth, move around the sun)*

★THINKING FURTHER: *Predicting* **What differences do you think the telescope would make in the study of astronomy?** *(the ability to see more objects in the sky and to see them closer)*

Discussing Observing the World Stress the shift from theory to observation.

- **Who was Galileo Galilei?** *(a mathematician, astronomer, inventor—a scientist)*

- **How did Galileo first prove Aristotle wrong about something?** *(by testing one of Aristotle's ideas and through observation proved it untrue)*

★THINKING FURTHER: *Cause and Effect* **What cause-and-effect relationships can you draw between Galileo's observations and later developments?** *(Disproving Aristotle led to calling into question other teachings based on Aristotle; discovering the regularity of pendulum swings led to the development of a pulse-measuring instrument, pendulum clocks.)*

CURRICULUM CONNECTION

LINKS TO SCIENCE Have a volunteer science research team study how a pendulum operates and explain its findings to the class. (An encyclopedia entry for *pendulum* is a good starting point.) A pendulum swings back and forth at a regular rate. Because of that regularity, many old clocks depended on pendulums.

SECOND-LANGUAGE SUPPORT

READING STRATEGIES Second-language learners will benefit by focusing their reading on Galileo and Newton. Have students develop summaries of the scientists' lives to keep for reference. In Lesson 2, students may create other summaries for inventors or explorers.

GLOBAL CONNECTION

MATHEMATICS ACROSS THE WORLD
- Mathematicians in ancient Egypt measured land after annual flooding. By 3000 B.C., Egyptians had a system of counting by groups of 10 (a decimal system).
- By 2100 B.C., Babylonians had developed a system of counting by 60. We use this system for measuring in hours, minutes, and seconds.
- The ancient Greeks raised mathematics from the purely practical to the abstract—or pure—mathematics.
- In India, the Hindus absorbed Greek ideas and made original contributions to arithmetic and algebra.
- The Arabs in turn adopted ideas from India, producing the Hindu-Arabic numbering system we use today.

EXPERIMENTS AND INVENTIONS

Help students to see that Galileo's inventions are important to us today.

- **What were some of Galileo's inventions?** *(thermometer, telescope)*

★**THINKING FURTHER:** *Compare and Contrast* **How would you contrast the use of the thermometer today with its use when Galileo invented it?** *(In contrast to no use in Galileo's time, the thermometer is used today in medicine, cooking, weather reporting and forecasting, and many lab and industrial uses.)*

Discussing A Look into Space Ask students to think of photos they may have seen of the moon seen through a telescope. Have them compare it to their view with the unaided eye on a clear night.

- **What discoveries did Galileo make through his new telescope?** *(a rough-surfaced moon; many more heavenly objects—stars and moons— and greater complexity than had been thought; evidence of Earth's rotation and movement around the sun, as well as that of other planets)*

- **How did these discoveries affect Galileo's view of the universe?** *(They convinced him that Copernicus's heliocentric view was correct and that the geocentric view was wrong.)*

- **How did Galileo's discoveries affect Church leaders?** *(They shocked and angered Church leaders.)*

★**THINKING FURTHER:** *Compare and Contrast* **How would you compare the development of the telescope with the development of Gutenberg's printing press nearly two centuries earlier?** *(Help students to recognize the power that technological breakthroughs like these can have in changing thought and behavior in wide-ranging ways.)*

Technology CONNECTION

VIDEODISC
Enrich Lesson 1 with the *Industrial Revolution* on the Videodisc.

Galileo (below) often worked on his telescope and other instruments in his room in Florence, Italy (left).

EXPERIMENTS AND INVENTIONS

Not long after he observed the swinging lamp, Galileo went on to study and to teach. Though he loved his new work as a teacher, he did not earn much money. So Galileo tried to come up with ideas for useful items that he could sell. He created the world's first thermometer. A thermometer measures temperature. It was 22 inches long and filled with water. No one had much use for the thermometer in the late 1500s, so it did not seem important then.

Galileo came up with a very successful device, however, in 1609. He learned that a maker of eyeglasses had invented an instrument that made distant things seem close. Galileo quickly made some changes and created his own model of a telescope. He gained wealth and success when he gave a telescope to the ruler of Venice. Commanders of the ruler's navy used the telescope for looking at far-off ships.

A Look into Space

The telescope brought changes to Galileo's life—and to the world—in another way. One night Galileo looked at the moon through the telescope. He expected to see the smooth surface that the ancient Greeks and many others had described. Instead, he saw that the moon was "rough and uneven, covered everywhere, just like Earth's surface, with huge mountains and deep valleys."

Galileo now began to study the sky carefully, night after night. He realized that it was far more complex than most people had ever realized. Far more stars existed than anyone had ever dreamed! Galileo discovered that another planet, Jupiter, also had moons orbiting it—just as the moon orbits Earth. Earth itself appeared to be slowly spinning, and moving around the sun.

458

CURRICULUM CONNECTION

LINKS TO MATH In 1623 Galileo described the importance of mathematics in unlocking the secrets of the universe:

- "Philosophy is written in this grand book—I mean the universe—which stands continually open to our gaze, but it cannot be understood unless one first learns to comprehend the language and interpret the characters in which it is written."

- "It is written in the language of mathematics, and its characters are triangles, circles, and other geometrical figures, without which it is humanly impossible to understand a single word of it; without these, one is wandering about in a dark labyrinth."

Galileo began to think that the long-held belief that Earth was at the center of the universe was wrong. His studies supported Copernicus' heliocentric idea.

Galileo made his findings public in 1610. At the time, it was as if a "new" universe had been discovered. Anyone could see it simply by looking through a telescope. Some people were shocked and surprised. Others, especially Church leaders, were angry.

Science and the Church

Leaders of the Catholic Church prepared to put Galileo on trial. They said that his views went against the Church's teachings. Earlier scientists had been sentenced to death because they wrote about heliocentric ideas.

Galileo, who was Roman Catholic, faced great danger. In 1633 the 69-year-old scientist was arrested and brought to Rome for trial. There Galileo was strongly advised to take back what he had said about the place of the sun in the universe.

Threatened with torture, Galileo finally stated, "I do not hold this opinion of Copernicus." Galileo was then taken back to his home in northern Italy. For the rest of his life, he was not allowed to leave his home. Galileo never publicly upheld the heliocentric view again. Before he died in 1642, though, he wrote:

I have two sources of comfort—first, that in my writings there cannot be found the faintest shadow of disobedience towards the Holy Church; and second, the truth of my own conscience, which only I and God in Heaven thoroughly know. And He knows that in this cause for which I suffer, none have spoken with more religious devotion or with greater enthusiasm for the Church than I.

DID YOU KNOW?

How have telescopes changed since Galileo's time?

Galileo's first telescope was about as long as his arm. It was made only of a tube and two-inch lenses.

By contrast, the Hubble Space Telescope, launched in 1990, is over 43 feet long. It uses mirrors over 7 feet wide and has a tangle of wires 26,000 miles long! The Hubble Telescope travels around Earth at a distance of 380 miles above the planet's surface. From there, the Hubble Telescope can spot stars *trillions* of miles away. Here's another way to put it: The Hubble could spot the punctuation mark at the end of this sentence from a mile away, or a dime from 20 miles away!

The Work of Isaac Newton

In the same year that Galileo died, Isaac Newton was born in the countryside of England. Newton grew up to become one of the world's giants in science. In fact, he built on Galileo's scientific legacy.

According to one story, the young Newton found a key to unlock these mysteries one day in 1675, when an apple fell on his head. The apple's fall from a tree led him to study the force of gravity. Gravity is the force that pulls things toward Earth. Newton calculated that the same force that pulls a falling apple toward Earth also pulls at the moon. Instead of falling to Earth's surface, the moon is kept moving in a circular path around the planet. Newton's study of gravity helped scientists in the late 1600s understand how a heliocentric universe actually worked.

459

BACKGROUND INFORMATION

ABOUT GALILEO'S QUIET AFFIRMATION Legend has it that at his trial, after he made his denial of the heliocentric view including the belief that Earth rotates, Galileo said in a very low, but defiant voice, "Nevertheless, it does move!"

CITIZENSHIP ★

UNDERSTANDING HEALTH AND ENVIRONMENTAL CONCERNS Encourage students to think about life in your community and what scientists have done and might do to improve it. Have students look for and discuss newspaper stories that concern matters of public health and the environment. Ask them how scientists might act as good citizens in dealing with such matters as these.

Discussing Science and the Church Explore Galileo's own conflict between his religion and science.

- *Why did the Roman Catholic Church try Galileo and threaten him with torture?* (His heliocentric view opposed the Church's geocentric view.)

- *What did Galileo decide to do in the face of this challenge?* (He denied believing in the heliocentric view, returned home, and never spoke publicly of it again.)

★ THINKING FURTHER: *Making Conclusions* **Based on the quote from Galileo in the text, how would you say that he dealt with the dilemma with the Church in his own mind?** *(Possible answer: He accepted public obedience to the Church, but privately believed that God knew his conscience was clear about his heliocentric belief.)*

Extending Did You Know? Point out to the class that the Hubble Telescope sends new information back to Earth every day. Invite a science research team to check recent editions of *Readers' Guide to Periodical Literature* for resources in which they can learn about Hubble's recent discoveries. Have them report their findings back to the class.

Exploring The Work of Isaac Newton Write *gravity* on the board.

- *Who was Isaac Newton?* (a scientist who built on the work of Galileo)

- *What is one of his greatest contributions to our scientific knowledge about Earth?* (He was the first to describe the idea of gravity.)

- *What is gravity? Why is it necessary to a heliocentric universe?* (The force of attraction between two objects; it is necessary to hold people and objects to a spinning Earth and to keep planets around the sun in orderly motion.)

★ THINKING FURTHER: *Making Conclusions* **Newton once said that he was able to make the discoveries he did "by standing upon the shoulders of Giants." What do you think he meant?** *(He built his scientific findings on the findings of earlier scientists.)*

3 CLOSE

WHY IT MATTERS

European discoveries in science had many results. They led to a new understanding of humanity's place in the universe and how that universe worked. Improvements in technology came about as well. For example, ship captains could now use telescopes to see faraway land, or to quickly spot enemy ships on the way. The pendulum clock helped people to measure time accurately.

European interest in learning about the natural world had another important result. It led to the development of what is called the scientific method. The scientific method is a way of questioning and studying things that occur in nature. With this method, an idea must be thoroughly tested before it is

This is a reconstruction of a clock part invented by Galileo. The swinging pendulum causes the gears to move.

460

accepted as true. This is what Galileo did when he carefully studied the motions of the stars and planets. His experiments, and the work of other scientists, led Europe and the rest of the world into a new age of science. Scientific advances in astronomy, medicine, and other fields continue to have great effects on the way we live and view the world.

Reviewing Facts and Ideas

MAIN IDEAS

- Most Europeans in the Middle Ages shared the ancient Greeks' belief that the universe was geocentric, or centered around Earth.

- In the early 1600s, Galileo Galilei built on the heliocentric, or sun-centered, ideas of Copernicus.

- Galileo's findings clashed with Catholic teachings. The Church supported geocentric ideas.

- Isaac Newton's studies of gravity in the late 1600s helped scientists to learn how a heliocentric system might work.

THINK ABOUT IT

1. How did the scientific method help both Galileo and Newton in their work?

2. Why was Newton's work with gravity important?

3. **FOCUS** How did scientists like Galileo and Newton change the way people thought about the world?

4. **THINKING SKILL** Explain some different *points of view* people held about the universe in the 1500s. What might account for each of these?

5. **WRITE** Write a paragraph explaining how science affects the way we live today.

CITIZENSHIP

MAKING A DIFFERENCE

Experimenting with Science

NEW YORK CITY, NEW YORK—Ever since Adam Exra Cohen was a small child, he's had the mind of an inventor. In third grade he would take home broken computers and televisions. He enjoyed taking them apart and figuring out how they worked. Adam also liked doing science experiments. "Sometimes," he explains, "my mother would bring home a whole fish for dinner. She would let me dissect it in the kitchen sink." His mother had only two rules. His experiments could not be dangerous and he had to clean up afterwards.

By the time Adam was in the fifth grade, he started keeping a notebook of his ideas for inventions. "I drew sketches and made written descriptions of each idea." Now he's up to 160 ideas.

Today, at age 18, this teenage science whiz has invented an amazing new way to build a type of electron microscope called a scanning tunneling microscope. Adam says that a person using this microscope can scratch as many as 50 words in a space the width of a human hair." It can also be used in making computer chips.

Adam built his award-winning microscope in his bedroom using modeling clay, legos, and bungee cord. "I used the cord," he explains, "to hang the microscope from the ceiling of my bedroom. This kept the microscope from jiggling around. Vibrations from the air make it harder for the machine

to do its work." His microscope also contains some very high-powered electronic parts, but the entire microscope only cost Adam about $100 for parts. Most scanning tunneling microscopes cost many thousands of dollars.

Not all of Adam's inventions work as well as his microscope. In fact, it wasn't until his third science fair that an invention of his was really successful. "I'm always doing lots and lots of experiments," he says. "Most of them don't work. This one did." Adam hopes some day to invent something that he says "will help other people lead easier lives." In the meantime, he has come advice for other young inventors. "Young kids have just as good ideas as grownups. Write down every idea and don't be discouraged. It could be very valuable some day."

"Young kids have just as good ideas as grownups."

461

LESSON 2
PAGES 462–465

Lesson Overview
The desire for trade with the East and advances in sailing technologies produced a great age of exploration.

Lesson Objectives
★ Explain why Europeans wanted to move out far beyond their continent.

★ Describe advances in sailing.

★ Identify the achievements of early European explorers.

⭐ 1 PREPARE

MOTIVATE Refer students to the lesson title. Ask them to put themselves in the shoes of explorers and "boldly go where no one has gone before." To set the mood, have two students do the *Read Aloud,* one to read the quote, the other as narrator.

SET PURPOSE Refer students to the picture of the caravel on this page and to the *Read to Learn* question. Who were these explorers? What made them go on dangerous quests? Encourage students to explore for answers. Preview the *Vocabulary.*

⭐ 2 TEACH

Understanding THE BIG PICTURE
As students work with the first paragraph, have them locate each place on a world map or desk map to reinforce their idea of different parts of the world.

● **What already tied many of these places together?** *(trade)*

● **Which cities were growing rich from trade?** *(certain Italian cities)*

★THINKING FURTHER: *Cause and Effect* **Why would long, expensive trade routes lead to exploration?** *(to find new, shorter trade routes)*

Resource **REMINDER**

Practice and Project Book: *p. 93*
Anthology: *Captain Cook's Journal, pp. 116–117*
Desk Map

Focus Activity

READ TO LEARN

How did European explorers bring distant parts of the world into contact with each other?

VOCABULARY

- caravel
- strait

PEOPLE

- Prince Henry
- Bartholomeu Dias
- Vasco da Gama
- Christopher Columbus
- Ferdinand Magellan

PLACES

- Strait of Magellan

462

| 1394 | 1522 | 1600 | 1700 | 1800 |

An Age of Exploration

Read Aloud
"They sent out a small boat in order to find the cape of the other sea, and they came back at the end of the third day and told how they had seen the cape of the great sea. And the Captain General wept with joy. And they named that cape Cape Desire because they had desired it for so long."

This description was written by a passenger on a ship captained by Ferdinand Magellan (muh JEL un). In the middle 1400s few Europeans had traveled far into the Atlantic Ocean. By 1520, though, European sailors were regularly crossing the Atlantic. One sailor, Magellan, was about to sail into the great Pacific Ocean. His goal was to sail around the world.

THE BIG PICTURE
In the middle 1400s the Aztec empire and its capital city, Tenochtitlán, were at the height of power and influence in Mexico. Across the Atlantic Ocean in western Africa, meanwhile, gold was flowing north from Mali to the coastal cities of North Africa. Cities in Italy were becoming rich from trade with Asia.

Soon trade would link these different parts of the world more closely. Already goods were moving between Asia, Africa, and Europe. However, the route to Asia was very long and expensive. In order to buy spices and other goods, European merchants would have to find another way to reach Asia. That search would bring the two hemispheres—East and West—into contact.

SHELTERED INSTRUCTION

READING STRATEGIES & LANGUAGE DEVELOPMENT

SEQUENCE Discuss how events occur in a specific sequence. To review the lesson concept, invite a volunteer to demonstrate getting ready for school. As the student acts out the events, jot them down on the board in scrambled order. Have the class number the events to show the correct sequence. Encourage students to trace the sequence of events as they read this chapter. **[SDAIE STRATEGY: BRIDGING]**

IDIOMS If you introduced students to idioms as suggested in Chapter 15, p. 434, remind them that idioms are informal expressions that add color to a language. Refer to the idiom *thanks to* on p. 463, which is just another way of saying "with the help of" or "owing to." Point out that its opposite is *no thanks to.*

TRAVEL FOR TRADE

uropean trade with Asia started to
row thanks largely to Marco Polo's
avels on the Silk Road. In 1295 Polo
eturned to Venice from China. Not
ong after, his tales of the Silk Road
nd China became widely known. Polo's
ccounts made many Europeans want
o take part in trade with Asia. Trade
long the Silk Road thrived for more
nan 100 years afterward.

One of the most profitable goods to
ring home was pepper. Since people
id not have refrigerators, meat quickly
poiled unless it was preserved with
alt. The salt, however, gave the meat
flavor that many people did
ot like. Europeans found that
dding pepper made meat taste
nuch better. Pepper became a
ery popular item.

A journey along the Silk Road
ometimes took years to complete
nd was expensive. Yet those who
eturned could make as much as
0 times the amount they had
pent making the journey. For this
eason, some European leaders
pent huge sums of money on the
earch for quicker, cheaper routes
o Asia.

The Search for a Shorter Route

Prince Henry of Portugal was
ne leader who supported the search
or such routes. He became known
s Henry the Navigator. Henry lived
etween 1394 and 1460. He wanted
o find a sea route to the gold mines
f western Africa. He provided money
nd help to Europe's finest sailors,
napmakers, and shipbuilders. These
eople improved the compass, updated
naps, and simplified the astrolabe,
vhich you read about in Chapter 10.

Most important, the people working
with Prince Henry designed a new kind
of boat called a caravel (KAR uh vel).
Caravels combined the smooth bodies
of European sailing ships and the three-
sided sails of Arab boats. These sails
allowed boats to sail into the wind. Earlier captains usually had to direct their
ships wherever the wind was blowing.
Now, for the first time, European ships
could go in almost any direction their
captain wished. You can see a type of
caravel on page 462.

The Granger Collection

**Prince Henry
helped navigators
improve the
compass. Italian
sailors used this
compass (right)
around 1580.**

463

Encourage students to try to sense the wonder of being the first to find a place.

More **MAP WORK**

Refer students to the map on this page. Have them work with the text and map.

- *In what directions did Vasco da Gama sail in his attempt?* (south down to the Cape of Good Hope, around Africa's southern tip, north up the east coast of Africa, and northeast across the Indian Ocean to India)

★THINKING FURTHER: *Cause and Effect* **What were the effects of the voyage of Vasco da Gama?** *(He found a new route to Asia, and his reaching India began a 400-year European rule there.)*

Exploring Across the Atlantic
Continue having students work back and forth between text and map.

- *Locate Columbus's route on the map and trace it with your finger. What was he trying to do and what feat did he accomplish?* (He was trying to reach Asia by sailing west across the Atlantic; he reached the Americas.)

- *What was Ferdinand Magellan's goal?* (to sail around the world)

★THINKING FURTHER: *Making Decisions* **On a scale of 1 to 10, how successful would you say these explorers were in opening up new trade routes to Asia?** *(Rankings may be high for success, but often, as with Magellan, at a terrible price.)*

EXPLORING AROUND THE WORLD

In 1469, nine years after Prince Henry died, Portuguese sailors became the first Europeans to reach the coast of western Africa. In 1488 a Portuguese captain became the first to sail around the southernmost tip of Africa, the Cape of Good Hope. This captain was Bartholomeu Dias (bahr tu lu MAY u DEE ush), whose achievement marked a turning point in the search for a new route to Asia. By sailing around Africa, Dias had discovered a possible sea route from Europe to the East.

Nine years later another Portuguese captain set sail for Asia. Vasco da Gama led a voyage that attempted to complete the trip around Africa to Asia. His success in reaching the coast of India made him the first European ever to sail so far east. Da Gama returned to India in 1502, bringing a navy to conquer rich port cities for Portugal. This began a period of European rule on th Indian subcontinent that would last for more than 400 years.

Across the Atlantic

Another explorer, Christopher Columbus, set out in 1492 to reach Asia by traveling in the opposite direction—west. Columbus did not reach Asia. However, as you will read in the next lesson, his voyage had tremendou effects on both Spain and the America

The wealth of Asia's spice-rich land continued to draw Europeans. In 1519 Spain sent Ferdinand Magellan on a westward journey to Asia. Neither Ma ellan nor anyone else had ever led suc a voyage. Magellan was trying to sail around the whole world!

Magellan and his crew made their way through a strait at the tip of Sout

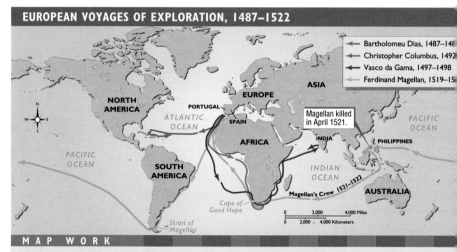

EUROPEAN VOYAGES OF EXPLORATION, 1487–1522

- Bartholomeu Dias, 1487–148
- Christopher Columbus, 1492
- Vasco da Gama, 1497–1498
- Ferdinand Magellan, 1519–15

Magellan killed in April 1521.

Magellan's Crew 1521–1522

M A P   W O R K

Beginning in the late 1400s, Europeans raced to find the shortest sea route to Asia.

1. Which explorer sailed along the east coast of Africa?

2. Which voyage did not reach the southernmost tip of Africa?

3. Which explorer's route did not have a return trip?

464   MAP WORK: **1.** Vasco da Gama **2.** Christopher Columbus **3.** Ferdinand Magellan

CITIZENSHIP ★

CITIZEN OF . . . , SAILING FOR . . . Both Bartholomeu Dias and Vasco da Gama were Portuguese-born and made expeditions for Portugal. Italian-born Christopher Columbus sailed for Spain (after being turned down by Portugal). Ferdinand Magellan, born in Portugal, set out on his round-the-world expedition in the service of Spain (after Portugal had denied a military pension he thought was due him). Magellan lost his life in a battle in the Philippines, in which he and 49 of his men helped a chief from Cebu, who had converted to Christianity, against a force of more than 1,000. "With lances of iron and of bamboo, . . . they slew our . . . light, our comfort, and our true guide," one of his men wrote.

VISUAL LITERACY

ABOUT THE PORTRAIT OF FERDINAND MAGELLAN This portrait of Magellan reflects the common admiration during the Italian Renaissance for great thinkers and achievers in the sciences, exploration, and the arts. Patrons of the arts, such as Lorenzo Medici from Florence, often paid artists to pursue their work. In some cases they also funded artists' self-portraits. Invite students to study the painting and share questions they might have liked to have asked Magellan about his life. Ask students: What famous person would you choose to paint?

Ferdinand Magellan studied astronomy and navigation for two years before leaving Europe with a fleet of five ships in 1519.

America. A strait is a narrow channel, or body of water, between two larger bodies of water. Find the Strait of Magellan on the map. After sailing through this strait, Magellan reached the calm waters of an ocean he called the *Pacific*, or "peaceful," Ocean.

For Magellan and his crew, the voyage on this ocean was anything but peaceful. Lack of food left the crew eating dust made from the wood on board and the leather from their gear to survive. In the Philippines, Magellan himself was killed in battle. The crew sailed on, finally reaching ports in Asia and then, in 1522, Spain. They were home at last after a three-year journey around the world.

Of 238 men and 5 ships that set out with Magellan, only 17 men and 1 ship returned. That single ship's cargo, or load, paid for the whole voyage, with money left over.

WHY IT MATTERS

New technology, together with human courage, added greatly to western Europe's knowledge of the world in the late 1400s and early 1500s. As ships sailed new sea routes again and again, different regions became more closely linked through trade and communication. Such links led to further exploration—and conquest. You will read about exploration and conquest in the Americas later in this chapter.

✓ Reviewing Facts and Ideas

MAIN IDEAS

- To find a cheaper route to Asia, Europeans explored sea routes south around Africa or west across the Atlantic Ocean.
- Portugal's Prince Henry helped develop the caravel.
- In the 1480s and 1490s, Portuguese explorers Bartholomeu Dias and Vasco da Gama discovered a route to Asia by sailing around Africa.
- Ferdinand Magellan set sail on a voyage around the world in 1519.

THINK ABOUT IT

1. How did the caravel help European explorers?

2. Why did Europeans want to find new routes to Asia?

3. **FOCUS** What were two major changes brought about by Europe's explorers in the 1400s and 1500s?

4. **THINKING SKILL** Make a *generalization* about the qualities explorers such as Dias, Da Gama, and Magellan must have needed to be successful.

5. **GEOGRAPHY** Describe some of the difficulties explorers faced in trying to reach Asia by sea.

465

Discussing **WHY IT MATTERS** Review the factors that opened up trade.

★ **THINKING FURTHER:** *Summarizing* **How would you summarize the reasons the European explorers were able to achieve what they did?** *(Summaries should reflect sailing technology, human courage, and the drive to keep pushing back the frontiers of what was known, as well as the desire for profit.)*

3 CLOSE

MAIN IDEAS

Call on students to come up to the board and write their answers.

- **What routes did explorers take to find cheaper ways to reach Asia?** *(around the tip of Africa into the Indian Ocean, west across the Atlantic)*

- **Who encouraged and supported the development of new sailing technology?** *(Henry the Navigator)*

- **Which Portuguese explorers developed a route to Asia around the tip of Africa?** *(Bartholomeu Dias and Vasco da Gama)*

EVALUATE
✓ **Answers to Think About It**

1. It gave them the ability to sail in any direction, even into the wind. *Recall Details*

2. They wanted cheaper ways to gain profits from trade with Asia. *Recall Details*

3. They reached known areas and areas they had not known existed and they established links among various world regions. *Summarize*

4. Generalizations should reflect such qualities as courage, skill, daring, persistence, and ability to deal with trouble and disappointment. *Form Generalizations*

5. storms, difficulties in navigating, sailing into the unknown *Five Themes of Geography: Human/ Environment Interactions*

Write About It Ask students to picture themselves as sailors aboard one of these explorers' ships and write a postcard message home describing an experience they had on a sailing expedition.

MEETING INDIVIDUAL NEEDS

RETEACHING (Easy) Have students review the lesson and choose the explorer whose achievements they admire the most. Have them write two reasons for their choice.

EXTENSION (Average) Have students choose one of the expeditions described and do further encyclopedia research on it. Have them create a "ship's log," describing important dates and events.

ENRICHMENT (Challenging) Human space exploration beginning in the 1960s has often been compared to the Age of Exploration that students have just studied. Have students do library research on space exploration and then write an essay comparing it with the explorations of the 1400s and 1500s, focusing on reasons for exploration, difficulties faced, and achievements made.

LESSON 3
PAGES 466–471

Lesson Overview
European expansion into the Americas brought about the destruction of Native American empires and transformed life in areas the Europeans occupied.

Lesson Objectives
★ Analyze how Europe claimed vast lands in the Americas.

★ Explain the downfall of the Aztec and Inca empires.

★ Describe life in Spanish America.

1 PREPARE

MOTIVATE Have two students do the *Read Aloud*, one as narrator, one as Pizarro who is shown in the picture on this page. Have the class briefly review what they know about life in the Americas before Columbus, specifically about the Aztec and Inca empires. Tell students that they will see how life will change for both Americans and Europeans.

SET PURPOSE How could this happen? Refer students to the *Read to Learn* question and encourage them to explore this lesson to find out. Preview the *Vocabulary*.

2 TEACH

Understanding THE BIG PICTURE
Set the stage by asking students to use desk maps of the world and—using the text—having them identify and locate sites of events across the world.

★THINKING FURTHER: *Compare and Contrast* **How did the world change in just 40 years after Columbus first reached the Americas?** *(heavy trans-Atlantic travel, exchange between Eastern and Western hemispheres, Spanish and Portuguese power enlarged.)*

Resource REMINDER

Practice and Project Book: *p. 94*

Anthology: *Battle of Tenochtitlán, pp. 118–119; Royal Commentaries of the Incas, p. 120; Tears of the Indians, pp. 121–122; The Legacy of Columbus, p. 123*

Desk Map

Focus Activity

READ TO LEARN
How did the empires of the Americas fall to Spain?

VOCABULARY
- Line of Demarcation
- conquistador
- missionary
- convert
- hacienda

PEOPLE
- Pedro Álvarez Cabral
- Hernando Cortés
- Moctezuma
- Francisco Pizarro
- Atahualpa

PLACES
- Hispaniola
- Cuzco
- New Spain
- Peru
- Mexico City
- Lima

466

1400	1500	1700	1800

Europeans in the Americas

Read Aloud
The commander of the exhausted men drew a line in the sand and challenged, "Here, you return to Panama to be poor; there, you may go on to Peru to be rich. Choose which best becomes you as good Spaniards!"

All but one man crossed the line in the sand with the commander, Francisco Pizarro (frahn SEES koh pih ZAHR oh). They went on to gain great fortunes at the expense of one of the world's largest empires—the Inca empire.

THE BIG PICTURE
Growth and change were taking place all around the world in the late 1400s. In western Africa the markets of Timbuktu were growing within the Songhai empire. China's Ming rulers were adding to the Great Wall, as Chinese workers produced more and more porcelain, a fine hand pottery, and silk. In the Americas, meanwhile, both the Aztec and Inca empires were growing larger than any civilizations that had yet developed in the Western Hemisphere.

In 1492, Christopher Columbus crossed the Atlantic Ocean, opening up the Americas to European exploration. Within 40 years the Atlantic Ocean had become a vast highway crisscrossed by ships filled with people, trade goods, and treasure. Most of this traffic was controlled by just two European countries—Spain and Portugal. Though these countries were small in size, their power stretched across the globe.

SHELTERED INSTRUCTION

READING STRATEGIES & LANGUAGE DEVELOPMENT

MAKING AND SUPPORTING GENERALIZATIONS Review with the class the steps in making and supporting a generalization: deciding on a topic, selecting supporting facts, making a generalization. Then present this topic: Exploration. Have students work in small groups to draw generalizations supported by at least three facts. Have students make and support generalizations about the Europeans in the Americas as they read this lesson. **[SDAIE STRATEGY: METACOGNITIVE DEVELOPMENT]**

HOMOGRAPHS Remind students that homographs are words that are spelled the same but may differ in meaning, origin, or pronunciation. Refer to several homographs in this lesson: *present, conduct, convert,* and *decrease.* Their pronunciations depend on whether they are nouns or verbs. Have students pronounce each as a noun and a verb.

EUROPEAN CLAIMS

In Lesson 2 you read that, in the late 1400s, Europe's race for new routes and territories was on. Portugal and Spain were in the lead. Their leaders believed that they had the right to claim whatever lands they explored. In 1494 the leaders of Spain and Portugal met to divide the lands of the Americas. They agreed upon an imaginary line, called the Line of Demarcation, across a map. Look at the map to see how this line affected claims in the Americas.

In 1493, Columbus had crossed the Atlantic for a second time. He brought more than 1,000 people with him to the island he called Hispaniola (his pun YOH luh). The Spanish were not coming simply to trade or explore—they meant to stay and colonize.

Portugal soon made its own claim in the Americas. Pedro Álvarez Cabral (PE droh AHL vah res kah BRAHL) set sail for India in 1500. A storm blew his ships west. So began a 300-year period of Portuguese rule in Brazil.

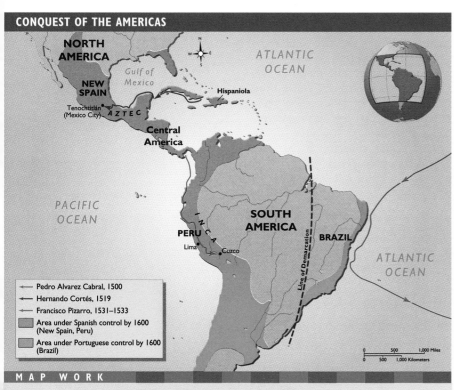

CONQUEST OF THE AMERICAS

- ← Pedro Alvarez Cabral, 1500
- ← Hernando Cortés, 1519
- ← Francisco Pizarro, 1531–1533
- Area under Spanish control by 1600 (New Spain, Peru)
- Area under Portuguese control by 1600 (Brazil)

MAP WORK

The Line of Demarcation divided control of lands in the Americas.

1. Which European power controlled Aztec and Inca lands?

2. Which explorer sailed to the east coast of South America?

3. About how far from the Line of Demarcation was Cuzco?

4. Which explorer reached Tenochtitlán?

MAP WORK: **1.** Spain **2.** Pedro Álvarez Cabral **3.** 1,500 miles (about 2,414 kilometers) **4.** Hernando Cortés

467

GLOBAL CONNECTION

DRAWING THE LINE OF DEMARCATION Before this line was drawn in 1494, Portugal and Spain had already been rivals over newly explored lands for some time. How could the two rival nations settle their dispute? They turned to Pope Alexander VI, the pope at the time. He drew a line for them, and the two countries proceeded to work out a compromise based on it. In June 1494, they signed the Treaty of Tordesillas, signaling agreement to the Line of Demarcation.

CURRICULUM CONNECTION

LINKS TO LANGUAGE ARTS Refer students to the map and the Line of Demarcation once again. What effect do they suppose this line had on the languages that are spoken in South America today? (Portuguese in Brazil; Spanish almost everywhere else)

EUROPEAN CLAIMS

Use this section to discuss the idea of one nation having a right to "claim" the land of another. Use modern examples, perhaps Iraq "claiming" the country of Kuwait, or one nation of the former Yugoslavia "claiming" the land of a neighboring nation.

- *Do people today believe that one nation has the right to "claim" the land of another?* (Most people do not, as reactions to both Iraq and the former Yugoslavia have proven.)

- *How did nations view the practice of claiming land in the 1500s?* (Conquerors believed they could claim others' lands.)

★THINKING FURTHER: *Making Conclusions* **How do you think you would react if another nation decided to "claim" all or part of the United States as its own?** (Use this question to help students recognize an attitudinal change over time and also to empathize with those whose land is "claimed.")

More MAP WORK

Refer the class to the map on this page.

- *By 1600 which two European nations had the major claims of the American territory shown?* (Spain and Portugal)

- *What boundary divided their claims?* (Line of Demarcation)

- *How did it divide their claims?* (East of the line was Portugal's; west was Spain's.)

- *Why was Portugal's claim the result of an accident?* (Have students refer to the map on p. 464 and view the Portuguese route southward down the west coast of Africa to see how easily Cabral could have been blown off course westward, to Brazil as shown here.)

- *Where did the Spanish begin settlement? the Portuguese?* (on the island of Hispaniola; in Brazil)

★THINKING FURTHER: *Predicting* **What do you predict these claims will mean for the people already in the Americas?** (probably a loss of their sovereignty)

THE CONQUISTADORS

Have students define *conquistadors* as "conquerors."

Discussing Cortés and the Aztec
Tell the class the story in the *Background Information* below to help them see why Moctezuma welcomed the invading Spanish.

- *Who was Hernando Cortés and why was he interested in the Aztec? (He was a Spaniard who had heard stories of Aztec gold in Mexico; he wanted it.)*

- *Why might you call Cortés's arrival in Mexico "an invasion"? (He brought a force of 500 soldiers with him.)*

- *Who was the Aztec leader and how did he react to Cortés's arrival? (Moctezuma had Cortés watched, but eventually he welcomed Cortés.)*

★THINKING FURTHER: *Cause and Effect* **How would you describe the cause and effect of Moctezuma's welcome?** *(Cause: perhaps the idea that Cortés was outnumbered. Effect: The Spanish destroyed the Aztec empire.)*

Learning about Pizarro and the Incas Have students locate the Inca territory on the map on p. 467.

★THINKING FURTHER: *Compare and Contrast* **How was Pizarro like Cortés?** *(He too was a Spanish military leader who wanted gold; he went to get it from the Inca empire in the Andes Mountains of South America.)*

Investigating The Death of Atahualpa Help students appreciate Pizarro's duplicity in dealing with the Inca.

- *Who was the Inca leader? (Atahualpa)*

- *How did Pizarro overcome Atahualpa? (Pizarro's men captured Atahualpa, whose ransom was paid; all the same, Pizarro ordered that he be killed.)*

★THINKING FURTHER: *Making Generalizations* **What generalizations can you make about the conquistadors' view of their mission?** *(They thought might made right and Europeans were superior.)*

THE CONQUISTADORS

Beginning in the early 1500s, Spain sent more men to explore and make claims in the Americas. These conquistadors (kon KEES tuh dawrz), or "conquerors," soon defeated the Aztec and Inca empires and took control of their lands and resources.

Cortés and the Aztec

Conquistador Hernando Cortés (er NAHN doh kor TES) and over 500 soldiers arrived in 1519 in the area that is now Mexico. Cortés had already lived in Spain's Caribbean colonies. He had heard stories of a powerful inland empire. This was the Aztec empire.

With the help of translators who knew both Spanish and the Aztec language, Cortés soon learned about the Aztec people. He was especially interested to learn that the Aztec empire had a great amount of gold.

After Cortés landed on the coast of Mexico, messengers of the Aztec ruler, Moctezuma (mahk tuh ZOO muh),

watched his movements. These messengers told the emperor that Cortés and his men were coming to the capital of the empire, Tenochtitlán.

When the Spaniards arrived in the city, Moctezuma welcomed them as guests. That welcome eventually proved the downfall of both Moctezuma and the Aztec empire. With the help of Indians who turned against the Aztec, the conquistadors kidnapped and killed Moctezuma. After a war that ended in 1521, Cortés destroyed Tenochtitlán and conquered the Aztec empire.

Pizarro and the Incas

Ten years after Cortés conquered the Aztec, another conquistador prepared to invade Inca lands. Recall that these lands were located to the south, in the Andes Mountains. Francisco Pizarro (fran SEES koh pee SAHR roh), like Cortés, was a military leader who had

Hernando Cortés (below right) led a large Spanish force in the conquest of Tenochtitlán, shown in the painting (below).

BACKGROUND INFORMATION

WAS CORTÉS QUETZALCOATL? When Moctezuma was told that a light-skinned bearded man had landed on Mexican shores, he was deeply troubled. Did this appearance mark the long-promised return of the light-skinned, bearded god Quetzalcoatl? Aztec belief held that Quetzalcoatl, a highly important god, had long ago been banished and had sailed off into the "eastern sea," swearing that one day he would return. Moctezuma wondered if that day had come. If so, how could he do anything but bid the newcomer welcome?

SECOND-LANGUAGE SUPPORT

MAKING CONNECTIONS Creating time lines that compare the different events in this chapter may help second-language learners create a more accurate context for this era. Provide a format for comparing events, such as *While Ming rulers in China were building the Great Wall, Christopher Columbus was preparing his ships.*

spent some time in the Americas. He too had heard stories of a kingdom filled with treasure.

Pizarro began his conquest of the Inca empire in 1531. The Inca were just ending a civil war that left Atahualpa (ah tah WAHL pah) emperor. As Atahualpa and his army traveled to the Inca capital of Cuzco (KOOZ koh), they heard news of some 160 strangers marching along a nearby coastal road. Meanwhile, Pizarro learned that Atahualpa was nearby. The conquistadors made their way to Atahualpa's camp. There, they were amazed to see the large number of tents that housed the new emperor's army.

The Death of Atahualpa

That night, Pizarro and his men talked about what they should do when they met with Atahualpa the next day. One soldier later wrote:

Few slept, and we kept watch in the square, from which the camp fires of the Indian army could be seen. It was a fearful sight. Most of them were on a hillside and close to one another: it looked like a brilliantly star-studded sky.

Pizarro chose to set a trap for the emperor and the thousands of Inca who would come with him to the meeting. During the meeting, the conquistadors captured Atahualpa. In exchange for his freedom, the emperor offered to fill the room in which he was held prisoner once with gold and twice with silver. The Inca honored Atahualpa's part of the bargain. Pizarro, nevertheless, ordered the emperor's death. Many bloody battles between the Spanish and the Inca followed. By 1535 much of the 3,000 mile-long Inca empire had fallen to the conquistadors.

This Inca codex, created in 1565, shows a battle between the Spanish and the Inca.

The Spread of Spanish Control

By the 1540s conquistadors had claimed land for Spain from what is today Kansas almost to the tip of South America. Spain's rulers divided this enormous area into two colonies, called New Spain and Peru.

New Spain stretched from southern Central America northward into what is now the southwestern United States. Its capital, Mexico City, was built over Tenochtitlán. The colony of Peru—today the name of a country—included most of South America except present-day Brazil. Peru's capital was the coastal city of Lima, built by Pizarro in 1535.

The street plan of Lima showed what life was like in the Americas under Spanish rule. Lima boasted majestic churches and a university. At the center of town stood the homes of Peru's most powerful citizens. Many of these people had been conquistadors like Pizarro. Top government jobs were held by men who were from Europe or had only European heritage. Neither Indians nor *mestizos*, people of both Indian and Spanish heritage, could get such jobs.

469

Exploring The Spread of Spanish Control Have the class refer to the map, p. 467, and study the extent of Spanish claim to land in the Americas by 1600.

- *What territory was included in the Spanish colony of New Spain? the colony of Peru?* (New Spain: from the present-day southwestern United States to Central America. Peru: nearly all of South America, except Portuguese Brazil.)

- *What was the capital of Peru and how was it laid out?* (Lima, which was laid out with religious and government buildings and with palaces where the wealthy and powerful lived)

- *Who held ruling power in Spanish America? Who did not?* (Only Europeans or people born of Europeans held power; Indians and mestizos— part Indian—held none.)

- *Look at a desk map of the world. How might the Spanish have sailed from Peru back to Spain?* (They would have sailed either west across the Pacific and Indian oceans into the Atlantic and north to Spain or north to the Isthmus of Panama, cross it by land, and then board another ship heading east across the Atlantic to Spain.)

★THINKING FURTHER: *Making Conclusions* **Locate Lima on the map on p. 467. Why do you suppose Pizarro and the Spanish who followed him made this Peru's capital city?** (Students should note that it lies on the coast, linking it by sea to Spain.)

CITIZENSHIP★

UNDERSTANDING GOVERNMENT Lima was the capital of Spain's empire in the Americas from 1535 to the early 1800s and the most prosperous city in Latin America.

- Lima was the seat of the viceroy of the colony of Peru. The viceroy was appointed by the King of Spain and the Council of the Indies, the colonies' governing body in Spain.

- The viceroy selected an *audiencia* to help him govern within the colony. An *audiencia* had both administrative and judicial powers within its region.

- Captains-general, or *presidencias*, were named to rule in regions far from Spain's capital cities in Latin America.

BACKGROUND INFORMATION

MORE ABOUT SPAIN'S SAILING ROUTES

- Spain used both trans-Atlantic and trans-Pacific sailing routes between the Americas and home.

- Squadrons of Spanish ships sailed west across the Pacific, into the Philippines, across the Indian Ocean, around the Cape of Good Hope, and northward up the Atlantic to the Iberian peninsula.

- Spanish treasure fleets from both South America and Mexico sailed up into the Gulf of Mexico to Havana, Cuba, through the often treacherous waters of the 95-mile passage between Cuba and the Florida Keys, and eastward across the Atlantic to Spain.

LIFE IN SPANISH AMERICA

Encourage students to picture the before and after of life in the Americas.

- **What do missionaries believe is their work?** (to convert, or change, other people to their own beliefs)

- **What did Spanish missionaries work to accomplish in the Americas?** (to convert and educate the Indians into the Roman Catholic religion and European ways of life)

★ **THINKING FURTHER:** *Making Generalizations* **What generalizations can you make about Spain's attitude toward colonizing?** *(Their ways were what others should follow. Others should be happy to learn their ways.)*

Discussing Indians at Work Have students briefly review what they learned in Chapter 12 about life on manors during the Middle Ages.

- **How did the Spanish introduce feudal manors into the Americas?** *(by setting up haciendas, which were run like feudal fiefs)*

★ **THINKING FURTHER:** *Compare and Contrast* **How was Indian life on the haciendas like that of peasants of the Middle Ages?** *(Haciendas were self-contained and self-supporting, Indians were bound to the land and to wealthy landowners, Indians owed service to landowners while having little use of land for their own needs.)*

Discussing Illness Strikes the Indians Students may identify modern counterparts of diseases new to an area.

- **What effects did European diseases have on the Indians? Why?** *(Since the Indians had no resistance to European diseases, millions died from diseases.)*

★ **THINKING FURTHER:** *Making Generalizations* **What generalizations can you make about Europeans' effects on Indians?** *(Indian cultures were altered, and European diseases were highly contagious to Indians who had no immunity.)*

This cathedral (left) in Lima is on the site of a church built by the Spanish in 1535. Churches are also found in Peru's rural areas.

LIFE IN SPANISH AMERICA

By the late 1500s it seemed nothing in Spanish America was as powerful as the Catholic Church. Most people who came to the Americas from Spain, whether conquistadors or craftworkers, were Catholic. Among them were missionaries, or people who worked to make others see the truth of their religion. Their main goal was to convert, or win over to Catholicism, the millions of Indians in the Americas.

Missionaries often achieved their goal through teaching. They built churches and schools throughout the colonies. Missionaries educated many Indians in the subjects that Europeans learned about. All schools in New Spain and Peru—including the university—were run by priests and nuns. At times though, the goal to convert Indians was achieved by force.

Indians at Work

Almost half of all Spaniards in the Americas lived in major cities like Lima or Mexico City. Most of the Indians, however, continued to live in the countryside. Many were forced to work on haciendas (ah see EN dahs) owned by Spaniards or the Catholic Church. *Hacienda* is Spanish for a large area of land used for agriculture.

Like the feudal manors of Europe, haciendas were like small towns. Indian families lived and worked there to raise wheat, grapes for wine, cattle, and other products that were sold in colonial cities. Although such products brought large profits to hacienda owners, Indians received low wages. To feed themselves, Indian workers raised corn and beans on small plots of land set aside for their use.

Indians also provided another source of wealth in Spanish America—silver. By law all Indian men had to spend some time working in the silver mines of Peru and New Spain. Men who had to carry the precious metal had the worst job of all. They worked in dark-

GLOBAL CONNECTION

THE COLUMBIAN EXCHANGE The Columbian exchange indeed had its "up" side, introducing new crops and animals from one side of the Atlantic to another. However, it also had its "down" side, the transfer of European diseases to the Indians, devastating them. Some diseases from the Americas also affected Europeans.

USING THE ANTHOLOGY

THE LEGACY OF COLUMBUS, page 123 Use this editorial as a starting point to discuss the *Columbian Exchange*, the movement of various goods and forms of culture between the Eastern and Western hemispheres.

ness, with candles tied to their fore-heads or little fingers for light. Carriers hauled as much as 300 pounds of silver at a time. Accidents often happened on what was sometimes a 60-story climb to the mine entrance.

Illness Strikes the Indians

Accidents and overwork caused many Indian deaths. Disease, however, caused an even greater number. Indians had no resistance to, or ability to over-come the effects of, several of the germs that caused diseases in Europe. Historians believe that in the 50 years following conquest, smallpox and measles were among the diseases that caused the most deaths. In those 50 years New Spain's Indian population may have fallen from about 25 million people to under three million. Peru's decreased from perhaps nine million people to under two million.

Hacienda owners, and those who ran the mines, saw a rapid drop in the number of available workers. They soon came up with a new source for cheap workers—enslaved Africans. You will read more about slavery in the Americas in the next lesson.

These children are a few of the more than five million people who live and work in Lima today.

WHY IT MATTERS

In 1519, on the eve of Hernando Cortés' journey into Mexico, the Aztec and Inca empires controlled vast stretches of land in the Americas. By the century's end, their lands had been conquered and many monuments destroyed. Many Indians died of disease or overwork.

In the place of the Indian empires, Spanish conquistadors created a new civilization with ties to Spain and Portu-gal. Many European legacies exist today in the Americas, including languages and the Catholic religion. Legacies of the Aztec and Inca continue, as well. These can be seen in customs, language and, most importantly, people.

✓ Reviewing Facts and Ideas

MAIN IDEAS

- In 1521 Hernando Cortés conquered the Aztec empire for Spain. Francisco Pizarro brought Spanish rule to the people of the Inca empire after 1531.
- Life for Indians in Spanish America was shaped by missionaries, mining, and farm work. Millions died from disease and overwork.

THINK ABOUT IT

1. What is a conquistador?
2. How did Pizarro gain control of the Inca empire?
3. **FOCUS** How did Spain's conquest of the Americas affect Indians there?
4. **THINKING SKILL** Support or deny the _generalization:_ "One person can change the world." Use evidence in the lesson.
5. **WRITE** Write a paragraph describing some ways in which Spain might have had trouble controlling its colonies in the faraway Americas.

471

Discussing WHY IT MATTERS En-courage students to consider the enor-mous change in a short time.

★**THINKING FURTHER:** _Compare and Contrast **How would you contrast the Americas before and after the arrival of Spain and Por-tugal?**_ (Before: home to Indian em-pires like the Aztec and Inca, many millions in population. After: Indian empires destroyed, European colo-nization and control of government and economy, more than 75 per-cent loss in Indian population.)

3 CLOSE

MAIN IDEAS
Call on students for answers.

- _**What was the fate of the Aztec empire? of the Inca empire?**_ (Aztec: conquest by Cortés, 1521. Inca: conquest by Pizarro, 1531.)

- _**How did European colonization and missionaries change life for the In-dians?**_ (destroyed their old way of life, tied them to haciendas or mines, missionized them, killed many people)

EVALUATE
✓ **Answers to Think About It**

1. a Spanish conqueror
Recall Details

2. by kidnapping and killing its leader Atahualpa, followed by many bloody battles
Recall Details

3. It destroyed their old way of life, put them under Spanish control, changed how and where they worked, missionized them, and killed off much of their population.
Steps in a Process

4. Students might cite the actions of anyone mentioned in this chapter as causing a major change in the world.
Form Generalizations

5. Paragraphs should reflect difficulty in trying to rule from far away.
Make Inferences

Write About It Ask students to pic-ture themselves as either a conquista-dor, an Aztec, or an Inca and write a journal entry describing a clash they had with the opposite side.

MEETING INDIVIDUAL NEEDS

RETEACHING (Easy) Refer students to the changes in New Spain's and Peru's Indian populations described on p. 470. Have them draw bar graphs illustrating those changes.

EXTENSION (Average) Divide the class in two. Have one half of the students think of themselves as Spanish colonizers. Have the other half think of themselves as Native Americans. Each student should write a paper expressing his or her right to land in the Americas. Papers might serve as the basis for a class debate.

ENRICHMENT (Challenging) Divide the class into groups and have each group research a different aspect of hacienda living, using the fol-lowing topics: land-owning families and how they lived, the work done on the hacienda, the Indian workers and how they lived. Then as a class activity, have them construct a model of a hacienda.

SKILLS LESSON

PAGES 472–473

Lesson Overview
Determining the credibility of sources calls for checking the expertise, point of view, and reliability.

Lesson Objective
★ Determine credibility of sources.

1 PREPARE

MOTIVATE Write the question: *Whom do you believe?* on the board. Remind students that people must often answer this question. Have students read *Why the Skill Matters.* Discuss the meaning of *credibility* and the role of accuracy.

SET PURPOSE How can we determine how credible a source is? Have students read *Helping Yourself* to preview the steps.

2 TEACH

Using the Skill Have a student read the quote aloud.

● **Who is the author of the source quoted here?** *(a well-respected Spaniard from the 1500s who traveled to Mexico City)*

● **Does he seem to have any reason to distort what he reports?** *(He would not have a reason to distort his report.)*

● **Do you have any reason to believe that he is given to lying about what he sees?** *(Nothing here suggests a lie, particularly since he was writing to a relative.)*

★**THINKING FURTHER:** *Making Decisions* **How would you rank him on expertise, bias, and reliability?** *(firsthand experience, no reason to lie, reputation for accuracy)*

Resource **REMINDER**

Practice and Project Book: *p. 95*
Transparency: *Graphic Organizer*

Thinking Skills

Determining the Credibility of a Source

VOCABULARY
credibility

WHY THE SKILL MATTERS

In the 1500s news of conquistadors in the Americas spread throughout Spain. Many Europeans learned about the Americas from sources such as books, reports, and letters. Did such sources give them honest and accurate information?

Being able to determine the credibility, or believability, of a source is an important skill. People use many types of sources to learn about unfamiliar things. How can we know which we can believe, and which, perhaps, are less believable?

The most important task in determining the believability of a source is learning as much as possible about its author. Does he or she have a reputation for being accurate? Does he or she have firsthand knowledge of the subject. Does he or she have something to gain by giving false or distorted information?

USING THE SKILL

Supppose that you came across a letter written in the 1500s by a well-respected traveler. The letter was written to a relative and contained this excerpt about the early Spanish settlement of Mexico City:

Upon my arrival, it was obvious that life is hard in this rough, new city. Furthermore, I soon saw the difficulty of adaptinf our farming techniques to the surrounding area.

Is this a credible source about life in Mexico City? To find out, apply the steps in the

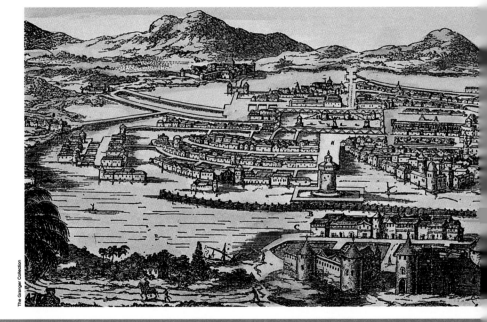

The Granger Collection

READING STRATEGIES & LANGUAGE DEVELOPMENT

PROBLEM AND SOLUTION Remind the class of the problem-and-solution organization that writers sometimes use. Explain that in this *Skills Lesson* they need to solve the big problem of how to determine credibility of a source. The task can be broken down into three small problems—How expert is the source? Does the source have a bias? How reliable is the source reputed to be? By answering each of these, they solve the problem of credibility.

SUFFIXES Refer the class to two terms that appear on this page—*credibility* and *believability.* Have them isolate the suffix of each and compare them. Explain that the first begins with *i (-ibility)* and the second with *a (-ability),* both meaning "acting in a certain way." Encourage students to check the dictionary for the correct spelling of this suffix in words they use.

Helping Yourself box. The author was a well-respected traveler. We can assume from this that he had a reputation for accuracy. The author visited Mexico City and therefore had firsthand knowledge of the subject. Since the author was writing to a relative, he doesn't appear to have had a reason to portray information inaccurately. From this we can conclude that the source is probably credible.

TRYING THE SKILL

Now consider a second example. Suppose a ship merchant from the 1500s who had never been to the Americas was planning to sail to Mexico City. He was hoping to pay for the passage by carrying passengers. He posted this

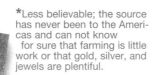

Helping yourself

- Determining the credibility of a source helps you to tell whether the information can be trusted.
- Determine if the source has a reputation for being accurate.
- Determine whether the author has firsthand or expert knowledge of the subject.
- Determine whether the author would have a reason to portray information inaccurately.

notice in the center of a Spanish town.

If you can afford the meager fare, you can join my expedition for Mexico City, where gold and silver glitter from the hills. The land is so fertile that farming is little work at all.

Is this a more or less credible source on Mexico City than the first? Why?*

REVIEWING THE SKILL

Use the Helping Yourself box to help you answer the questions below.

1. What are some factors in determining whether a source is credible?
2. How would firsthand knowledge of the author on a subject affect the credibility of his or her information?
3. What are some factors that might make a source less than credible?
4. How does determining the credibility of a source help you in the study of history?

*Less believable; the source has never been to the Americas and can not know for sure that farming is little work or that gold, silver, and jewels are plentiful.

This artwork (far left) shows Mexico City, built by the conquistadors on the site of Tenochtitlán.

Roswell Museum

473

Trying the Skill Tell students to review the steps in *Helping Yourself* before they begin this section.

- *Who is the source quoted here?* (a person who has never been to the place described)
- *Does the source have any reason to present such a glowing picture? Explain.* (Yes, he is trying to "sell" people to buy into his expedition.)
- *Should he be considered a reliable source?* (Speaking glowingly and knowingly about a place he has never seen does not make him seem reliable. Having a reason to color his statements also does not make him seem reliable.)

★THINKING FURTHER: *Making Decisions How would you rank this source on expertise, bias, and reliability and thus on his credibility as a source?* (Expertise: none. Bias and reliability: trying to "sell" something by coloring his statements. Credibility: very low.)

⭐ 3 CLOSE

SUM IT UP
Have students write a paragraph in which they explain why it is useful to be able to judge the credibility of a source.

EVALUATE
✓ **Answers to Reviewing the Skill**
1. Credible: having a reputation for accuracy, having firsthand knowledge or expertise in the subject, having no bias. Less credible; not having a reputation for accuracy, not having expertise, having a bias.
2. Firsthand knowledge would show that the author is most likely knowledgeable of the subject, which shows that the author is probably a credible source.
3. having a reputation for not being accurate, having little or no knowledge of the subject, having a bias
4. Determining credibility helps show which sources give the most accurate information on a particular historical period or event.

BACKGROUND INFORMATION

USING THE GRAPHIC ORGANIZER You may want to have students work with this Graphic Organizer transparency to help them organize their information.

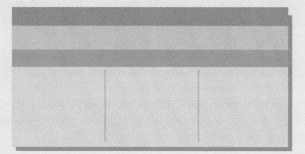

LESSON 4

PAGES 474–477

Lesson Overview

Beginning in the early 1500s, millions of Africans were enslaved to provide labor for plantations of West Indian colonies.

Lesson Objectives

★ Explain why the West Indian colonies caused widespread African enslavement.

★ Describe the horrors of the Middle Passage.

★ Explain the Triangular Trade.

1 PREPARE

MOTIVATE Have two students rehearse and do the *Read Aloud.* Tell students that as they listen, they should try to picture themselves as Olaudah Equiano, who is shown in the illustration. What is happening to him? How might you react if you experienced similar horrors?

SET PURPOSE Encourage students to review briefly examples of slavery they have already studied. Then refer them to the *Read to Learn* question. How will slavery in the Americas compare with other forms of slavery? Invite students to explore the lesson to find out. Refer to *Vocabulary* terms.

2 TEACH

Understanding THE BIG PICTURE
As students read this section, refer to the map on p. 475 to locate the West Indies.

● **Why did European colonization of the West Indies lead to enslavement of Africans there?** (Colonists needed a huge labor force to produce sugar.)

★ THINKING FURTHER: *Cause and Effect* **What were some effects of African slavery in the Americas?** (harsh and difficult lives for the enslaved, expanded world trade, new wealth for people on both sides of the Atlantic)

Resource REMINDER

Practice and Project Book: *p. 96*

Anthology: *Captured, pp. 124–125*

Outline Map

The Granger Collection

Focus Activity

READ TO LEARN

How did slavery develop in the Americas?

VOCABULARY

- sugarcane
- plantation
- Middle Passage
- triangular trade

PEOPLE

- Olaudah Equiano

PLACES

- West Indies
- Caribbean Sea
- Santo Domingo

474

1400   1505   1789

Africans in The Americas

Read Aloud

"Among the poor chained men, I found some from my own nation, which in a small way eased my mind. I asked what was to be done with us? They told me we were to be carried to the white people's country to work for them."

An African named Olaudah Equiano (AHL uh duh ih kwee AH nah) (left) wrote about his experiences in 1789. He was a captive on a slave ship bound for the Americas.

THE BIG PICTURE

The islands known as the West Indies were explored by Christopher Columbus in 1492. Later, ships loaded with silver from Lima and Mexico City sailed among these islands in the Caribbean Sea on their way back to Spain. In the early 1500s, Europeans began to establish colonies in the West Indies. The colonists learned that the region's tropical climate was ideal for growing sugar-producing plants. Enslaved persons were used to produce sugar for European markets.

You have read about slavery many times in this book. Nearly all the ancient empires in every part of the world kept people as property and forced them to work without pay. In the 1500s, however, a new form of slavery, based on an enormous demand for labor, took hold in the Americas. Millions of Africans were forced to lead harsh and difficult lives as slaves. Slavery in the Americas also had far-reaching effects on trade. This new form of slavery would create suffering as well as wealth for people on both sides of the Atlantic Ocean.

SDAIE SUPPORT

SHELTERED INSTRUCTION

READING STRATEGIES & LANGUAGE DEVELOPMENT

REREADING Remind the class of the benefits of rereading new material to be certain that they understand its meaning. Then have students write a question about each Vocabulary, People, and Places term. As students read, have them answer the questions. Remind them to reread passages to help them find the information they need. **[SDAIE STRATEGY: CONTEXTUALIZATION]**

WORD ROOTS AND PREFIXES Refer the class to the use of *exporting* and *importing* on p. 476 and write the words on the board. Explain that the word root *port* comes from the Latin word for "to carry." Then have them look up the prefixes *ex-* and *im-* to find that they mean "away from" and "toward," respectively. Help students to relate "carry away from" to *export* and "carry toward" to *import.*

WEST INDIAN COLONIES

The first West African slaves were brought to Spanish colonies in the Caribbean about 1505. Many were brought to Santo Domingo, a settlement in what is today the Dominican Republic. Santo Domingo had been established by the Spanish just nine years earlier, in 1496. You can see other European colonies on the map.

The islands' warm climate was perfect for growing sugarcane. Sugarcane is a tall grass with a thick, woody stem. It is a source of sugar. Many Europeans in the West Indies set up sugarcane plantations, or large farms. The region's Arawak Indians worked the plantations. However, like the Inca of South America, many Arawak soon died from diseases brought by the Europeans. Many were also killed in conflicts with the Spaniards.

Slavery in the Colonies

To take the place of the Arawak workers, enslaved people were brought from Africa to the colonies. Between 1500 and the middle 1800s, more than nine million Africans were shipped to the Americas.

Most West Africans who became slaves were kidnapped during surprise attacks led by European, Arab, and African traders. Captives were sold to other traders who would send them across the Atlantic Ocean to the West Indies. During the voyage across the Atlantic, captured Africans experienced many hardships. This part of the journey to the Americas became known as the Middle Passage. Captives were chained in crowded sections of ships. They were often given spoiled food and unclean water. Large numbers did not survive the voyage.

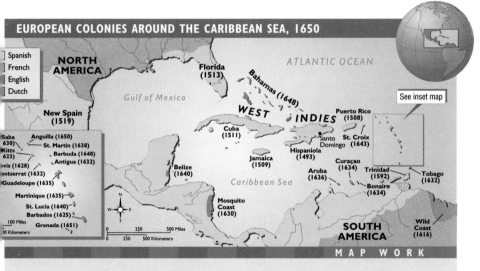

EUROPEAN COLONIES AROUND THE CARIBBEAN SEA, 1650

Spanish
French
English
Dutch

NORTH AMERICA
ATLANTIC OCEAN
Florida (1513)
Bahamas (1648)
Gulf of Mexico
See inset map
New Spain (1519)
WEST INDIES
Puerto Rico (1508)
Saba (1630)
Anguilla (1650)
St. Martin (1638)
Kitts (1623)
Barbuda (1648)
Cuba (1511)
nevis (1628)
Antigua (1632)
ontserrat (1632)
Guadeloupe (1635)
Belize (1640)
Jamaica (1509)
Hispaniola (1493)
Santo Domingo
St. Croix (1643)
Curaçao (1634)
Aruba (1636)
Trinidad (1592)
Tobago (1632)
Bonaire (1634)
Martinique (1635)
Caribbean Sea
St. Lucia (1640)
Barbados (1625)
100 Miles
00 Kilometers
Grenada (1651)
0 250 500 Miles
0 250 500 Kilometers
Mosquito Coast (1630)
SOUTH AMERICA
Wild Coast (1616)

MAP WORK

By 1650 most of the islands of the Caribbean Sea had been claimed as colonies by European powers.

1. Which power claimed the largest land area in the Americas?
2. Which European power claimed Nevis?
3. Which European power was best positioned to challenge Spain's Carribbean lands? Why?

MAP WORK: **1.** Spain **2.** England **3.** about 600 miles (about 966 kilometers) **4.** Cuba

475

GLOBAL CONNECTION

SUGAR'S JOURNEY TO THE WEST INDIES

- Growing sugarcane as a crop began in Southeast Asia and spread from there—to India, then to China and the ancient Arab world.
- Before the 1500s sugar was a rare luxury in Europe. But finding that it grew well in the Caribbean and South America changed all that. By 1600 European demand for sugar from the Americas made its production the richest industry in the world.

BACKGROUND INFORMATION

MORE ABOUT THE MIDDLE PASSAGE Its horrors also included cases of branding and of merciless floggings at sea. Death did not come just from inhuman treatment and disease—some people grew so desperate that they threw themselves over the side to drown.

WEST INDIAN COLONIES

Note that sugarcane was an alien crop.

- **Why were the West Indies a good place for growing sugarcane?** (warm climate)

- **Why would running a sugar plantation demand a lot of workers?** (Large farms required a great number of workers.)

★THINKING FURTHER: *Making Connections* **Why did the sugar plantations create hardships for both Arawak and Africans?** (They brought death to the Arawak and enslavement to the Africans.)

More **MAP WORK**

Refer the class to the map on this page.

- **Find the island of Hispaniola on the map. What colony was founded there in 1496?** (Santo Domingo)

- **What colony was founded that is today one of the U.S. states?** (Florida)

- **When was it founded? Who founded it?** (1513; the Spanish)

- **Who founded the colony of St. Martin? Martinique? Belize?** (the Dutch; the French; the English)

★THINKING FURTHER: *Making Conclusions* **What does this map tell you about how desirable the West Indies were to the Europeans? Why did the desire for slaves grow rapidly there?** (Several European countries set up colonies there; the more colonies, the more slaves were in demand.)

Exploring Slavery in the Colonies
Establish awareness of the bad treatment of enslaved Africans.

- **How many enslaved Africans were shipped to the Americas over a 300-year period?** (more than 9 million)

- **What was the Middle Passage?** (the voyage across the Atlantic made by captive Africans)

★THINKING FURTHER: *Cause and Effect* **Why was the death toll so high for enslaved Africans making the Middle Passage?** (crowding, being chained together, spoiled food, bad water)

Have students come up to the board to draw a flow chart of the steps in sugar production, as described in the text.

Discussing The Atlantic Routes
Give students outline maps of the world and have them label the continents, the oceans, the West Indies, and the Caribbean Sea. They will use them in an activity suggested below.

- **Why was sugar such a great boon to world trade?** (It vastly increased exports from the West Indies to the sugar markets of the world as well imports into the West Indies in the form of slaves and the goods that sugar profits could buy.)

★**THINKING FURTHER:** *Making Conclusions* **How would you illustrate on your outline map the triangular trade described in the text? Be sure to include the kinds of goods included in each leg of the triangle.** *(Have students trace the route described: West Indies→Europe→ Africa→West Indies. Invite them to suggest other possible triangular routes, for example, North America→ Africa→West Indies→North America or Europe→ North America→West Indies→ Europe.)*

MANY VOICES
PRIMARY SOURCE

Discussing the PRIMARY SOURCE

You may want to read this excerpt aloud to the class, because of some difficult words.

- **Who is speaking here?** *(Olaudah Equiano, the same man quoted in the Read Aloud)*

- **How desperate did Equiano's Middle Passage make him?** *(He wished for death.)*

- **What did he find in Jamaica?** *(harsh conditions for the enslaved, captured people from different parts of Africa)*

★**THINKING FURTHER:** *Making Conclusions* **Do you suppose Equiano spent the rest of his life in slavery? Why or why not?** *(He probably did not, since slaves would not usually be allowed to write books.)*

This painting shows slaves on a sugarcane plantation in Antigua bringing stalks from the field and preparing them for boiling.

PLANTATIONS AND THE SUGAR TRADE

Plantation owners depended on the hard work of enslaved Africans for success. Slaves cleared forests for planting. They hoed the soil and kept fields clear of weeds. At harvesttime they cut sugarcane all day in the hot sun. They also rushed the sugarcane stalks, or stems, to plantation mills. There liquid could be pressed out and boiled. During boiling, tiny crystals of sugar formed. Slaves filled barrel after barrel with the sugar.

The Atlantic Routes

Barrels of sugar were valuable trade goods. Sugar allowed plantation owners to buy expensive clothes, food, and furniture. Most important, sugar profits enabled planters to buy more slaves. Owners exported, or sold to other countries, sugar. Enslaved Africans were imported, or brought from other lands. This exporting and importing of sugar and slaves tightly linked plantations to the rest of the world.

476

Ships loaded with sugar traveled from the West Indies to Europe. Some returned to the West Indies loaded with fine furniture or cloth. Many, though, sailed to West Africa. There, European guns, cloth, and other goods were traded for slaves. Ships carrying slaves then sailed for the West Indies and English colonies in North America. The routes between Europe, Africa, and North America formed a triangle. For this reason, trade among these regions was known as the triangular trade.

One of the millions of Africans purchased in the triangular trade was Olaudah Equiano. He was kidnapped when he was 11 years old and sold in 1756. Read the following short piece from his autobiography, the story of his life. How was Equiano treated on the slave ship? How does he describe the way Africans lived in Jamaica?

CURRICULUM CONNECTION

LINKS TO READING Call for a volunteer research team to find out what later became of Olaudah Equiano. They might consult a book for young people by Karen Kennerly, *The Interesting Narrative of Olaudah Equiano: The Slave Who Bought His Freedom*, 1971, or a collection of biographies of African Americans. Students may also read an article "Middle Passage," in *American Heritage* magazine, February 1962.

SECOND-LANGUAGE SUPPORT

WORKING WITH A PEER Drawing and writing may help second-language learners understand the concepts in this lesson. Encourage students to think of themselves as if they were enslaved Africans, and create a picture and a diary entry to describe the experience. Encourage students to explain their items.

MANY VOICES
PRIMARY SOURCE

**Excerpt from
The Life of Olaudah Equiano,
written by himself, 1789.**

*The first object which saluted my eyes when I arrived on the [African] coast, was the sea, and a slave ship, which was then riding at anchor, and waiting for its cargo. . . . I was soon put down under the decks, and there . . . , with the **loathsomeness** of the **stench**, and crying together, I . . . wished for the last friend, death, to relieve me. . . .*

*I found Jamaica to be a very fine, large island. . . . There (were) a vast number of Negroes here, whom I found as usual, **exceedingly imposed** upon by the white people, and the slaves punished as in the other islands. . . . When I came to **Kingston**, I was surprised to see the number of Africans who were assembled together on Sundays. . . . Here each different nation of Africa meet and dance after the manner of their own country.*

loathsomeness: quality of being hateful or disgusting
stench: odor
exceedingly: to a large degree
imposed: to have had unfair demands made upon one
Kingston: a large town in Jamaica

WHY IT MATTERS

The civilization developed by Europeans in the West Indies affected not only that region but also the whole world. The demands of working on a sugarcane plantation cost the lives of thousands of Arawak Indians. Those Indian workers were replaced by enslaved people taken from their homes in Africa. Sugar from the plantations, and slaves themselves, became valuable and important goods in a triangle of trade that involved the West Indies, Europe, and Africa. By the 1800s the fortunes made in the sugar trade helped to make islands in the West Indies among the wealthiest and most powerful in the world. In time, as you will read in Chapter 17, those enslaved persons who made sugar plantations successful would fight for their own freedom.

✓ Reviewing Facts and Ideas

MAIN IDEAS

- The warm climate of islands in the West Indies was perfect for growing sugarcane.
- Sugarcane plantations in the West Indies depended on enslaved Africans for success.
- Between 1500 and the middle 1800s, more than nine million Africans were shipped to the Americas as slaves. They had been kidnapped from their homes and brought to slave ships.
- Trade of sugar, European goods, and slaves linked the West Indies, Africa, and Europe in the triangular trade.

THINK ABOUT IT

1. How did trade link the West Indies with other parts of the world?
2. How did many Africans become slaves?
3. **FOCUS** Why did slavery develop on sugarcane plantations in the West Indies?
4. **THINKING SKILL** Analyze the *credibility* of Olaudah Equiano as a source of information about slavery. What steps will you follow?
5. **GEOGRAPHY** Why was sugarcane a successful crop in the West Indies?

477

Discussing WHY IT MATTERS Reinforce the effects of slavery on various people.

> ★**THINKING FURTHER:** *Cause and Effect* **What effects did the development of sugar plantations have on the West Indies?** *(It helped kill off the Arawak, caused the importation of millions of enslaved Africans, made plantation owners and sugar traders wealthy, and made the West Indies a powerful world trade center.)*

★ 3 CLOSE

MAIN IDEAS
Call on students for answers.

- **What geographical fact accounted for the West Indies becoming a sugar-growing center?** *(a warm climate)*
- **How long did the African slave trade with the Americas continue and how many Africans were enslaved?** *(more than 300 years; more than 9 million)*
- **What was the triangular trade?** *(trade of sugar, European goods, and slaves that linked the West Indies, Europe, and Africa)*

EVALUATE
✓**Answers to Think About It**

1. Sugar was shipped from the West Indies in return for European goods and enslaved Africans.
   Make Conclusions
2. by being kidnapped from their homeland
   Recall Details
3. because sugarcane plantations required great numbers of workers
   Recall Details
4. Students will find that Equiano has expert knowledge, that he certainly had reason to portray things in a bleak light, and that they do not know his reputation for accuracy.
   Evaluate Fact and Opinion
5. It grew well in the warm climate.
   Five Themes of Geography: Place

Write About It Ask students to picture themselves as enslaved Africans who have just made the Middle Passage and write a short letter home describing the experience.

MEETING INDIVIDUAL NEEDS

RETEACHING (Easy) Have students draw a chart tracing cause and effect in the development of slavery in the Americas. (demand for sugar→dying out of Native Americans→enslavement of Africans)

EXTENSION (Average) As an offshoot of the activity suggested on p. 471, divide the class in two groups again, this time have one half take the part of plantation owners and the other of enslaved Africans. Have each student write a paper expressing his or her point of view on enslaving or being enslaved. Once again, a class debate might ensue.

ENRICHMENT (Challenging) As a class project, have students write and perform a play dramatizing the Middle Passage. Divide the class into groups for research, writing, backdrop and props, casting, and performing.

LESSON 5

Lesson Overview

The English originally colonized Australia as a place to send its convicts. In time, Australia became an important democratic nation.

Lesson Objectives

★ Identify reasons for the exploration and settlement of Australia.

★ Describe English settlement and its impact on Australia's aborigines.

★ Analyze the stages in Australia's developing democracy.

1 PREPARE

MOTIVATE Have students review Lesson 4 to recall the hardships many enslaved Africans endured in the West Indies. Then ask two volunteers to read the *Read Aloud*, one as the prisoner and the other as the narrator. How was the situation of the prisoner different from those of slaves in the West Indies?

SET PURPOSE Refer students to the *Read to Learn* question and ask them to compare and contrast the experiences of slaves and English convicts as suggested in the *Reading Strategy* below.

2 TEACH

Understanding THE BIG PICTURE
Invite students to imagine what hopes explorers might have had for the "unknown southern land."

- **What was an important reason for European exploration in the 1400s?** (the search for trade routes to the East)

- **What country founded the first European settlement in Australia?** (England)

> ★**THINKING FURTHER:** *Cause and Effect* **What were effects of the search for Australia?** (the founding of New South Wales and hardship for the aborigines)

Resource REMINDER

Practice and Project Book: *p. 97*

Anthology: *Jonathan Down Under pp.126–132*

Focus Activity

READ TO LEARN

How did democracy develop in Australia?

VOCABULARY

- aborigine
- convict
- emancipee

PEOPLE

- James Cook
- Elizabeth Veale
- Lachlan Macquarie

PLACES

- New South Wales

478

1400   1500   1606   1894

A European Colony in Australia

Read Aloud

"All the bondage I am under is to answer my name every Sunday before I goes to church, so you must not think that I am made a slave of. . . . I have got plenty to eat and drink as good as ever a gentleman in this country [has] . . . "

This letter was written in 1883 by a political prisoner serving his sentence in Australia. While some prisoners sent there were treated harshly, others saw Australia as a land of opportunity.

THE BIG PICTURE

As you read in Lesson 2, Europeans set out in the 1400s to find new trade routes to the East. In the 1500s, explorers also began to search for a legendary southern continent that had been rumored to exist for centuries. It was called the "terra australis incognita," which means "unknown southern land" in Latin.

Would the continent turn out to be as rich as the Americas? When explorers reached Australia, they were disappointed. To their eyes, much of the land was very dry and did not look promising.

In 1788, the English founded New South Wales, the first European settlement in Australia. At first, New South Wales was a prison colony. In time, the colony would become a thriving democracy in which both ex-prisoners and free settlers would have the right to vote. For Australia's original inhabitants, however, the coming of the English meant disaster.

SHELTERED INSTRUCTION

READING STRATEGIES & LANGUAGE DEVELOPMENT

COMPARE AND CONTRAST Draw four vertical columns under the heading: *Effect of European Settlement.* Label the columns: *Enslaved Africans (West Indies), Indians (New Spain), English Convicts (Australia), Aborigines (Australia).* Have students begin by filling in information in each column based on what they have already learned about these groups of people in this chapter. As they read this lesson, have them add information in the third and fourth columns to provide a basis for later comparisons and contrasts. [**SDAIE STRATEGY:** SCHEMA BUILDING]

WORD ORIGIN Refer the class to the Latin phrase *terra australis incognita,* meaning *unknown southern land,* on p. 478. Ask students to guess what each Latin word means. Encourage them to check the dictionary for English words that are related to the Latin words, such as *terrace* or *incognito.* Ask: what does *australis* mean? (southern)

A DIFFICULT LAND

Australia's first inhabitants were aborigines (ab or IH jin eez). The term aborigine means that they were the original people to live in this land. Historians believe that they arrived in Australia between 40,000 and 100,000 years ago from Indonesia and Asia.

The aborigines believed that the land was created by great spirits during a period called the "dreamtime." They also believed that the spirits created the "dream trails" across earth that connected important places for food and water. The aborigines' survival often depended on these trails, which could stretch over a thousand miles. They believed that land was a sacred gift and could not be owned.

This aboriginal art (above) was created with tree bark, ochre, and natural pigments.

In 1606, the Dutch landed on Australia—although historians think that Asian and Portuguese ships had probably visited Australia before this. The Dutch did not see any gold, only flat and dry land. Disappointed, they soon lost interest in Australia.

New South Wales

In 1768, England sent James Cook, a respected navigator, to explore the southern continent. In 1770, Cook claimed land for England on the East Coast of Australia, naming it New South Wales after a region of Great Britain.

Traveling with Cook was a young scientist named Joseph Banks. Banks sketched and labeled 1,600 species of Australian plants that were previously unknown to Europeans. He reported that the land was rich and fertile.

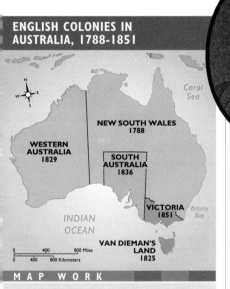

ENGLISH COLONIES IN AUSTRALIA, 1788-1851

WESTERN AUSTRALIA 1829

NEW SOUTH WALES 1788

SOUTH AUSTRALIA 1836

VICTORIA 1851

Coral Sea

Botany Bay

INDIAN OCEAN

VAN DIEMAN'S LAND 1825

0 400 800 Miles
0 400 800 Kilometers

MAP WORK

James Cook, right, landed in Botany Bay during his exploration of Australia.

1. What was the second colony to be founded, after New South Wales?

2. What was the second smallest colony in 1836?

MAP WORK: 1. Van Dieman's Land **2.** South Australia

479

A Difficult Land Help students see how the beliefs of the aborigines were connected to their idea of land ownership, and how these beliefs differed from those of Europeans.

● *Who were the original inhabitants of Australia?* (the aborigines)

● *What were "dream trails"?* (trails across the earth that connected places for food and water)

● *What does the length of the dream trails tell you about the land?* (In some places, food and water were very scarce.)

● *Why were the Dutch disappointed in Australia?* (They didn't see any gold or fertile land.)

More MAP WORK

Have students work with text and map.

● *How many colonies had been established in Australia by 1851?* (five)

● *Which settlement was the last to be named a colony?* (Victoria in 1851)

★THINKING FURTHER: *Making Conclusions James Cook called the bay where his ship landed Botany Bay in honor of Joseph Banks' work. How was this name an appropriate one?* (A botanist studies plants. Joseph Banks studied the plants of Australia.)

Discussing New South Wales
Have students locate New South Wales on the map.

● *New South Wales lay on which coast of Australia?* (the East Coast)

★THINKING FURTHER: *Cause and Effect How might Joseph Banks' reports of fertile land have influenced the settlement of New South Wales?* (It probably encouraged Europeans to move to Australia.)

Convicts In The New Colony

Have students look at the photograph of New South Wales and read the text to imagine what life might have been like for the convicts.

- **What is a convict?** *(A convict is someone found guilty of a crime and who is serving a sentence.)*

- **What effect did the American Revolution have on the settlement of Australia?** *(The American Revolution ended the transportation of English convicts to America. The English wanted to find a new place to send their prisoners and chose Australia.)*

- **What are some of the crimes that the convicts had committed?** *(violent robbery, pickpocketing, holding political beliefs in opposition to the government)*

- **What specific hardships did soldiers and convicts initially face in New South Wales?** *(lack of tools, unfamiliar land and climate, near-starvation)*

- **What future did convicts face once they had served their sentences?** *(some returned to England, others worked for themselves in the colony, some received land grants)*

- **What role did Elizabeth Veale play in the success of New South Wales?** *(She helped establish the wool industry by successfully raising sheep.)*

★**THINKING FURTHER:** *Making Connections* **What impact do you think the sentences of the convicts had on the growth of the colony?** *(Convicts were sentenced to work for the government or for free settlers. Their labor helped build up the colony.)*

CONVICTS IN THE NEW COLONY

For decades, England's jails had been overcrowded. Following a policy called "transportation," some prisoners had been sent to work in the American colonies. After the American Revolution, the English needed a new place to send its prison convicts. A convict is a person who has been found guilty by the government of committing a crime and has received a sentence for it. The English government decided to send many of its convicts to New South Wales.

The first ships carrying convicts arrived in Australia in January 1788 with 736 convicts and about 200 soldiers. The oldest convict was eighty-two years old. The youngest was nine. Some convicts had committed serious crimes such as violent robbery. Others were in chains for their political beliefs or for pickpocketing. One man was sentenced for destroying 12 cucumber plants. All convicts were sentenced to work for the new colony's government for at least seven years.

At first, soldiers and convicts struggled side by side to survive in New South Wales. They had few tools to build housing. Droughts and unfamiliar soil ruined crops. Many convicts and soldiers suffered from near-starvation.

During the 1790s, as the colony became more successful, the promise of land and a fresh start attracted free settlers to Australia. The convicts soon filled the important role of providing labor to the free settlers. Like slaves, the convicts' fates depended on the kindness or cruelty of their masters. Unlike slaves, convicts were never considered property. Some convicts who behaved well could return to England. Many, however, stayed in Australia to work for themselves or as laborers. Convicts were often given land when their sentences ended.

Many women, convict and free, helped build the colony's future. One such woman was Elizabeth Veale, who was married to a successful sheep owner named John Macarthur. Her husband spent much of his time outside the colony. As a result, she was often responsible for running their estate in Australia. She did this very successfully, and helped establish the production of wool as an important industry in Australia.

Convict laborers in New South Wales had rights often denied to slaves, such as the right to bring their master to court for ill-treatment.

CITIZENSHIP★

RECOGNIZING PERSPECTIVES People often have different views on which groups of people should have the right to participate in a democratic government. As convicts in New South Wales became free settlers, colonists debated the voting rights they should have.

- Divide students into two groups to debate the topic of voting rights for former convicts in New South Wales. Ask one group to represent the viewpoint of former convicts. Ask the second group to represent settlers who had never been convicts.

- Have students research magazines and newspaper articles to find current debates over voting rights.

CURRICULUM CONNECTION

LINKS TO SCIENCE Ask students to go to the library and research species of Australian plants or animals that explorers may have encountered in Australia. Possible animals, for example, would be the duckbilled platypus, the wallaby, the bandicoot, or the koala bear.

SECOND-LANGUAGE SUPPORT

TAKING NOTES Second-language students may help themselves to better understand the history of New South Wales by taking notes. Have students work in pairs to list the main points of the lesson. As they work through the lesson, have them write one detail for each of the main points that they have listed.

Lachlan Macquarie created a public works program and established a currency for New South Wales.

Conflict and Opportunity

As colonists settled new land, they clashed with the aborigines who had only simple weapons with which to defend themselves. Eventually, European diseases and guns would almost wipe out the aborigines.

Conflict also developed between groups of English settlers. One such group of settlers were emancipees (e MAN sih peez). Emancipees were convicts who had been freed from their sentence. Many landowners who had never been convicts did not want emancipees to have the rights they had.

Lachlan Macquarie (LAHK lan mak WAR ee), who favored the rights of emancipees, became governor of New South Wales in 1810. Once he invited some of the emancipees to dinner to show his support for them. Many of the non-convicted settlers were outraged. Macquarie also showed support by choosing Francis Greenaway, an ex-convict, as his architect when he built a hospital for the new colony.

As the colony grew, new British laws allowed the passage of the New South Wales Act of 1823. This enabled the colony to create a legislative body. In 1842 free settlers, including emancipees, won the right to vote for its members. Similar changes took place in other colonies, which were founded as British colonists settled more land in Australia.

Although unable to vote at this time, women would win the vote in the colony of South Australia in 1894. Australia was becoming one of the important democratic nations of the world.

WHY IT MATTERS

Convicts and soldiers struggled together to build a colony 15,000 miles across the ocean from their homes in England. Convicts arrived in chains, but they were not slaves. When their sentences ended, they were often granted land and the chance to participate in a democratic government.

As in the Americas, the original inhabitants of Australia did not fare well when the Europeans arrived. Currently, however, the Australian government is seeking to better recognize the aborigines' claims to their lands.

Reviewing Facts and Ideas

MAIN IDEAS

- Australia's first inhabitants were aborigines. The arrival of the colonists almost destroyed their way of life.
- After the American Revolution, England chose Australia as a new place to send its convicts.
- Australia's English settlers developed a democratic system of government.

THINK ABOUT IT

1. Why did European explorers begin to search for a southern continent?
2. Why was there conflict between the emancipees and the free settlers?
3. FOCUS What were the stages in Australia's development of democracy?
4. THINKING SKILL How might the different ideas of land ownership between colonists and aborigines have been a cause of their conflict?
5. GEOGRAPHY Where in Australia did the English discover fertile land?

481

Discussing WHY IT MATTERS
Review the impact of the colony's growth on the people of Australia.

★THINKING FURTHER: *Compare and Contrast* **How did the growth of the colony affect the former convicts differently than the aborigines?** *(Former convicts were often given land and the chance to participate in a growing democracy. The aborigines lost land and lives.)*

3 CLOSE

MAIN IDEAS
Call on students for answers.

- *What impact did English settlement have on the aborigines? (It almost destroyed their way of life.)*
- *What are two reasons why the English began to send convicts to Australia? (overcrowded jails, the American Revolution)*
- *What type of government was forming in New South Wales by 1842? (a democracy)*

EVALUATE
✓ Answers to Think About It

1. They had heard rumors of its existence and were looking for riches similar to those found in the Americas. *Summarize*
2. Landowners who had never been convicts did not want former convicts to share the same rights. They may have feared that former convicts would compete for land or threaten the system of free convict labor. *Make Inferences*
3. In 1823, the New South Wales Act allowed the colony to create a legislative body. In 1842, male free settlers were granted the right to vote. Women won the vote by 1894. *Sequencing*
4. Colonists would have claimed land and tried to keep others, including aborigines, from using it. Aborigines, who didn't believe that land could be owned, might have used it anyway. *Make Inferences*
5. The East Coast *Five Themes of Geography: Place*

WRITE ABOUT IT
Ask students to write a paragraph that compares the situation of English convicts in Australia with that of enslaved Africans in the West Indies.

MEETING INDIVIDUAL NEEDS

RETEACHING (Easy) Ask students to write a letter or journal entry from the viewpoint of a convict who was transported to New South Wales. Inform students that most people from that time had never been more than a few miles from their own homes and that the voyage alone lasted about eight months.

EXTENSION (Average) Refer students to the description of the aborigines' dream trails. Have students examine a map of Australia and note the distance and terrain that the trails may have crossed. Have them write sets of directions for a few possible dream trails.

ENRICHMENT (Challenging) Ask students to go to the library and do research on the early towns and cities in New South Wales. Students might want to construct models or recreate plans of the types of buildings that were designed for the growing colony.

DISCUSSING MAJOR EVENTS Use this time line to help students see the impact that one people can have on another.

- *Based on this time line, what major effects did European peoples have on the Americas?* (brought contact with the rest of the world, conquered the Aztec and the Inca, and began colonizing their land)

- *What effect did European peoples have on peoples of Africa?* (enslaved them and brought them to the Americas)

- *What impact did Columbus's, Magellan's, Galileo's, and Newton's feats have on all the peoples of the world?* (They vastly increased human knowledge.)

Answers to
THINKING ABOUT VOCABULARY

1. Middle Passage
2. telescope
3. strait
4. caravel
5. scientific method
6. plantations
7. credibility
8. conquistador
9. Line of Demarcation
10. geocentric

Answers to
Thinking About Facts

1. discovering gravity, which explained how a heliocentric universe worked

2. gaining control of Brazil for Portugal

3. The sugar of the West Indies linked them to European and American markets, which traded their goods for sugar, and to Africa, from which slaves were brought back to the West Indies.

Resource REMINDER

Practice and Project Book: *p. 98*

Assessment Book: *Chapter 16 Test*

Transparency: *Graphic Organizer, Main-Idea Pyramid*

CHAPTER 16 REVIEW

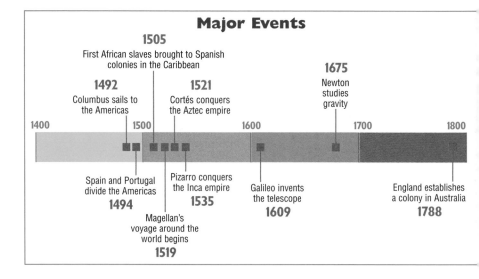

Major Events

1505 First African slaves brought to Spanish colonies in the Caribbean

1492 Columbus sails to the Americas

1521 Cortés conquers the Aztec empire

1675 Newton studies gravity

1400   1500   1600   1700   1800

Spain and Portugal divide the Americas **1494**

Magellan's voyage around the world begins **1519**

Pizarro conquers the Inca empire **1535**

Galileo invents the telescope **1609**

England establishes a colony in Australia **1788**

THINKING ABOUT VOCABULARY

Number a sheet of paper from 1 to 10. Beside each number write the word or term from the list below that best completes the sentence.

caravel
conquistador
credibility
geocentric
Line of Demarcation

Middle Passage
plantations
scientific method
strait
telescope

1. The _____ was a voyage that captured Africans were forced to make.

2. Galileo's invention of the _____ allowed him to study the sky more closely.

3. A _____ is a narrow waterway that connects two larger bodies of water.

4. The Portuguese ship that allowed explorers to sail into the wind was the _____.

5. Thoroughly testing an idea before accepting it as true is the _____.

6. Large farms in the West Indies where sugarcane was grown were called _____.

7. Somebody who can not be believed has lost his or her _____.

8. A _____ was a military person sent to the Americas to explore and gain land for Spain.

9. In 1494 Spain and Portugal drew the _____ to divide lands in the New World between them.

10. _____ means "centered around Earth."

THINKING ABOUT FACTS

1. What was Isaac Newton's main contribution to science?

2. What did Portuguese explorers accomplish in the New World?

3. How did colonial trade link the West Indies to other parts of the world?

4. What was one important result of England's system of transportation for convicts?

5. According to the time line above, which were the first two European countries to colonize the Americas?

482

SECOND-LANGUAGE SUPPORT

SELF-ASSESSMENT Ask students to make a K-W-L chart to outline what they knew about the topics covered in this chapter from their prior knowledge (WHAT I KNEW), what questions they wanted answered by the chapter (WHAT I WANTED TO KNOW), and what they learned from reading the chapter (WHAT I LEARNED). Encourage them to write general statements in each category. Discuss with students what they might do to answer questions that were not answered by the chapter.

PORTRAIT GALLERY Invite students to draw portraits of some of the outstanding scientists and explorers mentioned in the chapter. Attached to each portrait should be a paragraph explaining what the person did.

THINK AND WRITE ◄▭►

WRITING AN ESSAY

Write a short essay about differences between Spanish and English colonies that are discussed in this chapter. Mention what each country gained from its settlements. Also describe the way the colonists interacted with the original inhabitants of the land they settled.

WRITING BIOGRAPHICAL PARAGRAPHS

Write a paragraph about two of the following people: (1) Galileo (2) Henry the Navigator (3) Magellan (4) Cortés.

WRITING ABOUT PERSPECTIVES

Write about the different perspectives Native Americans and Europeans had toward each other in the 1500s. What do you think each thought of the other one? What do you think they might have found strange? What do you think they might have found appealing?

APPLYING THINKING SKILLS

EVALUATING THE CREDIBILITY OF A SOURCE

1. What is a credible source?
2. To evaluate the credibility of a source, what three things should you find out?
3. Reread the account of Olaudah Equiano on page 474. Do you find it credible? Why or why not?
4. Give an example of an account of the trip slaves were forced to make from Africa that would be less credible than Equiano's.
5. In what ways will this skill be helpful to you as a student?

4. Transportation encouraged the colonization of Australia
5. Spain and Portugal

Answers to APPLYING THINKING SKILLS

1. a source that can be trusted as accurate
2. whether the author has expert or first-hand knowledge of a subject, a reason to portray things in a certain way, and a reputation for accuracy
3. It seems credible because he was there, giving him expert knowledge, and even though he suffered, there seems no reason for him to distort the facts or for the reader to doubt his accuracy.
4. perhaps an account written by someone who wanted to whitewash the slave trade and deny its inhumanity, so that it would be allowed to continue
5. It will help to create a healthy skepticism about any sources of information and a desire first to test them for their accuracy and reliability.

Technology CONNECTION

VIDEODISC/VIDEO TAPE 5
Enrich Chapter 16 with the *Aztecs and Conquistadors* segment on the Videodisc.

Search Frame 41082 Side B

Summing Up the Chapter

Copy the main-idea pyramid below on a separate sheet of paper. Then review the chapter to find information to finish filling in the pyramid. When you have filled in the pyramid, use the information to answer the question "What were the main accomplishments of European scientists and explorers from the 1400s to the 1700s?"

Europeans from the 1400s to the 1700s made important discoveries in science and exploration.

Europeans explore the world and establish colonies	European scientists make important discoveries
Cortés - Mexico Pizarro - Peru Champlain - Quebec Columbus - Hispaniola	Galileo - proved heliocentric theory; used telescope Newton - law of gravity

483

SUGGESTIONS FOR SUMMING UP THE CHAPTER

Before students begin copying the main-idea pyramid on a piece of paper, have them read the main idea aloud. What are the two categories of achievements that it calls on you to identify? (science and exploration/colonization) When they have completed the copying, ask them to offer any pieces of information they think might belong in the pyramid. Have students discuss each suggestion. Suggested examples appear on the reproduced pupil page above. Then have them go back through the lesson, first for information for one category and then for another. When they have completed their pyramids, have them read the question posed aloud and then weave the information they have gathered into their answers.

ASSESSING THINK AND WRITE: *For performance assessment, see Assessment Book, Chapter 16, pp. T94–T96.*

CHAPTER 17

Revolutions Change the World

Pages 484–517

CHAPTER OVERVIEW

In 1789 the people revolted against the monarchy in the French Revolution. The fight for South American independence was led by Miguel Hidalgo in Mexico and Simón de Bolívar in Venezuela. Meanwhile, capitalism and scientific advances brought about the industrial revolution in Europe.

GEO ADVENTURES DAILY GEOGRAPHY ACTIVITIES

Use **Geo Adventures** Daily Geography activities to assess students' understanding of geography skills.

CHAPTER PLANNING GUIDE

LESSON 1	LESSON 2	Legacy
SUGGESTED PACING: 2 DAYS	SUGGESTED PACING: 2 DAYS	SUGGESTED PACING: 1 DAY
The French Revolution pp. 486–491	**The Colonies Gain Independence** pp. 492–497	**The United States Constitution** pp. 498–499
CURRICULUM CONNECTIONS Links to Language Arts, p. 490	**CURRICULUM CONNECTIONS** Links to Art, p. 495	
CITIZENSHIP Understanding Government, p. 487	**CITIZENSHIP** Recognizing Perspectives, p. 493	
RESOURCES Practice and Project Book, p. 99 ◉TECHNOLOGY *Adventure Time!* CD-ROM	**RESOURCES** Practice and Project Book, p. 100 Anthology, pp. 134–135 ▭Anthology, p. 133	

GEOGRAPHYSKILLS	LESSON 4	CITIZENSHIP
SUGGESTED PACING: 1 DAY	SUGGESTED PACING: 2 DAYS	SUGGESTED PACING: 1 DAY
Using Cartograms pp. 506–507	**The Rise Of Industrial Japan** pp. 508–513	**1853: What Did The Japanese Think About Opening Their Country To The West?** pp. 514–515
RESOURCES Practice and Project Book, p. 102 Transparency Map 19 ◉TECHNOLOGY *Adventure Time!* CD-ROM	**CURRICULUM CONNECTIONS** Links to Art, p. 511 Links to Math, p. 512	**CITIZENSHIP** Using Current Events, p. 515
	CITIZENSHIP Understanding Government, p. 510 Linking Past and Present, p. 511	
	RESOURCES Practice and Project Book, p. 103 Anthology, pp. 139–140 ◉TECHNOLOGY *Adventure Time!* CD-ROM	

LEARNING STYLE: Kinesthetic GROUP 30 MINUTES OR LONGER

Perform an "It Changed People's Lives" Skit

Objective: To prepare students to learn about revolutions that changed the world.

Materials: paper, art supplies

1. Have small groups of students choose an event that had a major impact on society—e.g., the use of polio vaccine in 1955 or the first moon walk in 1969.
2. Encourage students to research their group's event and to prepare a five-minute skit about it with a role for each student. Suggest that students create costumes also.
3. After the skits are performed for the class, discuss what the class learned from each skit.

LESSON 3

SUGGESTED PACING: 3 DAYS

The Industrial Revolution

p. 500–505

CITIZENSHIP
Understanding Government, p. 504

INFOGRAPHIC
Inventions of the Industrial Revolution, p. 503

FIELD TRIP
Visit an Industrial Museum, p. 503

RESOURCES
Project and Practice Book, p. 101
Anthology, pp. 136–137, 138
Desk Map

CHAPTER REVIEW

SUGGESTED PACING: 1 DAY

pp. 516–517

RESOURCES
Practice and Project Book, p. 104
TECHNOLOGY Videodisc/Video Tape 5
Assessment Book: Chapter 17 Test
Transparency: Graphic Organizer, Cause-and-Effect Map

SDAIE SUPPORT SHELTERED INSTRUCTION

READING STRATEGIES & LANGUAGE DEVELOPMENT

Cause and Effect/Words with Multiple Meanings, p. 486, Lesson 1
Problem and Solution/Homonyms, p. 492, Lesson 2
Making Conclusions/Synonyms, p. 500, Lesson 3
Context Clues/Word Origins, p. 506, Geography Skills
Sequence/Synonyms, p. 508, Lesson 4

SECOND-LANGUAGE SUPPORT

Reading Strategies, pp. 487, 510
Graphic Organizers, pp. 495, 504
Taking Notes/Dramatization, p. 516

MEETING INDIVIDUAL NEEDS

Reteaching, Extension, Enrichment, pp. 491, 497, 499, 505, 507, 513
McGraw-Hill Adventure Book

ASSESSMENT OPPORTUNITIES

Practice and Project Book, pp. 99–104
Write About It, pp. 491, 497, 499, 505, 513
Assessment Book: Assessing Think and Write, pp. T97–T99; Chapter 17 Tests: Content, Skills, Writing

Introducing the Chapter

Refer students to the chapter title. Ask what they think the term *Revolutions* here means? Help them use their knowledge about the American Revolution and the context clue *Change* to arrive at a definition (a sudden and great change).

THINKING ABOUT HISTORY AND GEOGRAPHY

Have students read the text on this page and have them trace each panel to the map to discover other parts of the world in which revolutions took place (Europe, Mexico, South America, Asia).

1789 PARIS, FRANCE

- **Where is the revolution shown here taking place?** *(France, in Europe)*

- **How long after the American Revolution began did this revolution take place?** *(1789 – 1783 = 6 years)*

★**THINKING FURTHER:** *Making Connections* ***Do you suppose one revolution might have had anything to do with the other? Explain.*** *(American ideas of liberty may have helped spur other people in the world to revolt against their governments.)*

1810 DOLORES, MEXICO

- **How much closer to the United States did this revolution take place?** *(just to the south, in Mexico)*

- **For what is this revolution being fought?** *(freedom)*

★**THINKING FURTHER:** *Compare and Contrast* ***With what American Revolutionary figures might you compare Miguel Hidalgo?*** *(Patrick Henry or George Washington or anyone else who argued for and/or led the American fight for freedom from Britain)*

Revolutions Change the World

THINKING ABOUT HISTORY AND GEOGRAPHY

In this chapter you will read about revolutions that changed the lives of people around the world. Follow the time line and the map to find out when and where these changes occurred. Some happened very quickly while others took longer. In each case, people's lives were changed, with effects that are still felt today.

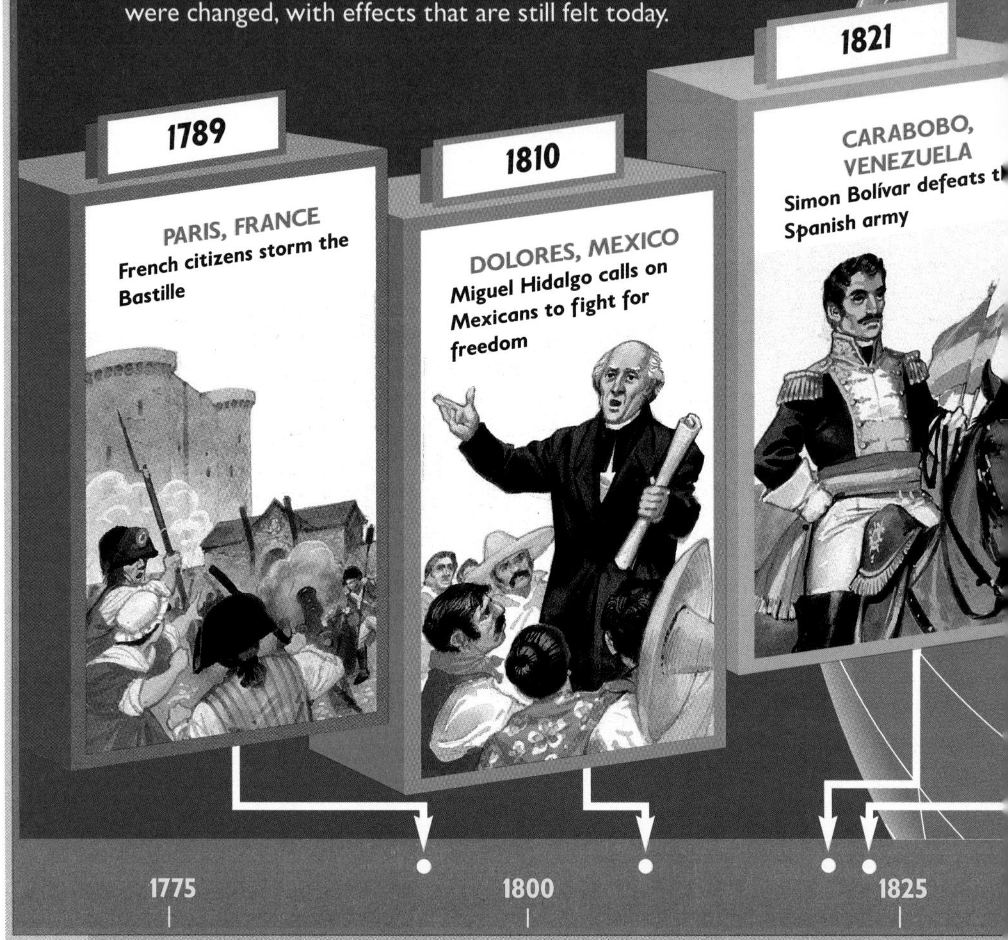

1789

PARIS, FRANCE
French citizens storm the Bastille

1810

DOLORES, MEXICO
Miguel Hidalgo calls on Mexicans to fight for freedom

1821

CARABOBO, VENEZUELA
Simon Bolívar defeats th[e] Spanish army

1775

1800

1825

BACKGROUND INFORMATION

LINKING THE MAP AND THE TIME LINE
- Because of its favorable position on the Seine River, a major commercial artery since Roman times, Paris had long been prosperous and populous and was a natural capital for France. Home of one of Europe's oldest universities, its intellectual life supported ideas about the natural rights of humankind.

- As a birthplace for a revolution, Dolores, Mexico, could not have been less like Paris. It was a quiet village, something of a backwater town on Mexico's Central Plateau. But its pastor, Father Miguel Hidalgo, had revolutionary ideas. In fact, he was probably sent to a small town because he clashed with his Church superiors over his ideas. Thus, the unlikely village of Dolores was thrust into history as a seat of rebellion.

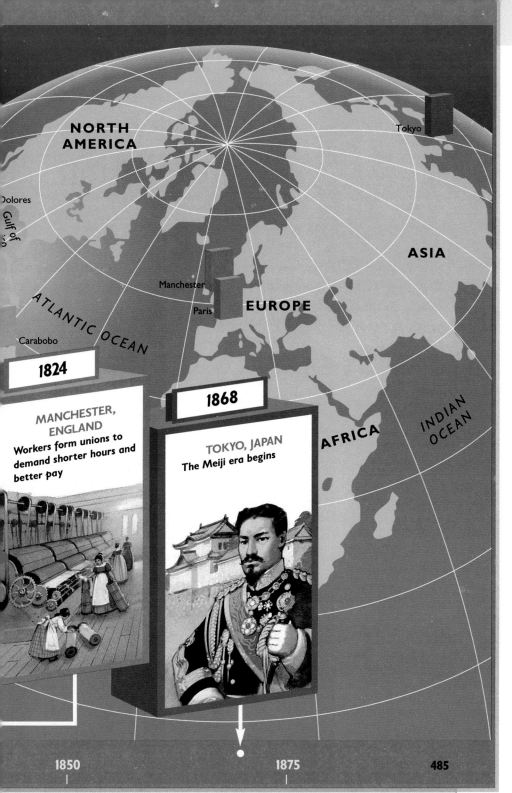

NORTH
AMERICA

Tokyo

Dolores

Gulf of
io

ASIA

ATLANTIC OCEAN

Manchester

Paris   EUROPE

Carabobo

1824

MANCHESTER,
ENGLAND
Workers form unions to
demand shorter hours and
better pay

1868

TOKYO, JAPAN
The Meiji era begins

AFRICA

INDIAN OCEAN

1850   1875   485

● **Where on the map is Carabobo located?** *(in northern South America)*

● **When is this revolution being fought? Against whom?** *(in 1821; the Spanish army)*

★**THINKING FURTHER:** *Making Conclusions* **Judging from what you learned in Chapter 16, how long had the Spanish been in control in South America when this revolution took place?** *(1821 – 1535 = 286 years)*

● **Where is Manchester located on the map?** *(in northwestern Europe)*

● **What does this panel say is happening here?** *(Factory workers are trying to form a union.)*

★**THINKING FURTHER:** *Compare and Contrast* **How is the revolution shown here different from those in the three earlier panels?** *(Those all seem to involve armed fights for freedom against governments while this one does not.)*

● **In what part of the world is Tokyo located?** *(Asia, in the archipelago of Japan off the continent's east coast)*

● **What does this panel say is happening?** *(A new era is beginning in Japan.)*

★**THINKING FURTHER:** *Predicting* **Based on the fact that this new era is included among revolutions, what do you predict it will be like?** *(It must change Japanese life in major ways.)*

BACKGROUND INFORMATION

LINKING THE MAP AND THE TIME LINE
● Carabobo was well protected by Spanish garrisons when Simón Bolívar attacked it with a force made up of a Venezuelan army and a British legion of veterans of the Napoleonic wars. Nevertheless, Bolívar was victorious there, freeing Venezuela from Spanish control.

● Perhaps no place was more suited to being the birthplace of the Industrial Revolution than Manchester in northwestern England. It had everything—nearness to coal for power and to the port of Liverpool for shipping and a history of textile making going back to the 1500s.

● Tokyo was well-situated to be the imperial capital of Meiji Japan. Unlike the landlocked Kyoto, it sat on a harbor that opened Japan to the sea and therefore the rest of the world.

LESSON 1

PAGES 486–491

Lesson Overview
The French Revolution brought sweeping changes to the government of France and to the rights of its citizens.

Lesson Objectives
★ Trace the changes in France's government from 1789 to 1815.

★ Describe the Reign of Terror.

★ Identify Napoleon and analyze how he affected France and Europe.

1 PREPARE

MOTIVATE Have two students rehearse and do the *Read Aloud* for the class, one dramatically reading the quote, the other the narrator's part. Invite students to tell what a revolution is and what suggests that this was a very bloody uprising. (call for killing the king)

SET PURPOSE Point out the illustration of storming the Bastille. What could have propelled the French people into such action? Refer the class to the *Read to Learn* question. Encourage students to explore the lesson to find out what led to revolution and what resulted from it. Preview the *Vocabulary*.

2 TEACH

Understanding THE BIG PICTURE Have students analyze pre-Revolutionary ideas.

● **How are divine right and absolute monarchy related?** *(The idea that a monarch's power to rule comes from God helps to justify the ruler's actions.)*

● **Who supported this idea?** *(monarchs themselves, nobles, church leaders)*

★**THINKING FURTHER:** *Compare and Contrast* **How would you contrast the belief in divine right with ordinary French citizens' beliefs?** *(Citizens rejected the idea and revolted against it and the people who held it.)*

Resource REMINDER

Practice and Project Book: *p. 99*

 Technology: *Adventure Time!* CD-ROM

| 1700 | 1750 | 1789 | 1815 | 1850 | 1900 |

The French Revolution

Read Aloud
Can you not hear in your hearts the voices of the citizens who died? Can you not see all the nations of the world, all the generations present and future, waiting until you show them whether the King has the right to murder citizens and groups without punishment; whether a monarch is a god whose actions must be blessed or a man whose crimes must be punished."

The words above were spoken by Jean Mailhe (MAY yuh) in France in 1792. As a member of the newly elected National Assembly, Mailhe was calling for the execution, or killing, of the king.

Focus Activity

READ TO LEARN

What conditions led to the French Revolution?

VOCABULARY

- absolute monarchy
- divine right
- revolution
- estates
- aristocracy
- peasants
- Declaration of the Rights of Man and of the Citizen
- Reign of Terror

PEOPLE

- Louis XVI
- Marie Antoinette
- Maximilien Robespierre
- Napoleon Bonaparte

PLACES

- Versailles
- Paris
- Bastille

486

THE BIG PICTURE
Just four years earlier King Louis XVI held firm control over his kingdom. France was an absolute monarchy. This means that the king had complete power to govern. His title, "Louis, by the Grace of God, King of France," showed the belief in his divine right. Divine right was a belief that a monarch's authority came from God. Now, in a sudden turn of events, the king faced the judgment of people he once ruled.

Throughout the continent, a system of rule based on the power of monarchs, nobles, and church leaders had been in place for centuries. Unhappiness with this system, however, was leading the people of France closer to a revolution. A revolution is a sudden or great change. The revolution in France would upset the old system of government and change Europe.

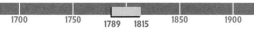

SHELTERED INSTRUCTION

READING STRATEGIES & LANGUAGE DEVELOPMENT

CAUSE AND EFFECT Explain how finding cause-and-effect relationships can help readers understand why things happen as they do. Have students create collaborative posters that reflect the ideas of the French fighting for freedom during the French Revolution. Encourage students to trace causes and effects of the French Revolution as they read this lesson. **[SDAIE STRATEGY: TEXT RE-PRESENTATION]**

WORDS WITH MULTIPLE MEANINGS Call students' attention to the following words in this lesson—*execution* (this page), *noble* (p. 487), and *tax* (p. 488). List them on the board and have students come up to write definitions of them, including *noble* as a noun and an adjective and *tax* as a noun and a verb. When students have entered all the definitions they can think of, have them consult a dictionary for any they may have missed.

AN AGE OF DISCONTENT

In many ways France in 1789 was not much different from France in the Middle Ages. Although feudalism no longer existed, most people still worked the land. By 1789, however, the population had been divided into three estates, or social classes. The chart on this page shows France's three estates.

The Three Estates

The First Estate was made up of the Catholic clergy. The clergy consists of people who perform religious services. About 130,000 of France's 26 million people belonged to the clergy. The wealthy Catholic Church owned nearly 15 percent of France's land and paid no regular taxes.

Aristocracy (ar uh STOHK ruh see) made up the Second Estate. The aristocracy included members of noble families. In the late 1700s nobles owned about 25 percent of the land in France. Most of them did not pay taxes. Although most nobles were rich, they had little power in government. In fact they were unhappy that the king held all political power in France. Even the richest nobles could not make laws.

The vast majority of people, nearly 98 percent, belonged to the Third Estate. This group included merchants and lawyers as well as craftworkers and peasants. Peasants are farm workers. A few members of the Third Estate were rich. Most, however, were poor.

Although many peasants owned land, they often did not have enough to support themselves and their families. One traveler described a seven-year-old peasant girl as "terribly ragged, if possible worse clad than if with no clothes at all." The different members of the Third Estate had two things in common. They paid taxes and had no say in how they were governed.

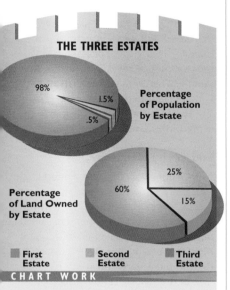

THE THREE ESTATES

Percentage of Population by Estate

98%
1.5%
.5%

Percentage of Land Owned by Estate

60%
25%
15%

■ First Estate   ■ Second Estate   ■ Third Estate

CHART WORK

The French social classes were called estates.

1. Which estate made up the largest percentage of the population?

2. How did the Third Estate's percentage of land compare to its percentage of the population?

This cartoon from 1789 shows the First and Second estates riding on the back of the Third Estate.

CHART WORK: **1.** Third **2.** It was much smaller.

487

AN AGE OF DISCONTENT
Help students understand the situation in France before the Revolution.

Discussing The Three Estates As students work with this section, have them draw a social pyramid on the board showing three levels of French society.

● *Who made up the First Estate?* (Catholic clergy)

● *What percentage of the population did they make up?* (Have students divide 130,000 by 26 million = .5%.)

● *Who made up the Second Estate?* (aristocracy)

● *How did the First and Second Estates compare in taxation?* (Neither was required to pay taxes.)

● *Who made up the Third Estate?* (everyone else—merchants, professionals, craftworkers, peasants)

● *What was the Third Estate's tax burden?* (They paid all the nation's taxes. As the political cartoon shows, they carried the whole tax burden.)

● *Which of the estates had lawmaking power?* (None of them—that power lay in the hands of the monarch.)

★THINKING FURTHER: *Compare and Contrast* **How would you contrast the political power of French nobles with that of English nobles?** (Remind students of the Magna Carta. Have them refer to pp. 326-327 to recall that English nobles had gained some political power while the French nobles had not.)

More CHART WORK

Refer students to the graphs on this page.

● *Which estate made up the greatest percentage of the population? What percentage was it?* (Third Estate; 98%)

● *What percentage of the land did they own?* (60%)

★THINKING FURTHER: *Making Conclusions* **Which estate owned the most land in relation to their percentage of the population?** (First)

CITIZENSHIP★

UNDERSTANDING GOVERNMENT Like other European governments of the time, the French government was full of corruption and inefficiency.

● There were no standards for weights, measures, or even coins.

● Laws were a mix of local customs, feudal law, and royal decrees.

● France had no forum where public policy could be discussed.

SECOND-LANGUAGE SUPPORT

READING STRATEGIES It may help second-language learners to view history as a story. Write *Characters* on the board and have students skim to find the names in the lesson. Then write *Setting* and have students find place names. Finally write *plot* and have students determine what the *problem* was in France, how people felt about it, and how it was resolved.

A STRUGGLE FOR LIBERTY

Help students to grasp the irony of the French monarchy bankrupting itself by backing the American Revolution, thus sowing the seeds of its own destruction.

Discussing The Revolution Begins
Help students link the tax problem with events that followed.

● **What was the Estates General?** *(a group made up of representatives of each of the three estates)*

● **Why was it called to meet?** *(The king hoped to get it to demand new taxes from an unwilling Second Estate.)*

★**THINKING FURTHER:** *Cause and Effect* **What unexpected consequence grew out of the meeting of the Estates General?** *(The Third Estate demanded political power and set out to get it by writing a constitution, forming the National Assembly, a new government body, thus leading to the Revolution.)*

Understanding Storming the Bastille
Refer the class to the illustrations of the storming of the Bastille on pp. 486 and 489.

● **What was the Bastille?** *(a stone prison fortress in Paris, the French capital)*

● **Why did citizens attack it?** *(to try to get weapons to fight a rumored attack by the king's troops on the National Assembly)*

● **When did they take this action?** *(July 14, 1789)*

★**THINKING FURTHER:** *Making Conclusions* **How did the successful storming of the Bastille show that the French king's ruling power was in grave danger?** *(The enforcers of the king's power, the army, deserted the king and helped the rebels.)*

A STRUGGLE FOR LIBERTY

By the late 1770s the French had been greatly influenced by the American Revolution. One French noblewoman said,

> The American cause seemed our own; we were proud of their victories, we cried at their defeats, we tore down bulletins and read them in our houses. None of us reflected on the danger that the New World could give to the Old.

France had given millions of dollars to support the American colonies in their war against the British. This expense, as well as the cost of the king's lifestyle, drained money from the French government. By 1789 there was no money left.

The Revolution Begins

King Louis XVI hoped to raise more money by taxing the nobles, or the Second Estate. The nobles refused. They demanded a meeting of the Estates General. The Estates General was a group made up of representatives from each of the three estates.

The Estates General met near the king's palace in Versailles (vair SIGH) in May of 1789. Members of the Third Estate wanted equal rights. They did not like being the least powerful group in France. A priest described the dissatisfaction of the Third Estate:

> What is the Third Estate? Everything. What has it been up 'til now in the political order? Nothing. What does it desire to be? Something.

Soon the members of the Third Estate began meeting to write a constitution. They formed a new law making body, called the National Assembly. The French Revolution had begun.

488

Storming the Bastille

Struggle for power between the estates and the king developed so quickly that rumors began to fly. One rumor was that the king was sending troops to break up the National Assembly. On July 14, 1789, about 800 people gathered in Paris, the capital of France. They marched to the big stone prison fortress called the Bastille (bas TEEL). They hoped to get weapons there to defend themselves. As people surrounded the prison, someone fired a cannon into the crowd.

Nearby, a citizen named Pierre Hulin convinced a group of 60 soldiers to help the crowd. "Do you not hear the cannons? Parisians are being slaughtered like sheep. Will you not march on the Bastille?" he said.

Although 98 people died, the marchers and soldiers captured the Bastille. This event became an important symbol of revolution to the French people. The anniversary of Bastille Day is still celebrated in France every July 14. The event also showed that even the army did not support the king.

End of the Monarchy

In August of 1789 the National Assembly issued a statement called the Declaration of the Rights of Man and of the Citizen. This statement called for fair taxation and freedom of religion. Most important, the Declaration said that all men were "born and remain free and equal in rights." Soon shouts of "Liberty! Equality! Fraternity [brotherhood]!" were heard across France.

Crowds also began singing a song, La Marseillaise (lah mahr say YEZ). It became France's national anthem. What does the song tell you about the point of view of the French people?

MANY VOICES
MUSIC

National Anthem of France

La Marseillaise

by
de Lisle

To arms,— to arms, ye brave! Th'a-veng-ing sword un-
sheathed! March on, march on!
All hearts re-solved on vic - to-ry or death.

489

Discussing End of the Monarchy
Help students analyze the shift in power.

● **Who issued the Declaration of the Rights of Man, and what was it?** *(The National Assembly issued it to declare the human rights of freedom and equality for all French citizens.)*

● **What was the rallying cry across France?** *(Liberty! Equality! Fraternity!)*

★**THINKING FURTHER:** *Compare and Contrast* **How would you contrast France's government before 1789 with the spirit of the Revolution?** *(Before: absolute ruling power in the hands of the monarch. After: ordinary people began believing in liberty and equality.)*

MANY VOICES
MUSIC

Discussing the PRIMARY SOURCE

Try to have a recording of "La Marseillaise" available so students can listen to its stirring melody.

● **Why is this song still important today?** *(It is France's national anthem.)*

● **What does it tell about what the French of 1789 wanted?** *(vengeance as well as victory over absolutist government, and if not victory, death)*

★**THINKING FURTHER:** *Making Conclusions* **What would you conclude were the major emotions in France when this song was first sung?** *(hatred of oppression, desire for revenge against oppressors, death-defying devotion to the cause of freedom and equality)*

GLOBAL CONNECTION

ABOUT MARIE ANTOINETTE'S AUSTRIAN BACKGROUND

● Marie Antoinette's name may sound French, but she was born in Austria, the daughter of Austrian rulers Maria Theresa and Francis I.

● After her marriage to the French prince who would become King Louis XVI, she was despised by an anti-Austrian faction in the French court. Because she often sought the advice of the Austrian ambassador to France, they suspected that she was spying on France for her home country.

● After the French Revolution began, she secretly urged the Austrians to declare war on France. Found out, she was tried and convicted of treason, which led to her execution in 1793.

● Her picture appears on p. 490.

 Technology CONNECTION

ADVENTURE TIME! CD-ROM
Enrich Lesson 1 with the *La Marseillaise* on the *Adventure Time!* CD-ROM.

NEW RULERS IN FRANCE

Help students recognize the change of power and the monarchs' reaction to it.

● *How did the king deal with the Declaration of the Rights of Man?* *(He was forced to approve it.)*

★THINKING FURTHER: *Cause and Effect How did the king's actions lead to his downfall?* *(Cause: He fled, showing his true feelings. Effect: The monarchy ended.)*

Discussing The Reign of Terror

Help students understand the meaning of "Reign of Terror"—that terror, not common sense, was ruling France.

● *How did the French Revolution punish the First and Second Estates and the king and queen?* *(by taking Church land, and executing aristocrats, nobles, and the monarchs)*

● *Who was Robespierre?* *(leader of the Reign of Terror, the most powerful person in France)*

● *How many French people died during the Reign of Terror?* *(40,000)*

★THINKING FURTHER: *Cause and Effect What would you say was the cause of the bloodshed?* *(the terrible anger of the Third Estate; people who had been oppressed under absolute rule)*

Investigating The Revolution Ends

Discuss the effects of the Revolution.

● *What effect did French disappointment with the Revolution have on the army?* *(People's desire for peace strengthened the army.)*

● *How did this in turn affect the fortunes of Napoleon Bonaparte?* *(The public was ready and eager to support a successful young general.)*

● *How did Napoleon use this support?* *(He made himself emperor of France, ending the French Republic.)*

★THINKING FURTHER: *Making Decisions Would you say that France under Napoleon I was better off, worse off, or about the same as it had been in pre-Revolution days? Explain.* *(Students may note that France had another absolute ruler, but ordinary people in the country were better off.)*

490

NEW RULERS IN FRANCE

The old France was gone. A new democratic government was rising in its place. The king was still leader of the government, but the National Assembly now had most of the power. In 1791 King Louis XVI was forced to approve the Declaration of the Rights of Man and of the Citizen.

After approving the Declaration, King Louis, Queen Marie Antoinette (muh REE an twuh NET), and their family tried to escape. They left Paris disguised as a family of tourists. They had not gone far, however, before someone recognized the king from his picture on money. The man tipped over a cart of furniture on a bridge to block the family's escape. Soldiers soon arrived and returned the royal family to Paris. In 1792 the monarchy was abolished and France became a republic.

The Reign of Terror

The change from a monarchy to a republic was not smooth for France. The Assembly angered many people by taking all land away from the Catholic Church. Priests who did not support the revolution lost their churches.

Maximilien Robespierre (MAX ih mihl yen ROHBZ pee air), a Revolution leader, became the most powerful man in the new government. He waged a war against enemies of the revolution by executing suspects. This period of cruelty became known as the Reign of Terror.

Robespierre's weapon was a machine, the guillotine (GEE oh teen),

490

Marie Antoinette (above), Queen of France and wife of Louis XVI, was beheaded in 1793. The guillotine (below) killed thousands during the revolution.

with a steel blade that chopped off people's heads. In January 1793 King Louis XVI was tried and executed by guillotine in a public square in Paris. Queen Marie Antoinette's execution by guillotine followed in October.

Aristocrats and nobles were targeted for death. However, it seemed no one was safe from the threat of execution. People feared execution for such "crimes" as giving sour wine to soldiers or weeping at the murder of a family member. When the Reign of Terror came to an end in 1794, about 40,000 French citizens had been killed. One of them was Robespierre himself.

The Revolution Ends

The time has come when people would ask for bread and be given corpses.

The woman who wrote this statement lived during the Reign of Terror.

CURRICULUM CONNECTION

LINKS TO LANGUAGE ARTS The guillotine had been used earlier in Scotland and elsewhere. Yet it is named for a French physician, Joseph Ignace Guillotin, who urged the National Assembly to adopt it for humane reasons, to make execution quick and painless.

BACKGROUND INFORMATION

ABOUT MAXIMILIEN ROBESPIERRE

● Robespierre was able to struggle out of a poverty-stricken youth to become a successful lawyer. Convinced of his own moral rightness, he crushed any opposition to his rule.

● In time, his uncompromising and dictatorial manner won him enemies who were able to rise up against him and have him arrested. He survived a suicide attempt but was himself put to the guillotine.

She summed up the disappointment that many people felt. Five years of revolution and bloodshed left many people hoping for peace and stability.

In this environment, the army gained more and more power. A 26-year-old general named Napoleon Bonaparte (nuh POH lee un BOH nuh pahrt), from the island of Corsica, became extremely popular. His success in a French war against Italy won him great support. When he returned to Paris in 1799, one newspaper reported: "Everyone is thrilled" by his victory.

Five years later, the young general had gained control of the new French Republic and crowned himself Emperor Napoleon I. Barely 10 years after the execution of Louis XVI, France had another absolute ruler. The French Republic was over.

After making himself emperor of France in 1804, Napoleon set out to conquer lands across Europe.

WHY IT MATTERS

Napoleon expanded French power across Europe. His armies conquered Holland, Germany, Italy, and Belgium, bringing new riches to the French.

Although France once again had a monarch, many of the changes that had come with the Revolution remained. For example, the old system of three estates was gone forever.

Napoleon's vast empire collapsed in 1815. The French began again to build a republic. They picked up many of the ideas that had fueled the revolution 25 years earlier. After the fateful events in France in 1789, the world would never be the same again. From India to Turkey to South America, the ideas of "Liberty, Equality, Fraternity" sparked national freedom movements around the world.

✔/ Reviewing Facts and Ideas

MAIN IDEAS

- Before the Revolution French society was divided into three "estates."
- The French Revolution began in 1789.
- Robespierre's Reign of Terror brought fear and disorder to France.
- Napoleon Bonaparte created a huge European empire.

THINK ABOUT IT

1. Who made up the Three Estates?
2. Why was a meeting of the Estates General called in 1789?
3. **FOCUS** List three reasons for the discontent among many French people before the Revolution.
4. **THINKING SKILL** What *effects* did the American Revolution have on France?
5. **WRITE** As a member of the Third Estate, write a paragraph describing changes you would like to see.

491

LESSON 2

Lesson Overview
Spurred by the American and French revolutions, in the 1800s several colonies throughout the world gained their independence from Europe.

Lesson Objectives
★ Explain how former European colonies gained their independence.
★ Describe the roles individual leaders played in the struggle.

1 PREPARE

MOTIVATE Refer the class to the lesson title and the Orozco painting of revolutionary Mexicans. Remind students that the United States was the first country in the Americas to be independent. How might this have affected other colonies throughout the world? Have two students do the *Read Aloud,* one as Bolívar, the other as narrator.

SET PURPOSE Have students recall how the U.S. gained independence. Refer to the *Read to Learn* question; encourage students to compare other colonies' struggles with that of the U.S. Preview the *Vocabulary.*

2 TEACH

Understanding THE BIG PICTURE
Explore the developing desire for liberty.

● **What is Latin America?** *(the cultural region south of the U.S., influenced by Spain, Portugal, and France)*

★**THINKING FURTHER:** *Cause and Effect* **How did the American and French revolutions inspire colonists in the Americas? How did the Napoleonic wars in Europe help their cause?** *(The revolutions made people want their own independence; Napoleonic wars had cost European countries too much to deal with American colonies.)*

Resource REMINDER

Practice and Project Book: *100*

Anthology: *Fighting for Freedom, p. 133; Letter from Jamaica, pp. 134–135*

Focus Activity

READ TO LEARN

How did European colonies gain independence?

VOCABULARY

- Latin America
- mestizo
- confederation

PEOPLE

- Toussaint L'Ouverture
- Miguel Hidalgo
- José María Morelos
- Agustín de Iturbide
- Simón Bolívar
- José de San Martín

PLACES

- Hispaniola
- Dolores
- Venezuela

492

1700   1750   1791   1867   1900

The Colonies Gain Independence

Read Aloud
"We are threatened with the fear of death, dishonor, and every harm; there is nothing we have not suffered at the hands of . . . Spain."

Simón Bolívar (see MOHN boh LEE vahr) wrote these words in a letter in 1815. He went on to free his native Venezuela and several other South American nations from Spanish rule. Freedom was a goal that inspired many people in colonies around the world.

THE BIG PICTURE
In the year 1800 the United States was the only independent country in the Americas. Yet the desire for independence was felt in colonies throughout the world. The American and French Revolutions caused others in the Americas to think about gaining their own rights. Many Spanish colonists said, "I am not a Spaniard, I am American." These feelings spread throughout Latin America. Latin America is a cultural region south of the United States that was strongly influenced by Spain, Portugal, and France.

Europe's costly wars with Napoleon made it possible for colonies to take control of their own governments. A period of 300 years of European rule in the Americas was ending. By 1830 North and South America were made up almost entirely of independent nations. Eventually, Australia would also begin the journey towards independence.

SHELTERED INSTRUCTION

READING STRATEGIES & LANGUAGE DEVELOPMENT

PROBLEM AND SOLUTION Remind students that they learned how they can often make sense of what they read by identifying problems and solutions. On the board, create a two-column chart. In the left column, write "Problems"; in the right, "Solutions." Have students work in teams to come up with problems and solutions for the topic: selling fast food in the school cafeteria. As they read, have students look for problems and solutions involving the colonists' struggle for independence from England. **[SDAIE STRATEGY: BRIDGING]**

HOMONYMS Refer students to the word *mines* on p. 493, and write *mine* on the board. Point out that *mine* has various homonyms that can be different parts of speech (noun, verb, possessive pronoun). Call for students to define *mine* in its use as each part of speech.

A SPIRIT OF FREEDOM

Although each colony in Latin America was unique, all had some things in common. For one, they felt that European nations were taking advantage of them. Europeans took minerals and crops, but gave little in return.

People born in the Latin American colonies struggled to grow crops or to work in mines for other people. Like the English colonists of North America, Latin Americans also had to pay taxes without having a voice in their government. One popular song expressed the Latin American colonists' viewpoint:

If anyone wants to know
Why I go shirtless
It's because of the taxes
Of the king.

Revolution in the Caribbean

The first rumblings of independence began on the large Caribbean island of Hispaniola (hihs pun YOH luh). Although Columbus had claimed Hispaniola for Spain in 1492, France controlled the western part of the island. In the French colony, called Saint Domingue (san duh MANG), enslaved Africans grew coffee and sugar on plantations.

When the French Revolution broke out across the Atlantic, distant cries of "Liberty, Equality, Fraternity" echoed in Saint Domingue. In 1791 a group of about 100,000 slaves rose up against plantation owners. This group was led by Toussaint L'Ouverture (too SAN loo ver TYUR). L'Ouverture believed that slavery was wrong. He and other former slaves forced the French to abolish it throughout Saint Domingue. In 1796 L'Ouverture took control of the colony's government.

In 1802 Napoleon Bonaparte tried to regain control of Saint Domingue. He sent a huge army to restart the practice of slavery on the island. This time L'Ouverture began a revolution to drive the French out completely.

Although L'Ouverture was captured and taken to France, the revolution became the first successful slave revolution in history. From it, the independent country of Haiti was born on Hispaniola in 1804.

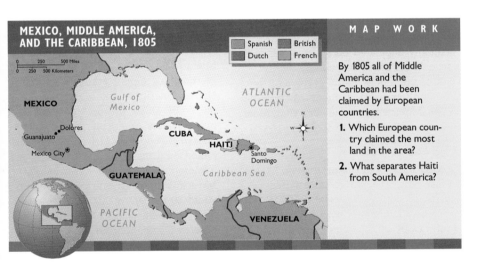

MEXICO, MIDDLE AMERICA, AND THE CARIBBEAN, 1805

MAP WORK

Spanish | British
Dutch | French

By 1805 all of Middle America and the Caribbean had been claimed by European countries.

1. Which European country claimed the most land in the area?

2. What separates Haiti from South America?

MEXICO — Gulf of Mexico — ATLANTIC OCEAN — Dolores — Guanajuato — Mexico City — CUBA — HAITI — Santo Domingo — GUATEMALA — Caribbean Sea — PACIFIC OCEAN — VENEZUELA

493

CITIZENSHIP ★

RECOGNIZING PERSPECTIVES What did "Liberty, Equality, Fraternity" mean to the people of the French colony of Saint Domingue, which became Haiti? It meant different things to different people.

- White planters believed that it meant they would now be represented in the French government in the French capital in Paris, representation they had previously lacked.

- Mulattos (children born to white plantation overseers and enslaved Africans) were already free, but they thought it would bring equality to all people of all colors on the island. They believed that if they were taxpayers, they could vote in the newly formed colonial legislature. When their leader, Victor Oge, tried to exercise this right, he was executed.

- Enslaved Africans believed it meant an end to slavery forever.

A SPIRIT OF FREEDOM

Note the recurring theme of taxation.

- **How did the Latin American colonies think they were being taken advantage of?** *(They supplied crops and minerals to Europe but got little in return.)*

★**THINKING FURTHER:** *Making Connections Why might Latin American colonists have agreed that "Taxation without representation is tyranny"?* *(They, too, paid taxes to a government and had no say.)*

More MAP WORK

Refer the class to the map on this page.

- **What different European nations had colonies in Latin America?** *(Spain, Netherlands, Britain, France)*

- **What two colonies make up the island of Hispaniola, which you studied earlier?** *(Haiti, Santo Domingo)*

- **Which of these was no longer a colony in 1805?** *(Haiti)*

★**THINKING FURTHER:** *Making Conclusions Why might Europeans want to hang onto their colonies?* *(wealth and power)*

Discussing Revolution in the Caribbean Locate Hispaniola on the map. (Haiti and Santo Domingo)

- **Who was Toussaint L'Ouverture?** *(a former slave who led a slave revolt in the French colony in Saint Domingue)*

- **Why did he and his followers think the time was right for revolt?** *(They believed that "Liberty, Equality, Fraternity" should extend to them.)*

- **What did the revolution in Saint Domingue accomplish?** *(the first successful slave revolt and creation of the independent country of Haiti)*

★**THINKING FURTHER:** *Cause and Effect How do you suppose their success might have affected other European colonial countries? other colonies of Latin America?* *(made them fearful for their colonies; emboldened them)*

REVOLUTION IN MEXICO

Have the class briefly identify the problems that Latin American colonists had in common and then identify Mexico's problems (mineral wealth going to Spanish king and widespread poverty).

Discussing The Call of Dolores
Have students locate the Mexican town of Dolores on the map on p. 493.

● **Who was Miguel Hidalgo?** *(a priest who led a revolt for Mexican independence from Spain)*

● **How did he begin his revolution?** *(by uttering the Call of Dolores to his parishioners, who were Native Americans or mestizos—part Native American and part European)*

● **What did he urge his followers to demand?** *(their land that the Spanish had seized, removal of Europeans from office, a better government,)*

● **How did people respond to his call?** *(Many in Mexico supported a revolutionary movement for independence.)*

★THINKING FURTHER: *Making Conclusions* **Why do you think some Mexicans of European descent supported independence?** *(Possible answers: They believed in the idea of liberty; they were also kept from positions in colonial government.)*

This painting by Mexican artist José Orozco shows Miguel Hidalgo rallying Mexicans to fight for independence from Spain.

REVOLUTION IN MEXICO

Six years after independence in Haiti, the bells of freedom began ringing in Mexico as well. The Spanish grip on New Spain, or Mexico, weakened when Napoleon conquered Spain in 1808.

Mexico was the richest of Spain's colonies. Remember that the colony's economy depended on silver mines and large farms called haciendas. Nearly half of the money made here went to the king's treasury in Spain. As a result, a few Mexicans became very rich. Most, though, were very poor.

The Call of Dolores

One Sunday morning in 1810, a priest, Miguel Hidalgo (mee GEL ee DAHL goh) was speaking to the poor people in the town of Dolores (doh LOHR es). Hidalgo felt a duty to improve life for Mexicans. He called upon his listeners to sweep the Europeans from office and create a better government. In this stirring speech, now known as *The Call of Dolores*, Hidalgo encouraged the local people to "recover from the hated Spaniards the land stolen from your forefathers."

The response to Hidalgo's speech was explosive. His words fueled a revolution that called for freedom from Spain and equality for all people. Most of Hidalgo's supporters were poor Native Americans and mestizos (me STEE sohs). Mestizos are people of mixed Native American and European ancestry. People of African descent also joined the cause.

Combined, the poor mestizos and Mexicans of African descent made up about 80 percent of Mexico's population. Some Mexicans of European descent also supported the movement for independence.

BACKGROUND INFORMATION

ABOUT MIGUEL HIDALGO
● He was born in 1753 in Guanajuato State, Mexico, to a moderately prosperous family of Spanish descent.
● Having distinguished himself as a student, he was ordained a priest in 1789 and dedicated himself to a career in teaching.
● In the early 1790s, he abandoned his academic career and became a parish priest. During this time, he began planning an independence movement.
● While he was a good speaker and a popular leader, he failed to win the support of enough of the better-off Mexicans to assure the success of his movement.

VISUAL LITERACY

ABOUT THE PAINTING BY JOSÉ OROZCO
José Clemente Orozco (1883–1949) has been a major influence on modern Mexican art. Orozco hoped that his paintings would make important political and humanist statements to the people of his country, including those who couldn't read. Particularly, he wanted to show the misery and futility of war. Orozco believed that art should belong to the people and painted many murals on public buildings. Some of his more controversial works were destroyed. Invite students to study Orozco's painting. Possible questions include: What different types of people does this painting show?

A Setback

The angry crowd in Dolores arrested Spanish officials and destroyed Spanish haciendas. The number of revolutionaries swelled to 25,000, and Hidalgo's army captured the nearby city of Guanajuato (gwah nah HWAH toh). As they moved on toward Mexico City, another 60,000 people joined in the march. Hidalgo called for equality for all groups. He also declared the end of slavery and the unfair taxes that the people had to pay the Spanish government.

Hidalgo's army never reached Mexico City. The Spanish army pursued the rebels, captured Hidalgo, and executed him in 1811. All hope for the Mexican war of independence seemed lost.

After Hidalgo's death, another priest, named José María Morelos (ho SE mah REE ah noh RE lohs), carried on the revolution. Morelos led a small army in central Mexico. He fought strong Spanish forces for several years. In 1813 Morelos called Mexico's first national congress and declared the colony's independence from Spain. In 1815, like Hidalgo before him, Morelos was captured and killed by Spanish soldiers.

An Independent Mexico

One of the soldiers who had fought against both Hidalgo and Morelos soon came to power. Agustín de Iturbide was an officer in the Spanish army. In 1821 Iturbide issued the *Plan de Iguala* (PLAHN DE ee GWAH lah). It described his own ideas about Mexico.

All inhabitants of New Spain, without any distinction between Europeans, Africans, and Indians, are citizens of this monarchy. . . . Behold the sweet chain that unites us; consider the bonds of friendship, interdependence of interest, education, language, and harmony of feelings. . . . The time has arrived . . . that our union should emancipate [free] America without need of foreign help. At the head of a brave and determined army, I [declare] the Independence of Northern America.

Finally, 11 years after Miguel Hidalgo rang the bell at his church in Dolores, Mexico was independent. However, Hidalgo's dream of liberty and equality for all Mexicans was lost. In 1822 Iturbide declared himself Emperor of Mexico. Five months later he dismissed the congress Morelos had started. Many years would pass before all Mexicans were given a say in their government.

This huge monument was built in honor of José Morelos.

495

Discussing A Setback Help students recognize the desire for freedom.

● **How many people eventually joined Hidalgo?** *(85,000)*

● **Who took up Hidalgo's struggle for Mexican independence?** *(José María Morelos, another priest)*

● **What fate did he share with Hidalgo?** *(capture by Spanish forces and execution)*

★**THINKING FURTHER:** *Making Decisions* **On a scale of 1 to 10, how would you rank the success of Hidalgo's and Morelos's efforts?** *(Ranks may be low for outright success, but students should recognize that both gained supporters and set in motion the idea of independence from Spain.)*

Discussing An Independent Mexico Note the ongoing struggle for freedom.

● **Why was Agustín de Iturbide in a better position than Hidalgo or Morelos to win the battle against Spain?** *(As an army officer, he was probably better equipped to defeat Spanish army forces.)*

● **What ideas did Iturbide profess?** *(that Europeans, Africans, and Indians should all be free, that Northern America should be independent)*

● **When did Mexico win its independence?** *(in 1821)*

★**THINKING FURTHER:** *Compare and Contrast* **What parallels can you draw between Napoleon and Iturbide?** *(Each appeared to support a republic, but each declared himself emperor.)*

BACKGROUND INFORMATION

ABOUT AGUSTÍN DE ITURBIDE

● He was born in 1783 in Mexico to a well-off family.

● He was not cut of the heroic cloth of his predecessors in the struggle for Mexican independence from Spain. In fact, he spent more than 10 years as an officer in the Spanish viceroy's army fighting against independence.

● The only reason he joined the independence side was that he was afraid Spain was about to reform its relationship with Mexico. He decided to declare independence rather than to let that happen.

● After being exiled in 1823, he tried to return to Mexico and recapture power there. Instead, he was tried and executed as a traitor in 1824.

CURRICULUM CONNECTION

LINKS TO ART Mexico City's public buildings are filled with murals by Diego Rivera, José Clemente Orozco, and David Alfaro Siqueiros showing scenes of Mexico's struggle for independence. Call for a team of volunteers to research art books to prepare a class presentation.

SECOND-LANGUAGE SUPPORT

GRAPHIC ORGANIZER Second-language learners may benefit from creating a time line of revolution in the Americas. Have students write on a time line the date, place name, and key people in each revolution they find in this chapter. Encourage groups of students to discuss why these may have occurred during that time period.

INDEPENDENCE MOVES

Introduce the class to the expression "an idea whose time has come." Have students discuss how independence from Europe was one such idea among the colonies of Latin America by the early 1800s.

Discussing The Liberator of South America Write *Simón Bolívar* on the board.

- **Who was Simón Bolívar and what were his goals?** *(a wealthy South American who fought for independence from Spain)*

- **Did he limit his ambitions to his homeland? Explain.** *(No, he believed he had to fight to liberate all colonial Latin America.)*

★**THINKING FURTHER:** *Making Decisions* **Do you think that Bolívar should be remembered as a genuine hero? Why or why not?** *(Students will probably see Bolívar as a man of principle who was willing to put his privileged life on the line to serve that principle.)*

More MAP WORK

Refer students to the map on this page. Encourage them to work back and forth between text and map.

- **How does the map show that Bolívar put his beliefs into action?** *(His route to oust the Spanish covers a great distance.)*

- **How did the lands of southern South America win their independence?** *(with the leadership of José de San Martín)*

Exploring Changes in Australia Have students describe Australia as they last studied it (under British control).

★**THINKING FURTHER:** *Compare and Contrast* **How would you contrast the ways Australia and Latin America won independence?** *(Australia gained independence peacefully, unlike many Latin American colonies, because self-government was practical. Once independent, Australia kept its ties to the British monarchy.)*

INDEPENDENCE MOVES

The forces of liberty soon pressed upon other parts of the world. Beginning in 1810 the Spanish-speaking colonies of South America began to revolt. Brazil, ruled by Portugal, was not far behind. On the other side of the world, Australia was also headed for change.

The Liberator of South America

The driving force behind independence in South America was Simón Bolívar. Bolívar was born into one of the richest families in Venezuela. He had read books by French writers explaining ideas of freedom. Liberty and equality served as the main goals of his struggle. Bolívar offered the hope of freedom from colonial rule to all people who joined his cause.

Bolívar spent ten years struggling to free his homeland from Spain. In 1821 a decade of leading armies through the rain forests and mountains of South America finally paid off. Bolívar's forces defeated the Spanish army in Venezuela. In a speech to his troops, Bolívar said:

But we cannot rest. Other obligations await us. And when our native land is entirely free, we shall go to fight the Spaniards in any part of America where they are in control, and we shall throw them into the sea. Freedom shall live protected by our swords!

Bolívar carried the revolution further into South America, freeing the areas now known as Colombia, Bolivia, Panama, Ecuador, and Peru from Spanish rule. His actions won him the nick-

ROUTES OF BOLÍVAR AND SAN MARTÍN, c. 1810–1821

MAP WORK

Bolívar and San Martín won independence for many of the lands of South America.

1. Which of these two liberators traveled farther south in South America?
2. How far is Santiago from Lima?

Simón Bolívar, a Venezuelan soldier, liberated much of northern South America.

name "Liberator of South America."

From the southern part of the continent came another liberator. His name was José de San Martín (ho SE DE sahn mahr TEEN). San Martín led revolutions in Argentina and Chile. Find his route on the map on this page.

Changes in Australia

Remember that in 1788 the English founded the colony of New South Wales in Australia. Eventually, other colonies such as Van Diemen's Land, South Australia, and Western Australia were also established.

GLOBAL CONNECTION

SIMÓN BOLÍVAR AND THE "FRENCH CONNECTION"

- Bolívar was born in 1783 and early in life had tutors who taught him about the French philosophers' views on the equality of humankind.

- A visit to France when Napoleon first came to power convinced Bolívar further of the rightness of the ideal of equality.

- Napoleon's conquest of Spain in 1808 gave Bolívar the chance he needed to rise up against a weakened Spain to fight for independence for his homeland and for the rest of Latin America.

- In his struggle against Spain, Bolívar was sometimes driven from South America, and twice fled to Haiti. By then, Haiti had thrown off its French masters, but Bolívar took comfort in its continuing belief in "Liberty, Equality, Fraternity."

The Parliament House in Canberra is the center of Australia's government.

It was difficult for England to govern these colonies from so far away. As a result, the Australian Colonies Government Act was passed in 1850. This allowed the colonies to create constitutions and legislative bodies.

Years later, as France and Germany became interested in lands near Australia, Australians began to see a need for a confederation that would help protect the colonies by unifying them. A confederation is a group of provinces or states under a central government. The Commonwealth of Australia came into existence on January 1, 1901. Although this new commonwealth kept the British monarch as its highest ruler, it was united and free to govern itself.

WHY IT MATTERS

The 1800s brought many freedoms to European colonists throughout the world. Sometimes the change came peacefully, as it did in Australia. Often, however, people had to fight for their freedom.

With liberty came responsibility. The young countries were now able to make decisions for themselves. Faraway kings and queens no longer took a large share of wealth. However, it was still difficult for the new nations to build strong economies. Often a few rich families controlled the country's land and money.

The peasants of Mexico often said their revolution "placed the same rider on a new mule." They meant that one group of rulers usually just replaced another. Although the colonies were free, freedom and equality for all people remained a distant promise.

✓// Reviewing Facts and Ideas

MAIN IDEAS

- In 1804 Haiti became the second independent country in the Americas, after the United States.
- Miguel Hidalgo led Mexicans in a revolt against Spain in 1810. Mexico became independent in 1821.
- Simón Bolívar and José de San Martín liberated much of South America from Spanish rule.
- An act passed in 1850 began self-rule in Australian colonies.

THINK ABOUT IT

1. How did Haiti gain independence?
2. From which social classes did Hidalgo gain most of his support?
3. **FOCUS** How did events in Europe influence the fight for independence in American colonies?
4. **THINKING SKILL** What steps would you take to *determine the credibility* of the quote by Iturbide on page 495?
5. **WRITE** Suppose you are a reporter recording the early events of the war of Mexican independence. Write a list of questions you could ask Miguel Hidalgo about his actions and his hopes for the future.

497

Discussing WHY IT MATTERS Review the enormous changes that took place.

- ***What problems did Latin Americans solve by gaining independence?*** *(They were no longer forced to ship their wealth overseas and they now had the political power to govern themselves.)*
- ***What new problems did this create?*** *(Many new nations still lacked equality and too often all power lay in the hands of the few wealthy people.)*

⭐ 3 CLOSE

MAIN IDEAS

Have students come up to the board to write their answers.

- ***What country was next after the U.S. in becoming an independent nation in the Americas?*** *(Haiti)*
- ***Who first led the struggle for Mexican independence?*** *(Miguel Hidalgo)*
- ***Who were the main liberators of South America?*** *(Simón Bolívar and José de San Martín)*
- ***What event started self-rule in Australian colonies?*** *(an act passed in 1850)*

EVALUATE
✓ **Answers to Think About It**

1. Slaves led by Toussaint L'Ouverture successfully overthrew the French. *Summarize*
2. from Native Americans and mestizos and from some Mexicans of European descent *Recall Details*
3. The French Revolution fostered a spirit of independence, and the Napoleonic wars prevented European nations from holding onto their colonies. *Make Conclusions*
4. Examine how much he knows about his subject, determine if he has a bias, and assess his reputation for accuracy. *Make Judgements and Decisions*
5. Questions should reflect Hidalgo's concern for Mexico's people and the form of government he desired. *Point of View*

Write About It Ask students to picture themselves as part of a liberating army and write a brief message home describing what they are fighting for.

MEETING INDIVIDUAL NEEDS

RETEACHING (Easy) Tell students to choose any one of the leaders in the struggle for independence whom they met in this lesson and reread his story. Then have them draw a color picture illustrating a moment in which he was involved in the struggle.

EXTENSION (Average) Have students choose one of the countries whose struggle for independence is described in this lesson. Have them do library research about that country's struggle and then create an illustrated time line of steps in the struggle.

ENRICHMENT (Challenging) Have students choose any one of the leaders they met in this lesson, do some further research on him and his beliefs, and then write a speech this leader might have given to his followers to stir them on in their struggle. Invite students to address the class with their speeches.

LEGACY

Lesson Overview

The U.S. Constitution has long served as a model for others.

Lesson Objective

★ Appreciate the power and influence of the U.S. Constitution.

1 PREPARE

MOTIVATE Have a student locate, rehearse, and read aloud the Preamble of the U.S. Constitution. Have students identify the reasons it spells out for having a constitution and ask them why they think the founders of our country thought such a document was necessary to the life of our country.

SET PURPOSE Tell students that a great English statesman—William Gladstone—called the Constitution "the most remarkable work known to me in modern times to have been produced by the human intellect." Encourage them to explore this *Legacy* to find out why.

2 TEACH

Understanding the Concept of a Legacy Have students read the text on this page.

● *How long ago was the U.S. Constitution written?* (in 1787, more than 200 years ago)

● *Why did it need to be written?* (As a new country that had gained its independence from Britain, the U.S. needed a new plan of government.)

● *What rights does the Constitution guarantee to the people of the United States?* (rights such as freedom of speech, religion, and peaceful assembly)

● *How is a constitution like a contract between the people and their government?* (Each is given something and each must give something in return.)

Legacy

LINKING PAST AND PRESENT

THE UNITED STATES CONSTITUTION

As you know from studying United States history, people in our country fought a revolution earlier than the ones in France and Latin America that you have read about. When the founders of our country wrote the Constitution in 1787, they made sure to protect the freedoms they had just won.

Because the United States had the first written constitution in the world, other countries used it as a model for their own constitutions. Many Latin American countries were especially influenced by the United States Constitution. In Costa Rica all citizens are considered equal before the law and can state political opinions freely.

In another part of the world, India's constitution protects freedom of religion, the right to assemble peaceably, and other rights. These freedoms have been guaranteed in the United States for over 200 years.

498

The first part of the United States Constitution states the goals and freedoms that the colonists sought. These students are looking at the Constitution in Washington, D.C.

BACKGROUND INFORMATION

ABOUT THE UNITED STATES CONSTITUTION

● It was written in Philadelphia during the often sweltering summer of 1787, behind closed doors and tightly shut windows. Secrecy was invoked so that its framers could speak out freely about what it should and should not contain.

● Thomas Jefferson, at the time in Paris where he was serving as American ambassador to France, said of the 55 delegates who framed the Constitution, "It was an assembly of demigods!" They were among the best-educated men in the country, steeped in knowledge of ancient Greek and Roman government.

● Chief Justice John Marshall said that the Constitution they wrote was "intended to endure for ages to come, and, consequently be adapted to the various crises in human affairs."

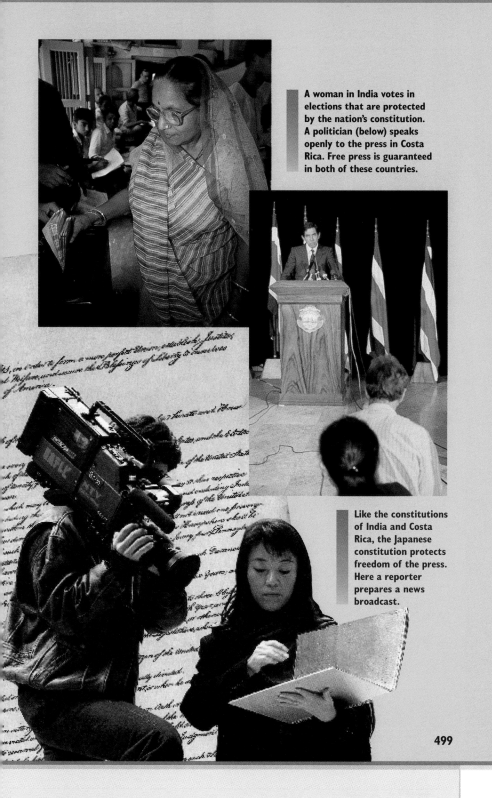

A woman in India votes in elections that are protected by the nation's constitution. A politician (below) speaks openly to the press in Costa Rica. Free press is guaranteed in both of these countries.

Like the constitutions of India and Costa Rica, the Japanese constitution protects freedom of the press. Here a reporter prepares a news broadcast.

499

★THINKING FURTHER: *Making Connections* **There is an old American saying, prim but still having the ring of truth, that "the O of obligation comes before the P of privilege." How does this saying relate to citizens and their constitution?** *(It says that citizens must be just as dedicated, or even more so, to fulfilling their responsibilities as citizens as they are to demanding their rights.)*

Examining the Illustrations Give students a few minutes to examine the illustrations and read their captions.

● **What are just three of the many countries that have used the U.S. Constitution as a model for their own constitutions?** *(Costa Rica, India, and Japan)*

● **What rights does the Indian constitution guarantee to Indian citizens.** *(freedom of religion; freedom to assemble peacefully and other rights)*

● **Which constitutional right does each of the photos here reflect and in which country?** *(the right to vote in India, freedom of the press in Japan, freedom of speech in Costa Rica)*

★THINKING FURTHER: *Making Decisions* **On a scale of 1 to 10, how would you rank the influence that the U.S. Constitution has had on constitutions elsewhere in the world? Why?** *(Students should give it a very high ranking because the freedoms it guarantees are now honored around the world.)*

3 CLOSE

SUM IT UP
Encourage students to compare the protections the U.S. Constitution guarantees its citizens with the pre-Revolutionary conditions for citizens in the countries they just studied.

EVALUATE
Write About It Have students write a short poem about what one of the constitutional freedoms means to them.

MEETING INDIVIDUAL NEEDS

RETEACHING (Easy) Tell students to choose a freedom that the U.S. Constitution guarantees and a responsibility it demands. Have them illustrate the freedom and the obligation side by side.

EXTENSION (Average) Tell students to picture themselves as political consultants called in to advise an emerging country on what should go into its constitution. Have them write a letter of advice identifying elements they consider most important to include.

ENRICHMENT (Challenging) Have students locate a copy of the Bill of Rights, the first ten amendments to the U.S. Constitution, and the beginning of India's constitution. Have them write a description of similarities that they find.

LESSON 3

PAGES 500–505

Lesson Overview

Beginning in the 1700s in England, the Industrial Revolution changed forever the way people lived and worked.

Lesson Objectives

★ Identify the technologies that produced the Industrial Revolution.

★ Analyze how the Industrial Revolution changed the ways people lived and worked.

★ 1 PREPARE

MOTIVATE Have students briefly recall ways that revolutions in France and Latin America changed people's lives. Then have two students do the *Read Aloud*, one as de Tocqueville, the other as narrator. Help the class see that revolutions may also bring about profound economic and social change.

SET PURPOSE Refer the class to the *Read to Learn* question, and examine the illustration of factory workers. Ask if anyone can identify the machine in the lower illustration on p. 501 (a cotton spinning mule). Encourage students to investigate how a revolution in technology can have effects as great as a revolution in government. Preview the *Vocabulary*.

★ 2 TEACH

Understanding THE BIG PICTURE As students read this section, invite them to picture in their minds the seemingly unchanging centuries of peasant life in Europe until the 1700s.

★ THINKING FURTHER: *Compare and Contrast* **How did life change suddenly?** (New farm technologies replaced old; the population doubled.)

Resource REMINDER

Practice and Project Book: *p. 101*

Anthology: *Working in the Mines, pp. 136–137; Progress in Industry, p. 138*

Desk Map

Focus Activity

READ TO LEARN

What changes were brought about by the Industrial Revolution?

VOCABULARY

- Industrial Revolution
- textile
- factory
- middle class
- working class
- socialism

PEOPLE

- John Kay
- James Hargreaves
- Richard Arkwright
- Edmund Cartwright
- James Watt
- Karl Marx

500

1700   1888 1900

The Industrial Revolution

Read Aloud

"From this foul drain the greatest stream of human industry flows out to fertilize the whole world. From this filthy sewer pure gold flows."

This is how French writer and historian Alexis de Tocqueville (a LEKS ihs dih tawk VEEL) described Manchester, England, in 1835. A revolution was taking place in Manchester and other European cities. This revolution did not cause the bloodshed that had taken place in France and Latin America. It did, however, permanently change the lives of people around the world.

THE BIG PICTURE

Before 1700 the most important event across Europe every year was the harvest. Most people lived and worked the land in rural areas. Many never traveled more than ten miles from their villages.

From 1700 to 1800, however, rural life throughout Europe began to change. New farming methods and technology—such as iron plows, crop rotation, and fertilizers—made farms much more productive. Europe's population exploded, nearly doubling to 190 million by 1800. No change, however, had as many effects as the one that began in England in the 1700s. The Industrial Revolution was a period of time when great technological advances changed the way goods were made and the ways people lived. Industry became the focus of economic activity. Unlike national revolutions, this revolution was felt around the world.

SHELTERED INSTRUCTION

READING STRATEGIES & LANGUAGE DEVELOPMENT

MAKING CONCLUSIONS Review with the class how they make conclusions by using facts in the text and what they already know about the subject. Write the term "Industrial Revolution" on the board and display products made possible as a result: mass-produced kitchen items, clothing, and toys, for example. Based on these items, have students make conclusions about the changes brought about by the Industrial Revolution. **[SDAIE STRATEGY: CONTEXTUALIZATION]**

SYNONYMS Refer students to the word *factories* on p. 501, and have them define it ("places where goods are produced"). Invite them to come up with other names people give to places where they make things (*plant, mill, shop,* and *studio.*)

THE GROWTH OF INDUSTRY

The Industrial Revolution started in Britain, spread across Europe, and reached the United States. It began in Britain for a number of reasons. British laws allowed people to start businesses, protect their property, and earn money. Britain also had a stable government and a rich supply of the raw materials coal and iron.

Work in the Country

The Industrial Revolution did not happen all at once. Industry first appeared in the countryside. Peasants produced thread and cloth on spinning wheels and looms in their homes. Peasants worked the fields in the summer. Then in the winter they spun yarn and made textiles. A textile is a cloth fabric that is either woven or knitted.

This type of work soon became an important source of income for rural families. As one Irish traveler observed:

The poor people spin a good deal of wool, and weave it into flannel for their own wear.

The Textile Boom

By the middle 1700s a growing population created more demand for textiles. New machines were invented that could make textiles more quickly and cheaply. Some of these machines are shown in the Infographic on

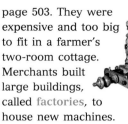

page 503. They were expensive and too big to fit in a farmer's two-room cottage. Merchants built large buildings, called factories, to house new machines.

Most of these new machines were made for weaving cotton. Cotton does not grow well in the cold, wet climate of Britain. However, it is cheaper than wool and has many uses. In the 1700s Britain became part of the triangular trade you read about in Chapter 16. The British found a vast source of cotton in the colonies of North America.

Soon a brisk trade developed. Raw cotton was shipped from America to the mills of Britain. Finished textiles were then shipped to Africa and traded for enslaved persons. Captured Africans were sent to work as slaves on cotton plantations in British colonies in America. British cities such as Liverpool soon became centers of textile manufacturing and shipping.

Before factories started, families made textiles at home (right). A hand-operated spinning wheel (above) was used to make thread.

Victoria & Albert Museum

501

THE GROWTH OF INDUSTRY

On a desk map, have students trace the path of the Industrial Revolution.

★**THINKING FURTHER:** *Classifying*
How would you classify geographic and political reasons that the Industrial Revolution began in Britain? *(Geographic: good roads, natural resources like coal and iron. Political: laws encouraging business, stable government.)*

Discussing Work in the Country
Explore the rural beginning of change.

● ***Where did the Industrial Revolution begin, in the country or the city? Why?*** *(in the country because people were able to make textiles at home)*

★**THINKING FURTHER:** *Predicting*
How do you predict this will change? Why? *(Students may predict new factories, as machinery and volume of work outgrows the home.)*

Investigating The Textile Boom
Discuss why the textile industry grew.

● ***How did larger, more powerful machines change textile manufacture?*** *(They made cloth faster and cheaper and moved work to factories.)*

● ***What was the main product of the early Industrial Revolution? From where did the raw material come?*** *(cotton; North American colonies)*

★**THINKING FURTHER:** *Cause and Effect* ***How did England's Industrial Revolution affect world trade?*** *(created a greater market for slaves, gave England new manufacturing centers)*

BACKGROUND INFORMATION

ABOUT THE PROGRESSION OF ENERGY SOURCES The Industrial Revolution increased the demand for energy sources to run machinery.

● Human and animal power had been the major sources of energy before the Industrial Revolution.

● Water power had also been harnessed. Fast-running streams or rivers turned grinding stones.

● Steam power, which required coal or wood to heat water, was developed during the Industrial Revolution, providing energy for heavy machinery.

● Electric power, created either by burning fossil fuels or harnessing the energy from running or falling water, gradually replaced steam power. Today, nuclear and solar energy are also used to create electric power.

USING THE ANTHOLOGY

WORKING IN THE MINES, pages 136–137 The *Anthology* selection will help bring general statements of working conditions to a more personal sense of how the conditions affected individual people. After students read the selection, ask them to think of themselves as people living at that time and to write letters to the editor of a newspaper about these conditions and what should to be done about them.

THE SPREAD OF INDUSTRY

Have students list the areas affected by the spreading Industrial Revolution.

★THINKING FURTHER: *Making Connections* **In addition to factory work, what occupations would have grown as a result of the Industrial Revolution?** *(coal and iron ore mining, iron making, machine manufacture, sales, and trading of goods)*

Discussing The Iron Horse Discuss the changes trains made in people's lives.

● **What were locomotives and what did they do?** *(steam-powered engines; pulled passenger and freight trains)*

★THINKING FURTHER: *Making Conclusions* **What changes do you suppose train transportation made in life?** *(Because people and goods could now travel farther, faster, and more easily, many people probably traveled much more often than before, on business or pleasure, and goods found new markets, enriching both their makers and their consumers.)*

Exploring More Products for Sale Have a student read the quote aloud.

★THINKING FURTHER: *Making Connections* **How did more people making more goods create more markets for goods? How did more markets for goods create more jobs for the people making them?** *(Help students see the circle that the Industrial Revolution created: more goods being supplied→more people being paid to make them→more people able to buy goods→more goods being supplied, and on and on. You may want to tell the class about Henry Ford, who in 1914 began paying the employees who built his cars $5 a day, which was then at least twice the pay of most factory workers. By making it possible for his workers to afford to buy a Ford, he was enlarging the market for his cars.)*

Ironworks produced large amounts of iron needed for railroads and other new inventions.

THE SPREAD OF INDUSTRY

The Industrial Revolution began mostly with cotton textiles. It soon included many textiles. The Industrial Revolution widened to cover other goods as well. In Britain coal and iron mines provided raw materials used to build machines and power factories.

The Iron Horse

No new machine created as much interest as the locomotive. These steam-powered railway engines hissed, belched, and squeaked along Britain's iron rails. The first passenger railroad, between Stockton and Darlington, opened in 1825. Within 15 years, more than 1,000 miles of track crisscrossed Europe. By 1870 the railroad had cut the travel time from London, England, to Edinburgh, Scotland, from 4 days to 12 hours! In 1888 the railroad, nicknamed the "iron horse," linked Europe from Calais, in France, to Istanbul. Passengers and goods could reach more distant places in less time than ever before.

502

More Products for Sale

As factories hummed and railroads chugged, the number of products people could buy increased. A pamphlet called *The Results of Machinery* gave one example in 1831:

> Two centuries ago not one person in a thousand wore stockings; one century ago not one person in five hundred wore them; now not one person in a thousand is without them.

This description was an exaggeration, since many workers could not even afford shoes. However, it shows an important change in the economy. Before the Industrial Revolution began, most people lived on farms that provided them with food and clothing. By 1800 about 20 percent of the population lived in cities.

The people who did move from farms to cities now worked in factories and were paid wages. New factory workers used this money to buy food, cotton clothing, and other goods.

GLOBAL CONNECTION

THE GLOBAL IMPLICATIONS OF THE INDUSTRIAL REVOLUTION The Industrial Revolution also affected the lives of people far from England.

● As industrialization spread and the demand for manufactured goods increased, England and other industrial countries looked to new sources in Africa, Asia, and the Americas for cheap natural resources.

● As a result of this quest for more resources, European countries extended political domination, in the form of colonialism, over many countries. For example, as students will see in Chapter 19, India became a major supplier of cotton for the English textile mills.

● English systems of government, transportation, commerce, and education were imposed on Indian people and dramatically changed the way they lived.

Infographic

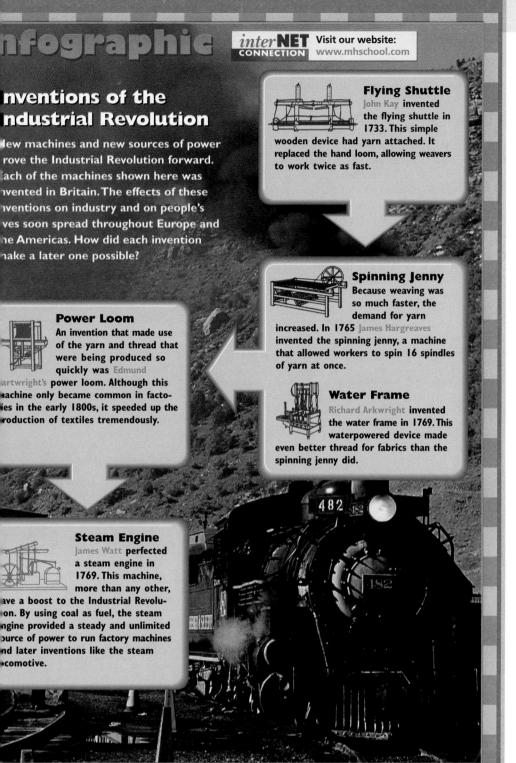

inter NET CONNECTION Visit our website: www.mhschool.com

Inventions of the Industrial Revolution

New machines and new sources of power drove the Industrial Revolution forward. Each of the machines shown here was invented in Britain. The effects of these inventions on industry and on people's lives soon spread throughout Europe and the Americas. How did each invention make a later one possible?

Flying Shuttle
John Kay invented the flying shuttle in 1733. This simple wooden device had yarn attached. It replaced the hand loom, allowing weavers to work twice as fast.

Spinning Jenny
Because weaving was so much faster, the demand for yarn increased. In 1765 James Hargreaves invented the spinning jenny, a machine that allowed workers to spin 16 spindles of yarn at once.

Water Frame
Richard Arkwright invented the water frame in 1769. This waterpowered device made even better thread for fabrics than the spinning jenny did.

Power Loom
An invention that made use of the yarn and thread that were being produced so quickly was Edmund Cartwright's power loom. Although this machine only became common in factories in the early 1800s, it speeded up the production of textiles tremendously.

Steam Engine
James Watt perfected a steam engine in 1769. This machine, more than any other, gave a boost to the Industrial Revolution. By using coal as fuel, the steam engine provided a steady and unlimited source of power to run factory machines and later inventions like the steam locomotive.

Infographic

Remind the class of humankind's first great revolution—the Agricultural Revolution—when hunters and gatherers first settle down to farm. Point out that the first revolution also began with new technologies, such as the plow and early methods of land irrigation. Here students can identify technologies that began the Industrial Revolution.

Discussing Inventions of the Industrial Revolution Give students a few minutes to read this page and to examine the illustrations and captions. Note that one new technology often spurs the next—greater speed and power prompt still greater speed and power.

- *What did the flying shuttle accomplish? (It made the weaving process nearly twice as fast as before.)*

- *What new need did this create? (for yarn to be spun more quickly)*

- *What answered this need? How? (the spinning jenny, which could spin yarn 16 times faster than before)*

- *What did the water frame accomplish? (It harnessed water power to spin a better quality thread.)*

- *How did both the spinning jenny and the water frame create a need for the power loom? (These technologies produced yarn and thread so fast that more powerful looms had to be built.)*

- *What technology gave a major power boost to many other kinds of technology? (the steam engine)*

★THINKING FURTHER: *Making Conclusions Why was the development of a technology like the steam engine likely during the Industrial Revolution? (A way had to be found to supply vast amounts of energy to run all the new technology.)*

EXPANDING THE INFOGRAPHIC

RESEARCHING AND PRESENTING Divide the class into five groups and assign each group one of the technologies pictured in this *Infographic*. Have each group research its assigned technology and then prepare an illustrated presentation of how it works to make to the class. You might suggest the following sources for research:

- Encyclopedia entries under *Industrial Revolution*.
- Library catalog entries under *Industry—History* or *Industrialization*.

FIELD TRIP

If you have any industrial museums in your area, try to arrange a class visit there. If not, make available Neil Grant's *The Industrial Revolution* for the class to examine.

A NEW SOCIAL PYRAMID

Call a student to the board to list England's social groupings (aristocrats and commoners) when they last studied the country, in Chapter 12.

- **In which of these social groupings would you place the middle class and the working class?** *(commoners)*

- **Why did the middle class become more numerous and more prosperous during the Industrial Revolution?** *(They supplied the skills and professions—merchants, lawyers, factory owners, bankers—that new business demanded.)*

- **Which was England's most populous social group?** *(the working class)*

★**THINKING FURTHER:** *Making Conclusions* **How would you draw a social pyramid of England after the Industrial Revolution?** *(from top down: monarch, aristocrats, middle class, working class)*

Discussing Working Conditions
Have one student read the first quote aloud and another read the second quote.

★**THINKING FURTHER:** *Compare and Contrast* **How would you compare and contrast working conditions described here with working conditions today?** *(Students should be aware that child labor is now barred, workdays are not 14 hours long, and laws and common sense reject unhealthy factory conditions.)*

Exploring An Idea for Change
Discuss the causes that led to unionizing.

- **Why did workers decide to unionize?** *(to use the strength of unity to improve their working conditions)*

- **To what did Karl Marx object, and what did he propose to correct it?** *(the fact that factory owners grew rich as workers remained poor; to give workers ownership and control of the factories)*

★**THINKING FURTHER:** *Summarizing* **How would you summarize Marx's idea of socialism?** *(Workers, not governments or rich people, should be in control.)*

A NEW SOCIAL PYRAMID

As the economy of Britain shifted from farms to factories, British society changed too. The middle class became more important as cities grew larger. The middle class was made up of business people, including merchants, lawyers, factory owners, and bankers. Although they did not have land or political power, the middle class increased trade and manufacturing. Some members of the middle class became rich.

The biggest group in British society was the working class. These men and women were mostly farmers who left farms to work in towns and cities. The rural lives they left behind were often difficult. However, many workers found life in the cities was sometimes worse.

Working Conditions

Working hours in the textile factories and mines were long and the conditions dangerous. Unlike farming or traditional craft work, factory work was boring and repetitive. One writer described what it was like:

They work fourteen hours per day, including the hour for dinner; the door is locked in working hours, except half an hour at tea time; the workpeople are not allowed to send for water to drink in the hot factory: and even the rain water is locked up, by the master's order, otherwise they would be happy to drink even that.

Many children worked in the narrow, wet, underground tunnels of the mines. Children as young as four years of age also worked in factories. Although children had always worked on farms, the conditions of the factories were severe. A French writer described a group of people leaving work, including

. . . young children, in greater numbers than the women, just as dirty, just as haggard, covered with rags which are thick with oil splashed over them as they toiled at the loom.

This painting (left) contrasts the middle class and the working class. Children often pulled carts through the narrow tunnels of coal mines (above).

CITIZENSHIP ★

UNDERSTANDING GOVERNMENT Students might be surprised to learn that child labor in the United States lasted into this century. Some states passed laws against child labor during the 1800s, but they often went unenforced. As late as the 1930s, it was not uncommon for children to go to work in factories or mines at the age of eight. Not until the Fair Labor Standards Act of 1938 did the federal government prohibit child labor.

SECOND-LANGUAGE SUPPORT

GRAPHIC ORGANIZERS Second-language learners will find organizing tools to be useful in understanding this lesson. Write on the board *The good news was* and *The bad news was*. As students read, have them identify and list "good" and "bad" changes that occurred as a result of the Industrial Revolution.

Karl Marx believed there had always been conflict between economic classes.

An Idea for Change

Conditions in factories led many workers to organize. They formed organizations called unions. Weak at first, these organizations were outlawed by the government until 1824.

Karl Marx, a German philosopher living in England, wrote about the workers. In *Das Kapital* he wrote, "The [workers] have nothing to lose but their chains; they have the world to gain." Marx believed that those who owned property became rich while those who did not remained poor. The solution, he felt, was for workers to own the factories.

Marx believed that the world was entering a new economic period when workers would rise up and take control. In time, Marx wrote, there would be no social classes, and government would disappear. Many people in Europe became interested in some of his ideas, which became known as socialism. Much later, in Russia, these ideas would form the basis of a new type of government.

WHY IT MATTERS

Thousands of years ago people experienced an economic revolution—agriculture. Farming meant that people no longer had to hunt and gather to meet their needs. The Industrial Revolution was another revolution that changed the way people met their needs.

The Industrial Revolution did not bring sudden change, as the French Revolution did. The term "Industrial Revolution" was not even used by the people who lived through it. Still, industry created new cities, bustling with activity and spewing clouds of smoke.

The Industrial Revolution spread from its birthplace in Britain throughout Europe and the Western Hemisphere. It would eventually change most of the planet. As these incredible changes took place, there would be no going back.

✓ Reviewing Facts and Ideas

MAIN IDEAS

- The Industrial Revolution began in Britain in the middle 1700s.
- New inventions in textile manufacturing led to the building of factories.
- The middle class gained much money and power during this period.
- Life for the working class was frequently difficult, with low wages and poor working conditions.
- The Industrial Revolution spread from Britain to Europe and the Americas.

THINK ABOUT IT

1. What work did peasants do in their homes before factories were built?
2. What was the first product of the Industrial Revolution?
3. **FOCUS** List some good and bad effects of the Industrial Revolution.
4. **THINKING SKILL** How might the *point of view* of a working class person differ from that of a middle class person?
5. **GEOGRAPHY** How might the invention of the steam engine allow factories to be built anywhere?

505

Discussing WHY IT MATTERS Call students' attention to expressions that are frequently used today: *You can't put the genie back in the bottle* and *You can't unring the bell.*

★**THINKING FURTHER:** *Making Connections* **How do such expressions describe the effects of the Industrial Revolution?** *(Whether for good or for ill, it changed the world in ways that can never be undone.)*

3 CLOSE

MAIN IDEAS
Have students write their answers on a piece of paper.

- *Where and about when did the Industrial Revolution begin?* (in Britain in the middle 1700s)
- *How did new inventions lead to the building of factories?* (Large machines demanded floor space to operate.)
- *Which social group probably gained the most from the Industrial Revolution?* (the middle class)
- *Which group frequently suffered low wages and poor working conditions?* (the working class)
- *What path did the Industrial Revolution cut across the world in the 1800s?* (from Britain to Europe and the Americas)

EVALUATE
✓ **Answers to Think About It**
1. spinning thread and weaving cloth
   Recall Details
2. textiles
   Recall Details
3. Good: more goods available, expanded trade, growing prosperity for the middle class, jobs and wages for the working class. Bad: expanded demand for slaves, poor working conditions, low wages, child labor.
   Compare and Contrast
4. A working-class person might say the classes were unequally rewarded.
   Point of View
5. Steam engine tracks can be built anywhere.
   Five Themes of Geography: Movement

Write About It Have students write a paragraph contrasting one aspect of life as it was before and after the Industrial Revolution.

SKILLS LESSON
PAGES 506–507

Lesson Overview
A *cartogram* is a map showing nations drawn to scale as they rank in any one factor.

Lesson Objective
★ Learn to interpret a cartogram.

1 PREPARE

MOTIVATE Refer to the cartogram and ask how it does and does not resemble other maps. Have students read *Why the Skill Matters* to learn why.

SET PURPOSE How do we interpret cartograms? Invite students to read *Helping Yourself.* Work on the *Vocabulary* terms. Point out that cartograms can show different kinds of statistics, making it possible to compare nations at a glance.

2 TEACH

Using the Skill Help students interpret this cartogram and reinforce the meaning of *gross domestic product* (GDP). Make sure that students understand that GDP includes the value of goods and services for which payment is exchanged. Many services—such as the work of homemakers and volunteers—are not part of GDP.

● **On a cartogram, what does it mean if a country is large? small?** *(It is rich in the factor measured; It is poor in it.)*

★**THINKING FURTHER:** *Making Conclusions* **Why does the cartogram distort the shapes and sizes of countries?** *(Real shape and size do not relate to comparative GDP.)*

Resource **REMINDER**

Practice and Project Book: *p. 102*
Transparency: *Map 19*
Technology: *Adventure Time!* CD-ROM

Geography Skills

Using Cartograms

VOCABULARY
gross domestic product
cartogram

WHY THE SKILL MATTERS

The Industrial Revolution had a great impact on the economy of Great Britain and eventually on the entire world. As more countries built factories and trade increased, the economies of the world became connected. A price increase on cotton in the Americas, for example, affected textile factories and buyers of textiles throughout the world.

To understand these effects it is important to be able to measure and compare economic information. Suppose that you want to learn about a country's gross domestic product, or GDP. GDP is the total value of goods and services produced by a country during a certain period, usually one year. You might look up a country's GDP on an economic table.

Suppose you want to compare the GDPs of different countries. You could use a cartogram. A cartogram is a special kind of map used to present economic and other kinds of information. Cartograms are especially useful for comparing information about many countries.

USING THE SKILL

Most maps show the shapes of land as they look from above. You read about the different ways map makers project these shapes onto flat surfaces in the Using Map Projections Skills Lesson, on page 432. Physical maps, political maps, and historical maps all show countries or continents in relation to their actual size. On a cartogram, however, the size of a country is not related to the country's physical size, but rather to the information that is being compared. For example, on a cartogram showing populations of countries, China would appear as the biggest country on the map. This is because China has the largest population in the world.

The cartogram on this page shows the GDP of all of the countries in the world. The larger a country appears on this map, the greater is the value of all the goods and services produced by its economy. We see on political maps that Russia is the largest country in physical size. Does Russia also have the greatest GDP?*

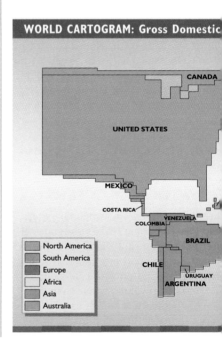

WORLD CARTOGRAM: Gross Domestic

CANADA

UNITED STATES

MEXICO

COSTA RICA

COLOMBIA

VENEZUELA

BRAZIL

CHILE

URUGUAY

ARGENTINA

- North America
- South America
- Europe
- Africa
- Asia
- Australia

506   *no

READING STRATEGIES & LANGUAGE DEVELOPMENT

CONTEXT CLUES Refer the class to the terms *gross domestic product,* or *GDP,* and *cartogram.* Help students see that each is defined by a declarative sentence after it is first named. Point out that there are other clues to broaden our understanding of these terms. We are told that GDP is available on an economic table, and we learn that cartograms are useful for comparing information. Explain to the class that it is important to look beyond direct definitions to recognize additional context clues to support word meanings and thus enrich our understanding of them.

WORD ORIGINS Once again, refer the class to *gross domestic product* and ask them to define *domestic.* Have them look it up in the dictionary to trace its origin (from the Latin *domus,* meaning "home") and have them relate *domestic* to "home."

Helping yourself

- **Cartograms are useful for studying and comparing information about different countries.**
- **The size of a country in a cartogram refers to information about that country.**
- **Compare information about countries by comparing their sizes.**

TRYING THE SKILL

In the last lesson you read that the Industrial Revolution began in Great Britain and then spread throughout Europe and to the Americas. You will read in the next lesson that it also spread to Japan. The influence of the Industrial Revolution is still felt today. For example, many of the countries with the greatest GDPs were among the first to build factories over 100 years ago. Which country has the largest GDP in the world? Which regions have countries with smaller GDPs? Why do you think this is so?*

REVIEWING THE SKILL

1. How are cartograms different from other kinds of maps?

2. How are cartograms useful for comparing countries?

3. Look at the cartogram on this page. Which country has the second-largest GDP?

4. Britain was the birthplace of the Industrial Revolution. Does this country still have the world's biggest GDP? Is its GDP greater or smaller than Germany's?

5. What other kinds of information could be presented in a cartogram?

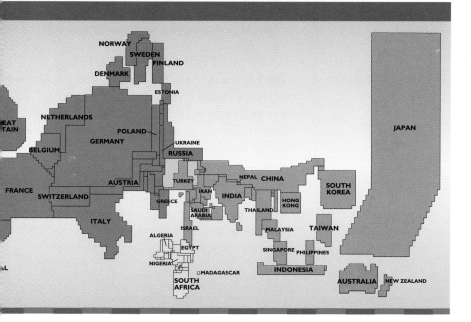

NORWAY
SWEDEN
FINLAND
DENMARK
ESTONIA
GREAT BRITAIN
NETHERLANDS
POLAND
GERMANY
BELGIUM
UKRAINE
RUSSIA
FRANCE
AUSTRIA
SWITZERLAND
TURKEY
NEPAL CHINA
IRAN
GREECE
INDIA
SAUDI ARABIA
THAILAND
HONG KONG
SOUTH KOREA
JAPAN
ITALY
ISRAEL
ALGERIA
EGYPT
MALAYSIA
TAIWAN
NIGERIA
SINGAPORE PHILIPPINES
MADAGASCAR
SOUTH AFRICA
INDONESIA
AUSTRALIA NEW ZEALAND

The United States; regions of the world which the Industrial Revolution reached later tend to have smaller GDPs.

507

Trying the Skill Again refer students to *Helping Yourself.*

- **How does the United States rank in GDP across the world? How do you know?** *(It has the largest GDP; it covers the largest space.)*

- **How does this cartogram show different continents?** *(It uses colors.)*

- **How do the continents of Europe, Africa, and South America rank in terms of actual land size? How do they rank in GDP?** *(1. Africa, 2. South America, 3. Europe; 1. Europe, 2. South America, 3. Africa)*

★**THINKING FURTHER:** *Making Connections* **What path did the Industrial Revolution follow? How does this cartogram reflect that path?** *(England to Europe to the United States; all areas with high GDPs)*

3 CLOSE

SUM IT UP

Call on students to make up a phrase to use when they interpret a cartogram (for example, "The larger the size, the richer in the factor measured. The smaller the size, the poorer in it.")

EVALUATE
✓ **Answers to Reviewing the Skill**

1. Other kinds of maps show countries in relation to actual size; cartograms show their size in relation to some other measurable factor.

2. They show at a glance how rich or poor countries are in some factor.

3. Japan

4. No; its GDP is smaller than Germany's.

5. Accept any factor that can be measured in numbers. (Examples: population, volume or value of goods that are manufactured or exported)

 Technology CONNECTION

ADVENTURE TIME! CD-ROM
Have students consider relative economic wealth of countries in *Explore* on the *Adventure Time!* CD-ROM.

MEETING INDIVIDUAL NEEDS

RETEACHING (Easy) Have students look in a current almanac to find the populations of Canada, the United States, and Mexico. Then have them draw a cartogram of the part of North America these nations fill, showing their size in relation to their populations.

EXTENSION (Average) Have students make up a fictitious continent on which there are at least six countries. Tell them to name the countries and to assign each one a population. Then have them draw a cartogram of their continent showing how the countries relate to one another in terms of size of population.

ENRICHMENT (Challenging) Refer students to South America on the cartogram. Have them find in an almanac the populations of the ten countries shown there, and then draw a cartogram showing their comparative populations.

LESSON 4

PAGES 508–513

Lesson Overview
In the latter half of the 1800s, Japan transformed itself from an isolated, feudal state into an industrial, imperial world power.

Lesson Objectives
★ Explain why Japan changed its course.

★ Describe the steps it took to transform itself.

⭐ 1 PREPARE

MOTIVATE Have students locate Japan on a map. Then ask them to recall Japan as described in Chapter 14. (It had isolated itself.) Have two students do the *Read Aloud,* one reading the quote, the other as narrator. What striking change does the quote reveal? (Japan was opening itself to the West.)

SET PURPOSE What could have brought on this about-face? Ask students if they can figure out what is shown in the illustration. (Commodore Perry's landing in Japan, a woodblock by Hiroshige) Refer students to the *Read to Learn* question; ask them to explore the lesson to find out how change occurred. Preview the *Vocabulary.*

⭐ 2 TEACH

Understanding THE BIG PICTURE
Help students see that contact brought change.

● **Did Japan open itself up again voluntarily? Explain.** *(No, in the 1850s, it was forced to reopen.)*

★**THINKING FURTHER:** *Predicting*
Based on the information on this page, how do you predict Japan will change? *(Possible answer: Japan will again borrow from other cultures.)*

Resource REMINDER

Practice and Project Book: *p. 103*

Anthology: *Clara's Diary, pp. 139–140*

Technology: *Adventure Time!* CD-ROM

Focus Activity

READ TO LEARN
How did Japan change during the Meiji Restoration?

VOCABULARY
- imperialism
  Meiji Restoration
- bureaucracy

PEOPLE
- Matthew C. Perry
- Meiji

PLACES
- Tokyo

508

| 1700 | 1750 | 1800 | 1854 | 1912 |

The Rise of Industrial Japan

Read Aloud
"We recognize the excellence of Western civilization. We value the Western theories of rights, liberty, and equality; and we respect Western philosophy and morals. . . . Above all, we esteem Western science, economics, and industry. These, however, ought not to be adopted simply because they are Western; they ought to be adopted only if they can contribute to Japan's welfare."

This statement was written in a Japanese newspaper in 1889. It expressed the feelings of many Japanese citizens at that time.

THE BIG PICTURE
In the 1630s, as you read in Chapter 14, the Tokugawa shogun had closed Japan to Western influences—influences of Europe and the United States. Only one Western ship was allowed to enter Japan each year. Japanese could not, under punishment of death, travel outside the country.

By the middle 1800s Western nations had adopted a policy of imperialism. Imperialism is the extension of a nation's power over other lands by military, political, or economic means. It was at this time, in the 1850s, that Japan was forced to reopen its borders.

SHELTERED INSTRUCTION

READING STRATEGIES & LANGUAGE DEVELOPMENT

SEQUENCE Review the definitions of *sequence* and *chronological order*. To help students review the lesson concept, have them skim the lesson and jot down the section headings and subheadings. Then have students create K-W-L charts to focus on facts they want to learn about the rise of industrial Japan. Encourage students to complete the chart as they read. **[SDAIE STRATEGY: METACOGNITIVE DEVELOPMENT]**

SYNONYMS Refer students to the *Read Aloud* and point out that the writer of the quote has used a device called parallel construction to make the key points—the first four independent clauses all begin with *we* as the subject of an active verb. Also point out that the parallelism is reinforced by the fact that three of the verbs—*value, respect, esteem*—are synonyms.

OPENING A CLOSED COUNTRY

After the 1630s almost every foreign ship that sailed to Japan for any reason was turned away. Although many ships from Europe and the United States sailed near Japan, few made contact with the Japanese.

Arrival of the Western Fleet

By the 1850s, however, the foreign pressure on Japan to reopen its borders increased. Many Western nations were seeking markets for new, factory-made goods. The United States, especially, wanted to sail its ships to Japan. During this time many American ships crossed the Pacific to hunt whales for oil. Japan would provide a perfect resting stop for these ships. The United States was also expanding its trade with China. Japan was located along the sea routes from California to China's ports.

In 1853 the United States government sent four warships to Japan. They were commanded by Commodore Matthew C. Perry. Perry carried a letter from President Millard Fillmore. The letter said that the United States wanted to be friends with Japan. "But no friendship can long exist," warned the letter, "unless Japan ceases to act toward Americans as if they were her enemies." Perry said he would return the next year for a response. Perry returned to Japan in 1854. This time he sailed eight warships into Edo Bay. The Japanese realized they could not match the firepower of these ships and agreed to meet with Commodore Perry.

Japanese leaders agreed to open two ports to American ships. The ships could stop at these ports to pick up supplies as they crossed the Pacific. Britain, France, Russia, and Holland also made trade agreements with the Japanese after Perry opened the door to trade with Japan.

The arrival of Matthew Perry (left) pushed Japan to negotiate a trade agreement with the United States.

The Granger Collection

OPENING A CLOSED COUNTRY

Point out to the class that not only did Japan turn away any ships that sailed to it, but it also treated any shipwrecked sailors who washed up on its shores very badly, often imprisoning them in cages. Nations whose sailors suffered shipwreck wanted the Japanese to treat their men more humanely.

Discussing Arrival of the Western Fleet Refer the class to the illustration of Perry's fleet arriving.

• *Why did the United States want Japan to reopen its borders?* (to turn Japan into a new market for U.S. goods and a safe haven where U.S. ships could resupply on long Pacific voyages)

• *What method did the U.S. use to persuade the Japanese?* (President Millard Fillmore sent Commodore Matthew C. Perry and four warships to make the request.)

• *How did the Japanese react to this request?* (They agreed to open two ports for trade and resupply.)

★THINKING FURTHER: *Making Decisions* **Would you say that President Fillmore's message might more accurately be called a request or a demand? Why?** *(Students will probably judge it a demand, since it was backed up by four, then eight warships with firepower Japan could not match.)*

BACKGROUND INFORMATION

ABOUT COMMODORE PERRY'S ARRIVAL

• Perry's fleet of ships that steamed into the harbor struck terror in the hearts of the Japanese, who called them "black ships of evil mien [look]" and were mystified about how these ships moved without sails or oars and why they belched black smoke.

• The fleet's arrival was not a total surprise to Japanese authorities. A Japanese spy had already informed them of Perry's mission.

• Nevertheless, thousands of Japanese fled Edo at the sight of the fleet, sure that the ships' guns trained on their city would destroy their homes.

• On Perry's second arrival, he brought with him not only a larger fleet but also a variety of gifts: a telegraph with almost a mile of wire, a telescope, several clocks, and a variety of firearms.

• By far, the most popular gift he brought was a miniature train, accurate in every detail. Its locomotive was one fourth the size of a real one and it ran on 370 feet of circular track. It created a sensation as Japanese dignitaries crowded into its little passenger car for a 20-mile-an-hour ride.

• The Japanese also were enthralled by Western dress, eagerly seeking "to possess themselves of anything that pertained to the dress of their visitors, and showed a particular passion for buttons."

509

THE MEIJI RESTORATION

To prepare the class for the "restoration," review with them what they learned in Chapter 14, that the shogun, not the emperor, was the real ruling power in Japan.

Discussing A New Government
Help students assess the revolution in Japan's society and government.

- *What Japanese leader had made the agreements to open Japan to Western countries?* (the shogun)

- *What happened to the shogun as a result?* (Samurai groups took away his power and gave it to the emperor, who was named Meiji.)

- *How was this action both a revolution and a restoration?* (It was a revolt against the shogun and a restoration of real ruling power to the emperor.)

- *What steps did Japan take to abolish feudalism?* (It bought lords' land and put it in the hands of the emperor, it made the lords regional governors under a central government, and it disbanded the samurai and created a modern army in their place.)

- *What happened to Japan's seat of government?* (The emperor moved from Kyoto into the former shogun's palace in Edo, renamed Tokyo.)

- *Who ran the new government?* (The emperor was its official head, and a bureaucracy of many ministers ran daily government business.)

- *What did the Charter Oath promise?* (that all Japanese would have a say in government and that old customs would be traded for new ones borrowed from the outside world)

★THINKING FURTHER: *Making Conclusions Why might you conclude that Japan was on its way to becoming a democratic country?* (It had a new constitution and a parliament, called the Diet.)

The emperor Meiji (above) moved to the imperial palace (left) in Tokyo after the shogun was overthrown in 1868.

THE MEIJI RESTORATION

The opening of Japan to foreign trade shook Japanese society. Many leaders opposed the shogun's agreements with Western countries. They believed Japan was giving too much away. A few Europeans and Americans living in Japan were attacked and killed.

A New Government

In 1868 the disagreement with the shogun grew into a revolt. Leaders of several samurai groups took over the shogun's palace in Kyoto. They returned control of Japan to the emperor, who had long been powerless in the Tokugawa government. Since the emperor's name was Meiji (MAY JEE), this event is known as the Meiji Restoration. While the uprising was really a revolution against the shogun, it was called a restoration because power was restored to the emperor.

The new Japanese government began to adopt foreign ways of governing. The feudal system was abolished. Lords became regional governors for the new central government. Lords also had to give all of their land to the emperor in exchange for money.

A modern army was created, and the samurai lost their special right to carry swords. Many samurai had to look for jobs as farmers or merchants. The emperor moved from Kyoto to what had been the shogun's palace in Edo. Edo was renamed Tokyo, which means "eastern capital" in Japanese.

Although the emperor was now the official head of Japanese government, leaders called ministers made most decisions. They controlled a large

510

CITIZENSHIP★

UNDERSTANDING GOVERNMENT Did Japan become a democracy?

- Japan became a constitutional monarchy with a two-house legislature, but only a small percentage of the people could vote.

- The prime minister and cabinet ministers were responsible, not to the people, but only to the emperor, who was regarded as divine.

- The army and navy had strong control over government policy.

SECOND-LANGUAGE SUPPORT

READING STRATEGIES An important skill for second-language learners is learning to skim for main ideas. Draw attention to p. 508. Read *The Big Picture* aloud, then model skimming techniques by looking for key people, dates, and events. Have students work with English-proficient partners to turn key words and phrases into main-idea statements.

bureaucracy. A bureaucracy is a large organization that runs the daily business of government. The new central government issued a declaration called the Charter Oath. This document declared that all Japanese would be given a say in their government. It also stated that old customs would be abandoned and "knowledge shall be sought throughout the world." In 1889 Japan had a new constitution and a parliament called the Diet (DIE et). The island nation was entering a new era.

Changes in Japan

This was not the first time that Japan looked to the outside for new ideas. Buddhism from China and Korea, and Confucianism from China, had been important parts of Japanese culture for centuries. Now, to learn about Western cultures, the Japanese government sent hundreds of students to the United States and Europe. Most studied such subjects as shipbuilding and navigation that would make Japan stronger. Some studied medicine and other subjects that would help Japanese people.

The Japanese government paid foreigners for expert advice on building railways, running factories, and sailing steamships. By 1889 telegraph lines and railroads linked all major cities. On steamships built in new shipyards, Japan began to export silk and tea to Europe and the United States. The first factories made silk textiles, but soon cotton mills were also built.

As contact with other cultures continued, styles of dress changed too. People began to wear suits or dresses instead of Japanese-style kimonos. In 1873 one person reported that he had seen a man wearing a samurai outfit in Tokyo. The man was stared at because

his clothes seemed so strange. The samurai hairstyle, with hair pulled up on top, quickly went out of style. The new government built buildings in Western styles of architecture. Some people even began to eat beef and other Western foods.

These changes broke down many Japanese feudal customs. For example, the strict separation between social classes became blurred. A foreign visitor described the attitude of many farmers:

In the old days the farmer did not complain; he thought his lot could not be changed. He was forbidden to adopt a new calling and he was restricted by law to a frugal way of living. Now farmers can be soldiers, merchants, or officials, and can live as they please. They begin to compare their standard of living with that of other callings.

Links to ART

From East to West

The flow of information between Japan and the West ran in both directions. Many artists in Europe and the United States became interested in Japanese art, particularly the colorful prints called Ukiyo-e. Artists such as Vincent van Gogh, Claude Monet, and James Whistler adapted many of the colors and styles of these prints. In fact, the French coined a term—*japonisme* (jap oh NEEZ mah)— to describe this use of Japanese artistic styles.

You can find art books in your library showing paintings by the artists listed above. Find also Japanese woodblock prints, such as the one by Hiroshige on page 514. How were European and Japanese styles similar and how were they different?

Discussing Changes in Japan Review the recurrent theme of Japan's cultural borrowing.

- *How was activity during the Meiji Restoration like a repetition of earlier Japanese history?* (Once again, as it had earlier done with China, Korea, and India, Japan sent people out to other parts of the world and brought experts in to teach new ideas.)

- *In what ways did Japan borrow from the Industrial Revolution and create its own industrial revolution?* (by finding out how to build and run railways, factories, steamships, and telegraph lines)

- *In what ways did social life change in Japan as a result of borrowing from the West?* (Clothing, hairstyles, and even diet changed to Western modes, and social class lines broke down.)

★THINKING FURTHER: *Compare and Contrast How would you compare and contrast Japan before and after Perry?* (Encourage students to put themselves in the place of the Japanese who lived before the Meiji Restoration and try to look at it through those eyes— the differences will be staggering.)

Technology CONNECTION

ADVENTURE TIME! CD-ROM
Enrich Chapter 17 with *Revolutions Change the World* on the *Adventure Time!* CD-ROM.

511

CURRICULUM CONNECTION

LINKS TO ART: FROM EAST TO WEST Encourage students to consult a library catalog to find art history books that tell them more about how Japanese art influenced Impressionist and Post-Impressionist painters and write brief reports.

BACKGROUND INFORMATION

ABOUT THE "CIVILIZATION BALL SONG" By 1879, the drive to Westernize was so strong that Japanese children were singing the "Civilization Ball Song." With each bounce of a ball, they sang out one of ten desirable Western things: gas lamps, steam engines, horse-drawn carriages, cameras, telegraphs, lightning rods, newspapers, schools, a postal service, and steamboats.

CITIZENSHIP★

LINKING PAST AND PRESENT The agents Japan sent out during the Meiji Restoration to learn what to adopt from the world were not the first, nor would they be the last.

- In the 1950s, Japan was eager to get into electronic technology, in which the U.S. was the world leader.

- The U.S. government encouraged American manufacturers to sell new electronic technology to Japan to help that war-torn nation get back on its economic feet.

- Soon Japanese engineers, jokingly called "antennas," spread out into American electronics firms in search of new technology. Within a dozen years, Japan had become a world leader in electronics manufacture.

EXPANSION OF JAPAN

Use the map on this page and the graph on p. 513 to reinforce the text.

Use the map on this page and the graph on p. 513 to reinforce the text.

More CHART WORK

Refer students to the line graph on p. 513 and encourage them to work back and forth between text and graph.

- **What impact did Japan have on world trade between 1883 and 1912?** *(It more than doubled the volume of world trade.)*

- **Based on the graph, about how much did Japan's GDP increase during roughly the same period?** *(It nearly doubled, from close to $2 billion to almost $4 billion.)*

- ★THINKING FURTHER: *Making Conclusions* **How did Japan show it knew its own economic power?** *(by demanding and getting fairer trade treaties from other nations)*

Discussing Military Activity Overseas Point out that Japan began seeking an empire as the Western powers had.

- **How did Japan put itself on the path to empire?** *(by attacking China and taking control of Korea and Taiwan)*

- **How did Japan prove itself to be a major naval power?** *(by defeating the powerful Russian navy)*

More MAP WORK

Refer students to the map; encourage them to work with the text and map.

- **Where was the most important battle of Japan's war with Russia fought?** *(the Tsushima Straits)*

- **What island prize did Japan take from Russia?** *(half of Sakhalin Island as well as land on the mainland)*

- **Where is it located on the map?** *(north of Japan's Hokkaido Island)*

- ★THINKING FURTHER: *Making Conclusions* **Why might you conclude that Japan was on its way to spreading its military power in Asia?** *(Its decade of conquest hints at its continuing on this path.)*

EXPANSION OF JAPAN

Japan changed quickly because of the Meiji Restoration. The country soon became a military and economic power. Between 1883 and 1912 an increase in Japanese exports more than doubled world trade. In the 1890s Japanese leaders began to change unequal trade treaties they had signed years before.

GROWTH OF JAPAN, 1870-1905

1870
1874-1875
1905

RUSSIA
SAKHALIN ISLAND
KURIL ISLANDS
HOKKAIDO
Sea of Japan
JAPAN
KOREA
HONSHU
CHINA
Tokyo
Korea Strait
Kyoto
KYUSHU
SHIKOKU
PACIFIC OCEAN
RYUKYU IS.
TAIWAN
0 250 500 Miles
0 250 500 Kilometers

MAP WORK

Japanese wealth and military power led to expansion into neighboring territories.

1. In which direction did Japan expand?
2. What body of water separates Japan from Korea?

Today bullet trains (right) run the length of the main Japanese island, Honshu.

512

Through all these changes Japan grew stronger and kept its own identity.

Military Activity Overseas

Japan soon began to show its power overseas. In 1894 Japan invaded Korea, which had long been occupied by China. China demanded that Japan remove its troops. Japan refused. Soon, Japan controlled most of the Korean Peninsula and the surrounding seas. Japan continued its push into Asia, attacking the Chinese mainland. In 1895 a treaty gave Japan control of Korea as well as the island of Taiwan.

In 1904 Japan entered into war against another neighbor—Russia. The most important battle of this war was in the stormy seas of the Tsushima (tsoo SHEE muh) Straits, which are part of the Korean Strait. There, Japan's navy destroyed the powerful Russian

CURRICULUM CONNECTION

LINKS TO MATH In the line graph, explain that when a figure is stated as 2,000 million, six zeros (for the million) must be added to it. Thus, 2,000 million becomes 2,000,000,000, or 2 billion.

GLOBAL CONNECTION

GOING FAR AFIELD FOR MILITARY EXPERTISE When Japan decided to create a new military to protect itself from, and compete with, the West, it sent out agents to find the best military models.

- It decided that Britain provided the best naval model, so it copied the British Navy in everything from ships to ranks to uniforms, and had British naval officers train naval personnel.
- It found that Germany provided the best army model, so it imported German officers to train army personnel.

havy. The war was costly for both sides, but the Japanese victory caused the rest of the world to notice Japan's new strength. When the two countries signed a peace treaty in 1905, Japan gained land from Russia on the Asian mainland as well as half of Sakhalin Island. Look at the map on page 512 to see new lands controlled by Japan.

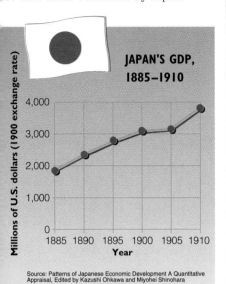

JAPAN'S GDP, 1885–1910

Source: Patterns of Japanese Economic Development A Quantitative Appraisal, Edited by Kazushi Ohkawa and Miyohei Shinohara

GRAPH WORK

After the Meiji Restoration Japan's economy began a period of rapid expansion.

1. Between which years shown did the Gross Domestic Product (GDP) increase the most?

2. By about how much did Japan's GDP increase between 1885 and 1910?

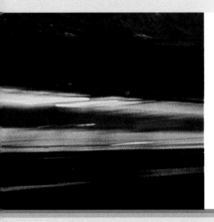

WHY IT MATTERS

The Emperor Meiji died in 1912, bringing to an end a remarkable era in Japanese history. During his nearly 50-year reign, Japan emerged from two centuries of isolation and feudal rule. It grew to become the most powerful military and economic force in Asia.

Japan's expansion did not end with the Meiji era. The small island nation grew even more powerful. When most of the world went to war in the 1940s, as you will read in Chapter 18, Japan played a major part in the conflict.

Reviewing Facts and Ideas

MAIN IDEAS

- In 1854 the United States forced Japan to reopen to outside trade.
- In 1868 the Meiji Restoration created a new central government, with the Emperor as its head.
- Japan rapidly modernized, borrowing many ideas from other cultures.
- By the 1890s Japan had become a powerful industrial country and began to expand into mainland Asia.

THINK ABOUT IT

1. Why did Japan have so little contact with the outside world under the Tokugawa Shogun?

2. How did Commodore Perry force Japan to begin trade with the West?

3. FOCUS What did Japan do to interact with the countries of the West?

4. THINKING SKILL In what ways did the establishment of a new government in 1868 *affect* Japan's relationship with other countries?

5. GEOGRAPHY How did Japan's island location help it first become isolated and later become industrialized?

513

Discussing WHY IT MATTERS Discuss the heritage of the Meiji restoration.

- **How long did Meiji rule last?** *(1912 minus 1868 = 44 years)*

★**THINKING FURTHER: Making Conclusions** *What does the national transformation accomplished in this short time tell you about Japan?* (that it is energetic, dedicated to change, adaptable, competitive, successful)

3 CLOSE

MAIN IDEAS
Call on students for answers.

- **How did the Meiji Restoration change Japan's government in 1864?** *(transferred power from the shogun to the emperor and created a central government)*

- **Why did Japan do a great deal of cultural borrowing in the late 1800s?** *(to modernize itself and strengthen itself economically and militarily)*

- **Where did Japan stand industrially and militarily by the 1890s?** *(It was industrialized and it began expanding through military force.)*

EVALUATE
√ **Answers to Think About It**

1. It had decided to isolate itself from all foreign contact.
Recall Details

2. by displaying a well-armed naval fleet
Make Conclusions

3. It began a period of cultural borrowing and heavy trade.
Form Generalizations

4. It opened the Japanese up to ideas and goods from other countries and set them on a path to trade, industrialization, and militarization.
Main Idea

5. As an archipelago, it was less accessible to people moving in on it. When it industrialized, its island location gave it water highways to anywhere on Earth.
Five Themes of Geography: Location

Write About It Ask students to write a paragraph in which they describe what they think was the single greatest change Japan made.

MEETING INDIVIDUAL NEEDS

RETEACHING (Easy) Have students choose some change that Japan underwent during the Meiji Restoration. Have them create a color drawing entitled "Japan: Before and After" illustrating that change; for example, a samurai warrior (before), a Japanese soldier (after).

EXTENSION (Average) Have students create a travel brochure entitled "Welcome to the New Japan." In it, have them illustrate and describe sights the traveler will see in Meiji Japan.

ENRICHMENT (Challenging) Divide the class into several groups and assign each group a different area of Japanese national life—government, industry, the military, trade, art, fashion. Have each group research their aspect to learn more about it before and after the Meiji Restoration. Have them prepare and give illustrated presentations of their assigned areas for the class.

CITIZENSHIP
Viewpoints
PAGES 514–515

Lesson Objective

★ Compare and contrast conflicting points of view on opening a culture to new influences.

Identifying the Issue Help students to see that people can honestly disagree about which is the better path for a country to take into the future.

● **Why was there heated debate over whether Japan should open itself to new influences in the 1850s?** *(Pressure from the West forced Japan to evaluate its own culture and determine what it wanted to be and what it might be allowed to be.)*

Discussing Three Different Viewpoints Have students read the *Viewpoints* on p. 515.

LORD II NAOSUKE

● **What does Lord Ii Naosuke mean by "foreign states"?** *(industrialized foreign countries of the West)*

● **What achievements of the West does he fear?** *(advanced ships and navigation as well as weapons and military forces that were far more powerful than Japan's)*

● **What does he think will happen if the West uses these strengths against Japan?** *(great calamity, disaster for Japan)*

AIZAWA SEISHISAI

● **Whom does Seishisai criticize in the debate?** *(those who would give in to foreign demands)*

● **What action does he think the government should take?** *(to order all citizens to resist and smash the foreign foes)*

CITIZENSHIP
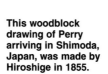
VIEWPOINTS

This woodblock drawing of Perry arriving in Shimoda, Japan, was made by Hiroshige in 1855.

1853: What did the Japanese think about opening their country to the West?

In July 1853, as you read in the last lesson, Commodore Matthew Perry sailed into Edo Bay and demanded that Japan be opened to trade with western nations. His arrival added urgency to a debate that had been going on in Japan for years.

Many Japanese people said that opening the country was too great a risk. They felt that their nation should maintain its own culture, without Western influences. A scholar named Fujita Toko wrote that once foreign ideas took hold there would be no way to restore Japanese traditions.

Japanese Lord Ii Naosuke believed that Japan should strengthen and protect itself by setting aside some of its feudal customs and learning from the West. He explained that the technology of Western nations made them strong enough to overpower Japan.

A Japanese writer stated that Japan should remain isolated. As you will read in the second viewpoint, he favored attacking Westerners who were in Japan.

Read and consider three viewpoints on this issue.

514

BACKGROUND INFORMATION

MORE ABOUT THE DEBATE

● As students have learned, the shogun lost power as a result of making agreements to open Japan to the West.

● The shogun's power had been weakened even before these agreements were made.

● When the controversy was just beginning, opponents of any concessions to the West had introduced the slogan "Revere the emperor, expel the barbarians!" signaling that power should be taken from the shogun and given to the emperor.

● By 1868, the emperor had reclaimed power, but the "barbarians" had not been expelled. Instead, Japan had begun to adopt many of their ways.

Three DIFFERENT Viewpoints

1 LORD II NAOSUKE
Feudal lord, Excerpt from a letter, 1847

The condition of foreign states is not what it once was: they have invented the steamship and introduced radical changes in the art of navigation. They have also built up their armies to a state of great efficiency and are possessed of war implements of great power and precision; in short, they have risen to be imposing powers. If we cling to our outdated systems, heaven only knows what mighty calamity may befall our empire.

2 AIZAWA SEISHISAI
Writer, Excerpt from New Proposals, 1825

Second-rate leaders, thinking only of easy peace, let the foreigners go unchecked. . . . They make the situation worse through half-hearted inaction. If, instead, the government issues orders to the entire nation to smash the foreigners whenever they come into sight and to treat them openly as our nation's foes, everyone high and low will push forward to enforce the order. This is a great opportunity. It must not be lost.

3 FUJITA TOKO
Scholar, 1849

Why should we not be able to defend our land against the invaders, though our defenses are not quite what we wish them to be? If once permitted, foreigners will soon try to win the hearts of the common people. If we suddenly find ourselves with the minds of our people loosened, our defenses neglected, the foreign religion (Christianity) gaining ground, what remedy would there be to reverse this awful state of things?

". . . our outdated systems . . ."

". . . treat them openly as our nation's foes . ."

". . . foreigners will soon try to win the hearts of the common people."

BUILDING CITIZENSHIP

1. What was the viewpoint of each person?
2. In what ways were some of the viewpoints alike? In what ways were they different?
3. What viewpoints might people have on this issue today?

SHARING VIEWPOINTS

Discuss what you agree with or disagree with about these viewpoints. Discuss why you think each speaker might feel as he did. Then as a class, write a statement that all three of the speakers might have agreed with in the Japanese debate over the opening of their country.

515

CITIZENSHIP ★

USING CURRENT EVENTS The conflict between pride and pragmatism is not so different from the conflict between cultural values and economic values that arose in the *Viewpoints* in Chapter 2 (pp. 38-39).

- Often one group wants to hang onto something in which it takes pride, while another group says it must be taken away to survive; for example, a sports team being sold from one city to another.
- Check the papers for any disputes that pit pride against pragmatism and bring the clippings in for class discussion and debate. Encourage students to offer any compromises they can think of that might resolve each conflict.

FUJITA TOKO

- **What does Toko fear will happen to the Japanese people if foreigners are admitted into Japan?** *(The Japanese people will begin to lose their culture.)*

- **What does he say Japan should do to prevent this?** *(resist the foreigners even in the face of superior forces)*

SUM IT UP
Encourage students to recognize that, even though the views differ, each person expresses an idea he believes is best for Japan.

EVALUATE
✓ **Answers to Building Citizenship**

1. Naosuke: accede to the more powerful foreigners to avoid disaster; Seishisai: take the opportunity to smash the foreigners; Toko: resist no matter what to save the culture.

2. Seishisai and Toko both vote for resistance as the only way to save Japanese culture; Naosuke says that resistance is useless and can bring only disaster to Japan.

3. While there are still isolationists in the world, probably most people would believe that it was neither wise nor even possible to cut themselves off from the "global village." The Japanese especially, with much of their wealth coming from foreign trade, probably would not want to be cut off from the rest of the world.

Sharing Viewpoints Invite students to offer their own viewpoints and help them identify and contrast the values that lie behind the speakers' viewpoints—the pragmatism of the speaker who bows to the inevitability of Western power, and the cultural pride that spurs the other speakers to preach resistance at any cost. All three speakers would probably agree that Japan has a culture that is well worth saving.

Debating Viewpoints As an extension, invite students to debate the values of pragmatism versus pride. When is resistance to the inevitable simply futile and when must people make a stand no matter what?

DISCUSSING MAJOR EVENTS Use the time line to reinforce the sequence in which major revolutionary events took place in the late 18th and the 19th century.

- *During what period did much of Latin America fight for independence from its European colonizers? (from 1791, with L'Ouverture's revolt, to 1821, with Mexico's independence)*

- *During what period did Japan undergo a major transformation? (from 1854, with its opening, to 1904, with its war against Russia, a major world power)*

- *What revolution, going on throughout this period, does the 1888 event reflect? How? (The railroad link reflects the Industrial Revolution, which made railroads possible.)*

Answers to THINKING ABOUT VOCABULARY

1. bureaucracy
2. Industrial Revolution
3. Latin America
4. absolute monarchy
5. cartogram
6. socialism
7. middle class
8. mestizo
9. aristocracy
10. revolution

Answers to THINKING ABOUT FACTS

1. Its meeting in 1789 triggered the Third Estate to write a constitution and form the National Assembly.

2. He spurred and led revolution in northern South America and became known as its "Liberator."

Resource **REMINDER**

Practice and Project Book: *p. 104*
Assessment Book: *Chapter 17 Test*
Technology: *Videodisc/*
Transparency: *Graphic Organizer, Cause-and-Effect Map*

CHAPTER 17 REVIEW

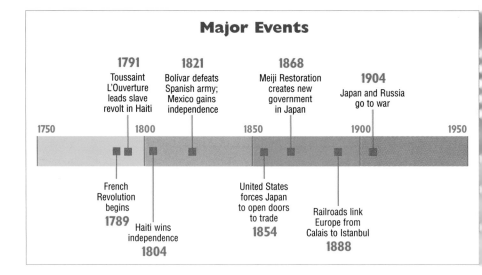

Major Events

1791 Toussaint L'Ouverture leads slave revolt in Haiti

1821 Bolívar defeats Spanish army; Mexico gains independence

1868 Meiji Restoration creates new government in Japan

1904 Japan and Russia go to war

1750 | 1800 | 1850 | 1900 | 1950

French Revolution begins **1789**

Haiti wins independence **1804**

United States forces Japan to open doors to trade **1854**

Railroads link Europe from Calais to Istanbul **1888**

THINKING ABOUT VOCABULARY

Number a sheet of paper from 1 to 10. Beside each number write the term from the list below that matches the statement.

absolute monarchy
aristocracy
bureaucracy
cartogram
Industrial Revolution

Latin America
mestizo
middle class
revolution
socialism

1. A large organization that runs the daily business of government
2. The period of rapid industrial and technological growth that began in England in the 1700s
3. The region south of the United States influenced by Spanish and Portuguese culture
4. A form of government in which a king or queen has complete power
5. A special map used to present economic and other kinds of information
6. A system of society based on ideas of Marx in which workers would own and control all property
7. A social class that includes merchants, lawyers, bankers, and business owners
8. A person of mixed Native American and European ancestry
9. A social class made up of nobles and their families
10. A sudden or great change

THINKING ABOUT FACTS

1. What role did the Estates General play in triggering the French Revolution?
2. What effect did Simón Bolívar have on South American history?
3. What were the main ideas of Karl Marx?
4. What part did Commodore Perry play in opening Japan to trade?
5. What does the time line above suggest about the possible influence of the French Revolution on events in Haiti and Latin America?

516

SECOND-LANGUAGE SUPPORT

TAKING NOTES Students should use their time lines as a way to organize the information in this chapter. Have students use their various graphic organizers, such as story maps *(p. 487)*, time lines, main idea statements *(p. 510)*, and semantic maps *(p. 504)* as they review the chapter. Ask students to evaluate how these graphic organizers helped them to understand the content of this chapter.

DRAMATIZATION Encourage second-language learners to take the story map they created about the French Revolution *(p. 487)* and dramatize part of it. They might create a scene written in their own words or form a tableau *(posed arrangement of characters with props and costumes)* to depict an important event.

THINK AND WRITE

WRITING AN ANALYSIS

Write a paragraph about the Industrial Revolution. Describe both the progress it brought and the social problems it created.

WRITING A JOURNAL ENTRY

Suppose you were alive during the French Revolution. Choose one event: (1) the meeting of the National Assembly (2) the storming of the Bastille or (3) the execution of the king and queen. Write a journal entry about what you saw or know happened.

WRITING AN EXPLANATION

Describe the changes that took place in Japan during the 45-year reign of the Emperor Meiji. Reread pages 510–511. Then write a short essay about the reasons behind the emergence of Japan from two centuries of isolation and feudal rule.

APPLYING GEOGRAPHY SKILLS

USING CARTOGRAMS

1. What is a cartogram?

2. Look at the cartogram on pages 506–507. Name in order the ten countries with highest GDPs. On which continents are they located?

3. According to the cartogram, which five countries in Africa have the highest GDPs? Is Algeria's GDP greater or less than Singapore's?

4. Is India's GDP greater or less than Argentina's? Than Great Britian? Than South Africa's?

5. Why are cartograms useful?

3. He believed that the workers should own and control the factories in a classless society for which government was unnecessary.

4. He commanded the American fleet that sailed to Japan and, with his naval guns trained on it, demanded that Japan open itself to the West.

5. It suggests that the French Revolution's ideas about liberty prompted leaders like L'Ouverture and Bolívvar to liberate their lands from their colonial rulers.

Answers to
APPLYING GEOGRAPHY SKILLS

1. a special kind of map used to present economic and other kinds of information

2. (1) U.S. (North America); (2) Japan (Asia); (3) Germany, (4) France, (5) Italy, (6) U.K., (7) Spain (all Europe); (8) Canada (North America); (9) Brazil (South America); (10) China (Asia)

3. South Africa, Algeria, Egypt, Nigeria, and Tunisia; and Algeria's GDP is less than Singapore's.

4. greater than Argentina; less than U.K.; greater than South Africa

5. They help us to compare some kinds of statistical information about countries.

Summing Up the Chapter

Copy the cause-and-effect chart below on a separate sheet of paper. Review the chapter and fill in at least two effects for each cause listed. When you have filled in the information, use it to answer the question "What important changes came about because of revolutions in Europe, the Americas, and Japan?"

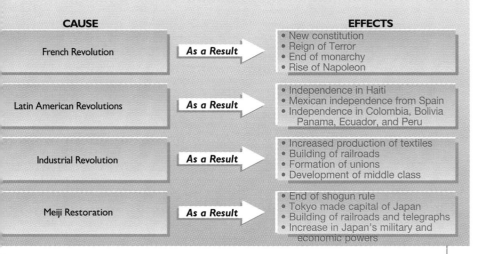

CAUSE		EFFECTS
French Revolution	As a Result	• New constitution • Reign of Terror • End of monarchy • Rise of Napoleon
Latin American Revolutions	As a Result	• Independence in Haiti • Mexican independence from Spain • Independence in Colombia, Bolivia Panama, Ecuador, and Peru
Industrial Revolution	As a Result	• Increased production of textiles • Building of railroads • Formation of unions • Development of middle class
Meiji Restoration	As a Result	• End of shogun rule • Tokyo made capital of Japan • Building of railroads and telegraphs • Increase in Japan's military and economic powers

517

Technology CONNECTION

VIDEODISC

Enrich Chapter 17 with the *Simón Bolívar* segment on the videodisc.

Search Frame 13293 Side B

SUGGESTIONS FOR SUMMING UP THE CHAPTER

After students have copied the cause-and-effect chart on a piece of paper, have them read each cause aloud and then discuss it briefly. Point out that the causes follow the same order as the lessons in the chapter. Suggested examples of effects appear on the reproduced pupil page above. When students have completed the cause-and-effect chart, encourage them to offer examples of what they have filled in. Which did they miss? Which might not really qualify as an effect? After this discussion, have students read the question posed aloud and then have them break it down into smaller questions, for example, How did the French Revolution change France? You may want to have students work together to produce a class answer to each question on the board or have them make up and write their own answers.

ASSESSING THINK AND WRITE: *For performance assessment, see Assessment Book, Chapter 17, pp. T97–T99.*

Answers to
THINKING ABOUT VOCABULARY

1. C	**6.** C
2. I, Triangular Trade	**7.** I, heliocentric
3. C	**8.** I, confederation
4. C	**9.** I, textile
5. Reign of Terror	**10.** I, missionary

Suggestions for
THINK AND WRITE

1. Have students reread the material on the Middle Passage on pages 474 and 475. Urge them to try to picture the scenes described and to put themselves in the place of an African living through them. Their perspectives might contrast those horrors with undisturbed village life back home.

2. Encourage students to reread whatever material they can about the life and times of the historical figure they choose. Urge them to think of themselves as TV interviewers, wanting to ask questions that would interest viewers. Have them first write these questions and then answer them, in character.

3. You may want to suggest that students contrast the riches and power of the First and Second Estates with the poverty and powerlessness of the Third to make their reasons for the French Revolution more compelling.

Suggestions for
BUILDING SKILLS

1. She is credible in that she has firsthand knowledge of the Reign of Terror, having lived through it, but her emotion perhaps causes her to exaggerate somewhat.

2. It suggests that the writer is much in favor of the Industrial Revolution and proud of its accomplishments.

3. Both writers show obvious distaste for conditions the Industrial Revolution created, stressing its drawbacks rather than accomplishments.

4. Answers may include the United States and Mexico, Brazil and its neighbors to its west, Costa Rica and its neighbor to its north, Thailand and its neighbor to its east.

UNIT 5 REVIEW

THINKING ABOUT VOCABULARY

Number a sheet of paper from 1 to 10. Decide whether the underlined word in each of the following statements correctly completes the sentence. If the word is correct, write **C** beside the number. If the word is incorrect, write **I** and then write the correct word to complete the sentence.

confederation	missionary
convert	Reign of Terror
divine right	sugarcane
heliocentric	textile
Meiji Restoration	Triangular Trade

1. The belief that a monarch's authority came from God was called <u>divine right</u>.

2. <u>Reign of Terror</u> is the name of the trade that developed between England, Africa, and North America in the 1600s.

3. To <u>convert</u> people is to win them over to one's point of view or beliefs.

4. The <u>Meiji Restoration</u> was the return to the throne of a Japanese emperor during a revolt against the shogun.

5. Enemies of the French Revolution were executed during a period called the <u>Triangular trade</u>.

6. <u>Sugarcane</u> is a tall grass with a thick, woody stem that contains the liquid source of sugar.

7. The <u>missionary</u> view, developed by Copernicus, Galileo, and Newton, states that the sun is the center of the universe.

8. A <u>textile</u> is a group of states that join together under a central government.

9. A <u>heliocentric</u> is a cloth that is woven or knitted.

10. A <u>confederation</u> tries to make other people see the truth of his or her religion.

518

THINK AND WRITE

WRITING ABOUT PERSPECTIVES

Suppose you were an African who crossed the Atlantic on a slave ship. Describe how your perspective would be different from an African who had never left home.

WRITING AN INTERVIEW

Suppose you could interview one person you read about in this unit. Write down your questions and his or her answers.

WRITING A PAMPHLET

Write a pamphlet explaining the reasons for the French revolution.

BUILDING SKILLS

1. **Analyzing credibility** How would you determine the credibility of the statement made by the woman who lived during the Reign of Terror? Look back at page 490.

2. **Analyzing credibility** Reread the excerpt on page 502. What does the point of view expressed suggest about the author?

3. **Analyzing credibility** Reread the two quotations on page 504. What is the point of view of these writers and how does it differ from the quote on page 502?

4. **Using cartograms** Look at the cartogram on page 506. Find three places in the world where rich and poor countries are located near each other.

5. **Using cartograms** The cartogram on page 506 shows the GDP of countries but *not* the average wealth of people in each country. Explain how people in a country with a relatively high GDP, like China, might actually be poorer than people in countries with lower GDPs but also fewer people. What kind of cartogram would give an accurate picture of the relative wealth of people in each country?

ONGOING UNIT PROJECT

OPTIONS FOR ASSESSMENT

This ongoing project, begun on page 450D, can be part of your assessment program, along with other forms of evaluation.

PLANNING Make sure children plan who the character is; where and when he/she lived; what he/she did. Set a time limit on length of scene—no more than 5 minutes.

SIGNS OF SUCCESS

- Children's scenes should show the main ideas in the lesson, how expansion of Europe and revolutions changed the world.

- Some costuming can be used, but the focus should be on the creativity of the story, characters, and dialogue. Children can pantomime some objects, and use paper/cardboard for others.

 FOR THE PORTFOLIO Scripts of the scenes and audience comments can be included in children's portfolios.

YESTERDAY, TODAY & *TOMORROW*

History has shown that some changes are brought about rapidly through revolution. Others are more gradual. What important changes do you think are taking place today? What changes do you think will take place in the future? What do you think the world will be like centuries from now? Explain your answers.

READING ON YOUR OWN

These are some books you might find at the library to help you learn more.

EXPLORER
by Rupert Matthews
This visual history with background information takes you from ancient to modern times through land, sea, air, and space.

THE INDUSTRIAL REVOLUTION
edited by John D. Clare
This illustrated book helps trace the technology that grew out of the Industrial Revolution.

THE MEIJI RESTORATION AND RISE OF MODERN JAPAN
by Monique Avakian
This book details Japan's transformation to a modern industrial and military power.

5. China's enormous population means that the GDP must support many more people than a country with half China's GDP but one tenth of its population. A cartogram showing wealth per person would give a more accurate picture.

Suggestions for YESTERDAY, TODAY & TOMORROW

To jog thinking about changes today, try to have pictures available of old telephones, typewriters, radios, and television sets as well as old trains, planes, and cars. This should prompt students to suggest major changes in communications and transportation. Also mention government, medicine, and science. For changes in the future, students may consider what they have seen or read in science fiction.

Suggestions for READING ON YOUR OWN

The first two of these books strongly reinforce the major social studies theme of change over time. The third captures the curiosity and spirit of adventure that drive humankind on to new knowledge about the world and the universe. Try to have these books on hand in class, as well as those included in the *Annotated Bibliography and Resources* in the Unit Organizer, p. 450B. Also encourage students to go to the library to find other books that treat similar themes. Ask each student to read one of the books and prepare a report on it. You may want to have students who have read books on the same theme, say, change over time, exploration, or explorers, to join together in a panel to discuss for the class's benefit how their different books dealt with the theme and what different approaches to it the books took.

UNIT 5 REVIEW PROJECT

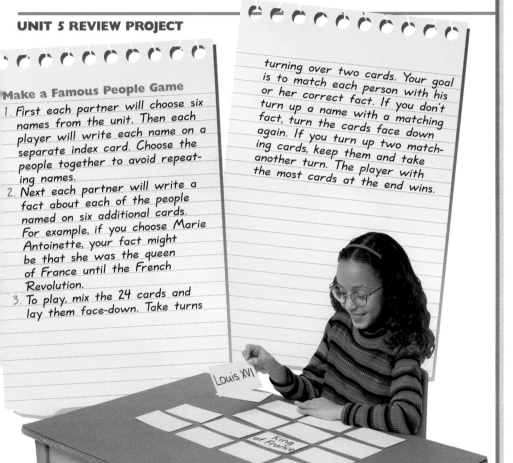

Make a Famous People Game

1. First each partner will choose six names from the unit. Then each player will write each name on a separate index card. Choose the people together to avoid repeating names.
2. Next each partner will write a fact about each of the people named on six additional cards. For example, if you choose Marie Antoinette, your fact might be that she was the queen of France until the French Revolution.
3. To play, mix the 24 cards and lay them face-down. Take turns turning over two cards. Your goal is to match each person with his or her correct fact. If you don't turn up a name with a matching fact, turn the cards face down again. If you turn up two matching cards, keep them and take another turn. The player with the most cards at the end wins.

UNIT 5 REVIEW PROJECT: *Make a Famous People Game*

COMPLETING AND PLAYING THE GAME
30 MINUTES OR LONGER *PARTNER*

OBJECTIVE: The game will encourage students to revisit the text and review what they have learned.

MATERIALS: index cards

- Have students pair up with partners. Give each pair 24 index cards, have them choose names of 12 famous people discussed in the unit and divide up the names so each one has 6.
- Explain that each partner will write the names of 6 people on 6 cards and a fact about each person on another 6 cards. Emphasize that the facts must be significant and specific enough so that each player will be able to

recognize matching names and facts. Each pair of students should have 24 cards.

- Instruct students to mix the cards and lay out the entire deck face down. Players take turns turning up two cards, attempting to match a name with a fact.

FOR THE PORTFOLIO Students may include selected names and facts in their portfolios.

OPTIONS FOR ASSESSMENT

This game can be part of your assessment program.

For more performance assessment and portfolio opportunities, see Assessment Book, Unit 5, p. T100.

6 UNIT ORGANIZER

A Century of Conflict

PAGES 520-635

UNIT OVERVIEW

Revolutions in Russia and China brought new communist governments to power. W
Wars I and II ended the old empires in Europe and began the Cold War between th
superpowers. New nations emerged from the European colonial possessions in Afr
India, and the Middle East. The end of the Cold War saw increased world economi
dependence.

ADVENTURES WITH NATIONAL GEOGRAPHIC
The Last Unknown Place **pp. 522-523**

UNIT PLANNING GUIDE

CHAPTER	SUGGESTED PACING	RESOURCES	ASSESSMENT
18 A World at War World Wars I and II ended the old empires and the rise of fascism in Europe, while revolutions in Russia and China brought communism to power, which resulted in the Cold War. pp. 524-563	10-11 days	• **Practice and Project Book,** pp. 105-111 • **Anthology,** pp. 142-157 • **Desk Map** • **Transparency:** Maps 20, Graphic Organizer, Sequence Train • **Technology:** Videodisc/Video Tape • **Technology:** *Adventure Time!* CD-ROM	• **Meeting Individual Needs,** pp. 531 539, 547, 549, 555, 561 • **Write About It,** 531, 539, 547, 549, 561 • **Chapter Review,** pp. 562-563 • **Assessment Book:** *Assessing Thin and Write, pp. T101-T103. Chapter Tests: Content, Skills, Writing*
19 New Nations Colonial possessions and new nations gained independence in Africa, India, and the Middle East, while the United States Army retreated from war in Vietnam. pp. 564-593	8-9 days	• **Practice and Project Book,** pp. 112-117 • **Anthology,** pp. 158-184 • **Desk Map** • **Transparency:** Graphic Organizer, Main-Idea Chart • **Technology:** Videodisc/Video Tape	• **Meeting Individual Needs,** pp. 571 573, 578, 585, 591 • **Write About It,** pp. 571, 578, 585, 5 • **Chapter Review,** pp. 592-593 • **Assessment Book:** *Assessing Thin and Write, pp. T104-T106. Chapter Tests: Content, Skills, Writing*
20 A Changing World The end of the Cold War brought together a divided Europe, while South Africa moved from apartheid to a majority-rule government. pp. 594-633	9-10 days	• **Practice and Project Book,** pp. 118-123 • **Anthology,** pp. 185-204 • **Transparency:** Graphic Organizer, Main-Idea Chart • **Technology:** Videodisc • **Technology:** *Adventure Time!* CD-ROM	• **Meeting Individual Needs,** pp. 603, 612, 621, 629 • **Write About It,** pp. 603, 612, 621, 6 • **Chapter Review,** pp. 632-633 • **Assessment Book:** *Assessing Thin and Write, pp. T107-T109. Chapter Tests: Content, Skills, Writing*
Unit 6 Review pp. 634-635	1-2 days	• **Geo Adventures Daily Geography Activities**	• **Unit 6 Project,** p. 635

McGRAW-HILL SCHOOL'S HOME PAGE at
☞ **http://www.mhschool.com**
contains on-line student activities
related to this unit.

FOR FURTHER SUPPORT
• **Language Support Handbook**
• **Standardized Test Support**

ANNOTATED BIBLIOGRAPHY

McGraw-Hill Adventure Books

Feldman, Eve. **Then and Now at Home.** The author traces popular inventions, entertainments, and other cultural phenomena of the twentieth century, decade by decade, from 1910 through the 1990s. **(Easy)**

Classroom Library

■ Toll, Nelly S. **Behind the Secret Window: A Memoir of a Hidden Childhood During World War Two.** New York: Dial Books, 1993. The autobiography of a young girl who survived Nazi-occupied Poland.

Student Books

Cooper, Floyd. **Mandela: From the Life of the South African Statesman.** New York: Philomel Books, 1996. A beautifully illustrated biography of one of the most influential political figures of our time. **(Average)**

■ Hautzig, Esther. **The Endless Steppe.** New York: HarperCollins Publishers, 1987. This story is about a family forced from their home in Poland, who live in exile for five years. **(Average)**

■ Hunter, Nigel. **Gandhi.** New York: Bookwright Press, 1986. This brief biography of Gandhi is accompanied by colorful photos. **(Easy)**

Huggett, Renee. **Growing Up in the First World War.** London: Batsford Academic and Educational, 1982. Photos and descriptions of events are presented by the people who experienced them. **(Challenging)**

Long, Cathryn J. **The Middle East in Search of Peace.** Brookfield, CT: The Millbrook Press, 1994. This book discusses the origins of the Arab-Israeli conflict and the hope for peace in the future. **(Average)**

■ Roberts, Jack L. **Nelson Mandela: Determined To Be Free.** Brookfield, CT: The Millbrook Press, 1995. Read about the man who became South Africa's first black president. **(Average)**

Whelan, Gloria. **Goodbye Vietnam.** New York: Alfred A. Knopf, 1992. A young girl and her family flee government terror. **(Average)**

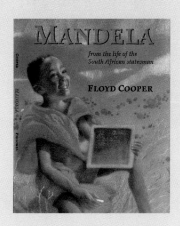

Teacher Books

Fritz, Jean. **China's Long March: 6,000 Miles of Danger.** G. P. Putnam's Sons, 1988. The Long March is described by the author, who interviewed survivors.

Kort, Michael. **The Cold War.** Brookfield, CT: The Millbrook Press, 1994. This is an examination of the long conflict between the communist world and the western democracies, from WW II until 1990.

Read Alouds

Haskett, Edythe Rance, ed. **Some Gold, a Little Ivory: Country Tales From Ghana and the Ivory Coast.** New York: The John Day Company, 1971. This collection of African folk tales reveals culture and traditions.

■ Nhuong, Huynh Quang. **The Land I Lost.** New York: Harper and Row, 1982. The author reminisces on life in Vietnam.

Technology Multimedia

The Firebird. Video. A Russian czar demands the Firebird and a princess. Story Lane Theater, Macmillan/McGraw-Hill. (800) 442–9685.

Number the Stars. Video. (Story 6) A family in Nazi-occupied Denmark helps a Jewish family to safety. Multimedia Literature. Macmillan/McGraw-Hill. (800) 442-9685.

The Middle East: A Closer Look. Videodisc. (17 min.) S95509-LASR. This is an overview of the geography and history of the Middle East. Society For Visual Education. (800) 829-1900.

The Rise and Fall of the Soviet Union. Video. No. XE1001. Learn about Russia, from Revolution through Cold War. Knowledge Unlimited. (800) 356-2303.

Free or Inexpensive Materials

For a free rental of a video called "Planting the Seeds of Peace," portraying teenagers and their perspectives on the Middle East conflict, send to: Church World Service; 28606 Phillips Street; P. O. Box 968; Elkhart, IN 46515.

■ *Book excerpted in the Anthology*

■ *Book featured in the student bibliography of the Unit Review*

☐ *National Geographic technology*

Ideas for Active Learning

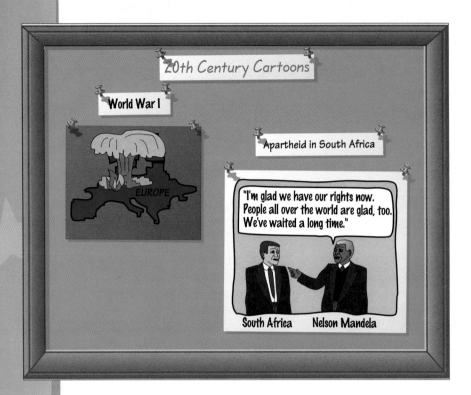

A Century of Conflict

Help students to create a bulletin board titled "20th Century Cartoons." Remind students that political cartoons often make fun of the leaders and ideologies involved in serious issues. Invite teams of students to create, or find and photocopy, political cartoons about some of the major conflicts that occurred from World War I to the present time. Students should post their cartoons on the bulletin board in chronological order. For each cartoon, ask volunteers to create a title on a piece of construction paper cut to the same size, and place it on the bulletin board at the top of the cartoon. Titles should give the name and date of the event to which the cartoon refers.

Thanks to: Myra Robinson, Ramirez Elementary, Lubbock, Texas

Cultural Fair Project

ON YOUR OWN   30 MINUTES OR LONGER

CURRICULUM CONNECTION   Language Arts

Materials: research books, index cards, notebooks, drawing paper, costumes, posterboard

1. Have students choose a culture to research for a project fair. They should write out goals of their research and choose a title.
2. Students should research information from library sources or museums, and from interviews. They should list all sources in a notebook to be displayed at the fair.
3. They should organize their findings into a 4-or-more-page report, with drawings, graphs, and other visuals and artifacts. They should compare the researched culture with their own. They may also include a book report based on a book about their researched culture. Students will need two posterboards to set up and complete their project.
4. On the day of the fair, students may dress up in costumes/clothes of their researched culture.
5. Award prizes, as in a science fair.

Enriching with Multimedia

RESOURCE: McGraw-Hill School's Home Page

- Have students go to McGraw-Hill School's home page at http://www.mhschool.com on the World Wide Web for projects related to this unit.

RESOURCE: *Adventure Time! CD-ROM*

- Enrich Unit 6 with the *Key People* and *Key Places* sections and Unit 6 Activities on the *Adventure Time!* CD-ROM.

SCHOOL-TO-HOME

A Century of Conflict

- Throughout the unit, students will have an opportunity to learn about changes and conflicts that have taken place in the twentieth century. With students, create two time lines with the headings "Then" and "Now." Then brainstorm a list of the countries discussed in the unit. List also some of the cultural, economic, or political changes that have occurred in each country between 1900 and 1965, and have students take the materials home.

- Students and their families can study the lists and prepare the time lines, adding information from their own knowledge and experience to the "Now" time line. Families can add the names of two other countries, and use the media and their own information to expand the chart.

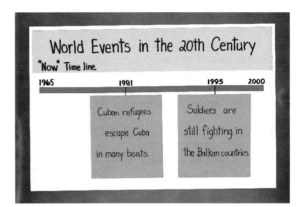

ONGOING UNIT PROJECT

Produce a Newsreel

CURRICULUM CONNECTION   Language Arts/Art

RESOURCE: Practice and Project Book p. 137.

Throughout this unit, students will be working individually and cooperatively to produce a newsreel that reflects a century of conflict and change.

1. After each chapter is completed, have each student draw a picture on 8 1/2" x 11" paper that illustrates one of the lessons' main ideas.
2. After all the drawings are completed, have students work in small groups to arrange and tape together the drawings in a sequence that shows conflict, struggle, and cooperation.
3. Provide each group with a cardboard box with an 8 1/2" x 11" opening. Cut a slit on each side of the box parallel to the length of the opening.
4. Guide students to pull the connected sheets gently through the slits while another group member narrates the scenes. The class can review the newsreels with the sheets provided.

Assessment suggestions for the activity appear on page 634.

UNIT SIX

Introducing the Unit

Refer students to the unit title and have them focus on the term *conflict*. Help them see that conflict is, unfortunately, another of history's recurring themes. Have them think back over this course and give examples of conflicts—of peoples and ideas. Then have them read *Why Does It Matter?* on p. 521 and examine the illustrations.

Exploring Prior Knowledge Ask students to identify any familiar subjects in the photographs.

- **Which of the photographs show subjects that are familiar to you? What do you know about them?** *(Encourage students to tell what they already know about the activities and subjects and explain how they came to learn it.)*

- **Is conflict the only theme of history that these photographs reflect? What other themes do they suggest?** *(No; they also reflect political development, advancing technology.)*

★**THINKING FURTHER:** *Making Conclusions* **Based on what you see here, what other titles could have been given to this unit?** *(Possible answers: "A Century of Conflict and Rapid Technological Development" or "A Century of Conflict and Political and Technological Change")*

Looking Ahead In this unit students will learn how the 20th century was the century in history during which the world changed the most—socially, politically, economically, and technologically.

UNIT CONTENTS

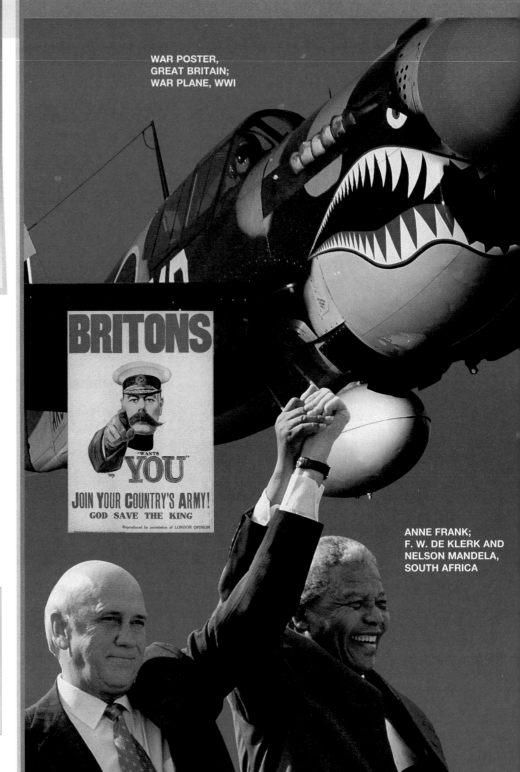

WAR POSTER, GREAT BRITAIN; WAR PLANE, WWI

BRITONS "WANTS" **YOU** JOIN YOUR COUNTRY'S ARMY! GOD SAVE THE KING
Reproduced by permission of LONDON OPINION

ANNE FRANK; F. W. DE KLERK AND NELSON MANDELA, SOUTH AFRICA

BACKGROUND INFORMATION

ABOUT THE PHOTOGRAPHS

- **WORLD WAR I WAR ENLISTMENT POSTER** Posters such as this one urged the British to join the war effort. Other countries involved in the war had similar enlistment efforts.

- **F.W. DE KLERK AND NELSON MANDELA** Apartheid sharply divided racial groups in the Republic of South Africa until free elections in 1994 made Nelson Mandela the first black president of the country. The governing power was transmitted peacefully from the previous president, F.W. de Klerk.

UNIT SIX

A Century of Conflict

"This cruelty too will end."

from The Diary of Anne Frank
See page 546.

Why Does It Matter?

A young girl, Anne Frank, wrote these words during a war that affected the entire world. In this, the second World War, as well as in the first World War, new weapons and fighting techniques caused tremendous loss of life.

Other struggles affected nations in the 1900s. Democratic beliefs and human rights were challenged. Colonies around the world struggled to gain independence.

As Anne Frank hoped, and as millions around the world continue to hope, conflicts have been giving way to greater peace, freedom, and cooperation. The technology that caused destruction has also been a source of life. New medicines and techniques have enabled people to live longer, more healthful lives. New ways of sharing information have also linked the whole world. People today share ideas that will shape the present and the future.

FIND OUT MORE!
Visit our website:
www.mhschool.com

*inter*NET
CONNECTION

521

BACKGROUND INFORMATION

ABOUT THE PHOTOGRAPHS

• **ANNE FRANK** This young girl's diary reflecting her experiences in hiding during World War II led many adults to consider improving efforts to keep the world safe for children.

• **FIGHTER PLANE FROM WORLD WAR II** Although aircraft were used during World War I, World War II was the first conflict in which aircraft played a major part.

Discussing the Photographs, Have students examine, identify, and classify each illustration.

★THINKING FURTHER: *Classifying*
How would you classify these photographs according to themes they reflect? *(Conflict: the World War I poster, the World War II fighter plane. Efforts toward peace: Nelson Mandela's election in South Africa; Anne Frank.)*

Discussing WHY DOES IT MATTER? Have a student read the quotation aloud and have the class review the passage that follows it.

• ***What various kinds of conflicts afflicted the world during the 1900s?*** *(world wars, revolutions, conflicts between colonizers and colonized, and conflicts to gain political power, economic power, and human rights)*

• ***What were some evil effects of these conflicts?*** *(Wars brought great damage and loss of life; democratic beliefs and human rights were often trampled; dictatorships came to power.)*

• ***What promising signs have emerged for the world?*** *(greater political freedom, more willingness among people to cooperate to solve problems, medical advances that make life more healthful, technologies that make life more comfortable and that link peoples around the world as never before, making cultural sharing and borrowing easier than ever)*

★THINKING FURTHER: *Making Conclusions* ***Do you suppose that a freer, more cooperative world is likely to be a more peaceful world? Why or why not?*** *(Encourage free discussion. Students will perhaps see cooperation as the most important prerequisite for peace; they may say that there are always those, free or not free, who want something their neighbor has and therefore will threaten peace. Perhaps only the cooperative effort of others can stop them.)*

Introducing
the Last Unknown Place

Exploring Prior Knowledge Students probably have a good deal of prior knowledge about space from what they have seen on television. Call on them to describe what were to them the most dramatic moments in space travel and exploration thus far. Encourage them to explain why they found these moments moving or important.

Links to the Unit In this unit, students will explore the 20th century, the century in which they were born, the century in which travel into space at last became a reality. The theme of space begins with the ancients looking up at the heavens and developing the science of astronomy. Later, the exploration of Earth and the rapid technological development of more recent centuries led to making space travel possible. The idea of space travel and exploration also serves as a bridge to the future.

The Last Unknown Place Have students read the text and examine the pictures. How does the lower right-hand inset differ from insets in this spot in previous *Adventures with National Geographic?* Help students to recognize that all the previous insets were drawn globes but that this shows the real thing—a photograph of Earth from the moon.

Call on students to explain what is going on in the major photograph on this spread (the launch of a U.S. space shuttle riding on rockets that carry it away from Earth and then drop off). Encourage students to share with the class anything that they know about space shuttles and the shuttle program. If there have been any recent shuttle missions, try to bring in news articles about them for students to discuss.

Resource **REMINDER**

National Geographic Poster
Geo Adventures *Daily Geography Activities*
Technology: *Adventure Time!* CD-ROM

BACKGROUND INFORMATION

MORE ABOUT SPACE EXPLORATION
While cutbacks in spending in the United States and the collapse of the Soviet Union have put severe limitations on space exploration, some projects are still discussed for future implementation, for example:

• continued unmanned space probes to other planets, to the Sun's outer atmosphere, and to other locations far out in deep space;

• the construction of a permanent base on the moon for deep-space observations and for mining;

• large-scale colonization in habitats constructed in space, each hosting hundreds or even thousands of inhabitants.

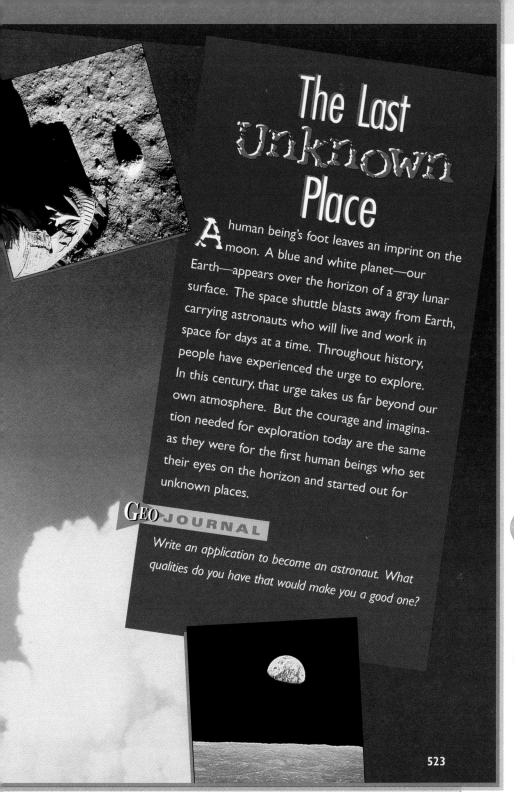

The Last Unknown Place

A human being's foot leaves an imprint on the moon. A blue and white planet—our Earth—appears over the horizon of a gray lunar surface. The space shuttle blasts away from Earth, carrying astronauts who will live and work in space for days at a time. Throughout history, people have experienced the urge to explore. In this century, that urge takes us far beyond our own atmosphere. But the courage and imagination needed for exploration today are the same as they were for the first human beings who set their eyes on the horizon and started out for unknown places.

GEO JOURNAL

Write an application to become an astronaut. What qualities do you have that would make you a good one?

523

Refer students to the lefthand inset and call on them to describe what is happening in it. (An astronaut is working outside a space shuttle.) You may want to explain that the first time an American went outside an orbiting spacecraft occurred in 1965 and was called the first "walk in space."

Point out to students the upper right-hand inset and call on them to identify what it shows. (A boot and imprint on the moon) How do you know for sure that it is the moon and not some other location in space? Help students to recognize that it has to be on the moon because that is the only place in space that human beings have reached so far.

Using the Geo Journal Before students begin their applications, call on the class to identify various qualities they think an astronaut should have and list them on the board. Have students use this list as a starting point for their applications.

 Technology CONNECTION

ADVENTURE TIME! CD-ROM
Enrich the discussion with the CD-ROM activity, *The Last Unknown Place.*

CURRICULUM CONNECTION

SCIENCE Space—"the final frontier"—is a major focus of current scientific research. Young people are part of this research, as evidenced by an article in the August 1944 issue of *National Geographic,* "Students With a Mission." The article describes the various CAN DO experiments in space that young students designed.

Have students form space research teams and help each team to choose some aspect of space research that they want to know more about. Have them do the research necessary and prepare an illustrated presentation of their findings to the class.

THEMES of GEOGRAPHY

As you work through Unit 6 with your students, consider the following themes:

PLACE Place refers to both the environmental and social features of a particular area. Discuss the physical characteristics of Russia as you read Lesson 2 of Chapter 18. Then discuss the social characteristics of Russia during the rise of Communism.

MOVEMENT People, goods, and ideas are moved around the world in many ways. As you read Chapter 19, discuss how movement affected life in Africa and Asia. In Chapter 20, discuss how the movement of ideas produced political and economic changes throughout the world.

18 A World At War

Pages 524–563

CHAPTER OVERVIEW

World War I ended the old empires of Europe and began the League of Nations in 1918. Revolutions in Russia and China brought communism to power there. World War II stopped the rise of fascism in Europe and resulted in the Cold War between the two superpowers: the USSR and the USA.

GEO ADVENTURES DAILY GEOGRAPHY ACTIVITIES

Use **Geo Adventures** Daily Geography activities to assess students' understanding of geography skills.

CHAPTER PLANNING GUIDE

LESSON 1	LESSON 2	LESSON 3
SUGGESTED PACING: 3 DAYS	SUGGESTED PACING: 2 DAYS	SUGGESTED PACING: 2 DAYS
The "Great War" pp. 526–531	**The Russian Revolution** pp. 532–539	**World War II** pp. 540–547
CURRICULUM CONNECTIONS Links to Language Arts, p. 527 Links to Math, p. 527 **CITIZENSHIP** Recognizing Point of View, p. 529 **INFOGRAPHIC** Weapons of World War I, p. 530 **RESOURCES** Practice and Project Book, p. 105 Anthology, pp. 142–143 ⦿TECHNOLOGY *Adventure Time!* CD-ROM Desk Map	**CURRICULUM CONNECTIONS** Links to Reading, p. 535 Links to Science, p. 535 **CITIZENSHIP** Understanding Government, pp. 534, 537 **RESOURCES** Practice and Project Book, p. 106 Anthology, pp. 144–145	**CURRICULUM CONNECTIONS** Links to Language Arts, p. 546 **CITIZENSHIP** The Citizen's Role on the Home Front, p. 543 Understanding Government, p. 545 **RESOURCES** Project and Practice Book, p. 107 Anthology, pp. 146–149, 150, 152, 153–154 ▭Anthology, p. 151

LESSON 4	LESSON 5	CHAPTER REVIEW
SUGGESTED PACING: 2 DAYS	SUGGESTED PACING: 2 DAYS	SUGGESTED PACING: 1 DAY
Communism In China pp. 550–555	**Cold War** pp. 556–561	pp. 562–563
CITIZENSHIP Using Current Events, p. 554 **RESOURCES** Practice and Project Book, p. 109 Anthology, p. 155–156	**CURRICULUM CONNECTIONS** Links to Science, p. 559 **CITIZENSHIP** Using Current Events, p. 560 **RESOURCES** Practice and Project Book, p. 110 Anthology, p. 157	**RESOURCES** Practice and Project Book, p. 111 ⦿TECHNOLOGY Videodisc Assessment Book: Chapter 18 Test Transparency: Graphic Organizer, Sequence Chain

LEARNING STYLE: Kinesthetic

PARTNER

30 MINUTES OR LONGER

Make a War Memorial

Objective: To prepare students to learn about World War I and World War II.

Materials: cartons, glue, markers, paint, paper towel tubes, cardboard, clay

1. Discuss with students the ways in which people commemorate, or remember, wars in which Americans fought and died in this century.
2. Have students, in pairs, choose a war memorial to research, write about, and recreate from art materials.
3. Invite students to write three questions about the war they studied and to share these questions with the class.

GEOGRAPHYSKILLS

SUGGESTED PACING: 1 DAY

Time Zone Maps pp. 548–549

RESOURCES

Practice and Project Book, p. 108
Transparency Map 20
TECHNOLOGY *Adventure Time!* CD-ROM

SHELTERED INSTRUCTION

READING STRATEGIES & LANGUAGE DEVELOPMENT

Rereading/Word Origin, p. 526, Lesson 1
Predicting/Word Origin and Homophones, p. 532, Lesson 2
Using Visuals/Contractions, p. 540, Lesson 3
Problem and Solution/Suffixes, p. 548, Geography Skills
Cause and Effect/Synonyms, p. 550, Lesson 4
Classifying/Compound Words, p. 556, Lesson 5

SECOND-LANGUAGE SUPPORT

Using Visuals, p. 527
Reader's Theater, p. 533
Graphic Organizers, pp. 541, 552
Taking Notes, p. 557
Retelling/Compare and Contrast, p. 562

MEETING INDIVIDUAL NEEDS

Reteaching, Extension, Enrichment, pp. 531, 539, 547, 549, 555, 561
McGraw-Hill Adventure Book

ASSESSMENT OPPORTUNITIES

Practice and Project Book, pp. 105–111
Write About It, pp. 531, 539, 547, 555, 561
Assessment Book: Assessing Think and Write, pp. T101–T103; Chapter 18 Tests: Content, Skills, Writing

Introducing the Chapter

Have students cast their minds back over what they have learned in this course and give examples of wars they have studied (Athens and Sparta, Rome and Carthage, for instance). Then refer them to the chapter title to get them thinking about war involving the entire world.

**THINKING ABOUT
HISTORY AND GEOGRAPHY**

Have students read the text on this page to pinpoint the kinds of conflict and change that marked the 20th century. Have students use their fingers to trace each panel to its location on the map.

1914 SARAJEVO, AUSTRIA-HUNGARY

- **What event preceded the beginning of World War I?** *(an assassination)*

- **In what part of Europe did it take place?** *(in southeastern Europe)*

★**THINKING FURTHER:** *Making Conclusions* **Do you think that a single assassination could be the only cause for plunging the world into war? Explain.** *(Students should conclude that there had to be more than a single event to start a world war.)*

1917 ST. PETERSBURG, RUSSIA

- **How does this panel tell you that revolution is taking place?** *(Protesters are bringing down a monarchy.)*

- **Where did this revolution take place? Locate it on the map.** *(in eastern Europe, St. Petersburg, Russia)*

★**THINKING FURTHER:** *Predicting* **Do you know anything that can help predict what form of government will replace the Russian monarchy?** *(Russia had a communist government for much of the 20th century.)*

Resource **REMINDER**

Technology: *Videodisc/Video Tape 2*

A World at War

**THINKING ABOUT
HISTORY AND GEOGRAPHY**

The twentieth century has been a time of great change and conflict. Old ways of governing were overthrown in many parts of the world. Two world wars were fought with weapons of great destruction. When the fighting ended, two superpowers with opposing goals sought to influence other nations. Follow these events on the map and on the time line.

1934

RUIJIN, CHINA
Communists begin their 6,000-mile Long March

1914

SARAJEVO, AUSTRIA-HUNGARY
World War I begins after Franz Ferdinand is killed

1917

ST. PETERSBURG, RUSSIA
Protesters end the rule of Russia's monarchy

1900   1915   1930

BACKGROUND INFORMATION

LINKING THE MAP AND TIME LINE

- Sarajevo was founded as a fortress in the early 1400s, but the Turks soon captured it. Because of its central location in Bosnia-Herzegovina, the Turks made it that area's capital in 1851, and Austria-Hungary renamed its capital when it captured the area in 1873. Franz Ferdinand was visiting Sarajevo in his role as Archduke of Austria-Hungary.

- St. Petersburg lies on the western border of Russia. As described in the *Citizenship* note on p. 534, it was built there to give Russia a "window on the West" and to replace Moscow as capital. In 1918 the capital was moved back to Moscow, which was more centrally located.

- **What is happening in this panel?** *(Communists in China are beginning their Long March.)*

- **Where in China did they begin?** *(in eastern China)*

- **What kind of government did China have when you last studied it?** *(dynasties ruled by emperors)*

★**THINKING FURTHER:** *Making Conclusions* **What political change in China does this panel suggest?** *(perhaps a change from dynasties to communism)*

- **What conflict does this panel illustrate?** *(World War II)*

- **Where is the invasion shown taking place?** *(in France in western Europe)*

★**THINKING FURTHER:** *Making Conclusions* **Which side will win this war, as hinted at in the caption?** *(the Allied side, since they are successfully invading France)*

- **What tells you that Berlin is a divided city in 1961?** *(There is East Berlin and West Berlin.)*

- **Where is Berlin?** *(eastern Europe)*

★**THINKING FURTHER:** *Making Conclusions* **Why do you suppose a wall was built between the two?** *(either to keep people in or keep them out)*

BACKGROUND INFORMATION

LINKING THE MAP AND THE TIME LINE

- The Long March cast a shadow over China for decades to come. From its survivors came not only Mao Zedong but also the inner core of China's communist leadership, the "Long March generation," that ruled China until the 1970s.

- Normandy was chosen for the Allied invasion from Britain precisely because it was *not* France's closest point to Britain. The Germans expected the invasion at Pas de Calais, which was the closest point, and they moved their strongest forces there.

- Berlin's central location led to its being named capital of Germany after the unification of Germany under Prussian leadership in 1871. West Germany moved its capital to Bonn, but East Germany retained Berlin as its capital.

Technology CONNECTION

VIDEODISC/VIDEO TAPE 2
Enrich Chapter 18 with the *China Today* segment on the Videodisc.

Search Frame 46510 Side A

525

Lesson Overview
Strong feelings of nationalism plunged the world into the deadliest war it had yet known—the Great War, or World War I.

Lesson Objectives
★ Explain how nationalism led to a series of national alliances.

★ Trace the steps that led to World War I.

★ Describe the war and its results.

1 PREPARE

MOTIVATE Have one student read the *Read Aloud* quote for the class and another the narrator's part. As they listen, have students close their eyes to visualize the scene. If possible, play some songs from World War I ("Over There") to set the mood of the time.

SET PURPOSE What conditions or events could have led to the sinking of the *Lusitania* (in the illustration) and the horrors of war that followed? Refer students to the *Read to Learn* question. Encourage them to read the lesson for answers. Preview the *Vocabulary*.

2 TEACH

Understanding THE BIG PICTURE
Help students link industrialization with competition that fueled a war.

● **What forces drove countries like Britain, Germany, and France into war?** *(Industrial development helped make them rivals for both economic markets and military superiority, a competition for power that led to war.)*

★**THINKING FURTHER:** *Predicting*
How do you predict that industrial development would make this war deadlier than earlier wars? *(Help students see that technology would produce more destructive weapons.)*

Resource REMINDER

Practice and Project Book: *p. 105*

Anthology: *All Quiet on the Western Front, pp. 142–143*

Technology: *Adventure Time!* CD-ROM

Desk Map

1890   1900   1918   1940   1965   1990

The "Great War"

Read Aloud
"I saw the ship go down. There was this huge lovely liner, and as I watched one [smokestack] went [under] and then the other and the other until the ship was gone and the sea was calm, and all you could see was bodies, and wreckage of furniture and everything that had been in the ship floating in the water."

This was how Alice Lines remembered the 1915 German submarine attack on the Lusitania, a ship crossing the Atlantic. The ship carried many American passengers. Lines was one of the few survivors. The 1,198 people who died were victims of an international conflict, the "Great War."

Focus Activity

READ TO LEARN

In what ways did nationalism affect the events leading to World War I?

VOCABULARY

- nationalism
- alliance
- Central Powers
- Allied Powers
- armistice
- League of Nations
- Treaty of Versailles
- World War I

PEOPLE

- Franz Ferdinand

PLACES

- Sarajevo
- Serbia

THE BIG PICTURE
The sinking of the *Lusitania* angered many people in the United States. Two years after that event, the country entered a war that had already involved many nations of the world. What forces and events led to the war?

In Chapter 17 you read about vast changes that swept through the world in the late 1700s and 1800s. Factories were built during the Industrial Revolution. Overland travel sped along with the help of railroads. Steamships crossed the Atlantic Ocean in just six days.

Countries such as Britain, Germany, and France grew economically because of the Industrial Revolution. The populations and military strength of many European countries also increased. This growth brought with it many new problems. European leaders wondered which countries would continue to strengthen. Which ones would eventually become the most powerful nations?

SHELTERED INSTRUCTION

READING STRATEGIES & LANGUAGE DEVELOPMENT

REREADING Review with students the advantages of rereading new material to be certain that they understand its meaning. Invite volunteers to model the process, using the Read Aloud. Then have students write a question about each Vocabulary, People, and Places term. As students read, have them answer the questions. Remind them to reread passages to find the information they need. **[SDAIE STRATEGY: CONTEXTUALIZATION]**

WORD ORIGIN Refer the class to the term *submarine* in the *Read Aloud* and point out that it is another example of a term that had to be made up to describe a newly developed object. Have them use the dictionary to discover the ancient words that were combined to create it (*sub* from Latin for "under" and *marine* from Latin *mare* for "sea").

EUROPE AT THE TURN OF THE CENTURY

In the early 1900s Europe was like a huge jigsaw puzzle. The "pieces" were nations. Some, such as Britain and France, had existed for centuries. Others, such as Italy and Germany, had been unified only in the 1800s.

In many of these European nations, a feeling of unity had grown among peoples who spoke the same language and shared a common history and culture. These feelings developed into the force that is known as nationalism (NASH uh nuh lihz um). Nationalism is a strong loyalty to one's own country and culture. Those who are influenced by nationalism want their countries to be more powerful than any others.

By the early 1900s nationalism had grown stronger in Europe. So had tensions between neighboring countries. To prepare for the possibility of war, countries trained large armies and formed alliances (uh LI un sez). An alliance is an agreement between countries that ties their interests together. Members of an alliance, called allies, pledge to defend each other if any of them are attacked.

Two Shots that Started a War

On June 28, 1914, Archduke Franz Ferdinand, the heir to the throne of Austria-Hungary, visited Sarajevo (sar uh YAY voh). This city had come under his empire's control. Sarajevo, capital of a region called Bosnia, shared ties with Serbia, a nearby kingdom. Many Serbian nationalists thought that Sarajevo and Bosnia should be part of Serbia. Some of them decided to send a message to the archduke's government.

As Ferdinand and his wife Sophie drove through Sarajevo, someone threw a bomb at them. The archduke knocked it away and the bomb exploded behind them. A wrong turn, however, took them in front of another Serbian nationalist. This man used a gun. He fired twice, killing them both.

Austria-Hungary, backed by Germany, declared war on Serbia in July. Serbia was aided by its ally, Russia. Russia's allies, France and Britain, also came to Serbia's aid. A British leader described Europe on the brink of war: "The lights are going out all over Europe. We shall not see them lit again in our lifetime." By August 1914 the "Great War" had begun.

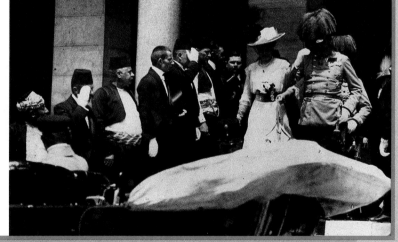

Archduke Franz Ferdinand and his wife Sophie were killed by a Serbian nationalist as they rode through Sarajevo. This photo shows them preparing for the ride.

EUROPE, 1914

Central powers
Neutral states
Allied powers

NORWAY
SWEDEN
North Sea
DENMARK
GREAT BRITAIN
NETHERLANDS
BELGIUM
GERMANY
RUSSIA
LUXEMBOURG
FRANCE
ATLANTIC OCEAN
SWITZERLAND
AUSTRIA-HUNGARY
RUMANIA
SERBIA
PORTUGAL
ITALY
Adriatic Sea
BULGARIA
SPAIN
MONTENEGRO
ALBANIA
GREECE
Mediterranean Sea
OTTOMAN EMPIRE
0   150   300 Miles
0   150   300 Kilometers

MAP WORK

The map shows how Europe was divided at the start of the "Great War."

1. Which nations made up the Central Powers?

2. Which neutral states bordered France?

3. The alliance of which neutral state would have best helped the Allied powers control the entrance to the Mediterranean Sea?

NATIONS AT WAR

As you can see on the map, Austria-Hungary, Germany, and their allies became known as the Central Powers. Serbia, Russia, France, Britain, and others were called the Allied Powers.

The Central Powers had some military success in the fall of 1914. Their armies forced their way deep into France and Russia. The Allied Powers, however, had a greater number of soldiers and more supplies. They were better equipped to survive a long war.

The Battlefront

Over the next four years the battlefront in France hardly changed. The battlefront, or front, is the place where opposing armies fight. Millions of soldiers died trying to push the front east or west. During many battles at the front, generals stuck to old-style war techniques. These ways of fighting were no match for the deadly technology now being used in war. Machine guns and poison gas could kill hundreds of enemy soldiers in a short time.

All across France, soldiers on both sides dug maze-like dirt trenches, or ditches, for protection. Soldiers camped in the trenches while waiting for orders. Bombs exploded nearby and bullets whizzed overhead. In winter, rain filled the trenches with puddles and mud. In summer, the heat and dust were almost unbearable. The worst times, though, were when the soldiers were ordered to go "over the top." This phrase meant climbing out of the trenches and into enemy machine-gun fire. How did one British soldier describe fighting at the front?

MAP WORK: **1.** Germany, Austria-Hungary, Bulgaria **2.** Spain, Switzerland **3.** Spain

528

GLOBAL CONNECTION

WHY WAS IT CALLED A "WORLD" WAR? Several European nations had colonized different areas of the world. When the European countries went to war, their colonies often became involved.

- In all, 27 nations fought in the war, so involvement in the war reached places far from Europe and the United States—such as Tokyo, Japan; Ottawa, Canada; Rio de Janeiro, Brazil; and Cape Town, South Africa.

- Japan took part by taking control of German colonial holdings in East Asia. Because of their former colonial ties, Canada and South Africa were two of the nations that entered the war with Britain. Brazil lent its support to Portugal, owing to their former colonial ties.

- Fighting took place in Asia (Turkey, Palestine, Syria, and Mesopotamia) and in Africa (Portuguese and German East Africa).

MANY VOICES
PRIMARY SOURCE

Excerpt from an interview
with British soldier, Charles Quinnell,
about the Battle of the Somme in 1916.

I gave the order "advance—up the ladders—over the top."... We went through, we got halfway across and then the two machine guns found us ... they played on us like spraying with a hose. At the finish I was the only man standing but I'm not one of those heroes who want to take on the German Army on my own and so I went to earth, I got down behind the lip of a big shell-hole.... The machine gun crew spotted me and they opened up on me. I ducked my head down ... and the dirt was just spraying down the back of my neck.

shell-hole: hole caused by an explosion

The Home Front

While millions of troops served in the war, people at home did what they could to help. People who worked to support the troops were said to be fighting on the "home front." Women and men worked in factories to make bullets, bombs, and airplanes. Others volunteered to serve as nurses or ambulance drivers at the war front.

In order to save food for the soldiers, governments controlled the amount of food people could buy. In Britain, laws for restaurants stated:

Two meatless days are to be observed. No milk may be served or consumed (drunk), except by children under 10 years of age.

In Germany and eastern European countries, food prices soared. Many people ate potato peels and watery soup given out by their government.

The United States Enters the War

Conditions were better for the Allied Powers because they received supplies from the United States. These supplies were sent on ships. In 1915 German submarines sank the *Lusitania*, which was carrying war supplies. The ship's passengers included 128 United States citizens. Many died in the attack. Attacks on ships outraged leaders and citizens of the United States. So did a secret message sent by Germany to Mexico that plotted an alliance against the United States.

In April 1917 the United States declared war on Germany and the other Central Powers. Large numbers of American soldiers, as well as vast amounts of money and supplies, greatly helped the Allied Powers. As you will read on page 531, the United States used posters and slogans to help send more than 2 million troops to Europe.

Out of their trenches, soldiers near the front went fully prepared for enemy attacks.

Learning about The Home Front
Help students see the need for civilian effort to support the military.

● ***What is the difference between the home front and the battle front?*** *(The home front supported the war effort but did not go to battle.)*

● ***How did people on the home front help the war effort?*** *(They made weapons and other supplies, sent medical help, and limited their own use of needed supplies, such as food)*

★THINKING FURTHER: *Compare and Contrast* **On which side's home front did the war take a greater toll? Explain.** *(The Central Powers suffered more, mainly because of greater food shortages.)*

Discussing The United States Enters the War Discuss U.S. efforts before the country entered the war.

● ***Why were shortages worse for the Central Powers than for the Allies?*** *(The U.S. sent supplies to the Allies.)*

● ***What drove the U.S. into the war?*** *(the sinking of the Lusitania followed by the German attempt to get Mexico to join Germany against the U.S.)*

★THINKING FURTHER: *Cause and Effect* **How did the U.S. entry affect the war?** *(The U.S. entry broke the stalemate in favor of the Allied Powers.)*

CITIZENSHIP★

RECOGNIZING POINT OF VIEW Not all Americans favored the U.S. entry into World War I. Many believed that the U.S. should remain isolated from European conflicts.

● One opponent was Jeanette Rankin of Montana, the first woman in the House of Representatives.

● She had promised during her campaign that she would keep the country out of war. When Congress was asked to declare war on Germany, she voted "no."

● Rankin's stand cost her reelection, but she later explained, "I felt at the time that the first time a woman had the chance to say 'no' to war she should say it." Ask students what they think Rankin meant by this remark.

BACKGROUND INFORMATION

ABOUT THE FOURTEEN POINTS U.S. President Woodrow Wilson proposed Fourteen Points for ending the war.

● Among his ideas were: "open covenants openly arrived at," removal of trade barriers, arms reduction, self-determination, and "adjustment of all colonial claims."

● One key idea was to form a "general association of nations," which later became the League of Nations.

● Wilson himself led the U.S. delegation to the Paris Peace conference in 1919.

● After many of the Fourteen Points were changed at Paris, the U.S. Senate rejected the Peace Treaty and refused to join the League of Nations.

Infographic

Remind the class of the Industrial Revolution and how it spurred the development of faster, more powerful technologies—new machines, new uses for chemistry. Help students see that it also spurred weapons technology—new machines and new gases that were much more deadly than earlier weapons.

Discussing Weapons of World War I Give students time to read the text and examine the photos and captions on this page. Invite them to think about how these weapons intensified earlier ways of making war.

● *Before World War I, soldiers often rode into battle on horses or chariots. What technology replaced these in World War I?* (tanks)

● *How did airplanes "extend the battlefield" and bring war to places it had never been fought before?* (Airplanes made bombing from the air possible and made the sky part of the battlefield.)

● *According to these photos, what other previously unknown weapon of war appeared in World War I? What was the only defense against it?* (Poisonous gases that could kill or disable soldiers; masks were needed to avoid inhaling the gases.)

★THINKING FURTHER: *Compare and Contrast* **Picture in your mind medieval knights going into battle or an army armed with bows, pikes, and a few muskets. How would you compare and contrast the destructive power of and dangers faced by these groups with those of World War I armies?** *(Encourage students to point out ways that tanks, aircraft, and poison gases greatly multiplied both the horrors of war and the number and power of ways to wage war.)*

Technology CONNECTION

ADVENTURE TIME! CD-ROM
Enrich the Infographic with the *Discoveries Time Lines* activity on the *Adventure Time!* CD-ROM.

Infographic

Weapons of World War I

Nations have always made use of the latest developments in technology to produce new weapons. Some of the weapons used during World War I were not only capable of tremendous destruction, but also changed the way wars were fought. How did the weapons shown change modern war?

TANKS were armored vehicles invented by the British to cross trenches. Soldiers inside fired guns.

AIRPLANES were used to drop bombs on enemy territory. Bombs were often carried under the wings.

GAS MASKS were worn by soldiers fighting at the front for protection from poison gas.

EXPANDING THE INFOGRAPHIC

RESEARCHING AND PRESENTING Divide the class into five groups and assign each group one of the weapon technologies illustrated here—tanks, airplanes, poison gas—as well as machine guns and submarines. Have each group research the World War I development, use, and effects of its assigned technology. Have each group prepare an illustrated report of its findings to present to the class.

You might suggest the following sources for research:

● Encyclopedia entries under the heading of the technology.

● Library catalog entries under the name of the technology and under *World War I*.

● Several books have been written for young people about this war, and students can use the books' indexes to find the topic.

● *American Heritage* has also produced solid sources on World War I.

AN END TO THE WAR

On November 11, 1918, Germany and the Allies signed an armistice (AHR muh stihs), or agreement to stop fighting. In January 1919, Allied leaders worked out terms for peace. As part of their treaty, they created the League of Nations, an international council that would work to prevent future wars. German leaders were forced to sign the Treaty of Versailles (vair SĪ) on June 28, 1919.

WHY IT MATTERS

The Treaty of Versailles caused great anger in Germany because it blamed that nation for the war. It also called for the payment of enormous fines to repair war damages. Even Ferdinand Foch, the commander of the Allied armies exclaimed, "This isn't peace! This is an armistice for 20 years!" Three months after those 20 years had passed, the nations of the world would again go to war. When that happened, the war that had been called the "Great War" became known as World War I.

Who was Uncle Sam?

Back in the War of 1812, merchant Samuel Wilson stamped "U.S." on all of his barrels headed for army troops. Wilson's workers teased him about that stamp. They said the letters "U.S." stood for his nickname, "Uncle Sam," rather than "United States." The legendary character "Uncle Sam" was born.

"Uncle Sam" became most famous in this World War I recruiting poster, which is still used today. The model for this "Uncle Sam" wasn't really anyone's uncle. He was the poster's artist, James Montgomery Flagg!

Reviewing Facts and Ideas

MAIN IDEAS

- Nationalism was a factor that led to World War I, which was fought from 1914 to 1918.
- Modern technology played a deadly new role in the trench, sea, and air battles of World War I.
- On the "home front" women and men worked in factories, and governments controlled food supplies to make sure troops were fed.
- United States supplies and troops played an important role in helping the Allied Powers win World War I.

THINK ABOUT IT

1. What role did technology play in World War I?
2. How did people on the "home front" contribute to the war effort?
3. **FOCUS** How did nationalism play a role in the start of World War I?
4. **THINKING SKILL** Make a *conclusion* about the impact alliances had on Europe in the early 1900s.
5. **WRITE** Read the excerpt from the interview with the soldier again. Write a letter to that soldier describing your reaction to his description of the front.

531

AN END TO THE WAR
Write *League of Nations* on the board.

- **How and when did the war end?** *(Allied victory, November 11, 1918)*

★**THINKING FURTHER: Cause and Effect** What was one peacekeeping effect of the war? *(creation of the League of Nations to prevent war)*

Discussing WHY IT MATTERS Write *Treaty of Versailles* on the board.

★**THINKING FURTHER: Cause and Effect** How did the Treaty of Versailles set the stage for a future war? *(It created great resentment in Germany.)*

Extending Did You Know? Try to have books on hand with war posters and slogans to show the importance of appeals for public support. Ask students to create their own posters and slogans.

3 CLOSE

MAIN IDEAS
Call on students for answers.

- **How did nationalism help bring on World War I?** *(It caused tensions among nations and led them to join alliances against one another.)*
- **How did modern technology make the war more deadly?** *(It produced more powerful and destructive weapons.)*
- **How did a home front help the battle front?** *(by supplying those fighting)*
- **What turned the tide for Allied victory?** *(U.S. entry into the war)*

EVALUATE
✓ **Answers to Think About It**
1. It provided more destructive weapons. *Make Conclusions*
2. by supplying the battle front *Make Inferences*
3. It raised tensions among nations, leading them into alliances for war. *Main Idea*
4. Conclusions should reflect creation of an "us against them" mentality. *Make Conclusions*
5. Encourage students to empathize with the soldier as they write to him. *Point of View*

Write About It Tell students to put themselves in this soldier's place and write a journal entry he might have written about a battle or life in the trenches.

MEETING INDIVIDUAL NEEDS

RETEACHING (Easy) Have students fill in an outline table of World War I by listing facts under these headings: *Europe Before World War I, The Event That Started It All, Central Powers, Allied Powers,* and *The End of the War.*

EXTENSION (Average) Tell students to picture themselves as the editor of an American newspaper in April 1917. Have them write an editorial in which they urge that the U.S. either enter or stay out of the war raging in Europe. Invite students to read their editorials to the class.

ENRICHMENT (Challenging) Divide the class into four groups and assign each group one of the following: Britain, Russia, Germany, the United States. Have each group research conditions on the home front for its country during World War I and report to the class.

LESSON 2

Lesson Overview

Revolution ended the Russian monarchy and created the communist-ruled Soviet Union.

Lesson Objectives

★ Describe life in tsarist Russia.

★ Trace the steps leading to revolution.

★ Analyze the development of Communist rule over the Soviet Union.

⭐ 1 PREPARE

MOTIVATE Have the class chant the slogan in the *Read Aloud*. Ask a student to read the rest aloud. Help students see the desperation of people who used the slogan.

SET PURPOSE Ask, "What caused such desperation? Where do you think it led?" Refer students to the illustration of the Russian Orthodox priest during the Russian Revolution on this page and the *Read to Learn* question. Invite them to explore the lesson to find out. Preview the *Vocabulary*.

⭐ 2 TEACH

Understanding THE BIG PICTURE
Direct students to the map on p. 533 to give them a sense of Russia's vast size and how size could make rule difficult.

● *In what part of Russia did most of its people live? What was their major industry?* (western Russia; farming)

● *On which side did Russia fight in World War I?* (It was an Allied Power.)

★THINKING FURTHER: *Making Conclusions* **Why might a war make a people more dissatisfied with their lives?** *(War takes resources from people and robs many of their lives.)*

Resource REMINDER

Practice and Project Book: *p. 106*
Anthology: *The Endless Steppe, pp. 144–145*

1890 1900 1940 1965 1990

The Russian Revolution

Focus Activity

READ TO LEARN

What were the causes and effects of the Russian Revolution?

VOCABULARY

- Russian Revolution
- tsar
- strike
- communism
- totalitarian

PEOPLE

- Alexander II
- Nicholas II
- Vladimir Ilyich Lenin
- Josef Stalin

PLACES

- Russia
- St. Petersburg
- Moscow
- Soviet Union

532

Read Aloud

"Peace! Land! Bread!"

This slogan summed up what ordinary Russians wanted most in the bloody, food-starved days of World War I. One group promised to give them all these things and more. Once in power, this group would transform Russia and affect the whole world.

THE BIG PICTURE

World War I was the peak of a long era of conflict and revolution. You have already read about political and industrial revolutions that rocked the world in the 1700s and 1800s. In the early 1900s, while the "Great War" still raged, yet another revolution broke out—in Russia. The Russian Revolution was an extremely important event in modern world history.

In 1900 the Russian empire stretched across parts of Europe and Asia. It included people of many different cultures. Most, though, lived in western Russia, where the land was better suited for the empire's main activity—farming. Most Russians were Christians. Muslims also lived in the empire, however, as well as many Jews.

World leaders took notice when revolutionaries overthrew Russia's leaders in 1917. Revolutionary leaders began to build a government around the ideas of Karl Marx, whom you read about in Chapter 17. The world watched and waited. What would happen in Russia? Would Russia continue to fight in World War I? How would the revolution affect other nations?

SHELTERED INSTRUCTION

READING STRATEGIES & LANGUAGE DEVELOPMENT

PREDICTING Remind the class that what they learned about different revolutions in the last chapter can help them make predictions about the Russian Revolution. Have students work in groups to brainstorm predictions about the Russian Revolution. Note their ideas on the board. Encourage students to revise their predictions as they read to evaluate their accuracy. **[SDAIE STRATEGY: BRIDGING]**

WORD ORIGIN AND HOMOPHONES Refer students to the term *serf* on p. 533. Explain to them that it is yet another word that comes to us from Latin, from *servus*, meaning "slave." Invite students to suggest how this word might describe the quality of a Russian serf's life. Ask them if they know a homophone for *serf* (the unrelated word *surf*).

GROWTH OF RUSSIA, 1360–1917

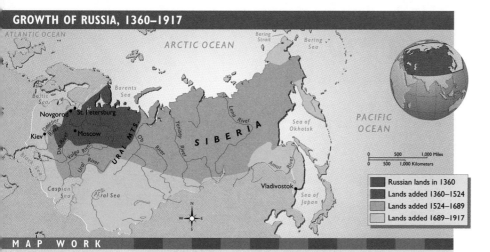

Russian lands in 1360
Lands added 1360–1524
Lands added 1524–1689
Lands added 1689–1917

MAP WORK

Russian tsars greatly expanded their nation's lands.

1. Which city was the center of Russia in 1360?
2. In which direction is St. Petersburg from Moscow?
3. During which years did Russian lands first reach the Caspian Sea?
4. What was the eastern boundary of Russia in 1524? In 1689?
5. After what year did Russian lands extend past the Ural Mountains?

RUSSIA UNDER THE TSARS

In the middle 1800s Russia was far from being a world power. While industry changed many parts of Europe, most Russians lived much as they had during the Middle Ages.

At the top of Russia's social pyramid was the tsar (ZAHR), or emperor. The tsar ruled with an iron hand. Anyone who displeased the tsar might be killed or sent to prison in Siberia. Find this frozen steppe region on the map.

Beneath the tsar were a handful of rich noble families. At the bottom of Russia's social pyramid were millions of poor farmers. Their crops fed the empire.

Russian Serfs

By the late 1700s France and other European countries no longer had serfs, or farmers, bound to the land. In the early 1800s, however, most Russians were still serfs. Russian law said serfs were the property of their owners, although serfs could not be sold.

By the middle 1800s serf revolts in Russia were increasing in number. Tsar Alexander II began to fear a revolution. He also wanted to shift Russia's work force away from farming and toward industry. Alexander decided to abolish serfdom in 1861. To abolish means to end a practice. The Tsar said: "It is better to abolish serfdom from above than to wait until the serfs begin to free themselves from below."

In exchange for freedom and small plots of land, the freed serfs had to pay heavy taxes. Paying the taxes was difficult, since many families were given small areas to farm.

MAP WORK: 1. Moscow 2. north 3. 1524–1689 4. Ural Mountains; Pacific Ocean and Sea of Okhatsk 5. 1524

533

RUSSIA UNDER THE TSARS

Have students recall social structures of other societies they studied.

★THINKING FURTHER: *Classifying How would you draw the social pyramid described in this section?* (Have a student draw it on the board: tsar—nobles—poor farmers)

More MAP WORK

Refer the class to the map on this page.

● *How long a period does this map cover?* (1360–1917, or 557 years)

● *From what two seas in the West to what three seas in the East did Russia stretch in 1917?* (West: Baltic Sea, Black Sea; East: Bering Sea, Sea of Okhotsk, Sea of Japan)

● *About how many miles across is it from sea to sea?* (5,000 miles)

● *What ocean does much of northern Russia border? What does this tell about its climate?* (Arctic; very cold)

● *During what period did Russia make its first land additions? What formed the eastern border for much of this addition?* (1360–1524; Ural Mts.)

★THINKING FURTHER: *Making Conclusions How does this map tell you that Russia was an imperial nation?* (The many additions of territory show that Russia was building an empire.)

Discussing Russian Serfs Stress that most Russians were serfs.

● *How does Russia of the early 1800s show that the Industrial Revolution and modern times had not yet reached it?* (Serfdom still existed and most Russians were engaged in agriculture, not industry.)

★THINKING FURTHER: *Making Conclusions How did the end of serfdom mean that the Russian people exchanged one form of oppression for another?* (They were no longer tied to the land, but they faced a heavy burden of taxes with few resources to pay the taxes.)

BACKGROUND INFORMATION

MORE ABOUT THE GROWTH OF RUSSIA

● 1360: Moscow became Russia's leading city. Moscow's Prince Yuri married into the ruling Mongol family and his family's wealth grew.

● 1524: Russia's maximum expansion under the princes before Ivan IV of Moscow was crowned the first tsar in 1547.

● 1689: Peter the Great's rule began. As children, he and his half-brother were crowned co-tsars, but his half-sister ruled until 1689.

SECOND-LANGUAGE SUPPORT

READER'S THEATER The dramatic events of Russian history lend themselves to interpretation by students who will pantomime actions and emotions of participants while other students read the lesson aloud. Students might also create tableaux of scenes described in the text.

533

Call on students to recall when the Industrial Revolution developed in Britain and other European countries (1700s and early 1800s) and have them contrast this to the time it reached Russia (not until the late 1800s).

Discussing Two Sides of a City
Ask for other examples students may know of cities with "two sides."

● *What tsar came to the throne in 1894?* (Nicholas II)

● *In what city was his capital and where in the city did he live?* (St. Petersburg, in the Winter Palace)

★THINKING FURTHER: *Compare and Contrast* **How would you compare and contrast the two sides of St. Petersburg?** *(Grand side: magnificent buildings and centers of culture. Industrial side: smoky factories, mills, overcrowded workers' apartments.)*

Exploring Workers Protest Ask students to analyze the tsar's role in conditions.

● *Why did St. Petersburg's industrial workers strike?* (for better conditions)

● *What happened on "Bloody Sunday"?* (Soldiers of the tsar fired on the strikers, killing over 100 of them.)

★THINKING FURTHER: *Cause and Effect* **What effects did "Bloody Sunday" have on Russia?** *(The tsar promised to share power with the elected Duma and make reforms, but he did not keep his promise.)*

Wealthy Russians like Tsar Nicholas and army officials owned expensive items like this egg by Fabergé (right).

WORLDS IN CONFLICT

By the late 1800s Russian cities were growing. Hard times in rural areas forced many former serfs to move to the cities in search of work. By the 1890s factories and mills of the Industrial Revolution were springing up in Russia's capital, St. Petersburg.

Two Sides of a City

To poor farmers St. Petersburg was a new world. They stared in wonder at the grand winter palace of Tsar Nicholas II, who began his rule in 1894. Dozens of mansions, churches, theaters, schools, and universities lined the streets of the city. More than one million people lived in St. Petersburg.

The city also had a less spectacular side. Away from the palace and other beautiful mansions, mills and factories clustered together. Smoke from their chimneys filled the air above the overcrowded apartment buildings where workers lived.

Workers Protest

Inside the factories and mills, conditions were often grim and workers were angry. A protest in 1897 won them a shortened work day—to 11½ hours. Factory workers protested again in 1905, shutting down the city with their strikes. A strike is a refusal to work in protest of unfair treatment.

On Sunday, January 22, 1905, thousands of striking workers marched toward the Winter Palace to speak with the tsar himself. The tsar's soldiers responded by shooting into the crowd. More than 100 people were killed. Many others were injured. The day became known as "Bloody Sunday."

A storm of revolts and strikes swept through the country after "Bloody Sunday." Tsar Nicholas II agreed to share some of his power with a new elected parliament, called the Duma. The Duma called for changes that would advance democracy and help the poor. The tsar refused. During the next nine years, Nicholas and the Duma were in constant conflict.

534

CITIZENSHIP ★

UNDERSTANDING GOVERNMENT
● Before Peter the Great became tsar in 1689, Russia's capital was Moscow. Peter wanted a new capital that would be Russia's "window on the West," from which Russia could see Europe and be seen.

● He chose its name, St. Petersburg, and location, at the mouth of the Neva River on the Baltic Sea.

● Building began in 1703 as countless thousands of Russians were drafted to do the labor. Some 200,000 of them died. The tsar also forced thousands of Russian nobles to build stone mansions in the city.

● In 1712 St. Petersburg was proclaimed capital, a status it retained for the next 206 years.

BACKGROUND INFORMATION

ABOUT TSAR NICHOLAS II AND HIS FAMILY
● Nicholas II was the last of the Romanovs, the dynasty that had ruled Russia since 1613.

● Like his predecessors, he was known to his people as "Little Father," a name that encouraged ordinary Russians to think of their tsar as a loving parent.

● Nicholas and his wife, Alexandra, had four daughters before their son, Alexi, a male heir to the throne. Alexi suffered from hemophilia, a sometimes fatal disease common to Europe's royal families at the time.

● Concern for Alexi's health brought the Romanovs under the influence of the infamous Rasputin, an influence that contributed to their unpopularity.

War and Hunger

In the years following "Bloody Sunday," unrest deepened in Russia. Things became even worse during World War I. More than a million Russian troops died on the battlefront. Some never even had guns or bullets to protect themselves, since weapons were in short supply. Most of the nation's railroads carried supplies to battle. Only a few trains were available to bring food and fuel to cities. As a result, factories and stores often closed. Many people were left without work. Goods that were already hard to get became even more scarce.

March of 1917 began as one of the coldest, snowiest months that many people in St. Petersburg could remember. The weather kept farmers and their food carts away from city markets. Within the city hungry workers lined up in the cold for hours. They hoped to spend what little money they had on small loaves of bread.

This photo from around 1900 shows workers on a farm in Russia. The lives of many Russian farmers were filled with hard work and hunger.

Revolution Begins

The skies cleared and the weather changed in time for a protest held by thousands of unhappy people. For four days, demonstrators jammed the streets of St. Petersburg. Shouts of "Down with the war!" and "Down with the government!" soon drowned out the simple cry for "Bread!"

The tsar's police called for help from soldiers who were staying in the city. Most of the soldiers, however, joined in the protest and turned on the police. With the soldiers' help the protest became a full-scale revolution against the government.

Tsar Nicholas, who was away meeting with his generals, had no idea of what was happening in his capital. By the time he set out to return home, the spirit of revolution had spread. Angry railroad workers forced his train to a standstill. On March 15, 1917, Nicholas II was forced to give up his role as tsar. Sixteen months later he, his wife Alexandra, and their children were executed. The rule of Russian tsars had come to an end. Who would rule the giant nation now?

Discussing War and Hunger Have students consider the effects of hard times on the Russian people.

- **By March 1917, how many years had passed since "Bloody Sunday"?** *(1917 – 1905 = 12 years)*

- **In what ways had life grown even worse for many Russians?** *(Over a million Russian troops had died in war, at least partly because they were ill-equipped; cities had food and fuel shortages; people were out of work; weather conditions kept food from reaching city people.)*

★**THINKING FURTHER:** *Summarizing* **What short phrases would you use to describe conditions in Russia?** *(Possible answers: sorrow and anger at losses of war, hunger, lack of work and wages, despair)*

Investigating Revolution Begins Have students list the people's demands.

- **How did the revolution begin?** *(with demonstrators in St. Petersburg demanding food and an end to the war and to the tsar's government)*

- **Why were the police and army unable to put down the demonstrations?** *(The army switched sides and joined the protesters.)*

★ **THINKING FURTHER:** *Cause and Effect* **What effect did the revolution in Russia have on the rule of the tsars?** *(It brought that rule to an end, with the execution of Tsar Nicholas II and his family.)*

GLOBAL CONNECTION

HOW WEATHER CAN AFFECT HISTORY Just as extremely cold weather helped to precipitate the Russian Revolution in 1917, so extreme weather conditions have affected events throughout history, for example:

- Typhoons saved Japan from Kublai Khan, as described in the *Global Connections*, p. 411.
- Napoleon invaded Russia in 1812 as part of his world conquest. When he tried to retreat, one of the coldest winters in Russian history set in, trapping his army. Only one-tenth of his men survived.
- In the 1930s, a severe and long drought set in on the American Great Plains, creating the Dust Bowl and worsening the already disastrous Great Depression.

CURRICULUM CONNECTION

LINKS TO READING Tell students of a haunting mystery. Did a member of the tsar's family, his daughter Anastasia, somehow escape? In his book *Seven League Boots*, adventurer Richard Halliburton raised the possibility in "The Massacre of the Romanovs." If this highly readable, though old, book is available, have a student read it and report on the mystery to the class.

LINKS TO SCIENCE In 1994 the Russian government allowed scientists to study the DNA of the royal family's remains. Have a student read the January 1995 *Discover* magazine article "Anastasia Nyet" and report to the class how science answers the Anastasia mystery.

A NEW GOVERNMENT

Have students discuss the possibilities and problems for a new government.

- **What body first tried to form a new government for Russia?** *(the Duma)*

- **What problems did the new government face?** *(continuing war, striking workers, hunger, low wages, farmers seizing land)*

- **What political group emerged with ideas for governing Russia? Who was its leader?** *(Bolsheviks; Lenin)*

- **On whose ideas did they base the form of government they wanted?** *(Karl Marx's ideas of socialism—review Marx's ideas, p. 505.)*

★ **THINKING FURTHER:** *Making Connections* **What ideas for government would Lenin and the Bolsheviks adopt from Marx?** *(The workers should own the factories and should take control.)*

Discussing The Bolsheviks Take Control Have students list effects of the new government.

- **What first step did the Bolsheviks take to gain control of the government?** *(They overthrew the Duma.)*

- **What did the Bolsheviks do about the war?** *(They withdrew Russian troops, negotiated for peace with Germany.)*

- **How did Bolsheviks change the life of workers and farmers?** *(They gave workers control of the factories and allowed farmers to continue using land they had seized from nobles.)*

- **What did they do about Russia's capital?** *(They moved it from St. Petersburg to Moscow. Have students trace this change with their fingers on the map on p. 533.)*

★ **THINKING FURTHER:** *Cause and Effect* **How did the revolution in Russia bring on a devastating civil war there?** *(Those who stood to lose by the new government—landowners, factory owners, and nobles—as well as various religious and ethnic groups opposed the Bolsheviks, bringing on two years of battle, disease, and starvation resulting in the death of millions.)*

In November 1917 soldiers marched to the Duma, where they helped the Bolsheviks gain control of government.

A NEW GOVERNMENT

After the revolution in March, the Duma chose leaders to run the country. Russia's many problems, however, continued. World War I was still underway and Russian military leaders demanded that their troops be withdrawn from the front. City workers went on striking in protest of even longer bread lines and lower wages. Many farmers, hungry and impatient for change, began seizing land for themselves.

Meanwhile a political group called the Bolsheviks was gaining strength. The Bolsheviks were led by a Russian lawyer named Vladimir Ilyich Lenin (VLAD uh meer IHL yitch LEN in). He believed that a different kind of revolution was necessary to change the government. The Bolsheviks planned a socialist revolution based on the ideas of Karl Marx whom you read about in Chapter 17. They wanted workers to control the government and own all property. Lenin promised Russians "Peace, Land, and Bread."

The Bolsheviks Take Control

With the support of the soldiers in St. Petersburg, Lenin and the Bolsheviks overthrew the Duma in November 1917. Soon after this second revolution they pulled Russian troops out of the Allied war effort. Russia began peace talks with Germany. The Bolsheviks allowed workers to control factories and farmers to use the farmland of wealthy nobles. The Bolsheviks also moved the capital of Russia south to the ancient city of Moscow.

The new Bolshevik government had many opponents. Landowners, factory owners, and nobles were losing their rights, as well as their wealth and power. Christians and different ethnic

536

MORE ABOUT VLADIMIR ILYICH LENIN

- He was born Vladimir Ilyich Ulyanov in 1870 to a well-to-do family, part of Russia's small middle class.

- His hatred of tsarism stemmed in part from the fate of his older brother, who was executed after participating in a plot to assassinate Tsar Alexander III in 1887.

- After that, he embraced Marxism fully and loudly, resulting in his arrest in 1895 and five-year imprisonment in Siberia.

- In 1900, he went abroad to continue his revolutionary activities, working out theories of revolution.

- When the Russian Revolution began in 1917, he was living in Switzerland. German officials shipped him back to Russia in a sealed train, hoping he would help Russia exit from the war.

roups also opposed the government. These people led a civil war against Lenin and the Bolsheviks.

The Russian people were already battered from world war and revolution. Their suffering became even greater, however, during this new civil war. Between 1918 and 1920, millions died from disease and starvation, as well as in violent battles.

Communism

Lenin wanted to create communism in Russia. Communism is a political and economic system in which all land and all businesses are controlled by the government.

In the months before the outbreak of the civil war, Lenin wrote, the Bolsheviks had left "one foot in socialism." In other words, they had been moving slowly toward a society controlled by workers. Now, though, Bolshevik leaders took harsh steps to achieve communism in Russia.

The Bolsheviks outlawed all private property, including farms. Farmers were forced to give all of their grain to the government. Lenin replaced factory workers' committees with new managers who were controlled by the Communist Party. Citizens were called upon to serve in the military. To break people's loyalty to religion, the Bolsheviks closed churches and arrested religious leaders. Lenin insisted that all loyalty be focused on the government.

Union of Soviet Socialist Republics

By 1920 the Bolsheviks had defeated their enemies. Two years later they renamed the old Russian empire. The new nation became known as the Union of Soviet Socialist Republics, or the Soviet Union. The soviets were councils of workers and soldiers formed during the revolution.

In 1922 Lenin became ill. He struggled to return to work, but another leader in the Soviet government was growing more powerful. His name was Josef Stalin.

Paintings such as this one of Lenin (left) and political posters (above) were used to urge people to support communism and join the military.

537

CITIZENSHIP ★

UNDERSTANDING GOVERNMENT Both *communism* and *socialism* refer to public ownership of land and business. Help students draw a distinction.

- Communist parties have considered socialism to be a stage in the formation of a true communist society. In this stage, a Communist party rules and most private property is abolished. However, the nation is probably not yet wealthy enough at this stage to provide all benefits for everyone. The government must use coercion, or force, to make people work hard.

- Communist parties have predicted that when a true communist society is achieved, the nation will be wealthy enough to satisfy people without coercion. Do students know of any "true communist society" yet achieved? (probably not)

Discussing Communism Help students recognize how Lenin departed from Marx's ideas of socialism to create communism. Again, have them review what they learned about Marx on p. 505.

- *In Karl Marx's socialism, who was to be in control of society?* (the workers)

- *What was supposed to happen to government under socialism?* (It was supposed to disappear entirely, along with the social class system.)

- *How did Lenin's communism depart from these ideas?* (Communism demanded that ownership and control of the political and economic system be controlled not by the workers but by a government acting in the workers' name.)

- *What steps did the Bolsheviks take to impose communism on Russia?* (Acting as the government, they claimed ownership of all property, replaced factory workers' committees with managers controlled by their own Communist Party, drafted people into the military, and acted to replace loyalty to religion with loyalty to government.)

★ THINKING FURTHER: *Making Decisions* **Do you think Karl Marx would or would not have approved of Russian communism? Explain.** (Students may decide that Russian communism did not give the workers what Marx wanted for them and it did not encourage the end of government.)

Exploring Union of Soviet Socialist Republics Help students see how the change of name was reflected in a substantial change in governing.

- *Who won Russia's civil war?* (the Bolsheviks)

- *What were the soviets?* (councils of workers and soldiers formed by the Bolsheviks during the revolution)

★THINKING FURTHER: *Making Conclusions* **What did Russia's new name indicate that the nation was now supposed to be?** (a union of workers and soldiers in a representative government under worker control)

STALIN'S RULE OF TERROR

Tell students that Lenin was suspicious of Stalin, whom Lenin did not choose as a successor.

- **Why was Stalin able to become the Soviet leader?** *(Lenin died, leaving Stalin free to become leader.)*

- **What did Stalin do to revolutionize agriculture in the Soviet Union?** *(He combined individual farms into collective farms on which farm families worked for the government.)*

- **What did he do to industrialize the Soviet Union?** *(He built up factories, mines, and railroads.)*

- **What kind of economy did the new government create?** *(a command economy)*

- **What is a command economy?** *(an economy that is controlled by the government)*

★ **THINKING FURTHER:** *Making Conclusions* **Why can you conclude that the Russian revolution was both a political and an economic revolution?** *(It changed government from tsarist to communist and it changed a mainly agricultural economy into a command economy with collective farms and industries.)*

Discussing Totalitarian Rule Write totalitarian on the board and ask students to identify a five-letter word within it *(total)*.

- **What does total have to do with totalitarian?** *(In a totalitarian society, a dictator has total control over all aspects of people's lives.)*

- **What totalitarian methods did Stalin use to build communism in the Soviet Union?** *(created fear and threatened arrest and imprisonment for dissent, used secret police to spy on people, denied all religious freedom, used political prisoners as forced labor, executed millions of "enemies of the state")*

STALIN'S RULE OF TERROR

Lenin died in 1924. Soon after, Josef Stalin became the new leader of the Soviet Union. In 1928 Stalin began working to make the Soviet Union stronger. He drew all power into the government. Stalin also created huge collective farms. Collective farms were run by the government and worked by many families. People not needed on farms were sent to work in mines and factories springing up across the nation. An economy completely controlled by government is called a command economy.

Within just 20 years the Soviet Union became one of the world's strongest industrial nations. Thousands of railroad lines crisscrossed the country, linking towns and cities that had never been connected before. Around 1900 many Russian farmers had never seen a tractor. By the 1940s Soviet factories were making more tractors than any other factories in the world.

Totalitarian Rule

People paid a huge price, however, for growth and change in the Soviet Union. Stalin used totalitarian (toh tal ih TAIR ee un) methods to rule the nation. In a totalitarian society, a dictator, often representing a single political party, controls all aspects of people's lives. Stalin and the Communist Party controlled the Soviet Union through fear and terror. For many, life was more difficult than it had been under the tsars. People were arrested for speaking their minds freely or for writing to friends in other countries. Many managers were killed because their factories or farms did not produce an expected amount. Stalin also ordered his secret police to arrest anyone who he thought challenged him in any way.

Many of those arrested were religious leaders. Their followers were forced to worship secretly or face arrest themselves. Stalin had more than 15 million people killed or sent to prison camps in Siberia. Almost half of them were Ukrainians. Many starved because the collective farms failed to produce enough food. Large numbers of people were sent to camps where religious

---

Stalin (below left) forced thousands of people to work on collective farms (below). Despite much hard work, many collective farms failed.

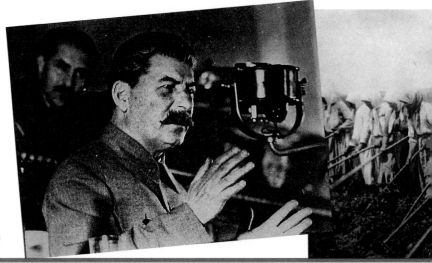

538

MORE ABOUT JOSEF STALIN

- He was born Iosif Vissarionovich Dzhugashvili in 1879 in Georgia, in European Russia, to a shoemaker and a washerwoman.

- At the age of 14, he entered a religious seminary. He later joined a Marxist group, which probably had something to do with his being expelled from the seminary in 1899.

- By 1917 he had been arrested and exiled several times for his writings as well as for his efforts to organize workers to strike.

- When he was in power, he had history books rewritten to say that he had worked closely with Lenin to overthrow the tsar.

- He took the name *Stalin* because in Russian it means "like steel".

eaders, teachers, workers, and others Stalin considered "enemies of the people" were imprisoned.

Oil, iron, timber—all the resources of the Soviet Union's new industry—were in great supply in Siberia. Since few people lived there, Stalin used political prisoners to help collect the resources.

One women's camp had the job of cutting down trees. One of the prisoners, a teacher, described the camp this way:

The cold and the hunger; the hunger and the cold. This must have been the blackest, the most [deadly], the most evil of all my winters in the camps.

WHY IT MATTERS

In the early 1900s life changed dramatically in Russia during a period of revolution. Many of the changes that took place became the foundation of a communist system of government. For this reason, the Russian Revolution is also known as a communist revolution. One of the revolution's many effects was the formation of the Soviet Union.

Revolutionary leaders had promised "peace, land, and bread." Under the

communist government, however, most people in the Soviet Union had none of these things. Millions were killed and sent to prison camps in Siberia by Josef Stalin. Stalin used totalitarian methods to rule the nation.

For many, suffering worsened when the Soviet Union and many other countries became involved in another world conflict. To the west of the Soviet Union, a dictator in Germany was making plans that would lead to war.

✔️ Reviewing Facts and Ideas

MAIN IDEAS

● Millions of serfs under Russia's tsars lived in poverty. The abolition of serfdom in 1861 gave farmers a limited amount of freedom.

● The Russian Revolution began in 1917 as a revolt against World War I, the tsar, and poor working and living conditions. Seven months later Lenin and the Bolsheviks seized control, bringing communism to the country they later renamed the Soviet Union.

● Under Stalin, the Communist Party controlled the Soviet Union using totalitarian methods.

THINK ABOUT IT

1. What were the policies of the Soviet Union regarding religious beliefs and practices?

2. Define the term *communism*.

3. **FOCUS** How were the governments led by Tsar Nicholas II and Josef Stalin similar? How were they different?

4. **THINKING SKILL** Describe Josef Stalin's *point of view* about the need to totally control the economy of the Soviet Union.

5. **GEOGRAPHY** Why might Stalin have chosen Siberia as a site for prisons?

539

Discussing WHY IT MATTERS On a map of the world, have students locate Russia's area in 1917. (See the map on p. 533.)

★ **THINKING FURTHER:** *Making Conclusions* **Why would a revolution covering this amount of land have a major effect on the world?** *(Help students realize that the revolution that turned Russia into the Soviet Union meant that communism now covered a vast area of the world and could affect the governments of other parts of the world.)*

⭐ 3 CLOSE

MAIN IDEAS
Have students write answers and exchange papers for correction.

● **What did the abolition of serfdom mean in Russia?** *(People who had been tied to the land, as in the Middle Ages, were given limited freedom.)*

● **What caused the Russian Revolution and what effect did it have?** *(Cause: World War I, tsarist rule, poor living and working conditions. Effect: creation of communist Soviet Union.)*

● **How did the Soviet Union become a totalitarian nation?** *(It came under the rule of the dictator Stalin and the Communist party.)*

EVALUATE
✔ **Answers to Think About It**

1. They were banned. *Summarize*

2. a system in which all land and businesses are controlled by the government in the name of workers *Make Inferences*

3. Similar: Both were dictatorships. Different: Tsars allowed religion and private ownership to exist. *Compare and Contrast*

4. He believed that total control was the only way to assure economic growth. *Point of View*

5. It was rich in resources, which forced labor could mine and gather. *Five Themes of Geography: Human/Environment Interactions*

Write About It Have students write a paragraph describing how the Russian Revolution changed life for Russian nobles.

MEETING INDIVIDUAL NEEDS

RETEACHING (Easy) Have students review "Two Sides of a City," p. 534, and tell them to use colored pens, pencils, or crayons to illustrate a scene from each, side by side.

EXTENSION (Average) Tell students to picture themselves as having lived through the Russian Revolution. Have them write a letter to a friend in another country describing how their lives have changed between the time of tsarist Russia to that of the communist Soviet Union.

ENRICHMENT (Challenging) To broaden students' knowledge about the Russian Revolution, divide the class into groups and assign each group one of the following: Alexander Kerensky, Mensheviks, Treaty of Brest Litovsk, Leon Trotsky. Have each group research its topic and report its findings to the class.

Lesson Overview
In an attempt to dominate the world, Germany, Italy, and Japan initiated World War II.

Lesson Objectives
★ Explain how Hitler fostered the rise of Nazism in Germany.

★ Sequence major events in World War II.

★ Analyze the causes and effects of the Holocaust.

1 PREPARE

MOTIVATE Have a student do the *Read Aloud* as Selassie, another as the narrator. Ask students to define *precedent* ("a decision that can guide later decisions") and to explain events in Ethiopia. Ask them for opinions about nations that are bullies. Should others try to stop them?

SET PURPOSE Ask students what, in their experience, happens when bullies are not stopped. Refer them to the *Read to Learn* question and encourage them to explore this lesson to answer it. Preview the *Vocabulary*.

2 TEACH

Understanding THE BIG PICTURE
Discuss the questions below.

● **What beliefs are key to fascism?** *(a powerful leader, totalitarian government, and extreme nationalism)*

● **What major fascist leaders emerged in Europe?** *(Benito Mussolini in Italy, Adolf Hitler in Germany)*

★ **THINKING FURTHER:** *Compare and Contrast* **How would you contrast fascism with democracy?** *(Fascism: people serve government. Democracy: government serves people.)*

Resource REMINDER

Practice and Project Book: *p. 107*

Anthology: *The Diary of Anne Frank, pp. 146–149; Defeating Nazi Germany, p. 150; Never Give Up the Fight, p. 151; Attack on Pearl Harbor, p. 152; When the A-Bomb Fell, pp. 153–154*

Focus Activity

READ TO LEARN

What conditions led to the outbreak of World War II?

VOCABULARY

- fascism
- inflation
- depression
- propaganda
- World War II
- Axis
- Allies
- concentration camp
- Holocaust

PEOPLE

- Adolf Hitler
- Winston Churchill
- Franklin Roosevelt
- Anne Frank

PLACES

- Pearl Harbor
- Normandy

540

| 1890 | 1915 | 1929 | 1945 | 1965 | 1990 |

World War II

Read Aloud
"I pray to Almighty God that He shall spare the nations the terrible sufferings that have just been [forced] on my people. . . . Are [you] going to set up the terrible precedent of bowing before force?"

In 1936 Ethiopian emperor Haile Selassie (HĪ lee suh LAS ee) appeared before the League of Nations to protest Italy's invasion of his African country. The League, however, did not come to Selassie's aid. Ethiopia would not regain its independence for nearly five years. During much of that time, the world was once again plunged into war.

THE BIG PICTURE
After the signing of the Treaty of Versailles, the countries that had fought in World War I turned to their own affairs. In the last lesson you read about the communist revolution in Russia. In 1922, the dictator Benito Mussolini and his Fascist (FASH ihst) party rose to power in Italy.

The Fascists believed in a powerful leader, totalitarian government, and an extreme form of nationalism. They supported a government whose goals they thought to be more important than those of individual people. This type of government came to be known as fascism. In some places fascism also came to mean hatred of certain ethnic groups.

After Italy took control of Ethiopia in 1936, Mussolini joined forces with another fascist dictator, Adolf Hitler of Germany. The people of nearby nations began to see that fascism was a serious threat to peace.

SHELTERED INSTRUCTION

READING STRATEGIES & LANGUAGE DEVELOPMENT

USING VISUALS Remind students how photographs can teach us much about history. Explain that World War II was the most visually recorded war at that time. Have small groups of students select a photograph they find especially dramatic, such as the photo of Hitler on p. 541, and write an "eyewitness" account of World War II, based on the visual they used. [SDAIE STRATEGY: TEXT RE-PRESENTATION]

CONTRACTIONS Write the term *contractions* on the board and ask the class what it means in connection with language ("shortened forms of phrases made by leaving letters out and replacing them with apostrophes"). Point out that we use contractions more in conversation and in informal writing, like letters or diaries, than in formal writing. Have them identify the contractions in the Anne Frank excerpt, p. 546, and the longer terms for which they stand.

GERMANY AFTER WORLD WAR I

In 1919 Germany began to live by the conditions of the Treaty of Versailles. The treaty stripped Germany of land and forced it to pay huge fines.

To meet these expenses the German government began printing large amounts of paper money. Before long Germany had printed so much money that it began to lose its value. The result was a period of inflation, or rising prices. Huge amounts of money were needed even to buy necessities such as food. By 1923 inflation had made German money practically worthless, and people's savings were gone.

In that year a bitter ex-soldier named Adolf Hitler led an attack against the German government in the state of Bavaria. Although the attack failed and Hitler was jailed, many Germans supported his actions. His followers were known as the Nazi (NAHT see) party.

Fascism in Germany

By the early 1930s, Germany and much of the world suffered a depression (di PRESH un). During a depression, fewer goods are produced, prices drop, many people lose their jobs, and money is hard to get.

During these hard times Hitler used propaganda (prahp uh GAN duh) to convince Germans that their nation could once again become powerful. Propaganda is the spreading of certain ideas or attitudes that have been exaggerated or falsified to advance a particular cause.

Hitler's propaganda spread the false idea that the Germans were a "master race," meant to rule the world. The Nazis wrongfully blamed Germany's Jews, along with the Treaty of Versailles, for the depression that was devastating the country. Promising to raise Germany back to glory, Hitler once again tried to gain control in 1933. This time he succeeded.

Hitler ruled as a fascist dictator, forming an alliance with Mussolini in Italy. He and the Nazis stirred up hatred against Jews. In five years the Nazis' plans would lead to the largest war in history.

Hitler (left) used propaganda methods to convince Germans that Germany would become powerful. His followers raised their arms and shouted "Hail Victory!"

541

GERMANY AFTER WORLD WAR I

Take the class back to the aftermath of World War I. All the warring nations were suffering, having lost millions of fighting men and having squandered their national treasure on war.

● *What additional burdens did Germany have to carry because of the Treaty of Versailles?* (It was stripped of land and armed forces and paid huge fines.)

★ THINKING FURTHER: *Sequencing How would you diagram the steps that led to Germany's terrible financial state?* (To pay fines, government prints too much money→money loses value→prices skyrocket→savings are wiped out→people cannot buy goods.)

Discussing Fascism in Germany
Discuss the events that led to unrest.

● *What happens when an economy suffers a depression?* (Production goes down, prices drop, people lose jobs, money is tight.)

● *Was Germany the only nation that suffered depression? Explain.* (No, much of the world suffered it.)

★ THINKING FURTHER: *Making Connections How did Hitler use propaganda to gain power?* (He used exaggerations and lies to tell Germans they were blameless in their fate, that Jews and the Treaty of Versailles were to blame, that Germans were a master race who should rule the world.)

A SECOND WORLD WAR

Review that the Treaty of Versailles stripped Germany of armed forces.

★THINKING FURTHER: *Compare and Contrast In what cases did Britain and France give in to Germany and when did they stand their ground?* (Gave in: when Germany entered Austria and Czechoslovakia. Stood ground: when Germany threatened Poland.)

Discussing The German Advance
Write *blitzkrieg* on the board and have students define it.

● *Why was Germany able to overrun Poland within weeks?* (because of its lightning military strikes and its treaty of friendship with the Soviet Union)

● *How did Britain and France respond to the attack on Poland?* (by declaring war on Germany)

● *How did Germany respond to that declaration?* (by turning its forces on France and defeating it in six weeks)

★THINKING FURTHER: *Compare and Contrast How would you compare and contrast Britain's situation regarding allies here with its situation at the beginning of World War I?* (Pre-WWI: France and Russia were major allies. Pre-WWII: Britain stood alone because the Soviet Union had sided with Germany and France had fallen.)

Exploring The Battle of Britain
Emphasize Britain's vulnerability.

● *Who was Britain's wartime leader?* (Prime Minister Winston Churchill)

● *How was the Battle of Britain fought?* (German planes bombed Britain every night, and British planes fought the German planes.)

● *How long did it last?* (almost a year)

★THINKING FURTHER: *Making Conclusions When the Battle of Britain ended, Winston Churchill said of Britain's Royal Air Force, "Never in the field of human conflict was so much owed by so many to so few." What do you suppose he meant?* (Help students to see that only the not-very-large RAF had stood between Britain and defeat.)

A SECOND WORLD WAR

In 1938 Hitler ordered Nazi troops to occupy neighboring Austria. With this command, Hitler knowingly broke the rules of the Treaty of Versailles. Then, in March 1939, Hitler seized control of Czechoslovakia. After years of trying to avoid war with Germany, the leaders of Britain and France promised to defend Hitler's next target—Poland. Europe was on the brink of war once again.

The German Advance

World War II began in Europe on September 1, 1939. On that day German tanks began a *blitzkrieg* (BLIHTZ kreeg), or "lightning war," in Poland. Hitler and Josef Stalin, whom you read about in Lesson 2, had recently signed a friendship treaty. With the help of the Soviet Union, Germany defeated Poland within weeks. Britain and France declared war on Germany but had not been able to defend their ally, Poland.

Eight months later German forces turned west. Hitler's armies quickly overran Belgium. They went on to seize Paris by June 1940. Hitler's fighting method of blitzkrieg was proving very effective. Germany had beaten France—a major world power—in only six weeks! With much of France under German control, Hitler made Britain the next Nazi target.

Many areas in London (left) were destroyed during the Battle of Britain. People often found their homes reduced to rubble by nightly bombings (above).

BACKGROUND INFORMATION

ABOUT THE "MIRACLE OF DUNKERQUE" (OR "DUNKIRK") Have students locate Dunkirk or Dunkerque in France on a map.

● British troops sailed to France to fight the Germans after World War II was declared.

● The Germans soon cornered about 350,000 British, French, and Belgian troops at Dunkirk. Escape seemed impossible.

● For the next six days, as the Royal Air Force fought off German planes above the field, a mixed assortment of 900 naval craft—from navy vessels to fishing boats—bravely crossed the Channel to bring the troops back to England. All but 30,000 of them made the miraculous return.

The Battle of Britain

The British people prepared for the worst. The country's leader, Prime Minister Winston Churchill, declared:

We shall fight on the seas and oceans, we shall fight with growing confidence and growing strength in the air, we shall defend our island, whatever the cost may be. . . . We shall never surrender.

Two months later, in August 1940, the Battle of Britain began. For almost a year German planes bombed the island nation every night. The British air force fought back. Although many sought safety in underground shelters, more than 12,000 British people were killed in the fighting. Despite the cost Britain did not surrender. The nation stood firm, as Churchill had predicted.

Weather Plays a Part

In June 1941 Hitler ended the bombing of Britain. Germany had lost more than 2,000 planes, along with their crews. Having failed in Britain, Hitler decided to break his treaty with Stalin. He ordered his armies to turn east and invade the Soviet Union. The Germans began what was to become a three-year struggle for control of major Soviet cities and supply centers. Millions of Soviet soldiers and civilians died during the struggle.

The Soviet Union now became an ally of Britain. In spite of their political differences, the British welcomed the Soviets in the fight against their common enemy, the Nazis. By November 1941 German troops were very close to one of their goals: the Soviet capital, Moscow. Soviet armies fought to defend their capital and their country. The German troops were finally stopped, however, by a deadly northern winter. On December 6, the near-frozen Germans began to retreat. It would not be the last time nature played a part in the outcome of the war.

An Attack on the United States

War had begun earlier in Asia than it had in Europe. Japan had hoped to create an empire with an endless supply of raw materials and labor for industry. By 1931 Japanese forces had invaded northern China. Later Japan conquered about one quarter of China and some islands off the coast of South Asia. Find the region of Japanese expansion on the map on pages 544–545.

In 1940 Japan formed an alliance with Germany. The conquests and the alliance created tension between Japan and the United States, which was against Japan's continuing expansionist policy. Japan was determined to stop the United States from involvement in its expansionist plans.

On December 7, 1941, Japan launched an attack without any warning or declaration of war. The target was the United States naval base at Pearl Harbor, Hawaii. More than 2,000 people died in the attack. The United States was now involved in World War II.

President Franklin Roosevelt declared war on Japan on December 8, 1941. Three days later, on December 11, Germany and Italy declared war on the United States. Japan, Germany, Italy, and their other allies were known as the Axis. The Allies included Britain, France, the Soviet Union, the United States, and China, among others. The United States had to fight Japan in Asia and Germany and Italy in Europe and Africa. As in World War I, United States forces would be very important to the Allied war effort.

543

CITIZENSHIP ★

THE CITIZEN'S ROLE ON THE HOME FRONT The U.S. government involved home-front Americans in the war effort as never before.

- Citizens were urged to buy war bonds, often at the urging of celebrities like film stars and recording stars. Essentially, these bonds were loans the people made to the government to fight the war. Adults bought bonds for $25 and up. Children bought war stamps for 10 cents apiece until they filled a book worth $25.

- Every citizen was issued a ration book. These books issued coupons for items like shoes, meat, and canned goods. A person could buy only as many of these items as the ration book coupons allowed.

- Young people, like Boy Scout and Girl Scout troops, collected scrap metal, newspapers, grease, old rubber tires, and tinfoil—anything that could be recycled into war materials.

Discussing Weather Plays a Part
On the board, have a student diagram the alliances before and after these events.

- *What two breaks did Britain get in 1941?* (Germany stopped its nightly bombing, and Hitler turned on the Soviet Union, which made the Soviet Union join Britain as an ally.)

- *How successful was Germany's invasion of the Soviet Union?* (Germany brought death and destruction to the Soviet Union, but was finally driven back by Soviet determination and by the deadly Russian winter.)

★THINKING FURTHER: *Making Conclusions Why do you suppose Hitler broke his pact with Stalin?* (Invite students to make any suppositions they can, perhaps that Hitler thought the Soviet Union was an easier target than Britain. Then explain that Hitler had always intended to invade the Soviet Union to gain additional "living room" he believed the growing German population needed.)

Investigating An Attack on the United States Turn to Japan's actions in the war.

- *What steps did Japan take in its drive to create an empire in Asia?* (1931: invasion of northern China, conquest of one-quarter of China and islands off Southeast Asia. 1940: alliance with Germany and Italy)

- *Why did tensions arise between Japan and the U.S.?* (U.S. opposed Japan's expansion into other Asian lands.)

- *What step did Japan take to stop the U.S. from interfering in its expansionist plans?* (Japan attacked the U.S. naval base at Pearl Harbor, Hawaii.)

★THINKING FURTHER: *Cause and Effect How would you diagram cause and effect from Pearl Harbor to full-scale world war?* (Pearl Harbor→U.S. declares war on Japan→ Japan's allies Germany and Italy declare war on U.S.→Allies-Britain, France, Soviet Union, U.S., and China→fight Axis→Germany, Italy, and Japan)

"THE LONGEST DAY"

Have the students locate Normandy on a map.

- **What was D-Day?** *(June 6, 1944, when the Allies landed from England in Normandy, France, to begin their invasion to defeat the Germans in Europe. Point out that the "D" stands for "day," as in "a red-letter day.")*

- **How did bad weather actually bene-fit the Allies?** *(It gave them the element of surprise because the Germans did not believe an attack was possible under such weather conditions.)*

More MAP WORK

Begin by having students locate the Axis Powers (orange) and the Allies (yellow) on the map on these pages to see that the war was truly global. Then have students concentrate on the Pacific theater of operations.

- **What part of the world did Japan control?** *(eastern and southeastern Asia and many islands of the Pacific)*

- **What territories that were connected with Allied nations did Japan control?** *(the [U.S.] Philippines, French Indochina, Netherlands Indies)*

- ★**THINKING FURTHER:** *Making Conclusions* **Why is it fair to say that Japanese control was spread very thin?** *(It was spread out over a very broad area.)*

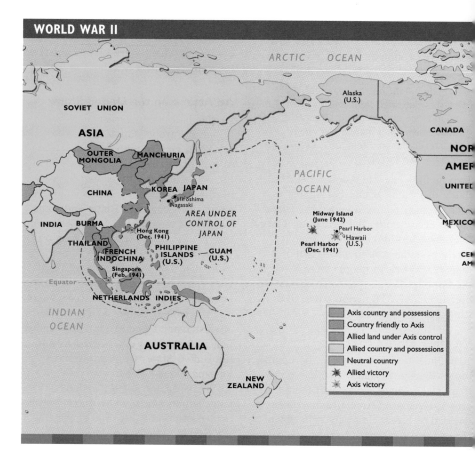

WORLD WAR II

"THE LONGEST DAY"

For three years the United States, Britain, and other Allies fought the Nazis in Europe and in North Africa. In that time, the Soviet Union struggled to push back and destroy the German invaders on its soil. Finally, Allied leaders prepared to put a risky plan into action. On the night of June 5, 1944, the Allies would begin a surprise invasion of Axis-held France. If they succeeded, Germany would be surrounded on three sides—west, east, and south. The Allies' code name for this operation was D-Day.

Allied leaders prepared their forces to land on the beaches of Normandy, France, at dawn on June 6. They would reach shore while the tide was low so that German weapons on the beach would be open to attack. Months earlier, weather experts had concluded that the best conditions for an attack would exist between June 5 and 7. On June 4, though, a terrible storm raged across the English Channel. Would nature stop the biggest sea invasion in history?

The storm actually helped the Allies. German commander Erwin Rommel believed that the Allies would not

544

BACKGROUND INFORMATION

ABOUT THE GRAND STRATEGY
- The Allies fought on two main fronts—in Europe and in the Pacific. In 1942 they agreed to concentrate on victory in Europe first because if Hitler won there, the United States would be left alone to fight the war.

- The Allies moved first against the Axis Powers in North Africa, where Italy, backed by Germany, was attempting to create a Mediterranean empire. There, the Allies defeated German General Erwin Rommel, known as the "Desert Fox" for his cunning and skill.

- In 1943 the Allies landed in Sicily to attack "the soft underbelly of Europe" and to work their way up the Italian peninsula into the heart of Europe.

- The Soviet Union had been fighting the Axis on the eastern front since Germany invaded it in 1941. By 1944 the Allies were ready to open a second, western front in Europe by landing in France on D-Day.

- Meanwhile the United States began its island-hopping campaign in the Pacific, capturing Japanese-held islands and turning them into air bases from which they could push the Japanese back to their homeland.

- By early 1945 the Soviet army began moving relentlessly on Germany from the east as the other Allies moved on it from the west, closing on it on the banks of the Elbe River in late April 1945.

- As war in Europe wound down, the Allies could turn their major attention to defeating the Japanese.

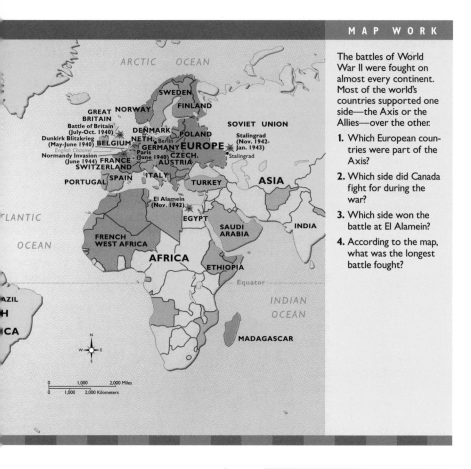

MAP WORK

The battles of World War II were fought on almost every continent. Most of the world's countries supported one side—the Axis or the Allies—over the other.

1. Which European countries were part of the Axis?

2. Which side did Canada fight for during the war?

3. Which side won the battle at El Alamein?

4. According to the map, what was the longest battle fought?

More MAP WORK

Continue referring to the map, having students concentrate on the European theater of operations on this page.

- *Over what Allied countries in Western Europe did the Axis gain control?* (France, Belgium, Norway, the Netherlands, Poland, Denmark)

- *Which side controlled most of Eastern Europe?* (Axis Powers)

- *Which side won the battle for Stalingrad in the Soviet Union?* (Allies)

- *How would Allied recapture of France help the Allies to move on the Axis Powers with a pincers movement?* (Help students see how the Allies Britain, France, and the U.S. moving from the west and the Soviet Union moving from the east would squeeze the Axis Powers in Central Europe into submission.)

- *How large a force did the Allies build up to make the D-Day landings?* (11,000 planes, more than 2,700 ships, 200,000 men)

★THINKING FURTHER: *Making Conclusions* **Why do you suppose D-Day seemed like "the longest day" to those who took part in it?** *(Invite students to tell about any D-Day movies they have seen, and help them to empathize with the troops charging up on shore, facing heavy fire and a strongly entrenched and heavily armed enemy.)*

nvade during such weather. He traveled home to Germany for a few days, ust when D-Day arrived. The Allies ttacked. Over 11,000 Allied planes dropped bombs and over 2,700 ships unloaded almost 200,000 men onto the beaches of Normandy. Find Normandy on the map.

Afterwards, an Allied soldier said D-Day seemed like "the longest day" of his life. At the end of that day, allied orces held the beaches. The Allies would now begin to push the Axis powers east across Europe and west from he Soviet Union.

On D-Day Allied soldiers gained control of the German-held beaches in Normandy, France, then moved inland to free Paris.

MAP WORK: 1. Germany, Austria, Italy 2. Allies 3. Allies 4. the Battle of Britain   **545**

CITIZENSHIP★

UNDERSTANDING GOVERNMENT Explain to the class that governments have reserved the right to draft able-bodied young people into military service. (Generally in the past, it has been young men, though some nations have drafted young women as well.)

- In World War II the American government drafted 10 million men into the U.S. armed services.

- Young men were ordered to register for the draft and, in an emergency, were called up to serve in the military.

Have students discuss why such a system might be necessary and why being a good citizen can call for willingness to serve one's country.

BACKGROUND INFORMATION

ABOUT CHIUNE SUGIHARA, A LIFE-SAVER

- In 1940 Japan assigned diplomat Chiune Sugihara to its consulate in Kaunas, Lithuania. He arrived as World War II began.

- Jewish refugees from Poland, whose lives were in danger, asked him for transit visas to leave Europe through Russia and Japan.

- Against his government's orders, Consul Sugihara issued about 6,000 visas, saving thousands of lives.

- In 1968, a diplomat from Israel, a man whose life had been saved, contacted Sugihara to thank him.

- Since that time many events have recognized Sugihara's courageous acts.

Have students assess the war's end.

● **How did World War II end in Europe?** *(The Allies defeated Germany.)*

● **How did the war end in Asia and the Pacific?** *(Japan surrendered after two atomic bombs were dropped.)*

★**THINKING FURTHER:** *Making Conclusions* **What can you conclude about conditions in Britain, France, Germany, the Soviet Union, China, and Japan as the war ended?** *(All suffered war damage, lost many lives, and used up vast resources.)*

Discussing The Terrible Effects of Fascism Have students recognize the wartime behavior of Axis countries.

● **What are concentration camps?** *(places where people are imprisoned and killed for their heritage, religion, or political views)*

● **How did the Japanese and Germans treat prisoners in their concentration camps?** *(tortured and often killed them)*

● **What was the Holocaust?** *(the Nazi murder of 6 million Jews and 6 million others)*

● **Who were some other peoples the Nazis murdered?** *(Gypsies, Poles, Russians, Slavs)*

★**THINKING FURTHER:** *Making Connections* **How can you relate Hitler's theory of the "master race" to the Holocaust?** *(Believing oneself to be master of others might lead to the belief that one has the right to exterminate them.)*

Discussing the PRIMARY SOURCE

Have a student read the excerpt aloud.

● **Who was Anne Frank?** *(a 15-year-old Holocaust victim)*

★**THINKING FURTHER:** *Compare and Contrast* **How would you compare and contrast what she saw around her with what she believed about human beings?** *(She saw evil yet held onto a belief in goodness.)*

THE END OF THE WAR

Less than a year after D-Day, Allied forces closed in around Germany. With the Soviet army already in the German capital of Berlin, Adolf Hitler killed himself to avoid capture on April 30, 1945. One week later, on May 7, 1945, Germany surrendered. Japan's leaders, however, refused to give up the struggle for power.

United States leaders considered using a newly developed bomb against the Japanese. Invading Japan could lead to many deaths on both sides. Could the tremendously powerful atomic bomb bring about Japan's surrender? On August 6, 1945, the United States dropped the first atomic bomb ever used in warfare on the Japanese city of Hiroshima (hihr uh SHEE muh). Most of the city was destroyed in seconds, and at least 80,000 people died.

Japan did not surrender. Three days later the United States dropped another atomic bomb on the city of Nagasaki (nah guh SAH kee). Japan surrendered on August 14, 1945. The most terrible war in history was finally over.

The Terrible Effects of Fascism

In the days before their defeat, German and Japanese commanders rushed to hide evidence of their concentration camps. Concentration camps are places where people are imprisoned because of their heritage, religious beliefs, or political views. Prisoners in Japanese and Nazi concentration camps were tortured and often killed. Millions of others were murdered as well.

The Nazis murdered about 6 million Jews, or two-thirds of Europe's Jewish

population, in concentration camps or by execution squads. These people, including women, children, and elderly people, had committed no crime. They were not soldiers. They were killed for no other reason than that they were Jewish. This deliberate destruction of human life is called the Holocaust (HOL uh kawst). About another 6 million people, among them Gypsies, Poles, Russians, and Slavs were also murdered in Nazi concentration camps.

One of the millions of young Jews who died in the camps was 15-year-old Anne Frank. She and her family spent two years hiding in the Netherlands before Nazi soldiers captured them. What did Anne Frank believe about people and about the future? Do you find her point of view surprising?

MANY VOICES

PRIMARY SOURCE

Excerpt from *The Diary of Anne Frank,* July 1944.

It's really a wonder that I haven't dropped all my ideals, because they seem so absurd and impossible to carry out. Yet I keep them, because in spite of everything I still believe that people are really good at heart. I simply can't build up my hopes on a foundation consisting of confusion, misery, and death. I see the world gradually being turned into a wilderness, I hear the ever approaching thunder, which will destroy us too, I can feel the sufferings of millions and yet, if I look up into the heavens, I think that it will all come [out] right, that this cruelty too will end, and that peace and tranquility will return again.

LINKS TO LANGUAGE ARTS Having the class read *The Diary of Anne Frank* can act as a catalyst for a variety of language arts activities.
● For example, have groups choose scenes from the book to dramatize and then perform for the class.
● Or have students choose their favorite parts of the book and then write poems in which they voice their reactions to those parts.
● Or have them research and write biographies of Anne Frank or write journal entries as if they were in her place themselves.

BACKGROUND INFORMATION

ABOUT THE HOLOCAUST Hitler called the extermination of all Jews "the final solution" to his hatred of them. Between 1939 and 1945, two-thirds of the Jews of Europe were killed by the Nazis.

Children like these brothers at the Auschwitz concentration camp were imprisoned by the Nazis. Prisoners in the camps were often tortured and killed.

WHY IT MATTERS

World War II was the largest war in history. Unlike World War I, which had been fought mostly in Europe, World War II took place in Europe, Asia, Africa, and the islands of the Pacific. While many battles took place on land, there were sea battles on the world's oceans, as well. The war left as many as 50 million people dead. Many millions more would be affected by its horrors throughout their lives.

People once again began to adjust to peace after a world war. It was not always easy. Destroyed roads, bridges, homes, and cities around the world had to be rebuilt. There were other serious problems, too.

Leaders of the United States and Western Europe feared the communist government of the Soviet Union. Soon the two most powerful Allies, the United States and the Soviet Union, would become bitter enemies. You will read about their conflict later in the chapter.

✔ Reviewing Facts and Ideas

MAIN IDEAS

- In the 1930s Nazi leader Adolf Hitler used propaganda to convince many Germans that their nation could return to its former power.

- A world depression in the 1930s caused suffering in many nations and helped to bring about the rise of fascist dictators, such as Hitler.

- The Nazis murdered about 6 million Jews in concentration camps. This became known as the Holocaust. There were also some 6 million other victims of the Holocaust, including Gypsies, Poles, Russians, and Slavs.

- Japan attacked and conquered parts of Southeast Asia and the Pacific. After Japan attacked Pearl Harbor, the United States entered World War II. The war came to an end after the United States used two atomic bombs on Japanese cities.

THINK ABOUT IT

1. How did the United States help the Allied war effort?

2. Why was D-Day an important battle?

3. **FOCUS** How did Hitler use the problems created by inflation, the depression, and unemployment to make himself dictator of Germany? How did he use this power to bring about World War II?

4. **THINKING SKILL** List three *facts* and one *opinion* about fascism.

5. **GEOGRAPHY** What role did the weather and time of attack play in the planning and outcome of D-Day?

547

Discussing WHY IT MATTERS Remind students that World War II was history's largest war.

★**THINKING FURTHER:** *Compare and Contrast* **How would you compare the size and effects of World War II with World War I?** *(Help students to recognize that in WWII more parts of the world were affected, there were a greater number of deaths, there was wider and more terrible destruction, and the need for recovery was much broader, among losers and winners.)*

3 CLOSE

MAIN IDEAS
Call on students for answers.

- **How did a worldwide economic condition of the 1930s make some nations ripe for fascism?** *(Worldwide depression threw people out of work; they believed that strong governments could solve their problems.)*

- **How many Jews were murdered in the Holocaust? How many others were killed?** *(6 million Jews, 6 million others)*

- **How did the fight between Japan and the United States begin and end?** *(Japanese bombed Pearl Harbor; the end came after the U.S. dropped atom bombs on Japan.)*

EVALUATE
✔ **Answers to Think About It**

1. with supplies and armed forces *Summarize*

2. It opened a western front against the Axis Powers. *Draw Conclusions*

3. He preyed on German fears, anger, and pride to convince the people that he could be their savior. *Main Idea*

4. Facts should focus on the beliefs and actions of fascism; opinions will focus on students' judgments. *Evaluate Fact/Opinion*

5. The bad weather and the attacking at dawn both added to the element of surprise, working for the Allies. *Five Themes of Geography: Human/Environment Interactions*

Write About It Tell students to picture themselves charging onto the beach at Normandy. Have them write a journal entry describing the experience.

MEETING INDIVIDUAL NEEDS

RETEACHING (Easy) Tell students to review the lesson and pick out the major events of World War II. Then have them create a chart in which they sequence these events and write a sentence about each.

EXTENSION (Average) Have students picture themselves as either American or other Allied military personnel fighting in either Europe or the Pacific during World War II. Have them write letters home explaining the ideals for which they are fighting.

ENRICHMENT (Challenging) Have students interview someone they know who lived through World War II and was old enough to have clear memories of it, either on the home front or in the military. Encourage students to prepare questions beforehand. Then have them write up their interviews as if they were preparing them as features for a newspaper.

SKILLS LESSON
PAGES 548–549

Lesson Overview
Time zone maps make it possible to determine time anywhere on Earth.

Lesson Objective
★ Learn to interpret a time zone map.

1 PREPARE

MOTIVATE Have a student hold a flashlight (the sun) over an area of a globe. Tell the class it is twelve noon at that spot. Rotate the globe a bit counterclockwise but keep the "sun" still. Ask students what time of day it is in the original area now? (afternoon) Have students read *Why the Skill Matters* to learn how time zone maps show different times across Earth.

SET PURPOSE Tell students to explore this lesson to learn how to tell what time it is at any given moment anywhere on Earth. Have them read *Helping Yourself* to preview methods.

2 TEACH

Using the Skill Refer the class to the map on this page.

- *Where does the prime meridian appear in this map?* (about center)

- *Is it later or earlier in the time zones right of the prime meridian? Why?* (It is later; Earth rotates eastward counterclockwise.)

Technology CONNECTION

ADVENTURE TIME! CD-ROM
Enrich the skills lesson with the *World Time Zones* map.

Resource REMINDER

Practice and Project Book: *p. 108*
Transparency: *Map 20*
 Technology: *Adventure Time! CD-ROM*

Geography Skills

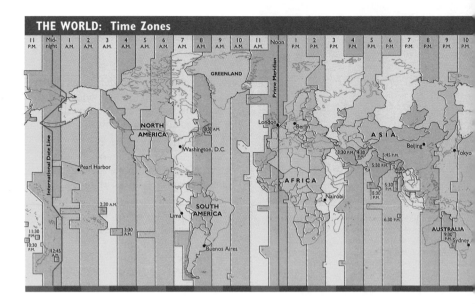

THE WORLD: Time Zones

Time Zone Maps

VOCABULARY
time zone
International Date Line

WHY THE SKILL MATTERS

Just before 8 A.M. on December 7, 1941, Japanese warplanes began bombing the United States naval base at Pearl Harbor, Hawaii. What time was it in Washington, D.C.? You can figure out the answer by reading a time-zone map.

Not everyone in the world is on the same time schedule. In fact, the world is divided into 24 time zones. Time zones were created by scientists in the 1800s to standardize timekeeping throughout the world. They based their work on the fact that Earth rotates 360° each day and that it always moves from west to east while rotating. Since Earth completes one rotation every 24 hours, the scientists divided 360° by 24. The result, 15°, is the amount that Earth rotates in one hour. Each time zone is a strip on a map about 15 degrees of longitude wide. As you can see from this time-zone map, though, some zones have been divided differently to make timekeeping easier for people living in certain regions.

USING THE SKILL

You can see Earth's 24 time zones marked in different colors on this map. As a line of reference, find the line of longitude called the prime meridian. The top of each zone tells what time it is when the time at the prime meridian is noon. Because Earth

548

READING STRATEGIES & LANGUAGE DEVELOPMENT

PROBLEM AND SOLUTION Explain to the class that the reason most people need to consult a time-zone map is to solve a problem. They know what time it is in one location but need to know what time it is at that same moment in another location somewhere else on Earth. The solution? Determine how many time zones away that other location is and whether it is later or earlier than the one they know. Then add or subtract hours as necessary. Encourage students to use this problem-and-solution method as they approach each situation.

SUFFIXES Refer students to the term *Japanese* on this page and have them identify its suffix (*-ese*). Ask for other words that have this suffix (*Chinese*, for example). What does this suffix mean in such words? ("of a certain country or place")

rotates eastward, zones east of the prime meridian have times that are later in the day. Zones to its west have times that are earlier in the day.

Find the zone in which Hawaii is located. Now find the zone in which Washington, D.C., is located. How many zones east of Pearl Harbor is Washington, D.C.? Since Washington, D.C., is 5 zones east, it is 5 hours ahead in time. The bombing of Pearl Harbor began at 7:55 A.M., Hawaii time, or 12:55 P.M. in Washington, D.C. President Franklin Roosevelt first received word of the bombing at 1:50 P.M., Washington, D.C., time. What time was that in Hawaii? Count west 5 zones and you know that it was 8:50 A.M., Hawaii time.

The tricky part begins when crossing the International Date Line. This is an imaginary line in the Pacific Ocean. The line marks the boundary between one day and the next. Whenever the International Date Line is crossed heading *east*, today becomes *yesterday!* Take the time difference between Japan and Hawaii, for example. Travelers from Japan add 5 hours to their watches when heading east to Hawaii. They also set back their calendars by one day! Imagine that it's 9:00 A.M. on Wednesday in Tokyo. What time and day would it be in Hawaii? It would be 2:00 P.M. on Tuesday.

What happens when travelers head west across the International Date Line? They count *backward* in the time of day, but *forward* one day. Travelers heading from Lima to Beijing, for example, would set their clocks back 11 hours, but move their calendars up one day.

*1:41 A.M., May 7, 1945; 10:41 A.M., May 7, 1945

Helping yourself

- A time-zone map shows how Earth's 24 **time zones** are divided.
- When traveling east, add hours to count time. When traveling west, subtract hours.
- When crossing the **International Date Line,** you subtract a day going east and add a day going west.

TRYING THE SKILL

At 2:41 A.M. on May 7, 1945, German leaders surrendered to Allied leaders in Berlin. Thus began V-E (Victory-in-Europe) Day. What time and date was it in London when V-E Day officially began? In Tokyo?*

REVIEWING THE SKILL

Use the Helping Yourself box to help determine the answers to the following questions.

1. What are time zone maps?

2. Why are time zones east of the prime meridian later than those to its west?

3. Why can crossing the International Date Line be tricky? What do travelers have to remember as they cross it heading east? Heading west?

4. What were your answers for the section above? How did you figure them out?

5. When might you need to read a time-zone map in your own life?

Airplanes like the Concorde can travel quickly through many time zones.

549

- *In which place is it later at any given moment—Berlin or Tokyo? Why?* (It is later in Tokyo because it is farther east than Berlin.)

- *What line appears at the far left on the map?* (International Date Line)

- *What happens if you have to cross this line in counting time zones?* (If you move east of it, you change the date to the day before. If you move west of it, you change the date to the next day. Help students to see that if the date did not change back in crossing the International Date Line from the east, hours would be added on endlessly.)

★THINKING FURTHER: *Making Conclusions* If it is June 10, 9:00 A.M. in Washington, D.C., what date and time is it in Beijing? (June 10, 10:00 P.M.)

Trying the Skill Refer students to *Helping Yourself.*

★THINKING FURTHER: *Making Conclusions* When did V-E Day begin in New York City? in San Francisco? in Sydney, Australia? (8:41 P.M. on May 6, 1945; 5:41 P.M. on May 6, 1945; 11:41 A.M. on May 7, 1945)

3 CLOSE

SUM IT UP

Invite students to make up their own problems for determining the time in one location based on a given time in another location. Then have them pose their problems to the class for solution.

EVALUATE
✓ **Answers to Reviewing the Skill**

1. maps that show Earth divided into 24 time zones

2. the sun remains stationary

3. Travelers must add a day when heading west or subtract a day when heading east.

4. 1:41 A.M. on May 7, 1945—by subtracting one hour; 10:41 A.M. on May 7, 1945—by adding eight hours

5. to know when you can phone someone in another place, to know what time your airplane will land in another city

---

MEETING INDIVIDUAL NEEDS

RETEACHING (Easy) Have students volunteer the names of American cities outside their time zone, and ask them to tell the time and day in each city: (a) at the time they do the activity; (b) if it is 11:00 P.M. Monday where they are.

EXTENSION (Average) Have students use the maps in the Atlas starting on page R3 to choose one city on each continent in the Eastern Hemisphere (Asia, Europe, Africa, Australia). Have them record the time and day in each city: (a) at the time they do the activity; (b) if it is 11:00 P.M. Monday where they are.

ENRICHMENT (Challenging) Have students research the time it takes for Earth to revolve around the sun, and explain how the revolution is related to a year and the passing of seasons. They should then explain why a leap year occurs every four years.

LESSON 4
PAGES 550–555

Lesson Overview
A long struggle for the right to rule China resulted in the emergence of the world's most populous communist nation.

Lesson Objectives
★ Explain how foreign and imperial rule ended in China.
★ Describe the ensuing struggle between Nationalists and Communists.
★ Analyze how communism changed China.

1 PREPARE

MOTIVATE Briefly review with students China as described in Chapter 14, with its imperial dynasties, grand cities, and millions of poor farmers and laborers. Then have two students read the *Read Aloud*, one as Soong Chingling and one as narrator. Ask students to compare China with prerevolutionary France or Russia.

SET PURPOSE Will such comparisons continue? Refer students to the *Read to Learn* question and encourage them to read to find answers to the questions. Preview the *Vocabulary*.

2 TEACH

Understanding THE BIG PICTURE
Tell students that many Chinese blamed foreigners for China's problems.

● **How was life wretched for China's poor?** (natural disasters, heavy taxes)

● **How had China's independence been lost?** (Foreign powers had gained control of parts of China.)

★THINKING FURTHER: *Making Conclusions* **Why might the Chinese have felt battered from within and without?** (China's government could not solve internal problems, and foreign governments had taken over.)

Resource REMINDER
Practice and Project Book: p. 109
Anthology: *No Tears for Mao*, pp. 155–156

Focus Activity

READ TO LEARN
What were the causes and effects of revolution in China?

VOCABULARY
- warlord
- Long March
- commune
- Cultural Revolution

PEOPLE
- Sun Yat-sen
- Chiang Kai-shek
- Mao Zedong

550

1890 1900   1976 1990

Communism In China

Read Aloud
"Many times my husband told me that it was in those early days, as a poor son of a poor peasant family, that he became a revolutionary. He was determined that the [life] of the Chinese peasant should not continue to be so wretched, that little boys in China should have shoes to wear and rice to eat."

Soong Chingling (SOONG CHING LING) wrote these words about her husband, Sun Yat-sen (SUN YAHT SEN), known also as the "father of modern China." He would help start an age of revolution in China.

THE BIG PICTURE
In the early 1900s Russia was not the only country on the edge of revolution. Like Russia, China had not kept pace with the technological and economic changes that were changing western societies. Most Chinese worked as farmers, just as they had since the Han dynasty. For poor farmers, survival was a daily struggle that could be lost when a flood, drought, or big tax bill hit.

By the early 1900s, however, change had come to China. Britain had seized control of Hong Kong, and forced China to open its markets to trade. Japan had taken over the island of Taiwan. Britain and other nations also set up zones within China that were subject to their laws, rather than China's. Many Chinese disliked the way their country was being treated by European nations. Some of these people believed the time had come for another change.

SHELTERED INSTRUCTION

READING STRATEGIES & LANGUAGE DEVELOPMENT

CAUSE AND EFFECT Review with the class how finding cause-and-effect relationships can help them understand why historical events unfold as they do, especially significant events such as massive social upheavals. Then bring in and display video clips, television dramatizations, and sound recordings to introduce students to the causes and effects of the revolution in China. As they read this lesson, guide students to trace causes and effects of the Chinese revolution. [SDAIE STRATEGY: CONTEXTUALIZATION]

SYNONYMS Refer the class to the word *said* on p. 551, and set them on a search for synonyms or near synonyms for this term in this lesson (*told*—p. 551, *proclaimed*—p. 553, *announced*—p. 554, *described*—p. 555). Discuss the use of a variety of synonyms to avoid monotonous repetition.

THE END OF DYNASTIES

During this time of unrest, the Qing (CHING) dynasty ruled China. The Qing were Manchus. They had come from the region of Manchuria, located north-east of China. During their 267-year reign, the Manchus saw several challenges to their rule. In the late 1800s, however, unhappiness with the Manchus was perhaps greater than in the past. Many people in China called for the government to be more democratic and less influenced by other nations. Strong leaders began to call for China to change. You read about one such leader in the Read Aloud.

A Voice of the People

Sun Yat-sen was born in 1866, near the southern city of Guangzhou (GWAHNG JO). However, he lived and studied in the Hawaiian Islands when he was young. That time spent away from China helped to shape Sun's views of how life could be improved in his own country.

After returning to China, Sun devoted much of his time to trying to change the government. Sun believed that his country needed to free itself of foreign rule in order to become great again. He said society would be fairer if ordinary citizens had a voice in their government. Finally, Sun told his audiences, China needed to focus on improving agriculture and industry. Many people agreed with his message. Sun once described his goal in this way:

> The real trouble is that China is not an independent country. She is the victim of foreign countries. . . . I set myself the object of the overthrow of the Qing dynasty and the establishment of a Chinese republic in its ruins.

The End of Imperial Rule

Sun and his supporters began a revolt against the Manchus in 1905. Six years later the Qing dynasty fell. It was the last of a series of dynasties that had begun ruling China more than 2,000 years earlier. On January 1, 1912, Sun Yat-sen and his Nationalist party took control of the government. They formed the new Republic of China.

Keeping the republic united turned out to be difficult. Strong local military leaders, called warlords, took advantage of China's unrest to seize power in their own areas. Nationalist forces struggled until 1927 to defeat many of the warlords. Even then it was only with the help of Chinese and Soviet communist allies that they succeeded. While Nationalist forces fought against the warlords, Sun Yat-sen died. Who would be the next leader of China?

Sun Yat-sen and Soong Chingling, his wife, helped China become a republic in 1912.

DIVIDED NATION

DIVIDED NATION

Explain to the class that though Chiang Kai-shek was a Nationalist, he had spent time in the Soviet Union as a military aide to his brother-in-law Sun Yat-sen and had gladly accepted aid from it in the fight against the Chinese warlords.

- **How did Chiang Kai-shek come to be the leader of the Republic of China?** *(He took over when Sun Yat-sen died.)*

- **Why did he turn on his former allies, the Communists?** *(He did not want China to become communist.)*

> ★THINKING FURTHER: *Cause and Effect* **How did this set up the possibility for civil war in China?** *(It set Nationalists against Communists.)*

Discussing The Long March Try to get students to appreciate the lasting effects of camaraderie for the marchers.

- **Why did the Long March begin?** *(Chiang moved his troops to surround the Communists in southern China, who tried to escape.)*

- **How large was the Communist army that made the Long March?** *(80,000)*

More MAP WORK

Refer students to the map. Encourage them to work with text and map.

- **In which direction did they march?** *(first to the west and then, looping around, to the north)*

- **What kinds of terrain did the Long March cross?** *(high mountains where the air was thin and cold, rainy marsh land, quicksand)*

- **In addition to rough and dangerous terrain, what challenges did the Communists have to face?** *(hunger, lack of clean water, lack of proper shoes, Nationalist air attacks, battles)*

- **Where did the Long March end?** *(Yan'an, in northern China)*

- ★THINKING FURTHER: *Making Conclusions* **Why can it be said that Chiang nearly fulfilled his desire to wipe out communism in China?** *(Only one tenth of the 80,000 Communists who began the march survived.)*

A Nationalist general became the next leader of the Republic of China. He was Sun's brother-in-law, Chiang Kai-shek (CHANG ki SHEK). Chiang did not want to keep lasting ties to the communist allies who had helped to defeat the warlords. Neither he nor his supporters wanted China to become communist, as the Soviet Union had. However, Communists were becoming a large political group in China. In 1927 Chiang turned on the Communists with force. A new period of civil war began in China.

The Long March

In 1934 Chiang ordered his troops to surround the Communists in southern China. The troops stopped food and supplies from getting through. Chiang hoped this plan would end the communist movement once and for all.

An army of 80,000 Communists, led by Mao Zedong (MOU DZE DUNG), broke past the Nationalist troops, however. This army began a long flight to safety in the north. The journey came to be known as the Long March. Men and women hiked and climbed almost 6,000 miles in about a year. On the map you can see the route the communists traveled in that time.

The Long March was equal to almost the entire length of a round trip across the mainland United States! During their flight the communists faced many Nationalist air attacks and battles. Also they traveled across harsh land. The marchers found it hard to cross the steep mountains. They were hungry and had little more than straw sandals for shoes. One man recalled:

> As we climbed higher, we were caught in a terrible hailstorm and the air became so thin we could hardly breathe. . . . Our breath froze and hands and lips turned blue. . . .

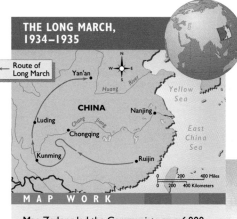

THE LONG MARCH, 1934–1935

Route of Long March

Yan'an

CHINA

Luding
Chongqing
Kunming
Nanjing
Ruijin

Huang River
Yellow Sea
East China Sea

0 200 400 Miles
0 200 400 Kilometers

MAP WORK

Mao Zedong led the Communists on a 6,000-mile march, trying to avoid Nationalist forces.

1. Where did the Long March start? Where did it end?

2. What major river did the Communists cross?

This poster shows Mao Zedong many years after the communists took control of China.

552

BACKGROUND INFORMATION

ABOUT CHINA'S SOONG SISTERS These three American-educated Chinese women were at the heart of the revolution in China. The oldest, Ailing, was married to H. H. Kung, who served briefly as president of China. The next, Chingling, was married to Sun Yat-sen. The youngest, Meiling, was married to Chiang Kai-shek. Only Chingling stayed on in mainland China after 1949.

SECOND-LANGUAGE SUPPORT

GRAPHIC OGANIZERS These students may better understand China's history on a time line. After reading *The Big Picture* aloud, write "1866—birth of Sun Yat-sen." Have students scan the chapter looking for important dates to add. Write the dates on the board; have students create a time line that explains the importance of each date.

Those who sat down to rest . . . froze to death on the spot.

Those who survived the mountains faced more hardships in the rainy marshes of northern China. There, quicksand could suck people down in minutes. Finding food and clean water was very difficult.

Only about one out of ten people who began the Long March arrived at the great bend of the Huang River. There, the survivors recovered from their journey and began to spread the ideas of communism.

Enemies Cooperate—Briefly

In 1937, two years before World War II began in Europe, Japan launched a full-scale invasion of China. The Communists and the Nationalists agreed to work together to fight the Japanese. In 1945, when Japan was defeated at the end of World War II, the two parties prepared to fight each other once again.

This time the Communists had an advantage. The Nationalist government had done most of the heavy fighting against the Japanese. They were also being blamed for inflation. Remember that inflation was a problem in Germany before Hitler took power.

The Communists, meanwhile, had become very popular in rural areas. Mao and his followers talked with thousands of people. The Communists also worked with farmers, showing them ways to produce more crops.

After two years of fighting, the Communists succeeded in driving the Nationalists from mainland China. Chiang and his

On Taiwan, Chiang Kai-shek (above) and the Nationalists established a government in exile.

followers retreated to the island of Taiwan. There they continued the Republic of China in exile from the mainland. In 1949 Mao and his followers created the People's Republic of China on the mainland. It was now the Communists' turn to try to lead China.

Recovering from Civil War

In October 1949 Mao proclaimed before cheering crowds, "China has stood up!" Gone were the warlords and Nationalist leaders. Many people believed that China's new Communist leaders would bring good government and good jobs to people everywhere.

The Communists quickly set out to rebuild their war-torn nation. They provided housing, medical care, and food supplies for city workers. They supported education for all, along with equal rights for women.

The changes brought by Mao and the Communists, however, had a great price. Between 1949 and 1952, the new government took over all businesses. As in the Soviet Union, landlords had all of their property taken away. As many as one million people were killed by the Communists during the takeover.

553

GLOBAL CONNECTION

U.S. AID FOR CHINA
- After Japan invaded China in 1937, the war there did not go well for China. In that year, a U.S. Army Air Service officer named Claire Chennault retired from that service so that he could become air adviser to Chiang Kai-shek.
- By 1941, before the U.S. entered the war, President Franklin D. Roosevelt wanted to find a way to help the beleaguered Chinese. He authorized the supply of P-40 airplanes to Chennault and encouraged American fighter pilots to join the American Voluntary Group (AVG)—the group Chennault organized to fly them.
- They became the famous and colorful fighting force called the Flying Tigers, whose planes were immediately recognizable by the ferocious, teeth-bared jaws painted on their noses.

Discussing Enemies Cooperate—Briefly Help students see that enemies may cooperate to fight a common enemy.

- *Did the end of the Long March end conflict between Nationalists and Communists? Explain* (No, communism continued to spread, and Nationalist–Communist rivalry continued.)

- *What made the Nationalists and Communists cooperate, even briefly?* (Japan's 1937 invasion of China made them unite against a common enemy.)

- *When did they resume their civil war?* (in 1945, after the defeat of Japan in World War II)

- *By this time, what advantages had the Communists gained over the Nationalists?* (The Nationalists were severely strained by fighting Japan, they were being blamed for high inflation, and the Communists had won popularity in rural areas.)

★THINKING FURTHER: *Cause and Effect* **How did the Communist victory lead to the creation of "two Chinas"?** (The Communists now controlled mainland China, which they called the People's Republic of China; the Nationalists set up a new government on the island of Taiwan, which they called the Republic of China.)

Exploring Recovering from Civil War Draw parallels with the Soviet Union.

- *Who was the first leader of the People's Republic?* (Mao Zedong)

- *What steps did the Communists take to rebuild the People's Republic of China?* (they provided housing, medical care, food, education, and equal rights for women.)

- *What price did China pay for Communist rule?* (the loss of private property as government took over ownership of businesses and land, death for as many as a million people)

★THINKING FURTHER: *Making Conclusions* **Do you think that life in Communist China was better or worse than life in pre-revolution China?** (Possible answer: Life probably changed little because China still faced staggering problems.)

CHINA UNDER MAO

Have students identify the problem Mao tried to address—the economy.

- *Why was Mao displeased with China's economy in the early 1950s?* (It was not growing as fast as he wanted.)

- *What step did he announce to bring more rapid growth?* (the "Great Leap Forward" to increase production)

★THINKING FURTHER: *Making Generalizations* **What factors do you think a country must have in place to make a national project like the Leap Forward succeed?** (vigorous support from the people, good planning, resources to complete the project)

Discussing Commune Life Help students form an idea of a commune.

- *What is a commune?* (an organized community in which all members share work and resources)

- *How were communes in China made up?* (by combining several villages into one unit, up to 20,000 people)

- *How did the communes change life in rural China?* (They made the government, not farmers, decide what to grow; they assigned members their work; they separated families into housing for men, women, and children.)

★THINKING FURTHER: *Compare and Contrast* **How would you contrast the aim of the Great Leap Forward with the actual results?** (It was supposed to produce more but it produced less and brought on major starvation.)

Exploring A New Revolution Discuss Mao's social engineering.

- *Why did Mao order the Cultural Revolution?* (to cleanse China of all ideas except communist ideas)

- *How did he trample on human rights to do so?* (by encouraging violence against anyone even suspected of anything but communist beliefs)

★THINKING FURTHER: *Making Decisions* **Think back to the conclusion you made at the end of p. 553. How accurate was it?** (Encourage full discussion.)

CHINA UNDER MAO

In the early 1950s the Chinese economy was growing, but not at a pace that pleased Mao. In 1957 he announced that it was time for China to take a "Great Leap Forward." There was no telling what China could do, he said, if people pitched in and worked harder. "More, faster, better, cheaper" became the slogan of the day. Factories worked around the clock to produce more steel, the building block of industry. Families tried to help by setting up tiny steel-making furnaces in their backyards.

Commune Life

Many farmers and their families were forced to join large communes (KAHM yoonz). A commune is an organized community in which all members share work and resources. Mao told people that by working together they would make the land more productive. Villages were combined to form single communes of up to 20,000 people. They could not choose the crops they wanted to farm. Instead the government assigned each commune a crop to produce. People in communes were also forced to build bridges, dams, and work on other projects for the government.

Family life in the commune was very different than it had been on small farms. People were expected to put loyalty to the government and commune ahead of loyalty to their families. At first, men, women, and children each slept in separate buildings. All residents of the commune ate together in large dining halls. Commune workers were divided into teams. Each team was responsible for a particular job such as cooking the meals, hoeing the fields, or schooling the children who lived on the commune.

Instead of producing more grain, communes produced less. This happened partly because farmers were so busy doing other things, such as making steel. China, however, lacked the resources to produce the steel it needed. Also, much of the steel produced could not be used because it was made incorrectly. Few Chinese workers had been trained in the modern ways of making steel.

In time Mao's plan for China failed. As many as 20 million people may have starved to death during a famine that followed the Great Leap Forward.

A New Revolution

Some regional leaders tried to help the situation by allowing farmers to once again own and control small pieces of land. Mao accused those leaders of "copying the West." In 1966 he removed them from power and put a new plan into action.

Mao began a ten-year period called the Cultural Revolution. He called for the destruction of all non-communist beliefs. These included many long-held religious and cultural beliefs. Any leaders critical of Mao were punished. With

---

CITIZENSHIP ★

USING CURRENT EVENTS
- Ever since 1919, students have gathered periodically in Beijing's Tiananmen Square to demonstrate for democracy and reforms of government policy.

- The largest and most famous demonstration took place in 1989, when a 30-foot-high plaster statue called the Goddess of Democracy was crushed by tanks sent to end the demonstration. An unknown number of demonstrators were killed in the action.

- The Chinese government responded to worldwide protests against its abuses of human rights by calling such charges improper interference in China's domestic affairs. Have students locate and bring to class current newspaper and magazine articles that deal with human rights in China and discuss them.

Mao Zedong's supporters wave his Little Red Book of teachings. Their banner says that they are building a new world.

government support, groups of students broke into people's homes. They destroyed Confucian books and ancient Chinese classics, as well as non-Chinese writings. Anyone with western-made clothing or a European-style haircut faced attack. Many innocent people were accused of being American spies. They were harshly punished.

One schoolgirl, Anchee Min, was forced to say her teacher was a spy. Anchee Min could not believe that her teacher, Autumn Leaves, was an enemy of China. But government leaders said that any teacher who asked students to read foreign literature was a traitor. Min later described how her teacher was treated by government officials.

Two strong men escorted Autumn Leaves onto the stage facing the crowd of 2,000 people. . . . Her arms were twisted behind her. . . . A rectangular board reading "Down with American Spy" hung from her neck. . . . Autumn Leaves kept silent. When kicked hard, she said that she had nothing to confess.

The dream of a China transformed by communism had turned into a nightmare.

WHY IT MATTERS

The Cultural Revolution ended in 1976 with the death of Mao Zedong. During Mao's 27-year rule, major changes had taken place in China. China had closed its doors to the United States and some other democratic nations until 1971. After Mao's death, though, some leaders who had been punished during the Cultural Revolution returned to power. They had new ideas for China. You will read about them in Chapter 20.

✓// Reviewing Facts and Ideas

MAIN IDEAS

- In the early 1900s many Chinese felt China should be free of foreign rule and should become more democratic.
- Sun Yat-sen led a revolt that overthrew the Qing dynasty in 1911. His Nationalist Party later fought the Communists for power.
- In 1949 the Nationalists retreated to Taiwan and the Communists created the People's Republic of China.
- Mao Zedong's Great Leap Forward and Cultural Revolution brought great unrest to China.

THINK ABOUT IT

1. Why was anti-foreign feeling so strong in China in the early 1900s?

2. What were the effects of the Cultural Revolution?

3. **FOCUS** List *causes* and *effects* of the communist victory in China.

4. **THINKING SKILL** *Determine the credibility of the source* on page 552. How did you reach your conclusion?

5. **GEOGRAPHY** How might geography have played a role in helping Mao and his followers escape Nationalist forces during the Long March?

555

Discussing **WHY IT MATTERS** Help students realize why Mao's plan failed.

★**THINKING FURTHER:** *Making Conclusions How did Mao close off cultural borrowing? How might China's opening up encourage it again? (The Cultural Revolution ended cultural borrowing while contacts outside would have encouraged it.)*

⭐ 3 CLOSE

MAIN IDEAS
Call on students for answers.

- *What united the Nationalists and Communists? What separated them again? (fights against the warlords and Japan; the wish to control Chinese government)*

- *How did "two Chinas" emerge? (After the Communists' People's Republic took control of mainland China, the Nationalists moved to Taiwan)*

- *Which two of Mao's programs battered China? (Great Leap Forward, Cultural Revolution)*

EVALUATE
✓ **Answers to Think About It**

1. because China was controlled by outsiders—a ruling dynasty from Manchuria, as well as various European countries and Japan
Summarize

2. starvation and violent assaults on human rights
Form Generalizations

3. Causes: dissatisfaction with the Nationalists, growing popularity of the Communists. Effects: government management, communes, persecution, starvation
Cause and Effect

4. Credibility should be high because the person was there and there is no evidence he had reason to lie.
Evaluate Fact and Opinion

5. The Nationalists would have been as challenged by the rough terrain as the Communists were.
Five Themes of Geography: Human/Environment Interactions

Write About It Have students picture themselves living through the Cultural Revolution. Have them write a journal entry describing an experience they had.

MEETING INDIVIDUAL NEEDS

RETEACHING (Easy) Have students choose a major event in China during the twentieth century. Have them create a colored illustration of a scene that might have occurred during it.

EXTENSION (Average) Have student choose one episode from this period in China and create a cartoon re-creation of it, with pictures and words.

ENRICHMENT (Challenging) Husband and wife teams loomed large in this period of Chinese history. Divide the class into six groups and assign each group one of the following: Sun Yat-sen, Chingling Soong (Madame Sun Yat-sen), Chiang Kai-shek, Meiling Soong (Madame Chiang Kai-shek), Mao Zedong, Chiang Ch'ing (Madame Mao Zedong). Have each group research and prepare a biography of its subject and present it to the class.

LESSON 5

PAGES 556-561

Lesson Overview

Cold War waged by two super-powers—the United States and the Soviet Union—gripped the world for over 40 years.

Lesson Objectives

★ Contrast two competing political and economic systems.

★ Trace major events in the Cold War.

★ Identify various ways that nations of the world try to protect themselves.

1 PREPARE

MOTIVATE Have two students read the *Read Aloud*, one as Churchill and one as the narrator. As the others listen, tell them to picture in their minds the image described. Refer to the photo of barbed wire in East Berlin on this page. Be sure students understand the lesson title; the *Cold War* did not have many armed battles, but had many battles of nerves.

SET PURPOSE Refer students to the *Read to Learn* question. Encourage them to explore the lesson to learn how their grandparents and parents faced many conflicts that could have set off World War III. Preview the *Vocabulary*.

2 TEACH

Understanding THE BIG PICTURE Have students evaluate the superpowers.

● **Which nations were superpowers after World War II?** (U.S., Soviet Union)

★**THINKING FURTHER:** *Compare and Contrast* **What basic differences between the two created tensions between them?** (US: free enterprise and democracy; Soviet Union: communism and totalitarianism)

Resource **REMINDER**

Practice and Project Book: P. 110
Anthology: *Charter of the United Nations, p. 157*

Focus Activity

READ TO LEARN

How did the Cold War develop after World War II?

VOCABULARY

- superpower
- free enterprise
- Cold War
- United Nations
- NATO
- Warsaw Pact
- Korean War
- nuclear arms race

PEOPLE

- Fidel Castro
- Nikita Khrushchev
- John F. Kennedy

PLACES

- Yalta
- Berlin

556

1890   1915   1940   1945   1989

Cold War

Read Aloud

"An iron curtain has descended across the Continent [of Europe]. Behind that line lie all the capitals of the ancient states of central and eastern Europe."

Winston Churchill, Prime Minister of Great Britain, said these words in 1946. He imagined an "iron curtain" that formed a dividing line between communist Europe in the East, and democratic Europe in the West. The idea of that "iron curtain" became a symbol of a new kind of war—one that would dominate world events for over 40 years.

THE BIG PICTURE

After World War II, several European countries had lost millions of people, had tremendous debts, and were in ruins. Although the Soviet Union had lost nearly 20 million people, its armies held most of Eastern Europe. Only the United States was stronger and richer than before the war. Yet about 300,000 Americans had died.

Because of their strength, the United States and the Soviet Union became known as superpowers. As you have read, the Soviet Union had a communist government. The United States supported free enterprise and democracy. A free enterprise economy, also called a market economy, is based on private ownership of land and businesses.

Tensions between the superpowers and their supporters developed into what became known as the Cold War. The Cold War was a struggle between the United States and the Soviet Union without the two nations fighting a full-scale war against each other.

 SHELTERED INSTRUCTION

READING STRATEGIES & LANGUAGE DEVELOPMENT

CLASSIFYING Discuss with students how classifying information can help clarify different elements in a text. Explain that this lesson explores how the Cold War developed after World War II. Have students list board games and video games they play and classify moves and countermoves they make during each one. As students read, have them list the moves and countermoves the Americans and Russians made during the Cold War. **[SDAIE STRATEGY: BRIDGING]**

COMPOUND WORDS Point out that compound words can be two words written together as one or hyphenated. A third variety is open compounds—two words separated by a space and having a specific meaning when combined (for example, *iron curtain*). Challenge students to find others in this lesson (*free enterprise* on this page, *machine guns* and *atomic bombs*, p. 559, *full alert*, p. 560).

NEW TENSIONS

In February 1945 the end of World War II in Europe was still three months away. Allied leaders met in the town of Yalta in the Soviet Union to discuss their plans. They agreed to create a United Nations organization. This world organization would be stronger than the League of Nations. It would work to prevent future conflicts.

The Allies also agreed to divide Germany into zones that the Allies would control for a period of time. Lastly, they agreed that the Eastern European nations taken over by Soviet troops when they defeated the Nazis there should be given the right to choose their own governments.

New Alliances

The Soviet Union's leader, Josef Stalin, quickly broke the agreement at Yalta. He refused to remove his troops from neighboring countries, including Poland, Czechoslovakia, and Romania. Soviet troops forced those nations to accept communist governments.

Fearful of further Soviet expansion, nations in western Europe and North America formed NATO, or the North Atlantic Treaty Organization, in 1949.

They pledged to defend each other if attacked. The Soviet Union and the communist countries of Eastern Europe signed a similar agreement called the Warsaw Pact in 1955.

War in Korea

A year after the creation of NATO, the Cold War heated up when a conflict with weapons took place in Asia. This conflict was the Korean War. After World War II, Korea had been freed from Japanese control. The Korean peninsula was then divided into two nations. The northern nation was communist and the southern nation was democratic.

In 1950 communist North Korea invaded democratic South Korea. To prevent the spread of communism, the United States sent thousands of troops to help United Nations troops fight North Koreans. The North Koreans were aided by the Chinese. The war lasted three years without a clear victory for either side. However, North Korean troops had been forced to withdraw from South Korea. At the war's conclusion, much of the Korean landscape was devastated and four million people were dead.

Allied leaders Winston Chuchill, Franklin Roosevelt, and Josef Stalin met in Yalta in 1945 to discuss the ending of World War II.

557

NEW TENSIONS
The "Big Three" at Yalta represented the U.S., Britain, and the Soviet Union.

- **What did the Yalta meeting intend the UN to be?** *(a world organization to prevent conflicts from leading to war)*

- **What did the meeting agree on about Germany and Eastern Europe?** *(Divide Germany and occupy it. Eastern European nations would choose their own governments.)*

★ **THINKING FURTHER:** *Making Conclusions* **Why do you think the Allies wanted to occupy Germany?** *(to form a democracy or prevent rearming)*

Discussing New Alliances Discuss events that led to forming NATO.

- **How did the Soviets break the Yalta agreement?** *(It forced communist governments on Eastern Europe.)*

★ **THINKING FURTHER:** *Cause and Effect* **How did Soviet actions lead to new alliances?** *(Soviet expansion led to NATO; NATO led to the Warsaw Pact.)*

Investigating War in Korea Point out that the Cold War sometimes grew hot.

- **How did war begin in Korea?** *(North Korea invaded South Korea.)*

- **Who supported each side?** *(North Korea: the Chinese; South Korea: the UN, with large U.S. forces)*

★ **THINKING FURTHER:** *Making Conclusions* **Did either side win the Korean War? Explain.** *(No land was exchanged, but communist expansion may have been discouraged.)*

TENSIONS BUILD UP

Point out to students that the Berlin Wall was built to keep East Berliners inside, not to keep others out.

- **How was Germany like Korea after World War II?** *(Both were divided, with the Soviet Union occupying one part and the U.S., Britain, and France occupying the other.)*

- **Who controlled the two parts of Germany?** *(Soviet Union: East Germany; U.S., Britain, and France: West Germany)*

- **In which part was Berlin? How was it occupied?** *(in East Germany; divided and occupied by the four nations)*

- **Why did Berlin become an escape route?** *(East Germans who did not want to live under communism went there to escape to West Berlin and from there to West Germany.)*

> ★ **THINKING FURTHER:** *Cause and Effect* **What did East Germany do to stop people leaving? Why did it take that action?** *(built the Berlin Wall; to keep its people from escaping)*

More MAP WORK

Refer students to the map, and have them work with the map and text.

- **Which countries did the Soviet Union take into the communist camp?** *(East Germany, Poland, Czechoslovakia, Hungary, Yugoslavia, Romania, Bulgaria, Albania)*

Discussing A Divided City Help students to understand what an ugly scar the Berlin Wall was on the once-great city, physically and as a symbol of political and economic imprisonment.

- **Did the Berlin Wall succeed in stopping flight from East Germany?** *(No.)*

> ★ **THINKING FURTHER:** *Making Conclusions* **What do these attempts tell you about the human drive for freedom?** *(To many people, freedom is stronger than the fear of arrest or death; indeed freedom is a matter of life and death itself.)*

MAP WORK: 1. East Germany, Poland, Soviet Union, Czechoslovakia, Hungary, Romania, Yugoslavia, Albania, Bulgaria **2.** Greece

TENSIONS BUILD UP

Korea was not the only country to be damaged by the Cold War. When World War II ended, Germany had been split. The Soviet Union was left in control of eastern Germany including the eastern part of Berlin, the capital city. Britain, France, and the United States controlled western Germany and the western part of Berlin.

By 1948 it was clear that the Soviet Union was not going to withdraw its troops from Germany. Soviet leaders established a communist government in the areas occupied by their troops. The communist part of Germany became the country of East Germany. The western part of Germany became the country of West Germany. The city of Berlin was split in the same way.

In the years that followed, thousands of East Germans who did not want to live in a communist nation moved to West Berlin. Such movement ended, however, in the early morning hours of August 13, 1961. While the people of Berlin slept, East German police built a barbed-wire fence between East and West Berlin. Over the next few days that fence became a concrete wall.

EUROPE, 1948–1989

Communist countries
Non-communist countries
— "Iron Curtain"

MAP WORK

After World War II Europe was divided between the mostly communist eastern countries and the mostly democratic western ones.

1. Which communist countries were east of the Iron Curtain?
2. What country bordered the Iron Curtain on the southeast?

The Berlin Wall was built in 1961 to stop the flow of East Germans crossing the border into democratic West Germany.

558

BACKGROUND INFORMATION

ABOUT THE BERLIN AIRLIFT The Berlin Wall did not mark the first time the people of Berlin found themselves cut off in some way. Thirteen years earlier, the Soviets had blockaded the city.

- In June 1948, the U.S., Britain, and France announced that they were going to combine their zones to create West Germany.
- Within days, to protest this action, the Soviets cut off access—roads, canals, railways—to Berlin from the West, hoping to drive the Western powers out of the city.
- The Western powers responded by taking to the skies to supply the blockaded city. World War II pilots were called back into service to fly cargo planes round the clock into Berlin. Over the next ten months they transported two million tons of food and supplies.
- Admitting failure, the Soviet lifted the blockade in May 1949.

A Divided City

The Berlin Wall divided backyards, streets, and even houses and churches. It was guarded by East German soldiers with machine guns. Escape became very difficult. Yet many people did make their way west. Some traveled in tiny tunnels or hot-air balloons. Others crossed the border hidden in coffins or secret car trunks. For every one person who made it, however, many more failed. At least 80 people were killed and hundreds more arrested while trying to leave East Berlin.

The Race to Build Nuclear Arms

A new competition between the superpowers began as Cold War tensions in Germany continued. In 1945 the United States had been the only nation with the ability to make atomic bombs. Remember the United States had used atomic bombs against Japan during World War II. By 1949, though, the Soviet Union also had these destructive weapons.

American scientists then developed the far more deadly hydrogen bomb. The Soviets matched this development a year later. The power for these weapons comes from nuclear energy. For this reason, the competition between the superpowers became known as the nuclear arms race.

In 1957 the Soviet Union's next development amazed the world. They launched *Sputnik*, a human-made satellite that orbited Earth. Scientists had come a long way since Isaac Newton first discovered how gravity held the planets in orbit. Western leaders became concerned. They were worried that *Sputnik*—and other satellites like it—could be used to launch nuclear weapons toward the West.

The Soviet Union often held military rallies like this one in Moscow's Red Square in 1988.

Preparing for Disaster

Many Americans feared that a Soviet nuclear attack could begin at any time. Students practiced what to do if a bomb exploded while they were at school. Some school principals handed out metal tags for children to wear. The tags would help them to be identified after an explosion. Thousands of families built small bomb shelters in their backyards. They stocked them with goods needed for survival.

559

Exploring The Race to Build Nuclear Arms Be sure students recognize the unique deadliness of atomic weapons.

- **As World War II ended, what weapon did the U.S. have that the Soviet Union did not have?** *(atomic bomb)*

- **How did the Soviet Union respond to this lack?** *(by developing atomic bombs "to level the playing field")*

- **How did the U.S. respond to the Soviet Union's development of the atomic bomb?** *(by developing the even more powerful hydrogen bomb)*

- **What kind of race developed between the U.S. and Soviet Union?** *(a nuclear arms race, for each to outdo the other in deadly nuclear power in case of war)*

- **In what other scientific area did they compete?** *(in the race for space, to create satellites to operate in space, and possibly launch nuclear weapons)*

★THINKING FURTHER: *Making Conclusions* **Some scholars describe postwar U.S.-Soviet Union relations as a "balance of terror." What do you think they meant by this phrase?** *(If two nations had such frightening weapons, neither would dare use them against the other.)*

Discussing Preparing for Disaster Ask students about reaction to the threat.

★THINKING FURTHER: *Making Conclusions* **How did people develop a wartime mentality?** *(They felt the threat of war affected them and sought ways to protect themselves.)*

GLOBAL CONNECTION

"THE NUCLEAR CLUB" The United States, Britain, and the Soviet Union were the first members of "the nuclear club." They were soon joined by France and China. In addition to Russia, several other former Soviet Republics were left with nuclear capability. By 1995, Israel, India, and Pakistan probably had it too, although not declared.

CURRICULUM CONNECTION

LINKS TO SCIENCE Call for a team of science research volunteers to gather information about the early space race, when the Soviet Union and U.S. vied to be first to put a satellite into space during the International Geophysical Year. Have them make a report to the class.

BACKGROUND INFORMATION

ABOUT U.S. REACTION TO SPUTNIK
- The U.S. was stunned when, with the launch of Sputnik on October 4, 1957, the Soviet Union put the very first satellite into space. Americans had no idea that Soviet technology had become so advanced.

- As a result, Congress established the National Aeronautics and Space Administration (NASA) to get an American satellite into orbit (which it did in 1958).

- Congress also passed the National Defense Education Act to provide millions of dollars to upgrade American education in the sciences, mathematics, and foreign languages, to ensure that the U.S. would not fall behind the Soviet Union in technology.

CUBAN MISSILE CRISIS

On a map, have students locate Cuba, just 90 miles south of Florida.

- **How and when did Cuba become communist?** *(Castro established a communist government in 1959.)*

- **What Soviet leader supported Castro? What American leader opposed him?** *(Khrushchev; Kennedy)*

★**THINKING FURTHER:** *Making Conclusions* **Why do you suppose the U.S. opposed Castro's rule?** *(It brought communism close to U.S. shores.)*

Discussing A Nuclear Target Be sure that students realize that each side believed the other would attack first.

- **What did the Soviet Union do that threatened the U.S.?** *(It placed nuclear missiles in Cuba.)*

- **How did this action bring the world to the brink of nuclear war?** *(Kennedy demanded the removal of the Soviet missiles and threatened a nuclear attack on the Soviet Union if the missiles in Cuba were fired.)*

More CHART WORK

Refer students to the chart on p. 561.

- **What is the form of government for the U.S.? What was it for the Soviet Union?** *(U.S.: democracy; Soviet Union: Communism)*

- **What is the type of economy in the U.S.? What was it for the Soviet Union?** *(U.S.: free enterprise; Soviet Union: command economy)*

Exploring The Crisis Ends Help students see that compromise was needed.

- **How did Kennedy and Khrushchev resolve this conflict?** *(Khrushchev removed missiles from Cuba, Kennedy removed missiles from Turkey and pledged not to attack Cuba.)*

★**THINKING FURTHER:** *Cause and Effect* **What cause-and-effect relationship can you draw between the Cuban Missile Crisis and the test-ban treaty?** *(The crisis scared both sides into reducing chances for a nuclear confrontation.)*

560

CUBAN MISSILE CRISIS

In 1959, Cuba's Fidel Castro succeeded in establishing the first communist government in the Americas. He won the support of Nikita Khrushchev, the Soviet leader who had come to power after Josef Stalin's death in 1953. The President of the United States, John F. Kennedy, tried—unsuccessfully—to end Castro's government in 1961. In 1962 a crisis arose over this island nation.

A Nuclear Target

Khrushchev sent nuclear weapons to Cuba in the summer of 1962. By October the weapons in Cuba were ready for use. Missiles far more powerful than the atom bombs used in Japan were now just a 20-minute flight away from the capital of the United States. Millions would die if the missiles were fired.

On October 22 Kennedy told Americans of the great danger. He warned that the United States would respond to the fire of any Cuban missile with an attack upon the Soviet Union. He also ordered Soviet ships to stay out of Cuban waters or risk the start of war.

On Saturday, October 27, the crisis reached a peak. American forces around the world were on full alert. In Cuba, over 40,000 Soviet and Cuban troops checked their weapons and missiles. In Washington, D.C., hundreds of people stood outside the White House—some shouting for peace, others for war. A single Soviet ship continued on a course toward Cuba.

To many, the end of the world seemed just around the corner. An adviser to the President of the United States later recalled,

> It was a beautiful fall evening . . . and I went up into the open air to look and to smell it, because I thought it was the last Saturday I would ever see.

An adviser to Khrushchev remembered,

> I went and telephoned my wife and told her to drop everything and get out of Moscow. I thought [United States] bombers were on the way.

Kennedy and Khrushchev met in 1962 (above) after Castro (above right) allowed Soviet missiles into Cuba.

560

CITIZENSHIP★

USING CURRENT EVENTS Whether they do or do not involve fighting, confrontations between nations are a recurring fact of life. They might center on land claims, trade policy, or environmental issues, to name just a few areas of contention.

- Have students look through newspapers or news magazines or take notes about reports on television or radio news about such confrontations.
- Have students identify who is involved, what the argument is about, and what actions each side has taken.
- Then have the class discuss possible ways the conflict might be resolved.

THE COLD WAR: GOVERNMENTS AND ECONOMIES

	Government	Economy
United States and Allies	**Democracy** Citizens elect their leaders and can influence government decisions. Rights are protected.	**Free Enterprise** Resources, property, and production are controlled by individuals and companies and the laws of supply and demand.
Soviet Union and Allies	**Communism** Totalitarian government controls nearly every aspect of people's lives.	**Command Economy** Government controls all resources and production. Citizens have little control over which goods and services are produced.

CHART WORK

The two superpowers had very different economies and ways of governing.

1. Which form of government gives citizens more rights?

2. Who controls resources and production in a command economy?

The Crisis Ends

As world leaders nervously watched and waited, Kennedy and Khrushchev reached an agreement. The United States promised not to invade Cuba. The Soviet Union's ships agreed to return home. The Soviet Union also removed its missiles from Cuba. In return the United States removed missiles based in Turkey.

The world had come dangerously close to a nuclear war. In the following year, 1963, the two superpowers signed a treaty banning most kinds of nuclear weapons testing. World leaders hoped that the treaty would reduce the chance that nuclear weapons would ever be used in war.

WHY IT MATTERS

For the next 25 years the United States and the Soviet Union continued their struggle. No part of the world was untouched by the Cold War. Conflicts between the ideas and values of communism and democracy took place around the globe. Look at the chart to compare the different systems that clashed in the Cold War. In the next chapter you will read about one such conflict in Vietnam. In the 1980s, however, Cold War tensions began to ease. You will read about that in Chapter 20.

Reviewing Facts and Ideas

MAIN IDEAS

- The Cold War was a struggle between the United States and the Soviet Union without the nations fighting a real war with each other.

- Josef Stalin forced some nations of Eastern Europe to accept communism.

- Communist attempts at expansion resulted in the division of Korea and Germany into separate communist and democratic nations.

- The nuclear arms race increased Cold War tensions. Nuclear war almost began after the Soviet Union placed missiles in Cuba in 1962.

THINK ABOUT IT

1. What factors led to the Cold War?

2. What was the Berlin Wall? Why was the wall such a powerful symbol of the Cold War?

3. FOCUS How did Cold War tensions affect the relationships between Eastern and Western nations?

4. THINKING SKILL What were some *causes* of the Cuban Missile Crisis? What were some of its *effects* on the United States and Soviet Union?

5. WRITE Suppose you are a journalist in Berlin at the end of World War II. Write an article describing the changes taking place in the city.

561

Discussing WHY IT MATTERS Help students understand the seemingly unresolvable nature of the Cold War.

> ★**THINKING FURTHER:** *Making Conclusions* **Why do you think that the two superpowers continually came into conflict?** *(Each side was so intent on making the world safe for its own ideas and values—which were opposite to the other's—that their peaceful coexistence seemed impossible.)*

3 CLOSE

MAIN IDEAS

Have students write their answers.

- **What was the Cold War?** *(a war of words and ideas between the U.S. and the Soviet Union with no direct war between them)*

- **Which Soviet leader forced Eastern Europe to accept communist governments after World War II?** *(Josef Stalin)*

- **How did communist expansion affect Korea and Germany?** *(It divided each in two—communist and democratic.)*

- **How did technology help to create a dangerous race between the superpowers?** *(It helped produce the nuclear arms race.)*

EVALUATE

✓ **Answers to Think About It**

1. Soviet expansion and differences between democratic and communist systems
Summarize

2. A wall built by East Germany to stop people from escaping to the West; it symbolized communist oppression.
Make Conclusions

3. Tensions divided nations into the Warsaw Pact and NATO.
Main Idea

4. each side posing nuclear threats to the other; Soviet expansion, U.S. action to stop that expansion; agreement to pull back the threat
Cause and Effect

5. Descriptions should include the division into zones and the different occupying force in each zone.
Point of View

Write About It Tell students to picture themselves visiting Berlin just after the Berlin Wall went up. Have them write a postcard home describing it.

MEETING INDIVIDUAL NEEDS

RETEACHING (Easy) Have students make a flow chart of major events in the Cold War, including a simple illustration of each event.

EXTENSION (Average) Have students choose a major event in the Cold War and picture themselves living through it. Have them write a letter to a friend describing the experience.

ENRICHMENT (Challenging) It was suggested in the *Enrichment* on p. 547 that students interview someone who lived through World War II. Have students conduct another interview, this time of someone who lived through the Cold War. Again, have them write up their interviews as features for the newspaper, but have them discuss their findings in class, comparing their subjects' reactions to and ideas about the two different eras.

DISCUSSING MAJOR EVENTS Use the time line to reinforce for students how crammed with world-shattering events the 20th century has been.

- **What major wars took place and how many years separated their starts?** (World War I and II; 25 years)

- **What major events reflected the rise and expansion of communism in the world?** (the Russian Revolution in 1917, China going communist in 1949, the Berlin Wall, and the Cuban Missile Crisis in 1962)

- **What alliances arose because of communism?** (NATO in 1949 and the Warsaw Pact in 1955)

Answers to THINKING ABOUT VOCABULARY

1. nationalism
2. superpower
3. propaganda
4. tsar
5. alliance
6. totalitarian
7. facism
8. commune
9. nuclear arms race
10. depression

Answers to THINKING ABOUT FACTS

1. The assassination of Archduke Franz Ferdinand of Austria-Hungary set off two opposing alliances against each other.

2. the overthrow of tsarist rule in Russia and the replacement of it with communist rule

3. Depression and its heavy unemployment caused Germans to accept a leader who promised to regain Germany's former pride.

Resource REMINDER

Practice and Project Book: *p. 111*
Assessment Book: *Chapter 18 Test*
Technology: *Videodisc*
Transparency: *Graphic Organizer, Sequence Chain*

CHAPTER 18 REVIEW

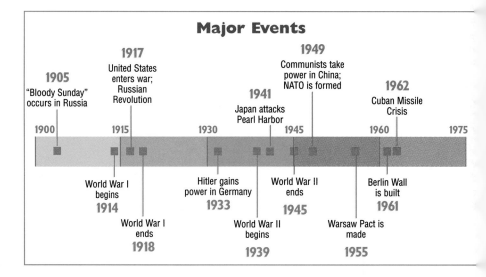

Major Events

1905 "Bloody Sunday" occurs in Russia

1917 United States enters war; Russian Revolution

1941 Japan attacks Pearl Harbor

1949 Communists take power in China; NATO is formed

1962 Cuban Missile Crisis

1900 — 1915 — 1930 — 1945 — 1960 — 1975

World War I begins 1914

World War I ends 1918

Hitler gains power in Germany 1933

World War II begins 1939

World War II ends 1945

Warsaw Pact is made 1955

Berlin Wall is built 1961

THINKING ABOUT VOCABULARY

Number a sheet of paper from 1 to 10. Beside each number write the word or term from the list below that matches the statement.

alliance	nuclear arms race
commune	propaganda
depression	superpower
fascism	totalitarian
nationalism	tsar

1. Strong loyalty to one's country and culture

2. A much stronger country than other countries

3. Exaggerated or false information used to persuade people to help advance a cause

4. Title of an emperor of Russia before the revolution

5. An agreement between countries to defend each other if attacked

6. A form of government in which a dictator controls all aspects of people's lives

7. A form of government in which the goals of a nation are more important than its individuals

8. An organized community where members share work and resources

9. The build-up of nuclear weapons by superpowers

10. An extended period of economic difficulties in a nation

THINKING ABOUT FACTS

1. How did World War I begin?

2. What was the Russian Revolution?

3. Why did Hitler gain power in Germany after World War I?

4. What was the Cultural Revolution? Why did Mao Zedong launch it? What were its consequences?

5. Look at the time line above. Which events listed after the end of World War II have to do with the Cold War? Explain.

SECOND-LANGUAGE SUPPORT

RETELLING Second-language students should work together to review the chapter. They can work in a group to share the graphic organizers they have created for the information in various lessons. They have been asked to create maps (p. 527), definitions of people, places, and vocabulary (p. 533), time lines, (p. 552), semantic maps (p. 541), outlines (p. 557), and sequence chains (p. 563). Pooling their resources and studying by retelling information in their own words should be beneficial to all students.

COMPARE AND CONTRAST Students may increase their understanding of important events in this chapter by making a "Good News" and "Bad News" chart. Under these headings, they should write the good results and bad results of these three events: World War I, the Russian Revolution, and World War II.

THINK AND WRITE

WRITING AN EXPLANATION

Briefly describe the conflicts that started World War I. Then explain why the United States entered it. What factors went into changing the American policy of neutrality. How did the United States help the Allied Powers to win the war?

WRITING A COMPARISON

Write two paragraphs in which you compare Hitler and Stalin. How were they alike? How were they different?

WRITING A REPORT

Write a report about the Cold War. Describe the nuclear arms race and several of the crises and conflicts that took place during this time.

APPLYING GEOGRAPHY SKILLS

TIME ZONE MAPS

1. What is a time zone map?

2. What is the International Date Line?

3. Look at the time zone map on page 548. As you can see, Africa is larger than the United States. How many time zones cross Africa?

4. What is the time difference between the East Coast and West Coast of the United States? If you lived in San Francisco and wanted to call somebody in Boston at noon, Boston time, what time would you make your call?

5. How are time zone maps useful?

4. a ten-year period of persecution and upheaval in China; to destroy all noncommunist beliefs in China; famine and violence, isolation from the rest of the world, setback for China's economic development.

5. All of them—NATO and the Warsaw Pact set up opposing noncommunist and communist alliances; China's becoming communist added to Cold War tensions, as did the Berlin Wall and the Cuban Missile Crisis.

Answers to
APPLYING GEOGRAPHY SKILLS

1. a map that shows the time in each of 24 zones into which Earth has been divided

2. an imaginary line in the Pacific Ocean that marks the boundary between one day and the next, or a date change

3. 4

4. three hours; 9:00 a.m.

5. to keep track of time when traveling, to know what time it is someplace else that one wants to contact

Summing Up the Chapter

Copy the sequence chains below on a separate sheet of paper. Review the chapter to find a chain of two events that led to the main event listed. When you have filled in the blanks, use the chains to answer the question "What are some of the conditions that led to the main conflicts of the twentieth century?"

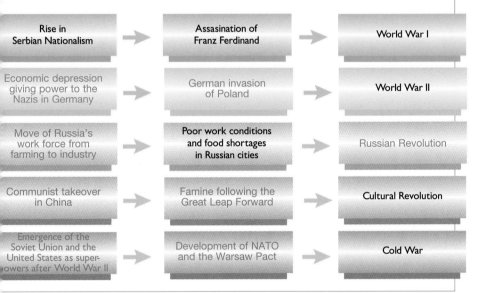

Rise in Serbian Nationalism	Assasination of Franz Ferdinand	World War I
Economic depression giving power to the Nazis in Germany	German invasion of Poland	World War II
Move of Russia's work force from farming to industry	Poor work conditions and food shortages in Russian cities	Russian Revolution
Communist takeover in China	Famine following the Great Leap Forward	Cultural Revolution
Emergence of the Soviet Union and the United States as superpowers after World War II	Development of NATO and the Warsaw Pact	Cold War

Technology CONNECTION

VIDEODISC

Enrich Chapter 18 with the *Change in China* segment on the videodisc.

Search 48074, Play To 50471 Side A

563

SUGGESTIONS FOR SUMMING UP THE CHAPTER

Before students copy the sequence chains on a piece of paper, discuss the format with them. Help them to differentiate the roles of the columns—the first two are for two events that led up to a main event in the third column. Point out that they sometimes need to identify lead-up events and a main event. Work through the first sequence chain, already completely filled in, with them to see that they understand the procedure. Then have them review the chapter to fill in the rest. Suggested examples of events appear on the reproduced pupil page above. You may want them to answer the question posed by calling on individuals in class to identify main conflicts and conditions that led to them. Or you may want to have students do this in writing.

ASSESSING THINK AND WRITE: *For performance assessment, see Assessment Book, Chapter 18, pp. T100–T103.*

CHAPTER 19 New Nations

Pages 564–593

CHAPTER OVERVIEW

European colonial possessions in Africa and India gained independence in the 20th century. New nations emerged in the Middle East and conflict developed between Israel and the Palestinians. In 1973 the United States military retreated from the war in Vietnam after years of public protest.

GEO ADVENTURES DAILY GEOGRAPHY ACTIVITIES

Use **Geo Adventures** Daily Geography activities to assess students' understanding of geography skills.

CHAPTER PLANNING GUIDE

LESSON 1	STUDYSKILLS	LESSON 2
SUGGESTED PACING: 2 DAYS	SUGGESTED PACING: 1 DAY	SUGGESTED PACING: 2 DAYS
Independence In Africa pp. 566–571	**Political Cartoons** pp. 572–573	**New Nations In The Middle East** pp. 574–578
CURRICULUM CONNECTIONS Links to Language Arts, p. 570	**RESOURCES** Practice and Project Book, p. 113	**CURRICULUM CONNECTIONS** Links to Math, p. 576
CITIZENSHIP Understanding Government, p. 568		**CITIZENSHIP** Using Current Events, p. 577
RESOURCES Practice and Project Book, p. 112 Anthology, pp. 158–159, 160–161, 162–165 ▦Anthology, pp. 166–167 Desk Map		**RESOURCES** Practice and Project Book, p. 114 ▦Anthology, pp. 168, 169–171, 172

LESSON 3	LESSON 4	CHAPTER REVIEW
SUGGESTED PACING: 2 DAYS	SUGGESTED PACING: 2 DAYS	SUGGESTED PACING: 1 DAY
India's Struggle For Independence pp. 580–585	**New Nations In Southeast Asia** pp. 586–591	pp. 592–593
CURRICULUM CONNECTIONS Links to Reading, p. 583	**CURRICULUM CONNECTIONS** Links to Language Arts, p. 587 Links to Reading, p. 590	**RESOURCES** Practice and Project Book, p. 117 ⦿TECHNOLOGY Videodisc/Video Tape 4
CITIZENSHIP Understanding Government, p. 582	**CITIZENSHIP** Recognizing Perspectives, p. 589	Assessment Book: Chapter 19 Test Transparency: Graphic Organizer, Main-Idea Chart
RESOURCES Project and Practice Book, p. 115 Anthology, pp. 173, 174, 175 ⦿TECHNOLOGY Videodisc	**RESOURCES** Practice and Project Book, p. 116 Anthology, pp. 176–179, 180–182 ▦Anthology, pp. 183–184 Desk Map	

LEARNING STYLE: AuObjectory ON YOUR OWN 30 MINUTES OR LONGER

Write a Leader's Speech

Objective: To prepare students to study the emergence of new nations.

Materials: paper, art supplies

1. Ask students to imagine they are leaders of new nations on their first day in power. They must speak to the people.
2. Have students make notes about ideas for their speeches: what are some goals and laws of the new government? Encourage students to make costumes or flags that reflect the ideals of the new nation.
3. Ask students to write their speeches and present them. Discuss the reasons new nations are formed.

CITIZENSHIP

SUGGESTED PACING: 1 DAY

Building Bridges To Friendship p. 579

CITIZENSHIP
Recognizing Perspectives, p. 579

SDAIE SUPPORT SHELTERED INSTRUCTION

READING STRATEGIES & LANGUAGE DEVELOPMENT

Main Idea and Details/Synonyms, p. 566, Lesson 1
Rereading/Word Origin, p. 572, Study Skills
Predicting/Word Family, p. 574, Lesson 3
Making and Supporting Generalizations/Word Roots, p. 580, Lesson 3
Compare and Contrast/Word Origins, p. 586, Lesson 4

SECOND-LANGUAGE SUPPORT

Graphic Organizers, p. 570
Making Connections, p. 575
Using Visuals, pp. 583, 589
Oral Practice/Interviewing, p. 592

MEETING INDIVIDUAL NEEDS

Reteaching, Extension, Enrichment, pp. 571, 573, 578, 585, 591
McGraw-Hill Adventure Book

ASSESSMENT OPPORTUNITIES

Practice and Project Book, pp. 112–117
Write About It, pp. 571, 578, 585, 591
Assessment Book: Assessing Think and Write, pp. T104–T106; Chapter 19 Tests: Content, Skills, Writing

Introducing the Chapter

Invite students to think back to the struggles of colonies for independence from colonial masters that they have already learned about—Latin American colonies fighting France and Spain, for example. Tell them that they will now explore a new round of such struggles.

THINKING ABOUT HISTORY AND GEOGRAPHY

Have students read the text to identify the scene of struggle for independence—Africa and Asia. They can trace each panel back to its location on the map.

1869 EGYPT

● **What is happening here?** *(The Suez Canal is being built in Egypt.)*

● **Looking at the map, where is the only logical place for a canal to be built in Egypt?** *(at the narrow isthmus joining Africa and Asia)*

★**THINKING FURTHER:** *Making Conclusions* **What do you think the advantages of such a canal might be?** *(Using a world map, help students see how a canal cut the distance from Europe to the Indian Ocean and thus to points in Asia.)*

1940S DELHI, INDIA

● **What colony is protesting against what colonial ruler here? When?** *(India is protesting Britain; 1940s.)*

● **Who led the protest?** *(Mohandas Gandhi)*

★**THINKING FURTHER:** *Compare and Contrast* **How do you suppose Gandhi's means to independence might differ from means Simón Bolívar used in South America?** *(Bolívar led military forces. Gandhi is leading protesters.)*

Resource REMINDER

💿 **Technology:** *Videodisc/Video Tape 1*

564

New Nations

THINKING ABOUT HISTORY AND GEOGRAPHY

In this chapter you will read how nations in many parts of the world gained independence from colonial powers in the 1900s. In places such as Ghana and India, strong leaders led the nationalist movements that broke colonial ties. For many, though, independence brought more war.

AFRICA

Accra

1869

EGYPT
The Suez Canal is built

1940s

DELHI, INDIA
Mohandas Gandhi leads protests against the rule of Britain

1850   1930   1950

BACKGROUND INFORMATION

LINKING THE MAP AND THE TIME LINE

● Because the 105-mile north-south length of the Suez Canal passes through level land, it has no need of locks, which the Panama Canal requires. The Suez Canal was not the first canal built in the area. As early as the 20th or 19th century B.C., a west-east canal was dug from the Nile River to the Red Sea. It operated on and off until the A.D. 700s.

● Delhi is located in a rather narrow passageway that commands the divide between the Indus Valley to the northwest and the Ganges Valley on the southeast. This location has made Delhi a great crossroads of the subcontinent of India, which is why the British chose it as the capital of the British Raj in 1912, and independent India retained New Delhi as its capital in 1947.

ASIA

Israel

Delhi

INDIAN OCEAN

Saigon

1957

1975

1990s

ACCRA, GHANA
Nkrumah declares Ghana's independence from Britain

SAIGON, VIETNAM
South Vietnam falls to communist forces

ISRAEL
Israelis and Palestinians move towards peace

1970

1990

565

1957 ACCRA, GHANA

★**THINKING FURTHER:** *Compare and Contrast* **What similarities and differences can you find between this panel and the previous one?** *(Similarities: Both reflect independence from Britain and both show a popular leader. Differences: This is Africa not Asia, 1957 not the 1940s, triumph not struggle.)*

1975 SAIGON, VIETNAM

● **On what continent and in what part of that continent did the action in this panel take place?** *(in southeastern Asia)*

● **What has happened?** *(South Vietnam has fallen to communist forces.)*

★**THINKING FURTHER:** *Making Conclusions* **From what you already know from other sources, did this happen as a result of a colonial war for independence or from some other cause?** *(Someone may know that it was a war fought between those who wanted to bring all of Vietnam under communist control and those who did not.)*

1990s ISRAEL

● **What is happening in this panel and when?** *(Two groups in conflict are trying to reach peace, 1990s.)*

● **Where has this struggle taken place?** *(in Israel, in southwestern Asia or the Middle East)*

★**THINKING FURTHER:** *Compare and Contrast* **How is what is happening here similar to the action in the third panel?** *(Both involve people striving for what they want.)*

BACKGROUND INFORMATION

LINKING THE MAP AND THE TIME LINE

● Accra is both the capital and the largest city of Ghana. Because of its coastal location on the Gulf of Guinea and its railroad connections to the cacao-growing areas of the country, it is an important commercial center.

● Located about 50 miles (80 km) from the South China Sea and linked to the Mekong River by canals, Saigon has long been the commercial center of southern Vietnam. When Vietnam was split in two in 1954, Saigon became capital of South Vietnam.

● The battle lines between the Israelis and the Palestinians were drawn in 1947 when the UN proposed to divide what had been Palestine into two states—Jewish Israel and Arab Palestine. The Arabs refused to accept this partition, and fighting began.

 Technology CONNECTION

VIDEODISC/VIDEO TAPE 1
Enrich Chapter 19 with the *Africa Today* segment on the Videodisc.

Search Frame 28735, Side A

565

LESSON 1

Lesson Overview

Europe turned Africa into a continent of European colonies, which then fought for independence from colonial rule.

Lesson Objectives

★ Explain the spread of European colonization across Africa.

★ Describe the rise of African nationalism and analyze its effects.

1 PREPARE

MOTIVATE Ask students to recall the resentment the 13 colonies felt toward the British just before the American Revolution and the resentment Latin American colonies felt toward Spain. Then have two students do the *Read Aloud,* one as Carlos Miranda, the other as narrator.

SET PURPOSE Ask what the natural outgrowth of such feeling would be. Students should recognize the desire for independence. Refer them to the *Read to Learn* question and encourage them to explore the lesson to trace African paths to independence, symbolized by the flags in the photo. Preview the *Vocabulary.*

2 TEACH

Understanding THE BIG PICTURE
Have students look at the map on p. 570 to view European colonization in Africa.

> ★**THINKING FURTHER: *Cause and Effect*** How would you expect Africans to react to the extent and the length of time of European control? *(Africans would want control over their own lands.)*

Resource REMINDER

Practice and Project Book: *p. 112*

Anthology: *Attack on the Congo River: One View, pp. 158–159; Attack on the Congo River: Another View, pp. 160–161; The Man Who Shared His Hut, pp. 162–165; The Vision That I See, pp. 166–167*

Desk Map

| 1800 | 1850 | 1874 | | 1995 | 2000 |

Independence in Africa

Read Aloud

"You ask what the difference between colonialism and independence means to me. . . . Before white and black did not talk. But now at this moment I have the pleasure of sitting with you, a white, and I speak to you like a man. That is all we fought for, the right to respect."

Carlos Miranda spoke these words to a writer after his country, Guinea-Bissau (GIHN ee bihs OW), gained independence from Portugal in 1974. Millions of other Africans shared his feelings about the long period of European rule in Africa.

Focus Activity

READ TO LEARN

How did countries in Africa gain independence from European rule?

VOCABULARY

• boycott

PEOPLE

• Kwame Nkrumah
• Gamal Abdel Nasser

PLACES

• Accra
• Ghana
• Egypt
• Suez Canal
• Cairo

566

THE BIG PICTURE

The Portuguese were the first Europeans to set up colonies in Africa. They built stone forts along the West African coast in 1482. By 1900, millions of Africans had come to be ruled by Europeans. Look at the map on page 570 to see how England, France, Portugal, Belgium, Germany, and Spain carved Africa into colonies. In 1914 Ethiopia and Liberia were the only independent nations south of the Sahara Desert. In some areas European colonists set up European-style communities and profited from the continent's natural resources.

During the 1900s many Africans spoke out against the European nations that had controlled their continent. In the decades that followed World War II, Africans once again began to control their own lands and lives. In this lesson you will read about two examples of nations struggling to gain independence.

SHELTERED INSTRUCTION

READING STRATEGIES & LANGUAGE DEVELOPMENT

MAIN IDEA AND DETAILS Remind students that finding the main ideas and details in a passage can help them understand the author's point. Explain how details support the main idea. To demonstrate visually, write *main idea* on the board. Sketch several boxes beneath and connect each to the words *main idea* with arrows. Have students read paragraph one on p. 567 and identify the main idea [The British established the Gold Coast colony] and details. Add them to the chart. Have students copy the chart and add to it as they read this lesson.
[SDAIE STRATEGY: SCHEMA BUILDING/TEXT RE-PRESENTATION]

SYNONYMS Have students note that *independence* is used several times on this page. Invite them to suggest words that convey a similar meaning *(freedom, liberty, self-rule).*

THE GOLD COAST

In 1874 the British established the colony they called the Gold Coast on Africa's west coast. The British named the colony after the gold that was plentiful in West Africa at the time. The Gold Coast is the area where the ancient African kingdoms of Ghana and Mali, which you read about in Chapter 13, were located.

As you read in Chapter 16, from the early 1500s to the middle 1800s, the Gold Coast had been a center of the slave trade. Both African and European slave traders raided villages of the region. Traders sold their captives for guns, cloth, and other goods.

Profits from Trade

Even after the British government outlawed slave trade, the Gold Coast continued to grow as an important center for British trade. By 1874, other European colonies in Africa and North America were already settled by British citizens. The Gold Coast, however, was run by fewer than 4,000 British soldiers and government officials. Profits gained in the Gold Coast were sent to Britain.

The supply of gold available in West Africa dwindled over time. The British colonists soon found a new source of income, though. The British planted cacao (kuh KAH oh) throughout large areas of the Gold Coast. The cacao tree produces seeds that are used to make chocolate. By 1920 half of the world's supply of cacao was grown in the Gold Coast.

Colonial Conflict

Many Africans in the Gold Coast had long resented British control of their land. Earlier, the British government of

Cacao beans (right) are used to make chocolate. This man in Ghana (above) is gathering dried beans.

the Gold Coast had also faced resistance from the Asante. These Africans, who lived in an independent kingdom to the north, had taken part in the slave trade along with the British and the Dutch in the 1700s. As the Asante gained wealth and power, they expanded the borders of their land. They resisted British rule until 1902.

Later, still others began to oppose British rule. Among them was a young man who studied philosophy in the United States. His name was Kwame Nkrumah (KWAHM ee en KROO muh). After leaving the United States in 1945 he wrote:

> I saw the Statue of Liberty with her arm raised as if in personal farewell to me. [I said silently] "You have opened my eyes to the true meaning of liberty. I shall never rest until I have carried your message to Africa."

567

Invite students to go back to Chapter 13 and thumb through the pages that describe and show the proud and prosperous days of Ghana and Mali.

> ★THINKING FURTHER: *Compare and Contrast* **How would you compare and contrast the glory days of Ghana and Mali with the later days of the Gold Coast?** *(African autonomy and prosperous trade have been replaced by foreign control of resources, including captured Africans enslaved and transported away.)*

Discussing Profits from Trade Reinforce the idea that profits from the Gold Coast resources went to Britain

- *In early colonial days, what were the two major sources of profits in the Gold Coast? (gold and slaves)*

- *Why did they stop earning profits? (Gold ran out; slave trade was outlawed.)*

- *What new profit source was introduced? (the cacao plant, for making chocolate. Have students identify where they learned about the plant—Chapter 11—and remind them that it was part of the Columbian Exchange, having been brought from Central and South America to Africa.)*

> ★THINKING FURTHER: *Compare and Contrast* **How did colonization in the Gold Coast differ from the colonizing of North America?** *(Unlike North America, the Gold Coast attracted few European settlers; only 4,000 British arrived to run the colony.)*

Exploring Colonial Conflict Be sure students recognize another case of the U.S. influence on desires for liberty.

- *What African group was able to resist British control? Why? (the Asante, who had grown wealthy in the slave trade and powerful enough to maintain an independent kingdom)*

> ★THINKING FURTHER: *Making Connections* **How did Kwame Nkrumah act as an agent of cultural borrowing?** *(He brought American ideas of liberty back to Africa with him in 1945.)*

BACKGROUND INFORMATION

"DR. LIVINGSTONE, I PRESUME?" At first Europeans colonized only coastal areas of Africa because they used these places for refueling their ships that trade in the East. Afterward missionaries and explorers traveled deep into the interior.

- One of the missionary-explorers was David Livingstone, a medical doctor, who in 1866 went in search of the source of the Nile River.

- In those pre-telecommunications days, after no word had been heard of Livingstone in five years, a New York newspaper decided he was lost and sent reporter Henry Morton Stanley to find him.

- After a ten-month search, Stanley learned of a white doctor who lived in an African community. Approaching the ailing, seemingly elderly man, Stanley removed his hat and spoke the words that have been quoted ever since: "Dr. Livingstone, I presume?"

THE RISE OF AFRICAN NATIONALISM

Have students begin listing the steps in the road to African independence.

- **How did African nationalists go about gaining support for independence?** *(by writing newspaper stories and by speaking to the African people)*

★ **THINKING FURTHER: *Making Conclusions*** **What method did Europeans use to try to resolve the conflict with the Africans?** *(Compromise—They gave Africans greater participation in government.)*

Discussing Economic Protest Help students recognize the increasing levels of pressure for independence.

- **What was Nkrumah's goal for the Gold Coast?** *(immediate, full independence from the British)*

- **What means did he use to reach this goal?** *(boycotts, refusal to buy goods)*

- **How would boycotts put pressure on the British?** *(Losing buyers of their goods would lose them money.)*

Understanding A Big Step Have students recognize gains and limits.

★ **THINKING FURTHER: *Cause and Effect*** **What effect did Nkrumah's actions have on the British?** *(The British allowed elections that made Nkrumah prime minister of the Gold Coast, but did not fully empower his government.)*

Exploring Independence at Last Discuss the importance of the nation's name.

- **What effect did the success of Ghana in winning independence have on other Africans living under colonial rule?** *(It inspired them and led the way to independence for most of Africa.)*

★ **THINKING FURTHER: *Making Conclusions*** **Why do you think Nkrumah and his people took the name Ghana for their nation?** *(to mark the start of a new African nation whose name echoed a proud heritage)*

THE RISE OF AFRICAN NATIONALISM

When Kwame Nkrumah returned home, he found a nationalist spirit already growing in the Gold Coast. Africa's nationalist leaders wrote for newspapers and talked with people in the colonies. In response the British gave some positions in the colonial government to Africans. Nearby French colonies did the same, giving Africans control of agriculture and education.

Economic Protest

Some African leaders were happy with the way change began to take root in the colonies. Others, like Nkrumah, wanted full independence right away. Nkrumah's slogan was "Self-Government Now." He began to organize boycotts of British goods. A boycott is a form of protest in which people join together and refuse to buy goods unless their demands are met. Nkrumah also led strikes against British companies in the Gold Coast.

DID YOU KNOW?

What is the origin of the word boycott?

The word boycott was first used in the 1880s in Ireland. Ireland was then a colony of Great Britain. Captain Charles Cunningham Boycott managed a large farm for the Earl of Erne in County Mayo. He was a cruel and demanding landlord who forced the farmers living on the earl's lands to pay high rents. In 1880 many farmers refused to pay the rent that Captain Boycott demanded. Soon the word boycott began to be used to describe this and other kinds of economic protest. The word and the protest were later used around the globe.

A Big Step

In time the British governor agreed to let the people of the Gold Coast elect a prime minister. In the 1951 election, Nkrumah's party won almost all the votes in the center of Accra, the capital city. The British governor asked Nkrumah to form a government. The governor did not, however, give the government full power immediately. Control of the colony remained in British hands for six more years.

Independence at Last

On March 6, 1957, the Gold Coast became a new African nation called Ghana. The new nation was named after the ancient kingdom of Ghana, which, as you have read, ruled part of West Africa from the 700s to the 1200s.

Africans living under colonial rule in Africa were inspired by the new nation. Kwame Nkrumah, now the new nation's prime minister, said:

> If we are to remain free, if we are to enjoy the full benefits of Africa's enormous wealth, we must unite to plan for the full [use] of our human and material resources in the interest of all our people.

Over the next 30 years, Africans in other nations gained control of their governments, ending European rule on most of the continent. Independence was not always won peacefully, though. Also, as in Ghana, independence did not always bring full democracy. The map on page 570 shows when each African nation gained independence from a European power.

Fight for Control of Egypt

Across the Sahara Desert, 2,500 miles northeast of Ghana, a struggle for independence was taking place in

---

CITIZENSHIP ★

UNDERSTANDING GOVERNMENT The hopes that Africa and much of the world had for the new nation of Ghana were soon dealt a blow.

- Because Kwame Nkrumah was educated in Britain and the U.S., people expected him to found a democratic government, probably based on the British parliamentary model and strong human rights.

- Soon after independence, Nkrumah muzzled the press to prevent any criticism of him and ruled as dictator over a one-party system.

- He also set his country on a disastrous economic course by ordering showy and expensive building projects and spending huge sums on the military.

- In 1966, that same military seized control of the government when he was out of the country.

- Nkrumah died in exile in 1972.

Kwame Nkrumah, center, is shown in 1957, just after Ghana gained independence from Britain.

gypt. The British had controlled this nd since the 1880s. Britain ruled gypt less directly than it did Ghana. ven so, the Egyptian leader had little ower to govern.

British colonists in Egypt developed n economic system based on cotton. he cotton was used to supply British extile factories. More important than otton, however, was the location of gypt. The point where Asia and Africa neet is in the northeast corner of gypt. There the Suez Canal Company, wned mostly by French and Egyptians, uilt the Suez Canal. Later the British ecame part of the company, and, long with the French, controlled he canal.

The Suez Canal connected the Mediterranean Sea and the Red Sea,

providing a shortcut for ships sailing between Europe and Asia. British ships sailing to the British colony of India could now pass through the Suez Canal instead of traveling around Africa. The canal cut 6,000 miles from the trip.

During World War I nationalist spirit in Egypt grew. Many Egyptians were angry over British demands for men and supplies. Continued unrest led Britain to give Egyptians limited power in their government in 1922. Although Egyptians elected a parliament, Britain appointed the king, Fuad (foo AHD) I. Fuad I ruled according to the wishes of the British. Europeans continued to control the Suez Canal.

A Republic is Born

Many Egyptians were angry that they had not truly been given a voice in their government. In 1952 a group of Egyptian officers in the British army seized control of the government. The group was led by Gamal Abdel Nasser (guh MAHL ahb DEL NAHS ur). The officers forced the king to leave Egypt. People celebrated in the streets of the capital city, Cairo, singing "Raise up your head my brother, the days of humiliation have passed."

In 1956 Nasser gained control of the Suez Canal.

> Today I seize the canal in the name of the people. . . . This night our canal shall be Egyptian, controlled by Egyptians!

The British and their allies sent an army to try to prevent Egypt from taking over the canal. However, governments around the world supported the Egyptians, and the British were forced to give up their claim to the canal. Finally British rule and political influence had come to an end in Egypt.

569

GLOBAL CONNECTION

THE SUEZ CANAL—LIFELINE OF WORLD SHIPPING

- The British were able to buy a controlling interest in the Suez Canal in 1875, six years after it opened, when the debt-ridden khedive of Egypt had to sell his holdings in it.
- European nations resented this British control (as students will see in the *Skills Lesson* on political cartoons on pp. 572–573), but in 1888, the British guaranteed freedom of passage through the canal to all ships in peace and war.
- As the canal's hundredth anniversary approached in the early 1960s, 15 percent of all the world's shipping passed through it, with the majority of ships carrying oil.

Extending Did You Know? Point out that a number of individuals' names have become English words—for example, *bloomers, leotards, quisling,* and *raglan.* Have students look up these words and learn their meanings and origins.

Discussing Fight for Control of Egypt Have students locate Egypt on the map on p. 570.

- **Which European country controlled Egypt?** *(Britain)*

- **Where is the Suez Canal located?** *(Have students point to that location on the map, at the northeastern corner of Egypt.)*

- **Why was the Suez Canal so important to Europeans?** *(It linked the Mediterranean Sea to the Red Sea, eliminating 6,000 miles for a ship to travel from Europe to Asia. On a desk map of the world, have a student trace the route from Europe to Asia around Africa and contrast it with the route through the Suez Canal.)*

★THINKING FURTHER: *Compare and Contrast* **How would you contrast the conflicting interests for Britain and Egypt in controlling Egypt?** *(Britain wanted to maintain control of the Suez Canal for economic and transportation reasons; Egyptian nationalists wanted independence.)*

Exploring A Republic Is Born Point out the connection between Egypt's gaining independence and its gaining control of the Suez Canal.

- **How did the Egyptians capture control of their land from Britain?** *(by a military coup led by Gamal Abdel Nasser that overthrew and exiled the British-chosen king)*

- **What action did Nasser then take?** *(He took control of the Suez Canal from the British.)*

- **Why were the British powerless to stop him?** *(World opinion was with Egypt's controlling its own land.)*

★THINKING FURTHER: *Making Conclusions* **How does this event show that colonialism was coming to an end in the world?** *(Most world nations thought colonialism was no longer acceptable.)*

MAP WORK

Help students recognize that two kinds of information are shown in this map.

- **What kind of information do the different shadings in this map show? How do you know?** *(The legend shows that each shade represents the areas that one European country once controlled.)*

- **What second kind of information does the map show?** *(the independent nations of Africa and the years they gained their independence)*

- **Which European power once controlled Nigeria? When did Nigeria gain independence?** *(Britain; 1960)*

- **Which European power once controlled Algeria? When did Algeria gain independence?** *(France; 1962)*

- **Which of today's African nations did Belgium control? Until when?** *(Congo, 1960; Rwanda, 1962)*

- **When did Namibia gain independence? From what African country?** *(1990, from South Africa)*

- **Which European nation once claimed today's Somalia? its neighbor Djibouti?** *(Italy; France)*

★**THINKING FURTHER:** *Making Conclusions* **During what time period did African nations gain their independence?** *(from 1951, Libya, to 1993, Eritrea)*

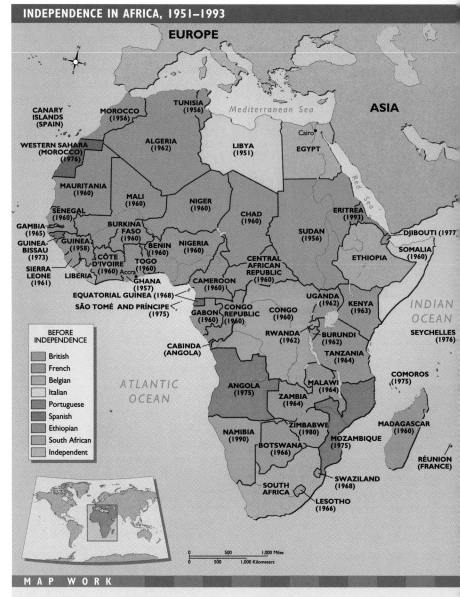

INDEPENDENCE IN AFRICA, 1951–1993

BEFORE INDEPENDENCE
- British
- French
- Belgian
- Italian
- Portuguese
- Spanish
- Ethiopian
- South African
- Independent

MAP WORK

Colonies in Africa gained independence from European rule beginning in 1951. Over a period of more than 40 years, many new nations emerged.

1. In what year did Tanzania gain independence?

2. Which country gained independence in 1951?

3. Which countries were formerly ruled by the Portuguese?

4. Which two European powers ruled the most land in Africa?

570

BACKGROUND INFORMATION

A HISTORY OF INDEPENDENCE—ETHIOPIA, LIBERIA

- Remind students that they have read about Ethiopia in Chapter 13 and in Chapter 18.

- Ethiopia regained its independence in 1941 when its emperor, Haile Selassie, returned to take the throne after the British expelled the Italians.

- Liberia was partially settled, beginning in the 1820s, by formerly enslaved people from America.

- The American Colonization Society began settling former enslaved people in the African community Monrovia.

- In 1847 Monrovia and other communities united to become Liberia, the first black republic in Africa.

CURRICULUM CONNECTION

LINKS TO LANGUAGE ARTS Students have learned that Africans renamed the Gold Coast Ghana to celebrate their African heritage. Have the class examine the map to find other ancient names (*Mali*, which had been called French West Africa, and *Zimbabwe*, which had been called Rhodesia).

SECOND-LANGUAGE SUPPORT

GRAPHIC ORGANIZERS Semantic mapping will help second-language learners follow this lesson. Have students write *African Independence* in the center of a paper. Then have them skim the lesson to find other major topics to cluster around the center. Encourage students to add details as they complete the lesson.

WHY IT MATTERS

European colonies in Africa were used to produce wealth for Europeans, rather than building the economy for the benefit of Africans. Europeans also created boundaries in Africa without considering that the continent's 2,000 different peoples had lived in certain areas for centuries. Often a new boundary divided an area where a group lived. When nations became independent, the borders were often the European boundaries. Many conflicts developed as people fought for land that had historically belonged to them but was now part of another nation.

By 1995 all of Africa had thrown off European rule and gained independence. However, many problems remained for its nations—the result of years of foreign rule. In recent years, several African nations have taken steps to solve those problems. In the next chapter you will read about one large African nation and how it achieved democracy and human rights.

President Abdel Nasser of Egypt addresses a crowd in 1958. In 1952 he had won control of the Egyptian government.

// Reviewing Facts and Ideas

MAIN IDEAS

● Beginning in the 1500s several European nations established colonies in Africa.

● In 1957 the Gold Coast became the first colony south of the Sahara to gain independence. The new nation was named Ghana.

● Following several steps towards independence, Egyptians gained control of their government in 1952.

● By 1995 all European colonies in Africa had become independent.

THINK ABOUT IT

1. How did European countries gain wealth from their African colonies?

2. How did the British respond to the activities of nationalist leaders in western Africa?

3. **FOCUS** How did the country of Ghana gain its independence from Britain?

4. **THINKING SKILL** Explain two *effects* of European colonialism on Africa.

5. **GEOGRAPHY** How did the Suez Canal affect the movement of people and goods between continents?

571

Discussing WHY IT MATTERS Discuss the long-lasting effects of European control.

★**THINKING FURTHER: Cause and Effect** **How did the way African boundaries were drawn cause potentially explosive problems for the independent nations?** *(The borders often divided a people's traditional lands, making land disputes between neighboring countries and peoples highly likely.)*

⭐ 3 CLOSE

MAIN IDEAS

Call on students for answers.

● **What major action did Europe take toward Africa beginning in the 1500s?** *(European countries began establishing colonies in Africa.)*

● **What happened in the British colony of Gold Coast in 1957?** *(It became the independent nation of Ghana.)*

● **Which African nation, claiming the Suez Canal, achieved independence in 1952?** *(Egypt)*

● **By 1995 what had become of European colonies in Africa?** *(They had all gained independence.)*

EVALUATE
✓ **Answers to Think About It**

1. by taking natural resources from them and selling goods to them
Summarize

2. They tried to compromise—to give Africans some power in government without full independence.
Recall Details

3. Nationalists pressured the British into granting elections and then independence after six years of partial power with an elected government.
Make Conclusions

4. Europeans did not build an African economy and they left behind highly disputable boundaries.
Form Generalizations

5. It eliminated 6,000 miles from a trip from Europe to southern and eastern Asia.
Five Themes of Geography: Movement

Write About It Have students write a paragraph describing a major change in Africa that took place between 1951 and 1980.

SKILLS LESSON

PAGE 572–573

Lesson Overview
A political cartoon uses symbols, exaggeration, and often humor to convey an opinion about a political matter.

Lesson Objective
★ Learn to interpret political cartoons.

1 PREPARE

MOTIVATE Have some current political cartoons on hand for the class to examine. Ask students to identify any symbols and people they recognize. Then have students read *Why the Skill Matters* to see how political cartoons can provide important clues to history.

SET PURPOSE Focus on how we can interpret the opinion a political cartoon expresses. Point out that such cartoons need to be decoded—they use picture symbols that readers are expected to understand. Invite students to explore this skills lesson to learn how to decode political cartoons. Have students preview the steps by reading *Helping Yourself.*

2 TEACH

Using the Skill Help students realize that they already know some symbols.

● **Describe some symbols that stand for your local sports teams. What are some symbols that stand for our country?** *(Use some familiar symbols to help students understand symbols and their use.)*

Resource REMINDER

Practice and Project Book: *p. 113*

Study Skills

Political Cartoons

VOCABULARY
political cartoon
symbol

WHY THE SKILL MATTERS

During the 1800s powerful European countries established colonies all over the world. Very often colonial powers had disagreements. People who lived in such countries as Britain and France also disagreed at times about whether their countries should establish colonies. Writers discussed these topics in magazines and newspapers.

Also during this time political cartoons began to appear more frequently in European magazines. Political cartoons are pictures that show an opinion about a political matter, such as a government action or an election. Political cartoons are useful historical sources. They tell the modern reader many things about cartoonists and people from the past for whom the cartoons were drawn.

USING THE SKILL

Cartoonists often use symbols in their cartoons to convey information. A symbol is a sign that stands for something else. For example, the character Uncle Sam is a symbol for the United States. The Statue of Liberty and the bald eagle are also symbols for the United States. Symbols provide an easy way for cartoonists to refer to a country such as the United States in a cartoon.

When you look at a political cartoon, study the symbols and try to figure out what they stand for. For example, look at Cartoon A on this page. This cartoon was published in a French magazine. The large figure is

572

This cartoon expresses the political viewpoint of many French who were angered by Britain's control of the canal.

John Bull, a symbol that stands for Great Britain. The smaller figures standing around John Bull are symbols that stand for other European countries.

It is also important to read any signs or captions that appear in the cartoon. In Cartoon A the words *Canal de Suez* are very important. These are the French words for Suez Canal. Remember what you read about Britain and the Suez Canal in Lesson 1.

Finally, think about the story or opinion that the cartoonist is trying to communicate. Cartoonists often use exaggeration to make their point. In Cartoon A, John Bull is much bigger than the other people. The cartoonist seems to be saying that Britain is over-exercising control of the canal.

READING STRATEGIES & LANGUAGE DEVELOPMENT

REREADING Explain to students that they need to be particularly careful in reading this skills lesson to be sure they understand the aims that creators of political cartoons have and the methods they use to achieve their aims. Encourage students to reread whenever they find it necessary in this lesson to learn how to do what they are asked to do. Point to three concepts that might bear rereading—what a political cartoon tries to do, the need to understand all the symbols and words that appear in it, and the need to call on knowledge one already has about a period.

WORD ORIGIN Explain that the word *cartoon* comes from the Italian *cartone,* or "cardboard," which at first referred to the original sketch made for a work of art—a painting or a fresco. Have students discuss how far this meaning is from today's animated cartoons.

he United States; fight in World
ar I **The title tells where the
gures are going and why; the
rtoonist supports American sol-
ers fighting in France;

the soldiers are led by the Statue
of Liberty and they are waving a
flag and looking very determined.

Helping yourself

- Political cartoons are useful for studying people's opinions in history.
- Cartoonists often use symbols to stand for something else.
- Study all the information to learn a cartoonist's point of view.

RYING THE SKILL

Cartoon B is from a United
tates newspaper. The title of
is cartoon is "To France!
917." It shows the Statue of
berty marching with a num-
er of soldiers. Look carefully
all of the information in the
rtoon. What do you think the
tatue of Liberty is a symbol
r? What do you think she
d the soldiers are headed
f to do?*

Remember what you read
earlier about World War I and
the role of the United States in
the war. How does the title of
Cartoon B help you under-
stand its meaning? What do
you think the cartoon "says"
about the cartoonist's feelings
about Americans fighting at the
battlefront in France? How can
you tell?**

REVIEWING THE SKILL

1. Why are political cartoons a useful source for studying history?

2. Why do cartoonists often use symbols?

3. Look at Cartoon A. How do you think an Egyptian would feel about this cartoon?

4. Look at Cartoon B. Do you think that people who lived in France would agree with the opinion of this cartoonist? Why or why not?

5. Find a political cartoon in your local newspaper. What does it tell you about how the cartoonist feels about the topic?

B

Political cartoons often rely on exaggerated representations or humor to express their viewpoints.

573

- **What does the big man in Cartoon A symbolize? the smaller figures?** *(Tell students that Angleterre is French for "England"; other European countries)*

- **What is each country holding? What does that symbol stand for?** *(a tiny ship; their shipping, which they want to send through the Suez Canal. Explain that the writing at the lower left means "Entry barred to the public.")*

★**THINKING FURTHER:** *Making Conclusions* **What opinion does this cartoon offer?** *(The British control the Suez Canal at Europe's expense.)*

Trying the Skill Have students review *Helping Yourself.*

- **What is the title of Cartoon B?** *("To France! 1917")*

- **What do the soldiers symbolize? How do you know?** *(the fighting and moral forces of the U.S.; from other symbols—the Statue of Liberty, the American flag)*

★**THINKING FURTHER:** *Making Conclusions* **Do you conclude that the cartoonist is in favor of this action or against it?** *(The look on the Statue of Liberty's face and the exploding light her torch throws off as well as the stern look of the soldiers indicate that the cartoonist agrees with America's joining the fight.)*

⭐ 3 CLOSE

SUM IT UP

Have students make a brief list to summarize the steps in interpreting political cartoons, for example: "Read caption, read words, decode symbols."

EVALUATE
√ **Answers to Reviewing the Skill**

1. They give clues to the time when they were drawn—how people thought and felt about issues then.

2. Symbols are a kind of shorthand, a way to express ideas in pictures.

3. An Egyptian might resent any European country's control of a canal through Egypt's territory.

4. Possible answer: They might agree that the U.S. was doing the right thing in joining on France's side.

5. Discuss the cartoons in class.

MEETING INDIVIDUAL NEEDS

RETEACHING (Easy) Have each student bring in a political cartoon clipped or copied from a newspaper or news magazine. Have students write brief statements identifying the cartoon's symbols and giving an interpretation of it. Then have students exchange the cartoons to see if they can agree on the interpretation.

EXTENSION (Average) Call on students to mention events currently in the news about which they have opinions. Have them use symbols and words to create their own cartoons that express their opinions.

ENRICHMENT (Challenging) The works of several major American cartoonists have been collected—Thomas Nast, Herblock (Herbert Block), Bill Mauldin, and Oliphant. Divide the class into groups and have each group research the work of one of these. Have the groups prepare illustrated presentations for the class.

LESSON 2

PAGES 574–578

Lesson Overview
The Jewish struggle for a homeland led to more than a half century of conflict between Israelis and Palestinians.

Lesson Objectives
★ Explain why Jews struggled for a homeland.

★ Describe the conflict between Israelis and Palestinians.

1 PREPARE

MOTIVATE Point out the photo of Yitzhak Rabin of Israel and Yasir Arafat of the Palestinian Liberation Organization shaking hands. To discover why they shook hands, have one student read the *Read Aloud* quote and another the narrator's part. Ask students to recall what they learned of ancient Israel in Chapter 5, Lesson 3. What do students think has taken place there in recent years? (conflict between Israelis and Palestinians)

Set Purpose Ask students what conditions might have led to conflict. Refer students to the *Read to Learn* question. Encourage them to explore the lesson to learn what has happened there lately. Preview the *Vocabulary*.

2 TEACH

Understanding THE BIG PICTURE
Have students sit in pairs, one with text open here, the other to the map, p. 576.

● *Where is the Middle East?* *(Have students locate it and name nations that are part of it.)*

★**THINKING FURTHER:** *Making Conclusions* **What ancient theme in human history lies behind the Israeli-Palestinian conflict?** *(two peoples claiming the same piece of land)*

Resource **REMINDER**

Practice and Project Book: *p. 114*

Anthology: *The Mountains in Israel, p. 168; Road to Peace, pp. 169–171; Poems for Peace, p. 172*

| 1800 | 1850 | 1874 | | 1995 | 2000 |

New Nations in The Middle East

Read Aloud
"The Government of the State of Israel and the . . . Palestinian people agree that it is time to put an end to decades of . . . conflict."

This is the opening of the Declaration of Principles, a special treaty written in 1993. After half a century of fighting, two peoples came to an agreement: the killing must stop. What caused their conflict?

Focus Activity

READ TO LEARN

What events led to the Israeli-Palestinian conflict?

VOCABULARY
- Zionism
- anti-semitism
- refugee
- Intifada

PEOPLE
- David Ben Gurion
- Yasir Arafat
- Anwar Sadat
- Yitzak Rabin

PLACES
- Middle East
- Palestine
- Turkey
- Iraq
- Israel
- Gaza
- Golan Heights
- West Bank

574

THE BIG PICTURE
Between the Mediterranean Sea and the western borders of Pakistan and Afghanistan is a region known as the Middle East. It spans all of western Asia and a small part of southeastern Europe. Find the 14 countries of the region on the map on page 576.

This region was the heart of the Baghdad Caliphate from the late 700s to the 1200s. From the 1500s until the end of World War I, the Middle East was ruled by the Ottoman empire. After 1918 Britain and France took control of most of the Middle East.

Along the western edge of the Middle East is a narrow wedge of land lying along the Mediterranean Sea. This land has had great impact on world events, and you have read about it more than once in this book. It has had many names: Canaan, Judea, Palestine, the Holy Land, Israel. Throughout history, it has been home to many peoples and cultures. In this lesson you will read about the struggle that developed between two of these peoples over a land that both claimed as their own.

SHELTERED INSTRUCTION

READING STRATEGIES & LANGUAGE DEVELOPMENT

PREDICTING Divide the class in half. Give one team three-quarters of the room; the other team, the remaining quarter. Have the teams brainstorm arguments to resolve this land dispute and then present their best points. Draw analogies between this situation and the land disputes in the Middle East. Have students skim the visuals and subheads to brainstorm predictions about the kind of information each section might contain. **[SDAIE STRATEGY: BRIDGING]**

WORD FAMILY Refer the class to the word *refugee* on p. 577. Write the word on the board and isolate the term *refuge* in it. Students should recognize a refuge as a place set aside for wildlife where animals can be safe. Have them relate what a *refuge* offers to what a *refugee* needs (safety).

A JEWISH HOMELAND

How did this struggle over the area that is today Israel develop? Part of the answer lies in the history of Zionism (ZI uh niz um). Zionism is a movement to establish a Jewish homeland, or nation. The word comes from Mount Zion, a mountain in Jerusalem.

An Ancient and Modern Hope

Modern Zionism began in the late 1800s. Its goal, in the words of a Hebrew song, was to make the Jews "a free people in our own land." Actually, the idea of a homeland for the Jewish people began much earlier. This idea began, in fact, in the time of the Diaspora. Remember from Chapter 5 that *Diaspora* means the "scattering" of the Jews from the land of Israel. This scattering began around 600 B.C., when the Babylonians conquered Judah. The Diaspora continued, but some Jews remained in the area. The Romans called it Palestine.

By the late 1800s, when modern Zionism began, Palestine was home to about 450,000 people. Most of them were Arabs. About 25,000 Jews also lived here. Most of the world's Jewish population lived outside of Palestine, in Europe and the rest of the world. However, they had never forgotten their ancient homeland. The yearly Passover seder always ends with the words: "Next year in Jerusalem!"

Troubles in Europe

The desire to return to Jerusalem grew stronger among many Jews in Europe. Feelings of nationalism had spread throughout the world since the French Revolution. Some European Jews, too, began hoping to have their own nation.

Also during this time anti-semitism grew stronger in Europe. Anti-semitism is discrimination against Jews. In Eastern European countries such as Russia and Poland where many Jews lived, Jews were often subjected to sudden, violent attacks. Many Jews left Europe for the United States and other regions, including Palestine.

These Jewish immigrants at a dock in Haifa reflect the desire of many Jews to return to the Jewish homeland and form their own nation.

A JEWISH HOMELAND

Point out that the suffix *-ism* often denotes a set of beliefs, as in *Judaism* and *Catholicism*. Then go on to have the class identify the belief of *Zionism* (that the Jews should have a homeland).

Discussing An Ancient and Modern Hope Have students locate Israel on the map on p. 576.

● *What caused the ancient scattering of the Jews from Israel?* (the Babylonian conquest in 586 B.C., which led to the exile of Jews to Babylon)

● *Who gave the area the name Palestine?* (the Romans)

● *How had the population of the area changed by the late 1800s?* (Its population of 450,000 was made up mostly of Arabs.)

● *Where did the rest of the Jews live?* (in Europe and other parts of the world)

★THINKING FURTHER: *Making Conclusions* What does the saying "Next year in Jerusalem" tell about the Jews' hopes? (For nearly 2,000 years, Jews had retained a desire to have their homeland back again.)

Exploring Troubles in Europe Help students relate events in Europe to nationalism and the Jews' desire to regain their homeland.

● *What is anti-semitism?* (discrimination against the Jews)

● *Where in Europe had anti-semitism subjected Jews to sudden, violent attacks?* (Russia and Poland)

● *Think back to chapter 18. What European leader came to power preaching anti-semitism?* (Adolf Hitler of Germany)

★THINKING FURTHER: *Making Conclusions* Why might modern anti-semitism in Europe be said to have caused a third Diaspora of the Jews? (It drove many from Europe to resettle in the United States or elsewhere, including Palestine.)

BACKGROUND INFORMATION

A JEWISH HOMELAND IN AFRICA? Britain facilitated the movement of Jews into Palestine when, in 1917, it approved the Balfour Declaration, which gave Jews permission to establish a homeland in Palestine. This was not the first homeland that Britain had proposed for the Jews. In 1905, it had offered the British colony Uganda, in Africa, as a Jewish homeland. Zionists did not accept that offer.

SECOND-LANGUAGE SUPPORT

MAKING CONNECTIONS The interest level for second-language learners will be heightened if they can relate this lesson to current events. Have students share current events articles from newspapers and magazines and reports from radio and television. Ask students to discuss what they knew about this region before reading the lesson.

CHANGES IN THE MIDDLE EAST

Encourage students to take up the thread of history following the collapse of the Ottoman empire.

● **What two European nations exercised control in the Middle East after the defeat of the Ottoman empire?** *(Britain and France)*

More ● **MAP WORK**

Refer students to the map on this page and encourage them to work back and forth between text and map.

● **Which European country exercised its limited control over a broader area?** *(Britain)*

● **Where did France exercise its limited control?** *(Syria and Lebanon, along the eastern Mediterranean)*

● **When did Turkey become an independent republic?** *(1923)*

★**THINKING FURTHER:** *Making Conclusions* **How does this map show that nationalists grew active in the Middle East after World War I just as nationalists grew active in Africa after World War II?** *(The dates on the maps show that several independent nations emerged shortly after World War I.)*

Discussing A Growing Population
Discuss the goals of conflicting nationalist interests.

● **By 1947 how had the makeup of Palestine's population changed since the late 1800s?** *(It had grown larger, and Jews were a third of the total.)*

● **How did growing nationalism create a conflict between Jews and Arabs in Palestine?** *(Jewish nationalists wanted to reclaim a Jewish homeland there and Palestinian Arabs wanted to create an independent nation there.)*

★**THINKING FURTHER:** *Making Conclusions* **What kinds of differences between peoples of Palestine seem certain to create bitter conflict?** *(ethnic background, religion, beliefs in the right to the land)*

MAP WORK: 1. Britain **2.** 1971 **3.** Syria, Iraq, Iran, Lebanon, Israel, Jordan, Saudi Arabia, Turkey

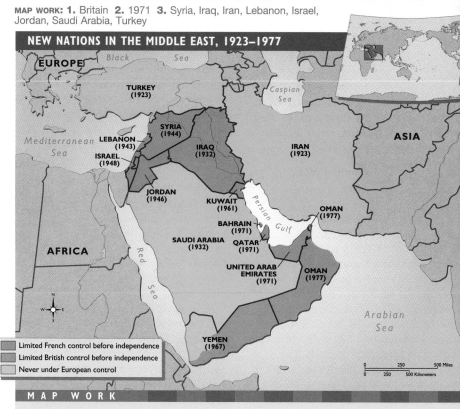

NEW NATIONS IN THE MIDDLE EAST, 1923–1977

MAP WORK

Beginning in 1923, many nations in the Middle East became independent.

1. Which European country had limited control of Iraq before independence?

2. In what year did Qatar become independent?

3. From looking at the map, what would be one reason that Iraq might want to conquer Kuiwait?

CHANGES IN THE MIDDLE EAST

After the defeat of the Ottoman empire in World War I, Britain and France took over much of the Middle East. By this time, however, nationalist movements were beginning to form in the region.

In 1923 nationalists in what was left of the Ottoman empire established an independent Republic of Turkey. It was only the first of several new nations in the Middle East. In 1932, after a period of British rule, the people of Iraq gained independence. Find these and other new nations on the map.

A Growing Population

Feelings of nationalism had been developing among both Arabs and Jew in British-controlled Palestine.

Growing numbers of Jews created tensions with Arabs who were already living in Palestine. Many Palestinian Arabs hoped to build new lives in an independent nation of Palestine. They feared that their own nationalist dreams would be lost.

576

CURRICULUM CONNECTION

LINKS TO MATH Use the population figures on pp. 575–576

● If the total population of Palestine in the late 1800s was 450,000 and 25,000 of them were Jews, how many were Arabs?

450,000 – 25,000 = 425,000

● What percentage did each group make up?

25,000 ÷ 450,000 = 6% Jews; 425,000 ÷ 450,000 = 94% Arabs

● What was the ratio of Arabs to Jews?

425,000 ÷ 25,000 = 17 to 1

● If in 1947, 650,000 Jews made up one third of the population, what was the total population? How many Arabs were there?

650,000 x 3 = 1,950,000 total; 1,950,000 – 650,000 = 1,300,000 Arabs

● How had the ratio of Arabs to Jew changed? (17 to 1 → 2 to 1)

World War II brought great changes to British Palestine. Many European Jews managed to escape Nazi oppression by immigrating to Palestine. After the war many survivors of Nazi concentration camps arrived in Palestine. By 1947 the number of Jews living in Palestine reached about 650,000, or about one-third of the population. The remaining two-thirds were Palestinian Arabs, most of whom were Muslims.

The Founding of Israel

After World War II the United Nations agreed to divide Palestine between Arabs and Jews. The Jews there accepted the plan. On May 14, 1948, they declared independence as the country of Israel. David Ben Gurion, a leader of the Jewish independence movement, became Israel's first prime minister.

War and Refugees

The day after Israel became an independent nation, armies from five Arab countries attacked the new nation. Jews fought to defend their new country. After more than six months of fighting, the Jews came out as victors. This war, however, was only the first of several wars that would be fought between Israel and Arab countries.

As the result of the Arab-Israeli conflict, as many as 750,000 Palestinian Arabs left Israel. Some fled out of fear. Some were forced to leave. Many settled in refugee camps in Jordan, Syria, and Lebanon. Refugees are people who have to flee their country for safety. About 600,000 Palestinians remained. Mahmoud Darwish, a Palestinian poet described his feelings about living in a homeland controlled by others:

You are my grief and my joy,
my wound and my rainbow,
my prison and my freedom.

In June 1967 war broke out again. In this conflict, the Six-Day War, Israel gained more land, including Gaza, the Golan Heights, and the West Bank. Find these areas on the map on page 578.

To gain back the land for Arabs, the Palestine Liberation Organization, or PLO, was formed in 1964. In 1968, under the leadership of Yasir Arafat, the PLO began to fight to get the land back from Israel.

The First Sign of Peace

Fighting between Arabs and Israelis continued on and off for years. Then in 1977 Egypt's President Anwar Sadat took a daring trip to Israel. For the first time an Arab leader publicly met with leaders of the Jewish nation. The Camp David agreement, signed by Egypt and Israel in 1978, established peaceful relations between those nations.

Golda Meir, Israeli prime minister from 1969 to 1974, greets Egyptian president Anwar Sadat in November 1977.

577

GLOBAL CONNECTION

PRESIDENTS FOR PEACE American Presidents sometimes take very active roles in working out peace agreements for other nations.

• In 1978 President Jimmy Carter brought Egypt and Israel together at the Presidential retreat at Camp David to help them work out their peace agreement, the Camp David Accords.

• In 1905 President Theodore Roosevelt brought representatives of Russia and Japan together in Portsmouth, New Hampshire, to help them work out a peace treaty to end their war (described in Chapter 17). Theodore Roosevelt won the Nobel Peace Prize as a result.

CITIZENSHIP★

USING CURRENT EVENTS Should the U.S. involve itself in mediating other nations' conflicts? Have students discuss why or why not.

Discussing The Founding of Israel
Point out that Arabs and Jews did not live in separate areas. Dividing Palestine would leave many Arabs and Jews in each other's part.

● *Who decided that the Jews and the Arabs should divide Palestine between them?* (the United Nations)

● *What was the immediate result of this decision?* (The independent nation of Israel was founded, with David Ben Gurion as its first prime minister.)

★THINKING FURTHER: *Predicting* *What do you predict would be the next result?* (Students might predict armed conflict between Jews and Arabs.)

Learning about War and Refugees
To verify students' predictions, read aloud the first paragraph of this section.

● *What support did the Palestinian Arabs receive to resist the formation of the nation of Israel?* (Five Arab countries attacked the new nation.)

● *When Israel was not defeated, what did the Palestinians there do?* (About 750,000 Palestinians left for refugee camps in neighboring countries and about 600,000 decided to stay.)

● *How did future Arab-Israeli wars make Arabs worse off?* (The Israelis captured Arab territories like Gaza, the Golan Heights, and the West Bank.)

★THINKING FURTHER: *Cause and Effect* *How did Israeli gains cause the PLO to form?* (The PLO formed to regain lost Arab lands.)

Exploring The First Sign of Peace
Help students appreciate Sadat's courage.

● *What was the first breakthrough toward peace between Jews and Arabs?* (the Egypt-Israel peace agreement in 1977)

★THINKING FURTHER: *Predicting* *Do you predict that Arab-Israeli peace will one day be achieved? Why or why not?* (Encourage free discussion identifying factors in favor—economic benefits of peace, for example—and against—long years of bitterness and hatred.)

More

MAP WORK

★ **THINKING FURTHER:** *Sequencing*
How would you sequence the events on the map? (Students should use the legend to create a sequence.)

Discussing WHY IT MATTERS Try to have on hand news articles that report on current Arab-Israeli relations, to bring the class up to date on their status.

★ **THINKING FURTHER:** *Making Decisions* **Do recent events in the Middle East encourage optimism or pessimism about the future there? Why?** *(Encourage open discussion.)*

★ 3 CLOSE

MAIN IDEAS

Have students write their answers and exchange papers to correct them.

● **Why did Jewish immigration to Palestine in this century alarm the people living there?** *(They wanted their own Arab nation there.)*

● **What hopeful signs began to take shape in the Middle East in the 1990s?** *(efforts toward Arab-Israeli peace)*

EVALUATE
✓ **Answers to Think About It**

1. to set up a homeland for the Jewish people, to escape severe anti-semitism in Europe
   Recall Details

2. to take back Arab lands captured by Israel
   Draw Conclusions

3. through world support for a Jewish homeland as reflected in the UN decision to allow one to be created
   Summarize

4. religious and ethnic differences and claim to the same land
   Main Idea

5. Its coastal location makes it open to attack by sea or land, it is virtually surrounded by Arab nations, it is very narrow.
   Five Themes of Geography: Location

Write About It If your students made predictions, as suggested in the *Reading Strategy* on p. 574, have them write an evaluation of one prediction.

ISRAEL AND TERRITORIES

- ☐ Areas occupied by Israel in Six-Day War, 1967
- ▨ Gradual Self-Rule, 1993
- • Gradual Self-Rule, 1996*
- * According to the 1995 Israeli-Palestinian Interim Agreement

LEBANON
ISRAEL SECURITY ZONE
SYRIA
GOLAN HEIGHTS
Mediterranean Sea
Jenin
Tulkarm
Qalqilya
Tel Aviv
Nablus
WEST BANK
Ramallah
Jerusalem
Jericho
Bethlehem
Dead Sea
GAZA STRIP
Gaza
Hebron
ISRAEL
JORDAN
EGYPT

N W E S

0   40   80 Miles
0   40   80 Kilometers

MAP WORK

In 1993 some Palestinian areas gained self-rule.
1. Which areas were the first to gain self-rule?
2. When did Jenin gain self-rule?

Palestinians show support for their leader Yasir Arafat in September 1988.

WHY IT MATTERS

The Camp David agreement did not end the struggle between Israel and the Palestinians. In 1987 Palestinians in Gaza and the West Bank began a revolt called the Intifada (ihn te FAH duh). *Intifada* means "shaking" in Arabic. Palestinians tried to "shake off" the rule of the Israelis.

Slowly, however, hopes for peace returned to this war-torn land. PLO leader Yasir Arafat and Yitzhak Rabin (YIHT zak rah BEEN), Prime Minister of Israel, signed agreements in 1993 and 1995. You read part of the 1993 agreement in this lesson's Read Aloud. They agreed that a Palestinian homeland would be established in Gaza and the West Bank.

Peace remains a difficult goal. In 1995 an Israeli opposed to the peace process *assassinated* Yitzhak Rabin. To assassinate means to kill for political reasons. Still, hope for peace remains, as Israelis and Palestinians continue to work together to solve their decades-old conflict.

✓ Reviewing Facts and Ideas

MAIN IDEAS

● In the 1900s Zionist immigration to Palestine concerned Palestinians, who desired a country of their own.

● In 1948 Arab armies attacked in an unsuccessful effort to destroy the new Jewish country of Israel. Palestinian refugees fled to other Arab lands.

● An uneasy peace began in the 1990s.

THINK ABOUT IT

1. What were two reasons for the creation of the Zionist movement?

2. Why was the PLO formed?

3. **FOCUS** How did modern Israel begin?

4. **THINKING SKILL** What were two *causes* for the Israeli-Palestinian conflict?

5. **GEOGRAPHY** Why might Israel's shape make it difficult to defend?

MEETING INDIVIDUAL NEEDS

RETEACHING (Easy) Have students review the lesson to identify the steps taken that gave the Jews Israel as their homeland. Have them draw a flow chart recording these steps.

EXTENSION (Average) Write the following quote from Anwar Sadat on signing the Egyptian-Israeli peace treaty in Washington, D.C. in 1979: "Let there be no more war or bloodshed between Arabs and Israelis. Let there be no more suffering or denial of rights. Let there be no more despair or loss of faith." Have students explain in writing why this statement can be a framework for peace anywhere.

ENRICHMENT (Challenging) To continue the "Class Almanac of Nations" (see p. 571), divide the class into groups and assign each group one of the Middle Eastern nations shown on the map on p. 576. Have each group research and write a page on its nation.

NEW NATIONS IN SOUTH ASIA, 1947–1972

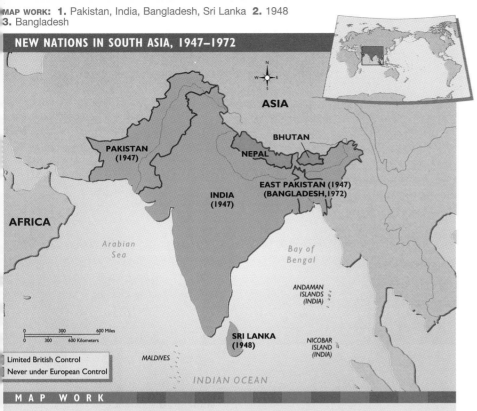

M A P   W O R K

Some nations in South Asia gained independence from European rule beginning in 1947. Others had never come under Euopean control.

1. Which nations were under British control?

2. In what year did Sri Lanka gain independence?

3. Which country became independent in 1972?

The Brink of Independence

In 1942 the Indian National Congress planned a new campaign to convince the British to leave. People shouted "Quit India" at British soldiers in India's cities. By 1947 the British were ready to give up control of India. Muslims feared that they would be treated poorly by a Hindu-led government. They demanded a separate country. On August 15, India and Pakistan gained independence.

Pakistan was made up of two separate areas in the northern corners of India. Many Muslims lived in these areas known as West and East Pakistan. The prime minister of Pakistan was Mohammad Ali Jinnah (muh HAM ud ah LEE JIHN ah). Jawaharlal Nehru (juh WAH hur ah NAY roo) was prime minister of India.

About ten million people moved across the border to be with people of their own faith. Nearly one million people died in violent conflicts between Hindus and Muslims. Gandhi was shot and killed in such a conflict in January 1948.

583

Discussing The Brink of Independence Once again, have the class return to Chapter 14, Lesson 3, to review the background for Muslim-Hindu tensions in India. (Muslim Moguls had introduced Islam into mainly Hindu India.)

● *What did Hindu-Muslims tensions lead to as India approached independence in 1947?* (the division into two independent countries—India and Pakistan)

● *What might you consider strange about the newly independent Pakistan?* (Possible answer: It had two unconnected parts—one in the northwest corner of the subcontinent and one in the northeast corner—and was separated by India.)

● *What serious human problems did the division of India create?* (uprooting of people, as millions of Hindus moved out of Muslim land and millions of Muslims moved out of Hindu territory, as well as bloody clashes between the two groups)

● *How did Gandhi himself become a victim of Muslim-Hindu conflict?* (He was assassinated.)

★THINKING FURTHER: *Making Conclusions* **Why might independence have been bittersweet for Gandhi, after the work he had done to win it?** (He had achieved his goal of independence, but not of Muslim-Hindu peace. Instead, that conflict had torn India apart and continued to rage on.)

More **MAP WORK**

● *Which two places in South Asia did not fall under European control at the time?* (Nepal, Bhutan)

★THINKING FURTHER: *Making Conclusions* **Looking at this map, what can you conclude has happened to West and East Pakistan?** (West Pakistan has now become Pakistan and East Pakistan has become Bangladesh.)

 Technology CONNECTION

VIDEODISC
Enrich Lesson 3 with *India's Independence.*
Search Frame 36707, Play to 39804 Side A

THE NEW NATIONS

On the board, create a scorecard with two columns for the newly emergent India and Pakistan and two rows, one labeled *Wins* and one *Losses.* As students discuss this section, have them come to the board and enter the events described appropriately.

Discussing India's Early Years
Discuss the achievements and short-comings of the two new nations.

● *What was the Green Revolution? How did it help India?* (program to increase crops dramatically; fed more people)

● *How did the untouchables win and lose?* (Their caste was abolished, but they still suffered discrimination.)

● *Did Indian women win or lose? Explain.* (They won the right to own property and to vote, and one, Indira Gandhi, became prime minister.)

● *How did Pakistan fare?* (It suffered both a war with India and a civil war, which split it in two—Pakistan and Bangladesh. See the map on p. 583.)

★**THINKING FURTHER:** *Making Generalizations* **What generalizations can you make about newly independent countries?** *(Independence is not necessarily a "happy ending." It brings many expected and unexpected problems.)*

THE NEW NATIONS

Although conflicts continued between India and Pakistan, the governments of both countries set about moving their countries forward. Achieving independence had been a huge challenge, but it was only the first of many.

India's Early Years

One of the many problems faced by independent India was raising enough food to feed the country's huge population. The government worked to make agriculture more productive. New types of wheat and rice crops were developed. The new focus on agriculture throughout the nation became known as the Green Revolution.

Other changes fulfilled many of the goals of Mahatma Gandhi. The untouchable caste was officially abolished, although discrimination against untouchables continued. Also, women gained new rights. In the 1940s and 1950s women were granted the right to own property and the right to vote.

In 1966 a woman, Indira Gandhi (ihn DEE rah GAHN dee), became India's prime minister. She was the daughter of Jawaharlal Nehru. Indira Gandhi continued many of her father's plans and policies. However, she also led India in a war against Pakistan. Trouble between East and West Pakistan led to civil war in 1971. In that year the Indian army helped East Pakistan. Soon after, the leaders of East Pakistan established the new independent country called Bangladesh. The Indian subcontinent, once the "jewel in the British crown," now contained three independent nations.

584

BACKGROUND INFORMATION

THE NEHRU-GANDHI DYNASTY For a while, it appeared that Jawaharlal Nehru had founded a dynasty to rule India.

● He served as prime minister from 1947 until 1964, when he suffered a stroke that ultimately killed him.

● Two years later, his daughter Indira Gandhi became prime minister, after having served as minister of information and broadcasting. Her rule was interrupted by a three-year loss of power, but she remained prime minister until she was assassinated in 1984.

● Her son Rajiv Gandhi succeeded her, but he lost office in 1989. When he campaigned again to become prime minister, he too was assassinated ending the family's rule after nearly 40 years.

GLOBAL CONNECTION

THE OPENING UP OF INDIA Since independence, India has moved sharply away from the colonial role of shipping out raw materials and buying foreign finished goods.

● India's government has encouraged the development of manufacturing to produce finished goods for sale to international markets. India has become a major producer of pharmaceuticals, electronics, and clothing.

● India has also become a major producer of educated professionals "for international markets." It has "exported" thousands of Indian engineers and technicians to work in other parts of the world, especially the Middle East. Thousands of Indian doctors now staff U.S. and U.K. hospitals.

Among the several programs that Indira Gandhi (left) started after she became India's prime minister in 1966, was one to make farming more productive (below).

WHY IT MATTERS

The Ganges, especially, is the river of India. . . . [It is] a symbol of India's age-long culture and civilizations, ever-changing, ever-flowing, and yet ever the same.

With these words, Jawaharlal Nehru summed up his feelings for India. He believed the flow of the Ganges River was as constant and lasting as the nation itself. Today India is the largest democracy in the world with a population of more than 900 million. Its history is long and varied. Great changes occurred in the subcontinent over the centuries. British colonialism had great effects on India in the 1800s and 1900s.

Change in India also influenced other parts of the world. As India struggled to free itself from British rule, other colonies around the world began to work toward independence, as well. Many people have been influenced by Gandhi's method of civil disobedience. In the United States, Martin Luther King, Jr., followed some of the teachings of Gandhi in the fight for civil rights. King described Gandhi with these words: "He lived, thought, and acted, inspired by the vision of humanity evolving toward a world of peace and harmony."

Reviewing Facts and Ideas

MAIN IDEAS

● The British East India Company began to establish trade with India in the 1600s.

● By the middle 1800s the British government had gained control of most of the Indian subcontinent.

● Mohandas Gandhi's civil disobedience program led India to independence.

● In 1947 British rule ended and the independent nations of India and Pakistan were formed.

THINK ABOUT IT

1. Describe three changes that the British East India Company brought to the Indian subcontinent.

2. Why did Indians boycott British-made cloth in 1905?

3. FOCUS How did India become an independent nation?

4. THINKING SKILL *Compare* India's struggle for independence with the struggle of a country in Africa or the Americas. How was it similar? How was it different?

5. WRITE Write an editorial describing how Gandhi's teachings might or might not be useful in solving problems in the world today.

585

Discussing WHY IT MATTERS Have a student read the Nehru quote aloud and help the class to recognize that it is an extended metaphor.

★THINKING FURTHER: *Making Conclusions* **Why is the Ganges a good metaphor for India?** *(Invite students to recall India's long history and to identify ways it has changed and ways it is unchanging.)*

3 CLOSE

MAIN IDEAS
Call on students for answers.

● *How long ago did the British East India Company begin its trade with India?* (nearly 400 years ago)

● *By what time had Britain gained control over most of India?* (the middle 1800s)

● *What policies did Mohandas Gandhi follow to gain independence?* (nonviolence, civil disobedience)

● *What effect did independence from Britain have on national boundaries on the Indian subcontinent?* (The subcontinent was divided into two countries—India and Pakistan.)

EVALUATE
✓ **Answers to Think About It**

1. Any three of the following: language, government, sports, transportation, food
Recall Details

2. to support India's textile industry
Summarize

3. through rebellion, civil disobedience including boycotts and nonpayment of taxes, and nonviolence
Recall Details

4. Similar: came from resentment against foreign rule, was won when Britain finally decided to grant it, as in Ghana. Different: nonviolent, as opposed to violent in America.
Compare and Contrast

5. Editorials should reflect the power of nonviolent moral persuasion.
Evaluate Fact and Opinion

Write About It Picture yourself at a celebration of India's independence. Write a postcard home describing the experience.

MEETING INDIVIDUAL NEEDS

RETEACHING (Easy) Have students review and identify the steps in India's long struggle for independence and illustrate them in the form of a stairway.

EXTENSION (Average) Have students picture themselves taking part in one of Mohandas Gandhi's peaceful demonstrations for independence from British rule. Have them write a letter to a friend describing the experience.

ENRICHMENT (Challenging) For further collection of material for the Class Almanac of Nations (see p. 571), divide the class into seven groups and assign each group one of the South Asia countries shown on the map on p. 583. Have each group research and write a page on its nation, to be included in the almanac when it is assembled.

LESSON 4

PAGES 586–591

Lesson Overview

French control over much of Southeast Asia provoked people there to fight for independence and to carve out Vietnam, Laos, and Cambodia.

Lesson Objectives

★ Describe French colonial control in Southeast Asia.

★ Trace the sequence of events before, during, and after the Vietnam War.

1 PREPARE

MOTIVATE Have a student read the *Read Aloud* to the class. Ask students to identify Ho Chi Minh. (a leader who declared the independence of Vietnam) What colonial power controlled Vietnam? (France) Ask students to explain why they expect independence will fail to bring peaceful development to Vietnam. (the end of the *Read Aloud*)

SET PURPOSE Refer students to the *Read to Learn* question. Encourage them to explore this lesson to discover how the struggle for independence from colonial rule grew in Southeast Asia and to compare and contrast it with events elsewhere. Preview the *Vocabulary.*

2 TEACH

Understanding THE BIG PICTURE Refer students to the map on p. 587 and have them locate the places mentioned here.

● **Where did the French colonize?** *(Vietnam, Laos, Cambodia)*

★**THINKING FURTHER:** *Making Conclusions* **What evidence might lead you to conclude that Vietnam would not easily surrender to a foreign foe?** *(its record of fighting off invaders)*

Resource REMINDER

Practice and Project Book: *p. 116*

Anthology: *Tank, the Water Buffalo, pp. 176–179; The War Years in Vietnam, pp. 180–182; Tet Trung, pp. 183–184*

Desk Map

Focus Activity

READ TO LEARN

How did nations in Southeast Asia gain independence?

VOCABULARY

• Vietnam War

PEOPLE

• Ho Chi Minh

PLACES

• Vietnam
• Southeast Asia
• Laos
• Cambodia
• Burma
• Thailand

586

1800   1858   1995   2000

New Nations in Southeast Asia

Read Aloud

In 1949 a leader named Ho Chi Minh declared the independence of his nation, Vietnam. This act followed over 100 years of colonial rule by the French. During those years many Vietnamese struggled to survive. Yet independence did not bring safety and peace to the new nation. Instead the Vietnamese continued to struggle through conflicts and war that divided the nation in many ways.

THE BIG PICTURE

Vietnam is located in Southeast Asia. In chapter 14 you read about the Khmer who lived in this region around A.D. 1000. For centuries Vietnam was invaded by neighbors such as the Khmer and the Ming of China.

In the middle 1800s, French ships began sailing into the port city of Da Nang. France established colonies in Vietnam and the neighboring countries of Laos and Cambodia. Around the same time, Britain took over parts of Burma, the westernmost kingdom in the region. Nearby Thailand remained one of the few independent areas in Southeast Asia. For about 100 years European powers would shape life for many people in the region. However, desire for the independence of the past grew very strong in Vietnam. This led to conflicts with other countries and within Vietnam.

 SHELTERED INSTRUCTION

READING STRATEGIES & LANGUAGE DEVELOPMENT

COMPARE AND CONTRAST Review how writers can organize facts by comparing and contrasting. Write *soccer* and *rollerblading* on the board and have students compare and contrast the two sports. Point out the Read to Learn question and invite students to create a chart as they read that compares and contrasts the struggle for independence among the nations in Southeast Asia to the independence struggle of another country students have studied. **[SDAIE STRATEGY: METACOGNITIVE DEVELOPMENT/SCHEMA BUILDING]**

WORD ORIGINS Refer the class to the word *armistice* on p. 588 and remind them that they saw the word in Chapter 18 when an armistice ended World War I. Explain that *armistice* is coined from two Latin words that mean "arms" and "put a stop to."

A COLONY OF FRANCE

In 1858 the French took control of Vietnam's coast. As French soldiers moved inland, local armies slowed their progress. By 1887 France succeeded in occupying Vietnam, Laos, and Cambodia, all of which they called Indochina.

The Colonists Prosper

Vietnam was an important source of raw materials. French colonists sent tons of rice, coal, and tin to France. While the French gained wealth, many of the people of Vietnam suffered. Before the French arrived, almost every family owned some land. By 1920, however, only French colonists and wealthy Vietnamese owned land. Many people were forced to work for others. One worker wrote:

> The larger parts of our wages are taken by the supervisors and foremen . . . [and] our salaries are already too low. . . . Food prices increase every day and we have become hungrier and hungrier.

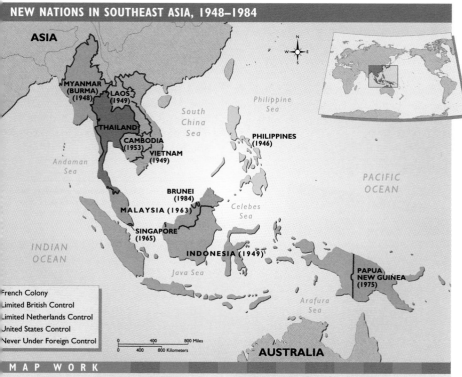

NEW NATIONS IN SOUTHEAST ASIA, 1948–1984

ASIA

MYANMAR (BURMA) (1948)
LAOS (1949)
THAILAND
CAMBODIA (1953)
VIETNAM (1949)
South China Sea
Philippine Sea
PHILIPPINES (1946)
BRUNEI (1984)
MALAYSIA (1963)
SINGAPORE (1965)
Andaman Sea
INDONESIA (1949)
Celebes Sea
PACIFIC OCEAN
INDIAN OCEAN
Java Sea
PAPUA NEW GUINEA (1975)
Arafura Sea
AUSTRALIA

French Colony
Limited British Control
Limited Netherlands Control
United States Control
Never Under Foreign Control

0   400   800 Miles
0   400   800 Kilometers

MAP WORK

Nations in Southeast Asia struggled for freedom from foreign rule. All succeeded in becoming independent.

1. Which nations became independent after 1950?

2. Which foreign power had control in the Philippines?

3. In what year did Malaysia gain independence?

MAP WORK: **1.** Cambodia, Brunei, Malaysia, Singapore, Papua New Guinea
2. United States **3.** 1963

587

CURRICULUM CONNECTION

LINKS TO LANGUAGE ARTS Like nations in Africa, nations in Southeast Asia changed their name over the years.

- Vietnam has not always been known as Vietnam. Historically, its large central portion was known as Annam, a land that extended for about 800 miles along the South China Sea.

- Up until 1939 the only Southeast Asian country to remain independent of colonial rule was known as Siam. In that year, it changed its name to Thailand, meaning "land of the free."

- The land long known in English as Cambodia came to be called Kampuchea after 1975, when Pol Pot (p. 590) came to power there.

- In May 1989 the military government that had taken power in Burma the previous year changed the country's name to Myanmar.

A COLONY OF FRANCE

Have students find the area on the map.

★**THINKING FURTHER:** *Making Conclusions* **Why do you suppose the French were able to occupy Vietnam when earlier invaders had been repelled?** *(Students might recall the experiences of the Aztec, the Inca, and the Japanese when these peoples faced much more powerful weapons than they themselves possessed.)*

Discussing The Colonists Prosper
Students should recognize the theme of colonies as sources of raw materials.

- *How did French colonizers fare in the area they called Indochina?* *(Very well—they exported rice, coal, tin, and rubber and became wealthy landowners.)*

- *How did the Vietnamese fare under French colonization?* *(Very poorly— they lost their land and had to work for whatever wages employers were willing to pay them.)*

★**THINKING FURTHER:** *Compare and Contrast* **How would you compare and contrast Vietnam's economy with other economies under colonization?** *(All were run to benefit the colonizing country, not the colonized people.)*

More **MAP WORK**

Refer students to the map on this page.

- *Which was the only country in Southeast Asia that never came under colonial control?* *(Thailand)*

- *Which areas came under limited British control?* *(Myanmar— Burma, Malaysia, Brunei, Papua New Guinea)*

- *Which area came under limited control of the Netherlands?* *(Indonesia)*

- *What nation took control in the Philippines?* *(the United States)*

★**THINKING FURTHER:** *Making Conclusions* **During what seven-year period did most of these lands gain independence and become new nations?** *(from 1946, Philippines, to 1953, Cambodia)*

587

FIGHTING COLONIAL RULE

Students should identify the 1920s as the start of Vietnam's independence movement.

- **How long after the French gained control of Vietnam did opposition to French rule begin in earnest?** *(1920s minus 1858 = about 60 years)*

- **What leader emerged?** *(Ho Chi Minh, leader of the Vietnamese communists)*

★**THINKING FURTHER:** *Compare and Contrast* **How would you compare his goal with those of nationalist leaders in other colonies?** *(It was the same—for independence, but he wanted a communist government, which many other leaders did not.)*

Discussing Independence Is Declared Help students realize that World War II simply changed the occupying country.

- **What effects did World War II have on Vietnam?** *(Japan captured it, took its crops and raw materials, and left two million people dead of starvation.)*

- **How did the defeat of Japan affect Vietnam?** *(It gave an army of Vietnamese communists, the Viet Minh, the chance to gain control of much of the country, especially the north, and caused Ho Chi Minh to declare Vietnam independent, with himself as head of a communist government.)*

- **How did the French react? What was the outcome?** *(The French went to war against the Viet Minh to retake the colony; the French were defeated and Vietnam was divided into communist North Vietnam and French-backed South Vietnam.)*

★**THINKING FURTHER:** *Compare and Contrast* **How would you compare and contrast the means the Vietnamese used to gain independence with those used in India?** *(The Vietnamese used similar methods like protests and strikes, but they also went to war against their colonizers, which the Indians did not do.)*

FIGHTING COLONIAL RULE

In the 1920s anti-French feeling began to take shape. Many Vietnamese people formed organizations that opposed French rule. One group, the Vietnamese communists, was led by Ho Chi Minh (HOH CHEE MIHN). His goal was to create an independent Vietnam. The Vietnamese communists worked toward that goal by planning protest marches and labor strikes against the French.

Independence Is Declared

In 1940, during World War II, the Japanese captured Vietnam and other French colonies in Southeast Asia. Japan immediately began to use Vietnam's resources to support its war effort. Rice was shipped from Vietnam to Japanese soldiers who were fighting the war. Little was left for the people of Vietnam to eat. More than two million starved to death.

Near the end of World War II, Japanese rule began to crumble in Southeast Asia. In 1945 an army of Vietnamese communists, called the Viet Minh (VEE et MIHN), took action. The Viet Minh gained control of many areas of the country, especially in the northern region. By September 1945 the communists controlled nearly all of Vietnam. Ho Chi Minh declared the nation's independence and became the head of a new communist government.

The French, however, were not ready to give up their claims to Vietnam. In 1946 the French, aided by the British, went to war against the communists. After eight years of fighting, the French lost an important struggle at the town of Dien Bien Phu (dyen byen FOO). In 1954 the two sides signed an armistice. The armistice called for Vietnam to be divided in half until elections to unify the nation could be held. The elections never happened. Communists continued to control North Vietnam. A government backed by the French controlled South Vietnam.

Ho Chi Minh (left) led the communist effort to gain Vietnam's independence. France signs the treaty recognizing Vietnam's independence in 1954 (below).

588

═══ BACKGROUND INFORMATION ═══

MORE ABOUT HO CHI MINH Like nationalists Kwame Nkrumah and Mohandas Gandhi, Ho Chi Minh had studied and lived away from his homeland for a time.

- He was born in 1890 in Annam (central Vietnam) but left there at age 19 to work on a French liner and then in a London hotel.

- He later moved to France, where he joined the Socialist party and agitated for the independence of Indochina. Later, he was a founding member of the French Communist party.

- In the 1920s he studied revolutionary methods in the Soviet Union. In 1941 he returned home to organize the Viet Minh, which led Vietnamese resistance to Japanese occupation.

- He died in 1969, six years before the Vietnam War ended and the communist government he had worked for took power.

From 1965 to 1973, American troops fought to try to prevent communist North Vietnam from taking over South Vietnam.

The United States in Vietnam

The armistice failed to bring peace to Vietnam. The communists wanted to unite South Vietnam with North Vietnam under their leadership. The leaders of South Vietnam, however, wanted to remain independent.

Many leaders in the United States were worried about the spread of communism from North Vietnam. By speaking out in favor of the government of South Vietnam, the United States stood firm against communism in the Cold War. American leaders wanted to keep communism from threatening democratic governments in other parts of Southeast Asia. This led the United States to take action in Vietnam. United States Secretary of State John Foster Dulles said that:

> [T]he United States should not stand passively by and see the extension of communism by any means into Southeast Asia.

War Breaks Out

South Vietnamese rebels, supported by North Vietnam, began a war against the government of South Vietnam. Later, North Vietnamese forces also moved into South Vietnam as they tried to spread communism and unite the nations.

The United States had begun to help the government of South Vietnam in 1954. The United States provided the country with money, weapons, and advisers. Then, in 1965, the United States sent troops and planes to help in the fighting. A war that became known as the Vietnam War was now raging. A million tons of United States supplies arrived in South Vietnam every month. By 1968, about half a million troops were stationed in Vietnam.

As American troops suffered losses in Vietnam, public opinion in the United States became divided. Some people believed the United States should be involved in the Vietnam War. Others, however, did not agree. In 1973 the United States began pulling its troops out of Vietnam. Two years later South Vietnam surrendered to North Vietnam. More than 58,000 Americans had died in the war. Nearly two million Vietnamese people had died.

589

FACING THE FUTURE

Discuss problems in post-war Vietnam.

● **What formidable problems did the Vietnamese face after the war ended?** *(loss of property and businesses to communist government, food shortages, war-scarred landscape, government unpopular to many)*

★**THINKING FURTHER:** *Cause and Effect* **What effect did these problems have on one million South Vietnamese?** *(They fled Vietnam for other countries.)*

Discussing Change in Southeast Asia Refer students to the map on p. 587 and have them locate Cambodia, noting its border with southern Vietnam.

● **Why were the people of Cambodia forced to live under a reign of terror after 1975?** *(The communist leader Pol Pot took power and put a tyrannical government in place, under which more than one million Cambodians perished.)*

● **How was this reign brought to an end?** *(Vietnam invaded Cambodia and forced Pol Pot and his supporters to flee. The UN helped Cambodians to take back their government.)*

★**THINKING FURTHER:** *Compare and Contrast* **What parallel can you draw between Vietnam and India after they became single, independent nations?** *(Both went to war against a neighbor—India against Pakistan and Vietnam against Cambodia.)*

After the Vietnam War, Vietnamese refugees (left) crowded into boats on a voyage to Hong Kong, where they sought freedom from communism.

FACING THE FUTURE

Vietnam faced serious problems after the war. Much of the country had been damaged by bombing and ground fighting. The communist government took control of property and businesses throughout the country after the war. Droughts and floods caused shortages of food. Planting new crops was dangerous because fields contained many unexploded bombs left from the war. Many Vietnamese were unhappy with communist government.

More than one million South Vietnamese people left their nation in overcrowded boats. They decided to risk their lives at sea to settle in free countries rather than live under a communist government. These Vietnamese eventually settled in countries throughout the world. More than 600,000 moved to the United States.

Change in Southeast Asia

Vietnam also had trouble with its neighbor Cambodia. Cambodia's communist leader, Pol Pot, had come to power in 1975 after leading a commu-

nist group against the government. During Pol Pot's rule there was a reign of terror. People were forced to leave the cities to live and work in rural camps. Educated Cambodians were considered enemies, and many of them were murdered. There was little food

590

USING THE ANTHOLOGY

THE WAR YEARS IN VIETNAM, pages 180-182 This selection reveals a Vietnamese girl's experience during the war. Have students discuss how her family's tradition helped her realize what was expected of her.

CURRICULUM CONNECTION

LINKS TO READING Students may want to do additional reading in one of the following:

● Dorothy Hoobler, *Vietnam, Why We Fought*, 1990.

● Eva Bunting, *The Wall*, 1990—a fictional story concerning the Vietnam Veterans Memorial.

● Stanek, *We Came From Vietnam*, 1985.

GLOBAL CONNECTION

WHY VIETNAM INVADED CAMBODIA

● Pol Pot feared that the Vietnamese would expand into Cambodia, or Kampuchea, as he called it. As a result, he ordered thousands of Vietnamese nationals who lived in Cambodia to be put to death. Then, beginning in 1976, he ordered attacks into Vietnam itself.

● In retaliation, the angry Vietnamese struck Cambodia with a lightning attack in December 1978. The next month, they captured the Cambodian capital of Phnom Penh and drove Pol Pot and his forces to the border of Thailand. With that accomplished, the Vietnamese installed a new government, more to their liking.

and no freedom. More than one million people were killed. Many others fled the country. In 1978 Vietnamese soldiers invaded Cambodia, forcing Pol Pot and his supporters to flee. After the United Nations supervised elections in 1993, Vietnamese troops left Cambodia, and a government including different political groups took power.

WHY IT MATTERS

When Vietnam gained independence, it became one of more than 100 new nations formed since 1943. Like many of the other new nations of the world, those in Southeast Asia faced difficult problems. Over 100 years of colonial rule and 30 years of war had harsh effects on Vietnam and on the other nations in Southeast Asia.

Today Hanoi (below), Vietnam's capital, is a busy industrial center, producing textiles, chemicals, and food products.

Since the end of the war in 1975, changes have begun to occur in Vietnam. For years Vietnam depended on the Soviet Union for aid. After the Soviet Union broke up, the leaders of Vietnam, as well as other Southeast Asian leaders, began to work toward an economy that allowed more free enterprise. Foreign companies have built factories in Vietnam. In 1995 Vietnam and the United States once again began to trade and have diplomatic relations.

 Reviewing Facts and Ideas

MAIN IDEAS

- In the middle 1800s the French began to establish a colony in Vietnam. By 1887 they had influence in much of Southeast Asia.
- The colony of Vietnam provided France with many raw materials.
- After World War II the Viet Minh, led by Ho Chi Minh and others, fought for independence from France.
- The United States fought with South Vietnam against communist forces of North Vietnam until 1973.
- In 1975 Vietnam became unified, but faced economic and social problems.

THINK ABOUT IT

1. Why were many Vietnamese people unhappy under French colonial rule?

2. How did World War II change colonial rule in Vietnam?

3. **FOCUS** How did the people of Vietnam finally gain independence?

4. **THINKING SKILL** Describe the *point of view* of United States official John Foster Dulles, quoted on page 589.

5. **WRITE** Write five questions that you might ask a United States soldier who served in Vietnam.

591

Discussing WHY IT MATTERS Discuss prospects for Vietnam's future.

> ★**THINKING FURTHER:** *Making Conclusions* **What details might lead you to conclude that Vietnam might take its place among the successful nations of the world?** *(It is now free of foreign dependence, it has taken steps toward free enterprise, it has potential for production and trade, and it has established new diplomatic relations.)*

3 CLOSE

MAIN IDEAS
Call on students for answers.

- **What raw materials did Vietnam supply to France?** *(rice, coal, tin)*

- **Who led the Viet Minh in their fight for independence from France?** *(Ho Chi Minh)*

- **For how long did the U.S. take a highly active role in fighting communist forces in Vietnam?** *(from 1965 until 1973—about eight years)*

- **When did Vietnam become unified?** *(1975)*

EVALUATE
✓ **Answers to Think About It**
1. They believed colonial France enriched itself at their expense. *Summarize*

2. It drove out the French, replacing them with Japanese colonial rule. *Recall Details*

3. by defeating the French who again tried to take colonial control *Summarize*

4. Communism must not be allowed to spread any further in Southeast Asia. *Point of View*

5. Questions will probably center on what the fighting was for, on personal experiences, and on opinions about the war. *Make Predictions*

Write About It Have students picture themselves as boat people. Have them write a letter home telling why they have taken this action and what they hope to find elsewhere.

MEETING INDIVIDUAL NEEDS

RETEACHING (Easy) Have students review *A Colony of France* on p. 587 and draw an illustration of a scene from the French colony.

EXTENSION (Average) Have students take the interview questions they made up for #5 in *Think About It* and use them to interview a Vietnam veteran. Have students write their interviews in question-answer form.

ENRICHMENT (Challenging) To complete work on the Class Almanac of Nations (see p. 571), divide the class into nine groups and assign each group one of the Southeast Asian nations shown on the map on p. 587. Have each group research its nation and write a page about it. Then have a committee collect all the pages created in this chapter and assemble them into a class book, perhaps using yarn to bind them and designing a cardboard cover. The completed Class Almanac of Nations can then become part of a classroom library.

DISCUSSING MAJOR EVENTS Help students focus on how major events progressed in different parts of the world.

- **Which of the events shown here took place in the Middle East?** *(Suez Canal—1869, British, French control — 1917, Turkey—1923, Iraq—1932, Israel—1948, Israel-Egypt peace— 1978, Arafat-Rabin treaty—1993)*

- **What progression do events involving India show?** *(British control— 1850, Indian National Congress begins to meet to press for independence—1885, republics of India and Pakistan—1947)*

- **What progression do events involving Vietnam show?** *(French control—1884, U.S. enters war there— 1965, U.S. leaves independent Vietnam—1973)*

Answers to
THINKING ABOUT VOCABULARY

1. refugee
2. civil disobedience
3. Vietnam War
4. boycott
5. anti-semitism

Answers to
THINKING ABOUT FACTS

1. the first leader of an independent Ghana in Africa

2. He helped make Egypt a republic independent of British control and seized the Suez Canal for Egypt.

3. mainly the U.S. and Palestine

4. The United Nations divided Palestine and formed a Jewish state—Israel—from one part of it.

5. the agreement between Israel and Egypt that pledged no more war between them

6. the Raj; because it put the right to rule them into British hands

Resource REMINDER

Practice and Project Book: *p. 117*
Assessment Book: *Chapter 19 Test*
Technology: *Videodisc/Video Tape 4*
Transparency: *Graphic Organizer, Main-Idea Chart*

CHAPTER 19 REVIEW

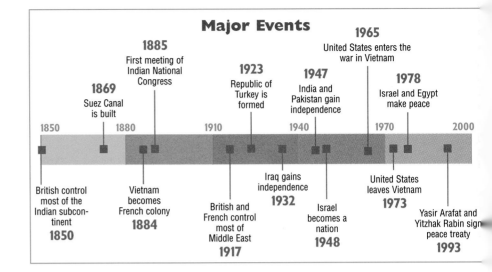

Major Events

1869 Suez Canal is built

1885 First meeting of Indian National Congress

1923 Republic of Turkey is formed

1947 India and Pakistan gain independence

1965 United States enters the war in Vietnam

1978 Israel and Egypt make peace

British control most of the Indian subcontinent **1850**

Vietnam becomes French colony **1884**

British and French control most of Middle East **1917**

Iraq gains independence **1932**

Israel becomes a nation **1948**

United States leaves Vietnam **1973**

Yasir Arafat and Yitzhak Rabin sign peace treaty **1993**

1850 1880 1910 1940 1970 2000

THINKING ABOUT VOCABULARY

Number a sheet of paper from 1 to 5. Beside each number write the word or term from the list below that best completes the sentence.

anti-semitism
boycott
civil disobedience
refugee
Vietnam War

1. A _____ is a person who flees his or her country for safety.

2. A nonviolent breaking of the law to protest something is called _____.

3. The _____ in Southeast Asia divided Americans against each other in the 1960s and early 1970s.

4. A _____ is the refusal to buy goods to protest something.

5. Discrimination against Jewish people is called _____.

THINKING ABOUT FACTS

1. Who was Kwame Nkrumah?

2. What role did Gamal Abdel Nasser play in Egyptian history?

3. Where did the Jews who left Russia and eastern Europe go to avoid persecution in the early 1900s?

4. How was Israel created?

5. What was the Camp David agreement? Why was it significant?

6. What was the British East India Company called? Why did most Indians dislike it?

7. Who was Mohandas Gandhi and what were his goals?

8. Why did the French colonize Vietnam, Laos, and Cambodia?

9. Who fought in the Vietnam War? What did each side hope to achieve?

10. Many new nations were created during the twentieth century. Look at the time line above and name as many newly formed nations as you can.

592

SECOND-LANGUAGE SUPPORT

ORAL PRACTICE Students will benefit from reading sections of this chapter aloud and making a tape to assess their own fluency and pronunciation. One method might be for an English-proficient student or the teacher to read a paragraph aloud and record it. Then students can practice reading along with the taped version until they feel ready to tape-record their own recitation.

INTERVIEWING "Enlist students' help in finding adults who might wish to speak to the class about personal experiences in the countries mentioned in this chapter. Encourage students to prepare questions to ask the speakers.

THINK AND WRITE ◄ ▤◗

WRITING AN INTERVIEW

Suppose you are going to interview Mohandas Gandhi. Write at least three questions you would ask him. Then list the answers you think he might give.

WRITING A REPORT

Write a report about the Vietnam War and the disagreements it caused in the United States. Explain arguments made by opponents and supporters of the war.

WRITING ABOUT PERSPECTIVES

Write about how Zionists and Palestinian nationalists have seen the situation in the Middle East during the past 40 years.

APPLYING STUDY SKILLS

POLITICAL CARTOONS

1. What is a political cartoon?

2. Look at Cartoon B on page 573. It shows in a positive light the American decision to send troops to fight against Germans during World War I. If a cartoon on the same subject had appeared in a German newspaper, what might it have shown?

3. Review Lesson 3. Describe what political cartoons about British control of India might show. How might the British show their presence in India? How might the Indians illustrate it?

4. How might American cartoonists who supported the Vietnam War have shown it? How might cartoonists who opposed the war have pictured it?

5. Look at Cartoon B in the skills lesson again. Why are the Statue of Liberty and the American flag important to the message of this cartoon?

Summing Up the Chapter

Copy the main-idea chart below on a separate sheet of paper. Then fill in the blanks in each column with information from the chapter. When you have filled in the blanks, write a paragraph that answers the question "What are some of the new countries in this century and how were they formed?"

MAIN IDEA In this century many new countries have emerged in Africa and Asia.

Region	New Countries	Leaders
Africa	Ghana Egypt	Nkrumah Nasser
Middle East	Israel	Ben Gurion
South Asia	India Pakistan	Gandhi Jinnah
Southeast Asia	Vietnam	Ho Chi Minh

593

---

7. the Indian leader who wanted an end to British rule, peace between Hindus and Muslims, fairness toward untouchables

8. to supply France with raw materials, rice

9. South Vietnamese rebels supported by North Vietnam against South Vietnam and the U.S.; the former wanted a unified, communist Vietnam and the latter, a noncommunist South Vietnam.

10. Turkey, Iraq, India, Pakistan, Israel, Vietnam (Egypt and Ghana were newly formed, but do not appear on time line.)

Answers to APPLYING STUDY SKILLS

1. a picture that shows an opinion about a political matter

2. It might show American troops as a murderous horde sent off by cravenlooking leaders, rather than as a cleancut force led by Lady Liberty.

3. British cartoons—noble British members of the Raj helping the "more primitive" Indians by ruling them; Indian cartoons—pompous, selfish British oppressing righteous Indians and stealing their resources

4. Support—selfless and noble Americans protecting the beleaguered South Vietnamese; opposition—heavily armed American troops attacking Vietnam villages, bringing death and destruction rather than salvation from communism

5. They appeal to the spirit of patriotism in Americans, to convince them that they are doing the right thing in entering the war.

Technology CONNECTION

VIDEODISC/VIDEO TAPE 4
Enrich Chapter 19 with *The Middle East Today* segment on the videodisc.

Search Frame 28735, Side A

SUGGESTIONS FOR SUMMING UP THE CHAPTER

As students copy the main-idea chart on a piece of paper, point out that the four regions it lists follow the order of and correspond to the four lessons in the chapter, to facilitate their chapter review. As they review to find the pieces of information they need for the chart (suggested examples appear on the reproduced pupil page above), urge them to reread the material about each nation and its leaders and take notes on how each nation was formed, to help them answer the question posed. As they approach writing their paragraphs, have them check their *how* notes. Encourage them to weave together details from those notes to construct their paragraphs.

ASSESSING THINK AND WRITE: *For performance assessment, see Assessment Book, Chapter 19, pp. T104–T106.*

20 A Changing World

Pages 564–593

CHAPTER OVERVIEW

The end of the Cold War brought together a divided Europe and the fall of the Berlin Wall reunited East and West Germany. South Africa moved from apartheid to a majority-rule government. The rise of trade in Asia and the Americas increased economic interdependence and communication.

GEO ADVENTURES DAILY GEOGRAPHY ACTIVITIES

Use **Geo Adventures** Daily Geography activities to assess students' understanding of geography skills.

CHAPTER PLANNING GUIDE

LESSON 1
SUGGESTED PACING: 2 DAYS

A Changing Europe
pp. 596–603

CURRICULUM CONNECTION
Links to Reading, p. 597
Links to Current Events, p. 602

CITIZENSHIP
Understanding Environmental Concerns, p. 601

INFOGRAPHIC
Economy of Europe, p. 602

RESOURCES
Practice and Project Book, p. 118
Anthology, pp. 185–186, 187–188
TECHNOLOGY *Adventure Time!* CD-ROM

THINKINGSKILLS
SUGGESTED PACING: 1 DAY

Evaluating Information For Accuracy pp. 604–605

RESOURCES
Practice and Project Book, p. 119
Transparency: Graphic Organizer

LESSON 2
SUGGESTED PACING: 2 DAYS

A Changing Africa pp. 606–612

CURRICULUM CONNECTIONS
Links to Music, p. 609

CITIZENSHIP
A First Taste of Democracy, p. 61

INFOGRAPHIC
Economy of Africa, p. 611

RESOURCES
Project and Practice Book, p. 12(
Anthology, pp. 189–191, 192–194
TECHNOLOGY *Adventure Tim* CD-ROM

LESSON 3
SUGGESTED PACING: 3 DAYS

A Changing Pacific Rim
pp. 614–621

CURRICULUM CONNECTIONS
Links to Math, p. 618

CITIZENSHIP
Understanding Government, p. 617
Using Current Events, p. 619

INFOGRAPHIC
Economy of Asia, p. 620

RESOURCES
Practice and Project Book, p. 121
Anthology, pp. 195, 196–197
TECHNOLOGY *Adventure Time!* CD-ROM

LESSON 4
SUGGESTED PACING: 3 DAYS

The Changing Americas
pp. 622–629

CURRICULUM CONNECTIONS
Links to Language Arts, p. 623
Links to Current Events, p. 627

CITIZENSHIP
Current Events, pp. 624, 626
Environmental Concerns, p. 625

INFOGRAPHIC
Economy of the Americas, p. 628

RESOURCES
Practice and Project Book, p. 122
Anthology, pp. 200–202
Anthology pp. 198–199, 203–204
TECHNOLOGY *Adventure Time!*

CITIZENSHIP
SUGGESTED PACING: 1 DAY

Why Should Nations Work Together to Protect the Environment?
pp. 630–631

CITIZENSHIP
Understanding Government, p. 63

ARNING STYLE: Visual

30 MINUTES
OR LONGER

ON YOUR
OWN

ake an International News Digest

bjective: To prepare students to learn about recent
hanges in the world.

aterials: newspapers, newsmagazines, paper, staplers

- Invite students to imagine they are editors of their own
  international news digests. Have them cut out three
  interesting news stories, each from a different country or
  region, and mount them on separate pieces of paper.
- Invite students to write a summary of each article and
  raise one question about it. Ask students how they think
  the events in their articles came about.
- Each digest should have a cover and stapled pages.

★ CITIZENSHIP

SUGGESTED PACING: I DAY

reparing for a New
outh Africa p. 613

ITIZENSHIP
Understanding Government, p. 613

CHAPTER REVIEW

SUGGESTED PACING: I DAY

p. 632–633

RESOURCES
Practice and Project Book, p. 123
 TECHNOLOGY Videodisc
Assessment Book: Chapter 20 Test
Transparency: Graphic Organizer,
Main-Idea Map

SDAIE SUPPORT — SHELTERED INSTRUCTION

READING STRATEGIES &
LANGUAGE DEVELOPMENT

Sequencing/Synonyms, p. 596, Lesson 1
Rereading/Word Origin, p. 604, Thinking Skills
Making Conclusions/Words with Multiple Meanings,
  p. 606, Lesson 2
Problem and Solution/Word History, p. 614, Lesson 3
Predicting/New Words, p. 622, Lesson 4

SECOND-LANGUAGE SUPPORT

Working with a Peer, pp. 597, 623
Making Connections, p. 608
Dialogues, p. 619
Debate/Response Journals, p. 632

MEETING INDIVIDUAL NEEDS

Reteaching, Extension, Enrichment, pp. 603, 612,
  621, 629
McGraw-Hill Adventure Book

ASSESSMENT OPPORTUNITIES

Practice and Project Book, pp. 118–123
Write About It, pp. 603, 612, 621, 629
Assessment Book: Assessing Think and Write,
  pp. T107–T109; Chapter 20 Tests: Content, Skills,
  Writing

Introducing the Chapter

Refer the class to the chapter title. Ask students what theme of history it reflects (change). Ask why things seem to change so quickly these days. (Help them to identify such causes as developments in technology and widespread desire for freedom and human rights.)

THINKING ABOUT HISTORY AND GEOGRAPHY

Encourage students to notice that the format of these opening pages is different from that of most of the preceding chapters. Instead of showing panels of events and their sites on a globe, this shows a globe and one single event.

- *What continents are shown and named on the globe?* (South America, North America, Asia, Australia, Africa, and Europe)

- *Is any continent missing? If so, why?* (Antarctica; probably because it is not a continent on which people live for most of their lives)

- *Do these continents look far apart or close together?* (They seem to be close together.)

★THINKING FURTHER: *Making Conclusions* **Why do you think it is appropriate for the continents to seem close together?** (As the paragraph on this page suggests, communication and travel are bringing most of the world closer and closer together.)

Resource REMINDER

Technology: *Videodisc/Video Tape 3*

A Changing World

THINKING ABOUT HISTORY AND GEOGRAPHY

Today communication and travel around the world are easier than at any other time in history. In this chapter you will read about some of the changes that have taken place in this shrinking world. Many of the changes have resulted in more freedom and opportunities. Others have left people struggling to meet challenges.

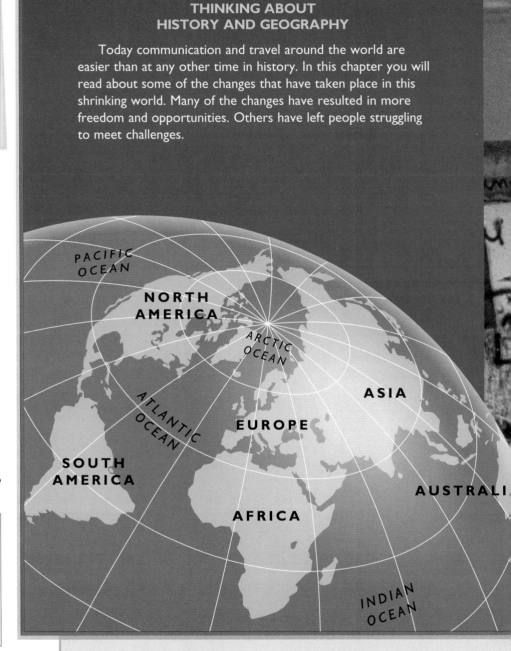

GLOBAL CONNECTION

A SMALL WORLD
- Columbus left Palos, Spain, on August 3, 1492, and touched land in the Americas on October 12, 1492, a little more than two months travel time.
- Modern airplanes can bring a traveler from Spain to the Americas in less than one-third of a day.
- Until recently, mail was carried on whatever transportation was available. The telegraph shortened communications time, and the telephone made shorter communications time more direct.
- Fax machines and e-mail (electronic mail) have made communications almost instantaneous throughout the world for people who have the necessary equipment.

Remains of the Berlin Wall

People everywhere celebrate the end of the Cold War.

595

The photograph on this page records one of the key events of the 20th century—the tearing down of the Berlin Wall. This act was one of the first events that led to the diminishing of communism throughout the world.

Tell students that shortly after the Berlin Wall came down, countries of Eastern Europe and republics of the Soviet Union began to abandon communism and claim independence.

● *Turn back to page 525. Who built the Berlin Wall? Why was it built?* (The East German police built the wall to keep people in East Germany from escaping to the west through West Berlin.)

● *Why would people everywhere celebrate the end of the Cold War?* (Help students understand that the Cold War affected almost all the countries of the world.)

★THINKING FURTHER: *Compare and Contrast* **What differences can you find between this picture and the one on page 525?** *(The picture on page 525 shows the wall going up, there is no graffiti; the picture on this page shows a portion of the wall that remains, it is full of graffiti and signs, and has a piece of sculpture balanced at the top.)*

Technology CONNECTION

VIDEODISC/VIDEO TAPE 3
Enrich Chapter 20 with the *Trade Today* segment on the Videodisc.

Search Frame 13293, Side B

BACKGROUND INFORMATION

THE UNIFICATION OF BERLIN AND GERMANY

● When the Berlin Wall came down in 1989, people could begin to travel freely between the east and west portions of Berlin, but East and West Germany were still separate countries.

● Germany was reunified in 1990, and the treaty of unification said that Berlin would again be its capital. Some people opposed moving the capital from Bonn to Berlin, citing the great expense.

● Those who wanted to reestablish Berlin as the capital of Germany cited the city's unique location as the geographic center of a Europe that stretches from Lisbon, Portugal, to Moscow, Russia.

LESSON 1
PAGES 596–603

Lesson Overview
The end of the Cold War profoundly changed the political and economic landscape of eastern Europe.

Lesson Objectives
★ Describe the Soviet Union's collapse.
★ Analyze the upheavals and conflicts in Europe as the Cold War ended.
★ Explain how the European Union is affecting the European economy.

1 PREPARE

MOTIVATE Read the *Read Aloud* to the class and ask students why they think this was "one of the most memorable days in the twentieth century." Remind them of the Cold War that existed for 40 years. How might this day relate to that?

SET PURPOSE Refer students to the photo of the opening of the Berlin Wall and the *Read to Learn* question to confirm the collapse of communism. What world-shaking effects would the collapse have? Encourage students to explore this lesson to find out. Preview the *Vocabulary*.

2 TEACH

Understanding THE BIG PICTURE
Discuss reasons for the Cold War's end.

● **What were some ways in which the Cold War put severe strains on the world?** *(money spent for nuclear and military buildups, governments crushed, lives lost in "hot wars")*

● **How was communism weakening?** *(It did not serve people's needs and had alienated many.)*

★**THINKING FURTHER:** *Cause and Effect* **What cause and effect relationship seems inevitable?** *(Communism did not work—it must end.)*

Resource **REMINDER**

Practice and Project Book: *p. 118*

Anthology: *New Year's Address, pp. 185–186; Speech Before the United Nations, pp. 187–188*

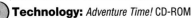 **Technology:** *Adventure Time!* CD-ROM

A Changing Europe

Read Aloud
In February 1989 an East German man was shot and killed trying to escape over the Berlin Wall. Just nine months later, hundreds of East Germans gathered on and around the wall. They were there to celebrate one of the most memorable days in the twentieth century. The Berlin Wall was about to come tumbling down.

Focus Activity

READ TO LEARN

How has Europe changed with the fall of communism?

VOCABULARY
• ethnic group
• per capita income
• European Union

PEOPLE
• Mikhail Gorbachev
• Ronald Reagan
• Lech Walesa
• Boris Yeltsin

PLACES
• Yugoslavia
• Balkan Peninsula

THE BIG PICTURE
By the middle 1980s the Cold War had been going on fo about 40 years. During that time the United States and the Soviet Union spent huge amounts of money to deve op nuclear weapons.

Each country also spent vast amounts on military struggles. In Chapter 19 you read about United States' efforts to stop the spread of communism in Vietnam. In the 1950s and 1960s, the Soviet Union used its army to crush movements for democracy in Hungary and Czechoslovakia. In the 1970s the Soviet Union invaded th South Asian nation of Afghanistan. The fighting in Afghanistan took its toll in many Soviet and Afghan lives and resources.

Problems were also growing within the Soviet Union and other Warsaw Pact countries. Government-run busi nesses could not provide enough food and other goods to meet people's needs. People could not discuss these problems without risking arrest. The communist system was not working well.

596

 SHELTERED INSTRUCTION

READING STRATEGIES & LANGUAGE DEVELOPMENT

SEQUENCE To help students review sequence, invite a volunteer to stack blocks as high as possible until they fall over and crash into other objects on the desk. Explain that Europe followed the same sequence: Once cracks appeared in the communist world, it began crashing down and sending shock waves across Europe. As students read, have them create a flowchart to trace this sequence of events. **[SDAIE STRATEGY: CONTEXTUALIZATION/SCHEMA BUILDING]**

SYNONYMS Refer students to *pact* as in Warsaw Pact on this page and challenge them to find a synonym for this word on p. 597 (*treaty*). Then invite them to offer other synonyms, perhaps by consulting a thesaurus. They may come up with *agreement, understanding, contract,* or perhaps a word they learned in Chapter 5—*covenant*.

CHANGES IN THE SOVIET UNION

President Mikhail Gorbachev (MIHK el GAWR buh chawf) was the first top Soviet leader born and raised in Soviet society. Earlier leaders had been born before the Russian Revolution. Gorbachev's grandfather had been imprisoned as an "enemy of the people." As you read in Chapter 18, Josef Stalin jailed and killed millions in the 1930s.

As a young man Gorbachev studied law in Moscow and gained a position in the Communist party. By 1985 he had become the leader of the Soviet Union. One of his early actions was to point out the country's need for *perestroika* (per es TROY kuh), or rebuilding the failing Soviet economy. Gorbachev soon concluded however, that perestroika could not succeed without *glasnost* (GLAS nohst). Glasnost was his new policy of permission to speak freely.

The communist economy was controlled by the government. Workers had almost no voice in planning. There was little reason for them to work hard or carefully. Wages stayed much the same no matter how hard people worked. Some workers joked, "They pretend to pay us and we pretend to work."

Greater Freedom

Gorbachev believed that workers' views would change only when people had the freedom to speak up. He thought they should have some say in their government. Gorbachev said:

> Wide, prompt, and frank information is evidence of [the government's] confidence in the people. . . . It enhances the resourcefulness of the working people.

In the new era of glasnost, political prisoners were released. Some religious freedom was also allowed.

Soviet relations with the United States also began to improve. In 1987 Gorbachev signed a treaty with United States President Ronald Reagan. Both countries agreed to reduce nuclear weapons stockpiles. The Soviet Union also agreed to begin pulling troops out of its unpopular war with Afghanistan.

Food shortages in the Soviet Union led to long lines for food (left). Such problems caused Mikhail Gorbachev (above) to begin his policy of perestroika.

597

CHANGES IN THE SOVIET UNION

Point out that new Soviet leaders did not remember the Russian Revolution.

- **How was Mikhail Gorbachev different from the Soviet leaders who had preceded him, like Stalin and Khrushchev?** *(He had never lived in tsarist Russia; his entire life had been lived under the Soviet Union.)*

- **What did Gorbachev believe the Soviet Union needed? What did he call this process?** *(rebuilding of the failing Soviet economy; perestroika)*

- **What human right did he believe Soviet people needed to achieve his goal? What did he call it?** *(the right to speak freely; glasnost)*

★ **THINKING FURTHER:** *Making Decisions* **Do you agree or disagree that freedom to speak out was necessary for rebuilding the economy? Explain.** *(Students should note that the government controlled the economy, which was failing. To change it, people would need to be able to say what was wrong and how it might be changed. To do that, people had to believe that the government would not punish them for speaking.)*

Discussing Greater Freedom Read aloud the quote from Gorbachev.

- **What steps did the Soviet government take to encourage greater freedom for people?** *(It released political prisoners and eased restrictions on religion.)*

- **What steps did the Soviet government take to improve its relations with other nations of the world?** *(It withdrew troops from Afghanistan and agreed to a reduction of nuclear weapons.)*

★ **THINKING FURTHER:** *Predicting* **How do you predict that people under Soviet control would be likely to react to a taste of freedom?** *(Possible answer: A taste could make them want more freedom, possibly more than the Soviet government intended.)*

A "YEAR OF MIRACLES"

Have students use the opening paragraph to verify or correct their predictions.

Discussing Spring Thaw Encourage students to recall what they learned about the Russian Revolution in 1917.

- *How did Russian soldiers help the revolution succeed in 1917?* (They refused to fire on the protesters, as they had in 1905.)

- *What parallel can you draw to Soviet soldiers' actions in 1917 and in Hungary in 1989?* (They did not stand in the way of the Hungarians seeking freedom, as they had in 1956.)

> ★ **THINKING FURTHER:** *Compare and Contrast How would you contrast Poland before and after 1989?* (Protester Lech Walesa and Solidarity had virtually disappeared, but free elections won them many seats in Poland's parliament.)

Exploring Season of Fall Encourage students to recognize similar events.

> ★ **THINKING FURTHER:** *Compare and Contrast What parallel can you draw between the East German experience in throwing off communist rule and the Hungarian experience?* (In both, soldiers did not move to stop anti-government activities of the people.)

Investigating Winter's Discontent Help students understand that violence occurred in some countries.

- *How was Czechoslovakia's path to freedom marred?* (Police beat hundreds of protesting students.)

- *What was the outcome of the Czechoslovaks' struggle against their communist government?* (They threw it out and replaced it with officials who had been active against communism.)

> ★ **THINKING FURTHER:** *Making Conclusions Why is it fair to call 1989 a "Year of Miracles"?* (Within this one year, Eastern Europe was able to throw off 40 years of communist rule.)

A "YEAR OF MIRACLES"

The ideas of glasnost and perestroika soon spread to neighboring eastern European nations controlled by the Soviet Union. In just one year—1989—these movements helped overturn more than 40 years of Communist rule.

Spring Thaw

In January 1989 Hungary planned its own elections. In 1956 a Hungarian revolt for more democracy had resulted in a fierce Soviet crackdown. Now Soviet troops stood by as Hungarians moved towards democracy. In May Hungarians tore down an electric fence separating Hungary from democratic Austria. In the months to come, many eastern Europeans used this hole in the "Iron Curtain" to escape to western Europe.

In Poland a workers' group called Solidarity won recognition from the government in March 1989. Eight years earlier shipworker Lech Walesa (LEK wuh LEN suh) and other Solidarity leaders had been jailed for protesting poor living conditions. Their group had been outlawed and almost disappeared under government pressure. In June 1989, however, the Solidarity party won many seats in both houses of Poland's Parliament.

Season of Fall

Still more changes took place in East Germany in the fall. Thousands of East Germans jammed city squares to demand changes in their government. East Germany's leader, Erich Honecker, ordered the army to break up the crowds. His command, however, was not followed. On October 15 Honecker stepped down. Twenty one days later East Berlin opened its gates to West Berlin.

Winter's Discontent

The "Year of Miracles," as 1989 has been called, did not end without bloodshed. In November students in Czechoslovakia protested for democracy. When they sang the American civil rights song, "We Shall Overcome," police beat hundreds of the students. By December, however, the communist government had been overthrown. Citizens elected two new leaders. Both had served time in prison for speaking against the communist government. One year later, nearly all of eastern Europe had freed itself of communism.

Lech Walesa (right) helped end communist rule by defending workers' rights. Boris Yeltsin (below) spoke out against the actions of communists in Russia.

BACKGROUND INFORMATION

CZECHOSLOVAKIA SPLITS APART

- Like several other European countries, Czechoslovakia had been created by diplomats in Paris who carved up Europe after World War I. Often, these nation creators combined incompatible peoples under one government. To create Czechoslovakia, they lumped together the Slovak-inhabited part of Hungary with the Czech-inhabited lands of Bohemia, Moravia, and Silesia.

- The Slovaks felt dominated by the Czechs whom they resented, but the nation was held together following World War II by the iron hand of communism.

- With freedom that forced bond ended. In 1992, the people of Czechoslovakia elected to split into two separate nations—the Czech Republic and Slovakia.

The Soviet Collapse

After the "Year of Miracles," the Soviet Union also began to change. You read in Chapter 18 that the Soviet Union's full name was the Union of Soviet Socialist Republics. Many different ethnic groups lived in its 15 republics. An ethnic group is a group of people who share a heritage of common customs, values, and language.

In 1990 and 1991, many republics broke away from Soviet control. This began with the republics of Latvia, Lithuania, and Estonia. In 1991 Russia, the biggest republic of all, held a democratic election. The Russians elected Boris Yeltsin to be their president.

These changes angered some Communist leaders. In August 1991 they tried to overthrow Gorbachev and take power themselves, moving tanks into Moscow. Before glasnost, these actions would have terrified citizens. Now, however, the Soviet people rallied behind Yeltsin, who, standing on top of a tank in Moscow, called these acts illegal. Soldiers refused to follow Communist orders. Without force to back them up, the communists had no chance of success. Yeltsin warned them:

> You can build a throne of bayonets but you cannot sit on it for very long. There is no return to the past, nor will there be.

Three days after it began, the revolt came to an end. Just as Yeltsin had predicted, there was no returning to the past. One by one Soviet republics declared their independence. In December 1991, Gorbachev stepped down and the Soviet Union ceased to exist. In its place stood 15 independent republics. Find these new nations on the map.

COUNTRIES OF THE FORMER SOVIET UNION

⊛ National capital

MAP WORK

Many of the republics that once made up the Soviet Union are now independent nations.

1. Which is the largest of these nations?

2. What is the capital of Ukraine?

3. Of which nation is Minsk the capital?

4. Which countries shown only have access to the Black Sea?

MAP WORK: 1. Russia 2. Kiev 3. Belarus 4. Georgia (green) and Ukraine (pink)   **599**

Discussing The Soviet Collapse

Refer students to the map on this page and have them locate the area on a map of the world, to help them recognize the great expanse of land the Soviet Union once covered and how many different peoples and cultures it included.

- *What are ethnic groups?* (They are groups of people who share a common heritage and culture.)

- *Why would there have been a great number of different ethnic groups in the Soviet Union?* (It covered such a broad area.)

- *Why were these ethnic groups and their republics able to begin breaking away from the Soviet Union in 1990 and 1991?* (Help students to see that once glasnost had begun, the taste for freedom could not be limited.)

- *What happened to Russia, the largest of all the republics?* (It held a democratic election, and chose as president Boris Yeltsin, who helped put down the attempts of hard-line communists to return to communism.)

★ **THINKING FURTHER:** *Compare and Contrast* **How would you contrast the Soviet Union before and after 1991?** *(Before: a central communist government with power to rule and plan the economy of a collection of ethnic groups. After: 15 independent republics with control over their own governments and economies.)*

More **MAP WORK**

Refer students to the map on this page.

- *Where are Latvia, Lithuania, and Estonia located?* (along the western border of Russia, on the Baltic Sea)

- *What large country borders Russia, southeast of Moscow?* (Kazakhstan)

- *In what country is St. Petersburg?* (Russia)

BACKGROUND INFORMATION

ABOUT INDEPENDENCE FOR LATVIA, LITHUANIA, AND ESTONIA

- Long dominated by German barons and then taken over by tsarist Russia, these three small Baltic states gained their independence following World War I.

- Their status as independent states did not last long.

- In 1940, the Soviet Union occupied them and declared them to be soviet republics of the Union of Soviet Socialist Republics.

- The United States never recognized the Soviet takeover and continued to recognize the three as independent republics.

- All three finally became independent in 1991.

AFTER THE FALL

Help students weigh the good and bad effects of the fall of communism.

★THINKING FURTHER: *Cause and Effect* **What good news did the end of the Cold War bring? What bad news?** *(Good news: triumph of democracy and free enterprise. Bad news: nationalist and ethnic conflicts)*

Discussing Local Wars Have a student write on the board the countries named.

● **What former Soviet republics fought each other for territory?** *(Armenia and Azerbaijan)*

● **What major cultural difference separates the people of these two republics?** *(Religion: Armenia is Christian and Azerbaijan is Muslim.)*

More MAP WORK

Refer students to the map on p. 601 and have them use the map and text.

● **Where are Belarus and Ukraine located?** *(Belarus is southeast of Lithuania and Latvia, and Ukraine is south of Belarus.)*

● **Where was the former nation of Yugoslavia?** *(along the east coast of the Adriatic, across the water from Italy)*

● **How was it shattered?** *(It broke up into five republics, torn apart by religion and disputes over land.)*

★THINKING FURTHER: *Compare and Contrast* **How did the Cold War's end hurt some people?** *(Some ethnic groups made war against others.)*

AFTER THE FALL

There was much to cheer about as the Soviet Union broke apart. The Cold War had ended and the countries of the Warsaw Pact were turning toward democracy. Democracy and free enterprise had won the conflict with communism. Yet now there was much to worry about. Conflicts over nationalism and ethnic differences had replaced Cold War tensions.

Local Wars

One conflict resulting from these differences has involved the former Soviet republics of Armenia and Azerbaijan (ah zur bi JAHN). Armenia, mostly Christian, and Azerbaijan, mostly Muslim, fought a war over territory in 1993. Thousands of people left their homes as the borders shifted during the fighting.

Another place torn apart by war is the area that made up Yugoslavia until 1991. The area is part of the Balkan Peninsula, which has had a long history of ethnic and religious conflict. In 1991 Yugoslavia began to break apart. By 1992, the country had split into five separate republics. One of these republics is still called Yugoslavia. It includes Serbia and Montenegro. The other republics are Bosnia and Herzegovina, Croatia, Macedonia, and Slovenia. Find the republics on the map.

Since this breakup, many ethnic conflicts have flared in the republics. A civil war began in 1991 in Croatia between two ethnic groups, Croats and Serbs. Some of the worst fighting began in 1992 in the tiny country of Bosnia. There Bosnian Serbs, who are Orthodox Christians, and the mostly Muslim government battled for control. The fighting has had terrible effects for every group involved. Cities and towns have been destroyed. Thousands of people have been killed or forced to flee. In 1995, however, the region's leaders signed a peace agreement. Today this agreement helps to maintain some peace in the area.

The war in Bosnia has left thousands of people homeless and hungry. Many refugees have fled areas of heavy fighting.

600

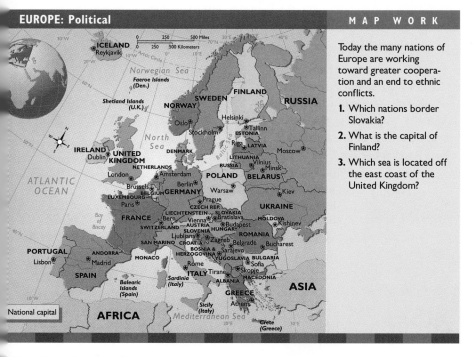

EUROPE: Political

MAP WORK

Today the many nations of Europe are working toward greater cooperation and an end to ethnic conflicts.

1. Which nations border Slovakia?
2. What is the capital of Finland?
3. Which sea is located off the east coast of the United Kingdom?

Discussing Life after Communism

On the board, write the following: *Heritage of the Cold War.* Then as students identify various problems, have them come to the board and list them under this head.

- ***What problems does the world face as a result of the Cold War?*** *(local wars in Europe brought on by nationalist and ethnic conflicts, poor economies and outdated factories, nuclear weapons that might fall into the hands of people who will use them, widespread pollution)*

- ***What is per capita income?*** *(the amount of money each person in a country would have if the country divided its income equally among its people)*

- ***Why is this a good way to measure the wealth of a country?*** *(It measures everyone across the world in the same way, whether they come from countries with large or small populations or with high or low national incomes. It shows how large or small each person's share of the world economic pie is and how much of a cut his or her country has.)*

- ***In which section of Europe is the per capita income higher—eastern or western? Why?*** *(western, where free enterprise rather than communism ruled the economy since World War II)*

- ***What organization has helped western Europe toward higher per capita income? How?*** *(the European Union; by encouraging countries to cooperate in their economic growth, to make profitable trade between countries easier, to lower barriers between ethnic groups and bring them into closer and easier contact)*

Life after Communism

Conflicts such as the one in Bosnia are among the toughest that European leaders face today. How far should nations go to help their neighbors? Ethnic conflicts in Europe and the debate over how to deal with them threaten to continue in the future. The issue is made more complicated by the reality of nuclear weapons. How can leaders be kept from using these weapons, left from the Cold War, if war breaks out?

Another concern for Europe is the continued struggle of eastern European economies. Years of communist rule left many old factories in need of complete rebuilding. Pollution from uncontrolled industry needs to be cleaned up. Costly rebuilding and repair efforts are moving along slowly, though. Today there is still a huge gap between the nations of western and eastern europe in per capita income. Per capita income is the amount of money each person of a country would have if that country's total income were divided equally among its people. Look at the Infographic on page 602 to learn more about economies in Europe.

In 1995 the most powerful organization in Europe, the European Union (EU), agreed to consider allowing eastern European nations to join. The EU is a group of western European nations working to build a common economy throughout Europe. The EU has already broken down many barriers to trade and movement in western Europe. For example, cars and trucks can now travel freely between the nations of western Europe. German students can apply to British or French universities as easily as to colleges in their hometowns.

601

★THINKING FURTHER: *Making Conclusions* **How do you think that eastern Europe could benefit by becoming part of the European Union?** *(Cooperation and the encouragement of trade should help economic growth, and more contact between ethnic groups could help to ease those tensions.)*

BACKGROUND INFORMATION

MORE ABOUT THE EUROPEAN UNION The European Union began after World War II as the European Economic Community. It has also been called European Common Market and the European Community.

CITIZENSHIP★

UNDERSTANDING ENVIRONMENTAL CONCERNS Tales of serious pollution have arisen from Eastern Europe and the former Soviet Union. An enormous amount of money will be needed to clean up these areas.

- In Magnitka, a Russian steelmaking city, one third of the inhabitants suffer from respiratory ailments, such as asthma and bronchitis.

- At one site in Lithuania, people can skim kerosene to heat their homes from the springwater because petroleum products have seeped out of faulty underground tanks.

Infographic

Ask students if they have ever heard of *Leading Economic Indicators*. Explain that these are measurements taken to see how well our economy is doing and how it is likely to do in the near future.

Discussing the Economy of Europe Give students time to read the text and examine the illustrations and captions.

- *What different kinds of graphics do you see here?* (bar graph, pie chart, photos of economic activities)

- *What is Gross Domestic Product, or GDP?* (the total value of goods and services a nation produces in a year)

- *Which two European countries have the highest GDP?* (Germany and France)

- *What would GDP indicate about a nation's economy?* (how much income it could get each year by selling goods and services produced)

- *Which two countries have the most similar GDPs?* (United Kingdom and Italy)

- *What is the ratio of people who live in urban areas to people who live in rural areas in Europe?* (about 3:1)

Technology CONNECTION

ADVENTURE TIME! CD-ROM
Enrich Infographic with the *Discoveries Time Lines* activity on the *Adventure Time!* CD-ROM.

Economy of Europe

New businesses and methods of agriculture have strengthened the economies of many nations in Europe. Look at the graph to see the gross domestic product of five European nations. Remember the GDP is the total value of goods and services produced in one year. Which is highest?

With 8.8 million people, Moscow is Europe's largest city and an important Russian economic center.

German marks

ZEHN DEUTSCHE MARK
DD6248255N6

Rural-Urban Population

Rural 27 %

Urban 73 %

Coal (above) is an important natural resource for many European countries. It is used for heating and by industries. Cheese from Switzerland (below) is among many products of Europe's vast and profitable agriculture industry.

GDP: Largest Five Economies

GDP in billions of United States dollars (1995)

- GERMANY 2,416
- FRANCE 1,536
- UNITED KINGDOM 1,106
- ITALY 1,087
- SPAIN 559

2,000 / 1,500 / 1,000 / 500 / 0

Source: World Development Indicators 1997 CD-ROM, World Bank

EXPANDING THE INFOGRAPHIC

RESEARCHING AND WRITING Refer students to the bar graph showing Europe's five leading GDP countries. Then turn to the map on p. 601 and have students or pairs of students each choose a different country of Europe whose GDPs are not among the leading five.

- Assign groups of students to construct an economic profile of these other countries, including such information as GDP, per capita GDP (reached by dividing the population into GDP), the amount of money spent on agricultural programs, and other facts about its economy like balance of imports to exports and the ratio of televisions sets and telephones to persons.

- Explain that these will become part of a class book "Economies Around the World" they will assemble at the end of this chapter.

- A good source for the information is the current *World Almanac*.

CURRICULUM CONNECTION

LINKS TO CURRENT EVENTS: THE EUROPEAN UNION
After students have done their research, have them work in pairs to create bar graphs similar to the one shown in the *Infographic*. Remind them that their graphs should include the amount spent by each country on agricultural programs.

WHY IT MATTERS

The EU's pledge to help its eastern neighbors has led many to believe that all of Europe might someday be united. Supporters see much to be gained from strong bonds between European countries. Former enemies like France and Germany have become close partners through the EU. An economic alliance with Western Europe could help the countries of Eastern Europe solve some of their economic problems.

Peace and prosperity in Eastern Europe also depends on its relationship with the rest of the world. In March of 1997 Yeltsin met with United States' President Bill Clinton in Helsinki, Finland. There they signed an agreement aimed at improving Russian economic growth and helping Russia join the global economy. Many people feel that agreements such as this are a positive step into the twenty-first century.

Links to CURRENT EVENTS

The European Union

What does the European Union do?

The European Union distributes funds collected from its member states to improve the economies of Europe. In 1996 the European Union committed 48% of its budget, amounting to $52 billion, to various agriculture programs. The European Union also helps develop poor areas of Europe, funds research and environmental programs, and assists the restructuring of Eastern European countries.

Find out how EU programs are helping the development of Europe today. Use current newspapers or the Internet in your research. Write a paragraph describing the effects of these programs.

Reviewing Facts and Ideas

MAIN IDEAS

- Mikhail Gorbachev's program of glasnost sparked pro-democracy movements in the Soviet Union and eastern Europe in the late 1980s.

- Communist governments throughout eastern Europe fell in 1989, called the "Year of Miracles."

- The Cold War ended when the Soviet Union ceased to exist in 1991. However, new conflicts rooted in national, ethnic, and religious differences arose in Europe.

- The European Union has created a strong partnership between many European nations.

THINK ABOUT IT

1. Why has 1989 been called a "Year of Miracles" in Europe?

2. What problems and conflicts have arisen in the Soviet Union and the nations of eastern Europe since the fall of communism?

3. **FOCUS** What are some of the challenges that Europe faces since the Cold War has ended?

4. **THINKING SKILL** *Make Conclusions* about how ordinary people brought about the end of the Cold War.

5. **WRITE** Use what you have learned about European history this year to explain why the European Union can be called a bold experiment in the continent's history.

603

MEETING INDIVIDUAL NEEDS

RETEACHING (Easy) Have students thumb through this lesson to choose a country and an event that occurred on its path to freedom. Have them illustrate a scene that might have occurred during that event.

EXTENSION (Average) Refer students to the illustration on p. 596 showing the Berlin Wall being torn down. Tell them to picture themselves as witnesses to this event and have them write a letter home describing the experience.

ENRICHMENT (Challenging) Divide the class into four groups and assign each one of the following people who made a difference: Mikhail Gorbachev, Boris Yeltsin, Lech Walesa, and Vaclav Havel of Czechoslovakia. Have each group research the life of its subject and prepare a biographical presentation for the class.

Discussing WHY IT MATTERS Ask students to consider Europe's future.

> ★**THINKING FURTHER:** *Making Decisions* **Do you think that a European Union can ever bring all of Europe together in cooperation and peace? Why or why not?** *(Encourage free discussion of chances for and against, but insist that students support their opinions with evidence from history, both recent and far back in time.)*

3 CLOSE

MAIN IDEAS

Call on students for answers.

- **What effects did Gorbachev's policy of glasnost have on the Soviet Union and Eastern Europe?** *(It sparked pro-democracy movements there.)*

- **What changed about Eastern European governments during the "Year of Miracles"?** *(They overthrew communist governments.)*

- **How did the Cold War end? What conflicts then came about?** *(The Soviet Union ceased to exist; national, ethnic, and religious differences, held in check by communism, flared up.)*

- **Why was the European Union created?** *(to bring about cooperation instead of rivalry among European nations)*

EVALUATE
✓ **Answers to Think About It**

1. Eastern Europe ended communism. *Main Idea*

2. Nationalist, ethnic, and religious groups have fought one another for land and power. *Recall Details*

3. local wars, struggling economies, pollution, nuclear weapons *Summarize*

4. Conclusions will probably center on the threat that freedom poses to oppression—once some freedom is won, it is hard to cut off the desire for more. *Form Generalizations*

5. After centuries of national rivalry and war, nations are pulling together for their mutual benefit. *Main Idea*

Write About It Ask students to write a paragraph expressing their wishes for the future of the European Union.

603

SKILLS LESSON

Lesson Overview
Evaluating information for accuracy involves identifying point of view and analyzing credibility.

Lesson Objective
★ Follow steps in evaluation.

1 PREPARE

MOTIVATE On the board, again write the question suggested for the *Analyzing the Credibility of a Source* skill on p. 472: *Whom do you believe?* Remind students of steps they learned to practice that skill, and tell them they will use those steps again to practice this one. Have them read *Why the Skill Matters* and briefly review the *Determining Point of View* skill on pp. 328–329 and the *Analyzing Credibility* skill on pp. 472–473.

SET PURPOSE How can we combine these skills to develop another skill—to evaluate information for accuracy? Invite students to preview the steps by reading *Helping Yourself*.

2 TEACH

Using the Skill Have students read the sources.

● *How would you describe the points of view in these reports?* (greatly concerned, sympathetic)

● *Look at the names of the second and third source. Do you have any reason to believe they would not hire expert reporters? That they would be biased in their reporting? That they might just make things up?* (Probably not—they seem straightforward and factual.)

Resource REMINDER

Practice and Project Book: *p. 119*

Transparency: *Graphic Organizer*

Thinking Skills

Evaluating Information for Accuracy

VOCABULARY
evaluate
accuracy

WHY THE SKILL MATTERS

In the last lesson you read about the civil war that is raging in Bosnia. Like most historical events, this conflict is complicated and difficult to understand. Many people have said many different things about this war. How will you know which information regarding this issue is accurate?

Being able to **evaluate** the **accuracy** of information is crucial to understanding history. To *evaluate* means to judge something. *Accuracy* refers to the truth of a statement. When we evaluate information for accuracy, we make a judgment about whether the information is true.

Historians constantly evaluate information for accuracy. "History," in fact, is always an interpretation based on the most accurate information available.

The skill of evaluating information for accuracy combines some of the Thinking Skills presented in this book. For example, you must determine the credibility of the source. To do this, you must also determine the author's point of view. Other Thinking Skills are called on as well, such as comparing information between different sources and distinguishing facts from opinions. You might want to review these skills before going on.

604

USING THE SKILL

Read these excerpts regarding Bosnia's civil war. Bosnia used to be part of Yugoslavia, but became a republic when Yugoslavia split apart in 1992. Since the Cold War had ended, ethnic differences had caused much tension in the area. The civil war in Bosnia resulted mainly from tensions between two groups, the Bosnian Serbs and the primarily Muslim government. As you read, consider the following questions: What are the points of view of the authors? Does the author have a reason to portray information inaccurately? Does the source have a reputation for being accurate? Does the information agree with information from other sources? Is the information fact or opinion?

Hundreds of thousands of Serbs have been killed for no reason.

from a Serbian Soldier

More than 17,000 have been killed and 110,000 wounded [in Sarajevo].

Time

About 130,000 people in Sarajevo have been killed or injured, including children and women.

from an international news bulletin

READING STRATEGIES & LANGUAGE DEVELOPMENT

REREADING Help students to see that they are given quite a lot of information in this skills lesson and they are asked to review information from previous skills lessons. Tell them to pause after they read each paragraph and ask themselves what its main idea was. If they cannot answer, encourage them to reread the paragraph until they can.

WORD ORIGIN Refer the class to the word *accuracy* and have them look up its origin in the dictionary. When they discover that it comes from the Latin for "to take care of," ask them to relate "taking care" with being "accurate." (They should recognize that one needs to "take care" when presenting information so that no falsity creeps in and thus the information is accurate.)

*She does not seem to have a reason to give inaccurate information; her information agrees with the other sources that many people are dying, includ-

How can you determine the accuracy of each piece of information? First, determine the points of view of the authors. The first excerpt is from someone directly involved in the fighting. As a result, he might tend to give less than accurate information so that others would favor his side of the conflict.

Next, determine if the source has a reputation for being accurate and if the information agrees with other credible sources. Only the last two excerpts are from sources that would seem to have a reputation for accuracy. Furthermore, only these two sources agree on the number of people killed and injured in Sarajevo.

Finally, determine if the information presented is fact or opinion. The last two excerpts present only solid facts that can be proven. The first excerpt is mainly an opinion.

Considering all these factors, we can conclude that the second and third excerpts probably contain more accurate information than the first.

Helping yourself

- **Evaluating for accuracy** determines which statements can be considered true.
- Determine the author's point of view.
- Analyze the credibility of the source.
- Compare the source to other credible sources.
- Identify facts and opinions.
- Evaluate for accuracy.

ing children; the death of Eldin from bombing is fact; "innocent victim," "disgusting war," and "sweet, good boy" are opinions; this information seems accurate.

TRYING THE SKILL

Now evaluate the accuracy of this information. Its teenage author, Zlata Filipovic, lived her whole life in Sarajevo until the war forced her and her family to leave. In May 1993 she wrote in her diary:

I have another sad piece of news for you. A boy in my drama club got killed! . . . A shell fell in front of the community center and a horrible piece of shrapnel [metal] killed him. His name was Eldin and he was a refugee from Grbavica.

Another innocent victim of this disgusting war, another child among thousands of other children killed in Sarajevo. I feel so sorry, he was a sweet, good boy.

Does the author have a reason to give inaccurate information? Does she provide information that agrees with excerpts from the previous page? What information does she give that is fact? What is opinion? How accurate do think this information is?*

REVIEWING THE SKILL

1. Why is it important to evaluate information for accuracy? How can you do so?
2. How did you determine the accuracy of the information in Zlata Filipovic's statement?
3. How does this skill combine other Thinking Skills you learned about earlier in the book?
4. How can the ability to evaluate information for accuracy help you in your own life?

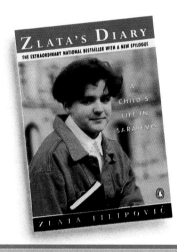

605

- *Do the various reports contradict one another or do they seem to agree?* (They agree on the desperation of the situation, but each offers a different facet.)

★ **THINKING FURTHER:** *Making Conclusions* **How do you evaluate the accuracy of these reports on Bosnia?** (probably high—they pass the tests of expertise, lack of bias, reliability, and backing one another up)

Trying the Skill Have students review *Helping Yourself* before going on.

- *What is the author's point of view?* (It is that of one who has lived through terrible experiences and feels deep emotions about them.)
- *How would you rank her expertise on her subject?* (very high since she lived through it)
- *Have you seen any other sources that might confirm the kind of thing she reports?* (yes, the news sources on conditions in Bosnia)

★ **THINKING FURTHER:** *Making Conclusions* **How accurate do you believe the information is that she presents?** (Though she is understandably emotional about what she reports and gives opinions, the facts stated appear to be accurate.)

⭐ 3 CLOSE

SUM IT UP

Have groups of students write a paragraph in which they explain why it is useful to be able to evaluate the accuracy of information in interpreting current events.

EVALUATE
✓ **Answers to Reviewing the Skill**

1. to be able to tell the difference between truth and falsity; by identifying the source's point of view and analyzing its credibility
2. identified her point of view, checked her expertise and reliability, looked for backup for what she says
3. It uses steps in identifying point of view and in analyzing credibility.
4. It should save you from being fooled and should give you a sound basis on which to make decisions and take or not take actions.

BACKGROUND INFORMATION

USING THE GRAPHIC ORGANIZER You may want to have students work with the sequence chain Graphic Organizer transparency to help them organize their information.

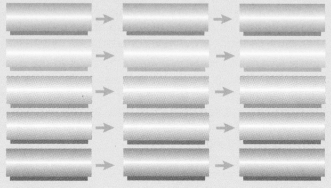

LESSON 2

Lesson Overview

Black South Africans, long ruled by a white minority that separated their country's races with apartheid, won a long struggle for ruling power.

Lesson Objectives

★ Describe the policy of apartheid and the struggle to end it.

★ Identify problems that South Africa is working to overcome.

1 PREPARE

MOTIVATE Have a student read the Mandela quote in the *Read Aloud* and another read the narrator's part. Ask students to put themselves in Mandela's place as they listen to his words and look at his photo. What might his emotions have been? What had at last been achieved in South Africa?

Set Purpose Refer students to the *Read to Learn* question to confirm their answer that South Africa had achieved democracy. Have them notice that democracy did not come until 1994, and encourage them to explore the lesson to find out why. Preview the *Vocabulary*.

2 TEACH

Understanding THE BIG PICTURE
Help students recognize the problem.

● **What two European groups made up South Africa's white population?** (British and Dutch, or Afrikaners)

● **How large is the white minority in South Africa? the nonwhite majority?** (19 percent; 81 percent)

★THINKING FURTHER: *Making Conclusions* **What do you conclude the black African population wanted in South Africa?** (economic and political power in their country)

Resource REMINDER

Practice and Project Book: *p. 120*

Anthology: *Long Walk to Freedom, pp. 189–191; Why the Tortoise's Shell Is Not Smooth, pp. 192–194*

Technology: *Adventure Time!* CD-ROM

A Changing Africa

Focus Activity

READ TO LEARN

What did South Africans do to achieve democracy?

VOCABULARY

- apartheid
- township
- sanction

PEOPLE

- Nelson Mandela
- Frederik Willem de Klerk

PLACES

- Cape Town
- Soweto
- Johannesburg

606

Read Aloud

"When I walked to the voting station, my mind dwelt on the heroes who had fallen so that I might be where I was that day, the men and women who had made the ultimate sacrifice for a cause that was now finally succeeding. . . . I did not go into that voting station alone on April 27 [1994]; I was casting my vote with all of them."

Nelson Mandela wrote these words in his auto-biography. Mandela and millions of other South Africans had finally voted in their nation's first democratic election.

THE BIG PICTURE

Democracy once seemed like a dream in South Africa. Europeans had ruled much of South Africa since the 1700s. Dutch settlers formed a colony at Cape Town. Find Cape Town on the map on page 607. Their descendants are called Afrikaners. Afrikaners make up 60 percent of South Africa's white population today. However, whites are only about 19 percent of the population. Most of the people are black.

The British took control from the Dutch in 1814. By 1900 Britain had established rule over all of South Africa. A large European population lived in the colony. When South Africa won full independence from Britain in 1961, the white minority continued to rule. Blacks like Nelson Mandela faced a future without freedom or a voice in government.

SHELTERED INSTRUCTION

READING STRATEGIES & LANGUAGE DEVELOPMENT

MAKING CONCLUSIONS Divide the class into small groups to quiz each other on the process of making conclusions. As they work, have students read the second paragraph of *The Big Picture* and find the facts that support the conclusion in the last sentence. Encourage students to make additional conclusions as they read about a changing Africa.
[SDAIE STRATEGY: METACOGNITIVE DEVELOPMENT/TEXT RE-PRESENTATION]

WORDS WITH MULTIPLE MEANINGS Refer the class to the word *sanctions* on p. 608. Point out that it not only has multiple meanings but that two of its meanings seem to have opposite meanings. Have them define the word as it is used here ("penalties against a nation"). Then have them look it up in the dictionary to find an opposite meaning ("official approval of something").

AFRICA: Political

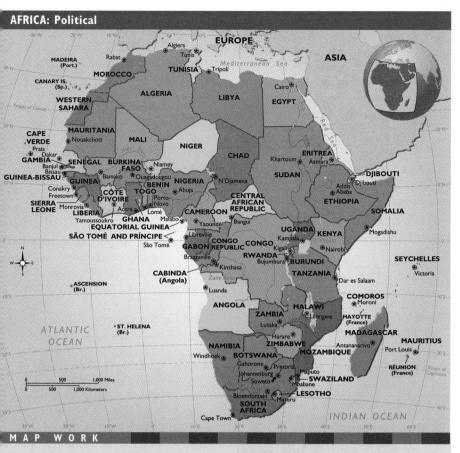

MAP WORK

More than 50 nations are found on the continent of Africa today.

1. What is the capital of Gabon?

2. Which nations border Sudan to the east?

3. Which country has access to two seas shown on the map?

SOUTH AFRICA DIVIDED

Refer the class to *The Big Picture* to identify when South Africa gained full independence from Britain (1961).

● *If South Africa got its independence then, why were South Africans still trying to gain democracy?* (Only white South Africans, not black South Africans, had rights.)

● *What policy did white leaders put into action in 1948? What did the policy do?* (Apartheid; it strictly segregated whites, blacks, and other nonwhites. Areas were designated white or black, and blacks were forced to give up their lands and move out of any white areas. They were forced to live in black areas called townships where services including education were poor or nonexistent.)

★ **THINKING FURTHER:** *Making Connections How were black Africans like a colonial people even after South Africa ceased to be a colony?* (Their land was taken from them and they had no say in how they were governed.)

More MAP WORK

You may wish to have students work with this map later in the lesson, for example, just before work begins on the *Infographic* on p. 611.

● *Why is the Central African Republic aptly named? What countries surround it?* (It is in the center of the continent; Cameroon, Chad, Sudan, Congo, Congo Republic)

● *In what part of Africa do several small countries line the coastline?* (the bottom of the "hump" of western Africa, from Senegal to Benin)

● *What countries form the "horn" of Africa, to the east?* (Eritrea, Djibouti, Somalia, Ethiopia)

● *Which is the largest country of North Africa, bordering the Mediterranean Sea? What is its capital?* (Algeria; Algiers)

SOUTH AFRICA DIVIDED

Even after independence, blacks did not gain many rights or freedoms. They could not vote, own land, or move freely in the country. In 1948 white leaders created a system of laws called apartheid (uh PAHR tid). In the Afrikaans (af ri KAHNZ) language spoken by Afrikaners, *apartheid* means "apartness."

Under apartheid, millions of blacks were forced to give up their land to whites and live in townships, crowded areas for blacks in or near cities. Blacks and other nonwhites could not live or go to school in white neighborhoods. Township schools and services were of poor quality. In some cases, these services did not exist.

607

BACKGROUND INFORMATION

ABOUT SOUTH AFRICA'S PATH TOWARD INDEPENDENCE

● In 1909, the Afrikaner and British states united to form the Union of South Africa, a dominion of Britain.

● In 1931, Britain granted the Union of South Africa a new status, as part of the British Commonwealth of Nations, which also included Canada, Australia, and New Zealand. These nations were held together by loyalty to the crown, a common language, and common traditions.

● In 1961, when other members opposed its racial policies, the Union of South Africa withdrew from the Commonwealth. It then proclaimed itself the Republic of South Africa.

Have students review the population breakdown in South Africa—19 percent white, 81 percent black and nonwhite.

- **Why would the policy of apartheid require a large police force to uphold it?** *(People who wanted apartheid were greatly outnumbered by those against it.)*

- **What means did black South Africans use to try to end apartheid?** *(protests and protest organizations, like the African National Congress, or ANC)*

- **How did the South African government respond to protest against it?** *(It put down protests with violence, banned the ANC, and imprisoned ANC leader Mandela for 27 years.)*

★**THINKING FURTHER:** *Making Connections* **What famous American saying do Mandela's words echo?** *(Patrick Henry's "Give me liberty or give me death!")*

Discussing Growing Tensions Ask students if violence helped or hurt.

- **Why didn't blacks benefit from the boom economy in the 1960s and 1970s?** *(Their wages were kept low.)*

- **What uprising set off the violent struggle against apartheid?** *(the Soweto protest demanding better education opportunities for blacks)*

★**THINKING FURTHER:** *Predicting* **Why might you predict that the struggle against apartheid had to be violent?** *(Neither side would retreat, and peaceful compromise was impossible.)*

Exploring Working for Change Ask students to think about when domestic policies become international issues.

- **How did other countries join the fight to end apartheid?** *(by calling for sanctions against South Africa, to penalize it until it ended its policy)*

★**THINKING FURTHER:** *Making Decisions* **Do you think other countries had a right to intrude in South Africa's affairs? Why or why not?** *(Encourage discussion of whether or when such intrusions are or are not justified.)*

The South African police often used force to uphold apartheid. The threat of violence did not stop many black South Africans from protesting, however. An important leader in the fight to end apartheid was lawyer Nelson Mandela. In 1960 the government banned Mandela's group, the African National Congress (ANC), along with other protest organizations. Four years later Mandela was accused of planning to destroy the government. He was put on trial and sentenced to life in jail. Before Mandela was put in jail he declared:

> I have cherished the ideal of a democratic and free society in which all persons live together in harmony and with equal opportunities. It is an ideal which I hope to live for and to achieve. But if needs be, it is an ideal for which I am prepared to die.

Nelson Mandela was kept in prison for 27 years.

Thousands of blacks in South Africa took part in protests against apartheid. **The police often acted with violence to end protests.**

Growing Tensions

During the 1960s and 1970s, sales of diamonds, gold, and other valuable resources increased. In spite of the growing economy, mining companies and other employers kept wages for black workers low. South African police continued to enforce apartheid.

In the late 1970s, tensions between blacks and police increased in South Africa. In 1976 thousands of young black students led a protest for better education in Soweto. Soweto is the name for the "South-West Townships" outside the city of Johannesburg. Police fired at the protesters, killing one student and wounding hundreds more. The bloodshed triggered years of protests and violence across the country.

Working for Change

In the 1980s countries set up sanctions against the South African government because of its apartheid laws. Sanctions are penalties placed against a nation to make it change its policies. In this case the United States and many other countries decided to boycott South African goods. In addition, South African athletes were banned from international sports events like the Olympics. World leaders hoped that these sanctions would convince the South African government to end its policy of apartheid.

The struggle for freedom continued in South Africa. Blacks often sang a song called *N'kosi Sikelel'i Afrika* (n KAW see see keh LEH lee AH free kah), or "Prayer for Africa." Groups such as the African National Congress adopted it as an anthem. What similarities can you find in the words of *N'kosi Sikelel'i Afrika* and the United States' national anthem?

GLOBAL CONNECTION

MORE ABOUT INTERNATIONAL SANCTIONS Nations and individual groups can penalize a nation—usually by "pocketbook diplomacy"
- by cutting off all trade, neither buying its goods nor selling it goods.
- by refusing to invest in any of that nation's corporations.
- by refusing to buy the goods of any corporations that operate there.
Because sanctions take a long time to work, their success is debatable.

SECOND-LANGUAGE SUPPORT

MAKING CONNECTIONS Second-language learners will benefit from making connections with current events in Africa. Encourage students to cut out any newspaper articles they find, or present summaries of broadcast news items, and write a sentence or two connecting the current events with the changes they are reading about in the lesson.

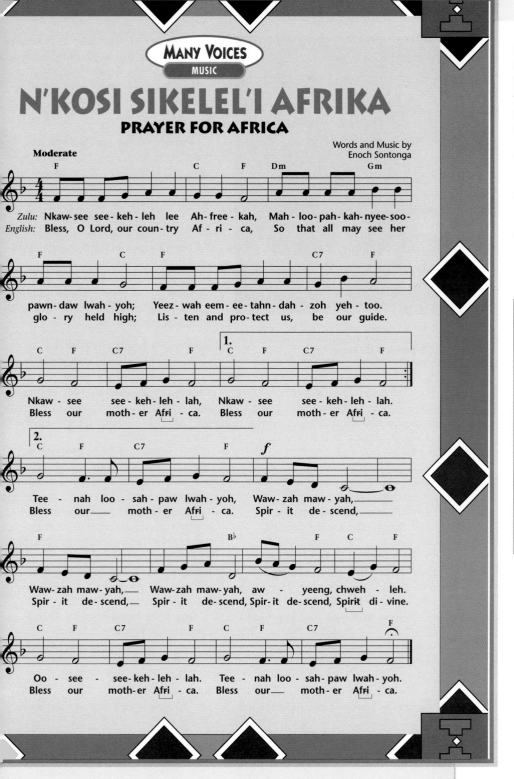

MANY VOICES
MUSIC

N'KOSI SIKELEL'I AFRIKA
PRAYER FOR AFRICA

Words and Music by
Enoch Sontonga

Moderate

Zulu: Nkaw-see see-keh-leh lee Ah-free-kah, Mah-loo-pah-kah-nyee-soo-
English: Bless, O Lord, our coun-try Af-ri-ca, So that all may see her

pawn-daw lwah-yoh; Yeez-wah eem-ee-tahn-dah-zoh yeh-too.
glo-ry held high; Lis-ten and pro-tect us, be our guide.

1.
Nkaw-see see-keh-leh-lah, Nkaw-see see-keh-leh-lah.
Bless our moth-er Afri-ca. Bless our moth-er Afri-ca.

2.
Tee-nah loo-sah-paw lwah-yoh, Waw-zah maw-yah,
Bless our moth-er Afri-ca. Spir-it de-scend,

Waw-zah maw-yah, Waw-zah maw-yah, aw-yeeng, chweh-leh.
Spir-it de-scend, Spir-it de-scend, Spir-it de-scend, Spirit di-vine.

Oo-see see-keh-leh-lah. Tee-nah loo-sah-paw lwah-yoh.
Bless our moth-er Afri-ca. Bless our moth-er Afri-ca.

Discussing "Prayer for Africa"
Give students a few minutes to examine the anthem—to read its lyrics and try to follow its melody. If you have a musical instrument available, pick out its notes.

- *In what African language is this anthem written?* (Zulu)

- *To whom is the prayer addressed?* (a divine spirit)

- *For what are people who sing it asking?* (for blessings on Africa, for protection and guidance, for the divine spirit to descend on their land)

★**THINKING FURTHER:** *Making Conclusions* **Why do you suppose the white South African government objected to people singing "Prayer for Africa"?** (Help students to see that songs can unite people in a cause by reminding them of "We Shall Overcome" in the civil rights movement and "This Land Is Your Land" in the environmental movement. Songs can bring people together and give them a common focus and emotion. Anyone who opposes that focus or emotion will not want to hear that song.)

BACKGROUND INFORMATION

ABOUT THE ZULU LANGUAGE
- Just as Europe has its Romance languages, so Africa has its Bantu languages. They number about 700, and Zulu is one of them.

- Zulu is the language of the Zulu people, who settled in southern Africa before the Europeans began arriving. In the early 1800s, under their leader Shaka, they created the powerful Zulu nation in what is today South Africa.

- By the end of the 19th century, warfare with European settlers had severely weakened the Zulu and they became wage earners in white-owned businesses.

- Today, there are about 5 million Zulu speakers.

CURRICULUM CONNECTION

LINKS TO MUSIC To give students some insight into life in the South African townships under apartheid, you might want to play them the cast recording of the musical *Sarafina* and explain the following:

- *Sarafina* treats life under apartheid in the South African township of Soweto. It focuses on a girl named Sarafina and her high school classmates.

- The show's cast of 22, ages 14 and up, was recruited from townships like Soweto. Prior to their appearance in the show—which took them to New York, Tokyo, and London—the actors had never lived under any system free from apartheid.

609

AFRICA TODAY

- **What evidence can you find that international sanctions worked in South Africa?** *(The white government finally abolished apartheid laws and called for elections in which both blacks and whites could vote.)*

> ★**THINKING FURTHER:** *Cause and Effect* **What was the effect of free elections?** *(With 72 percent of the population, black Africans were able to win the presidency, for Nelson Mandela, and many seats in the government, for African National Congress members.)*

Discussing Life in South Africa
Have students identify benefits and problems.

- **What advances have been made in South Africa?** *(It is now a representative democracy, housing for the poor is being built, and chances for blacks to be educated have opened somewhat.)*

- **What problems remain to be solved?** *(providing all the housing needed and better education for blacks)*

> ★**THINKING FURTHER:** *Making Conclusions* **Why might these problems be considered economic problems?** *(They require huge sums of money to solve.)*

Exploring Facing the Future in Africa
If you have not yet done the *Map Work* on p. 607, you may want to do it at the end of this section.

- **What is the major challenge facing Africa today?** *(widespread poverty resulting from inadequately developed economies)*

- **What might give Africans the opportunity to develop better economies?** *(rich natural resources)*

> ★**THINKING FURTHER:** *Making Conclusions* **What steps do you think Africans must take to develop countries that are successful politically and economically?** *(Possible answers: good educational systems, development of well-run industries to make the best possible use of natural resources)*

Nelson Mandela and F. W. de Klerk greeted a crowd of South Africans after Mandela became president of the nation.

AFRICA TODAY

In 1989 Frederik Willem de Klerk became the president of South Africa. De Klerk thought that the time had come for change in South Africa. In 1990 he released Nelson Mandela, then 72 years old, from prison. In 1991 De Klerk abolished most apartheid laws. As a result international sanctions against South Africa were stopped.

Even bigger changes followed in 1993. De Klerk, Mandela, and other leaders agreed that national elections should be held the following year. They would be the first in the nation's history in which all South Africans, black and white, would have the right to vote.

Despite threats of violence by extreme groups opposed to democracy, the elections were held peacefully in April 1994. Black citizens, who made up 72 percent of the total population, lined up and cast the first votes of their lives Nelson Mandela was elected president. Members of the African National Congress won many other positions in government as well.

Life in South Africa

Democracy has put down strong new roots in South Africa. The nation, however, still faces many challenges. The challenge of overcoming the effects of apartheid will be a difficult one and will likely take years. The government is now building thousands of new homes for poor people. Many more are needed. Formerly all-white schools have been opened to students of all races. However, most black students in South Africa still attend overcrowded, poorly equipped schools.

Facing the Future in Africa

South Africa is not alone in facing such great challenges. Other African nations are also working for change. Many hope to move toward democracy after years of dictatorships and government corruption.

The greatest problem facing most African nations is poverty. As you read in Chapter 19, the economies of colonies in Africa were built to create wealth for Europe. The end of colonialism left many African nations economically weak. Now these nations are struggling to build strong businesses and develop industry. As their economies grow, African nations continue to strengthen through international trade.

One advantage for many African countries is a wealth of natural resources. Botswana produces even more diamonds each year than its neighbor, South Africa. Nigeria pumps thousands of gallons of oil each day and Algeria is rich in natural gas.

CITIZENSHIP★

A FIRST TASTE OF DEMOCRACY The emotion Nelson Mandela expressed election day April 1994 (p. 606) was echoed across South Africa.

- As Anglican Archbishop Desmond Tutu, the short, feisty fighter for democracy, stepped out of the voting station, he said gleefully, "I am about two inches taller than before I arrived."

- Said bricklayer Julius Molawa, "My heart tells me this is the best day of my life."

- In many places across the country, voters stood in lines a mile or more long and waited patiently for their first chance to vote.

- For farmer Gladys Mswele, the wait was seven hours. "Voting is hard labor," she said. "But we have done our duty."

nfographic

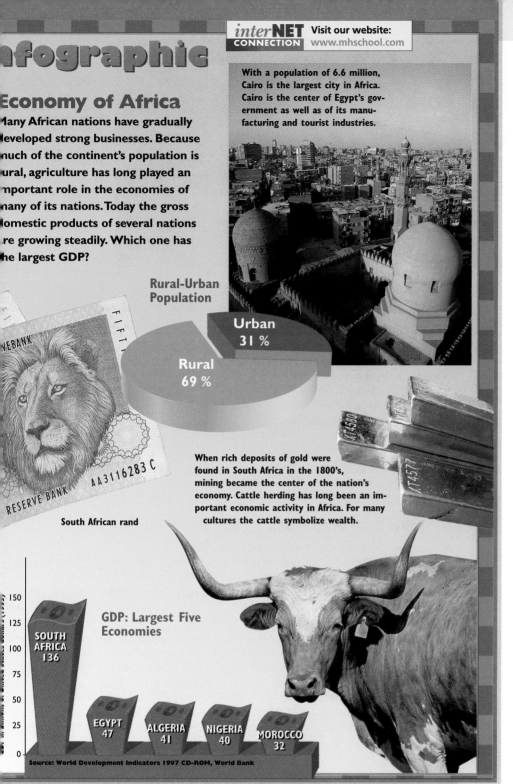

inter**NET** CONNECTION Visit our website: www.mhschool.com

Economy of Africa

Many African nations have gradually developed strong businesses. Because much of the continent's population is rural, agriculture has long played an important role in the economies of many of its nations. Today the gross domestic products of several nations are growing steadily. Which one has the largest GDP?

With a population of 6.6 million, Cairo is the largest city in Africa. Cairo is the center of Egypt's government as well as of its manufacturing and tourist industries.

Rural-Urban Population

Urban 31 %

Rural 69 %

South African rand

When rich deposits of gold were found in South Africa in the 1800's, mining became the center of the nation's economy. Cattle herding has long been an important economic activity in Africa. For many cultures the cattle symbolize wealth.

GDP: Largest Five Economies

150
125
100
75
50
25
0

SOUTH AFRICA 136
EGYPT 47
ALGERIA 41
NIGERIA 40
MOROCCO 32

Source: World Development Indicators 1997 CD-ROM, World Bank

EXPANDING THE INFOGRAPHIC

RESEARCHING AND WRITING Refer the class to the map on p. 607 and have students or pairs of students each choose a different African country that is not among the leading five GDP producers. As suggested with the last lesson's *Infographic*, assign them to construct an economic profile of their country—GDP, per capita GDP, balance of imports and exports, and ratios of televisions and telephones to persons—which will be part of the class book "Economies Around the World." They may use the *World Almanac* to find needed information.

USING THE ANTHOLOGY

LONG WALK TO FREEDOM, pages 189–191 Students may gain a better understanding of the struggle for freedom in South Africa by reading this selection by Nelson Mandela.

Infographic

Review the idea of economic indicators introduced with the *Infographic* on the European economy on p. 602. Have students sit in pairs with one text open here and the other to p. 602. Encourage them to recall what they have already learned about African economies (had been operated to benefit European colonists and not Africans; now often poorly developed, which makes poverty a major challenge).

Discussing the Economy of Africa Give students time to read and examine the illustrations and captions.

- *What glaring difference between Africa and Europe do the pie charts make clear?* (Africa is roughly the opposite of Europe as to where the population lives, with Africa about two-thirds rural and Europe about two-thirds urban.)

- *What does this tell you about how most Africans make their livings?* (Theirs is mainly an agricultural, not an industrial, economy.)

- *Where does Nigeria rank in GDP in Africa? What have you already learned about Nigeria that might account for this high ranking?* (Fourth; it is an oil-producing country.)

- *How does Africa's highest GDP compare with Europe's highest?* (At $136 billion, South Africa's is about 1/18 of Germany's $2,416 billion.)

★THINKING FURTHER: *Making Conclusions* **Why do you think that a highly agricultural economy produces less income from goods and services than an industrialized economy?** (Help students see that in agricultural economies farm families often grow only enough for their own needs. They do not produce the surpluses that would gain income from goods sold, which would enlarge GDP.)

 Technology CONNECTION

ADVENTURE TIME! CD-ROM
Enrich the Infographic with the *Discovery Time Lines* activity on the *Adventure Time!* CD-ROM.

LOOKING TO THE FUTURE
Have students consider the future.

★THINKING FURTHER: *Making Conclusions* **In what ways might African nations that join economic forces contribute to Africa's development?** *(by encouraging trade and profitable use of resources for mutual benefit, by lessening chances of wars between countries)*

Discussing WHY IT MATTERS Discuss the improvements in Africa.

★THINKING FURTHER: *Making Conclusions* **Why might Africans have better experience in the future than they have had in the past?** *(self-rule and control of their own resources instead of colonialism)*

3 CLOSE

MAIN IDEAS
Call on students for answers.

● **What happened in 1994 in South Africa that showed it had become a democracy?** *(free elections that brought in a majority president)*

● **What challenges from their histories do African nations face?** *(the effects of colonialism, economic problems)*

EVALUATE
✓ **Answers to Think About It**
1. a system of laws that segregated people by race and oppressed blacks *Summarize*

2. Their wise development and use can be the basis of sound economies. *Draw Conclusions*

3. through protests and sanctions; free elections, a democratic government *Recall Details*

4. desire for better education; more acts of protest and world support for an end to apartheid *Cause and Effect*

5. It is located on the coast where the Indian Ocean meets the Atlantic Ocean. *Five Themes of Geography: Location*

Write About It Ask students to picture themselves as observers of the April 1994 elections in South Africa and write home describing the experience.

612

After years of unequal schooling for blacks, children of all races now attend classes together in South African cities.

LOOKING TO THE FUTURE

Just as Europeans formed the European Union (EU), in 1980 many southern African nations formed the Southern African Development Community (SADC). Economies of the SADC member nations are not yet as closely linked as those in the European Union. Many experts, however, believe that southern Africa's natural resources and growing democratic movements hold great promise for the economies of individual nations and for the region as a whole.

WHY IT MATTERS

It may take many years for Africans to overcome their histories of colonialism and economic problems. Yet events such as the end of apartheid and the election of a democratic government in South Africa have given many people hope. Throughout the coming years many of the peoples of Africa's diverse nations hope to continue the development of democratic governments. By gaining, protecting, and practicing new rights and freedoms, people in Africa will shape their own futures.

612

✔ Reviewing Facts and Ideas

MAIN IDEAS

● After gaining independence from British rule, South Africa was ruled by a white minority.

● In 1994 South African apartheid ended. Black and other nonwhite citizens voted in a national election for the first time, electing Nelson Mandela president.

● Many African nations are moving to overcome years of colonialism and economic problems.

THINK ABOUT IT

1. What was apartheid?

2. Why are natural resources so important to Africa's future?

3. **FOCUS** How did South Africans succeed in ending apartheid? What did their success mean to the nation?

4. **THINKING SKILL** What was the *cause* of the Soweto students' uprising of 1976? What were some of its *effects*?

5. **GEOGRAPHY** Locate Cape Town, South Africa, on a globe. Write a paragraph explaining why Dutch settlers may have chosen this spot for a colony.

MEETING INDIVIDUAL NEEDS

RETEACHING (Easy) Have students review the material on Nelson Mandela and have them design a campaign poster for him for the April 1994 elections in South Africa. Invite their use of slogans.

EXTENSION (Average) Tell students that they want to convince a white friend in South Africa to work to end apartheid. Have them write a letter to this friend presenting their case.

ENRICHMENT (Challenging) As a cooperative learning project entitled "Life Under Apartheid," divide the class into five groups and assign each group one of the following: the laws of apartheid, life as a black under apartheid, life as a white under apartheid, economic effects of apartheid, political effects of apartheid. Have each group research its topic and prepare a presentation of their findings for the class.

CITIZENSHIP

MAKING A DIFFERENCE

Preparing for a New South Africa

CAPE TOWN, SOUTH AFRICA— Peter Volmink (VOHL mihnk) grew up under apartheid in South Africa. Opportunities for his parents were limited. "My dad worked for the township government. He dug holes and worked in the department of sewers. My mom was a tea lady, she made tea for the bosses in an oil company." In the 1970s, as a student, Volmink protested apartheid and studied law. Once Peter became a lawyer in the 1980s, he continued protesting apartheid and worked on human right cases.

In 1989, Volmink began teaching young people about human rights. "For me," says Volmink, "human rights is respect for the dignity of all people of all races." He taught human rights to teenagers using theater, music, art and dance. He also helped prisoners in South African jails learn about their legal rights and started education projects in remote areas of South Africa.

Now he is taking his message to teachers and young children, ages 7–10, in South Africa's elementary schools. "My materials for young children," says Volmink, "reflect core values of the African experience: compassion for the less fortunate, working together, and mutual respect." When teaching in the classroom, Volmink uses the traditional African teaching tool of storytelling. One of the stories he uses, *Jubalani and the Lion*, shows the importance of treating everyone fairly and not

returning good with evil. Volmink also encourages the students to make songs, dances, and plays from the ideas that he presents.

Volmink believes human rights should be an important part of the school curriculum in the new South Africa. "A truly great nation," he says, "is one in which the majority of its citizens believe in the dignity and worth of all people regardless of any differences. Young children must learn the values of fairness and respect for human life at a very early age if our democracy is to succeed."

". . . human rights is respect for the dignity of all people of all races."

Peter Volmink

613

Lesson Objective
★ Recognize that people often learn about human rights on the grass-roots level.

Identifying the Focus Help students to see how Volmink used his skills as a teacher and storyteller to involve people in human rights issues.

● *How does Volmink define human rights?* (respect for the dignity of all people)

● *How does Volmink define a "truly great nation?"* (a nation in which the citizens believe in the dignity and worth of all people)

Point out that people often form their values and ideals at a young age. Discuss how Volmink's work with young people today may affect his country in the years to come.

Why It Matters Remind students that nations exist that often do not respect basic human rights. Discuss how basic human rights affect the quality of life for a nation's citizens.

● *Who are some of the people that Volmink has educated?* (young children, teenagers, and prisoners)

● *According to Volmink, what are the core values of the African experience?* (compassion, working together, and mutual respect)

★**THINKING FURTHER:** *Making Conclusions* **How is maintaining a successful democracy difficult when the government doesn't respect the basic human rights of its citizens?** (Without basic human rights, citizens would be less likely to voice their opinions about the government. The voicing of opinions is an important part of democracy.)

CITIZENSHIP★

UNDERSTANDING GOVERNMENT It is often difficult for people with few legal rights to protect their basic human rights.

● Under South Africa's current constitution, all people have legal rights, a change that represents a substantial achievement in the human rights struggle. However, when apartheid ended, many people either did not know they had acquired legal rights or could not afford legal representation. This situation has improved with the establishment of community law centers where legal advice is offered at no cost to those who cannot afford it.

● In the United States, anyone accused of a crime who asks for legal counsel in a criminal case must be granted it. This landmark Supreme Court decision was made in the 1963 case of *Gideon v Wainwright.*

LESSON 3

PAGES 614–621

Lesson Overview
Since World War II, nations of the Pacific Rim have rebuilt themselves into leading economic powers in the world.

Lesson Objectives
★ Describe Japan's economic rebirth.

★ Analyze the rapid economic development of other Pacific Rim countries.

★ Describe China's political struggles and economic successes.

1 PREPARE

MOTIVATE As you read the *Read Aloud* to students, suggest they close their eyes and try to picture the scenes described. Invite them to contrast these with scenes of those same locales today—skyscrapers, prosperous-looking office workers, humming factories.

SET PURPOSE Point out the photo of modern Hong Kong. How did this amazing change occur? What are its effects? Refer students to the *Read to Learn* question. Have them read this lesson to find out. Preview the *Vocabulary*.

2 TEACH

Understanding THE BIG PICTURE
Explore the changes in war-torn lands.

● **Why are nations often in poor economic shape after a war?** *(government bankruptcy from the money spent on war, widespread destruction, lack of money to rebuild, individual poverty and despair)*

★ THINKING FURTHER: *Making Conclusions* **What do you think war-torn nations must have in order to rebuild?** *(people with the will and skill to rebuild, money to get started again, sound plans for how to rebuild)*

Resource REMINDER

Practice and Project Book: *p. 121*

Anthology: *Massacre at Tiananmen Square,* p. 195; *Japanese School Days,* pp. 196–197

 Technology: *Adventure Time!* CD-ROM

Focus Activity

READ TO LEARN

How has economic growth affected the peoples of eastern Asia?

VOCABULARY
• Pacific Rim

PEOPLE
• Deng Xiaoping

PLACES
• Japan
• South Korea
• Singapore
• Tiananmen Square
• Hong Kong

614

A Changing Pacific Rim

Read Aloud
World War II left big stretches of Asia in ruins. China, Hong Kong, and other areas conquered by Japanese forces lay in shambles. Much of Japan had also been destroyed. Most buildings in its major cities had been turned to ashes by Allied bombs. People wearing rags hunted for scraps to eat. In 1946 few would have guessed that Japan and other countries of Asia would become economic giants within a few decades.

THE BIG PICTURE
In Chapter 18 you read that the Cold War began in Europe in the middle 1940s. Before long the conflict between communist and democratic governments deeply divided Asia as well. Communists took control of North Korea in 1948, mainland China in 1949, and North Vietnam in 1954. Both communist and non-communist nations throughout Asia faced similar challenges. How could they build strong governments and economies after years of war?

You have already read about Mao Zedong's attempts to meet such challenges in China. His programs, known as the Great Leap Forward and Cultural Revolution, led to some disastrous results for the Chinese people. Meanwhile, other nations in East Asia tried different methods to build stable governments and industries. Perhaps most successful of all in its efforts to rebuild after war was Japan.

SHELTERED INSTRUCTION

READING STRATEGIES & LANGUAGE DEVELOPMENT

PROBLEM AND SOLUTION Review how students can make sense of what they read by identifying problems and solutions. Explain that each of the war-torn countries in eastern Asia faced the same problem: How could they rebuild their government and economy and be self-supporting? Groups of students can make posters to show possible solutions to this problem. **[SDAIE STRATEGY: TEXT RE-PRESENTATION]**

WORD HISTORY Help students to see how knowing the history of a word can give it greater depth of meaning for us. For example, the word *shambles* in the *Read Aloud* on this page originally described a display of butchered meat. Invite them to research the history of other words in this lesson, for example, *disastrous* (ill-starred), *cash* (money box), *luxuries* (excess), *hamburgers* (meat patties originating in Hamburg, Germany) and *slogan* (army cry).

THE REBUILDING OF JAPAN

Between 1945 and 1952 the United States, which occupied Japan after World War II, oversaw the rebuilding of Japan. Under United States direction, a new Japanese constitution was written. The new constitution gave Japanese women equal rights as citizens for the first time. The new constitution also stated that Japan could not go to war. United States supervision of Japan ended in 1952.

Building Japan's Economy

In Chapter 18 you read that the United States sent thousands of troops to fight in Korea between 1950 and 1953. Japan became the main United States base. At its closest point Japan is only 100 miles away from Korea. Thanks partly to the huge American military demand for everything from trucks to sleeping bags, bandages, and bootlaces, Japan's economy boomed.

After the Korean war ended, the Japanese government took steps to keep businesses growing. Schools taught business and technical skills so students would become good industrial workers. The government encouraged companies to produce goods for export. As more cash came in from trade, money was invested in new factories. More cash and new factories led to an increase in Japanese exports.

By the 1960s Japan's economy was expanding at a very fast rate. In 1950 Japan's Gross Domestic Product had been smaller than the GDP of any western country. By 1965 it had grown larger than those of Britain and France. Today the United States' GDP is still the world's largest, followed by that of Japan.

Manufacturing and shipping contributed greatly to Japan's economic expansion.

615

THE REBUILDING OF JAPAN

Have students review the things they believe a nation must have in order to rebuild. Encourage them to see how many of these things Japan had.

● **What changes occurred in Japan as a result of the U.S. postwar direction?** *(a new constitution, equal rights for women, resolve not to go to war again)*

★THINKING FURTHER: *Making Conclusions* **How might these factors help Japan to rebuild?** *(A stable government might encourage economic development, and no more war-making would mean that it was not necessary to spend scarce resources on arms, freeing funds for investment in more profitable areas.)*

Discussing Building Japan's Economy Identify external and internal causes of Japan's economic growth.

● **How was the Korean war good for Japan's economy?** *(The U.S. demand for a wide variety of Japanese goods aided Japanese industry, causing it to expand and prosper.)*

● **What steps did the Japanese government take to encourage further economic expansion?** *(It strengthened education to provide good industrial workers and it encouraged industries to expand exports, making them more profitable.)*

● **What has all this Japanese economic expansion done to Japan's GDP?** *(It has made it the second highest economy in the world, after the U.S.)*

★THINKING FURTHER: *Making Conclusions* **You may have heard the expression "It takes money to make money." How did Japan use money to make money?** *(Help students realize that sound reinvestment of profits in industry is the fuel that causes industries to grow—profits reinvested create more production, which creates more profits to reinvest, which creates more production, and on and on.)*

BACKGROUND INFORMATION

A JAPANESE "RIP VAN WINKLE" Perhaps no one found the rapid transformation of Japan more stunning and bewildering than Hiroo Onoda, a World War II Japanese Army Intelligence officer.

● For nearly 30 years following the end of the war, Onoda, a lone sharpshooter in a Japanese army uniform, had terrorized villagers on the island of Lubang in the Philippines.

● He knew the war had ended but he never gave up: "Only in case my commanding officer tells me to will I surrender." His old commanding officer was located and Onoda was read his order, after which he finally surrendered.

● In 1974, Onoda returned to a Japan he had not seen since 1942. The changes he saw were too much for him, so he exiled himself once again, this time to a quiet, remote area in Brazil.

615

JAPAN AND THE PACIFIC RIM

Introduce students to the idea that producing finished goods is more profitable than producing raw materials. For example, Japan makes much more money by producing cars than, say, Nigeria makes by producing oil to fuel Japan's car manufacturing. This "value added" is key to Japan's favorable balance of trade—that is, Japan gains much more income from its exports than it spends for what it imports.

- **What are examples of finished goods that Japan produces?** *(cars, computer parts, televisions, cameras)*

- **Why are such goods more valuable than, say, the raw steel that goes into them?** *(They employ people and high technology to create them, and these steps add to their value.)*

★ **THINKING FURTHER:** *Making Decisions* **On a scale of 1 to 10, how would you rank Japan's ability to produce goods the world wants?** *(As students decide on their rankings, encourage them to identify products from Japan that they use—the names of Japanese cars as well as Sony, Sega, and Nintendo will probably lead to high rankings.)*

More MAP WORK

Refer students to the map on these pages and have them locate and point to the countries with fast-growing economies mentioned in the second paragraph of Japan and the Pacific Rim.

- **In addition to Japan, what are other Pacific Rim places with highly successful economies?** *(South Korea, Taiwan, Hong Kong, Singapore, Thailand)*

- **What geographic feature do all of these countries share? Hint: Think water.** *(location on the sea)*

★ **THINKING FURTHER:** *Making Conclusions* **Why would this be an advantage to an economy?** *(shipping—the ability to get needed raw materials in and send finished goods out to world markets)*

ASIA AND AUSTRALIA: Political

MAP WORK

Many Asian nations have developed strong economies based on industry. Several nations support large populations.

1. Which nations border Pakistan to the north?

2. Of which nation is Port Moresby the capital?

3. Which country shown is furthest from a sea or an ocean?

616 MAP WORK: **1.** Afghanistan, China **2.** Papua New Guinea **3.** Kyrgyzstan

---

BACKGROUND INFORMATION

THE SOCIAL COST OF RAPID ECONOMIC GROWTH Japan's rapid growth has not been achieved without a high social cost.

- As noted on p. 625, Tokyo–Yokohama is the most populous city in the world; it is packed with 38,000 people per square mile. Families there often live in tiny apartments of no more than 400 square feet. Even in the suburbs, a family bungalow may be no larger than a two-car garage.

- Hours of work for men—and increasingly for women—entering the work force, are long and strained. Long commutes add to the time workers must spend away from their families.

- Pressure on young people to succeed in school is intense. After their regular day in school, many students spend several hours more in special cramming schools, so they can get into college.

The modern buildings of downtown Singapore (right) reflect the wealth of the city and its businesses.

JAPAN AND THE PACIFIC RIM

The big push to industrialize made Japan wealthy. Though Japan is poor in natural resources, its workers turned imported raw materials into expensive goods such as cars, computer parts, televisions, and cameras.

Today other nations along the Pacific Rim—the ring of countries surrounding the Pacific Ocean—have grown economically as well. Among them are South Korea, Taiwan, Hong Kong, Singapore, and Thailand. South Korea, in particular, quickly and successfully rebuilt its economy after the Korean War of the early 1950s. Look at the map on page 616 to locate these countries.

The Rise of the Pacific Rim

The economic growth in the Pacific Rim has led to a shift in the power of the world's regions. For hundreds of years much of world trade and power centered around the Atlantic Ocean. With the growth of Pacific Rim nations, however, a new region of wealth and power has emerged whose economies compete with those of the West.

The tiny republic of Singapore is a Pacific Rim country that has become a giant in world trade. The electronics industry provides many high-paying jobs. Many homes have televisions and other appliances that are considered luxuries throughout much of Asia.

Growth in Australia

Another member of the Pacific Rim, Australia, has been gaining increasing prominence in the world. In 1951 it formed an economic and political partnership with the United States. It has been actively involved with international peacekeeping missions and has supported economic advancement in Asia.

With ideal land for grazing sheep, Australia is the world leader in wool production. It also has a strong economy in mineral exports. In recent years Australia has moved toward other areas of production as well. It exports large amounts of computer parts to Japan, Hong Kong, and South Korea. It is also a pioneer in solar research.

617

CITIZENSHIP★

UNDERSTANDING GOVERNMENT While the jobs and incomes of Pacific Rim citizens may be similar to our own, their laws and punishments are often quite different, as 18-year-old American Michael Fay learned while living in Singapore.

• Convicted in 1993 of defacing cars with spray-paint, Fay was sentenced not only to a fine and a prison stay, but also to six lashes with a cane on his bare backside. The cane was sure to draw blood.

• Fay's parents protested the harshness of the caning and went to the U.S. press and President Clinton to try and stop it.

• But the caning took place anyway in May 1994, though Fay got four lashes, not six. Said a Singapore government minister, Singapore's institutions would lose all credibility "if its citizens see the government giving in to U.S. press pressure."

CHANGE COMES TO CHINA

China also tries to spur growth with limited human rights.

- **How much of the world's population lives in China?** *(one person in five)*

- **Why does this large proportion interest business leaders of the world?** *(They see China as a huge market in which to sell goods.)*

- **Why does it cause concern to military planners?** *(It could produce a massive army, larger than any other country's.)*

★**THINKING FURTHER:** *Making Decisions* **In an earlier part of the quote cited in this section, Napoleon called China "a sleeping giant." Reread the quote. Do you agree or disagree with Napoleon? Explain.** *(Students will probably agree, citing the effect that such a large nation could have on the rest of the world.)*

Discussing A Changing Economy
Help students recognize that there are degrees of tight government control.

★**THINKING FURTHER:** *Compare and Contrast* **How would you compare and contrast China under Mao Zedong and Deng Xiaoping?** *(Mao: collective farms under direct control of the government, isolation from outside cultural influences and rooting out of any already present; Deng: degree of economic freedom for farmers, encouragement of cultural borrowing in both education and business)*

CHANGE COMES TO CHINA

Should jobs and the economy be more important in society than citizens' rights and freedoms? What is too high a price to pay for economic growth? People in the wealthy, capitalist nation of Singapore are not the only ones debating such questions. People in China have also been facing this complex issue.

According to legend the French leader Napoleon Bonaparte declared in the 1800s, "when China wakes, it will shake the world." Today about one out of every five people on Earth lives in China. To business leaders in other countries, China's huge population means a huge number of customers. To military planners, it means a possibly massive army. To world leaders, this population means that China's decisions could have huge effects on the rest of the world.

A Changing Economy

After the death of Mao Zedong in 1976, a power struggle began among China's top leaders. It ended when Deng Xiaoping (DUNG SHOW PING) won control of the government in 1978. Deng was a veteran of the Long March.

In 1989, thousands of students (above) gathered in Beijing to demonstrate for democracy. About one month after they began, the Chinese government brought in tanks (right) to end the protests.

618

---

nd a victim of the Cultural Revolution. When Deng gained power, his government moved away from Mao's strict style of communism.

Farmers were given more control over their work. They were allowed to sell surplus crops for profit. Mao had tried to root out everything foreign in China. Deng, on the other hand, encouraged students to study abroad. He hoped they would learn new science skills that could help China. Foreign companies began to do business in China, selling everything from airplanes to hamburgers.

A Movement For Democracy

Deng's changes led to strong economic growth. By the spring of 1989—the "Year of Miracles" in Europe—many Chinese hoped that glasnost would spread to China. In May 1989 about one million students gathered to protest for democracy in an immense square in Beijing. Tiananmen (TYEN AHN MEN) Square is at the heart of the Chinese central government area. It leads into the Forbidden City, which you read was built for China's emperors during the Ming dynasty.

Deng refused to let supporters of glasnost and democracy take over Tiananmen Square. That June the government ordered dozens of tanks into the square to destroy the democracy movement. Hundreds of student protesters were killed. Many more were wounded, and their leaders were thrown in prison. Deng succeeded in ending the democracy movement in China for the time being.

In February of 1997, Deng passed away. Many people wondered if his successor, Jiang Zemin [JAHNG ZU min], would be able to continue Deng's

Deng Xiaoping (above) encouraged free enterprise in China even after crushing the 1989 democracy movement.

methods of modernizing China. Other countries had imposed trade sanctions, or penalties, against China for its actions in Tiananmen Square. Would the communist party be able to maintain control while encouraging interaction with the rest of the world?

Uncertainty in Hong Kong

One place where people are especially interested in the changes in China is Hong Kong. This thriving city, a center for international trade, had been a British colony since the 1800s. In 1984 Britain agreed to return Hong Kong to Chinese control in 1997. On July 1, 1997, Hong Kong officially became reunited with China.

Many people in Hong Kong are concerned that the Chinese government will restrict their freedoms. China's actions in Tiananmen Square raised many of these concerns. Some of these people left Hong Kong before July of 1997 to settle in Canada and the United States. Others have stayed to see what changes will take place under China's control.

619

Discussing A Movement for Democracy Compare events in China to events in Eastern Europe and the Soviet Union.

- *How did Deng's loosening up of Mao's strict control backfire?* (Cultural influences from the outside, like glasnost, made 1 million students stage a protest for democracy.)

- *How did Deng react to this democracy movement?* (He ordered it put down with tanks and troops, causing the death of hundreds of protesters.)

★THINKING FURTHER: *Compare and Contrast How would you compare and contrast Deng's policies toward economic freedom and political freedom?* (Economic freedom: in favor, to achieve growth; Political freedom: opposed to any degree)

Exploring Uncertainty in Hong Kong Discuss the problems that arise from an uncertain future.

- *What caused uncertainty in Hong Kong?* (its return to China's control in 1997)

- *What worries the people of Hong Kong?* (whether or not China will honor its promise to let them keep their laws and free enterprise system)

★THINKING FURTHER: *Making Conclusions What might make China keep its promise? What might make it break it?* (Keep: benefits of Hong Kong's prosperity; Break: not wanting one part of the country to be treated differently from another)

CITIZENSHIP★

USING CURRENT EVENTS Now that the "sleeping giant" is stirring, stories about China frequently appear in the news, often centering on the condition of human rights or on economic matters. Have students find and bring to class newspaper and magazine articles that deal with China for a "China Watch" discussion.

SECOND-LANGUAGE SUPPORT

DIALOGS Second-language learners may be helped by listening to talks by community members who have immigrated from Asia. Encourage students to prepare questions about how the changes described in the lesson may have affected the speakers or their families.

BACKGROUND INFORMATION

ABOUT HONG KONG

- Hong Kong is made up of Hong Kong Island, which covers about 29 square miles, and Kowloon, a peninsula on mainland China that covers about 404 square miles. A one-mile-wide strait separates the two and gives Hong Kong a fine deep-water harbor.

- Hong Kong was once a center of the incense trade. This gave it the name Hong Kong, which in Cantonese means "incense harbor" or "fragrant harbor."

- Hong Kong came under British control during the 1800s, when European nations and Japan were carving China into their own spheres of influence. In 1898, the British signed a 100-year lease for Hong Kong.

Infographic

Before the class turns to this *Infographic* on the economy of Asia, invite them to make predictions about what it will contain. Which five Asian nations might have the highest GDPs? In what order? Is Asia mainly rural or urban? Have students write their predictions on the board. Then have the class sit in pairs and open one book to this page and the other to p. 602.

Discussing the Economy of Asia
Give students time to read the text on this page and examine the illustrations and their captions.

- *How accurate were your predictions? Are there any surprises? Explain.* (Have students compare the GDP graph and the pie chart to their predictions on the board.)

- *How much larger is Japan's GDP than the runner-up?* (It is about 7 1/3 times larger than China's.)

- *How does it compare with the largest GDP in Europe?* (It is close to 2 times larger than Germany's.)

- *How does Asia's urban-rural split of the population compare with that of Europe?* (They are very similar.)

★**THINKING FURTHER:** *Problem Solving* **Japan has a population of about 126 million while India has about 952 million people. How does per capita GDP differ between the two?** (Japan: $5.1 trillion ÷ 126 million = $40,476 and change; India: $324 billion ÷ 952 million = $340 and change)

Technology CONNECTION

ADVENTURE TIME! CD-ROM
Enrich the Infographic with the *Discoveries Time Lines* activity on the *Adventure Time!* CD-ROM.

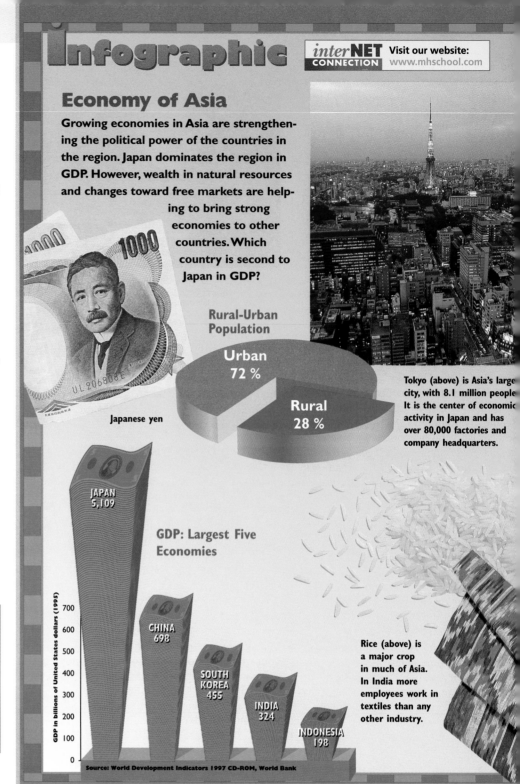

Infographic

| interNET CONNECTION | Visit our website: www.mhschool.com |

Economy of Asia

Growing economies in Asia are strengthening the political power of the countries in the region. Japan dominates the region in GDP. However, wealth in natural resources and changes toward free markets are helping to bring strong economies to other countries. Which country is second to Japan in GDP?

Japanese yen

Rural-Urban Population

Urban 72 %

Rural 28 %

Tokyo (above) is Asia's large city, with 8.1 million people It is the center of economic activity in Japan and has over 80,000 factories and company headquarters.

GDP: Largest Five Economies

GDP in billions of United States dollars (1995)

JAPAN 5,109
CHINA 698
SOUTH KOREA 455
INDIA 324
INDONESIA 198

700
600
500
400
300
200
100
0

Source: World Development Indicators 1997 CD-ROM, World Bank

Rice (above) is a major crop in much of Asia. In India more employees work in textiles than any other industry.

EXPANDING THE INFOGRAPHIC

RESEARCHING AND WRITING Refer the class to the map on p. 616 and have students or pairs of students choose countries of Asia that are not among the top GDP producers. As suggested for *Infographics* in earlier lessons in this chapter, assign them to construct an economic profile of their country—GDP, per capita GDP, balance of imports and exports, and ratios of televisions and telephones to persons—to become part of the class book "Economies Around the World." Suggest that they use the *World Almanac* to find the information they need.

WHY IT MATTERS

In only about 50 years, the nations around Asia's Pacific Rim have grown from areas devastated by war to major economic powers. The rapid economic growth of the nations in this region is likely to continue well into the twenty-first century. Such growth assures that the power of that part of Asia will continue to increase.

As economies develop and become more connected, whatever happens in one nation or continent will have great impact in other parts of the world. Because of this, observers around the world watch carefully to detect signs of what is in store for the most populous continent.

When did European explorers arrive in Australia?

Before it was named, the Dutch landed on Australia's West Coast in 1616. The British explored and colonized the East Coast in 1788.

It wasn't until the early 1800s, however, that explorers knew that the East and West Coasts did, in fact, belong to the same body of land. From 1801 to 1803 two British navigators, George Bass and Matthew Flinders, sailed around the entire continent and mapped the southern coastline. This proved that the Dutch and English had landed on the same land mass. Matthew Flinders suggested calling this land Australia, and by the 1820s this had become the accepted name.

Reviewing Facts and Ideas

MAIN IDEAS

- The growing nations of the Pacific Rim make up an important new region of economic power.
- Japan's industrialization was helped by United States involvement and the Korean War. Growth was also dependent on Japanese government policies and education.
- For many Pacific Rim countries, such as Singapore, economic growth has been stressed over democracy.

THINK ABOUT IT

1. How did the Korean War affect the Japanese economy?

2. What is the Pacific Rim? Why can its growth be described as a major shift in world history?

3. **FOCUS** How has economic growth changed life for Asians since the end of World War II?

4. **THINKING SKILL** What steps would you take to *evaluate the accuracy* of the GDP graph on page 620?

5. **WRITE** Should concern about jobs and the economy have priority over the protection of individual rights? Write a paragraph describing your view of this issue.

621

MEETING INDIVIDUAL NEEDS

RETEACHING (Easy) Have students review the lesson to find a subject for a poster that might appear in one of the Asian countries they have just studied, perhaps one celebrating an economic success or urging better performance in school or in the workplace. Have each student create a poster.

EXTENSION (Average) Invite students to picture themselves as Chinese students pleading with their government for democracy. Have each student write a short speech making the case for it.

ENRICHMENT (Challenging) Explain that the 20th century has sometimes been called "the American century" and that today some thinkers suggest that the 21st century may be called "the Pacific Rim century." Have students write a paper explaining why they think this prediction may or may not come true.

Extending Did You Know? Students may want to do research on how some local places got their names.

Discussing WHY IT MATTERS Make students aware of the need to be alert to changes in world economies.

★**THINKING FURTHER:** *Making Conclusions* **How does the growth of Pacific Rim economies increase how much different parts of the world depend on one another?** *(Increasingly one part of the world needs raw materials from another part, and relies on markets elsewhere in the world to buy manufactured goods.)*

3 CLOSE

MAIN IDEAS

Have students write their answers and exchange papers for correction.

- *Why has the Pacific Rim become a powerful region of the world recently?* (rapid economic growth)

- *To what factors can Japan's phenomenal postwar economic growth be attributed?* (U.S. need for Japanese production during the Korean War, Japanese policies favoring business, reinvestment of profits, strong education system)

- *What has been suppressed to achieve economic growth in some Asian countries, like China?* (democracy)

EVALUATE

√ **Answers to Think About It**

1. It brought on a boom because the U.S. needed Japanese products. *Recall Details*

2. Countries that ring the Pacific Ocean; it has shifted economic power from the Atlantic to the Pacific. *Draw Conclusions*

3. It has changed the work that many do, given them better education, and made many more of them urban dwellers. *Main Idea*

4. check it out with a variety of other sources and news articles *Make Judgements and Decisions*

5. Encourage students to identify the pros and cons of each position before they begin writing. *Point of View*

Write About It Have students write a one-paragraph before-and-after sketch of Japan, 1945 and 1965.

LESSON 4

PAGES 622–629

Lesson Overview

Since World War II, the nations of the Americas have become more industrialized, urbanized, democratic, and interdependent.

Lesson Objectives

★ Identify major changes that the Americas have undergone in the past half century.

★ Identify major challenges that the Americas face in the future.

1 PREPARE

MOTIVATE Remind the class of the European Union and the South African Development Community and have students review the purpose of regional groups. Then have a student do the *Read Aloud*. What ties the nations of the Americas together?

SET PURPOSE Refer students to the *Read to Learn* question and encourage them to explore the lesson to learn about problems of the nations of the Americas and how cooperation can help solve them. Preview the *Vocabulary*.

2 TEACH

Understanding THE BIG PICTURE
Elicit information students already have.

● **How has industrialization changed the Americas since World War II?** *(Before: only the U.S. and Canada were industrialized. Now: other American nations have industrialized.)*

★ **THINKING FURTHER:** *Cause and Effect* **How has increased trade among nations of the Americas made them interdependent?** *(They now depend very much on one another to supply their wants and needs.)*

Resource REMINDER

Practice and Project Book: *p. 122*

Anthology: *Ode to an Artichoke, pp. 198–199; A Tale of Disappearance, pp. 200–202; De Lanterna na Mão, pp. 203–204*

Technology: *Adventure Time! CD-ROM*

The Changing Americas

Read Aloud

The future is the great common thread tying together Americans." To Mexican poet Octavio Paz, the "thread" that will tie people of the Americas together is not just the trade of exports and imports. It is also the free trade of ideas and cultural traditions.

Focus Activity

READ TO LEARN

In what ways are the nations of the Americas working together on common problems?

VOCABULARY

- interdependent
- urbanization
- NAFTA
- bilingual
- Internet

PEOPLE

- Jean-Bertrand Aristide

PLACES

- Brazil
- Canada
- United States
- Haiti
- Dominican Republic
- Mexico
- Mexico City
- Nunavut

622

THE BIG PICTURE

Earlier in this chapter you read about the great changes sweeping through Europe, Africa, and Asia in the second half of the 1900s. These include political revolutions, industrial revolutions, and a movement toward greater unity among nations. It should not surprise you to learn that change has been transforming the nations of the Americas as well.

Before World War II, the United States and Canada were the only major industrial nations in the Americas. The other nations were mainly rural. In the past Brazil imported most of its manufactured goods such as clothes and cars. Today, however, Brazilian factory workers make everything from blue jeans to armored cars. Some of their most important buyers are other nations of the Americas such as Canada and the United States.

Trade has made the nations of the Americas increasingly interdependent. This means that they count on each other to meet the needs and wants of their peoples. Agreements about trade and politics have made countries like the United States, Mexico, and Canada closer neighbors.

SHELTERED INSTRUCTION

READING STRATEGIES & LANGUAGE DEVELOPMENT

PREDICTING To help students grasp the lesson concept, have them create a graphic organizer. On the left side of their paper, have students write *predictions*; on the right side, *revisions*. Then direct students to skim this lesson, noting visuals, headings, and subheadings, and write down their predictions. As students read the lesson, have them revise their predictions and add to their charts. **[SDAIE STRATEGY: SCHEMA BUILDING]**

NEW WORDS Remind students that our language is constantly expanding because new inventions and methods demand new words to name them. Refer the class to two terms on p. 627—*fax machines* and *cellular phones*. Ask students to explain what each is, then report that just a few years ago, both terms were unknown to the general public, but now both are a common part of everyday life.

NATIONS OF THE AMERICAS

The Western Hemisphere includes two cultural regions. The United States and Canada make up Anglo-America. This region was influenced strongly by British culture. Latin America includes Mexico, Central America, the Caribbean islands, and South America. It was influ enced by Spain, Portugal, and France.

Many Caribbean islands have gained independence from European control since the 1800s. Haiti in 1804 and the Dominican Republic in 1844 were the first. As you can see on the map, these nations are both located on one island—Hispaniola. Most Caribbean nations became independent after World War II.

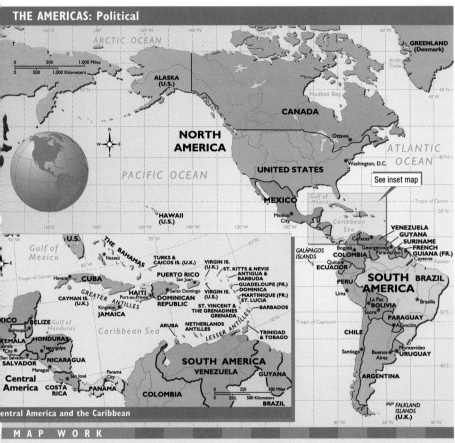

THE AMERICAS: Political

Central America and the Caribbean

MAP WORK

The two cultural regions of the Americas have been shaped by European influences. Today the many nations of these regions continue to develop new and unique traditions.

1. Of which nation is Montevideo the capital? In which of the Americas is this city located?
2. Which is farther west—Mexico City or Washington, D.C.?
3. What is the capital of Jamaica?

MAP WORK: 1. Uruguay; South America 2. Mexico City 3. Kingston   623

NATIONS OF THE AMERICAS

Link the different cultures to the different histories of the areas.

- **Into what two cultural regions may the Americas be divided?** *(Anglo America and Latin America)*

- **What countries make up each group?** *(Anglo America: the United States and Canada; Latin America: all countries south of the United States, including Mexico and countries of Central and South America and the Caribbean)*

- **How did each of these groups get their names?** *(Latin American countries were influenced strongly by European nations—Spain, Portugal, and France—that speak languages that come from Latin. Anglo American nations were strongly influenced by British culture—the term Anglo is derived from "England.")*

★THINKING FURTHER: *Making Conclusions* **Can you think of any cases in which Latin overlaps Anglo?** *(Students may recall the French influence on Quebec in Canada—people there still speak French—and the Spanish influence on the Southwest of the United States.)*

More MAP WORK

Refer the class to the map on this page.

- **How far south in latitude does Anglo America extend in the Western Hemisphere?** *(at its farthest, nearly to the Tropic of Cancer)*

- **How far north to south in latitude does Latin American extend?** *(from about 35°N nearly to the South Pole)*

- **Which is Latin America's largest country?** *(Brazil)*

- **In which 30 degrees of latitude are the greatest number of American nations found?** *(from the equator to 30° N, which includes Mexico, the nations of Central America, the Caribbean, and northern South America)*

★THINKING FURTHER: *Making Conclusions* **Where are the island nations of the Americas located?** *(mostly in the Caribbean Sea)*

CURRICULUM CONNECTION

LINKS TO LANGUAGE ARTS Point out to the class that relations between the United States and Latin America have not always been smooth. Latin Americans have often been suspicious of their powerful neighbor to the north. Around 1900, a Uruguayan writer called the U.S. the "Colossus of the North." Have students refer to the *Infographic* on p. 216 to see why *Colossus* suggests great size.

SECOND-LANGUAGE SUPPORT

WORKING WITH A PEER Second-language learners may be helped by working with a partner to put together a multimedia presentation for the class about this lesson. Have students use their map skills, time line skills, and art skills to prepare the presentation for display. Encourage second-language students to explain their display.

LATIN AMERICA TODAY

Have students locate Mexico on the map on p. 623.

- **What problem did Mexico face after World War II?** *(lack of manufactured goods)*

- **What did this lack cause Mexico to do?** *(industrialize so it could produce the goods it needed for itself)*

★THINKING FURTHER: *Making Connections* **How did this decision parallel decisions being made elsewhere in the world at that time?** *(Asian nations and others were industrializing as a way to build strong new national economies.)*

Discussing Mexico City Help students realize that *urbanization*, defined on p. 625, is a result of industrialization.

- **How did industrialization and the discovery of oil affect Mexico City?** *(Both created new businesses, which caused millions to move to Mexico City from rural areas to fill new jobs.)*

★THINKING FURTHER: *Making Conclusions* **How are industrialization and urbanization related?** *(Industries need people working in one place, which creates or enlarges cities.)*

Discussing Need for Jobs Help students realize that some Mexicans have not gained from industrialization.

★THINKING FURTHER: *Cause and Effect* **What have been the unintended consequences of industrialization for Mexico?** *(not enough jobs or housing; flight to the U.S. to find jobs)*

Exploring Jobs and the Environment Have students locate Brazil on the map on p. 623.

- **How has Brazil tried to increase available land?** *(by opening the Amazon rain forest to farming, logging, mining, and ranching)*

★THINKING FURTHER: *Cause and Effect* **How did this policy cause new problems?** *(It encouraged clearing of vast areas of the rain forest, and destroyed an environment and its native people, animals, and plants.)*

LATIN AMERICA TODAY

Mexico, a country of 92 million people, has become one of the world's major industrial powers. It is an important producer of such items as oil, electronic goods, and cars.

Mexico's industrial revolution began during World War II. A decline in world trade left Mexico with a shortage of manufactured goods. Because of this shortage and the need for more money, Mexican leaders decided to industrialize their nation.

Mexico City

After World War II, hundreds of new factories began to fill Mexico City, the nation's capital. New jobs brought about three million people there from rural areas between 1940 and 1970.

Oil drilling (above) became important in Mexico when vast oil reserves were found.

624

During the 1970s oil was discovered in southern Mexico. This "black gold" helped pay for more businesses in Mexico City and other cities. By the early 1990s Mexico City had become the world's second-largest urban area— behind Tokyo, Japan.

Need for Jobs

Mexico's economic growth has created riches for a few, but has not helped all Mexicans. Many in Mexico City have a hard time finding work and housing. One woman remembered:

> When we arrived in Mexico City, we lived in cardboard boxes and [searched] for food from the garbage dump. I cried. This is not what I had dreamed of.

Many thousands of Mexicans cross the United States border each year, legally and illegally. These Mexicans can go from making about $4 a day to $4 an hour. Living costs, however, are much higher in the United States than in Mexico.

Jobs and the Environment

Other Latin American countries face similar economic problems. In the 1980s Brazil's government offered poor people free land in the Amazon rain forest for farming. Thousands of families moved to this fragile environment. People set fires to clear land for crops. The rain forest land was ill-suited for growing rice or beans, however. Many people soon left their farms, though much damage had already been done to the land, the animals, and the Indians who had long lived there. This damage was then made worse by the arrival of new logging, mining, and ranching businesses.

One Brazilian scientist, Jacques Marcovitch, called for a new approach to this difficult problem:

CITIZENSHIP★

UNDERSTANDING CURRENT EVENTS The growth in immigration into the United States, legal and illegal, from Mexico and elsewhere, has sparked a national debate over what U.S. immigration policy should be.

- In the 1950s, about 250,000 immigrants entered the United States annually. By the middle 1990s, that figure was 1 million.

- By the mid-1990s, there were an estimated 4 million illegal immigrants living in the United States

- Today's immigrants into the United States are on average less well educated than the people born here, and they earn 32 percent less than those born here. Encourage students to bring in news clippings dealing with the immigration debate, and discuss them in class.

We need strategies that are both economically productive and environmentally sound....You cannot talk about ecology to people who are struggling to survive.

Today Brazil's government is working with other nations in the Americas to preserve the rain forests. Some United States companies are trying to build a demand for rain forest products such as nuts and oils. This demand helps to create jobs in the Amazon that are friendly to the environment.

Fighting the Drug Problem

Another difficult problem facing nations of the Americas is the drug trade. Farmers in Colombia, Peru, and Bolivia raise coca plants, which are used to make cocaine. This illegal and dangerous drug brings little money to farmers. Most profits go to crime organizations that sell the drugs around the world. The United States has joined other nations to try to stamp out the drug trade. Their efforts include destroying coca fields and helping farmers to raise other crops.

Growth of Democracy

During much of the 1900s most Latin American countries were ruled by dictators. In the 1980s democratic movements swept through the Americas, overturning most of the dictatorships. The people of Chile, for example, elected a democratic government in 1988.

Two years later, Haitians elected Jean-Bertrand Aristide (JAHN BAIR trahnd AH rihs teed) to be their president. Military leaders overthrew him the following year. With the help of the United States, Aristide regained his office in 1994.

In 1997, democratic elections in Mexico resulted in the defeat of a political party that had dominated the Mexican government for nearly 70 years. As a result, other political parties and views gained a greater opportunity to shape Mexico's future.

Growing Cities

Just as in Mexico City, millions of job-seekers have moved to cities throughout Latin America. In the 1970s in Brazil, 30 million people moved from the countryside to urban areas. Find the percentage of people now living in rural and urban areas in the Americas on the Infographic on page 628.

Urbanization, or growth of cities, has brought other challenges. As you can see on the chart on this page, two out of the five largest cities in the world are in Latin America.

THE WORLD'S FIVE LARGEST CITIES

Tokyo-Yokohama, Japan	28,447,000 population / 1,089 sq. miles
Mexico City, Mexico	23,913,000 population / 522 sq. miles
São Paulo, Brazil	21,539,000 population / 451 sq. miles
Seoul, South Korea	19,065,000 population / 342 sq. miles
New York, United States	14,638,000 population / 1,247 sq. miles

Note: City populations include populations for metropolitan areas.
Source: 1997 Information Please Almanac

CHART WORK

The world's five largest cities are located in Asia and the Americas.

1. What is the population of Tokyo-Yokohama?
2. Which city is located in Brazil?

Exploring Fighting the Drug Problem Explain to the class that the farmers who grow coca get relatively little money, but sometimes it is their only cash crop.

★**THINKING FURTHER:** *Making Conclusions* **For what reasons do you think the drug problem is so hard to solve?** *(Unfortunately, there is a large market for drugs, and farmers are willing to grow coca for the little cash it brings them, while criminal groups make billions from drugs.)*

Discussing Growth of Democracy Review the meaning of *dictator* and the history of governments in the Americas.

★**THINKING FURTHER:** *Making Decisions* **On a scale of 1 to 10, how would you rank the growth of democracy in the Americas?** *(From the examples cited, students should rank it high.)*

Discussing Growing Cities Students should be encouraged to see the trend to urbanization as a worldwide trend.

★**THINKING FURTHER:** *Making Conclusions* **Why is urbanization likely to keep growing in Latin America?** *(because industrialization continues to increase.)*

More **CHART WORK**

Refer the class to the chart on this page.

● **How many of the world's five largest cities are in the Americas? Which are they?** *(three; Mexico City; São Paulo in Brazil; New York City)*

● **In what single region are the other two largest cities located?** *(Asia)*

CITIZENSHIP ★

UNDERSTANDING ENVIRONMENTAL CONCERNS To underscore the rain forest's importance, read to students what one botanist said in 1988:

● "It appears likely that no fewer than 1.2 million species, at least a quarter of the biological diversity existing in the mid-1980s, will vanish during this quarter-century or soon thereafter, and that a much higher proportion of the total will follow by the second half of the next century as the remaining forest refuges are decimated."

● Point out that just one of the many unfortunate effects of destroying the rain forest is the loss of plants that may have medicinal value. Today, about one quarter of all the ingredients used in prescription drugs come from the rain forest. It is possible that many more might never be discovered before they are gone forever.

INTO THE FUTURE

Write *NAFTA* on the board.

● **What is NAFTA?** *(It is the North American Free Trade Agreement, signed by the U.S., Canada, and Mexico, to increase trade among these countries by lowering taxes on their goods.)*

★THINKING FURTHER: *Making Conclusions* **Why might nations' lowering taxes on their goods increase trade?** *(Taxes add to the prices of goods—the lower the taxes, the lower the prices and therefore the greater the quantity of goods demanded.)*

Discussing Canadian Provinces
Refer the class to the map on p. 623 and have students locate Canada on it.

● **Europeans from which country originally settled in Canada?** *(France)*

● **How is Quebec different from the rest of Canada?** *(It is rooted in the French language and traditions while the other provinces' roots are British.)*

● **How does this difference threaten Canada's unity?** *(Many French Canadians want Quebec to become a separate country.)*

★THINKING FURTHER: *Making Conclusions* **What might be the consequences of such a split?** *(self-rule for French Canadians, a national economy torn apart, perhaps bad feelings typical of a divided family)*

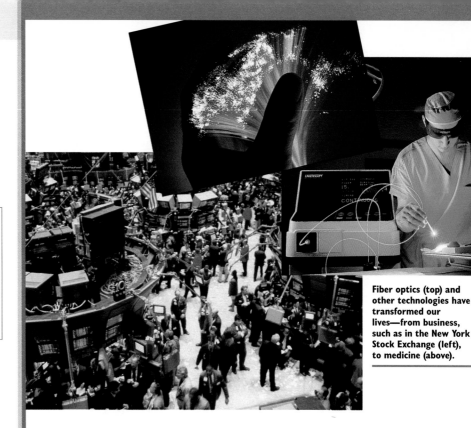

Fiber optics (top) and other technologies have transformed our lives—from business, such as in the New York Stock Exchange (left), to medicine (above).

INTO THE FUTURE

The three largest countries of North America—the United States, Canada, and Mexico, are working to develop strong ties. In 1993 the North American Free Trade Agreement, NAFTA, went into effect. Its goal is to increase trade among these nations.

Canadian Provinces

Canada was originally settled by the French. Today, in the province of Quebec, most people are bilingual—able to speak two languages. The French Canadians speak both French and English, but follow French customs.

Canada's other provinces are mainly rooted in the English language and British traditions. Many French Canadians tried to make Quebec

a separate country in 1995. But after a close vote, Quebec has remained part of Canada.

Many people in Canada have ancestors who were here long before the Europeans. In 1999 the Canadian government plans to create a vast new territory to be known as Nunavut (NUH nuh vut). This territory is for the Inuit, who are native to northern Canada.

World Role for the United States

As the remaining superpower, the United States continues to play an active role in world affairs. In 1991 the United States led an alliance of nations that sent troops to the Persian Gulf region. They forced Iraq to withdraw its troops from neighboring Kuwait. Iraq

626

GLOBAL CONNECTION

FIRST THE EUROPEAN UNION, THEN NAFTA
● The impetus to connect the United States, Canada, and Mexico in NAFTA came to a large degree from observing the European Union (p. 601).
● As North American leaders saw the powerhouse market of 442 million people that the European Union was creating for its members, they wanted to create something similar for northern North America.
● As presently constituted, NAFTA creates an internal market of more than 360 million people.
● Other nations of North America may join at a later time.

CITIZENSHIP★

USING CURRENT EVENTS Explain that the movement to separate Quebec from the rest of Canada is not new.

● In 1976 the Parti Quebecois, which advocated separation from the rest of Canada, won election in Quebec. Its leader, René Levesque, became premier of that province.
● In 1980, Quebec held a referendum to see if its people wanted to separate, but the voters said no. That was not the end, however.
● From time to time, the movement is revived. Call for a research team to check recent *Readers' Guides* to see if it is again in the news. Have the team report to the class on the current status of Quebec's separatist movement.

had invaded Kuwait and wanted to make it part of Iraq.

In the 1990s the United States assisted the United Nations in efforts to bring food to starving citizens in the African country of Somalia. In the last lesson you read about the civil war in Bosnia in the Balkan Peninsula. This war also brought calls for world response. Within the United States these world crises have led to heated debate. Many disagree over what the country's role in world politics should be in the future. Should it continue to act as protector of democracy and human rights as it often did during the Cold War?

New Technologies

As the United States considers its world role, it is undergoing great changes in technology at home. Scientific advances in medicine enable people to live longer, healthier lives. The average person born in the United States in 1900 lived to be only 42 years old. The average person born in this country in 1996 can expect to live more than thirty years longer, reaching 76 years of age.

Space satellites now send information back to Earth. This relay has helped scientists update their knowledge about climate and the environment. Other technological improvements have made it possible for people to communicate instantly. Fax machines and cellular phones bring the world closer together than ever before.

All of these developments are part of an "information revolution" that has changed the way we work, learn, and communicate. A big part of this revolution is the Internet. The Internet is a constantly growing group of interconnected computers around the world.

They are part of an "information superhighway"—new ways for people to share ideas.

The Internet had its start during the Cold War. United States technology experts began connecting government and research computers. They hoped that this link would allow the government to keep running in case of a nuclear attack. The network, which later grew into the Internet, has become one of the most important legacies of the Cold War. Instead of being used in war, it has united people around the world.

Today more than 40 million people from over 160 nations use the Internet. People are able to read the latest news without opening a newspaper. They can "talk" to each other without telephones or shop without going to a store. With access to the Internet, much of the world is no farther than a computer screen away.

Links to CURRENT EVENTS

What's happening now?

With today's computer technology and the help of the Internet, you can find out what is happening around the world right now. You do not need to wait for this evening's news or tomorrow's newspaper. The Internet allows you to read about things right after they happen. You might also have conversations with people from other countries about an event while it is taking place.

Ask your teacher or librarian for help using the Internet to find a news article about something that happened today. Why might it be useful to learn about events while they are happening, rather than after they are over?

627

CURRICULUM CONNECTION

LINKS TO CURRENT EVENTS: WHAT'S HAPPENING NOW? To reinforce the idea of how far-reaching the effects of new technologies are, explain to the class that, in the past, when there was an uprising in a country, one major concern was the control of broadcasting facilities, which controlled the information that did or did not reach the outside world.

- When the student uprising took place in Beijing's Tiananmen Square in 1989, the Chinese government blacked out broadcast coverage of it to prevent the world from seeing what was going on.
- When hard-line Russian communists tried to overthrow Gorbachev in 1991, they took control of the broadcasting facilities.
- Neither the Chinese nor the Russians realized that witnesses of the events were sending faxes and electronic mail throughout the world to describe what was happening.

Discussing World Role for the United States Write on the board: *Policeman to the World.*

- *What are examples of how the U.S. has involved itself in world actions since the end of the Cold War?* (Persian Gulf War, food to Somalia, trying to bring peace to Bosnia)

★THINKING FURTHER: *Making Decisions* **Refer the class to the expression on the board. Ask: Should the U.S. act as policeman to the world today? Why or why not?** (Encourage students to debate this question by first discussing such questions as: What are the costs, in both money and the lives of our fighting men and women? Can we afford these costs and do we want to? What are the costs of not doing it? Do we risk letting small problems grow into bigger more dangerous ones? At the end, have the class try to reach a consensus.)

Exploring New Technologies As you discuss this topic, ask students if they have used any of these new technologies.

- *What is the "information superhighway"?* (It is a new way for people to communicate, by using electronic connectors like fax machines, cellular telephones, and networked computers.)

- *How is the Internet linking people across the world as never before?* (by letting them send and receive information almost instantaneously by computer links)

★THINKING FURTHER: *Predicting* **What predictions can you make for the future of the "information highway"? What new developments do you foresee for it? What effects will it have on our lives—in how we learn, how we do our jobs, how we conduct our personal lives, in how countries deal with one another?** (Encourage any and all predictions, no matter how fanciful. After all, many of the technological developments we now take for granted would have been pure fancy not so many years ago.)

Once again, have students make predictions about the economy of the Americas. Which five American countries will have the highest GDPs? In what order will they rank? Are the Americas more rural than urban or more urban than rural? Have students note their predictions on the board. Then have them sit in fours, with one text opened to each of the following—pp. 602, 611, 620, and this page.

Discussing the Economy of the Americas Give students time to read this page and examine the illustrations.

● *How accurate were your predictions? (Have students compare the list on the board with the GDP graph and the circle graph.)*

● *To what do you attribute these five nations' having the highest GDP? (Students will probably note both size and industrialization for the U.S. and Canada, perhaps size for Brazil, size and industrialization for Argentina, and industrialization and oil for Mexico.)*

● *Are the Americas more rural or more urban? (urban by 72% to 28%)*

● *As you compare the rural/urban split on all four Infographics, does any coincidence strike you? (Europe, Asia, and the Americas have nearly identical percentages of urban over rural, and Africa has nearly identical percentages of rural over urban.)*

● *How much larger is the U.S. GDP than that of the country with the next largest GDP in the world? (nearly 1 2/5 times the GDP of Japan)*

● *Which nations rank third and fourth in GDP in the world? (Germany, France)*

★ THINKING FURTHER: *Making Decisions* **Which of the four economies shown do you think has the most potential for growth? Why?** *(Encourage any response that has a sound reason behind it, for example, Africa because it is currently the lowest but has vast natural resources.)*

Technology CONNECTION

ADVENTURES CD-ROM
Enrich the Infographic with the *Discoveries Time Lines* activity on the Adventures CD-ROM.

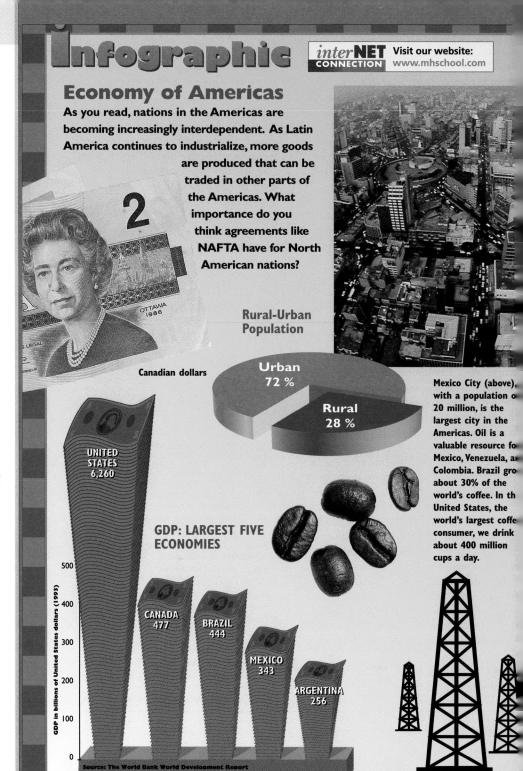

Infographic

interNET CONNECTION · Visit our website: www.mhschool.com

Economy of Americas

As you read, nations in the Americas are becoming increasingly interdependent. As Latin America continues to industrialize, more goods are produced that can be traded in other parts of the Americas. What importance do you think agreements like NAFTA have for North American nations?

Canadian dollars

Rural-Urban Population

Urban 72 %
Rural 28 %

GDP: LARGEST FIVE ECONOMIES

GDP in billions of United States dollars (1993)

UNITED STATES 6,260
CANADA 477
BRAZIL 444
MEXICO 343
ARGENTINA 256

Source: The World Bank World Development Report

Mexico City (above), with a population of 20 million, is the largest city in the Americas. Oil is a valuable resource for Mexico, Venezuela, and Colombia. Brazil grows about 30% of the world's coffee. In the United States, the world's largest coffee consumer, we drink about 400 million cups a day.

EXPANDING THE INFOGRAPHIC

RESEARCHING AND WRITING Refer the class to the map on p. 623 and have students or pairs of students choose a different nation of the Americas that is not among the top GDP producers. As suggested for earlier *Infographics* in this chapter, have students construct an economic profile of the selected country—GDP, per capita GDP, balance of imports and exports, and ratios of televisions and telephones to persons. When the profiles are complete, have a committee assemble the sets of economic profiles for the four lessons in this chapter into a class book entitled "Economies Around the World" and have them add it to the class library. As earlier, suggest that students look for the information they need in the *World Almanac*.

WHY IT MATTERS

Throughout history the world has been shaped by technological, governmental, social, and cultural change. The first agricultural revolution began over 8,000 years ago. People began to build cities and specialize in the work they did. Improvements in agriculture have continued to this day. Crops like wheat, rice, corn, and potatoes were once grown in only small parts of the world. Today these crops are grown around the globe, helping to feed millions of people.

The world's urban revolution began in places like ancient Catal Huyuk. It eventually led to the creation of large, modern cities like New York City and Buenos Aires. Political revolutions of the past few centuries brought greater democracy and sometimes, losses of freedom. The Industrial Revolution began in Britain in the 1700s. It is continuing today, reaching some parts of the world for the first time.

New technological advances continue to change the ways people live. Today the world has only just begun a new "information revolution." These advances build on earlier inventions of paper and printed books. Many everyday objects in our lives may become old-fashioned in the twenty-first century. Some people believe books and newspapers could be replaced by computers. What do you think?

It is possible that you—as a future inventor, teacher, or leader in business or government—will help influence future change. In doing so you can change history and the world.

Many students of today will become the leaders of tomorrow.

✓ Reviewing Facts and Ideas

MAIN IDEAS

- Industrial growth after World War II resulted in job opportunities and overcrowded cities in Latin America.
- Democratic governments have replaced dictators throughout much of Latin America.
- The North American Free Trade Agreement (NAFTA) went into effect in 1993.
- A powerful "information revolution" now links people around the world.

THINK ABOUT IT

1. What was one way the Brazilian government tried to solve the problems of urbanization? What problems have resulted?

2. What has been the United States' role in recent world events?

3. **FOCUS** In what ways are nations of the Americas interdependent?

4. **THINKING SKILL** Make and support at least two _conclusions_ about how life in the Americas has changed since World War II.

5. **GEOGRAPHY** How has the Internet affected the movement of ideas in the world?

Discussing WHY IT MATTERS Encourage students to look to the future.

> ★**THINKING FURTHER:** _Summarizing_ **How would you summarize the major revolutions that have shaped our world?** _(agricultural, urban, political, industrial, information)_

MAIN IDEAS
Call on students to answer.

- _**What effects did industrial growth have on Latin America after World War II?**_ _(greater job opportunities, overcrowded cities)_

- _**How has government changed in Latin America in recent years?**_ _(replacement of some dictatorships with democracies)_

- _**What is the aim of NAFTA?**_ _(free trade among the U.S., Canada, and Mexico)_

- _**What effect is the "information revolution" having on the world?**_ _(It is linking people as never before through communication.)_

EVALUATE
✓ **Answers to Think About It**

1. Opening up the Amazon rain forest for work and housing; destruction of an entire environment
Cause and Effect

2. It has involved itself in humanitarian aid, war, and peace-making.
Make Inferences

3. They rely on other nations in the Americas for raw materials to produce goods and for markets to sell goods. _Form Generalizations_

4. Conclusions will probably include greater industrialization, urbanization, democratization, communication, and interdependence.
Make Conclusions

5. It has made possible nearly instantaneous communication.
Five Themes of Geography: Movement

Write About It Ask students to write a paragraph in which they make three wishes for the world—three things they would like to happen on Earth in the future.

Lesson Objective
★ Analyze why nations need to cooperate with one another to protect the
environment.

Identifying the Issue Help students
understand that nations often have different views on problems and solutions
concerning the environment.

● **What are some of the environmental issues that nations are working
on individually?** (reducing pollution,
protecting endangered species, reducing soil erosion and flooding)

● **What is one environmental concern
that is considered a serious issue
for all nations?** (the buildup of
gases, which causes global warming)

**Discussing Three Different View-
points** Give students time to read the
viewpoints on p. 631.

<hr>

SMRUTI KOPPIKAR

● **What does Koppikar believe needs
to stop in order to properly address environmental problems
worldwide?** (the finger-pointing between nations)

● **What does Koppikar see as an important factor in how a nation
views environmental problems?**
(the health of its economy and the
availability of jobs for its people)

<hr>

ADAM RIVAS WYZKOWSKI

● **According to Wyzkowski, what
problems do Venezuelans place
ahead of environmental protection?** (jobs and education)

● **What does Wyzkowski think needs
to change among the attitudes of
Venezuelans?** (Environmental problems need to become equal in importance to other problems.)

CITIZENSHIP
VIEWPOINT

In 1997, at the
Earth Summit II
in New York,
delegates from
around the world
met to discuss
important
environmental
issues.

How should nations work together to protect the environment?

Today, the nations of the world face many threats to the
environment. Some nations are trying to clean up pollution and
protect endangered species. Others are working to reduce soil
erosion and flooding due to the loss of forests. Many nations
consider global warming, the buildup of gases that is causing
Earth's climate to slowly change, to be a serious issue worldwide.

At the 1992 Earth Summit in Rio de Janeiro, Brazil, delegates
from all over the world met to discuss these and other
environmental issues. Then, in 1997, Earth Summit II was held at
the United Nations in New York City. They agreed that international
cooperation is needed to solve many of these problems. However,
finding a way to cooperate is difficult because nations often blame
each other for the pollution. Also, the leaders of some nations see
cleaning up the environment as a luxury they cannot afford. They
say finding jobs for their citizens must come first. Many poorer
nations need the help of industrialized countries in developing
technology that can reduce pollution. Consider these viewpoints on
this issue and answer the questions that follow.

630

<hr>

ABOUT THE EARTH SUMMIT OF 1992 One of the major issues during
the Earth Summit was the differing views between the already industrialized countries and the developing countries.

● Some delegates felt that industrial nations, which had been free of
environmental regulations when they built their own industries, were
insisting that developing nations operate under a strict new set of
rules when building their industries. Developing countries argued that
industrial nations should help them pay the cost of environmental
protection, especially since industrial nations were responsible for
causing many of the problems in the first place.

● Nonetheless, despite serious conflicts, delegates from 178 countries
arrived at agreement on some of the issues, including forest preser-
vation.

Three DIFFERENT Viewpoints

1 SMRUTI KOPPIKAR
Journalist, India
Excerpt from interview, 1997

Right now nations are blaming each other for our environmental problems. This finger-pointing has to stop. Each nation has its own needs and priorities. If your stomach is full and your economy is growing, you look at problems in one way. In my country, India, environment is an issue of livelihood. . . . We have to find common ground.

"Each nation has its own needs . . . "

2 ADAM RIVAS WYZYKOWSKI
Teacher, Venezuela
Excerpt from interview, 1997

We must first change the way Venezuelans think about the environment. Cleaning up the environment must become a high priority, because right now we have other problems we consider more important such as jobs and education. We must get people to think of the environment as a serious problem equal in importance to other problems.

"Cleaning up the environment must become a high priority . . . "

3 EVELYN TENG
Government worker, Malaysia
Excerpt from interview, 1997

Countries like Malaysia don't have the money to develop the clean and green technologies that industrial nations already have. We need cooperation between richer and poorer nations to exchange information and share technologies that will help us run our factories without hurting our environment. Without cooperation, it's a lose-lose situation for all nations. . . . Everyone has to work together.

"We need cooperation between richer and poorer nations . . . "

BUILDING CITIZENSHIP

1. What is the viewpoint of each person?
2. In what ways are some of the viewpoints alike? In what ways are they different? What might be the reasons each person has his or her viewpoint on this issue?
3. What other viewpoints might people have on global cooperation concerning the environment?

SHARING VIEWPOINTS

Discuss what you agree with or disagree with about these viewpoints. Discuss why you think the speakers might feel as they do. Then as a class, write two statements that all of you can agree with about global cooperation on environmental issues.

631

CITIZENSHIP ★

UNDERSTANDING GOVERNMENT The need for environmental protection is a subject of constant controversy in the United States.

- Under a 1906 law, the Federal government is allowed to set aside land for national monuments and parks and to forbid development in these areas.

- In some cases, however, Federal agencies will disagree among themselves about the wisdom of restricting development. For example, the Bureau of Land Management may regard development of a wilderness area as a positive step, while the Fish and Wildlife Service may fight for conservation.

Ask students to choose a national park or monument and to research its inception. What conflicts, if any, surrounded its creation and its continued existence?

- **What does Teng say that poor and rich nations need to do?** *(They need to exchange information and share technologies.)*

- **What do you think Teng means by "clean and green technologies"?** *(technologies that don't cause pollution or harm the environment)*

SUM IT UP
Ask students to list at least three ways that nations can work together to solve environmental problems.

EVALUATE
✓ **Answers to Building Citizenship**

1. Koppikar: There must be respect for each nation's own needs and priorities. Wyzkowski: Venezuelans must see the environment as a high priority. Teng: Rich nations should share their knowledge and technology.

2. All viewpoints reflect the opinion that each nation has its own problems that may conflict with protecting the environment. The viewpoints differ in what they consider those problems to be. Each point of view is most likely shaped by the individual's own concerns and the problems of his or her country.

3. Students may want to research the issue in newspapers, magazines, or on the Internet. Some feel, for example, that national interests must come before global cooperation.

Sharing Viewpoints Agreed-upon statements might include: 1) There should be consideration of each nation's unique concerns. 2) Industrial nations need to help developing nations achieve environmental protection.

Debating Viewpoints Remind students that disagreement can exist within a country as well as among different countries. For example, environmentalists and loggers have long disagreed about the necessity of protecting the spotted owl's habitat in the American northwest. Ask students to research this issue and debate the pros and cons of protecting the spotted owl.

Answers to
THINKING ABOUT VOCABULARY

1. T

2. F, NAFTA is an agreement signed by the U.S., Canada, and Mexico to increase trade among the three countries.

3. T

4. F, A person able to speak two languages is bilingual.

5. T

6. T

7. T

8. F, Sanctions are penalties other nations place against a nation to make it change its policies.

9. F, Interdependent means that nations count on one another to meet needs and wants of their peoples.

10. T

Answers to
THINKING ABOUT FACTS

1. Communism lost its hold on Hungary, Poland, East Germany, Czechoslovakia, and Romania.

2. They ended apartheid and held elections in which both black and white South Africans could vote, bringing blacks into major government positions.

3. a 1-million-student protest for democracy in China, which was crushed by the government

4. As freely elected president of Haiti, he was first overthrown by the military but restored to office in 1994.

5. late 1991, brought on by the collapse of the Soviet Union; expanded democracy, German reunification, greater unity among nations through the European Union

Resource REMINDER

Practice and Project Book: p. 123

Assessment Book: Chapter 20 Test

Technology: Videodisc

Transparency: Graphic Organizer, Main-Idea Map

CHAPTER 20 REVIEW

THINKING ABOUT VOCABULARY

Each of the following statements contains an underlined vocabulary word. Number a sheet of paper from 1 to 10. Beside each number write **T** if the statement is true and **F** if the statement is false. If the statement is false, rewrite the sentence using the vocabulary word correctly.

1. The Pacific Rim is the ring of countries that surrounds the Pacific Ocean.

2. NAFTA is a military alliance that involves European nations.

3. The crowded areas inside or near cities in South Africa where many blacks live are called townships.

4. A person unable to speak more than one language is bilingual.

5. Ethnic groups have a language, customs, and a heritage in common.

6. The Internet is a constantly expanding network of interconnected computers around the world.

7. The system of laws once used to keep the races separate in South Africa was called apartheid.

8. Sanctions are trade agreements that countries make with each other.

9. Interdependent means having the ability to stand alone without getting help from other countries.

10. The amount of money each person would have if a country's total income was divided evenly among its people is called per capita income.

THINKING ABOUT FACTS

1. Why was 1989 considered a "Year of Miracles" in Europe?

2. How did Nelson Mandela and F.W. de Klerk transform South Africa in the first half of the 1990s?

3. What events took place at Tiananmen Square in June of 1989?

4. Who is Jean-Bertrand Aristide? What has his role been in Haiti since 1990?

5. When did the Cold War end? What helped to bring about the end? How did Europe change as a result?

6. Why did Gorbachev feel that glasnost would be an important part of rebuilding the Soviet Union's economy?

7. What are some of the economic and political problems that South Africans face now that apartheid has been abolished?

8. What changes have taken place in China under the leadership of Deng Xiaoping?

9. What did people in Hong Kong fear would happen when China took control in 1997?

10. How does NAFTA affect North American trade? How does it affect the ties between the United States, Mexico, and Canada?

632

SECOND-LANGUAGE SUPPORT

DEBATE Have second-language learners work with a partner or in a small group to make a chart comparing the "Good News" and the "Bad News" about any of the important changes that are described in this chapter. Then have student groups compare their lists and defend their decisions about events.

RESPONSE JOURNAL Encourage students to write in their response journals about how changes in the world over the last few years have affected their own lives or lives of people they know about. If students have no personal knowledge on this topic, ask them to find *Zlata's Diary* in the library, read a section, and respond in their journals.

THINK AND WRITE ◀ ▭▶

WRITING A JOURNAL ENTRY

Suppose you were a Russian living in Moscow in 1990. Write a journal entry about the changes taking place as the Soviet Union collapses and moves toward democracy.

WRITING A PAMPHLET

Write a pamphlet about Nelson Mandela. Describe his early work for the African National Congress. Tell about his arrest, imprisonment, and release. Then describe his election as the first president of South Africa.

WRITING ON THE INTERNET

Suppose you could send a message on the Internet to thousands of students around the world. Write a message and two answers you might receive from South America, Africa, the Middle East, or East Asia.

APPLYING THINKING SKILLS

EVALUATING INFORMATION FOR ACCURACY

1. What does evaluating information for accuracy mean?

2. Compare this skill with the skill of analyzing the credibility of a source you learned in Chapter 16 on pages 472–473. How are they similar? How are they different?

3. Choose an article from a national news magazine or newspaper. What are some of the things that had to be evaluated before the information was printed?

4. Review the account of the Vietnamese worker's conditions under the French, quoted on page 587. How would you go about evaluating this source for accuracy?

5. Why is evaluating information for accuracy important for the study of history?

Summing Up the Chapter

Copy the main idea map below on a separate sheet of paper. Review the chapter for information to complete the map. When you have filled in the main idea map, use the information to answer the question "What important changes have taken place in the world recently?"

Changes in Europe
- Fall of Communism
- Organization of European Union
- Ethnic war in Bosnia

Changes in the Pacific Rim
- Industrializing in Japan
- Growth of Pacific Rim economies
- Demonstrations for democracy in China

MAIN IDEA
Around the world the old is giving way to the new.

Changes in the Americas
- Urbanization in Latin America
- Signing of NAFTA
- Development of new technologies

Changes in Africa
- Free elections in South Africa
- Apartheid ends in South Africa
- Organization of South African Development Community

633

SUGGESTIONS FOR SUMMING UP THE CHAPTER

After students have copied the spider chart on a piece of paper, have them read its main idea aloud. Let them know that there has been more change in the period they have just studied than in any other period in the history of the world—and THEY WERE THERE!, at least for part of it. Spend a few minutes going over the categories—pointing out that they correspond to the lessons in the chapter—and discuss the answers already filled in, to give them a better sense of what they should look for to complete the chart. If necessary, you may want to give them a few more clues from the answers reproduced on the pupil page above. When they have completed their charts, you may want to have them answer the question posed aloud or in writing. In either case, have them choose the changes they consider most important and give the reasons for their choices.

ASSESSING THINK AND WRITE: *For performance assessment, see Assessment Book, Chapter 20, pp. T107–T110.*

6. He believed the freedom to speak freely would give the people who best knew how to rebuild the economy the chance to give their input.

7. overcoming economic poverty with its attendant problems of poor housing and education; developing a truly democratic government in which all citizens know their rights and responsibilities

8. movement away from strict communism, with some individual economic freedom; encouragement of study abroad; increased international trade

9. that their democracy would be restricted and their laws and free enterprise system interfered with

10. It lowers taxes on goods both imported and exported; it strengthens economic ties among the three nations.

Answers to APPLYING THINKING SKILLS

1. judging information about whether it is true or untrue

2. Evaluating information for accuracy involves all the steps that analyzing the credibility of a source does and in addition calls for the comparison of one source with another on the same subject.

3. The answers to Who? What? When? Where? Why? and perhaps How? all had to be evaluated, as did any other factual information included.

4. Perhaps first identify the farmer's point of view as that of someone who feels victimized, recognize that he has firsthand knowledge, compare what he says with a source that records wage and price information of the time, and then make an evaluation based on all this.

5. Because the study of history is a search for truth about the past, being able to distinguish truth from untruth is crucial to it.

Technology CONNECTION

VIDEODISC

Enrich Chapter 20 with *The Information Revolution* on the Videodisc.

Search Frame 22911, Play To 24016 Side B

Answers to
THINKING ABOUT VOCABULARY

1. urbanization
2. European Union
3. warlords
4. Middle East
5. sanctions
6. concentration camp
7. armistice
8. Zionism
9. communism
10. strike

Suggestions for
THINK AND WRITE

1. Have students first write their two or three choices on a piece of paper. Then have them review what they have learned about each and note under each his/her major accomplishments and qualities worthy of admiration. When students have written their essays based on these notes, have some presented in class and have students choose a Class Hall of Fame including the most popular figures.

2. Perspectives should locate where Sarajevo is in Europe and identify it as an area that different empires have claimed over time and where several often unfriendly ethnic groups were once lumped together as one nation.

3. Urge students to begin by creating a very strong and detailed picture of their subjects in their minds. What do they find most intriguing about them? Encourage them to base their interview questions on this question and then write their answers, in character.

Suggestions for
BUILDING SKILLS

1. Answers will depend on the time zone of your area.

2. That person has crossed the International Date Line heading east, which means he/she has to count back a day in time.

3. Answers will depend on the cartoons students find and will reflect how recognizable the symbols are and how clearly they convey a political opinion.

4. Cartoons should make as much use of symbols as possible and present a simple enough idea to be conveyed by a cartoon.

UNIT 6 REVIEW

THINKING ABOUT VOCABULARY
Number a sheet of paper from 1 to 10. Beside each number write the word or term from the list below that matches the statement.

armistice	sanctions
communism	strike
concentration camp	urbanization
European Union	warlords
Middle East	Zionism

1. The growth of cities
2. An organization of western European nations working to build a common economy in Europe
3. Local military leaders in China who took advantage of political unrest in the early 1900s to seize power in their regions
4. The region between the Mediterranean Sea and the western borders of Pakistan and Afghanistan
5. Penalties placed on a nation to make it change its behavior
6. A camp where people are imprisoned because of their heritage, religious beliefs, or political views
7. An agreement to stop fighting
8. The movement to establish a Jewish homeland or nation
9. A political system in which the government owns everything in name of the workers
10. The refusal to work in protest of unfair treatment

THINK AND WRITE

WRITING AN ESSAY
Write a short essay about two or three people in the twentieth century you most admire. Describe what they accomplished and what you admire about them.

634

WRITING ABOUT PERSPECTIVES
The Bosnian city of Sarajevo has been at the center of conflict more than once in this century. In 1914 the assassination there of the Austrian archduke Franz Ferdinand was the spark that ignited World War I. In the 1990s the war raging between ethnic groups in the nation hit the city particularly hard. Write about the two conflicts and the links, if any, between them.

WRITING AN INTERVIEW
Choose two leaders from wars in the twentieth century. Write questions you would ask them if you could interview them. Then write the responses they might have given.

BUILDING SKILLS

1. **Time zone maps** Look at the time zone map on page 548. When it is noon where you live, what time is it in Honolulu? Montreal? Rome? Bombay? Hong Kong?

2. **Time zone maps** Explain why it is possible for somebody to fly from Tokyo on May 2 and arrive in the United States on May 1?

3. **Political cartoons** Find a political cartoon in a newspaper or news magazine. Explain what it means. How does the cartoon make its point?

4. **Political cartoons** Choose a political event that you read about in this book. Then make a political cartoon about the event. Draw simple stick figures if you like and use words to fill out the meaning of the cartoon.

5. **Evaluating information** Choose an article from a newspaper, magazine, or newsletter or take a passage from a book. How would you evaluate the information you find there for its accuracy?

ONGOING UNIT PROJECT

OPTIONS FOR ASSESSMENT
This ongoing project, begun on page 520D, can be part of your assessment program, along with other forms of evaluation.

PLANNING Inform children that their drawings should show an important idea about conflict and/or cooperation learned in each lesson.

SIGNS OF SUCCESS

• Children's drawings and narrations should reflect a major change presented in each lesson. For example, in Chapter 18, narration should show the relationship between World War I and World War II.

• Group members should work well together to select and arrange drawings in sequence telling a story of a century of change.

• Narration should carefully match or reinforce the images on screen.

 FOR THE PORTFOLIO Individual drawings can be placed in each child's portfolio.

YESTERDAY, TODAY &
TOMORROW

The United Nations was created at the end of World War II to promote peace and help countries develop. In 1995 the UN celebrated its 50th anniversary. What role do you think the United Nations will play in the next 50 years? Do you think the United Nations should be doing more? If so, what?

READING ON YOUR OWN

These are some books you might find at the library to help you learn more.

BEHIND THE SECRET WINDOW
by Nelly Toll
This book reveals the memories and paintings of a young Jewish girl in hiding during World War.

GANDHI
by Nigel Hunter
This brief biography of Ghandi is accompanied by colorful photos.

NELSON MANDELA: DETERMINED TO BE FREE
by Jack L. Roberts
This biography describes the man who struggled against apartheid and became South Africa's first black president.

5. Evaluations should reflect identification of the author's point of view, determination of credibility, and comparison with credible sources on the same subject.

Suggestions for
YESTERDAY, TODAY & TOMORROW

Help students to identify UN accomplishments in its first 50 years—its work with refugees, UNICEF, the World Health Organization, the World Court, UN peacekeeping efforts in world trouble spots, UN opposition to North Korea's invasion of South Korea, for example. To answer what its future role may be and what, if anything, it should be doing more of, have students identify current world problems and discuss what actions the UN might take to deal with them.

Suggestions for
READING ON YOUR OWN

World War II seems to hold a certain fascination for many young people these days, so the first two books listed here should generate real reading interest. Try to have them available in class as well as the books included in the *Annotated Bibliography and Resources* on page 520B, in the Unit Organizer. Also have a library search team go to the library to find and bring back additional books for young people on World War II. You may want to have students prepare dramatic readings from the eyewitness accounts included in *A Child's War: World War II Through the Eyes of Children* and then hold a discussion of that war by all those students who have read a book on it. Other students might concentrate on the inspiring Mandela biography or other biographies of this unit's figures that the library provides. Have them mount a discussion for the class too.

UNIT 6 REVIEW PROJECT

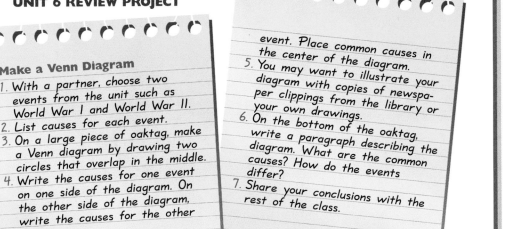

Make a Venn Diagram

1. With a partner, choose two events from the unit such as World War I and World War II.
2. List causes for each event.
3. On a large piece of oaktag, make a Venn diagram by drawing two circles that overlap in the middle.
4. Write the causes for one event on one side of the diagram. On the other side of the diagram, write the causes for the other event. Place common causes in the center of the diagram.
5. You may want to illustrate your diagram with copies of newspaper clippings from the library or your own drawings.
6. On the bottom of the oaktag, write a paragraph describing the diagram. What are the common causes? How do the events differ?
7. Share your conclusions with the rest of the class.

Venn Diagram

World War I — An attack on Austria–Hungry leader Franz Ferdinand

nationalism / alliances / attacks on American people

World War II — propoganda from Germany's leader Adolf Hitler / a depression / the treaty of Versailles

Comparing Causes of World Wars

635

UNIT 6 REVIEW PROJECT *Make a Venn Diagram*

COMPLETING THE DIAGRAM

 GROUP — 15 TO 30 MINUTES

OBJECTIVE: Making a Venn diagram will encourage students to return to the text and to apply analytical skills to what they have learned in the unit.

MATERIALS: oaktag

• Have students pair up with partners.

• Instruct partner pairs to choose two events from the unit. One partner might list the causes for each event before the two work together to decide which causes apply to both events and which to only one.

• Review how to make a Venn diagram. Provide each pair a sheet of oaktag. Instruct students to make and fill in their diagrams, illustrate them with newspaper clippings or original drawings, and write a paragraph explaining respective types of causes.

• Schedule class time for sharing diagrams and paragraphs.

 FOR THE PORTFOLIO Students may include copies of their paragraphs in their portfolios.

OPTIONS FOR ASSESSMENT

This project can be part of your assessment program.

For more performance assessment and portfolio opportunities, see Assessment Book, Unit 6, p. T110.

REFERENCE SECTION

The Reference Section has many parts,
each with a different type of information.
Use this section to look up people,
places, and events as you study.

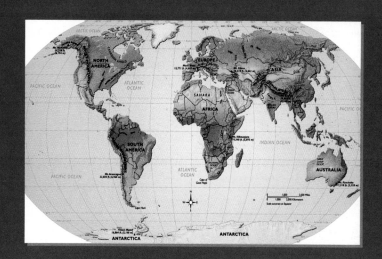

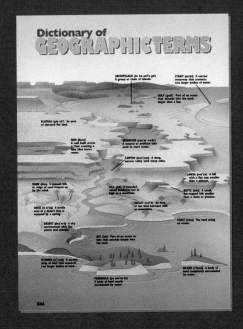

Atlas

An atlas is a collection of maps. An atlas

can be a book or a separate section

within a book. This Atlas is a separate

section with maps to help you study

the history and geography

presented in this book.

MAP BUILDER
The World: Climate and Population

The map on the facing page is a special kind of map. Each transparent overlay shows a different aspect of the world's climate and population. You can see where in the world similar climates exist and how climates relate to latitude. You can also compare population density around the world and see in which climates people live. Start by lifting all of the transparent overlays and observe the base map of the continents and oceans of the world. Then cover the base map with the first overlay and study the climates shown. In which climate do you live?

Allow the second overlay to cover the first and consider how climates are related to latitude. What latitude lines divide the zones shown? What kinds of climates are generally found nearest the equator? Finally, let down the third overlay and compare population densities around the world. Which areas of North America are the most densely populated? In which climates do the fewest people live?

R4

The World: Climates

GROUP

15 TO 30 MINUTES

HOW ARE THEY DIFFERENT? HOW ARE THEY ALIKE?
Objective: To practice reading climate maps.

1. Refer the class to the climate key and give them time to match the map colors to it. Point out how climate regions fall in bands around the world.

2. Ask questions calling for differences and similarities in climate regions—for example, "How are climate regions near a pole different from those near the equator?" "How are climate regions of much of Europe like those of the eastern United States?" Ask students to make up and offer such questions too.

GROUP

30 MINUT OR LONG

HAVE A NICE VACATION
Objective: To recognize traits of climate regions.

Materials: paper, pens, crayons or colored pencils, travel pictures, glue

1. Divide the class into six groups and assign each group one of the regions in the climate key.

2. Tell each group to prepare a travel brochure for a vacation in that region. Invite groups to draw or gather pictures showing scenes from their region and to brainstorm things that would be fun to do there.

3. Have the groups write and illustrate their vacation brochures and present them to the class.

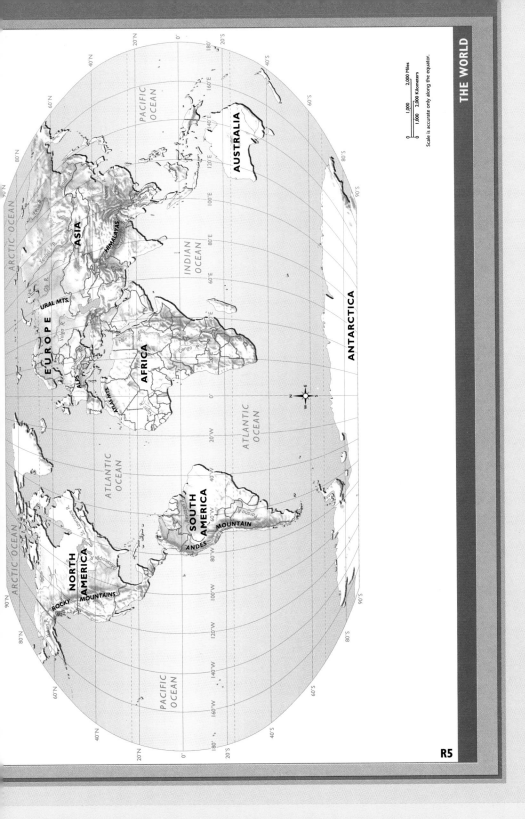

THE WORLD

0   1,000   2,000 Miles
0   1,000   2,000 Kilometers
Scale is accurate only along the equator.

ARCTIC OCEAN

PACIFIC
OCEAN

ASIA

HIMALAYAS

EUROPE

URAL MTS.

ALPS

ATLAS MTS.

AFRICA

INDIAN
OCEAN

AUSTRALIA

ANTARCTICA

ATLANTIC
OCEAN

ATLANTIC
OCEAN

SOUTH
AMERICA

MOUNTAIN

ANDES

NORTH
AMERICA

ROCKY   MOUNTAINS

PACIFIC
OCEAN

ARCTIC OCEAN

R5

The World: Population

MOST POPULOUS, LEAST POPULOUS

Objective: To practice reading population maps.

Materials: paper, pencil

1. Refer the class to the population map key and have them identify examples of each symbol on the map.

2. Have students write two headings on a piece of paper—MOST POPULOUS, LEAST POPULOUS. Under the appropriate heading have them list the three most populous areas of the world, by area of continent—for example, Eastern Asia—and three of the least populous.

3. Call on students to compare and discuss their lists.

RELATE DENSITY TO CLIMATE

Objective: To relate population and climate.

Materials: paper, pencil

1. Tell students to choose a most or least populous area of the world and then identify the climate region/regions it occupies.

2. Have them write a paragraph in which they identify their chosen area, describe its climate or climates, and then explain the role that climate probably plays in helping to make it heavily or lightly populated.

3. Call on students to read their paragraphs in class and invite other students' comments on their reasoning.

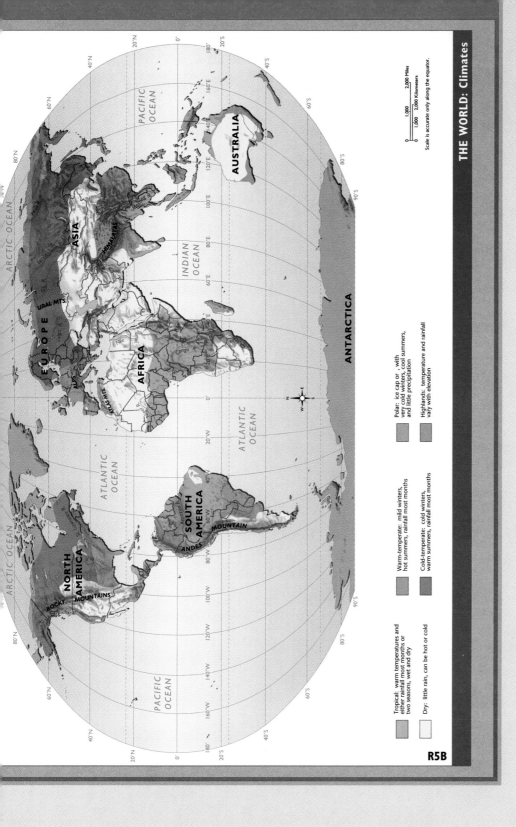

THE WORLD: Climates

R5B

Tropical: warm temperatures and either rainfall most months or two seasons, wet and dry

Dry: little rain, can be hot or cold

Warm-temperate: mild winters, hot summers, rainfall most months

Cold-temperate: cold winters, warm summers, rainfall most months

Polar: ice cap or , with very cold winters, cool summers, and little precipitation

Highlands: temperature and rainfall vary with elevation

0   1,000   2,000 Miles
0   1,000   2,000 Kilometers
Scale is accurate only along the equator.

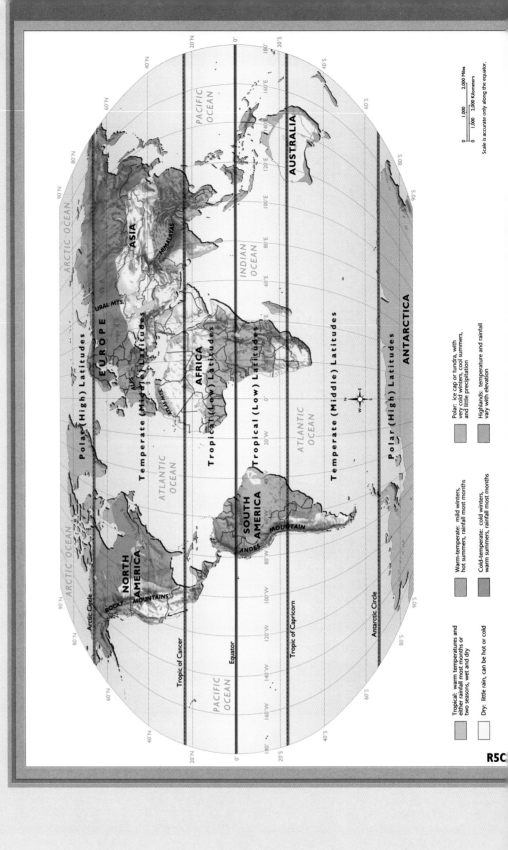

Tropical: warm temperatures and either rainfall most months or two seasons, wet and dry

Dry: little rain, can be hot or cold

Warm-temperate: mild winters, hot summers, rainfall most months

Cold-temperate: cold winters, warm summers, rainfall most months

Polar: ice cap or tundra, with very cold winters, cool summers, and little precipitation

Highlands: temperature and rainfall vary with elevation

Scale is accurate only along the equator.

0   1,000   2,000 Miles
0   1,000   2,000 Kilometers

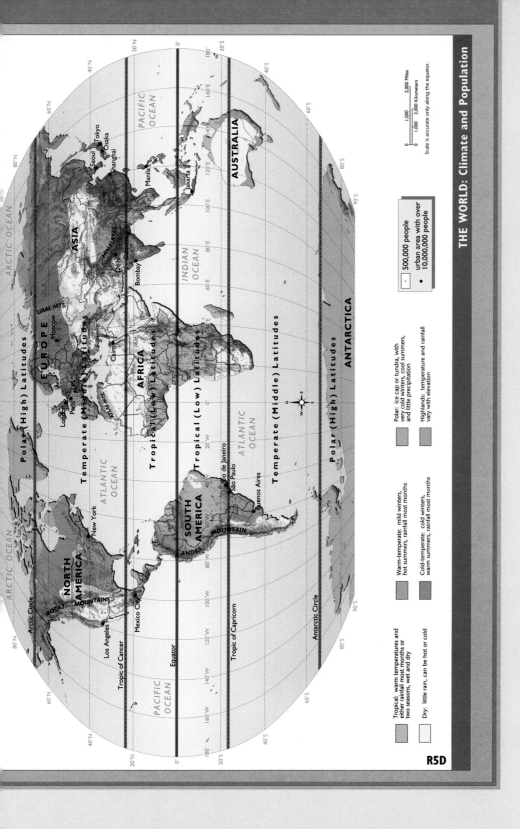

THE WORLD: Climate and Population

Tropical: warm temperatures and either rainfall most months or two seasons, wet and dry

Dry: little rain, can be hot or cold

Warm-temperate: mild winters, hot summers, rainfall most months

Cold-temperate: cold winters, warm summers, rainfall most months

Polar: ice cap or tundra, with very cold winters, cool summers, and little precipitation

Highlands: temperature and rainfall vary with elevation

500,000 people

urban area with over 10,000,000 people

0   1,000   2,000 Miles

0   1,000   2,000 Kilometers

Scale is accurate only along the equator.

R5D

EUROPE: Political

ASIA

RUSSIA

UKRAINE

Legend:
- National capital
- Other city

0   250   500 Miles
0   250   500 Kilometers

R6

Europe: Political Map

FIND THE CAPITAL

Objective: To locate and identify national capitals.

Students can use the European political map to play a guessing game based on geographic clues.

1. The game begins when one students says, "I am thinking of a national capital in [southwestern Europe]."

2. To narrow the choices, students might ask, "Does it lie near a major body of water or does it lie far inland?" "Is it south of the Bay of Biscay?"

3. The student who guesses correctly gives a clue to a new mystery capital and answers questions about it.

USE THE GRID

Objective: To locate political boundaries by latitude and longitude.

Materials: pencils, paper

1. Have each group choose three countries in Europe and use the map grid to estimate roughly each country's political borders by latitude and longitude.

2. Have them list the three grid locations on a piece of paper with a blank space following each. Then have them exchange their lists with another group.

3. Challenge the groups to use the map here to fill in the countries that fit the locations they received.

EUROPE: Physical

R7

Europe: Physical Map

NATURAL BOUNDARIES/POLITICAL BORDERS

Objective: To compare physical and political maps.

Students can use the two European maps to identify cases in which natural boundaries—like water or mountains—create political borders.

1. Have each pair of students compare the two maps to locate one case where a natural boundary also serves as the political border between two or more countries or forms most or all of one country's political borders.

2. Have each pair write a paragraph describing the case they have found, naming the natural boundary and the borders it creates.

3. Invite the partners to present their cases in class.

MAKE A JIGSAW PUZZLE

GROUP

Objective: To map and locate major landforms of Europe.

Materials: construction paper, pencils, scissors

30 MINUTES OR LONGER

1. Have each group draw an outline of this physical map of Europe and label the following by name: peninsulas, major islands, mountain ranges, major plains areas.

2. Have them cut their maps apart, jigsaw fashion, around the named geographic features. The groups should then exchange sets of puzzle pieces.

3. At the call of "Go," have each group work against the clock to reassemble Europe. The group that completes the task correctly in the best time wins.

AFRICA: Political

Africa: Political Map

LOCATE PORT CAPITALS
Objective: To link city importance to port location.

Materials: paper, pencil

1. Direct students to the map legend and have them identify the symbol for national capitals.

2. Have students examine the map to locate national capitals that are ports on major bodies of water.

3. Call on students to identify national capitals and their countries. As they identify each, have students list the capitals and their countries on a piece of paper. When they complete their lists, have them discuss why they suppose so many national capitals in Africa are port cities.

SET UP AN ITINERARY
Objective: To trace routes and measure distance.

Materials: outline map of Africa, pencil, paper

1. Invite students to choose three cities/countries in Africa that they would like to visit.

2. Have them list their cities/countries on a piece of paper and exchange papers with a partner.

3. Invite students to locate and label their partners' choices on the outline map of Africa, draw the land or sea route they would use to get from one place to the next, and use the map scale to list the distance covered on each leg of the trip.

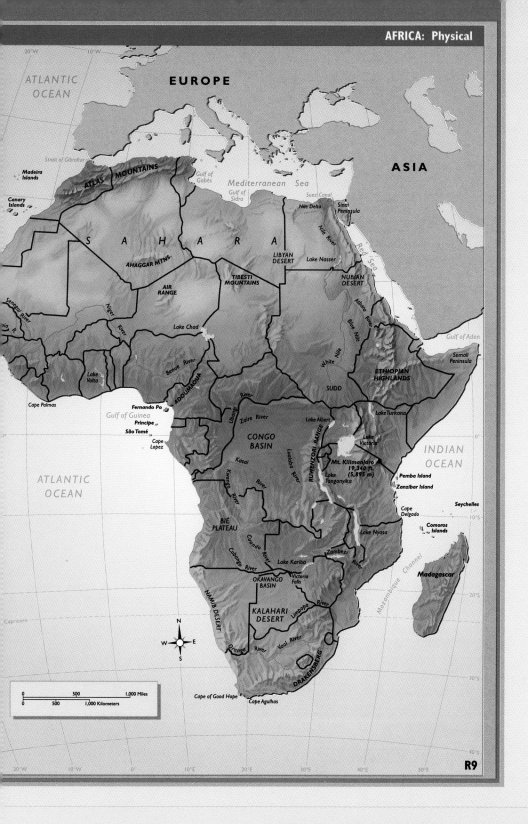

AFRICA: Physical

EUROPE

ASIA

ATLANTIC OCEAN

Strait of Gibraltar

Madeira Islands

Canary Islands

ATLAS MOUNTAINS

Gulf of Gabès

Mediterranean Sea

Gulf of Sidra

Suez Canal

Nile Delta

Sinai Peninsula

Red Sea

S A H A R A

AHAGGAR MTNS.

LIBYAN DESERT

Lake Nasser

TIBESTI MOUNTAINS

AIR RANGE

NUBIAN DESERT

Senegal River

Niger River

Lake Chad

Benue River

Atbara River

Blue Nile

White Nile

ETHIOPIAN HIGHLANDS

Gulf of Aden

Somali Peninsula

Cape Palmas

Gulf of Guinea

Fernando Po

Príncipe

São Tomé

Cape Lopez

Lake Volta

ADOUMAOUA

Ubangi

Zaire River

CONGO BASIN

Kasai

Kwango River

River

Lualaba River

RUWENZORI RANGE

SUDD

Lake Albert

Lake Turkana

Lake Victoria

Mt. Kilimanjaro 19,340 ft. (5,895 m)

Lake Tanganyika

Pemba Island

Zanzibar Island

INDIAN OCEAN

ATLANTIC OCEAN

BIÉ PLATEAU

Cuando River

Cubango River

Lake Kariba

Zambezi River

Victoria Falls

OKAVANGO BASIN

Lake Nyasa

Cape Delgado

Comoros Islands

Seychelles

Mozambique Channel

Madagascar

NAMIB DESERT

KALAHARI DESERT

Limpopo River

Orange River

Vaal River

DRAKENSBERG

Capricorn

N W E S

0°

10°S

20°S

30°S

40°S

Cape of Good Hope

Cape Agulhas

0 500 1,000 Miles
0 500 1,000 Kilometers

20°W 10°W 0° 10°E 20°E 30°E 40°E 50°E

R9

Africa: Physical Map

PLEASE SEND HELP!

Objective: To identify places based on geographic clues.

Materials: paper, pencil

1. Have students examine the physical map of Africa and picture themselves in a downed plane somewhere on it.

2. Have them write a description of their location based on clues on the map: for example, "I'm on a peninsula facing the Indian Ocean, near the equator."

3. Students should look for the location on the physical map and then find the country at that location on the political map. The student who identifies the country correctly reads the description of his or her location.

WHERE AM I GOING?

Objective: To trace a route based on geographic clues.

Materials: paper, pencil

1. Have each student choose one geographic feature in Africa as a starting point for an overland expedition and another as the ending point.

2. Have students write the names of these locations—for example, "Atlas Mountains/Cape of Good Hope"—on a piece of paper and exchange it with a partner.

3. Invite students to trace a route connecting the two places on the map and then write a list of the geographic features the expedition will travel through.

PARTNER

15 TO 30 MINUTES

ASIA: Political

R10

Asia: Political Map

HOW FAR IS IT?

GROUP

15 TO 30 MINUTES

Objective: To use a map scale to measure distances.

Materials: poster board, pencil, scissors

1. Refer the class to the map scale. Have them cut a strip of posterboard and draw on it a sort of "ruler" based on the map scale.

2. Invite a student to pose a question about the distance between two cities on the map—for example, "How far is it from India's capital to China's?"

3. Have students use their "rulers" to measure each distance called for. The student who gives the answer correctly gets to pose the next distance question.

HOWDY, NEIGHBOR

Objective: To identify where Asian countries are located in relation to one another.

Materials: paper, pencil

1. Have each group choose three countries on the map and list them on a piece of paper.

2. For each country, have them write a statement telling with which countries it shares political borders—for example, "My neighbors are China, Laos, and Cambodia."

3. Have groups read their statements and invite the rest of the class to identify the correct countries.

PARTN

15 TO MINU

ASIA: Physical

R11

Asia: Physical Map

 FIND THE COUNTRY

Objective: To compare physical and political maps.

Students can play a guessing game that calls for them to locate a named place on the physical map and then locate and name its country on the political map.

1. Tell students to find a place on the physical map—for example, "The Deccan Plateau in southern Asia."

2. When a student identifies the country for the place, he or she makes up a similar clue to another place, giving the place name and general area. The game continues as each student answering correctly gives the next clue.

 WHAT AM I?

Objective: To locate various geographic features.

Materials: index cards, pencils

1. Assign each group one form or feature—peninsulas, islands, plateaus, plains, mountain ranges, deserts.

2. Have each group choose three examples of their type from the map. Have them write clues to the location of each example on a separate card—for example, "I am a peninsula bordered by the Red Sea and the Persian Gulf." Have them include the answers.

3. Collect and shuffle the cards. Read each "I am ..." statement and call on students to identify each place.

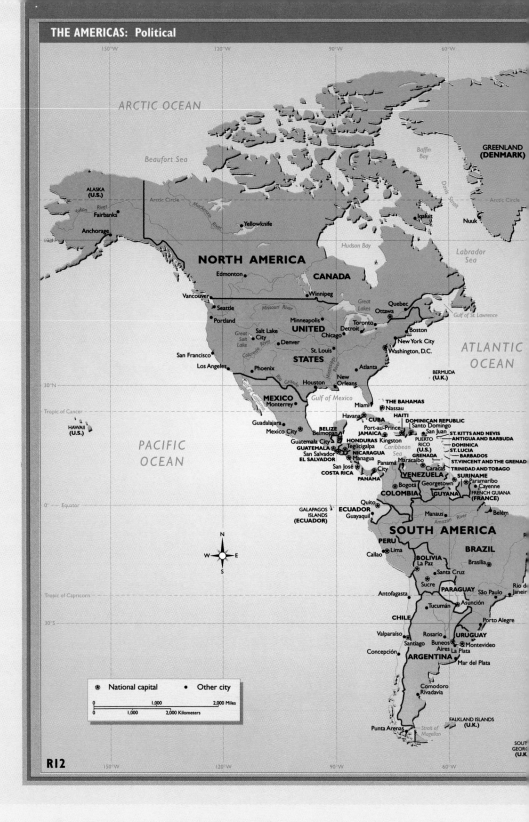

THE AMERICAS: Political

ARCTIC OCEAN

Beaufort Sea

Baffin Bay

GREENLAND (DENMARK)

ALASKA (U.S.)
Fairbanks
Anchorage

Arctic Circle

Mackenzie River

Yellowknife

Iqaluit

Nuuk

Arctic Circle

Davis Strait

Hudson Bay

Labrador Sea

NORTH AMERICA

Edmonton

CANADA

Vancouver
Seattle
Portland

Winnipeg

Great Lakes

Quebec
Ottawa

Gulf of St. Lawrence

Missouri River

Minneapolis
Salt Lake City
Denver

UNITED
Chicago
St. Louis

Detroit
Toronto

Boston
New York City
Washington, D.C.

ATLANTIC OCEAN

San Francisco
Los Angeles
Phoenix

Great Salt Lake

Colorado River

STATES

Atlanta

BERMUDA (U.K.)

30°N

Tropic of Cancer

HAWAII (U.S.)

Houston
New Orleans

Rio Grande

MEXICO
Monterrey

Gulf of Mexico

Miami

THE BAHAMAS
Nassau

Mississippi River

PACIFIC OCEAN

Guadalajara
Mexico City

Havana
CUBA
BELIZE
Belmopan
Guatemala City
GUATEMALA
San Salvador
EL SALVADOR

Port-au-Prince
HONDURAS Kingston
Tegucigalpa
NICARAGUA
Managua

HAITI
JAMAICA

DOMINICAN REPUBLIC
Santo Domingo
San Juan ST. KITTS AND NEVIS
PUERTO   ANTIGUA AND BARBUDA
RICO   ST. LUCIA
(U.S.)   DOMINICA
GRENADA   BARBADOS
ST. VINCENT AND THE GRENAD

Caribbean Sea

San José
COSTA RICA

Panamá
City
PANAMA

Maracaibo

Caracas
VENEZUELA
Bogotá Georgetown
COLOMBIA GUYANA

TRINIDAD AND TOBAGO
SURINAME
Paramaribo
Cayenne
FRENCH GUIANA
(FRANCE)

0° Equator

GALAPAGOS ISLANDS (ECUADOR)

Quito
ECUADOR
Guayaquil

Amazon River

Manaus

Belém

N
W   E
S

PERU

SOUTH AMERICA

Callao
Lima

BOLIVIA
La Paz

BRAZIL

Brasilia

Tropic of Capricorn

Antofagasta

Sucre
Santa Cruz

PARAGUAY
Tucumán Asunción

São Paulo

Rio de Janeiro

CHILE

Porto Alegre

30°S

Valparaíso
Santiago
Concepción

Rosario
Buenos
Aires La Plata
ARGENTINA

URUGUAY
Montevideo

Mar del Plata

Comodoro
Rivadavia

Punta Arenas Strait of Magellan

FALKLAND ISLANDS (U.K.)

SOUT
GEORG
(U.K

National capital   Other city

0   1,000   2,000 Miles
0   1,000   2,000 Kilometers

R12

150°W   120°W   90°W   60°W

The Americas: Political Map

CATALOG THE AMERICAS

Objective: To recognize the countries of the Americas and their capitals.

Materials: paper, pencil

1. Have students create a chart with the following heads—North America, Central America, the Caribbean, South America.

2. Under each heading, have them list its countries, with the capital shown next to each one. (Include only the larger Caribbean countries.)

3. Invite students to decorate each list with a symbol for that part of the Americas.

CAPITALS OF THE AMERICAS

Objective: To identify capitals and countries.

Materials: index cards, pen

Create a game of *Jeopardy* using student panels.

GROUP

30 MINUT OR LONG

1. For each country in the Americas (only the larger ones in the Caribbean), prepare an index card with a country name on one side and its capital on the other.

2. Call up a series of panels to play. As you name a country or a capital, the panelists should try to answer with the correct match. Offer 10 points for a correct answer and an additional 5 points for the correct part of the Americas—North, South, and so on.

THE AMERICAS: Physical

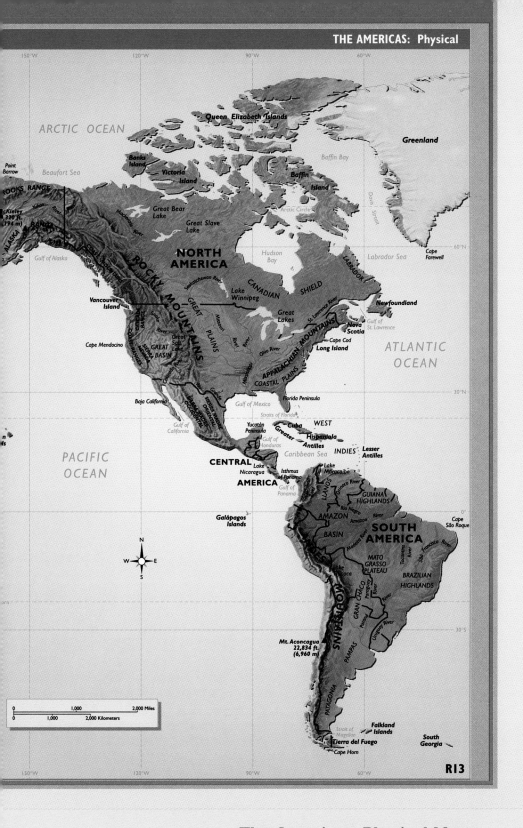

ARCTIC OCEAN

Point Barrow

Beaufort Sea

BROOKS RANGE

McKinley 20,320 ft (6,194 m)

ALASKA RANGE

Yukon River

Gulf of Alaska

Banks Island

Victoria Island

Queen Elizabeth Islands

Great Bear Lake

Mackenzie River

Great Slave Lake

NORTH AMERICA

ROCKY MOUNTAINS

GREAT PLAINS

Saskatchewan River

Lake Winnipeg

CANADIAN SHIELD

Hudson Bay

Arctic Circle

Baffin Island

Baffin Bay

Greenland

Davis Strait

60°N

Labrador Sea

Cape Farewell

LABRADOR

Vancouver Island

COAST RANGE

Snake River

Columbia River

GREAT BASIN

SIERRA NEVADA

Great Salt Lake

Missouri River

Platte River

Great Lakes

St. Lawrence River

APPALACHIAN MOUNTAINS

Newfoundland

Nova Scotia

Gulf of St. Lawrence

Cape Mendocino

Cape Cod

Long Island

Colorado River

Ohio River

Mississippi River

COASTAL PLAINS

ATLANTIC OCEAN

Baja California

Rio Grande

SIERRA MADRE OCCIDENTAL

SIERRA MADRE ORIENTAL

Florida Peninsula

30°N

Gulf of Mexico

Straits of Florida

Gulf of California

Yucatán Peninsula

Cuba

Greater Antilles

Hispaniola

WEST

Gulf of Honduras

CENTRAL AMERICA

Lake Nicaragua

Isthmus of Panama

Gulf of Panama

Caribbean Sea

INDIES

Lesser Antilles

Galápagos Islands

Lake Maracaibo

Orinoco River

LLANOS

GUIANA HIGHLANDS

AMAZON BASIN

Rio Negro

Amazon River

SOUTH AMERICA

Cape São Roque

Madeira River

MATO GRASSO PLATEAU

Tocantins River

São Francisco River

BRAZILIAN HIGHLANDS

ANDES MOUNTAINS

Lake Titicaca

GRAN CHACO

Paraguay River

Paraná River

PACIFIC OCEAN

Mt. Aconcagua 22,834 ft. (6,960 m)

PAMPAS

Uruguay River

30°S

PATAGONIA

Strait of Magellan

Falkland Islands

Tierra del Fuego

Cape Horn

South Georgia

N
W E
S

0   1,000   2,000 Miles
0   1,000   2,000 Kilometers

150°W   120°W   90°W   60°N

R13

The Americas: Physical Map

WHERE IS IT FROM HERE?

Objective: To practice using directions.

Materials: paper, pencil

GROUP

30 MINUTES

Students can create directional questions and challenge one another to work out the correct answers.

1. Refer the class to the *N* compass direction on the map and have them deduce the other directions from it.

2. Tell each student to choose two places shown on the map and write a question about what direction the places are from each other.

3. Invite a student to read aloud his or her question. The student who answers it correctly asks the next question.

PLAN A VACATION

Objective: To relate geography to real life.

Materials: paper, pens, crayons, periodicals

GROUP

30 MINUTES OR LONGER

1. Divide the class into groups and assign each group one of the following—skiing, lake fishing, jungle river travel, mountain climbing, tropical swimming.

2. Have each group locate a place in the Americas where such a vacation could be taken. Have them clip or draw pictures of the area and create an illustrated travel brochure showing vacation possibilities there.

3. Have the groups exchange brochures for examination and then create a bulletin board display of them.

THE UNITED STATES: Political

R14

The United States: Political

ESTABLISH U.S. BORDERS

GROUP

Objective: To locate the borders of the U.S.

Materials: paper, pencil

15 TO 30 MINUTES

1. Have students create worksheets by listing the following on a piece of paper—Alaska, Hawaii, Contiguous 48 States. Opposite each they should label and leave a space for the four borders of each—North, East, South, West.

2. Tell students to work with the map to fill in each space, using natural barriers like oceans, lakes, gulfs, or rivers where they apply and longitude or latitude where it applies.

MAKE A JIGSAW PUZZLE

Objective: To practice locating states in the U.S.

Materials: blowup of map, posterboard, scissors, outline map of U.S. borders in same size as blowup

1. Blow up this map of the U.S. to twice its size here. Cut it in quarters and give one quarter to each group.

2. Have groups mount their quarters on posterboard and then cut the states apart. You may want them to treat smaller states as one unit, for example: Mass., Conn., R.I.

3. Invite students to take turns as individuals or in small groups to reassemble the states where they belong on the outline map.

The United States: Political

KNOW YOUR NEIGHBORS

Objective: To practice using map key and scale.

Materials: posterboard, scissors, pencil

1. Have students identify the symbols in the map key and have them cut out and make posterboard "rulers" based on the map scale.

2. Call on students to locate your state and to identify your neighboring states. Have them also identify these states' capitals and other cities.

3. Invite them to make up questions about distances between these cities. Have them use their "rulers" to measure distances. Each correct answerer asks the next question.

WHAT'S THE STATE CAPITAL?

Objective: To identify state capitals.

Materials: index cards, pen

Point out that the category State Capitals often comes up on *Jeopardy.* Here students can play it themselves.

1. Make up, or have students make up, 50 cards with a state on one side and its capital on the other.

2. Call up a series of panels to play. You may name either the state and or the capital and have the panel vie to identify its capital or state.

3. Score 10 points for each correct answer. The highest individual scorer or scorers is/are *Jeopardy* Champion.

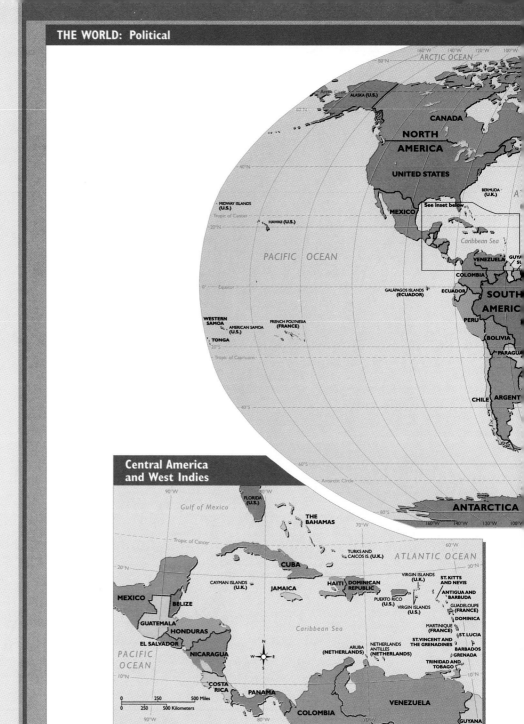

THE WORLD: Political

R16

**Central America
and West Indies**

The World: Political Map

DIFFERENTIATE BETWEEN MAP SCALES
GROUP

Objective: To understand the purpose of map insets.

Materials: posterboard, pencil, scissors

15 TO 30 MINUTES

1. Refer the class to the two inset areas on the large map and have them relate the enlarged inset maps to these areas of the map. Discuss why this inset method is used—to be able to show and label place names in "crowded" areas.

2. To reinforce the idea that insets enlarge an area, have students cut out two strips of posterboard and draw "rulers" based on the two different scales shown.

3. Have students compare the two scales and work out the small-scale to large-scale ratio (about 4:1).

USE MAP SCALES
PARTNE

Objective: To measure distances using map scales.

Materials: posterboard "rulers"

15 TO 3 MINUTE

1. Refer the class to the Abbreviation Key and to the Caribbean map inset. Explain that some countries hold political control over areas far from their shores.

2. Have students find examples of such areas in the Caribbean map inset—for example, Martinique (FR.). Invite a student to name such a territory and ask the class how far it is located from its mainland country.

3. The first student to measure the distance correctly gets to name the next area.

Europe

R17

The World: Political Map

WHAT'S BECOME OF THE FORMER SOVIET UNION?

Objective: To identify countries based on map clues.

1. Explain to the class that much of easternmost Europe and all of Northern Asia were once part of the Soviet Union.

2. Describe the old Soviet Union borders—all the land east of the Poland-Slovakia-Romania eastern border and the land east of the Black Sea about as far south as latitude 40°N to the China-Mongolia border and east to the Pacific.

3. Call on students to name the countries that this area now includes—Russia, Estonia, Tajikistan, and so on.

COUNTRIES OF THE WORLD

Objective: To identify countries by continent.

Materials: index cards, pencils

1. Divide the class into five groups and assign each one of the following—North America and the Caribbean, Central and South America, Europe, Asia, Africa.

2. Have the groups write the name of each of the countries in their area on one side of an index card and its continent (or the Caribbean) on the other.

3. Make a pack of the cards and shuffle them. Line the class up for a kind of "spell-down," calling out country names and having students identify their continent.

The World: Physical Map

CHART THE WORLD

Objective: To identify major geographic features.

Materials: paper, pencil, crayons or colored pencils

1. Explain that this map labels the major geographic features of the world that everyone should know.

2. Invite students to chart the information on this map by making headings of its major categories—mountain ranges, major rivers, deserts, plateaus—and listing the appropriate names and their continents under each.

3. Encourage students to illustrate their charts.

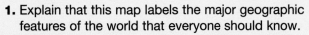

15 TO 30 MINUTES

PLOT A TRIP AROUND THE WORLD

Objective: To map a route and measure distances.

Materials: outline maps of the world, pencils

1. Invite pairs of students to picture themselves having the opportunity to take a trip around the world.

2. Have partners agree where they would want to stop along the way and have them trace their route on the outline map. Have them label the continents on which they would stop and the oceans they would cross.

3. Finally, they should measure and note on the map the distance covered in each leg of the trip. Encourage them to make a bulletin board display of their work.

PARTNE

30 MINU OR LONG

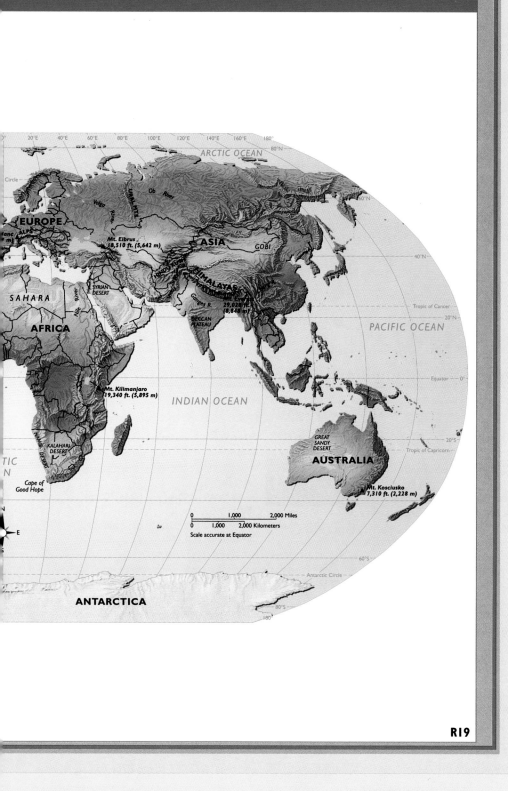

R19

The World: Physical Map

WHERE IS IT IN RELATION TO...?

Objective: To practice using directions.

Materials: none

1. Refer the class to the *N* compass direction and have them deduce the other directions based on it. Remind them that this map is a flat version of a round Earth.

2. Pose directional questions—for example, "If you were on the Canadian Shield, in which direction would you travel to get to Cape Horn?" "What direction would take you from the Cape of Good Hope to Australia?"

3. Encourage students to make up such questions themselves and pose them to the class.

WHERE IN THE WORLD AM I?

Objective: To identify location based on a variety of geographic clues.

Material List: paper, pencil

1. Have students pick two locations anywhere on this map and write them on a piece of paper.

2. For each, students should write down three geographic clues. Clues can be anything—relation to another place, latitude and longitude, ocean nearby, type of landform or other geographic feature.

3. Call on a student for one set of clues. The student who names the location correctly gives the next set.

ON YOUR OWN

15 TO 30 MINUTES

COUNTRIES of the WORLD

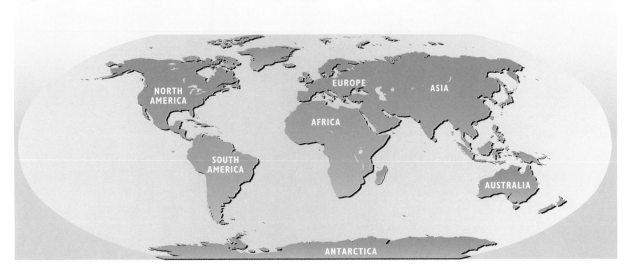

AFGHANISTAN

CAPITAL ★ Kabul

POPULATION: 22.7 million

MAJOR LANGUAGES: Pashtu and Afghan Persian

AREA: 250,000 sq mi; 647,500 sq km

LEADING EXPORTS: fruit, natural gas, and carpets

CONTINENT: Asia

ALBANIA

CAPITAL ★ Tiranë

POPULATION: 3.2 million

MAJOR LANGUAGES: Albanian and Greek

AREA: 11,100 sq mi; 28,748 sq km

LEADING EXPORTS: asphalt, petroleum products, and minerals

CONTINENT: Europe

ALGERIA

CAPITAL ★ Algiers

POPULATION: 29.2 million

MAJOR LANGUAGES: Arabic, Berber, and French

AREA: 919,595 sq mi; 2,381,751 sq km

LEADING EXPORTS: oil and natural gas

CONTINENT: Africa

ANDORRA

CAPITAL ★ Andorra la Vella

POPULATION: 68,000

MAJOR LANGUAGES: Catalan, French, and Castilian Spanish

AREA: 175 sq mi; 453 sq km

LEADING EXPORTS: electricity, tobacco products, and furniture

CONTINENT: Europe

ANGOLA

CAPITAL ★ Luanda

POPULATION: 10.3 million

MAJOR LANGUAGES: Portuguese and Bantu

AREA: 481,350 sq mi; 1,246,700 sq km

LEADING EXPORTS: oil, coffee, diamonds, and fish

CONTINENT: Africa

ANTIGUA AND BARBUDA

CAPITAL ★ St. John's

POPULATION: 66,000

MAJOR LANGUAGE: English

AREA: 171 sq mi; 442 sq km

LEADING EXPORTS: petroleum products and machinery

CONTINENT: North America

ARGENTINA

CAPITAL ★ Buenos Aires

POPULATION: 34.7 million

MAJOR LANGUAGES: Spanish, English, and Italian

AREA: 1,072,067 sq mi; 2,766,654 sq km

LEADING EXPORTS: meat, grain, hides, and wool

CONTINENT: South America

ARMENIA

CAPITAL ★ Yerevan

POPULATION: 3.5 million

MAJOR LANGUAGE: Armenian

AREA: 11,500 sq mi; 29,800 sq km

LEADING EXPORTS: machinery and processed food items

CONTINENT: Asia

AUSTRALIA

CAPITAL ★ Canberra
POPULATION: 18.2 million
MAJOR LANGUAGES: English and aboriginal languages
AREA: 2,966,150 sq mi; 7,682,300 sq km
LEADING EXPORTS: coal, gold, wool, and alumina
CONTINENT: Australia

AUSTRIA

CAPITAL ★ Vienna
POPULATION: 8.0 million
MAJOR LANGUAGE: German
AREA: 32,375 sq mi; 83,851 sq km
LEADING EXPORTS: iron and steel products, and timber
CONTINENT: Europe

AZERBAIJAN

CAPITAL ★ Baku
POPULATION: 7.7 million
MAJOR LANGUAGES: Azeri, Russian, and Armenian
AREA: 33,430 sq mi; 86,600 sq km
LEADING EXPORTS: oil and chemicals
CONTINENT: Asia

THE BAHAMAS

CAPITAL ★ Nassau
POPULATION: 0.3 million
MAJOR LANGUAGES: English and Creole
AREA: 5,380 sq mi; 13,939 sq km
LEADING EXPORTS: crawfish, medicine, and cement
CONTINENT: North America

BAHRAIN

CAPITAL ★ Manama
POPULATION: 0.6 million
MAJOR LANGUAGES: Arabic, English, Farsi, and Urdu
AREA: 240 sq mi; 620 sq km
LEADING EXPORTS: oil, petroleum products, and aluminum
CONTINENT: Asia

BANGLADESH

CAPITAL ★ Dhaka
POPULATION: 123.1 million
MAJOR LANGUAGES: Bangla and English
AREA: 55,598 sq mi; 143,998 sq km
LEADING EXPORTS: textiles, jute, leather, and seafood
CONTINENT: Asia

BARBADOS

CAPITAL ★ Bridgetown
POPULATION: 0.3 million
MAJOR LANGUAGE: English
AREA: 166 sq mi; 431 sq km
LEADING EXPORTS: sugar, molasses, and electrical components
CONTINENT: North America

BELARUS

CAPITAL ★ Minsk
POPULATION: 10.4 million
MAJOR LANGUAGES: Byelorussian and Russian
AREA: 80,200 sq mi; 207,600 sq km
LEADING EXPORTS: machinery and chemicals
CONTINENT: Europe

BELGIUM

CAPITAL ★ Brussels
POPULATION: 10.1 million
MAJOR LANGUAGES: Flemish and French
AREA: 11,781 sq mi; 30,518 sq km
LEADING EXPORTS: machinery, iron, steel, and diamonds
CONTINENT: Europe

BELIZE

CAPITAL ★ Belmopan
POPULATION: 0.2 million
MAJOR LANGUAGES: English and Spanish
AREA: 8,867 sq mi; 22,965 sq km
LEADING EXPORTS: sugar, molasses, clothing, and lumber
CONTINENT: North America

BENIN

CAPITAL ★ Porto-Novo
POPULATION: 5.7 million
MAJOR LANGUAGES: French and Fon
AREA: 43,483 sq mi; 12,622 sq km
LEADING EXPORTS: crude oil, cotton, palm products, and cocoa
CONTINENT: Africa

BHUTAN

CAPITAL ★ Thimphu
POPULATION: 1.8 million
MAJOR LANGUAGES: Dzongkha and Nepali
AREA: 18,000 sq mi; 46,620 sq km
LEADING EXPORTS: cardamom, gypsum, timber, and handicrafts
CONTINENT: Asia

BOLIVIA

CAPITALS ★ Sucre (judicial) and La Paz (administrative)
POPULATION: 7.2 million
MAJOR LANGUAGES: Spanish, Quechua, and Aymará
AREA: 424,162 sq mi; 1,098,581 sq km
LEADING EXPORTS: metals, natural gas, soybeans, and timber
CONTINENT: South America

COUNTRIES of the WORLD

BOSNIA AND HERZEGOVINA

CAPITAL ★ Sarajevo
POPULATION: 2.7 million
MAJOR LANGUAGE: Serbo-Croatian
AREA: 19,741 sq mi; 51,129 sq km
LEADING EXPORTS: (not available)
CONTINENT: Europe

BOTSWANA

CAPITAL ★ Gaborone
POPULATION: 1.5 million
MAJOR LANGUAGES: English and Setswana
AREA: 231,800 sq mi; 600,360 sq km
LEADING EXPORTS: diamonds, copper, and nickel
CONTINENT: Africa

BRAZIL

CAPITAL ★ Brasília
POPULATION: 162.7 million
MAJOR LANGUAGES: Portuguese, Spanish, French, and English
AREA: 3,286,470 sq mi; 8,511,957 sq km
LEADING EXPORTS: coffee, iron ore, and soybeans
CONTINENT: South America

BRUNEI

CAPITAL ★ Bandar Seri Begawan
POPULATION: 0.3 million
MAJOR LANGUAGES: Malay, English, and Chinese
AREA: 2,226 sq mi; 5,765 sq km
LEADING EXPORT: oil
CONTINENT: Asia

BULGARIA

CAPITAL ★ Sofia
POPULATION: 8.6 million
MAJOR LANGUAGE: Bulgarian
AREA: 42,823 sq mi; 110,912 sq km
LEADING EXPORTS: machinery, minerals, and agricultural products
CONTINENT: Europe

BURKINA FASO

CAPITAL ★ Ouagadougou
POPULATION: 10.6 million
MAJOR LANGUAGES: French and Sudanic languages
AREA: 105,870 sq mi; 274,200 sq km
LEADING EXPORTS: oilseeds and cotton
CONTINENT: Africa

BURUNDI

CAPITAL ★ Bujumbura
POPULATION: 5.9 million
MAJOR LANGUAGES: Kirundi, French, and Swahili
AREA: 10,747 sq mi; 27,834 sq km
LEADING EXPORTS: coffee, tea, cotton, and hides
CONTINENT: Africa

CAMBODIA

CAPITAL ★ Phnom Penh
POPULATION: 10.6 million
MAJOR LANGUAGES: Khmer and French
AREA: 69,884 sq mi; 181,035 sq km
LEADING EXPORTS: rubber, rice, pepper, and raw timber
CONTINENT: Asia

CAMEROON

CAPITAL ★ Yaoundé
POPULATION: 14.3 million
MAJOR LANGUAGES: English and French
AREA: 183,569 sq mi; 475,442 sq km
LEADING EXPORTS: coffee, cocoa, timber, and petroleum products
CONTINENT: Africa

CANADA

CAPITAL ★ Ottawa
POPULATION: 29.9 million
MAJOR LANGUAGES: English and French
AREA: 3,851,809 sq mi; 9,976,186 sq km
LEADING EXPORTS: newsprint, wood pulp, and timber
CONTINENT: North America

CAPE VERDE

CAPITAL ★ Praia
POPULATION: 0.4 million
MAJOR LANGUAGES: Portuguese and Crioulo
AREA: 1,557 sq mi; 4,033 sq km
LEADING EXPORTS: fish, bananas, and salt
CONTINENT: Africa

CENTRAL AFRICAN REPUBLIC

CAPITAL ★ Bangui
POPULATION: 3.3 million
MAJOR LANGUAGES: French and Sango
AREA: 241,313 sq mi; 625,000 sq km
LEADING EXPORTS: diamonds, cotton, timber, coffee, and tobacco
CONTINENT: Africa

CHAD

CAPITAL ★ N'Djamena
POPULATION: 7.0 million
MAJOR LANGUAGES: French and Arabic
AREA: 495,752 sq mi; 1,284,000 sq km
LEADING EXPORTS: cotton, cattle, fish, and textiles
CONTINENT: Africa

CHILE

CAPITAL ★ Santiago
POPULATION: 14.3 million
MAJOR LANGUAGE: Spanish
AREA: 292,132 sq mi; 756,622 sq km
LEADING EXPORTS: copper, fish, metals, and minerals
CONTINENT: South America

CHINA

CAPITAL ★ Beijing
POPULATION: 1,210 million
MAJOR LANGUAGES: Mandarin and local Chinese dialects
AREA: 3,691,521 sq mi; 9,561,000 sq km
LEADING EXPORTS: manufactured goods, footwear, and toys
CONTINENT: Asia

COLOMBIA

CAPITAL ★ Bogotá
POPULATION: 36.8 million
MAJOR LANGUAGE: Spanish
AREA: 439,735 sq mi; 1,138,910 sq km
LEADING EXPORTS: coffee, petroleum, coal, and bananas
CONTINENT: South America

COMOROS

CAPITAL ★ Moroni
POPULATION: 0.6 million
MAJOR LANGUAGES: French, Arabic, and Comoran
AREA: 690 sq mi; 1,787 sq km
LEADING EXPORTS: vanilla, cloves, perfume oil, and copra
CONTINENT: Africa

CONGO REPUBLIC

CAPITAL ★ Brazzaville
POPULATION: 2.5 million
MAJOR LANGUAGES: French, Kikongo, Lingala, and other African languages
AREA: 132,046 sq mi; 342,000 sq km
LEADING EXPORTS: crude oil, lumber, coffee, and cocoa
CONTINENT: Africa

COSTA RICA

CAPITAL ★ San José
POPULATION: 3.5 million
MAJOR LANGUAGES: Spanish and English
AREA: 19,652 sq mi; 50,898 sq km
LEADING EXPORTS: coffee, bananas, textiles, and sugar
CONTINENT: North America

CÔTE D'IVOIRE (Ivory Coast)
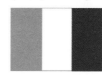
CAPITAL ★ Yamoussoukro
POPULATION: 14.8 million
MAJOR LANGUAGES: French and many African languages
AREA: 124,502 sq mi; 322,462 sq km
LEADING EXPORTS: cocoa, coffee, tropical woods, and petroleum
CONTINENT: Africa

CROATIA

CAPITAL ★ Zagreb
POPULATION: 5 million
MAJOR LANGUAGE: Serbo-Croatian
AREA: 21,829 sq mi; 56,537 sq km
LEADING EXPORTS: machinery, transport equipment, and other manufactures
CONTINENT: Europe

CUBA

CAPITAL ★ Havana
POPULATION: 11 million
MAJOR LANGUAGE: Spanish
AREA: 44,218 sq mi; 114,524 sq km
LEADING EXPORTS: coffee, sugar, nickel, shellfish, and tobacco
CONTINENT: North America

CYPRUS

CAPITAL ★ Nicosia
POPULATION: 0.7 million
MAJOR LANGUAGES: Greek, Turkish, and English
AREA: 3,572 sq mi; 9,251 sq km
LEADING EXPORTS: fruit, cement, and clothing
CONTINENT: Asia

CZECH REPUBLIC

CAPITAL ★ Prague
POPULATION: 10.3 million
MAJOR LANGUAGES: Czech and Slovak
AREA: 30,464 sq mi; 78,902 sq km
LEADING EXPORTS: manufactured goods and machinery
CONTINENT: Europe

COUNTRIES of the WORLD

DEMOCRATIC REPUBLIC OF CONGO

CAPITAL ★ Kinshasa

POPULATION: 46.5 million

MAJOR LANGUAGES: French, English, Swahili, Lingala and other Bantu dialects

AREA: 905,365 sq mi; 2,344,885 sq km

LEADING EXPORTS: copper, cobalt, diamonds, oil, and coffee

CONTINENT: Africa

DENMARK

CAPITAL ★ Copenhagen

POPULATION: 5.2 million

MAJOR LANGUAGES: Danish and Faroese

AREA: 16,631 sq mi; 43,075 sq mi

LEADING EXPORTS: food, machinery, and chemicals

CONTINENT: Europe

DJIBOUTI

CAPITAL ★ Djibouti

POPULATION: 0.4 million

MAJOR LANGUAGES: Arabic and French

AREA: 8,490 sq mi; 22,000 sq km

LEADING EXPORTS: hides and skins

CONTINENT: Africa

DOMINICA

CAPITAL ★ Roseau

POPULATION: 0.1 million

MAJOR LANGUAGES: English and Creole

AREA: 290 sq mi; 751 sq km

LEADING EXPORTS: bananas, coconuts, soap, and vegetables

CONTINENT: North America

DOMINICAN REPUBLIC

CAPITAL ★ Santo Domingo

POPULATION: 8.1 million

MAJOR LANGUAGES: Spanish

AREA: 18,704 sq mi; 48,442 sq km

LEADING EXPORTS: sugar, coffee, cocoa, gold, and ferronickel

CONTINENT: North America

ECUADOR

CAPITAL ★ Quito

POPULATION: 10.7 million

MAJOR LANGUAGES: Spanish and Quechua

AREA: 106,822 sq mi; 276,670 sq km

LEADING EXPORTS: oil, coffee, bananas, and cocoa

CONTINENT: South America

EGYPT

CAPITAL ★ Cairo

POPULATION: 63.6 million

MAJOR LANGUAGES: Arabic, English, and French

AREA: 386,900 sq mi; 1,002,000 sq km

LEADING EXPORTS: cotton, oil, and textiles

CONTINENT: Africa

EL SALVADOR

CAPITAL ★ San Salvador

POPULATION: 5.8 million

MAJOR LANGUAGES: Spanish and Nahua

AREA: 8,260 sq mi; 21,393 sq km

LEADING EXPORTS: coffee, cotton, sugarcane, and shrimp

CONTINENT: North America

EQUATORIAL GUINEA

CAPITAL ★ Malabo

POPULATION: 0.4 million

MAJOR LANGUAGES: Spanish, Fang, and Bubi

AREA: 10,830 sq mi; 28,051 sq km

LEADING EXPORTS: cocoa, timber, and coffee

CONTINENT: Africa

ERITREA

CAPITAL ★ Asmara

POPULATION: 3.9 million

MAJOR LANGUAGES: Tigrinya and Arabic

AREA: 45,754 sq mi; 121,300 sq km

LEADING EXPORTS: (not available)

CONTINENT: Africa

ESTONIA

CAPITAL ★ Tallinn

POPULATION: 1.5 million

MAJOR LANGUAGES: Estonian, Latvian, Lithuanian, and Russian

AREA: 18,370 sq mi; 47,549 sq km

LEADING EXPORTS: food products, textiles, vehicles, and metals

CONTINENT: Europe

ETHIOPIA

CAPITAL ★ Addis Ababa

POPULATION: 57.2 million

MAJOR LANGUAGES: Amharic, English, and local languages

AREA: 446,952 sq mi; 1,157,585 sq km

LEADING EXPORTS: coffee, leather products, gold, and petroleum products

CONTINENT: Africa

FIJI

CAPITAL ★ Suva

POPULATION: 0.8 million

MAJOR LANGUAGES: Fijian, Hindi, and English

AREA: 7,078 sq mi; 18,333 sq km

LEADING EXPORTS: sugar, copra, fish, lumber, and gold

CONTINENT: Islands in the Pacific Ocean

FINLAND

CAPITAL ★ Helsinki

POPULATION: 5.1 million

MAJOR LANGUAGES: Finnish and Swedish

AREA: 130,558 sq mi; 338,145 sq km

LEADING EXPORTS: paper and wood

CONTINENT: Europe

FRANCE

CAPITAL ★ Paris

POPULATION: 58.3 million

MAJOR LANGUAGE: French

AREA: 211,208 sq mi; 547,030 sq km

LEADING EXPORTS: manufactured goods and machinery

CONTINENT: Europe

GABON

CAPITAL ★ Libreville

POPULATION: 1.2 million

MAJOR LANGUAGES: French, Fang, and Bantu dialects

AREA: 103,346 sq mi; 267,667 sq km

LEADING EXPORTS: crude oil, manganese, and timber

CONTINENT: Africa

THE GAMBIA

CAPITAL ★ Banjul

POPULATION: 1.0 million

MAJOR LANGUAGES: English and Mandinka

AREA: 4,093 sq mi; 10,600 sq km

LEADING EXPORTS: peanut products, fish, and cotton lint

CONTINENT: Africa

GEORGIA

CAPITAL ★ Tbilisi

POPULATION: 5.2 million

MAJOR LANGUAGES: Georgian and Russian

AREA: 26,900 sq mi; 69,700 sq km

LEADING EXPORTS: agricultural products and machinery

CONTINENT: Asia

GERMANY

CAPITAL ★ Berlin

POPULATION: 83.5 million

MAJOR LANGUAGE: German

AREA: 137,826 sq mi; 356,970 sq km

LEADING EXPORTS: machinery and manufactured goods

CONTINENT: Europe

GHANA

CAPITAL ★ Accra

POPULATION: 17.7 million

MAJOR LANGUAGES: English and African languages

AREA: 92,100 sq mi; 238,537 sq km

LEADING EXPORTS: cocoa, gold, timber, and tuna

CONTINENT: Africa

GREECE

CAPITAL ★ Athens

POPULATION: 10.7 million

MAJOR LANGUAGES: Greek, English, and French

AREA: 50,961 sq mi; 131,990 sq km

LEADING EXPORTS: manufactured goods and food products

CONTINENT: Europe

GRENADA

CAPITAL ★ St. George's

POPULATION: 0.1 million

MAJOR LANGUAGES: English and French patois

AREA: 133 sq mi; 344 sq km

LEADING EXPORTS: nutmeg, cocoa, bananas, and mace

CONTINENT: North America

GUATEMALA

CAPITAL ★ Guatemala City

POPULATION: 11.3 million

MAJOR LANGUAGES: Spanish and Mayan dialects

AREA: 42,042 sq mi; 108,889 sq km

LEADING EXPORTS: coffee, sugar, and bananas

CONTINENT: North America

GUINEA

CAPITAL ★ Conakry

POPULATION: 7.4 million

MAJOR LANGUAGES: French, Soussou, and Manika

AREA: 94,925 sq mi; 245,857 sq km

LEADING EXPORTS: bauxite, alumina, diamonds, and food products

CONTINENT: Africa

GUINEA-BISSAU

CAPITAL ★ Bissau

POPULATION: 1.2 million

MAJOR LANGUAGES: Portuguese and Crioulo

AREA: 13,948 sq mi; 36,125 sq km

LEADING EXPORTS: peanut products, fish, and palm kernels

CONTINENT: Africa

GUYANA

CAPITAL ★ Georgetown

POPULATION: 0.7 million

MAJOR LANGUAGES: English, Hindi, and Urdu

AREA: 83,000 sq mi; 214,969 sq km

LEADING EXPORTS: sugar, bauxite, rice, timber, and shrimp

CONTINENT: South America

COUNTRIES *of the* WORLD

HAITI

CAPITAL ★ Port-au-Prince

POPULATION: 6.7 million

MAJOR LANGUAGES: French and French Creole

AREA: 10,714 sq mi; 27,750 sq km

LEADING EXPORTS: coffee and assembled lighting products

CONTINENT: North America

HONDURAS

CAPITAL ★ Tegucigalpa

POPULATION: 5.6 million

MAJOR LANGUAGE: Spanish

AREA: 43,872 sq mi; 112,492 sq km

LEADING EXPORTS: coffee, lumber, bananas, shrimp, and lobster

CONTINENT: North America

HUNGARY

CAPITAL ★ Budapest

POPULATION: 10.0 million

MAJOR LANGUAGE: Hungarian

AREA: 35,919 sq mi; 93,030 sq km

LEADING EXPORTS: raw materials, chemicals, and consumer goods

CONTINENT: Europe

ICELAND

CAPITAL ★ Reykjavik

POPULATION: 0.3 million

MAJOR LANGUAGE: Icelandic

AREA: 39,709 sq mi; 102,846 sq km

LEADING EXPORTS: fish, animal products, and aluminum

CONTINENT: Europe

INDIA

CAPITAL ★ New Delhi

POPULATION: 952.1 million

MAJOR LANGUAGES: Hindi, English, and 14 other official languages

AREA: 1,229,737 sq mi; 3,185,019 sq km

LEADING EXPORTS: gems and jewelry, clothing, engineering goods, and fabric

CONTINENT: Asia

INDONESIA

CAPITAL ★ Jakarta

POPULATION: 206.6 million

MAJOR LANGUAGES: Bahasa Indonesian, English, Dutch, and Javanese

AREA: 735,268 sq mi; 1,904,344 sq km

LEADING EXPORTS: oil, gas, timber, rubber, and coffee

CONTINENT: Asia

IRAN

CAPITAL ★ Tehran

POPULATION: 66.1 million

MAJOR LANGUAGES: Farsi, Turkic, and Kurdish

AREA: 636,293 sq mi; 1,648,000 sq km

LEADING EXPORTS: oil, carpets, and fruits

CONTINENT: Asia

IRAQ

CAPITAL ★ Baghdad

POPULATION: 21.4 million

MAJOR LANGUAGES: Arabic and Kurdish

AREA: 168,920 sq mi; 434,913 sq km

LEADING EXPORT: oil and chemicals

CONTINENT: Asia

IRELAND

CAPITAL ★ Dublin

POPULATION: 3.6 million

MAJOR LANGUAGES: English and Irish

AREA: 27,136 sq mi; 70,282 sq km

LEADING EXPORTS: live animals, dairy products, and machinery

CONTINENT: Europe

ISRAEL

CAPITAL ★ Jerusalem

POPULATION: 5.2 million

MAJOR LANGUAGES: Hebrew and Arabic

AREA: 8,020 sq mi; 20,772 sq km*

LEADING EXPORTS: diamonds, fruits, and textiles

CONTINENT: Asia

*does not include the 2,402 sq mi of the Gaza Strip and the West Bank

ITALY

CAPITAL ★ Rome

POPULATION: 57.5 million

MAJOR LANGUAGE: Italian

AREA: 116,500 sq mi; 301,278 sq km

LEADING EXPORTS: clothing, metals, machinery, and chemicals

CONTINENT: Europe

JAMAICA

CAPITAL ★ Kingston

POPULATION: 2.6 million

MAJOR LANGUAGES: English and Jamaican Creole

AREA: 4,411 sq mi; 11,424 sq km

LEADING EXPORTS: alumina, bauxite, sugar, and bananas

CONTINENT: North America

JAPAN

CAPITAL ★ Tokyo
POPULATION: 125.6 million
MAJOR LANGUAGE: Japanese
AREA: 145,874 sq mi; 377,815 sq km
LEADING EXPORT: machinery
CONTINENT: Asia

JORDAN

CAPITAL ★ Amman
POPULATION: 4.2 million
MAJOR LANGUAGE: Arabic
AREA: 34,573 sq mi; 89,544 sq km
LEADING EXPORTS: phosphates
and agricultural products
CONTINENT: Asia

KAZAKHSTAN

CAPITAL ★ Almaty
POPULATION: 16.9 million
MAJOR LANGUAGES: Kazakh and
Russian
AREA: 1,049,000 sq mi; 2,717,300 sq
km
LEADING EXPORTS: oil, metals,
chemicals, wool, and grain
CONTINENT: Asia

KENYA

CAPITAL ★ Nairobi
POPULATION: 28.2 million
MAJOR LANGUAGES: English and
Swahili
AREA: 224,960 sq mi; 582,646 sq km
LEADING EXPORTS: tea, coffee, and
petroleum products
CONTINENT: Africa

KIRIBATI

CAPITAL ★ Tarawa
POPULATION: 80,900
MAJOR LANGUAGES: Gilbertese
and English
AREA: 280 sq mi; 726 sq km
LEADING EXPORTS: fish and copra
CONTINENT: Islands in the Pacific
Ocean

KOREA, NORTH

CAPITAL ★ Pyongyang
POPULATION: 23.9 million
MAJOR LANGUAGE: Korean
AREA: 46,768 sq mi; 121,129 sq km
LEADING EXPORTS: minerals and
agricultural products
CONTINENT: Asia

KOREA, SOUTH

CAPITAL ★ Seoul
POPULATION: 45.5 million
MAJOR LANGUAGE: Korean
AREA: 38,031 sq mi; 98,392 sq km
LEADING EXPORTS: agricultural
products, electronics, machinery, and
clothing
CONTINENT: Asia

KUWAIT

CAPITAL ★ Kuwait
POPULATION: 2.0 million
MAJOR LANGUAGE: Arabic
AREA: 6,880 sq mi; 17,820 sq km
LEADING EXPORT: oil
CONTINENT: Asia

KYRGYZSTAN

CAPITAL ★ Bishkek
POPULATION: 4.5 million
MAJOR LANGUAGES: Kyrgyz and
Russian
AREA: 76,000 sq mi; 198,500 sq km
LEADING EXPORTS: wool,
chemicals, cotton, metals, and shoes
CONTINENT: Asia

LAOS

CAPITAL ★ Vientiane
POPULATION: 4.9 million
MAJOR LANGUAGES: Lao, French,
and English
AREA: 91,429 sq mi; 236,800 sq km
LEADING EXPORTS: electricity,
timber, tin, and coffee
CONTINENT: Asia

LATVIA

CAPITAL ★ Riga
POPULATION: 2.5 million
MAJOR LANGUAGES: Latvian and
Russian
AREA: 25,400 sq mi; 65,786 sq km
LEADING EXPORTS: timber, metals,
machinery, and fish
CONTINENT: Europe

LEBANON

CAPITAL ★ Beirut
POPULATION: 3.8 million
MAJOR LANGUAGES: Arabic and
French
AREA: 4,015 sq mi; 10,400 sq km
LEADING EXPORTS: fruits, textiles,
and chemicals
CONTINENT: Asia

LESOTHO

CAPITAL ★ Maseru
POPULATION: 2.0 million
MAJOR LANGUAGES: Sesotho and
English
AREA: 11,720 sq mi; 30,355 sq km
LEADING EXPORTS: wool, mohair,
wheat, cattle, peas, and beans
CONTINENT: Africa

COUNTRIES of the WORLD

LIBERIA

CAPITAL ★ Monrovia
POPULATION: 2.1 million
MAJOR LANGUAGES: English and Niger-Congo languages
AREA: 43,000 sq mi; 111,370 sq km
LEADING EXPORTS: iron ore, rubber, timber, and coffee
CONTINENT: Africa

LIBYA

CAPITAL ★ Tripoli
POPULATION: 5.4 million
MAJOR LANGUAGES: Arabic, Italian, and English
AREA: 679,536 sq mi; 1,759,998 sq km
LEADING EXPORTS: oil, peanuts, and natural gas
CONTINENT: Africa

LIECHTENSTEIN

CAPITAL ★ Vaduz
POPULATION: 31,000
MAJOR LANGUAGE: German
AREA: 61 sq mi; 157 sq km
LEADING EXPORTS: machinery, dental products, stamps, and hardware
CONTINENT: Europe

LITHUANIA

CAPITAL ★ Vilnius
POPULATION: 3.7 million
MAJOR LANGUAGES: Lithuanian, Russian, and Polish
AREA: 25,212 sq mi; 65,300 sq km
LEADING EXPORTS: textiles, chemicals, and mineral products
CONTINENT: Europe

LUXEMBOURG

CAPITAL ★ Luxembourg
POPULATION: 0.4 million
MAJOR LANGUAGES: Luxembourgisch, German, French, and English
AREA: 999 sq mi; 2,586 sq km
LEADING EXPORTS: steel products, chemicals, rubber products, and glass
CONTINENT: Europe

MACEDONIA

CAPITAL ★ Skopje
POPULATION: 2.1 million
MAJOR LANGUAGES: Macedonian and Albanian
AREA: 9,928 sq mi; 25,713 sq km
LEADING EXPORTS: manufactured goods, machinery, and transport equipment
CONTINENT: Europe

MADAGASCAR

CAPITAL ★ Antananarivo
POPULATION: 13.7 million
MAJOR LANGUAGES: French and Malagasy
AREA: 226,660 sq mi; 587,050 sq km
LEADING EXPORTS: coffee, cloves, vanilla, and sugar
CONTINENT: Africa

MALAWI

CAPITAL ★ Lilongwe
POPULATION: 9.5 million
MAJOR LANGUAGES: English and Chichewa
AREA: 45,747 sq mi; 118,484 sq km
LEADING EXPORTS: tobacco, sugar, tea, coffee, and peanuts
CONTINENT: Africa

MALAYSIA

CAPITAL ★ Kuala Lumpur
POPULATION: 20.0 million
MAJOR LANGUAGES: Malay, English, and Chinese dialects
AREA: 128,328 sq mi; 332,370 sq km
LEADING EXPORTS: rubber, palm oil, tin, and timber
CONTINENT: Asia

MALDIVES

CAPITAL ★ Malé
POPULATION: 0.3 million
MAJOR LANGUAGE: Divehi
AREA: 115 sq mi; 298 sq km
LEADING EXPORTS: fish and clothing
CONTINENT: Asia

MALI

CAPITAL ★ Bamako
POPULATION: 9.7 million
MAJOR LANGUAGES: Bambara and French
AREA: 478,819 sq mi; 1,240,142 sq km
LEADING EXPORTS: cotton, livestock, and gold
CONTINENT: Africa

MALTA
CAPITAL ★ Valletta
POPULATION: 0.4 million
MAJOR LANGUAGES: Maltese and English
AREA: 122 sq mi; 316 sq km
LEADING EXPORTS: clothing, textiles, and footwear
CONTINENT: Europe

MARSHALL ISLANDS

CAPITAL ★ Majuro
POPULATION: 58,000
MAJOR LANGUAGES: English, Marshallese dialects, and Japanese
AREA: 70 sq mi; 181 sq km
LEADING EXPORTS: coconut oil, fish, live animals, and trichus shells
CONTINENT: Islands in the Pacific Ocean

MAURITANIA

CAPITAL ★ Nouakchott
POPULATION: 2.3 million
MAJOR LANGUAGES: Arabic and Wolof
AREA: 397,953 sq mi; 1,030,700 sq km
LEADING EXPORTS: iron ore and fish
CONTINENT: Africa

MAURITIUS

CAPITAL ★ Port Louis
POPULATION: 1.1 million
MAJOR LANGUAGES: English, Creole, and French
AREA: 787 sq mi; 2,040 sq km
LEADING EXPORTS: sugar, light manufactures, and textiles
CONTINENT: Africa

MEXICO

CAPITAL ★ Mexico City
POPULATION: 95.8 million
MAJOR LANGUAGE: Spanish
AREA: 761,600 sq mi; 1,972,547 sq km
LEADING EXPORTS: motor vehicles, consumer electronics, cotton, and shrimp
CONTINENT: North America

MICRONESIA

CAPITAL ★ Palikir
POPULATION: 125,000
MAJOR LANGUAGES: English, Trukese, Yapese, and Kosrean
AREA: 271 sq mi; 703 sq km
LEADING EXPORT: copra
CONTINENT: Islands in the Pacific Ocean

MOLDOVA

CAPITAL ★ Kishinev
POPULATION: 4.5 million
MAJOR LANGUAGES: Moldovan, Russian, and Gagauz
AREA: 13,000 sq mi; 33,700 sq km
LEADING EXPORTS: food, wine, tobacco, and textiles
CONTINENT: Europe

MONACO

CAPITAL ★ Monaco
POPULATION: 31,000
MAJOR LANGUAGES: French, Monégasque, and English
AREA: 0.7 sq mi; 1.9 sq km
LEADING EXPORTS: (not available)
CONTINENT: Europe

MONGOLIA

CAPITAL ★ Ulaanbaatar
POPULATION: 2.5 million
MAJOR LANGUAGES: Khalkha Mongolian, Turkic, Russian, and Chinese
AREA: 604,250 sq mi; 1,565,000 sq km
LEADING EXPORTS: copper, cashmere, and livestock
CONTINENT: Asia

MOROCCO

CAPITAL ★ Rabat
POPULATION: 29.8 million
MAJOR LANGUAGES: Arabic, Berber, and French
AREA: 172,413 sq mi; 446,550 sq km
LEADING EXPORTS: food, beverages, consumer goods, and phosphates
CONTINENT: Africa

MOZAMBIQUE

CAPITAL ★ Maputo
POPULATION: 17.9 million
MAJOR LANGUAGES: Portuguese and African languages
AREA: 303,073 sq mi; 799,380 sq km
LEADING EXPORTS: cashew nuts, sugar, and shrimp
CONTINENT: Africa

MYANMAR (Burma)

CAPITAL ★ Yangon
POPULATION: 50.0 million
MAJOR LANGUAGE: Burmese
AREA: 261,220 sq mi; 678,560 sq km
LEADING EXPORTS: rice, teak, oilseeds, and metals
CONTINENT: Asia

NAMIBIA

CAPITAL ★ Windhoek
POPULATION: 1.7 million
MAJOR LANGUAGES: English, Afrikaans, and German
AREA: 318,261 sq mi; 824,296 sq km
LEADING EXPORTS: diamonds, metals, and livestock
CONTINENT: Africa

COUNTRIES of the WORLD

NAURU

CAPITAL ★ Yaren

POPULATION: 10,000

MAJOR LANGUAGES: Nauruan and English

AREA: 8 sq mi; 21 sq km

LEADING EXPORT: phosphates

CONTINENT: Islands in the Pacific Ocean

NEPAL

CAPITAL ★ Kathmandu

POPULATION: 22.1 million

MAJOR LANGUAGE: Nepali

AREA: 54,463 sq mi; 141,059 sq km

LEADING EXPORTS: clothing, carpets, leather goods, and grain

CONTINENT: Asia

NETHERLANDS

CAPITAL ★ Amsterdam

POPULATION: 15.5 million

MAJOR LANGUAGE: Dutch

AREA: 16,033 sq mi; 41,526 sq km

LEADING EXPORTS: foodstuffs, natural gas, and chemicals

CONTINENT: Europe

NEW ZEALAND

CAPITAL ★ Wellington

POPULATION: 3.5 million

MAJOR LANGUAGES: English and Maori

AREA: 103,884 sq mi; 270,534 sq km

LEADING EXPORTS: meat, dairy products, and wool

CONTINENT: Islands in the Pacific Ocean

NICARAGUA

CAPITAL ★ Managua

POPULATION: 4.3 million

MAJOR LANGUAGE: Spanish

AREA: 50,180 sq mi; 130,000 sq km

LEADING EXPORTS: coffee, cotton, and foodstuffs

CONTINENT: North America

NIGER

CAPITAL ★ Niamey

POPULATION: 9.1 million

MAJOR LANGUAGES: French, Hausa, and Djerma

AREA: 489,206 sq mi; 1,267,044 sq km

LEADING EXPORTS: uranium ore, cowpeas, and livestock products

CONTINENT: Africa

NIGERIA

CAPITAL ★ Abuja

POPULATION: 103.9 million

MAJOR LANGUAGES: English, Hausa, Yoruba, Ibo, and Fulani

AREA: 356,700 sq mi; 923,853 sq km

LEADING EXPORTS: oil and cocoa

CONTINENT: Africa

NORWAY

CAPITAL ★ Oslo

POPULATION: 4.3 million

MAJOR LANGUAGE: Norwegian

AREA: 125,049 sq mi; 323,877 sq km

LEADING EXPORTS: oil, natural gas, fish, and ships

CONTINENT: Europe

OMAN

CAPITAL ★ Muscat

POPULATION: 2.2 million

MAJOR LANGUAGE: Arabic

AREA: 82,030 sq mi; 212,458 sq km

LEADING EXPORTS: oil and fish

CONTINENT: Asia

PAKISTAN

CAPITAL ★ Islamabad

POPULATION: 129.3 million

MAJOR LANGUAGES: Urdu, Punjabi, and English

AREA: 310,400 sq mi; 803,936 sq km

LEADING EXPORTS: cotton, rice, and textiles

CONTINENT: Asia

PALAU

CAPITAL ★ Koror

POPULATION: 16,952

MAJOR LANGUAGES: Palauan and English

AREA: 196 sq mi; 508 sq km

LEADING EXPORTS: trochus, tuna, and copra

CONTINENT: Islands in the Pacific Ocean

PANAMA

CAPITAL ★ Panama City

POPULATION: 2.7 million

MAJOR LANGUAGES: Spanish and English

AREA: 29,761 sq mi; 77,082 sq km

LEADING EXPORTS: bananas, sugar, shrimp, and coffee

CONTINENT: North America

PAPUA NEW GUINEA

CAPITAL ★ Port Moresby

POPULATION: 4.2 million

MAJOR LANGUAGES: Pidgin English, English, and Motu

AREA: 178,704 sq mi; 462,840 sq km

LEADING EXPORTS: gold, copper, coffee, palm oil, and copra

CONTINENT: Islands in the Pacific Ocean

PARAGUAY

CAPITAL ★ Asunción

POPULATION: 5.5 million

MAJOR LANGUAGES: Spanish and Guarani

AREA: 157,047 sq mi; 406,752 sq km

LEADING EXPORTS: cotton, soybeans, and meat products

CONTINENT: South America

PERU

CAPITAL ★ Lima

POPULATION: 24.5 million

MAJOR LANGUAGES: Spanish, Quechua, and Aymará

AREA: 496,222 sq mi; 1,285,216 sq km

LEADING EXPORTS: copper, fish products, and cotton

CONTINENT: South America

PHILIPPINES

CAPITAL ★ Manila

POPULATION: 74.5 million

MAJOR LANGUAGES: Filipino, Tagalog, and English

AREA: 115,830 sq mi; 300,000 sq km

LEADING EXPORTS: electronics, coconut products, and chemicals

CONTINENT: Asia

POLAND

CAPITAL ★ Warsaw

POPULATION: 38.6 million

MAJOR LANGUAGE: Polish

AREA: 120,727 sq mi; 312,683 sq km

LEADING EXPORTS: coal, machinery, chemicals, and metals

CONTINENT: Europe

PORTUGAL

CAPITAL ★ Lisbon

POPULATION: 9.9 million

MAJOR LANGUAGE: Portuguese

AREA: 35,550 sq mi; 92,075 sq km

LEADING EXPORTS: cotton, textiles, and cork

CONTINENT: Europe

QATAR

CAPITAL ★ Doha

POPULATION: 0.5 million

MAJOR LANGUAGES: Arabic and English

AREA: 4,000 sq mi; 11,437 sq km

LEADING EXPORTS: oil, steel, and fertilizers

CONTINENT: Asia

ROMANIA

CAPITAL ★ Bucharest

POPULATION: 21.7 million

MAJOR LANGUAGES: Romanian, Hungarian, and German

AREA: 91,700 sq mi; 237,500 sq km

LEADING EXPORTS: machinery, metals, chemicals, and timber

CONTINENT: Europe

RUSSIA

CAPITAL ★ Moscow

POPULATION: 148.2 million

MAJOR LANGUAGE: Russian

AREA: 6,592,800 sq mi; 17,075,400 sq km

LEADING EXPORTS: petroleum, natural gas, wood, and coal

CONTINENTS: Europe and Asia

RWANDA

CAPITAL ★ Kigali

POPULATION: 6.9 million

MAJOR LANGUAGES: Kinyarwanda, French, and Kiswahili

AREA: 10,169 sq mi; 26,338 sq km

LEADING EXPORTS: coffee and tea

CONTINENT: Africa

ST. KITTS AND NEVIS

CAPITAL ★ Basseterre

POPULATION: 41,000

MAJOR LANGUAGE: English

AREA: 65 sq mi; 169 sq km

LEADING EXPORTS: sugar, electronics, and stamps

CONTINENT: North America

ST. LUCIA

CAPITAL ★ Castries

POPULATION: 158,000

MAJOR LANGUAGES: English and French patois

AREA: 238 sq mi; 616 sq km

LEADING EXPORTS: bananas, cocoa, clothing, and vegetables

CONTINENT: North America

ST. VINCENT AND THE GRENADINES

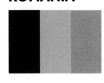

CAPITAL ★ Kingstown

POPULATION: 118,000

MAJOR LANGUAGE: English

AREA: 150 sq mi; 389 sq km

LEADING EXPORTS: bananas, arrowroot starch, taro, and tennis racquets

CONTINENT: North America

SAMOA

CAPITAL ★ Apia
POPULATION: 214,000
MAJOR LANGUAGES: Samoan and English
AREA: 1,093 sq mi; 2,831 sq km
LEADING EXPORTS: copra, cocoa, coconut oil, and cream
CONTINENT: Islands in the Pacific Ocean

SAN MARINO

CAPITAL ★ San Marino
POPULATION: 25,000
MAJOR LANGUAGE: Italian
AREA: 23 sq mi; 62 sq km
LEADING EXPORTS: lime, chestnuts, and wheat
CONTINENT: Europe

SÃO TOMÉ AND PRÍNCIPE

CAPITAL ★ São Tomé
POPULATION: 144,000
MAJOR LANGUAGE: Portuguese
AREA: 370 sq mi; 958 sq km
LEADING EXPORTS: cocoa, coffee, copra, and palm oil
CONTINENT: Africa

SAUDI ARABIA

CAPITAL ★ Riyadh
POPULATION: 19.4 million
MAJOR LANGUAGE: Arabic
AREA: 865,000 sq mi; 2,250,070 sq km
LEADING EXPORT: oil
CONTINENT: Asia

SENEGAL

CAPITAL ★ Dakar
POPULATION: 9.1 million
MAJOR LANGUAGES: French and Wolof
AREA: 75,954 sq mi; 196,722 sq km
LEADING EXPORTS: peanuts, phosphates, and canned fish
CONTINENT: Africa

SEYCHELLES

CAPITAL ★ Victoria
POPULATION: 78,000
MAJOR LANGUAGES: Creole, English, and French
AREA: 175 sq mi; 453 sq km
LEADING EXPORTS: fish, canned tuna, copra, and cinnamon bark
CONTINENT: Africa

SIERRA LEONE

CAPITAL ★ Freetown
POPULATION: 4.8 million
MAJOR LANGUAGES: English, Mende, Temne, and Krio
AREA: 27,925 sq mi; 73,326 sq km
LEADING EXPORTS: diamonds, rutile, bauxite, and cocoa
CONTINENT: Africa

SINGAPORE

CAPITAL ★ Singapore
POPULATION: 3.4 million
MAJOR LANGUAGES: Chinese, English, Malay, and Tamil
AREA: 247 sq mi; 639 sq km
LEADING EXPORTS: petroleum products, rubber, and computer equipment
CONTINENT: Asia

SLOVAKIA

CAPITAL ★ Bratislava
POPULATION: 5.4 million
MAJOR LANGUAGES: Slovak and Hungarian
AREA: 18,917 sq mi; 48,995 sq km
LEADING EXPORTS: machinery, chemicals, fuels, and minerals
CONTINENT: Europe

SLOVENIA

CAPITAL ★ Ljubljana
POPULATION: 2.0 million
MAJOR LANGUAGE: Slovenian
AREA: 7,819 sq mi; 20,251 sq km
LEADING EXPORTS: manufactured goods and chemicals
CONTINENT: Europe

SOLOMON ISLANDS

CAPITAL ★ Honiara
POPULATION: 0.4 million
MAJOR LANGUAGES: English, Pidgin English, and Melanesian
AREA: 11,500 sq mi; 29,785 sq km
LEADING EXPORTS: fish, timber, copra, and palm oil
CONTINENT: Islands in the Pacific Ocean

SOMALIA

CAPITAL ★ Mogadishu
POPULATION: 9.6 million
MAJOR LANGUAGES: Somali and Arabic
AREA: 246,199 sq mi; 637,655 sq km
LEADING EXPORTS: live animals, hides, and bananas
CONTINENT: Africa

SOUTH AFRICA

CAPITALS ★ Pretoria, Cape Town, and Bloemfontein
POPULATION: 41.7 million
MAJOR LANGUAGES: Afrikaans, English, Zulu and other African languages
AREA: 471,440 sq mi; 1,221,030 sq km
LEADING EXPORTS: gold, other minerals, and metals
CONTINENT: Africa

SPAIN

CAPITAL ★ Madrid

POPULATION: 38.8 million

MAJOR LANGUAGES: Spanish and Catalan

AREA: 199,365 sq mi; 505,992 sq km

LEADING EXPORTS: cars and trucks, machinery

CONTINENT: Europe

SRI LANKA

CAPITAL ★ Colombo

POPULATION: 18.5 million

MAJOR LANGUAGES: Sinhala, Tamil, and English

AREA: 25,332 sq mi; 65,610 sq km

LEADING EXPORTS: textiles, tea, rubber, and petroleum products

CONTINENT: Asia

SUDAN

CAPITAL ★ Khartoum

POPULATION: 31.1 million

MAJOR LANGUAGES: Arabic, Nubian and Sudanic languages

AREA: 967,491 sq mi; 2,505,802 sq km

LEADING EXPORTS: cotton, peanuts, gum arabic, and sesame

CONTINENT: Africa

SURINAME

CAPITAL ★ Paramaribo

POPULATION: 0.4 million

MAJOR LANGUAGES: Dutch, English, and Hindi

AREA: 63,251 sq mi; 163,820 sq km

LEADING EXPORTS: bauxite, alumina, rice, and shrimp

CONTINENT: South America

SWAZILAND

CAPITAL ★ Mbabane

POPULATION: 1.0 million

MAJOR LANGUAGES: Siswati and English

AREA: 6,704 sq mi; 17,363 sq km

LEADING EXPORTS: sugar, wood products, asbestos, and citrus

CONTINENT: Africa

SWEDEN

CAPITAL ★ Stockholm

POPULATION: 8.9 million

MAJOR LANGUAGE: Swedish

AREA: 173,800 sq mi; 449,964 sq km

LEADING EXPORTS: machinery, motor vehicles, and wood products

CONTINENT: Europe

SWITZERLAND

CAPITAL ★ Bern

POPULATION: 7.0 million

MAJOR LANGUAGES: German, French, Italian, and Romansch

AREA: 15,941 sq mi; 41,288 sq km

LEADING EXPORTS: machinery, metal products, and textiles

CONTINENT: Europe

SYRIA

CAPITAL ★ Damascus

POPULATION: 15.6 million

MAJOR LANGUAGES: Arabic and Kurdish

AREA: 71,498 sq mi; 185,180 sq km

LEADING EXPORTS: oil, textiles, cotton, fruits, and vegetables

CONTINENT: Asia

TAIWAN

CAPITAL ★ Taipei

POPULATION: 21.3 million

MAJOR LANGUAGES: Mandarin, Taiwanese, and Hakka dialects

AREA: 13,895 sq mi; 35,988 sq km

LEADING EXPORTS: textiles, electronic products, and information products

CONTINENT: Asia

TAJIKISTAN

CAPITAL ★ Dushanbe

POPULATION: 5.9 million

MAJOR LANGUAGES: Tajik and Russian

AREA: 55,300 sq mi; 143,100 sq km

LEADING EXPORTS: aluminum, cotton, and fruit

CONTINENT: Asia

TANZANIA

CAPITAL ★ Dar es Salaam

POPULATION: 29.1 million

MAJOR LANGUAGES: Swahili and English

AREA: 364,879 sq mi; 945,037 sq km

LEADING EXPORTS: coffee, cotton, sisal, and cloves

CONTINENT: Africa

THAILAND

CAPITAL ★ Bangkok

POPULATION: 58.9 million

MAJOR LANGUAGES: Thai and English

AREA: 198,455 sq mi; 514,000 sq km

LEADING EXPORTS: machinery and food

CONTINENT: Asia

COUNTRIES *of the* WORLD

TOGO

CAPITAL ★ Lomé

POPULATION: 4.6 million

MAJOR LANGUAGES: French, Kabye, Ewe, Mina, and Dagomba

AREA: 21,925 sq mi; 56,785 sq km

LEADING EXPORTS: phosphates, cocoa, coffee, and cotton

CONTINENT: Africa

TONGA

CAPITAL ★ Nuku'alofa

POPULATION: 106,000

MAJOR LANGUAGES: Tongan and English

AREA: 290 sq mi; 751 sq km

LEADING EXPORTS: copra, coconut oil, bananas, and fruits

CONTINENT: Islands in the Pacific Ocean

TRINIDAD AND TOBAGO

CAPITAL ★ Port-of-Spain

POPULATION: 1.3 million

MAJOR LANGUAGES: English, Hindi, and French

AREA: 1,980 sq mi; 5,128 sq km

LEADING EXPORTS: oil and steel products

CONTINENT: North America

TUNISIA

CAPITAL ★ Tunis

POPULATION: 9.0 million

MAJOR LANGUAGES: Arabic and French

AREA: 63,170 sq mi; 163,610 sq km

LEADING EXPORTS: textiles, agricultural products, and chemicals

CONTINENT: Africa

TURKEY

CAPITAL ★ Ankara

POPULATION: 62.5 million

MAJOR LANGUAGES: Turkish, Kurdish, and Arabic

AREA: 300,947 sq mi; 779,452 sq km

LEADING EXPORTS: agricultural products and textiles

CONTINENTS: Asia and Europe

TURKMENISTAN

CAPITAL ★ Ashgabat

POPULATION: 4.1 million

MAJOR LANGUAGES: Turkmen, Russian, and Uzbek

AREA: 188,500 sq mi; 488,100 sq km

LEADING EXPORTS: gas, oil, chemicals, and cotton

CONTINENT: Asia

TUVALU

CAPITAL ★ Funafuti

POPULATION: 10,000

MAJOR LANGUAGES: Tuvaluan and English

AREA: 10 sq mi; 26 sq km

LEADING EXPORT: copra

CONTINENT: Islands in the Pacific Ocean

UGANDA

CAPITAL ★ Kampala

POPULATION: 20.2 million

MAJOR LANGUAGES: English, Luganda, Swahili, and Bantu languages

AREA: 91,459 sq mi; 236,880 sq km

LEADING EXPORTS: coffee, cotton, and tea

CONTINENT: Africa

UKRAINE

CAPITAL ★ Kiev

POPULATION: 50.9 million

MAJOR LANGUAGES: Ukrainian, Russian, Romanian, and Polish

AREA: 233,000 sq mi; 603,700 sq km

LEADING EXPORTS: coal, electric power, and metals

CONTINENT: Europe

UNITED ARAB EMIRATES

CAPITAL ★ Abu Dhabi

POPULATION: 3.1 million

MAJOR LANGUAGES: Arabic, Persian, English, Hindi, and Urdu

AREA: 32,000 sq mi; 82,880 sq km

LEADING EXPORTS: oil and natural gas

CONTINENT: Asia

UNITED KINGDOM

CAPITAL ★ London

POPULATION: 58.5 million

MAJOR LANGUAGES: English, Welsh, and Scottish Gaelic

AREA: 94, 247 sq mi; 244, 100 sq km

LEADING EXPORTS: machinery and chemicals

CONTINENT: Europe

UNITED STATES

CAPITAL ★ Washington, D.C.

POPULATION: 265.1 million

MAJOR LANGUAGES: English and Spanish

AREA: 3,536,341 sq mi; 9,159,123 sq km

LEADING EXPORTS: machinery, chemicals, aircraft, and military equipment

CONTINENT: North America

URUGUAY

CAPITAL ★ Montevideo

POPULATION: 3.2 million

MAJOR LANGUAGES: Spanish and Brazilero

AREA: 68,040 sq mi; 176,224 sq km

LEADING EXPORTS: meat and wool

CONTINENT: South America

UZBEKISTAN

CAPITAL ★ Tashkent

POPULATION: 23.4 million

MAJOR LANGUAGES: Uzbek, Russian, and Tajik

AREA: 172,700 sq mi; 447,400 sq km

LEADING EXPORTS: cotton, gold, textiles, and chemicals

CONTINENT: Asia

VANUATU

CAPITAL ★ Port-Vila

POPULATION: 178,000

MAJOR LANGUAGES: Bislama, English, and French

AREA: 5,700 sq mi; 14,763 sq km

LEADING EXPORTS: copra, cocoa, coffee, and fish

CONTINENT: Islands in the Pacific Ocean

VATICAN CITY (The Holy See)

CAPITAL ★ Vatican City

POPULATION: 830

MAJOR LANGUAGES: Italian and Latin

AREA: 0.17 sq mi; 0.44 sq km

LEADING EXPORTS: (not available)

CONTINENT: Europe

VENEZUELA

CAPITAL ★ Caracas

POPULATION: 22.0 million

MAJOR LANGUAGES: Spanish and Indian dialects

AREA: 352,143 sq mi; 912,050 sq km

LEADING EXPORTS: oil, iron ore, and bauxite

CONTINENT: South America

VIETNAM

CAPITAL ★ Hanoi

POPULATION: 74.0 million

MAJOR LANGUAGES: Vietnamese, French, Chinese, English, and Khmer

AREA: 127,246 sq mi; 329,566 sq km

LEADING EXPORTS: agricultural products, minerals, and marine products

CONTINENT: Asia

YEMEN

CAPITAL ★ San'a

POPULATION: 13.5 million

MAJOR LANGUAGE: Arabic

AREA: 203, 850 sq mi; 527,970 sq km

LEADING EXPORTS: cotton, coffee, hides, and vegetables

CONTINENT: Asia

YUGOSLAVIA

CAPITAL ★ Belgrade

POPULATION: 10.6 million

MAJOR LANGUAGES: Serbo-Croatian and Albanian

AREA: 39,449 sq mi; 102,169 sq km

LEADING EXPORTS: machinery and transport equipment

CONTINENT: Europe

ZAMBIA

CAPITAL ★ Lusaka

POPULATION: 9.2 million

MAJOR LANGUAGES: English and about 70 Bantu dialects

AREA: 290,586 sq mi; 752,618 sq km

LEADING EXPORTS: copper, zinc, lead, cobalt, and tobacco

CONTINENT: Africa

ZIMBABWE

CAPITAL ★ Harare

POPULATION: 11.3 million

MAJOR LANGUAGES: English, Shona, and Sindebele

AREA: 150,698 sq mi; 390,308 sq km

LEADING EXPORTS: gold, tobacco, and asbestos

CONTINENT: Africa

SOURCE: population, languages, area, exports—*Information Please Almanac*, 1997; additional information on languages—*The World Almanac and Book of Facts*, 1997

EUROPE

	paint the walls of caves near Avignon, France		other parts of the continent
10,000 B.C.	Early Europeans make tiny blades, called *microliths*, out of flint	**5500 B.C.**	Early pottery decorated with patterned lines is made through much of the continent
7000 B.C.	Farming begins in southern Europe, as Greek farmers raise wheat and herd sheep and goats		

	appear in southern France
4500 B.C.	Stone axes are traded and used to clear forest land for farming

AFRICA

10,000 B.C.	People begin to build villages along the Nile River	**6000 B.C.**	Farmers build irrigation ditches along the Nile River
8000 B.C.	People along the Nile use reed nets to catch fish	**6000 B.C.**	People use barbed harpoons to catch fish in Africa's rivers and lakes
6500 B.C.	Rock paintings in the Sahara Desert show animals long gone from the region, such as buffalo, giraffes and elephants		

5000 B.C.	Farmers grow wheat and barley in Egypt
4500 B.C.	Nubian artisans make pottery in what is now Sudan

ASIA AND AUSTRALIA

40,000 years ago	Aborigines settle in Australia after arriving from Indonesia and Asia	**6000 B.C.**	Early agriculture begins at Catal Huyuk, in what is today Turkey
8000 B.C.	Hunter-gatherers use wild rice in East and Southeast Asia		
7000 B.C.	Before the development of pottery, early people in western Asia make "white ware" from lime and ash		

5000 B.C.	First towns settled in Sumer
5000 B.C.	Early settlements emerge in China
5000 B.C.	Copper used in Mesopotamia

THE AMERICAS

40,000 years ago	Asian hunters begin to cross the Beringia land bridge	**5000 B.C.**	Cochise and Chumash cultures develop in southwestern North America
15,000 years ago	People have spread throughout the Americas	**5000 B.C.**	Chinchorros people build settlements in what is today northern Chile
7000 B.C.	Native American craftworkers use stone tools for woodworking		

5000 B.C.	Early maize farming begins in what is today Mexico
4500 B.C.	Indians use weighted nets to fish the waters of the American northwest

The Ancient World

4000–3000 B.C.		3000–2000 B.C.		2000–1000 B.C.	
4000 B.C.	Farmers cultivate crops in the British Isles	3000 B.C.	Artisans on Crete use bronze and gold	2000 B.C.	Minoan palace civilization begins to flourish in Crete
3500 B.C.	New Stone Age period begins in western Europe	3000 B.C.	Loom weaving begins in Europe	1600 B.C.	Mycenaeans gain power in Aegean region
3300 B.C.	"Iceman" takes his last hike into the Alps	3000 B.C.	Huge stone structures built at Stonehenge, England	1500 B.C.	Minoan culture ends in Crete
		2200 B.C.	Bronze Age begins in Ireland	1400 B.C.	Mycenaean culture spreads to Greece
4000 B.C.	The sail is first used on boats on the Nile River	2772 B.C.	Egyptians create a calendar of 365 days	2000 B.C.	Kushite culture develops along the Upper Nile
4000 B.C.	Artisans make pottery in Ghana, West Africa	2600 B.C.	Pharaoh Khufu orders construction of the Great Pyramid	1550 B.C.	Egyptians defeat the Hyksos and begin the New Kingdom period
3200 B.C.	Egyptians begin to develop hieroglyphic writing	2500 B.C.	Egyptians build the Great Sphinx at Giza	1500 B.C.	Queen Hatshepsut is pharaoh
3100 B.C.	Menes unites Upper and Lower Egypt	2500 B.C.	First libraries are built in Egypt	1362–1352 B.C.	Tutankhamun is pharaoh
				1250 B.C.	Possible date of Moses' Exodus
4000 B.C.	Sumerians begin to settle in the Fertile Crescent	3000 B.C.	City-states begin in Sumer	1800 B.C.	Code of Hammurabi recorded
3500 B.C.	City of Ur founded in Mesopotamia	3000 B.C.	Plow first used in China	1700 B.C.	Babylonians conquer Sumer and more of Mesopotamia
3500 B.C.	Cuneiform writing appears in Sumer	2500 B.C.	Writing and trade begin in Indus Valley	1700 B.C.	Possible date of Abraham's journey to Canaan
3100 B.C.	Bronzework begins in Mesopotamia	2300 B.C.	Mohenjo-Daro and Harappa flourish in Indus River Valley	1700 B.C.	The Shang gain control of the Huang Valley
		2250 B.C.	Ziggurat built at Ur	1500 B.C.	Aryans migrate into Indus River Valley
3500 B.C.	Villagers in what is now Peru use the llama as a pack animal	2000 B.C.	Inuit people hunt caribou and seals in the Arctic	2000 B.C.	Andean settlements thrive in Peru
3500 B.C.	Cotton becomes an important crop in what is now Peru			1400 B.C.	Farming villages develop in Central America and southwestern North America
3500 B.C.	Haida culture begins on northwest coast of what is now Canada			1200 B.C.	Olmec civilization begins in Mexico

R37

WORLD HISTORY TIME LINE

	1000–750 B.C.		750–500 B.C.		500–250 B.C.	
EUROPE	900 B.C.	Etruscans settle north of the Tiber River, in what is now Italy	700 B.C.	According to Roman legend, Romulus and Remus found the city on seven hills	499 B.C.	Persian Wars begin
	900 B.C.	Greek city-state of Sparta is founded	700 B.C.	Homer creates the first Greek epics	450 B.C.	Twelve Tables become basis of Roman Law
	776 B.C.	First Olympic Games are held in Greece	600–560 B.C.	Aesop tells fables in ancient Greece	431 B.C.	Peloponnesian Wars begin
			509 B.C.	Patricians take power in Rome	399 B.C.	Socrates is on trial
			500 B.C.	Greeks build the Parthenon to house statues of gods and goddesses	336 B.C.	Alexander the Great spreads Greek culture
AFRICA	900 B.C.	Nok people of Nigeria use terra cotta	700 B.C.	Iron tools made in Egypt	305 B.C.	Ptolemy II founds library in Alexandria
	900 B.C.	Kushite kingdom in Sudan thrives	671 B.C.	Assyrians overrun Egypt	300 B.C.	Kushite kingdom expands and develops extensive trade networks
	814 B.C.	Phoenician traders found colony at Carthage	600 B.C.	Nok people of Nigeria mine iron		
			600 B.C.	Carthaginian explorers sail southward from North Africa		
ASIA AND AUSTRALIA	950(?)–928 B.C.	King Solomon rules Israel	689 B.C.	Assyrians invade Babylonia and sack Babylon	500 B.C.	Indian traders bring Hindu ideas to Southeast Asia
	911 B.C.	Rise of Assyrian power in Mesopotamia	586 B.C.	Armies of New Babylonia conquer Judah and exile Jews	400 B.C.	Buddhism spreads through Asia
			539 B.C.	Persia's Cyrus the Great conquers Babylon and frees exiled Jews	400 B.C.	Confucius teaches about duty in China
			528 B.C.	Possible date that Siddhartha Gautama, founder of Buddhism, begins teaching in India	322 B.C.	Chandragupta founds Mauryan empire in India
					273 B.C.	Asoka spreads Buddhist teaching and religious tolerance in India
THE AMERICAS	1000 B.C.	La Venta becomes center of Olmec culture in Mexico	600 B.C.	Oaxaca culture begins to dominate Olmec civilization in Mexico	500 B.C.	Farmers in Ohio Valley construct burial mounds
	850 B.C.	Peruvians build temple at Chavín de Huantar in Andes			300–100 B.C.	City of Teotihuacán develops in Mexico

250 B.C.–A.D. 1		A.D. 1–250		A.D. 250–500	
73–71 B.C.	Spartacus leads slave revolt in Rome	A.D. 29	Jesus' religious teachings become the foundation for Christianity	A.D. 306	Constantine rules Roman empire
45 B.C.	Julius Caesar becomes dictator of Rome	A.D. 80	Roman Colosseum is completed	A.D. 312	Christianity tolerated in Roman empire
27 B.C.	Augustus Caesar begins Pax Romana in Roman empire	A.D. 100	Network of Roman roads increases trade and travel through the empire	A.D. 445	Attila the Hun attacks western Europe
				A.D. 476	Rome falls to Germanic invaders
250 B.C.	Kush begins Golden Age, which lasts for about 300 years	A.D. 238	North Africans revolt against Roman empire	A.D. 300	Ptolemy describes Earth-centered universe
202 B.C.	Roman army defeats Hannibal's army at Zama			A.D. 300	Gold-salt trade develops in Ghana
30 B.C.	Egypt becomes Roman province			A.D. 324	King Ezana of Ethiopia becomes a Christian
				A.D. 350	Defeated by Aksum, Kushite civilization at Meroe ends
				A.D. 400	St. Augustine spreads Christianity in North Africa
250 B.C.	Kingdom of Parthia emerges in eastern Persia	A.D. 50	St. Paul spreads Christianity	A.D. 320	Gupta empire emerges in Ganges Valley, India
215 B.C.	Shihuangdi's Qin dynasty begins construction of the Great Wall of China	A.D. 70	Romans destroy Jerusalem, beginning Jewish diaspora	A.D. 330	Constantinople becomes new capital of Roman empire
206 B.C.	Han Dynasty begins in China, adopting many Confucian ideas	A.D. 101	Chinese invent paper	A.D. 400	Chinese manufacture steel
		A.D. 120	Chinese invent seismograph		
		A.D. 220	Fall of Han Dynasty in China		
200 B.C.	Maya culture begins to develop in Central America	A.D. 100	Hopewell culture flourishes on upper Mississippi	A.D. 250	Classic period of Maya civilization in Guatemala, Honduras, and eastern Mexico
200 B.C.	Nazca culture begins in southern Peru	A.D. 100–200	Oaxaca culture reaches height	A.D. 500	Hopewell culture builds burial mounds and makes pottery and iron weapons
100 B.C.	Anasazi culture emerges in southwestern United States				

A.D. 529–534	Byzantine Emperor Justinian issues Codes of Law
A.D. 670	Bulgars from Russia settle near Danube River
A.D. 715	Muslims conquer most of Spain
A.D. 732	Charles Martel, king of Franks, stops Muslim advance into France

A.D. 800	First castles built in western Europe
A.D. 843	Charlemagne's Frankish empire breaks up
A.D. 885–886	Vikings raid Paris, France
A.D. 900	Feudalism is widespread social and economic system
A.D. 986	Viking explorer Eric the Red founds colony in Greenland

A.D. 500	Kingdom of Ghana rises to power in West Africa
A.D. 640–641	Islamic leader Caliph Omar conquers Egypt
A.D. 642	Arabs build first mosque in al-Fustat, new capital of Muslim Egypt
A.D. 711	Arab empire conquers North Africa

A.D. 800	Arabs and Persians explore East African coast and set up trading stations
A.D. 800–950	Christianity continues in Ethiopia after decline of Aksum
A.D. 950–1050	Igbo-Ukwu culture thrives in eastern Nigeria
A.D. 969	Fatimid dynasty conquers Egypt and builds Cairo
A.D. 970	Fatimids build one of the world's first universities in Cairo
A.D. 970	Ghana empire flourishes in West Africa

A.D. 552	Buddhism spreads to Japan from China and Korea
A.D. 595	Indian mathematicians use decimal system
A.D. 605–610	Sui emperors build Grand Canal in China
A.D. 610	According to Muslim sources, the date that Muhammad founds Islam in Arabia
A.D. 622	According to Muslim sources, Muhammad makes the migration, or hijra, from Mecca to Medina

A.D. 700–1100	Baghdad is capital of Arab empire
A.D. 794–1184	Heian period in Japan
A.D. 802	Jayavarman II rules the Khmer throne
A.D. 868	Chinese use wood blocks to print books
A.D. 889	Khmers build capital at Angkor, in what is today Cambodia
A.D. 907–26	Mongols conquer inner Mongolia and northern China
A.D. 970	Chinese introduce paper money

A.D. 500	Polynesians from Southeast Asia settle in Hawaiian Islands
A.D. 600	Height of Maya civilization
A.D. 650	Teotihuacán thrives as trade center in Mexico

A.D. 900	Maya civilization in southern Mexico mysteriously collapses
A.D. 900–1000	Pueblo settlements thrive in North America
A.D. 990	Toltec people take over Maya city of Chichén Itzá in Mexico

A.D. 1000–1250	A.D. 1250–1500
A.D. 1054 Church in Constantinople breaks with Church of Rome	**A.D. 1348–1352** Bubonic plague (Black Death) devastates Europe
A.D. 1066 Normans defeat English at Battle of Hastings	**A.D. 1350** Renaissance begins in Italy
A.D. 1095 Pope Urban calls for the First Crusade	**A.D. 1429** Joan of Arc leads French against the English at Orléans
A.D. 1150 Chartres cathedral built	**A.D. 1448** John Gutenberg develops the printing press
A.D. 1209 St. Francis of Assisi founds Franciscan religious order	**A.D. 1453** Ottomans capture Constantinople; end of Byzantine empire
A.D. 1215 King John of England signs Magna Carta	**A.D. 1478–1492** Renaissance art patron Lorenzo de Medici rules Italy
	A.D. 1492 Columbus sails from Spain to America
	A.D. 1497–1499 Portuguese explorer Vasco da Gama sails around Africa to India

A.D. 1000–1250	A.D. 1250–1500
A.D. 1000 Bantu-speaking kingdoms emerge in southern Africa	**A.D. 1300** Timbuktu is a major trading center
A.D. 1000 Kingdoms in West Africa flourish from gold trade	**A.D. 1324** Mansa Musa, emperor of Mali, goes on pilgrimage to Mecca, Arabia
A.D. 1100 Swahili city-states develop trade with Arabia and India	**A.D. 1350** Kingdom of Great Zimbabwe thrives on gold trade
A.D. 1200 City-state of Kilwa prospers	**A.D. 1352–1353** Ibn Batuta writes an account of his travels across Africa
A.D. 1235 Sunjata founds Mali empire in West Africa	**A.D. 1420** Portuguese sailors begin to explore west coast of Africa
	A.D. 1488 Bartholomeu Dias sails around tip of Africa
	A.D. 1490 Songhai empire begins in West Africa

A.D. 1000–1250	A.D. 1250–1500
A.D. 1000 Chinese perfect gunpowder	**A.D. 1271** Marco Polo sets out for China
A.D. 1000 Murasaki Shikibu writes *Tale of Genji*	**A.D. 1279** Kublai Khan founds Yuan Dynasty
A.D. 1076 Muslim Seljuk Turks capture Jerusalem	**A.D. 1301** Osman I founds Ottoman dynasty in Turkey
A.D. 1099 Crusaders from Europe recapture Jerusalem	**A.D. 1368** Mongols are driven from China; Ming dynasty begins
A.D. 1100 Samurai dominate Japan	**A.D. 1453** Ottoman Turks conquer Constantinople, renaming the city *Istanbul*
A.D. 1100 Angkor Wat is built in what is now Cambodia	
A.D. 1192 Yoritomo becomes first shogun in Japan	
A.D. 1209 Genghis Khan leads Mongols to conquer China	

A.D. 1000–1250	A.D. 1250–1500
A.D. 1000 Viking explorer Leif Erickson reaches America	**A.D. 1300** Incas expand their empire throughout the central Andes
A.D. 1100 Anasazi people in North America build cliff dwellings at Mesa Verde	**A.D. 1325** Aztecs found city of Tenochtitlán in what is today Mexico City
A.D. 1200 Incas in Peru settle at Cuzco	**A.D. 1450** Inca city of Machu Picchu built in Peru
	A.D. 1486–1521 Aztec empire at its height
	A.D. 1497 John Cabot claims land in North America for England

A.D. 1517	Martin Luther nails the 95 Theses on a church door in Germany
A.D. 1519–1522	Ferdinand Magellan's crew completes sailing voyage around the world
A.D. 1534	Henry VIII of England makes himself head of English church
A.D. 1541–1564	John Calvin leads church reforms in Switzerland
A.D. 1550	Reformation spreads throughout Europe
A.D. 1558–1603	Elizabeth I reigns in England
A.D. 1588	English warships fight the Spanish Armada
A.D. 1595	William Shakespeare writes *Romeo and Juliet*
A.D. 1643–1715	Louis XIV rules France
A.D. 1653–1658	Oliver Cromwell is Lord Protector of Britain, replacing monarchy with parliamentary rule
A.D. 1682–1725	Peter the Great rules Russia
A.D. 1687	Isaac Newton publishes his "laws of gravity"
A.D. 1689	England's Parliament drafts a Bill of Rights, limiting the power of the monarchy

AFRICA

A.D. 1500	Songhai empire reaches height
A.D. 1575	Portugese begin colonization of Angola
A.D. 1590–591	Moroccan army overthrows Songhai empire
A.D. 1598	Dutch set up trading posts in western Africa
A.D. 1652	Dutch found Cape Town
A.D. 1680	Asante kingdom begins in West Africa

ASIA AND AUSTRALIA

A.D. 1520–1566	Ottoman empire reaches height under Süleyman
A.D. 1556–1605	Mogul emperor Akbar reforms government in India
A.D. 1600–1614	English, Dutch, Danish, and French East India Companies founded
A.D. 1603	Tokugawa period begins in Japan
A.D. 1603	Japan begins to restrict foreign contacts
A.D. 1616	Dutch explorer Dirk Hartog lands on the West Coast of Australia
A.D. 1627	Manchus conquer Korea
A.D. 1632–1648	Shah Jahan builds the Taj Mahal
A.D. 1644	Manchus conquer Beijing and found the Qing dynasty
A.D. 1683	Chinese control Formosa, what is today called Taiwan

THE AMERICAS

A.D. 1500	Pedro Cabral claims Brazil for Portugal
A.D. 1521	Hernando Cortés conquers Aztecs
A.D. 1531–1535	Francisco Pizarro conquers Inca empire
A.D. 1534	Jacques Cartier claims what is now Canada for France
A.D. 1549	Coronado conquers Zuñi pueblos
A.D. 1580	Iroquois League unites Five Nations
A.D. late 1500s	Powhatan confederacy organized
A.D. 1607	The English establish the Jamestown settlement in Virginia
A.D. 1608	French settlers found Quebec
A.D. 1610	Henry Hudson explores Hudson Bay
A.D. 1620	Pilgrims sail to Plymouth in the *Mayflower*
A.D. 1636	Puritans found Harvard University
A.D. 1664	English capture Dutch colony of New Amsterdam and rename it New York
A.D. 1681	Quaker William Penn founds Pennsylvania

A.D. 1700–1800		A.D. 1800–1900	
A.D. 1700	Industrial Revolution begins	A.D. 1804	Napoleon crowns himself emperor
A.D. 1769	James Watt perfects the steam engine	A.D. 1815	Napoleon defeated at Waterloo
A.D. 1776	Adam Smith writes *The Wealth of Nations*	A.D. 1825	The Industrial Revolution spreads to Germany, Belgium, and France
A.D. 1789	French Revolution begins	A.D. 1827	First photograph taken
A.D. 1793	Louis XVI is executed	A.D. 1848	Karl Marx publishes *Communist Manifesto*
A.D. 1799	Napoleon overthrows the French government	A.D. 1861	Serfdom is abolished in Russia
		A.D. 1895	Lumière brothers invent the film projector
		A.D. 1895	Marconi invents radio

A.D. 1720	Yoruba kingdom of Oyo prospers	A.D. 1822	Liberia is founded as home for freed United States slaves
A.D. 1730	More than 50,000 Africans are shipped each year to the Americas as slaves, in the Triangular Trade	A.D. 1840	Zanzibar becomes a commercial center, exporting cloves and other spices
A.D. 1795	British seize Cape Colony from the Dutch	A.D. 1850	Slave trading is abolished in most countries
A.D. 1800	Benin City becomes a center for West African slave trade	A.D. 1853–1856	British explorer Dr. Livingstone crosses Africa
		A.D. 1867	Diamonds discovered in South Africa
		A.D. 1869	The Suez Canal is opened in Egypt
		A.D. 1872	Britain grants Cape Colony self-government

A.D. 1750	Japanese arts and commerce flourish under Tokugawa shogunate	A.D. 1823	The New South Wales Act allows the New South Wales colony in Australia to create a legislative body
A.D. 1750	Rice production in China increases greatly	A.D. 1842	After a war with Britain, China is forced to open its ports to Western traders
A.D. 1770	England's Captain Cook explores eastern coast of Australia	A.D. 1853	Matthew C. Perry enters Edo Bay
A.D. 1784	United States begins to trade with China	A.D. 1854	United States opens Japan to trade
A.D. 1788	The first fleet of ships carrying convicts from England arrives in Australia; the English colony of New South Wales is founded in Australia	A.D. 1868–1912	Meiji restoration in Japan brings industrialization; capital moves to Edo, present-day Tokyo
		A.D. 1894	Women win the right to vote in the Australian colony of South Australia

A.D. 1700	Sugar plantations flourish in Caribbean	A.D. 1804–1806	Louis and Clark explore Louisiana Territory
A.D. 1754–1763	French and Indian War is fought	A.D. 1821	Bolívar frees northern South America
A.D. 1775	American Revolution begins at Lexington	A.D. 1821	San Martín wins independence for Peru
A.D. 1776	Declaration of Independence signed	A.D. 1821	Mexico wins independence from Spain
A.D. 1781	British surrender to Americans at Yorktown	A.D. 1823	Monroe Doctrine opposes European interference in the Western Hemisphere
A.D. 1789	George Washington becomes first President of the United States	A.D. 1836	Texas gains independence from Mexico
A.D. 1791	Toussaint L'Ouverture leads revolt against French in Haiti	A.D. 1861–1865	United States Civil War is fought
		A.D. 1867	Canada's provinces unite
		A.D. 1869	Transcontinental Railroad completed
		A.D. 1876	Alexander Graham Bell invents telephone
		A.D. 1883	Thomas Edison invents lightbulb

A.D. 1914	World War I begins		

		A.D. 1933	...television

EUROPE

A.D. 1914	World War I begins
A.D. 1917	Russian Revolution ends Tsarist rule and brings Communist Party to power
A.D. 1919	Treaty of Versailles ends World War I
A.D. 1920	League of Nations founded
A.D. 1924	Joseph Stalin becomes dictator of Soviet Union

A.D. 1933	Adolf Hitler rises to power in Germany
A.D. 1933–1945	About 6 million European Jews are killed during the Holocaust
A.D. 1939	Germany invades Poland; World War II begins
A.D. 1944	Allies land at Normandy, France on D-Day to free Europe from Hitler's advance
A.D. 1945	World War II ends
A.D. 1945	The United Nations is created
A.D. 1949	As Cold War intensifies, Western nations organize NATO

AFRICA

A.D. 1912	The African National Congress is founded in the Union of South Africa
A.D. 1914	European powers control nearly all of Africa
A.D. 1922	Howard Carter discovers King Tut's tomb
A.D. 1923	Ethiopia joins League of Nations

A.D. 1931	South Africa gains independence from Britain
A.D. 1931	First trans-African railway completed
A.D. 1942	Battle of El Alamein fought in Egypt during World War II
A.D. 1948	Apartheid system begins in South Africa

ASIA AND AUSTRALIA

A.D. 1901	The Commonwealth of Australia comes into existence as a new nation
A.D. 1910	Japan invades Korea
A.D. 1911–1912	Manchu dynasty ends in China; Sun Yat-Sen establishes a republic
A.D. 1913	Indian poet Rabindranath Tagore receives Nobel Prize for Literature
A.D. 1920	Mohandas Gandhi begins nonviolent protest against British rule in India

A.D. 1931	Japanese occupy Chinese province of Manchuria
A.D. 1932	Abd al-Aziz ibn Saud unifies a new kingdom called Saudi Arabia
A.D. 1934	Mao Zedong leads Chinese Communists on the Long March
A.D. 1937–1945	War breaks out between China and Japan
A.D. 1945	United States drops first atomic bombs on Hiroshima and Nagasaki
A.D. 1947	India and Pakistan gain independence from Britain
A.D. 1948	Israel gains independence
A.D. 1949	Mao Zedong establishes communist rule in China

THE AMERICAS

A.D. 1903	Wright Brothers make first successful airplane flight
A.D. 1908	Henry Ford produces first Model T car
A.D. 1914	Panama Canal opens
A.D. 1918	President Wilson proposes "Fourteen Points" as a plan for lasting world peace
A.D. 1920	Women gain voting rights in the United States

A.D. 1929	Great Depression begins with the New York stock market crash
A.D. 1933	Franklin Roosevelt launches the New Deal to help end the Great Depression
A.D. 1941	Japanese bomb Pearl Harbor; United States enters World War II
A.D. 1945	United States scientists build first atomic bomb
A.D. 1948–1951	The United States' Marshall Plan helps Europe recover from the war

A Century of Conflict

A.D. **1955**	Communist countries sign the Warsaw Pact	A.D. **1979**	Margaret Thatcher becomes first female prime minister of Britain
A.D. **1956**	Eastern European countries revolt against communism	A.D. **1980**	Lech Walesa leads a strike by Polish workers and starts the Solidarity movement
A.D. **1957**	Russians launch *Sputnik* space mission	A.D. **1985**	Soviet leader Mikhail Gorbachev introduces *glasnost*
A.D. **1961**	Berlin Wall is built	A.D. **1989**	Berlin Wall is torn down
		A.D. **1991**	Cold War ends as the Soviet Union collapses
		A.D. **1991**	Yugoslavia breaks up; civil war begins
		A.D. **1997**	President Bill Clinton and Soviet leader Boris Yeltsin sign an agreement in Finland aimed at helping Russia join the global economy

A.D. **1952**	Egypt gains independence from Britain	A.D. **1986**	Severe droughts hit Africa, especially Ethiopia
A.D. **1956**	Egypt takes control of the Suez Canal	A.D. **1986**	Western nations put pressure on South Africa to abolish apartheid
A.D. **1957**	Ghana gains independence from Britain	A.D. **1992**	Foreign troops bring aid to Somalia
A.D. **1958**	Sékou Touré used boycotts to help Guinea gain independence from France	A.D. **1993**	Apartheid ends in South Africa
A.D. **1963–1990**	Nelson Mandela imprisoned in South Africa	A.D. **1994**	Nelson Mandela is elected president of South Africa
A.D. **1974**	Nigeria becomes leading oil producer in Africa		

A.D. **1950–1953**	Korean War is fought	A.D. **1978**	Israel and Egypt hold peace-talks at Camp David in the United States
A.D. **1951**	Australia forms an economic and political partnership with the United States	A.D. **1980**	Iran-Iraq war begins
A.D. **1960**	Arab nations form the Organization of Petroleum Exporting Countries, or OPEC	A.D. **1989**	Chinese students protest for democracy in Beijing's Tiananmen Square
A.D. **1964**	Palestinians found the Palestine Liberation Organization, or PLO	A.D. **1990–1991**	Persian Gulf War is fought
A.D. **1966**	Indira Gandhi becomes prime minister of India	A.D. **1993**	Palestinian and Israeli leaders sign agreement in United States for Palestinian self-rule
A.D. **1965–1975**	Vietnam War is fought	A.D. **1997**	Jiang Zemin becomes the leader of China after the death of Deng Xiaoping
A.D. **1966–1969**	Mao Zedong begins Cultural Revolution in China	A.D. **1997**	Hong Kong becomes reunited with China after being a British colony since the 1800s
A.D. **1970**	Japan becomes second-largest economic power in the world		

A.D. **1960–1965**	Martin Luther King, Jr., leads civil rights movement in the United States	A.D. **1980–1992**	Civil war breaks out in El Salvador
A.D. **1962**	The United States faces down the Soviet Union in the Cuban Missile Crisis, a tense moment of the Cold War	A.D. **1987**	Oscar Arias Sánchez is first Latin American to win Nobel Peace Prize
A.D. **1962**	Jamaica gains independence from Britain	A.D. **1990–1991**	United States leads fight against Iraq in Persian Gulf War
A.D. **1969**	American Neil Armstrong becomes the first person on the moon	A.D. **1993**	Floods in Mississippi River basin destroy homes and crops
		A.D. **1995**	Canadians in Quebec narrowly vote to remain a part of Canada

Dictionary of GEOGRAPHICTERMS

ARCHIPELAGO (är kə pel'ə gō) A group or chain of islands.

STRAIT (strāt) A narrow waterway that connects two larger bodies of water.

GULF (gulf) Part of an ocean that extends into the land; larger than a bay.

PLATEAU (pla tō') An area of elevated flat land.

DAM (dam) A wall built across a river, creating a lake that stores water.

RESERVOIR (rez'ər vwär) A natural or artificial lake used to store water.

CANYON (kan'yən) A deep, narrow valley with steep sides.

MESA (mā'sə) A hill with a flat top; smaller than a plateau.

DUNE (dün) A mound, hill, or ridge of sand heaped up by the wind.

HILL (hil) A rounded, raised landform; not as high as a mountain.

BUTTE (būt) A small, flat-topped hill; smaller than a mesa or plateau.

OASIS (ō ā'sis) A fertile area in a desert that is watered by a spring.

VALLEY (val'ē) An area of low land between hills or mountains.

DESERT (dez'ərt) A dry environment with few plants and animals.

COAST (cōst) The land along an ocean.

BAY (bā) Part of an ocean or lake that extends deeply into the land.

ISTHMUS (is'məs) A narrow strip of land that connects two larger bodies of land.

ISLAND (ī'lənd) A body of land completely surrounded by water.

PENINSULA (pə nin'sə lə) A body of land nearly surrounded by water.

VOLCANO (vol kā′nō) An opening in Earth's surface through which hot rock and ash are forced out.

MOUNTAIN (moun′tən) A high landform with steep sides; higher than a hill.

PEAK (pēk) The top of a mountain.

GLACIER (glā′shər) A huge sheet of ice that moves slowly across the land.

HARBOR (här′bər) A sheltered place along a coast where boats dock safely.

CANAL (kə nal′) A channel built to carry water for irrigation or navigation.

LAKE (lāk) A body of water completely surrounded by land.

PORT (pôrt) A place where ships load and unload their goods.

TRIBUTARY (trib′yə ter ē) A smaller river that flows into a larger river.

SOURCE (sôrs) The starting point of a river.

TIMBERLINE (tim′bər līn) A line beyond which trees do not grow.

RIVER BASIN (riv′ər bā′sin) All the land that is drained by a river and its tributaries.

WATERFALL (wô′tər fôl) A flow of water falling vertically.

MOUNTAIN RANGE (moun′tən rānj) A row or chain of mountains.

PLAIN (plān) A large area of nearly flat land.

RIVER (riv′ər) A stream of water that flows across the land and empties into another body of water.

BASIN (bā′sin) A bowl-shaped landform surrounded by higher land.

DELTA (del′tə) Land made of silt left behind as a river drains into a larger body of water.

MOUNTAIN PASS (moun′tən pas) A narrow gap through a mountain range.

MOUTH (mouth) The place where a river empties into a larger body of water.

FJORD (fyôrd) A deep, narrow inlet of an ocean between high, steep cliffs.

OCEAN (ō′shən) A large body of salt water; oceans cover much of Earth's surface.

R47

Gazetteer

This Gazetteer is a geographical dictionary that will help you to pronounce and locate the places discussed in this book. Latitude and longitude are given for cities and some other places. The page numbers tell you where each place appears on a map or in the text.

A

Aachen (ä′khən) Capital of Charlemagne's empire, c. 800; a city in present-day Germany; 51°N, 6°E. (m. 321, t. 321)

Accra (ə krä′) The capital and largest city of Ghana; 6°N, 0°. (m. 570, t. 568)

Acropolis (ə krop′ə lis) A hill in ancient Athens that became a religious center and meeting place; site of the Parthenon. (t. 205)

Africa (af′ri kə) The world's second-largest continent, lying south of Europe between the Atlantic and Indian oceans. (m. 607, t. 354)

Agra (ä′grə) A city in north-central India; capital of the Mogul empire around 1564–1658; 27°N, 78°E. (m. 393, t. 394)

Aksum (äk′süm) A powerful African kingdom and trading center, about 350–900, located in what is today Ethiopia. (m. 359, t. 359)

Alexandria (al ig zan′drē ə) A city in Egypt founded c. 332 B.C. by Alexander the Great; 31°N, 30°E. (m. 214, t. 214)

Alps (alps) Europe's highest mountains, extending in an arc from the Mediterranean coast to the Balkan peninsula. (m. 33, t. 33)

Anatolia (an ə tō′lē ə) Asia Minor; a peninsula in western Asia. (m. 390, t. 388)

Andes Mountains (an′dēz moun′tənz) The world's longest mountain chain, stretching along the west coast of South America. (m. 423, t. 422)

Angkor (ang′kôr) Ruined city in Cambodia; capital of the Khmer around 850–1430; 14°N, 104°E. (m. 399, t. 400)

Antarctica (ant ärk′ti kə) An ice-covered continent surrounding the South Pole. (m. G5)

Anyang (än′yäng) The ancient Chinese capital of the Shang dynasty; 36°N, 114°E. (m. 165, t. 165)

Apennine Mountains (ap′ə nīn moun′tənz) A mountain range on the Italian peninsula. (m. 225, t. 225)

Arabia (ə rā′bē ə) A large peninsula in southwestern Asia. (m. 263, t. 262)

Arabian Sea (ə rā′bē ən sē) A body of water that lies between Arabia and India; the northwestern part of the Indian Ocean. (m. 263, t. 263)

Arctic Ocean (ärk′tik ō′shən) The body of water north of the Arctic Circle and surrounding the North Pole. (m. G5)

Asia (ā′zhə) The largest continent, bounded on the west by Europe and Africa, on the south by the Indian Ocean, and on the east by the Pacific. (m. 616, t. 586)

Athens (ath′ənz) For many centuries the most powerful of all ancient Greek city-states; capital of present-day Greece; 38°N, 23°E. (m. 198, t. 197)

Atlantic Ocean (at lan′tik ō′shən) The body of water separating Europe and Africa from North and South America. (m. G5, t. 317)

Attica (at′i kə) A peninsula in east-central Greece on the Aegean Sea on which Athens was built. (m. 193, t. 193)

Australia (ôs trāl′yə) The world's smallest continent, bounded by the Indian and Pacific oceans; also a country. (m. 616, t. 478)

B

Babylonia (bab ə lō′nē ə) An ancient Mesopotamian empire that extended throughout the Fertile Crescent in the 1700s B.C. (m. 110, t. 112)

Baghdad (bag′dad) Capital and cultural center of the Muslim caliphate from A.D. 762 to 1100; present-day capital of Iraq; 33°N, 44°E. (m. 273, t. 272)

Balkan Peninsula (bôl′kən pə nin′sə lə) A peninsula in southern Europe, bounded by the Black, Aegean, and Adriatic seas. (m. 601, t. 600)

pronunciation key

a	at	ī	ice	u	up	th	thin
ā	ape	îr	pierce	ū	use	th	this
ä	far	o	hot	ü	rule	zh	measure
âr	care	ō	old	ù	pull	ə	about, taken,
e	end	ô	fork	ûr	turn		pencil, lemon,
ē	me	oi	oil	hw	white		circus
i	it	ou	out	ng	song		

Bangladesh (bän glə desh′) A nation established in 1971 on the Indian subcontinent, and mostly surrounded by India; formerly known as East Pakistan. (m. 583, t. 584)

Bastille (bas tēl′) A prison fortress in Paris that was attacked and destroyed on July 14, 1789, at the start of the French Revolution. (t. 488)

Beijing (bā′jing′) The capital of the People's Republic of China; first became China's capital during the reign of Kublai Khan in the 1200s; 40°N, 116°E. (m. 403, t. 403)

Beringia (bə rin′jē ə) A land bridge that connected North America and Asia during the Ice Age; located where the Bering Strait is today. (m. 285, t. 286)

Berlin (bər lin′) The capital of Germany, divided from 1945 to 1990 into West Berlin and East Berlin; 53°N, 13°E. (m. 601, t. 558)

Bethlehem (beth′lə hem) A small town south of Jerusalem where Jesus is said to have been born; 31°N, 35°E. (m. 247, t. 247)

Border Cave (bôr′dər kāv) A major archaeological site in Zululand, South Africa and home of Old Stone Age hunters and gatherers; 27°S, 32°E. (m. 47, t. 46)

Bowating (bō′ä ting) An Ojibwa village that was located on an island in the river connecting lakes Superior and Huron; 46°N, 83°W. (m. 441, t. 441)

Brazil (brə zil′) The largest nation in South America, on the northeastern part of the continent. (m. 623, t. 622)

Burma (bər′mə) A nation in Southeast Asia on the Bay of Bengal; now known as Myanmar. (m. 587, t. 586)

Byzantine empire (bi′zən tēn em′pīr) The name by which the eastern half of the Roman empire became known some time after A.D. 400. (m. 254, t. 255)

C

Cairo (kī′rō) The capital of modern Egypt and the largest city in Africa; 30°N, 31°E. (m. 570, t. 569)

Cambodia (kam bō′dē ə) A nation in Southeast Asia. (m. 587, t. 586)

Canada (kan′ə də) A country in North America bordering the United States. (m. 623, t. 622)

Canadian Shield (kə nā′dē ən shēld) A large rocky plain in northern Canada that was formed by glaciers during the Ice Age. (m. 423, t. 423)

Cape Town (kāp toun) Seaport city in South Africa, settled by the Dutch in the late 1600s; 34°S, 18°E. (m. 607, t. 606)

Caribbean Sea (kar ə bē′ən sē) A sea bounded on the north and east by the West Indies, and by Central and South America on the west and south. (m. 475, t. 474)

Carthage (kär′thij) An ancient city on the north coast of Africa; 37°N, 10°E. (m. 234, t. 234)

Central Plateau (sen′trəl pla tō′) A high plateau extending throughout central Mexico and bounded by high mountain ranges. (m. 287, t. 287)

Chartres (shärt) A city in northwestern France, noted for its cathedral; 48°N, 1°E. (m. 334, t. 332)

China (chī′nə) A nation in East Asia, and the most populous country in the world. (m. 616, t. 618)

Colosseum (kä lə sē′əm) A large stadium in ancient Rome where athletic events took place. (t. 241)

Constantinople (kon stan tə nō′pəl) A city established as the new eastern capital of the Roman empire by the emperor Constantine in A.D. 330, now called Istanbul; 41°N, 29°E. (m. 254, t. 254)

Copán (kō pän′) An ancient city of Middle America, in what is now Honduras, that was a center of classic Maya culture; 15°N, 89°W. (m. 299, t. 299)

Crete (krēt) A Greek island in the Mediterranean Sea, southeast of Greece. (m. 193, t. 193)

Cuzco (küs′kō) A city in southern Peru; capital of the Inca empire from the 1200s to the 1500s; 14°S, 72°W. (m. 435, t. 435)

D

Dolores (də lôr′əs) A city in central Mexico where Miguel Hidalgo began Mexico's independence movement in 1810; 29°N, 108°W. (m. 493, t. 494)

Dominican Republic (də min′i kən ri pub′lik) A Caribbean nation, on the eastern part of Hispaniola, that gained independence in 1844. (m. 623, t. 623)

E

Edo (ed′ō) The former name of Tokyo, Japan; became capital under the rule of the Tokugawa shoguns in the 1600s; 36°N, 140°E. (m. 411, t. 412)

Egypt (ē′jipt) A country in northeast Africa; birthplace of ancient Egyptian civilization. (m. 570, t. 569)

England (ing′glənd) Part of the United Kingdom, on the island of Great Britain. (m. 321, t. 326)

Ethiopia (ē thē ō′pē ə) A country in eastern Africa. (m. 607, t. 358)

Euphrates River (ū frā′tēz riv′ər) A river in southwestern Asia that flows through the southern part of the Fertile Crescent. (m. 105, t. 104)

Eurasia (yù rā′zhə) A large land mass that includes the continents of Europe and Asia. (t. 316)

Europe (yür′əp) The continent north of Africa between Asia and the Atlantic Ocean. (m. 601, t. 316)

Gazetteer

F

Fertile Crescent (fûrt′əl kres′ənt) A fertile region in southwestern Asia that includes the region of Mesopotamia. (m. 105, t. 104)

Florence (flôr′əns) A city in present-day Italy; one of the great centers of Renaissance art; 44°N, 11°E. (m. 334, t. 337)

Forbidden City (fər bid′ən sit′ē) A walled area in Beijing built 1417–1420, during the Ming dynasty, that contained the palaces of the emperors. (t. 404)

Forum (for′əm) The city market and meeting place in the center of ancient Rome. (t. 233)

G

Gaul (gôl) An ancient region and Roman province that included most of present-day France. (m. 240, t. 237)

Gaza (gä′zə) A territory between Egypt and Israel on the southeastern coast of the Mediterranean Sea. Controlled by Israel from 1967 to 1994, after which it began to return to Palestinian control. (m. 578, t. 577)

Ghana (gä′nə) An empire, about 400–1235, located at the southwestern edge of the Sahara Desert; a present-day country in western Africa on the Gulf of Guinea. (m. 364, t. 363)

Gobi Desert (gō′bē dez′ərt) A large desert in east-central Asia. (m. 385, t. 386)

Golan Heights (gō′län hīts) Land occupied by Israel after the Six-Day War. 1967 (m. 578, t. 577)

Great Lakes (grāt lāks) A group of five large freshwater lakes on the border between the United States and Canada. (m. 423, t. 422

Great Rift Valley (grāt rift val′ē) A series of cliffs and canyons caused by powerful prehistoric earthquakes that extends from Mozambique in southeastern Africa north to the Red Sea. (m. 355, t. 355)

Great Wall of China (grāt wôl əv chī′nə) A long defensive wall extending 1,500 miles (2,415 km) through northern China; built between 1300 and 1600. (m. 172, t. 170)

Great Zimbabwe (grāt zim bäb′wā) A city in southern Africa that rose to power in the 1300s through gold mining and trading; 20°S, 30°E. (m. 377, t. 376)

H

Haiti (hā′tē) A Caribbean nation, on the western part of Hispaniola, that gained independence from France in 1804. (m. 623, t. 623

Harappa (hə ra′pə) A city of the ancient Harappan civilization, c. 2500–1600 B.C., located in the Indus Valley of South Asia; 31°N, 73°E. (m. 135, t. 135)

Himalayas (him ə lā′əz) The world's highest mountain range, forming the northern border of the Indian subcontinent. (m. 131, t. 131)

Hispaniola (his pən yō′lə) A Caribbean island settled by Spaniards in 1493; a present-day island that is divided into the Dominican Republic and Haiti. (m. 467, t. 467)

Hong Kong (häng käng) A large city and center of international trade developed as a British colony in mainland China; 22°N, 114°E. (m. 616, t. 619)

Huang River (hwäng riv′ər) [Yellow River] A river that flows from the Tibetan plateau, across northern China, and into the Yellow Sea. (m. 161, t. 160)

I

India (in′dē ə) The largest nation of the Indian subcontinent; became independent from British rule in 1947. (m. 583, t. 580)

Indian Ocean (in′dē ən ō′shən) The body of water south of Asia, between Africa and Australia. (m. G5, t. 372)

Indus Plain (in′dəs plān) A vast, dry region south of the Himalayas that is made fertile by deposits of silt from the Indus River; birthplace of the ancient Harappan civilization. (m. 131, t. 131)

Indus River (in′dəs riv′ər) A river that flows from Tibet, through the Himalayas and Hindu Kush into the Arabian Sea. (m. 131, t. 130)

Iraq (i rak′) A nation of western Asia that became independent in 1932. (m. 576, t. 576)

Israel (iz′rē əl) A country in western Asia, created in 1948 as a home for the Jews; ancient kingdom of Israelites. (m. 576, t. 577)

Istanbul (is tan bül′) Largest city in present-day Turkey; formerly the ancient city of Constantinople and later the capital of the Ottoman empire; 41°N, 29°E. (m. 390, t. 388)

J

Japan (jə pan′) An island nation off the eastern Asia mainland. (m. 616, t. 614)

Jerusalem (jə rü′sə ləm) An ancient city in western Asia; capital of present-day Israel; 31°N, 35°E. (m. 121, t. 124)

Johannesburg (jō han′əs bərg) The largest city in South Africa; 26°S, 28°E. (m. 607, t. 608)

Judea (jü dē′ə) The land in the eastern Mediterranean region populated by Jews at the time of the Roman empire. (m. 247, t. 246)

K

Kosala (kō sa′lə) An ancient kingdom in northern India where Siddhartha Gautama is said to have been born. (t. 151)

Kush (kush) An ancient kingdom in northeastern Africa, conquered by Egypt. It later regained independence and flourished through trade between c. 500 B.C. and A.D. 150. (m. 86, t. 86)

Kyoto (kyō′tō) A city in Japan; formerly the emperor's capital during the rule of the shoguns; 35°N, 136°E. (m. 411, t. 413)

L

La Venta (lə vent′ə) An ancient island town of Middle America on the east coast of what is now Mexico; center of Olmec culture in 1000 B.C.; 18°N, 94°W. (m. 293, t. 294)

Lake Texcoco (lāk tā skō′kō) A lake in what is now Central Mexico on which the Aztec built Tenochtitlán. (t. 427)

Laos (lä′ōs) A nation in Southeast Asia, between northern Thailand and northern Vietnam. (m. 587, t. 586)

Latium (lā′shē əm) A plain on the west coast of Italy on which the city of Rome was built. (m. 225, t. 225)

Lima (lē′mə) The capital of Peru, founded by Francisco Pizarro in 1535; 12°S, 77°W. (m. 467, t. 469)

Lower Egypt (lō′ər ē′jipt) The northern part of ancient Egypt. (m. 71, t. 71)

M

Macedonia (mas i dō′nē ə) An ancient kingdom ruled by Alexander the Great that conquered Greece and the Persian empire in the 300s B.C. (m. 214, t. 213)

Machu Picchu (mäch′ü pēk′chü) The site of a ruined Inca city on a mountain in the Andes northwest of Cuzco, Peru; 13°S, 72°W. (m. 435, t. 438)

Mali (mä′lē) African empire that flourished between the 1200s and 1400s; a present-day country in West Africa. (m. 364, t. 364)

Mecca (mek′ə) An Arabian oasis city believed to be the birthplace of Muhammad; 21°N, 40°E. (m. 267, t. 267)

Medina (mə dē′nə) An Arabian oasis town to which, according to Muslim writings, Muhammad migrated in A.D. 622; 24°N, 40°E. (m. 267, t. 268)

Mediterranean Sea (med i tə rā′nē ən sē) A large, almost landlocked arm of the Atlantic Ocean touching Europe, Asia, and Africa. (m. 193, t. 192)

Mekong River (mā′kong′ riv′ər) A river in Southeast Asia that flows from Tibet to the South China Sea. (m. 399, t. 398)

Memphis (mem′fis) Capital of Egypt's Old Kingdom, located on the Nile near present-day Cairo; 29°N, 31°E. (m. 76, t. 76)

Mesopotamia (mes ə pə tā′mē ə) The region between the Tigris and Euphrates rivers; birthplace of the Sumerian and Babylonian civilizations. (m. 105, t. 105)

Mexico (mek′si kō) A nation in North America, south of the United States. (m. 623, t. 624)

Mexico City (mek′si kō sit′ē) The capital and largest city of Mexico; formerly Tenochtitlán, it became the capital of New Spain after the Spanish conquered the Aztec in the 1500s; 19°N, 99°W. (m. 467, t. 469)

Middle America (mid′əl ə mer′i kə) An ancient region of North America that included southern Mexico and much of Central America. It was the birthplace of the ancient Olmec and Maya civilizations. (m. 287, t. 286)

Middle East (mid′əl ēst) A region of southwestern Asia that stretches from Turkey to Iran. (m. 576, t. 574)

Mogadishu (mōg ə dish′ü) A coastal city that dominated African gold trade between about 1000 and 1300; the present-day capital of Somalia; 2°N, 45°E. (m. 373, t. 374)

Mohenjo-Daro (mō hen′jō där′ō) A city of the ancient Harappan civilization, located in the Indus Valley; 27°N, 68°E. (m. 135, t. 135)

Mombasa (mom bä′sä) An important Swahili city-state and trading center between 1100 and 1500; the main port of Kenya on the Indian Ocean; 4°N, 40°E. (m. 373, t. 374)

Morocco (mə rok′ō) A country in northwestern Africa on the Atlantic Ocean and Mediterranean Sea. (m. 570, t. 367)

Moscow (mäs′kou) The capital and largest city of Russia; 56°N, 38°E. (m. 533, t. 536)

Mount Everest (mount ev′ər əst) The tallest mountain in the world, located in the Himalayas on the border between Nepal and Tibet; 28°N, 87°E. (m. 385, t. 385)

Mount Kilimanjaro (mount kil ə mən jär′ō) The tallest mountain in Africa, located in northeastern Tanzania; 3°S, 37°E. (m. 355, t. 355)

pronunciation key

a **at**; ā **ape**; ä **far**; âr **care**; e **end**; ē **me**; i **it**; ī **ice**; îr **pierce**; o **hot**; ō **old**; ô **fork**; oi **oil**; ou **out**; u **up**; ū **use**; ü **rule**, u̇ **pull**; ûr **turn**; hw **white**; ng **song**; th **thin**; t̲h̲ **this**; zh **measure**; ə **about, taken, pencil, lemon, circus**

Mount Olympus (mount ə lim′pəs) The highest mountain in Greece, where the ancient Greeks believed many of their gods and goddesses lived; 40°N, 22°E. (m. 198, t. 200)

N

Nazareth (na′ zə rəth) A small town in northern Judea where, according to the New Testament, Jesus grew up; 32°N, 35°E. (m. 247, t. 247)

New Delhi (nü del′ē) The capital of India and one of the most populous cities in the world; 29°N, 77°E. (m. 15, t. 15)

New South Wales (nü south wālz) English Colony founded on the East Coast of Australia in 1788; currently a state of Australia. (m. 479, t. 478)

New Spain (nü spān) Spanish colony in North America including Mexico, Central America, the southwest United States, and many of the Caribbean Islands from the 1500s to the 1800s. (m. 467, t. 469)

Niger River (nī′jər riv′ər) A river flowing from western Africa into the Gulf of Guinea. (m. 355, t. 355)

Nile River (nīl riv′ər) The world's longest river, which flows northward through East Africa into the Mediterranean Sea. (m. 71, t. 70)

Normandy (nôr′mən dē) A region in northwestern France on the English Channel. (m. 545, t. 326)

North America (nôrth ə mâr′i kə) The third-largest continent, located in the Western Hemisphere. (m. 623, t. 440)

North China Plain (nôrth chī′nə plān) A large, lowland region of eastern China that is watered by the Huang River; birthplace of Chinese civilization. (m. 161, t. 160)

North European Plain (nôrth yür ə pē′ən plān) A large, fertile area that extends from the Atlantic Ocean to the Ural Mountains. (m. 317, t. 318)

North Sea (nôrth sē) A large arm of the Atlantic Ocean, between Great Britain and continental Europe. (m. 317, t. 317)

Nubia (nü′bē ə) An ancient kingdom south of Egypt. (m. 86, t. 84)

Nunavut (nü′ nü vüt) A territory in Canada that is to be created for the Inuit in 1999. (t. 626)

P

Pacific Ocean (pə sif′ik ō′shən) The world's largest body of water, bounded by the Americas on the east and Asia and Australia on the west. (m. G5, t. 410)

Pakistan (pak′i stan) One of two independent nations formed in 1947 on the Indian subcontinent. (m. 583, t. 583)

Palestine (pal′ə stīn) Region in southwestern Asia that became the ancient home of the Jews; the ancient Roman name for Judea; in recent times, the British protectorate that became Israel in 1947. (m. 254, t. 253)

Pantheon (pan′thē on) A large, domed temple built in ancient Rome to honor many gods and goddesses. (t. 241)

Paris (par′is) Capital and largest city of France; 49°N, 2°E. (m. 601, t. 488)

Parthenon (pär′thə non) A temple to the goddess Athena, built 447–432 B.C. on the Acropolis in Athens. (t. 205)

Pearl Harbor (pûrl här′bər) A United States naval base in Hawaii that was bombed by the Japanese in 1941, causing the United States to enter World War II; 21°N, 158°W. (m. 544, t. 543)

Peloponnesus (pel ə pə nē′səs) A mountainous peninsula in southern Greece, between the Ionian and Aegean seas. (m. 193, t. 193)

Persian Gulf (pûr′zhən gulf) A body of water east of the Arabian peninsula that separates Arabia from Iran. (m. 263, t. 263)

Peru (pə rü′) Colonial lands held by Spain in South America from the 1500s to the 1800s; present-day country in western South America. (m. 467, t. 469)

Petra (pē′trə) The ancient Arabian capital of Nabataea, in what is today Jordan; 30°N, 35°E. (t. 264)

Phnom Penh (pə nom′ pen′) The capital of Cambodia; first became capital during the Khmer rule in the 1400s; 12°N, 105°E. (m. 399, t. 401)

Phoenicia (fə nē′shə) An ancient seafaring civilization located on the eastern shore of the Mediterranean Sea. (m. 193, t. 195)

Pompeii (pom pā′) An ancient city in southwestern Italy that was buried by the eruption of Mount Vesuvius in A.D. 79; 41°N, 14°E. (m. 240, t. 242)

Punt (punt) An ancient Egyptian name for an area of Africa south of Egypt. (m. 86, t. 87)

Q

Qin (chin) An ancient province in northern China that rose to power under Emperor Shihuangdi in 221 B.C. (m. 169, t. 168)

Qinling Mountains (chin′ling′ moun′tənz) A mountain range in north-central China. (m. 169, t. 169)

R

Red Sea (red sē) A narrow sea between Arabia and northeastern Africa. (m. 263, t. 263)

Rhodes (rōdz) A Greek island, lying east of Crete in the Aegean Sea. (m. 193, t. 193)

Rocky Mountains (rok'ē moun'tənz) A mountain range in North America that stretches from Alaska into Mexico. (m. 423, t. 422)

Rome (rōm) The former center of both the ancient Roman Republic and the Roman empire; capital of present-day Italy; 42°N, 12°E. (m. 225, t. 224)

Russia (rush'ə) A country in eastern Europe and northern Asia; the largest country in the world; a republic of the Soviet Union from 1922 to 1991. (m. 533, t. 532)

S

Sahara Desert (sə har'ə dez'ərt) The largest desert in the world, covering most of northern Africa. (m. 355, t. 355)

Sahel (sə həl') The dry, grassy region south of the Sahara Desert, extending from Senegal to the Sudan. (m. 355, t. 355)

Santo Domingo (san'tō də ming'gō) A Spanish colony established on Hispaniola in 1496; the capital of the Dominican Republic; 19°N, 70°W. (m. 475, t. 475)

Sarajevo (sar ə yā'vō) The site of assassination that led to World War I; present-day capital of Bosnia; 44°N, 18°E. (m. 601, t. 527)

Seine River (sān riv'ər) A river that flows from eastern France northward into the English Channel. (m. 317, t. 319)

Serbia (sûr'bē ə) A country in eastern Europe. (m. 528, t. 527)

Sicily (sis'ə lē) An island in the Mediterranean Sea off the southwest tip of the Italian peninsula. (m. 225, t. 225)

Singapore (sing'ə pôr) A city and independent republic in Southeast Asia; 1°N, 104°E. (m. 616, t. 617)

Sofala (sō fäl'ə) A seaport village in eastern Mozambique; in the 1300s, an important trading center for the gold miners of Great Zimbabwe; 19°S, 35°E. (m. 377, t. 378)

Songhai (sông'hī) The most powerful empire in West Africa from about 1490 to 1590. (m. 364, t. 367)

South America (south ə mâr'i kə) The fourth-largest continent, located in the Western Hemisphere. (m. 623, t. 491)

South Korea (south kə rē'ə) A country in East Asia on the southern part of the Korean Peninsula; also a Pacific Rim nation. (m. 616, t. 617)

Southeast Asia (south ēst' ā'zhə) A region of southern Asia bounded by the Indian and Pacific Oceans. (m. 587, t. 586)

Soviet Union (sō'vē et ūn'yən) The name commonly used for the Union of Soviet Socialist Republics, which was a country in eastern Europe and northern Asia; the largest country in the world from 1922–1991. (m. 544, t. 537)

Soweto (sə wē'tō) A black African township just outside Johannesburg, South Africa; 26°S, 28°E. (m. 607, t. 608)

Sparta (spär'tə) The largest ancient Greek city-state, located on the southern Peloponnesus; 37°N, 22°E. (m. 198, t. 198)

St. Petersburg (sānt pē'tərz bûrg) A Russian port city on the Baltic Sea; formerly the capital of Russia, it was called Leningrad when Russia was part of the Soviet Union; 60°N, 30°E. (m. 533, t. 534)

Strait of Magellan (strāt əv mə jel'ən) A narrow waterway at the southern tip of South America, linking the Atlantic and Pacific oceans. (m. 464, t. 465)

Suez Canal (sü ez' kə nal') A canal in northeastern Egypt connecting the Mediterranean and Red seas. (t. 569)

Sumer (sü'mər) A group of ancient city-states in southern Mesopotamia; the earliest civilization in Mesopotamia. (m. 110, t. 108)

T

Taj Mahal (täzh mə häl') A grand tomb in Agra, India, built by Mogul emperor Shah Jahan to honor his wife. (t. 396)

Tenochtitlán (te noch tēt län') The capital of the Aztec empire, founded around 1325 on the site of present-day Mexico City; 19°N, 99°W. (m. 427, t. 426)

Thailand (tī'land) A nation in Southeast Asia, formerly called Siam. (m. 587, t. 586)

Thebes (thēbz) An ancient city in Upper Egypt that became the capital of the New Kingdom; 26°N, 33°E. (m. 76, t. 81)

Tiananmen Square (tyen'än men skwâr) A square in Beijing, China where government troops killed hundreds of people who were demonstrating for democratic reform in 1989. (t. 619)

Tiber River (tī′bər riv′ər) A river flowing southward from north-central Italy across the Latium plain, and into the Tyrrhenian Sea. (m. 225, t. 225)

Tibetan Plateau (ti bet′ən pla tō′) A high mountain plateau in Asia. (m. 385, t. 385)

Tigris River (tī′gris riv′ər) A river in southwestern Asia that flows through the eastern part of the Fertile Crescent. (m. 105, t. 104)

Timbuktu (tim buk tü′) A trade and cultural center of the Songhai empire in the 1400s; a present-day town in the West African country of Mali; 16°N, 3°W. (m. 364, t. 364)

Tokyo (tō′kyō) The capital and largest city in Japan; formerly called Edo; 36°N, 140°W. (m. 411, t. 412)

Tonle Sap (tän lā′ sap′) A lake in western Cambodia. (m. 399, t. 399)

Turkey (tür′kē) A nation established in 1923 in western Asia and southeastern Europe. (m. 576, t. 576)

U

United States (ū nī′tid stāts) A nation mainly in North America consisting of fifty states, the District of Columbia, and several territories. (m. 623, t. 622)

Upper Egypt (up′ər ē′jipt) The southern part of ancient Egypt. (m. 71, t. 71)

V

Valley of Mexico (val′ē əv mek′si kō) A fertile valley between two mountain chains in central Mexico. (t. 427)

Valley of the Kings (val′ē əv <u>the</u> kingz) West of Thebes in ancient Egypt, the burial place of 30 New Kingdom pharaohs; 26°N, 33°E. (m. 93, t. 88)

Venezuela (ven ə zwā′lə) A country in northern South America on the Caribbean Sea. (m. 493, t. 496)

Versailles (vâr sī′) A historic city in north-central France that contains the grand palace of Louis XIV; 49°N, 2°E. (t. 488)

Vietnam (vē et näm′) A nation in Southeast Asia that was divided from 1954 until 1975 into North Vietnam and South Vietnam. (m. 581, t. 586)

W

West Bank (west bangk) An area in western Asia west of the Jordan River; controlled by Israel from 1967 to 1995, after which Palestinians gained partial control. (m. 578, t. 577)

West Indies (west in′dēz) An archipelago stretching from Florida to Venezuela, separating the Caribbean Sea from the Atlantic Ocean. (m. 475, t. 474)

X

Xianyang (shē än′yang) Capital city of the Qin dynasty during the rule of the emperor Shihuangdi; 34°N, 109°E. (m. 169, t. 169)

Y

Yalta (yôl′tə) A resort city in Ukraine; site of meeting between Franklin Roosevelt, Winston Churchill, and Joseph Stalin in 1945; 44°N, 34°E. (t. 557)

Yemen (yem′ən) A present-day country in the mountainous southwestern area of Arabia; location of the ancient Sabaean civilization. (m. R10, t. 264)

Yugoslavia (yū gō slä′ vē ə) A nation that also included the republics of Bosnia and Herzegovina, Croatia, Macedonia, and Slovenia until 1991. (m. 601, t. 600)

Z

Zama (zä′mə) Site in northern Africa where the Roman army defeated the Carthaginian army in 202 B.C.; 36°N, 8°E. (m. 234, t. 235)

Zambezi River (zam bē′zē riv′ər) A river in southern Africa, flowing east through Zimbabwe and Mozambique into the Indian Ocean. (m. 355, t. 355)

Zanzibar (zan′zə bär) An important Swahili city-state and trading center between 1100 and 1500; an island port in Tanzania in the Indian Ocean; 6°S, 39°E. (m. 373, t. 374)

Biographical Dictionary

Biographical Dictionary

The Biographical Dictionary tells you about the people you have learned about in this book. The Pronunciation Key tells you how to say their names. The page numbers tell you where each person first appears in the text.

A

Abraham (ā'brə ham), 1700s B.C. Founder of Judaism who, according to the Bible, led his family from Ur to Canaan in obedience to God's command. (p. 121)

Ahmose (äm'ōs), d. 1546 B.C. New Kingdom pharaoh who drove the Hyksos out of the Nile Delta and reunited Egypt. (p. 85)

Akbar (ak'bär), A.D. 1542–1605 Ruler of the Mogul empire in India from A.D. 1556 to 1605. (p. 392)

Alexander II (al ig zan'dər), A.D. 1818–1881 Russian tsar who abolished serfdom in 1861. (p. 533)

Alexander the Great (al ig zan'dər), 356–323 B.C. King of Macedonia who conquered Greece, Persia, Egypt, and the Indus Valley; his conquests spread Greek culture throughout parts of three continents. (p. 212)

Amanishakhete (ä män ə shäk'hə tē), 100s B.C. Queen of Kush whose lavish tomb at Meroe reflects the richness of the Kingdom of Kush. (p. 359)

Arafat, Yasir (ar'ə fat), A.D. 1929– Leader of the Palestine Liberation Organization. (p. 577)

Aristide, Jean Bertrand (är'is tēd), A.D. 1953– Elected president of Haiti in 1990. (p. 625)

Aristotle (ar'ə stot əl), 384–322 B.C. Greek philosopher who was the private teacher of Alexander the Great. (p. 211)

Atahualpa (ä tə wäl'pə), A.D. 1502?–1533 The last Inca emperor, captured and killed by Francisco Pizarro. (p. 469)

Augustus (ô gus'təs), 63 B.C.–A.D. 14 First Roman emperor; won the civil war following Julius Caesar's assassination and went on to unify the empire and establish the Pax Romana. (p. 236)

Avicenna (av ə sen'ə), A.D. 980–1037 Persian philosopher and physician; wrote a medical encyclopedia that became a standard text in North Africa, western Asia, and Europe. (p. 274)

B

Ben-Gurion, David (ben gùr'ē ən), A.D. 1886–1973 Israeli prime minister from 1949 to 1953 and from 1955 to 1963; he proclaimed Israel to be a new and independent country on May 14, 1948. (p. 577)

Benedict (ben'i dikt), A.D. 480?–547 Italian monk; founder of the Benedictine order. (p. 331)

Bolívar, Simón (bō lē'vär, sē mōn'), A.D. 1783–1830 Leader of the struggle for independence in South America; his armies freed Colombia, Venezuela, and Peru from Spanish rule. (p. 492)

C

Cabral, Pedro Álvarez (kə bräl'), A.D. 1467?–1520? Portuguese navigator who landed on the coast of Brazil in 1500 and claimed it for Portugal. (p. 467)

Caesar, Julius (sē'zər, jül'yəs), 100–44 B.C. Roman general who became the republic's dictator in 45 B.C. (p. 237)

Castro, Fidel (kas'trō), A.D. 1926– Cuban revolutionary leader; premier of Cuba since 1959. (p. 560)

Charlemagne (shär'lə mān), A.D. 742–814 King of the Franks from 768 to 814, and emperor of Rome from 800 to 814. (p. 321)

Chiang Kai-shek (chang'kī shek'), A.D. 1887–1975 Chinese Nationalist leader and president of Taiwan from 1950 to 1975. (p. 552)

Churchill, Winston (chûr'chil), A.D. 1874–1965 British prime minister from 1940 to 1945 and 1951 to 1955. He led Britain during World War II. (p. 543)

Cleopatra (klē ə pa'trə), 69–30 B.C. Ruler of the Egyptian government in Alexandria who backed Caesar in the civil war he waged from 49 to 45 B.C. (p. 237)

Columbus, Christopher (kə lum' bəs), A.D. 1451?–1506 Italian explorer in the service of Spain who arrived in the Americas in 1492. (p. 464)

Confucius (kən fū'shəs), 551–479 B.C. Chinese philosopher who stressed the need to respect tradition; his teachings discussed the right and wrong uses of power. (p. 174)

Constantine (kon'stən tēn), A.D. 280–337 Roman emperor who founded Constantinople as the new eastern capital of the Roman empire. (p. 254)

pronunciation key

a	at	ī	ice	u	up	th	thin
ā	ape	îr	pierce	ū	use	th	this
ä	far	o	hot	ü	rule	zh	measure
âr	care	ō	old	ù	pull	ə	about, taken,
e	end	ô	fork	ûr	turn		pencil, lemon,
ē	me	oi	oil	hw	white		circus
i	it	ou	out	ng	song		

Cook, James (kůk, jāmz), A.D. 1728–1779 A navigator and ship captain who explored and claimed land in Australia for England in 1770. (p. 479)

Copernicus, Nicolaus (kə pûr'ni kəs), A.D. 1473–1543 Polish astronomer; in 1514 he discovered that Earth and the other planets revolve around the sun. (p. 339)

Cortés, Hernando (kôr tes', er nän'dō), A.D. 1485–1547 Spanish conquistador who defeated the Aztec in 1521. (p. 468)

D

Da Gama, Vasco (də gä'mə, väs'cō), A.D. 1460?–1524 Portuguese navigator who in 1498 sailed from Europe around Africa to Asia. (p. 464)

Da Vinci, Leonardo (də vin'chē, lē ə när'dō), A.D. 1452–1519 Italian Renaissance artist, inventor, and scientist. (p. 338)

De Klerk, F.W. (də klerk'), A.D. 1936– South African president from 1989 to 1994. He worked for a peaceful transition from the policy of apartheid to majority rule in South Africa. (p. 610)

Deng Xiaoping (dung' shou'ping'), A.D. 1904–1997 Chairman of the Chinese Communist Party and of the People's Republic of China. (p. 618)

Dias, Bartholomeu (dē'ash, bâr tù lù mã'ù), A.D. 1450?–1500 Portuguese ship captain whose voyage around the southern tip of Africa in 1487 led to the opening of a sea route between Europe and Asia. (p. 464)

Diocletian (dī ə klē'shən), A.D. 245–313 Roman emperor who divided the empire in two and oversaw the eastern part. (p. 253)

E

Elizabeth I (i liz'ə bəth), A.D. 1533–1603 Queen of England from 1558 to 1603; the English Renaissance flourished during her reign. (p. 346)

Equiano, Olaudah (i kwē ä'nō, ōl'ə dä), A.D. 1750–1797 Enslaved African writer. In 1789 he wrote an autobiography describing his life in slavery. (p. 476)

Erasmus (i raz'məs), A.D. 1466?–1536 Dutch writer and humanist; he favored reform of the Catholic Church but came to oppose the Protestant Reformation. (p. 343)

F

Francis of Assisi (fran'sis əv ə sē'zē), A.D. 1181–1226 Italian monk who founded the Franciscan order; he devoted his life to serving the poor and sick. (p. 332)

Frank, Anne (frangk), A.D. 1929–1945 Dutch-Jewish girl who, with other Jews, hid from the Nazis from 1942 to 1944; she was found and sent to a concentration camp where she died. (p. 546)

Franz Ferdinand (franz fur'də nand), A.D. 1863–1914 Archduke of Austria whose assassination led to the outbreak of World War I. (p. 527)

Fu Hao (fü'hou'), 1100s B.C. A Chinese king's wife who led troops to war. Her tomb contained records of her life and times. (p. 166)

G

Galilei, Galileo (gal ə lā'ē, gal ə lā'ō), A.D. 1564–1642 Italian astronomer, mathematician, and physicist. His telescopes proved the sun is the center of the solar system. (p. 456)

Gandhi, Indira (gän'dē), A.D. 1917–1984 Prime minister of India from 1966 to 1977 and from 1980 to 1984. (p. 17)

Gandhi, Mohandas (gän'dē), A.D. 1869–1948 Indian political and religious leader; he supported the use of nonviolent methods to bring about change. (p. 580)

Genghis Khan (geng'gəs kän'), A.D. 1162?–1227 Mongol conqueror. At its peak, his empire included China, western Asia, and parts of eastern Europe. (p. 403)

Gorbachev, Mikhail (gôr'bə chəf), A.D. 1931– Soviet secretary general of the Communist Party from 1985 to 1990, and last president of the Soviet Union, 1990–1991. (p. 597)

Gutenberg, Johannes (gü'tən bûrg), A.D. 1400?–1468 German printer; in 1448 he invented a printing press that used movable type. (p. 344)

H

Hammurabi (hä mù rä'bē), 1800?–1750? B.C. King of the Babylonian empire; creator of the Code of Hammurabi, one of the world's oldest codes of law. (p. 112)

Han Gaozu (hän'gou'zü'), 200s B.C. A farmer-turned-general who, in 206 B.C., overthrew the Qin dynasty; he founded the Han dynasty. (p. 174)

Hannibal (han'ə bəl), 247?–183? B.C. General of Carthage who marched his army from Spain to Rome in the Second Punic War. (p. 234)

Hargreaves, James (här'grēvz), A.D. 1720–1778 English inventor of the spinning jenny. (p. 503)

Hatshepsut (hat shep'süt), 1520?–1482 B.C. One of the few women Egyptian pharaohs; organized a trade expedition to Egypt's southern neighbor, Punt. (p. 87)

Henry VIII (hen′rē), A.D. 1491–1547 King of England from 1509 to 1547 and founder of the Church of England; he broke with the Catholic Church because the pope would not grant him a divorce. (p. 345)

Henry, Prince (hen′rē), A.D. 1394–1460 Portuguese prince who directed the search for a sea route to the gold mines of western Africa. He also designed a fast, steerable ship known as a caravel. (p. 463)

Hidalgo, Miguel (ē däl′gō), A.D. 1753–1811 Mexican priest and revolutionary who led a revolt that started the Mexican war of independence. (p. 494)

Hitler, Adolf (hit′lər), A.D. 1889–1945 German dictator. He founded the National Socialist (Nazi) Party, which led Germany during World War II. (p. 540)

Ho Chi Minh (hō′chē′min′), A.D. 1890–1969 Communist leader in Vietnam who became head of the communist government in 1945. (p. 586)

Homer (hō′mûr), 700s B.C. Ancient Greek poet. (p. 200)

Iturbide, Agustin de (ē tür bē′de), A.D. 1783–1824 Mexican soldier and leader; he won Mexican independence from Spain and became ruler of Mexico from 1822 to 1823. (p. 495)

Jayavarman II (jä yä vär′män), A.D. 800s One of the first Khmer kings of Cambodia. (p. 399)

Jesus (jē′zəs), 4? B.C.–A.D. 29? Religious leader and founder of Christianity. (p. 247)

Jinnah, Mohammad Ali (jin′ə), A.D. 1876–1948 First president of Pakistan from 1947 to 1948. (p. 583)

John I (jon), A.D. 1167?–1216 King of England from A.D. 1199 to 1216; in 1215 he signed the Magna Carta, giving more rights to British nobles. (p. 326)

Kay, John (kā), A.D. 1704–1764 English watchmaker who invented the flying shuttle used in weaving. (p. 503)

Kennedy, John F. (ken′i dē), A.D. 1917–1963 The 35th President of the United States from 1961 to 1963. He successfully negotiated the removal of Soviet nuclear missiles from Cuba. (p. 560)

Khadija (ka dē′jä), d. A.D. 619 A wealthy merchant who became the first wife of Muhammad. (p. 267)

Khrushchev, Nikita (krüsh′chef), A.D. 1894–1971 Secretary general of the Soviet Communist Party from 1958 to 1964. (p. 560)

Khufu (kü fü′), 2650?–2600? B.C. Egyptian pharaoh who built the Great Pyramid. (p. 81)

Kublai Khan (kü′blə kän′), A.D. 1215–1294 Grandson of Genghis Khan, founder of China's Yuan Dynasty. (p. 403)

Lady Murasaki Shikibu (mur ä säk′ē shē kē′bü), A.D. 978?–1026? Japanese author who wrote *The Tale of Genji*, which is thought to be the world's first novel. (p. 414)

Lalibela (lä′lē be lä), b. A.D. 1100s Zagwe king who ruled Ethiopia from about A.D. 1185 to 1225. (p. 360)

Lenin, Vladimir Ilyich (len′in), A.D. 1870–1924 Bolshevik leader and founder of the Soviet Union. (p. 536)

Livy (liv′ē), 59 B.C.–A.D. 17 Historian of the Roman Republic who wrote about the struggle between plebeians and patricians of Rome. (p. 231)

Louis XVI (lü′ē), A.D. 1754–1793 King of France from 1774 to 1792; executed during the French Revolution. (p. 486)

Luther, Martin (lüth′ər), A.D. 1483–1546 German monk and leader of the Protestant Reformation. (p. 342)

Macquarie, Lachlan (mak wôr′ ē, läk län), A.D. 1761–1824 Governor of the English colony of New South Wales in Australia from 1810 to 1821. He supported the rights of the emancipees in New South Wales. (p. 481)

Magellan, Ferdinand (mə jel′ən), A.D. 1480?–1521 Portuguese explorer in the service of Spain; he set out to find a route to Asia by sailing around the southern tip of South America. (p. 462)

Mandela, Nelson (man del′ə), A.D. 1918– South African civil rights leader who became president of South Africa in 1994. (p. 606)

Mansa Musa (män′sä mü′sä), A.D. 1297?–1337? Emperor of Mali from 1312 to 1337, when the kingdom was at its peak of wealth and power. (p. 366)

Mao Zedong (mou′dze′dùng′), A.D. 1893–1976 Chinese communist leader and founder of the People's Republic of China. (p. 552)

Marie Antoinette (mə rē′ an twə net′), A.D. 1755–1793 Queen of France from 1774 to 1792, who was executed during the French Revolution. (p. 490)

Marx, Karl (märks), A.D. 1818–1883 German philosopher and economist. His ideas, called Marxism, formed the basis of communism. (p. 505)

Medici, Lorenzo (med'i chē), A.D. 1449–1492 Ruler of Florence during the Renaissance and patron of artists such as Michelangelo. (p. 337)

Meiji (mā'jē'), A.D. 1852–1912 Japanese emperor from 1867 to 1912 who led Japan into a period of rapid modernization. (p. 510)

Menes (mē'nēz), 3100? B.C. King of Upper Egypt who united Upper and Lower Egypt. (p. 75)

Michelangelo (mī kəl an'jə lō), A.D. 1475–1564 Italian Renaissance sculptor, painter, architect, and poet. (p. 338)

Moctezuma (mäk tə zü'mə), A.D. 1468?–1520 Aztec emperor defeated and killed by the Spanish conquistador Hernando Cortés in 1520. (p. 468)

Morelos, José María (mō re'lōs), A.D. 1765–1815 Mexican priest and revolutionary who succeeded Miguel Hidalgo as rebel leader and issued a declaration of independence from Spain in 1813. He was captured and killed by Spanish soldiers in 1815. (p. 495)

Moses (mō'ziz), 1200s B.C. Prophet who led the Israelites out of slavery in Egypt. (p. 122)

Muhammad (mù ham'əd), A.D. 570?–632? Founder of Islam whose words are recorded in the Quran. (p. 267)

Mumtaz Mahal (mùm täz' mä häl'), A.D. 1592–1631 Wife of Shah Jahan, emperor of India; the Taj Mahal in Agra, India, was built in her memory. (p. 396)

N

Napoleon Bonaparte (nə pō'lē ən bō'nə pärt), A.D. 1769–1821 French revolutionary general who became Emperor Napoleon I of France in 1804. (p. 491)

Nasser, Gamal Abdel (nas'ər), A.D. 1918–1970 First President of Egypt from 1956 to 1958, and of the United Arab Republic from 1958 to 1970. (p. 569)

Nehru, Jawaharlal (nā'rü), A.D. 1889–1964 Prime minister of India from 1947 to 1964 and father of Indira Gandhi; close associate of Mohandas Gandhi. (p. 583)

Newton, Isaac (nü'tən), A.D. 1642–1727 English scientist who studied gravity. (p. 459)

Nicholas II (nik'ə ləs), A.D. 1868–1918 Last Russian tsar from 1894 to 1917. Discontent with his policies led to the Russian Revolution of 1917. (p. 534)

Nkrumah, Kwame (en krü'mə), A.D. 1909–1972 Leader in the liberation of the Gold Coast from British rule and first president of Ghana from 1960 to 1966. (p. 567)

O

Osman (äs män'), A.D. 1258–1326? Founder of the Ottoman empire. (p. 389)

P

Pachakuti Inca (pä chä kü'tē), d. A.D. 1471 Inca emperor from 1438 to 1471; he greatly extended Inca borders in 1438 and became known as Sapa Inca, or Supreme Inca. (p. 435)

Paul (pôl), A.D. 11?–67? Follower of Jesus who helped spread Christianity throughout the Roman world. (p. 250)

Pericles (per'i klēz), 495?–429 B.C. Athenian general who led Athens during the war with Sparta; he made sure that poor as well as rich citizens could take part in government. (p. 206)

Perry, Matthew (per'ē), A.D. 1794–1858 U.S. naval officer who sailed to Japan in 1853 with a demand that Japanese ports be opened to U.S. trade. (p. 509)

Peter (pē'tər), A.D. 5?–67? One of the 12 apostles of Jesus; Roman Catholics consider him to be the first pope, or bishop of Rome. (p. 248)

Petrarch (pē'trärk), A.D. 1304–1374 Italian Renaissance poet and humanist. (p. 338)

Pizarro, Francisco (pē sär'rō), A.D. 1471?–1541 Spanish conquistador who in 1532 defeated the Inca emperor Atahualpa. (p. 468)

Plato (plā'tō), 428?–347? B.C. Greek philosopher and student of Socrates. (p. 201)

Polo, Marco (pō'lō), A.D. 1254–1324 Italian merchant who traveled to China, where he lived for 17 years, at times serving as diplomat for Kublai Khan. (p. 403)

Pope Urban II (ur'bən), A.D. 1042–1099 Pope who called for the First Crusade to reclaim Jerusalem from the Muslims. (p. 332)

R

Rabin, Yitzhak (rä bēn'), A.D. 1922–1995 Prime minister of Israel who negotiated a peace plan with Palestinians in the West Bank and Gaza. (p. 578)

Robespierre, Maximilien (rōbz'pē âr), A.D. 1758–1794 French revolutionary. He sent suspected traitors to the guillotine during the Reign of Terror from 1793 until his own death by guillotine in 1794. (p. 490)

Roosevelt, Franklin Delano (rō'zə velt), A.D. 1882–1945 The 32nd President of the United States. He led the nation against the Axis powers in World War II. (p. 543)

S

Sadat, Anwar (sə dat'), A.D. 1918–1981 Egyptian president who established peaceful relations with Israel in 1978. (p. 577)

San Martín, José de (sän mär tēn'), A.D. 1778–1850 Argentine soldier who led revolutions that freed Argentina and Chile from Spanish rule. (p. 496)

Sargon (sär′gon), died 2279? B.C. King of the city-state Kish; united the city-states of Sumer to create an empire. (p. 111)

Schliemann, Heinrich (shlē′män, hīn′rikh), A.D. 1822–1890 German archaeologist and discoverer of the remains of Troy. (p. 30)

Scipio (sip′ē ō), 234?–183? B.C. Roman general who defeated Hannibal in the Battle of Zama outside Carthage, North Africa, in 202 B.C. (p. 235)

Shah Jahan (shä jə hän′), A.D. 1592–1666 Mogul emperor of India; he built the Taj Mahal in Agra, India, in memory of his wife Mumtaz Mahal. (p. 396)

Shakespeare, William (shāk′spēr), A.D. 1564–1616 English dramatist and poet; considered one of the greatest writers in the English language. (p. 346)

Shihuangdi (shē′hwäng dē), 259?–210 B.C. Chinese emperor who founded the Qin dynasty and unified China with a standardized system of writing and money; his tomb contained the famous "clay army." (p. 168)

Siddhartha Gautama (sid där′tə gô′tə mə), 563?–483? B.C. Ancient Indian religious leader known as the Buddha, or Enlightened One, who founded Buddhism. (p. 150)

Sinan (sə nän′), A.D. 1489–1588 Süleyman's chief architect; he designed more than 300 buildings, including the mosque in Istanbul. (p. 390)

Socrates (sok′rə tēz), 470?–399 B.C. Greek philosopher who discussed laws, customs, values, and religion with students; accused of urging young people to revolt, he was sentenced to death. (p. 206)

Spindler, Konrad (shpin′dlər), A.D. 1939– German archaeologist who analyzed the 5,000–year–old "Iceman" body found in the Alps in 1991. (p. 33)

Stalin, Josef (stä′lin), A.D. 1879–1953 Soviet revolutionary and dictator who ruled the Soviet Union from 1924 to 1953. (p. 537)

Süleyman (sü′lä män), A.D. 1495?–1566 Sultan of the Ottoman empire during its peak from 1520 to 1566. (p. 389)

Sun Yat-sen (sùn′ yät sen′), A.D. 1866–1925 Leader of the Chinese Nationalists and founder of the Republic of China in 1912. (p. 550)

Sunjata (sän jä′tä), d. A.D. 1255 King of Mali who conquered all of Ghana. (p. 364)

Suryavarman II (sur yə vär′mən), A.D. 1100s Khmer king who filled his capital city of Angkor with magnificent Hindu temples. (p. 400)

T

Tokugawa Ieyasu (tō kù gä′wä ē yä′sü), A.D. 1543–1616 Shogun, or military commander, of the Tokugawa dynasty from 1603 to 1605; his family's shogunate kept Japan peaceful for more than 200 years. (p. 412)

Toussaint L'Ouverture (tü san′ lü vər tyùr′), A.D. 1743?–1803 Haitian general; in 1802 he led a successful slave revolution, leading to the independence of Haiti in 1804. (p. 493)

Tutankhamun (tü täng kä′mən), 1371?–1352 B.C. Egyptian pharaoh who ruled from about the ages of 7 to 17; his tomb remained nearly untouched until its discovery in 1922. (p. 88)

V

Veale, Elizabeth (vēl, i liz′ ə bəth), A.D. 1767–1850 Early colonist of the English colony of New South Wales in Australia who helped establish the production of wool as an important Australian industry. (p. 480)

W

Walesa, Lech (wə len′sə), A.D. 1943– Polish labor leader who became the first president of democratic Poland in 1990. (p. 598)

Watt, James (wot), A.D. 1736–1819 Scottish engineer and inventor who developed a steam engine that burned coal in 1765. (p. 503)

William the Conqueror (wil′yəm), A.D. 1027–1087 Norman king; in 1066 he defeated Harold, the Anglo-Saxon king, to become the first Norman king of England. (p. 326)

Wudi (wü′dē′), 100s B.C. Han emperor who ruled China from 140 B.C. to 87 B.C.; he set up a system of schools that prepared students for government jobs. (p. 176)

Y

Yeltsin, Boris (yel′tsin), A.D. 1931– Russian politician; in 1991 he became the first president of post-Soviet Russia. (p. 599)

Yoritomo (yōr ē tō′mō), A.D. 1147–1199 Japanese shogun, or military commander; in 1192 he attained supreme power from the emperor and ruled the country as a military dictator. (p. 411)

pronunciation key

a at; ā ape; ä far; âr care; e end; ē me; i it; ī ice; îr pierce; o hot; ō old; ô fork; oi oil; ou out; u up; ū use; ü rule, ù pull; ûr turn; hw white; ng song; th thin; <u>th</u> this; zh measure; ə about, taken, pencil, lemon, circus

Glossary

Glossary

This Glossary will help you to pronounce and understand the meanings of the vocabulary in this book. The page number at the end of the definition tells where the word first appears.

A

aborigine (ab′ ə rij′ ə nē) A person belonging to, or descending from, the group of people who first inhabited Australia. (p. 479)

absolute monarchy (ab′sə lüt   mon′ər kē) A form of government headed by a ruler, or monarch, with unlimited power. See **divine right**. (p. 486)

accuracy (ak′yər ə sē) Being true or correct. (p. 604)

acropolis (ə krop′ə lis) A large hill in ancient Greece where city residents sought shelter and safety in times of war and met to discuss community affairs. (p. 197)

agora (ag′ər ə) A central area in Greek cities used both as a marketplace and as a meeting place. (p. 197)

agriculture (ag′ri kul chər) The raising of crops and animals for human use. (p. 52)

algebra (al′je brə) A type of mathematics to which Muslims made great contributions. (p. 275)

alliance (ə lī′əns) An agreement between countries to work together in war or trade. (p. 527)

Allied Powers (al′īd pou′ərz) In World War I, the nations allied against the Central Powers; included Serbia, Russia, France, Britain, and the United States. (p. 528)

Allies (al′īz) In World War II, the nations allied against the Axis powers, including Britain, France, the Soviet Union, the United States, and China. (p. 543)

anti-semitism (an tē sem′i tiz əm) Discrimination against and hatred of Jews. (p. 575)

apartheid (ə pär′tīd) The government policy of strict and unequal segregation of the races as practiced in South Africa from 1948 to the early 1990s. (p. 607)

apostle (ə pos′əl) One of the 12 closest followers of Jesus, chosen by him to help him teach. (p. 248)

aqueduct (ak′wə dukt) A high, arched structure built to carry water over long distances. (p. 238)

archaeology (är kē ol′ə jē) The study of the remains of past cultures. (p. 32)

archipelago (är kə pel′ə gō) A large group of islands. (p. 385)

architecture (är′ki tek chər) The science of planning and constructing buildings. (p. 257)

aristocracy (ar ə stok′rə sē) The class of a society made up of members of noble families, usually the most powerful group. (p. 487)

armada (är mä′də) A fleet of warships. (p. 346)

armistice (är′mə stis) An agreement to stop fighting; a truce. (p. 531)

artifact (är′tə fakt) An object made by someone in the past. (p. 25)

assembly (ə sem′blē) A lawmaking body of government made up of a group of citizens. (p. 206)

astrolabe (as′trə lāb) An instrument invented by Muslims that is used to determine direction by figuring out the position of the stars. (p. 275)

Axis (ak′sis) In World War II, the nations who fought the Allies, including Japan, Germany, and Italy. (p. 543)

B

bilingual (bī ling′gwəl) Able to speak two languages. (p. 626)

bishop (bish′ əp) A church official who leads a large group of Christians in a particular region. (p. 251)

boycott (boi′kot) A form of protest in which people join together to refuse to buy goods. (p. 568)

Buddhism (bùd′iz əm) A religion founded in India by Siddhartha Gautama which teaches that the most important thing in life is to reach peace by ending suffering. (p. 150)

bureaucracy (byù rok′rə sē) The large organization that runs the daily business of government. (p. 511)

pronunciation key

a	at	ī	ice	u	up	th	thin
ā	ape	îr	pierce	ū	use	th	this
ä	far	o	hot	ü	rule	zh	measure
âr	care	ō	old	ù	pull	ə	about, taken,
e	end	ô	fork	ûr	turn		pencil, lemon,
ē	me	oi	oil	hw	white		circus
i	it	ou	out	ng	song		

C

caliph (kā′lif) A Muslim leader who had both political and religious authority. (p. 273)

caravan (kar′ə van) A group of people and animals traveling together for safety, especially through a desert. (p. 264)

caravel (kar′ə vel) A sailing ship developed in Portugal in the 1400s that had greater directional control than earlier ships and could sail great distances more safely. (p. 463)

cardinal directions (kärd′ən əl di rek′shənz) The directions north, south, east, and west. (p. G6)

cartogram (kär′tə gram) A special kind of map that distorts the shapes and sizes of countries or other political regions to present economic or other kinds of data for comparison. (p. 506)

caste system (kast sis′təm) The social system in Hindu society in which a person's place is determined by the rank of the family into which he or she is born. (p. 144)

cathedral (kə thē′drəl) A large or important Christian church. (p. 332)

cause (kôz) Something that makes something else happen. *See* **effect.** (p. 118)

census (sen′səs) A periodic count of all the people living in a country, city, or other region. (p. 239)

Central Powers (sen′trəl pou′ərz) In World War I, the nations who fought against the Allied Powers, including Austria-Hungary and Germany. (p. 528)

chinampas (chin äm′paz) One of the floating islands made by the Aztec around Tenochtitlán for growing crops. (p. 427)

Christianity (kris chē an′i tē) A religion based on the teachings of Jesus, as recorded in the New Testament. (p. 246)

circa (sûr′kə) A Latin word, often abbreviated "c." that means "about" or "around." (p. 59)

citadel (sit′ə dəl) A walled fort that protects a city. (p. 135)

citizen (sit′ə zən) A person with certain rights and responsibilities in his or her country or community. (p. 197)

city-state (sit′ē stāt) A self-governing city, often with surrounding lands and villages. (p. 110)

civil disobedience (siv′əl dis ə bē′dēəns) A means of protest by refusing to obey a law that is considered to be unjust. (p. 582)

civil war (siv′əl wōr) An armed conflict between groups within one country. (p. 237)

civilization (siv ə lə zā′shən) A culture that has developed systems of specialization, religion, learning, and government. (p. 55)

Classic Period (klas′ik pêr′ē əd) A time of great cultural achievement for a civilization. (p. 299)

climate (klī′ mit) The weather pattern of an area over a long period of time. (p. 9)

climograph (klī′mə graf) A graph that shows the temperature and precipitation in a place over a period of months. (p. 290)

code of law (kōd uv lô) A written set of laws that apply to everyone under a government. (p. 113)

codex (kō′deks) A manuscript page such as the kind used by the Aztec to record historical, religious, governmental and scientific knowledge. (p. 430)

Cold War (kōld wôr) A term used for the battle of words and ideas that developed between the democratic nations of the West and the Soviet Union and Eastern Europe from about 1945 to 1990. (p. 556)

colony (kol′ ə nē) A territory or community that is under the control of another country. (p. 201)

commune (kom′ūn) A community in which resources, work, and living space are shared by all members of the group. (p. 554)

communism (kom′yə niz əm) A system in which the government owns all property and makes nearly all decisions for its citizens. (p. 537)

compass rose (kum′pəs rōz) A drawing on a map that shows directions. (p. G6)

concentration camp (kon sən trā′shən kamp) A place where people are imprisoned because of their heritage, religious beliefs, or political views. (p. 546)

conclusion (kən klü′zhən) A final statement or opinion reached by putting together information about a subject. (p. 210)

confederation (kən fed ə rā′shən) A group of states or provinces under a central government. (p. 497)

Confucianism (kən fū′shə niz əm) In China, a system of beliefs and behavior based on the teachings of Confucius, who said that people should lead good lives by studying ancient traditions; stressed the importance of respecting one's family and ancestors. (p. 175)

conquistador (kon kēs′tə dôr) A Spanish conqueror who came to the Americas to search for gold, land, and glory. (p. 468)

consul (kon′səl) One of two elected officials of the Roman Republic who commanded the army and were supreme judges. (p. 232)

continent (kon′tə nənt) One of Earth's seven large bodies of land. (p. G4)

convent (kon′vent) A religious community in which women, or nuns, live and pray. *See* **nun.** (p. 331)

convert (kən vürt′) To adopt or cause someone to adopt a new religion. (p. 470)

convict (kon′ vikt) A person who has been found guilty by the government of committing a crime and receives a sentence of punishment. (p. 480)

credibility (kre də bi′lə tē) Believability. (p. 472)

Crusade (krü säd′) Any of the journeys and battles undertaken by European Christians between 1095 and 1270, to win control of the Holy Land (Palestine) from the Muslims. (p. 332)

Cultural Revolution (kul′chər əl rev ə lü′shən) A campaign in China, 1966–1976, when the Communist Party under Mao Zedong called for the destruction of all noncommunist beliefs. (p. 554)

culture (kul′ chər) The way of life of a group of people at a particular time, including their daily habits, beliefs, and arts. (p. 10)

cuneiform (kū nē′ ə fōrm) A system of writing that used wedge-shaped symbols to represent sounds, ideas, and objects; developed in ancient Sumer. (p. 108)

custom (kus′təm) A way of living that people of the same culture practice regularly over time. (p. 14)

D

decision (di sizh′ən) a choice made from a number of alternatives. *See* **conclusion.** (p. 30)

Declaration of the Rights of Man and of the Citizen (dek lə rā′shən) A statement issued by the French National Assembly in August 1789 that all men were "born and remain free and equal in rights." (p. 488)

deforestation (dē for ə stā′shən) The process of clearing the land of forests, often to make space for farms and cities. (p. 318)

degree (di grē′) In geography, a unit of measurement that indicates the distance between lines of latitude and longitude; a unit of measurement for temperature. (p. 12)

delta (del′tə) The flat, fan-shaped land made of silt deposited at the mouth of a river. (p. 71)

demand (di mand′) In economics, people's desire for a particular item. *See* **supply.** (p. 363)

democracy (di mok′rə sē) A system of government in which citizens vote to make governmental decisions. (p. 199)

depression (di presh′ən) A severe slowdown in business characterized by high unemployment and falling prices. (p. 541)

dharma (där′me) In Hinduism, the laws and duties that guide the behavior of each caste member. (p. 145)

Diaspora (dī as′pər ə) The scattering of Jews to many parts of the world. (p. 125)

dictator (dik′tā tər) A ruler who has absolute power. (p. 237)

distortion (di stôr′shən) In cartography, or map-making, the unavoidable inaccuracy caused by stretching or cutting parts of the globe to fit them onto a flat map. (p. 432)

distribution map (dis trə bū′shən map) A special purpose map that shows how a particular feature such as population density is spread over an area. (p. G11)

diversity (di vûr′si tê) Differences; variety. (p. 440)

divine right (di vīn′ rīt) The belief that a monarch received authority to rule from God and therefore could not be questioned. *See* **absolute monarchy.** (p. 486)

domesticate (də mes′ti kāt) To train plants or animals to be useful to people. (p. 53)

drought (drout) A long period of dry weather. (p. 105)

dynasty (dī′nə stê) A line of rulers who belong to the same family. (p. 164)

E

Eastern Orthodox Christianity (ēs′tərn ôr′thə doks kris chē an′i tē) A branch of Christianity that developed in the Byzantine Empire and that did not recognize the pope as its supreme leader. (p. 255)

economy (i kon′ə mē) The way people manage money and resources for the production of goods and services. (p. 77)

effect (i fekt′) Something that happens as a result of a cause. *See* **cause.** (p. 118)

Eightfold Path (āt′fōld path) In Buddhism, the basic rules of behavior and belief leading to an end of suffering. *See* **Four Noble Truths.** (p. 153)

elevation (el ə vā′shən) Height above sea level. (p. 228)

elevation map (el ə vā′shən map) A map that shows the height of land above sea level. (p. G10)

emancipee (i man′ sə pē) A person who has been freed, or emancipated, from a sentence of punishment given to him or her by the government. (p. 481)

emperor (em′pər ər) The supreme ruler of an empire. (p. 168)

empire (em′pīr) A group of lands and peoples ruled by one government. (p. 86)

equal-area projection (ē'kwəl ār'ē ə prə jek'shən) A map that is useful for comparing sizes of land masses, on which shapes at the center are fairly accurate but are very distorted at the edges of the map. (p. 432)

equator (i kwā'tər) An imaginary line circling Earth halfway between the North and South poles and dividing Earth into Northern and Southern Hemispheres. (p. G4)

erosion (i rō'zhən) The gradual wearing away of soil and rock by wind, glaciers, or water. (p. 162)

estates (e stāts') The three social classes into which France was divided before the French Revolution, including the clergy, the aristocracy, and the common people. (p. 487)

ethnic group (eth'nik grüp) A people who share a heritage of common customs, values, and language. (p. 599)

European Union (EU) (yür ə pē'ən ün'yən) A group of European nations working to build a common economy and create cultural ties throughout Europe. (p. 601)

evaluate (i val'ū āt) To judge. (p. 31)

excavate (eks' kə vāt') To dig or to scoop out earth. (p. 32)

expedition (ek spi dish'ən) A group of people who go on a trip for a specific reason. (p. 87)

F

factory (fak'tə rē) A building in which machines used to manufacture goods are located. (p. 501)

famine (fam'in) A widespread lack of food resulting in hunger and starvation. (p. 162)

fascism (fash'iz əm) A totalitarian government that promotes a form of nationalism in which the goals of the nation are more important than those of the individual. (p. 540)

feudalism (fū'də liz əm) Starting in Europe around A.D. 800, a system for organizing and governing society, based on land and service. *See* **fief, lord, vassal.** (p. 322)

fief (fēf) In the Middle Ages, a property given to a vassal in exchange for his loyalty. (p. 322)

Five Pillars (fīv pil'ərz) The five basic duties of all Muslims. (p. 269)

Four Noble Truths (fôr nō'bəl trüthz) In Buddhism, the principles that rule life and promise an end to suffering. *See* **Eightfold Path.** (p. 153)

free enterprise (frē en'tər prīz) The economic system of private ownership of land and businesses that allows people to make their own economic decisions and profit from their own work. (p. 556)

G

generalization (jen ər ə lə zā'shən) A broad statement that points out a common feature shared by different kinds of examples. (p. 408)

geocentric (jē ō sen'trik) Based on the idea that Earth is the center of the universe and that the sun, stars, and planets revolve around Earth. (p. 456)

geography (jē og'rə fē) The study of Earth's environment and how it shapes people's lives and how Earth is shaped in turn by people's activities. (p. 8)

glacier (glā'shər) A great sheet of ice that moves slowly over a land surface. *See* **Ice Age.** (p. 286)

gladiator (glad'ē ā tər) A Roman athlete, usually a slave, criminal, or prisoner of war, who was forced to fight for the entertainment of the public. (p. 240)

global grid (glō'bəl grid) Pattern formed on a map or globe by the crossing of parallels and meridians. This pattern makes it possible to pinpoint exact locations. (p. 13)

glyph (glif) A writing symbol, often carved into stone, that stands for an object or a sound. *See* **stela.** (p. 302)

Grand Canal (grand kə nal') A waterway in China connecting Beijing with cities to the south. (p. 403)

Grand School (grand skül) A school begun by Confucian scholars in China that trained students for government jobs. (p. 176)

grand mufti (grand muf'tē) A religious leader of the Ottoman empire responsible for interpreting the laws of Islam. (p. 389)

gravity (grav'i tē) The force that pulls objects toward Earth and that draws planets into orbits around the sun. (p. 459)

Green Revolution (grēn rev ə lü'shən) A campaign by the government of India in the 1950s to increase agricultural productivity. (p. 584)

griot (grē'ō) An oral historian and musician who became important in western Africa in the 1500s and still carries on oral traditions today. (p. 367)

gross domestic product (grōs də mes'tik prod'ukt) The total value of goods and services produced by a country during a year. (p. 506)

pronunciation key

a at; ā ape; ä far; âr care; e end; ē me; i it; ī ice; îr pierce; o hot; ō old; ô fork; oi oil; ou out; u up; ū use; ü rule; ù pull; ûr turn; hw white; ng song; th thin; <u>th</u> this; zh measure; ə about, taken, pencil, lemon, circus

guild (gild) In the Middle Ages, an organization of workers in a trade or craft that set standards and protected the interests of its members. (p. 324)

H

hacienda (hä sē en′də) A large agricultural estate owned by Spaniards or the church in Spain's American colonies. (p. 470)

harbor (här′bər) A sheltered place along a coast used to protect boats and ships. (p. 193)

heliocentric (hē lē ō sen′trik) Based on Copernicus's idea that the Earth and the other planets revolve around the sun. (p. 457)

hemisphere (hem′is fîr) One of the halves of Earth. (p. G4)

hieroglyphics (hī ər ə glif′iks) The ancient Egyptian system of writing that used symbols to stand for objects, ideas, or sounds. (p. 78)

hijra (hij′rə) The migration of Muhammad from Mecca to Medina in A.D. 622, marking the founding of Islam. (p. 268)

Hinduism (hin′dü iz əm) The religion of India that grew out of the beliefs of the ancient Aryan peoples; it stresses that one main force connects all of life. (p. 142)

historical map (hi stôr′i kəl map) A map that shows information about the past. (p. 280)

history (his′tə rē) The story or record of what has happened in the past. (p. 24)

Holocaust (hol′ə kôst) The deliberate killing of 6 million Jews solely because they were Jewish by the Nazis during World War II. (p. 546)

humanism (hū′mə niz əm) An idea important to the Renaissance that focused on human values and what people can achieve in this world. (p. 336)

hunter-gatherer (hun′tər gath′ər ər) A person of the Old Stone Age who met needs by hunting animals and gathering plants. (p. 46)

I

Ice Age (īs āj) Any of the periods of time in the past lasting for millions of years when glaciers spread to cover nearly half of Earth's land. (p. 286)

imperialism (im pîr′ē ə liz əm) The extension of a nation's power over other lands by military, political, or economic means. (p. 508)

indulgence (in dul′jəns) A pardon or forgiveness given by the Roman Catholic Church to people who act against Christian teachings. (p. 343)

Industrial Revolution (in dus′ trē əl rev ə lü′ shən) A time when great technological advances changed the way goods were made and the ways people lived; it began in England in the 1700s and then spread throughout Europe and the United States. (p. 500)

inflation (in flā′shən) A period of rising prices. (p. 541)

interaction (in tər ak′shən) The exchange of ideas and customs among cultures. (p. 16)

interdependent (in tər di pen′dənt) Depending upon one another to meet needs and wants. (p. 622)

intermediate directions (in tər mē′dē it di rek′shənz) The directions halfway between the cardinal directions; northeast, southeast, southwest, and northwest. (p. G6)

International Date Line (in tər nash′ə nəl dāt līn) An imaginary line in the Pacific Ocean marking the boundary between one day and the next. (p. 549)

Internet (in′ tər net) A constantly growing international group of interconnected computers. (p. 627)

Intifada (in tə fä′də) The Palestinian uprising against Israeli rule that began in 1987. (p. 578)

irrigation (ir i gā′shən) The watering of dry land by means of canals or pipes. (p. 72)

Islam (is läm′) The religion of Muslims based on the teachings of the prophet Muhammad in the A.D. 600s. (p. 266)

isthmus (is′məs) A narrow strip of land that connects two larger land masses. (p. 423)

J

Judaism (jü′dē iz əm) The religion of the Jewish people. (p. 120)

jury (jür′ē) A group of citizens chosen to hear evidence and make a decision in a court of law. (p. 206)

K

Kaaba (kä′bə) A religious temple in Mecca that became sacred to Muslims. (p. 267)

karma (kär′mə) In Hinduism and Buddhism, the end result of all of a person's good and bad acts, which determines his or her rebirth. (p. 152)

Korean War (kə rē′ən wôr) A war fought between communist North Korea, aided by China, and South Korea, aided by United Nations members, during 1950–1953. (p. 557)

L

landform (land′fôrm) A feature of Earth's surface, such as a mountain range, plain, or plateau. (p. 9)

large-scale map (lärj skāl map) A map that provides many details about a small area by measuring lesser distances in small units. (p. 92)

Latin America (lat′in ə mer′i kə) The cultural region including Mexico, the Caribbean, and South America that has been strongly influenced by Spain and Portugal. (p. 492)

latitude (lat′i tüd) Distance north or south of the equator, measured by a set of imaginary lines, or parallels, that run east and west around Earth. *See* **parallel.** (p. G4, 12)

League of Nations (lēg əv nā′shənz) An international council created in 1920 by the Allied Powers to try to prevent future wars. (p. 531)

levee (lev′ē) A wall built along a river bank to prevent flooding. (p. 162)

Line of Demarcation (lin əv dē mär kā′shən) An imaginary line drawn across North and South America in 1494 to divide the claims of Spain and Portugal. (p. 467)

locator (lō′kāt ər) A small map that shows where the subject area of a main map is located. (p. G8)

loess (les) A fine, yellow soil that is easily carried by wind and rain, found in China. (p. 161)

longitude (lon′ji tüd) Distance east or west of the prime meridian measured by a set of imaginary lines, or meridians, that run north and south from Earth's poles. *See* **meridian.** (p. G4)

lord (lôrd) In the Middle Ages, a noble who owned and controlled all activities on his manor. *See* **vassal.** (p. 322)

M

Magna Carta (mag′nə kär′tə) A legal document written by English lords in 1215 that stated certain rights and limited the power of the king. (p. 326)

maize (māz) Corn; a crop first grown in Middle America about 5,000 B.C. (p. 300)

Mandate of Heaven (man′dāt uv hev′ən) The belief that the Chinese emperor's right to rule came from the gods. (p. 175)

manor (man′ər) In the Middle Ages, a large self-sufficient estate granted to a lord and worked by serfs. (p. 320)

map key (map kē) A list of map symbols that tells what each symbol stands for. (p. G8)

Meiji Restoration (mā′ jē′ res tə rā′ shən) The overthrow of Japan's shogun in 1868 and restoration of power to the emperor Meiji. (p. 510)

mercator projection (mər kä′tər prə jek′shən) A map that shows accurate shapes of land masses and correct straight-line directions, but which is distorted for areas near the poles. (p. 432)

meridian (mə rid′ē ən) Any line of longitude east or west of Earth's prime meridian. *See* **parallel.** (p. G4)

Messiah (mə sī′ə) A special leader the Jewish people believe will be sent by God to guide them and set up God's rule on Earth. Christians believe Jesus to be the Messiah. (p. 247)

mestizo (me stē′zō) A person of mixed Native American and Spanish ancestry. (p. 494)

Middle Ages (mid′əl āj′əz) A period in European history between A.D. 500 and about the 1500s. (p. 320)

Middle Passage (mid′əl pas′ij) The difficult voyage made by enslaved Africans across the Atlantic Ocean to the West Indies where they were sold. (p. 475)

Middle Way (mid′əl wā) In Buddhism, a way of life, neither too strict nor too easy, that results from following the Eightfold Path. (p. 153)

middle class (mid′əl klas) During the Industrial Revolution, the new class of business people. (p. 504)

migrate (mī′grāt) To move from one place to another to live, especially a large group of people. (p. 138)

missionary (mish′ə ner ē) A person who teaches his or her religion to people with different beliefs. (p. 470)

monarchy (mon′ər kē) A government ruled by a king or queen. (p. 197)

monastery (mon′ə ster ē) A community in which monks lead lives devoted to religion. *See* **convent.** (p. 331)

monk (mungk) A man who devotes his life to a religious group, often giving up all he owns. *See* **monastery.** (p. 151)

monotheism (mon′ə thē iz əm) A belief in one God. *See* **polytheism.** (p. 123)

monsoon (mon sün′) A seasonal wind that blows across South Asia bringing dry weather in the winter and heavy rains in the summer. (p. 386)

mosque (mosk) A Muslim place of worship. (p. 273)

N

NAFTA (naf′tə) The North American Free Trade Agreement, which went into effect in 1993, allowing free trade for many goods traded between Canada, Mexico, and the United States. (p. 626)

nationalism (nash′ə nə liz əm) A strong loyalty to one's own country and culture. (p. 527)

pronunciation key

a **at**; ā **ape**; ä **far**; âr **care**; e **end**; ē **me**; i **it**; ī **ice**; îr **pierce**; o **hot**; ō **old**; ô **fork**; oi **oil**; ou **out**; u **up**; ū **use**; ü **rule**; u̇ **pull**; ûr **turn**; hw **white**; ng **song**; th **thin**; <u>th</u> **this**; zh **measure**; ə **about, taken, pencil, lemon, circus**

NATO (nā′tō) The North Atlantic Treaty Organization, a military alliance formed in 1949 by nations in western Europe and North America. (p. 557)

navigable (nav′i gə bəl) Able to be traveled by boats or ships. (p. 318)

New Stone Age (nü stōn āj) The period of human prehistory that lasted from 12,000 years ago to about 6,000 years ago, during which people still depended mainly on stone tools and began experimenting with agriculture. (p. 52)

New Testament (nü tes′tə mənt) The second part of the Christian Bible, containing descriptions of the life and teachings of Jesus and of his early followers. (p. 246)

noble (nō′bəl) A member of a ruling family or one of high rank. *See* **aristocracy.** (p. 165)

nuclear arms race (nü′klē ər ärmz rās) The Cold War competition between superpowers to develop more powerful and greater numbers of nuclear weapons. (p. 559)

nun (nun) A woman who devotes her life to religion, often living in a convent. *See* **convent.** (p. 331)

⊙

oasis (ō ā′sis) A well-watered area in a desert. (p. 263)

Old Stone Age (ōld stōn āj) The period of human prehistory that lasted until about 12,000 years ago, during which stone tools were the most common technology used by humans. (p. 45)

oligarchy (ol′i gär kē) A type of government in which a small group of citizens control decision-making. (p. 197)

oracle bone (ôr′ə kəl bōn) In ancient China, a cattle or sheep bone used to predict the future. (p. 167)

oral tradition (ôr′əl trə dish′ən) The passing on of history, beliefs, or customs by word of mouth. (p. 25)

ℙ

Pacific Rim (pə sif′ik rim) The ring of countries surrounding the Pacific Ocean. (p. 616)

papyrus (pə pī′rəs) A kind of paper made from papyrus, a reed plant growing along the Nile, that the ancient Egyptians used for writing. (p. 79)

parable (par′ə bəl) A simple story that contains a message or truth. (p. 248)

parallel (par′ə lel) In geography, any line of latitude north or south of the equator; parallels never cross or meet. *See* **meridian.** (p. G4)

patrician (pə trish′ən) A member of the noble families who controlled all power in the early years of the Roman Republic. (p. 231)

patron (pā′trən) A supporter of the arts. (p. 337)

Pax Romana (paks rō mä′nə) A period of peace for the Roman Empire that began with the rule of Augustus in about 27 B.C. and lasted around 200 years. (p. 236)

peasant (pez′sənt) A small farm owner or farm worker. (p. 487)

Peloponnesian War (pel ə pə nē′zhən wôr) A war fought between Athens and Sparta in the 400s B.C., ending in a victory for Sparta. (p. 208)

peninsula (pə nin′sə lə) An area of land almost entirely surrounded by water. (p. 193)

per capita income (pūr kap′i tə in′kum) The amount of money each person would have if his or her country's total income were divided equally among its people. (p. 601)

pharaoh (fâ′rō) The title used by the rulers of ancient Egypt. (p. 75)

philosophy (fə los′ə fē) The study of or search for truth, wisdom, and the right way to live. (p. 206)

physical map (fiz′i kəl map) A map that primarily shows natural features of Earth, such as lakes, rivers, mountains, and deserts. (p. G10)

pilgrimage (pil′grə mij) A journey for religious purposes. (p. 269)

plague (plāg) A terrible disease that spreads quickly and kills many people. (p. 334)

plantation (plan tā′shən) A large farming estate where mainly a single crop is grown; until the mid-1800s slaves often worked on plantations. (p. 475)

plateau (pla tō′) An area of flat land that rises above the surrounding land. (p. 105)

plebeian (pli bē′ən) A common farmer, trader, or craftworker in ancient Rome. (p. 231)

point of view (point əv vū) The position of someone toward the world or a subject, shaped by his or her thinking, attitudes, and feelings. (p. 328)

polar projection (pō′lər prə jek′shən) A map projection that shows the area around the North or South Pole. (p. 432)

polis (pō′lis) A city-state in ancient Greece. (p. 196)

political cartoon (pə lit′i kəl kär tün′) A drawing that states an opinion about a political matter. (p. 572)

political map (pə lit′i kəl map) A map mainly showing political divisions, such as national or state boundaries, cities, and capitals. (p. G9)

polytheism (pol′ē thē iz əm) The belief in many gods and goddesses. *See* **monotheism.** (p. 111)

pope (pōp) The bishop, or church leader, of Rome and head of the Roman Catholic Church. (p. 251)

population density (pop yə lā′shən den′si tê) The number of people living in a given space. (p. 370)

prehistory (prē his′tə rē) The period before events were recorded in writing. (p. 33)

prime meridian (prīm mə rid′ē ən) The line of longitude marked 0° on the world map, from which longitude east and west are measured. (p. G4)

primary source (prī′mer ē sôrs) A first-hand account of an event or an artifact created during the period of history being studied. *See* **secondary source.** (p. 26)

profile (prō′fil) In geography, a map showing a cross-section of a land surface. (p. 228)

projection (prə jek′shən) A way of placing parts of Earth onto a flat map. (p. 432)

propaganda (prop ə gan′də) The spreading of persuasive ideas or attitudes that are often exaggerated or falsified in order to help or hurt a particular cause or group. (p. 541)

Protestantism (prot′ə stən tiz əm) The beliefs of Christians who opposed, or protested against, the Roman Catholic Church in the 1500s; the beliefs of people who follow a Protestant religion today. (p. 344)

province (prov′ins) A division of land within an empire or country. (p. 169)

Punic Wars (pū′nik wôrz) A series of conflicts between Rome and Carthage in the 200s B.C., ending in a victory for Rome. (p. 234)

Q

quipu (kē′pü) A knotted cord used for record-keeping by the Inca. (p. 437)

Quran (kü rän′) The most holy book of Islam, believed to contain the teachings of Allah, or God, to Muhammad. (p. 266)

R

rain forest (rān fōr′ist) A warm, wet forest that receives more than 80 inches of rain per year. (p. 288)

Raj (räj) The period in India from the 1850s to 1947 when it was ruled by the British. (p. 581)

reform (ri fôrm′) To change. (p. 343)

Reformation (ref ər mā′shən) A movement beginning in Europe in the 1500s, to bring reform to the Roman Catholic Church, and leading to Protestantism. (p. 344)

refugee (ref yü jē′) A person who flees his or her country for safety. (p. 577)

region (rē′jən) An area with common features that set it apart from other areas. (p. 9)

Reign of Terror (rān əv ter′ər) The period 1793–1794 in revolutionary France when suspected traitors were beheaded in great numbers. (p. 490)

reincarnation (rē in kär na′shən) A Hindu belief that people move in a constant cycle of life, death, and rebirth. (p. 144)

relief map (ri lēf′ map) A map that shows changes in elevation. (p. G10)

Renaissance (ren ə säns′) A period of great cultural and artistic change that began in Italy around 1350 and spread throughout Europe. (p. 336)

representative (rep ri zen′tə tiv) A person who is elected by citizens to speak or act for them. *See* **Republic.** (p. 232)

republic (ri pub′lik) A form of government in which citizens elect representatives to speak or act for them. (p. 231)

revolution (rev ə lü′shən) The overthrow of an existing government and its replacement with another; any sudden or very great change. (p. 486)

Roman Catholicism (rō′mən kə thol′ə siz əm) A branch of Christianity that developed in the western Roman empire and that recognized the Pope as its supreme head. (p. 257)

Russian Revolution (rush′ən rev ə lü′shən) Beginning in 1917, the events leading up to the overthrow of tsarist rule and the eventual establishment of the Soviet government led by Vladimir Ilyich Lenin and the Bolsheviks. (p. 532)

S

Sabbath (sab′əth) A weekly day of rest, prayer, and study. (p. 124)

saint (sānt) A woman or man considered by a religious group to be especially holy. (p. 332)

samurai (sam′ü rī) A class of soldiers in fuedal Japan who were loyal only to their lords. (p. 411)

sanction (sangk′shən) A penalty placed against a nation to make it change its behavior, such as a refusal to buy its goods or sell it products. (p. 608)

savanna (sə van′ə) A broad, grassy, plain with few trees, found especially in large parts of Africa. (p. 356)

pronunciation key

a **at**; ā **ape**; ä **far**; âr **care**; e **end**; ē **me**; i **it**; ī **ice**; îr **pierce**; o **hot**; ō **old**; ô **fork**; oi **oil**; ou **out**; u **up**; ū **use**; ü **rule**, u̇ **pull**; ûr **turn**; hw **white**; ng **song**; th **thin**; th **this**; zh measure; ə **about**, taken, pencil, lemon, circus

scale (skāl) A unit of measure on a map, such as an inch, that is used to represent a distance on Earth. (p. G7)

scientific method (sī ən tif'ik meth'əd) A way of studying things through questioning and thorough testing. (p. 460)

scribe (skrīb) A professional writer who kept records and copied letters and official documents. (p. 78)

secondary source (sek'ən der ē sôrs) A record of the past, based on information from primary sources. (p. 27)

seismograph (sīz'mə graf) A scientific instrument that could detect earthquakes hundreds of miles away, invented during the Han dynasty. (p. 177)

Senate (sen'it) The lawmaking body and most powerful branch of government in ancient Rome's Republic. (p. 232)

serf (sûrf) In the Middle Ages, a person who was bound to work on a noble's manor. (p. 320)

Shinto (shin'tō) A Japanese religion marked by the belief in the spirits of nature. (p. 410)

shogun (shō'gən) The ruler of feudal Japan from the 1100s to the 1800s who, although appointed by the emperor, ruled the country as a military dictator. (p. 411)

silt (silt) A mixture of tiny bits of soil and rock carried and deposited by a river. (p. 71)

slash and burn (slash and bûrn) A farming method involving the cutting of trees, then the burning of them to provide ash-enriched soil for the planting of crops. (p. 293)

slavery (slā'və rē) The practice of one person owning another person. (p. 95)

small-scale map (smôl skāl map) A map that shows a big area in less detail by measuring its greater distance in large units. (p. 92)

social pyramid (sō'shəl pir'ə mid) A diagram illustrating the divisions within a culture; usually showing the most powerful person or group at the peak and the least powerful groups at the bottom. (p. 95)

socialism (sō'shə liz əm) An economic and political system based on collective or government ownership and control of all resources and industry; also a political philosophy based on the writings of Karl Marx. (p. 505)

specialization (spesh ə lə zā'shən) Training to do a particular kind of work. (p. 55)

stela (stē'lə) A tall, flat stone, often carved with writing, used to mark an important historical event. (p. 302)

steppe (step) A dry, grassy, treeless plain found in Asia and eastern Europe. (p. 163)

strait (strāt) A narrow channel, or body of water, connecting two larger bodies of water. (p. 464)

strike (strīk) A refusal to work as a protest against unfair treatment. (p. 534)

subcontinent (sub kon'tə nənt) A large landmass that is connected to the rest of a continent. (p. 131)

sugarcane (shug'ər kān) A tall grass with a thick, woody stem containing a liquid that is a source of sugar. (p. 475)

sultan (sult' ən) Supreme ruler of the Ottoman empire. (p. 389)

summary (sum'ə rē) A brief statement of main ideas. (p. 172)

superpower (sü'pər pou ər) A term used for the world's strongest nations—the United States, China, and the Soviet Union—during the Cold War. (p. 556)

supply (sə plī') In economics, the available quantity of a good, product, or resource. See **demand.** (p. 363)

surplus (sûr'plus) An extra supply of something, such as crops that are not needed immediately for food. (p. 55)

symbol (sim'bəl) Anything that stands for something else. (p. G8)

T

technology (tek nol'ə jē) The use of skills and tools to meet practical human needs. (p. 45)

telescope (tel'ə skōp) An optical instrument for making distant objects, such as planets and stars, appear nearer and larger. (p. 457)

temperate (tem'pər it) Mild; moderate in temperature. (p. 317)

Ten Commandments (ten kə mand'mənts) According to the Hebrew Bible, the laws God gave to Moses on Mount Sinai. (p. 123)

terrace (ter'is) A level platform of earth built into a hillside, usually used for farming. (p. 437)

textile (teks'tīl) A cloth fabric that is either woven or knitted. (p. 501)

Three Fires Council (thrē fīrz koun'səl) A league or cooperative group formed by the Ojibwa and the neighboring Potawatomi and Ottawa to promote trade. (p. 441)

timberline (tim'bər līn) An imaginary line on high mountains or in the arctic; above or beyond it trees cannot grow. (p. 424)

time line (tīm līn) A diagram that shows when events took place during a given period of time. (p. 58)

time zone (tīm zōn) A geographic region where the same standard time is used. (p. 548)

topic sentence (top'ik sen'təns) A sentence that contains the main idea of a paragraph, often the first sentence in that paragraph. (p. 172)

Torah (tôr'ə) The first five books of the Hebrew Bible containing the laws and teachings of Judaism. (p. 123)

totalitarian (tō tal i târ'ē ən) A government in which a dictator or a small group of leaders control all aspects of people's lives. (p. 538)

township (toun'ship) A segregated area where blacks in South Africa were forced to live under apartheid. (p. 607)

trade (trād) The exchange of goods between peoples. (p. 56)

Treaty of Versailles (trē'tē əv vâr sī') The treaty that the Allied Powers forced Germany to sign at the end of World War I. (p. 531)

Triangular Trade (trī ang'gyə lər trād) From the 1500s to the mid-1800s, the triangular-shaped trade routes between the Americas, England, and Africa, which involved the buying and selling of captive Africans as well as guns, sugar, and iron goods. (p. 476)

tribune (trib'ūn) An elected leader of ancient Rome who represented the interests of the plebeians. (p. 232)

tribute (trib'ūt) A tax, often in the form of crops, paid by one ruler to another, usually to ensure peace or protection. (p. 428)

Triple Alliance (trip'əl ə lī'əns) The pact that the army of the Aztec made with the forces of Texcoco and Tlacopan in 1428 in order to gain control of the Valley of Mexico. (p. 428)

tropical (trop'i kəl) Of or relating to the area of Earth between the Tropic of Cancer (23.5°N) and the Tropic of Capricorn (23.5°S). (p. 287)

tsar (zär) In pre-revolution Russia, the emperor. (p. 533)

tundra (tun'drə) A vast, treeless plain in arctic or subarctic places such as Alaska and northern Canada. (p. 422)

Twelve Tables (twelv tā'belz) The earliest written collection of Roman laws, drawn up by patricians about 450 B.C., that became the foundation of Roman law. (p. 233)

unification (ū nə fi kā'shən) The joining of separate parts, such as kingdoms, into one. (p. 75)

United Nations (ū nī'tid nā'shənz) An organization founded in 1945 whose members include most of the world's nations. It works to preserve world peace, settle disputes, and aid international cooperation. (p. 557)

urbanization (ur bən ə zā'shən) The growth of cities. (p. 625)

V

values (val'ūz) Ideals or beliefs that guide the way people live. (p. 16)

vassal (vas'əl) In the Middle Ages, a noble who usually was given a fief by his lord in exchange for loyalty. (p. 322)

Vedas (vā'dəz) In Hinduism, the ancient books of sacred songs on which much of its religious beliefs are based. (p. 143)

Vietnam War (vē et näm' wôr) A civil war fought between South Vietnam, aided by the United States, and communist North Vietnam during 1954–1975. (p. 589)

W

warlord (wôr'lôrd) In China, 1912–1927, a strong local military leader who took advantage of political unrest to seize power in the area. (p. 551)

Warsaw Pact (wôr'sô pakt) A military alliance formed in 1955 by the Soviet Union and seven eastern European nations. (p. 557)

wigwam (wig'wom) A dome-shaped dwelling built by the Ojibwa and other Native Americans made of birch bark, cattail reeds, and wooden poles. (p. 443)

working class (wûrk'ing klas) People who work for wages, such as factory workers. (p. 504)

World War I (wûrld wôr) Called the "Great War" at the time, the war of 1914–1918 in which the Allied Powers defeated the Central Powers. (p. 531)

World War II (wûrld wôr) The war of 1939–1945 in which the Allies defeated the Axis powers. (p. 542)

Z

ziggurat (zig'ū rat) A large temple located in the centers of ancient Sumerian cities. (p. 111)

Zionism (zī'ə niz əm) A movement to create a national homeland for the Jewish people. (p. 575)

index

This Index lists many topics that appear in the book, along with the pages on which they are found. Page numbers after an m refer you to a map. Page numbers after a p indicate photographs, artwork, or charts.

CREDITS

(continued from page ii)

Acknowledgments

Extract from **Children of the World** by E. Blauer, D.K. Wright, G. Holland, B.R. Rogers. Published by Gareth Stevens, Inc., Milwaukee, WI. Reprinted by permission.

From **The Sumerians: Their History, Culture and Character** by Samuel Noah Kramer. Copyright 1963 by The University of Chicago. Reprinted by permission of the publisher.

From **Pharaoh's People** by T.G.H. James. Copyright 1984 by T.G.H. James. Reprinted by permission of The University of Chicago Press.

From **God's Country: America in the Fifties** by J. Ronald Oakley. Copyright 1986 by J.

Ronald Oakley. Red Dembner Enterprises Corp., New York.

From **Television** by Michael Winship. Copyright 1988 by Educational Broadcasting Corporation and Michael Winship. Random House, New York.

From **Monsoons**, edited by Jay S. Fein, Pamela L. Stephens. Copyright 1987 by John Wiley & Sons, Inc. A. Wiley-Interscience Publication, John Wiley & Sons, Inc.

From **The Ancient Civilization of Angkor** by Christopher Pym. Copyright 1968 by Christopher Pym. A Mentor Book published by The New American Library, N.Y. & Toronto.

From **Angkor Heart of an Asian Empire** by Bruno Dagens. English translation copyright 1995 by Harry N. Abrams, Inc., N.Y. and Thames and Hudson Ltd., London. Harry N. Abrams, Inc., Publishers.

From **The Travels of Marco Polo**, a modern translation by Teresa Waugh from the Italian by Maria Bellonci. Translation copyright 1984 by Sadgwick and Jackson Limited. Facts on File Publications, N.Y.

From **The Longest Walk: An Odyssey of the Human Spirit** by George Meegan. Copyright 1988 by George Meegan. Dodd, Mead & Company, N.Y.

From **The Way of the Earth: Encounters with Nature in Ancient and Contemporary Thought** by T.C. McLuhan. Copyright 1994 by T.C. McLuhan. Simon & Schuster, N.Y.

From "The land is everything." quote printed in **Native Peoples Magazine** Vol. 6, Number 3, Spring 1993, quote from Gerald Vizenor. Copyright 1993 by Media Concepts Group, Inc. Media Concepts Group, Inc., AZ.

From **Coming of Age in the Milky Way** by Timothy Ferris. Copyright 1988 by Timothy Ferris. An Anchor Book published by Doubleday, a division of Bantam Doubleday Dell Publishing Group, Inc., N.Y. The Anchor Books Edition was published by arrangement with William Morrow and Company.

From **The Diary of a Young Girl: The Definitive Edition** by Anne Frank. Otto H. Frank & Mirjam Pressler, Editors, translated by Susan Massotty. Translation copyright © 1995 by Doubleday, a division of Bantam Doubleday Dell Publishing Group, Inc. Used by permission of Doubleday, a division of Bantam Doubleday Dell Publishing Group, Inc.

From **Red Azalea** by Anchee Min. Copyright 1994 by Anchee Min. Pantheon Books, a division of Random House, N.Y.

From **China: The Long March** by Anthony Lawrence. Copyright 1986 by Intercontinental Publishing Corp., China National Publishing Industry Trading Corp. and China Photographic Publishing House, London.

From **Mme Sun Yat-sen** by Jung Chang with Jon Halliday. Copyright 1986 by Jung Chang and Jon Halliday. Penguin Books.

From **The Cold War** by Martin Walker. Copyright 1993 by Walker & Watson Ltd. A John Macrae Book, Henry Holt and Company, N.Y.

From **The Africans** by David Lamb. Copyright 1983 by David Lamb. Vintage Books, a division of Random House, N.Y.

From **Holy War: The Crusades and Their Impact on Today's World** by Karen Armstrong. Copyright 1988, 1991 by Karen Armstrong. Papermac, a division of Macmillan Publishers Limited, London.

From **Long Walk to Freedom: The Autobiography of Nelson Mandela** by Nelson Mandela. Copyright 1994 by Nelson Rolihlahla Mandela. Little, Brown and Company.

From **Zlata's Diary: A Child's Life in Sarajevo** translated with notes by Christina Pribichevich-Zoric. Translation Copyright by Fixot et editions Robert Laffont, 1994. Viking, published by the Penguin Group, Penguin Books USA Inc., N.Y.

From **Self-Made Man: Human Evolution from Eden to Extinction** by Jonathan Kingdon. Copyright 1993 by Jonathan Kingdon. John Wiley & Sons, Inc.

From **Mesopotamian Myths** by Henrietta McCall. Copyright by The Trustees of the British Museum. British Museum Publications, Ltd.

From **Legacy of the Indus: A Discovery of Pakistan** by Samina Quraeshi. Copyright 1974 by Samina Quraeshi. Poem on pg. 8 Copyright 1974 by Salman Tarik Kureshi. John Weatherhill, Inc.

From **The Vedic Experience Mantramanjari**, edited and translated with introductions and notes by Raimundo Panikkar. Copyright 1977 by Raimundo Panikkar. University of California Press.

From **Four-Dimensional Man: Meditations Through the Rg Veda** by Antonio T. de Nicolas. Copyright 1976 by Nicolas Hays, Ltd. Nicolas Hays Ltd.

From **The Wisdom of the Buddha**, by Jean Boisselier. Copyright 1993 by Gallimard. English translation Copyright 1994 Harry N. Abrams, Inc., N.Y. Harry N. Abrams, Inc., New York.

From **The Odyssey of Homer** a new verse translation by Allen Mandelbaum. Copyright 1990 by Allen Mandelbaum. University of California Press.

From **God's Bits of Wood**, Sembene Ousmane translated by Francis Price. Copyright 1962 Doubleday & Company Inc. Heinemann Educational Books Ltd.

From **Serowe Village of the Rain Wind** by Bessie Head. Copyright 1981 by Bessie Head. Heinemann Educational Books Ltd.

From **The Search for Africa**, by Basil Davidson. Copyright 1994 by Basil Davidson. Times Books/Random House.

From **Corpus of early Arabic sources for West African history**, translated by J.F.P. Hopkins, edited and annotated by N. Levtzion & J.F.P. Hopkins. Copyright 1981 by University of Ghana, International Academic Union, Cambridge University Press. Cambridge University Press.

From "China-the End of an Era" from The Nation Magazine by Orville Schell. The Nation Magazine, July 17/24, 1995.

DEDUCTION AND OUTSIDE KNOWLEDGE

Most of the multiple-choice exams you take will include charts, graphs, maps, time lines, and political cartoons. For some questions, you will need to look at this data to find the answer. The process of looking at the information provided, finding the answer to the question, and choosing the correct answer from among the answer choices is called DEDUCTION.

Not all the answers to the questions will be in the data, however. Sometimes, multiple-choice tests ask you to remember a fact that you learned in social studies class. You won't be able to find the correct answer on a map, chart, graph, or drawing; the correct answer will be in your memory. We call these OUTSIDE KNOWLEDGE questions.

Look at the map below, and then answer questions 1 and 2.

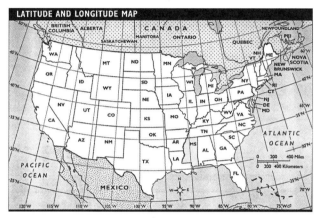

1 Which state is closest to 40°N latitude?

A   Florida
B   West Virginia
C   Maine
D   North Carolina

2 The weather in Texas is warmer than the weather in Wisconsin because Texas is

F   closer to the equator
G   a larger state
H   closer to a body of water
J   west of Wisconsin

Remember: Do not write in your textbook.   **TP 1**

Remind students not to write in their textbooks before beginning this section. Students will have a separate answer sheet when taking standardized tests. For the exercises that follow, they should respond aloud or on a separate piece of paper.

The types of questions introduced on these pages are given as general guidelines, to help students become familiar with the questions they will see on standardized tests. Many questions, however, fall into more than one category.

DEDUCTION AND OUTSIDE KNOWLEDGE

OBJECTIVES:
• To familiarize students with two basic types of questions they are likely to see on nationally administered standardized tests.
• To alert students to the fact that some questions will require students to remember information they have learned in class.

Teaching suggestions: Read the first two paragraphs of the page aloud to students. Then have students answer the two sample questions on their own.

1. **B** This question can be answered with the map. Students should place one finger on the 40°N latitude line. They should then locate each of the four states included among the answer choices. They should notice that the line runs through the state of West Virginia, the correct answer.

2. **F** This question requires outside knowledge. Students' knowledge of the climatic characteristics of U.S. regions is frequently tested on national standardized tests at this grade level. Students should know that the U.S. climate is warmer in the south than in the north.

PROCESS OF ELIMINATION

OBJECTIVES:
- To make students aware of valid alternate strategies to problem solving.
- To teach students to use process of elimination on multiple-choice tests when they are unsure of the correct answer.

Teaching suggestions: Read the first three paragraphs aloud to students. Then read the questions aloud and ask students to use process of elimination to eliminate answers that cannot be correct. Go through the answers, asking, **Is it possible the Pan American Highway could run from Mexico to Italy? Is it possible the Pan American Highway could run from Mexico to Cuba?** Encourage students to consider all answer choices, even when they believe they have found the correct answer before considering all choices. Say: **Let's look at the other answers to make sure that we have selected the best one.**

This skill will serve students well throughout their standardized test-taking careers.

1. **D** This question is a simple but effective illustration of how to use the process of elimination. Students probably do not know the southern destination of the Pan American Highway; however, they should be able to eliminate all of the incorrect answers based on their knowledge of world geography (and their understanding that highways cannot cross oceans). Go through the answers as indicated above.

2. **H** Students may not be able to eliminate ALL of the incorrect answers. They should remember from class that Christianity and Judaism originated in the Middle East. Students should be encouraged to eliminate as many as possible, and guess from among the remaining answers.

PROCESS OF ELIMINATION

When you take a multiple-choice test, you have an advantage that you don't have on other tests. On most tests, you must come up with the answers to the questions all on your own. For example, a test might ask "What is the capital of the United States?" You would then have to write the name "Washington D.C." on your answer sheet.

On a multiple-choice test, however, the correct answer is already written down for you; it is among the answer choices! All you have to do is figure out which of the answer choices is the correct one.

This is good news for you! It means that you can still answer a question correctly *even if you can't come up with the correct answer on your own*. That's because you can ELIMINATE choices that you know are *incorrect*. Eliminating answers this way will be especially helpful on OUTSIDE KNOWLEDGE questions. Sometimes you will be able to eliminate all of the choices except one. When that happens, it means that you have found the best answer by the PROCESS OF ELIMINATION.

Try using the process of elimination to answer this question:

1 The Pan American Highway extends from the northern tip of Mexico to the southern tip of—

A Italy
B Cuba
C Egypt
D Chile

Were you able to eliminate any *incorrect* answers? How many?

Now try using process of elimination To answer this question:

2 Which religion originated in India?

F Christianity
G Islam
H Buddhism
J Judaism

Sometimes process of elimination will help you eliminate ALL the incorrect answers. Sometimes it will only help you eliminate one or two. On a multiple-choice exam, it ALWAYS helps to use the process of elimination when you are unsure about which answer is correct, no matter what type of question you are working on.

 Remember: Do not write in your textbook.

THINKING SKILLS

Some multiple-choice questions require you to use critical thinking skills to find the answer. These critical thinking skills may include:

- drawing conclusions
- evaluating information
- making generalizations

Read the quotation, then answer question 1.

"The good person is satisfied and calm; the mean person is always full of distress."
—Confucius, Chinese scholar and teacher, 500 B.C.

1 Confucius would probably have agreed with which of the following statements?

A Justice is its own reward.

B Might makes right.

C A little white lie never hurt anyone.

D There's a sucker born every minute.

Study the graph. Then answer question 2.

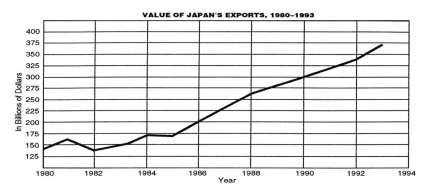

VALUE OF JAPAN'S EXPORTS, 1980–1993

2 Which of the following most likely caused the increase in the value of Japanese exports in 1987 and 1988?

F Japanese companies stopped advertising their products overseas in 1987.

G Japanese factories reduced production of goods in 1987.

H Prosperous nations like the United States increased the amount of Japanese goods they imported in 1987.

J Many Japanese factories closed in 1987.

Remember: Do not write in your textbook.

Teaching suggestions: Read the first paragraph of the page aloud to the class. Discuss the skills listed. If necessary, review these skills with students to make sure they understand them. Point out that sometimes we use a combination of these or other critical thinking skills in order to answer questions.

Have students read the questions and choose the correct answers.

1. **A** Process of elimination should help students eliminate all the incorrect answers. The quote from Confucius states that "the good person is satisfied and calm." Confucius extols goodness. Each of the incorrect answers advocates unvirtuous behavior.

2. **H** The question asks for an explanation of the increase in value of Japanese exports. Again, students should be encouraged to use process of elimination, working through each answer. Each of the incorrect answers would best explain a decrease in value of Japanese exports. Had the Japanese stopped advertising products overseas, for example, one would expect sales of Japanese products to decrease, since fewer consumers would know about Japanese goods.

OBJECTIVE:

- To familiarize students with one type of reading question that they are likely to see on nationally administered standardized tests.

Teaching suggestions: Often the questions on standardized tests that are text-heavy will require students to keep several short texts in mind, to compare or contrast people or things. Read the first paragraph aloud to students. Choose four students to read the four narratives accompanying the portraits of historical figures. Have students complete the two questions on their own.

1. **C** Golda Meir and Kublai Khan were government leaders; Pablo Neruda served as a diplomat. Of the four biographical sketches, only Peter Ilyich Tchaikovsky's makes no mention of political or governmental involvement.

2. **F** Neruda was a Nobel Prize winning poet; Tchaikovsky was a great composer. To answer correctly, students must understand that composers and poets work in the arts; therefore students should be able to infer that these people would be MOST interested in the arts.

Some test questions specifically test your ability to read and understand what you have read. These questions may also require you to compare and contrast the people or things you read about.

Read about the four famous people. Then answer questions 1 and 2.

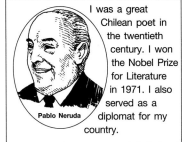

I was a great Chilean poet in the twentieth century. I won the Nobel Prize for Literature in 1971. I also served as a diplomat for my country.

Pablo Neruda

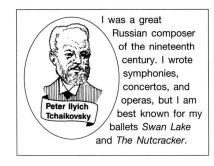

I was a great Russian composer of the nineteenth century. I wrote symphonies, concertos, and operas, but I am best known for my ballets *Swan Lake* and *The Nutcracker*.

Peter Ilyich Tchaikovsky

After helping create the state of Israel, I was elected its leader in 1969. I served as prime minister until 1974.

Golda Meir

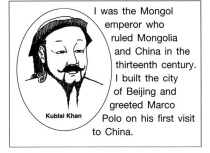

I was the Mongol emperor who ruled Mongolia and China in the thirteenth century. I built the city of Beijing and greeted Marco Polo on his first visit to China.

Kublai Khan

1 Which of these people was probably LEAST involved in politics and government?

  A Pablo Neruda
  B Golda Meir
  C Peter Ilyich Tchaikovsky
  D Kublai Khan

2 Which two people were probably MOST interested in the arts?

  F Pablo Neruda and Peter Ilyich Tchaikovsky
  G Golda Meir and Pablo Neruda
  H Kublai Khan and Peter Ilyich Tchaikovsky
  J Peter Ilyich Tchaikovsky and Kublai Khan

Remember: Do not write in your textbook.

MAPS

The ability to read and understand maps is an important skill in social studies. Many of the multiple-choice tests you take will require you to read a map.

Look carefully at all the parts of a map. Maps contain a lot of information. Whenever you see a map, you should ask yourself questions like these:

- What do the titles of the maps tell you?
- Where are the map keys?
- What symbols are on the map keys? What do they stand for?
- Where is the compass rose on each map?
- Is there a map scale?

Study the two maps of Alberta, Canada. Then do questions 1 and 2.

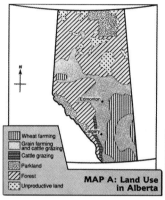

MAP A: Land Use in Alberta

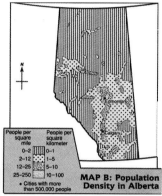

MAP B: Population Density in Alberta

1 The land surrounding both of Alberta's major cities is primarily used as

   A wheat farms
   B grain farms and cattle ranches
   C forests
   D parkland

2 Which of the following best explains the population density of northern Alberta?

   F The weather in northern Alberta is too cold to support a large population.
   G Alberta's biggest cities are in its northern section.
   H Wheat farming in northern Alberta attracts a large number of workers to the region.
   J Most residents of Alberta prefer to live in the forest.

Remember: Do not write in your textbook.

OBJECTIVES:
- To reinforce map skills learned in class.
- To familiarize students with one type of map-reading question that they are likely to see on nationally administered standardized tests.

Teaching suggestions: Read the first half of the page out loud. Call on students to read and answer each of the questions concerning the various features of the maps of Alberta.

1. **B** The phrase "land . . . is primarily used" should cue students to consult the "Land Use in Alberta" map. Instruct students to first locate Edmonton and Calgary on the map, then consult the key to determine the land use of the surrounding area. All the information needed to answer the question is in the map.

2. **F** This question directs students to consult the "Population Density in Alberta" map. It also requires students to draw an inference based on common sense, or use their knowledge of Canada's climate. Students can also use process of elimination on this question; answer **G** is clearly false, as both Edmonton and Calgary are in the southern half of Calgary; answer **H** is false since the population density is lower in the northern part of Alberta than in the southern part; **J** goes against common sense and is contradicted by the population density map, which shows the greatest population density in the south.

GRAPHS

Teaching suggestions: Read the first two paragraphs of the page aloud to the class. As you read paragraph one, ask students to think of examples of the different types of graphs discussed. Perhaps some are displayed in the classroom. You might also ask students to point out examples of the different types of graphs in their textbooks.

Have students read the questions and choose the correct answers.

1. **C** Some students might become confused by the fact the Belo Horizonte is not among the answer choices. Students should be reminded that, on a multiple-choice test, they must consider the answer choices before committing to an answer. Although the chart shows that Belo Horizonte has a population of nearly 4 million, Belo Horizonte cannot be the correct answer for the simple reason that it is not among the answer choices. Further consideration should lead students to the insight that the population of Rio de Janeiro is also very nearly 4,000,000.

2. **G** Services constitute 40 percent of Brazilian jobs in 1990.

3. **D** This question requires students to apply outside knowledge. Farmers (answer **B**) and cattle ranchers (answer **C**) fall under the category of agricultural workers; factory workers (answer **A**) fall under the category of industrial workers.

GRAPHS

Different types of graphs are used to present numerical information. A **line graph** shows how something changes over time. A line graph might be used to show how the population of the United States has grown over the years. A **bar graph** compares amounts. A **bar graph** might show the population of different United States cities. A **circle graph** shows how a whole is divided into smaller parts. For example, a circle graph might show how the government divides its budget to pay for roads, defense, education, and other services.

On some multiple-choice tests, you will see a set of questions accompanied by more than one graph. Each question will contain clues to tell you which graph you should read to find the answer. Take the extra time to make sure you are looking at the correct graph. This will help you avoid careless errors.

Use the graphs and your own knowledge to do questions 1 through 3.

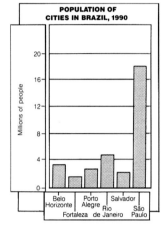

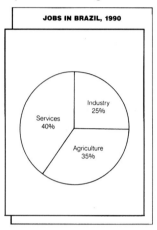

1 According to the graph, which city in Brazil had a population closest to 4,000,000 in 1990?

A	Fortaleza	**C**	Rio de Janiero
B	Salvador	**D**	Sao Paulo

2 In 1990, what part of the economy provided the greatest number of jobs to Brazilians?

F	Industry	**H**	Agriculture
G	Services	**J**	Arts and Entertainment

3 Which of the following jobs would fall under the category of "services"?

A	Factory worker	**C**	Cattle rancher
B	Farmer	**D**	Waitress

Remember: Do not write in your textbook.

POLITICAL CARTOONS

Some tests will ask you to look at and interpret a political cartoon. A political cartoon is an illustration or drawing that expresses a political point of view.

When you look at a political cartoon, ask yourself the following questions:

- What do the images in the cartoon represent? Are they *symbols* for something else? Uncle Sam is an example of a symbol. When he appears in a cartoon, he is being used as a symbol of the United States.
- What is the cartoonist's *point of view*? Is the cartoonist for or against the political issue that is the subject of the drawing? Look carefully at the details of the drawing. Do they provide hints about the artist's point of view?

Study the cartoon. Then do Numbers 1 through 3.

1 In the cartoon, the people under the umbrella represent

    A members of the United States Congress

    B citizens of the United States

    C Europeans who would like to move to the United States

    D foreign nations asking for financial assistance from the United States

2 The cartoonist would probably agree that the United States Constitution is

    F foolish   **H** important

    G difficult to understand   **J** outdated

3 Which of these would provide the most factual information about the United States Constitution?

    A a textbook about the United States government

    B a campaign poster for a Presidential candidate

    C a fictional movie about the American space program

    D an advertisement for a trip to Washington DC

Remember: Do not write in your textbook.   **TP 7**

POLITICAL CARTOONS

OBJECTIVE:
- To familiarize students with one type of question that they are likely to see on nationally administered standardized tests.

Teaching suggestions: Read aloud all text preceding the political cartoon. Direct the bulleted questions to students and ask for their responses. If possible, present another political cartoon as an illustration, and use it to answer the bulleted questions. You might use a newspaper or news magazine cartoon. You might also select a political cartoon from the textbook.

Have students read the questions and choose the correct answers.

1. **B** The people under the umbrella are protected from 'injustice' and 'tyranny' which are symbolized by rain. The umbrella, which symbolizes the U.S. Constitution, protects citizens from injustice and tyranny.

2. **H** The cartoon clearly holds the Constitution in high regard. Each of the three incorrect answers indicate that the cartoonist's attitude toward the Constitution is a negative one.

3. **A** This is an outside knowledge question. It tests students' familiarity with reference sources, a commonly tested area on nationally administered standardized tests.

TIME LINES

Teaching suggestions: Have students practice locating information on a time line. Ask them what occurred in 45 B.C. (Julius Caesar became dictator of Rome).

1. **C** The Colosseum is completed in A.D. 80, which is halfway through the time line. Julius Caesar and Augustus only rule for portions of the time covered by the time line, as well. The Pax Romana covers almost all of the time represented on the time line, so that would be the best title.

2. **H** Students need only find "Augustus dies" on the time line.

TIME LINES

Historical information is sometimes presented in a time line. A time line shows events in the order in which they occurred. It should be read from left to right, like a sentence. Sometimes a time line is presented vertically, in which case it should be read from top to bottom.

Some questions may ask you to find information on a time line. They may also ask you to remember outside knowledge about the subject of the time line.

Look at the time line below. Then answer questions 1 and 2.

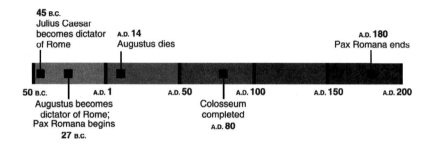

1 The best title for this time line would be:

    A The Building of the Colosseum

    B The Rule of Julius Caesar

    C The Pax Romana

    D The Rule of Augustus

2 In what year did Augustus die?

    F 45 B.C.

    G 27 B.C.

    H A.D. 14

    J A.D. 80

Remember: Do not write in your textbook.

Worksheet 1: Using a Global Grid

USING A GLOBAL GRID

You can locate places on a map by using a grid of latitude and longitude lines. Use the global grid map below to complete the activities on this page. Write the letter of the answer on the line. For help, you can refer to pages G4–G11 in your textbook.

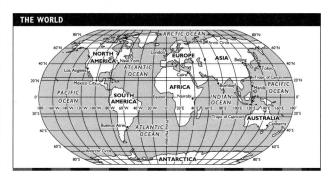

THE WORLD

_c_ 1. What are the lines that run north and south on the map called?
  a. latitude lines
  b. polar lines
  c. longitude lines

_a_ 2. Latitude lines measure distance in degrees north and south of this.
  a. equator
  b. prime meridian
  c. Western Hemisphere

_c_ 3. On the grid above, which longitude line is closest to Mexico City?
  a. 120°W
  b. 140°E
  c. 100°W

_c_ 4. What does the latitude line, or parallel, 60°S run through?
  a. three continents
  b. Antarctica
  c. three oceans

_b_ 5. Which city is nearest to 40°N, 120°E?
  a. Los Angeles
  b. Beijing
  c. Tokyo

_c_ 6. What is the approximate location of Nairobi?
  a. 40°N, 0°
  b. 0°, 40°W
  c. 0°, 40°E

Worksheet 2: Using Maps of Different Scales

USING MAPS OF DIFFERENT SCALES

The maps below show the same area using different scales. Use the maps to complete the activities that follow. For help, you can refer to pages G4–G11 in your textbook.

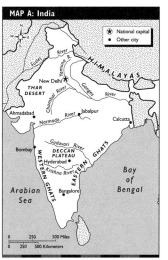

MAP A: India   **MAP B: India**

1. How does the scale on Map A compare with the scale on Map B?
   One inch stands for fewer miles on Map A than on Map B.

2. Which map shows a larger land area? Map B

3. Make a scale strip by placing the edge of a strip of paper under the scale lines on Map A. Then mark the distances in miles and kilometers.
   a. How many miles is Ahmadabad from New Delhi? about 500 miles
   b. Which city is about 300 miles northeast of Bangalore? Hyderabad

4. On Map B which city in southern India is about 1,000 miles from Calcutta?
   Bangalore

Worksheet 3: Exploring Mexico's Resources

EXPLORING MEXICO'S RESOURCES

The map below shows some of Mexico's natural resources. Use the map to answer the questions that follow. For help, you can refer to pages G4–G11 in your textbook.

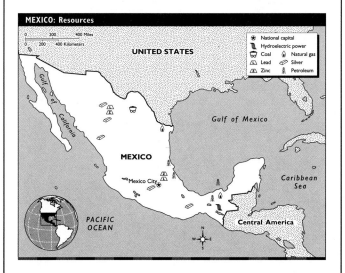

MEXICO: Resources

1. What does the locator map show?
   The locator map shows Mexico's location in the Western Hemisphere.

2. Why is the map key important to the map above?
   The map key tells what the symbols on the map mean.

3. What symbol is used for hydroelectric power? falling water

4. What resource is located along the Gulf of Mexico coast? petroleum

5. In what part of Mexico is coal mined? in the northern part of Mexico

---

Worksheet 4: Reading an Elevation Map

READING AN ELEVATION MAP

The map below shows the elevation of China. Study the map and the map key. Then put an **X** next to each sentence that is correct. For help, you can refer to pages G4–G11 in your textbook.

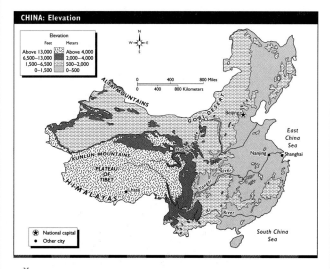

CHINA: Elevation

_X_ 1. The map of China is a physical map.

____ 2. The elevation along the eastern coast of China is about 7,000 feet.

_X_ 3. The southwestern part of China is higher than 13,000 feet.

_X_ 4. The capital city of China has an elevation between 0 and 500 meters.

____ 5. The city of Lhasa has a much lower elevation than Shanghai.

_X_ 6. Shanghai and Beijing have about the same elevation.

____ 7. The elevation of most of China is less than 700 feet.

_X_ 8. The elevation of China increases as you travel west.

INDIAN EMPIRES

The map below shows the Indian empires that developed in the Americas. Use the information in the map to answer the questions that follow. If you need help, refer to pages G4–G11 in your textbook.

INDIAN EMPIRES

Legend: Maya, Aztec, Inca

1. What type of map is this?
   It is an historical map.

2. What continents are shown on this map?
   North and South America

3. What three empires are shown on the map?
   Maya, Aztec, and Inca
   empires

4. By the year 1500 the city of Tenochtitlán was twice as large as London, England. What Indian group built this magnificent city?
   the Aztec

5. Today many tourists visit the ruins of Machu Picchu. Who built this city?
   the Inca

ONE COUNTRY'S REGIONS

Below is a profile of the physical, climate, and cultural regions found in one country. Use the information provided to answer the questions that follow. Then write the name of the country on the final line.

Location:	North America
Climate:	mostly temperate, but varies from tropical to arctic; arid to semiarid in west
Landforms:	vast central plain, mountains in west, hills and low mountains in east
Natural Borders:	Atlantic Ocean on the east, Gulf of Mexico to the south, Pacific Ocean on the west, Great Lakes to the north
Language:	predominately English; sizable Spanish-speaking minority
Ethnic Groups:	73% Caucasian, 12% African American, 10% Hispanic, 3% Asian, 1% Native American, 1% other
Major Religions:	93 mil. Protestant, 60 mil. Roman Catholic, 6 mil. Jewish, 4 mil. Mormon, 3 mil. Muslim, 3 mil. Eastern Orthodox
Government:	federal republic; strong democratic traditions; executive, legislative, and judicial branches
Administrative Divisions:	50 states and 1 district

Source: Information Please Almanac 1997

1. What physical regions make up the geography of this country?
   mountainous regions, plains, and hills

2. What climate regions are found in this country?
   temperate, tropical, arctic, arid, and semiarid climate regions

3. What political regions make up the country?
   50 states and 1 district

4. What are the majority of the people who live in this country like?
   The majority of the people are Caucasian, Protestant, and
   English-speaking.

   Name of Country: United States of America

USING LATITUDE AND LONGITUDE

Plan a trip in which you will visit each of the capital cities listed here. Use latitude and longitude to locate each city. Then label the city according to the letter on the right. For help, you can refer to pages 12–13 in your textbook.

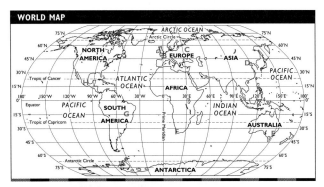

WORLD MAP

CITY	LOCATION	LABEL
Washington, D.C., U.S.A.	38°N, 77°W	A
Paris, France	48°N, 2°E	B
Moscow, Russia	55°N, 37°E	C
Beijing, China	40°N, 116°E	D
Canberra, Australia	35°S, 149°E	E
Cape Town, South Africa	34°S, 18°E	F
Brasília, Brazil	15°S, 47°W	G
Mexico City, Mexico	19°N, 99°W	H

A degree is a unit of measurement that describes the distance between lines of latitude and longitude. What is the approximate distance in degrees between the Tropic of Cancer and the Tropic of Capricorn?
about 47 degrees

FINDING CLUES TO INDIAN CULTURE

Details of everyday life can reveal a great deal about the culture in which people live. Use the pictures on the right to complete the activities on this page. For help, you can refer to pages 14–19 in your textbook.

1. Draw a line to the picture that shows a custom unique to the culture of India. What are other important parts of Indian culture?
   Hinduism, family temples, the
   mridanga, traditional foods such as
   uttapam

2. Draw a line to the picture that suggests the importance of language in Indian culture. What are four of the many languages spoken in India?
   English, Hindu, Sanskrit, Bengali

3. Draw a line to the picture that shows the interaction of Asian and European cultures. What are two examples of change in the Indian culture?
   style of chess, more freedom for
   women, Chinese and American foods

4. What are some similarities between Indian and American culture?
   Both countries are representative democracies, women have
   more rights than they did in the past, and families live together
   and share values and customs.

USING NEW WORDS

Use the words in the box to complete the puzzle below. For help, you can refer to the lessons in Chapter 1 in your textbook.

| climate |
| geography |
| landform |
| culture |
| region |
| custom |
| interaction |
| values |

Across

2. a Greek word meaning "Earth writing"

5. a natural feature, such as a mountain or a plain

6. the exchange of ideas and customs

8. the things people believe are most important in life

Down

1. an area with common features that set it apart from other areas

3. a way of life of a group of people, including daily habits, beliefs, and art

4. a way of living that people practice regularly over time

7. the weather pattern that an area has over a long period of time

---

LEARNING FROM A PRIMARY SOURCE

Below is a primary source from 1949. This advertisement called television a "miracle" that was "undreamed of 150 years ago." What can you learn about American culture in the 1940s from this ad?

1. What does this ad tell you about Americans' attitude toward television in the 1940s?
   Possible answer: Americans viewed television as an exciting technological "miracle."

2. What does the ad suggest about families and family values in the 1940s?
   Possible answer: The average family consisted of a mother, father, and two children, and families enjoyed doing things together, such as watching television.

3. How might people in today's society view this ad?
   Possible answer: People might find the ad old-fashioned because it no longer represents American society and family life today.

4. Why is this ad considered a primary source?
   The ad was created during a specific period of time in American history, and it is not based on another source.

DECISION MAKING ABOUT ARTIFACTS

One of the most important tasks of historians is decision making. Below is a story about a scholar's decision that made headlines in May 1995. Answer the questions that follow the story. If you need help, refer to pages 30–31 in your textbook.

Dr. Kent Weeks is a scholar at the American University in Cairo, Egypt. His main goal is to find and preserve every possible artifact that exists in the Valley of the Kings. This valley, which is located on the west bank of the Nile River in Upper Egypt, is where most of the tombs of ancient Egyptian kings have been found.

In 1988 Dr. Weeks had a difficult decision to make. A site known as Tomb 5 had been identified as a good place to build a parking lot for tourists. When the site was first explored in 1820, a British scholar concluded that all the artifacts had been uncovered. Dr. Weeks, however, wasn't so sure. Should he explore the site one more time, or should he begin a new dig in a completely different part of the Valley of the Kings?

Dr. Weeks decided to explore Tomb 5 again. After seven years of slow, careful digging, he was finally able to pry open a stone door that had remained shut for thousands of years. There, before his eyes, was the discovery of a lifetime: a long corridor with ten doors on each side and at the end a statue of Osiris, the god of the afterlife. This and other artifacts led Dr. Weeks to conclude that he had found the last resting place of as many as 50 sons of Rameses II, the greatest of all the ancient Egyptian kings.

Michael D. Lemonick, "Secrets of the Lost Tomb," *Time*, May 29, 1995.

1. What was Dr. Weeks's goal?
   Dr. Weeks's goal was to find and preserve every possible artifact in the Valley of the Kings.

2. What alternatives did he consider?
   He considered reexploring Tomb 5 or digging in a different part of the Valley of the Kings.

3. What decision did he make? Why did he choose this alternative?
   Dr. Weeks chose to reexplore Tomb 5 because he realized that existing artifacts would be lost forever if a parking lot was built on the site.

WORKING AS AN ARCHAEOLOGIST

Suppose that you are an archaeologist like Konrad Spindler. You are studying the Iceman and his belongings that have been uncovered from a glacier in the Alps. Other archaeologists have decided to join you in your work. Summarize your findings for your colleagues by explaining what you think each of the artifacts reveals about the Iceman. If you need help, you can refer to pages 32–37 in your textbook.

An archaeologist at work

1. traces of grain in the melted snow and ice
   The Iceman had contact with farmers.

2. small net with wide spaces in the mesh
   The Iceman used the net to catch birds.

3. knife blades, rope, and hunting arrows
   When mountain climbing, the Iceman carried survival gear.

4. tiny crystals of sulfur and iron attached to black fungus
   The Iceman probably used the fungus to start fires.

5. two small beads of fungus on a leather strap
   This was probably the Iceman's medicine.

6. 2,000 grains of pollen from alder and pine trees
   The Iceman died in autumn.

7. amount of wear on the Iceman's teeth
   The Iceman was about 35 or 40 years old at death.

8. results of carbon dating of skin samples
   The Iceman lived between 5,000 and 5,300 years ago.

SOME WORDS ABOUT THE PAST

Answer each question in the space provided. For help, you can refer to the lessons in Chapter 2 in your textbook.

1. What is **history**?
   History is the story of the past.

2. How does an **oral tradition** help us remember our history?
   History is passed on from generation to generation by word of mouth.

3. Will the computer you are using today be an **artifact** in 50 years? Explain.
   Yes; any object made by a person or produced by a company in the past is an artifact.

4. What is the difference between **primary sources** and **secondary sources**?
   Primary sources are materials or texts created during a period of time under study, and secondary sources are based on studies of primary sources.

5. Is your social studies textbook a **primary source** or a **secondary source**?
   It is a secondary source.

6. What is the significant difference between **prehistory** and **history**?
   Prehistory produced no written records.

7. What major clues to the past are studied in the science of **archaeology**?
   Historical sites, artifacts, and human remains are clues to the past.

8. What does it mean to **excavate**?
   To excavate is to uncover by digging carefully.

EARLY DISCOVERIES

How did early people discover the uses of fire? Read the possible explanation below and then answer the questions that follow. If you need help, refer back to pages 44–49 in your textbook.

> They learned to carry it from the wilds, where it appeared when a volcano erupted, when lightning struck in the dry grass of the plains, or when some outcrop of coal or shale oil burst into flames by spontaneous combustion. Having captured fire, the first men learned to keep it going in their hearths. . . .
>
> Besides the protection it afforded, fire was a key to survival in other ways. Once Homo erectus discovered the art of cooking—perhaps by accident as a slab of meat fell onto a flaming hearth and was eaten—he seems to have cooked much of what he caught. . . .
>
> Besides cooking with fire, Homo erectus discovered other practical uses for it. It broadened his choice of tools and weapons. The observation that bone or antler grew hard in the heat of a campfire or that green wood did not always burn completely and instead hardened must have led him to employ fire in toolmaking.

Editors of Time-Life Books, *The First Men* (New York: Time-Life Books, 1973), pages 20–21.

1. How did hunter-gatherers discover possible uses for fire?
   First they learned how to keep fire going and then accidently learned how to use it to cook with and make weapons.

2. How did the technology of fire building change life in the Old Stone Age?
   Fire building made it possible for people to cook food, survive the cold, and improve their tools.

3. What other technology did hunter-gatherers use to meet their needs?
   They used sharp stone tools to kill animals and cut through their hides, and they used plants and seeds as medicine.

4. What do ancient rock paintings and carvings reveal about early people?
   They had found a way to express themselves through art, and they most probably valued beauty.

WRITING ABOUT AN EARLY COMMUNITY

You are an archaeologist who has uncovered the remains shown below during a dig. What conclusions can you draw from these remains about the community you have discovered and the people who lived there? Use the questions below to write a report on your findings.

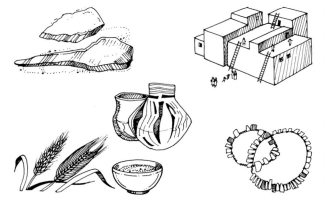

1. What kind of technology did the people use?
   They pounded stones to make sharp tools that they used for cutting animal hides and chopping wood, and they used fire to bake clay pottery.

2. What were their homes like?
   The brick homes had walls and several levels.

3. What kinds of food did they eat? How did they get this food?
   They ate wheat and barley, which had been planted.

4. Did the group practice specialization? How can you tell?
   Yes; in addition to farmers, there were craftsworkers who made pottery and jewelry.

USING A TIME LINE

The time line below shows important events in the development of sports and games. Use the time line to answer the questions. If you need help, look back at pages 58–59 in your textbook.

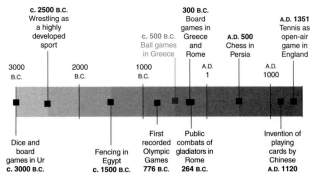

Bernard Grun, *Timetables of History*, and *Guinness Book of Records*, 1990.

1. What period of time does the time line cover? Are most of the listed events B.C. or A.D.?
   The time line covers the period from 3000 B.C. to A.D. 1500; B.C.

2. When did the first recorded Olympic Games take place?
   776 B.C.

3. About how many years passed between the appearance of board games in Ur and board games in Greece and Rome?
   about 2,700 years

4. Which appeared earlier, gladiator combats in Rome or fencing in Egypt?
   fencing in Egypt

5. Which came later, the invention of playing cards or open-air tennis in England?
   open-air tennis in England

6. The Greeks began playing ball games about 500 B.C. Write this event in the correct place on the time line.

USING NEW WORDS

Choose a word from the box to complete each sentence. For help, you can refer to the lessons in Chapter 3 of your textbook.

civilization	agriculture	technology
New Stone Age	surplus	specialization
Old Stone Age	trade	domesticate

1. The earliest human beings lived during the <u>Old Stone Age</u>, which began over 2 million years ago.

2. They were hunters and gatherers who used simple <u>technology</u>, such as stone tools and fire building, to meet their needs.

3. About 12,000 years ago people began practicing <u>agriculture</u>, the raising of crops and animals for human use.

4. The world's first farmers learned to <u>domesticate</u> animals, such as wild goats, cattle, and sheep.

5. Early farmers, unlike their hunting-gathering ancestors, began to produce an oversupply, or <u>surplus</u>, of food.

6. Demands on farmers' time led to <u>specialization</u>, people training for specific tasks, such as turning wheat into bread flour.

7. During the <u>New Stone Age</u>, which ended about 6,000 years ago, towns and cities developed.

8. Complex changes in the way people lived and worked sparked the development of <u>civilization</u>, cultures with systems of religion, learning, and government.

9. People began to <u>trade</u>, or exchange goods, with people from faraway places.

THE NILE RIVER

You have been asked to write an entry about the Nile River for the *Geography Book of Records*. Use the outline map and the categories below to write your entry. For help, refer to pages 70–73 in your textbook.

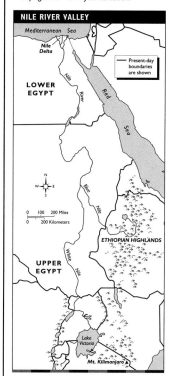

NILE RIVER VALLEY

LENGTH: <u>The Nile is the world's longest river, flowing over 4,000 miles.</u>

LOCATION: <u>East Africa</u>

DIRECTION IT FLOWS: <u>It flows northward from the mountains of East Africa.</u>

WHERE IT EMPTIES: <u>Mediterranean Sea</u>

FLOOD SEASON: <u>The Nile floods its banks from July through October.</u>

IMPORTANCE TO ANCIENT EGYPT: <u>The Nile provided fertile soil, water for irrigation, and a means of transportation.</u>

LANDSCAPE OF NILE REGION: <u>To the north is a fertile delta. To the south, in Upper Egypt, the Nile flows through stone cliffs and desert sands.</u>

THE ROLE OF THE PHARAOHS IN THE OLD KINGDOM

Complete the diagram below to explain how the pharaoh was the center of Egyptian civilization in the Old Kingdom. One entry has been done for you in each section. Then use the diagram to answer the question that follows. If you need help, refer to pages 74–81 in your textbook.

In Government
The pharaoh decided how Egypt's affairs should be run at all levels.
<u>Area governors reported to the pharaoh.</u>
<u>The pharaoh depended on scribes to keep written records.</u>

Role of the Pharaoh

In Religion
The pharaoh owned all the temples.
<u>The pharaoh was worshiped as a child of the sun god. Massive pyramids were built as tombs to house the pharaoh in the afterlife.</u>

In the Economy
All things belonged to the pharaoh.
<u>The pharaoh collected taxes on everything produced in Egypt. Craftworkers and artists depended on the pharaoh for jobs.</u>

Why did local leaders revolt against the pharaohs' government?
<u>Massive government building projects strained the Egyptian economy and angered the people and their local government leaders.</u>

EXPANSION AND TRADE IN ANCIENT EGYPT

You are a reporter for *Egypt Today*. Your job is to write a brief paragraph to go with each newspaper headline below. For help, refer to pages 84–91 in your textbook.

EGYPTIANS DEFEAT HYKSOS

<u>Led by Pharaoh Ahmose, the Egyptians drove out the Hyksos and regained control of the Delta. This victory marks the beginning of the New Kingdom.</u>

EGYPTIAN TRADERS BRING BACK AFRICAN RICHES

<u>Caravans continue to bring back ebony, ivory, gold, precious stones, and other riches from the wealthy kingdoms of Africa. Trade routes between Egypt and these kingdoms opened up when Nubia became part of the Egyptian empire.</u>

HATSHEPSUT SENDS GREAT EXPEDITION TO PUNT

<u>Today Pharaoh Hatshepsut sent five ships and a caravan of scribes, soldiers, artists, and attendants on a journey south to open trade with the kingdom of Punt. This may be the pharaoh's biggest expedition yet.</u>

TUTANKHAMUN IS BURIED IN SPLENDOR

<u>Pharaoh Tutankhamun, who ruled from the age of 9 to 19, was buried today in a magnificent tomb with numerous objects from his household. They reveal much about Egyptian culture.</u>

EGYPT GAINING FAME FOR NEW IDEAS AND SKILLS

<u>Scribes are recording vast amounts of medical knowledge. Priest-scientists are busy writing down the mathematical rules that made possible the building of the pyramids and the study of the stars.</u>

USING MAPS AT DIFFERENT SCALES

A map scale is a unit of measure, such as an inch, used to represent a distance on Earth. Use the maps below to answer the questions. If you need help, refer to pages 92–93 in your textbook.

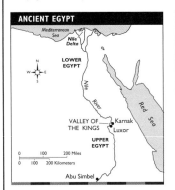

ANCIENT EGYPT

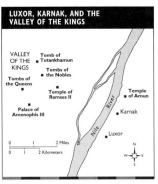

LUXOR, KARNAK, AND THE VALLEY OF THE KINGS

1. What does one inch represent on the map of ancient Egypt? **200 miles**

   On the map of the Valley of the Kings? **2 miles**

2. Compare the two maps. Which map is a small-scale map?
   map of ancient Egypt

3. Which map would you use to trace the route of the Nile River?
   map of ancient Egypt

4. Which map would you use to plan a walking tour of temples and royal tombs?
   map of Luxor, Karnak, and the Valley of the Kings

5. What is the distance from Abu Simbel to Luxor? **about 225 miles**
   Which map did you use to find the distance? **map of ancient Egypt**

6. Is the Tomb of Tutankhamun east or west of the Nile River? **west**
   Which map did you use to find the answer?
   map of Luxor, Karnak, and the Valley of the Kings

EGYPTIAN SOCIETY

Write a job description for the Egyptians in each picture below. If you need help, refer to pages 94–99 in your textbook.

1. Farmer

dig up fields for planting; dig canals and haul water for irrigation; grow and harvest crops

4. Homemaker

get water from local canal; bake and cook; go to market

2. Children

scatter seed during planting time; cut and carry at harvest time; perform chores

5. Woodcutter
build plows and make furniture

3. Scribe

measure crops and take away shares claimed by the pharaoh

6. Slave
assist farmers to dig canals and prepare land for planting; mine gold; work as house servant

---

RELATING WORDS TO ANCIENT EGYPT

Choose a word or phrase from the box to match each clue. For help, you can refer to the lessons in Chapter 4 in your textbook.

slavery	social pyramid	delta
pharaoh	irrigation	expedition
unification	papyrus	empire
economy	hieroglyphics	scribe
silt		

1. fertile, fan-shaped land created where Nile empties into Mediterranean Sea   **delta**

2. bits of soil and rock carried off by the Nile River   **silt**

3. technology used by Egyptian farmers to water their crops   **irrigation**

4. joining of Upper Egypt and Lower Egypt into one kingdom   **unification**

5. the way a country's people manage money and resources for the production of goods and services   **economy**

6. a writer who kept records in Egypt   **scribe**

7. name given to Egyptian rulers   **pharaoh**

8. system of writing made up of about 800 picture-signs   **hieroglyphics**

9. reed plant growing along the Nile used to make paper   **papyrus**

10. group of lands and peoples ruled by Egyptian government   **empire**

11. caravan of people sent to trade with Egypt's neighbors   **expedition**

12. practice of one person owning another person   **slavery**

13. how Egyptian society was shaped   **social pyramid**

TWO RIVERS: TIGRIS AND EUPHRATES

Use the map below to answer the questions. For help, refer to pages 104–107 in your textbook.

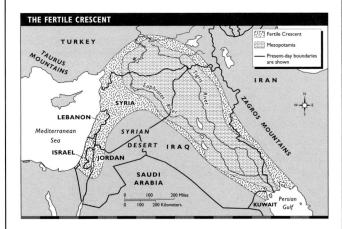

THE FERTILE CRESCENT

1. What two important rivers are shown on the map?
   Tigris and Euphrates rivers

2. Into what body of water do these rivers flow?
   into the Persian Gulf

3. In ancient times what civilization developed between the Tigris and Euphrates rivers?
   Mesopotamia

4. Parts of what countries make up the region once known as the Fertile Crescent?
   Iraq, Syria, Lebanon, Israel, Iran, Jordan, Kuwait, Turkey

5. How did ancient farmers in this region make their land productive?
   They used canal systems to control flooding and make the land fertile.

THE CODE OF HAMMURABI

The Code of Hammurabi contained over 200 laws. Read some of the laws listed below and answer the questions that follow. If you need help, refer to pages 108–115 in your textbook.

If a citizen has stolen property of the temple or of the crown, that man shall die, and whosoever receives the stolen goods from his hand shall die.

If a citizen steals the child of a citizen, he shall die.

If a citizen has committed a robbery and is caught, that man shall die.

If a son has struck his father, they shall cut off his hand.

If a citizen has destroyed the eye of one of citizen status, they shall destroy his eye.

If he has destroyed the eye of a vassal, he shall pay one mina (17.5 ounces) of silver.

If he has destroyed the eye of a slave of a citizen, he shall pay half of his market value.

1. What kinds of behavior did the above laws punish?
robbery, kidnapping, causing physical injury

2. What punishment did the law require if a father complained that his son hit him during a quarrel?
The son's hand would be cut off.

3. Was everyone treated equally under Hammurabi's laws? Explain.
No; the punishment for blinding a slave was less severe than the punishment for blinding a citizen.

4. What are the advantages to society of having a written code?
Possible answer: All citizens know what the laws are and the penalties for breaking them.

IDENTIFYING CAUSE AND EFFECT

The passage below describes the fall of Sumer. As you read, look for cause and effect connections. A cause is something that makes something else happen. What happens as the result of a cause is an effect. If you need help, refer to pages 118–119 in your textbook.

For over 1,000 years the city-states of Sumer were at war with each other. From 3000 B.C. to 2000 B.C., one city-state after another had its brief moment of glory and power. Constant rebellion weakened the vast Sumerian empire. City-states could no longer fight off attacks from their enemies, all of whom wanted the riches of the empire. Finally, nomadic warriors from the deserts and the hills surrounding Sumer scaled the walls of Ur and destroyed the city-state. Other city-states were similarly destroyed.

The Sumerians never recovered from the attacks on their cities. Although the Sumerian empire was physically destroyed, its ideas lived on. Other empires developed in Mesopotamia, and the leaders of these empires adopted Sumerian ways. They built ziggurats, used cuneiform writing, and irrigated their fields.

1. What was the effect of constant warfare among the city-states of Sumer?
Constant warfare made the city-states too weak to fight off attacks from their enemies.

2. Why did nomadic warriors want to conquer the city-states of Sumer?
They wanted the riches of the empire.

3. What was the final cause of the fall of the Sumerian empire?
The empire never recovered from the attacks on its city-states.

4. How did Sumerian civilization affect other empires that developed in Mesopotamia?
These empires adopted Sumerian ideas, such as cuneiform writing and irrigation.

5. Why do historians study cause-effect connections?
They want to understand why events happened the way they did.

JUDAISM YESTERDAY AND TODAY

You have been asked to prepare a Question & Answer almanac entry on the Jewish religion. Below are the questions your editor has asked you to answer. Fill in the spaces with the answers. If you need help, refer to pages 120–125 in your textbook.

Q: What special agreement marked the beginning of Jewish history?
A: The covenant God made with Abraham in Canaan is considered to be the beginning of Jewish history.

Q: Who were the first Jews?
A: The descendants of Abraham, later called the Israelites, were the first Jews.

Q: What role did Moses play in Jewish history?
A: Moses, with the help of God, led the enslaved Israelites from Egypt.

Q: What laws were among those Moses received from God at Mount Sinai?
A: The Ten Commandments were among the laws Moses received at Mount Sinai.

Q: Why is the Torah so important to the Jewish people?
A: The Torah is the five books of laws and teachings God gave to Moses. It is the basis of life and faith for the Jewish people.

Q: What belief set the Israelites apart from other groups living in the Fertile Crescent?
A: The Israelites believed in only one God and practiced monotheism.

Q: Why is the city of Jerusalem so important to Jews today?
A: The city was once the capital of the kingdom of Israel and the site of a great temple built by Solomon. Today the city is a center of religious and political life.

USING NEW WORDS

Write the letter of the term that matches each definition. For help, refer to the lessons in Chapter 5 in your textbook.

a. city-state	f. Judaism	j. Sabbath
b. code of law	g. monotheism	k. drought
c. cuneiform	h. plateau	l. Torah
d. Diaspora	i. polytheism	m. ziggurat
e. Ten Commandments		

___l___ 1. first five books of the Hebrew Bible

___c___ 2. system of writing invented in Sumer

___d___ 3. scattering of Jews to many parts of the world

___g___ 4. belief in only one god

___h___ 5. area of flat, elevated land

___b___ 6. written set of laws that apply to everyone under a government

___k___ 7. long period of dry weather

___m___ 8. large building with a temple on its peak

___a___ 9. self-governing city and its surrounding villages

___i___ 10. belief in many gods and goddesses

___e___ 11. laws given by God to Moses at Mount Sinai

___f___ 12. religion of the Jewish people

___j___ 13. weekly day of rest, prayer, and study

Write a sentence about Sumer or Babylon. Use two words from the box in your sentence.
Possible answer: Sumerians practiced polytheism and worshiped their gods in a ziggurat.

Write a sentence about the beginnings of Judaism. Use two or more words from the box in your sentence.
Possible answer: Among the laws that God gave the Israelites, who believed in monotheism, were the Ten Commandments.

THE JOURNEY OF THE INDUS RIVER

Use the map to answer questions 1–4. If you need help, refer to pages 130–133 in your textbook.

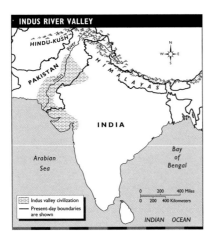

INDUS RIVER VALLEY

HINDU-KUSH

PAKISTAN

INDIA

Arabian Sea

Bay of Bengal

Indus valley civilization
Present-day boundaries are shown

INDIAN OCEAN

0   200   400 Miles
0   200   400 Kilometers

1. In what mountains does the Indus River originate?

Himalayas

2. Into what body of water does the Indus River flow?

Arabian Sea

3. Through what country does the Indus River mainly flow?

Pakistan

4. In what ways does the Indus River resemble the Nile, Tigris, and Euphrates rivers?

All carry silt and make farming possible in dry regions, and the valleys of all these rivers were centers of early civilizations.

INTERPRETING CLUES TO EARLY INDIAN CIVILIZATION

Archaeologists have pieced together a picture of India's ancient past from the artifacts that they have uncovered in the ruins of Harappa and Mohenjo-Daro. Descriptions of the ruins and some of the artifacts are listed in the box below. Write the letter of the description next to the information it revealed about life in ancient India. If you need help, refer to pages 134–139 in your textbook.

Ruins and Artifacts

a. jewelry made of lapis lazuli from Afghanistan

b. large warehouse used for storing grain

c. a sewer system and paved streets laid out in grid pattern

d. painted pottery, carved stone figures, bronze statues

e. stone seals with writing

f. massive fort with thick walls

Stone seal

Conclusions

_c_ **1.** Cities were carefully planned and built.

_b_ **2.** Farmers harvested crops and were able to set aside surplus grain.

_e_ **3.** A system of marking belongings was used.

_a_ **4.** Harappans traded with their neighbors.

_d_ **5.** Craftworkers were highly skilled.

_f_ **6.** The city was protected from enemy attacks and from floods.

COMPARING DIFFERENT KINDS OF MAPS

Comparing maps helps you to see relationships that you would not be able to see by looking at maps separately. Compare the maps below to answer the questions. If you need help, refer to pages 140–141 in your textbook.

INDIA: POLITICAL

Present-day boundaries are shown

New Delhi, Kanpur, Ahmadabad, Calcutta, Bombay, Hyderabad, Bangalore, Madras

Arabian Sea

Bay of Bengal

0   200   400 Miles
0   200   400 Kilometers

INDIA: PHYSICAL

Present-day boundaries are shown

THAR DESERT, INDO-GANGETIC PLAIN, Ganges River, VINDHYA MTS., Narmada River, DECCAN PLATEAU, WESTERN GHATS, EASTERN GHATS

Arabian Sea

Bay of Bengal

INDIAN OCEAN

0   200   400 Miles
0   200   400 Kilometers

1. What are some physical features of India?

Physical features include mountains, plateaus, plains, deserts, and rivers.

2. On what kinds of physical features are most cities located?

They are located on plains and in valleys along rivers.

3. In what areas are the fewest cities (or no cities) located?

mountain regions

4. What conclusions can you draw about the effect of physical features on the development of cities in India?

Possible answer: Cities have developed in river valleys and on the plains and plateaus of India where the land is the most fertile and transportation is available.

HINDUISM YESTERDAY AND TODAY

Hinduism is one of the world's major religions, and 80 percent of the people in India are Hindus. The pictures below show some aspects of Hinduism. Use the pictures and pages 142–147 in your textbook to answer the questions.

1. What are the names of three gods and goddesses worshiped by different groups of Hindus today?

Vishnu, Devi, Shiva

Which one is considered the "Mother of Creation"?

Devi

2. Where do Hindus worship their favorite gods?

They worship at home, in temples, and at special festivals.

3. What are the Vedas and two important Hindu beliefs presented in them?

The Vedas are the "Books of Knowledge" that tell Hindus how they should live. The Vedas introduced the ideas of reincarnation, castes, and dharma.

BUDDHISM YESTERDAY AND TODAY

Use the information below to complete the boxes of the diagram. One item has been completed in boxes 1–4. For help, you can refer to pages 150–155 in your textbook.

> Hindus believe in karma, a force caused by a person's good and bad acts.
> The Middle Way of life was meant to be neither too strict nor too easy.
> Suffering is caused by people's wants.
> Suffering can be ended if people stop wanting things.
> To stop wanting, people must follow eight basic laws.
> One ends suffering by following the Eightfold Path.

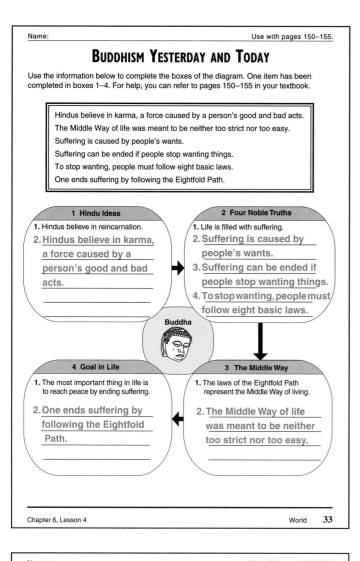

1 Hindu Ideas
1. Hindus believe in reincarnation.
2. Hindus believe in karma, a force caused by a person's good and bad acts.

2 Four Noble Truths
1. Life is filled with suffering.
2. Suffering is caused by people's wants.
3. Suffering can be ended if people stop wanting things.
4. To stop wanting, people must follow eight basic laws.

Buddha

4 Goal in Life
1. The most important thing in life is to reach peace by ending suffering.
2. One ends suffering by following the Eightfold Path.

3 The Middle Way
1. The laws of the Eightfold Path represent the Middle Way of living.
2. The Middle Way of life was meant to be neither too strict nor too easy.

USING NEW WORDS

Use the words in the box to complete the sentences below. For help, you can refer to the lessons in Chapter 6 in your textbook.

Buddhism	Four Noble Truths	migrate
caste system	Hinduism	monk
citadel	karma	reincarnation
dharma	Middle Way	subcontinent
Eightfold Path	Vedas	

1. At Mohenjo-Daro archaeologists have found the remains of a large fort or citadel _____.

2. Around 1500 B.C. the Aryans began to migrate _____ to the Indian subcontinent _____, bringing their language, called Sanskrit.

3. The beginnings of the religion called Hinduism _____ are found in the ancient Aryan songs called the "Books of Knowledge," or the Vedas _____.

4. In the caste system _____ a person's place in society is set by the rank that he or she is born into.

5. The Vedas state that people move in a constant cycle of life, death, and rebirth, which is called reincarnation _____.

6. The Hindu religion includes hundreds of laws and duties called the dharma _____, outlined in the "Books of Knowledge."

7. Siddhartha Gautama, the founder of the religion called Buddhism _____, left his home and became a monk _____.

8. The Buddha believed in karma _____, a force caused by a person's good and bad acts that affects future lives.

9. The Buddha's ideas that suffering is central to life were expressed in Four Noble Truths _____.

10. The Buddha taught that the way to end suffering was to follow the Eightfold Path _____. These instructions outlined a way of living, neither too strict nor too easy, called the Middle Way _____.

A RIVER IN CHINA

Use the clues and the words in the box to complete the puzzle below. Write one letter of each word on a blank line. If you need help, refer back to pages 160–163 in your textbook.

Words

Ordos Desert
erosion
grapes
delta
famine
levees
plateau
loess
civilizations
North China Plain

Clues

1. major landform in China flooded by the Huang River
2. huge landform in Tibet where the Huang River begins
3. land feature created by deposits of silt
4. time of crop failure and starvation
5. crop harvested by Huang farmers
6. wearing away of soil by wind or water
7. what ancient farming communities developed into
8. earth walls farmers built to hold back the Huang
9. dusty, yellow soil deposited by wind
10. dry region around which the Huang curves

What is another name for the Yellow River? Huang River

1. N O R T H C H I N A P L A I N
2. P L A T E A U
3. D E L T A
4. F A M I N E
5. G R A P E S
6. E R O S I O N
7. C I V I L I Z A T I O N S
8. L E V E E S
9. L O E S S
10. O R D O S D E S E R T

CHINESE WRITING: PAST AND PRESENT

The earliest Chinese writing had characters that were pictographs; they looked like pictures of objects. By the time of the Shang dynasty, the symbols in Chinese writing were simpler and could stand for objects or ideas. Answer the questions about Chinese writing below. If you need help, refer to pages 164–167 in your textbook.

1. Before the Shang dynasty, an early writing system had developed along which river?
   the Huang River

2. What objects with writing on them have been found from the Shang period? Circle the correct answers.
   (stones)   (bronze pots)   (oracle bones)

3. In the time of the Shang kings, how was writing on objects used to predict the future?
   Oracle bones with writing on them were heated until they cracked, and priests interpreted the cracks to find answers to questions.

Today there are different kinds of Chinese characters. Some are greatly simplified pictures. Others are formed by combining two or more pictographs. Each character stands for a word.

4. The Chinese character for the word *up* is on the left. Look at the one on the right. Can you guess its meaning? down

上　下

THE QIN EMPIRE

Some of Shihuangdi's ideas about how a government should be run are listed below. Explain how each idea helped him create a strong, unified empire. If you need help, refer to pages 168–171 in your textbook.

Shihuangdi's Idea	How It Helped Unify the Empire
He set up a single system of writing.	1. helped local leaders communicate with the capital and helped the government to record and collect taxes
He ordered farmers to build highways.	2. linked the cities of the empire
He collected taxes from farmers.	3. made the empire rich
He allowed farmers to own land.	4. weakened the power of the nobles; ensured that there would be food for the empire
He ordered farmers to strengthen walls along the northern border.	5. kept people from the northern steppes from coming into the empire

6. What geographical features helped Shihuangdi win control of the Qin region?

the Huang River and the Quinling Mountains

7. Which of Shihuangdi's ideas would become lasting legacies?

His centralized systems of writing, government, and money would live on for centuries.

WRITING A SUMMARY

A summary briefly states the main ideas contained in a piece of writing. As you read the selection below, look for the main idea in each paragraph. Then complete the activities that follow. For help, refer to pages 172–173 in your textbook.

The Han rulers wanted educated people for government jobs. Wudi was the first strong emperor of the Han dynasty. His rule lasted from 140 B.C. to 87 B.C. Wudi created schools to prepare students for government service. These schools were run by Confucian teachers.

Under Wudi's government, schools were set up in each province in China. The schools taught Chinese literature to students who would serve in local government. Very good students were sometimes sent to the best school in the empire. This was the Grand School.

More and more people were educated for government service. During Wudi's rule only 50 students were allowed to study at the Grand School. By A.D. 200 the school had more than 30,000 students. For one year students learned about ancient China's poetry, history, proper behavior, and folk songs. The teachers were China's most brilliant Confucian scholars. At the end of the year, students at the Grand School took a long test. If they passed, they earned jobs as government workers or as teachers in province schools. They also won great respect in society because they were so well educated.

1. Write the topic sentence of each of the paragraphs.

The Han rulers wanted educated people for government jobs. Under Wudi's government, schools were set up in each province in China. More and more people were educated for government service.

2. Write a summary of the selection in three or four sentences.

The Han emperors set up a system of schools to educate people for government service. In local schools and the Grand School, students studied Chinese literature. The education system grew, providing the empire with well-respected government officials and teachers.

THE TEACHINGS OF CONFUCIUS

Confucius was an important Chinese teacher and scholar. Some of his teachings, which his students wrote down in a book called *The Analects*, are listed below. Use his teachings and the information on pages 174–178 in your textbook to answer the questions.

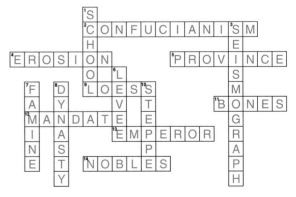

- Daily I examine myself on three points: Have I worked hard? Have I been loyal to my friends? Have I shared what I have learned?

- Do not worry about having an important job; worry about doing your job well.

- The good person is satisfied and calm; the mean person is always full of distress.

- When we see good and kind people, we should think of following their example; when we see criminal and greedy people, we should look at ourselves.

1. According to Confucius, what are the traits of a good person?

A good person is satisfied, calm, hardworking, loyal to friends, and shares knowledge.

2. What are the traits of a good worker?

A good worker works hard and is concerned about doing the job well rather than about the importance of the job.

3. What did Confucius mean when he advised people to think of themselves when they saw a criminal or a greedy person?

Possible answer: People should look for their own negative traits and try to correct them.

4. How did Confucian ideas influence the Han dynasty?

Confucian emphasis on education resulted in increased knowledge and remarkable inventions during the Han dynasty. The Han emperor Wudi started Confucian schools to educate government workers.

USING NEW WORDS

Use the words in the box to complete the crossword puzzle below. For help, you can refer to the lessons in Chapter 7 in your textbook.

Confucianism	dynasty	Mandate of Heaven
emperor	Grand School	levee
loess	famine	oracle bones
erosion	nobles	province
seismograph	steppe	

(crossword grid)

2. C O N F U C I A N I S M
4. E R O S I O N   5. P R O V I N C E
9. L O E S S   11. B O N E S
12. M A N D A T E   13. E M P E R O R
14. N O B L E S

Across

2. teachings of Confucius
4. wearing away of soil
5. political division of land in the empire
9. dusty, yellow soil
11. used to predict future (1 of 2 words)
12. god-given right to rule (1 of 3 words)
13. supreme ruler of an empire
14. rich, powerful relatives of the king

Down

1. Grand _____, best place for Chinese to be educated
3. machine that detects earthquakes
6. wall that keeps a river within its banks
7. time when people starve
8. line of rulers from the same family
10. dry, treeless plain

THE GEOGRAPHY OF ANCIENT GREECE

Use the map to answer the questions below. For help, you may refer to pages 192–195 in your textbook.

ANCIENT GREECE

1. What seas border Greece?
   Aegean Sea, Mediterranean Sea, Ionian Sea

2. On what peninsula is Sparta located? **Peloponnesus**

3. On what peninsula is Athens located? **Attica**

4. What is the name of the biggest Greek island? **Crete**

5. Why has it always been difficult to travel by land in Greece?
   Nine out of every ten acres are hilly or mountainous.

COMPARING ATHENS AND SPARTA

The two Greek city-states of Athens and Sparta shared a common culture yet differed from each other in many ways. Read the sentences below carefully. If the sentence describes life in Athens, circle **A**. If the sentence describes life in Sparta, circle **S**. If the sentence describes both Athenian and Spartan life, circle **A** and **S**. If you need help, refer back to pages 196–201 in your textbook.

1. Only free men were citizens of their polis. — (A) (S)
2. Athletes participated in the Olympic Games. — (A) (S)
3. People honored Athena as their special protector and provider. — (A) S
4. People gathered at temples to worship Zeus, the most powerful Greek god. — (A) (S)
5. Life revolved around an agora and an acropolis. — (A) (S)
6. Boys spent a lot of time training to be soldiers. — A (S)
7. Girls practiced sports and were trained to be strong mothers of strong children. — A (S)
8. Girls stayed at home to help their mothers. — (A) S
9. Boys worked with their fathers in the fields or in craft shops. — (A) S
10. Women and slaves had few rights. — (A) (S)
11. The government changed from an oligarchy to a democracy. — (A) S
12. Here people enjoyed hearing the stories of Homer. — (A) (S)

THE GOLDEN AGE OF ATHENS

The pictures below show important people and places in Athenian life. Write a caption for each picture explaining how the person or place reflected the "Golden Age" of Greece. If you need help, refer back to pages 204–209 in your textbook.

Parthenon

Possible answer: The Parthenon lay at the center of the Acropolis, which was the largest in Greece and reflected the power and wealth of Athens.

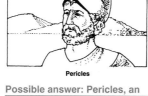

Pericles

Possible answer: Pericles, an Athenian leader, arranged for citizens to be paid when they held an office or served on a jury.

Agora

Possible answer: People bought and traded goods in Athens' busy agora.

Plato

Possible answer: Plato, a famous philosopher, wrote down the teachings of Socrates.

MAKING CONCLUSIONS

Making a conclusion involves pulling together pieces of information so that they have meaning. Practice making a conclusion by reading the passage below and completing the activity that follows. If you need help, refer back to pages 210–211 in your textbook.

> *The Athenian philosopher Socrates was tried and condemned to death for disturbing the public peace. Here is part of his speech to the jury after he received the death penalty, as reported by his student Plato.*
>
> There is great reason to hope that death is a good, for one of two things: either death is a state of nothingness and utter unconsciousness, or . . . there is a change and migration of the soul from this world to another. Now if you suppose that there is no consciousness, but a sleep like the sleep of him who is undisturbed even by the sight of dreams. . . . Now if death is like this, I say that to die is gain; for eternity is then only a single night. But if death is the journey to another place, and there, as men say, all the dead are, what good, O my friends and judges, can be greater than this. . . . I . . . shall have a wonderful interest in a place where I can converse *[talk]* with Palamedes, and Ajax the son of Telamon, and the other heroes of old. . . . Above all, I shall be able to continue my search into true and false knowledge; as in this world, so also in that; I shall find out who is wise, and who pretends to be wise, and is not.

Mark **X** next to each statement that is a reasonable conclusion based on the information you have just read.

_____ 1. Socrates hoped that death would end his suffering.
__X__ 2. Socrates had no fear of death.
_____ 3. Socrates had difficulty sleeping.
__X__ 4. To Socrates, death could only be a good thing.
__X__ 5. Socrates believed that even in death he could continue his search for the truth.
_____ 6. When he slept, Socrates had disturbing dreams.
__X__ 7. In death Socrates hoped to be reunited with friends, judges, and heroes from the past.
_____ 8. Socrates believed that in the afterlife all people were wise.
_____ 9. Socrates was a popular teacher.
__X__ 10. Wisdom and knowledge were important to Socrates.

THE GREEK ALPHABET

The great library at Alexandria contained hundreds of thousands of books written in Greek. Suppose that you have found a piece of one of these books, a scroll written on a papyrus roll. To find the meaning of the words on the scroll, use the Greek alphabet as shown here. Below each Greek letter write its English equivalent.

Modern

A B C D E F H I K L M N O P Q R S T V X Z

Greek

A B Γ Δ E F ⊕ S X Λ M N O Γ Φ R S T Y X I

1. ΓΟΛSE

polis

2. ΔΓRΟΓΟΛSE

acropolis

3. SOΓRΔTES

Socrates

4. When Alexander the Great conquered the Persian empire, he spread Greek culture from Egypt to India. In addition to the Greek alphabet, what other Greek legacies did Alexander spread throughout his empire?

The cities that Alexander built mirrored a Greek polis; they had an agora, a theater, temples, and a stadium. In these cities citizens took part in democratic assemblies. Alexander spread Greek achievements in math and science by building a library to house the scholarly work of Greek experts.

USING NEW WORDS

Choose a term from the box to answer each question. For help, you can refer to the lessons in Chapter 8 of your textbook.

acropolis	democracy	Peloponnesian War
agora	harbor	peninsula
assembly	jury	philosophy
citizen	monarchy	polis
colony	oligarchy	

1. What is the Greek word for a city-state? **polis**

2. Where did the ancient Greeks meet and conduct business? **agora**

3. What kind of government is headed by one ruler? **monarchy**

4. In what lawmaking body did people vote on issues that helped to shape the future of the city? **assembly**

5. What was the name of the conflict between Athens and Sparta and their allies? **Peloponnesian War**

6. Where do ships find a sheltered place along a coast? **harbor**

7. Who hears evidence and makes decisions in a court of law? **jury**

8. What is the name for the large hill around which Greek city-states were built? **acropolis**

9. What area of land is nearly surrounded by water? **peninsula**

10. What kind of government is run by a small group of people? **oligarchy**

11. Who has certain rights and responsibilities in his or her country or community? **citizen**

12. In what form of government do people vote to make decisions? **democracy**

13. If you wanted to search for wisdom and the right way to live, what would you study? **philosophy**

14. What is the name for a group of people who lived apart from Greece but kept economic ties with it? **colony**

THE GEOGRAPHY OF ANCIENT ITALY

Use the map to answer the questions. Refer to pages 224–227 in your textbook.

ANCIENT ITALY

1. What are two ways in which the geography of Italy is similar to that of Greece?
Both are peninsulas in the Mediterranean Sea, and both are mountainous with fertile plains.

2. What mountain range separates Italy from the rest of Europe? the Alps

3. What mountain range runs down the center of Italy? Apennine Mountains

4. What large island is part of southern Italy? Sicily

5. What two geographic features made the location of Rome a favorable one?
Possible answers: The hills helped to protect the city from attack; the plain of Latium had fertile soil; the Tiber River provided a means of transportation to the sea.

READING ELEVATION MAPS AND PROFILES

An elevation map shows the height of land above sea level. A profile map shows a cross section of a region. Use the maps below to answer the questions that follow. Refer back to pages 228–229 in your textbook.

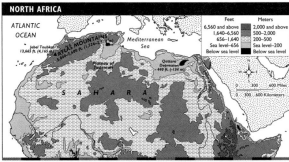

NORTH AFRICA

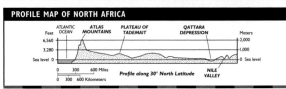

PROFILE MAP OF NORTH AFRICA

1. What land features are shown on both maps? Nile Valley, Qattara Depression, Plateau of Tademait, Atlas Mountains

2. On the profile map, what is the elevation of the Plateau of Tademait? about 1,700 feet

3. What is the highest peak in North Africa? Jebel Toubkal

4. On which map is it easier to see differences in elevation?
Differences in elevation are easier to see on the profile map.

5. Which map would you use to show the relative location of landforms in the region?
You would use the elevation map.

THE ROMANS AT WAR

In 390 B.C. an army of Gauls attacked Rome. The Roman historian Livy tells how the Gauls tried to surprise the Romans one night. Read the passage below and answer the questions that follow. For help, you may refer to pages 230–235 in your textbook.

> The Capitol of Rome was meantime in great danger; for the Gauls had [observed] the easy ascent [to it] by the rock at the Temple of Carmentis. On a moonlight night, after they had first sent ahead a man unarmed to test the way . . . they gained the summit all in silence. Not merely had they escaped the [sight] of the [guards], but even the dogs, sensitive as they are to noises at night, had not been alarmed. But they did not escape the notice of the geese; for these creatures were sacred to [the goddess] Juno, and had been accordingly spared despite the scarcity of food.
>
> Thus it befell that Marcus Manlius, who had been consul three years earlier, and who was a [respected] warrior, was awakened by their hissing and the flapping of their wings. He snatched his arms, and calling loudly to his fellows, ran to the spot. Here he [hit] with . . . a shield a Gaul who had already gained a foothold on the summit, and tumbled him headlong. . . . Manlius also slew certain others who in their alarm had cast aside their weapons and were clinging to the rocks. By this time the rest [of the Romans] had rushed together, and crushed the enemy with darts and stones, so that the whole band, dislodged from their foothold, were hurled down the precipice in general ruin.

1. Describe the Gauls' plan to attack the Romans.
   They planned to surprise the Romans by silently climbing the
   rock at the Temple of Carmentis at night.

2. How did the Romans find out that the Gauls were attacking?
   The Romans were awakened by the sound of geese hissing
   and flapping their wings.

3. What did Marcus Manlius do when he realized that the Gauls were attacking?
   He alerted his fellow soldiers and led the Romans in fighting.

4. Rome's army defeated the Gauls. Later, Roman soldiers fought in the Punic Wars and in the Battle of Zama. What was the outcome of each of these conflicts for Rome?
   Rome won both conflicts, gained control of Carthage's
   territory, and became the most powerful nation in the
   Mediterranean region.

PAX ROMANA

Explain how each of the following helped to keep the Roman empire together during the 200 years of the Pax Romana. For help, you may refer to pages 236–243 in your textbook.

1. **Army**
   The Roman army defended
   the empire against bandits,
   built the empire's roads,
   and helped enforce laws.

3. **Tax collectors**
   Tax collectors collected
   taxes from craftworkers and
   merchants to pay for
   the upkeep of the empire.

2. **Roads**
   A network of roads helped
   to make communication,
   trade, and travel possible
   throughout the vast empire.

4. **Laws**
   Roman governors, who also
   acted as judges, enforced
   Roman laws throughout the
   empire.

THE BEGINNINGS OF CHRISTIANITY

The first four books of the New Testament, known as the Gospels, give different kinds of information about Jesus. Read the excerpts below and answer the questions that follow. For help, you may refer to pages 246–251 in your textbook.

A. Jesus was born in the town of Bethlehem in Judea, during the time when Herod was king.

Matthew 2:1

C. But I tell you who hear me: Love your enemies, do good to those who hate you, bless those who curse you, and pray for those who mistreat you.

Luke 6:27–28

B. They crossed the lake and came to land at Gennesaret, where the people recognized Jesus. So they sent for the sick people in all the surrounding country and brought them to Jesus. They begged him to let the sick at least touch the edge of his cloak; and all who touched it were made well.

Matthew 14:34–36

D. What do you think a man does who has one hundred sheep and one of them gets lost? He will leave the other ninety-nine grazing on the hillside and go and look for the lost sheep. When he finds it, I tell you, he feels far happier over this one sheep than over the ninety-nine that did not get lost. In just the same way, your Father in heaven does not want any of these little ones to be lost.

Matthew 18:12–14

1. Which passage tells about Jesus as a historical person? **A**
2. Which passage tells about Jesus as a healer? **B**
3. Which passage shows Jesus teaching people the right way to live? **C**
4. Which passage presents a story that Jesus told? **D**
5. What is the name for the kind of story Jesus told? a parable

---

THE SHIFT FROM WEST TO EAST

Use the map to complete the activities below. Refer to pages 252–257 in your textbook.

THE ROMAN EMPIRE, A.D.284

1. In A.D. 284 the emperor Diocletian divided the empire into two halves. Why?
   The empire was too big to be ruled by one leader.

2. Circle the parts of the empire over which Diocletian ruled.
   (Greece) (Egypt) Spain Italy (Palestine) Britain

3. Locate and name the new capital city built by Constantine.
   Constantinople

4. Give two reasons why Constantine located his capital on this site.
   Constantinople was located on a major trade route, was easy
   to protect, and was far from Rome.

5. The western half of the Roman empire collapsed in the 400s, but the eastern half continued for another 1,000 years. What was the name of the eastern empire?
   the Byzantine empire

6. What two forms of Christianity developed in the divided empire?
   Roman Catholicism developed in the west, and Eastern
   Orthodox Christianity developed in the east.

SOME WORDS ABOUT ROME

Cross out the word in each group that does not belong. Then write a sentence telling how the remaining three words are related. If you need help, refer back to the lessons in Chapter 9 of your textbook.

1. Forum   patricians   ~~Messiah~~   Twelve Tables
   Possible answer: The patricians agreed to write Roman laws
   down on the Twelve Tables and post them in the city's Forum.

2. republic   ~~architecture~~   consuls   Senate
   Possible answer: The powerful Senate and the consuls were
   two branches of Rome's republic.

3. representatives   tribunes   plebeians   ~~Punic Wars~~
   Possible answer: Representatives in the assembly elected
   tribunes who worked to gain rights for Rome's plebeians.

4. ~~apostles~~   Pax Romana   aqueducts   census
   Possible answer: During the period known as Pax Romana, the
   emperor ordered the building of aqueducts and the taking of a
   census every five years.

5. Christianity   New Testament   parables   ~~gladiators~~
   Possible answer: The story of the birth of Christianity and the
   parables of Jesus can be found in the New Testament.

6. Eastern Orthodox Christianity   ~~dictator~~   Roman Catholicism   pope
   Possible answer: In the western half of the empire, Christianity
   became known as Roman Catholicism, and the pope was its
   leader; in the eastern half the religion became known as
   Eastern Orthodox Christianity.

7. Choose two of the words that you crossed out. Write two sentences explaining how each word relates to the history of ancient Rome.
   Possible answer: After defeating Carthage in the Punic Wars,
   Rome became the greatest power in the Mediterranean region.
   Julius Caesar was a dictator of Rome.

THE GEOGRAPHY OF ARABIA

Use the map to complete the activities below. Refer to pages 262–265 in your textbook.

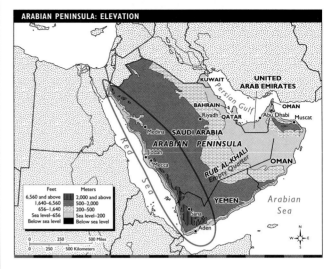

ARABIAN PENINSULA: ELEVATION

1. The Arabian peninsula is bounded by the Persian Gulf to the east, the Arabian Sea to the south, and the Red Sea to the west. Locate and label these waters on the map.

2. Which city on the map above has the highest elevation? Sana

3. Locate and circle the Jabal Al-Hijaz mountains of western Arabia.

4. In what areas of the Arabian peninsula did towns and cities develop?
   in fertile regions, at desert edges, and at oases

5. Name three modern nations that are located on the Arabian peninsula.
   Saudia Arabia, Yemen, Oman, United Arab Emirates, Kuwait,
   Qatar

THE RELIGION OF ISLAM

The pictures below show important parts of the Islamic religion. Use the pictures and the information on pages 266–271 in your textbook to answer the questions that follow.

1. What is the holy city of Islam?
   Mecca

2. Why is the year 622 important to Muslims?
   It is the starting point of the Islamic calendar.

3. What are the five basic duties of all Muslims?
   a. belief in one god, Allah
   b. prayer five times a day
   c. giving to those in need
   d. fasting during the month of Ramadan
   e. a religious pilgrimage to Mecca

4. What is the name of the sacred book containing these five duties?
   the Quran

5. What do Muslims believe is the origin of this sacred book?
   Muslims believe the Quran contains the holy teachings that Muhammad received from Allah.

A MUSLIM CALIPHATE

The caliphs of Baghdad built a huge library called the House of Wisdom. There Arab scholars translated and studied Greek, Roman, and Indian works. They also wrote books in the fields of medicine, math, science, and literature. Use each picture to answer the question that follows. For help, you may refer to pages 272–277 in your textbook.

A Persian doctor wrote a famous medical textbook. What was his name?
Ibn Sina or Avicenna

You use a system of numbers invented by Muslim mathematicians. What is the name for a type of mathematics these scholars developed?
algebra

People today still read a collection of folktales originally written in Arabic. What is the name of this book?
The Arabian Nights

Muslim scholars studied the stars and developed a calendar. What was the name of the instrument they used to figure out position from the stars?
astrolabe

T14

READING HISTORICAL MAPS

Historical maps show places or events from the past. There are many of these maps in your textbook. Use the historical map below to complete the activities that follow. Refer to pages 280–281 in your textbook for help.

THE ISLAMIC WORLD, 750

Muslim lands
Christian lands

ATLANTIC OCEAN
ENGLAND
EUROPE
FRANCE
SPAIN
ITALY
Rome
Constantinople
Carthage
Mediterranean Sea
Asia Minor
Black Sea
Caspian Sea
ASIA
PERSIA
INDIA
Alexandria
Jerusalem
Damascus
Baghdad
Persian Gulf
EGYPT
ARABIA
Medina
Mecca
Red Sea
AFRICA
Arabian Sea

0   500   1,000 Miles
0   500   1,000 Kilometers

1. Name two cities in Africa that were part of the Islamic world.
   Carthage and Alexandria

2. Name the European country that was Islamic by 750. **Spain**

3. Circle the names of the regions to which Islam had spread by 750.
   (Northern Africa)   Asia Minor   Italy   (Arabian Peninsula)   (Persia)

4. By 750, was the Islamic world double or more than double the size of the Christian world?
   more than double the size of the Christian world

USING NEW WORDS

Use the words in the box to complete the activity below. For help, you can refer to the lessons in Chapter 10 in your textbook.

algebra	Five Pillars	mosque
astrolabe	hijra	oasis
caliph	Islam	pilgrimage
caravan	Kaaba	Quran

Rearrange the letters to spell the word that fits the definition. Use capital letters where needed.

	Word	**Definition**
1. pailch	c a l i p h	Muslim ruler
2. quesom	m o s q u e	Muslim place of worship
3. elbagar	a l g e b r a	a type of mathematics
4. blastearo	a s t r o l a b e	instrument used to find position from stars
5. soisa	o a s i s	place with water in the desert
6. ranavac	c a r a v a n	group of people and animals traveling together
7. mails	I s l a m	Muslim religion
8. narqu	Q u r a n	sacred book of Islam
9. abaka	K a a b a	temple in Mecca
10. rajih	h i j r a	Muhammad's move from Mecca to Medina
11. veif sliplar	F i v e P i l l a r s	a Muslim's basic duties
12. miggrapile	p i l g r i m a g e	journey for religious purposes

---

CLIMATE REGIONS IN MIDDLE AMERICA

In Middle America there are three climate zones, each largely determined by elevation. Use the information in the diagram below to answer the questions that follow. If you need help, refer back to pages 286–289 in your textbook.

Climate Regions in Middle America

Elevation/Feet
Tierra Fría
—6,000—
Tierra Templada
—3,000—
Tierra Caliente
0

B = Bananas
BE = Beans
CA = Cacao
CF = Coffee
CO = Cotton
CR = Corn
P = Potatoes
S = Sugarcane
T = Tobacco
W = Wheat

1. a. What is the hottest region in Middle America called?
   tierra caliente

   b. What is the elevation of this region?
   sea level to 3,000 feet

   c. What crops grow in this region?
   bananas, tobacco, cotton, corn, sugarcane, cacao, coffee

2. a. In what region is the climate mild?
   tierra templada

   b. What is the elevation of this region?
   from 3,000 to 6,000 feet

   c. What crops grow in this region?
   bananas, tobacco, cotton, corn, sugarcane, cacao, coffee

3. a. In what region is the climate usually cold?
   tierra fría

   b. What is the elevation of this region?
   above 6,000 feet

   c. What crops grow in this region?
   wheat, corn, potatoes, beans

4. What do all the climate regions have in common?
   All the climate regions have a rainy season; they all grow corn.

COMPARING CLIMOGRAPHS

Study the climographs below. Then answer the questions. For help, you may refer to pages 290–291 in your textbook.

CLIMATE: SAN JOSÉ, COSTA RICA

Inches / °F
Average Monthly Temperature
Average Monthly Precipitation
JAN. MAR. MAY JULY SEP. NOV.
FEB. APR. JUNE AUG. OCT. DEC.

CLIMATE: TEGUCIGALPA, HONDURAS

Inches / °F
Average Monthly Temperature
Average Monthly Precipitation
JAN. MAR. MAY JULY SEP. NOV.
FEB. APR. JUNE AUG. OCT. DEC.

1. a. What does the bar graph of each climograph show?
   average monthly precipitation in inches

   b. What does the line graph show?
   average monthly temperature in degrees Fahrenheit

2. a. During which month does each city get the most precipitation?
   San José **September**   Tegucigalpa **May**

   b. What is the average temperature during this month?
   San José **about 70°F**   Tegucigalpa **about 70°F**

3. How are the climates of San José and Tegucigalpa similar?
   The temperatures are similar and do not vary much during the year, and both have a rainy season.

4. How does the climate of San José differ from that of Tegucigalpa?
   San José gets more precipitation than Tegucigalpa.

THE MYSTERIOUS OLMEC

Archaeologists have found the artifacts pictured below. In the space provided write the clues that each one reveals about the Olmec civilization. For help, you may refer to pages 292–296 in your textbook.

1. Carved head

Possible answer: The Olmec had specialized skills to carve out a large piece of sculpture. The large head may be a statue of an Olmec ruler.

2. Jaguar carving

Possible answer: The Olmec believed that certain animals had special powers and that the jaguar was the most powerful of all.

3. Rubber ball

Possible answer: The Olmec lived in an area where there were many rubber trees.

4. What do historians want to find out about the Olmec?

Historians want to learn what they called themselves and why their civilization declined.

THE WORLD OF THE MAYA

Read the descriptions and look at the pictures. Then complete the activity below. For help, you may refer to pages 298–303 in your textbook.

1. This is a pyramid temple at Copán.
What other types of buildings have archaeologists found at Copán?
a ball court, palaces

2. Maya writing is one source of information about the Maya.
On what did the Maya write?
stone buildings and stelae, books

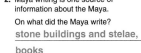
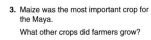

3. Maize was the most important crop for the Maya.
What other crops did farmers grow?
beans, squash, peppers, cacaos, avocados, papayas

4. The Maya studied the stars and planets.
What did the study of astronomy help them to do?
develop an accurate calendar and record the exact dates of events

5. Why do we know more about the Maya civilization than about the Olmec civilization?
We can read their writing, and descendants of the Maya speak a version of the ancient language and preserve many of the traditions.

SOME WORDS ABOUT MIDDLE AMERICA

Use the clues and the words in the box to complete the puzzle below. Write one letter of the word in each square. The mystery box in the puzzle spells out the name of a country in Middle America. For help, you may refer to the lessons in Chapter 11 in your textbook.

Words

Classic Period
Ice Age
slash and burn
glacier
maize
stela
glyph
rain forest
tropical

Clues

1. sheet of ice

2. farming method in which jungle is cleared and burned

3. important time of cultural achievement for a civilization

4. tall, flat stone

5. wooded area that receives more than 80 inches of rain per year

6. corn

7. period when ice covered nearly half of Earth's land mass

8. symbol used in Maya writing

9. located near the equator where the climate is usually warm

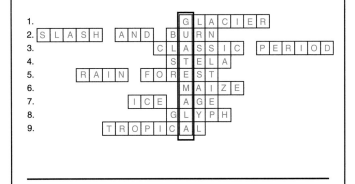

1.   G L A C I E R
2. S L A S H   A N D   B U R N
3.   C L A S S I C   P E R I O D
4.   S T E L A
5.   R A I N   F O R E S T
6.   M A I Z E
7.   I C E   A G E
8.   G L Y P H
9.   T R O P I C A L

THE GEOGRAPHY OF EUROPE

Use the map to answer the questions below. For help, you may refer to pages 316–319 in your textbook.

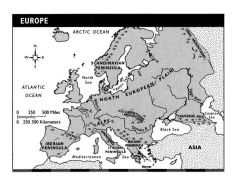

1. a. Name the largest peninsula in northern Europe.
Scandinavian Peninsula

b. Name the largest peninsula in southern Europe.
Iberian Peninsula

2. a. What major river empties into the North Sea?
Rhine River

b. What river flows through central Europe to the Black Sea?
Danube

3. a. What ocean lies to the north of Europe?
Arctic Ocean

b. What sea forms the southern boundary of Europe?
Mediterranean Sea

4. a. What two mountain ranges separate the continent of Europe from Asia?
Ural and Caucasus mountains

b. What landform covers over 50 percent of Europe?
North European Plain

LIFE IN THE MIDDLE AGES

Follow the directions and complete the activities below. For help, you may refer to pages 320–327 in your textbook.

1. Draw a line to the picture of a vassal.

What did a vassal do for his lord?
He served as a knight in the lord's army.

What did the lord give the vassal?
The lord gave each vassal a fief.

What word describes the relationship between lords and vassals?
feudalism

2. Draw a line to the picture of a serf.

Where did a medieval serf live?
A serf lived on a manor.

What did a serf have to do for his lord?
The serf worked on the lord's land and paid rent and taxes.

3. Draw a line to the picture of a craftworker.

Where did craftworkers live in the Middle Ages?
Craftworkers lived primarily in towns.

What was the name for a group of craftworkers?
a guild

DETERMINING POINT OF VIEW

As you read the following passages, try to determine the writer's point of view. For help, you may refer to pages 328–329 in your textbook.

> *Charlemagne fought many wars with neighboring peoples in order to establish the Frankish empire. The Saxons were one of these peoples. Charlemagne's secretary and close friend, Einhard, wrote a book in which he described Charlemagne's war with the Saxons:*
>
> No war ever undertaken by the Franks was waged with such persistence and bitterness, or cost so much labor, because the Saxons, like almost all Germans, were a ferocious folk, . . . hostile to our Faith, and they did not consider it dishonorable to transgress and violate all law—be it human or divine.
>
> William Stearns Davis, *Readings in Ancient History* (Boston: Allyn and Bacon, 1913), page 374.

1. How does Einhard view the Saxons?
He views them as ferocious, anti-Christian, and dishonorable.

2. What words or phrases reveal Einhard's feelings?
ferocious, hostile to our Faith

3. What helped to shape Einhard's point of view?
The Saxons and the Franks were enemies and had fought each other in a war.

> *Here is how Einhard describes Charlemagne:*
>
> The upper part of his head was round, his eyes very large and animated, nose a little long, hair fair, and face laughing and merry. Thus his appearance was always stately and dignified, whether he was standing or sitting; although his neck was thick and somewhat short, and his belly rather prominent; but the symmetry of the rest of his body concealed these defects.
>
> Einhard, *The Life of Charlemagne* (Ann Arbor, MI: Ann Arbor Paperbacks, The University of Michigan Press, 1960), page 50.

4. How does Einhard view Charlemagne? Do you think that he likes or dislikes him?
Einhard appears to admire and respect Charlemagne but recognizes some of his physical shortcomings.

5. What words or phrases reveal Einhard's feelings about Charlemagne?
animated, laughing and merry, stately and dignified

THE CALL FOR THE FIRST CRUSADE

Read the passage below and answer the questions. For help, you may refer to pages 330–335 in your textbook.

> *In 1095 the Byzantine emperor appealed for help against the Turks, who had captured Jerusalem and were threatening Constantinople. Pope Urban II called Christians to join a crusade against the Turks. Here is part of his speech:*
>
> For your brethren who live in the east are in urgent need of your help, and you must hasten to give them the aid which has often been promised them. For, as most of you have heard, the Turks and Arabs have attacked them. . . . They have killed and captured many, and have destroyed the churches and devastated the empire. If you permit them to continue . . . the faithful of God will be much more widely attacked by them. On this account I, or rather the Lord, beseech you as Christ's heralds to publish this everywhere and to persuade all people of whatever rank, footsoldiers and knights, poor and rich, to carry aid promptly to those Christians and to destroy that vile race from the lands of our friends. . . . Moreover, Christ commands it.
>
> Oliver J. Thatcher and Edgar H. McNeal, *A Source Book for Mediaeval History* (New York: Charles Scribner's Sons, 1905).

3. a. What armies did the Crusaders fight? What was their religion?
the Seljuk Turks, who were Muslim

b. Did the first Crusaders succeed in capturing Jerusalem?
yes

1. Whom did Pope Urban ask to go on the Crusade?
Christians of all ranks, both rich and poor

2. What did Urban say to persuade people to join the Crusade?
He said Christ commanded them.

4. During the Middle Ages how did people express their devotion to religion?
They worshiped in village churches, built cathedrals, made pilgrimages, and honored saints. Some people entered monasteries.

LEONARDO DA VINCI: A RENAISSANCE MAN

Leonardo da Vinci, who described himself as a "disciple of experiment," had many interests and talents. In a letter to the duke of Bari and Milan, he told what he could do for the duke. Read four parts of his letter and complete the activities that follow. For help, you may refer to pages 336–341 in your textbook.

> **A.** I have a sort of extremely light and strong bridges, adapted to be most easily carried, and with them you may pursue, and at any time flee from the enemy.
> **B.** I will make covered chariots, safe and unattackable, which, entering among the enemy with their artillery, there is no body of men so great but they would break them.
> **C.** In time of peace I believe I can give perfect satisfaction and to the equal of any other in architecture and the composition of buildings public and private.
> **D.** I can carry sculpture in marble, bronze, or clay, and also I can do in painting whatever may be done, as well as any other, be he who he may.
>
> Jean Paul Richter and Irma A. Richter, editors, *The Literary Works of Leonardo da Vinci* (London: Oxford University Press, 1936).

1. a. In which statement does Leonardo describe himself as an artist? D
b. Name the patron in Florence who invited Leonardo to set up a studio in his house.
Lorenzo Medici

2. a. In which statement does Leonardo describe himself as an inventor? B
b. Name three things that Leonardo planned or designed.
submarine, parachute, machine gun, flying machine

3. a. In which statement does Leonardo describe himself as an engineer? A
b. Why would the duke be interested in Leonardo's engineering ability?
Leonardo says he could help the duke be successful in war.

4. a. In which statement does Leonardo describe himself as an architect? C
b. Name another Renaissance artist who was an architect as well as a painter and sculptor.
Michelangelo

5. In what way was the Renaissance both a time of looking back and a time of looking forward?
The Renaissance looked back to the classical achievements of Greece and Rome and forward to future achievements and discoveries in art, literature, and science.

THE REFORMATION

Each pair of sentences below states a cause-effect relationship. Write **C** next to the sentence that states a cause and **E** next to the sentence that states an effect. If you need help, refer to pages 342–347 in your textbook.

C 1. Humanism gains popularity among Europe's scholars.

E   Some Christians begin to question the authority of the Pope.

E 2. Erasmus begins to criticize Church policy.

C   Priests grant indulgences, or pardons, to people who pay the Church to be forgiven.

E 3. The Reformation movement begins in Germany.

C   Martin Luther posts 95 Theses on a Wittenberg church door.

C 4. Johannes Gutenberg invents a printing press that uses movable type.

E   Luther's criticism of the Roman Church and a translation of the Bible into German spread quickly.

E 5. German leaders protect Martin Luther from the Church.

C   German leaders, loyal to their homeland, want to keep the taxes intended for Rome.

C 6. Catholic Church leaders meet in Trent.

E   The Catholic Church reforms some of its practices.

C 7. The Pope refuses to give King Henry VIII permission to divorce his queen.

E   Henry starts a new Protestant church, the Church of England.

Now it is your turn. Write a cause-effect sentence pair about the reign of Queen Elizabeth I. Tell which sentence states a cause and which sentence states an effect.

Possible answer: Cause—Spain hopes to return England to the

Catholic faith. Effect—King Philip II sends a Spanish armada to

attack England.

USING NEW WORDS

Write the letter of the correct word from the box next to its meaning. For help, you may refer to the lessons in Chapter 12 of your textbook.

a. armada	**h.** guild	**o.** monastery	**v.** Reformation
b. cathedral	**i.** humanism	**p.** navigable	**w.** Renaissance
c. convent	**j.** indulgence	**q.** nun	**x.** saint
d. Crusade	**k.** lord	**r.** patron	**y.** serf
e. deforestation	**l.** Magna Carta	**s.** plague	**z.** temperate
f. feudalism	**m.** manor	**t.** Protestantism	**aa.** vassal
g. fief	**n.** Middle Ages	**u.** reform	

p 1. deep enough for boat travel

i 2. concern with human interests and values

u 3. improve by making changes

g 4. manor given to a vassal by a lord

x 5. holy person

c 6. religious community of nuns

e 7. process of clearing forests

k 8. noble who owned a manor

l 9. English charter guaranteeing rights

z 10. mild climate

w 11. historical period of great creativity

aa 12. person who served a lord

t 13. branch of Christianity that broke away from Roman Catholicism

a 14. fleet of warships

s 15. terrible disease

v 16. movement that brought reform to the Church

j 17. pardon for sins

y 18. person who lived and worked on a manor

n 19. period between ancient Roman times and the 1400s

b 20. grand and beautiful church

q 21. woman who devotes her life to religion

m 22. large estate owned by a noble

f 23. way of organizing society based on land and military service

o 24. religious community of monks

r 25. person who supports the arts

d 26. first journey to gain control of Jerusalem

h 27. group of craftworkers

THE GEOGRAPHY OF AFRICA

You are planning a television documentary called "Amazing Africa." Use the map below to name the natural features you plan to film. For help, you may refer to pages 354–357 in your textbook.

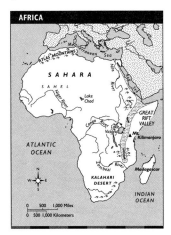

1. The world's largest desert region:
   Sahara

2. The world's longest river:
   Nile River

3. The highest mountain in Africa:
   Mt. Kilimanjaro

4. This river flows through southern Africa, emptying into the Indian Ocean:
   Zambezi River

5. The narrow, dry grassland along the Sahara's southern edge:
   Sahel

6. A gigantic valley, extending almost 3,000 miles:
   Great Rift Valley

7. Two seas and two oceans that border Africa:
   Mediterranean Sea, Red Sea, Atlantic Ocean, Indian Ocean

CIVILIZATIONS OF NORTHEASTERN AFRICA

Use the pictures below and the information on pages 358–361 in your textbook to answer the questions.

Coins from Aksum

Kushite pyramid

Church at Lalibela

1. **a.** What city was the capital of the kingdom of Kush?
   Meroe

   b. How do we know that the Kushite kings were wealthy?
   Remains of large palaces, temples, and pyramid-shaped tombs, and large amounts of gold in a royal tomb.

2. **a.** What do gold coins reveal about the kingdom of Aksum?
   The cross shows the rulers were Christians, and gold shows the kingdom was wealthy.

   b. How did Aksum become a wealthy kingdom?
   Aksum controlled major cities and trade routes.

3. **a.** In what modern country is this church located?
   Ethiopia

   b. During whose rule were these stone churches built?
   during the rule of Zagwe king Lalibela

WEST AFRICAN GOLD

Answer the questions on the lines provided. For help, you may refer to pages 362–367 in your textbook.

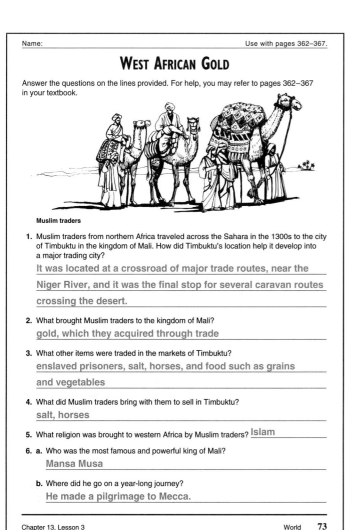

Muslim traders

1. Muslim traders from northern Africa traveled across the Sahara in the 1300s to the city of Timbuktu in the kingdom of Mali. How did Timbuktu's location help it develop into a major trading city?

   It was located at a crossroad of major trade routes, near the
   Niger River, and it was the final stop for several caravan routes
   crossing the desert.

2. What brought Muslim traders to the kingdom of Mali?

   gold, which they acquired through trade

3. What other items were traded in the markets of Timbuktu?

   enslaved prisoners, salt, horses, and food such as grains
   and vegetables

4. What did Muslim traders bring with them to sell in Timbuktu?

   salt, horses

5. What religion was brought to western Africa by Muslim traders? Islam

6. a. Who was the most famous and powerful king of Mali?

   Mansa Musa

   b. Where did he go on a year-long journey?

   He made a pilgrimage to Mecca.

READING A DISTRIBUTION MAP

A distribution map shows how one feature is spread over an area. The distribution map below shows the population density of northeastern Africa. Use the map to answer the questions. If you need help, refer to pages 370–371 in your textbook.

NORTHEASTERN AFRICA: POPULATION DENSITY

People per square mile	People per square kilometer
0–25	0–10
25–250	10–100
250–500	100–200
over 500	over 200

● Major city

1. Which country is more densely populated, Ethiopia or Somalia?

   Ethiopia

2. What is the population density of Cairo?

   over 500 people per square mile

3. What is the population density of most of Ethiopia?

   25–250 people per square mile

4. What is the most densely populated area in Sudan?

   area along the Nile River

5. Why is most of northern Africa uninhabited?

   The Sahara covers most of northern Africa.

THE SWAHILI CITIES

The English word *safari* comes from a Swahili word meaning "journey." In the early history of eastern Africa, many people journeyed to the Swahili cities along the coast. Traders from Asia and India came to the cities by ship. People from the inland areas of Africa came bearing products of the mines and forests. What goods and ideas were traded? Use the words in the box to fill in the chart below. If you need help, refer to pages 372–375 in your textbook.

cloth	leopard skins
fine pottery	metal tools
glass containers	rhinoceros horns
gold	tortoise shells
ivory	wheat
Islamic religion	Arabic words

What the traders brought from Asia	What the traders took away from eastern Africa
cloth	gold
fine pottery	ivory
glass containers	leopard skins
Islamic religion	rhinoceros horns
metal tools	tortoise shells
wheat	
Arabic words	

GREAT ZIMBABWE

In 1868 explorers found the ruins of Great Zimbabwe. Since that time, archaeologists have excavated the ruins, but there are still many mysteries about Great Zimbabwe. Read the following list. If the information listed is known about Great Zimbabwe, mark the item with a **K**. If the item remains a mystery, mark it with an **M**. For help, you may refer to pages 376–379 in your textbook.

K 1. type of stone used to build the walls

K 2. height of the stone walls

M 3. reason stone walls were built

M 4. lifestyle of the leaders of Great Zimbabwe

M 5. reason why one section of the city was called "the house of the great woman"

K 6. importance of gold as a source of wealth

K 7. trading partners of Great Zimbabwe

K 8. type of pottery made by the people of Great Zimbabwe

K 9. type of jewelry made by craftworkers

K 10. crops grown by Zimbabwe farmers

K 11. type of metal used by the people to make tools

M 12. reason why the city declined

M 13. reason why the city was abandoned

M 14. oral traditions of the people of Great Zimbabwe

K 15. size of the city's population during the early 1400s

Why do we know so little about Great Zimbabwe?

The people left no oral traditions or written records, only artifacts
that have been found and interpreted by archaeologists.

USING NEW WORDS

Write a word from the box next to its definition. Then locate and circle the words in the puzzle below. For help you may refer to the lessons in Chapter 13 in your textbook.

| demand | supply |
| griot | savanna |

```
Z  S  G  J  K  O  D  L  C  D  S  J  G
M  U  T  T  U  E  L  E  O  A  A  P  R
E  P  X  S  N  M  U  P  M  B  R  W  I
U  P  M  A  B  R  J  C  D  A  P  N  O
T  L  V  X  W  O  R  X  W  O  N  H  T
W  Y  H  O  T  X  E  M  T  V  A  D  G
P  O  R  S  A  V  A  N  N  A  W  R  P
```

__savanna__   1. a grassy, tree-dotted plain

__supply__   2. a quantity of some good, product, or resource

__griot__   3. a person who tells stories that describe historical events

__demand__   4. people's desire for a particular good, product, or resource

---

GEOGRAPHY OF ASIA

Use the map to complete the activities below. Refer to pages 384–387 in your textbook.

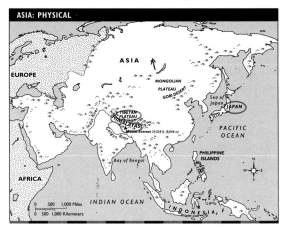

1. Locate and circle the Himalayas. Explain how they influence the climate of Asia.
   They block clouds that blow north from the Indian Ocean. As a result, there is a lot rain on the ocean-facing side of the mountains and very little rain on the northern side.

2. Locate and circle the large plateau on the northern border of the Himalayas.
   a. What is the name of this plateau? Tibetan Plateau
   b. What river begins in this plateau and flows through India into the Bay of Bengal?
   Ganges River

3. Locate and circle Japan, a country that is made up of 3,400 islands.
   a. What is the name for a group or chain of islands? archipelago
   b. Locate and name another group of islands in Asia. Philippine Islands, Indonesia

---

THE OTTOMAN EMPIRE

Read the following passage and answer the questions below. For help, you may refer to pages 388–391 in your textbook.

> In 1453 the Ottomans tried to capture the Byzantine city of Constantinople. The city had thick stone walls, with moats and ditches, and was surrounded on three sides by water. The Ottomans could not sail into the harbor because the Byzantines had blocked it with a heavy iron chain.
> The Ottoman leader, Muhammad II, had 70 light ships built and dragged on rollers overland to the Black Sea. The ships were then loaded with soldiers and guns. The Ottomans sailed the ships up to the city and attacked from the rear. They broke through the walls and captured the city. The last Byzantine emperor, Constantine, was killed.

1. Why was the city of Constantinople difficult to attack?
   It was surrounded on three sides by water and had thick stone walls, moats, and ditches; the Byzantines blocked the harbor with a chain.

2. How were the Ottomans able to capture the city?
   They attacked the city from boats that had been dragged on rollers overland to the Black Sea.

3. Why is the year 1453 considered a turning point in European history?
   The fall of Constantinople in 1453 ended the Byzantine empire and began a new era of Muslim rule in part of Europe.

4. Name two ways in which the Ottoman empire differed from the Byzantine empire.
   The Ottoman empire was Muslim, not Christian, and significantly larger and more prosperous than the Byzantine empire.

5. a. Under whose rule did the Ottoman empire reach its peak?
   under the rule of Sultan Süleyman

   b. How long did the Ottoman empire last?
   from 1453 to 1922

INDIA UNDER THE MOGULS

The following statements describe the Mogul emperor Akbar. On the lines provided write two facts that support each statement. For help, you may refer to pages 392–397 in your textbook.

1. Akbar was a successful military leader.
   He almost never lost a battle.
   He expanded the Mogul empire.

2. Akbar helped the farmers and businesspeople living in his empire.
   He created a unified money system. He varied the amount of taxes farmers had to pay and had canals and wells built.

3. Akbar made changes to improve life for the Hindus in the empire.
   He included Hindus in his government and abolished the special tax on non-Muslims. He allowed Hindus to build new temples.

4. Akbar was interested in learning about other religions.
   He built a special building where religious leaders of different faiths could meet. He participated in the heated debates.

5. Although he couldn't read, Akbar was interested in learning.
   He had a big library with custom-made translations of classics. He had someone read to him every day.

6. Akbar was a patron of the arts.
   He brought Asia's best artists to his palace and visited their workshops. He worked with the craftworkers, discussed paintings, and played the drums.

Akbar

T20

ANGKOR WAT: A CAPITAL CITY

Read the passage below and answer the questions. Refer to pages 398–401 in your textbook for more information about Angkor Wat.

> In January 1860 a young Frenchman, Henri Mouhot, was traveling by canoe and on foot through thick forests in Southeast Asia. He saw in the distance a huge stone building with five towers: the temple of Angkor at Angkor Wat. Exploring the ruins, he found sculptures of lions and elephants, huge walls of stone, and collapsed towers. The deserted ruins were overgrown by large trees and vines. "The howling of wild animals, and the cries of a few birds, alone disturb the solitude," he wrote.
>
> Mouhot caught a tropical fever and died in the forest, without ever knowing that he had discovered the largest religious monument in the world. His notebook, with sketches of Angkor Wat, was recovered and published in Europe, leading others to explore the ruins and eventually restore some of them.
>
> Mouhot had many questions about his discovery. Now the answers to these questions are known. Can you answer them?

1. Who built Angkor Wat?
   the king of the Khmer,
   Suryavarman II

2. Who discovered its remains in 1860?
   Henri Mouhot

3. What was Angkor Wat?
   a huge complex of temples,
   sculptures, and walls that
   expressed the Hindu religion

4. When and where was it built?
   in the early 1100s, in
   Cambodia, near the "Great
   Lake," or Tonle Sap

5. How was Angkor Wat designed?
   The temple was designed so
   that in spring the sun lit up
   the walls, which told stories
   about creation, and in winter
   the sun highlighted scenes
   describing death.

6. Why does Angkor Wat today contain both Buddhist and Hindu statues?
   Over time, Khmer rulers,
   beginning with Jayavarman
   VII, honored Buddhist
   beliefs.

KUBLAI KHAN

Compare and contrast two great empires of China. Complete the chart below by writing each item from the box in the correct column. For help, refer to pages 402–407 in your textbook.

> • 1368: rebel Chinese forces drove out Mongols
> • 1209–1227: Mongols gained control of northern China
> • expansion of Grand Canal
> • Kublai Khan
> • first all-paper money system
> • Forbidden City
> • porcelain and silk products
> • emperors
> • extension of Great Wall
> • made Silk Road safe for travel

	YUAN DYNASTY	MING DYNASTY
ORIGIN	1209–1227: Mongols gained control of northern China	1368: rebel Chinese forces drove out Mongols
LEADERS	Kublai Khan	emperors
BUILDING PROJECTS	expansion of Grand Canal	Forbidden City; extension of Great Wall
ACHIEVEMENTS	first all-paper money system; made Silk Road safe for travel	porcelain and silk products

Kublai Khan

Ming vase

MAKING GENERALIZATIONS

Practice making generalizations by completing the activities below. For help, you may refer to pages 408–409 in your textbook.

A. Marco Polo wrote the following about Kublai Khan's capital city.

> • The city . . . is a center from which many roads radiate to many provinces.
> • In every suburb . . . there are many fine hostels which provide lodging for merchants coming from different parts [of the world].
> • It is a fact that every day more than 1,000 cart-loads of silk enter the city; for much cloth of gold and silk is woven here.
> • More precious and costly wares are imported into [the city] than into any other city in the world.
> Translated by Ronald Latham, *The Travels of Marco Polo* (New York: Penguin Books).

Put an X in front of each generalization that is supported by the above information.

_____ Kublai Khan's capital was the biggest city in the world.

___X___ Kublai Khan's capital had many roads connecting it to the provinces.

___X___ Kublai Khan's capital was an important center of trade.

B. Marco Polo described how the nobles behaved in Kublai Khan's presence.

> • All those who are within half a mile from the Great Khan . . . show their reverence for his majesty by conducting themselves . . . peaceably, and quietly.
> • Every . . . nobleman continually carries with him a little vessel of pleasing design into which he spits so long as he is in the hall, so that no one may make so bold as to spit on the floor.
> • They have handsome slippers of white leather, which they carry about with them. When they have come to court . . . they put on these white slippers . . . so as not to dirty the beautiful and elaborate carpets of silk.
> Translated by Ronald Latham, *The Travels of Marco Polo* (New York: Penguin Books).

Write one generalization that is supported by the above information.

Possible answers: There were strict rules for proper behavior at
Kublai Khan's court; there were rules to keep Kublai Khan's court
quiet and clean.

LIFE IN FEUDAL JAPAN

Below is a social pyramid of feudal Japan. Explain the role of each person or group in the life of feudal Japan. If you need help, refer back to pages 410–415 in your textbook.

Feudal Japan

Emperor — ruled Japan in name only

Shoguns — ruled country as military dictators

Lords — controlled large pieces of land; served the shogun

Samurai — protected lords and their lands

Commoners — produced goods; showed respect to those above them

Culture flourished in feudal Japan. A popular form of poetry that was created at this time is called *haiku*. This is a short, unrhymed verse of three lines containing a total of 17 syllables in a 5, 7, and 5 pattern. Here is one example of haiku:

In the morning light
Purple rays of dawn creep down
Covering the earth.

On your own, or with a partner, write your own haiku.

Answers will vary.

USING NEW WORDS

Write each word or term from the box in front of its definition. For help, you may refer to the lessons in Chapter 14 in your textbook.

archipelago	grand mufti	samurai	shogun
Grand Canal	monsoon	Shinto	sultan

1. <u>a r c h i p e l a g o</u> group or chain of islands

2. <u>m o n s o o n</u> seasonal wind that brings rain

3. <u>s u l t a n</u> supreme ruler of Ottoman empire

4. <u>g r a n d m u f t i</u> Muslim religious leader

5. <u>G r a n d C a n a l</u> link between Huang and Chang rivers

6. <u>S h i n t o</u> Japanese religion

7. <u>s h o g u n</u> Japanese military commander

8. <u>s a m u r a i</u> Japanese soldier

GEOGRAPHY OF THE AMERICAS

Use the places listed in the box to complete the passage below. For help, you may refer to pages 422–425 in your textbook.

Amazon
Andes Mountains
Atlantic
Canadian Shield
Great Lakes
Isthmus of Panama
Pacific
Rocky Mountains

THE AMERICAS

The <u>Isthmus of Panama</u> connects North and South America. The two continents are similar in important ways. Both are bordered by the <u>Atlantic</u> Ocean on the east and the <u>Pacific</u> Ocean on the west. Both have extensive seacoasts with many harbors. Along the western side of each continent is a range of mountains. In North America the mountains are called the <u>Rocky Mountains</u>. In South America the mountains are called the <u>Andes Mountains</u>.

There are also differences between the two continents. In South America the mountains are higher and steeper than those in North America, so travel in South America is more difficult. South America has the world's largest rain forest, along the <u>Amazon</u> River. In North America there is a large area of rocky land, not suitable for farming, called the <u>Canadian Shield</u>. There are also large lakes. The five <u>Great Lakes</u> were carved out by glaciers, centuries ago.

THE AZTEC CULTURE

The picture shows an Aztec man and woman preparing for a feast. Use the picture and pages 426–431 in your textbook to answer the questions.

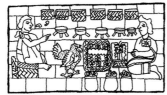

1. What kind of house did the people probably live in?
   a one-room stone or mud house

2. What kind of food might have been served at the feast?
   squash, tomatoes, chili peppers, and maize

3. Where did the people of the Aztec capital of Tenochtitlán grow their food?
   on chinampas, human-made islands, and along the shores of
   Lake Texcoco

4. What other source of food did the Aztec have?
   Conquered peoples were forced to send food as tribute.

5. The man and woman in the picture were probably members of the largest social group in Aztec society.

   a. What people were members of this group?
   farmers, merchants, craftworkers, and soldiers

   b. What groups had the lowest status in Aztec society?
   poor, landless farmers and slaves

   c. Who was at the top of Aztec society?
   the emperor

6. How important was religion to the Aztec?
   Religion played a central role in the lives of the Aztec. They
   built a Great Temple to honor their sun god and their rain god.

USING MAP PROJECTIONS

A projection is a way of placing parts of Earth on a flat map. Use the map below to answer the questions. For help, you may refer to pages 432–433 in your textbook.

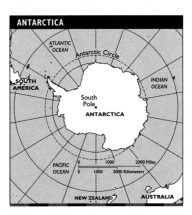

ANTARCTICA

1. a. Which continent is shown in the center of the map?
   Antarctica

   b. What other continents are shown on the map?
   Australia and South
   America

2. What three oceans are shown on the map?
   Atlantic, Pacific, Indian
   oceans

3. What is in the center of the map?
   the South Pole

4. a. What is this kind of map called?
   a polar projection map

   b. Who uses this type of map projection?
   navigators on airplanes
   that fly over the North or
   South Pole

5. What kind of map projection would you use to show the sizes of land masses?
   equal-area projection

THE INCA EMPIRE

Explain why each of the following items was important to the Inca. For help, you may refer to pages 434–439 in your textbook.

Cuzco

1. a. Why was Cuzco important?
It was the center of the Inca empire.

b. How did the Inca use their building skills to hold their empire together?
They built roads so people and news could travel quickly throughout the empire.

Quipu

2. a. What was the quipu used for?
keeping records

b. How did the quipu help the Inca rule their empire?
The quipu was a convenient and portable way to keep and transport records.

Mountain farming

3. a. How were the Inca able to grow food on hilly mountain slopes?
They constructed terraces, level platforms of earth that climbed each hill like a staircase.

b. What are some of the crops the Inca grew?
potatoes, maize, and peppers

Llamas

4. How did the Inca use the llama?
The llama was used as a pack animal to carry goods.

PEOPLES OF NORTH AMERICA: THE OJIBWA

The Ojibwa moved their villages to a different place each season of the year. Listed below are some of their other activities. Complete the calendar by matching each activity with the appropriate season. For help, you may refer to pages 440–445 in your textbook.

- collecting maple sap
- making maple syrup
- hunting deer, moose, bear, and fox
- fishing
- gathering nuts and berries
- harvesting wild rice
- smoking meat
- growing corn, beans, and squash
- making clothes out of animal skins

SPRING
collecting maple sap; making maple syrup

FALL
harvesting wild rice

SUMMER
fishing; gathering nuts and berries; growing corn, beans, and squash

WINTER
hunting deer, moose, bear, and fox; smoking meat; making clothes out of animal skins

---

USING NEW WORDS

Use the words in the box to answer the questions below. For help, you may refer to the lessons in Chapter 15 in your textbook.

chinampas	terraces	Triple Alliance
codex	Three Fires Council	tundra
diversity	timberline	wigwams
isthmus	tribute	quipus

1. What narrow strip of land connects North and South America? _isthmus_

2. What is the name of the treeless plain located in Alaska? _tundra_

3. Above what place on a mountain can trees not grow? _timberline_

4. Where did the Aztec grow food for the people who lived in Tenochtitlán?
chinampas

5. What did the Aztec force conquered people to pay them? _tribute_

6. The army of what group gained control of the entire Valley of Mexico?
Triple Alliance

7. What did the Aztec use to record information about their history, religion, and government? _codex_

8. What did the Inca build to help them grow crops on hilly slopes? _terraces_

9. What league was formed by the Ojibwa, the Potawatomi, and the Ottawa?
Three Fires Council

10. In what kind of homes did the Ojibwa live? _wigwams_

11. What word best describes the peoples who lived in North and South America before the arrival of the Europeans? _diversity_

12. What did the Inca use to keep records of trade throughout the empire?
quipus

EXPLORING THE UNIVERSE

Use the pictures below to answer the questions on this page. For help, you can refer to pages 456–460 in your textbook.

A. 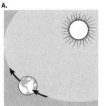 **B.**  **C.**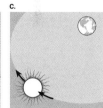

1. Which picture illustrates the geocentric theory? _C_

Why did most Europeans in the Middle Ages support this view?
The sun did appear to "rise" and "set" each day, while Earth didn't seem to move.

2. Which picture illustrates Copernicus's heliocentric theory? _A_

How did Galileo support this theory after he invented the telescope?
Viewing the stars and planets more closely through his telescope, Galileo concluded that Earth and other planets were spinning in orbit around the sun.

3. Which picture illustrates the force of gravity? _B_

How did Isaac Newton's studies of gravity help support the heliocentric theory?
Newton's studies helped to explain how the same force of gravity that pulled objects, such as an apple, toward Earth also pulled on the moon and kept it in orbit.

4. What were the long-term consequences of these scientific discoveries?
Scientific discoveries led to a new understanding of the universe, improvements in technology, and the development of the scientific method.

VOYAGES OF EXPLORATION

Use the map below to complete the activities that follow. For help, you can refer to pages 462–465 in your textbook.

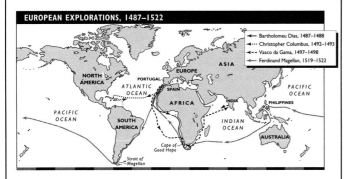

EUROPEAN EXPLORATIONS, 1487–1522

→ Bartholomeu Dias, 1487–1488
←••• Christopher Columbus, 1492–1493
←•– Vasco da Gama, 1497–1498
←– Ferdinand Magellan, 1519–1522

1. Write the name of the explorer next to the description of his voyage.
   a. Portugal to the southernmost tip of Africa **Bartholomeu Dias**
   b. Portugal around the Cape of Good Hope to India **Vasco da Gama**
   c. Spain through a strait at the tip of South America to the Pacific Ocean to the Philippines **Ferdinand Magellan**
   d. Spain to the Caribbean islands **Christopher Columbus**

2. How did the invention of the caravel help European explorers?
   The caravel enabled explorers to sail in almost any direction
   they wished.

3. Why were European explorers so eager to find an all-water route to Asia?
   Europeans wanted to find a trade route to Asia that was easier
   and faster than the land route along the Silk Road.

EXPLORING THE AMERICAS

Use the information in the box below to complete the chart. One entry has been filled in for you. Then answer the questions that follow. For help, you can refer to pages 466–471 in your textbook.

Pedro Álvarez Cabral	Francisco Pizarro	Hernando Cortés
present-day Mexico	near present-day Brazil	Christopher Columbus
conquest of Inca empire	conquest of Aztec empire	Hispaniola
beginning of Portuguese rule in Brazil	Andes Mountains	beginning of Spanish colonization in Americas

EXPLORER	LAND CLAIM	OUTCOME OF VOYAGE
Christopher Columbus	Hispaniola	beginning of Spanish colonization in Americas
Pedro Álvarez Cabral	near present-day Brazil	beginning of Portuguese rule in Brazil
Hernando Cortés	present-day Mexico	conquest of Aztec empire
Francisco Pizarro	Andes Mountains	conquest of Inca empire

1. What was the main goal of Spanish missionaries in the Americas?
   The missionaries wanted to convert the Indians to Catholicism.

2. What was life like for Indians who lived in the Spanish Americas?
   Many were forced to work on haciendas or in silver mines, and
   millions died of diseases brought over from Europe.

3. By the 1540s what two Spanish colonies dominated the Americas?
   New Spain and Peru

DETERMINING THE CREDIBILITY OF A SOURCE

Read the passages below. Then answer the questions to help determine the credibility of each source. Can the source be trusted for accuracy? For help, you can refer to pages 472–473 in your textbook.

A. Suppose that the following letter was written in the late 1500s by a Catholic priest asking to join a Spanish mission in the Americas.

I have heard from different sources that the Native Americans desire to serve our beloved Spain. The Indians, I have been told, are hungering for Christianity as well as Spanish culture. They are so anxious to become citizens of our honorable empire that they are begging for instruction. I pray that you will honor my request to join the mission and bless me in my great endeavor.

B. Suppose that the following letter was written in the late 1500s by a Catholic missionary in the Americas to a close friend in Spain.

We strive to bring the Native Americans into our villages to protect them from slave hunters and to teach them Christianity. Yet I am not so sure they understand what we are trying to do for them. I am not sure I understand myself. I always thought our goal was to save souls, but now I think the goal is to extend the realm of our empire.

1. Does the author have firsthand experience with the Native Americans? Explain.
   No, the author's information
   comes from other sources.

2. Does the author have a specific goal in mind? Explain.
   Yes, the author's goal is to
   convince the reader to let
   him join a mission.

3. Do you think the author's information about the Native Americans is credible? Explain.
   No, the author has never
   met the Native Americans
   and is portraying them in a
   certain way.

4. Does the author have firsthand experience with Native Americans? Explain.
   Yes, the author teaches
   them Christianity.

5. Does the author have a specific goal in mind? Explain.
   No, the author is confiding
   in a friend.

6. Do you think the author's information about the Native Americans is credible? Explain.
   Yes, the author is writing
   from firsthand experience
   and has no reason to give
   false or distorted
   information.

THE TRIANGULAR TRADE

The Triangular Trade was a network of trade routes. Use the map below to help you answer the questions that follow. Refer to pages 474–477 in your textbook.

TRIANGULAR TRADE ROUTES

1. What areas of the world were linked by the Triangular Trade routes?
   North America, West Indies, Europe, and West Africa

2. For what European goods did some West Indian plantation owners trade sugar?
   They traded sugar for fine furniture or cloth.

3. What part of the Triangular Trade route was the Middle Passage?
   the voyage from Africa's west coast across the Atlantic Ocean
   to the West Indies

4. What were conditions like for kidnapped slaves who traveled along the Middle Passage?
   They were chained up in overcrowded sections of the ship and
   fed spoiled food and unclean water. Many did not survive the
   journey.

5. Why were enslaved Africans important to colonies in the West Indies?
   Sugarcane plantations depended on slave labor to clear forests
   for planting, hoe the soil, harvest the sugarcane, and load
   barrels with sugar.

THE SUCCESS OF NEW SOUTH WALES

Answer the following questions about the colonization of New South Wales and discover how Australia became an important democracy in the Southern Hemisphere. Refer to pages 478–481 in your textbook.

1. Who was James Cook and what did he do?

   James Cook was a respected English navigator who searched for Australia and claimed land for Great Britain there, naming it New South Wales.

2. Why were many people sent to New South Wales at first?

   English jails were overcrowded and the government decided to send many of its prison convicts to work there.

3. What were some of the beliefs of the aborigines and how were these people affected by the arrival of the colonists?

   The aborigines believed in the "dreamtime" and that land could not be owned by just one person. They were almost wiped out by the guns and diseases that the settlers brought with them from Europe.

4. Who were the emancipated people and who helped them win rights in the new colony?

   The emancipated people were former convicts from England who had been freed from their sentences in Australia. Governor Lachlan Macquarie supported them in their efforts to win their rights.

5. What two events led to the development of democracy in Australia?

   The creation of a legislative body with the New South Wales Act of 1823 and the right for free settlers and emancipated people to vote in 1842.

6. When and where did women win the right to vote in Australia?

   The women of South Australia won the right to vote in 1894.

SOME WORDS ABOUT EUROPEAN EXPANSION

Answer each question on the lines provided. For help, you can refer to Chapter 16 in your textbook.

1. a. How do the **heliocentric** and **geocentric** views of the universe differ?

   In the heliocentric view the sun is the center of the universe; in the geocentric view Earth is the center.

   b. How did Galileo's **telescope** and Newton's studies of **gravity** help support the heliocentric view of the universe?

   The telescope enabled scientists to study the movement of the stars and planets; gravity helped explain how a heliocentric universe works.

2. What is the **scientific method**?

   The scientific method is a way of learning about nature by questioning, studying, and thoroughly testing an idea.

3. How did Prince Henry's **caravel** help explorers?

   The caravel enabled explorers to sail in almost any direction.

4. What is a **strait**? **A strait is a narrow channel between two larger bodies of water.**

5. Who tried to **convert** the Native Americans—**conquistadors** or the **missionaries**?

   the missionaries

6. What was the purpose of the **Line of Demarcation**?

   to divide Spain's and Portugal's land claims in the Americas

7. Was **sugarcane** grown on **haciendas** or on **plantations**?

   Sugarcane was grown on plantations in the West Indies.

8. What role did the **Middle Passage** play in the **Triangular Trade**?

   The Middle Passage was the part of the Triangular Trade that carried enslaved Africans to the West Indies.

9. Was an **emancipee** formerly an **aborigine** or a **convict**?

   a convict

THE EVENTS OF THE FRENCH REVOLUTION

Something that makes something else happen is a cause. What happens as the result of a cause is called an effect. Fill in the missing cause or effect in the sentence pairs below. If you need help, refer to pages 486–491 in your textbook.

1. **Cause:** **The king has complete power to govern.**

   Effect: The three estates, or social classes, in France become dissatisfied with the king and his government.

2. **Cause:** The king wants to raise money by taxing the nobles.

   Effect: **The nobles refuse and demand a meeting of the Estates General.**

3. **Cause:** People think the king is sending troops to break up the National Assembly.

   Effect: **The people storm the Bastille to get weapons to defend themselves.**

4. **Cause:** The National Assembly issues the Declaration of the Rights of Man and of the Citizen.

   Effect: **The absolute monarchy is abolished, and France becomes a republic.**

5. **Cause:** **Catholic priests and others angered by the Assembly refuse to support the revolution.**

   Effect: Robespierre wages a Reign of Terror against his enemies.

6. **Cause:** The Reign of Terror leaves many people hoping for peace and stability.

   Effect: **The army gains power, and Napoleon takes control of the republic.**

Write another cause and effect sentence pair about the French Revolution.

Possible answer: Cause—The ideas of "Liberty, Equality, Fraternity" spread throughout the world. Effect—National freedom movements begin in many countries.

REVOLUTIONS IN THE AMERICAS

Use the information in the box below to complete the chart. Then answer the questions that follow. For help, you can refer to pages 492–497 in your textbook.

Bolivia	Chile	Haiti
Mexico	Panama	Ecuador
Venezuela	Colombia	Argentina Peru
end slavery		
freedom from France		
freedom from Spain		

REVOLUTIONARY LEADER	COUNTRY OR COUNTRIES	REASON OR REASONS FOR REVOLUTION
Toussaint L'Ouverture	Haiti	end slavery freedom from France
Miguel Hidalgo	Mexico	end slavery freedom from Spain
José de San Martín	Argentina, Chile	freedom from Spain
Simón Bolívar	Venezuela, Colombia, Bolivia, Panama, Ecuador, Peru	freedom from Spain

1. What complaints against European nations did many Latin American colonies share?

   The Europeans took their minerals and crops and gave little in return. The colonies also disliked paying taxes without having a say in the government.

2. What change occurred in Canada in 1867?

   The Canadian provinces formed a confederation that was free to govern itself, although ultimate authority rested with the British crown.

REVOLUTIONIZING INDUSTRY AND SOCIETY

Use the pictures on the left and the information on pages 500–505 in your textbook to complete the activities below.

1. Explain how textile machines helped revolutionize industry.

   Machines made it possible for workers to produce textiles quickly and cheaply.

2. Give a reason why factories were built.

   Factories were needed to house the new machines, which were too big to fit into a farmer's cottage.

3. Explain how the locomotive contributed to the spread of industry.

   It increased trade because goods could be shipped greater distances in less time.

4. Describe the contributions of the middle and working classes to the British economy.

   The middle class increased trade and manufacturing by running businesses and services; the working class helped manufacture goods.

USING CARTOGRAMS

A cartogram is a special kind of map used to compare information about countries. On a cartogram the size of a country is related to the information that is being compared. Use the cartogram below to answer the questions. Refer to pages 506–507 in your textbook.

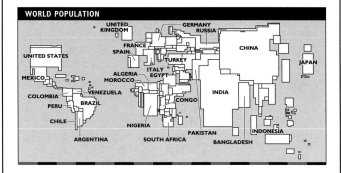

WORLD POPULATION

1. What information does the cartogram show?

   populations of countries

2. How can you tell that India has a larger population than the United States?

   India's size is larger than that of the United States.

3. Which country has the largest population in the world?

   China

4. Which nation has more people, Argentina or Brazil?

   Brazil

5. What additional information would you need to tell whether Russia is more crowded than Japan?

   the area of both Russia and Japan in relation to their populations

6. Which African country has the largest population?

   Nigeria

A CHANGING JAPAN

Japan experienced rapid changes in its government, military, economy, and culture from the mid-1800s to the early 1900s. Complete the diagram by writing each activity from the box below in the appropriate category. Refer to pages 508–513 in your textbook.

Meiji Restoration	Feudal customs break down
Japan invades Korea	Charter Oath is issued
Diet is created	Japan attacks Chinese
Railroads link major cities	mainland
Japanese begin to wear	Japan exports silk and tea
suits or dresses	Japan enters into war
Western-style architecture	against Russia
becomes popular	Cotton mills are built

Government

Meiji Restoration

Charter Oath is issued

Diet is created

Military

Japan invades Korea

Japan attacks Chinese mainland

Japan enters into war against Russia

A Changing Japan

Economy

Railroads link major cities

Japan exports silk and tea

Cotton mills are built

Culture

Japanese begin to wear suits or dresses

Western-style architecture becomes popular

Feudal customs break down

REVOLUTIONS AROUND THE WORLD

Write the letter of the term that is not related to the other three. Then write a sentence to show how the three remaining terms are related. For help, you can refer to the lessons in Chapter 17 of your textbook.

d 1. **a.** divine right   **b.** revolution   **c.** absolute monarchy   **d.** socialism

Possible answer: The absolute monarchy in France and the king's belief in the divine right to rule led to revolution in France.

b 2. **a.** peasants   **b.** Meiji Restoration   **c.** aristocracy   **d.** estates

Possible answer: The peasants and aristocracy belonged to different estates, or social classes, in France.

c 3. **a.** Reign of Terror   **b.** Bastille   **c.** imperialism   **d.** Declaration of the Rights of Man and of the Citizen

Possible answer: Three important events of the French Revolution were the storming of the Bastille, the writing of the Declaration of the Rights of Man and of the Citizen, and the Reign of Terror.

d 4. **a.** Latin America   **b.** mestizos   **c.** revolutions   **d.** bureaucracy

Possible answer: Many revolutions in Latin America were carried out by mestizos.

c 5. **a.** textiles   **b.** factories   **c.** confederation   **d.** Industrial Revolution

Possible answer: During the Industrial Revolution the demand for textiles led to the building of factories.

c 6. **a.** middle class   **b.** working class   **c.** aristocracy   **d.** Industrial Revolution

Possible answer: As a result of the Industrial Revolution, the middle class became more important and life for the working class became more difficult.

CAUSES AND EFFECTS OF WORLD WAR I

Each sentence pair below states a cause-effect relationship. Write **C** next to the sentence that states the cause and **E** next to the sentence that states the effect. For help, you can look back at pages 526–531 in your textbook.

1. __C__ **a.** Nationalism and tensions among European countries increased in the early 1900s.

   __E__ **b.** To prepare for the possibility of war, the countries of Europe trained armies and formed alliances.

2. __C__ **a.** A Serbian nationalist assassinated Archduke Franz Ferdinand, heir to the throne of Austria-Hungary.

   __E__ **b.** Austria-Hungary and its ally, Germany, declared war on Serbia.

3. __C__ **a.** German submarines sank the *Lusitania,* and German diplomats plotted an alliance with Mexico against the United States.

   __E__ **b.** The United States declared war on Germany and the other Central Powers.

4. __E__ **a.** Bloody battles were fought in trenches, at sea, and in the air.

   __C__ **b.** During World War I most warring nations had access to modern technology.

5. __E__ **a.** Germans were angry and felt alienated from the rest of Europe.

   __C__ **b.** The Treaty of Versailles blamed Germany for the war and forced the country to pay enormous fines.

Write a cause-effect sentence pair about life on the "home front" during World War I.

Possible answer: Daily life on the home front changed.

Governments controlled food supplies; people went hungry as a

result of high food prices; women went to work in the factories.

FROM RUSSIA TO THE SOVIET UNION

The sentences in the box describe conditions and changes in Russia before and after the Revolution of 1917. Write each sentence in the appropriate column. Then add a sentence of your own to each column. For help, refer to pages 532–539 in your textbook.

- Wealthy nobles owned most of the farmland.
- Private property, including farms, was outlawed.
- Moscow was the capital.
- St. Petersburg was the capital.
- Collective farms were created.
- Serfdom was abolished.
- Communist leaders established a totalitarian society.
- Tsars ruled as absolute monarchs.
- Factory workers protested grim working conditions.
- The nation became an industrial power.

Before the Russian Revolution	**After the Russian Revolution**
Wealthy nobles owned most of the farmland.	Private property, including farms, was outlawed.
St. Petersburg was the capital.	Moscow was the capital.
Serfdom was abolished.	Collective farms were created.
Tsars ruled as absolute monarchs.	Communist leaders established a totalitarian society.
Factory workers protested grim working conditions.	The nation became an industrial power.
Possible answer: Most Russians lived as they had in the Middle Ages.	Possible answer: Churches were closed and religious leaders arrested.

WORLD WAR II HEADLINES

The newspaper headlines below relate to events that occurred before, during, and after World War II. Answer the questions beneath each headline. For help, refer to pages 540–547 in your textbook.

Hitler and Nazis Gain Control of Germany

a. In which year would this headline have been written? 1933

b. Which factors aided Hitler's rise to power?

Germany was economically depressed, and the Germans

longed to make their country great again.

German Tanks Roll into Poland! Britain and France Declare War on Germany!

a. In what month and year would this headline have been written? September 1939

b. Who were the Allies and the Axis nations?

The Allies included Britain, France, the Soviet Union, China, and

the United States; the Axis included Japan, Germany, and Italy.

Japanese Bomb Pearl Harbor

a. In which month and year would this headline have been written? December 1941

b. How did the United States react to this attack?

The United States entered World War II on the side of the Allies.

Concentration Camp Prisoners Freed

a. In which two countries were concentration camps built during World War II?

Germany and Japan

b. To what does the term Holocaust refer?

The Holocaust refers to the deliberate destruction of human

life in Nazi concentration camps.

Write two newspaper headlines that might have been printed during World War II.

Possible answers: Allied Forces Invade Normandy; U.S. Bombs

Hiroshima; Japan Surrenders.

USING TIME ZONE MAPS

The world is divided into 24 time zones. Use the map to answer the questions on this page. For help, refer to pages 548–549 in your textbook.

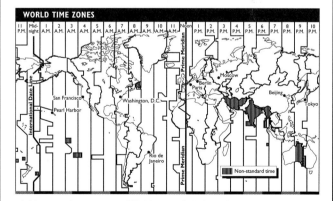

1. How many time zones east of Washington, D.C., is Berlin, Germany?

   six time zones

2. When German leaders surrendered in Berlin at 2:41 A.M. on May 7, 1945, what were the time and date in Washington, D.C.?

   8:41 P.M., May 6, 1945

3. When the Japanese bombed Pearl Harbor in Hawaii at about 8:00 A.M. on December 7, 1941, what were the time and date in Tokyo, Japan?

   3:00 A.M., December 8, 1941

4. Why would people traveling from Tokyo to Honolulu find that they were traveling "back in time"?

   When you travel east across the International Date Line, you

   subtract a day so that today becomes yesterday.

5. When it is 4:00 A.M. in San Francisco, what time is it in Washington, D.C.?

   In Paris, France? 7:00 A.M. in Washington; 1 P.M. in Paris

T27

THE BELIEFS OF MAO ZEDONG

The quotations below are from Mao Zedong, founder of Communist China. Read the quotations carefully. Then complete the activities that follow. For help, you can look back at pages 550–555 in your textbook.

> War is the highest form of struggle for resolving contradictions when they have developed to a certain state, between classes, nations, states, or political groups, and it has existed ever since the emergence of private property and of classes.
>   We are advocates of the abolition of war; we do not want war, but war can only be abolished through war, and in order to get rid of the gun it is necessary to take up the gun. . . . When classes and states are eliminated there will be no more wars.
>
> George Seldes, "Quotations from Chairman Mao," *The Great Thoughts* (New York: Ballantine Books, 1985).

1. Put an **X** next to each sentence that describes Mao Zedong's beliefs about war.
   - __X__ **a.** The only way to end a war is to fight the war.
   - _____ **b.** War is the worst way to resolve problems.
   - __X__ **c.** Social classes and private property are responsible for causing wars.
   - __X__ **d.** Peace can be achieved by eliminating classes and states.

2. When and how did Mao and his Communist followers gain control of China?
   After years of civil war, Mao and the Communists drove the Nationalists from mainland China to the island of Taiwan.

3. How did Mao's "Great Leap Forward" affect life in China?
   Farmers and their families were forced to join communes and take on additional tasks such as steel production. The plan failed, and economic conditions worsened.

4. What were some effects of the Cultural Revolution?
   Many Chinese people were terrorized, and traditional religious and cultural beliefs were destroyed.

FANNING THE COLD WAR

Listed below are five problems that caused tension between the United States and the Soviet Union. How did the superpowers react in each Cold War situation? Complete each box below. For help, you can look back at pages 556–561 in your textbook.

1. **Problem:** Stalin forces Eastern European countries to accept communist government.
   United States Reaction: United States and European allies form NATO.

2. **Problem:** North Korea invades South Korea.
   United States Reaction: United States sends troops to help United Nations troops fight North Koreans.

3. **Problem:** Thousands of East Germans move to West Berlin.
   Soviet Reaction: East German police build a concrete wall between East and West Berlin.

4. **Problem:** Soviet leader Khrushchev sends nuclear missiles to Cuba.
   United States Reaction: President Kennedy orders Soviet ships to stay out of Cuban waters and places American forces on full alert.

WARS AND REVOLUTIONS

Write the letter of the term that is not related to the other three. Then write a sentence using the remaining three related terms. Refer to the lessons in Chapter 18.

__c__ 1. **a.** nuclear arms race   **b.** superpowers   **c.** free enterprise   **d.** Cold War
   During the Cold War the superpowers engaged in a nuclear arms race.

__a__ 2. **a.** warlord   **b.** NATO   **c.** Warsaw Pact   **d.** United Nations
   Despite growing tensions, the member nations of the Warsaw Pact and NATO remained members of the United Nations.

__b__ 3. **a.** Long March   **b.** alliance   **c.** communes   **d.** Cultural Revolution
   Mao Zedong led the Long March, created communes, and began the Cultural Revolution in China.

__a__ 4. **a.** tsar   **b.** inflation   **c.** depression   **d.** fascism
   High inflation and economic depression helped bring about the rise of fascism in post-World War I Europe.

__d__ 5. **a.** World War II   **b.** Axis   **c.** Allies   **d.** Korean War
   The Axis Powers fought the Allies during World War II.

__d__ 6. **a.** propaganda   **b.** nationalism   **c.** communism   **d.** strike
   Propaganda and nationalism helped advance communism.

__a__ 7. **a.** Russian Revolution   **b.** Central Powers   **c.** World War I   **d.** Allied Powers
   In World War I the Central Powers fought the Allied Powers.

__c__ 8. **a.** Treaty of Versailles   **b.** League of Nations   **c.** totalitarian   **d.** armistice
   After the armistice that ended World War I, the Treaty of Versailles was signed and the League of Nations was formed.

__b__ 9. **a.** Holocaust   **b.** alliance   **c.** concentration camps   **d.** World War II
   During World War II millions of Jews died in concentration camps in what became known as the Holocaust.

INDEPENDENCE IN AFRICA

Use the information in the box and the maps to complete the sections below. For help, you can look back at pages 566–571 in your textbook.

- Accra
- Suez Canal
- Cairo
- cotton
- slave trade
- military control of government
- boycotts of British goods
- strikes against British companies
- seizure of Suez Canal
- Kwame Nkrumah
- Gamal Abdel Nasser
- gold
- cacao

GHANA

EGYPT

Importance to Britain: slave trade, gold, cacao

Leader of independence movement: Kwame Nkrumah

Methods used to gain independence: boycotts of British goods, strikes against British companies

Capital city: Accra

Importance to Britain: cotton, Suez Canal

Leader of independence movement: Gamal Abdel Nasser

Methods used to gain independence: military control of government, seizure of Suez Canal

Capital city: Cairo

T28

INTERPRETING POLITICAL CARTOONS

The political cartoon below was drawn by Thomas Nast, an artist who lived in the United States in the late 1800s. Look at the words and symbols in the cartoon. Then answer the questions that follow. For help, look at pages 572–573 in your textbook.

"Peaceful Neutrality: The Position of England and France on the Suez Canal"

1. You read about the Suez Canal in Lesson 1. Why was it so important to European countries?

   The Suez Canal connects the Red Sea and the Mediterranean

   Sea, thus providing a short route for ships sailing between

   Europe and Asia.

2. What are the two countries arguing about?

   control over the Suez Canal

3. The pyramid in the picture is used to represent Egypt. Why is the British leader standing on Egypt's side of the Suez Canal?

   Egypt was a British colony.

4. The caption to the cartoon reads "Peaceful Neutrality: The Position of England and France on the Suez Canal." Do you think the cartoonist felt that the countries were really at peace?

   Possible answer: No; Nast portrayed the countries as

   mistrustful and ready to fight to defend their claims.

HISTORY OF THE MIDDLE EAST

Use the information in the box to complete the chart below. Then answer the question at the bottom of the page. For help, you can look back at pages 574–578 in your textbook.

- Yasir Arafat and Yitzhak Rabin sign a peace agreement.
- The PLO begins its fight to regain land from Israel.
- The Republic of Turkey is established.
- Israel becomes an independent nation.
- Egypt and Israel sign the Camp David agreement.
- Israel gains Gaza, the Golan Heights, and the West Bank.
- Iraq becomes an independent nation.
- Palestinians in Gaza and the West Bank begin the Intifada.
- Yitzhak Rabin is assassinated.

CHANGES IN THE MIDDLE EAST	
YEAR	EVENT
1923	The Republic of Turkey is established.
1932	Iraq becomes an independent nation.
1948	Israel becomes an independent nation.
1967	Israel gains Gaza, the Golan Heights, and the West Bank.
1968	The PLO begins its fight to regain land from Israel.
1977	Egypt and Israel sign the Camp David agreement.
1987	Palestinians in Gaza and the West Bank begin the Intifada.
1993	Yasir Arafat and Yitzhak Rabin sign a peace agreement.
1995	Yitzhak Rabin is assassinated.

What is a primary cause of conflict between Palestinians and Jews over the area that is today Israel?

Both groups want to create a nation in the area that was once

their ancient homeland.

INDEPENDENCE IN INDIA

You have been asked to write an entry about independence in India for an almanac titled *The World Book of Facts*. The editor of the almanac has asked you to write answers to the following questions. For help, you can refer to pages 580–585 in your textbook.

The Great Mutiny

Q: In what year did the Great Mutiny spread across India?
A: 1857

Q: Prior to the Great Mutiny, who controlled most of India?
A: the East India Company, known as the Raj

Q: Why was India such a desirable colony?
A: India provided raw materials for British industries and a market for British goods.

Mohandas Gandhi

Q: When did Gandhi become an important leader in India?
A: 1915

Q: What were Gandhi's three goals for India?
A: independence from British rule, peace between Muslims and Hindus, and an end to mistreatment of the untouchables

Q: What are two examples of how Indians practiced civil disobedience?
A: The Indians boycotted British goods and refused to pay taxes.

Independence

Q: On what day did India and Pakistan gain independence?
A: August 15, 1947

Q: Why were two independent countries formed?
A: As a result of Hindu-Muslim conflicts, the Muslims were granted their own country—Pakistan.

Q: What changes took place in India after independence?
A: The Green Revolution boosted agriculture, the untouchable caste was abolished, and women gained new rights.

BEFORE AND AFTER THE VIETNAM WAR

Use the events in the box to complete the columns below. Then answer the questions that follow. For help, you can refer to pages 586–591 in your textbook.

- United States withdraws from Vietnam.
- Vietnam becomes French colony.
- Ho Chi Minh leads communist revolt.
- Communists seize control of South Vietnam.
- South Vietnamese flee communism.
- Vietnamese invade Cambodia.
- Vietnam is divided into North and South Vietnam.
- United States sends advisers to South Vietnam.

Before the Vietnam War	After the Vietnam War
Vietnam becomes French colony.	United States withdraws from Vietnam.
Ho Chi Minh leads communist revolt.	Communists seize control of South Vietnam.
Vietnam is divided into North and South Vietnam.	South Vietnamese flee communism.
United States sends advisers to South Vietnam.	Vietnamese invade Cambodia.

1. Why did the United States participate in the Vietnam War?

   The United States wanted to prevent the spread of

   communism.

2. How did the relationship between Vietnam and the United States change in the 1990s?

   In 1995 Vietnam and the United States began to trade and have

   diplomatic relations.

PUZZLING WORDS

Use the terms in the box and the clues to complete the crossword puzzle below. For help, you can refer to the lessons in Chapter 19 in your textbook.

Vietnam War	boycott	refugee
civil disobedience	Zionism	Raj
Green Revolution	anti-Semitism	Intifada

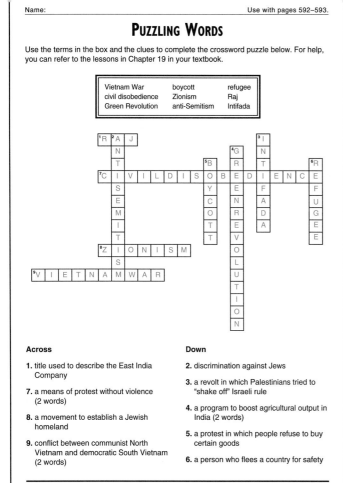

Across

1. title used to describe the East India Company

7. a means of protest without violence (2 words)

8. a movement to establish a Jewish homeland

9. conflict between communist North Vietnam and democratic South Vietnam (2 words)

Down

2. discrimination against Jews

3. a revolt in which Palestinians tried to "shake off" Israeli rule

4. a program to boost agricultural output in India (2 words)

5. a protest in which people refuse to buy certain goods

6. a person who flees a country for safety

THE FALL OF COMMUNISM IN EUROPE

Fill in the diagram below. Using the events in the box, explain what "miracle" happened in each of the countries in 1989, the "Year of Miracles." Then answer the question that follows. For help, you can refer back to pages 596–603 in your textbook.

Hungary
Soviet troops stand by as the country plans free elections in January.
In May people tear down an electric fence separating their country from democratic Austria.

Czechoslovakia
In November police beat students who were singing "We Shall Overcome."
By December citizens freely elect two new leaders who had been imprisoned.

1989: Year of Miracles

Poland
Workers' group, led by Lech Walesa, is recognized by government.
Solidarity party wins many seats in Parliament.

Germany
Erich Honecker steps down from office.
East Berlin opens its gates to West Berlin.

- In November police beat students who were singing "We Shall Overcome."
- By December citizens freely elect two new leaders who had been imprisoned.
- Soviet troops stand by as the country plans free elections in January.
- In May people tear down an electric fence separating their country from democratic Austria.
- Workers' group, led by Lech Walesa, is recognized by government.
- Solidarity party wins many seats in Parliament.
- Erich Honecker steps down from office.
- East Berlin opens its gates to West Berlin.

Describe three changes that took place in Eastern Europe after the "Year of Miracles."

The Soviet republics declared their independence, ethnic conflicts broke out in Yugoslavia, and the European Union pledged to help its eastern neighbors build their economies.

EVALUATING INFORMATION FOR ACCURACY

The excerpt below is from a newspaper article written by reporter Mike O'Connor. The article discusses the progress of peace in Bosnia-Herzegovina since the Dayton peace accord ended the war there. Read the article. Then answer the questions that follow to evaluate the information for accuracy. For help, refer to pages 604–605 in your textbook.

KRUSCICA, Bosnia-Herzegovina—Hundreds of Bosnian Muslims who had returned to homes they fled in the war have been driven out again, officials said Sunday.

Over the last two weeks, the people of this village, who had been forced to leave by Bosnian Croats in 1993, have been coming back. . . . Sunday, though, the end of the short success story became clear. By the end of the day, the last of the Muslims had been forced to leave by groups of Croatian thugs.

. . . U.N. officials said they were puzzled by both the sudden opening and the just-as-sudden end of cooperation. . . . "Croat politicians can help to implement the peace agreement or they can shut the whole thing down," said a U.N. official, speaking on condition of anonymity.

Mike O'Connor, "Bosnian Muslims Driven Out of Homes a Second Time," *The New York Times*, August 4, 1997.

1. What is the reporter's purpose in writing this article?

to describe the difficulties faced by these Bosnian Muslims and to show the problems of the peace agreement

2. How does the reporter view the situation of the Bosnian Muslims? How does he view the Bosnian Croats?

He thinks the Muslims are being treated unfairly and that the Croats are being uncooperative and cruel to the Muslim refugees.

3. Which words in the article show the reporter's opinion of the Bosnian Croats?

Croatian thugs

4. What are two facts that the reporter states in the article?

Possible answers: Muslims had been forced to leave their homes in 1993; the Muslim refugees were forced to leave again on Sunday.

5. What other sources could you use to determine the accuracy of the article?

Possible answer: articles written by other newspaper and magazine reporters as well as other observers of the war

---

DEMOCRACY IN SOUTH AFRICA

Write the events listed in the box in the correct place on the chart. Then answer the questions that follow. For help, you can refer back to pages 606–612 in your textbook.

- Black students lead protest in Soweto.
- The government bans the African National Congress (ANC).
- South Africa gains full independence from Britain.
- De Klerk abolishes most apartheid laws.
- World leaders begin to impose sanctions against South African government.
- South Africans elect Nelson Mandela president.
- President Frederik Willem de Klerk releases Nelson Mandela from prison.
- White leaders create system of apartheid.

CHANGES IN SOUTH AFRICA	
YEAR	**EVENT**
1948	White leaders create system of apartheid.
1960	The government bans the African National Congress (ANC).
1961	South Africa gains full independence from Britain.
1976	Black students lead protest in Soweto.
1980s	World leaders begin to impose sanctions against South African government.
1990	President Frederik Willem de Klerk releases Nelson Mandela from prison.
1991	De Klerk abolishes most apartheid laws.
1994	South Africans elect Nelson Mandela president.

1. How did the system of apartheid discriminate against blacks in South Africa?

Blacks lost their land and were forced into townships; blacks could not attend white schools; black workers received poor wages.

2. What changes have occurred in South Africa since apartheid was ended?

The government is building new homes for poor people; all-white schools have been opened to all races; all South African citizens can vote.

THE PACIFIC RIM NATIONS

The chart below describes the economic growth of some countries in the Pacific Rim. Complete the chart by writing the name of the country next to the entries that tell about it. Use the names on the map. If you need help, refer to pages 614–621 in your textbook.

PACIFIC RIM NATIONS

COUNTRY	FACTORS THAT AIDED THE ECONOMY	ECONOMY TODAY
Japan	demand for goods during Korean War; United States aid; good schools; government policies and investment	second highest GDP in world
South Korea	factories produced inexpensive clothes and shoes; complex technology	builds cars, electronics, and steel products
Singapore	tight government controls over society	giant in world trade; prosperous electronics industry
China	foreign companies set up businesses; farmers were given more control over their work	communist, but moving to free enterprise
Hong Kong	center for international trade as a former British colony	thriving, but future uncertain under Chinese control since 1997
Australia	ideal sheep grazing land; strong mineral exports; partnership with United States	large exports of computer parts; pioneer in solar research

---

WORKING TOGETHER IN THE AMERICAS

Listed below are challenges facing the Americas in the second half of the 1900s. Explain what the different countries in the Americas have done, or are doing, to meet each challenge. Refer to pages 622–629 in your textbook.

THE AMERICAS

1. **Challenge:** Many Latin countries were ruled by dictatorships.
   Action: In the 1980s democratic movements swept through the Americas, overthrowing the dictatorships.

2. **Challenge:** Much of Brazil's rain forest was destroyed by farming, logging, mining, and ranching.
   Action: Brazil's government is working with other nations to preserve the rain forests and to create jobs in the Amazon that are friendly to the environment.

3. **Challenge:** Crime organizations are involved in an illegal drug trade that brings little money to farmers who raise the coca plants used to make cocaine.
   Action: The United States and other nations are trying to stamp out the drug trade by destroying coca fields and helping farmers raise other crops.

4. **Challenge:** There is a need for closer ties and greater unity among the United States, Canada, and Mexico.
   Action: In 1993 NAFTA went into effect to increase trade by lowering taxes on goods traded among these countries.

What are some of the challenges the Americas face in the year 2000?

Possible answer: Latin American countries face the challenge of improving life for its people, many of whom are poor, unemployed, and living in overcrowded cities. Canada faces a challenge from French Canadians who want Quebec to form a separate country. The United States must define its role as a world power.

TERMS FROM THE MODERN WORLD

Match the terms with their meanings. Write the letter of the correct term next to its definition. For help, you can refer to the lessons in Chapter 20 in your textbook.

a. ethnic group	**d.** apartheid	**g.** European Union	**j.** NAFTA
b. per capita income	**e.** township	**h.** Internet	**k.** Pacific Rim
c. interdependent	**f.** bilingual	**i.** urbanization	**l.** sanction
	m. gross domestic product (GDP)		

___b___ 1. the amount of money each person of a country would have if that country's total income were equally apportioned

___g___ 2. a group of Western European nations working to build a common economy

___l___ 3. a penalty placed against a nation to make it change its policies

___d___ 4. a system of laws that discriminated against black South Africans

___e___ 5. crowded areas in which South African blacks were forced to live

___k___ 6. the ring of countries surrounding the Pacific Ocean

___c___ 7. the dependence of countries on each other to meet the needs and wants of their peoples

___a___ 8. people who share a heritage of common customs, values, and language

___i___ 9. the growth of cities

___h___ 10. a group of interconnected computers around the world

___f___ 11. the ability to speak two languages

___j___ 12. agreement among the United States, Canada, and Mexico designed to increase trade

___m___ 13. goods and services produced in a country

CONTENT

Fill in the circle before the correct answer.

1. Culture is a people's _____.
   ⓐ way of life   ⓑ technology   ⓒ region   ⓓ geography

2. A *climate region* is marked by similarities in _____.
   ⓐ customs   ⓑ landforms   ⓒ longitude   ⓓ weather

3. What is one thing that helps make up a cultural region?
   ⓐ physical boundaries   ⓒ weather
   ⓑ language   ⓓ economy

4. Which fact about the boy Azeez shows what is meant by a *custom*?
   ⓐ He lives in a city.   ⓒ He never eats meat.
   ⓑ He is Indian.   ⓓ He has a brother.

5. Which is an example of cultural change in India?
   ⓐ Some Indian families now have temples in their homes.
   ⓑ Indian schoolchildren are learning to play musical instruments.
   ⓒ Indian women, especially in cities, have more freedom than before.
   ⓓ Many Indians speak Hindi.

Write the word or phrase from the box that best answers each question.

representative democracy	physical region	English
political region	cultural value	

6. What kind of region is the Mississippi River valley? _physical region_

7. In 1990, when East and West Germany joined to become the Federal Republic of Germany, what type of region was changed? _political region_

8. Most Hindus believe that all living things have souls. This is an example of a _cultural value_.

9. From what you learned in this chapter, what do many people in both Ireland and Canada speak? _English_

10. What kind of government does India have? _representative democracy_

SKILLS

Latitude and longitude are sometimes used to set boundaries between countries, states, and other areas. Use the map below to answer the questions. Write your answers on the lines.

LATITUDE AND LONGITUDE MAP

1. The southwestern corner of Tennessee is located at _35° N, 90° W_.

2. 110°W marks the boundary between which two Canadian provinces?
   Alberta and Saskatchewan

3. The point 40°N, 100°W lies on the boundary between what two states?
   Kansas and Nebraska

4. The southernmost point in the continental United States shown on this map lies in what state and at about what latitude and longitude?
   Florida; 25° N, 80° W

5. What three states meet at about 42°N, 120°W?
   Oregon, California, and Nevada

WRITING

Write a short paragraph to answer each question. If you need more room, continue writing on the back of this page.

1. Use the map below to describe the continent of Australia in terms of climate regions.

CLIMATE REGIONS OF AUSTRALIA

See answer at right.

_____
_____
_____
_____
_____
_____

2. What is the difference between customs and culture? Give examples of each in your answer.
   See answer at right.

_____
_____
_____
_____
_____
_____

WRITING ANSWERS

1. An adequate response will describe the five climate regions of Australia with some indication of their location. (Example: The northernmost parts of Australia have a tropical climate. The central part of Australia has desert and semi-dry climate regions. Two parts of the southern coast have a warm and rainy climate with a dry summer, and the eastern coast has a warm and rainy climate.) An excellent response will also describe the kinds of weather most likely to be found in these climate regions. (Examples: The tropical region is hot and humid. The desert and semi-dry regions are hot and dry.)

2. An adequate response will explain that culture is a people's way of life, while customs are things that people practice regularly. It will also give at least one example of each. For example, many of the peoples of Latin America share a common culture because they speak Spanish and share the same religion. Examples of customs might include types of food that people eat, how they dress, holidays they celebrate, and religious practices. An excellent response will further explain that culture is largely based on a people's beliefs, values, and ethnic heritage, and customs are daily or regular habits that reflect cultural values. Also, all cultures are made up of many different customs.

CONTENT

Fill in the circle before the correct answer.

1. Which is a *primary source* for learning about pioneer life?
   - Ⓐ a history textbook
   - Ⓒ a book based on pioneers' stories
   - Ⓑ an encyclopedia article
   - Ⓓ a letter by a pioneer woman

2. What is one problem faced by people who study ancient history?
   - Ⓐ Many important sources have been destroyed or lost.
   - Ⓑ There are no written records from ancient times.
   - Ⓒ Most of the sources are primary sources.
   - Ⓓ The original purpose of most artifacts is unknown.

3. What information about an archaeological sample can be obtained by carbon-14 testing?
   - Ⓐ how old it is
   - Ⓒ what it is made of
   - Ⓑ how quickly it decayed
   - Ⓓ what climate it is from

4. What made the "Iceman" discovery so interesting to archaeologists?
   - Ⓐ The man had died in an accident.
   - Ⓑ The man's clothing and possessions were preserved with him.
   - Ⓒ The body was the first ever found in the Alps.
   - Ⓓ The man's ax was made of copper and chipped stone.

5. How did archaeologists figure out what the Iceman's net was used for?
   - Ⓐ They found prehistoric pictures of people using that kind of net.
   - Ⓑ They studied the objects discovered near it.
   - Ⓒ They compared it to a kind of net still in use in the region today.
   - Ⓓ They tried fishing and catching birds with it.

Write the letter of the definition that best fits each term.

6. __d__ excavate

7. __c__ oral tradition

8. __b__ artifact

9. __e__ archaeology

10. __a__ prehistory

a. the time before writing was developed

b. an object made by someone in the past

c. the practice of passing on history from one person to another by word of mouth

d. to uncover by digging carefully

e. the study of the remains of past cultures

SKILLS

Read the following journal entry. It tells about a new site an archaeologist has come upon by accident. Then write your answer to each question.

> I was out for a hike when I came upon a large rock that had been moved by the recent heavy rains. Where the rock had been was the entrance to a cave. I looked in and could hardly believe my eyes! In a hollowed-out place in the back wall were a number of scrolls. One had fallen to the floor and was partly open, but I could not see clearly enough to identify the writing. I was very excited. What if the scrolls were made by the same people as those we had found earlier?
>
> I debated whether or not to enter. Entering could be dangerous, especially since erosion from the rains could have weakened the cave walls. On the other hand, if the cave collapsed or became flooded, the scrolls could be lost forever. If I went in, I could at least look at the writing and make some drawings. I did not have any equipment with me, not even my camera. To remove the scrolls without first mapping the site would break one of the first rules of archaeology.
>
> I finally decided to run back to the village and alert the rest of the team. They arranged for the needed equipment while I returned to the cave with my camera and began taking pictures from the entrance.

1. What was the archaeologist's goal after discovering the new site?

   to examine the scrolls, or to find out who made the scrolls

2. What decision did the archaeologist have to make?

   whether or not to enter the cave

3. What were two things that were considered in making the decision?

   the hazards of entering the cave, the risk of losing the scrolls if the cave

   collapsed or flooded, and whether or not to remove the scrolls

4. What did the archaeologist eventually decide to do?

   go for help, then return to the cave (with a camera)

5. Do you think the right decision was made? Tell why or why not.

   Answers will vary but should be supported by reasonable arguments and

   information from the journal entry.

WRITING

Read the selection. Then write a short paragraph to answer each question. If you need more room, continue writing on the back of this page.

As a boy, Alex Haley heard many family stories about a long-ago ancestor named Kinte [kin-tay]. "The African" had been kidnapped while out cutting wood, shipped across the ocean, and sold into slavery in America. He never resigned himself to being a slave; when he later had a daughter, he told her about Africa and taught her his words for everyday things. The daughter told her children, and they told their children, and so on through the years.

In 1965, Haley decided to find out if the stories were true. His main clues were the African words passed down through the family. This evidence led him to a village in Gambia, where he found an old man who could recite the history of the Kinte clan. Haley listened in amazement as the man told of a young man named Kunta Kinte, who in 1767 had gone out to cut wood and never been seen again. Haley had found his ancestor's people!

Haley could not stop there. He kept hunting through historic documents such as ships' logs and plantation records. Eventually he learned the name of the ship that had brought Kinte to America. He even found the papers recording Kinte's sale to a new master! Haley's 1976 book *Roots* tells the story, from Kunta Kinte's boyhood through Haley's own birth in 1921. Haley combined the facts, the family stories, and details from his own imagination to come up with a powerful tale from American history.

1. Describe the sources Alex Haley used in learning about his family's history. Tell what kind of source each one was and how it helped him.

   See answer at right.

2. Suppose that 1,000 years from now, archaeologists discover a copy of *Roots*. Do you think it would be a good source of information about American history? Tell why or why not.

   See answer at right.

WRITING ANSWERS

1. An adequate response will mention at least one example of oral tradition and at least one primary source, and it will explain how these sources helped Haley. An excellent response will cite more examples of oral tradition and primary sources. Examples: (a) The family stories were oral tradition. They gave him basic information and the clues needed to start his research. (b) The African man who knew the clan history was also part of oral tradition. His information told Haley where his ancestor came from. (c) The historic documents (ships' logs, plantation records, sales record) were primary sources. They helped prove that the stories were true.

2. An adequate response will tell whether *Roots* would be a good source or not and give at least two supporting reasons. An excellent response will consider both sides of the argument, make a decision one way or another, and support the decision with several examples. Points in favor of *Roots* as a source include its basis in fact and the number of years of history it covers. Points against it include the facts that much of it is based on Haley's imagination and that it tells one family's story from one point of view.

T34

CONTENT

Fill in the circle before the correct answer.

1. About how many years ago did the New Stone Age begin?
   ⓐ 12 thousand   ⓑ 40 thousand   ⓒ 600 thousand   ⓓ 2 million

2. Once people learned to build fires, they were able to _____.
   ⓐ hunt animals for food   ⓒ make their homes in caves
   ⓑ survive in cold climates   ⓓ make tools

3. Art from ancient times becomes especially important when _____.
   ⓐ there are no written records from those times
   ⓑ it shows what people looked like
   ⓒ it is in excellent condition
   ⓓ no one has seen it before

4. The surplus food produced by agriculture meant that _____.
   ⓐ less land was needed for farming use
   ⓑ farmers had more time for other activities
   ⓒ everyone had to become farmers
   ⓓ nonfarmers were free to develop other important skills

5. Stone Age people used technology when they _____.
   ⓐ saw lightning start a fire   ⓒ shaped stones to use in hunting
   ⓑ found shelter in caves   ⓓ gathered grass for bedding

Write the letter of the conclusion about Stone Age life that best fits each clue.

6. __e__ Animal bones were found together with Old Stone Age tools.

7. __a__ The Border Cave people made beads.

8. __c__ Many of Catal Huyuk's buildings were temples.

9. __d__ The people of Catal Huyuk produced woven wool cloth.

10. __b__ Obsidian products from Catal Huyuk were found in Syria, and Syrian pottery was found in Catal Huyuk.

a. The Border Cave people valued beautiful objects, not just useful ones.

b. The people of Catal Huyuk traded with the people of Syria.

c. Religion was an important part of daily life.

d. People had domesticated sheep or had learned to breed sheep for thicker wool.

e. People had learned how to hunt.

SKILLS

Use the time line to answer the questions.

EARLY BREAKTHROUGHS IN FARMING

10,000 B.C.   8000 B.C.   6000 B.C.   4000 B.C.

First crops planted c. 9000 B.C.   Cattle domesticated c. 7000 B.C.   Irrigation invented c. 6000 B.C.   Plow invented c. 4000 B.C.

1. About how many years does this time line cover?   6,000 years

2. About how many years passed between the first crops planted and the invention of irrigation?   3,000 years

3. What name do archaeologists use for the period covered by most of this time line?   New Stone Age

4. When was the plow invented?   4,000 B.C.

5. Put an X beside the conclusion you can draw from this time line.
   _____ People did not use cattle for food after 7000 B.C.
   _____ Cattle were domesticated between 10,000 B.C. and 7000 B.C.
   __X__ Before 9000 B.C. people did not grow their own food.
   _____ Before irrigation was invented, people did not plant crops.

WRITING

Write a short paragraph to answer each question. If you need more room, continue writing on the back of this page.

1. This drawing from a prehistoric rock carving in Arizona shows a group of people and some sheep. What do you think is happening in the picture? What conclusions can you draw from the picture?

Source: *Canyon de Chelly: Its People and Rock Art* by Campbell Grant, University of Arizona Press, 1978

   See answer at right. _____
   _____
   _____
   _____
   _____

2. Imagine that you are a New Stone Age hunter-gatherer. You have never seen a city until, one day, you come upon Catal Huyuk. Describe what you see when you enter the city. What is most surprising or interesting to you? How do you feel about it?

   See answer at right. _____
   _____
   _____
   _____
   _____

WRITING ANSWERS

1. An adequate response will note that the people seem to be herding sheep and therefore had begun to domesticate animals, and that they used tools (rocks and something like a whip). An excellent response will draw further conclusions. Examples: The people of that culture had learned to work together. Also, they liked to create art to depict such scenes.

2. An adequate response will mention the number or structure of the buildings and the existence of craftworkers. The response should include both literal details and subjective impressions. An excellent response will include more detail and show a greater awareness of the contrast between the nomadic hunter-gatherer life and early city life.

CONTENT AND SKILLS

Fill in the circle before the correct answer.

1. To understand Earth better, geographers divide it into different types of _____.
   ⓐ landforms   ⓑ regions   ⓒ customs   ⓓ peoples

2. Contact between two cultures that often leads to cultural change is called _____.
   ⓐ cultural interaction   ⓒ cultural region
   ⓑ oral history   ⓓ values

3. A surplus is _____.
   ⓐ an extra supply   ⓒ a group of farmers
   ⓑ an early harvest   ⓓ an ancient settlement

4. The work of historians is similar to that of detectives because they both _____.
   ⓐ display artifacts in museums   ⓒ use clues to solve mysteries
   ⓑ create primary sources   ⓓ study ancient cultures

5. Archaeologists knew that people at Border Cave had made contact with people from the coast when they found _____.
   ⓐ stone tools   ⓒ animal bones
   ⓑ a seashell bead   ⓓ a painting of the ocean

6. Why did archaeologists working at the Iceman site melt the snow and filter the water?
   ⓐ They wanted to see if the water was clean.
   ⓑ They did not want to lose any evidence.
   ⓒ They needed drinking water.
   ⓓ They wanted to clean the Iceman.

7. Bits of sulfur and iron, which are used to make matches, were found in a piece of fungus carried by the Iceman. This suggests that the Iceman _____.
   ⓐ was a miner   ⓒ traded with other people
   ⓑ invented matches   ⓓ knew how to make fire

8. What important development began in the New Stone Age?
   ⓐ agriculture   ⓑ cave painting   ⓒ stone tools   ⓓ fire

9. People training to do different kinds of work is an example of _____.
   ⓐ archaeology   ⓑ specialization   ⓒ technology   ⓓ agriculture

10. Archaeologists learn about the people of the Stone Ages by studying _____.
    ⓐ oral history   ⓑ maps   ⓒ diaries   ⓓ artifacts

CONTENT AND SKILLS

Suppose that you are studying the history of your community. Match the type of source to each example of information by writing the letter on the line.

11. __b__ primary source
12. __d__ secondary source
13. __a__ oral tradition
14. __c__ artifact

a. a story of long ago told by a resident of the area
b. a diary written by one of the founders of the community
c. an object from the past found at a construction site
d. a TV documentary about people who lived in the area

Use the map to answer questions 15–17.

15. What type of region does this map illustrate?
    physical

16. What is the location (longitude and latitude) of Caracas?
    about 10° N, 70° W

17. What kind of landform would you find in Bogotá?
    mountains

Write the term that best fits each description on the left.

18. refers to the years since Jesus' birth __A.D.__   B.C.

19. refers to the years before Jesus' birth __B.C.__   A.D.

20. means "around" or "about" __circa__   circa

WRITING

Write a short paragraph to answer each question. If you need more room, continue writing on the back of this page.

1. Look at this sketch of a prehistoric archaeological site. What can you tell about the culture of the people who once lived in this settlement?

See answer at right.
_____
_____
_____
_____
_____

2. Suppose that you have to make a decision about whether or not to spend next summer working at an archaeological dig. Describe the steps you would take to make the decision.

See answer at right.
_____
_____
_____
_____
_____
_____

WRITING ANSWERS

1. An adequate response should note that the people (a) raised grain and animals (indicated by the grain storage building and animal pens); (b) had developed a formal religion (indicated by the temple); and (c) had begun to develop specialization, or crafts (indicated by the workshops). An excellent response will connect these observations to other concepts and/or include more complex observations and speculations. Examples: The existence of agriculture and specialization indicates a New Stone Age (or later) site; the size of the temple complex indicates the importance of religion; the orderly arrangement of the public buildings suggests cooperation or planning in constructing that part of the settlement.

2. An adequate response will indicate that the student would set a goal, consider alternatives, and make a decision. An excellent response will apply these steps to the question of whether or not to work at an archaeological dig for the summer.

T36

CONTENT

Fill in the circle before the correct answer.

1. Hieroglyphics helped Egyptian scribes keep records of _____.
   - (a) history
   - (b) speeches
   - (c) flooding
   - (d) taxes

2. Egyptian farmers used irrigation to _____.
   - (a) water their crops
   - (b) make the soil more fertile
   - (c) control flood waters
   - (d) travel among villages

3. In Egypt's Old Kingdom what did craftworkers and artists receive in return for the objects they made for the pharaohs?
   - (a) land
   - (b) clothes and food
   - (c) money
   - (d) golden bowls and stone statues

4. The Middle Kingdom is best described as a time when Egypt _____.
   - (a) first developed a written language
   - (b) began to use irrigation techniques
   - (c) increased contact with other cultures
   - (d) became a wealthy empire

5. In ancient Egypt most of the land and farms were owned by _____.
   - (a) hard-working farmers
   - (b) skilled craftworkers
   - (c) Nubians and Syrians
   - (d) government officials

Write the letter of the description that best fits each pharaoh.

6. __c__ Hatshepsut
7. __b__ Menes
8. __e__ Ahmose
9. __a__ Khufu
10. __d__ Tutankhamun

a. ordered the construction of the Great Pyramid

b. unified Egypt by overthrowing the king of Lower Egypt and became the first pharaoh

c. organized a two-year expedition to Punt, expanding trade beyond the Egyptian empire

d. ruled as a wealthy young pharaoh from about age 9 to 19

e. studied the Hyksos and used their weapons to drive them back out of Lower Egypt

---

SKILLS

Use the maps to answer the questions. Write your answers on the lines.

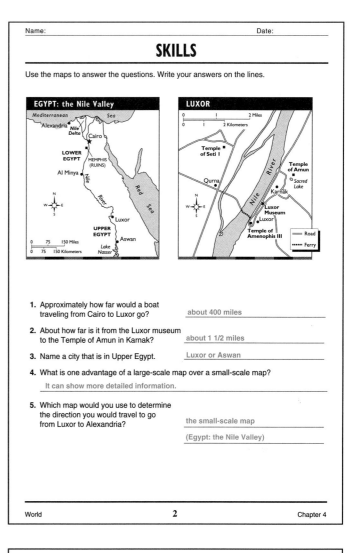

EGYPT: the Nile Valley

LUXOR

1. Approximately how far would a boat traveling from Cairo to Luxor go?

   about 400 miles

2. About how far is it from the Luxor museum to the Temple of Amun in Karnak?

   about 1 1/2 miles

3. Name a city that is in Upper Egypt.

   Luxor or Aswan

4. What is one advantage of a large-scale map over a small-scale map?

   It can show more detailed information.

5. Which map would you use to determine the direction you would travel to go from Luxor to Alexandria?

   the small-scale map

   (Egypt: the Nile Valley)

WRITING

Write a short paragraph to answer each question. If you need more room, continue writing on the back of this page.

1. How did the development of hieroglyphics affect ancient Egyptian culture? Tell what hieroglyphs were used for and how hieroglyphics changed Egyptian culture.

   See answer at right.
   _____
   _____
   _____
   _____

2. Look at the map of Egypt. Where would you expect to find the best farmland? Tell why.

   EGYPT

   See answer at right.
   _____
   _____
   _____
   _____

WRITING ANSWERS

1. An adequate response will explain that hieroglyphs were used for recording taxes and making calculations. These uses changed Egyptian culture by making complex accounting possible and by extending government control over its people. An excellent response will mention other uses of hieroglyphs (such as, writing letters and recording medical procedures and treatments). It will also explain other ways in which the use of hieroglyphs changed Egyptian culture. For example, it made possible the building of the pyramids, communicating over long distances, developing sophisticated medical knowledge, and inventing a calendar.

2. An adequate response will specify that the best farmland can be found along the Nile River, especially in the delta area of Lower Egypt, and will tell why. For example, the river brings down silt to fertilize the land and water for irrigating fields. An excellent response will also analyze the potential of other areas. For example, the land around Lake Nasser does not receive the benefits of flooding, but at least there is water. Much of the rest of Egypt is desert that offers neither good soil nor water.

CONTENT

Fill in the circle before the correct answer.

1. In ancient Sumer each city-state had a ziggurat where people went to _____.
   - (a) learn to write cuneiform
   - (b) worship a special god or goddess
   - (c) trade with people from other cities
   - (d) buy clothes and food

2. What factor made it especially difficult to farm in southern Mesopotamia?
   - (a) unskilled laborers
   - (b) droughts and irregular floods
   - (c) not enough sunshine
   - (d) rocky, infertile soil

3. The Code of Hammurabi was a _____.
   - (a) set of laws
   - (b) form of writing
   - (c) type of alphabet
   - (d) system of taxes

4. The Israelites left Canaan and went to Egypt in order to _____.
   - (a) escape slavery
   - (b) conquer Egypt
   - (c) find food
   - (d) own land

5. Nineveh was important because it became the _____.
   - (a) capital city of Babylonia
   - (b) only city that defeated Egypt
   - (c) birthplace of Judaism
   - (d) first city-state in Sumer

Read each sentence and write the name from the box of the person it describes.

| Gilgamesh | Sargon | Hammurabi | Abraham | Moses |

6. This king of Babylon dammed parts of the Euphrates River and attacked the Sumerians. **Hammurabi**

7. According to the Bible, this Hebrew prophet grew up in Egypt and traveled to Mount Sinai, where he was given the Torah. **Moses**

8. He was an important hero to the Sumerians. **Gilgamesh**

9. This king of Kish used cuneiform to expand his empire and unite the other city-states. **Sargon**

10. According to the Bible, the history of the Jewish people began when this man traveled to Canaan and made a covenant, or agreement, with God. **Abraham**

SKILLS

Read the passage. Then complete the chart below by writing in the missing causes and effects.

The Sumerians lived in an environment with limited resources. Southern Mesopotamia was very hot and dry, receiving hardly any rain each year. Trees cannot grow in such a place. Even rocks were hard to find. The Sumerians needed to find another material from which to build shelter. Fortunately, sunshine and clay were plentiful. As a result, the Sumerians packed moist clay into molds and left it to dry in the sun. Since the flat bricks could then be stacked, they were used to form the walls of buildings.

Because the Sumerians were not happy with the way the sun-dried bricks eventually crumbled, they found a better way to work with the clay. They found out that if they baked the bricks, they were harder and lasted longer. Using a natural material called asphalt to join the bricks, they could make a long-lasting wall. The Sumerians built massive and long-lasting ziggurats, parts of which have survived four thousand years. As a result, archaeologists can study these remains to learn about the Sumerians.

CAUSES	EFFECTS
1. They had plenty of materials for making clay, or they did not have any other materials for building.	1. The Sumerians made buildings out of clay.
2. The Sumerians made flat bricks that could be stacked.	2. They were used to form walls.
3. The sun-dried bricks eventually crumbled.	3. The Sumerians experimented with baked bricks.
4. The Sumerians used asphalt to join the bricks.	4. They made long-lasting walls.
5. Parts of the ziggurats they built have lasted four thousand years.	5. Archaeologists can study about the Sumerians from their remains.

WRITING

Write a short paragraph to answer each question. If you need more room, continue writing on the back of this page.

1. Describe the contributions of ancient Mesopotamian culture to our world today.

   See answer at right.

2. Much of Mesopotamia is now called Iraq. Today most of Iraq's people live in cities, some live in villages, and a few travel with their herds of animals (mostly sheep). Look at the map of Iraq. Based on what you have learned about farming and the development of cities, where would you expect most of the people of Iraq to live? Tell why.

IRAQ

   See answer at right.

WRITING ANSWERS

1. An adequate response will mention that the people of Mesopotamia developed a system of writing and a code of laws, and they invented both the wheel and irrigation. An excellent response will mention less obvious contributions, such as the development of schools, literature, and science.

2. An adequate response will indicate that most of the population lives in the lower plains along the major rivers and will give a logical reason. For example, towns and cities tend to prosper in areas where there is plenty of food, and farmers in Iraq are much more likely to succeed along the rivers than in other areas. An excellent response will provide more detail. For example, it might indicate that the population would be considerably smaller in the mountains where the soil is poor or in the desert where there is no water for crops. It might also refer to ancient Mesopotamia and the fact that it developed between the Tigris and Euphrates rivers, which still provide water and transportation.

CONTENT

Fill in the circle before the correct answer.

1. Archaeologists say that Mohenjo-Daro and Harappa might have been abandoned because of _____.

   (a) war (b) drought (c) invaders (d) an earthquake

2. Much of the water that floods the Indus River comes from _____.

   (a) tides in the Arabian Sea (c) rain falling on the Indus Plain

   (b) snow in the Himalayas (d) streams in the Hindu Kush Mountains

3. What clue makes historians think that Mohenjo-Daro had a strong government?

   (a) sewer system design (c) location of the city

   (b) weavers' use of cotton (d) skill of the metalworkers

4. Why do historians know less about the Harappan civilization than they know about ancient Egyptian or Mesopotamian civilization?

   (a) People of the Harappan civilization did not trade with other cultures.

   (b) The written records have not been translated.

   (c) The Harappans did not construct large buildings.

   (d) No written records have survived the harsh climate.

5. Buddhism differs from Hinduism in that Buddhists believe _____.

   (a) all people go through a cycle of life, death, and rebirth

   (b) karma is a force based on people's behavior and affects their future lives

   (c) the most important goal is to reach peace by ending suffering

   (d) there is one powerful force that connects all life

Write the term that best completes each sentence: Vedas, caste, dharma, monk, Buddhism.

6. The laws and duties of members of each caste described in the Vedas are called dharma .

7. A special group within Hindu society is called a caste .

8. A monk is a man who gives up his possessions and devotes his life to a religious group.

9. Ancient Aryan songs that became the beginnings of Hinduism were written down in the Vedas .

10. The teachings of Siddhartha Gautama became the basis of Buddhism .

SKILLS

Use the maps to answer the questions. Write your answers on the lines.

INDIA: PHYSICAL MAP

INDIA: AGRICULTURAL MAP

1. What is a primary use of the land along the Ganges River in northern India?

   farming

2. What is a primary use of land around Calcutta?

   farming

3. In which area of India is cotton the main crop?

   Deccan Plateau

4. What important crops are grown on the Northern Plains?

   cattle, barley, sugarcane

5. Where are the main areas of unused land in India located?

   in the northwest (Thar Desert) and far north (Himalayan Mountains)

WRITING

Write a short paragraph to answer each question. If you need more room, continue writing on the back of this page.

1. Look at the information about Pakistan's industries today. What similarities do you see between the economy of the ancient Indus Valley civilization and the economy of the country that exists in the same area today?

   CHIEF INDUSTRIES IN PAKISTAN TODAY

   • **Wheat**—the country's most important crop—is grown by farmers to feed their families

   • **Cotton-cloth manufacturing**—the country's second most important crop

   • **Food processing**—for example, milling grains, refining sugar, and producing vegetable oil

   • **Fertilizer production**

   • **Cigarettes**

   • **Carpets**

   • **Steel**

   See answer at right.

2. Describe the growth of agriculture in the ancient Indus Valley civilization.

   See answer at right.

WRITING ANSWERS

1. An adequate response should indicate the similarity between the importance of food and cotton production in ancient times and modern times. An excellent response will address each of the industries in the chart. Example: As in ancient times, Pakistani farmers grow food to feed their families. Cotton was and is a very important crop. Residents of the ancient cities were also involved with weaving cloth from cotton. The industries of fertilizer production, cigarette making, carpet making, and steel production were not a part of ancient life, although metalworkers did exist. Other craftworkers existed, just as part of the population in modern Pakistan works in manufacturing.

2. An adequate response will mention at least three features of life in the Indus Valley. Example: In the Indus Valley, farmers were usually able to use irrigation to grow two crops each year. Animals were domesticated and their use enabled farmers to plow larger fields. Cotton was grown and used to make cloth for the first time. An excellent response will detail other crops, such as rice, bananas, black pepper, mustard, and sesame. It will also note that farming began in the Indus Valley around 6000 B.C.

CONTENT

Fill in the circle before the correct answer.

1. In ancient China oracle bones were used by the Shang people to _____.
   - ⓐ record history
   - ⓒ win wars
   - ⓑ cure illnesses
   - ⓓ predict the future

2. During which time period did rulers first apply Confucian ideas about fairness and learning?
   - ⓐ Qin dynasty
   - ⓒ Han dynasty
   - ⓑ Shang dynasty
   - ⓓ Huang civilization

3. What was the main form of agriculture on the steppes north of the Huang Valley?
   - ⓐ herding sheep and cattle
   - ⓒ raising horses
   - ⓑ growing rice and other grains
   - ⓓ cultivating fruits

4. Loess created problems for Huang Valley farmers because it _____.
   - ⓐ poisoned the water
   - ⓒ left fine silt on the fields
   - ⓑ clogged irrigation ditches
   - ⓓ soaked up all the rainwater

5. The ancient huts uncovered by archaeologists at Anyang were once used for _____.
   - ⓐ workshops
   - ⓑ prisons
   - ⓒ storehouses
   - ⓓ temples

Read each sentence and write the name from the box of the person it describes.

Fu Hao	Shihuangdi	Han Gaozu	Confucius	Wudi

6. This emperor of the Han dynasty created schools to prepare people for government jobs.   **Wudi**

7. This teacher said that rulers must be wise and good, just as their subjects must be respectful.   **Confucius**

8. Archaeologists found the tomb of this woman, who was a leader of troops, a ruler of her town, and a king's wife.   **Fu Hao**

9. Although he was successful in creating a strong government, China's first emperor is remembered for his harsh rule.   **Shihuangdi**

10. This general was originally a farmer, before he led rebel armies to overthrow the Qin dynasty.   **Han Gaozu**

SKILLS

Read the passage below. Then answer the questions about writing a summary.

China is so large that many different forms of Chinese are spoken within its borders. People in one part of the country might not be able to understand people in another part. To help his people understand one another, an emperor named Shihuangdi set up a single system of writing that everyone in his empire could read. This form of writing, which is still used today, contains about 50,000 characters. It does not have an alphabet. In an alphabet each character stands for a sound. In Chinese each character stands for a thing or an idea, such as *house* or *down*. Using these characters, people in China could communicate with one another, even if they could not understand one another's spoken words. This standard form of writing helped Shihuangdi unite the people in such a vast region. It is one of the reasons the ancient nation of China has endured for so many centuries.

1. Which is the topic sentence of this passage?
   "To help his people understand one another, an emperor named Shihuangdi set up a single system of writing that everyone in his empire could read."

2. What supporting details tell you that the emperor's system of writing was important to China?
   It helped unite the people, and it has helped China endure for centuries.

3. Which sentence or sentences do not directly relate to the topic?
   "It does not have an alphabet. In an alphabet each character stands for a sound."

4. What is the purpose of the first sentence of this paragraph?
   It explains why people in China do not always understand one another.

5. Write one or two sentences to summarize this passage.
   Example: Shihuangdi developed a standard written form of Chinese so that people across his empire could communicate with one another.

WRITING

Write a short paragraph to answer each question. If you need more room, continue writing on the back of this page.

1. Explain how government was organized during the Han dynasty.
   See answer at right.

2. The three maps below make it clear that the growth of China was tied to control of the Huang and Chang rivers. Why was control of the rivers so important?

CHINA: Three Dynasties
— Boundary of present-day China
1200 B.C.   SHANG DYNASTY
221 B.C.   QIN DYNASTY
A.D. 100   HAN DYNASTY
0 500 1,000 Miles
0 500 1,000 Kilometers
East China Sea   Bay of Bengal   South China Sea

   See answer at right.

WRITING ANSWERS

1. An adequate response will describe how during the Han dynasty, emperors adopted some of the ideas of Confucianism, such as the view that a subject must respect the ruler, but the ruler must be wise and good. Han emperors also wanted to lessen the power of nobles and rule fairly. An excellent response will explain how the Han emperor Wudi created schools to prepare people for government service, so educated people—not just nobles—got government jobs.

2. An adequate response will explain that control of the rivers was important because the rivers made farming successful and served as protective geographic boundaries. An excellent response will explain these reasons in more detail. For example, the success of farming was important because it allowed for greater population and more farmers to help build and defend the growing empire. It may also mention that control of the rivers allowed rulers to control trade and transportation in and out of the empire.

CONTENT AND SKILLS

Fill in the circle before the correct answer.

1. The ancient Egyptians filled the tombs of their pharaohs with treasures to _____.
   - (a) use the tombs as museums
   - (b) take with them to the afterlife
   - (c) keep the treasures safe from looters
   - (d) show them respect

2. Menes was known as the pharaoh who _____.
   - (a) unified Egypt
   - (b) conquered Mesopotamia
   - (c) invented hieroglyphs
   - (d) destroyed Egyptian culture

3. In the ancient world of the Fertile Crescent, the Israelites' religion was different because they believed in _____.
   - (a) an afterlife
   - (b) many gods
   - (c) only one God
   - (d) reincarnation

4. Egypt's economy was based on _____.
   - (a) religion
   - (b) banking
   - (c) manufacturing
   - (d) farming

5. Farming in Mesopotamia was made possible by _____.
   - (a) two rivers
   - (b) constant rain
   - (c) many lakes
   - (d) a dry climate

6. Based on the layout of the city and its advanced engineering, historians believe that Mohenjo-Daro had _____.
   - (a) good schools
   - (b) strong local government
   - (c) frequent wars
   - (d) problems with earthquakes

7. The teachings of Siddhartha Gautama were the basis of _____.
   - (a) Hinduism
   - (b) Confucianism
   - (c) Buddhism
   - (d) Christianity

8. During the Shang dynasty in ancient China, land was owned by the _____.
   - (a) nobles
   - (b) farmers
   - (c) monks
   - (d) soldiers

9. Shihuangdi helped to unify China by setting up a single system of _____.
   - (a) farming
   - (b) irrigation
   - (c) schools
   - (d) writing

10. During the Han dynasty in China, great schools of learning were created by _____.
    - (a) Shihuangdi
    - (b) Han Gaozu
    - (c) Wudi
    - (d) Fu Hao

CONTENT AND SKILLS

For questions 11–16 choose the term from the box that best completes each sentence.

Moses	Rosetta Stone	Hammurabi	Aryans	Abraham	Vedas

11. The Bible describes how __Abraham__ traveled from Mesopotamia to Canaan and made a covenant with God.

12. __Hammurabi__ established a code of law in the Babylonian empire.

13. __Aryans__ migrated to India around 1500 B.C.

14. The __Rosetta Stone__ was the key that helped historians understand hieroglyphics.

15. According to the Bible, __Moses__ led the Israelites out of slavery in Egypt.

16. Among Hindus the __Vedas__ are the "Books of Knowledge."

For questions 17–20 write your answer to each question on the lines.

17. Name two religions based on a belief in reincarnation.

    Hinduism and Buddhism

18. Write a summary of one or two sentences telling how the use of hieroglyphics and cuneiform changed the cultures of the ancient Egyptians and Sumerians.

    Hieroglyphics and cuneiform enabled the Egyptians and Sumerians to keep

    records of surpluses and taxes and communicate across long distances.

19. If you planned to walk around a city to visit its historic sites, what kind of map would give you the best level of detail?

    large-scale map

20. Write a summary telling why loess was a blessing and a curse to Chinese farmers.

    It made the soil very fertile, but it washed away easily; it also caused flooding

    and blocked canals.

WRITING

Write a short paragraph to answer each question. If you need more room, continue writing on the back of this page.

1. Look at the physical map of river valley civilizations in parts of the ancient world. Explain why the Shang people in ancient China probably did not have contact with the people of other cultures, such as those on the Mediterranean Sea, the Red Sea, and the Indus River.

RIVER VALLEY CIVILIZATIONS

   See answer at right.

   _____
   _____
   _____
   _____

2. In what ways did flooding affect agriculture in the ancient civilizations of Egypt, Mesopotamia, the Indus River valley, and China? What advantages did the floods offer? What were the disadvantages?

   See answer at right.

   _____
   _____
   _____
   _____
   _____
   _____

WRITING ANSWERS

1. An adequate response should state that the distance and physical barriers made contact unlikely, and it will identify at least two barriers. An excellent response will also compare the travel routes among other civilizations to those of China. Example: The distance from the Huang River to the other rivers is very great. In addition, huge physical barriers including high mountains (Himalayas), large deserts, and vast bodies of water (Pacific and Indian oceans) made contact unlikely. The people of the Indus Valley, for example, could sail to the Arabian Sea and on to the Middle East, but the people of the Huang Valley could not use that route.

2. An adequate response should mention at least two advantages and two disadvantages of floods. Examples: Floods deposited silt, created fertile farmland, and provided plenty of water for irrigation. Floods also posed the dangers of drowning, of losing homes, and of losing crops. An excellent response will apply these advantages and disadvantages to specific civilizations. Example: The mineral-rich silt in Mesopotamia made the soil very fertile, enabling farmers to grow surplus crops. The Nile River generally flooded at a predictable time before crops were planted and softened the soil, which made it easier to start plants. Along the other rivers, however, flooding was more unpredictable. People sometimes lost their homes or lives during the floods. When floods along the Indus River came before the crops were harvested, they could destroy the crops, and people died during the famine that followed. Along the Huang River, uncontrolled floods easily eroded the loess, leaving unproductive land behind.

CONTENT

Fill in the circle before the correct answer.

1. The landscape of Greece is made up mostly of _____.
   - ⓐ mountains and hills
   - ⓒ large stretches of plains
   - ⓑ a wide river valley
   - ⓓ a gently rising plateau

2. An oligarchy is governed by _____.
   - ⓐ a single ruler or king
   - ⓒ a small group of wealthy, powerful men
   - ⓑ leaders elected by all the people
   - ⓓ a respected scholar or teacher

3. Which of these was a result of the Peloponnesian Wars?
   - ⓐ No single polis maintained control over Greece.
   - ⓑ Athens became the leading city-state.
   - ⓒ Greece was taken over by Persia.
   - ⓓ The Greek Golden Age began.

4. The city-state of Sparta was especially concerned with _____.
   - ⓐ strengthening its military
   - ⓒ acquiring more land for farming
   - ⓑ building democracy
   - ⓓ trading with other city-states

5. The Seven Wonders of the World were alike in that they were all _____.
   - ⓐ located in Greece
   - ⓒ made by people
   - ⓑ portraits of gods
   - ⓓ government buildings

Write the name from the box that best fits each description.

Homer	Pericles	Alexander	Socrates	Herodotus

6. an Athenian leader who worked to allow poor citizens to take part in government .... Pericles

7. a philosopher who questioned Athenian laws, customs, and religion .... Socrates

8. a poet whose works were part of the culture shared by all of Greece .... Homer

9. an historian who wrote about ancient Greece and its culture .... Herodotus

10. a Macedonian king who conquered Greece and made it part of his empire .... Alexander

---

SKILLS

For each question circle the letter of the conclusion that can be made based on the information given.

1. Greek tragedies are part of the legacy we have inherited from ancient Greece. Although many Greek tragedies have been lost, works by Sophocles, Euripides, and Aeschylus have survived.
   - ⓐ Tragedies written by ancient Greeks are still performed today.
   - b. The works of Sophocles are more entertaining than those of Euripides.

2. In *Oedipus Rex*, a Greek tragedy written by Sophocles, the main character is an admirable person who faces a difficult choice. As in most Greek tragedies, this character has a fault that eventually leads to his downfall.
   - a. Sophocles did not write many plays about admirable people.
   - ⓑ The main character in most Greek tragedies has faults.

3. In ancient Greece only two or three actors performed in a tragedy, and they often had to play more than one character. The actors were always men, and they played both male and female roles.
   - ⓐ Greek tragedies were performed in a way that is different from the way most plays are performed today.
   - b. The women of ancient Greece did not have any talent for acting.

4. Sophocles and Euripides wrote tragedies to help audiences feel better about their own lives. As they watched a tragedy, the audience felt pity for the main character's downfall or death.
   - a. Every play written by Sophocles or Euripides had a happy ending.
   - ⓑ The purpose of a tragedy was to relieve the audience's feelings of fear or self-pity by showing them the suffering of the play's main character.

5. Plays in ancient Greece were performed in open-air theaters during religious festivals. Every theater had an altar to honor Dionysus or another god or goddess.
   - ⓐ Plays in ancient Greece were produced to honor a god or goddess.
   - b. Performances were often canceled because of bad weather.

WRITING

Write a short paragraph to answer each question. If you need more room, continue writing on the back of this page.

1. In about 600 B.C. how were Athens and Sparta similar, and how were they different?

   See answer at right.

   _____
   _____
   _____
   _____
   _____

2. How might the geography of Greece have led to the development of many separate city-states rather than a single, united empire? Use the map below to help answer the question.

ANCIENT GREECE: 450 B.C.

   See answer at right.

   _____
   _____
   _____
   _____

WRITING ANSWERS

1. An adequate response will explain that both Athens and Sparta were city-states. Life in both Athens and Sparta revolved around an agora and an acropolis, and the people in both places worshiped the same gods and goddesses. The major difference between them was that Athens emphasized farming and education, while Sparta emphasized military power. An excellent response will point out other similarities and other differences. For example, in both city-states leaders had to be citizens. Women and slaves were not considered citizens and had few rights. Sparta had many more slaves than Athens. In Sparta boys trained to be soldiers, and girls trained to be strong mothers of strong children. In Athens girls worked at home, while boys went to school and worked in farming or craftmaking. Also, in Athens the government began developing as a democracy.

2. An adequate response will describe at least one geographical feature (e.g., mountainous terrain, peninsulas, islands, lack of fertile valleys for farming) and explain how this feature made it difficult for ancient Greece to become a united empire. Example: Most of Greece is covered with mountains and hills. These features create natural boundaries, which must have made it difficult to travel from place to place. As a result, separate city-states grew up in these areas that were isolated from one another. An excellent response will give more than one feature and explain the results in more detail.

CONTENT

Fill in the circle before the correct answer.

1. Roman citizens included plebians and _____.
   (a) gladiators   (b) patricians   (c) slaves   (d) Gauls

2. In the Roman republic the Senate was controlled by _____.
   (a) all men and women of Rome   (c) members of Rome's noble families
   (b) workers and merchants   (d) army commanders and soldiers

3. In the Punic Wars, Rome became the most powerful Mediterranean nation by defeating _____.
   (a) Greece   (b) Carthage   (c) Persia   (d) Etruria

4. When Constantine became emperor, he made his capital in _____.
   (a) Rome   (b) Gaul   (c) Carthage   (d) Constantinople

5. The Roman governors of Judea feared the growing popularity of Jesus because they thought he might _____.
   (a) punish the Jews   (c) defeat the armies of Rome
   (b) criticize Roman gods   (d) lead a revolt

Look at the time line and read the events below. Then write the correct letter next to each event to show when it happened.

History of the Roman Empire

a. 494 B.C.   b. 202 B.C.   c. 45 B.C.   d. A.D. 180   e. A.D. 284

500 B.C.   250 B.C.   A.D. 1   A.D. 250   A.D. 500

6. __c__ Julius Caesar becomes dictator of Rome

7. __a__ Roman plebians rebel, leading to the creation of the republic

8. __e__ Diocletian divides the Roman empire into two parts

9. __d__ Armies from northern Europe begin to invade the Roman empire

10. __b__ Rome defeats Carthage in the Battle of Zama

SKILLS

Use the elevation map of Italy to answer the questions.

ITALY: ELEVATION

Feet	Meters
7,000–14,000	2,000–4,000
1,500–7,000	500–2,000
700–1,500	200–500
0–700	0–200

1. In what part of Italy are the highest elevations?
   in the Alps, or in the north

2. What is the elevation of Venice?
   0 ft. – 700 ft.

3. What is the elevation of the Apennines?
   about 1,500 ft. – 7,000 ft.

4. How is this elevation map similar to a profile map?
   It shows differences in the height of land areas.

5. What could a profile map of Italy show better than this elevation map?
   It could show relative height better than an elevation map can.

WRITING

Write a short paragraph to answer each question. If you need more room, continue writing on the back of this page.

1. Read this version of a speech that Julius Caesar made to the Roman Senate in 63 B.C.

   Our ancestors were good at planning and full of courage in action. They also imitated whatever was worthwhile in the culture of other nations. For example, they copied the armor and weapons of the Samnites. Their official robes and symbols came from the Etruscans. In fact, they eagerly imitated any promising idea, whether it came from a friend or an enemy.

   Think of two "promising ideas" developed by the Romans that are imitated or used by people today. Describe each idea and explain why it is still useful and important to modern people.

   See answer at right.

2. In your opinion were most Romans better off during the years of the republic or during the Pax Romana? Give reasons to support your answer.

   See answer at right.

WRITING ANSWERS

1. An adequate response will mention two legacies or achievements of Roman civilization. Example: Romans developed the republican form of government, in which citizens elect government leaders to represent them. The Romans were also the first to make cement by mixing sand, lime, and stone. An excellent response will mention two or more legacies and explain why each is still important today. Examples: The republican form of government is widely used today, including in the United States. We still use concrete in the construction of modern buildings and roads. Other legacies include the Roman alphabet and Latin-based languages, aqueducts to bring water to cities, a mail system, the use of arches in buildings, a national census, and an advanced road system.

2. An adequate response will give persuasive reasons for stating that Romans were better off during the years of the republic or during the Pax Romana. Example: Romans were better off during the Pax Romana than during the years of the republic. Although citizens were no longer able to participate in government, their emperors helped to improve living conditions by building new roads, water systems, and public buildings. They also maintained strong armies for protection. An excellent response will explain in more detail why Romans were better off in one period than in the other.

CONTENT

Fill in the circle before the correct answer.

1. Much of the inner part of the Arabian peninsula is made up of _____.
   - (a) mountains
   - (b) valleys
   - (c) deserts
   - (d) forests

2. Why did the Nabatean civilization grow rich?
   - (a) It had the largest area of fertile farmland in Arabia.
   - (b) Its capital was an important place of worship for Muslims.
   - (c) Its leaders conquered many colonies in the Mediterranean area.
   - (d) Its capital was an important stop on a busy trade route.

3. The main activity of the Bedouin people was _____.
   - (a) trading
   - (b) farming
   - (c) herding
   - (d) hunting

4. The center of the Muslim world community is _____.
   - (a) Mecca
   - (b) Petra
   - (c) Baghdad
   - (d) Medina

5. In the early 1000s a Muslim named Avicenna made which of these contributions?
   - (a) He described how diseases can spread through air and water.
   - (b) He invented a tool for determining the position of the stars.
   - (c) He developed the number system that we use today.
   - (d) He designed and built important Muslim monuments.

Write the word or term from the box that best completes each sentence.

| Quran | Mecca | Islam | Five Pillars | mosque |

6. The religion of Muslim people is called Islam.

7. According to Muslim belief, Mecca is the city where Muhammad began teaching about Allah.

8. Muslims believe that the Quran contains Allah's teachings to Muhammad.

9. The five basic duties of all Muslims are known as the Five Pillars.

10. A mosque is a place of worship where Muslims gather for prayer.

SKILLS

Look at the map. Beside each city listed below write the name of the leader or leaders who made it part of the caliphate: Muhammad, the first four caliphs, the Umayyad caliphs.

EXPANSION OF THE CALIPHATE: A.D. 622–750

1. Sana — Muhammad
2. Cordoba — Umayyad caliphs
3. Damascus — first four caliphs
4. Al-Fustat — first four caliphs
5. Ghazni — Umayyad caliphs

WRITING

Write a short paragraph to answer each question. If you need more room, continue writing on the back of this page.

1. Look at the map below. Find the route from Mecca to Damascus and the route from Mecca to Muscat. Which route do you think would be easier for a trader to travel? Support your answer using facts you have learned about the geography and climate of the Arabian peninsula.

ARABIAN TRADE ROUTES: 8TH CENTURY

See answer at right.

_____
_____
_____
_____

2. The Muslim caliphate thrived from the late 700s to the 1200s. What were some of the major achievements of the caliphate?

See answer at right.

_____
_____
_____
_____
_____

WRITING ANSWERS

1. An adequate response will specify one of the two trade routes and explain why it would be easier to travel, mentioning facts about climate and geography. Example: It would be easier to travel from Mecca to Muscat. Even though most of this land is hot, dry desert, there are probably oases along the way. An excellent response will contrast the two routes in more detail. Example: This route does not have the mountainous terrain of the route between Mecca and Damascus, which makes traveling difficult.

2. An adequate response will describe several of the caliphs' achievements. For example, the caliphs gathered and preserved writings from many parts of the world in a library in Baghdad. Avicenna and other Muslim doctors developed medical textbooks and standard procedures in medicine. Muslim scholars in the caliphate developed Arabic numbers and made great advancements in algebra and other areas of mathematics. They made advancements in astronomy and mapmaking and improvements in the use of the astrolabe for navigation. They also made advancements in architecture in the process of building mosques. An excellent response will further explain some of the reasons for these developments. For example, the caliphs valued education and learning. The spread of Islam helped support the effort to seek and spread knowledge.

CONTENT

Fill in the circle before the correct answer.

1. Beringia is the name of the land bridge that connected North America to _____.
   - (a) Europe
   - (b) Asia
   - (c) Africa
   - (d) South America

2. The climate throughout Middle America is characterized by _____.
   - (a) hot summers and cold winters
   - (c) heavy precipitation all year long
   - (b) mild temperatures all year long
   - (d) a rainy season between May and October

3. What helped form the land bridge to Asia?
   - (a) glaciers
   - (b) volcanoes
   - (c) mud slides
   - (d) rain forest expansion

4. Which of these was an agricultural method used by the Olmec?
   - (a) rotating types of crops
   - (c) enriching the soil with ashes
   - (b) irrigating crops with canals
   - (d) using work animals to plow

5. The Maya were the first people of Middle America to _____.
   - (a) create a widely used written language
   - (b) invent practical uses for rubber
   - (c) carve stone statues of their rulers
   - (d) make and play musical instruments

Read each sentence and decide whether it tells about the Olmec, the Maya, or both groups. Write **Olmec**, **Maya**, or **both** on the line.

6. They planted crops including corn, beans, and squash. _____both_____

7. They developed an accurate calendar by studying the night sky. _____Maya_____

8. They made jewelry, which they traded with people from other parts of Middle America. _____Olmec_____

9. Yum Kax, the maize god, was an important part of their religion. _____Maya_____

10. Most of the people worked as farmers. _____both_____

SKILLS

Use the climographs to answer the questions. Write your answers on the lines.

Climograph A: San José, Costa Rica
Elevation: 3,759 feet/ 1,146 meters

Average Monthly Temperature
Average Monthly Precipitation

inches / °F

Jan. Feb. Mar. Apr. May June July Aug. Sept. Oct. Nov. Dec.

Source: *Great International Atlas*

Climograph B: New Orleans, Louisiana
Elevation: 4 feet/ 1.22 meters

Average Monthly Temperature
Average Monthly Precipitation

inches / °F

Jan. Feb. Mar. Apr. May June July Aug. Sept. Oct. Nov. Dec.

Source: *World Almanac and Book of Facts, 1995*

1. In which city does the amount of precipitation vary the most throughout the year? _____San José_____

2. Which city has temperatures below 60°F during some months? _____New Orleans_____

3. In which month does New Orleans have the least precipitation? _____October_____

4. Which city has temperatures above 80°F in July and August? _____New Orleans_____

5. In which month does San José have the least precipitation? _____February_____

WRITING

Write a short paragraph to answer each question. If you need more room, continue writing on the back of this page.

1. The map below shows the areas settled by the Olmec and the Maya. Compare and contrast the Olmec and Maya civilizations. How were they alike, and how were they different?

OLMEC AND MAYA CIVILIZATIONS

NORTH AMERICA

Gulf of Mexico

Chichén Itzá

La Venta

Copán

PACIFIC OCEAN

Olmec
Maya

0   200   400 Miles
0   200   400 Kilometers

See answer at right.

2. Imagine that you are part of a group living in Middle America at the time of the Olmec civilization. Based on your knowledge of the area's climate and natural resources, describe the type of shelter you would need and the materials you would use to build it.

See answer at right.

WRITING ANSWERS

1. An adequate response will explain at least two similarities and two differences between the Olmec and the Maya. Similarities: Both civilizations centered on agriculture, both practiced polytheism, both developed products from rubber and played games with rubber balls, and both developed crafts, such as stone carving. Differences: The Olmec used the slash-and-burn method for farming, and they grew mainly corn, beans, and squash. The Maya developed many other crops, such as maize, peppers, and cacao. The Olmec believed that certain animals (especially the jaguar) had special powers; the Maya studied the stars and planets as part of their religion. The Olmec made huge stone carvings; the Maya built pyramids and palaces from stone blocks. An excellent response will explain other differences and similarities from an archaeological or historical perspective. For example, the Olmec flourished from 1200 to 400 B.C., while the Maya flourished from A.D. 250 to about 900. The Olmec left no written records of their civilization; the Maya developed a written language and left many records carved in stone. No one knows for sure why these two civilizations died out. The Olmec left artifacts behind; although the Maya civilization faded away, many people descended from the Maya still live in the region and practice Maya traditions.

2. An adequate response will describe a shelter that Middle Americans might have constructed with available materials and which is appropriate for the warm climate with dry and rainy seasons. Example: Since there are many trees and plants, it would be possible to build a shelter frame with branches and then cover the top with a roof of woven grasses and leaves. An excellent response will explain the advantages of such a shelter in more detail. For example, this shelter would give protection during the rainy season, but it would still let in breezes when the weather is hot.

CONTENT AND SKILLS

Fill in the circle before the correct answer.

1. In what ancient civilization did democracy have its beginnings?
   (a) Rome   (b) Greece   (c) Persia   (d) Phoenicia

2. The expansion of Alexander's empire led to the spread of _____.
   (a) democracy   (b) Islam   (c) Christianity   (d) Greek culture

3. In the Punic Wars, Rome defeated _____.
   (a) Carthage   (b) Sparta   (c) Persia   (d) Rome

4. Which type of map would best show how the boundaries of the Roman empire changed over several centuries?
   (a) elevation   (b) profile   (c) historical   (d) physical

5. Which type of visual would best show the average precipitation and average temperature in a certain area?
   (a) bar graph   (b) climograph   (c) time line   (d) profile map

6. The Roman governors of ancient Judea feared the growing popularity of _____.
   (a) Jesus   (b) Julius Caesar   (c) Hannibal   (d) Constantine

7. According to Muslim beliefs, what city is the center of Islam?
   (a) Baghdad   (b) Medina   (c) Petra   (d) Mecca

8. During the time of the caliphate, Avicenna made great advancements in the study and practice of _____.
   (a) Latin   (b) music   (c) medicine   (d) architecture

9. Which civilization developed the first system of writing in Middle America?
   (a) Olmec   (b) Aztec   (c) Maya   (d) Inca

10. The Olmec may have died out when their agriculture failed. The Olmec did not leave any written records. What conclusion can you make from these two statements?
   (a) No one knows how or why the Olmec civilization ended.
   (b) The Olmec were more successful farmers than the Maya.
   (c) Archaeologists have found books produced by the Olmec.
   (d) The Maya civilization faded as a result of many wars.

CONTENT AND SKILLS

Write the name from the box that best fits each description.

Sparta	Copán	Constantinople
Baghdad	Alexander	Muhammad
Socrates	Constantine	Augustus
Pompeii		

11. an important philosopher in the city-state of Athens — Socrates

12. a Roman city buried in the eruption of Mount Vesuvius in A.D. 79 — Pompeii

13. an important center of Maya culture during the Classic Period — Copán

14. a ruler of the Roman empire during the Pax Romana — Augustus

15. the first leader of the religion of Islam — Muhammad

16. the capital of the Muslim caliphate, located on the Tigris River — Baghdad

17. the largest city-state and strongest military power in ancient Greece — Sparta

18. a ruler who granted freedom to Christians living in the Roman empire — Constantine

19. a ruler who conquered the Greek city-states and the empire of Persia — Alexander

20. the new capital of the Roman empire after the western empire collapsed — Constantinople

---

WRITING

Write a short paragraph to answer each question. If you need more room, continue writing on the back of this page.

1. Read the situations below. Tell which situation is an example of a democracy and which is an example of an oligarchy. Give reasons for your answers.

   Situation 1

   The Acme Company is considering a change in work hours. Some of the company's workers favor changing to a four-day work week of ten hours per day. Other workers want to work six days per week for only six hours per day. The three owners of the company announce that the new work week will be four ten-hour days. When some workers complain, the owners state, "The decision is final. We've made up our minds."

   Situation 2

   Mr. Yang's sixth-grade class is trying to decide whether they will take a field trip to the science museum or the art museum. "Let's take a vote," suggests Mr. Yang. After the students vote, Mr. Yang announces, "The science museum wins by a vote of 17 to 12."

   See answer at right.
   _____
   _____
   _____
   _____
   _____

2. Compare and contrast the achievements of the Muslim caliphate and the Maya civilization.

   See answer at right.
   _____
   _____
   _____
   _____
   _____
   _____

WRITING ANSWERS

1. An adequate response will state that Situation 1 illustrates an oligarchy and Situation 2 illustrates a democracy, and it will explain why. Example: Situation 1 is an oligarchy because the three owners of the company make the decisions. Situation 2 is a democracy because the students vote. An excellent response will explain the principles of each form of government and apply them to the situation. Example: Situation 1 is an oligarchy because the owners, who are the most powerful members of the group, make decisions for the entire group. Situation 2 is a democracy because all the members of the class take part in making a decision that affects them.

2. An adequate response will mention at least two important achievements of each civilization. An excellent response will present two or more achievements of each civilization as direct comparisons. Examples: The Muslims gathered, translated, and preserved many books in a library; the Maya developed a system of writing and a calendar. The Muslims made great advancements in medicine, created a system of Arabic numbers, and made advancements in mathematics, especially algebra. The Maya developed a system of glyphs to represent numbers, which they used to keep track of historical events and trade. The Muslims used astronomy and an improved version of the astrolabe for navigation, and they built mosques facing Mecca with great precision of measurement. The Maya used astronomy and mathematics to build pyramids and palaces that reflected changes in seasons with great precision.

CONTENT

Fill in the circle before the correct answer.

1. Most of Europe has a temperate climate because _____.
   - (a) it is near the Arctic Circle
   - (b) it has many powerful rivers
   - (c) most of the land is at high elevations
   - (d) warm winds blow in from the ocean

2. When the Magna Carta was written, it was important mainly because it _____.
   - (a) freed slaves
   - (b) limited the king's powers by law
   - (c) gave lands to vassals
   - (d) established the Christian Church

3. Under feudalism serfs were mainly responsible for _____.
   - (a) working the fields
   - (b) protecting the vassals
   - (c) defending the manor
   - (d) traveling with lords

4. During the later Middle Ages in Europe, Christian townspeople in many communities expressed their religious beliefs by _____.
   - (a) becoming saints
   - (b) building grand churches
   - (c) becoming Protestants
   - (d) making pilgrimages to Mecca

5. What was one reason the Renaissance began in Florence?
   - (a) Artists and scholars found classical works in the city's museums.
   - (b) Queen Elizabeth supported playwrights and poets.
   - (c) The Medicis paid artists and scholars to pursue their work.
   - (d) The Pope brought the Roman Church great wealth, which was spent on art.

Write the letter of the person best described by each sentence.

6. __e__ He urged Europeans to capture Jerusalem.

7. __c__ This monarch was one of the most powerful and popular ever to rule England.

8. __a__ This leader of the Franks was crowned emperor by Pope Leo III.

9. __b__ He designed a flying machine in Renaissance Italy.

10. __d__ He believed it was wrong to pay indulgences to gain forgiveness from the Church.

a. Charlemagne
b. Leonardo da Vinci
c. Queen Elizabeth I
d. Martin Luther
e. Pope Urban II

SKILLS

Read the passage below. Then answer the questions about determining point of view. Write your answers on the lines.

> I work most days in my lord's fields to grow his fancy herbs and vegetables. Come evening I drag my sore body home for a dish of porridge, rye bread, and buttermilk. Meanwhile, my lord enjoys a feast of foods I only dream of eating. The cooks say that his favorites are roast venison [deer], fresh trout from his pond fried in butter with almonds, roast peacock, and pears cooked with cinnamon, cloves, and honey.
>
> As much as I long to eat those fancy foods, I'll try to avoid the mistake my cousin made. Last winter, when food was running out, he couldn't resist helping himself to a deer. When my lord kills a deer, it's called hunting. If we kill one, it's poaching [stealing], and poor cousin paid the price with his life.
>
> All the same, I am luckier than some. We grow grains, onions, garlic, cabbage, and lettuce in our garden. Our cow keeps us well supplied with milk, cheese, and butter. Sometimes we have some bacon or pickled pork, although our faith forbids us from eating meat on Wednesdays, Fridays, and Saturdays. We can trade for salted or dried fish. We manage to get by, and as long as there isn't a drought, we are all right.

1. What is the subject of this passage?
   life as a serf, life in the Middle Ages, or one man's life compared with that of his lord

2. From whose point of view is this passage written? _a serf_

3. What is the author's opinion of the lord?
   He envies the lord; he also feels some contempt or scorn toward him.

4. Write one or two sentences from the passage that show how the author feels about his lord.
   Examples: "Meanwhile, my lord enjoys a feast of foods I only dream of eating."
   "When my lord kills a deer, it's called hunting. If we kill one, it's poaching."

5. Write two examples of words or phrases in the passage that show how the author feels about his own life.
   Examples: drag my sore body, luckier than some, well supplied, manage to get by

WRITING

Write a short paragraph to answer each question. If you need more room, continue writing on the back of this page.

1. What were the Crusades, and how did they bring change to Europe? Use the map of the First Crusade below to help answer the question.

THE FIRST CRUSADE 1096–1099

Christian lands
Muslim lands
Routes of the First Crusade, 1095

British Isles
ATLANTIC OCEAN
EUROPE
Venice
Genoa
Rome
Black Sea
Constantinople
ASIA
AFRICA
Mediterranean Sea
HOLY LAND
Jerusalem
0 250 500 Miles
0 250 500 Kilometers

See answer at right.

2. How did Gutenberg's invention of a printing press with movable type contribute to the Reformation?

See answer at right.

1. An adequate response will explain that the Crusades were attempts by European Christians to capture Jerusalem from the Seljuk Turks. It would also state at least two changes brought about by the Crusades. For example, the Crusaders passed through the Italian port cities of Genoa, Venice, and Rome, which brought trade and growth to those cities. When the Crusaders returned, they brought products and new knowledge from Asia and Africa. An excellent response will further explain that the Christians held Jerusalem for 100 years but eventually lost control of it. It will also describe how Crusaders, in their march across Europe, attacked many non-Christians, raiding Jewish communities in France and Germany.

2. An adequate response will explain that Gutenberg's press made printing cheaper and easier and that the use of the press helped to spread Martin Luther's criticism of the Roman Church and his translation of the Bible. An excellent response will further explain that before the invention of Gutenberg's press, almost everything was written in Latin. Luther wrote in German, and the wide distribution of his works in German, as well as a translation of the Bible into German, helped unite many German-speaking people on his side.

CONTENT

Fill in the circle before the correct answer.

1. About 4,000 years ago Africans began farming in the _____.
   ⓐ Sahel   ⓑ rain forests   ⓒ Sahara   ⓓ savannas

2. After the fall of Kush, important cities and trade routes in Ethiopia were controlled by the kingdom of _____.
   ⓐ Meroe   ⓑ Aksum   ⓒ Zagwe   ⓓ Punt

3. Both Ghana and Mali became very rich by controlling the _____.
   ⓐ Red Sea   ⓑ Sahara Desert   ⓒ gold trade   ⓓ ivory trade

4. For hundreds of years merchant-sailors from Asia traveled to the port cities of East Africa to buy _____.
   ⓐ ivory   ⓑ wheat   ⓒ salt   ⓓ metal tools

5. Why are historians uncertain what life was like in Great Zimbabwe?
   ⓐ No ruins of the city were able to withstand the harsh environment.
   ⓑ No artifacts remain because Great Zimbabwe was not wealthy.
   ⓒ The people of Great Zimbabwe did not trade with people from other cultures.
   ⓓ There are no stories or written documents that have survived.

Write **true** or **false** next to each statement.

6. Lalibela was a Zagwe king who ruled Ethiopia from 1185 to 1225.   true

7. Mansa Musa was a Mali leader who conquered all of Ghana in the 1200s.   false

8. Songhai was a kingdom that replaced Mali as the most powerful kingdom in West Africa in about 1490.   true

9. Kush was a busy center of trade in the Mali empire.   false

10. Swahili was a civilization that developed in the coastal cities of East Africa.   true

---

SKILLS

Use the map of Africa to answer the questions. Write your answers on the lines.

MAJOR RELIGIONS IN AFRICA TODAY

1. How can you tell that this is a distribution map?
   It shows how one particular feature (religion) is distributed, or spread, over an area.

2. What religion dominates northern Africa? Islam

3. How would you describe the religions of Madagascar?
   The eastern coast has an area of Christianity, but most of the island has other religions.

4. Which city is located in an area that is primarily Christian? Cape Town

5. How would you describe the religions of central Africa?
   There is a mix of Christianity, Islam, and other religions.

WRITING

Write a short paragraph to answer each question. If you need more room, continue writing on the back of this page.

1. How did gold affect the rise of early kingdoms in West Africa?
   See answer at right.

2. How did the Swahili city-states become important international trade centers? Use the map below to help answer the question.

SWAHILI CITIES OF EAST AFRICA 1000–1500

See answer at right.

WRITING ANSWERS

1. An adequate response will explain that several early African kingdoms became wealthy because they controlled the gold trade. They became powerful by controlling trade routes to other parts of Africa, Europe, and Asia. Each fell to a greater power that wanted to control the valuable gold trade. An excellent response will give specific examples to support these ideas. Examples: Ghana controlled West Africa's supply of gold for over 500 years. It controlled the value of gold by keeping the supply scarce. In the 1300s gold became more valuable, and Mali also grew rich by controlling the gold trade. The empire of Songhai took over the gold trade in West Africa in about 1490, but it was later conquered by Morocco, whose leaders wanted to gain control of the gold.

2. An adequate response will explain that the Swahili city-states became trade centers because gold, ivory, and other goods produced in Zimbabwe were bought and sold in the Swahili port cities, which established trade routes to Asia. An excellent response will further explain that many Arab traders traveled to the Swahili ports to buy gold and ivory, and many of them settled there. Through these Arab settlers and other foreign merchants, the Swahili cities grew and established control over important international trade routes.

CONTENT

Fill in the circle before the correct answer.

1. Which of these separates India and Nepal from China?
   (a) Gobi Desert   (b) Himalayas   (c) Indian Ocean   (d) Mekong River

2. The Byzantine empire came to an end as a result of the _____.
   (a) fall of Constantinople   (c) birth of Süleyman
   (b) fall of Rome   (d) invasion by Moguls

3. Akbar ended the tax on all people in the Mogul empire who were _____.
   (a) Muslims   (b) enslaved   (c) non-Muslims   (d) Chinese

4. The rulers of the ancient Khmer people were considered to be _____.
   (a) priests   (b) emperors   (c) saints   (d) god-kings

5. Kublai Khan established control over all of China mainly by _____.
   (a) building canals to connect the Huang and Chang rivers
   (b) having Mongols oversee the government
   (c) creating jobs for people who had been farmers
   (d) protecting merchants on the Silk Road

Read each sentence below and write the name of the person from the box that it describes.

Shah Jahan   Genghis Khan   Kublai Khan   Süleyman   Yoritomo

6. This leader united the Mongols to conquer China.   **Genghis Khan**

7. Under this sultan the Ottoman empire reached its peak.   **Süleyman**

8. He built the Taj Mahal to honor his wife and Islamic beliefs.   **Shah Jahan**

9. This man was Japan's first shogun.   **Yoritomo**

10. This Mongol leader developed the world's first all-paper money system.   **Kublai Khan**

SKILLS

Read the facts below. Then answer the questions about making generalizations. Write your answers on the lines.

> a. Rice is a principal agricultural product of India.
> b. Rice is the most important food in the diet of the people of China.
> c. The most important agricultural product in Japan is rice.
> d. Rice fields require flooding by irrigation or periods of heavy rainfall, both of which are found in many parts of Asia.

1. What is a generalization?
   a broad statement of observation that can be applied to different kinds of examples

2. After you have selected examples, what is the next step in making a generalization?
   compare and contrast the examples

3. What topic is addressed by the facts listed above?
   the importance of rice in Asia

4. What generalization can you make from these facts?
   The countries of Asia depend mainly on rice, or rice is the most important agricultural product in Asia.

5. Which facts support your generalization?
   letters a, b, c

WRITING

Write a short paragraph to answer each question. If you need more room, continue writing on the back of this page.

1. What important changes did Akbar bring to the Mogul empire in India? Read the passage below to help answer the question.

> **Akbar** (1556–1605) was the most celebrated Mogul emperor. He greatly expanded the territories of the Mogul empire and established an efficient system of government. In an effort to put an end to the hatred between Hindus and Muslims, he tried to establish a new religion combining the religious beliefs of the two groups, but his efforts were unsuccessful.

See answer at right.
_____
_____
_____
_____
_____
_____
_____

2. How did Japan change under the rule of the Tokugawa shoguns?
   See answer at right.
_____
_____
_____
_____
_____
_____
_____

WRITING ANSWERS

1. An adequate response will give three examples of changes that Akbar brought about. Examples: He included Hindus in his government, ended the tax on non-Muslims, and allowed Hindus to build temples. An excellent response will also conclude that under Akbar's rule, Hindus were treated more fairly, and the result of his changes was an era of harmony between the Hindu majority and the ruling Muslim minority.

2. An adequate response will state that Japan became unified and remained at peace for over 200 years under the Tokugawa shoguns. It also became isolated from other countries because foreign contact was forbidden. An excellent response will describe other ways in which Japan changed during this period. Examples: The Tokugawa shoguns established control over the country by forcing all of the lords to live in Edo (Tokyo). This brought about changes in Japan's feudal society; for example, samurais no longer fought wars, and many farmers moved to towns and cities. The development of Edo also brought about new traditions, such as Kabuki theater.

CONTENT

Fill in the circle before the correct answer.

1. The Great Lakes were formed by the movement of _____.
   - (a) glaciers
   - (b) volcanoes
   - (c) rivers
   - (d) storms

2. The Aztec took control of areas in the _____.
   - (a) Isthmus of Panama
   - (c) Canadian Shield
   - (b) Valley of Mexico
   - (d) Andes Mountains

3. The Aztec built chinampas to _____.
   - (a) perform religious rituals
   - (c) increase the land for building
   - (b) improve the drinking water
   - (d) create vegetable gardens

4. What was most important to keeping the Inca empire together?
   - (a) quipus
   - (c) farming on terraces
   - (b) a huge network of roads
   - (d) raising llamas

5. What was the main purpose of the Three Fires Council formed by Native Americans in the Great Lakes region?
   - (a) religion
   - (b) boat building
   - (c) trade
   - (d) cooperative farming

Write the letter of the name that best fits each description.

6. __c__ a mountaintop city built by the Inca

7. __d__ a trading center founded by the Ojibwa

8. __a__ a supreme ruler of the Inca in the 1400s

9. __b__ the capital city of the Aztec empire

10. __e__ the village in Peru in which the Inca empire began

a. Pachakuti

b. Tenochtitlán

c. Machu Picchu

d. Bowating

e. Cuzco

SKILLS

Look at the maps below. Then answer the questions about map projections.

MAP A: EQUAL-AREA PROJECTION	MAP B: MERCATOR PROJECTION	MAP C: POLAR PROJECTION

1. Why are maps of the world less accurate representations of Earth than a globe?
   A globe, like Earth, is a sphere, so cartographers must stretch and cut parts of it to make it fit onto flat paper.

2. Why do cartographers use projections to create complete maps of Earth?
   It is a way of showing parts of Earth on a flat map.

3. Which map projection distorts sizes the farther you move from the equator?
   Map B

4. Which map projection would be most useful for comparing the sizes of North America and South America? Map A

5. Which map shows about half the globe? Map C

WRITING

Write a short paragraph to answer each question. If you need more room, continue writing on the back of this page.

1. In what ways was the government of the Inca similar to the government of the Aztec?
   See answer at right.

2. The map below shows where the Ojibwa first settled. How did the Ojibwa use their natural environment?

OJIBWA LANDS: 1400–1500

Ojibwa

Lake Superior (Kitchigami)

Bowating

Ottawa

St. Lawrence River

Lake Ontario

Lake Huron

Lake Michigan

Lake Erie

Potawatomi

Ojibwa lands
Present-day boundaries are shown.

0   500   1,000 Miles
0   500   1,000 Kilometers

ATLANTIC OCEAN

See answer at right.

WRITING ANSWERS

1. An adequate response will explain at least two similarities between the Inca and Aztec systems of government. An excellent response will explain more than two similarities. Examples: Both were ruled by powerful emperors. Both had similar classes of people: nobles, craftworkers/merchants, and farmers. In both empires nobles were responsible for helping to run the empire.

2. An adequate response will give three or more examples of how the Ojibwa used their environment. Examples: They lived in wigwams built of wooden poles and birch bark. They lived near a lake during the summer. They fished and hunted, gathered nuts and berries, and grew vegetables. In the fall they moved to the marshes and gathered wild rice. In the winter they moved to areas where they could hunt. In spring they moved again to collect the sap of maple trees for making maple sugar. An excellent response will further explain that the Ojibwa depended to a great extent on the lakes and rivers in the region. They often traveled and traded by boat (canoes made from birch bark), and their most important villages were located on the shores of lakes or, like Bowating, on rivers that connected lakes.

CONTENT AND SKILLS

Fill in the circle before the correct answer.

1. Starting around A.D. 800 a system began in Europe that was called _____.
   - ⓐ monarchy
   - ⓑ feudalism
   - ⓒ Reformation
   - ⓓ Protestantism

2. The Middle Ages began after the _____.
   - ⓐ end of the western Roman empire
   - ⓒ First Crusade
   - ⓑ fall of the Ottoman empire
   - ⓓ Renaissance

3. Many of the early kingdoms of Africa became wealthy by _____.
   - ⓐ demanding tribute from serfs
   - ⓒ controlling the gold trade
   - ⓑ collecting taxes from merchants
   - ⓓ building large navies

4. Which kind of map shows how one particular feature is spread over an area?
   - ⓐ elevation
   - ⓑ physical
   - ⓒ distribution
   - ⓓ polar projection

5. A broad statement of observation applied to different kinds of examples is _____.
   - ⓐ an opinion
   - ⓑ a fact
   - ⓒ a point of view
   - ⓓ a generalization

6. The stretching and cutting that cartographers must do to make a flat map of a globe causes _____.
   - ⓐ distortion
   - ⓑ polarization
   - ⓒ generalization
   - ⓓ distribution

7. Which civilization was established in the land now called Cambodia?
   - ⓐ Songhai
   - ⓑ Kush
   - ⓒ Mogul
   - ⓓ Khmer

8. Which civilization settled in the Valley of Mexico?
   - ⓐ Inca
   - ⓑ Ojibwa
   - ⓒ Aztec
   - ⓓ Swahili

9. The Inca built their empire along the _____.
   - ⓐ Amazon River
   - ⓒ Isthmus of Panama
   - ⓑ Andes Mountains
   - ⓓ Gulf of Mexico

10. Which empire expanded over parts of three continents?
    - ⓐ Ottoman
    - ⓑ Inca
    - ⓒ Aztec
    - ⓓ Mogul

CONTENT AND SKILLS

Write the name from the box that best fits each description.

Copernicus	Lorenzo Medici	Charlemagne
Genghis Khan	Martin Luther	Johannes Gutenberg
Süleyman	Akbar	Tokugawa Ieyasu
Jayavarman II		

11. This astronomer discovered that Earth orbits the sun once each year.

_____ Copernicus _____

12. This ruler of Florence paid artists and scholars to pursue their work.

_____ Lorenzo Medici _____

13. The Ottoman empire reached its peak under this ruler.

_____ Süleyman _____

14. This leader of the Franks conquered much of Europe in the 700s and 800s.

_____ Charlemagne _____

15. This leader established the Mogul empire in India.

_____ Akbar _____

16. This leader united the Mongols to conquer China.

_____ Genghis Khan _____

17. He helped to unify Japan in the 1600s.

_____ Tokugawa Ieyasu _____

18. His criticism of the Roman Church led to the Reformation.

_____ Martin Luther _____

19. He invented a printing press with movable type.

_____ Johannes Gutenberg _____

20. He was one of Cambodia's first kings.

_____ Jayavarman II _____

WRITING

Write a short paragraph to answer each question. If you need more room, continue writing on the back of this page.

1. Use the map below to describe the Ottoman conquest of Constantinople. Why was this important to Europe and Asia?

THE OTTOMAN EMPIRE: 1500s

See answer at right.

_____

_____

_____

_____

_____

_____

2. Describe the feudal system that existed in Japan from the 1200s to the 1600s.

See answer at right.

_____

_____

_____

_____

_____

_____

WRITING ANSWERS

1. An adequate response will explain that Constantinople lay at the point that connected Europe and Asia. When a Turkish army conquered Constantinople in 1453 (eventually renaming it Istanbul), this event marked the fall of the Byzantine empire and the rise of the Ottoman empire as a power on three continents. An excellent response will further explain that Constantinople was built by the Roman emperor Constantine (in A.D. 330) and was a center of Christianity for more than 1,000 years. The fall of Constantinople signaled more than the fall of the Byzantine empire; it also marked the growth and expansion of Islam from the Middle East toward Europe.

2. An adequate response will describe at least two aspects of life under feudalism. Examples: In Japan lords controlled the land and served the emperor and shogun, while the samurai protected the lords. Below were the farmers, merchants, and craftworkers. An excellent response will note that in feudal Japan, the emperor was head of the country, but the shogun ruled as military dictator. It will also note that the Tokugawa shoguns changed feudal Japanese society by concentrating their power over the lords.

CONTENT

Fill in the circle before the correct answer.

1. Galileo's belief in the heliocentric view angered some people because it _____.
   - (a) stated that Earth was the center of the universe
   - (b) contradicted the teachings of the Catholic Church
   - (c) stated there was no God
   - (d) contradicted the teachings of Aristotle

2. The Line of Demarcation separated lands claimed by _____.
   - (a) Spain and Portugal
   - (c) England and France
   - (b) North America and South America
   - (d) the United States and Mexico

3. Which European conquered the empire of the Inca?
   - (a) Magellan
   - (b) Cortés
   - (c) da Gama
   - (d) Pizarro

4. In the triangular trade, ships sailed from West Africa to the West Indies with a cargo of _____.
   - (a) cloth
   - (b) guns
   - (c) gold
   - (d) enslaved people

5. Which country lost control over its colony in North America as a result of the French and Indian War?
   - (a) France
   - (b) Spain
   - (c) Portugal
   - (d) Great Britain

Write the name from the box that best fits each description.

James Cook	Galileo Galilei	Bartholomeu Dias
Isaac Newton	Pedro Álvarez Cabral	

6. He created a thermometer and a telescope. **Galileo Galilei**

7. He was the first European to sail around the Cape of Good Hope. **Bartholomeu Dias**

8. He was a navigator who claimed the east coast of Australia for England. **James Cook**

9. He conducted studies of gravity in the late 1600s. **Isaac Newton**

10. His voyage to South America began a period of Portuguese rule in Brazil. **Pedro Álvarez Cabral**

SKILLS

Read the passage below. Then answer the questions. Write your answers on the lines.

> In April of 1519, an Aztec traveler looked out over the Gulf of Mexico and saw a huge object in the sea. He was so shocked by the sight, he walked many miles to tell Emperor Moctezuma that he had seen a "small mountain floating in the midst [middle] of the water, and moving here and there without touching the shore."
>
> Moctezuma immediately sent his own messengers to the coast. When they returned, they reported: "in the middle of the water [was] a house from which appeared white men, their faces white and their hands likewise. They have long thick beards and their clothing is of all colors."
>
> On hearing this, the emperor sent back gifts of gold, featherwork, and beautiful stones and instructed the messengers to give them to the strange visitors.

Source for quotes: *The Mighty Aztecs* by Gene S. Stuart, National Geographic Society, Washington, D.C., 1981

1. Do you think the first messenger was a credible source? Tell why or why not.
   Example: He is not a credible source because he is an unknown traveler and has no reputation for accuracy.

2. Why did Moctezuma send his own men to the coast?
   to verify the report or check its accuracy

3. How can you determine whether the emperor's second source was credible?
   Example: Decide whether the source has expert knowledge of the subject, determine whether they have a reason to portray things in a certain way, or determine if they have a reputation for accuracy.

4. Do you think the first messenger had a reason to tell about what he had seen in a certain way? Explain why or why not.
   Examples: Yes, he wanted to make sure his story stirred interest; or no, he had no interest in lying about what he thought he saw.

5. How do you know that Moctezuma trusted the accuracy of his messengers' report?
   He responded to their report by sending gifts to the visitors.

WRITING

Write a short paragraph to answer each question. If you need more room, continue writing on the back of this page.

1. What were the major reasons for European explorations of the Americas in the 1400s and 1500s?
   See answer at right.

2. The map below shows the triangular trade route. Why did this route develop, and what did ships carry on each leg of the trip?

TRIANGULAR TRADE: 1600–1750

See answer at right.

WRITING ANSWERS

1. An adequate response will explain that the Europeans were searching for ways to reach Asia in order to increase trade or to gain wealth. Europeans sailed west across the Atlantic Ocean looking for a sailing route to Asia. Later they explored more of the Americas to gain lands, to find wealth (especially gold and furs), and to increase their own power. An excellent response will explain in more detail. For example, Europeans sought new routes to Asia because the current routes, such as the Silk Road, were long and expensive. They also sought faster routes because they knew they could make enormous profits with products from Asia, such as silk and pepper. Spaniards explored many parts of the Americas in search of wealth and the power they would gain from control of these areas. Another reason they explored the Americas was to bring Christianity to the native inhabitants. France and England explored the Americas to gain colonies and wealth, especially through the fur trade.

2. An adequate response will explain that triangular trade developed in order to transport sugar to European markets and bring enslaved Africans to North America and the West Indies. Ships from the West Indies carried sugar to Europe. Then they sailed from Europe to West Africa with guns, cloth, and other goods, which were traded for enslaved people. Ships sailed from West Africa to the West Indies with captives. An excellent response will further explain the reasons for triangular trade. For example, Europeans found that the West Indies was an ideal place to grow sugar, and they used Indians as forced labor. Because of disease and harsh working conditions, many Indians died. The triangular trade route developed as a way for plantation owners to bring more slaves to their plantations.

CONTENT

Fill in the circle before the correct answer.

1. Which was a major cause of the French Revolution?
   - (a) The Third Estate wanted equal rights.
   - (b) The people did not support Napoleon.
   - (c) The First Estate seized most of the land in France.
   - (d) Robespierre conducted a Reign of Terror.

2. Simón Bolívar fought mainly to free South Americans from _____.
   - (a) high taxes
   - (b) the Catholic Church
   - (c) colonial rule
   - (d) military obligations

3. Some of Karl Marx's ideas about what would happen to the world's economy became known as _____.
   - (a) absolute monarchy
   - (b) imperialism
   - (c) the Industrial Revolution
   - (d) socialism

4. In 1853 President Millard Fillmore sent four United States warships to Japan with a letter asking the Japanese to _____.
   - (a) buy Chinese products
   - (b) open its borders to trade
   - (c) allow whale hunting
   - (d) go to war

5. The Meiji Restoration was a revolution against _____.
   - (a) Commodore Perry
   - (b) the Diet
   - (c) the shoguns
   - (d) the bureaucracy

Write the name from the box that best completes each sentence.

Toussaint L'Ouverture	José de San Martín	James Hargreaves
Maximilien Robespierre	Miguel Hidalgo	

6. _Maximilien Robespierre_ executed suspected enemies of the revolution in France.

7. _James Hargreaves_ invented the spinning jenny.

8. _Toussaint L'Ouverture_ led a revolution against slavery in Saint Domingue.

9. _José de San Martín_ led revolutions in Argentina and Chile.

10. _Miguel Hidalgo_ tried to lead Mexico to independence from Spain.

SKILLS

Use the cartogram below to answer the questions.

World Population by Region: 1850

WORLD POPULATION BY REGION: 1850

NORTH AMERICA · EUROPE · ASIA · SOUTH AMERICA · AFRICA · AUSTRALIA

Source: World Almanac, 1996.

1. What does this cartogram show?
   It shows the relative populations of world regions in 1850.

2. How is this different from a typical map of the world?
   The size of each continent is based on population, not physical size.

3. Which region had the largest population in 1850?
   Asia.

4. How did the population of North America compare with that of Europe?
   It was quite a bit smaller (about one tenth of the size).

5. What is one advantage of using a cartogram to show information?
   Examples: You can compare information about many countries; it can give a
   clear, quick picture of the information presented.

WRITING

Write a short paragraph to answer each question. If you need more room, continue writing on the back of this page.

1. How did the French Revolution and the American Revolution affect the desire for independence in Latin America? Use the time line below to help answer the question.

1760 — 1780 — 1800 — 1820 — 1840

1810 Call of Dolores

American Revolution 1776
French Revolution 1789
Haiti gains independence 1804
Argentina wins independence 1816
Chile wins independence 1818
Mexico & Venezuela become independent 1821

See answer at right.
_____
_____
_____
_____

2. How did Japan change and expand during the Meiji era?
   See answer at right.
_____
_____
_____
_____

WRITING ANSWERS

1. An adequate response will explain that many Latin American countries were influenced by the United States Constitution. It will also explain that the French Revolution caused people in Latin America to think about gaining their own rights, and it will give some examples from the time line. The spirit of "Liberty, Equality, Fraternity" spread to Latin America and encouraged the people of several countries to fight for independence. Toussaint L'Ouverture led the struggle against slavery in Saint Domingue and eventually helped drive out the French to make Haiti an independent country. José de San Martín helped win independence for Argentina and Chile. Simón Bolívar helped gain independence for Venezuela and several other nations. Mexico, led by Hidalgo and Morelos, rebelled against Spain and finally won independence in 1821. An excellent response will explain the reasons for these revolutions in more detail. For example, the people in Latin America rebelled against colonial rule for many of the same reasons that the French people rebelled: they came to believe that their leaders should be accountable to the people, they wanted more of a say in their own governments, and they wanted equal rights. Many Latin American countries were able to gain their independence at that time because the wars with Napoleon kept their European rulers occupied.

2. An adequate response will describe three or more important changes that occurred during this era. For example, the new government put an end to feudalism, opened up the country to foreigners, gave its people a say in government, implemented advancements in technology and other subjects learned from foreign countries, and expanded its borders by invading Korea and attacking China and Russia. An excellent response will give more specific examples of these changes. For example, many Japanese adopted Western dress, customs, and styles of architecture, and the government built factories and expanded trade with other countries, especially in tea and silk. Japanese conquests in Asia led to the country's control of Korea, Taiwan, and land taken from Russia.

T53

CONTENT AND SKILLS

Fill in the circle before the correct answer.

1. Who developed the telescope and helped prove the heliocentric theory?
   - (a) Copernicus
   - (b) Newton
   - (c) Hargreaves
   - (d) Galileo

2. Which European conquered the Aztec?
   - (a) Pizarro
   - (b) Cortés
   - (c) Cabral
   - (d) Dias

3. Which explorer led the first voyage around the world?
   - (a) Magellan
   - (b) Dias
   - (c) da Gama
   - (d) Prince Henry

4. Many Europeans brought enslaved Africans to the West Indies to _____.
   - (a) fight the Arawak
   - (b) spread Christianity
   - (c) work on sugar plantations
   - (d) dig for gold and silver

5. Who was known as the "Liberator of South America"?
   - (a) Simón Bolívar
   - (b) Miguel Hidalgo
   - (c) José María Morelos
   - (d) Agustín de Iturbide

6. Before the French Revolution who held most of the political power in France?
   - (a) the Church
   - (b) the army
   - (c) the king
   - (d) the Third Estate

7. The French Republic ended with the rise to power of _____.
   - (a) Robespierre
   - (b) Napoleon
   - (c) King Louis XVI
   - (d) Marie Antoinette

8. What event brought about revolutionary changes in Japan?
   - (a) the Meiji Restoration
   - (b) the rise of the Tokugawa shogun
   - (c) the invasion of Korea
   - (d) the Chinese invasion of Japan

9. A written source of information is most likely to be credible if its author has _____.
   - (a) a personal interest in the subject
   - (b) expert knowledge in the subject
   - (c) reason to portray things a certain way
   - (d) knowledge of what the reader believes

10. What type of visual would be most useful for showing the relative sizes of populations among European countries?
    - (a) time line
    - (b) line graph
    - (c) historical map
    - (d) cartogram

CONTENT AND SKILLS

Choose the term from the box that best fits each description. Write the term on the line.

Reign of Terror	Industrial Revolution	triangular trade
Charter Oath	Call of Dolores	Toussaint L'Ouverture
José de San Martín	Elizabeth Veale	Atahualpa
Lachlan Macquarie	James Watt	

11. an Inca emperor who was captured by Pizarro — Atahualpa

12. a governor of New South Wales who favored the rights of the freed convicts — Lachlan Macquarie

13. the inventor of the steam engine — James Watt

14. a statement by the government of Japan declaring that all Japanese would have a say in their government — Charter Oath

15. Maximilien Robespierre's war against enemies of the French Revolution — Reign of Terror

16. a period during which new inventions rapidly changed the world — Industrial Revolution

17. the leader of a revolution that led to the founding of Haiti as an independent nation — Toussaint L'Ouverture

18. a system in which sugar was transported to Europe and enslaved captives were transported to North America — triangular trade

19. the liberator of Argentina and Chile — José de San Martín

20. a statement by Miguel Hidalgo that stirred up revolution in Mexico — Call of Dolores

21. a manager of an estate who helped establish the production of wool as an important industry in Australia — Elizabeth Veale

---

WRITING

Write a short paragraph to answer each question. If you need more room, continue writing on the back of this page.

1. By 1770 which European countries controlled territories in the Americas, and why did they establish colonies in these areas?

TERRITORIES CONTROLLED BY EUROPEAN COUNTRIES: 1770

NORTH AMERICA

BAHAMA ISLANDS
WEST INDIES
CUBA
JAMAICA
HAITI
SANTO DOMINGO
LESSER ANTILLES

SOUTH AMERICA

Legend:
Spanish
Portuguese
English
French

See answer at right.

2. Where did the Industrial Revolution begin, and what kinds of changes did it bring?

See answer at right.

WRITING ANSWERS

1. An adequate response will explain which European countries controlled what parts of the Americas and will give at least two reasons why these countries established colonies. Example: Spain controlled much of South America, except the region of Brazil. Spain also controlled all of Central America, southwestern North America, and Florida. Britain controlled most of eastern North America and some small areas in the Caribbean. France had only small colonies in the Caribbean, such as Haiti. All of these countries established colonies in the Americas to gain wealth and to expand their own trade and power. An excellent response will give more detailed reasons. For example, Spain established colonies to gain wealth, especially gold, and to spread Christianity. Britain established colonies to gain wealth from the fur trade and other natural resources in North America.

2. An adequate response will explain that the Industrial Revolution began in Britain and will give at least two examples of major changes it brought about. An excellent response will explain why it began in Britain and will mention three or more changes. Example: The Industrial Revolution began in Britain because British laws allowed people to start businesses, protect their property, and earn money. Britain also had a rich supply of coal and iron, and a stable government. The Industrial Revolution brought about many changes: the invention of machines made certain kinds of work much faster and cheaper, especially in the textile industry; advancements in production made more products available; inventions such as the steam engine made transportation much faster; the growth of factories over cottage industries brought about a change in jobs and population centers from rural farms to factories in the cities. The Industrial Revolution also increased the importance of the middle class and the size of the working class. Difficult working conditions eventually brought about demands for change, which led to the formation of unions and the development of new ideas, such as socialism.

CONTENT

Fill in the circle before the correct answer.

1. The United States entered World War I as a result of _____.
   - (a) the Treaty of Versailles
   - (b) German attacks on United States ships
   - (c) the League of Nations
   - (d) the assassination of Archduke Ferdinand

2. The Bolshevik Revolution of 1917 was led by _____.
   - (a) Tsar Alexander II
   - (b) Vladimir Lenin
   - (c) Tsar Nicholas II
   - (d) Joseph Stalin

3. What event marked the beginning of World War II in Europe?
   - (a) invasion of Poland
   - (b) Battle of Britain
   - (c) invasion of the Soviet Union
   - (d) occupation of Austria

4. At a meeting in Yalta in 1945, the Allied leaders agreed to _____.
   - (a) join the Warsaw Pact
   - (b) expand communism in Europe
   - (c) ban all nuclear weapons
   - (d) create the United Nations

5. In China the goal of the Cultural Revolution was to _____.
   - (a) make factories more productive
   - (b) overthrow the Qing dynasty
   - (c) destroy all noncommunist beliefs
   - (d) defeat the Nationalist army

Write the letter of the phrase that best describes each person.

6. __d__ Joseph Stalin

7. __c__ Nikita Khrushchev

8. __e__ Mao Zedong

9. __a__ Franz Ferdinand

10. __b__ Adolf Hitler

a. his murder led to the beginning of World War I

b. Nazi dictator who led Germany into World War II

c. reached an agreement with President John F. Kennedy that ended the Cuban missile crisis

d. leader of the Soviet Union during World War II

e. led the Communists to victory in China in 1949

SKILLS

Use the time zone map to answer the questions.

TIME ZONES

1. When the President arrives in his office in Washington, D.C., at 8:00 A.M. on Monday, what time and day is it in Moscow?

   4:00 P.M. on Monday

2. When it is 12:00 noon in London, what time is it in Moscow?

   3:00 P.M.

3. When it is 9:00 P.M. in Tokyo on Monday, what time and day is it in Los Angeles?

   4:00 A.M. on Sunday

4. If you are traveling from London to New York, what change should you make to your watch?

   set it back 5 hours

5. When you travel east across the International Date Line, what change should you make to the date indicator on your watch?

   subtract a day

WRITING

Write a short paragraph to answer each question. If you need more room, continue writing on the back of this page.

1. How did the rise of nationalism contribute to the outbreak of both world wars?

   See answer at right.

2. What was the Cuban missile crisis, and how was it resolved? Use the map below for reference.

CUBAN MISSILE CRISIS

   See answer at right.

WRITING ANSWERS

1. An adequate response will note that both world wars were started largely because of strong feelings of nationalism and the many alliances that European countries had established. An excellent response will give specific examples from both World War I and World War II. For example, in the early 1900s nationalism and tension between neighboring countries in Europe were on the rise. Countries formed alliances to help each other in case of war. When a Serbian nationalist killed Archduke Franz Ferdinand of Austria and his wife, Austria-Hungary and Germany (an ally) declared war on Serbia. Soon other allies of Serbia, including Russia, France, and Britain, entered the fighting, and World War I had begun. As for World War II, Hitler's extreme nationalism, called Nazism, was a major factor in his decision to occupy Austria and invade Poland, which led Great Britain and France to declare war on Germany. In Asia, Japan's nationalism led to invasions of China and Korea, which threatened United States interests in the region. To keep the United States from involvement in its expansionist plans, Japan attacked Pearl Harbor, which drew the United States into World War II.

2. An adequate response will explain that the Cuban missile crisis occurred when the United States discovered that Soviet missiles had been placed in Cuba and were just a short flight from the United States. President Kennedy blockaded Cuba. He threatened to attack the Soviet Union if any missiles were fired from Cuba. Khrushchev eventually removed the missiles. An excellent response will explain the event in historical context and provide more detail. Example: During the Cold War the Soviet Union and the United States were each concerned about the power that nuclear weapons gave the other and feared a nuclear attack. After the United States tried to end Castro's communist government in Cuba (the first communist government in the Americas), Khrushchev sent nuclear weapons to Cuba. This placed Soviet missiles very close to the United States and was thus very threatening. As part of the agreement that ended the crisis, the Soviet Union removed the missiles and the United States agreed to remove its missiles from Turkey.

CONTENT

Fill in the circle before the correct answer.

1. Britain wanted to maintain its power in Egypt in order to keep control of the _____.
(a) ancient ruins (b) gold mines (c) Suez Canal (d) Red Sea

2. Who was the first Arab leader to meet publicly with Israeli leaders to work toward peace?
(a) Yasir Arafat (b) Anwar Sadat (c) Yitzhak Rabin (d) David Ben Gurion

3. Which term refers to the Palestinian revolt to "shake off" Israeli rule?
(a) anti-Semitism (b) Zionism (c) boycott (d) Intifada

4. In India the goal of the Green Revolution was to _____.
(a) make farms more productive (c) define women's rights
(b) gain independence from Britain (d) abolish the caste system

5. Who led the communists during Vietnam's fight for independence after World War II?
(a) Chiang Kai-shek (c) Ho Chi Minh
(b) Mao Zedong (d) Pol Pot

Write the letter of the phrase that best describes each place.

6. ___b___ Pakistan
7. ___c___ Vietnam
8. ___e___ Gold Coast
9. ___a___ Palestine
10. ___d___ Gaza

a. a land that was divided by the United Nations to form the independent nation of Israel

b. a country formed by Muslims who feared they would be treated poorly in a Hindu-led India

c. a former colony of France that became a battleground when the United States tried to stop the spread of communism

d. a part of the land that is to be used to establish a Palestinian homeland according to a 1993 agreement

e. the former name of Ghana, when it was the first colony south of the Sahara to gain independence

---

SKILLS

Study the political cartoon published earlier in this century. Use the cartoon to answer the questions below.

The Meaning of America

1. Who do you think the figure in the cartoon represents?
Uncle Sam, or the United States of America; the government of the United States.

2. What is the figure doing?
He is breaking the chains of tyranny for the world.

3. What is this cartoon about?
It is probably about the role the United States has played in defeating tyrannies or defending freedom in the world.

4. What specific events might the cartoon be referring to?
United States participation in World War I, World War II, and the Cold War

5. Write a sentence describing the cartoonist's point of view.
The cartoonist believes that the role of the United States is a defender of freedom.

WRITING

Write a short paragraph to answer each question. If you need more room, continue writing on the back of this page.

1. Why do you think it is difficult to resolve the conflict between the Jews in Israel and the Palestinians?
See answer at right.
_____
_____
_____
_____
_____

2. How did India gain its independence from Britain? Use the time line below to help describe the major events and the results of India's struggle for independence.

1857	1885	1915	1947
Great Mutiny	First Indian National Congress	Gandhi returns to India	India & Pakistan gain independence

1850 — 1900 — 1950

See answer at right.
_____
_____
_____
_____
_____
_____

WRITING ANSWERS

1. An adequate response will note that both the Jews and the Palestinians have long considered the land in Israel to be their homeland. Both groups have strong feelings of nationalism, and when the Jews established the State of Israel, it created tension with the Palestinian Arabs who want their own independent nation in the same area. An excellent response will explain historical roots of the conflict. Example: The Jews were originally driven from Jerusalem when the Babylonians conquered the city and the Diaspora began. Later, the Romans took the city. Some Jews remained in the area. Those in exile never forgot their ancient homeland, and when anti-Semitism in Europe grew, many Jews became influenced by Zionism and moved to Palestine. This immigration increased after World War II, as many survivors from Nazi concentration camps arrived. Their return caused tension with Arabs who lived in Palestine because they feared their own dream for a nation would be lost. After war broke out in 1948 between Israel and its Arab neighbors, about 750,000 Palestinians left their home in Israel and became refugees.

2. An adequate response will describe the Great Mutiny, Gandhi's efforts to gain independence for India, and the birth of an independent India in 1947. An excellent response will describe other events, such as the First Indian National Congress, and the reason for the creation of Pakistan. Example: In 1857 Indian soldiers in the British army revolted against the Raj, but the revolt was put down. In 1885, at the first Indian National Congress, Indians demanded more involvement in the government. In 1905 the Congress began a boycott of British cloth. Beginning in 1915, Gandhi led the nonviolent effort to oust Britain, and in 1947 the British finally left. India became an independent nation. Because Muslims living in India were concerned about their fate in a nation under Hindu control, the separate nation of Pakistan was established at the same time.

CONTENT

Fill in the circle before the correct answer.

1. In the late 1980s the Soviet Union and many Eastern European countries moved toward _____.
   (a) democracy   (b) colonialism   (c) communism   (d) fascism

2. In the 1980s countries around the world set up sanctions against the government of South Africa in an effort to _____.
   (a) end the violent protests   (c) spur economic development
   (b) oppose the move to democracy (d) end apartheid

3. South Korea is a Pacific Rim nation that has _____.
   (a) become poorer in recent years (c) limited its trade
   (b) industrialized rapidly   (d) turned to communism

4. In Mexico during the 1970s, many new businesses and economic growth were financed by the discovery of _____.
   (a) coal   (b) diamonds   (c) oil   (d) gold

5. In the 1980s Brazil's government tried to help the economy by _____.
   (a) giving families tropical rain forest land to farm
   (b) outlawing mining and logging in the Amazon rain forest
   (c) encouraging families to move to other countries
   (d) helping farmers establish coca farms

Write the term from the box that best completes each sentence.

| apartheid | European Union | NAFTA | Pacific Rim | per capita income |

6. The __European Union__ is working to build a common economy throughout Europe.

7. The economic growth of countries such as Japan and Singapore has led to a shift in power toward the __Pacific Rim__.

8. The South African system of laws called __apartheid__ treated people of different races differently.

9. By signing __NAFTA__, the United States, Canada, and Mexico agreed to lower taxes on goods traded among them in an effort to increase trade.

10. The amount of money each person of a country would have if that country's total income were divided equally among its people is the __per capita income__.

SKILLS

In 1989 Solidarity won recognition from the government of Poland, and Lech Walesa became president of Poland in 1990. In 1995 Walesa ran for reelection. Read the articles about the results of the election. Then answer the questions below.

When a triumphant Lech Walesa became President of Poland in 1990, European communism appeared to be finished for good. . . . Now, barely five years later, ex-communists have returned to power across much of Eastern Europe, and last week the mighty Walesa himself fell victim to the comrades' comeback. Aleksander Kwasniewski, 41, a minister in the last communist Polish government, defeated the old Solidarity warhorse in a runoff presidential election. . . . The good news, however, is that nearly all those former communists, including Kwasniewski, appear to have abandoned their Marxist past. All reached power through free and democratic elections, they are pursuing policies of privatization and market economics, and they are clamoring [calling] for membership in both NATO and the European Union.
Source: Time, December 4, 1995

The confrontation politics that gripped Poland in the 1980s may be on the way back, a result of the narrow presidential victory that ex-Communist Alexander Kwasniewski scored last week over Lech Walesa. . . . Walesa vows to "strike back," but his capacity to stir trouble seems limited. Kwasniewski is committed to democracy, backs free-market reforms and favors membership in NATO and the European Union.
Source: U.S. News & World Report, December 4, 1995

1. Is the underlined sentence a statement of fact or opinion? Tell how you know.
   It is an opinion because it cannot be proven true.

2. How could you verify the information about Walesa in these articles?
   You could check the facts in other sources.

3. What is Time's point of view about Kwasniewski?
   He is not really a communist anymore.

4. What reason might Time have to describe events from a certain point of view?
   Time might describe an event from a certain point of view because of the writer's
   American bias, to attract readers, or to express an opinion that might appeal to its
   readers. On the other hand, the article was written by a reporter whose job it is to
   tell people about world events.

5. Do you think the information in these articles is accurate? Tell why you think so.
   The information in these articles is probably accurate because it appeared in
   established newsmagazines, and both sources reported the same information.

WRITING

Write a short paragraph to answer each question. If you need more room, continue writing on the back of this page.

1. How did Japan develop into an economic power after World War II?
   See answer at right.

2. What happened in Eastern Europe during 1989, the "Year of Miracles," and why did it happen? Describe what happened in several of the countries identified in the map below.

EASTERN EUROPE: 1989

See answer at right.

WRITING ANSWERS

1. An adequate response will explain that Japan was rebuilt after the war with help from the United States, and it developed a strong economy by importing raw materials, turning them into expensive goods for export, and selling these goods to other nations. An excellent response will include other important factors. For example, Japan's economy began to grow rapidly during the Korean War, when United States troops were based in Japan and the Japanese provided them with many basic goods. Japan also helped develop its own economy by emphasizing business and technical skills in school to train young people for jobs in industry.

2. An adequate response will explain that all of these countries in Eastern Europe overthrew their communist governments and moved toward democracy and free enterprise. This movement began because when Gorbachev took power in the Soviet Union, he instituted the policies of glasnost and perestroika. These policies spread to other communist nations. An excellent response will give more detailed explanations of what happened in specific countries. For example, Hungary opened up its border with Austria, and many Eastern Europeans used this opening to escape to Western Europe. Solidarity won recognition from the government in Poland and then, in an election, won many seats in that nation's parliament. East Germany overthrew Erich Honecker and took down the Berlin Wall. Czechoslovakia overthrew its communist government and replaced it with elected leaders.

CONTENT AND SKILLS

Fill in the circle before the correct answer.

1. To understand Earth better, geographers divide it into different types of _____.
   - (a) landforms
   - (b) regions
   - (c) customs
   - (d) peoples

2. Contact between two cultures that often leads to cultural change is called _____.
   - (a) cultural interaction
   - (c) cultural region
   - (b) oral history
   - (d) values

3. A surplus is _____.
   - (a) an extra supply
   - (c) a group of farmers
   - (b) an early harvest
   - (d) an ancient settlement

4. The work of historians is similar to that of detectives because they both _____.
   - (a) display artifacts in museums
   - (c) use clues to solve mysteries
   - (b) create primary sources
   - (d) study ancient cultures

5. Archaeologists knew that people at Border Cave had made contact with people from the coast when they found _____.
   - (a) stone tools
   - (c) animal bones
   - (b) a seashell bead
   - (d) a painting of the ocean

6. Why did archaeologists working at the Iceman site melt the snow and filter the water?
   - (a) They wanted to see if the water was clean.
   - (b) They did not want to lose any evidence.
   - (c) They needed drinking water.
   - (d) They wanted to clean the Iceman.

7. Bits of sulfur and iron, which are used to make matches, were found in a piece of fungus carried by the Iceman. This suggests that the Iceman _____.
   - (a) was a miner
   - (c) traded with other people
   - (b) invented matches
   - (d) knew how to make fire

8. What important development began in the New Stone Age?
   - (a) agriculture
   - (b) cave painting
   - (c) stone tools
   - (d) fire

9. People training to do different kinds of work is an example of _____.
   - (a) archaeology
   - (b) specialization
   - (c) technology
   - (d) agriculture

10. Archaeologists learn about the people of the Stone Ages by studying _____.
    - (a) oral history
    - (b) maps
    - (c) diaries
    - (d) artifacts

CONTENT AND SKILLS

Write the name from the box that best completes each sentence.

Vladimir Lenin	Cultural Revolution
Yasir Arafat	Nelson Mandela
Jean-Bertrand Aristide	Gamal Abdel Nasser
Mohandas Gandhi	League of Nations
Cold War	Deng Xiaoping

11. In an attempt to prevent future wars, after World War I the Allied Powers established an international council called the _League of Nations_.

12. _Vladimir Lenin_ led the Bolshevik Revolution in Russia and founded the Union of Soviet Socialist Republics.

13. The _Cultural Revolution_ is the period in Chinese history when Mao called for the destruction of all noncommunist beliefs.

14. _Cold War_ refers to the struggle based on distrust between the United States and the Soviet Union.

15. _Yasir Arafat_ led the Palestine Liberation Organization in its struggle against Israel.

16. In 1952 _Gamal Abdel Nasser_ helped seize control of Egypt and led the country to independence.

17. _Mohandas Gandhi_ advocated the use of civil disobedience in India's fight for independence.

18. Because of his efforts to end apartheid, _Nelson Mandela_ was imprisoned for 27 years and was later elected the president of South Africa.

19. _Deng Xiaoping_ allowed more free enterprise in China than Mao had but crushed the protest for democracy in Tiananmen Square.

20. Military leaders overthrew _Jean-Bertrand Aristide_, the elected president of Haiti, in 1991, but the United States helped him regain his position in 1994.

WRITING

Write a short paragraph to answer each question. If you need more room, continue writing on the back of this page.

1. What was a major cause of World War II?

   See answer at right.

   _____

   _____

   _____

   _____

   _____

2. Study the political cartoon below. It was published in 1957. What do you think the cartoon is about, and what point of view does it convey?

   See answer at right.

   _____

   _____

   _____

   _____

WRITING ANSWERS

1. An adequate response will discuss at least one major cause of World War II. Example: A major cause of World War II was nationalism. Germany, Italy, and Japan all wanted to expand their borders and strengthen their own countries. An excellent response will describe specific events that caused the war. Example: Britain and France declared war on Germany when Hitler invaded Poland. When the Soviet Union was invaded by Germany, it also entered the war. The United States declared war on Japan after the bombing of Pearl Harbor and also joined the Allies when the Axis powers declared war on it.

2. An adequate response will note that the cartoon shows the United States public being protected from injustice and tyranny by the United States Constitution. An excellent response will note that the man holding the umbrella is Uncle Sam, often a symbol of the United States, and that the umbrella is a symbol for the protection that the Constitution offers. The point of view of the cartoon is pro-Constitution and suggests that the United States is a country where freedom is protected.